THE MICHELIN GUIDE

GREAT BRITAIN | IRELAND

2018

THE MICHELIN GUIDE'S COMMITMENTS

EXPERIENCED IN QUALITY!

Whether they are in Japan, the USA, China or Europe, our inspectors apply the same criteria to judge the qualit of each and every hotel and restaurant that they visit. The Michelin guide commands a worldwide reputation thanks to the commitments we make to our readers – and we reiterate these below:

Anonymous inspections

Our inspectors make regular and anonymous visits to hotel and restaurants to gauge the quality of products and service offered to an ordinary customer. They settle their own bill an may then introduce themselves and ask for more informatio about the establishment. Our readers' comments are als a valuable source of information, which we can follow up wit a visit of our own.

Independence

To remain totally objective for our readers, the selectio is made with complete independence. Entry into the guide i free. All decisions are discussed with the Editor and our highes awards are considered at a European level.

Our famous one ✽, two ✽✽ and three ✽✽✽ stars identify establishments serving the highest quality cuisine – taking into account the quality of ingredients, the mastery of techniques and flavours, the levels of creativity and, of course, consistency.

Selection and choice

The guide offers a selectio of the best hotels and res taurants in every categor of comfort and price. This i only possible because all th inspectors rigorously appl the same methods.

✿✿✿ THREE MICHELIN STARS

Exceptional cuisine, worth a special journey!

Our highest award is given for the superlative cooking of chefs at the peak of their profession. The ingredients are exemplary, the cooking is elevated to an art form and their dishes are often destined to become classics.

✿✿ TWO MICHELIN STARS

Excellent cooking, worth a detour!

The personality and talent of the chef and their team is evident in the expertly crafted dishes, which are refined, inspired and sometimes original.

✿ ONE MICHELIN STAR

High quality cooking, worth a stop!

Using top quality ingredients, dishes with distinct flavours are carefully prepared to a consistently high standard.

BIB GOURMAND

Good quality, good value cooking.

'Bibs' are awarded for simple yet skilful cooking for under £28 or €40.

THE MICHELIN PLATE

Good cooking

Fresh ingredients, carefully prepared: simply a good meal.

Annual updates

All the practical information, classifications and awards are revised and updated every year to give the most reliable information possible.

Consistency

The criteria for the classifications are the same in every country covered by the MICHELIN guide.

The sole intention of Michelin is to make your travels safe and enjoyable.

Follow our anonymous inspectors: @MichelinGuideUK

DEAR READER

We are delighted to present the 2018 edition of the MICHELIN guide to Great Britain and Ireland – a guide to the best places to eat and stay in England, Wales, Scotland, Northern Ireland and the Republic of Ireland.

- ***The guide caters for every type of visitor, from business traveller to families on holiday, and lists the best establishments across all categories of comfort and price – from cosy bistros and intimate townhouses to celebrated restaurants and luxurious hotels. So, whether you're visiting for work or pleasure, you'll find something that's right for you.***

- ***All of the establishments in the guide have been selected by our team of famous Michelin inspectors, who are the eyes and ears of our readers. They always pay their own bills and their anonymity is key to ensuring that they receive the same treatment as any other guest. Each year, they search for new establishments to add to the guide – and only the best make it through. Once the annual selection has been made, the 'best of the best' are then recognised with awards: our famous One ✿, Two ✿✿ and Three ✿✿✿ Stars and our value-for-money Bib Gourmands ☺.***

- ***Regular readers will notice that the guide has a different look this year. The most significant change is that the restaurants - our readers' favourite part - now appear at the front of each locality, with the hotels following afterwards. Restaurants are also now ordered according to the quality of their food, with the awards that you already know and love (Michelin Stars and Bib Gourmands) being placed at the top. The rest of the restaurants in our selection are then identified by a new symbol: The Michelin Plate ⑩. Being chosen by the Michelin Inspectors for inclusion in the guide is a guarantee of quality in itself and the plate symbol highlights restaurants where you will have a good meal.***

- ***The presentation of the guide may have changed but our mission is still the same: to help you find the best restaurants and hotels on your travels. Please don't hesitate to contact us, as we are keen to hear your opinions on the establishments listed within these pages, as well as those you feel could be of interest for future editions.***

- ***We trust you will enjoy travelling with the 2018 edition of our Great Britain & Ireland guide.***

CONTENTS

ivanastar/iStock

A CULINARY HISTORY

Britain hasn't always been known for its vibrant culinary scene – indeed, the food of the 'masses' started out dull and dreary, with meals driven by need rather than desire. So how did we get to where we are today? Well, it took quite a few centuries...

There's no place like Rome

The Romans kick-started things with their prolific road building, opening up the country and allowing goods to be transported more easily, country-wide. The Vikings brought with them new smoking and drying techniques for preserving fish, and the Saxons, who were excellent farmers, cultivated a wide variety of herbs – used not only for flavouring but to bulk-out stews. They also made butter, cheese and mead (a drink made from fermented honey); with the lack of sugar to sweeten things, honey was very important, and bees were kept in every village. The Normans introduced saffron, nutmeg, pepper, ginger and sugar – ingredients used in the likes of plum pudding, hot cross buns and Christmas cake. They also encouraged the drinking of wine. Meat was a luxury reserved for those with money, so the poor were left with bread, cheese and eggs as their staple diet.

The Middle Ages saw the wealthy eating beef, mutton, pork and venison, along with a great variety of birds, including blackbirds, greenfinches, herons and swans; and when the church decreed that meat couldn't be eaten on certain days, they turned to fish. Breakfast was eaten in private; lunch and dinner, in the great hall; and on special occasions they held huge feasts and banquets with lavish spectacles, musicians

flyfloor/iStock

and entertainment. The poor, meanwhile, were stuck with their simple, monotonous fare: for lunch, cheese and coarse, dark bread made from barley or rye; and in the evening, pottage, a type of stew made by boiling grain, vegetables and, on occasion, some rabbit – if they could catch one.

Sugar and spice...

Things really began to take off in Tudor times, with spices being brought back from the Far East, and sugar from the Caribbean. Potatoes and turkeys were introduced from north America; the latter were bred almost exclusively in Norfolk, then driven to London in flocks of 500 or more and fattened up for several days before being sold. The poor baked bread, salted meat, preserved vegetables, made pickles and conserves, and even brewed their own beer. As the water was so dirty, the children drank milk, the adults drank ale, cider or perry, and the rich drank wine.

Little changed until the rise of the British Empire, when new drinks such as tea, coffee and chocolate appeared, and coffee houses started to spring up – places where professionals could meet to read the newspaper and 'talk shop'. More herbs and spices were brought back, this time from India, and exotic fruits such as bananas and pineapples came onto the scene. Despite improvements in farming, the poor continued to eat bread, butter, cheese, potatoes and bacon; butcher's meat remained a luxury.

byheaven/iStock

Import–ant times

Advancements continued to pick up pace in Victorian times. The advent of the railways and steamships made it possible to import cheap grain from North America, and refrigeration units allowed meat to be brought in from Argentina and Australia. The first fish and chip shops opened in the 1860s and the first convenience food in tins and jars went on sale. The price of sugar also began to drop and sweets such as peanut brittle, liquorice allsorts and chocolate bars came into being.

In the early 20C, the cost of food fell dramatically: in 1914 it accounted for up to 60% of a working class family's income and by 1937, just 35%. Then, as things were beginning to look up, the war intervened and staple food items such as meat, sugar, butter, eggs and tea were rationed until long after the war had ended.

The late 20C saw a surge in technological and scientific advancements, and the creation of affordable fridges, freezers and microwave ovens meant that food could be stored for longer and cooked more easily. In an increasingly time-pressured world, convenience and time-saving became key, increasing the popularity of the 'ready meal' and takeaway outlets.

As immigration increased, so too did the number of restaurants serving cuisine from different nations. What started as a handful of Indian and Chinese restaurants, has now moved on in the 21C to cover everything from Thai to Turkish, Jamaican to Japanese.

Not only has the range of dining establishments increased but, with the opening up of European borders and the ease of travel and transport, many supermarkets have also started to stock a range of foreign products, from pierogi to paneer.

The British Aisles

Supermarkets may now offer an endless choice of products but at the same time, an increased interest in health and wellbeing has sparked a trend for using seasonal ingredients from small, local producers – with a focus on reducing food miles. With increasing concerns about the origins of produce and the methods used in mass-production, many people are now turning back to the traditional 'farmers' market' or opting for 'organic' alternatives, where the consumer can trace the product back to its source or be assured of a natural, ethical or sustainable production method.

This can be seen in a true British institution – the pub. Take the traditional Sunday roast, one of the country's favourite meals; some chewy meat and microwaved veg won't cut it anymore – consumers now want to see top quality seasonal ingredients on their plate, sourced from the nearby farmer or the local allotment, and freshly prepared in the kitchen. And chefs are rising to the challenge: exploring new ways of using British ingredients, and reviving and reinventing traditional regional recipes.

In the past Britain may have lagged behind its European neighbours, due, in part, to its having a largely industrial economy. But what is in no doubt today, is that it's certainly making up for lost time. It may not have such a clear culinary identity as say, France or Italy, but it now offers greater choice and diversity by providing chefs with the freedom and confidence to take inspiration from wherever they wish and bring together flavours from across the globe.

SEEK AND SELECT...

HOW TO USE THIS GUIDE

RESTAURANTS

Restaurants are listed by award.

Within each award category, they are ordered by comfort, from XXXXX to X.

Within each comfort category, they are then ordered alphabetically.

Awards:

- ✿✿✿ **Three Stars:** Exceptional cuisine, worth a special journey!
- ✿✿ **Two Stars:** Excellent cooking, worth a detour!
- ✿ **One Star:** High quality cooking, worth a stop!
- **Bib Gourmand:** Good quality, good value cooking.
- **The Michelin Plate:** Good cooking.

Comfort:

Level of comfort, from XXXXX to X, followed by for pubs.

Red: our most delightful places.

ENGLAND

BEAULIEU

Hampshire – Pop. 726 – Brockenhur
London 55 mi – Coventry 88 mi -

✿ **Scott's**

FRENCH • CLASSIC XXX This
18C inn; head to the terrace
and efficient, and only top qu
dishes. Cooking has a classic
➜Spiced scallops with cau
Roast duck breast, smoked
soufflé with Sichuan spiced
Menu £30/50 (dinner on
Town plan: D1-a – *Palace Ln*
www.Scotts.com – Closed De

Sea Grill N

MEATS AND GRILLS • BISTR
lage, this laid-back bar-resta
classic. The eggs are from th
nearby farms.
Menu £28 (weekday dinr
Town plan: D1-c – *12 Robert*
www.seagrill.co.uk – Closed D

Manor of Roses

ROMANTIC • STYLISH With i
this charming 18C inn has a ti
marry antique furniture with
lised. The wicker-furnished c
18 rooms – †£62/ £120
Town plan: D1-a – *Palace Ln*
✿ **Scott's** –See restaurant lis

Wentworth

FRIENDLY • COSY Ivy-clad
the bedrooms; some are tr
bright and modern. 19C resta
28 rooms – † £61/106
Town plan: D1-c – *35 Charles*
www.wentworth.com – Close

HOTELS

Hotels are listed by comfort, from to , followed by for guesthouses.

Within each comfort category, they are then ordered alphabetically.

Red: our most delightful places.

Locating the establishment

Location and coordinates on the town plan, with main sights.

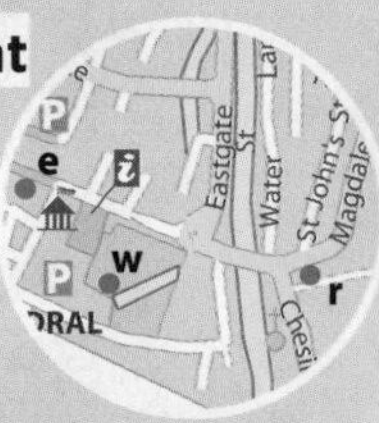

Key words

Each entry comes with two keywords, making it quick and easy to identify the type of establishment and/or the food that it serves.

n°6-B2
ester 74 mi – Norwich 61 mi

found at the heart of an alluring lovely gardens. Service is polite n the refined, precisely prepared ouches.

coriander and cumin velouté. eamed potatoes. Seville orange

) 612 324 (booking essential) –

e red-brick inn in a delightful vil- ot for a pint and a home-cooked meats are free range and from

'0 7491 2622 –

et floors and old wood panelling, itional country house bedrooms service is discreet and persona- ce overlook the lovely gardens.

0 612 324 – www.roses.com

rved wooden staircase leads to mahogany furniture, others are rary furnishings.

suites

20 7491 2622 –

Other Special Features

- Particularly interesting wine list
- Notable cocktail list
- Great view
- Peaceful establishment

Facilities & services

- Restaurant or pub with bedrooms
- Hotel with a restaurant
- Lift (elevator) • Wheelchair access
- Air conditioning (in all or part of the establishment)
- Outside dining available
- Open for breakfast • Small plates
- Restaurant offering vegetarian menus
- Restaurant offering lower priced theatre menus
- No dogs allowed
- Wellness centre
- Sauna • Exercise room
- Swimming pool: outdoor or indoor
- Garden or park • Tennis court
- Golf course
- Conference room
- Private dining room
- Car park • Garage
- Credit cards not accepted
- Nearest Underground station (London)
- New establishment in the guide

Prices

- Prices are given in £ sterling, and in € euros for the Republic of Ireland.
- All accommodation prices include both service and V.A.T. Restaurant prices include V.A.T. and service is also included when an **s** appears after the prices.

Restaurants		**Hotels**	
Menu £13/28	Fixed price menu. Lowest/highest price.	† £50/90 †† £100/120	Lowest/highest price for single and double room.
Carte £20/35	À la carte menu. Lowest/highest price.	☕†† £100/120	Bed & breakfast rate.
s	Service included.	☕ £5	Breakfast price where not included in rate.

2018...NEW AWARDS IN THIS YEAR'S GUIDE

STARS...

✿✿✿

London	Westminster/Mayfair	**The Araki**

✿✿

London	Kensington & Chelsea/Chelsea	**Claude Bosi at Bibendum**

✿

London	City of London	**La Dame de Pic**
	Kensington & Chelsea/Chelsea	**Elystan St**
	Kensington & Chelsea/Chelsea	**Vineet Bhatia London**
	Westminster/Mayfair	**Jamavar**
	Westminster/Mayfair	**The Square**
	Westminster/St James's	**Aquavit**
	Westminster/Victoria	**A. Wong**
England	Ascot	**Coworth Park**
	Aughton	**Moor Hall**
	Bagshot	**Matt Worswick at The Latymer**
	Bristol	**Paco Tapas**
	Lympstone	**Lympstone Manor**
	Malmesbury	**The Dining Room**
	Marlow	**The Coach**
	Ripley	**Clock House**
Scotland	Skye (Isle of)/Stein	**Loch Bay**
Republic of Ireland	Lisdoonvarna	**Wild Honey Inn**

A complete list of Stars and Bib Gourmands 2018 are at the beginning of each region.

... AND BIB GOURMANDS 

London

Hackney/Shoreditch	**Popolo**
Islington/Holloway	**Westerns Laundry**
Islington/Islington	**Plaquemine Lock**
Tower Hamlets/Bethnal Green	**Smokestak**
Tower Hamlets/Spitalfields	**The Frog**
Tower Hamlets/Spitalfields	**Madame. D.**
Westminster/Regent's Park & Marylebone	**Clipstone**
Westminster/Soho	**Kiln**
Westminster/Soho	**Kricket**
Westminster/Strand & Covent Garden	**Cinnamon Bazaar**

England

Ewell	**Dastaan**
Hadleigh	**Hadleigh Ram**
Howe Street	**Green Man**
Newcastle-upon-Tyne/Ponteland	**Haveli**
North Shields	**Staith House**
Sheffield	**Jöro**
South Ferriby	**Hope & Anchor**
York	**Skosh**

Wales

Aberthin	**Hare & Hounds**

Northern Ireland

Holywood	**Noble**

Republic of Ireland

Doonbeg	**Morrissey's**
Dublin	**Bastible**
Dublin	**Richmond**
Dublin/Ranelagh	**Forest & Marcy**
Dublin/Terenure	**Craft**
Galway	**Kai**
Sallins	**Two Cooks**

Starred establishments 2018

London — This location has at least one 3 star restaurant ✻✻✻

Dublin — This location has at least one 2 star restaurant ✻✻

Edinburgh — This location has at least one 1 star restaurant ✻

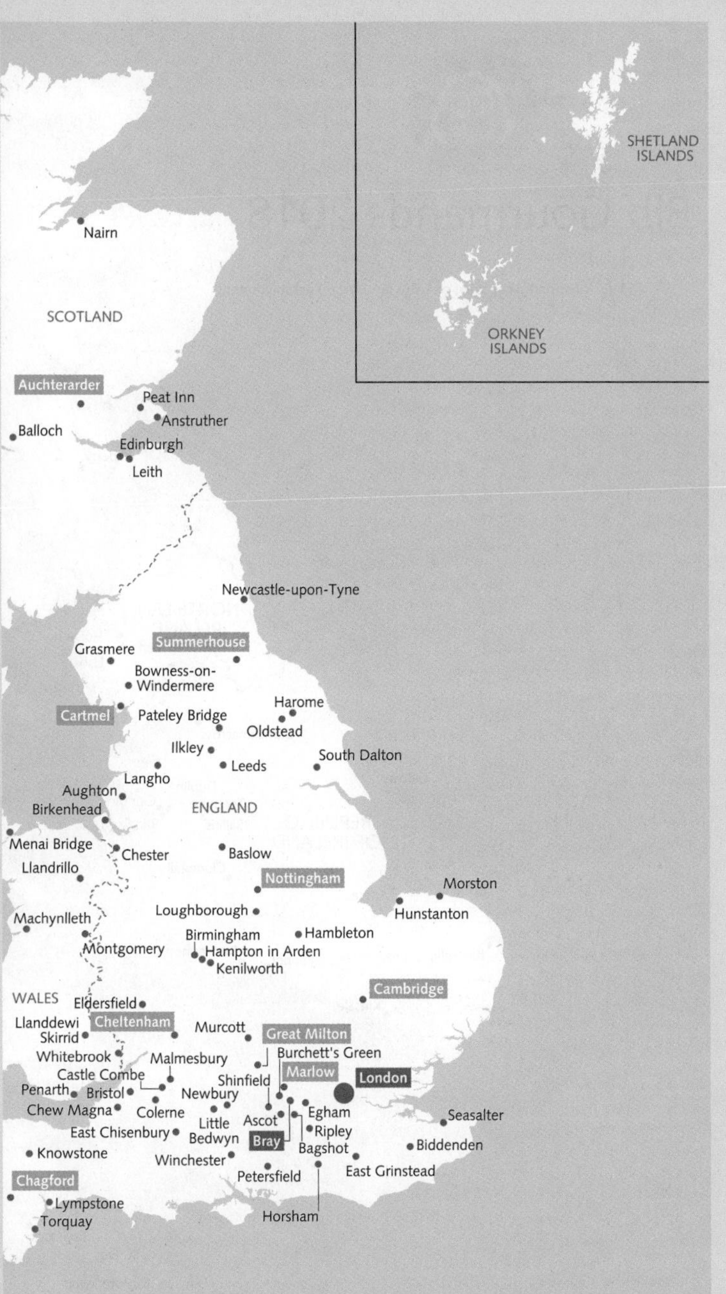
SHETLAND ISLANDS
ORKNEY ISLANDS
Nairn
SCOTLAND
Auchterarder
Peat Inn
Anstruther
Balloch
Edinburgh
Leith
Newcastle-upon-Tyne
Grasmere
Summerhouse
Bowness-on-Windermere
Cartmel
Pateley Bridge
Harome
Oldstead
Ilkley
Leeds
South Dalton
Langho
Aughton
Birkenhead
ENGLAND
Menai Bridge
Chester
Baslow
Llandrillo
Nottingham
Morston
Hunstanton
Loughborough
Machynlleth
Birmingham
Hambleton
Montgomery
Hampton in Arden
Kenilworth
Cambridge
WALES
Eldersfield
Llanddewi Skirrid
Cheltenham
Murcott
Great Milton
Whitebrook
Malmesbury
Burchett's Green
Castle Combe
Marlow
London
Shinfield
Penarth
Bristol
Newbury
Chew Magna
Colerne
Egham
Seasalter
Little Bedwyn
Ascot
Ripley
East Chisenbury
Bray
Bagshot
Biddenden
Knowstone
Winchester
East Grinstead
Petersfield
Chagford
Lympstone
Torquay
Horsham

Bib Gourmands 2018

• This location has at least one Bib Gourmand establishment

SHETLAND
ISLANDS
ORKNEY
ISLANDS
SCOTLAND
Glasgow
Edinburgh
Peebles
Ponteland
North Shields
Newcastle-
upon-Tyne
Maltby
Lower Dunsforth
Thornton
York
Fence
Drighlington
Bury
Manchester
South Ferriby
Stockport
Sheffield
Chester
Nottingham
Derby
Thorpe Market
Ingham
Wymondham
WALES
ENGLAND
Bury St. Edmunds
Welland
Hadleigh
Aldeburgh
Brecon
Cirencester
Ashendon
Hunsdon
Howe Street
Upper South Wraxall
Butlers Cross
Oxford
Ripley
Hullbridge
Aberthin
Cookham
London
Long Ashton
Bristol
Gerrards Cross
Ewell
Mells
Clyst Hydon
Donhead-
St-Andrew
Old Alresford
West Hoathly
Tenterden
Brighton and Hove
Seaview

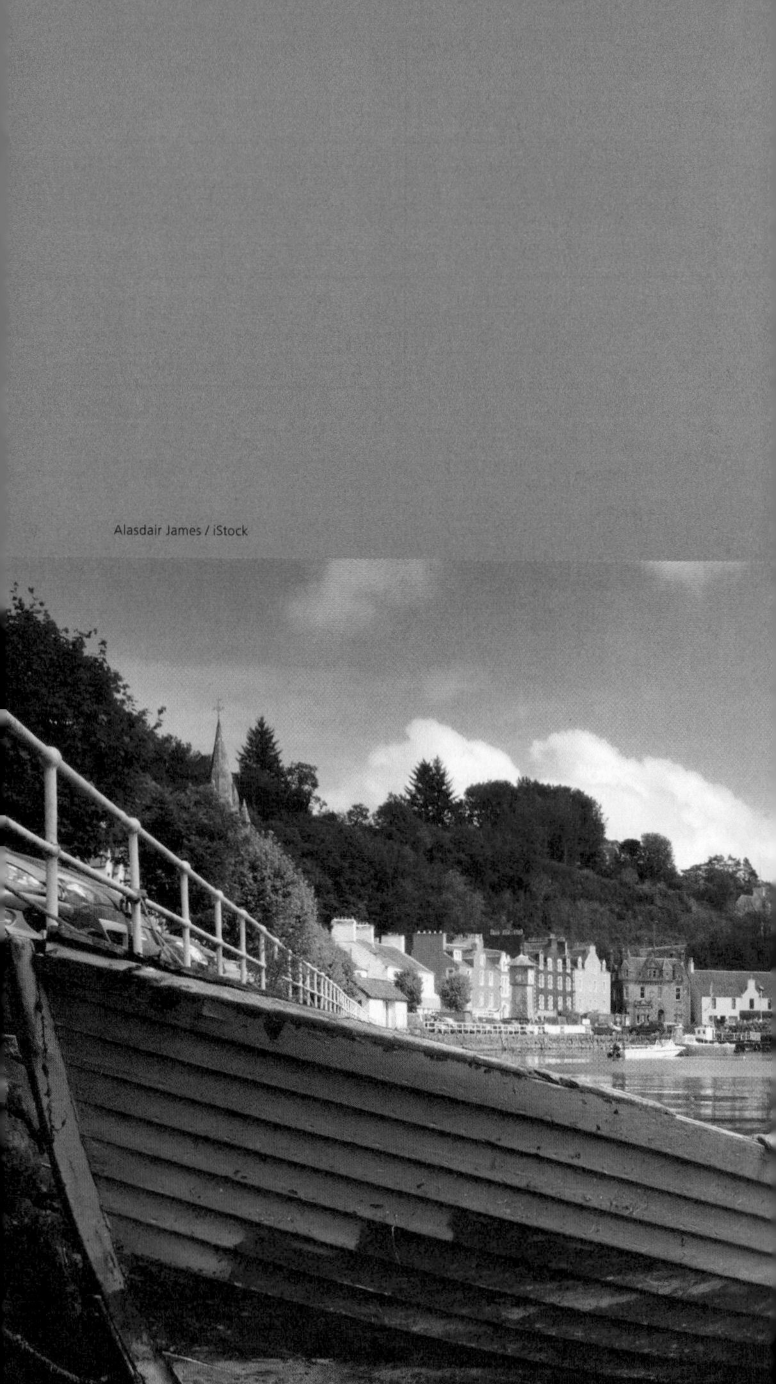
Alasdair James / iStock

GREAT BRITAIN

Great Britain & Ireland

3
Alderney
Guernsey
Jersey
Channel Islands

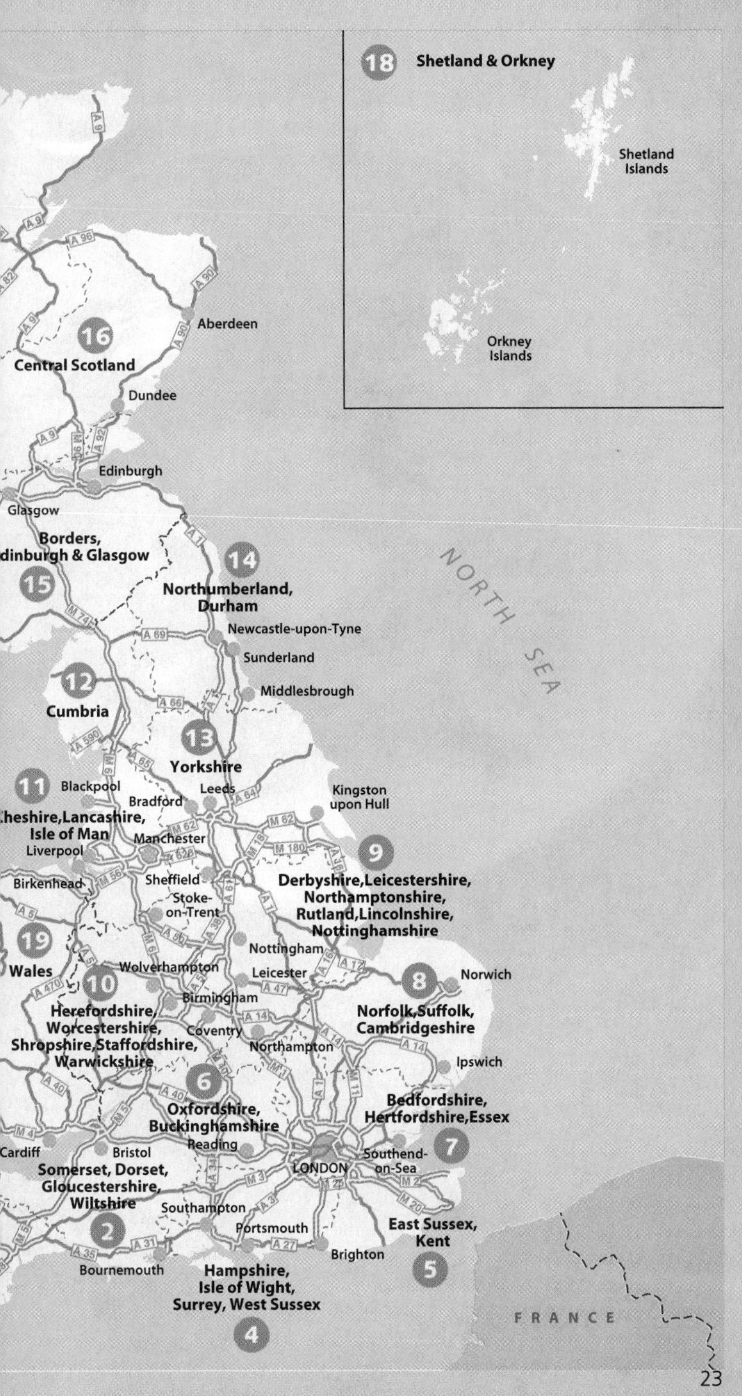

18
Shetland & Orkney
Shetland Islands
Orkney Islands
16
Central Scotland
Aberdeen
Dundee
Edinburgh
Glasgow
Borders,
dinburgh & Glasgow
15
14
Northumberland, Durham
Newcastle-upon-Tyne
Sunderland
Middlesbrough
NORTH SEA
12
Cumbria
13
Yorkshire
11
Blackpool
Bradford
Leeds
Kingston upon Hull
:heshire,Lancashire, Isle of Man
Manchester
Liverpool
Birkenhead
Sheffield
Stoke-on-Trent
9
Derbyshire,Leicestershire, Northamptonshire, Rutland,Lincolnshire, Nottinghamshire
Nottingham
19
Wales
10
Wolverhampton
Leicester
8
Norwich
Birmingham
Herefordshire, Worcestershire, Shropshire,Staffordshire, Warwickshire
Coventry
Norfolk,Suffolk, Cambridgeshire
Northampton
Ipswich
6
Oxfordshire, Buckinghamshire
Bedfordshire, Hertfordshire,Essex
Cardiff
Bristol
Reading
7
LONDON
Southend-on-Sea
Somerset, Dorset, Gloucestershire, Wiltshire
Southampton
Portsmouth
East Sussex, Kent
2
Brighton
Bournemouth
Hampshire, Isle of Wight, Surrey, West Sussex
5
4
FRANCE

LONDON

London is one of the most cosmopolitan, dynamic, fashionable and cultured cities on earth, home not only to such iconic images as Big Ben, Tower Bridge and bear-skinned guards, but also Bengali markets, speedboat rides through the Docklands and stunning views of the city from the top of the very best of 21C architecture. From Roman settlement to banking centre to capital of a 19C empire, the city's pulse has never missed a beat; it's no surprise that a dazzling array of theatres, restaurants, museums, markets and art galleries populate its streets.

The city is one of the food capitals of the world, where you can eat everything from Turkish to Thai and Polish to Peruvian; diners here are an eclectic, well-travelled bunch who gladly welcome all-comers and every style of cuisine. Visit one of the many food markets like Borough or Brixton to witness the capital's wonderfully varied produce, or pop into a pop-up to get a taste of the latest trends. If it's traditional British you're after, try one of the many pubs in the capital; this was, after all, where the gastropub movement began.

- Michelin Road map n° 504
- Michelin Green Guide: London

NOT TO BE MISSED

STARRED RESTAURANTS

Exceptional cuisine, worth a special journey!

Excellent cooking, worth a detour!

High quality cooking, worth a stop!

Five Fields

BIB GOURMAND RESTAURANTS

Good food, good value cooking

ALPHABETICAL LIST OF RESTAURANTS

C

Simon Harvey Photography / Pied a Terre

Michelin

P

Gymkhana

Q

R

S

T

Yauatcha

RESTAURANTS BY CUISINE TYPE

Argentinian

Asian

Austrian

Barbecue

Basque

Chinese

Classic cuisine

Creative

Creative British

Creative French

Creole

Fish and chips

French

Greek

Indian

Barrafina

Italian

Japanese

Korean

Lebanese

Meats and grills

Mediterranean cuisine

Mexican

Middle Eastern

Modern British

Modern French

Modern cuisine

Moroccan

North African

North American

Peruvian

Jason Lowe / Yauatcha

Trishna

Polish

Portuguese

Provençal

Scandinavian

Scottish

Seafood

South Indian

Spanish

Thai

Traditional British

Traditional cuisine

Turkish

Vegetarian

Vietnamese

World cuisine

OUR TOP PICKS

RESTAURANTS WITH OUTSIDE DINING

Araki

M

N-O

P-R

S

T

V-Y-Z

Jan Macuch/istock

THE BEST PUBS

ALPHABETICAL LIST OF HOTELS

N-O

P-R

S

T

W-Z

loveguli/iStock

OUR MOST DELIGHTFUL HOTELS

Boroughs and areas

Greater London is divided, for administrative purposes, into 32 boroughs plus **the City:** these sub-divide naturally into minor areas, usually grouped around former villages or quarters, which often maintain a distinctive character.

BRENT

Church End

Shayona

INDIAN • FAMILY Opposite the striking Swaminarayan Temple is this simple, sattvic restaurant: it's vegetarian and 'pure' so avoids onion or garlic. Expect curries from the north, dosas from the south and Mumbai street food. No alcohol so try a lassi.

Menu £10 (weekday lunch) – Carte approx. £19

Town plan: 2C3-a – *54-62 Meadow Garth ✉ NW10 8HD – ⊖ Stonebridge Park – ✆ 020 8965 3365 – www.shayonarestaurants.com – Closed 7-8 November and 25 December*

Kensal Green

Paradise by way of Kensal Green

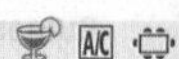

MODERN BRITISH • PUB Less a pub, more a veritable fun palace. Music, comedy and film nights happen upstairs; the bar and restaurant are wonderfully quirky; staff are contagiously enthusiastic and the European themed food is prepared with genuine care.

Carte £28/41

Town plan: 16L4-x – *19 Kilburn Ln ✉ W10 4AE – ⊖ Kensal Green. – ✆ 020 8969 0098 – www.theparadise.co.uk – dinner only and lunch Saturday-Sunday*

Parlour

MODERN BRITISH • PUB A fun, warmly run and slightly quirky neighbourhood hangout. The menu is a wonderfully unabashed mix of tradition, originality and reinvention, and dishes are beautifully fresh, full of flavour and such great value. Don't miss the cow pie which even Dan, however Desperate, would struggle to finish.

Menu £15/25 – Carte £20/41

Town plan: 16L4-r – *5 Regent St ✉ NW10 5LG – ⊖ Kensal Green – ✆ 020 8969 2184 – www.parlourkensal.com – Closed 1 week late August, 1 week Christmas-New Year and Monday*

Queen's Park

Ostuni

ITALIAN • NEIGHBOURHOOD The cuisine of Puglia, the red hot heel in Italy's boot, is celebrated at this rustic local restaurant. Don't miss the olives, creamy burrata, fava bean purée, the sausages and bombette, or the orecchiette – the ear-shaped pasta.

Carte £16/40

Town plan: 10M3-b – *43-45 Lonsdale Rd ✉ NW6 6RA – ⊖ Queen's Park – ✆ 020 7624 8035 – www.ostuniristorante.co.uk – Closed 25 December*

BROMLEY

Farnborough

Chapter One

MODERN CUISINE • FRIENDLY XXX Long-standing restaurant with many regulars, its stylish bar leading into an elegant, modern dining room. Wide-ranging menus offer keenly priced, carefully prepared modern European dishes; cooking is light and delicate, mixing classic and modern flavours. Assured service.

Menu £ 22 (weekday lunch) – Carte £ 30/40

Town plan: 8G6-c – *Farnborough Common, Locksbottom ✉ BR6 8NF – ✆ 01689 854848 – www.chapteronerestaurant.co.uk – Closed 2-4 January*

Keston

Herbert's

MODERN CUISINE • FASHIONABLE X A neat, contemporary restaurant in shades of grey, occupying a pleasant spot overlooking the Common. The European cooking is modern but the combinations of ingredients are reassuringly familiar.

Carte £ 23/51

Town plan: 8G6-x – *6 Commonside ✉ BR2 6BP – ✆ 01689 855501 – www.thisisherberts.co.uk – Closed Sunday dinner and Monday*

Orpington

Xian

CHINESE • NEIGHBOURHOOD XX Stylish, modern dining room with banquette seating, bamboo matting on the walls and six super lithographs of the famous Terracotta Warriors of Xian. Appealing menu offers flavoursome, authentic Chinese dishes, with something for everyone.

Menu £ 10 (weekday lunch)/20 – Carte £ 15/26

Town plan: 8G6-a – *324 High St. ✉ BR6 0NG – ✆ 01689 871881 – Closed 1 week October, Christmas, Easter, Sunday lunch and Monday*

Petts Wood

Indian Essence

INDIAN • NEIGHBOURHOOD XX Atul Kochhar of Benares is one of the owners of this smart and contemporary Indian restaurant. Everything is made in-house, from the masala paste to the kulfi; dishes are vibrant and flavoursome and the prices are good.

Menu £ 19 (weekday lunch)/25 – Carte £ 26/39

Town plan: 8G5-e – *176-178 Petts Wood Rd ✉ BR5 1LG – ✆ 01689 838700 – www.indianessence.co.uk*

Sundridge Park

Cinnamon Culture

INDIAN • NEIGHBOURHOOD XX Former Victorian pub; now a smart Indian restaurant serving carefully prepared, imaginative dishes. Various menus include tasting and vegetarian options; there's a shorter lunch menu as well as a monthly menu focusing on one Indian region.

Menu £ 22 (weekday dinner) – Carte £ 24/40

Town plan: 8G5-z – *46 Plaistow Ln ✉ BR1 3PA – ✆ 020 8289 0322 – www.cinnamonculture.com – Closed 26 December and Monday*

Céleste

CAMDEN

Belsize Park

ꕀ Hazara

INDIAN • NEIGHBOURHOOD XX At this keenly run, modern Indian restaurant, the adventurous diner will find specialities from all regions. Game and fish stand out – the owner goes personally to Smithfield and Billingsgate to ensure the quality of the produce.

Menu £ 20 – Carte £ 16/31

Town plan: 11N2-n – *44 Belsize Ln ✉ NW3 5AR – ⊖ Belsize Park – ✆ 020 7433 1147 – www.hazararestaurant.com – dinner only and lunch Saturday-Sunday – Closed 25-26 December and 1 January*

Retsina

GREEK • RUSTIC X Family-run restaurant whose unapologetically traditional menu offers all the Greek classics but the charcoal grill makes souvla, kebabs and cutlets the best choices. Simple, bright and airy room with a friendly atmosphere.

Carte £ 24/34

Town plan: 11N2-n – *48-50 Belsize Ln ✉ NW3 5AR – ⊖ Belsize Park – ✆ 020 7431 5855 – www.retsina.squarespace.com – Closed 25-26 December, 1 January, Monday lunch and bank holidays*

Tandis

WORLD CUISINE • NEIGHBOURHOOD X Persian and Middle Eastern food whose appeal stretches way beyond the Iranian diaspora. The specialities are the substantial and invigorating khoresh stew and the succulent kababs; end with Persian sorbet with rosewater.

Carte £ 19/31

Town plan: 11P2-x – *73 Haverstock Hill ✉ NW3 4SL – ⊖ Chalk Farm – ✆ 020 7586 8079 – www.tandisrestaurant.com – Closed 25 December*

Bloomsbury

✿ Pied à Terre

CREATIVE • ELEGANT XXX For over 25 years, David Moore's restaurant has stood apart in Charlotte Street, confident in its abilities and in the loyalty of its regulars. Subtle decorative changes keep it looking fresh and vibrant, while Andrew McFadden delivers refined, creative, flavoursome cooking.

→ Scallop ceviche with hazelnut, black radish and truffle. Suckling pig with parsnip and cider. Coconut rice pudding, sweet cheese, sake and yoghurt.

Menu £ 30/80

Town plan: 31AN1-a – *34 Charlotte St ✉ W1T 2NH – ⊖ Goodge Street – ✆ 020 7636 1178 (booking essential) – www.pied-a-terre.co.uk – Closed last week December-5 January, Saturday lunch, Sunday and bank holidays*

Hakkasan Hanway Place

CHINESE • TRENDY XX There are now Hakkasans all over the world but this was the original. It has the sensual looks, air of exclusivity and glamorous atmosphere synonymous with the 'brand'. The exquisite Cantonese dishes are prepared with care and consistency by the large kitchen team; lunch dim sum is a highlight.

➜ Dim sum platter. Grilled Chilean sea bass in honey. Chocolate and olive oil ganache.

Menu £ 38/128 - Carte £ 29/98

Town plan: 31AP2-y - *8 Hanway Pl. ✉ W1T 1HD - ⊖ Tottenham Court Road - ✆ 020 7927 7000 - www.hakkasan.com - Closed 24-25 December*

Kitchen Table at Bubbledogs (James Knappett)

MODERN CUISINE • FASHIONABLE XX Fight through the crowds enjoying a curious mix of hotdogs and champagne and head for the curtain - behind it is a counter for 19 diners. Chef-owner James prepares a no-choice menu of around 12 dishes. The produce is exemplary; the cooking has a clever creative edge; and the dishes have real depth.

➜ Lobster and tomatoes with lemon verbena. Duck, cherry and turnips. Strawberries, black pepper meringue, tarragon and milk.

Menu £ 98 - tasting menu only

Town plan: 31AN1-g - *70 Charlotte St ✉ W1T 4QG - ⊖ Goodge Street - ✆ 020 7637 7770 (booking essential) - www.kitchentablelondon.co.uk - dinner only - Closed 1-14 January, 17 August-2 September, 23-27 December and Sunday-Tuesday*

The Ninth (Jun Tanaka)

MEDITERRANEAN CUISINE • BRASSERIE X Jun Tanaka's first restaurant - the ninth in which he has worked - is this neighbourhood spot with a lively downstairs and more intimate first floor. Cooking uses classical French techniques with a spotlight on the Med; dishes look appealing but the focus is firmly on flavour. Vegetables are a highlight.

➜ Sea bass carpaccio with salsa verde and pickled kohlrabi. Chargrilled sea bream with lemon confit, miso and fennel salad. Pain perdu with vanilla ice cream.

Menu £ 25 (weekday lunch) - Carte £ 32/57

Town plan: 31AN1-j - *22 Charlotte St ✉ W1T 2NB - ⊖ Goodge Street - ✆ 020 3019 0880 - www.theninthlondon.com - Closed Christmas-New Year, Sunday and bank holidays*

Barbary

WORLD CUISINE • TAPAS BAR X A sultry, atmospheric restaurant from the team behind Palomar: a tiny place with 24 non-bookable seats squeezed around a horseshoe-shaped, zinc-topped counter. The menu of small sharing plates lists dishes from the former Barbary Coast. Service is keen, as are the prices.

Carte £ 16/32

Town plan: 31AQ2-k - *16 Neal's Yard ✉ WC2H 9DP - ⊖ Covent Garden (bookings not accepted) - www.thebarbary.co.uk - Closed dinner 24-26 December*

Barrica

SPANISH • TAPAS BAR X All the staff at this lively little tapas bar are Spanish, so perhaps it's national pride that makes them run it with a passion lacking in many of their competitors. When it comes to the food, authenticity is high on the agenda.

Carte £ 17/36

Town plan: 31AN1-x - *62 Goodge St ✉ W1T 4NE - ⊖ Goodge Street - ✆ 020 7436 9448 (booking essential) - www.barrica.co.uk - Closed 25-31 December, 1 January, Easter, Sunday and bank holidays*

Honey & Co

WORLD CUISINE • SIMPLE X The husband and wife team at this sweet little café were both Ottolenghi head chefs so expect cooking full of freshness and colour. Influences stretch beyond Israel to the wider Middle East. Open from 8am; packed at night.

Menu £ 33 – Carte £ 25/31

Town plan: 18Q4-c – *25a Warren St ✉ W1T 5LZ – ⊖ Warren Street – ☎ 020 7388 6175 (booking essential) – www.honeyandco.co.uk – Closed 24-26, 31 December, 1 January and Sunday*

Salt Yard

MEDITERRANEAN CUISINE • TAPAS BAR X A ground floor bar and buzzy basement restaurant specialising in good value plates of tasty Italian and Spanish dishes, ideal for sharing. Ingredients are top-notch; charcuterie is a speciality. Super wine list and sincere, enthusiastic staff.

Carte £ 18/28

Town plan: 31AN1-d – *54 Goodge St. ✉ W1T 4NA – ⊖ Goodge Street – ☎ 020 7637 0657 – www.saltyard.co.uk – Closed dinner 24 and 25, 31 December and 1 January*

Mere N

MODERN CUISINE • FASHIONABLE XX Monica Galetti's first collaboration with her husband, David, is an understatedly elegant basement restaurant flooded with natural light. Global, ingredient-led cooking features French influences with a nod to the South Pacific.

Menu £ 35 (weekday lunch) – Carte £ 44/67

Town plan: 31AN1-r – *74 Charlotte St ✉ W1T 4QH – ⊖ Goodge Street – ☎ 020 7268 6565 – www.mere-restaurant.com – Closed Sunday and bank holidays*

Mon Plaisir

FRENCH • FAMILY XX This proud French institution opened in the 1940s. Enjoy satisfyingly authentic classics in any of the four contrasting rooms, full of Gallic charm; apparently the bar was salvaged from a Lyonnais brothel.

Menu £ 16 (weekdays)/28 – Carte £ 26/55

Town plan: 31AQ2-g – *19-21 Monmouth St. ✉ WC2H 9DD – ⊖ Covent Garden – ☎ 020 7836 7243 – www.monplaisir.co.uk – Closed 25-26 December, Easter and bank holidays*

Roka

JAPANESE • FASHIONABLE XX The original Roka, where people come for the lively atmosphere as much as the cooking. The kitchen takes the flavours of Japanese food and adds its own contemporary touches; try specialities from the on-view Robata grill.

Carte £ 42/75

Town plan: 31AN1-k – *37 Charlotte St ✉ W1T 1RR – ⊖ Goodge Street – ☎ 020 7636 5228 – www.rokarestaurant.com – Closed 25 December*

Cigala

SPANISH • NEIGHBOURHOOD X Longstanding Spanish restaurant, with a lively and convivial atmosphere, friendly and helpful service and an appealing and extensive menu of classics. The dried hams are a must and it's well worth waiting the 30 minutes for a paella.

Menu £ 25 (weekdays) – Carte £ 29/43

Town plan: 32AR1-a – *54 Lamb's Conduit St. ✉ WC1N 3LW – ⊖ Russell Square – ☎ 020 7405 1717 (booking essential) – www.cigala.co.uk – Closed 25-26 December, 1 January, Easter Sunday and Monday*

Drakes Tabanco

SPANISH • SIMPLE X Taking advantage of our newfound fondness for fino is this simple tabanco, from the people behind nearby Barrica and Copita. The small, Andalusian-inspired tapas menu uses imported produce from Spain alongside British ingredients.

Carte £ 16/37

Town plan: 31AN1-t – *3 Windmill St ✉ W1T 2HY – ⊖ Goodge Street – ✆ 020 7637 9388 – www.drakestabanco.com – Closed Sunday and bank holidays*

Flesh & Buns

ASIAN • TRENDY X A fun, frenetic basement spot next to The Donmar. The mostly Japanese dishes are fairly priced and full of flavour; star billing goes to the gua bao bun – soft, steamed pillows of delight that sandwich your choice of meat or fish filling.

Menu £ 22/40 – Carte £ 16/46

Town plan: 31AQ2-q – *41 Earlham St ✉ WC2H 9LX – ⊖ Covent Garden – ✆ 020 7632 9500 (booking advisable) – www.bonedaddies.com – Closed 24-25 December*

Noble Rot

TRADITIONAL BRITISH • RUSTIC X A wine bar and restaurant from the people behind the wine magazine of the same name. Unfussy cooking comes with bold, gutsy flavours; expect fish from the Kent coast as well as classics like terrines, rillettes and home-cured meats.

Carte £ 30/43

Town plan: 18R4-r – *51 Lamb's Conduit St ✉ WC1N 3NB – ⊖ Russell Square – ✆ 020 7242 8963 (booking advisable) – www.noblerot.co.uk – Closed 25-26 December and Sunday*

Talli Joe

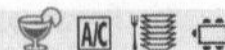

INDIAN • FASHIONABLE X Talli means 'tipsy' in Hindi and this lively place was inspired by India's dive bars. Cocktails and tapas-style small plates are the order of the day; some dishes are old family favourites of the chef, while others have a Western edge.

Menu £ 10 (weekday lunch)/35 – Carte £ 16/26

Town plan: 31AP2-r – *152-156 Shaftesbury Ave ✉ WC2H 8HL – ⊖ Covent Garden – ✆ 020 7836 5400 – www.tallijoe.com – Closed 1-15 January, 25-26 December, bank holidays and Sunday*

Covent Garden

LUXURY • DESIGN Popular with those of a theatrical bent. Boldly designed, stylish bedrooms, with technology discreetly concealed. Boasts a very comfortable first floor oak-panelled drawing room with its own honesty bar. Easy-going menu in Brasserie Max.

52 rooms – †£ 240/378 ††£ 240/378 – ☕ £ 18

Town plan: 31AP2-x – *10 Monmouth St ✉ WC2H 9HB – ⊖ Covent Garden – ✆ 020 7806 1000 – www.firmdalehotels.com*

Camden Town

York & Albany

MODERN CUISINE • INN XX This handsome 1820s John Nash coaching inn was rescued by Gordon Ramsay a few years ago after lying almost derelict. It's a moot point whether it's still an inn or more a restaurant; the food is sophisticated and the service is bright.

Menu £ 25 (weekday lunch) – Carte £ 27/56

9 rooms ☕ – †£ 145/175 ††£ 175/305

Town plan: 12Q3-s – *127-129 Parkway ✉ NW1 7PS – ⊖ Camden Town – ✆ 020 7592 1227 – www.gordonramsayrestaurants.com/york-and-albany*

Dartmouth Park

Bull & Last

TRADITIONAL BRITISH • NEIGHBOURHOOD A busy Victorian pub with plenty of charm and character; the upstairs is a little quieter. Cooking is muscular, satisfying and reflects the time of year; charcuterie is a speciality.

Carte £ 32/42

Town plan: 12Q1-a – *168 Highgate Rd ✉ NW5 1QS – ⊖ Tufnell Park.*
– ✆ 020 7267 3641 (booking essential) – www.thebullandlast.co.uk – Closed 23-25 December

Hatton Garden

Anglo

CREATIVE BRITISH • RUSTIC X As its name suggests, British produce is the mainstay of the menu at this pared-down, personally run restaurant, with 'home-grown' ingredients often served in creative ways. Cooking is well-executed with assured flavours.

Menu £ 39/45 – Carte lunch £ 34/53

Town plan: 32AS1-o – *30 St Cross St ✉ ECIN 8UH – ⊖ Farringdon*
– ✆ 020 7430 1503 – www.anglorestaurant.com – Closed 22 December-4 January, Sunday and Monday lunch

Holborn

Great Queen Street

MODERN BRITISH • RUSTIC X The menu is a model of British understatement and is dictated by the seasons; the cooking, confident and satisfying with laudable prices and generous portions. Lively atmosphere and enthusiastic service. Highlights include the shared dishes like the suet-crusted steak and ale pie for two.

Menu £ 18 (weekday lunch) – Carte £ 19/42

Town plan: 31AQ2-c – *32 Great Queen St ✉ WC2B 5AA – ⊖ Holborn*
– ✆ 020 7242 0622 (booking essential) – www.greatqueenstreetrestaurant.co.uk – Closed Christmas-New Year, Sunday dinner and bank holidays

Margot

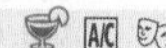

ITALIAN • ELEGANT XXX Bucking the trend of casual eateries is this glamourous, elegant Italian, where a doorman greets you, staff sport tuxedos and the surroundings are sleek and stylish. The seasonal, regional Italian cooking has bags of flavour and a rustic edge.

Menu £ 25 (lunch and early dinner) – Carte £ 30/53

Town plan: 31AQ2-m – *45 Great Queen St ✉ WC2 5AA – ⊖ Holborn*
– ✆ 020 3409 4777 – www.margotrestaurant.com – Closed 25 December

Rosewood London

HISTORIC • ELEGANT A beautiful Edwardian building that was once the HQ of Pearl Assurance. The styling is very British and the bedrooms are uncluttered and smart. Cartoonist Gerald Scarfe's work adorns the walls of his eponymous bar. A classic brasserie with a menu of British favourites occupies the former banking hall.

306 rooms – £ 378/882 £ 378/882 – 44 suites

Town plan: 32AR1-x – *252 High Holborn ✉ WC1V 7EN – ⊖ Holborn*
– ✆ 020 7781 8888 – www.rosewoodhotels.com/london

The Hoxton

TOWNHOUSE • CONTEMPORARY When the room categories are Shoebox, Snug, Cosy and Roomy, you know you're in a hip hotel. A great location and competitive rates plus a retro-style diner, a buzzy lobby and a 'Chicken Shop' in the basement.

174 rooms – £ 109/229 £ 189/389

Town plan: 31AQ1-h – *199 - 206 High Holborn ✉ WC1V 7BD – ⊖ Holborn*
– ✆ 020 7661 3000 – www.thehoxton.com

Kentish Town

Beef & Brew

MEATS AND GRILLS • SIMPLE X The name says it all. A fun place that looks not unlike a butcher's shop. Prices are kept down by using lesser cuts of meat, like onglet or flat iron, and beers are from small artisan brewers. Don't miss the brisket jam nuggets.

Carte £ 18/31

Town plan: 12Q2-t – *323 Kentish Town Rd ✉ NW5 2TJ – ⊖ Kentish Town – ✆ 020 7998 1511 (bookings advisable at dinner) – www.beef-and-brew.co.uk – Closed Monday lunch*

Chicken Shop

MEATS AND GRILLS • RUSTIC X Simply great chicken – marinated, steamed and finished over wood and charcoal – with a choice of sides and three desserts. It all happens in a noisy, mildly chaotic basement but it's great fun and good value. Be ready to queue.

Carte £ 16/21

Town plan: 12Q2-c – *79 Highgate Rd ✉ NW5 1TL – ⊖ Kentish Town – ✆ 020 3310 2020 (bookings not accepted) – www.chickenshop.com – dinner only and lunch Saturday-Sunday*

Primrose Hill

Michael Nadra Primrose Hill

MODERN CUISINE • NEIGHBOURHOOD XX Michael Nadra went north for his second branch and took over this unusual, modern building. The menu resembles his Chiswick operation, which means flavours from the Med but also the odd Asian note. The bar offers over 20 martinis.

Menu £ 23/39

Town plan: 12Q3-m – *42 Gloucester Ave ✉ NW1 8JD – ⊖ Camden Town – ✆ 020 7722 2800 – www.restaurant-michaelnadra.co.uk/primrose – Closed 24-28 December and 1 January*

Odette's

MODERN CUISINE • NEIGHBOURHOOD XX A long-standing local favourite. Warm and inviting interior, with chatty yet organised service. Robust and quite elaborate cooking, with owner passionate about his Welsh roots. Good value lunch menu.

Menu £ 22 (lunch) – Carte £ 31/53

Town plan: 11P3-b – *130 Regent's Park Rd. ✉ NW1 8XL – ⊖ Chalk Farm – ✆ 020 7586 8569 – www.odettesprimrosehill.com – Closed Christmas-New Year, Monday and dinner Sunday*

L'Absinthe

FRENCH • BISTRO X A classic French bistro offering a great atmosphere, a roll-call of favourites from cassoulet to duck confit, and a terrific wine list where only corkage is charged on the retail price. Ask for a table on the ground floor.

Carte £ 20/30

Town plan: 11P3-s – *40 Chalcot Rd ✉ NW1 8LS – ⊖ Chalk Farm – ✆ 020 7483 4848 – www.labsinthe.co.uk – Closed 1 week Christmas, Sunday and dinner Monday*

Swiss Cottage

Bradley's

MODERN CUISINE • NEIGHBOURHOOD XX A stalwart of the local dining scene and ideal for visitors to the nearby Hampstead Theatre. The thoughtfully compiled and competitively priced set menus of mostly classical cooking draw in plenty of regulars.

Menu £ 24 (lunch and early dinner) – Carte £ 34/44

Town plan: 11N2-e – *25 Winchester Rd. ✉ NW3 3NR – ⊖ Swiss Cottage – ✆ 020 7722 3457 – www.bradleysnw3.co.uk – Closed Sunday dinner and bank holidays*

Michelin

CITY OF LONDON

Restaurants

✿ City Social

MODERN CUISINE • ELEGANT XXX Jason Atherton's dark and moody restaurant with an art deco twist, set on the 24th floor of Tower 42; the City views are impressive, especially from tables 10 and 15. The flexible menu is largely European and the cooking manages to be both refined and robust at the same time.

➜ Yellowfin tuna tataki with cucumber salad and radish with ponzu dressing. Cornish sea bass with deep-fried oyster, cucumber, cauliflower and oyster velouté. Hazelnut plaisir sucré with chocolate syrup, biscuit and milk ice cream.

Carte £ 43/68

Town plan: 33AW2-s – *Tower 42 (24th floor), 25 Old Broad St ✉ EC2N 1HQ – ⊖ Liverpool Street – ✆ 020 7877 7703 – www.citysociallondon.com – Closed Sunday and bank holidays*

✿ La Dame de Pic Ⓝ

MODERN FRENCH • DESIGN XX A high-ceilinged, columned room in the impressive Beaux-Arts style Four Seasons Hotel at Ten Trinity Square; a charming brasserie deluxe with a spacious, stylish feel. Pic's cuisine is feminine and highly original: firmly rooted in classic French techniques yet delivered in a modern manner; relying on exciting flavour combinations of top quality ingredients.

➜ Berlingots with smoked Pélardon cheese, wild mushrooms and Voatsiperifery pepper. Wild turbot with beetroot, lovage sabayon and saffron. The white millefeuille.

Menu £ 39 (weekday lunch) – Carte £ 65/102

Town plan: 34AY3-d – *Four Seasons Hotel London at Ten Trinity Square, 10 Trinity Sq ✉ EC3N 4AJ – ⊖ Tower Hill – ✆ 020 3297 3790 – www.ladamedepiclondon.co.uk – Closed Sunday dinner*

✿ Club Gascon (Pascal Aussignac)

FRENCH • INTIMATE XX The gastronomy of Gascony and France's southwest are the starting points but the assured and intensely flavoured cooking also pushes at the boundaries. Marble and huge floral displays create suitably atmospheric surroundings.

➜ Flamed duck and smoked pine with aromatic razor clams. Barbecued 'white gold' fish with maize, truffle and bacon sauce. 'Millionaire' 72% Colombian chocolate with black olive, lemon gel and thyme ice cream.

Menu £ 45/80 – Carte £ 50/70

Town plan: 33AU1-z – *57 West Smithfield ✉ EC1A 9DS – ⊖ Barbican – ✆ 020 7600 6144 (booking essential) – www.clubgascon.com – Closed August, Christmas-New Year, Saturday lunch, Sunday-Monday and bank holidays*

Mei Ume

ASIAN • ELEGANT XXX Within the impressive surroundings of the Four Seasons Hotel; an elegant, high ceilinged room with subtle Asian touches, including some beautiful themed friezes. The menu focuses on Chinese dishes but also incorporates some Japanese elements; dishes come with a pleasing refinement and a lightness of touch.

Menu £ 29 (lunch) – Carte £ 42/75

Town plan: 34AY3-d – *Four Seasons Hotel London at Ten Trinity Square, 10 Trinity Sq ✉ EC3N 4AJ – ⊖ Tower Hill – ☏ 020 3297 3799 – www.meiume.com – Closed Sunday*

Lutyens

MODERN CUISINE • ELEGANT XXX The unmistakable influence of Sir Terence Conran: timeless and understated good looks mixed with functionality, and an appealing Anglo-French menu with plenty of classics such as Cornish lamb cassoulet and game in season.

Menu £ 33 (weekday lunch) – Carte £ 31/61

Town plan: 32AT2-c – *85 Fleet St. ✉ EC4Y 1AE – ⊖ Blackfriars – ☏ 020 7583 8385 – www.lutyens-restaurant.com – Closed Christmas, Saturday, Sunday and bank holidays*

Barbecoa

MEATS AND GRILLS • DESIGN XX Set up by Jamie Oliver, to show us what barbecuing is all about. The prime meats, butchered in-house, are just great; go for the pulled pork shoulder with cornbread on the side. By dessert you may be willing to share.

Menu £ 27 (weekday lunch) – Carte £ 32/64

Town plan: 33AV2-v – *20 New Change Passage ✉ EC4M 9AG – ⊖ St Paul's – ☏ 020 3005 8555 (booking essential) – www.barbecoa.com – Closed 25-26 December and 1 January*

Bird of Smithfield

MODERN CUISINE • CONTEMPORARY DÉCOR XX Five floors of fun include a cocktail bar, lounge, rooftop terrace and small, friendly restaurant – it feels like a private members' club but without the smugness. Carefully executed classic French dishes have a subtle modern edge.

Menu £ 18 (lunch and early dinner) – Carte £ 28/53

Town plan: 33AU1-s – *26 Smithfield St ✉ EC1A 9LB – ⊖ Farringdon – ☏ 020 7559 5100 (booking essential) – www.birdofsmithfield.com – Closed Christmas, New Year, Sunday and bank holidays*

Bread Street Kitchen

MODERN CUISINE • TRENDY XX Gordon Ramsay's take on NY loft-style dining comes with a large bar, thumping music, an open kitchen and enough zinc ducting to kit out a small industrial estate. For the food, think modern bistro dishes with an element of refinement.

Carte £ 31/63

Town plan: 33AV2-e – *10 Bread St ✉ EC4M 9AJ – ⊖ St Paul's – ☏ 020 3030 4050 (booking advisable) – www.breadviewkitchen.com*

The Chancery

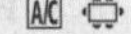

MODERN CUISINE • CHIC XX An elegant restaurant that's so close to the law courts you'll assume your fellow diners are barristers, jurors or the recently acquitted. The menu is appealingly concise; dishes come with a classical backbone and bold flavours.

Menu £ 40 (weekdays)/65

Town plan: 32AS2-a – *9 Cursitor St ✉ EC4A 1LL – ⊖ Chancery Lane – ☏ 020 7831 4000 – www.thechancery.co.uk – Closed 23 December-4 January, Saturday lunch, Sunday and bank holidays*

Chiswell Street Dining Rooms

MODERN BRITISH • BRASSERIE XX This Martin brothers' restaurant is set in a corner spot of the old Whitbread Brewery and comes alive in the evening, thanks to its busy bar. The menu makes good use of British produce and dishes are gutsy, satisfying and full of flavour.

Menu £ 38 – Carte £ 31/57

Town plan: 33AV1-r – *Montcalm London City Hotel, 56 Chiswell St ✉ EC1Y 4SA – ⊖ Barbican – ✆ 020 7614 0177 – www.chiswellstreetdining.com – Closed 25-26 December, 1 January, Saturday and Sunday*

Cigalon

FRENCH • ELEGANT XX Hidden away among the lawyers offices on Chancery Lane, this bright, high-ceilinged restaurant pays homage to the food and wine of Provence. Expect flavoursome French classics like salade niçoise and bouillabaisse.

Menu £ 22/37 – Carte lunch £ 29/39

Town plan: 32AS2-x – *115 Chancery Ln ✉ WC2A 1PP – ⊖ Chancery Lane – ✆ 020 7242 8373 – www.cigalon.co.uk – Closed Christmas, New Year, Saturday, Sunday and bank holidays*

Cinnamon Kitchen

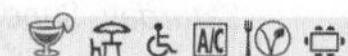

INDIAN • TRENDY XX A buzzing Indian restaurant with contemporary styling, a terrace and a trendy bar. The cooking is creative and original, with punchy flavours and arresting presentation. Meat dishes are a highlight – watch the action from the Grill Bar.

Menu £ 21 (lunch) – Carte £ 27/52

Town plan: 34AX1-2-e – *9 Devonshire Sq ✉ EC2M 4YL – ⊖ Liverpool Street – ✆ 020 7626 5000 – www.cinnamon-kitchen.com – Closed Saturday lunch, Sunday and bank holidays*

Fenchurch

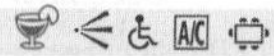

MODERN CUISINE • DESIGN XX Arrive at the 'Walkie Talkie' early so you can first wander round the Sky Garden and take in the views. The smartly dressed restaurant is housed in a glass box within the atrium. Dishes are largely British and the accomplished cooking uses modern techniques.

Menu £ 35 (weekday lunch) – Carte £ 49/69

Town plan: 34AX3-a – *Level 37, 20 Fenchurch St ✉ EC3M 3BY – ⊖ Monument – ✆ 0333 772 0020 (booking advisable) – www.skygarden.london – Closed 25-26 December*

Kenza

LEBANESE • EXOTIC DÉCOR XX Exotic basement restaurant, with lamps, carvings, pumping music and nightly belly dancing. Lebanese and Moroccan cooking are the menu influences and the food is authentic and accurate.

Carte £ 31/38

Town plan: 34AX2-c – *10 Devonshire Sq. ✉ EC2M 4YP – ⊖ Liverpool Street – ✆ 020 7929 5533 – www.kenza-restaurant.com – Closed 24-25 December, Saturday lunch and bank holidays*

New St Grill

MEATS AND GRILLS • FRIENDLY XX D&D converted an 18C warehouse to satisfy our increasing appetite for red meat. They use Black Angus beef: grass-fed British, aged for 28 days, or corn-fed American, aged for 40 days. Start with a drink in the Old Bengal Bar.

Menu £ 29 (weekdays) – Carte £ 30/85

Town plan: 34AX2-n – *16a New St ✉ EC2M 4TR – ⊖ Liverpool Street – ✆ 020 3503 0785 – www.newstreetgrill.com – Closed 25 December-3 January except dinner 31 December*

Sauterelle

MODERN CUISINE • HISTORIC XX This D&D restaurant has an impressive location on the mezzanine floor of the Royal Exchange, overlooking what was once the original trading floor – now a Grand Café by day and a cocktail bar by night. Contemporary, Italian-inspired menus.

Menu £ 25 (weekdays) – Carte £ 36/52

Town plan: 33AW2-a – *The Royal Exchange, Threadneedle St ✉ EC3V 3LR – ⊖ Bank – ✆ 020 7618 2480 – www.royalexchange-grandcafe.co.uk – Closed Christmas, Easter, Saturday, Sunday and bank holidays*

Vanilla Black

VEGETARIAN • INTIMATE XX A vegetarian restaurant where real thought has gone into the creation of dishes, which deliver an array of interesting texture and flavour contrasts. Modern techniques are subtly incorporated and while there are some original combinations, they are well-judged.

Menu £ 27 (weekday lunch)/55

Town plan: 32AS2-e – *17-18 Tooks Ct. ✉ EC4A 1LB – ⊖ Chancery Lane – ✆ 020 7242 2622 (booking essential) – www.vanillablack.co.uk – Closed 2 weeks Christmas and bank holidays*

Yauatcha City

CHINESE • FASHIONABLE XX A more corporate version of the stylish Soho original, with a couple of bars and a terrace at both ends. All the dim sum greatest hits are on the menu but the chefs have some work to match the high standard found in Broadwick Street.

Carte £ 26/67

Town plan: 34AX1-w – *Broadgate Circle ✉ EC2M 2QS – ⊖ Liverpool Street – ✆ 020 3817 9880 – www.yauatcha.com – Closed 24 December-3 January and bank holidays*

Cabotte (N)

FRENCH • WINE BAR X A bistro de luxe with a stunning wine list – owned by two master sommeliers who share a passion for the wines of Burgundy. Cooking comes with the same regional bias and the accomplished classics are simple in style and rich in flavour.

Carte £ 30/44

Town plan: 33AV2-c – *48 Gresham St ✉ EC2V 7AY – ⊖ Bank – ✆ 020 7600 1616 (booking essential) – www.cabotte.co.uk – Closed Saturday and Sunday*

Fish Market

SEAFOOD • FRIENDLY X How to get to the seaside from Liverpool Street? Simply step into this bright fish restaurant, in an old warehouse of the East India Company, and you'll almost hear the seagulls. The menu is lengthy and the cooking style classic.

Menu £ 20 – Carte £ 29/50

Town plan: 34AX2-f – *16b New St ✉ EC2M 4TR – ⊖ Liverpool Street – ✆ 020 3503 0790 (booking advisable) – www.fishmarket-restaurant.com – Closed 25-26 December, 1 January, Sunday dinner and bank holidays*

Hawksmoor

MEATS AND GRILLS • TRADITIONAL DÉCOR X Fast and furious, busy and boisterous, this handsome room is the backdrop for another testosterone filled celebration of the serious business of beef eating. Nicely aged and rested Longhorn steaks take centre-stage.

Menu £ 28 (lunch and early dinner) – Carte £ 23/63

Town plan: 33AV2-a – *10-12 Basinghall St ✉ EC2V 5BQ – ⊖ Bank – ✆ 020 7397 8120 (booking essential) – www.thehawksmoor.com – Closed 24 December-2 January, Saturday, Sunday and bank holidays*

James Cochran EC3

MODERN CUISINE • SIMPLE A spacious, simply furnished restaurant where the eponymous chef offers original combinations of interesting ingredients in an array of gutsy, good value small plates. The 6 course evening tasting menu is available with matching wines.

Carte £ 26/46

Town plan: 34AX2-v - *19 Bevis Marks ✉ EC3A 7JA - ⊖ Liverpool Street - ✆ 020 3302 0310 (booking essential at lunch) - www.jcochran.restaurant - Closed Christmas, Saturday lunch, Sunday and bank holidays*

José Pizarro

SPANISH • TAPAS BAR The eponymous chef's third operation is a good fit here: it's well run, flexible and fairly priced - and that includes the wine list. The Spanish menu is nicely balanced, with the fish and seafood dishes being the standouts.

Menu £ 25/35 - Carte £ 15/40

Town plan: 34AX1-p - *36 Broadgate Circle ✉ EC2M 1QS - ⊖ Liverpool Street - ✆ 020 7256 5333 - www.josepizarro.com - Closed Sunday*

Mac & Wild

SCOTTISH • TRENDY Sister to the Fitzrovia original, this fun spot offers good service, good value and prime Scottish ingredients, with a focus on wild game, seafood and whisky. Dishes come with subtle contrasts and great flavours.

Carte £ 22/31

Town plan: 34AX2-w - *9a Devonshire Sq ✉ EC2M 4YN - ⊖ Liverpool Street - ✆ 020 7637 0510 - www.macandwild.com - Closed Sunday*

Paternoster Chop House

TRADITIONAL BRITISH • BRASSERIE Appropriately British menu in a restaurant lying in the shadow of St Paul's Cathedral. Large, open room with full-length windows; busy bar attached. Kitchen uses thoughtfully sourced produce.

Menu £ 24 (lunch and early dinner) - Carte £ 25/63

Town plan: 33AU2-x - *Warwick Ct., Paternoster Sq. ✉ EC4M 7DX - ⊖ St Paul's - ✆ 020 7029 9400 - www.paternosterchophouse.co.uk - Closed 26-30 December, 1 January, lunch Saturday and dinner Sunday*

Temple and Sons

TRADITIONAL BRITISH • BISTRO In a glass cube next to Tower 42 is this relaxed restaurant styled on a Victorian grocer's shop, with a bar serving home-canned cocktails, and a menu of traditional British dishes like sausage and mash and sticky toffee pudding.

Carte £ 19/62

Town plan: 33AW2-s - *22 Old Broad St ✉ EC2N 1HQ - ⊖ Liverpool Street - ✆ 020 7877 7710 - www.templeandsons.co.uk - Closed Sunday*

28°-50° Fetter Lane

MODERN CUISINE • WINE BAR From the owner of Texture comes this cellar wine bar and informal restaurant. The terrific wine list is thoughtfully compiled and the grills, cheeses, charcuterie and European dishes are designed to allow the wines to shine.

Menu £ 25 (weekday lunch) - Carte £ 32/53

Town plan: 32AS2-s - *140 Fetter Ln ✉ EC4A 1BT - ⊖ Temple - ✆ 020 7242 8877 - www.2850.co.uk - Closed Saturday, Sunday and bank holidays*

Jugged Hare

TRADITIONAL BRITISH • PUB Vegetarians may feel ill at ease - and not just because of the taxidermy. The atmospheric dining room, with its open kitchen down one side, specialises in stout British dishes, with meats from the rotisserie a highlight.

Menu £ 25 (early dinner) - Carte £ 27/58

Town plan: 33AV1-x - *42 Chiswell St ✉ EC1Y 4SA - ⊖ Barbican. - ✆ 020 7614 0134 (booking essential) - www.thejuggedhare.com - Closed 25-26 December*

Hotels

Four Seasons H. London at Ten Trinity Square

HISTORIC BUILDING • ELEGANT This extraordinary building, built in 1922, is the former headquarters of The Port of London Authority and boasts many original features including the impressive rotunda lounge with its domed ceiling and plaster reliefs. Classically furnished bedrooms; choose an Executive for more space and a contemporary look. Accomplished French cooking in La Dame du Pic. Asian dishes in Mei Ume.

100 rooms – £ 390/700 £ 390/700 – £ 24 – 7 suites

Town plan: 34AY3-d – *10 Trinity Sq ✉ EC3N 4AJ – Tower Hill – 020 3297 9200 – www.fourseasons.com*

La Dame de Pic • **Mei Ume** – See restaurant listing

Andaz Liverpool Street

BUSINESS • DESIGN A contemporary and stylish interior hides behind the classic Victorian façade. Bright and spacious bedrooms boast state-of-the-art facilities. Various dining options include a brasserie specialising in grilled meats, a compact Japanese restaurant and a traditional pub.

267 rooms – £ 169/699 £ 169/699 – £ 28 – 14 suites

Town plan: 34AX2-t – *40 Liverpool St ✉ EC2M 7QN – Liverpool Street – 020 7961 1234 – www.andazliverpoolstreet.com*

The Ned

HISTORIC BUILDING • CONTEMPORARY The former Midland bank headquarters, designed and built by Sir Edwin Lutyens in 1926; now a hotel and members club offering relaxed luxury and considerable style. Edwardian-style bedrooms feature rug-covered wooden floors and beautiful furniture. There are numerous restaurants housed in the vast hall; pay a visit to the former bank vaults – now a quirky bar.

252 rooms – £ 180/500 £ 180/500 – £ 15

Town plan: 33AW2-n – *27 Poultry ✉ EC2R 8AJ – Bank – 020 3828 2000 – www.thened.com*

Montcalm London City at The Brewery

BUSINESS • CONTEMPORARY The majority of the stylish, modern bedrooms are in the original part of the Whitbread Brewery, built in 1714; ask for a quieter one overlooking the courtyard, or one of the 25 found in the 4 restored Georgian townhouses across the road. Enjoy a meal in the Chiswell Street Dining Rooms or The Jugged Hare.

236 rooms – £ 147/400 £ 187/500 – 7 suites

Town plan: 33AV1-r – *52 Chiswell St ✉ EC1Y 4SA – Barbican – 020 7614 0100 – www.themontcalmlondoncity.co.uk*

Chiswell Street Dining Rooms – See restaurant listing

Threadneedles

HISTORIC BUILDING • CONTEMPORARY A converted bank, dating from 1856, with a smart, boutique feel and a stunning stained-glass cupola in the lounge. Individually styled bedrooms feature Egyptian cotton sheets, iPod docks and thoughtful extras. Spacious Wheeler's with its marble, pillars and panelling specialises in grills and seafood.

74 rooms – £ 149/599 £ 149/599 – £ 15

Town plan: 33AW2-y – *5 Threadneedle St. ✉ EC2R 8AY – Bank – 020 7657 8080 – www.hotelthreadneedles.co.uk*

The sun's out? Enjoy eating outside on the terrace: .

CROYDON

South Croydon

Albert's Table

MODERN CUISINE • NEIGHBOURHOOD XX Named after the chef-owner's grandfather, this restaurant has a loyal local following. Gutsy, full-flavoured dishes use the best ingredients from Surrey, Sussex and Kent. Portions are generous and combinations rooted in the classics.

Menu £ 23 - Carte £ 33/50

Town plan: 7E6-x - *49b South End ✉ CR0 1BF - ✆ 020 8680 2010 - www.albertstable.co.uk - Closed Sunday dinner and Monday*

Karnavar

INDIAN • NEIGHBOURHOOD X This simple neighbourhood restaurant is passionately run and service is helpful and friendly; take their advice and try some of the Karnavar Signature dishes. Cooking - from all over India - is tasty and authentic with a modern twist.

Menu £ 10 (weekday lunch) - Carte £ 20/37

Town plan: 7E6-r - *62 South End ✉ CR0 1DP - ✆ 020 8686 2436 - www.karnavar.com - Closed 2 January and Monday lunch except bank holidays*

EALING

Acton Green

Le Vacherin

FRENCH • BRASSERIE XX Authentic feel to this comfortable brasserie, with its brown leather banquette seating, mirrors and belle époque prints. French classics from snails to duck confit; beef is a speciality.

Menu £ 25 (weekdays) - Carte £ 25/53

Town plan: 6C4-f - *76-77 South Par ✉ W4 5LF - ⊖ Chiswick Park - ✆ 020 8742 2121 - www.levacherin.com - Closed Monday lunch*

Duke of Sussex

MEDITERRANEAN CUISINE • PUB Bustling Victorian pub, whose striking dining room was once a variety theatre complete with proscenium arch. Stick to the Spanish dishes; stews and cured meats are the specialities. BYO on Mondays.

Carte £ 24/31

Town plan: 6C4-f - *75 South Par ✉ W4 5LF - ⊖ Chiswick Park. - ✆ 020 8742 8801 - www.realpubs.co.uk*

Ealing

Charlotte's W5

MODERN CUISINE • NEIGHBOURHOOD X It's all about flexibility at this converted stable block - you can come for a drink, a snack or a full meal. Every dish is available in a choice of three sizes and every bottle of wine is offered by the glass or carafe. The charming service team add to the buzz.

Menu £ 15 - Carte £ 28/32

Town plan: 1B3-c - *Dickens Yard, Longfield Ave ✉ W5 2UQ - ⊖ Ealing Broadway - ✆ 020 3771 8722 - www.charlottes.co.uk*

Charlotte's Place

MODERN CUISINE • BISTRO X Warmly run neighbourhood restaurant opposite the Common; divided between bright ground floor room and cosier downstairs. Menu is an appealing mix of British and Mediterranean influences.

Menu £ 23/39

Town plan: 2C3-c - *16 St Matthew's Rd ✉ W5 3JT - ⊖ Ealing Common - ✆ 020 8567 7541 - www.charlottes.co.uk - Closed 26 December and 1 January*

Kerbisher & Malt

FISH AND CHIPS • SIMPLE The fish and chip shop reinvented... fresh, sustainably sourced fish is cooked to order in rapeseed oil; chips are made from British spuds and fried separately; and packaging is biodegradable. There's another branch in Hammersmith.

Carte approx. £ 16

Town plan: 2C3-m - *53 New Broadway ✉ W5 5AH - ⊖ Ealing Broadway - ✆ 020 8840 4418 - www.kerbisher.co.uk - Closed Christmas and New Year*

Kiraku

JAPANESE • FRIENDLY The name of this cute little Japanese restaurant means 'relax and enjoy' - easy with such charming service. Extensive menu includes zensai, skewers, noodles, rice dishes and assorted sushi; ask if you want them in a particular order.

Carte £ 14/40

Town plan: 2C3-v - *8 Station Par, Uxbridge Rd. ✉ W5 3LD - ⊖ Ealing Common - ✆ 020 8992 2848 - www.kiraku.co.uk - Closed Christmas-New Year*

Shikumen

CHINESE • BRASSERIE Sister to the restaurant of the same name in Shepherd's Bush: this branch serves dim sum only – four choices are about right but if you're feeling hungry do order a rice bowl. Well-spaced tables and a dark, moody atmosphere.

Carte £ 20/50

Town plan: 2C3-s - *26-42 Bond St ✉ W5 5AA - ⊖ Ealing Broadway - ✆ 020 8567 2770 - www.shikumen.co.uk*

South Ealing

Ealing Park Tavern

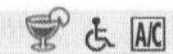

MODERN BRITISH • TRENDY An impressive Arts and Crafts property, dating from 1886 and brought up to date thanks to a splendid refurbishment from the Martin Brothers. Cooking is robust yet with a refined edge. The pub also boasts its own brewery at the back.

Carte £ 22/35

Town plan: 6C4-e - *222 South Ealing Rd ✉ W5 4RL - ⊖ South Ealing - ✆ 020 8758 1879 - www.ealingparktavern.com*

GREENWICH

Craft London

MODERN BRITISH • DESIGN Chef Stevie Parle has created a striking space beside the O2 that includes a coffee shop, a cocktail bar, and a restaurant championing seasonal British produce. They do their own curing and smoking, and roast their own coffee.

Menu £ 35 - Carte £ 32/50

Town plan: 7F4-f - *Peninsula Sq ✉ SE10 0SQ - ⊖ North Greenwich - ✆ 020 8465 5910 - www.craft-london.co.uk - dinner only and Saturday lunch - Closed Christmas-New Year, Sunday and Monday*

HKK London

HACKNEY

Dalston

Jidori

JAPANESE • BISTRO A sweet, unadorned yakitori-style restaurant serving succulent skewers of chicken, cooked on a charcoal-fired Kama-Asa Shoten grill imported from Japan. Charming staff and a good selection of cocktails, sake and craft beers.

Carte £ 17/28

Town plan: 14U2-y – *89 Kingsland High St ✉ E2 8BP – ⊖ Dalston Kingsland – ✆ 020 7686 5634 (bookings not accepted) – www.jidori.co.uk – dinner only and lunch Wednesday-Friday – Closed 25-26 December, 1 January, bank holiday Mondays and Sunday*

Rotorino

ITALIAN • SIMPLE A stylish yet down to earth Italian serving Southern Italian specialities like caponata, gnudi and Sasso chicken. Staff are welcoming and knowledgeable; ask for one of the booths at the back.

Menu £ 15 (early dinner) – Carte £ 18/33

Town plan: 14U3-w – *434 Kingsland Rd ✉ E8 4AA – ⊖ Dalston Junction – ✆ 020 7249 9081 – www.rotorino.com – dinner only and Saturday-Sunday lunch – Closed 23 December-2 January*

The Richmond

MODERN BRITISH • NEIGHBOURHOOD Seafood is the focus at this former pub but there's also plenty to please carnivores, such as the 35 day aged Longhorn steaks. Bold red décor gives the place a fashionable look, prices are sensible and staff are charm personified.

Carte £ 21/35

Town plan: 14U3-n – *316 Queensbridge Rd ✉ E8 3NH – ⊖ Dalston Junction – ✆ 020 7241 1638 (booking advisable) – www.therichmondhackney.com – dinner only and lunch Saturday-Sunday – Closed 25-26 December*

Hackney

Legs

MODERN BRITISH • NEIGHBOURHOOD An urban, no-frills bistro with a lively atmosphere, charming staff and food bursting with freshness and flavour. Lunch offers interesting sandwiches; dinner is a daily selection of small plates for sharing – and they also do brunch on Saturdays. The wine list focuses on organic wines from small producers.

Carte £ 19/36

Town plan: 14V2-s – *120 Morning Ln ✉ E9 6LH – ⊖ Hackney Central – ✆ 020 3441 8765 – www.legsrestaurant.com – Closed Sunday dinner, Monday and Tuesday*

Laughing Heart

MODERN CUISINE • WINE BAR A wine bar for our age and as joyful as the name suggests. It comes with a great vibe, lovely service and a flexible menu of cleverly paired seasonal ingredients with occasional Asian flavours. Natural wines are the focus of the wine list and the small wine shop downstairs.

Carte £ 19/40

Town plan: 14U3-s – *277 Hackney Rd ✉ E2 8NA – ⊖ Hoxton – ✆ 020 7686 9535 – www.thelaughingheartlondon.com – dinner only and Sunday lunch*

Hoxton

Beagle

TRADITIONAL BRITISH • RUSTIC Occupying three vast converted railway arches: one houses the bar; one the dining room; and the third is the kitchen. The British menu, with touches of Italian, changes twice a day and its contents are determined by the seasons.

Carte £ 27/46

Town plan: 20U4-a – *397-400 Geffrye St ✉ E2 8HZ – ⊖ Hoxton – ✆ 020 7613 2967 – www.beaglelondon.co.uk – Closed Sunday dinner*

Morito

SPANISH • SIMPLE Sam and Sam Clark's second Morito has all the utilitarianism of its older sister but much more space. Small plates draw their influences from Spain, North Africa and the Eastern Mediterranean, including the chef's homeland, Crete.

Carte £ 25/40

Town plan: 14U3-o – *195 Hackney Rd ✉ E2 8JL – ⊖ Hoxton – ✆ 020 7613 0754 – www.moritohackneyroad.co.uk – Closed Christmas, Monday lunch and bank holidays*

Sardine

FRENCH • FASHIONABLE A trendy, compact restaurant with a communal table at the heart of proceedings. The food comes from Southern France, and dishes are rustic, unfussy and very tasty; try the lamb à la ficelle, cooked over an open fire.

Carte £ 26/40

Town plan: 19T4-r – *Parasol Art Gallery, 15 Micawber St ✉ N1 7TB – ⊖ Old Street – ✆ 020 7490 0144 (booking essential) – www.sardine.london – Closed Christmas-New Year and Monday lunch*

M by Montcalm

BUSINESS • DESIGN Contemporary hotel with a designer style, set within a striking modern building. Appropriately for a hotel in Tech City, you can control the bedroom lighting, music, etc. from the bedside iPad. Relaxed ground floor restaurant with a mezzanine cocktail bar; modern British brasserie with city views.

269 rooms – †£ 140/330 ††£ 180/400

Town plan: 19T4-m – *151-157 City Rd ✉ EC1V 1JH – ⊖ Old Street – ✆ 020 3837 3000 – www.mbymontcalm.co.uk*

London Fields

Ellory (Matthew Young)

MODERN CUISINE • SIMPLE On the ground floor of Netil House is this unpretentious, stripped back restaurant with an open kitchen and a turntable. No-frills menu of Mediterranean-influenced small plates; unfussy modern dishes are perfectly balanced and rich in flavour. Well-priced European wine list with a good selection by the glass.

→ Chicory with walnut and Ossau-Iraty cheese. Brill with lovage and parsley root. Pear sorbet, parmesan and olive oil.

Menu £ 30/42 – Carte £ 32/43

Town plan: 14V3-e – *Netil House, 1 Westgate St ✉ E8 3RL – ⊖ London Fields – ✆ 020 3095 9455 – www.ellorylondon.com – dinner only and lunch Saturday-Sunday – Closed 23 December-3 January*

Hill & Szrok

MEATS AND GRILLS • NEIGHBOURHOOD X Butcher's shop by day; restaurant by night, with a central marble-topped table, counters around the edge and a friendly, lively feel. Daily blackboard menu of top quality meats, including steaks aged for a minimum of 60 days. No bookings.

Carte £ 20/57

Town plan: 14V3-z - *60 Broadway Market ✉ E8 4QJ - ⊖ Bethnal Green - ✆ 020 7254 8805 (bookings not accepted) - www.hillandszrok.co.uk - dinner only and Sunday lunch - Closed 23 December-3 January*

Lardo

ITALIAN • BISTRO X A delightful Italian eatery with a big open kitchen and a faux industrial look; housed in the striking 1930s Arthaus building. Daily menu of tasty small plates; try the succulent home-cured meats and the terrific pizzas.

Carte £ 26/43

Town plan: 14V2-h - *197-205 Richmond Rd ✉ E8 3NJ - ⊖ Hackney Central - ✆ 020 8985 2683 - www.lardo.co.uk - Closed 24 December-2 January*

Market Cafe

MEDITERRANEAN CUISINE • NEIGHBOURHOOD X This former pub by the canal appeals to local hipsters with its retro looks, youthful service team and Italian-influenced menu. Cooking is fresh and generous and uses some produce from the local market; homemade pasta a feature.

Carte £ 19/31

Town plan: 14V3-m - *2 Broadway Mkt ✉ E8 4QG - ⊖ Bethnal Green - ✆ 020 7249 9070 - www.market-cafe.co.uk - Closed 25 December*

Pidgin

MODERN BRITISH • NEIGHBOURHOOD X A cosy, single room restaurant with understated décor and a lively atmosphere, tucked away on a residential Hackney street. The no-choice four course menu of modern British dishes changes weekly, as does the interesting wine list.

Menu £ 45 - tasting menu only

Town plan: 14V2-d - *52 Wilton Way ✉ E8 1BG - ⊖ Hackney Central - ✆ 020 7254 8311 (booking essential) - www.pidginlondon.com - dinner only and lunch Saturday and Sunday - Closed Christmas-New Year, Monday and Tuesday*

Shoreditch

HKK

CHINESE • ELEGANT XX Cantonese has always been considered the finest of the Chinese cuisines and here at HKK it is given an extra degree of refinement. Expect classic flavour combinations delivered in a modern way. The room is elegant and graceful; the service smooth and assured.

➜ Dim sum platter. Jasmine tea-smoked Chilean wagyu beef. Century egg with hazelnut, sesame and coffee.

Menu £ 94 (dinner) - Carte lunch £ 30/65

Town plan: 34AX1-h - *88 Worship St ✉ EC2A 2BE - ⊖ Liverpool Street - ✆ 020 3535 1888 - www.hkklondon.com - Closed Sunday and bank holidays*

Clove Club (Isaac McHale)

MODERN CUISINE • TRENDY X The smart, blue-tiled open kitchen takes centre stage in this sparse room at Shoreditch Town Hall. Menus showcase expertly sourced produce in dishes that are full of originality, verve and flair - but where flavours are expertly judged and complementary; fish and seafood are a highlight.

➜ Raw Orkney scallop with mandarin, hazelnut and Périgord truffle. Grilled red mullet with new season onions, cinnamon and curry leaf sauce. Amalfi lemonade and Kampot pepper ice cream.

Menu £ 75/110 - Carte lunch £ 35/56

Town plan: 20U4-c - *380 Old St ✉ EC1V 9LT - ⊖ Old Street - ✆ 020 7729 6496 (bookings advisable at dinner) - www.thecloveclub.com - Closed 2 weeks Christmas-New Year, August bank holiday, Monday lunch and Sunday*

Lyle's (James Lowe)

MODERN BRITISH • SIMPLE The young chef-owner is an acolyte of Fergus Henderson and delivers similarly unadulterated flavours from seasonal British produce, albeit from a set menu at dinner. This pared-down approach extends to a room that's high on functionality, but considerable warmth comes from the keen young service team.

→ Monkfish liver with blood orange. Red mullet with cured roe and turnip tops. Sleightlett cheese ice cream with burnt pear and goat's whey.

Menu £ 55 (dinner) - Carte lunch £ 37/47

Town plan: 20U4-g - *Tea Building, 56 Shoreditch High St ✉ E1 6JJ - ⊖ Shoreditch High Street - ✆ 020 3011 5911 - www.lyleslondon.com - Closed Sunday and bank holidays*

Popolo

MEDITERRANEAN CUISINE • TRENDY Skimmed concrete floors and exposed brick walls give this restaurant a utilitarian feel; sit at the counter and chat to the chefs as they work. Italian, Spanish and North African influences feature on the menu of small plates. Pasta is a highlight and classic, simply cooked dishes allow the ingredients to shine.

Carte £ 22/35

Town plan: 19T4-c - *26 Rivington St ✉ EC2A 3DU - ⊖ Old Street - ✆ 020 7729 4299 (bookings not accepted) - www.popoloshoreditch.com - Closed Sunday and Monday*

L'Anima

ITALIAN • FASHIONABLE Very handsome room, with limestone and leather creating a sophisticated, glamorous environment. Appealing menu is a mix of Italian classics and less familiar dishes, with the emphasis firmly on flavour. Service is smooth and personable.

Carte £ 36/70

Town plan: 34AX1-a - *1 Snowden St, Broadgate West ✉ EC2A 2DQ - ⊖ Liverpool Street - ✆ 020 7422 7000 (booking essential) - www.lanima.co.uk - Closed 25-26 December, Sunday and bank holidays*

Eyre Brothers

SPANISH • ELEGANT Sleek, confidently run and celebrating all things Iberian, as well as drawing on the brothers' memories of their childhood in Mozambique. Delicious hams; terrific meats cooked over lumpwood charcoal. If in a larger group, pre-order paella or a whole suckling pig. Tapas is served in the bar.

Carte £ 29/54

Town plan: 19T4-k - *70 Leonard St ✉ EC2A 4QX - ⊖ Old Street - ✆ 020 7613 5346 - www.eyrebrothers.co.uk - Closed 24 December-4 January, Saturday lunch, Sunday and bank holidays*

L'Anima Café

ITALIAN • BRASSERIE A baby sister to L'Anima around the corner but more than a mere café: this is a big, bright restaurant with a busy bar and deli. The fairly priced menu includes plenty of pizza and pasta dishes. A DJ plays on Thursdays and Fridays.

Carte £ 15/32

Town plan: 34AX1-h - *10 Appold St ✉ EC2A 2AP - ⊖ Liverpool Street - ✆ 020 7422 7080 - www.lanimacafe.co.uk - Closed Saturday, Sunday and bank holidays*

Merchants Tavern

TRADITIONAL BRITISH • BRASSERIE The 'pub' part - a Victorian warehouse - gives way to a large restaurant with the booths being the prized seats. The cooking is founded on the sublime pleasures of seasonal British cooking, in reassuringly familiar combinations.

Carte £ 29/48

Town plan: 20U4-t - *36 Charlotte Rd ✉ EC2A 3PG - ⊖ Old Street - ✆ 020 7060 5335 - www.merchantstavern.co.uk - Closed 25-26 December and 1 January*

Andina

PERUVIAN • SIMPLE Andina may be smaller and slightly more chaotic that its sister Ceviche, but this friendly picantería with live music is equally popular. The Peruvian specialities include great salads and skewers, and ceviche that packs a punch.

Carte £13/28

Town plan: 20U4-w - *1 Redchurch St ✉ E2 7DJ - ⊖ Shoreditch High Street - ✆ 020 7920 6499 (booking essential) - www.andinalondon.com*

Oklava

TURKISH • BISTRO An oklava is a traditional Turkish rolling pin used to make pastries and pides, both of which appear on the menu; for the chef is a Turkish Cypriot and cooks her 'small plate' interpretations of classic dishes from these countries.

Menu £18 (weekday lunch) - Carte £17/30

Town plan: 20U4-r - *74 Luke St ✉ EC2A 4PY - ⊖ Old Street - ✆ 020 7729 3032 (booking essential) - www.oklava.co.uk - Closed Saturday lunch, Sunday dinner, Monday and bank holidays*

Tramshed

MEATS AND GRILLS • BRASSERIE A 1905 Grade II warehouse is home to Mark Hix's cavernous brasserie. The Damien Hirst cow and cockerel in formaldehyde give a clue to the menu - it's all about chicken and beef. Swainson House Farm chickens and Glenarm steaks are accurately cooked and delicious.

Carte £20/65

Town plan: 20U4-d - *32 Rivington St ✉ EC2A 3LX - ⊖ Old Street - ✆ 020 7749 0478 - www.chickenandsteak.co.uk - Closed 25 December*

Princess of Shoreditch

TRADITIONAL BRITISH • PUB There has been a pub on this corner site since 1742 but it is doubtful many of the previous incarnations were as busy or as pleasant as the Princess is today. The best dishes are those with a rustic edge, such as goose rillettes or chicken pie.

Menu £25/32 - Carte £26/38

Town plan: 19T4-a - *76-78 Paul St ✉ EC2A 4NE - ⊖ Old Street - ✆ 020 7729 9270 (booking essential) - www.theprincessofshoreditch.com - Closed 24-26 December*

Ace Hotel

BUSINESS • MINIMALIST What better location for this achingly trendy hotel than hipster-central itself - Shoreditch. Locals are welcomed in, the lobby has a DJ, urban-chic rooms have day-beds if you want friends over and the minibars offer everything from Curly Wurlys to champagne. British favourites in the stylish brasserie.

258 rooms - 🚹£179/359 🚹🚹£230/409 - ☕£15 - 3 suites

Town plan: 20U4-p - *100 Shoreditch High St ✉ E1 6JQ - ⊖ Shoreditch High Street - ✆ 020 7613 9800 - www.acehotel.com*

Courthouse H. Shoreditch (N)

HISTORIC BUILDING • CONTEMPORARY Former magistrates' court and police station; a quirky mix of original features and modern amenities including a cinema, bowling alley and roof terrace. Contemporary bedrooms boast high levels of facilities. The Kray twins were once incarcerated in what is now the bar - and tried in the panelled dining room.

128 rooms ☕ - 🚹£179/600 🚹🚹£179/600 - 42 suites

Town plan: 20U4-v - *335-337 Old St ✉ EC1V 9LL - ⊖ Old Street - ✆ 020 3310 5555 - www.shoreditch.courthouse-hotel.com*

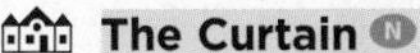

The Curtain

BUSINESS · TRENDY A trendy, fun hotel which used to be a warehouse used for raves. The stylish, comfortable bedrooms feature original art and steam showers. Enjoy a taco and tequila in Tienda Roosteria, soul food from Harlem in Red Rooster or brasserie dishes in rooftop Lido. Live music in members club, LP.

120 rooms – £ 200/260 £ 200/260 – £ 24 – 5 suites

Town plan: 20U4-e – *45 Curtain Rd ✉ EC2A 3PT – ⊖ Old Street – ✆ 020 3146 4545 – www.thecurtain.com*

Nobu H. Shoreditch

BUSINESS · DESIGN The UK's first Nobu hotel is an impressive modern building with a super-stylish interior, hidden away in the streets of Shoreditch. Comfortable bedrooms have a subtle industrial feel and offer state-of-the-art TVs. The 35th branch of the renowned Nobu restaurant serves its modern Japanese cuisine in the basement.

150 rooms – £ 315/409 £ 315/409 – 4 suites

Town plan: 19T4-h – *10-50 Willow St ✉ EC2A 4BH – ⊖ Old Street – ✆ 020 7683 1200 – www.nobuhotelshoreditch.com*

Boundary

LUXURY · DESIGN Owned by Sir Terence Conran, this converted warehouse boasts individually styled bedrooms, studios and duplex loft suites which are cool, stylish and bursting with personality. Basement Tratra for rustic French-inspired cooking; Rooftop has a relaxed Mediterranean flavour; Albion is an all-day café with something for everyone.

17 rooms – £ 190/600 £ 190/600 – £ 12 – 5 suites

Town plan: 20U4 – *2-4 Boundary St ✉ E2 7DD – ⊖ Shoreditch High Street – ✆ 020 7729 1051 – www.theboundary.co.uk*

The Hoxton

BUSINESS · QUIRKY Industrial-style urban lodge with a rakish, relaxed air, youthful clientele and even younger staff. Bedrooms are compact but have some nice touches; choose a 'concept' room for something different. Open-plan restaurant with American menu and great cocktails.

210 rooms – £ 99/299 £ 99/299

Town plan: 19T4-x – *81 Great Eastern St. ✉ EC2A 3HU – ⊖ Old Street – ✆ 020 7550 1000 – www.thehoxton.com*

South Hackney

Empress

TRADITIONAL BRITISH · PUB An 1850s neighbourhood pub with a short, simple and pleasingly seasonal menu of traditional British dishes with the occasional Mediterranean influence. Service is friendly and you can bring your own bottle on Tuesday nights.

Carte £ 24/34

Town plan: 3F3-d – *130 Lauriston Rd, Victoria Park ✉ E9 7LH – ⊖ Homerton. – ✆ 020 8533 5123 – www.empresse9.co.uk – Closed 25-27 December and Monday lunch except bank holidays*

Michelin

HAMMERSMITH and FULHAM

Fulham

Harwood Arms

MODERN BRITISH • PUB Its reputation may have spread like wildfire but this remains a proper, down-to-earth pub that just happens to serve really good food. The cooking is very seasonal, proudly British, full of flavour and doesn't seem out of place in this environment. Service is suitably relaxed and friendly.

→ Cornish crab and herb muffin. Braised shoulder of venison, smoked bone marrow tart and beets. Lemon curd doughnuts with Earl Grey cream.

Menu £ 36/43

Town plan: 22M7-a - *Walham Grove ✉ SW6 1QP - ⊖ Fulham Broadway. - ✆ 020 7386 1847 (booking essential) - www.harwoodarms.com - Closed 24-27 December, 1 January and Monday lunch except bank holidays*

Claude's Kitchen

MODERN CUISINE • BISTRO Two operations in one converted pub: 'Amuse Bouche' is a well-priced champagne bar; upstairs is an intimate dining room with a weekly changing menu. The cooking is colourful and fresh, with the odd challenging flavour combination.

Menu £ 20 - Carte £ 29/39

Town plan: 22M8-a - *51 Parsons Green Ln ✉ SW6 4JA - ⊖ Parsons Green. - ✆ 020 3813 3223 (booking essential) - www.amusebouchelondon.com - dinner only - Closed Sunday*

Koji

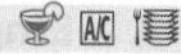

JAPANESE • WINE BAR A fun, contemporary wine bar serving Japanese food. The menu mixes the modern and the classic, with tempura and dishes from the robata grill particularly popular; food is full of flavour and the kitchen clearly know their craft.

Carte £ 40/65

Town plan: 22NZH-e - *58 New King's Rd ✉ SW6 4LS - ⊖ Parsons Green - ✆ 020 7731 2520 - www.koji.restaurant - Closed 24-26 December and Monday*

Manuka Kitchen

MODERN CUISINE • RUSTIC The two young owners run their simple little restaurant with great enthusiasm and their prices are keen. Like the magical Manuka honey, the chef is from New Zealand; his menu is varied and his food is wholesome and full of flavour.

Menu £ 15 (weekday lunch) - Carte £ 26/37

Town plan: 22M8-k - *510 Fulham Rd ✉ SW6 5NJ - ⊖ Fulham Broadway - ✆ 020 7736 7588 - www.manukakitchen.com - Closed 25-26 December, Sunday dinner and Monday lunch*

Tendido Cuatro

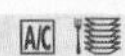

SPANISH • NEIGHBOURHOOD X Along with tapas, the speciality is paella. Designed for a hungry two, they vary from seafood to quail and chorizo; vegetarian to cuttlefish ink. Vivid colours used with abandon deck out the busy room.

Menu £30 (lunch and early dinner) – Carte £16/41

Town plan: 22M8-x – *108-110 New Kings Rd ✉ SW6 4LY – ⊖ Parsons Green – ☎ 020 7371 5147 – www.cambiodetercio.co.uk – Closed 2 weeks Christmas*

Tommy Tucker

TRADITIONAL BRITISH • PUB The old Pelican pub was revamped by the owners of nearby Claude's Kitchen. It's bright and open plan, with an unstructured menu divided under headings of 'meat', 'fish' and 'fruit and veg'. The cooking is rustic and satisfying.

Carte £19/39

Town plan: 22M8-s – *22 Waterford Rd ✉ SW6 2DR – ⊖ Fulham Broadway. – ☎ 020 7736 1023 – www.thetommytucker.com*

Hammersmith

River Café (Ruth Rogers)

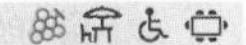

ITALIAN • FASHIONABLE XX It's more than 30 years since this iconic restaurant opened, and superlative ingredients are still at the centre of everything they do. Dishes come in hearty portions and are bursting with authentic Italian flavours. The on-view kitchen with its wood-fired oven dominates the stylish and buzzing riverside room.

→ Calamari ai ferri. Wood-roasted Dover sole with marjoram, lemon and artichoke alla Romana. Chocolate Nemesis.

Carte £61/85

Town plan: 21K7-c – *Thames Wharf, Rainville Rd ✉ W6 9HA – ⊖ Barons Court – ☎ 020 7386 4200 (booking essential) – www.rivercafe.co.uk – Closed Christmas-New Year and Sunday dinner*

Azou

NORTH AFRICAN • NEIGHBOURHOOD X Silks, lanterns and rugs add to the atmosphere of this personally run, North African restaurant. Most come for the excellent tajines with triple steamed couscous. Much is designed for sharing.

Carte £21/38

Town plan: 21J7-u – *375 King St ✉ W6 9NJ – ⊖ Stamford Brook – ☎ 020 8563 7266 (booking essential) – www.azou.co.uk – dinner only – Closed 1 January and 25 December*

L'Amorosa

ITALIAN • NEIGHBOURHOOD X Former Zafferano head chef Andy Needham has created a warm and sunny Italian restaurant – one that we'd all like to have in our high street. The quality of the produce shines through and homemade pasta dishes are a highlight.

Menu £17 (weekday lunch) – Carte £25/39

Town plan: 21K7-s – *278 King St ✉ W6 0SP – ⊖ Ravenscourt Park – ☎ 020 8563 0300 – www.lamorosa.co.uk – Closed 1 week August, 1 week Christmas, Sunday dinner, Monday and bank holidays*

Indian Zing

INDIAN • NEIGHBOURHOOD XX Chef-owner Manoj Vasaikar seeks inspiration from across India. His cooking balances the traditional with the more contemporary and delivers many layers of flavour – the lamb dishes and breads are particularly good. The restaurant is always busy yet service remains courteous and unhurried.

Menu £14/27 – Carte £21/44

Town plan: 21K7-a – *236 King St. ✉ W6 0RF – ⊖ Ravenscourt Park – ☎ 020 8748 5959 – www.indianzing.co.uk*

Brackenbury 

MEDITERRANEAN CUISINE • NEIGHBOURHOOD X A much loved neighbourhood restaurant given a new lease of life. The kitchen looks to Italy, France and the Med for inspiration and doesn't waste time on presentation; dishes feel instinctive and flavours marry well.

Menu £ 16 (weekday lunch) – Carte £ 23/47

Town plan: 15K6-c – *129 - 131 Brackenbury Rd ✉ W6 0BQ – ⊖ Ravenscourt Park – ✆ 020 8741 4928 – www.brackenburyrestaurant.co.uk – Closed Christmas, New Year, Easter, August bank holiday, Sunday and Monday*

Anglesea Arms 

MODERN BRITISH • NEIGHBOURHOOD One of the daddies of the gastropub movement. The seasonal menu gives the impression it's written by a Brit who occasionally holidays on the Med – along with robust dishes are some that display a pleasing lightness of touch.

Carte £ 24/36

Town plan: 15K6-e – *35 Wingate Rd ✉ W6 0UR – ⊖ Ravenscourt Park – ✆ 020 8749 1291 – www.angleseaarmspub.co.uk – Closed 24-26 December*

Shepherd's Bush

Shikumen

CHINESE • INTIMATE XX Impressive homemade dim sum at lunch and excellent Peking duck are the standouts at this unexpectedly sleek Cantonese restaurant in an otherwise undistinguished part of Shepherd's Bush.

Carte £ 19/48

Town plan: 15K6-s – *58 Shepherd's Bush Grn ✉ W12 8QE – ⊖ Shepherd's Bush – ✆ 020 8749 9978 – www.shikumen.co.uk – Closed 25 December*

HARINGEY

Crouch End

Bistro Aix 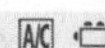

FRENCH • BISTRO X Dressers, cabinets and contemporary artwork lend an authentic Gallic edge to this bustling bistro, a favourite with many of the locals. Traditionally prepared French classics are the highlights of an extensive menu.

Menu £ 19/24 – Carte £ 25/50

Town plan: 3E2-v – *54 Topsfield Par, Tottenham Ln ✉ N8 8PT – ⊖ Crouch Hill – ✆ 020 8340 6346 – www.bistroaix.co.uk – dinner only and lunch Saturday-Sunday – Closed 24, 26 December and 1 January*

HARROW

Pinner

Friends

TRADITIONAL BRITISH • COSY XX This characterful, low-beamed restaurant has been proudly and personally run for over 20 years – and has a history stretching back over 500 more. Cooking is classical and carefully done, and the service is well-paced and friendly.

Menu £ 18 (weekday lunch) – Carte £ 28/46

Town plan: 1B2-a – *11 High St ✉ HA5 5PJ – ⊖ Pinner – ✆ 020 8866 0286 – www.friendsrestaurant.co.uk – Closed 25-26 December, 26-27 May, Sunday dinner, Monday and bank holidays*

HEATHROW AIRPORT

Mr Todiwala's Kitchen

INDIAN • FRIENDLY XX Secreted within the Hilton is Cyrus Todiwala's appealingly stylish, fresh-looking restaurant. The choice ranges from street food to tandoor dishes, Goan classics to Parsee specialities; order the 'Kitchen menu' for the full experience.

Carte £ 25/55

Hilton London Heathrow Airport Terminal 5 Hotel, Poyle Rd, Colnbrook ⊠ SL3 OFF - West : 2.5 mi by A 3113 - ✆ 01753 766482 - www.hilton.com/heathrowt5 - dinner only - Closed Christmas and Sunday

Hilton London Heathrow Airport Terminal 5

BUSINESS • MODERN A feeling of light and space pervades this modern, corporate hotel. Soundproofed rooms are fitted to a good standard; the spa offers wide-ranging treatments. Open-plan Gallery for British comfort food.

350 rooms - †£ 139/345 ††£ 159/375 - 4 suites

Poyle Rd, Colnbrook ⊠ SL3 OFF - West : 2.5 mi by A 3113 - ✆ 01753 686860 - www.hilton.com/heathrowt5

Mr Todiwala's Kitchen - See restaurant listing

Sofitel

BUSINESS • CONTEMPORARY Smart and well-run contemporary hotel, designed around a series of atriums, with direct access to T5. Crisply decorated, comfortable bedrooms with luxurious bathrooms. Choice of restaurant: international or classic French cuisine.

605 rooms - †£ 169/329 ††£ 199/359 - 27 suites

Town plan: 5A4-a - *Terminal 5, Heathrow Airport ⊠ TW6 2GD - ⊖ Heathrow Terminal 5 - ✆ 020 8757 5029 - www.sofitelheathrow.com*

HOUNSLOW

Chiswick

Hedone (Mikael Jonsson)

MODERN CUISINE • DESIGN XX Mikael Jonsson, former lawyer turned chef, is not one for complacency, so his restaurant continues to evolve. The content of his surprise menus is governed entirely by what ingredients are in their prime - and it is this passion for produce which underpins the superlative and very flavoursome cooking.

→ Devon crab with velvet crab consommé, hazelnut mayonnaise and Granny Smith apple. Hare à la royale. Vanilla millefeuille with balsamic vinegar.

Menu £ 95/135 - surprise menu only

Town plan: 6C4-g - *301-303 Chiswick High Rd ⊠ W4 4HH - ⊖ Chiswick Park - ✆ 020 8747 0377 (booking essential) - www.hedonerestaurant.com - dinner only and lunch Friday-Saturday - Closed 2 weeks summer, 2 weeks Christmas-New Year, Sunday and Monday*

La Trompette

MODERN BRITISH • NEIGHBOURHOOD XX Chez Bruce's sister is a delightful neighbourhood restaurant that's now a little roomier. The service is charming and the food terrific. Dishes at lunch are quite simple but great value; the cooking at dinner is a tad more elaborate.

→ Raw bream, bonito, shimeji, shiso cress and English wasabi. Crisp suckling pig shoulder, creamed polenta, grapes, cavolo nero and chilli. Banana soufflé with gingerbread and passion fruit ice cream.

Menu £ 35 (weekday lunch)/55

Town plan: 21J7-y - *5-7 Devonshire Rd ⊠ W4 2EU - ⊖ Turnham Green - ✆ 020 8747 1836 (booking essential) - www.latrompette.co.uk - Closed 24-26 December and 1 January*

Charlotte's Bistro

MODERN CUISINE • NEIGHBOURHOOD XX A pleasant, unpretentious bistro; run by a friendly team, with a well-priced menu of flavoursome, well-prepared dishes of largely European provenance. Little sister to Charlotte's Place in Ealing.

Menu £ 25/35

Town plan: 21J7-a – *6 Turnham Green Terr ✉ W4 1QP – ⊖ Turnham Green – ✆ 020 8742 3590 (booking advisable) – www.charlottes.co.uk*

Michael Nadra

MODERN CUISINE • NEIGHBOURHOOD XX Half way down a residential side street is this intimate little place where the closely set tables add to the bonhomie. Dishes are modern, colourful and quite elaborate in their make-up; it's worth going for the sensibly priced set menu and the chosen wines.

Menu £ 28/39

Town plan: 21J7-z – *6-8 Elliott Rd ✉ W4 1PE – ⊖ Turnham Green – ✆ 020 8742 0766 – www.restaurant-michaelnadra.co.uk – Closed 24-28 December, 1 January and Sunday dinner*

High Road Brasserie

FRENCH • FASHIONABLE X An authentic brasserie with mirrors, panelling, art deco lighting and a menu that offers something for everyone. Despite the high volume of customers, the classic dishes are prepared with care and staff cope well with being busy.

Carte £ 20/36

Town plan: 21J7-e – *High Road House Hotel, 162 Chiswick High Rd. ✉ W4 1PR – ⊖ Turnham Green – ✆ 020 8742 7474 (booking essential) – www.highroadhouse.co.uk*

Smokehouse Chiswick

TRADITIONAL BRITISH • NEIGHBOURHOOD A sizeable pub with a delightful rear garden is the site of the second Smokehouse. The Belted Galloway burgers with pulled pork fly out of the kitchen but the winning dish is the short rib Bourguignon with creamy mash.

Carte £ 26/34

Town plan: 6C4-s – *12 Sutton Ln North ✉ W4 4LD – ⊖ Chiswick Park. – ✆ 020 3819 6066 – www.smokehousechiswick.co.uk – dinner only and lunch Friday to Sunday*

High Road House

TOWNHOUSE • MINIMALIST A cool, sleek hotel and club; the latter a slick place to lounge around or play games. Light, bright bedrooms come with crisp linen and good facilities. This is a carefully appointed and fairly-priced destination.

14 rooms – †£ 140/285 ††£ 140/285 – ☕ £ 22

Town plan: 21J7-e – *162 Chiswick High Rd ✉ W4 1PR – (High Rd House Hotel) – ⊖ Turnham Green – ✆ 020 8742 1717 – www.highroadhouse.co.uk*

High Road Brasserie – See restaurant listing

Michelin

ISLINGTON

Archway

500

ITALIAN • FRIENDLY X Small, fun and well-priced Italian that's always busy. Good pastas and bread; the veal chop and rabbit are specialities. The passion of the ebullient owner and keen chef are evident.

Carte £ 26/34

Town plan: 12R1-y – *782 Holloway Rd ✉ N19 3JH – ⊖ Archway – ✆ 020 7272 3406 (booking essential) – www.500restaurant.co.uk – dinner only and lunch Friday-Sunday – Closed 2 weeks summer and 2 weeks Christmas-New Year*

St John's Tavern

MODERN CUISINE • PUB A Junction Road landmark with friendly service and a great selection of artisan beers. Tapas is served in the front bar; head to the vast, hugely appealing rear dining room for well-crafted British and Mediterranean dishes.

Carte £ 21/36

Town plan: 12Q1-s – *91 Junction Rd ✉ N19 5QU – ⊖ Archway. – ✆ 020 7272 1587 (booking advisable) – www.stjohnstavern.com – Closed 25-26 December and Monday lunch*

Canonbury

Primeur

MODERN CUISINE • SIMPLE X A relaxed neighbourhood restaurant whose concertina doors fold back to reveal a quirky interior with counter seating around the edges and a huge communal table. Plates are small and designed for sharing; understated but packed with flavour – simplicity is key, allowing the ingredients to really shine.

Menu £ 30/35 – Carte £ 16/33

Town plan: 13T2-p – *116 Petherton Rd ✉ N5 2RT – ⊖ Canonbury – ✆ 020 7226 5271 – www.primeurn5.co.uk – Closed Christmas, Sunday dinner, Monday and Tuesday-Thursday lunch*

Trullo

ITALIAN • NEIGHBOURHOOD X A neighbourhood gem split over two floors; its open kitchen serving an ingredient-led daily menu. Harmonious, tried-and-tested combinations create rustic, full-flavoured Italian dishes, including meats and fish cooked on the charcoal grill and delicious fresh pasta, hand-rolled before each service.

Carte £ 28/45

Town plan: 13S2-t – *300-302 St Paul's Rd ✉ N1 2LH – ⊖ Highbury & Islington – ✆ 020 7226 2733 (booking essential) – www.trullorestaurant.com – Closed 25-26 December and Sunday dinner*

Canonbury Kitchen

ITALIAN • NEIGHBOURHOOD A bright, local Italian with seating for just 40; exposed brick walls and painted floorboards add to the fresh feel. The kitchen keeps things simple and the menu pricing is prudent.

Menu £ 14 – Carte £ 27/37

Town plan: 13S3-c – *19 Canonbury Ln ✉ N1 2AS – ⊖ Highbury & Islington – ✆ 020 7226 9791 – www.canonburykitchen.com – dinner only and lunch Saturday-Sunday – Closed Sunday dinner*

Smokehouse

MODERN CUISINE • PUB You can smell the oak chips in the smoker as you approach this warm, modern pub. Meat is the mainstay – the peppered ox cheeks are a firm favourite – but whilst flavours are gutsy, the smoking and barbecuing is never overpowering.

Carte £ 28/35

Town plan: 13T3-h – *63-69 Canonbury Rd ✉ N1 2DG – ⊖ Highbury & Islington. – ✆ 020 7354 1144 (booking advisable) – www.smokehouseislington.co.uk – Closed 24-26 December and lunch Monday-Thursday except bank holidays*

Clerkenwell

St John

TRADITIONAL BRITISH • SIMPLE A glorious celebration of British fare and a champion of 'nose to tail' eating. Utilitarian surroundings and a refreshing lack of ceremony ensure the food is the focus; it's appealingly simple, full of flavour and very satisfying.

→ Roast bone marrow with parsley salad. Pigeon and trotter pie. Dr Henderson ice cream.

Carte £ 27/61

Town plan: 33AU1-k – *26 St John St ✉ EC1M 4AY – ⊖ Farringdon – ✆ 020 7251 0848 (booking essential) – www.stjohnrestaurant.com – Closed Christmas-New Year, Saturday lunch, Sunday dinner and bank holidays*

Comptoir Gascon

FRENCH • BISTRO A buzzy, well-priced restaurant; sister to Club Gascon. Rustic and satisfying specialities from the SW of France include wine, bread, cheese and plenty of duck, with cassoulet and duck rillettes perennial favourites and the duck burger popular at lunch. There's also produce on display to take home.

Carte £ 18/34

Town plan: 32AT1-a – *61-63 Charterhouse St. ✉ EC1M 6HJ – ⊖ Farringdon – ✆ 020 7608 0851 (booking essential) – www.comptoirgascon.com – Closed Christmas-New Year, Sunday, Monday and bank holidays*

Luca N

ITALIAN • DESIGN Owned by the people behind The Clove Club, but less a little sister, more a distant cousin. There's a cheery atmosphere, a bar for small plates and a frequently changing menu of Italian dishes made with quality British ingredients.

Menu £ 55 – Carte £ 32/52

Town plan: 33AU1-c – *88 St. John St ✉ EC1M 4EH – ⊖ Farringdon – ✆ 020 3859 3000 (booking essential) – www.luca.restaurant – Closed Sunday*

Sosharu

JAPANESE • FASHIONABLE The seventh London restaurant from Jason Atherton and the first serving Japanese food is this bustling operation with a chic, understated style. Six small plates with a large rice pot or a 'classic' between two will do nicely.

Menu £ 30 (lunch and early dinner) – Carte £ 28/50

Town plan: 32AT1-s – *64 Turnmill St ✉ EC1M 5RR – ⊖ Farringdon – ✆ 020 3805 2304 – www.sosharulondon.com – Closed Sunday and bank holidays except Good Friday*

Foxlow

MEATS AND GRILLS • NEIGHBOURHOOD ꭗ From the clever Hawksmoor people comes this fun and funky place where the staff ensure everyone's having a good time. There are steaks available but plenty of other choices too, with influences from Italy, Asia and the Middle East.

Menu £ 18 – Carte £ 22/39

Town plan: 33AU1-b – *69-73 St John St ✉ EC1M 4AN – ⊖ Farringdon – ✆ 020 7680 2702 – www.foxlow.co.uk – Closed 24 December-1 January and bank holidays*

Granger & Co. Clerkenwell

MODERN CUISINE • FAMILY ꭗ Aussie food writer and restaurateur Bill Granger's 2nd London branch is a stylish affair. His food is inspired by his travels, with the best dishes being those enlivened with the flavours of SE Asia; his breakfasts are also renowned.

Carte £ 13/39

Town plan: 19S4-y – *50 Sekforde St ✉ EC1R 0HA – ⊖ Farringdon – ✆ 020 7251 9032 – www.grangerandco.com – Closed 24-26 December and Sunday dinner*

Hix Oyster and Chop House

TRADITIONAL BRITISH • BISTRO ꭗ Appropriately utilitarian surroundings put the focus on seasonal and often underused British ingredients. Cooking is satisfying and unfussy, with plenty of oysters and aged beef served on the bone.

Menu £ 15 (lunch) – Carte £ 15/48

Town plan: 33AU1-e – *36-37 Greenhill Rents ✉ EC1M 6BN – ⊖ Farringdon – ✆ 020 7017 1930 – www.hixoysterandchophouse.co.uk – Closed 25-29 December and bank holidays*

Palatino (N)

ITALIAN • DESIGN ꭗ Stevie Parle's latest restaurant is an airy, canteen-like, all-day spot with an open kitchen, yellow booths and an industrial feel. The seasonal Italian menu has a strong emphasis on Rome, with dishes like rigatoni with veal pajata.

Carte £ 18/38

Town plan: 19T4-p – *71 Central St ✉ EC1V 8AB – ⊖ Old Street – ✆ 020 3481 5300 – www.palatino.london – Closed Sunday*

Polpo Smithfield

ITALIAN • FRIENDLY ꭗ For his third Venetian-style bacaro, Russell Norman converted an old meat market storage facility; it has an elegantly battered feel. Head first for the Negroni bar downstairs; then over-order tasty, uncomplicated dishes to share.

Menu £ 28 – Carte £ 20/30

Town plan: 33AU1-u – *3 Cowcross St ✉ EC1M 6DR – ⊖ Farringdon. – ✆ 020 7250 0034 – www.polpo.co.uk – Closed Christmas, New Year and Sunday dinner*

Malmaison

TOWNHOUSE • MODERN Striking early 20C red-brick building overlooking a pleasant square. Stylish, comfy public areas. Bedrooms in vivid, bold colours, with plenty of extra touches. Modern brasserie with international menu; grilled meats a highlight.

97 rooms – †£ 119/350 ††£ 119/420 – ☕ £ 15

Town plan: 33AU1-q – *18-21 Charterhouse Sq ✉ EC1M 6AH – ⊖ Barbican – ✆ 020 7012 3700 – www.malmaison.com*

The Rookery

TOWNHOUSE • PERSONALISED A row of charmingly restored 18C houses which remain true to their roots courtesy of wood panelling, flagstone flooring, open fires and antique furnishings. Highly individual bedrooms have feature beds and Victorian bathrooms.

33 rooms – †£ 205/235 ††£ 235/349 – ☕£ 12 – 3 suites

Town plan: 33AU1-p – *12 Peters Ln, Cowcross St ✉ EC1M 6DS – ⊖ Farringdon – ✆ 020 7336 0931 – www.rookeryhotel.com*

Finsbury

Angler

SEAFOOD • ELEGANT XX It's built into the eaves of D&D's South Place hotel, but this 7th floor room feels very much like a stand-alone entity and is bright, elegant and intimate. Fish is the mainstay of the menu; its quality is supreme and the kitchen has a light, yet assured touch.

➜ Tartare of yellowfin tuna with avocado, wasabi and shiso. Cornish turbot with crab and Jersey Royals. Seville orange soufflé with toasted brioche ice cream and marmalade.

Menu £ 38 (weekday lunch) – Carte £ 61/72

Town plan: 33AW1-v – *South Place Hotel, 3 South Pl ✉ EC2M 2AF – ⊖ Moorgate – ✆ 020 3215 1260 (booking advisable) – www.anglerrestaurant.com – Closed 26-30 December, Saturday lunch and Sunday*

Morito

SPANISH • TAPAS BAR X From the owners of next door Moro comes this authentic and appealingly down to earth little tapas bar. Seven or eight dishes between two should suffice but over-ordering is easy and won't break the bank.

Carte £ 14/29

Town plan: 19S4-b – *32 Exmouth Mkt ✉ EC1R 4QE – ⊖ Farringdon – ✆ 020 7278 7007 – www.morito.co.uk – Closed 24 December-2 January, Sunday dinner and bank holidays*

The Modern Pantry Finsbury Square

WORLD CUISINE • BRASSERIE XX Spacious, elegant dining room on the ground floor of the imposing Alphabeta Building, with a lively bar counter for 'global tapas' and sherry liveners. Extensive menu of internationally influenced dishes; puddings are a highlight.

Carte £ 26/37

Town plan: 33AW1-m – *14 Finsbury Sq ✉ EC2A 1AH – ⊖ Moorgate – ✆ 020 3696 6565 – www.themodernpantry.co.uk – Closed 25 December and Sunday dinner*

Quality Chop House

TRADITIONAL BRITISH • COSY X In the hands of owners who respect its history, this 'progressive working class caterer' does a fine job of championing gutsy British grub; game is best but steaks from the butcher next door are also worth ordering. The terrific little wine list has lots of gems. The Grade II listed room, with its trademark booths, has been an eating house since 1869.

Carte £ 24/49

Town plan: 19S4-h – *92-94 Farringdon Rd ✉ EC1R 3EA – ⊖ Farringdon – ✆ 020 7278 1452 (booking advisable) – www.thequalitychophouse.com – Closed 24-31 December, Sunday dinner and bank holidays*

Caravan

WORLD CUISINE • TRENDY X A discernible Antipodean vibe pervades this casual eatery, from the laid-back charm of the service to the kitchen's confident combining of unusual flavours. Cooking is influenced by the owner's travels – hence the name.

Carte £ 18/35

Town plan: 19S4-c – *11-13 Exmouth Market ✉ EC1R 4QD – ⊖ Farringdon – ✆ 020 7833 8115 (booking advisable) – www.caravanrestaurants.co.uk – Closed 25-26, 31 December and 1 January*

Ceviche Old St

PERUVIAN • BRASSERIE Sister to the Soho original is this buzzy Peruvian restaurant in the former Alexandra Trust Dining Rooms, built by tea magnate Sir Thomas Lipton. Start with ceviche and a pisco sour; dishes are easy to eat, vibrant and full of flavour.

Menu £ 20/50 - Carte £ 15/37

Town plan: 19T4-s - *2 Baldwin St ✉ EC1V 9NU - ⊖ Old Street - ✆ 020 3327 9463 - www.cevicheuk.com*

Clerkenwell Kitchen

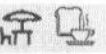

MODERN CUISINE • FRIENDLY The owner of this simple, friendly, tucked away eatery worked with Hugh Fearnley-Whittingstall and is committed to sustainability. Daily changing, well-sourced produce; fresh, flavoursome cooking.

Carte £ 15/28

Town plan: 19S4-v - *27-31 Clerkenwell Cl ✉ EC1R 0AT - ⊖ Farringdon - ✆ 020 7101 9959 (booking advisable) - www.theclerkenwellkitchen.co.uk - lunch only - Closed Christmas-New Year, Saturday, Sunday and bank holidays*

The Modern Pantry Clerkenwell

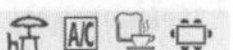

WORLD CUISINE • DESIGN Fusion cooking that uses complementary flavours to create vibrant, zesty dishes. The simple, crisp ground floor of this Georgian building has the buzz; upstairs is more intimate. Clued-up service.

Menu £ 26 (weekday lunch) - Carte £ 25/38

Town plan: 19S4-k - *47-48 St John's Sq. ✉ EC1V 4JJ - ⊖ Farringdon - ✆ 020 7553 9210 (booking advisable) - www.themodernpantry.co.uk - Closed August bank holiday and 25-26 December*

Moro

MEDITERRANEAN CUISINE • FRIENDLY It's the stuff of dreams - pack up your worldly goods, drive through Spain, Portugal, Morocco and the Sahara, and then back in London, open a restaurant and share your love of Moorish cuisine. The wood-fired oven and chargrill fill the air with wonderful aromas and food is vibrant and colourful.

Carte £ 32/42

Town plan: 19S4-m - *34-36 Exmouth Mkt ✉ EC1R 4QE - ⊖ Farringdon - ✆ 020 7833 8336 (booking essential) - www.moro.co.uk - Closed dinner 24 December-2 January, Sunday dinner and bank holidays*

South Place

BUSINESS • DESIGN Restaurant group D&D's first venture into the hotel business is a stylish affair; unsurprising as its interior was designed by Conran & Partners. Bedrooms are a treat for those with an eye for aesthetics and no detail has been forgotten. The ground floor hosts 3 South Place, a bustling bar and grill.

80 rooms - †£ 195/350 ††£ 195/350 - ☕ £ 25 - 1 suite

Town plan: 33AW1-v - *3 South Pl ✉ EC2M 2AF - ⊖ Moorgate - ✆ 020 3503 0000 - www.southplacehotel.com*

✿ **Angler** - See restaurant listing

Montcalm Royal London House (N)

BUSINESS • MODERN A modern business hotel overlooking Finsbury Square, stylish bedrooms come with their own aromatherapy machines and smart phones. Burdock bar features craft beers and some unique shuffleboard tables. 10th floor Aviary serves classic grill dishes and has a superb panorama of the city skyline from its terrace.

253 rooms - †£ 140/367 ††£ 200/552 - ☕ £ 25 - 16 suites

Town plan: 33AW1-h - *22-25 Finsbury Square ✉ EC2A 1DX - ⊖ Moorgate - ✆ 020 3873 4000 - www.montcalmroyallondoncity.co.uk*

Zetter

TOWNHOUSE • MODERN A trendy and discreet converted 19C warehouse with well-equipped bedrooms that come with pleasant touches, such as Penguin paperbacks. The more idiosyncratic Zetter Townhouse across the square is used as an overflow.

59 rooms – †£ 113/266 ††£ 113/266 – £ 16

Town plan: 19S4-s – *St John's Sq, 86-88 Clerkenwell Rd. ✉ EC1M 5RJ – ⊖ Farringdon – ✆ 020 7324 4444 – www.thezetter.com*

Highbury

Au Lac

VIETNAMESE • FRIENDLY X Sweet, long-standing Vietnamese restaurant run by two brothers. New dishes are regularly added to the already lengthy but authentic and keenly priced menu, whose dishes exhibit plenty of fresh and lively flavours.

Carte £ 12/24

Town plan: 13T1-b – *82 Highbury Park ✉ N5 2XE – ⊖ Arsenal – ✆ 020 7704 9187 – www.aulac.co.uk – dinner only and lunch Thursday-Friday – Closed 24-26 December, 1-2 January and 1 week early August*

Holloway

Westerns Laundry (N)

SEAFOOD • FASHIONABLE X Sister to Primeur and with the same industrial feel; set on the ground floor of a former laundry, with a pleasant front terrace. Sit at the kitchen counter or at one of the communal tables. The fish-focused menu is accompanied by natural wines and the confidently executed dishes are full of flavour.

Carte £ 25/33

Town plan: 13S2-w – *34 Drayton Pk ✉ N5 1PB – ⊖ Holloway Road – ✆ 020 7700 3700 (booking essential) – www.westernslaundry.com – Closed Monday, lunch Tuesday-Thursday and Sunday dinner*

Islington

Bellanger

FRENCH • BRASSERIE XX All-day brasserie, with the sumptuous style of an authentic grand café, modelled on those opened in Paris by the Alsatians at the turn of the century. Regional French and Alsatian-inspired fare is served from breakfast until late.

Menu £ 18 (lunch) – Carte £ 21/43

Town plan: 13S3-d – *9 Islington Grn ✉ N1 2XH – ⊖ Angel – ✆ 020 7226 2555 (bookings advisable at dinner) – www.bellanger.co.uk*

Drapers Arms

TRADITIONAL BRITISH • NEIGHBOURHOOD An imposing neighbourhood pub with warming fires, shabby-chic styling, a relaxed, unpretentious feel, a bevy of eager-to-please staff and a courtyard garden. They offer gutsy and satisfying seasonal British dishes, a great selection of regional ales and a well-thought-out wine list.

Carte £ 22/34

Town plan: 13S3-x – *44 Barnsbury St ✉ N1 1ER – ⊖ Highbury & Islington. – ✆ 020 7619 0348 (bookings advisable at dinner) – www.thedrapersarms.com – Closed 25-26 December*

Plaquemine Lock (N)

CREOLE • COSY A unique and very colourful pub named after a small city in Louisiana and with a menu centred around Creole and Cajun traditions. Dishes like gumbo with okra, blackened chicken, and crawfish with corn and potatoes are carefully cooked and packed with flavour. Big Easy style cocktails add to the fun.

Carte £ 20/30

Town plan: 13S3-e – *139 Graham St ✉ N1 8LB – ⊖ Angel – ✆ 020 7688 1488 – www.plaqlock.com – Closed 25 December*

Galley

SEAFOOD • BRASSERIE A smart, colourful seafood restaurant with a brasserie feel; there's a bar at the front and a few prized booths, but the best seats in the house are at the kitchen counter. The hot or cold seafood platters are great to share.

Menu £ 15 (weekday lunch) – Carte £ 22/57

Town plan: 13S3-a – *105-106 Upper St ✉ N1 1QN – ⊖ Highbury & Islington – ✆ 020 3670 0740 – www.galleylondon.co.uk – Closed 1 January*

Oldroyd

MODERN BRITISH • INTIMATE The eponymous Oldroyd is Tom, who left his role with the Polpo group to open this busy little bistro. It's all about small plates – ingredients are largely British, influences are from within Europe and dishes are very easy to eat.

Menu £ 19 (weekday lunch) – Carte £ 20/31

Town plan: 13S3-w – *344 Upper St ✉ N1 0PD – ⊖ Angel – ✆ 020 8617 9010 – www.oldroydlondon.com – Closed 25-26 December*

Ottolenghi

MEDITERRANEAN CUISINE • FASHIONABLE Two communal tables form the centrepiece of this coolly decorated deli/restaurant. The frequently changing menu offers fresh, vibrant flavours from the Med, North Africa and Middle East; three dishes each is about right.

Carte £ 23/45

Town plan: 13S3-k – *287 Upper St. ✉ N1 2TZ – ⊖ Highbury & Islington – ✆ 020 7288 1454 (booking essential) – www.ottolenghi.co.uk – Closed 25-26 December, Sunday dinner and bank holidays*

Radici

ITALIAN • RUSTIC Its name means roots and cooking is based around hearty Southern Italian classics inspired by chef Francesco Mazzei's childhood. The room has a rustic look, a wood-fired oven for pizzas and a wine lounge packed with Italian bottles.

Menu £ 18 (lunch and early dinner) – Carte £ 21/41

Town plan: 13S3-r – *30 Almeida St ✉ N1 1AD – ⊖ Angel – ✆ 020 7354 4777 – www.radici.uk – Closed 25 December, Sunday dinner and Monday*

Pig and Butcher

TRADITIONAL BRITISH • PUB Dating from the mid-19C, when cattle drovers taking livestock to Smithfield Market would stop for a swift one, and now fully restored. There's a strong British element to the daily menu; meat is butchered and smoked in-house.

Carte £ 28/50

Town plan: 13S3-e – *80 Liverpool Rd ✉ N1 0QD – ⊖ Angel. – ✆ 020 7226 8304 (booking advisable) – www.thepigandbutcher.co.uk – dinner only and lunch Friday-Sunday – Closed 24-26 December*

Marcus Wareing Restaurants

KENSINGTON and CHELSEA (ROYAL BOROUGH OF)

Chelsea

✿✿✿ Gordon Ramsay

FRENCH • ELEGANT XxxX Gordon Ramsay's flagship restaurant is a model of composure and professionalism. The service is discreet and highly polished, yet also warm and reassuring. The cooking bridges both classical and modern schools and is executed with considerable poise, a lightness of touch and remarkable attention to detail.

➜ Pan-fried scallops with apple, walnuts, celery and cider. Poached halibut, king crab and lime with ras el hanout infused broth. Earl Grey parfait, Yorkshire rhubarb and lemon balm.

Menu £ 65/110

Town plan: 37AJ8-c – *68-69 Royal Hospital Rd. ✉ SW3 4HP – ⊖ Sloane Square – ✆ 020 7352 4441 (booking essential) – www.gordonramsayrestaurants.com – Closed 21-28 December, Saturday and Sunday*

✿✿ Claude Bosi at Bibendum (N)

FRENCH • ELEGANT XxX Claude Bosi has breathed new life into Bibendum, on the first floor of Michelin's former London HQ. With a clean, contemporary look and an iconic stained glass window, the handsome interior cannot fail to impress. Expect high-end traditional French cooking with creative modern touches; dishes are poised and well-balanced with bold, assured flavours.

➜ Frogs' legs with girolles and vin jaune. Somerset kid, razor clams and sea beets sauce. Pistachio soufflé with banana ice cream.

Menu £ 37/85

Town plan: 37AH7-s – *Michelin House, 81 Fulham Road ✉ SW3 6RD – ⊖ South Kensington – ✆ 020 7581 5817 (booking essential) – www.bibendum.co.uk – Closed dinner 24-26 December, 2-4 January, Sunday dinner, Monday and Tuesday*

✿ Five Fields (Taylor Bonnyman)

MODERN CUISINE • NEIGHBOURHOOD XxX A formally run yet intimate restaurant, with a discreet atmosphere and a warm, comfortable feel. Modern dishes are skilfully conceived, quite elaborate constructions; attractively presented and packed with flavour. Produce is top-notch and often comes from the restaurant's own kitchen garden in East Sussex.

➜ Foie gras with shimeji mushrooms and beetroot. Roe deer with morels, artichoke and truffle. Apple with caramel, vanilla cream and panna cotta.

Menu £ 65/85

Town plan: 37AJ7-s – *8-9 Blacklands Terr ✉ SW3 2SP – ⊖ Sloane Square – ✆ 020 7838 1082 (booking essential) – www.fivefieldsrestaurant.com – dinner only – Closed Christmas-mid January, 2 weeks August, Saturday-Sunday and bank holidays*

Outlaw's at The Capital

SEAFOOD • INTIMATE XX An elegant yet informal restaurant in a personally run hotel. The seasonal menus are all about sustainable seafood, with fish shipped up from Cornwall on a daily basis. The original modern cooking is delicately flavoured and ingredient-led, with the spotlight on the freshness of the produce.

➜ Lobster risotto, orange and basil. John Dory, Porthilly sauce and cabbage. Strawberry ice cream sandwich with lime and elderflower.

Menu £ 29/62

Town plan: 37AJ5-a – *The Capital Hotel, 22-24 Basil St. ✉ SW3 1AT – ⊖ Knightsbridge – ☎ 020 7591 1202 (booking essential) – www.capitalhotel.co.uk – Closed Sunday*

Elystan Street (N) (Philip Howard)

MODERN BRITISH • ELEGANT XX After 25 years at The Square in Mayfair, Philip Howard opened this elegant, understated restaurant in 2016. Cooking is relaxed and unfussy with a focus on vegetables and salads. Many dishes have Mediterranean influences and flavours are well-defined and eminently satisfying. Desserts are a highlight.

➜ Ravioli of langoustines with barbecue dressing, cabbage and pumpkin. Breast and spring roll of duck with pistachio, cherries, turnip and greens. Orange cheesecake with caramelised white chocolate and cardamom ice cream.

Menu £ 43 (weekday lunch) – Carte £ 45/92

Town plan: 37AH7-e – *43 Elystan St ✉ SW3 3NT – ⊖ South Kensington – ☎ 020 7628 5005 (booking essential) – www.elystanstreet.com – Closed 25-26 December and 1 January*

Vineet Bhatia London (N)

INDIAN • ELEGANT XX Intimate, discreetly lit restaurant in an archetypal Chelsea townhouse. The 7 course tasting menu is informed by the owners' Mumbai heritage and global travels, and dishes are detailed, delicately spiced and colourful, with a stunning array of textures and flavours. A lack of carbs keeps things light.

➜ Chilli cod. Kapi lamb chop. Clementine kulfi.

Menu £ 105 – tasting menu only

Town plan: 37AJ7-v – *10 Lincoln St ✉ SW3 2TS – ⊖ Sloane Square – ☎ 020 7225 1881 (booking essential) – www.vineetbhatia.london – dinner only – Closed 25-27 December, 1-3 January and Monday*

One-O-One

SEAFOOD • INTIMATE XXX Smart ground floor restaurant; it might be lacking a little in atmosphere but the seafood is good. Much of the excellent produce is from Brittany and Norway; don't miss the King crab legs which are the stars of the show.

Menu £ 20 (lunch and early dinner) – Carte £ 43/106

Town plan: 37AJ5-t – *Park Tower Knightsbridge Hotel, 101 Knightsbridge ✉ SW1X 7RN – ⊖ Knightsbridge – ☎ 020 7290 7101 – www.oneoonerestaurant.com*

Colbert

FRENCH • BRASSERIE XX With its posters, chessboard tiles and red leather seats, Colbert bears more than a passing resemblance to a Parisian pavement café. It's an all-day, every day operation with French classics from croque monsieur to steak Diane.

Carte £ 21/56

Town plan: 38AK7-t – *50-52 Sloane Sq ✉ SW1W 8AX – ⊖ Sloane Square – ☎ 020 7730 2804 (booking advisable) – www.colbertchelsea.com – Closed 25 December*

Bluebird
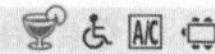

MODERN BRITISH • DESIGN XX It boasts an épicerie, a café, a terrace and even a clothes shop, but the highlight is the first floor restaurant with its marble-topped horseshoe bar, bold print banquettes and abundance of foliage. A Mediterranean menu and super cocktails.

Carte £ 30/55

Town plan: 36AF8-n - *350 King's Rd. ✉ SW3 5UU - ⊖ South Kensington - ✆ 020 7559 1000 - www.bluebird-restaurant.co.uk*

Le Colombier

FRENCH • NEIGHBOURHOOD XX Proudly Gallic corner restaurant in an affluent residential area. Attractive enclosed terrace. Bright and cheerful surroundings and service; traditional French cooking.

Menu £ 25 (lunch) - Carte £ 36/63

Town plan: 37AG7-e - *145 Dovehouse St. ✉ SW3 6LB - ⊖ South Kensington - ✆ 020 7351 1155 - www.le-colombier-restaurant.co.uk*

Good Earth
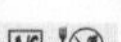

CHINESE • ELEGANT XX The menu might appear predictable but this long-standing Chinese has always proved a reliable choice in this area. Although there's no particular geographical bias, the cooking is carefully executed and dishes are authentic.

Menu £ 12 (weekday lunch) - Carte £ 26/46

Town plan: 37AH6-h - *233 Brompton Rd. ✉ SW3 2EP - ⊖ Knightsbridge - ✆ 020 7584 3658 - www.goodearthgroup.co.uk - Closed 23-31 December*

Hawksmoor

MEATS AND GRILLS • BRASSERIE XX The Hawksmoor people turned to rarefied Knightsbridge for their 5th London branch. Steaks are still the star of the show but here there's also plenty of seafood. Art deco elegance and friendly service compensate for the basement site.

Menu £ 28 (weekday lunch) - Carte £ 23/69

Town plan: 37AH6-r - *3 Yeoman's Row ✉ SW3 2AL - ⊖ South Kensington - ✆ 020 7590 9290 - www.thehawksmoor.com - Closed 24-26 December and 1 January*

il trillo

ITALIAN • FRIENDLY XX The Bertuccelli family have been making wine and running a restaurant in the Tuscan Hills for over 30 years. Two of the brothers now run this smart local which showcases the produce and wine from their region. Delightful courtyard.

Menu £ 31 - Carte £ 36/60

Town plan: 36AE8-s - *4 Hollywood Rd ✉ SW10 9HY - ⊖ Earl's Court - ✆ 020 3602 1759 - www.iltrillo.net - dinner only and lunch Saturday-Sunday - Closed Monday*

Ivy Chelsea Garden
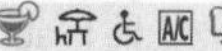

TRADITIONAL BRITISH • FASHIONABLE XX A sophisticated restaurant with a lively atmosphere; start with a cocktail, then head down to the orangery or out to the garden. The menu covers all bases; from breakfast through to lunch, afternoon tea and dinner, with brunch at weekends.

Carte £ 27/61

Town plan: 37AH8-c - *197 King's Rd ✉ SW3 5ED - ⊖ South Kensington - ✆ 020 3301 0300 (booking essential) - www.theivychelseagarden.com*

Maze Grill Park Walk

MEATS AND GRILLS • FASHIONABLE XX The site of Aubergine, where it all started for Gordon Ramsay, now specialises in steaks. Dry-aged in-house, the meats are cooked on a fierce bit of kit called a Montague grill. There's another Maze Grill close by in Royal Hospital Road.

Menu £ 19/40 - Carte £ 25/75

Town plan: 36AF8-x - *11 Park Walk ✉ SW10 0AJ - ⊖ South Kensington - ✆ 020 7255 9299 - www.gordonramsayrestaurants.com/maze-grill-park-walk*

Medlar

MODERN CUISINE • NEIGHBOURHOOD XX A charming, comfortable and very popular restaurant with a real neighbourhood feel, from two alumni of Chez Bruce. The service is engaging and unobtrusive; the kitchen uses good ingredients in dishes that deliver distinct flavours in classic combinations.

Menu £ 35/49

Town plan: 23N7-x - *438 King's Rd ✉ SW10 0LJ - ⊖ South Kensington - ✆ 020 7349 1900 - www.medlarrestaurant.co.uk - Closed 24-26 December and 1 January*

Bandol

PROVENÇAL • DESIGN X Stylishly dressed restaurant with a 100 year old olive tree evoking memories of sunny days spent on the French Riviera. Sharing plates take centre stage on the Provençal and Niçoise inspired menu; seafood is a highlight.

Menu £ 15 (weekday lunch) - Carte £ 26/57

Town plan: 36AE8-b - *6 Hollywood Rd ✉ SW10 9HY - ⊖ Earl's Court - ✆ 020 7351 1322 - www.barbandol.co.uk - Closed 24-26 December and 1 January*

Bo Lang

CHINESE • TRENDY X It's all about dim sum at this diminutive Hakkasan wannabe. The kitchen has a deft touch but stick to the more traditional combinations; come with friends for the cocktails and to mitigate the effects of some ambitious pricing.

Menu £ 15 (lunch) - Carte £ 30/50

Town plan: 37AH7-a - *100 Draycott Ave ✉ SW3 3AD - ⊖ South Kensington - ✆ 020 7823 7887 - www.bolangrestaurant.com*

Dinings SW3 Ⓝ

JAPANESE • INTIMATE X Head to the basement dining area with its closely spaced tables and brightly lit marble-topped bar – the best place to sit to enjoy the kitchen's signature sushi and sashimi, made with top quality sustainable seafood mostly from UK waters.

Carte £ 19/65

Town plan: 37AH6-s - *Walton House, Lennox Garden Mews (off Walton St.) ✉ SW3 2JH - ⊖ Sloane Square - ✆ 020 7723 0666 (booking advisable) - www.diningssw3.co.uk - Closed 24-26, 31 December and 1 January*

Rabbit

MODERN BRITISH • RUSTIC X The Gladwin brothers have followed the success of The Shed with another similarly rustic and warmly run restaurant. Share satisfying, robustly flavoured plates; game is a real highlight, particularly the rabbit dishes.

Menu £ 14 (weekday lunch)/28 - Carte £ 21/31

Town plan: 37AH7-r - *172 King's Rd ✉ SW3 4UP - ⊖ Sloane Square - ✆ 020 3750 0172 (pre-book at weekends) - www.rabbit-restaurant.com - Closed 22 December-2 January*

Jumeirah Carlton Tower

BUSINESS • MODERN Imposing international hotel overlooking a leafy square and just yards from all the swanky boutiques. Well-equipped rooftop health club has great views. Generously proportioned bedrooms boast every conceivable facility.

216 rooms - †£ 342/835 ††£ 342/835 - ☕ £ 32 - 58 suites

Town plan: 37AJ6-r - *Cadogan Pl ✉ SW1X 9PY - ⊖ Knightsbridge - ✆ 020 7235 1234 - www.jumeirah.com/jct*

The Capital

LUXURY • CLASSIC A fine, thoroughly British hotel, known for its discreet atmosphere and its conscientious and attentive service. Comfortable, immaculately kept bedrooms are understated in style. Enjoy afternoon tea in the intimate Sitting Room.

49 rooms – 🚹£ 265/395 🚹🚹£ 315/495 – ☕£ 17 – 1 suite

Town plan: 37AJ5-a – *22-24 Basil St.* ✉ *SW3 1AT* – ⊖ *Knightsbridge* – ☏ *020 7589 5171* – *www.capitalhotel.co.uk*

✿ **Outlaw's at The Capital** – See restaurant listing

Draycott

TOWNHOUSE • PERSONALISED Charming 19C house with elegant sitting room overlooking tranquil garden for afternoon tea. Bedrooms are individually decorated in a country house style and are named after writers or actors.

35 rooms – 🚹£ 190/240 🚹🚹£ 380/522 – ☕£ 22

Town plan: 37AJ7-c – *26 Cadogan Gdns* ✉ *SW3 2RP* – ⊖ *Sloane Square* – ☏ *020 7730 6466* – *www.draycotthotel.com*

Egerton House

TOWNHOUSE • CLASSIC Compact but comfortable townhouse in a very good location, well-maintained throughout and owned by the Red Carnation group. High levels of personal service make the hotel stand out.

28 rooms – 🚹£ 295/425 🚹🚹£ 295/425 – ☕£ 29

Town plan: 37AH6-e – *17-19 Egerton Terr* ✉ *SW3 2BX* – ⊖ *South Kensington* – ☏ *020 7589 2412* – *www.egertonhousehotel.com*

Knightsbridge

LUXURY • PERSONALISED Charming and attractively furnished townhouse in a Victorian terrace, with a very stylish, discreet feel. Every bedroom is immaculately appointed and has a style all of its own; fine detailing throughout.

44 rooms – 🚹£ 240/342 🚹🚹£ 270/366 – ☕£ 19

Town plan: 37AH6-s – *10 Beaufort Gdns* ✉ *SW3 1PT* – ⊖ *Knightsbridge* – ☏ *020 7584 6300* – *www.knightsbridgehotel.com*

The Levin

TOWNHOUSE • CLASSIC Little sister to The Capital next door. Impressive façade, contemporary interior and comfortable bedrooms in a subtle art deco style, with marvellous champagne mini bars. Simple dishes served all day down in the basement restaurant.

12 rooms – 🚹£ 245/379 🚹🚹£ 245/379 – ☕£ 13

Town plan: 37AJ5-c – *28 Basil St.* ✉ *SW3 1AS* – ⊖ *Knightsbridge* – ☏ *020 7589 6286* – *www.thelevinhotel.co.uk*

No.11 Cadogan Gardens

TOWNHOUSE • PERSONALISED Townhouse hotel fashioned out of four red-brick houses and exuberantly dressed in bold colours and furnishings. Theatrically decorated bedrooms vary in size from cosy to spacious. Intimate basement Italian restaurant with accomplished and ambitious cooking.

56 rooms – 🚹£ 295/395 🚹🚹£ 395/495 – ☕£ 24 – 7 suites

Town plan: 37AJ7-n – *11 Cadogan Gdns* ✉ *SW3 2RJ* – ⊖ *Sloane Square* – ☏ *020 7730 7000* – *www.11cadogangardens.com*

Earl's Court

K + K George

BUSINESS • MODERN In contrast to its period façade, this hotel's interior is stylish, colourful and contemporary. The hotel is on a quiet street, yet close to the Tube and has a large rear garden where you can enjoy breakfast in summer. Comfortable bar/lounge and a spacious restaurant serving a wide-ranging menu.

154 rooms ☕ – 🚹£ 190/280 🚹🚹£ 200/300

Town plan: 35AC7-s – *1-15 Templeton Pl* ✉ *SW5 9NB* – ⊖ *Earl's Court* – ☏ *020 7598 8700* – *www.kkhotels.com*

Twenty Nevern Square

TOWNHOUSE • PERSONALISED Privately owned townhouse overlooking an attractive Victorian garden square. It's decorated with original pieces of hand-carved Indonesian furniture; breakfast in a bright conservatory. Some bedrooms have their own terrace.

25 rooms – £ 75/160 £ 85/215

Town plan: 35AC7-u – *20 Nevern Sq ✉ SW5 9PD – ⊖ Earl's Court – ✆ 020 7565 9555 – www.mayflowercollection.com*

Kensington

Kitchen W8

MODERN CUISINE • NEIGHBOURHOOD XX A joint venture between Rebecca Mascarenhas and Philip Howard. Not as informal as the name suggests but still refreshingly free of pomp. The cooking has depth and personality and prices are quite restrained considering the quality of the produce and the kitchen's skill.

→ Smoked eel with grilled mackerel, golden beetroot and sweet mustard. Roast rump of veal with bulgur wheat, charred lettuce, hazelnuts and shiitake. Muscovado financiers with salted peanut ice cream, bitter chocolate and banana.

Menu £ 28/30 (early weekday dinner) – Carte £ 40/55

Town plan: 35AC5-a – *11-13 Abingdon Rd ✉ W8 6AH – ⊖ High Street Kensington – ✆ 020 7937 0120 – www.kitchenw8.com – Closed 24-26 December and bank holidays*

Launceston Place

MODERN CUISINE • NEIGHBOURHOOD XXX A favourite of many thanks to its palpable sense of neighbourhood, pretty façade and its nooks and crannies which make it ideal for trysts or tête-à-têtes. The menu is fashionably terse and the cooking is quite elaborate, with dishes big on originality and artfully presented.

Menu £ 25/75

Town plan: 36AE5-a – *1a Launceston Pl ✉ W8 5RL – ⊖ Gloucester Road – ✆ 020 7937 6912 (bookings advisable at dinner) – www.launcestonplace-restaurant.co.uk – Closed 25-30 December, 1 January, Tuesday lunch and Monday*

Min Jiang

CHINESE • ELEGANT XXX The cooking at this stylish 10th floor Chinese restaurant covers all provinces, but Cantonese and Sichuanese dominate. Wood-fired Beijing duck is a speciality. The room's good looks compete with the great views of Kensington Gardens.

Menu £ 40/80 – Carte £ 30/99

Town plan: 36AD5-c – *Royal Garden Hotel, 2-24 Kensington High St (10th Floor) ✉ W8 4PT – ⊖ High Street Kensington – ✆ 020 7361 1988 – www.minjiang.co.uk*

Babylon

MODERN CUISINE • FASHIONABLE XX Found on the 7th floor and affording great views of the city skyline and an amazing 1.5 acres of rooftop garden. Stylish modern décor in keeping with the contemporary British cooking.

Menu £ 24 (weekday lunch) – Carte £ 38/59

Town plan: 36AD5-n – *The Roof Gardens, 99 Kensington High St ✉ W8 5SA – (entrance on Derry St) – ⊖ High Street Kensington – ✆ 020 7368 3993 – www.roofgardens.virgin.com – Closed 24-30 December, 1-2 January and Sunday dinner*

Don't expect guesthouses to provide the same level of service as a hotel. They are often characterised by a warm welcome and décor which reflects the owner's personality. Those shown in red are particularly charming.

Clarke's

MODERN CUISINE • NEIGHBOURHOOD XX A forever popular restaurant, which has enjoyed a loyal local following for over 30 years. Sally Clarke uses only the freshest seasonal ingredients and her cooking is confidently executed with a pleasing lightness of touch.

Menu £ 27/39 – Carte £ 40/60

Town plan: 27AC4-c – *124 Kensington Church St ✉ W8 4BH – ⊖ Notting Hill Gate – ✆ 020 7221 9225 (booking advisable) – www.sallyclarke.com – Closed 2 weeks August, Christmas-New Year, Sunday January-September and bank holidays*

Malabar

INDIAN • NEIGHBOURHOOD XX Opened in 1983 in a residential Notting Hill street, but keeps up its appearance, remaining fresh and good-looking. Balanced menu of carefully prepared and sensibly priced Indian dishes. Buffet lunch on Sunday.

Carte £ 18/37 **s**

Town plan: 27AC3-e – *27 Uxbridge St. ✉ W8 7TQ – ⊖ Notting Hill Gate – ✆ 020 7727 8800 – www.malabar-restaurant.co.uk – dinner only and lunch Saturday-Sunday – Closed 1 week Christmas*

Yashin

JAPANESE • DESIGN XX Ask for a counter seat to watch the chefs prepare the sushi; choose 8, 11 or 15 pieces, to be served together. The quality of fish is clear; tiny garnishes and the odd bit of searing add originality.

Carte £ 45/89

Town plan: 35AC5-c – *1a Argyll Rd. ✉ W8 7DB – ⊖ High Street Kensington – ✆ 020 7938 1536 (booking essential) – www.yashinsushi.com – Closed 24, 25 and 31 December and 1 January*

Zaika 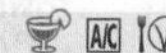

INDIAN • EXOTIC DÉCOR XX The cooking focuses on the North of India and the influences of Mughal and Nawabi, so expect rich and fragrantly spiced dishes. The softly-lit room makes good use of its former life as a bank, with its wood-panelling and ornate ceiling.

Menu £ 19 (lunch) – Carte £ 32/67

Town plan: 36AD5-r – *1 Kensington High St. ✉ W8 5NP – ⊖ High Street Kensington – ✆ 020 7795 6533 – www.zaikaofkensington.com – Closed 25-26 December, 1 January and Monday lunch*

Kensington Place

SEAFOOD • NEIGHBOURHOOD X 2017 marked the 30th birthday of this iconic brasserie which helped change London's dining scene forever. Fish is the focus of the fairly priced menu which mixes classics like prawn cocktail and fish pie with more modern dishes.

Menu £ 20 (lunch and early dinner) – Carte £ 25/52

Town plan: 27AC3-z – *201-209 Kensington Church St. ✉ W8 7LX – ⊖ Notting Hill Gate – ✆ 020 7727 3184 – www.kensingtonplace-restaurant.co.uk – Closed Sunday dinner, Monday lunch and bank holidays*

Mazi

GREEK • FRIENDLY X It's all about sharing at this simple, bright Greek restaurant where traditional recipes are given a modern twist to create vibrant, colourful and fresh tasting dishes. The garden terrace at the back is a charming spot in summer.

Menu £ 15 (weekday lunch) – Carte £ 28/43

Town plan: 27AC3-a – *12-14 Hillgate St ✉ W8 7SR – ⊖ Notting Hill Gate – ✆ 020 7229 3794 – www.mazi.co.uk – Closed 24-25 December and 1-2 January*

The Shed

MODERN BRITISH • RUSTIC It's more than just a shed but does have a higgledy-piggledy charm and a healthy dose of the outdoors. One brother cooks, one manages and the third runs the farm which supplies the produce for the earthy, satisfying dishes.

Carte £ 21/32

Town plan: 27AC3-s - *122 Palace Gardens Terr ✉ W8 4RT - ⊖ Notting Hill Gate - ✆ 020 7229 4024 - www.theshed-restaurant.com - Closed Monday lunch and Sunday*

Royal Garden

BUSINESS • MODERN A tall, modern hotel with many of its rooms enjoying enviable views over the adjacent Kensington Gardens. All the modern amenities and services, with well-drilled staff. Bright, spacious Park Terrace offers an international menu as well as afternoon tea for which you're accompanied by a pianist.

394 rooms - †£ 170/460 ††£ 210/520 - £ 25 - 17 suites

Town plan: 36AD5-c - *2-24 Kensington High St ✉ W8 4PT - ⊖ High Street Kensington - ✆ 020 7937 8000 - www.royalgardenhotel.co.uk*

Min Jiang - See restaurant listing

The Milestone

LUXURY • PERSONALISED Elegant and enthusiastically run hotel with decorative Victorian façade and a very British feel. Charming oak-panelled sitting room is popular for afternoon tea; snug bar in former stables. Meticulously decorated bedrooms offer period detail. Ambitious cooking in discreet Cheneston's restaurant.

62 rooms - †£ 330/500 ††£ 450/1500 - 6 suites

Town plan: 36AE5-u - *1-2 Kensington Ct ✉ W8 5DL - ⊖ High Street Kensington - ✆ 020 7917 1000 - www.milestonehotel.com*

Baglioni

LUXURY • PERSONALISED It's opposite Kensington Palace and there's no escaping the fact that this is an Italian-owned hotel. The interior is bold and ornate and comes with a certain swagger. Stylish bedrooms have a masculine feel and boast impressive facilities. Italian classics are served in the ground floor restaurant.

67 rooms - †£ 315/660 ††£ 315/660 - 15 suites

Town plan: 36AE5-e - *60 Hyde Park Gate ✉ SW7 5BB - ⊖ High Street Kensington - ✆ 020 7368 5718 - www.baglionihotels.com*

North Kensington

Ledbury (Brett Graham)

MODERN CUISINE • NEIGHBOURHOOD Brett Graham's husbandry skills and close relationship with his suppliers ensure the quality of the produce shines through and flavour combinations linger long in the memory. This smart yet unshowy restaurant comes with smooth and engaging service. Only a tasting menu is served at dinner on weekends.

→ Clay-baked golden beetroot with English caviar, smoked and dried eel. Dorset Sika deer with hen-of-the-wood, pickled wild hops and smoked bone marrow. Chocolate, dark chocolate Chantilly and mint.

Menu £ 75/145

Town plan: 27AB2-c - *127 Ledbury Rd. ✉ W11 2AQ - ⊖ Notting Hill Gate - ✆ 020 7792 9090 - www.theledbury.com - Closed 25-26 December, August bank holiday and lunch Monday-Tuesday*

Flat Three

CREATIVE • DESIGN Basement restaurant blending the cuisines of Scandinavia, Korea and Japan. Not everything works but there's certainly ambition. They make their own soy and miso and serve more foraged ingredients than you'll find in Ray Mears' pocket.

Carte £ 40/66

Town plan: 27AA4-k - *120-122 Holland Park Ave ✉ W11 4UA - ⊖ Holland Park - ✆ 020 7792 8987 - www.flatthree.london - dinner only and lunch Friday-Saturday - Closed 21 December-4 January, 21 August-1 September, Sunday and Monday*

Dock Kitchen

MEDITERRANEAN CUISINE • DESIGN X Set in an open-plan former Victorian goods yard where steel girders and exposed brick create an industrial feel. The cooking relies on quality ingredients and simple, natural flavours; look out for the themed set menus.

Carte £25/40

Town plan: 16L4-k – *Portobello Dock, 342-344 Ladbroke Grove ✉ W10 5BU – ⊖ Ladbroke Grove – ✆ 020 8962 1610 – www.dockkitchen.co.uk – Closed Christmas, Sunday dinner and bank holidays*

Electric Diner

MEATS AND GRILLS • RUSTIC X Next to the iconic Electric Cinema is this loud, brash and fun all-day operation with an all-encompassing menu; the flavours are as big as the portions. The long counter and red leather booths add to the authentic diner feel.

Carte £17/34

Town plan: 27AB2-e – *191 Portobello Rd ✉ W11 2ED – ⊖ Ladbroke Grove – ✆ 020 7908 9696 – www.electricdiner.com – Closed 30-31 August and 25 December*

Granger and Co. Notting Hill

MODERN CUISINE • FRIENDLY X When Bill Granger moved from sunny Sydney to cool Notting Hill he opened a local restaurant too. He brought with him that delightful 'matey' service that only Aussies do, his breakfast time ricotta hotcakes and a fresh, zesty menu.

Carte £19/41

Town plan: 27AC2-x – *175 Westbourne Grove ✉ W11 2SB – ⊖ Bayswater – ✆ 020 7229 9111 (bookings not accepted) – www.grangerandco.com – Closed August bank holiday weekend and 25 December*

108 Garage N

MODERN BRITISH • NEIGHBOURHOOD X A former garage with a utilitarian look that's more Hackney than Kensington; all bare brick, exposed ducting and polished concrete. Sit at the counter and chat to the affable chef; modern dishes are colourful and vibrant and change daily.

Menu £35/45 – Carte £28/46

Town plan: 16L4-e – *108 Golborne Rd ✉ W10 5PS – ⊖ Westbourne Park – ✆ 020 8969 3769 (booking essential) – www.108garage.com – Closed 2 weeks August, 2 weeks Christmas, Sunday and Monday*

Six Portland Road

FRENCH • NEIGHBOURHOOD X An intimate and personally run neighbourhood restaurant owned by Oli Barker, previously of Terroirs. The menu changes frequently and has a strong French accent; dishes are reassuringly recognisable, skilfully constructed and very tasty.

Menu £19 (weekday lunch) – Carte £30/52

Town plan: 27AA4-n – *6 Portland Rd ✉ W11 4LA – ⊖ Holland Park – ✆ 020 7229 3130 – www.sixportlandroad.com – Closed Christmas-New Year, last 2 weeks August, Sunday dinner and Monday*

Zayane

MOROCCAN • NEIGHBOURHOOD X An intimate neighbourhood restaurant owned by Casablanca-born Meryem Mortell and evoking the sights and scents of North Africa. Carefully conceived dishes have authentic Moroccan flavours but are cooked with modern techniques.

Menu £25 – Carte £24/38

Town plan: 16L4-z – *91 Golborne Rd ✉ W10 5NL – ⊖ Westbourne Park – ✆ 020 8960 1137 – www.zayanerestaurant.com – Closed 26 August-3 September*

The Portobello

TOWNHOUSE • PERSONALISED An attractive Victorian townhouse in an elegant terrace, with original, theatrical décor, charming staff and a home-from-home feel. Circular beds, half-testers, Victorian baths: no two bedrooms are the same.

21 rooms – £ 175 £ 180/395

Town plan: 27AB2-n – *22 Stanley Gdns. W11 2NG – Notting Hill Gate – 020 7727 2777 – www.portobellohotel.com*

South Kensington

Bombay Brasserie

INDIAN • EXOTIC DÉCOR XXX A well-run, well-established and comfortable Indian restaurant, featuring a very smart bar and conservatory. Creative dishes sit alongside more traditional choices on the various menus and vegetarian are well-catered for.

Menu £ 27 (weekday lunch) – Carte £ 36/52

Town plan: 36AE6-y – *Courtfield Rd. SW7 4QH – Gloucester Road – 020 7370 4040 (bookings advisable at dinner) – www.bombayb.co.uk – Closed 25 December*

Cambio de Tercio

SPANISH • COSY XX A long-standing, ever-improving Spanish restaurant. Start with small dishes like the excellent El Bulli inspired omelette, then have the popular Pluma Iberica. There are super sherries and a wine list to prove there is life beyond Rioja.

Menu £ 45 – Carte £ 21/69 **s**

Town plan: 36AE7-a – *163 Old Brompton Rd. SW5 0LJ – Gloucester Road – 020 7244 8970 – www.cambiodetercio.co.uk – Closed 2 weeks December and 2 weeks August*

L'Etranger

MODERN FRENCH • NEIGHBOURHOOD XX A moody, atmospheric restaurant serving an eclectic menu which mixes French dishes with techniques and flavours from Japanese cooking. Impressive wine and sake lists and a great value set menu. Ask for a corner table.

Menu £ 25/30 – Carte £ 30/57

Town plan: 36AE6-c – *36 Gloucester Rd. SW7 4QT – Gloucester Road – 020 7584 1118 (booking essential) – www.etranger.co.uk*

Ognisko

POLISH • ELEGANT XX Ognisko Polskie – The Polish Hearth Club – was founded in 1940 in this magnificent townhouse; its elegant restaurant serves traditional dishes from across Eastern Europe and the cooking is without pretence and truly from the heart.

Menu £ 22 (lunch and early dinner) – Carte £ 27/37

Town plan: 37AG5-r – *55 Prince's Gate, Exhibition Rd SW7 2PN – South Kensington – 020 7589 0101 – www.ogniskorestaurant.co.uk – Closed 24-26 December and 1 January*

Ours

MODERN CUISINE • FASHIONABLE XX An immense restaurant featuring trees, a living plant wall of 1,200 flower pots and a mezzanine level bar-lounge. The modern menu offers seasonal, ingredient-led dishes with a fresh, light style. Keen service; weekend brunches.

Carte £ 35/77

Town plan: 37AH6-o – *264 Brompton Rd SW3 2AS – South Kensington – 020 7100 2200 (booking advisable) – www.restaurant-ours.com – dinner only and Saturday lunch – Closed 24-28 December, Sunday and Monday*

Yashin Ocean House

JAPANESE • CHIC XX The USP of this chic Japanese restaurant is 'head to tail' eating, although, as there's nothing for carnivores, 'fin to scale' would be more precise. Stick with specialities like the whole dry-aged sea bream for the full umami hit.

Carte £ 20/86

Town plan: 36AF7-y – *117-119 Old Brompton Rd ✉ SW7 3RN – ⊖ Gloucester Road – ✆ 020 7373 3990 – www.yashinocean.com – Closed Christmas*

Capote y Toros

SPANISH • TAPAS BAR X Expect to queue at this compact and vividly coloured spot which celebrates sherry, tapas, ham... and bullfighting. Sherry is the star; those as yet unmoved by this most underappreciated of wines will be dazzled by the variety.

Menu £ 25 – Carte £ 24/64

Town plan: 36AE7-v – *157 Old Brompton Road ✉ SW5 0LJ – ⊖ Gloucester Road – ✆ 020 7373 0567 – www.cambiodetercio.co.uk – dinner only – Closed 2 weeks Christmas, Sunday and Monday*

Go-Viet Ⓝ

VIETNAMESE • CONTEMPORARY DÉCOR X A Vietnamese restaurant from experienced chef Jeff Tan. Lunch concentrates on classics like pho and bun, while dinner provides a more sophisticated experience, offering interesting flavourful dishes with a distinct modern edge.

Carte £ 20/74

Town plan: 36AF7-v – *53 Old Brompton Rd ✉ SW7 3JS – ⊖ South Kensington – ✆ 020 7589 6432 – www.vietnamfood.co.uk – Closed 24-26 December*

Margaux

MEDITERRANEAN CUISINE • TRENDY X France and Italy are the primary influences at this modern bistro, where classics feature alongside more unusual dishes. The wine list provides a good choice of varietals and the ersatz industrial look is downtown Manhattan.

Menu £ 15 (weekday lunch) – Carte £ 32/57

Town plan: 36AE7-m – *152 Old Brompton Rd ✉ SW5 0BE – ⊖ Gloucester Road – ✆ 020 7373 5753 – www.barmargaux.co.uk – Closed 24-26 December, 1 January and lunch August*

Blakes

LUXURY • DESIGN Behind the Victorian façade is one of London's first 'boutique' hotels. Dramatic, bold and eclectic décor, with oriental influences and antiques from around the world. International dishes in the spacious ground floor restaurant.

45 rooms – †£ 235/255 ††£ 345/395 – ☕ £ 23 – 7 suites

Town plan: 36AF7-n – *33 Rowland Gdns ✉ SW7 3PF – ⊖ Gloucester Road – ✆ 020 7370 6701 – www.blakeshotels.com*

Enjoy good food without spending a fortune!
Look out for the Bib Gourmand symbol to find restaurants offering good food at great prices!

The Pelham

LUXURY • ELEGANT Great location if you're in town for museum visiting. It's a mix of English country house and city townhouse, with a panelled sitting room and library with honesty bar. Sweet and intimate basement restaurant with Mediterranean menu.

52 rooms – ♦£ 200/350 ♦♦£ 200/350 – ☕ £ 15 – 2 suites

Town plan: 37AG6-z – *15 Cromwell Pl* ✉ *SW7 2LA* – ⊖ *South Kensington* – ✆ *020 7589 8288* – *www.pelhamhotel.co.uk*

Number Sixteen

TOWNHOUSE • ELEGANT Elegant 19C townhouses in a smart neighbourhood; well-run by charming, helpful staff. Tastefully furnished lounges feature attractive modern art. First floor bedrooms benefit from large windows and balconies; basement rooms are the quietest and two have their own terrace. Airy Orangery restaurant for afternoon tea and light meals overlooking the pretty garden.

41 rooms – ♦£ 180/240 ♦♦£ 276/342 – ☕ £ 20

Town plan: 36AF7-d – *16 Sumner Pl.* ✉ *SW7 3EG* – ⊖ *South Kensington* – ✆ *020 7589 5232* – *www.firmdalehotels.co.uk*

The Gore

TOWNHOUSE • PERSONALISED Idiosyncratic, hip Victorian house close to the Royal Albert Hall, whose charming lobby is covered with pictures and prints. Individually styled bedrooms have plenty of character and fun bathrooms. Bright and casual bistro.

50 rooms – ♦£ 190/500 ♦♦£ 190/500 – ☕ £ 18

Town plan: 36AF5-n – *190 Queen's Gate* ✉ *SW7 5EX* – ⊖ *Gloucester Road* – ✆ *020 7584 6601* – *www.gorehotel.com*

The Exhibitionist

TOWNHOUSE • DESIGN A funky, design-led boutique hotel fashioned out of several 18C townhouses. The modern artwork changes every few months and the bedrooms are individually furnished – several have their own roof terrace.

37 rooms – ♦£ 199/599 ♦♦£ 199/899 – ☕ £ 20 – 3 suites

Town plan: 36AF6-b – *8-10 Queensberry Pl* ✉ *SW7 2EA* – ⊖ *South Kensington* – ✆ *020 7915 0000* – *www.theexhibitionisthotel.com*

KING'S CROSS ST PANCRAS

Gilbert Scott

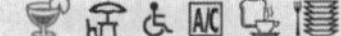

TRADITIONAL BRITISH • BRASSERIE XX Named after the architect of this Gothic masterpiece and run under the aegis of Marcus Wareing, this restaurant has the splendour of a Grand Salon but the buzz of a brasserie. The appealing menu showcases the best of British produce, whilst incorporating influences from further afield.

Menu £ 21 (lunch) – Carte £ 28/61

Town plan: 18R4-d – *St Pancras Renaissance Hotel, Euston Rd* ✉ *NW1 2AR* – ⊖ *King's Cross St Pancras* – ✆ *020 7278 3888* – *www.thegilbertscott.co.uk*

Granger & Co. King's Cross

MODERN CUISINE • FRIENDLY X The third London outpost for Aussie chef Bill Granger is a bright, buzzing place serving small plates, barbecue dishes, and bowls and grains, with plenty of South East Asian flavours. Dishes are vibrant, fresh and uplifting.

Carte £ 18/39

Town plan: 12R3-c – *Stanley Building, 7 Pancras Sq.* ✉ *N1C 4AG* – ⊖ *King's Cross St Pancras* – ✆ *020 3058 2567* – *www.grangerandco.com* – *Closed 25 December*

St Pancras Renaissance

BUSINESS • ELEGANT This restored Gothic jewel was built in 1873 as the Midland Grand hotel and reopened in 2011 under the Marriott brand. A former taxi rank is now a spacious lobby and all-day dining is in the old booking office. Luxury suites in Chambers wing; Barlow wing bedrooms are a little more functional.

245 rooms - †£ 250/400 ††£ 400/550 - ☕ £ 18 - 10 suites

Town plan: 18R4-d - *Euston Rd ✉ NW1 2AR - ⊖ King's Cross St Pancras - ☎ 020 7841 3540 - www.stpancraslondon.com*

Gilbert Scott - See restaurant listing

Great Northern H. London

HISTORIC BUILDING • CONTEMPORARY Built as a railway hotel in 1854 and reborn as a stylish townhouse; it's connected to King's Cross' western concourse and just metres from the Eurostar check-in. Bespoke furniture features in each of the modern bedrooms. Classic British dishes in the intimate first floor bistro; start with a drink in the GNH bar.

91 rooms - †£ 249/299 ††£ 249/379 - ☕ £ 25 - 1 suite

Town plan: 12R3-n - *Pancras Rd ✉ N1C 4TB - ⊖ King's Cross St Pancras - ☎ 020 3388 0818 - www.gnhlondon.com*

KINGSTON UPON THAMES

Surbiton

The French Table

MEDITERRANEAN CUISINE • NEIGHBOURHOOD XX Husband and wife run this lively local: he cooks and she runs the show, assisted by her team of friendly staff. Expect zesty and satisfying French-Mediterranean cooking, as well as great bread, as they also run the bakery next door.

Menu £ 25/45

Town plan: 6C5-a - *85 Maple Rd ✉ KT6 4AW - ☎ 020 8399 2365 - www.thefrenchtable.co.uk - Closed last 2 weeks August, 25 December-5 January, Sunday and Monday*

LAMBETH

Brixton

Boqueria

SPANISH • TAPAS BAR X Contemporary tapas bar, named after Barcelona's famous food market. Sit at the counter rather than in the unremarkable dining room. Highlights include the assorted cured hams and an excellent Crema Catalana.

Carte £ 12/25

Town plan: 24R9-x - *192 Acre Ln. ✉ SW2 5UL - ⊖ Clapham North - ☎ 020 7733 4408 - www.boqueriatapas.com - dinner only and lunch Saturday-Sunday - Closed 24-27 December and 1 January*

Nanban

JAPANESE • SIMPLE X A ramen-bar-cum-izakaya, tucked away at the back of Brixton Market and owned by former MasterChef winner, Tim Anderson. Food is fresh and full of flavour; the spicy, super-crispy chicken karaage will have you coming back for more.

Carte £ 19/29

Town plan: 25S9-n - *426 Coldharbour Ln ✉ SW9 8LF - ⊖ Brixton - ☎ 020 7346 0098 - www.nanban.co.uk - Closed 25 December and Monday lunch*

Clapham Common

Trinity

MODERN CUISINE • FASHIONABLE XX Adam Byatt's Trinity and Clapham Old Town are a perfect fit. This bright, warmly run and contemporary restaurant has a genuine neighbourhood feel and the cooking is sophisticated yet easy to eat. This is a kitchen at the top of its game.

→ Tuna tartare with crab salad, avocado and pickled cucumber. Pot-roast Anjou pigeon with salt-baked celeriac and red wine salsify. Salted caramel custard tart.

Menu £ 39 (lunch) – Carte £ 47/63

Town plan: 24Q9-a – *4 The Polygon ✉ SW4 0JG – ⊖ Clapham Common – ✆ 020 7622 1199 – www.trinityrestaurant.co.uk – Closed 24-30 December and 1-2 January*

Bistro Union

MODERN BRITISH • NEIGHBOURHOOD X The little sister to Trinity restaurant is fun and affordable, with a welcoming feel and sweet staff. The menu is appealingly flexible, whether you're here for brunch or a full dinner; eschew starters in favour of their great 'snacks'.

Menu £ 26 (weekday dinner) – Carte £ 25/47

Town plan: 7E4-s – *40 Abbeville Rd ✉ SW4 9NG – ⊖ Clapham South – ✆ 020 7042 6400 (booking advisable) – www.bistrounion.co.uk – Closed 24-27 December*

Upstairs (at Trinity)

MODERN BRITISH • FASHIONABLE X The open-plan kitchen is the focus of this more relaxed room upstairs from Trinity. It's all about sharing the visually appealing, flavoursome and reasonably priced plates, which bring a hint of the Mediterranean with them.

Carte £ 21/37

Town plan: 24Q9-a – *4 The Polygon ✉ SW4 0JG – ⊖ Clapham Common – ✆ 020 3745 7227 – www.trinityrestaurant.co.uk – dinner only – Closed 24-30 December, 1-2 January, Sunday and Monday*

Dairy

CREATIVE BRITISH • RUSTIC X The higgledy-piggledy, homemade look of this fun, lively restaurant adds to its charm. What you don't expect is such innovative cooking. The earthy, easy-to-eat food is driven by seasonality – some produce is grown on the roof. You can also try their pintxos bar next door.

Menu £ 25 (weekday lunch) – Carte £ 22/33

Town plan: 24Q9-d – *15 The Pavement ✉ SW4 0HY – ⊖ Clapham Common – ✆ 020 7622 4165 (booking essential at dinner) – www.the-dairy.co.uk – Closed Christmas, Sunday dinner, Monday and lunch Tuesday*

The Manor

CREATIVE BRITISH • NEIGHBOURHOOD X Fans of The Dairy will like The Manor – they share ownership and menu formats and have similar cuisine styles. With its distressed looks and young, informed service, it certainly captures the zeitgeist. The innovative cooking uses modern techniques and bursts with flavour.

Menu £ 30 – Carte £ 20/28

Town plan: 24Q9-b – *148 Clapham Manor St ✉ SW4 6BX – ⊖ Clapham Common – ✆ 020 7720 4662 – www.themanorclapham.co.uk – Closed 21-27 December, 1 January, Sunday dinner, Tuesday lunch and Monday*

May the Fifteenth

MEDITERRANEAN CUISINE • RUSTIC X Formerly Abbeville Kitchen – the chef took over this bistro and christened it after the date he signed the forms. The food remains as was: gutsy and wholesome, with fair prices and plenty of choice.

Menu £ 20 (weekday lunch) – Carte £ 23/43

Town plan: 7E4-a – *47 Abbeville Rd ✉ SW4 9JX – ⊖ Clapham South – ✆ 020 8772 1110 (bookings advisable at dinner) – www.maythe15th.com – dinner only and lunch Friday-Sunday – Closed 24-27 December and 1 January*

Herne Hill

Llewelyn's

TRADITIONAL BRITISH • NEIGHBOURHOOD X A neighbourhood restaurant in a village-like location. Cooking is British with Mediterranean influences and dishes to share are a feature. Expect quality ingredients in hearty portions, with no unnecessary elaboration.

Carte £ 24/33

Town plan: 7E4-n – *293-295 Railton Rd ✉ SE24 0JP – ⊖ Herne Hill – ✆ 020 7733 6676 (bookings advisable at dinner) – www.llewelyns-restaurant.co.uk – Closed 22 December-4 January, Sunday dinner and Monday*

Kennington

Kennington Tandoori

INDIAN • NEIGHBOURHOOD XX Kowsar Hoque runs this contemporary Indian restaurant with great pride and his eagerness and professionalism filters through to his staff. The food is prepared with equal care – try the seasonal specialities and the excellent breads.

Carte £ 20/34

Town plan: 40AS8-a – *313 Kennington Rd ✉ SE11 4QE – ⊖ Kennington – ✆ 020 7735 9247 (booking advisable) – www.kenningtontandoori.com – dinner only and lunch Saturday and Sunday – Closed 25-26 December*

Southbank

Skylon

MODERN CUISINE • DESIGN XXX Ask for a window table here at the Royal Festival Hall. Informal grill-style operation on one side, a more formal and expensive restaurant on the other, with a busy cocktail bar in the middle.

Menu £ 30/35 – Carte £ 39/58

Town plan: 32AR4-a – *1 Southbank Centre, Belvedere Rd ✉ SE1 8XX – ⊖ Waterloo – ✆ 020 7654 7800 – www.skylon-restaurant.co.uk – Closed 25 December*

London Marriott H. County Hall

BUSINESS • MODERN Occupying the historic County Hall building on the banks of the River Thames. Bedrooms are spacious, stylish and modern; many enjoy river and Parliament outlooks. Impressive leisure facilities. World famous views too from wood-panelled Gillray's, which specialises in steaks.

206 rooms – †£ 260/600 ††£ 260/900 – ☕ £ 17 – 5 suites

Town plan: 40AR5-a – *Westminster Bridge Rd ✉ SE1 7PB – ⊖ Westminster – ✆ 020 7928 5200 – www.marriott.co.uk/lonch*

Stockwell

Canton Arms

TRADITIONAL BRITISH • PUB An appreciative crowd of all ages come for the earthy, robust and seasonal British dishes which suit the relaxed environment of this pub so well. Staff are attentive and knowledgeable.

Carte £ 19/33

Town plan: 24R8-a – *177 South Lambeth Rd ✉ SW8 1XP – ⊖ Stockwell. – ✆ 020 7582 8710 (bookings not accepted) – www.cantonarms.com – Closed Christmas-New Year, Monday lunch, Sunday dinner and bank holidays*

Don't confuse the classification X with the Stars ✿!
The number of X denotes levels of comfort and service, while Stars are awarded solely for the cooking.

Vauxhall

℩O Pharmacy 2

MODERN BRITISH • DESIGN XX Pharmacy was the place to be in the '90s and in 2016 Damien Hirst revived the name for the restaurant in his Newport Street Gallery. The medicinally-themed decoration is familiar yet more vivid. For the food he paired up with Mark Hix – the best dishes are the more British ones.

Carte £ 29/65

Town plan: 40AR7-v – *Newport Street Gallery, Newport St ✉ SE11 6AJ – ⊖ Vauxhall – ✆ 020 3141 9333 – www.pharmacyrestaurant.com – Closed Christmas, Sunday dinner and Monday*

LEWISHAM

Forest Hill

℩O Babur

INDIAN • NEIGHBOURHOOD XX Good looks and innovative cooking make this passionately run and long-established Indian restaurant stand out. Influences from the south and north west feature most and seafood is a highlight - look out for the 'Treasures of the Sea' menu.

Menu £ 32/56 – Carte £ 28/36

Town plan: 7F4-s – *119 Brockley Rise ✉ SE23 1JP – ⊖ Honor Oak Park – ✆ 020 8291 2400 – www.babur.info – Closed 26 December*

Lewisham

℩O Sparrow N

MODERN BRITISH • FRIENDLY X A bright and buzzing neighbourhood spot whose name symbolises the culinary diversity of its globally influenced menus, as well as one of the owners' Sri Lankan heritage. Weekend brunches also offer an eclectic choice of dishes.

Carte £ 22/33

Town plan: 7F4-w – *2 Rennell St ✉ SE13 7HD – ⊖ Lewisham – ✆ 020 8318 6941 – www.sparrowlondon.co.uk – dinner only and weekend brunch – Closed 2 weeks August, Christmas, Sunday dinner and Monday*

MERTON

Wimbledon

℩O Light House

MEDITERRANEAN CUISINE • NEIGHBOURHOOD X A neighbourhood favourite offering Mediterranean cooking in smart, comfortable surroundings. The food is wholesome and confident, with plenty of bold flavours; Italian dishes and puddings are the highlights and staff are calm and cheery.

Menu £ 17 (weekdays) – Carte £ 26/42

Town plan: 6D5-u – *75-77 Ridgway ✉ SW19 4ST – ⊖ Wimbledon – ✆ 020 8944 6338 – www.lighthousewimbledon.com – Closed 25-26 December, 1 January and Sunday dinner*

℩O Light on the Common 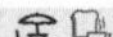

TRADITIONAL BRITISH • NEIGHBOURHOOD X All-day neighbourhood restaurant offering an extensive menu to take you through from breakfast until dinner. Staff are helpful and friendly and the setting bright and modern; ask for a seat in the conservatory at the back.

Menu £ 23 (weekdays) – Carte £ 23/33

Town plan: 6D5-c – *48 High St ✉ SW19 5AX – ⊖ Wimbledon – ✆ 020 8946 3031 – www.lightwimbledon.co.uk – Closed 25 December and Sunday dinner*

Takahashi

JAPANESE • FRIENDLY X The eponymous chef-owner of this sweet spot is a Nobu alumnus and his wife runs the service with a personal touch. Mediterranean ingredients bring a creative edge to the pure, delicately flavoured dishes. Sushi and sashimi are a highlight.

Menu £ 20/40 – Carte £ 22/47

Town plan: 6D5-s – *228 Merton Rd ✉ SW19 1EQ – ⊖ South Wimbledon – ✆ 020 8540 3041 (booking essential) – www.takahashi-restaurant.co.uk – dinner only and lunch Saturday-Sunday – Closed Monday and Tuesday*

White Onion

MODERN CUISINE • BISTRO X A relaxed bistro deluxe with a handsome marble-topped bar and an attentive young team. Flavoursome classic French cooking has clever modern touches. Great value set lunch and a terrific selection of wine by the glass and carafe.

Menu £ 23 (lunch) – Carte dinner £ 29/48

Town plan: 6D5-w – *67 High St ✉ SW19 5EE – ⊖ Wimbledon – ✆ 020 8947 8278 – www.thewhiteonion.co.uk – Closed first 2 weeks August, 25 December-4 January, Monday, lunch Tuesday-Wednesday and Sunday dinner*

Hotel du Vin

BUSINESS • CONTEMPORARY A charming part-Georgian house surrounded by over 30 acres of parkland. Dine in the light and airy Orangery or in the restaurant overlooking an Italian sunken garden; French-influenced menus offer something for everyone. Bedrooms are comfortable and well-equipped; ask for one with views of the park.

48 rooms – †£ 145/264 ††£ 155/264 – 2 suites

Town plan: 6C5-x – *Cannizaro House, West Side, Wimbledon Common ✉ SW19 4UE – ✆ 0330 024 0706 – www.hotelduvin.com*

REDBRIDGE

South Woodford

Grand Trunk Road

INDIAN • CONTEMPORARY DÉCOR XX Named after one of Asia's oldest and longest routes, which provided inspiration for the menu. Dishes are well-balanced and original with a modern touch; breads come from a charcoal-fired tandoor and vegetable dishes are a highlight.

Menu £ 23 (weekday lunch) – Carte £ 27/57

Town plan: 4G2-w – *219 High Rd ✉ E18 2PB – ⊖ South Woodford – ✆ 020 8505 1965 (booking essential at dinner) – www.gtrrestaurant.co.uk – Closed 25-26 December, 1 January and Monday*

Wanstead

Provender

FRENCH • BISTRO X A modern, busy and bustling neighbourhood bistro courtesy of experienced restaurateur Max Renzland. The well-priced French cooking is pleasingly rustic and satisfying, with great charcuterie, appealing salads and well-timed grills.

Menu £ 17 (lunch and early dinner) – Carte £ 20/45

Town plan: 4G2-x – *17 High St ✉ E11 2AA – ⊖ Snaresbrook – ✆ 020 8530 3050 – www.provenderlondon.co.uk*

Five Fields

RICHMOND-UPON-THAMES

Barnes

Rick Stein (N)

SEAFOOD • FASHIONABLE XX In a stunning spot beside the Thames; its glass extension offering the best views. Dishes from the celebrity chef's travels inform the menu, so expect Indonesian seafood curry alongside old favourites like cod and chips with mushy peas.

Menu £ 25 (weekday lunch) – Carte £ 26/77

Town plan: 21J8-r – *Tideway Yard, 125 Mortlake High St ✉ SW14 8SN – ☎ 020 8878 9462 (booking advisable) – www.rickstein.com – Closed 25 December*

Riva

ITALIAN • NEIGHBOURHOOD X A restaurant built on customer loyalty; the regulars are showered with attention from the eponymous owner. Gutsy, no-nonsense dishes, full of flavour. Interesting all-Italian wine list.

Carte £ 33/52

Town plan: 21K8-a – *169 Church Rd. ✉ SW13 9HR – ☎ 020 8748 0434 – Closed 2 weeks August, Easter, Christmas-New Year, bank holidays and Saturday lunch*

Sonny's Kitchen

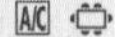

MEDITERRANEAN CUISINE • NEIGHBOURHOOD X A longstanding and much-loved neighbourhood spot with a bright, relaxed feel and some striking art on the walls; co-owned by Barnes residents Rebecca Mascarenhas and Phil Howard. Menus are all-encompassing and portions generous.

Menu £ 20 (weekday lunch) – Carte £ 26/38

Town plan: 21K8-x – *94 Church Rd ✉ SW13 0DQ – ☎ 020 8748 0393 – www.sonnyskitchen.co.uk – Closed 25-26 December, 1 January and bank holiday Mondays*

Brown Dog

MODERN BRITISH • PUB Concealed in a maze of residential streets is this homely, relaxed pub with a lived-in feel. The balanced menu offers traditional and flavoursome fare like venison pie or haddock fishcake; all done 'properly'.

Carte £ 20/40

Town plan: 21J8-9-b – *28 Cross St ✉ SW13 0AP – ⊖ Barnes Bridge (Rail). – ☎ 020 8392 2200 – www.thebrowndog.co.uk – Closed 25 December*

East Sheen

Victoria

MODERN BRITISH · PUB A proper local, with a lived-in feel, especially in the bars; if you're here to eat head for the conservatory, which overlooks a terrace. The appealing menu offers a good range of dishes and comes with a distinct Mediterranean slant, with Middle Eastern influences never far away.

Carte £ 27/47

7 rooms - £ 135 £ 135

Town plan: 6C4-h - *10 West Temple Sheen SW14 7RT - Mortlake (Rail). - 020 8876 4238 - www.thevictoria.net*

Kew

The Glasshouse

MODERN CUISINE · FASHIONABLE XX The Glasshouse is the very model of a modern neighbourhood restaurant and sits in the heart of lovely, villagey Kew. Food is confident yet unshowy - much like the locals - and comes with distinct Mediterranean flavours along with the occasional Asian hint. Service comes with the eagerness of youth.

→ Roast duck breast with charred salsify, pickled rhubarb and samphire. Monkfish, Fowey mussels, sea beets, parsnips, blood orange and verjus sauce. Passion fruit meringue with coconut ice cream and caramelised mango.

Menu £ 35 (weekday lunch)/70

Town plan: 6C4-z - *14 Station Par. TW9 3PZ - Kew Gardens - 020 8940 6777 - www.glasshouserestaurant.co.uk - Closed 24-26 December and 1 January*

Richmond

Bingham Restaurant

MODERN CUISINE · DESIGN XX Its riverside setting adds to the charm of this comfortable and enthusiastically run hotel restaurant. The various menus provide plenty of choice; the cooking is a blend of the modern and the classical and dishes are nicely balanced.

Menu £ 17 (lunch) - Carte £ 30/48

Town plan: 6C4-c - *Bingham Hotel, 61-63 Petersham Rd. TW10 6UT - Richmond - 020 8940 0902 - www.thebingham.co.uk - Closed Sunday dinner*

Dysart Petersham

MODERN CUISINE · INTIMATE XX A pub built in the 1900s as part of the Arts and Crafts movement but now run as quite a formal restaurant. The kitchen uses top-notch ingredients and adds subtle Asian tones to a classical base. Occasional music recital suppers.

Menu £ 25 (weekdays) - Carte £ 38/75

Town plan: 6C4-d - *135 Petersham Rd TW10 7AA - 020 8940 8005 (booking advisable) - www.thedysartpetersham.co.uk - Closed Sunday dinner, Monday and Tuesday*

Petersham Nurseries Café

MODERN CUISINE · RUSTIC X On a summer's day there can be few more delightful spots for lunch, whether that's on the terrace or in the greenhouse. The kitchen uses the freshest seasonal produce in unfussy, flavoursome dishes that have a subtle Italian accent.

Carte £ 28/43

Town plan: 6C4-k - *Church Ln (off Petersham Rd) TW10 7AB - 020 8940 5230 (booking essential) - www.petershamnurseries.com - lunch only - Closed 24-27 December and Monday*

Matsuba

JAPANESE • DESIGN Family-run Japanese restaurant with just 11 tables; understated but well-kept appearance. Extensive menu offers wide range of Japanese dishes, along with bulgogi, a Korean barbecue dish.

Menu £ 25/45 – Carte £ 30/45

Town plan: 6C4-n – *10 Red Lion St* ✉ *TW9 1RW* – ⊖ *Richmond* – *020 8605 3513* – *www.matsuba-restaurant.com* – *Closed 25-26 December, 1 January and Sunday*

Swagat

INDIAN • BISTRO A very likeable little Indian restaurant, run by two friends who met while training with Oberoi hotels in India. One partner organises the warm service; the other prepares dishes with a pleasing degree of lightness and subtlety.

Menu £ 30 – Carte £ 20/32

Town plan: 6C4-b – *86 Hill Rise* ✉ *TW10 6UB* – ⊖ *Richmond* – *020 8940 7557 (booking essential)* – *www.swagatindiancuisine.co.uk* – *dinner only* – *Closed 25 December*

Petersham

HISTORIC • CLASSIC Extended over the years, a fine example of Victorian Gothic architecture, with Portland stone and self-supporting staircase. The most comfortable bedrooms overlook the Thames. Formal restaurant in which to enjoy a mix of classic and modern cooking; ask for a window table for terrific park and river views.

58 rooms – £ 115/165 £ 135/215 – 1 suite

Town plan: 6C4-j – *Nightingale Ln* ✉ *TW10 6UZ* – ⊖ *Richmond* – *020 8940 7471* – *www.petershamhotel.co.uk* – *Closed 25-26 December*

Bingham

TOWNHOUSE • MODERN A pair of conjoined and restored Georgian townhouses; a short walk from Richmond centre. Ask for a room overlooking the river and garden. Contemporary bedrooms; some with four-posters.

15 rooms – £ 129/309 £ 165/325 – £ 17

Town plan: 6C4-c – *61-63 Petersham Rd.* ✉ *TW10 6UT* – ⊖ *Richmond* – *020 8940 0902* – *www.thebingham.co.uk*

Bingham Restaurant – See restaurant listing

Teddington

Simply Thai

THAI • NEIGHBOURHOOD Simple Thai restaurant offering a huge array of dishes. Cooking is adjusted for Western tastes but makes commendable use of British ingredients; the signature dishes are a good bet. Come on a Sunday for good value street food.

Menu £ 30 (weekdays) – Carte £ 20/32

Town plan: 5B5-x – *196 Kingston Rd.* ✉ *TW11 9JD* – ⊖ *Hampton Wick (Rail)* – *020 8943 9747* – *www.simplythai-restaurant.co.uk* – *dinner only* – *Closed 25-26 December*

Prices quoted after the symbol refer to the lowest rate for a single room in low season, followed by the highest rate in high season. The same principle applies to the symbol for a double room.

Twickenham

A Cena

ITALIAN • NEIGHBOURHOOD XX The menu at this bigger-than-you-first-think restaurant covers all parts of Italy but there's more of a northern bias in winter; pasta is a highlight. The owners may not be Italian but you can't fault their passion and enthusiasm.

Menu £ 10 (weekday lunch) – Carte £ 20/45

Town plan: 6C4-p – *418 Richmond Rd. ✉ TW1 2EB – ⊖ Richmond – ✆ 020 8288 0108 – www.acena.co.uk – Closed 2 weeks August, Sunday dinner, Monday lunch and bank holidays*

Crown

TRADITIONAL BRITISH • PUB Relaxed, stylish pub with parquet floors and feature fireplaces; sit in the airy, elegant rear restaurant, with its high vaulted ceiling and garden view. Global, bound-to-please menus offer fresh, tasty, amply-sized dishes.

Carte £ 23/43

Town plan: 5B4-c – *174 Richmond Rd, St Margarets ✉ TW1 2NH – ⊖ St Margarets (Rail). – ✆ 020 8892 5896 – www.crowntwickenham.co.uk – Closed 26 December*

HKK London

SOUTHWARK

Bermondsey

✿ Story (Tom Sellers)

MODERN CUISINE • DESIGN XX Tom Sellers offers a 6 or 10 course lunch and a 12 course dinner menu; serving just 12 tables in what used to be a public toilet and now looks like a Nordic eco-lodge. Modern techniques and a light touch result in food with a back-to-nature feel and strong earthy flavours. Dishes are colourful, playful and easy to eat.

→ Crab with avocado and sea vegetables. Herdwick lamb with sheep's curd. Almond and dill.

Menu £ 45 (weekday lunch)/120 – tasting menu only

Town plan: 42AY5-s – *199 Tooley St ✉ SE1 2JX – ⊖ London Bridge – ☏ 020 7183 2117 (booking essential) – www.restaurantstory.co.uk – Closed 2 weeks Christmas-New Year, Sunday dinner and Monday lunch*

José

SPANISH • MINIMALIST X Standing up while eating tapas feels so right, especially at this snug, lively bar that packs 'em in like boquerones. The vibrant dishes are intensely flavoured – five per person should suffice; go for the daily fish dishes from the blackboard. There's a great list of sherries too.

Carte £ 14/28

Town plan: 42AX5-v – *104 Bermondsey St ✉ SE1 3UB – ⊖ London Bridge – ☏ 020 7403 4902 (bookings not accepted) – www.josepizarro.com – Closed 24-26 December and Sunday dinner*

Le Pont de la Tour

FRENCH • ELEGANT XXX Few restaurants can beat the setting, especially when you're on the terrace with its breathtaking views of Tower Bridge. For its 25th birthday it got a top-to-toe refurbishment, resulting in a warmer looking room in which to enjoy the French-influenced cooking.

Menu £ 24/55 – Carte £ 33/62

Town plan: 34AY4-c – *36d Shad Thames, Butlers Wharf ✉ SE1 2YE – ⊖ London Bridge – ☏ 020 7403 8403 – www.lepontdelatour.co.uk – Closed 1 January*

Aqua Shard

MODERN CUISINE • FASHIONABLE XX The Shard's most accessible restaurant covers all bases by serving breakfast, brunch, lunch, afternoon tea and dinner. If you don't mind queuing, you can even come just for a drink. The contemporary cooking makes good use of British ingredients and comes with a degree of finesse in flavour and looks.

Menu £ 32 (weekday lunch) – Carte £ 49/82

Town plan: 33AW4-e – *Level 31, The Shard, 31 St Thomas St, ✉ SE1 9RY – ⊖ London Bridge – ☏ 020 3011 1256 (booking advisable) – www.aquashard.co.uk – Closed 25 December*

Oblix

MEATS AND GRILLS • TRENDY XX A New York grill restaurant on the 32nd floor of The Shard; window tables for two are highly prized. Meats and fish from the rotisserie, grill and Josper oven are the stars of the show; brunch in the lounge bar at weekends.

Menu £55 (weekday lunch) – Carte £30/164

Town plan: 33AW4-e – *Level 32, The Shard, 31 St Thomas St. ✉ SE1 9RY – ⊖ London Bridge – ☎ 020 7268 6700 – www.oblixrestaurant.com*

Antico

ITALIAN • NEIGHBOURHOOD X A former antiques warehouse, with a fun atmosphere. Straightforward Italian food has its focus on comfort; homemade pasta dishes are a highlight. The downstairs cocktail bar offers over 80 gins and their own brand of tonic water.

Menu £18 (lunch and early dinner) – Carte £23/39

Town plan: 42AX6-e – *214 Bermondsey St ✉ SE1 3TQ – ⊖ London Bridge – ☎ 020 7407 4682 – www.antico-london.co.uk – Closed 24-26 December, 1 January and Monday*

Butlers Wharf Chop House

TRADITIONAL BRITISH • BRASSERIE X Grab a table on the terrace in summer and dine in the shadow of Tower Bridge. Rustic feel to the interior; noisy and fun. The menu focuses on traditional English ingredients and dishes; grilled meats a speciality.

Menu £29 – Carte £28/69

Town plan: 34AY4-n – *36e Shad Thames, Butlers Wharf ✉ SE1 2YE – ⊖ London Bridge – ☎ 020 7403 3403 – www.chophouse-restaurant.co.uk – Closed 1 January*

Cantina Del Ponte

ITALIAN • RUSTIC X This Italian stalwart offers an appealing mix of classic dishes and reliable favourites from a sensibly priced menu, in pleasant faux-rustic surroundings. Its pleasant terrace takes advantage of its riverside setting.

Menu £20 (weekday lunch) – Carte £31/42

Town plan: 34AY4-c – *36c Shad Thames, Butlers Wharf ✉ SE1 2YE – ⊖ London Bridge – ☎ 020 7403 5403 – www.cantina.co.uk – Closed 26-27 December*

Casse Croûte

FRENCH • BISTRO X Squeeze into this tiny bistro and you'll find yourself transported to rural France. A blackboard menu offers three choices for each course but new dishes are added as others run out. The cooking is rustic, authentic and heartening.

Carte £30/36

Town plan: 42AX5-t – *109 Bermondsey St ✉ SE1 3XB – ⊖ London Bridge – ☎ 020 7407 2140 (booking essential) – www.cassecroute.co.uk – Closed Sunday dinner*

Pique-Nique (N)

FRENCH • BISTRO X Set in a converted 1920s park shelter is this fun French restaurant with a focus on rotisserie-cooked Bresse chicken. Concise menu of French classics; go for the 6 course 'Menu autour du poulet de Bresse' which uses every part of the bird.

Menu £38 – Carte £32/39

Town plan: 42AX5-n – *Tanner St. Pk ✉ SE1 3LD – ⊖ London Bridge – ☎ 020 7403 9549 (booking essential) – www.pique-nique.co.uk*

Pizarro

MEDITERRANEAN CUISINE • NEIGHBOURHOOD José Pizarro has a refreshingly simple way of naming his establishments: after José, his tapas bar, comes Pizarro, a larger restaurant a few doors down. Go for the small plates, like prawns with piquillo peppers and jamón.

Carte £ 28/42

Town plan: 42AX6-r – *194 Bermondsey St ✉ SE1 3UW – ⊖ London Bridge – ✆ 020 7378 9455 – www.josepizarro.com – Closed 24-28 December*

St John Maltby

TRADITIONAL BRITISH • BISTRO An austere, industrial-style dining space, tucked under a railway arch in deepest Bermondsey. Cooking is tasty, satisfying and as British as John Bull and the earthy, original selection of wines are also available to take away.

Carte £ 31/35

Town plan: 42AY5-x – *41 Ropewalk, Maltby St ✉ SE1 3PA – ⊖ London Bridge – ✆ 020 7553 9844 (booking advisable) – www.stjohngroup.uk.com – dinner only and lunch Friday-Sunday – Closed Christmas, New Year and Sunday dinner-Tuesday*

Village East

MODERN CUISINE • TRENDY Counter dining is the focus in the main room; those celebrating can tuck themselves away in a separate bar. Cooking mixes contemporary dishes with Mediterranean-inspired plates; the confit turkey leg is the house speciality.

Carte £ 22/50

Town plan: 42AX5-a – *171-173 Bermondsey St ✉ SE1 3UW – ⊖ London Bridge – ✆ 020 7357 6082 – www.villageeast.co.uk – Closed 24-26 December*

Garrison

MEDITERRANEAN CUISINE • PUB Known for its charming vintage look, booths and sweet-natured service, The Garrison boasts a warm, relaxed vibe. Open from breakfast until dinner, when a Mediterranean-led menu pulls in the crowds.

Carte £ 26/39

Town plan: 42AX5-z – *99-101 Bermondsey St ✉ SE1 3XB – ⊖ London Bridge. – ✆ 020 7089 9355 (booking essential at dinner) – www.thegarrison.co.uk – Closed 25 December*

Shangri-La

LUXURY • ELEGANT When your hotel occupies floors 34-52 of The Shard, you know it's going to have the wow factor. The pool is London's highest and north-facing bedrooms have the best views. An East-meets-West theme includes the restaurant's menu and afternoon tea when you have a choice of traditional English or Asian.

202 rooms – †£ 350/725 ††£ 350/875 – ☕ £ 32 – 17 suites

Town plan: 33AW4-s – *The Shard, 31 St Thomas St ✉ SE1 9QU – ⊖ London Bridge – ✆ 020 7234 8000 – www.shangri-la.com/london*

Bermondsey Square

BUSINESS • MODERN Cleverly designed hotel in a regenerated square, with subtle '60s influences and a hip feel. Relaxed public areas; well-equipped bedrooms include stylish loft suites.

90 rooms ☕ – †£ 150/450 ††£ 160/480

Town plan: 42AX6-n – *Bermondsey Sq, Tower Bridge Rd ✉ SE1 3UN – ⊖ London Bridge – ✆ 020 7378 2450 – www.bermondseysquarehotel.co.uk*

East Dulwich

Palmerston

MEDITERRANEAN CUISINE • PUB A brightly run Victorian pub that has a comfortable, lived-in feel and lies at the heart of the local community. The cooking has a satisfying, gutsy edge with meat dishes, especially game, being the highlight.

Menu £ 14 (weekday lunch) – Carte £ 26/44

Town plan: 26U9-x – *91 Lordship Ln ✉ SE22 8EP – ⊖ East Dulwich (Rail). – ✆ 020 8693 1629 – www.thepalmerston.co.uk – Closed 25-26 December and 1 January*

Peckham

Artusi

ITALIAN • NEIGHBOURHOOD X An enthusiastically run Italian restaurant which shows Peckham is on the rise. The kitchen displays clear respect for the seasonal ingredients, dishes are kept honest and the prices are more than fair.

Carte £ 20/40

Town plan: 26U9-a – *161 Bellenden Rd ✉ SE15 4DH – ⊖ Peckham Rye – ✆ 020 3302 8200 (booking essential at dinner) – www.artusi.co.uk – Closed 1 week Christmas*

Southwark

Elliot's

MODERN CUISINE • RUSTIC X A lively, unpretentious café which sources its ingredients from Borough Market, in which it stands. The appealing menu is concise and the cooking is earthy, pleasingly uncomplicated and very satisfying. Try one of the sharing dishes.

Carte £ 25/33

Town plan: 33AV4-h – *12 Stoney St, Borough Market ✉ SE1 9AD – ⊖ London Bridge – ✆ 020 7403 7436 (booking advisable) – www.elliotscafe.com – Closed Sunday and bank holidays*

Padella

ITALIAN • BISTRO X This lively little sister to Trullo offers a short, seasonal menu where hand-rolled pasta is the star of the show. Sauces and fillings are inspired by the owners' trips to Italy and prices are extremely pleasing to the pocket. Sit at the ground floor counter overlooking the open kitchen.

Carte £ 12/22

Town plan: 33AW4-d – *6 Southwark St, Borough Market ✉ SE1 1TQ – ⊖ London Bridge (bookings not accepted) – www.padella.co – Closed 25-26 December, Sunday dinner and bank holidays*

Oxo Tower

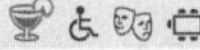

MODERN CUISINE • FASHIONABLE XXX Set on top of an iconic converted factory and providing stunning views of the Thames and beyond. Stylish, minimalist interior with huge windows. Expect quite ambitious, mostly European, cuisine.

Menu £ 35 (lunch) – Carte £ 38/81

Town plan: 32AS3-a – *Oxo Tower Wharf (8th floor), Barge House St ✉ SE1 9PH – ⊖ Southwark – ✆ 020 7803 3888 – www.oxotower.co.uk – Closed 25 December*

Oxo Tower Brasserie – See restaurant listing

Baltic

WORLD CUISINE • BRASSERIE XX A bright, buzzing restaurant with wooden trussed ceilings, skylights and sleek styling. The menu specialises in Eastern European food, from Poland, Russia, Bulgaria and even Siberia. Dumplings and meat dishes stand out – and the vodkas will warm the heart.

Menu £ 22 (lunch and early dinner) – Carte £ 26/38

Town plan: 32AT4-e – *74 Blackfriars Rd ✉ SE1 8HA – ⊖ Southwark – ✆ 020 7928 1111 (bookings advisable at dinner) – www.balticrestaurant.co.uk – Closed 24-27 December and Monday lunch*

Rabot 1745

MODERN CUISINE • DESIGN XX Want something different? How about cocoa cuisine? Rabot 1745 is from the owners of Hotel Chocolat and is named after their estate in St Lucia. They take the naturally bitter, spicy flavours of the bean and use them subtly in classically based dishes. The chocolate mousse dessert is pretty good too!

Carte £ 25/43

Town plan: 33AW4-c - *2-4 Bedal St, Borough Market ✉ SE1 9AL - ⊖ London Bridge - ✆ 020 7378 8226 - www.rabot1745.com - Closed 25-30 December, Sunday and Monday*

Roast

MODERN BRITISH • FRIENDLY XX Known for its British food and for promoting UK producers – not surprising considering the restaurant's in the heart of Borough Market. The 'dish of the day' is often a highlight; service is affable and there's live music at night.

Menu £ 30 (weekdays) – Carte £ 31/63

Town plan: 33AV4-e - *The Floral Hall, Borough Market ✉ SE1 1TL - ⊖ London Bridge - ✆ 020 3006 6111 (booking essential) - www.roast-restaurant.com - Closed 25-26 December, 1 January and Sunday dinner*

Union Street Café

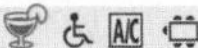

ITALIAN • TRENDY XX Occupying a former warehouse, this Gordon Ramsay restaurant has been busy since day one and comes with a New York feel, a faux industrial look and a basement bar. The Italian menu keeps things simple and stays true to the classics.

Menu £ 26 (lunch) – Carte £ 31/55

Town plan: 33AU4-u - *47-51 Great Suffolk St ✉ SE1 0BS - ⊖ London Bridge - ✆ 020 7592 7977 - www.gordonramsayrestaurants.com*

Arabica Bar & Kitchen

WORLD CUISINE • RUSTIC X The owner-chef once sold mezze in Borough Market so it's no surprise he opened his Levantine-inspired restaurant under a railway arch here. This fun, cavernous place serves sharing plates from Egypt, Syria, Iraq, Jordan and Lebanon.

Carte £ 21/36

Town plan: 33AV4-s - *3 Rochester Wk. Borough Market ✉ SE1 9AF - ⊖ London Bridge - ✆ 020 3011 5151 (bookings advisable at dinner) - www.arabicabarandkitchen.com - Closed 25-27 December and 1 January*

Bala Baya (N)

MIDDLE EASTERN • DESIGN X A friendly, lively restaurant which celebrates the Middle Eastern heritage of its passionate owner. Dishes are fresh, vibrant and designed for sharing and the bright, modern interior is inspired by the Bauhaus architecture of Tel Aviv.

Menu £ 20 (lunch) – Carte £ 22/41

Town plan: 33AU4-a - *Arch 25, Old Union Yard Arches, 229 Union St ✉ SE1 0LR - ⊖ Southwark - ✆ 020 8001 7015 (bookings advisable at dinner) - www.balabaya.co.uk - Closed 25-26 December and Sunday dinner*

El Pastór (N)

MEXICAN • TRENDY X A lively, informal restaurant under the railway arches at London Bridge; inspired by the taquerias of Mexico City. Flavours are beautifully fresh, fragrant and spicy; don't miss the Taco Al Pastór after which the restaurant is named.

Carte £ 12/20

Town plan: 33AV4-r - *7a Stoney St, Borough Market ✉ SE1 9AA - ⊖ London Bridge (bookings not accepted) - www.tacoselpastor.co.uk - Closed 25-26 December, 1-2 January and Sunday*

Hawksmoor

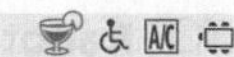

MEATS AND GRILLS • BRASSERIE Hawksmoor's lively 7th branch is a stone's throw from Borough Market, and its Market Specials menu makes good use of its produce. Chargrilled, grass-fed, 35 day dry-aged British steaks are properly cooked and rested and very, very tasty.

Menu £ 25 (lunch and early dinner) – Carte £ 23/68

Town plan: 33AV4-a – *16 Winchester Walk ✉ SE1 9AQ – ⊖ London Bridge – ✆ 020 7234 9940 – www.thehawksmoor.com – Closed 24-26 December and 1 January*

Lobos

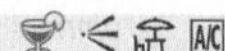

SPANISH • TAPAS BAR A dimly lit, decidedly compact tapas bar under the railway arches – sit upstairs to enjoy the theatre of the open kitchen. Go for one of the speciality meat dishes like the leg of slow-roasted Castilian milk-fed lamb.

Carte £ 18/45

Town plan: 33AW4-a – *14 Borough High St ✉ SE1 9QG – ⊖ London Bridge – ✆ 020 7407 5361 – www.lobostapas.co.uk – Closed 25-26 December and 1 January*

Oxo Tower Brasserie

MODERN CUISINE • DESIGN Less formal but more fun than the next-door restaurant. The open-plan kitchen produces modern, colourful and easy-to-eat dishes with influences from the Med. Great views too from the bar.

Menu £ 30 (lunch) – Carte £ 27/49

Town plan: 32AS3-a – *Oxo Tower Wharf (8th floor), Barge House St ✉ SE1 9PH – ⊖ Southwark – ✆ 020 7803 3888 – www.oxotower.co.uk – Closed 25 December*

Tapas Brindisa

SPANISH • TAPAS BAR A blueprint for many of the tapas bars that subsequently sprung up over London. It has an infectious energy and the well-priced, robust dishes include Galician-style octopus and black rice with squid; try the hand-carved Ibérico hams.

Carte £ 25/32

Town plan: 33AV4-k – *18-20 Southwark St, Borough Market ✉ SE1 1TJ – ⊖ London Bridge – ✆ 020 7357 8880 (bookings not accepted) – www.brindisatapaskitchens.com*

Tate Modern (Restaurant)

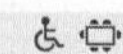

MODERN BRITISH • DESIGN A contemporary, faux-industrial style restaurant on the ninth floor of the striking Switch House extension. Modern menus champion British ingredients; desserts are a highlight and the wine list interesting and well-priced.

Carte £ 27/56

Town plan: 33AU3-s – *Switch House (9th floor), Tate Modern, Bankside ✉ SE1 9TG – ⊖ Southwark – ✆ 020 7401 5621 – www.tate.org.uk – lunch only and dinner Friday-Saturday – Closed 24-26 December*

Wright Brothers

SEAFOOD • COSY Originally an oyster wholesaler; now offers a wide range of oysters along with porter, as well as fruits de mer, daily specials and assorted pies. It fills quickly and an air of contentment reigns.

Carte £ 28/38

Town plan: 33AV4-m – *11 Stoney St, Borough Market ✉ SE1 9AD – ⊖ London Bridge – ✆ 020 7403 9554 (booking advisable) – www.thewrightbrothers.co.uk – Closed bank holidays*

Anchor & Hope 

MODERN BRITISH • PUB As popular as ever thanks to its congenial feel and lived-in looks but mostly because of the appealingly seasonal menu and the gutsy, bold cooking that delivers on flavour. No reservations so be prepared to wait at the bar.

Menu £ 17 (weekday lunch) – Carte £ 19/45

Town plan: 32AT4-n – *36 The Cut ✉ SE1 8LP – ⊖ Southwark. – ✆ 020 7928 9898 (bookings not accepted) – www.anchorandhopepub.co.uk – Closed Christmas-New Year, Sunday dinner, Monday lunch and bank holidays*

Hilton London Bankside

BUSINESS • MODERN A sleek, design-led hotel with faux industrial touches; ideally situated for visiting the attractions of the South Bank. Spacious, contemporary bedrooms are furnished in a minimalist style. Impressive pool in the basement. OXBO serves a range of British dishes including meats from the Josper grill.

292 rooms – †£ 270/369 ††£ 270/369 – ☕ £ 30 – 30 suites

Town plan: 33AU4-b – *2-8 Great Suffolk St ✉ SE1 0UG – ⊖ Southwark – ✆ 020 3667 5600 – www.londonbankside.hilton.com*

Mondrian London

BUSINESS • DESIGN The former Sea Containers house now has slick, stylish look evoking the golden age of the transatlantic liner. Rooms come with a bright splash of colour; Suites have balconies and Superiors, a river view. Globally influenced small plates in the smart restaurant, with meat and fish from the grill & clay oven.

359 rooms – †£ 232/515 ††£ 350/930 – ☕ £ 16 – 5 suites

Town plan: 32AT3-x – *20 Upper Ground ✉ SE1 9PD – ⊖ Southwark – ✆ 020 3747 1000 – www.mondrianlondon.com*

SUTTON

Sutton

Brasserie Vacherin

FRENCH • BRASSERIE Relaxed, modern French brasserie with tiled walls, art nouveau posters and deep red banquettes. Good value midweek set price menu and à la carte of French classics. Diligent service.

Menu £ 20 (lunch and early dinner) – Carte £ 22/41

Town plan: 6D6-x – *12 High St ✉ SM1 1HN – ✆ 020 8722 0180 – www.brasserievacherin.co.uk*

TOWER HAMLETS

Bethnal Green

Brawn

MODERN CUISINE • NEIGHBOURHOOD Unpretentious and simply kitted out, with a great local atmosphere and polite, helpful service. The name captures the essence of the cooking perfectly: it is rustic, muscular and makes very good use of pig. Interesting wine list with a focus on natural and organic wines.

Carte £ 25/44

Town plan: 20U4-z – *49 Columbia Rd. ✉ E2 7RG – ⊖ Bethnal Green – ✆ 020 7729 5692 – www.brawn.co – Closed Christmas-New Year, Sunday dinner, Monday lunch and bank holidays*

Paradise Garage

TRADITIONAL BRITISH • BISTRO X This north-of-the-river sister to Clapham's Manor and Dairy is set under the railway arches in lively Bethnal Green and shares a menu format with its older siblings. The constantly evolving collection of small plates are British at heart and come with compelling contrasts in temperature, texture and flavour.

Menu £ 20 (weekdays) – Carte £ 26/39

Town plan: 20V4-a – *Arch 254, Paradise Row ✉ E2 9LE – ⊖ Bethnal Green – ✆ 020 7613 1502 – www.paradise254.com – Closed 2 weeks Christmas-New Year, Sunday dinner, Monday and lunch Tuesday-Friday*

Smokestak

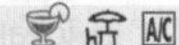

MEATS AND GRILLS • RUSTIC X A buzzing barbecue restaurant with an open kitchen and an industrial feel. Highlights include the brisket and ribs: these are brined, oak smoked, coated with sweet and sour BBQ sauce and chargrilled – the results being unctuous and incredibly satisfying. The charming staff are happy to guide you.

Carte £ 18/30

Town plan: 20U4-f – *35 Sclater St ✉ E1 6LB – ⊖ Shoreditch High Street – ✆ 020 3873 1733 – www.smokestak.co.uk*

Typing Room

MODERN CUISINE • FASHIONABLE XX The room once home to the town hall's typing pool is now dominated by an open kitchen. The 5 course menu offers earthy and elaborate cooking that's heavily influenced by new Nordic cuisine. The tone and style of the service suit the place perfectly.

Menu £ 27 (weekdays)/65 – tasting menu only

Town plan: 20V4-x – *Town Hall Hotel, Patriot Sq ✉ E2 9NF – ⊖ Bethnal Green – ✆ 020 7871 0461 – www.typingroom.com – Closed Sunday dinner, Monday and lunch Tuesday/Wednesday*

Bistrotheque

FRENCH • NEIGHBOURHOOD X When the exterior is as irredeemably bleak as this, you just know it's going to be painfully cool inside. This bustling space in a converted sweatshop is great fun; its menu is French-bistro in style. Live music at weekend brunch.

Menu £ 25 (early dinner) – Carte £ 31/50

Town plan: 14V3-s – *23-27 Wadeson St ✉ E2 9DR – ⊖ Bethnal Green – ✆ 020 8983 7900 (booking advisable) – www.bistrotheque.com – dinner only and lunch Saturday-Sunday – Closed 24-26 December*

Blanchette

FRENCH • BISTRO X Sister to the Soho original with the same lively buzz, funky music and tasty French dishes, but this time the menu heads further south, with a few North African influences too. 3 or 4 plates per person should suffice.

Menu £ 15 (lunch) – Carte £ 14/38

Town plan: 20U4-h – *204 Brick Ln ✉ E1 6SA – ⊖ Shoreditch High Street – ✆ 020 7729 7939 (booking advisable) – www.blanchettelondon.co.uk – Closed 24-26 December*

Good quality cooking at a great price?
Look out for the Bib Gourmand.

Corner Room

CREATIVE • INTIMATE Hidden upstairs in the old town hall is this bright, intimate space – first have a drink in the little bar. The core ingredient of each dish is British and the assured cooking makes you feel you're getting a real taste of nature.

Carte £ 28/35

Town plan: 20V4-x – *Town Hall Hotel, Patriot Sq E2 9NF – Bethnal Green – 020 7871 0461 (bookings advisable at dinner) – www.cornerroom.co.uk*

Sager + Wilde

MEDITERRANEAN CUISINE • RUSTIC Friendly neighbourhood restaurant – a former wine bar – set underneath a railway arch. Tasty, well-priced, creative dishes have a Mediterranean heart and an eye-catching modern style, with some interesting combinations.

Carte £ 19/33

Town plan: 20V4-s – *250 Paradise Row E2 9LE – Bethnal Green – 020 7613 0478 – www.sagerandwilde.com – dinner only and lunch Friday-Sunday – Closed Monday*

Marksman

TRADITIONAL BRITISH • FRIENDLY With its quirky, brown-tiled façade, this pub has long been a local landmark; the wood-panelled bar retains the feel of a traditional boozer, while the first floor dining room is more modern. Simply cooked, seasonal British dishes are wonderfully fresh, well-balanced and full of flavour.

Carte £ 30/40

Town plan: 20U3-m – *254 Hackney Rd E2 7SJ – Hoxton. – 020 7739 7393 – www.marksmanpublichouse.com – dinner only and lunch Saturday-Sunday – Closed 25 December and 1 January*

Town Hall

LUXURY • DESIGN Grand Edwardian and Art Deco former council offices converted into a stylish, trendy hotel, whilst retaining many original features. Striking, individually decorated bedrooms come with retro furnishings and frequently changing art.

97 rooms – †£ 170/457 ††£ 190/532 – 57 suites

Town plan: 20V4-x – *Patriot Sq E2 9NF – Bethnal Green – 020 7871 0460 – www.townhallhotel.com*

Typing Room • **Corner Room** – See restaurant listing

Spitalfields

Galvin La Chapelle

FRENCH • ELEGANT With its vaulted ceiling, arched windows and marble pillars, this restaurant remains as impressive now as when it first opened nearly a decade ago. Service is professional and the atmosphere, relaxed and unstuffy. Cooking is assured, with a classical French foundation and a sophisticated modern edge.

→ Lasagne of Dorset crab with beurre Nantais. Tagine of Bresse pigeon with couscous and harissa sauce. Tarte Tatin with crème fraîche.

Menu £ 35 (lunch and early dinner) – Carte £ 48/76

Town plan: 34AX1-v – *35 Spital Sq E1 6DY – Liverpool Street – 020 7299 0400 – www.galvinrestaurants.com – Closed 25-26 December and 1 January*

Blixen

MEDITERRANEAN CUISINE • DESIGN A charmingly run and good-looking restaurant with lots of natural light; set in a former bank. The appealing European menu offers keenly priced modern dishes. Service is enthusiastic, the atmosphere's buzzing and you'll want to return for breakfast, or cocktails in the basement bar.

Menu £ 24 (lunch) – Carte £ 23/38

Town plan: 34AY1-w – *65a Brushfield St E1 6AA – Liverpool Street – 020 7101 0093 – www.blixen.co.uk – Closed Sunday dinner*

The Frog

MODERN CUISINE • NEIGHBOURHOOD X Ambitious young chef Adam Caxton is making a splash with his restaurant, set in the old Truman brewery; the décor may be neutral but the food is modern and creative, with vibrant flavour combinations. Craft beers and cocktails add to the fun.

Carte £ 17/32

Town plan: 34AY1-f – *2 Ely's Yard, Old Truman Brewery, Hanbury St. ✉ E1 6QR – ⊖ Shoreditch High Street – ✆ 020 3813 9832 (booking essential) – www.thefrogrestaurant.com – Closed Sunday and Monday*

Gunpowder

INDIAN • SIMPLE X A loud, buzzy restaurant with just ten tightly packed tables, serving vibrant small plates from across the Indian regions. The name is a reference to the chef's daily-made spice mix and his menu takes its influence from old family recipes. Standout dishes include deep-fried crab and crispy pork ribs.

Carte £ 15/31

Town plan: 34AY1-g – *11 White's Row ✉ E1 7NF – ⊖ Liverpool Street – ✆ 020 7426 0542 (bookings not accepted) – www.gunpowderlondon.com – Closed Sunday*

Madame. D. (N)

WORLD CUISINE • SIMPLE X Sister to Gunpowder, with a focus on Himalayan cuisine and including dishes from Nepal, Tibet, Northern India and China. The concise menu is made up of great-tasting, nicely spiced small plates; tables, like dishes, are for sharing.

Carte £ 15/30

Town plan: 34AY1-d – *76 Commercial St ✉ E1 6LY – ⊖ Liverpool Street – ✆ 020 7247 1341 (bookings not accepted) – www.madame-d.com – dinner only – Closed Monday*

St John Bread and Wine

TRADITIONAL BRITISH • BISTRO X An appealing restaurant with a stripped back style. The highly seasonal menu offers starter-sized dishes perfect for sharing and the cooking is British, uncomplicated and very satisfying. Breakfast includes a wonderful rare breed bacon sandwich.

Carte £ 26/40

Town plan: 34AY1-a – *94-96 Commercial St ✉ E1 6LZ – ⊖ Liverpool Street – ✆ 020 7251 0848 – www.stjohngroup.uk.com – Closed 25-26 December and 1 January*

Taberna do Mercado

PORTUGUESE • SIMPLE X An appealingly modest little place from Nuno Mendes, serving small plates of Portuguese classics. You'll see staples elevated to a higher level: alheira, Bísaro pork and prawn rissois all deliver wonderful flavours. The wine list, staff, crockery and cutlery are all Portuguese too.

Menu £ 15 (weekday lunch) – Carte £ 16/38

Town plan: 34AY1-m – *Old Spitalfields Market, 107b Commercial St ✉ E1 6BG – ⊖ Liverpool Street – ✆ 020 7375 0649 – www.tabernamercado.co.uk – Closed 24 December-3 January*

Hawksmoor

MEATS AND GRILLS • FRIENDLY X A buzzy, relaxed restaurant with friendly staff. It's not really about the starters or the puds here – the star is the great British beef, hung for 35 days, which comes from Longhorn cattle in the heart of the Yorkshire Moors.

Menu £ 25 (lunch and early dinner) – Carte £ 23/75

Town plan: 34AY1-s – *157a Commercial St ✉ E1 6BJ – ⊖ Shoreditch High Street – ✆ 020 7426 4850 (booking essential) – www.thehawksmoor.com – Closed 24-26 December*

Ottolenghi

MEDITERRANEAN CUISINE • DESIGN X A cross between the original Islington shop and Nopi, their Soho restaurant. The room's bright white look reminds you that the food's all about freshness. Dishes are as flavoursome as they are colourful and sharing is encouraged.

Carte £ 26/67

Town plan: 34AY1-e - *50 Artillery Ln ✉ E1 7LJ - ⊖ Liverpool Street - ✆ 020 7247 1999 (booking essential) - www.ottolenghi.co.uk - Closed dinner 24-27 and 31 December, 1-2 January, 2 April and Sunday dinner*

Som Saa

THAI • RUSTIC X Som Saa's success took it from pop-up to permanent restaurant, with a lively atmosphere and a rustic, industrial look. Menus showcase the diversity of Thai cuisine. 4 or 5 dishes between two are recommended – and do try a cocktail or two!

Carte £ 18/31

Town plan: 34AY1-t - *43a Commerical St ✉ E1 6BD - ⊖ Aldgate East - ✆ 020 7324 7790 (bookings advisable at dinner) - www.somsaa.com - Closed Christmas, bank holiday Mondays, Sunday and Monday lunch*

Batty Langley's

TOWNHOUSE • ELEGANT It looks and feels like a Georgian house, thanks to the antique furniture and attention to detail, yet even the façade was rebuilt. The luxurious rooms come with flowing drapes, reproduction fireplaces and lovely bathrooms. An oasis of composed elegance.

29 rooms - †£ 200/240 ††£ 200/340 - ☕ £ 12 - 1 suite

Town plan: 34AY1-y - *12 Folgate St ✉ E1 6BX - ⊖ Liverpool Street - ✆ 020 7377 4390 - www.battylangleys.com*

Whitechapel

Cafe Spice Namaste

INDIAN • NEIGHBOURHOOD XX Fresh, vibrant and fairly priced Indian cuisine from Cyrus Todiwala, served in a colourfully decorated room that was once a magistrate's court. Engaging service from an experienced team.

Carte £ 24/35

Town plan: 34AZ3-z - *16 Prescot St. ✉ E1 8AZ - ⊖ Tower Hill - ✆ 020 7488 9242 - www.cafespice.co.uk - Closed Saturday lunch, Sunday and bank holidays*

WANDSWORTH

Balham

Lamberts

MODERN BRITISH • NEIGHBOURHOOD X Locals come for the relaxed surroundings, hospitable service and tasty, seasonal food. Sunday lunch is very popular. The enthusiasm of the eponymous owner has rubbed off on his team.

Menu £ 17 (weekday dinner) - Carte £ 24/39

Town plan: 6D5-h - *2 Station Par, Balham High Rd. ✉ SW12 9AZ - ⊖ Balham - ✆ 020 8675 2233 - www.lambertsrestaurant.com - Closed 25-27 December, Sunday dinner and Monday*

Battersea

Chada

THAI • FRIENDLY XX A much loved local Thai restaurant which opened back in 1986 and is still run with considerable charm by its owner. The extensive menu includes a selection of 'small eats' representing refined street food.

Carte £ 19/37

Town plan: 23P8-x - *208-210 Battersea Park Rd. ✉ SW11 4ND - ⊖ Clapham Junction - ✆ 020 7622 2209 - www.chadathai.com - dinner only - Closed Sunday and bank holidays*

London House

MODERN BRITISH • NEIGHBOURHOOD XX One doesn't always associate neighbourhood restaurants with Gordon Ramsay but London House is an appealing place. It's comfortable and well run and the classically-based dishes come with modern touches and ingredients that marry well.

Menu £ 17 (weekday lunch) - Carte £ 29/47

Town plan: 23N8-h - *7-9 Battersea Sq, Battersea Village ✉ SW11 3RA - ⊖ Clapham Junction - ✆ 020 7592 8545 - www.gordonramsayrestaurants.com/london-house*

Boqueria

SPANISH • TAPAS BAR X Occupying a converted bank and smarter than the first branch in Brixton but still delivering the true flavours of Spain. Try the dishes unique to here, like the classic Mallorcan dish Coca Mallorquina and the island sausage Sobrasada.

Carte £ 11/19

Town plan: 24Q8-a - *278 Queenstown Rd ✉ SW8 4LT - ⊖ Clapham Junction - ✆ 020 7498 8247 - www.boqueriatapas.com - Closed 25 December*

Gastronhome (N)

MODERN FRENCH • INTIMATE X A cosy restaurant run by two young Frenchmen. Bi-monthly changing menus offer regional French dishes which come with a very modern, almost Scandic touch. The Gallic wine list has prices right across the scale.

Menu £ 24 (lunch) - Carte £ 45/52

Town plan: 24Q9-e - *59 Lavender Hill ✉ SW11 5QN - ✆ 020 3417 5639 (booking essential at dinner) - www.gastronhome.co.uk*

Nutbourne (N)

MODERN BRITISH • NEIGHBOURHOOD X The 3rd restaurant from the Gladwin brothers; named after the family farm and vineyards in West Sussex. British produce drives the eclectic daily menu, with meats cooked on the open fire; dishes are hearty, wholesome and full of flavour.

Menu £ 20 (weekday lunch) - Carte £ 25/45

Town plan: 23P8-n - *Unit 29, Ransomes Dock, 35-37 Parkgate Rd ✉ SW11 4NP - ✆ 020 7350 0555 (booking advisable) - www.nutbourne-restaurant.com - Closed Christmas, New Year, Sunday dinner and Monday*

Sinabro

MODERN CUISINE • NEIGHBOURHOOD X The main room feels almost kitchen-like, courtesy of a wall of stainless steel; sit at the wooden counter - made by the chef-owner's father. Confidently prepared dishes rely largely on classic French flavours but are modern in style.

Carte £ 30/45

Town plan: 23P9-r - *28 Battersea Rd ✉ SW11 1EE - ⊖ Clapham Junction - ✆ 020 3302 3120 - www.sinabro.co.uk - Closed 13-28 August, 25 December, 1 January, Sunday and Monday*

Soif

FRENCH • NEIGHBOURHOOD X A busy bistro-cum-wine-shop with a great atmosphere. The satisfying French food takes regular excursions across the border into Italy and the thoughtfully compiled wine list includes plenty of natural wines from artisan winemakers.

Menu £ 20 (weekday lunch) - Carte £ 29/40

Town plan: 23P9-c - *27 Battersea Rise ✉ SW11 1HG - ⊖ Clapham Junction - ✆ 020 7223 1112 (booking essential at dinner) - www.soif.co - Closed Christmas, New Year, Sunday dinner, Monday lunch and bank holidays*

Putney

Bibo

ITALIAN • BISTRO X A fun neighbourhood Italian which comes with an appealing vibe, clued up service and well-priced food that's effortlessly easy to enjoy. Its name means 'to drink' and the Italian wine list is well worth exploring.

Menu £ 17 (lunch) – Carte £ 30/38

Town plan: 22L9-b – *146 Upper Richmond Rd* ✉ *SW15 2SW* – ⊖ *East Putney* – ☏ *020 8780 0592* – *www.biborestaurant.com* – *Closed 25-26 December, Sunday dinner, Monday and bank holidays*

Wandsworth

Chez Bruce (Bruce Poole)

FRENCH • BRASSERIE XX Flavoursome, uncomplicated French cooking with hints of the Mediterranean, prepared with innate skill; well-organised, personable service and an easy-going atmosphere – some of the reasons why Chez Bruce remains a favourite of so many.

→ Tuna tartare with spiced onions, lime and coriander. Barbary duck breast with wild garlic butter and asparagus. Lemon and mascarpone Swiss roll with Yorkshire rhubarb.

Menu £ 35/55

Town plan: 6D5-e – *2 Bellevue Rd* ✉ *SW17 7EG* – ⊖ *Tooting Bec* – ☏ *020 8672 0114 (booking essential)* – *www.chezbruce.co.uk* – *Closed 24-26 December and 1 January*

Benares

WESTMINSTER (City of)

Bayswater and Maida Vale

Hereford Road

TRADITIONAL CUISINE • NEIGHBOURHOOD X Converted butcher's shop specialising in tasty British dishes without frills, using first-rate, seasonal ingredients; offal a highlight. Booths for six people are the prized seats. Friendly and relaxed feel.

Menu £ 16 (weekday lunch) – Carte £ 24/32

Town plan: 27AC2-s – *3 Hereford Rd ✉ W2 4AB – ⊖ Bayswater – ☎ 020 7727 1144 (booking essential) – www.herefordroad.org – Closed 24 December-3 January and August bank holiday*

Kateh

MEDITERRANEAN CUISINE • NEIGHBOURHOOD X Booking is imperative if you want to join the locals who have already discovered what a little jewel they have in the form of this buzzy, busy Persian restaurant. Authentic stews, expert chargrilling and lovely pastries and teas.

Carte £ 21/35

Town plan: 28AE1-a – *5 Warwick Pl ✉ W9 2PX – ⊖ Warwick Avenue – ☎ 020 7289 3393 (booking essential) – www.katehrestaurant.co.uk – dinner only and lunch Friday-Sunday – Closed 25-26 December*

Angelus

FRENCH • BRASSERIE XX Hospitable owner has created an attractive French brasserie within a 19C former pub, with a warm and inclusive feel. Satisfying and honest French cooking uses seasonal British ingredients.

Menu £ 23/41 – Carte £ 39/70

Town plan: 29AG2-c – *4 Bathurst St ✉ W2 2SD – ⊖ Lancaster Gate – ☎ 020 7402 0083 – www.angelusrestaurant.co.uk – Closed 24-25 December and 1 January*

Marianne

FRENCH • COSY XX The eponymous Marianne was a finalist on MasterChef. Her restaurant is a sweet little place with just 6 tables. Concise daily lunch menu and seasonal tasting menu; cooking is classically based but keeps things quite light.

Menu £ 35/95 – tasting menu only

Town plan: 27AC1-m – *104a Chepstow Rd ✉ W2 5QS – ⊖ Westbourne Park – ☎ 020 3675 7750 (booking essential) – www.mariannerestaurant.com – dinner only and lunch Friday-Sunday – Closed 22 December-4 January , August bank holiday and Monday*

Kurobuta Marble Arch

JAPANESE • NEIGHBOURHOOD X The Aussie owner-chef's fun Japanese restaurant was influenced by an izakaya. The robata grill provides the sticky BBQ pork belly for the pork buns; the black pepper soft shell crabs fly out of the kitchen; and the yuzu tart is good.

Carte £ 17/32

Town plan: 29AH2-m - *17-20 Kendal St ✉ W2 2AW - ⊖ Marble Arch - ✆ 020 3475 4158 - www.kurobuta-london.com - Closed 25 December*

Pomona's

WORLD CUISINE • NEIGHBOURHOOD X A large neighbourhood restaurant with bright décor, an airy, open feel and a fun, laid-back Californian vibe. All-day menus offer soulful, colourful cooking with breakfast, smoothies, salads, house specials and small plates.

Carte £ 23/51

Town plan: 27AC2-a - *47 Hereford Rd ✉ W2 5AH - ⊖ Bayswater - ✆ 020 7229 1503 - www.pomonas.co.uk - Closed 25 December*

Salt & Honey Bistro

MODERN CUISINE • BISTRO X A cosy neighbourhood restaurant in a residential area just north of Hyde Park. Well-priced, colourful, boldly flavoured dishes use the best British ingredients; expect Mediterranean and Middle Eastern flavours - and plenty of Manuka honey.

Menu £ 15 (weekday lunch) - Carte £ 26/39

Town plan: 29AG2-a - *28 Sussex Pl ✉ W2 2TH - ⊖ Lancaster Gate - ✆ 020 7706 7900 (bookings advisable at dinner) - www.saltandhoneybistro.com - Closed 25-26 December, 1 January and Monday*

Belgravia

Marcus

MODERN CUISINE • ELEGANT XXXX Marcus Wareing's flagship - now run by two long-serving protégés of the MasterChef judge - is elegant, stylish and eminently comfortable. The menu is flexible and dishes come with a refreshing lack of complication; they rely instead on excellent ingredients and accurate techniques to deliver well-defined flavours.

→ Tropea onion with truffle, Old Winchester cheese and wild garlic. Goosnargh duck with chickweed, cauliflower and cumin. Yorkshire rhubarb, vanilla, mascarpone and pistachio.

Menu £ 55/120

Town plan: 38AK5-e - *Berkeley Hotel, Wilton Pl ✉ SW1X 7RL - ⊖ Knightsbridge - ✆ 020 7235 1200 - www.marcusrestaurant.com - Closed Sunday*

Céleste

CREATIVE FRENCH • ELEGANT XXXX The Lanesborough Hotel's restaurant is dressed in opulent Regency clothes; its vast chandeliers, Wedgwood blue friezes and fluted columns giving it a luxurious, formal feel. Classic French cuisine is delivered in an original, modern style; the richness of the dishes reflecting the opulence of the décor.

→ Pressed foie gras terrine, corn-fed chicken, mustard vinaigrette and brioche. Stone bass with globe artichoke, mussels and seaweed butter. Fudge ice cream with roast almonds, caramel and fudge sauce.

Menu £ 38 (lunch) - Carte £ 77/107

Town plan: 38AK5-c - *The Lanesborough Hotel, Hyde Park Corner ✉ SW1X 7TA - ⊖ Hyde Park Corner - ✆ 020 7259 5599 - www.lanesborough.com*

Pétrus

FRENCH • ELEGANT XXX Gordon Ramsay's Belgravia restaurant is a sophisticated and elegant affair. The service is discreet and professional, and the cooking is rooted in classical techniques but isn't afraid of using influences from further afield. The superb wine list has Château Pétrus going back to 1928.

➜ Curried Orkney scallop with egg sabayon, braised kombu and bacon. Poulet de Bresse with pancetta, foie gras, morels and leeks. 'Black Forest', Kirsch mousse and Morello cherry sorbet.

Menu £ 38/85

Town plan: 38AK5-v - *1 Kinnerton St ✉ SW1X 8EA - ⊖ Knightsbridge - ☎ 020 7592 1609 - www.gordonramsayrestaurants.com/petrus - Closed 21-27 December, 1 January and Sunday*

Amaya

INDIAN • DESIGN XXX A decade and a half on and Amaya is still as bright and lively as ever, thanks to the buzz of excited diners and the theatre of its open kitchen. Order a selection of small dishes from the tawa, tandoor or sigri grill and finish with a curry or biryani. Dishes are aromatic, visually appealing and very satisfying.

➜ Black pepper chicken tikka. Smoked chilli lamb chops. Almond and saffron crème brûlée.

Menu £ 26 (weekday lunch) - Carte £ 34/78

Town plan: 37AJ5-k - *Halkin Arcade, 19 Motcomb St ✉ SW1X 8JT - ⊖ Knightsbridge - ☎ 020 7823 1166 - www.amaya.biz*

Ametsa

CREATIVE • ELEGANT XXX Whilst the father and daughter team from the celebrated Arzak restaurant in San Sebastián are behind it, Ametsa has its own style. Most ingredients are sourced from within the British Isles but the flavours, combinations and colours are typically Basque and the dishes are wonderfully vibrant.

➜ Scallops with hemp seeds. Sea bass 'Tamal'. Chocolate emeralds and strata.

Menu £ 29/110 - Carte £ 60/85

Town plan: 38AK5-b - *COMO The Halkin Hotel, 5 Halkin St ✉ SW1X 7DJ - ⊖ Hyde Park Corner - ☎ 020 7333 1234 - www.comohotels.com/thehalkin - Closed 24-26 December, lunch 31 December, Sunday and lunch Monday*

Zafferano

ITALIAN • FASHIONABLE XXX The immaculately coiffured regulars continue to support this ever-expanding, long-standing and capably run Italian restaurant. They come for the reassuringly familiar, if rather steeply priced dishes from all parts of Italy.

Carte £ 37/84

Town plan: 37AJ5-f - *15 Lowndes St ✉ SW1X 9EY - ⊖ Knightsbridge - ☎ 020 7235 5800 (booking essential) - www.zafferanorestaurant.com - Closed 25 December*

The Alfred Tennyson

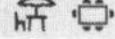

MODERN BRITISH • PUB A cosy, enthusiastically run pub with a busy first-come-first-served ground floor and a more formal upstairs dining room. Classic dishes have light, modern touches; expect smoked mackerel, duck and venison alongside steaks, burgers and pies.

Carte £ 30/43

Town plan: 38AK5-d - *10 Motcomb St ✉ SW1X 8LA - ⊖ Knightsbridge. - ☎ 020 7730 6074 (booking advisable) - www.thealfredtennyson.co.uk - Closed 26 December-4 January*

Berkeley

GRAND LUXURY · ELEGANT A discreet and very comfortable hotel with spacious, modern, immaculately kept bedrooms; several of the suites have their own balcony. Relax over afternoon tea in the gilded, panelled Collins Room or have a drink in the ice cool Blue Bar. Standards of service are second to none.

190 rooms – †£ 330/780 ††£ 390/900 – ☕£ 38 – 27 suites

Town plan: 38AK5-e – *Wilton Pl ✉ SW1X 7RL – ⊖ Knightsbridge – ✆ 020 7235 6000 – www.the-berkeley.co.uk*

✿✿ **Marcus** – See restaurant listing

The Lanesborough

GRAND LUXURY · ELEGANT A multi-million pound refurbishment has restored this hotel's Regency splendour; its elegant Georgian-style bedrooms offering bespoke furniture, beautiful fabrics, tablet technologies and 24 hour butler service. Opulent Céleste serves rich French cooking under its domed glass roof.

93 rooms – †£ 500/700 ††£ 500/700 – ☕£ 38 – 46 suites

Town plan: 38AK5-c – *Hyde Park Corner ✉ SW1X 7TA – ⊖ Hyde Park Corner – ✆ 020 7259 5599 – www.lanesborough.com*

✿ **Céleste** – See restaurant listing

COMO The Halkin

LUXURY · ELEGANT A discreet hotel for those in the know: opened in 1991 as one of London's first boutique hotels and still looking sharp today. Stylish, thoughtfully conceived bedrooms with silk walls and marble bathrooms; those overlooking the garden at the back are particularly quiet. Attentive service; butlers available.

41 rooms – †£ 385/760 ††£ 385/760 – ☕£ 25 – 6 suites

Town plan: 38AK5-b – *5 Halkin St ✉ SW1X 7DJ – ⊖ Hyde Park Corner – ✆ 020 7333 1000 – www.comohotels.com/thehalkin*

✿ **Ametsa** – See restaurant listing

The Wellesley

TOWNHOUSE · ART DÉCO Stylish, elegant townhouse inspired by the jazz age, on the site of the famous Pizza on the Park. Impressive cigar lounge and bar with a super selection of whiskies and cognacs. Smart bedrooms have full butler service; those facing Hyde Park are the most prized. Modern Italian food in the discreet restaurant.

36 rooms – †£ 325/445 ††£ 375/505 – ☕£ 35 – 14 suites

Town plan: 38AK5-w – *11 Knightsbridge ✉ SW1X 7LY – ⊖ Hyde Park Corner – ✆ 020 7235 3535 – www.thewellesley.co.uk*

Hari

BUSINESS · MODERN An elegant and fashionable boutique-style hotel with a relaxed atmosphere and a hint of bohemia. Uncluttered, decently proportioned bedrooms come with oak flooring and lovely marble bathrooms. Cigar bar and terrace featuring a retractable roof. Italian dishes are served in the stylish restaurant.

85 rooms ☕ – †£ 230/500 ††£ 242/512 – 9 suites

Town plan: 38AK6-c – *20 Chesham Pl ✉ SW1X 8HQ – ⊖ Knightsbridge – ✆ 020 7858 0100 – www.thehari.com*

Hyde Park and Knightsbridge

✿✿ Dinner by Heston Blumenthal

TRADITIONAL BRITISH · DESIGN XXX Don't come expecting 'molecular gastronomy' – this is all about respect for, and a wonderful renewal of, British food, with just a little playfulness thrown in. Each one of the meticulously crafted and deceptively simple looking dishes comes with a date relating to its historical provenance.

→ Mandarin, chicken liver parfait and grilled bread (c.1500). Hereford rib-eye with mushroom ketchup and triple cooked chips (c.1830). Tipsy cake with spit-roast pineapple (c.1810).

Menu £ 45 (weekday lunch) – Carte £ 58/121

Town plan: 37AJ5-x – *Mandarin Oriental Hyde Park Hotel, 66 Knightsbridge, ✉ SW1X 7LA – ⊖ Knightsbridge – ✆ 020 7201 3833 – www.dinnerbyheston.com – Closed 17-31 October*

Bar Boulud

FRENCH • BRASSERIE XX Daniel Boulud's London outpost is fashionable, fun and frantic. His hometown is Lyon but he built his considerable reputation in New York, so charcuterie, sausages and burgers are the highlights.

Menu £ 19 (weekday lunch) – Carte £ 26/57

Town plan: 37AJ5-x – *Mandarin Oriental Hyde Park Hotel - 66 Knightsbridge ✉ SW1X 7LA – ⊖ Knightsbridge – ✆ 020 7201 3899 – www.mandarinoriental.com/london*

The Magazine

MODERN CUISINE • DESIGN XX Designed by the late Zaha Hadid, the Serpentine Sackler Gallery comprises a restored 1805 gunpowder store and a modern tensile extension. The Magazine is a bright open space with an easy-to-eat menu of dishes whose influences are largely from within Europe.

Menu £ 26/35 – Carte £ 26/40

Town plan: 29AG4-t – *Serpentine Sackler Gallery, West Carriage Dr, Kensington Gardens ✉ W2 2AR – ⊖ Lancaster Gate – ✆ 020 7298 7552 – www.magazine-restaurant.co.uk – lunch only – Closed Monday except bank holidays*

Rivea

MEDITERRANEAN CUISINE • DESIGN XX Elegant basement restaurant where blues and whites make reference to warmer climes – and also to its sister in St Tropez. Precise, unfussy cooking focuses on the French and Italian Riviera, with an interesting range of vibrant small plates.

Menu £ 26 (lunch) – Carte £ 39/51

Town plan: 37AH5-k – *Bulgari Hotel, 171 Knightsbridge ✉ SW7 1DW – ⊖ Knightsbridge – ✆ 020 7151 1025 – www.rivealondon.com*

Zuma

JAPANESE • FASHIONABLE XX Now a global brand but this was the original. The glamorous clientele come for the striking surroundings, bustling atmosphere and easy-to-share food. Go for the more modern dishes and those cooked on the robata grill.

Menu £ 76/124 – Carte £ 26/193

Town plan: 37AH5-m – *5 Raphael St ✉ SW7 1DL – ⊖ Knightsbridge – ✆ 020 7584 1010 (booking essential) – www.zumarestaurant.com – Closed 25 December*

Mandarin Oriental Hyde Park

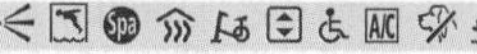

GRAND LUXURY • CONTEMPORARY This celebrated hotel, dating from 1889, is a London landmark; to ensure it remains as such, improvements are constantly being made – this time to the spacious bedrooms, many of which have views of Hyde Park. Enjoy afternoon tea in the charming Rosebery salon or relax in the luxurious spa with its 17m pool. Service remains as strong as ever.

181 rooms – †£ 540/1080 ††£ 540/1080 – ☕ £ 36 – 25 suites

Town plan: 37AJ5-x – *66 Knightsbridge ✉ SW1X 7LA – ⊖ Knightsbridge – ✆ 020 7235 2000 – www.mandarinoriental.com/london*

✿✿ **Dinner by Heston Blumenthal** • **Bar Boulud** – See restaurant listing

Bulgari

LUXURY • ELEGANT Impeccably tailored hotel making stunning use of materials like silver, mahogany, silk and marble. Luxurious bedrooms with sensual curves, sumptuous bathrooms and a great spa – and there is substance behind the style. Down a sweeping staircase to the Alain Ducasse restaurant.

85 rooms – †£ 550/835 ††£ 550/835 – ☕ £ 34 – 23 suites

Town plan: 37AH5-k – *171 Knightsbridge ✉ SW7 1DW – ⊖ Knightsbridge – ✆ 020 7151 1010 – www.bulgarihotels.com/london*

Rivea – See restaurant listing

Mayfair

✿✿✿ Alain Ducasse at The Dorchester

FRENCH • ELEGANT XXXXX Elegance, luxury and attention to detail are the hallmarks of Alain Ducasse's London outpost, where the atmosphere is warm and relaxed. The kitchen uses the best seasonal produce, whether British or French, to create visually striking, refined modern dishes. The 'Table Lumière' with its shimmering curtain affords an opulent, semi-private dining experience.

→ Dorset crab, celeriac and caviar. Dry aged beef, artichoke and bone marrow. 'Baba like in Monte Carlo'.

Menu £ 65/105

Town plan: 30AK4-a – *Dorchester Hotel, Park Ln ✉ W1K 1QA – ⊖ Hyde Park Corner – ✆ 020 7629 8866 (booking essential) – www.alainducasse-dorchester.com – Closed 3 weeks August, first week January, 26-30 December, Easter, Saturday lunch, Sunday and Monday*

✿✿✿ The Araki (Mitsuhiro Araki)

JAPANESE • INTIMATE XX Behind the beautiful 9-seater cypress counter stands Mitsuhiro Araki, one of Japan's great Sushi Masters. He closed his Three Star sushi restaurant in Tokyo to move to London for a fresh challenge, which included using largely European fish. He has spent time adjusting his Edomae methods and techniques and the results are extraordinary.

→ Cornish squid with albino caviar. Salmon roe with seaweed. Medium fatty tuna in two servings.

Menu £ 300 – tasting menu only

Town plan: 30AM3-e – *12 New Burlington St ✉ W1S 3BF – ⊖ Oxford Circus – ✆ 020 7287 2481 (booking essential) – www.the-araki.com – dinner only – Closed August, Christmas-first week January and Monday*

✿✿ Hélène Darroze at The Connaught

MODERN CUISINE • LUXURY XXXX From a Solitaire board of 13 marbles, each bearing the name of an ingredient, you choose 5, 7 or 9 (courses); this highlights the quality of produce used. The cooking is lighter these days yet still with the occasional unexpected flavour. The warm service ensures the wood-panelled room never feels too formal.

→ Norfolk lobster with almond, peach, mint and bottarga. Duck with beetroot, cherry and buckwheat. Strawberry, vanilla, thyme and olive oil.

Menu £ 52/95

Town plan: 30AL3-e – *Connaught Hotel, Carlos Pl. ✉ W1K 2AL – ⊖ Bond Street – ✆ 020 7107 8880 (booking essential) – www.the-connaught.co.uk*

✿✿ Sketch (The Lecture Room & Library)

FRENCH • LUXURY XXXX Mourad Mazouz and Pierre Gagnaire's 18C funhouse is awash with colour, energy and vim and the luxurious 'Lecture Room & Library' provides the ideal setting for the sophisticated French cooking. Relax and enjoy artfully presented, elaborate dishes that provide many varieties of flavours and textures.

→ Perfume of the Earth. Wild turbot on the bone with plankton butter and broccoli. Pierre Gagnaire's 'grand dessert'

Carte £ 110/143

Town plan: 30AM2-h – *9 Conduit St (1st floor) ✉ W1S 2XG – ⊖ Oxford Circus – ✆ 020 7659 4500 (booking essential) – www.sketch.london – Closed 25 December, 1 January, 2 weeks late August-early September, Sunday, Monday and lunch Tuesday to Thursday.*

An important business lunch or dinner with friends?
The symbol ⇔ indicates restaurants with private rooms.

✿✿ Le Gavroche (Michel Roux Jnr)

FRENCH • INTIMATE XXXX Classical, rich and indulgent French cuisine is the draw at Michel Roux's renowned London institution. The large, smart basement room has a clubby, masculine feel; service is formal and structured but also has charm.
→ Lobster mousse with champagne and caviar butter sauce. Loin and cheek of Dingley Dell pork with heritage beetroot and confit lemon. Bitter chocolate and praline with gold leaf.

Menu £ 67/160 **s** – Carte £ 67/197 **s**

Town plan: 30AK3-c – *43 Upper Brook St ✉ W1K 7QR – ⊖ Marble Arch – ✆ 020 7408 0881 (booking essential) – www.le-gavroche.co.uk – Closed 2 weeks Christmas, Saturday lunch, Tuesday lunch, Sunday, Monday and bank holidays*

✿✿ Greenhouse

CREATIVE • FASHIONABLE XXX Chef Arnaud Bignon's cooking is confident, balanced and innovative and uses the best from Europe's larder; his dishes exude an exhilarating freshness. The breadth and depth of the wine list is astounding. This is a discreet, sleek and contemporary restaurant with well-judged service.
→ Native lobster with Green Chartreuse, rhubarb and puntarella. Welsh lamb with aubergine, gomasio, harissa and soya. Garrigue honey with gavotte biscuit and Greek yoghurt.

Menu £ 40/100

Town plan: 30AL3-m – *27a Hay's Mews ✉ W1J 5NY – ⊖ Hyde Park Corner – ✆ 020 7499 3331 – www.greenhouserestaurant.co.uk – Closed Saturday lunch, Sunday and bank holidays*

✿✿ Umu

JAPANESE • FASHIONABLE XXX Stylish, discreet interior using natural materials, with central sushi bar. Extensive choice of Japanese dishes; choose one of the seasonal kaiseki menus for the full experience. Over 160 different labels of sake.
→ Sake-steamed abalone sunomono. Charcoal-grilled quail with sake kasu egg and sansho pepper. Gariguette strawberry, sakura mousse and yomogi.

Menu £ 45/155 – Carte £ 46/151

Town plan: 30AL3-k – *14-16 Bruton Pl. ✉ W1J 6LX – ⊖ Bond Street – ✆ 020 7499 8881 – www.umurestaurant.com – Closed Christmas, New Year, Easter, Sunday and bank holidays*

✿ Fera at Claridge's

CREATIVE BRITISH • ELEGANT XXXX Elegant without stuffiness, this is one of the most striking rooms in the capital and the attentive, personable service is a good match to the setting. There's an impressive purity and originality to the seasonal ingredients, and dishes are deftly executed and wonderfully balanced, with layers of texture and flavour. Tasting menus only, Thurs-Sat.
→ White asparagus with veal sweetbread, curd and smoked egg. Belted Galloway beef with globe artichoke, tomato and sea greens. Chocolate and sweet clover mousse with goat's cheese and apricot.

Menu £ 42/110 (lunch) – Carte £ 61/83

Town plan: 30AL2-c – *Claridge's Hotel, Brook St ✉ W1K 4HR – ⊖ Bond Street – ✆ 020 7107 8888 (booking advisable) – www.feraatclaridges.co.uk*

✿ Alyn Williams at The Westbury

MODERN CUISINE • DESIGN XXXX Confident, cheery service ensures the atmosphere never strays into terminal seriousness; rosewood panelling and a striking wine display add warmth. The cooking is creative and even playful, but however elaborately constructed the dish, the combinations of flavours and textures always work.
→ Roast lobster with guacamole and green gazpacho. Herdwick lamb with preserved green walnut and borage. Strawberry pavlova with sweet cicely.

Menu £ 30/80

Town plan: 30AM3-z – *Westbury Hotel, 37 Conduit St ✉ W1S 2YF – ⊖ Bond Street – ✆ 020 7183 6426 – www.alynwilliams.com – Closed first 2 weeks January, last 2 weeks August, Sunday and Monday*

The Square

CREATIVE FRENCH • ELEGANT XXXX A landmark restaurant now under the ownership of Marlon Abela. Chef Yu Sugimoto brings a greater degree of originality to the cooking as well as more unusual flavour combinations. Service remains as smooth and as well organised as ever and the wine list is now even longer.

→ Marinated langoustine sandwich with mushroom, apple and coral mayonnaise. Pyrenean milk-fed lamb, Roscoff onion, Tokyo turnip and tarragon. Jura whisky chestnut cake with buckwheat praline and toasted malt ice cream.

Menu £ 40/105

Town plan: 30AM3-v - *6-10 Bruton St.* ✉ *W1J 6PU* - ⊖ *Green Park* - ✆ *020 7495 7100* - *www.squarerestaurant.com* - *Closed 24-26 December and Sunday*

Benares (Atul Kochhar)

INDIAN • CHIC XXX No Indian restaurant in London enjoys a more commanding location or expansive interior. Atul Kochhar's influences are many and varied; his spicing is deft and he makes excellent use of British ingredients like Scottish scallops and New Forest venison. The Chef's Table has a window into the kitchen.

→ Chilli, lime and ginger marinated mackerel with gem lettuce salad, garlic and tomato raita. Venison with sorrel, oyster mushrooms and chocolate curry. Peanut butter parfait with almond cake, cumin marshmallow and jaggery ice cream.

Menu £ 25 (lunch and early dinner)/98 - Carte £ 52/68

Town plan: 30AL3-q - *12a Berkeley Square House, Berkeley Sq.* ✉ *W1J 6BS* - ⊖ *Green Park* - ✆ *020 7629 8886* - *www.benaresrestaurant.com* - *Closed 25 December, 1 January and Sunday lunch*

Galvin at Windows

MODERN CUISINE • FRIENDLY XXX The cleverly laid out room makes the most of the spectacular views across London from the 28th floor. Relaxed service takes the edge off the somewhat corporate atmosphere. The bold cooking uses superb ingredients and the classically based food comes with a pleasing degree of flair and innovation.

→ Raw scallop with nori emulsion, blood orange, sweet soy and shiso. Beef fillet with foie gras, mushrooms and truffle. Pistachio and chocolate éclair, poached pear and vanilla ice cream.

Menu £ 37 (weekday lunch)/82

Town plan: 30AL4-e - *London Hilton Hotel, 22 Park Ln (28th floor)* ✉ *W1K 1BE* - ⊖ *Hyde Park Corner* - ✆ *020 7208 4021* - *www.galvinatwindows.com* - *Closed Saturday lunch and Sunday dinner*

Kai

CHINESE • INTIMATE XXX There are a few classics on the menu but Chef Alex Chow's strengths are his modern creations and re-workings of Chinese recipes. His dishes have real depth, use superb produce and are wonderfully balanced. The interior is unashamedly glitzy and the service team anticipate their customers' needs well.

→ Pork belly open bao and char siew with BBQ glaze, crispy bao and pickled cucumber. Roasted Chilean sea bass with sweet lime, chilli and lemongrass sambal. 'Chocolate does grow on trees'.

Carte £ 44/199

Town plan: 30AK3-n - *65 South Audley St* ✉ *W1K 2QU* - ⊖ *Hyde Park Corner* - ✆ *020 7493 8988 (booking essential)* - *www.kaimayfair.co.uk* - *Closed 25-26 December and 1 January*

Murano (Angela Hartnett)

ITALIAN • FASHIONABLE XXX Angela Hartnett's Italian-influenced cooking exhibits an appealing lightness of touch, with assured combinations of flavours, borne out of confidence in the ingredients. This is a stylish, elegant room run by a well-organised, professional and friendly team who put their customers at ease.

→ Manzo di pozza with ricotta, broad beans, spring onion and hazelnuts. Hake, crab and ginger raviolo with savoy cabbage, baby leek and ginger velouté. Honey panna cotta with macadamia clusters and brown bread ice cream.

Menu £ 33/70

Town plan: 30AL4-b - *20 Queen St* ✉ *W1J 5PP* - ⊖ *Green Park* - ✆ *020 7495 1127* - *www.muranolondon.com* - *Closed Christmas and Sunday*

Tamarind

INDIAN • CHIC XXX Makes the best use of its basement location through smoked mirrors, gilded columns and a somewhat exclusive feel. The appealing northern Indian food is mostly traditionally based; kebabs and curries are the specialities, the tandoor is used to good effect and don't miss the carefully judged vegetable dishes.

→ Pudhina chops with dried mint and tomato & coriander chutney. Murgh tikka masala with dried fenugreek leaves. Mango kulfi.

Menu £ 25 (weekday lunch)/75 – Carte £ 37/66

Town plan: 30AL4-h – *20 Queen St. ✉ W1J 5PR – ⊖ Green Park – ☎ 020 7629 3561 – www.tamarindrestaurant.com – Closed 25-26 December and 1 January*

Bonhams

MODERN CUISINE • MINIMALIST XX Established in 1793, Bonhams is now one of the world's largest fine art and antique auctioneers. Its restaurant is bright, modern and professionally run. Dishes are elegant and delicate and there is real clarity to the flavours. The wine list has also been very thoughtfully compiled by Bonhams' own wine department.

→ Scallops, smoked roe, peas and endive. Lamb with ratatouille, olive and anchovy. Chocolate sabayon tart with vanilla ice cream and sour cherry.

Carte £ 47/59

Town plan: 30AL2-n – *101 New Bond St ✉ W1S 1SR – ⊖ Bond Street – ☎ 020 7468 5868 (booking advisable) – www.bonhamsrestaurant.com – Closed 2 weeks Christmas, 2 weeks mid August, Saturday, Sunday, dinner Monday-Tuesday and bank holidays*

Gymkhana

INDIAN • INTIMATE XX If you enjoy Trishna then you'll love Karam Sethi's Gymkhana – that's if you can get a table. Inspired by Colonial India's gymkhana clubs, the interior is full of wonderful detail and plenty of wry touches; ask to sit downstairs. The North Indian dishes have a wonderful richness and depth of flavour.

→ Dosa, Chettinad duck and coconut. Wild muntjac biryani with pomegranate and mint raita. Mango kheer.

Menu £ 25 (weekday lunch) – Carte £ 25/71

Town plan: 30AM3-a – *42 Albemarle St ✉ W1S 4JH – ⊖ Green Park – ☎ 020 3011 5900 (booking essential) – www.gymkhanalondon.com – Closed 1-3 January, 25-27 December and Sunday*

Hakkasan Mayfair

CHINESE • MINIMALIST XX If coming for lunchtime dim sum then sit on the ground floor; for dinner ask for a table in the moodily lit and altogether sexier basement. The Cantonese cuisine uses top quality produce and can be delicate one minute; robust the next. There are also specialities specific to this branch.

→ Supreme dim sum platter. Black pepper rib-eye beef with merlot. Banana and caramel délice.

Menu £ 38 (lunch and early dinner)/128 – Carte £ 37/110

Town plan: 30AL3-a – *17 Bruton St ✉ W1J 6QB – ⊖ Green Park – ☎ 020 7907 1888 (booking essential) – www.hakkasan.com – Closed 24-25 December*

Jamavar (N)

INDIAN • EXOTIC DÉCOR XX Leela Palaces & Resorts are behind this smartly dressed Indian restaurant. The menus, including vegetarian, look to all parts of India, although there's a bias towards the north. The 'small plates' section includes jewels like Malabar prawns, and kid goat shami kebab; from the tandoor the stone bass tikka is a must; and biryanis are also good.

→ Malabar prawns with turmeric, onion and curry leaves. Tulsi chicken tikka with sweet basil, pickled radish and raita. Port-poached pear with chocolate and pink peppercorn kulfi.

Menu £ 25 (lunch and early dinner) – Carte £ 34/54

Town plan: 30AL3-v – *8 Mount St ✉ W1K 3NF – ⊖ Bond Street – ☎ 020 7499 1800 (booking essential at dinner) – www.jamavarrestaurants.com – Closed 25 December, 1 January and Sunday*

Pollen Street Social (Jason Atherton)

CREATIVE • FASHIONABLE XX The restaurant where it all started for Jason Atherton when he went solo. Top quality British produce lies at the heart of the menu and the innovative dishes are prepared with great care and no little skill. The room has plenty of buzz, helped along by the 'dessert bar' and views of the kitchen pass.

→ Pine-smoked quail, 'English breakfast'. Loin & braised shoulder of lamb hotpot with spiced tomato and mint sauce. Bitter chocolate pavé, olive biscuit and olive oil ice cream.

Menu £ 37 (lunch) - Carte £ 62/87

Town plan: 30AM2-c - *8-10 Pollen St ✉ W1S 1NQ - ⊖ Oxford Circus - ✆ 020 7290 7600 (booking essential) - www.pollenstreetsocial.com - Closed Sunday and bank holidays*

Veeraswamy

INDIAN • DESIGN XX It may have opened in 1926 but this celebrated Indian restaurant just keeps getting better and better! The classic dishes from across the country are prepared with considerable care by a very professional kitchen. The room is awash with colour and it's run with great charm and enormous pride.

→ Tandoori green prawns. Hyderabadi lamb biryani. Coconut and palm sugar crème brûlée.

Menu £ 34/45 - Carte £ 33/75

Town plan: 31AN3-t - *Victory House, 99 Regent St ✉ W1B 4RS - Entrance on Swallow St. - ⊖ Piccadilly Circus - ✆ 020 7734 1401 - www.veeraswamy.com*

Cut

MEATS AND GRILLS • DESIGN XXX The first European venture from Wolfgang Puck, the US-based Austrian celebrity chef, is this very slick, stylish and sexy room where glamorous people come to eat meat. The not-inexpensive steaks are cooked over hardwood and charcoal and finished off in a broiler.

Menu £ 45 (weekday lunch) - Carte £ 55/185

Town plan: 30AK4-r - *45 Park Lane Hotel, 45 Park Ln ✉ W1K 1PN - ⊖ Hyde Park Corner - ✆ 020 7493 4545 (booking essential) - www.dorchestercollection.com*

Park Chinois

CHINESE • EXOTIC DÉCOR XXX Old fashioned glamour, strikingly rich surroundings and live music combine to great effect at this sumptuously decorated restaurant. The menu traverses the length of China, with dim sum at lunchtimes and afternoon tea at weekends.

Menu £ 30 (lunch) - Carte £ 37/107

Town plan: 30AM3-f - *17 Berkeley St ✉ W1J 8EA - ⊖ Green Park - ✆ 020 3327 8888 (booking essential) - www.parkchinois.com - Closed 25 December*

Scott's

SEAFOOD • FASHIONABLE XXX Scott's is proof that a restaurant can have a long, proud history and still be fashionable, glamorous and relevant. It has a terrific clubby atmosphere and if you're in a two then the counter is a great spot. The choice of prime quality fish and shellfish is impressive.

Carte £ 37/83

Town plan: 30AK3-h - *20 Mount St ✉ W1K 2HE - ⊖ Bond Street - ✆ 020 7495 7309 - www.scotts-restaurant.com - Closed 25-26 December*

Amaranto

ITALIAN • FASHIONABLE XXX It's all about flexibility here, as the Italian-influenced menu is served in the stylish bar, in the comfortable lounge, on the great terrace or in the restaurant, which is decorated in the vivid colours of the amaranth plant.

Carte £ 38/78

Town plan: 30AL4-v - *Four Seasons Hotel, Hamilton Pl, Park Ln ✉ W1J 7DR - ⊖ Hyde Park Corner - ✆ 020 7319 5206 - www.fourseasons.com/london/dining*

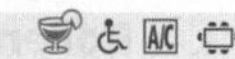

China Tang

CHINESE • FASHIONABLE XXX Sir David Tang's atmospheric, art deco-inspired Chinese restaurant, downstairs at The Dorchester, is always abuzz with activity. Be sure to see the terrific bar, before sharing the traditional Cantonese specialities.

Menu £ 30 (lunch) – Carte £ 28/79

Town plan: 30AK3-e – *Dorchester Hotel, Park Ln ✉ W1K 1QA – ⊖ Hyde Park Corner – ✆ 020 7629 9988 – www.chinatanglondon.co.uk – Closed 24-25 December*

Corrigan's Mayfair

MODERN BRITISH • ELEGANT XXX Richard Corrigan's flagship celebrates British and Irish cooking, with game a speciality. The room is comfortable, clubby and quite glamorous and feels as though it has been around for years.

Menu £ 28 (weekday lunch) – Carte £ 48/81

Town plan: 30AK3-a – *28 Upper Grosvenor St. ✉ W1K 7EH – ⊖ Marble Arch – ✆ 020 7499 9943 – www.corrigansmayfair.com – Closed 25-30 December, Saturday lunch and bank holidays*

The Grill

FRENCH • ELEGANT XXX The Grill is relaxed yet formal, with an open kitchen and a striking, hand-blown Murano glass chandelier as its centrepiece. Grill favourites sit alongside modern day classics on the menu; sharing dishes are a good choice, as are the speciality soufflés. Service is smooth and highly professional.

Menu £ 40 (weekday lunch) – Carte £ 38/87

Town plan: 30AK4-a – *Dorchester Hotel, Park Ln ✉ W1K 1QA – ⊖ Hyde Park Corner – ✆ 020 7317 6531 (booking advisable) – www.dorchestercollection.com*

Hix Mayfair

TRADITIONAL BRITISH • TRADITIONAL DÉCOR XXX This wood-panelled dining room is lightened with the work of current British artists. Mark Hix's well-sourced menu of British classics will appeal to the hunter-gatherer in every man.

Menu £ 35 (dinner) – Carte £ 29/110

Town plan: 30AM3-d – *Brown's Hotel, 33 Albemarle St ✉ W1S 4BP – ⊖ Green Park – ✆ 020 7518 4004 – www.hixmayfair.com*

Sartoria

ITALIAN • CHIC XXX A long-standing feature on Savile Row but now looking much more dapper. Francesco Mazzei, formerly of L'Anima, hooked up with D&D to take the reins and the place now feels more energised. There are hints of Calabria but the menu covers all Italian regions and keeps things fairly classical.

Menu £ 27 (weekday lunch) – Carte £ 38/61

Town plan: 30AM3-c – *20 Savile Row ✉ W1S 3PR – ⊖ Oxford Circus – ✆ 020 7534 7000 – www.sartoria-restaurant.co.uk – Closed 25-26 December, Saturday lunch, Sunday except lunch September-June and bank holidays*

34

MEATS AND GRILLS • BRASSERIE XXX A wonderful mix of art deco styling and Edwardian warmth makes it feel like a glamorous brasserie. A parrilla grill is used for fish, game and beef – choose from Scottish dry-aged, US prime, organic Argentinian and Australian Wagyu.

Menu £ 28 (weekdays) – Carte £ 34/60

Town plan: 30AK3-b – *34 Grosvenor Sq (entrance on South Audley St) ✉ W1K 2HD – ⊖ Marble Arch – ✆ 020 3350 3434 – www.34-restaurant.co.uk – Closed 25-26 December, dinner 24 December and lunch 1 January*

Colony Grill Room

TRADITIONAL BRITISH • BRASSERIE XX Based on 1920s London and New York grill restaurants, The Beaumont's Colony Grill comes with leather booths, striking age-of-speed art deco murals and clever lighting. By making the room and style of service so defiantly old fashioned, Chris Corbin and Jeremy King have created somewhere effortlessly chic.

Carte £ 28/68

Town plan: 30AK2-x - *The Beaumont Hotel, Brown Hart Gdns. ✉ W1K 6TF - ⊖ Bond Street - ✆ 020 7499 9499 (booking essential) - www.colonygrillroom.com*

Momo

MOROCCAN • EXOTIC DÉCOR XX An authentic Moroccan atmosphere comes courtesy of the antiques, kilim rugs, Berber artwork, bright fabrics and lanterns – you'll feel you're eating near the souk. Go for the classic dishes: zaalouk, briouats, pigeon pastilla, and tagines with mountains of fluffy couscous.

Menu £ 19 (weekday lunch) - Carte £ 29/81

Town plan: 30AM3-n - *25 Heddon St. ✉ W1B 4BH - ⊖ Oxford Circus - ✆ 020 7434 4040 - www.momoresto.com - Closed 25 December*

Sketch (The Gallery)

MODERN CUISINE • TRENDY XX The striking 'Gallery' has a smart look from India Mahdavi and artwork from David Shrigley. At dinner the room transmogrifies from art gallery to fashionable restaurant, with a menu that mixes the classic, the modern and the esoteric.

Carte £ 38/79

Town plan: 30AM2-h - *9 Conduit St ✉ W1S 2XG - ⊖ Oxford Circus - ✆ 020 7659 4500 (booking essential) - www.sketch.london - dinner only - Closed 25 December and 1 January*

Bentley's

SEAFOOD • TRADITIONAL DÉCOR XX This hundred year old seafood institution comes in two parts: upstairs is the more formal and smartly dressed Grill, with seafood classics and grilled meats; on the ground floor is the Oyster Bar which is more fun and does a good fish pie.

Menu £ 25 (weekday lunch) - Carte £ 35/72

Town plan: 31AN3-c - *11-15 Swallow St. ✉ W1B 4DG - ⊖ Piccadilly Circus - ✆ 020 7734 4756 - www.bentleys.org - Closed 25 December, 1 January, Saturday lunch and Sunday*

Black Roe (N)

WORLD CUISINE • TRENDY XX Poke, made famous in Hawaii, is the star here. You can choose traditional ahi over the sushi rice or something more original like scallop and octopus. Other options include dishes with assorted Pacific Rim influences, along with others cooked on the Kiawe wood grill.

Carte £ 26/66

Town plan: 30AM2-b - *4 Mill St ✉ W1S 2AX - ⊖ Oxford Circus - ✆ 020 3794 8448 - www.blackroe.com*

Chucs Bar and Grill

ITALIAN • ELEGANT XX Like the shop to which it's attached, Chucs caters for those who summer on the Riviera and are not afraid of showing it. It's decked out like a yacht and the concise but not inexpensive menu offers classic Mediterranean dishes.

Carte £ 40/71

Town plan: 30AM3-r - *30b Dover St. ✉ W1S 4NB - ⊖ Green Park - ✆ 020 3763 2013 (booking essential) - www.chucsrestaurant.com - Closed 25-26 and dinner 24 and 31 December, 1 January and bank holidays*

Coya

PERUVIAN • FRIENDLY XX A lively, loud and enthusiastically run basement restaurant that celebrates all things Peruvian, from the people behind Zuma and Roka. Try their ceviche and their skewers, as well as their pisco sours in the fun bar.

Menu £ 31 (weekday lunch) – Carte £ 27/66

Town plan: 30AL4-d – *118 Piccadilly ✉ W1J 7NW – ⊖ Hyde Park Corner – ☎ 020 7042 7118 (booking advisable) – www.coyarestaurant.com – Closed 24-26 December and 1 January*

Galvin at the Athenaeum

MODERN CUISINE • BRASSERIE XX The ground-floor restaurant of the Athenaeum hotel is now run by the Galvin brothers. Forget the name tags and the turgid music – this is a keenly run room with good food. The ingredients are mostly British but the best dishes are the French ones, like cassoulet and Floating Island.

Menu £ 25 – Carte £ 22/48

Town plan: 30AL4-a – *Athenaeum Hotel,116 Piccadilly ✉ W1J 7BJ – ⊖ Hyde Park Corner – ☎ 020 7640 3333 – www.athenaeumhotel.com*

Goodman Mayfair

MEATS AND GRILLS • BRASSERIE XX A worthy attempt at recreating a New York steakhouse; all leather and wood and macho swagger. Beef is dry or wet aged in-house and comes with a choice of four sauces; rib-eye the speciality.

Carte £ 28/89

Town plan: 30AM2-e – *26 Maddox St ✉ W1S 1QH – ⊖ Oxford Circus – ☎ 020 7499 3776 (booking essential) – www.goodmanrestaurants.com – Closed Sunday and bank holidays*

Hawksmoor

MEATS AND GRILLS • FASHIONABLE XX The best of the Hawksmoors is large, boisterous and has an appealing art deco feel. Expect top quality, 35-day aged Longhorn beef but also great seafood, much of which is charcoal grilled. The delightful staff are well organised.

Menu £ 28 (lunch and early dinner) – Carte £ 23/58

Town plan: 30AN3-m – *5a Air St ✉ W1J 0AD – ⊖ Piccadilly Circus – ☎ 020 7406 3980 (booking advisable) – www.thehawksmoor.com – Closed 24-26 December*

Heddon Street Kitchen

MODERN CUISINE • BRASSERIE XX Gordon Ramsay's follow up to Bread Street is spread over two floors and is all about all-day dining: breakfast covers all tastes, there's weekend brunch, and an à la carte offering an appealing range of European dishes executed with palpable care.

Menu £ 23 (lunch and early dinner) – Carte £ 26/63

Town plan: 30AM3-y – *3-9 Heddon St ✉ W1B 4BE – ⊖ Oxford Circus – ☎ 020 7592 1212 – www.gordonramsayrestaurants.com – Closed 25 December*

Hush

MODERN CUISINE • FASHIONABLE XX If there's warmth in the air then tables on the large courtyard terrace are the first to go. The ground floor serves brasserie classics prepared with care; there's a stylish cocktail bar upstairs, along with smart private dining rooms.

Carte £ 27/64

Town plan: 30AL2-v – *8 Lancashire Ct., Brook St. ✉ W1S 1EY – ⊖ Bond Street – ☎ 020 7659 1500 (booking essential) – www.hush.co.uk – Closed 25 December and 1 January*

Keeper's House

MODERN BRITISH · INTIMATE XX Built in 1860 and fully restored, this house is part of the Royal Academy. Two intimate dining rooms are lined with green baize and hung with architectural casts. The emphasis is on seasonality, freshness and contrasts in textures.

Menu £ 21 (lunch) – Carte £ 28/39

Town plan: 30AM3-x – *Royal Academy of Arts, Burlington House, Piccadilly ✉ W1J 0BD – ⊖ Green Park – ✆ 020 7300 5881 – www.keepershouse.org.uk – Closed 25-26 December and Sunday*

Kiku

JAPANESE · NEIGHBOURHOOD XX For over 35 years this earnestly run, authentically styled, family owned restaurant has been providing every style of Japanese cuisine to its homesick Japanese customers, from shabu shabu to sukiyaki, yakitori to teriyaki.

Menu £ 26 (weekday lunch) – Carte £ 37/125

Town plan: 30AL4-g – *17 Half Moon St. ✉ W1J 7BE – ⊖ Green Park – ✆ 020 7499 4208 – www.kikurestaurant.co.uk – Closed 25-27 December, 1 January and lunch Sunday and bank holidays*

Maze

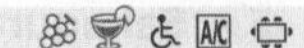

MODERN CUISINE · FASHIONABLE XX This Gordon Ramsay restaurant still offers a glamorous night out, thanks to its great cocktails, effervescent atmosphere and small plates of Asian-influenced food. Three or four dishes per person is about the going rate.

Menu £ 30 – Carte £ 33/53

Town plan: 30AK2-z – *London Marriott Hotel Grosvenor Square, 10-13 Grosvenor Sq ✉ W1K 6JP – ⊖ Bond Street – ✆ 020 7107 0000 – www.gordonramsayrestaurants.com*

Maze Grill Mayfair

MEATS AND GRILLS · FASHIONABLE XX Next door to Maze and specialising in steaks cooked on the Josper grill. Expect a good range of aged meat, including Aberdeen Angus (28 days), Dedham Vale (31), USDA Prime (36) and Wagyu 9th Grade (49), served on wooden boards.

Menu £ 23 – Carte £ 26/105

Town plan: 30AK2-a – *London Marriott Hotel Grosvenor Square, 10-13 Grosvenor Sq ✉ W1K 6JP – ⊖ Bond Street – ✆ 020 7495 2211 – www.gordonramsayrestaurants.com*

Nobu

JAPANESE · FASHIONABLE XX Nobu restaurants are now all over the world but this was Europe's first and opened in 1997. It retains a certain exclusivity and is buzzy and fun. The menu is an innovative blend of Japanese cuisine with South American influences.

Menu £ 33 (lunch) – Carte £ 24/73

Town plan: 30AL4-c – *Metropolitan by COMO Hotel, 19 Old Park Ln ✉ W1Y 1LB – ⊖ Hyde Park Corner – ✆ 020 7447 4747 (booking essential) – www.noburestaurants.com*

Nobu Berkeley St

JAPANESE · FASHIONABLE XX This branch of the glamorous chain is more of a party animal than its elder sibling at The Metropolitan. Start with cocktails then head upstairs for Japanese food with South American influences; try dishes from the wood-fired oven.

Menu £ 33 (lunch) – Carte £ 30/92

Town plan: 30AM3-b – *15 Berkeley St. ✉ W1J 8DY – ⊖ Green Park – ✆ 020 7290 9222 (booking essential) – www.noburestaurants.com – Closed 25 December and Sunday lunch except December*

Ormer Mayfair

MODERN BRITISH · TRADITIONAL DÉCOR XX Run in partnership with Shaun Rankin, chef-owner of Ormer in Jersey. The Channel Islands provide much of the produce in the carefully crafted dishes. The restaurant may suffer a little from its lower floor hotel location but is run with care and enthusiasm.

Menu £ 30 (lunch) – Carte £ 50/70

Town plan: 30AL4-m – *Flemings Hotel, 7-12 Half Moon St ✉ W1J 7BH – ⊖ Green Park – ✆ 020 7016 5601 – www.flemings-mayfair.co.uk – Closed Sunday and lunch Monday*

Roka

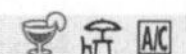

JAPANESE · ELEGANT XX London's third Roka ventured into the rarefied surroundings of Mayfair and the restaurant's seductive looks are a good fit. All the favourites from their modern Japanese repertoire are here, with the robata grill taking centre stage.

Carte £ 24/99

Town plan: 31AN1-k – *30 North Audley St ✉ W1K 6HP – ⊖ Bond Street – ✆ 020 7305 5644 – www.rokarestaurant.com – Closed Christmas-New Year*

Sakagura

JAPANESE · EXOTIC DÉCOR XX A contemporary styled Japanese restaurant part owned by the Japan Centre and Gekkeikan, a sake manufacturer. Along with an impressive drinks list is an extensive menu covering a variety of styles; highlights include the skewers cooked on the robata charcoal-grill.

Menu £ 30/80 – Carte £ 27/55

Town plan: 30AM3-s – *8 Heddon St ✉ W1B 4BS – ⊖ Oxford Circus – ✆ 020 3405 7230 – www.sakaguralondon.com – Closed 25 December*

Sexy Fish

SEAFOOD · DESIGN XX Everyone will have an opinion about the name but what's indisputable is that this is a very good looking restaurant, with works by Frank Gehry and Damien Hirst, and a stunning ceiling by Michael Roberts. The fish comes with various Asian influences but don't ignore the meat dishes like the beef rib skewers.

Menu £ 36 (weekday lunch) – Carte £ 34/147

Town plan: 30AL3-w – *Berkeley Sq. ✉ W1J 6BR – ⊖ Green Park – ✆ 020 3764 2000 – www.sexyfish.com – Closed 25-26 December*

StreetXO

CREATIVE · TRENDY XX The menu at Madrid chef David Muñoz's London outpost is inspired by European, Asian and even South American cuisines. Dishes are explosions of colour and a riot of different flavours, techniques and textures. The quasi-industrial feel of the basement room adds to the moody, noisy atmosphere.

Menu £ 25/90 – Carte £ 38/54

Town plan: 30AM3-t – *15 Old Burlington St ✉ W1S 2JL – ⊖ Oxford Circus – ✆ 020 3096 7555 – www.streetxo.com – Closed 22-26 December*

Theo Randall

ITALIAN · CLASSIC DÉCOR XX A lighter, less formal look to the room was unveiled in 2016 to celebrate Theo's 10 years at the InterContinental. The lack of windows and the corporate nature of the hotel have never helped but at least there is now greater synergy between the room and the rustic Italian fare, made with prime ingredients.

Menu £ 29 (weekdays) – Carte £ 34/65

Town plan: 30AL4-k – *InterContinental London Park Lane Hotel, 1 Hamilton Pl, Park Ln ✉ W1J 7QY – ⊖ Hyde Park Corner – ✆ 020 7318 8747 – www.theorandall.com*

Tokimeitē

JAPANESE • CHIC XX Yoshihiro Murata, one of Japan's most celebrated chefs, teamed up with the Zen-Noh group to open this good looking, intimate restaurant on two floors. Their aim is to promote Wagyu beef in Europe, so it's understandably the star of the show.

Carte £ 28/143

Town plan: 30AM3-k - *23 Conduit St ✉ W1S 2XS - ⊖ Oxford Circus - ✆ 020 3826 4411 - www.tokimeite.com - Closed 25 December, 1-3 January and Sunday*

Wild Honey

MODERN CUISINE • DESIGN XX The elegant wood panelling and ornate plasterwork may say 'classic Mayfair institution' but the personable service team keep the atmosphere enjoyably easy-going. The kitchen uses quality British ingredients and a French base but is not afraid of the occasional international flavour.

Menu £ 35 (lunch and early dinner) - Carte £ 33/55

Town plan: 30AM2-w - *12 St George St. ✉ W1S 2FB - ⊖ Oxford Circus - ✆ 020 7758 9160 - www.wildhoneyrestaurant.co.uk - Closed 25-26 December, 1 January, Sunday and bank holidays except Good Friday*

Le Boudin Blanc

FRENCH • RUSTIC X Appealing, lively French bistro in Shepherd Market, spread over two floors. Satisfying French classics and country cooking are the draws, along with authentic Gallic service. Good value lunch menu.

Menu £ 19 (lunch) - Carte £ 28/55

Town plan: 30AL4-q - *5 Trebeck St ✉ W1J 7LT - ⊖ Green Park - ✆ 020 7499 3292 - www.boudinblanc.co.uk - Closed 24-26 December and 1 January*

Little Social

FRENCH • BISTRO X Jason Atherton's lively French bistro, opposite his Pollen Street Social restaurant, has a clubby feel and an appealing, deliberately worn look. Service is breezy and capable and the food is mostly classic with the odd modern twist.

Menu £ 21 (weekday lunch) - Carte £ 37/56

Town plan: 30AM2-r - *5 Pollen St ✉ W1S 1NE - ⊖ Oxford Circus - ✆ 020 7870 3730 (booking essential) - www.littlesocial.co.uk - Closed Sunday and bank holidays*

Kitty Fisher's

MODERN CUISINE • BISTRO X Warm, intimate and unpretentious restaurant - the star of the show is the wood grill which gives the dishes added depth. Named after an 18C courtesan, presumably in honour of the profession for which Shepherd Market was once known.

Carte £ 30/63

Town plan: 30AL4-s - *10 Shepherd Mkt ✉ W1J 7QF - ⊖ Green Park - ✆ 020 3302 1661 (booking essential) - www.kittyfishers.com - Closed Christmas, New Year, Easter, Sunday and bank holidays*

Mayfair Chippy

FISH AND CHIPS • VINTAGE X There are chippies, and there is the Mayfair Chippy. Here you can get cocktails, wine, oysters, starters and dessert but, most significantly, the 'Mayfair Classic' - fried cod or haddock with chips, tartar sauce, mushy peas and curry sauce.

Carte £ 21/38

Town plan: 30AK2-e - *14 North Audley St ✉ W1K 6WE - ⊖ Marble Arch - ✆ 020 7741 2233 - www.eatbrit.com - Closed 25 December and 1 January*

Neo Bistro

MODERN BRITISH · RUSTIC A rustic two floored former pub which offers a tasting menu alongside its concise and ever-evolving à la carte. The easy-eating, vividly coloured dishes are not only aesthetically pleasing but also packed with flavour.

Menu £ 42 (dinner) – Carte £ 31/37

Town plan: 30AL2-m – *11 Woodstock St ✉ W1C 2AE – ⊖ Bond Street – ☎ 020 7499 9427 – www.neobistro.co.uk – Closed Christmas, Sunday, Monday and lunch Tuesday*

Peyote

MEXICAN · TRENDY From the people behind Zuma and Roka comes a 'refined interpretation of Mexican cuisine' at this fun, glamorous spot. There's an exhilarating freshness to the well-judged dishes; don't miss the great guacamole or the cactus salad.

Menu £ 25 (weekday lunch) – Carte £ 32/63

Town plan: 30AM3-m – *13 Cork St ✉ W1S 3NS – ⊖ Green Park – ☎ 020 7409 1300 (booking essential) – www.peyoterestaurant.com – Closed Saturday lunch and Sunday*

Claridge's

GRAND LUXURY · CLASSIC Claridge's has a long, illustrious history dating back to 1812 and this iconic and very British hotel has been a favourite of the royal family over generations. Its most striking decorative feature is its art deco. The hotel also moves with the times, with its modern restaurant Fera proving a perfect fit.

197 rooms – †£ 480/1140 ††£ 480/1140 – ☕ £ 34 – 62 suites

Town plan: 30AL2-c – *Brook St ✉ W1K 4HR – ⊖ Bond Street – ☎ 020 7629 8860 – www.claridges.co.uk*

✿ **Fera at Claridge's** – See restaurant listing

Connaught

GRAND LUXURY · CLASSIC One of London's most famous hotels, the Connaught offers effortless serenity and exclusivity and an elegant British feel. All the luxurious bedrooms come with large marble bathrooms and butler service; some overlook a small oriental garden, others look down onto mews houses. Refined French cooking in Hélène Darroze; eclectic dishes in relaxed, all-day Jean-Georges.

121 rooms – †£ 540/990 ††£ 630/1110 – ☕ £ 38 – 25 suites

Town plan: 30AL3-e – *Carlos Pl. ✉ W1K 2AL – ⊖ Bond Street – ☎ 020 7499 7070 – www.the-connaught.co.uk*

✿✿ **Hélène Darroze at The Connaught** – See restaurant listing

Dorchester

GRAND LUXURY · CLASSIC One of the capital's iconic properties offering every possible facility and exemplary levels of service. The striking marbled and pillared promenade provides an elegant backdrop for afternoon tea. Bedrooms are eminently comfortable; some overlook Hyde Park. The Grill is for all things British; Alain Ducasse waves Le Tricolore; China Tang celebrates the cuisine of the Orient.

250 rooms – †£ 410/895 ††£ 480/1085 – ☕ £ 34 – 51 suites

Town plan: 30AK4-a – *Park Ln ✉ W1K 1QA – ⊖ Hyde Park Corner – ☎ 020 7629 8888 – www.dorchestercollection.com*

✿✿✿ **Alain Ducasse at The Dorchester** • **The Grill** • **China Tang** – See restaurant listing

Four Seasons

GRAND LUXURY · MODERN It raised the bar for luxury hotels: a striking red and black lobby sets the scene, while the spacious, sumptuous and serenely coloured bedrooms have a rich, contemporary look and boast every conceivable comfort. Italian influenced menu in Amaranto, with its outdoor terrace. Great views from the stunning rooftop spa.

193 rooms – †£ 480/930 ††£ 480/930 – ☕ £ 30 – 33 suites

Town plan: 30AL4-v – *Hamilton Pl, Park Ln ✉ W1J 7DR – ⊖ Hyde Park Corner – ☎ 020 7499 0888 – www.fourseasons.com/london*

Amaranto – See restaurant listing

45 Park Lane

LUXURY • MODERN It was the original site of the Playboy Club and used to be a car showroom, before being reborn as The Dorchester's sister hotel. The bedrooms, all with views over Hyde Park, are wonderfully sensual and the marble bathrooms are beautiful.

46 rooms – **†**£ 495/695 **††**£ 495/695 – ☕£ 32 – 10 suites

Town plan: 30AK4-r – *45 Park Ln ✉ W1K 1PN* – *⊖ Hyde Park Corner* – *✆ 020 7493 4545* – *www.45parklane.com*

Cut – See restaurant listing

The Beaumont

LUXURY • ART DÉCO From a 1926 former garage, restaurateurs Chris Corbin and Jeremy King fashioned their first hotel; art deco inspired, it's stunning, stylish and exudes understated luxury. The attention to detail is exemplary, from the undeniably masculine bedrooms to the lively, cool cocktail bar and busy brasserie.

73 rooms ☕ – **†**£ 395/825 **††**£ 395/825 – 10 suites

Town plan: 30AK2-x – *Brown Hart Gdns ✉ W1K 6TF* – *⊖ Bond Street* – *✆ 020 7499 1001* – *www.thebeaumont.com*

Colony Grill Room – See restaurant listing

Brown's

LUXURY • CLASSIC Opened in 1837 by James Brown, Lord Byron's butler. This urbane and very British hotel with an illustrious past offers a swish bar with Terence Donovan prints, bedrooms in neutral hues and a classic English sitting room for afternoon tea.

115 rooms – **†**£ 500/1000 **††**£ 500/1000 – ☕£ 36 – 33 suites

Town plan: 30AM3-d – *33 Albemarle St ✉ W1S 4BP* – *⊖ Green Park* – *✆ 020 7493 6020* – *www.roccofortehotels.com*

Hix Mayfair – See restaurant listing

Westbury

BUSINESS • MODERN As stylish now as when it opened in the 1950s. Smart, comfortable bedrooms with terrific art deco inspired suites. Elegant, iconic Polo bar and bright, fresh sushi bar. All the exclusive brands are outside the front door.

225 rooms ☕ – **†**£ 300/529 **††**£ 300/529 – 13 suites

Town plan: 30AM3-z – *Bond St ✉ W1S 2YF* – *⊖ Bond Street* – *✆ 020 7629 7755* – *www.westburymayfair.com*

✿ **Alyn Williams at The Westbury** – See restaurant listing

Chesterfield

TOWNHOUSE • CLASSIC There's an assuredly English feel to this Georgian house. The discreet lobby leads to a clubby bar and wood panelled library. Individually decorated bedrooms, with some antique pieces. Intimate and pretty restaurant.

107 rooms ☕ – **†**£ 195/390 **††**£ 220/510 – 4 suites

Town plan: 30AL3-f – *35 Charles St ✉ W1J 5EB* – *⊖ Green Park* – *✆ 020 7491 2622* – *www.chesterfieldmayfair.com*

Flemings (N)

TOWNHOUSE • CONTEMPORARY Made up of a series of conjoined townhouses, this hotel was re-launched in 2016 following a comprehensive refit. Bedrooms are very pleasantly decorated and the keen team provide charming and attentive service.

129 rooms – **†**£ 228/276 **††**£ 282/456 – ☕£ 27 – 10 suites

Town plan: 30AL4-m – *7-12 Half Moon St ✉ W1J 7BH* – *⊖ Green Park* – *✆ 020 7499 0000* – *www.flemings-mayfair.co.uk*

Ormer Mayfair – See restaurant listing

Regent's Park and Marylebone

✿ Locanda Locatelli (Giorgio Locatelli)

ITALIAN • FASHIONABLE XXX Giorgio Locatelli's Italian restaurant may be well into its second decade but it still looks as dapper as ever. The service is smooth and the room was designed with conviviality in mind. The hugely appealing menu covers all regions; unfussy presentation and superb ingredients allow natural flavours to shine.

→ Scallops with saffron. Linguine with Cornish lobster, tomato, garlic and sweet chilli. Warm apple with sultanas, Grand Marnier and yoghurt.

Carte £ 38/69

Town plan: 29AJ2-r – *8 Seymour St. ✉ W1H 7JZ – ⊖ Marble Arch – ✆ 020 7935 9088 – www.locandalocatelli.com – Closed 24-26 December and 1 January*

✿ Texture (Agnar Sverrisson)

CREATIVE • DESIGN XX Technically skilled but light and invigorating cooking from an Icelandic chef-owner, who uses ingredients from his homeland. Bright restaurant with high ceiling and popular adjoining champagne bar. Pleasant service from keen staff, ready with a smile.

→ Chargrilled Anjou pigeon with sweetcorn, shallots, bacon popcorn and red wine essence. Salted cod with Jersey Royals, avocado and romanesco. Icelandic skyr with rye bread and Yorkshire rhubarb.

Menu £ 34/95 – Carte £ 60/92

Town plan: 30AK2-p – *34 Portman St ✉ W1H 7BY – ⊖ Marble Arch – ✆ 020 7224 0028 – www.texture-restaurant.co.uk – Closed first 2 weeks August, 1 week Easter, Christmas-New Year, Sunday, Monday and lunch Tuesday*

✿ Lima Fitzrovia

PERUVIAN • NEIGHBOURHOOD X Lima Fitzrovia is one of those restaurants that just makes you feel good about life – and that's even without the pisco sours. The Peruvian food at this informal, fun place is the ideal antidote to times of austerity: it's full of punchy, invigorating flavours and fantastically vivid colours.

→ Black bream ceviche with avocado, sweet potato and chilli. Suckling pig, chicharrón, sesame and celeriac. Elderberry with avocado mousse, 75% chocolate and rocoto pepper.

Carte £ 41/57

Town plan: 31AN1-h – *31 Rathbone Pl ✉ W1T 1JH – ⊖ Goodge Street – ✆ 020 3002 2640 – www.limalondongroup.com/fitzrovia – Closed 24-26 December, 1 January, Monday lunch and bank holidays*

✿ Portland

MODERN CUISINE • INTIMATE X A no-frills, pared-down restaurant that exudes honesty. One look at the menu and you know you'll eat well: it twists and turns on a daily basis and the combinations just sound right together. Dishes are crisp and unfussy but with depth and real understanding – quite something for such a young team.

→ Isle of Mull scallop, carrots, macadamia nuts and ramson. Denham Estate venison with brassica tops, burnt bread and black garlic jam. Gariguette strawberries with yoghurt sorbet, lemon curd and tarragon.

Menu £ 39/65 – Carte dinner £ 43/55

Town plan: 30AM1-p – *113 Great Portland St ✉ W1W 6QQ – ⊖ Great Portland Street – ✆ 020 7436 3261 (booking essential) – www.portlandrestaurant.co.uk – Closed 23 December-3 January and Sunday*

Trishna (Karam Sethi)

INDIAN • NEIGHBOURHOOD X A double-fronted, modern Indian restaurant dressed in an elegant, understated style. The coast of southwest India provides the influences and the food is vibrant, satisfying and executed with care - the tasting menus provide a good all-round experience, and much thought has gone into the matching wines.

→ Aloo tokri chaat. Seafood pilau with pink peppercorn raita. Chocolate mousse chikki.

Menu £ 35/70 - Carte £ 38/53

Town plan: 30AK1-r - *15-17 Blandford St. ✉ W1U 3DG - ⊖ Baker Street - ☎ 020 7935 5624 - www.trishnalondon.com - Closed 25-27 December and 1-3 January*

Clipstone

MODERN CUISINE • FASHIONABLE X Another wonderful neighbourhood spot from the owners of Portland, just around the corner. The great value sharing menu is a lesson in flavour and originality; choose one charcuterie dish, one from the seasonal vegetable-based section, one main and a dessert. Cocktails and 'on-tap' wine add to the fun.

Carte £ 24/38

Town plan: 30AM1-n - *5 Clipstone St ✉ W1W 6BB - ⊖ Great Portland Street - ☎ 020 7637 0871 (booking advisable) - www.clipstonerestaurant.co.uk - Closed Sunday dinner*

Foley's

WORLD CUISINE • NEIGHBOURHOOD X Cosy up in one of the ground floor booths or head downstairs to the engine room of this lively, well-run restaurant, with its busy open kitchen and counter seating, and its barrel-vaulted caves for six. Vibrant, original small plates reflect the international spice trail; 3 or 4 dishes will suffice.

Carte £ 17/28

Town plan: 30AM1-f - *23 Foley St ✉ W1W 6DU - ⊖ Goodge Street - ☎ 020 3137 1302 (booking advisable) - www.foleysrestaurant.co.uk - Closed Christmas-New Year, Easter and Sunday*

Picture Fitzrovia

MODERN BRITISH • SIMPLE X An ex Arbutus and Wild Honey triumvirate created this cool, great value restaurant. The look may be a little stark but the delightful staff add warmth. The small plates are vibrant and colourful, and the flavours are assured.

Menu £ 22 (lunch) - Carte £ 27/33

Town plan: 30AM1-t - *110 Great Portland St. ✉ W1W 6PQ - ⊖ Oxford Circus - ☎ 020 7637 7892 - www.picturerestaurant.co.uk - Closed Sunday and bank holidays*

Orrery

MODERN CUISINE • NEIGHBOURHOOD XXX These are actually converted stables from the 19C but, such is the elegance and style of the building, you'd never know. Featured is elaborate, modern European cooking; dishes are strong on presentation and come with the occasional twist.

Menu £ 28/60 - Carte lunch £ 34/73

Town plan: 18Q4-a - *55 Marylebone High St ✉ W1U 5RB - ⊖ Regent's Park - ☎ 020 7616 8000 (booking essential) - www.orrery-restaurant.co.uk*

Roux at The Landau

FRENCH • ELEGANT XXX Grand, oval-shaped hotel restaurant run under the aegis of the Roux organisation. Classical, French-influenced cooking is the order of the day, but a lighter style of cuisine using the occasional twist is also emerging.

Menu £ 39 - Carte £ 41/95

Town plan: 30AM1-n - *Langham Hotel, 1c Portland Pl., Regent St. ✉ W1B 1JA - ⊖ Oxford Circus - ☎ 020 7636 1000 - www.rouxatthelandau.com - Closed Saturday lunch*

Archipelago

CREATIVE • EXOTIC DÉCOR XX A true one-off, with eccentric decoration that makes you feel you're in a bazaar. 'Exploring the exotic' is their slogan and the menu reads like an inventory at a safari park; it could include crocodile, zebra and wildebeest.

Carte £ 30/46

Town plan: 30AM1-e – *53 Cleveland St* ✉ *W1T 4JJ* – ⊖ *Goodge Street* – ✆ *020 7637 9611* – *www.archipelago-restaurant.co.uk* – *Closed 23-26 December, Saturday lunch, Sunday and bank holidays*

L'Autre Pied

MODERN CUISINE • DESIGN XX This sibling of Pied à Terre in Charlotte Street has a more relaxed feel and a real sense of neighbourhood; ask for a table by the window to better enjoy the local 'village' feel. The European-influenced food is modern without being unfamiliar.

Menu £ 24/50

Town plan: 30AK1-d – *5-7 Blandford St.* ✉ *W1U 3DB* – ⊖ *Bond Street* – ✆ *020 7486 9696* – *www.lautrepied.co.uk* – *Closed 4 days Christmas, 1 January and Sunday dinner*

Beast

MEATS AND GRILLS • ELEGANT XX An underground banquet hall with three exceedingly long tables set for communal dining. Mains include a perfectly cooked hunk of rib-eye steak and a large platter of succulent King crab. Bring a big appetite and a fat wallet.

Carte £ 49/110

Town plan: 30AL2-d – *3 Chapel Pl* ✉ *W1G 0BG* – ⊖ *Bond Street* – ✆ *020 7495 1816* – *www.beastrestaurant.co.uk* – *Closed Sunday, lunch Monday-Wednesday and bank holidays*

Bernardi's

ITALIAN • NEIGHBOURHOOD XX A modern neighbourhood Italian: chic yet relaxed and with a friendly atmosphere. Pop in for breakfast, brunch, lunch, dinner or cicchetti and cocktails; everything is homemade and dishes are vibrantly flavoured, with a lightness of touch.

Menu £ 18 (weekday lunch) – Carte £ 31/56

Town plan: 29AJ2-x – *62 Seymour St* ✉ *W1H 5BN* – ⊖ *Marble Arch* – ✆ *020 3826 7940* – *www.bernardis.co.uk*

Berners Tavern

MODERN BRITISH • BRASSERIE XX What was once a hotel ballroom is now a very glamorous restaurant, with every inch of wall filled with gilt-framed pictures. Jason Atherton has put together an appealing, accessible menu and the cooking is satisfying and assured.

Menu £ 25 (lunch) – Carte £ 34/76

Town plan: 31AN2-b – *The London Edition Hotel, 10 Berners St* ✉ *W1T 3NP* – ⊖ *Tottenham Court Road* – ✆ *020 7908 7979* – *www.bernerstavern.com*

Chiltern Firehouse

WORLD CUISINE • FASHIONABLE XX How appropriate – one of the hottest tickets in town is a converted fire station. The room positively bursts with energy but what makes this celebrity hangout unusual is that the food is rather good. Nuno Mendes' menu is full of vibrant North and South American dishes that are big on flavour.

Carte £ 37/74

Town plan: 30AK1-a – *Chiltern Firehouse Hotel, 1 Chiltern St* ✉ *W1U 7PA* – ⊖ *Baker Street* – ✆ *020 7073 7676* – *www.chilternfirehouse.com*

Fischer's

AUSTRIAN • BRASSERIE XX An Austrian café and konditorei that summons the spirit of old Vienna, from the owners of The Wolseley et al. Open all day; breakfast is a highlight – the viennoiserie are great. Schnitzels are also good; upgrade to a Holstein.

Carte £ 23/59

Town plan: 30AK1-b – *50 Marylebone High St ✉ W1U 5HN – ⊖ Baker Street – ✆ 020 7466 5501 – www.fischers.co.uk – Closed 25 December*

Galvin Bistrot de Luxe

FRENCH • BISTRO XX Firmly established modern Gallic bistro with ceiling fans, globe lights and wood-panelled walls. Satisfying and precisely cooked classic French dishes from the Galvin brothers. The elegant basement cocktail bar adds to the comfy feel.

Menu £ 20/22 – Carte £ 30/68

Town plan: 30AK1-f – *66 Baker St. ✉ W1U 7DJ – ⊖ Baker Street – ✆ 020 7935 4007 – www.galvinrestaurants.com – Closed dinner 24, 25-26 December and 1 January*

Latium

ITALIAN • NEIGHBOURHOOD XX An Italian stalwart with warm, welcoming service, a contemporary look and a loyal following. The menu focuses on Lazio but travels the length of Italy for inspiration; 'fatto a casa' is their motto and fresh pasta, their speciality.

Menu £ 18 (weekdays) – Carte £ 29/50

Town plan: 31AN1-n – *21 Berners St. ✉ W1T 3LP – ⊖ Oxford Circus – ✆ 020 7323 9123 – www.latiumrestaurant.com – Closed 25-26 December, 1 January and Sunday lunch*

Les 110 de Taillevent

FRENCH • ELEGANT XX Ornate high ceilings and deep green banquettes create an elegant look for this brasserie deluxe. Dishes are firmly in the French vein and they offer 110 wines by the glass: 4 different pairings for each dish, in 4 different price brackets.

Menu £ 20 – Carte £ 31/64

Town plan: 30AL2-f – *16 Cavendish Sq ✉ W1G 9DD – ⊖ Oxford Circus – ✆ 020 3141 6016 – www.les-110-taillevent-london.com – Closed 25 December and 1 January*

Lurra

BASQUE • DESIGN XX Its name means 'land' in Basque and reflects their use of the freshest produce, cooked over a charcoal grill. Choose tasty nibbles or sharing plates like 14 year old Galician beef, whole grilled turbot or slow-cooked shoulder of lamb.

Menu £ 20 (weekday lunch) – Carte £ 31/70

Town plan: 29AJ2-c – *9 Seymour Pl ✉ W1H 5BA – ⊖ Marble Arch – ✆ 020 7724 4545 – www.lurra.co.uk – Closed Monday lunch and Sunday dinner*

Meraki (N)

GREEK • FASHIONABLE XX A lively Greek restaurant from the same owners as Roka and Zuma; its name a fitting reference to the passion put into one's work. Contemporary versions of classic Greek dishes; much of the produce is imported from Greece, including the wines.

Carte £ 25/60

Town plan: 30AM1-m – *80-82 Great Titchfield St ✉ W1W 7QT – ⊖ Goodge Street – ✆ 020 7305 7686 – www.meraki-restaurant.com – Closed Sunday dinner and Christmas*

Percy & Founders

MODERN CUISINE • BRASSERIE XX Where Middlesex hospital once stood is now a residential development that includes this all-day operation. It's a mix between a smart pub and a modern brasserie and the kitchen brings quite a refined touch to the seasonal menu.

Carte £ 26/49

Town plan: 31AN1-f - *1 Pearson Sq, (off Mortimer St) ✉ W1T 3BF - ⊖ Goodge Street - ☎ 020 3761 0200 - www.percyandfounders.co.uk*

The Providores

CREATIVE • TRENDY XX Tables and tapas are shared in the buzzing ground floor; head to the elegant, slightly more sedate upstairs room for innovative fusion cooking, with ingredients from around the world. New Zealand wine list; charming staff.

Carte £ 25/54

Town plan: 30AK1-y - *109 Marylebone High St. ✉ W1U 4RX - ⊖ Bond Street - ☎ 020 7935 6175 - www.theprovidores.co.uk - Closed Easter, dinner 24 and 31 December and 25-26 December*

Royal China

CHINESE • EXOTIC DÉCOR XX Barbequed meats, assorted soups and stir-fries attract plenty of large groups to this smart and always bustling Cantonese restaurant. Over 40 different types of dim sum served during the day.

Menu £ 34/38 - Carte £ 25/100

Town plan: 30AK1-h - *24-26 Baker St ✉ W1U 7AB - ⊖ Baker Street - ☎ 020 7487 4688 - www.royalchinagroup.co.uk - Closed 23-25 December*

Royal China Club

CHINESE • ELEGANT XX 'The Club' is the glittering bauble in the Royal China chain but along with the luxurious feel of the room comes an appealing sense of calm. Their lunchtime dim sum is very good; at dinner try their more unusual Cantonese dishes.

Carte £ 35/80

Town plan: 30AK1-c - *40-42 Baker St ✉ W1U 7AJ - ⊖ Baker Street - ☎ 020 7486 3898 - www.royalchinagroup.co.uk - Closed 25-27 December*

The Wallace

MODERN BRITISH • FRIENDLY XX Large glass-roofed courtyard on the ground floor of Hertford House, home to the splendid Wallace Collection. Menu of Modern British dishes, with plenty to please vegetarians. The ambience is sedate and service is smooth and unruffled.

Carte £ 32/49

Town plan: 30AK1-2-k - *Hertford House, Manchester Sq ✉ W1U 3BN - ⊖ Bond Street - ☎ 020 7563 9505 - www.peytonandbyrne.co.uk - lunch only and dinner Friday-Saturday - Closed 24-26 December and Easter Sunday*

Bonnie Gull

SEAFOOD • SIMPLE X Sweet Bonnie Gull calls itself a 'seafood shack' - a reference perhaps to its modest beginnings as a pop-up. Start with something from the raw bar then go for classics like Cullen skink, Devon cock crab or fish and chips. There's another branch in Soho.

Carte £ 27/45

Town plan: 30AM1-b - *21a Foley St ✉ W1W 6DS - ⊖ Goodge Street - ☎ 020 7436 0921 (booking essential) - www.bonniegull.com - Closed 25 December-3 January*

Dinings

JAPANESE • COSY It's hard not to be charmed by this sweet little Japanese place, with its ground floor counter and basement tables. Its strengths lie with the more creative, contemporary dishes; sharing is recommended but prices can be steep.

Carte £ 21/65

Town plan: 29AH1-c – *22 Harcourt St. ✉ W1H 4HH – ⊖ Edgware Road – ✆ 020 7723 0666 (booking essential) – www.dinings.co.uk – Closed Christmas*

Donostia

BASQUE • TAPAS BAR The two young owners were inspired by the food of San Sebastián to open this pintxos and tapas bar. Sit at the counter for Basque classics like cod with pil-pil sauce, chorizo from the native Kintoa pig and slow-cooked pig's cheeks.

Carte £ 20/43

Town plan: 29AJ2-s – *10 Seymour Pl ✉ W1H 7ND – ⊖ Marble Arch – ✆ 020 3620 1845 – www.donostia.co.uk – Closed Christmas, New Year and Monday lunch*

Jikoni (N)

INDIAN • ELEGANT Indian tablecloths and colourful cushions create a homely feel at this idiosyncratic restaurant. Born in Kenya of Indian parents and brought up in London, chef Ravinder Bhogal takes culinary inspiration from these sources and more.

Menu £ 20 (weekday lunch) – Carte £ 26/45

Town plan: 30AK1-d – *19-21 Blandford St ✉ W1U 3DH – ⊖ Baker Street – ✆ 020 7034 1988 – www.jikonilondon.com – Closed Saturday lunch and Sunday dinner*

Mac & Wild

SCOTTISH • FRIENDLY The owner of this 'Highland restaurant' is the son of an Ardgay butcher – it is all about their wild venison and top quality game and seafood from Scotland. Don't miss the 'wee plates' like the deliriously addictive haggis pops. There's also a choice of over 100 whiskies.

Carte £ 23/50

Town plan: 30AM1-a – *65 Great Tichfield St ✉ W1W 7PS – ⊖ Oxford Circus – ✆ 020 7637 0510 – www.macandwild.com – Closed Sunday dinner*

Opso

GREEK • NEIGHBOURHOOD A modern Greek restaurant which has proved a good fit for the neighbourhood – and not just because it's around the corner from the Hellenic Centre. It serves small sharing plates that mix the modern with the traditional.

Carte £ 17/53

Town plan: 30AK1-s – *10 Paddington St ✉ W1U 5QL – ⊖ Baker Street – ✆ 020 7487 5088 – www.opso.co.uk – Closed 23 December-3 January*

Picture Marylebone

MODERN BRITISH • DESIGN This follow-up to Picture Fitzrovia hit the ground running. The cleverly created à la carte of flavoursome small plates lists 3 vegetable, 3 fish and 3 meat choices, followed by 3 desserts – choose one from each section.

Menu £ 22 (lunch) – Carte £ 27/33

Town plan: 30AL1-m – *19 New Cavendish St ✉ W1G 9TZ – ⊖ Bond Street – ✆ 020 7935 0058 – www.picturerestaurant.co.uk – Closed Sunday and bank holidays*

Riding House Café

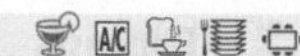

MODERN CUISINE • RUSTIC It's less a café, more a large, quirkily designed, all-day New York style brasserie and cocktail bar. The small plates have more zing than the main courses. The 'unbookable' side of the restaurant is the more fun part.

Carte £ 25/46

Town plan: 30AM1-k - *43-51 Great Titchfield St ✉ W1W 7PQ - ⊖ Oxford Circus - ✆ 020 7927 0840 - www.ridinghousecafe.co.uk - Closed 25-26 December*

Social Wine & Tapas

MEDITERRANEAN CUISINE • NEIGHBOURHOOD From the Jason Atherton stable, and the name says it all. Urban styling, with wines on display; sit in the moodily lit basement. A mix of Spanish and Mediterranean dishes, with some Atherton classics too; desserts are a highlight.

Menu £ 16 (lunch) - Carte £ 15/34

Town plan: 30AK2-t - *39 James St ✉ W1U 1DL - ⊖ Bond Street - ✆ 020 7993 3257 (bookings not accepted) - www.socialwineandtapas.com - Closed bank holidays*

Vinoteca

MODERN CUISINE • WINE BAR A fun place with a great selection of wines, fresh flavourful cooking and enthusiastic staff. Influences from sunnier parts of Europe, along with some British dishes. Great value midweek lunch menu; try the themed monthly wine flight.

Menu £ 16 (weekday lunch) - Carte £ 22/36

Town plan: 29AJ2-v - *15 Seymour Pl. ✉ W1H 5BD - ⊖ Marble Arch - ✆ 020 7724 7288 (booking advisable) - www.vinoteca.co.uk - Closed Christmas, bank holidays and Sunday dinner*

Zoilo

ARGENTINIAN • FRIENDLY It's all about sharing so plonk yourself at the counter and discover Argentina's regional specialities. Typical dishes include braised pig head croquettes or grilled scallops with pork belly, and there's an appealing all-Argentinian wine list.

Menu £ 15 (weekday lunch) - Carte £ 25/53

Town plan: 30AK2-z - *9 Duke St. ✉ W1U 3EG - ⊖ Bond Street - ✆ 020 7486 9699 - www.zoilo.co.uk*

Portman

MODERN CUISINE • PUB The condemned on their way to Tyburn Tree gallows would take their last drink here. Now it's an urbane pub with a formal upstairs dining room. The ground floor is more fun for enjoying the down-to-earth menu.

Carte £ 26/46

Town plan: 29AJ2-n - *51 Upper Berkeley St ✉ W1H 7QW - ⊖ Marble Arch. - ✆ 020 7723 8996 - www.theportmanmarylebone.com*

Langham

LUXURY • ELEGANT Was one of Europe's first purpose-built grand hotels when it opened in 1865. Now back to its best, with its famous Palm Court for afternoon tea, its stylish Artesian bar and bedrooms that are not without personality and elegance.

380 rooms - †£ 400/600 ††£ 400/600 - ☕ £ 34 - 31 suites

Town plan: 30AM1-n - *1c Portland Pl, Regent St ✉ W1B 1JA - ⊖ Oxford Circus - ✆ 020 7636 1000 - www.langhamhotels.com*

Roux at The Landau - See restaurant listing

The London Edition

BUSINESS • DESIGN Formerly Berners, a classic Edwardian hotel, strikingly reborn through a partnership between Ian Schrager and Marriott – the former's influence most apparent in the stylish lobby and bar. Slick, understated rooms; the best ones have balconies.

173 rooms – †£ 295/500 ††£ 295/500 – ☕ £ 26 – 7 suites

Town plan: 31AN2-b – *10 Berners St ✉ W1T 3NP – ⊖ Tottenham Court Road – ✆ 020 7781 0000 – www.editionhotels.com/london*

Berners Tavern – See restaurant listing

Charlotte Street

GRAND LUXURY • CONTEMPORARY Stylish interior designed with a charming, understated English feel. Impeccably kept and individually decorated bedrooms. Popular in-house screening room. Colourful restaurant whose terrace spills onto Charlotte Street; grilled meats a highlight.

52 rooms – †£ 276/396 ††£ 276/612 – ☕ £ 18 – 3 suites

Town plan: 31AN1-e – *15 Charlotte St ✉ W1T 1RJ – ⊖ Goodge Street – ✆ 020 7806 2000 – www.charlottestreethotel.co.uk*

Chiltern Firehouse

TOWNHOUSE • GRAND LUXURY From Chateau Marmont in LA to The Mercer in New York, André Balazs' hotels are effortlessly cool. For his London entrance, he sympathetically restored and extended a Gothic Victorian fire station. The style comes with an easy elegance; it's an oasis of calm and hardly feels like a hotel at all.

26 rooms – †£ 455/545 ††£ 720/950 – ☕ £ 25 – 10 suites

Town plan: 30AK1-a – *1 Chiltern St ✉ W1U 7PA – ⊖ Baker Street – ✆ 020 7073 7676 – www.chilternfirehouse.com*

Chiltern Firehouse – See restaurant listing

Sanderson

LUXURY • MINIMALIST Originally designed by Philippe Starck and his influence is still evident. The Purple Bar is dark and moody; the Long Bar is bright and stylish. Bedrooms are crisply decorated and come complete with all mod cons.

150 rooms – †£ 219/459 ††£ 219/459 – ☕ £ 22

Town plan: 31AN1-c – *50 Berners St ✉ W1T 3NG – ⊖ Oxford Circus – ✆ 020 7300 1400 – www.morganshotelgroup.com*

Zetter Townhouse Marylebone

TOWNHOUSE • ELEGANT A stylish Georgian townhouse, with a sumptuously decorated lounge and cocktail bar and beautifully appointed bedrooms; the best features a roll-top bath on its rooftop terrace. Friendly, professional staff and impressive eco credentials.

24 rooms – †£ 290/570 ††£ 290/570 – ☕ £ 14

Town plan: 29AJ2-b – *28-30 Seymour St ✉ W1H 7JB – ⊖ Marble Arch – ✆ 020 7324 4544 – www.thezettertownhouse.com*

Dorset Square

TOWNHOUSE • CONTEMPORARY Having reacquired this Regency townhouse, Firmdale refurbished it fully before reopening it in 2012. It has a contemporary yet intimate feel and visiting MCC members will appreciate the cricketing theme, which even extends to the cocktails in their sweet little basement brasserie.

38 rooms – †£ 180/234 ††£ 240/504 – ☕ £ 18

Town plan: 17P4-s – *39-40 Dorset Sq ✉ NW1 6QN – ⊖ Marylebone – ✆ 020 7723 7874 – www.dorsetsquarehotel.co.uk*

LONDON ENGLAND

Durrants

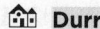

TRADITIONAL • CLASSIC Traditional, privately owned hotel with friendly, long-standing staff. Bedrooms are now brighter in style but still retain a certain English character. Clubby dining room for mix of British classics and lighter, European dishes.

92 rooms – £ 195 £ 250 – £ 20 – 4 suites

Town plan: 30AK1-e – *26-32 George St ✉ W1H 5BJ – ⊖ Bond Street – ✆ 020 7935 8131 – www.durrantshotel.co.uk*

Marble Arch by Montcalm

TOWNHOUSE • CONTEMPORARY Bedrooms at this 5-storey Georgian townhouse come with the same high standards of stylish, contemporary design as its parent hotel opposite, the Montcalm, but are just a little more compact.

42 rooms – £ 250/395 £ 265/395 – £ 20

Town plan: 29AJ2-a – *31 Great Cumberland Pl ✉ W1H 7TA – ⊖ Marble Arch – ✆ 020 7258 0777 – www.themarblearch.co.uk*

No. Ten Manchester Street

TOWNHOUSE • MODERN Converted Edwardian house in an appealing, central location. A discreet entrance leads into a little lounge and an Italian-themed bistro; the semi-enclosed cigar bar is also a feature. Neat, well-kept bedrooms.

44 rooms – £ 180/385 £ 180/385 – £ 15 – 9 suites

Town plan: 30AK1-v – *10 Manchester St ✉ W1U 4DG – ⊖ Baker Street – ✆ 020 7317 5900 – www.tenmanchesterstreethotel.com*

Sumner

TOWNHOUSE • PERSONALISED Two Georgian terrace houses in a great central location. There's a stylish sitting room, a basement breakfast room and well-kept, comfortable bedrooms; the largest of which – 101 and 201 – benefit from having full-length windows.

19 rooms – £ 140/300 £ 140/300

Town plan: 29AJ2-c – *54 Upper Berkeley St ✉ W1H 7QR – ⊖ Marble Arch – ✆ 020 7723 2244 – www.thesumner.com*

St James's

Ritz Restaurant

CLASSIC CUISINE • LUXURY XxXxX Thanks to the lavishness of its Louis XVI decoration, there is nowhere grander than The Ritz. The classic cuisine uses extravagant ingredients along with subtle contemporary elements to lift dishes to new heights while still respecting their heritage. The formal service is now more youthful and enthusiastic.

→ Norfolk crab with pickled cucumber, egg yolk and oscietra caviar. Fillet of veal with wild mushrooms and smoked bone marrow. Crêpes Suzette.

Menu £ 52 (weekday lunch) – Carte £ 75/136

Town plan: 30AM4-c – *Ritz Hotel, 150 Piccadilly ✉ W1J 9BR – ⊖ Green Park – ✆ 020 7300 2370 – www.theritzlondon.com*

Seven Park Place

MODERN CUISINE • COSY XxX William Drabble's cooking is all about the quality of the produce, much of which comes from the Lake District, and his confident cooking allows natural flavours to shine. This diminutive restaurant is concealed within the hotel and divided into two; ask for the warmer, gilded back room.

→ Warm salad of poached native lobster tail with spring vegetables. Saddle of Lune Valley lamb with garlic and rosemary. Passion fruit soufflé with dark chocolate sauce.

Menu £ 33/71

Town plan: 30AM4-k – *St James's Hotel and Club, 7-8 Park Pl ✉ SW1A 1LS – ⊖ Green Park – ✆ 020 7316 1615 (booking essential) – www.stjameshotelandclub.com – Closed Sunday and Monday*

Aquavit

SCANDINAVIAN • BRASSERIE XX Unlike the original in NYC, this Aquavit comes in the form of a warmly lit, relaxed brasserie. The Scandinavian cooking may also be less intricate but it's still immeasurably appealing. Kick things off by heading straight to the smörgåsbord section and some wonderful herring or shrimp.

→ Smoked eel with charred spring cabbage. Boned trout, dill, almond and capers. Arctic bird's nest.

Menu £ 29 (lunch) – Carte £ 26/67

Town plan: 31AN3-d – *St James's Market, 1 Carlton St ✉ SW1Y 4QQ – ⊖ Piccadilly Circus – ✆ 020 7024 9848 – www.aquavitrestaurants.com – Closed 24-26 December and 1 January*

Chutney Mary

INDIAN • ELEGANT XXX One of London's pioneering Indian restaurants, in the heart of St James's; the elegant surroundings feature bold art and a smart bar. Spicing is understated; classics are done well; and some regional dishes have been subtly updated.

Menu £ 28 (weekday lunch) – Carte £ 34/77

Town plan: 30AM4-c – *73 St James's St ✉ SW1A 1PH – ⊖ Green Park – ✆ 020 7629 6688 – www.chutneymary.com – Closed 25 December*

Milos

SEAFOOD • ELEGANT XXX London's branch of this international group of Greek seafood estiatorios makes the most of the grand listed building it occupies. Choose from the impressive display of fish flown in daily from Greek waters – and prepare for a sizeable bill.

Menu £ 29/49 – Carte £ 58/131

Town plan: 31AP3-k – *1 Regent St ✉ SW1Y 4NR – ⊖ Piccadilly Circus – ✆ 020 7839 2080 – www.milos.ca – Closed 25 December and 1 January*

The Wolseley

MODERN CUISINE • FASHIONABLE XXX This feels like a grand and glamorous European coffee house, with its pillars and high vaulted ceiling. Appealing menus offer everything from caviar to a hot-dog. It's open from early until late and boasts a large celebrity following.

Carte £ 23/69

Town plan: 30AM3-q – *160 Piccadilly ✉ W1J 9EB – ⊖ Green Park – ✆ 020 7499 6996 (booking essential) – www.thewolseley.com*

Al Duca

ITALIAN • FRIENDLY XX Cooking which focuses on flavour continues to draw in the regulars at this warm and spirited Italian restaurant. Prices are keen when one considers the central location and service is brisk and confident.

Menu £ 17 (dinner) – Carte £ 26/45

Town plan: 31AN3-r – *4-5 Duke of York St ✉ SW1Y 6LA – ⊖ Piccadilly Circus – ✆ 020 7839 3090 – www.alduca-restaurant.co.uk – Closed Easter, 25-26 December, 1 January, Sunday and bank holidays*

Avenue

MODERN CUISINE • ELEGANT XX Mayfair meets Manhattan at this buzzing, all-American restaurant with a light, bright interior designed by Russell Sage. Enjoy buttermilk pancakes at brunch and grain-fed USDA New York strip for dinner; cocktails add to the fun.

Menu £ 25 – Carte £ 32/80

Town plan: 31AN4-y – *7-9 St James's St. ✉ SW1A 1EE – ⊖ Green Park – ✆ 020 7321 2111 – www.avenue-restaurant.co.uk – Closed Sunday dinner and bank holidays*

Boulestin

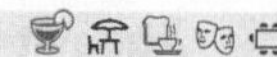

FRENCH • ELEGANT XX Nearly a century after Xavier Marcel Boulestin opened his eponymous restaurant showcasing 'Simple French Cooking for English Homes', his spirit has been resurrected at this elegant brasserie, with its lovely courtyard terrace.

Menu £30 – Carte £40/61

Town plan: 31AN4-s – *5 St James's St ✉ SW1A 1EF – ⊖ Green Park – ✆ 020 7930 2030 – www.boulestin.com – Closed Sunday and bank holidays*

Brumus

MODERN CUISINE • FASHIONABLE XX Pre-theatre dining is an altogether less frenzied activity when you can actually see the theatre from your table. This is a modern, elegant space with switched-on staff. Stick to the good value set menu or the 'dish of the day'.

Menu £20 – Carte £24/62

Town plan: 31AP3-x – *Haymarket Hotel, 1 Suffolk Pl ✉ SW1Y 4HX – ⊖ Piccadilly Circus – ✆ 020 7470 4000 – www.haymarkethotel.com*

Cafe Murano

ITALIAN • FASHIONABLE XX Angela Hartnett and her chef have created an appealing and flexible menu of delicious North Italian delicacies – the lunch menu is very good value. It's certainly no ordinary café and its popularity means prebooking is essential.

Menu £23 (lunch and early dinner) – Carte £26/43

Town plan: 30AM4-m – *33 St. James's St ✉ SW1A 1HD – ⊖ Green Park – ✆ 020 3371 5559 (booking essential) – www.cafemurano.co.uk – Closed Sunday dinner*

Le Caprice

MODERN CUISINE • FASHIONABLE XX For over 35 years Le Caprice's effortlessly sophisticated atmosphere and surroundings have attracted a confident and urbane clientele. The kitchen is well-practised and capable and there's something for everyone on their catch-all menu.

Menu £25 (lunch and early dinner) – Carte £33/64

Town plan: 30AM4-h – *Arlington House, Arlington St. ✉ SW1A 1RJ – ⊖ Green Park – ✆ 020 7629 2239 – www.le-caprice.co.uk – Closed 24-26 December*

45 Jermyn St

MODERN BRITISH • BRASSERIE XX What was Fortnum & Mason's Fountain restaurant for 60 years is now a bright, contemporary brasserie. The sodas, coupes and floats pay tribute to its past and cooking has a strong British element. Prices can be steep but, in contrast, the well-chosen wine list has very restrained mark-ups.

Menu £30 (weekday dinner) – Carte £24/67

Town plan: 31AN3-f – *45 Jermyn St. ✉ SW1 6DN – ⊖ Piccadilly Circus – ✆ 020 7205 4545 – www.45jermynst.com – Closed 25-26 December*

Franco's

ITALIAN • TRADITIONAL DÉCOR XX Open from breakfast until late, with a café at the front leading into a smart, clubby restaurant. The menu covers all parts of Italy and includes a popular grill section and plenty of classics.

Menu £26/36 – Carte £28/66

Town plan: 30AM3-i – *61 Jermyn St ✉ SW1Y 6LX – ⊖ Green Park – ✆ 020 7499 2211 (booking essential) – www.francoslondon.com – Closed Sunday and bank holidays*

Game Bird

MODERN BRITISH • CLASSIC DÉCOR XX A hotel dining room is not for everyone but the warmth of the service, the discreet atmosphere and the classic British dishes prepared with care and understanding make this a worthwhile choice. Smoked and cured salmon and game are specialities.

Menu £ 25 – Carte £ 32/72

Town plan: 30AM4-u – *Stafford Hotel, 16-18 St James's Pl. ✉ SW1A 1NJ – ⊖ Green Park – ✆ 020 7493 0111 – www.thestaffordlondon.com*

Ginza Onodera

JAPANESE • ELEGANT XX Re-fitted and re-launched in 2017 on the site of what was Matsuri for over 20 years. A staircase leads down to the smart restaurant and the three counters: for sushi, teppanyaki and the robata grill. The emphasis is on traditional Japanese cuisine and top-end ingredients.

Menu £ 23 (lunch) – Carte £ 25/70

Town plan: 31AN4-w – *15 Bury St ✉ SW1Y 6AL – ⊖ Green Park – ✆ 020 7839 1101 – www.onodera-group.com – Closed 25 December and 1 January*

Quaglino's

MODERN CUISINE • DESIGN XX This colourful, glamorous restaurant manages to be cavernous and cosy at the same time, with live music and a late night bar adding a certain sultriness to proceedings. The kitchen specialises in contemporary brasserie-style food.

Menu £ 23 (weekdays)/33 – Carte £ 37/68

Town plan: 30AM4-j – *16 Bury St ✉ SW1Y 6AJ – ⊖ Green Park – ✆ 020 7930 6767 – www.quaglinos-restaurant.co.uk – Closed Easter Monday and Sunday dinner*

Sake No Hana

JAPANESE • MINIMALIST XX A modern Japanese restaurant within a Grade II listed '60s edifice – and proof that you can occasionally find good food at the end of an escalator. As with the great cocktails, the menu is best enjoyed when shared with a group.

Menu £ 31 – Carte £ 24/121

Town plan: 30AM4-n – *23 St James's ✉ SW1A 1HA – ⊖ Green Park – ✆ 020 7925 8988 – www.sakenohana.com – Closed 25 December and Sunday*

Veneta

ITALIAN • BRASSERIE XX Operated by the Salt Yard Group so expect the same small plates formula, but with more of an Italian slant and a particular emphasis on specialities from Venice. More comfortable than their other branches but perhaps not quite as fun.

Carte £ 17/36

Town plan: 31AN3-b – *3 Norris St., St James's Market ✉ SW1Y 4RJ – ⊖ Piccadilly Circus – ✆ 020 3874 9100 – www.saltyardgroup.co.uk*

Chop Shop

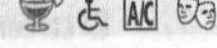

MEATS AND GRILLS • SIMPLE X Spread over two floors and with an ersatz-industrial look, this lively spot could be in Manhattan's Meatpacking district. Start with a cocktail, then order 'jars', 'crocks' or 'planks' of mousses, meatballs and cheeses; then it's the main event – great steaks and chops.

Menu £ 22 (lunch and early dinner) – Carte £ 21/50

Town plan: 31AP3-c – *66 Haymarket ✉ SW1Y 4RF – ⊖ Piccadilly Circus – ✆ 020 7842 8501 – www.chopshopuk.com*

Portrait

MODERN CUISINE • DESIGN Set on the top floor of National Portrait Gallery with rooftop local landmark views: a charming spot to dine or enjoy breakfast or afternoon tea. Carefully prepared modern European dishes; good value pre-theatre and weekend set menus.

Menu £ 32 – Carte £ 36/48

Town plan: 31AP3-n – *National Portrait Gallery (3rd floor), St Martin's Pl. ✉ WC2H 0HE – ⊖ Charing Cross – ✆ 020 7312 2490 (booking essential) – www.npg.org.uk/portraitrestaurant – lunch only and dinner Thursday-Saturday – Closed 24-26 December*

Shoryu

JAPANESE • SIMPLE Owned by the Japan Centre opposite and specialising in Hakata tonkotsu ramen. The base is a milky broth made from pork bones to which is added hosomen noodles, egg and assorted toppings. Its restorative powers are worth queuing for. There are two larger branches in Soho.

Carte £ 15/33

Town plan: 31AN3-s – *9 Regent St. ✉ SW1Y 4LR – ⊖ Piccadilly Circus – ✆ 020 3405 1391 (bookings not accepted) – www.shoryuramen.com – Closed 25 December and 1 January*

Ritz

GRAND LUXURY • CLASSIC World famous hotel, opened in 1906 as a fine example of Louis XVI architecture and decoration. Elegant Palm Court famed for its afternoon tea. Many of the lavishly appointed and luxurious rooms and suites overlook the park.

136 rooms – †£ 430/1130 ††£ 430/1130 – ☕ £ 39 – 24 suites

Town plan: 30AM4-c – *150 Piccadilly ✉ W1J 9BR – ⊖ Green Park – ✆ 020 7493 8181 – www.theritzlondon.com*

✿ **Ritz Restaurant** – See restaurant listing

Haymarket

LUXURY • PERSONALISED Smart and spacious hotel in John Nash Regency building, with a stylish blend of modern and antique furnishings. Large, comfortable bedrooms in soothing colours. Impressive basement pool is often used for private parties.

50 rooms – †£ 276/648 ††£ 276/648 – ☕ £ 14 – 3 suites

Town plan: 31AP3-x – *1 Suffolk Pl. ✉ SW1Y 4HX – ⊖ Piccadilly Circus – ✆ 020 7470 4000 – www.haymarkethotel.com*

Brumus – See restaurant listing

Sofitel London St James

LUXURY • ELEGANT Great location for this international hotel in a Grade II former bank. The triple-glazed bedrooms are immaculately kept; the spa is one of the best around. The bar is inspired by Coco Chanel; the lounge by an English rose garden. Balcon is a grand brasserie in a former banking hall.

183 rooms – †£ 350/663 ††£ 350/683 – ☕ £ 25 – 18 suites

Town plan: 31AP3-a – *6 Waterloo Pl. ✉ SW1Y 4AN – ⊖ Piccadilly Circus – ✆ 020 7747 2200 – www.sofitelstjames.com*

Dukes

TRADITIONAL • CLASSIC The wonderfully located Dukes has been steadily updating its image over the last few years, despite being over a century old. Bedrooms are now fresh and uncluttered and the atmosphere less starchy. GBR restaurant offers an all-day menu of British dishes and also serves afternoon tea.

90 rooms – †£ 376/540 ††£ 376/540 – ☕ £ 24 – 6 suites

Town plan: 30AM4-f – *35 St James's Pl. ✉ SW1A 1NY – ⊖ Green Park – ✆ 020 7491 4840 – www.dukeshotel.com*

Stafford

LUXURY • ELEGANT Styles itself as a 'country house in the city'; its bedrooms are divided between the main house, converted 18C stables and a more modern mews. The legendary American bar is certainly worth a visit.

104 rooms – †£ 348/678 ††£ 390/720 – ☕ £ 31 – 15 suites

Town plan: 30AM4-u – *16-18 St James's Pl.* ✉ *SW1A 1NJ* – ⊖ *Green Park* – ☎ *020 7493 0111* – *www.thestaffordlondon.com*

Game Bird – See restaurant listing

St James's Hotel and Club

BUSINESS • MODERN 1890s house, formerly a private club, in a wonderfully central yet quiet location. Modern, boutique-style interior with over 300 European works of art from the '20s to the '50s. Fine finish to the compact but well-equipped bedrooms.

60 rooms – †£ 295/580 ††£ 295/580 – ☕ £ 20 – 10 suites

Town plan: 30AM4-k – *7-8 Park Pl.* ✉ *SW1A 1LS* – ⊖ *Green Park* – ☎ *020 7316 1600* – *www.stjameshotelandclub.com*

✿ **Seven Park Place** – See restaurant listing

Soho

✿ Yauatcha Soho

CHINESE • DESIGN XX It's been here almost 15 years but still manages to feel fresh and contemporary, with its bright ground floor and moody basement, featuring low banquettes, an aquarium bar and a star-lit ceiling. Dishes are colourful with strong flavours and excellent texture contrasts; dim sum is the highlight – try the venison puff.

→ Venison puff. Stir-fried rib-eye beef. Raspberry délice.

Menu £ 30 (lunch) – Carte £ 29/67

Town plan: 31AN2-k – *15 Broadwick St* ✉ *W1F 0DL* – ⊖ *Tottenham Court Road* – ☎ *020 7494 8888* – *www.yauatcha.com* – *Closed 25 December*

✿ Barrafina

SPANISH • TAPAS BAR X In 2016 the original Barrafina moved to this brighter, roomier site fashioned out of what was previously a part of Quo Vadis restaurant. Dishes burst with flavour – do order some dishes from the blackboard specials – the staff are fun and the L-shaped counter fills up quickly, so be prepared to wait.

→ Pluma Iberica with confit potatoes. Rump of milk-fed lamb. Santiago tart.

Carte £ 18/44

Town plan: 31AP2-v – *26-27 Dean St* ✉ *W1D 3LL* – ⊖ *Tottenham Court Road* – ☎ *020 7440 1456 (bookings not accepted)* – *www.barrafina.co.uk* – *Closed bank holidays*

✿ Social Eating House

MODERN CUISINE • FASHIONABLE X There's something of a Brooklyn vibe to this Jason Atherton restaurant, with its bare brick and raw plastered walls and its speakeasy bar upstairs. It's great fun, very busy and gloriously unstuffy; the menu is an eminently good read, with the best dishes being the simplest ones.

→ Scorched mackerel and tartare with pickled walnuts, apple and chicory. Roast rack of lamb, braised neck, baby gem, cured lamb and rocket. Caramelised milk and brown sugar tart with ginger wine and fromage frais sorbet.

Menu £ 27 (lunch and early dinner) – Carte £ 39/56

Town plan: 31AN2-t – *58 Poland St* ✉ *W1F 7NR* – ⊖ *Oxford Circus* – ☎ *020 7993 3251 (booking advisable)* – *www.socialeatinghouse.com* – *Closed Christmas, Sunday and bank holidays*

Brasserie Zédel

FRENCH • BRASSERIE XX A grand French brasserie, which is all about inclusivity and accessibility, in a bustling subterranean space restored to its original art deco glory. Expect a roll-call of classic French dishes and some very competitive prices.

Menu £ 13/20 – Carte £ 18/44

Town plan: 31AN3-q – *20 Sherwood St ✉ W1F 7ED – ⊖ Piccadilly Circus – ✆ 020 7734 4888 (booking advisable) – www.brasseriezedel.com – Closed 25 December*

Dehesa

MEDITERRANEAN CUISINE • TAPAS BAR X Repeats the success of its sister restaurant, Salt Yard, by offering flavoursome and appealingly priced Spanish and Italian tapas. Busy, friendly atmosphere in appealing corner location. Terrific drinks list too.

Carte £ 14/36

Town plan: 30AM2-i – *25 Ganton St ✉ W1F 9BP – ⊖ Oxford Circus – ✆ 020 7949 4170 – www.dehesa.co.uk – Closed 25 December*

Bao

ASIAN • SIMPLE X There are some things in life worth queueing for – and that includes the delicious eponymous buns here at this simple, great value Taiwanese operation. The classic bao and the confit pork bao are standouts, along with 'small eats' like trotter nuggets. There's also another Bao in Windmill St.

Carte £ 17/27

Town plan: 31AN2-f – *53 Lexington St ✉ W1F 9AS – ⊖ Tottenham Court Road – ✆ 020 3011 1632 (bookings not accepted) – www.baolondon.com – Closed 23 December-3 January and Sunday*

Copita

SPANISH • TAPAS BAR X Perch on one of the high stools or stay standing and get stuck into the daily menu of small, colourful and tasty dishes. Staff add to the atmosphere and everything on the Spanish wine list comes by the glass or copita.

Carte £ 19/32

Town plan: 31AN2-h – *27 D'Arblay St ✉ W1F 8EP – ⊖ Oxford Circus – ✆ 020 7287 7797 (bookings not accepted) – www.copita.co.uk – Closed Sunday and bank holidays*

Hoppers

SOUTH INDIAN • SIMPLE X Street food inspired by the flavours of Tamil Nadu and Sri Lanka features at this fun little spot from the Sethi family (Trishna, Gymkhana). Hoppers are bowl-shaped pancakes made from fermented rice and coconut – ideal with a creamy kari. The 'short eats' are great too, as are the prices, so expect a queue.

Carte £ 15/25

Town plan: 31AP2-z – *49 Frith St ✉ W1D 4SG – ⊖ Tottenham Court Road – ✆ 020 3011 1021 (bookings not accepted) – www.hopperslondon.com – Closed 25-27 December and 1-3 January.*

Kiln (N)

THAI • SIMPLE X Sit at the far counter to watch chefs prepare fiery Thai food in clay pots, woks and grills. The well-priced menu includes influences from Laos, Myanmar and Yunnan – all prepared using largely British produce. The counter is for walk-ins only but parties of four can book a table downstairs.

Carte £ 14/20

Town plan: 31AN3-k – *58 Brewer St ✉ W1F 9TL – ⊖ Piccadilly Circus (bookings not accepted) – www.kilnsoho.com*

Kricket

INDIAN • SIMPLE From Brixton pop-up to a permanent spot in Soho; not many Indian restaurants have a counter, an open kitchen, sharing plates and cocktails. The four well-priced dishes under each heading of 'Meat, 'Fish' and 'Veg' are made with home-grown ingredients. Bookings are only taken for groups of 4 or more at the communal tables downstairs.

Carte £ 12/34

Town plan: 31AN3-t – *12 Denman St ✉ W1D 7HH – ⊖ Piccadilly Circus – ✆ 020 7734 5612 (bookings not accepted) – www.kricket.co.uk*

Palomar

WORLD CUISINE • TRENDY A hip slice of modern-day Jerusalem in the heart of theatreland, with a zinc kitchen counter running back to an intimate wood-panelled dining room. Like the atmosphere, the contemporary Middle Eastern cooking is fresh and vibrant.

Carte £ 26/33

Town plan: 31AP3-s – *34 Rupert St ✉ W1D 6DN – ⊖ Piccadilly Circus – ✆ 020 7439 8777 (booking advisable) – www.thepalomar.co.uk – Closed dinner 24-26 December*

Polpetto

ITALIAN • SIMPLE Re-opened by Russell Norman in bigger premises. The style of food is the perfect match for this relaxed environment: the small, seasonally inspired Italian dishes are uncomplicated, appealingly priced and deliver great flavours.

Carte £ 12/21

Town plan: 31AN2-u – *11 Berwick St ✉ W1F 0PL – ⊖ Tottenham Court Road – ✆ 020 7439 8627 – www.polpetto.co.uk*

Quo Vadis

TRADITIONAL BRITISH • TRADITIONAL DÉCOR Annexed in 2016 to accommodate Barrafina, this Soho institution is now limited to one room – upstairs is a private members' dining club. The cooking, though, remains as robust and forthright as ever.

Menu £ 23 – Carte £ 36/50

Town plan: 31AP2-v – *26-29 Dean St ✉ W1D 3LL – ⊖ Tottenham Court Road – ✆ 020 7437 9585 – www.quovadissoho.co.uk – Closed 25-26 December, 1 January, Sunday and bank holidays*

Gauthier - Soho

FRENCH • INTIMATE Detached from the rowdier elements of Soho is this charming Georgian townhouse, with dining spread over three floors. Alex Gauthier offers assorted menus of his classically based cooking, with vegetarians particularly well looked after.

Menu £ 24/75

Town plan: 31AP2-k – *21 Romilly St ✉ W1D 5AF – ⊖ Leicester Square – ✆ 020 7494 3111 – www.gauthiersoho.co.uk – Closed Monday, Sunday and bank holidays except Good Friday*

Imperial China

CHINESE • ELEGANT Sharp service and comfortable surroundings are not the only things that set this restaurant apart: the Cantonese cooking exudes freshness and vitality, whether that's the steamed dumplings or the XO minced pork with fine beans.

Menu £ 20/46 – Carte £ 15/57

Town plan: 31AP3-e – *White Bear Yard, 25a Lisle St ✉ WC2H 7BA – ⊖ Leicester Square – ✆ 020 7734 3388 (booking advisable) – www.imperialchina-london.com – Closed 25 December*

Red Fort

INDIAN • EXOTIC DÉCOR XXX A smart, stylish and professionally run Indian restaurant that has been a feature in Soho since 1983. Cooking is based on the Mughal Court and uses much UK produce such as Welsh lamb; look out for more unusual choices like rabbit.

Menu £ 15/49 – Carte £ 31/59

Town plan: 31AP2-z – *77 Dean St. ✉ W1D 3SH – ⊖ Tottenham Court Road – ✆ 020 7437 2525 (bookings advisable at dinner) – www.redfort.co.uk – Closed Sunday*

Bob Bob Ricard

MODERN CUISINE • VINTAGE XX Everyone needs a little glamour now and again and this place provides it. The room may be quite small but it sees itself as a grand salon – ask for a booth. The menu is all-encompassing – oysters and caviar to pies and burgers.

Carte £ 37/90

Town plan: 31AN2-s – *1 Upper James St ✉ W1F 9DF – ⊖ Oxford Circus – ✆ 020 3145 1000 – www.bobbobricard.com*

Dean Street Townhouse Restaurant

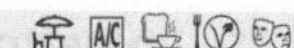

MODERN BRITISH • BRASSERIE XX A Georgian house that's home to a fashionable bar and restaurant which is busy from breakfast onwards. Appealingly classic British food includes some retro dishes and satisfying puddings.

Menu £ 29 – Carte £ 29/44

Town plan: 31AP2-t – *Dean Street Townhouse Hotel, 69-71 Dean St. ✉ W1D 3SE – ⊖ Piccadilly Circus – ✆ 020 7434 1775 (booking essential) – www.deanstreettownhouse.com*

Ham Yard

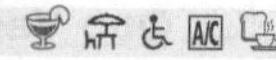

MODERN CUISINE • BRASSERIE XX An exuberantly decorated restaurant; start with a cocktail – the bitters and syrups are homemade with herbs from the hotel's roof garden. The menu moves with the seasons and the kitchen has the confidence to keep dishes simple.

Menu £ 20 (dinner) – Carte £ 28/46

Town plan: 31AN3-p – *Ham Yard Hotel, 1 Ham Yard, ✉ W1D 7DT – ⊖ Piccadilly Circus – ✆ 020 3642 1007 – www.firmdalehotels.com*

Hix

TRADITIONAL BRITISH • FASHIONABLE XX The exterior may hint at exclusivity but inside this big restaurant the atmosphere is fun, noisy and sociable. The room comes decorated with the works of eminent British artists. Expect classic British dishes and ingredients.

Menu £ 20 (lunch and early dinner) – Carte £ 25/68

Town plan: 31AN3-l – *66-70 Brewer St. ✉ WIF 9UP – ⊖ Piccadilly Circus – ✆ 020 7292 3518 – www.hixsoho.co.uk – Closed 25-26 December*

MASH

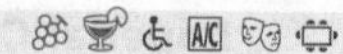

MEATS AND GRILLS • BRASSERIE XX A team from Copenhagen raised the old Titanic and restored the art deco to create this striking 'Modern American Steak House', offering Danish, Nebraskan and Uruguayan beef. A great bar and slick service add to the grown up feel.

Menu £ 30 (lunch) – Carte £ 30/96

Town plan: 31AN3-i – *77 Brewer St ✉ W1F 9ZN – ⊖ Piccadilly Circus – ✆ 020 7734 2608 – www.mashsteak.co.uk – Closed 24-26 December and Sunday lunch*

100 Wardour St

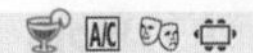

MODERN CUISINE • CONTEMPORARY DÉCOR XX D&D have reinvented the space formerly occupied by Floridita and the original Marquee Club. At night, head downstairs for cocktails, live music and a modern menu with Japanese and South American influences. In the daytime stay on the ground floor for an all-day menu, a bar and a pop-in/plug-in lounge.

Menu £ 15/35 – Carte £ 27/59

Town plan: 31AN2-v – *100 Wardour St ✉ W1F 0TN – ⊖ Tottenham Court Road – ✆ 020 7314 4000 – www.100wardourst.com – Closed 25-26 December and Sunday-Monday*

Plum Valley

CHINESE • DESIGN XX Its striking black façade makes this modern Chinese restaurant easy to spot in Chinatown. Mostly Cantonese cooking, with occasional forays into Vietnam and Thailand; dim sum is the strength.

Menu £ 38 – Carte £ 19/37

Town plan: 31AP3-i – *20 Gerrard St. ✉ W1D 6JQ – ⊖ Leicester Square – ✆ 020 7494 4366 – Closed 23-24 December*

Refuel

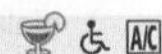

MODERN BRITISH • FASHIONABLE XX At the heart of the cool Soho hotel is their aptly named bar and restaurant. With a menu to suit all moods and wallets, from burgers to Dover sole, and a cocktail list to lift all spirits, it's a fun and bustling spot.

Menu £ 23/30 – Carte £ 30/62

Town plan: 31AN2-n – *Soho Hotel, 4 Richmond Mews ✉ W1D 3DH – ⊖ Tottenham Court Road – ✆ 020 7559 3007 – www.firmdalehotels.com*

Tamarind Kitchen (N)

INDIAN • EXOTIC DÉCOR XX A more relaxed sister to Tamarind in Mayfair, this Indian restaurant comes with endearingly earnest service and a lively buzz. There's a nominal Northern emphasis to the fairly priced menu, with Awadhi kababs a speciality, but there are also plenty of curries and fish dishes.

Carte £ 21/36

Town plan: 31AN2-m – *167-169 Wardour St ✉ W1F 8WR – ⊖ Tottenham Court Road – ✆ 020 7287 4243 – www.tamarindkitchen.co.uk – Closed 25-26 December, 1 January*

Temper (N)

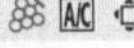

BARBECUE • CONTEMPORARY DÉCOR XX A fun, basement restaurant all about barbecue and meats. The beasts are cooked whole, some are also smoked in-house and there's a distinct South African flavour to the salsas that accompany them. Kick off with some tacos – they make around 1200 of them every day.

Carte £ 16/37

Town plan: 31AN2-r – *25 Broadwick St ✉ W1F 0DF – ⊖ Oxford Circus – ✆ 020 3879 3834 – www.temperrestaurant.com – Closed 25-26 December and 1 January*

Vasco and Piero's Pavilion

ITALIAN • FRIENDLY XX Regulars and tourists have been flocking to this institution for over 40 years; its longevity is down to a twice daily changing menu of Umbrian-influenced dishes rather than the matter-of-fact service or simple decoration.

Carte £ 27/49

Town plan: 31AN2-q – *15 Poland St ✉ W1F 8QE – ⊖ Oxford Circus – ✆ 020 7437 8774 (booking essential at lunch) – www.vascosfood.com – Closed Saturday lunch, Sunday and bank holidays*

Nopi

MEDITERRANEAN CUISINE • DESIGN ✕ The bright, clean look of Yotam Ottolenghi's charmingly run all-day restaurant matches the fresh, invigorating food. The sharing plates take in the Mediterranean, the Middle East and Asia and the veggie dishes stand out.

Carte £ 21/50

Town plan: 31AN3-g – *21-22 Warwick St. ✉ W1B 5NE – ⊖ Piccadilly Circus – ✆ 020 7494 9584 – www.nopi-restaurant.com – Closed bank holidays*

Antidote

MODERN CUISINE • INTIMATE ✕ A cute, busy little wine bar on the ground floor offers charcuterie, cheese and mostly biodynamic and organic French wines. Upstairs is a more comfy restaurant with sharing plates of largely European dishes.

Carte £ 25/38

Town plan: 31AN2-j – *12a Newburgh St ✉ W1F 7RR – ⊖ Oxford Circus – ✆ 020 7287 8488 (booking advisable) – www.antidotewinebar.com – Closed Sunday and bank holidays*

Baozi Inn

CHINESE • RUSTIC ✕ Buzzy, busy little place that's great for a quick bite, especially if you like pork buns, steaming bowls of noodles, a hit of Sichuan fire and plenty of beer or tea. You'll leave feeling surprisingly energised and rejuvenated.

Carte £ 15/22

Town plan: 31AP3-r – *25-26 Newport Court ✉ WC2H 7JS – ⊖ Leicester Square – ✆ 020 7287 6877 (bookings not accepted) – Closed 24-25 December*

Barshu

CHINESE • EXOTIC DÉCOR ✕ The fiery and authentic flavours of China's Sichuan province are the draw here; help is at hand as the menu has pictures. It's decorated with carved wood and lanterns; downstairs is better for groups.

Carte £ 26/58

Town plan: 31AP2-g – *28 Frith St. ✉ W1D 5LF – ⊖ Leicester Square – ✆ 020 7287 8822 (booking advisable) – www.barshurestaurant.co.uk – Closed 24-25 December*

Beijing Dumpling

CHINESE • NEIGHBOURHOOD ✕ This relaxed little place serves freshly prepared dumplings of both Beijing and Shanghai styles. Although the range is not as comprehensive as the name suggests, they do stand out, especially varieties of the famed Siu Lung Bao.

Menu £ 18 – Carte £ 10/40

Town plan: 31AP3-e – *23 Lisle St. ✉ WC2H 7BA – ⊖ Leicester Square – ✆ 020 7287 6888 – Closed 24-25 December*

Bibigo

KOREAN • FRIENDLY ✕ The enthusiastically run Bibigo represents Korea's largest food company's first foray into the UK market. Watch the kitchen send out dishes such as kimchi, Bossam (simmered pork belly) and hot stone galbi (chargrilled short ribs).

Menu £ 13 – Carte £ 18/27

Town plan: 31AN2-x – *58-59 Great Marlborough St ✉ W1F 7JY – ⊖ Oxford Circus – ✆ 020 7042 5225 – www.bibigouk.com – Closed 25 December and 1 January*

Blanchette

FRENCH • SIMPLE ✕ Run by three frères, Blanchette takes French bistro food and gives it the 'small plates' treatment. It's named after their mother – the ox cheek Bourguignon is her recipe. Tiles and exposed brick add to the rustic look.

Menu £ 15 (lunch) – Carte £ 14/28

Town plan: 31AN2-c – *9 D'Arblay St ✉ W1F 8DR – ⊖ Oxford Circus – ✆ 020 7439 8100 (booking essential) – www.blanchettesoho.co.uk*

Bocca di Lupo

ITALIAN • TAPAS BAR Atmosphere, food and service are all best when sitting at the marble counter, watching the chefs at work. Specialities from across Italy come in large or small sizes and are full of flavour and vitality. Try also their gelato shop opposite.

Carte £ 26/45

Town plan: 31AN3-e – *12 Archer St ✉ W1D 7BB – ⊖ Piccadilly Circus – ✆ 020 7734 2223 (booking essential) – www.boccadilupo.com – Closed 25 December and 1 January*

Bone Daddies

ASIAN • FASHIONABLE Maybe ramen is the new rock 'n' roll. The charismatic Aussie chef-owner feels that combinations are endless when it comes to these comforting bowls. Be ready to queue then share a table. It's a fun place, run by a hospitable bunch.

Carte £ 17/27

Town plan: 31AN2-o – *31 Peter St ✉ W1F 0AR – ⊖ Piccadilly Circus – ✆ 020 7287 8581 (bookings not accepted) – www.bonedaddies.com – Closed 25 December*

Casita Andina

PERUVIAN • RUSTIC Respect is paid to the home-style cooking of the Andes at this warmly run and welcoming Peruvian picanteria. Dishes are gluten-free and as colourful as the surroundings of this 200 year old house.

Carte £ 13/25

Town plan: 31AN3-n – *31 Great Windmill St ✉ W1D 7LP – ⊖ Piccadilly Circus – ✆ 020 3327 9464 – www.andinalondon.com/casita*

Cây Tre

VIETNAMESE • MINIMALIST Bright, sleek and bustling surroundings where Vietnamese standouts include Cha La Lot (spicy ground pork wrapped in betel leaves), slow-cooked Mekong catfish with a well-judged sweet and spicy sauce, and 6 versions of Pho (noodle soup).

Menu £ 25 – Carte £ 23/32

Town plan: 31AP2-m – *42-43 Dean St ✉ W1D 4PZ – ⊖ Tottenham Court Road – ✆ 020 7317 9118 (booking advisable) – www.caytresoho.co.uk*

Ceviche Soho

PERUVIAN • FRIENDLY Based on a Lima Pisco bar, Ceviche is as loud as it is fun. First try the deliriously addictive drinks based on the Peruvian spirit pisco, and then share some thinly sliced sea bass or octopus, along with anticuchos skewers.

Carte £ 18/26

Town plan: 31AP2-w – *17 Frith St ✉ W1D 4RG – ⊖ Tottenham Court Road – ✆ 020 7292 2040 (booking essential) – www.cevicheuk.com/soho*

Cinnamon Soho

INDIAN • FRIENDLY Younger and more fun than its sister the Cinnamon Club. Has a great selection of classic and more modern Indian dishes like Rogan Josh shepherd's pie. High Chai in the afternoon and a pre-theatre menu that's a steal.

Menu £ 15 (lunch and early dinner) – Carte £ 16/32

Town plan: 31AN2-3-a – *5 Kingly St ✉ W1B 5PF – ⊖ Oxford Circus – ✆ 020 7437 1664 – www.cinnamonsoho.com*

Duck & Rice

CHINESE • INTIMATE Alan Yau is one of our most innovative restaurateurs and once again he's created something different – a converted pub with a Chinese kitchen. Beer is the thing on the ground floor; upstairs is for Chinese favourites and comforting classics.

Carte £ 18/31

Town plan: 31AN2-w – *90 Berwick St ✉ W1F 0QB – ⊖ Tottenham Court Road – ✆ 020 3327 7888 – www.theduckandrice.com – Closed 25 December*

Ember Yard

MEDITERRANEAN CUISINE • TAPAS BAR Those familiar with the Salt Yard Group will recognise the Spanish and Italian themed menus – but their 4th fun outlet comes with a focus on cooking over charcoal or wood. There's even a seductive smokiness to some of the cocktails.

Carte £ 14/25

Town plan: 31AN2-e – *60 Berwick St* ✉ *W1F 8DX* – ⊖ *Oxford Circus* – *☎ 020 7439 8057 (booking advisable)* – *www.emberyard.co.uk* – *Closed 25-26 December and 1 January*

Haozhan

CHINESE • DESIGN Interesting fusion-style dishes, with mostly Cantonese but other Asian influences too. Specialities like jasmine ribs or wasabi prawns reveal a freshness that marks this place out from the plethora of Chinatown mediocrity.

Menu £ 14 – Carte £ 15/43

Town plan: 31AP3-u – *8 Gerrard St* ✉ *W1D 5PJ* – ⊖ *Leicester Square* – *☎ 020 7434 3838* – *www.haozhan.co.uk* – *Closed 24-25 December*

Jinjuu

ASIAN • DESIGN American-born celebrity chef Judy Joo's restaurant is a celebration of her Korean heritage. The vibrant dishes, whether Bibimbap bowls or Ssam platters, burst with flavour and are as enjoyable as the fun surroundings. There's another branch in Mayfair.

Menu £ 17 (weekday lunch) – Carte £ 29/41

Town plan: 31AN2-d – *15 Kingly St* ✉ *W1B 5PS* – ⊖ *Oxford Circus* – *☎ 020 8181 8887* – *www.jinjuu.com* – *Closed 25 December*

Koya Bar

JAPANESE • SIMPLE A simple, sweet place serving authentic Udon noodles and small plates; they open early for breakfast. Counter seating means everyone has a view of the chefs; bookings aren't taken and there is often a queue, but the short wait is worth it.

Carte £ 12/25

Town plan: 31AP2-c – *50 Frith St* ✉ *W1D 4SQ* – ⊖ *Tottenham Court Road* – *☎ 020 7494 9075 (bookings not accepted)* – *www.koyabar.co.uk* – *Closed 24-25 December and 1 January*

Mele e Pere

ITALIAN • FRIENDLY Head downstairs – the 'apples and pears'? – to a vaulted room in the style of a homely Italian kitchen, with an appealing vermouth bar. The owner-chef has worked in some decent London kitchens but hails from Verona so expect gutsy Italian dishes.

Menu £ 23 (lunch and early dinner) – Carte £ 23/44

Town plan: 31AN3-h – *46 Brewer St* ✉ *W1F 9TF* – ⊖ *Piccadilly Circus* – *☎ 020 7096 2096* – *www.meleepere.co.uk* – *Closed 25-26 December and 1 January*

Oliver Maki

JAPANESE • MINIMALIST A small, eagerly run corner restaurant from a group with branches in Kuwait and Bahrain. The modern Japanese food has a more pronounced fusion element than similar types of place – not everything works but the confident kitchen uses good produce.

Menu £ 12/65 – Carte £ 22/56

Town plan: 31AP2-a – *33 Dean St* ✉ *W1D 4PW* – ⊖ *Leicester Square* – *☎ 020 7734 0408* – *www.olivermaki.co.uk* – *Closed 23-30 December*

Polpo Soho

ITALIAN • TAPAS BAR X A fun and lively Venetian bacaro, with a stripped-down, faux-industrial look. The small plates, from arancini and prosciutto to fritto misto and Cotechino sausage, are so well priced that waiting for a table is worth it.

Carte £ 14/28

Town plan: 31AN2-g - *41 Beak St ✉ W1F 9SB - ⊖ Oxford Circus - ✆ 020 7734 4479 - www.polpo.co.uk*

Rosa's Soho

THAI • SIMPLE X The worn-in, pared-down look of this authentic Thai café adds to its intimate feel. Signature dishes include warm minced chicken salad and a sweet pumpkin red curry. Tom Yam soup comes with a lovely balance of sweet, sour and spice.

Menu £ 20 - Carte £ 18/30

Town plan: 31AP2-j - *48 Dean St ✉ W1D 5BF - ⊖ Leicester Square - ✆ 020 7494 1638 (booking advisable) - www.rosasthaicafe.com - Closed 25-26 December*

Spuntino

NORTH AMERICAN • RUSTIC X Influenced by Downtown New York, with its no-booking policy and industrial look. Sit at the counter and order classics like mac 'n' cheese or mini burgers. The staff, who look like they could also fix your car, really add to the fun.

Carte £ 12/30

Town plan: 31AN3-j - *61 Rupert St. ✉ W1D 7PW - ⊖ Piccadilly Circus (bookings not accepted) - www.spuntino.co.uk - Closed dinner 24 December, 25-26, 31 December and 1 January*

Tonkotsu

JAPANESE • RUSTIC X Some things are worth queuing for. Good ramen is all about the base stock: 18 hours goes into its preparation here to ensure the bowls of soup and wheat-based noodles reach a depth of flavour that seems to nourish one's very soul.

Carte £ 17/26

Town plan: 31AP2-q - *63 Dean St ✉ W1D 4QG - ⊖ Tottenham Court Road - ✆ 020 7437 0071 (bookings not accepted) - www.tonkotsu.co.uk*

Zelman Meats

MEATS AND GRILLS • RUSTIC X Those clever Goodman people noticed a lack of affordable steakhouses and so opened this fun, semi-industrial space. They serve three cuts of beef: sliced picanha (from the rump), Chateaubriand, and a wonderfully smoky short rib.

Carte £ 18/49

Town plan: 31AN2-y - *2 St Anne's Ct ✉ W1F 0AZ - ⊖ Tottenham Court Rd - ✆ 020 7437 0566 - www.zelmanmeats.com - Closed Monday lunch and bank holidays*

Café Royal

GRAND LUXURY • HISTORIC One of the most famous names of the London social scene for the last 150 years is now a luxury hotel. The bedrooms are beautiful, elegant and discreet and the wining and dining options many and varied - they include the gloriously rococo Oscar Wilde bar, once home to the iconic Grill Room.

160 rooms - †£ 440/600 ††£ 440/600 - ☕ £ 32 - 16 suites

Town plan: 31AN3-r - *68 Regent St ✉ W1B 4DY - ⊖ Piccadilly Circus - ✆ 020 7406 3333 - www.hotelcaferoyal.com*

Ham Yard

LUXURY • ELEGANT This stylish hotel from the Firmdale group is set around a courtyard – a haven of tranquillity in the West End. Each of the rooms is different but all are supremely comfortable. There's also a great roof terrace, a theatre, a fully stocked library and bar... and even a bowling alley.

91 rooms – †£ 260/380 ††£ 260/380 – ☕£ 14 – 2 suites

Town plan: 31AN3-p – *1 Ham Yard, ✉ W1D 7DT – ⊖ Piccadilly Circus – ✆ 020 3642 2000 – www.firmdalehotels.com*

Ham Yard – See restaurant listing

Soho

LUXURY • PERSONALISED Stylish and fashionable hotel that mirrors the vibrancy of the neighbourhood. Boasts two screening rooms, a comfortable drawing room and up-to-the-minute bedrooms; some vivid, others more muted but all with hi-tech extras.

96 rooms – †£ 264/408 ††£ 264/408 – ☕£ 18 – 7 suites

Town plan: 31AN2-n – *4 Richmond Mews ✉ W1D 3DH – ⊖ Tottenham Court Road – ✆ 020 7559 3000 – www.firmdalehotels.com*

Refuel – See restaurant listing

Dean Street Townhouse

TOWNHOUSE • CLASSIC In the heart of Soho and where bedrooms range from tiny to bigger; the latter have roll-top baths in the room. All are well designed and come with a good range of extras. Cosy ground floor lounge.

39 rooms – †£ 200/450 ††£ 220/470 – ☕£ 15

Town plan: 31AP2-t – *69-71 Dean St. ✉ W1D 3SE – ⊖ Piccadily Circus – ✆ 020 7434 1775 – www.deanstreettownhouse.com*

Dean Street Townhouse Restaurant – See restaurant listing

Hazlitt's

TOWNHOUSE • HISTORIC Dating from 1718, the former house of essayist and critic William Hazlitt still welcomes many a writer today in its role as a charming townhouse hotel. It has plenty of character and is warmly run. No restaurant so breakfast in bed really is the only option – and who is going to object to that?

30 rooms – †£ 205/235 ††£ 255/750 – ☕£ 12 – 3 suites

Town plan: 31AP2-u – *6 Frith St ✉ W1D 3JA – ⊖ Tottenham Court Road – ✆ 020 7434 1771 – www.hazlittshotel.com*

Strand and Covent Garden

L'Atelier de Joël Robuchon

FRENCH • ELEGANT Ground floor L'Atelier, with counter dining and chefs on view; La Cuisine upstairs offers table dining in an intimate setting just a few nights a week. Assured, accomplished cooking with an emphasis on the Mediterranean; dishes are creative and well-balanced, with a pleasing simplicity to their presentation.

→ Langoustine and truffle ravioli with savoy cabbage. Fillet of beef with Malabar pepper and spring vegetables. Passion fruit soufflé with exotic fruit sorbet.

Menu £ 45 (lunch and early dinner) – Carte £ 64/119

Town plan: 31AP2-n – *13-15 West St. ✉ WC2H 9NE – ⊖ Leicester Square – ✆ 020 7010 8600 – www.joelrobuchon.co.uk*

Cinnamon Bazaar Ⓝ

INDIAN • EXOTIC DÉCOR Vivek Singh's latest venture provides relaxed, all-day contemporary Indian dining in the heart of Covent Garden, with a bright and colourful interior evoking a marketplace. Menus are influenced by the trade routes of the subcontinent, with twists that encompass Afghanistan, the Punjab and the Middle East.

Menu £ 16/24 – Carte £ 20/31

Town plan: 31AQ3-b – *28 Maiden Ln ✉ WC2E 7JS – ⊖ Leicester Square – ✆ 020 7395 1400 – www.cinnamon-bazaar.com*

Delaunay

MODERN CUISINE • ELEGANT XXX The Delaunay was inspired by the grand cafés of Europe but, despite sharing the same buzz and celebrity clientele as its sibling The Wolseley, is not just a mere replica. The all-day menu is more mittel-European, with great schnitzels and wieners.

Carte £ 27/70

Town plan: 32AR2-x – *55 Aldwych ✉ WC2B 4BB – ⊖ Temple – ✆ 020 7499 8558 (booking essential) – www.thedelaunay.com – Closed 25 December*

The Ivy

TRADITIONAL BRITISH • FASHIONABLE XXX This landmark restaurant has had a facelift and while the glamorous clientele remain, it now has an oval bar as its focal point. The menu offers international dishes alongside the old favourites and personable staff anticipate your every need.

Menu £ 24 (weekday lunch) – Carte £ 31/70

Town plan: 31AP2-p – *9 West St ✉ WC2H 9NE – ⊖ Leicester Square – ✆ 020 7836 4751 – www.the-ivy.co.uk – Closed 25 December*

J.Sheekey

SEAFOOD • FASHIONABLE XX Festooned with photographs of actors and linked to the theatrical world since opening in 1890. Wood panels and alcove tables add famed intimacy. Accomplished seafood cooking.

Carte £ 36/58

Town plan: 31AP3-v – *28-32 St Martin's Ct ✉ WC2N 4AL – ⊖ Leicester Square – ✆ 020 7240 2565 (booking essential) – www.j-sheekey.co.uk – Closed 25-26 December*

Rules

TRADITIONAL BRITISH • TRADITIONAL DÉCOR XX London's oldest restaurant boasts a fine collection of antique cartoons, drawings and paintings. Tradition continues in the menu, specialising in game from its own estate.

Carte £ 36/64

Town plan: 31AQ3-n – *35 Maiden Ln ✉ WC2E 7LB – ⊖ Leicester Square – ✆ 020 7836 5314 (booking essential) – www.rules.co.uk – Closed 25-26 December*

Spring

ITALIAN • FASHIONABLE XX Spring occupies the 'new wing' of Somerset House that for many years was inhabited by the Inland Revenue. It's a bright, feminine space under the aegis of chef Skye Gyngell. Her cooking is Italian-influenced and ingredient-led.

Menu £ 32 (lunch) – Carte £ 39/67

Town plan: 32AR3-c – *New Wing, Somerset House, Strand ✉ WC2R 1LA – Entrance on Lancaster Pl – ⊖ Temple – ✆ 020 3011 0115 (booking advisable) – www.springrestaurant.co.uk – Closed Sunday*

Balthazar

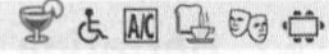

FRENCH • BRASSERIE XX Those who know the original Balthazar in Manhattan's SoHo district will find the London version of this classic brasserie uncannily familiar in looks, vibe and food. The Franglais menu keeps it simple and the cocktails are great.

Menu £ 20 (lunch and early dinner) – Carte £ 31/62

Town plan: 31AQ2-t – *4-6 Russell St. ✉ WC2B 5HZ – ⊖ Covent Garden – ✆ 020 3301 1155 (booking essential) – www.balthazarlondon.com – Closed 25 December*

Cafe Murano

ITALIAN • NEIGHBOURHOOD XX The second Cafe Murano is in the heart of Covent Garden, in a space much larger than the St James's original; head for the smart marble-topped counter at the back. Appealing menu of Northern Italian dishes cooked with care and respect.

Menu £ 17 (weekdays) - Carte £ 19/38

Town plan: 32AR3-o - *36 Tavistock St ✉ WC2E 7PB - ⊖ Charing Cross - ✆ 020 7240 3654 - www.cafemurano.co.uk - Closed Sunday dinner*

Clos Maggiore

FRENCH • CLASSIC DÉCOR XX One of London's most romantic restaurants - but be sure to ask for the enchanting conservatory with its retractable roof. The sophisticated French cooking is joined by a wine list of great depth. Good value and very popular pre/post theatre menus.

Menu £ 28 (weekday lunch) - Carte £ 39/81

Town plan: 31AQ3-a - *33 King St ✉ WC2E 8JD - ⊖ Leicester Square - ✆ 020 7379 9696 - www.closmaggiore.com - Closed 24-25 December*

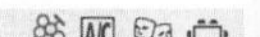

Eneko at One Aldwych

BASQUE • DESIGN XX Set in the One Aldwych Hotel, this stylish, ultra-modern restaurant features curved semi-private booths and a bar which seems to float above like a spaceship. Menus offer a refined reinterpretation of classic Basque dishes.

Menu £ 25 (lunch and early dinner) - Carte £ 30/39

Town plan: 32AR3-r - *One Aldwych Hotel, 1 Aldwych ✉ WC2B 4BZ - ⊖ Temple - ✆ 020 7300 0300 - www.eneko.london - Closed 2 weeks January*

Ivy Market Grill

TRADITIONAL BRITISH • DESIGN XX Mere mortals can now experience a little of that Ivy glamour by eating here at the first of their diffusion line. Breakfast, a menu of largely British classics and afternoon tea keep it busy all day. There's another branch in Chelsea.

Menu £ 21 (early dinner) - Carte £ 27/61

Town plan: 31AQ3-z - *1 Henrietta St ✉ WC2E 8PS - ⊖ Covent Garden - ✆ 020 3301 0200 - www.theivymarketgrill.com*

Roka

JAPANESE • FASHIONABLE XX This is the fourth and largest Roka in the group. It shares the same stylish look, efficient service and modern Japanese food, although there are some dishes unique to this branch. Consider the tasting menu for a good all-around experience.

Menu £ 31 (weekday lunch) - Carte £ 32/85

Town plan: 32AR2-v - *71 Aldwych ✉ WC2B 4HN - ⊖ Temple - ✆ 020 7294 7636 - www.rokarestaurant.com - Closed 25 December*

J.Sheekey Atlantic Bar

SEAFOOD • INTIMATE X An addendum to J. Sheekey restaurant. Sit at the bar to watch the chefs prepare the same quality seafood as next door but at slightly lower prices; fish pie and fruits de mer are the popular choices. Open all day.

Carte £ 25/38

Town plan: 31AP3-v - *33-34 St Martin's Ct. ✉ WC2 4AL - ⊖ Leicester Square - ✆ 020 7240 2565 (booking advisable) - www.j-sheekey.co.uk - Closed 25-26 December*

Barrafina

SPANISH • TAPAS BAR X The second Barrafina is not just brighter than the Soho original - it's bigger too, so you can wait inside with a drink for counter seats to become available. Try more unusual tapas like ortiguillas, frit Mallorquin or the succulent meats.

Carte £ 15/41

Town plan: 31AQ3-x - *10 Adelaide St ✉ WC2N 4HZ - ⊖ Charing Cross - ✆ 020 7440 1456 (bookings not accepted) - www.barrafina.co.uk - Closed Christmas, New Year and bank holidays*

Barrafina

SPANISH • TAPAS BAR X The third of the Barrafinas is tucked away at the far end of Covent Garden; arrive early or prepare to queue. Fresh, vibrantly flavoured fish and shellfish dishes are a real highlight; tortillas y huevos also feature.

Carte £ 28/41

Town plan: 31AQ2-a - *43 Drury Ln ✉ WC2B 5AJ - ⊖ Covent Garden - ✆ 020 7440 1456 (bookings not accepted) - www.barrafina.co.uk - Closed bank holidays*

Dishoom

INDIAN X A facsimile of a Bombay café, of the sort opened by Persian immigrants in the early 20C. Try baked roti rolls with chai, vada pav (Bombay's version of the chip butty), a curry or grilled meats. There's another branch in Shoreditch.

Carte £ 12/26

Town plan: 31AP2-j - *12 Upper St Martin's Ln ✉ WC2H 9FB - ⊖ Leicester Square - ✆ 020 7420 9320 (booking advisable) - www.dishoom.com - Closed 24 December dinner, 25-26 December and 1-2 January*

Frenchie

MODERN CUISINE • BISTRO X A well-run modern-day bistro – younger sister to the Paris original, which shares the name given to chef-owner Greg Marchand when he was head chef at Fifteen. The adventurous, ambitious cooking is informed by his extensive travels.

Menu £ 26 (weekday lunch) - Carte £ 43/58

Town plan: 31AQ3-c - *16 Henrietta St ✉ WC2E 8QH - ⊖ Covent Garden - ✆ 020 7836 4422 (booking advisable) - www.frenchiecoventgarden.com - Closed 25-26 December and 1 January*

Hawksmoor

MEATS AND GRILLS • RUSTIC X Steaks from Longhorn cattle lovingly reared in North Yorkshire and dry-aged for at least 35 days are the stars of the show. Atmospheric, bustling basement restaurant in former brewery cellars.

Menu £ 25 (weekdays) - Carte £ 25/75

Town plan: 31AQ2-f - *11 Langley St ✉ WC2H 9JG - ⊖ Covent Garden - ✆ 020 7420 9390 - www.thehawksmoor.com - Closed 24-26 December*

Henrietta N

MODERN CUISINE • FASHIONABLE X An informal, lounge-style hotel restaurant and cocktail bar. The ingredient-led menu follows the seasons and cooking has an appealing modern style, with well-defined yet delicate flavours. Madeleines make an excellent end to the meal.

Carte £ 29/47

Town plan: 31AQ3-r - *Henrietta Hotel, 14-15 Henrietta St ✉ WC2E 8QH - ⊖ Covent Garden - ✆ 020 3794 5314 (booking advisable) - www.henriettahotel.com*

Lima Floral

PERUVIAN • FASHIONABLE X This second Lima branch has a light and airy feel by day and a cosy, candlelit vibe in the evening; regional Peruvian dishes are served alongside the more popular causa and ceviche. Basement Pisco Bar for Peruvian tapas and Pisco sours.

Menu £ 20 (early dinner) - Carte £ 33/52

Town plan: 31AQ3-k - *14 Garrick St ✉ WC2E 9BJ - ⊖ Leicester Square - ✆ 020 7240 5778 - www.limalondongroup.com/floral - Closed 25-27 December, 1-2 January and bank holiday Mondays*

Opera Tavern

MEDITERRANEAN CUISINE • TAPAS BAR X Another in the Salt Yard stable, this former pub has a lively ground floor and a quieter first floor dining room. Spanish-Italian menus follow the seasons, with a selection of flavourful small plates designed for sharing.

Menu £ 21 (lunch) - Carte £ 14/29

Town plan: 31AQ2-y - *23 Catherine St. ✉ WC2B 5JS - ⊖ Covent Garden - ✆ 020 7836 3680 - www.operatavern.co.uk - Closed 25 December and 1 January*

Polpo Covent Garden

ITALIAN • SIMPLE X First Soho, then Covent Garden got a fun Venetian bacaro. The small plates are surprisingly filling, with delights such as pizzette of white anchovy vying with fennel and almond salad; fritto misto competing with spaghettini and meatballs.

Carte £ 13/21

Town plan: 31AQ3-p - *6 Maiden Ln. ✉ WC2E 7NA - ⊖ Leicester Square - ✆ 020 7836 8448 - www.polpo.co.uk - Closed 25-26 December*

Terroirs

MEDITERRANEAN CUISINE • WINE BAR X Flavoursome French cooking, with extra Italian and Spanish influences and a thoughtfully compiled wine list. Eat in the lively ground floor bistro/wine bar or in the more intimate cellar, where they also offer some sharing dishes like rib of beef for two.

Carte £ 26/72

Town plan: 31AQ3-h - *5 William IV St ✉ WC2N 4DW - ⊖ Charing Cross - ✆ 020 7036 0660 - www.terroirswinebar.com - Closed 25-26 December, 1 January, Sunday and bank holidays*

Tredwell's

MODERN BRITISH • BRASSERIE X A modern brasserie from Marcus Wareing, with an art deco feel. Cooking is best described as modern English; dishes show a degree of refinement, and a commendable amount of thought has gone into addressing allergen issues.

Menu £ 30 (lunch and early dinner) - Carte £ 27/56

Town plan: 31AP2-s - *4a Upper St Martin's Ln ✉ WC2H 9EF - ⊖ Leicester Square - ✆ 020 3764 0840 - www.tredwells.com - Closed 24-26 December and 1 January*

Savoy

GRAND LUXURY • ART DÉCO One of the grande dames of London's hotel scene. Luxurious bedrooms come in Edwardian or Art Deco styles; many have magnificent views over the Thames and the stunning suites pay homage to past guests. Enjoy tea in the Thames Foyer; sip a cocktail in the iconic American Bar or elegant Beaufort bar. Dine in the famous Savoy Grill or enjoy seafood and steaks in Kaspar's.

267 rooms - †£ 420/1500 ††£ 420/1500 - ☕ £ 35 - 45 suites

Town plan: 31AQ3-s - *Strand ✉ WC2R 0EU - ⊖ Charing Cross - ✆ 020 7836 4343 - www.fairmont.com/savoy*

One Aldwych

GRAND LUXURY • MODERN A stylish, modern hotel featuring over 400 pieces of contemporary artwork. Bedrooms are understated in style with fine linen, iPod docking stations, and fresh fruit and flowers daily. Charlie and the Chocolate Factory themed afternoon tea. Gluten and dairy-free British dishes in Indigo; Basque cooking in Eneko.

105 rooms - †£ 324/576 ††£ 324/576 - ☕ £ 29 - 12 suites

Town plan: 32AR3-r - *1 Aldwych ✉ WC2B 4BZ - ⊖ Temple - ✆ 020 7300 1000 - www.onealdwych.com*

Eneko at One Aldwych - See restaurant listing

Waldorf Hilton

HISTORIC • ELEGANT Impressive curved and columned façade: an Edwardian landmark in a great location. Stylish, contemporary bedrooms in calming colours have superb bathrooms and all mod cons. Tea dances in the Grade II listed Palm Court Ballroom. Stylish 'Homage' is popular for afternoon tea and relaxed brasserie style dining.

298 rooms – †£ 289/600 ††£ 289/600 – £ 25 – 12 suites

Town plan: 32AR2-s – *Aldwych ✉ WC2B 4DD – ⊖ Temple – ✆ 020 7836 2400 – www.waldorf.hilton.com*

St Martins Lane

LUXURY • DESIGN The unmistakable hand of Philippe Starck is evident at this most contemporary of hotels. Unique and stylish, from the starkly modern lobby to the state-of-the-art bedrooms, which come in a blizzard of white.

204 rooms – †£ 219/399 ††£ 219/459 – £ 18 – 2 suites

Town plan: 31AP-AQ3-e – *45 St Martin's Ln ✉ WC2N 3HX – ⊖ Charing Cross – ✆ 020 7300 5500 – www.morganshotelgroup.com*

Henrietta (N)

BOUTIQUE HOTEL • DESIGN Cosy boutique townhouse in the heart of Covent Garden; stylish, contemporary bedrooms offer good facilities including Bluetooth speakers and Nespresso machines. Ask for one of the quieter rooms at the back; 18, with its balcony and city views, is best. Cocktail bar and restaurant serving original modern dishes.

18 rooms – †£ 220/500 ††£ 220/500 – £ 20

Town plan: 31AQ3-r – *14-15 Henrietta St ✉ WC2E 8QH – ⊖ Covent Garden – ✆ 020 3794 5313 – www.henriettahotel.com*

Henrietta – See restaurant listing

Victoria

Dining Room at The Goring

TRADITIONAL BRITISH • ELEGANT XXX A paean to all things British and the very model of discretion and decorum – the perfect spot for those who 'like things done properly' but without the stuffiness. The menu is an appealing mix of British classics and lighter, more modern dishes, all prepared with great skill and understanding.

→ Cured sea bream with pickled lemon, iced celery and cucumber. Roast squab with Tokyo turnip, crispy leg parcel and cider vinegar sauce. Gianduja chocolate with Williams pear, caramelised hazelnut and sweet cream cheese.

Menu £ 35/60

Town plan: 38AL6-a – *Goring Hotel, 15 Beeston Pl ✉ SW1W 0JW – ⊖ Victoria – ✆ 020 7396 9000 – www.thegoring.com – Closed Saturday lunch*

Quilon

INDIAN • DESIGN XXX A meal here will remind you how fresh, vibrant, colourful and healthy Indian food can be. Chef Sriram Aylur and his team focus on India's southwest coast, so the emphasis is on seafood and a lighter style of cooking. The room is stylish and comfortable and the service team, bright and enthusiastic.

→ Chargrilled scallops with pawpaw, poppy seeds and chilli relish. Pan-fried duck breast with coconut cream sauce. Hot vermicelli kheer with rose ice cream.

Menu £ 31/60 – Carte £ 42/57

Town plan: 39AN5-6-e – *St James' Court Hotel, 41 Buckingham Gate ✉ SW1E 6AF – ⊖ St James's Park – ✆ 020 7821 1899 – www.quilon.co.uk – Closed 25 December*

The Michelin Plate highlights restaurants where you can get a good meal. Simply being selected for inclusion in the guide is an award in itself.

A. Wong (Andrew Wong)

CHINESE • NEIGHBOURHOOD A modern Chinese restaurant with a buzzy ground floor and a sexy basement. The talented eponymous chef reinvents classic Cantonese dishes using creative, modern techniques; retaining the essence of a dish, whilst adding an impressive lightness and intensity of flavour. Service is keen, as are the prices.

→ Hong Kong egg waffle with marinated scallop salad. 'Gold Fish' dumpling with foie gras, dried pork and chive flower oil. Poached meringue with lychee granité, mango purée, orange sorbet and lotus root.

Carte £ 18/42

Town plan: 38AM7-w - *70 Wilton Rd ✉ SW1V 1DE - ⊖ Victoria - ✆ 020 7828 8931 (booking essential) - www.awong.co.uk - Closed 23 December-4 January, Sunday and lunch Monday*

The Cinnamon Club

INDIAN • HISTORIC Locals and tourists, business people and politicians - this smart Indian restaurant housed in the listed former Westminster Library attracts them all. The fairly elaborate dishes arrive fully garnished and the spicing is quite subtle.

Menu £ 26 (weekday lunch) - Carte £ 35/69

Town plan: 39AP6-c - *30-32 Great Smith St ✉ SW1P 3BU - ⊖ St James's Park - ✆ 020 7222 2555 - www.cinnamonclub.com - Closed 2 April, 27 August and bank holidays*

Grand Imperial

CHINESE • ELEGANT Grand it most certainly is, as this elegant restaurant is in the Grosvenor Hotel's former ballroom. It specialises in Cantonese cuisine, particularly the version found in Hong Kong; steaming and frying are used to great effect.

Menu £ 16/26 - Carte £ 24/78

Town plan: 38AL6-u - *Grosvenor Hotel, 101 Buckingham Palace Rd ✉ SW1W 0SJ - ⊖ Victoria - ✆ 020 7821 8898 - www.grandimperiallondon.com - Closed 25-26 December*

Roux at Parliament Square

MODERN CUISINE • ELEGANT Light floods through the Georgian windows of this comfortable restaurant within the offices of the Royal Institute of Chartered Surveyors. Carefully crafted, elaborate and sophisticated cuisine, with some interesting flavour combinations.

Menu £ 42/59

Town plan: 39AP5-x - *Royal Institution of Chartered Surveyors, Parliament Sq. ✉ SW1P 3AD - ⊖ Westminster - ✆ 020 7334 3737 (bookings advisable at lunch) - www.rouxatparliamentsquare.co.uk - Closed Christmas, Saturday, Sunday and bank holidays*

Santini

ITALIAN • FASHIONABLE This elegant restaurant is still pulling in the crowds over thirty years after it opened, thanks to its reliable, confident cooking and impeccable service. Classic Italian dishes have a Venetian accent and pasta's the star of the show.

Carte £ 33/81

Town plan: 38AL6-e - *29 Ebury St ✉ SW1W 0NZ - ⊖ Victoria - ✆ 020 7730 4094 - www.santinirestaurant.com - Closed 25-26 December, 1 January dinner*

Rex Whistler

MODERN CUISINE • CLASSIC DÉCOR A hidden gem, tucked away on the lower ground floor of Tate Britain; its most striking element is Whistler's restored mural, 'The Expedition in Pursuit of Rare Meats', which envelops the room. The menu is stoutly British and the remarkably priced wine list has an unrivalled 'half bottle' selection.

Menu £ 35

Town plan: 39AP7-w - *Tate Britain, Millbank ✉ SW1P 4RG - ⊖ Pimlico - ✆ 020 7887 8825 - www.tate.org.uk - lunch only - Closed 24-26 December*

Aster

MODERN CUISINE • CONTEMPORARY DÉCOR XX Aster has a deli, a café, a bar and a terrace, as well the restaurant; a stylish, airy space on the first floor. The Finnish chef brings a Nordic slant to the modern French cuisine, with dishes that are light, refined and full of flavour.

Carte £ 29/58

Town plan: 38AM6-a - *150 Victoria St ✉ SW1E 5LB - ⊖ Victoria - ✆ 020 3875 5555 - www.aster-restaurant.com - Closed Sunday*

Enoteca Turi

ITALIAN • NEIGHBOURHOOD XX In 2016 Putney's loss was Pimlico's gain when, after 25 years, Giuseppe and Pamela Turi had to find a new home for their Italian restaurant. They brought their warm hospitality and superb wine list with them, and the chef has introduced a broader range of influences from across the country.

Menu £ 25 (lunch) - Carte £ 31/61

Town plan: 38AK7-s - *87 Pimlico Rd ✉ SW1W 8PU - ⊖ Sloane Square - ✆ 020 7730 3663 - www.enotecaturi.com - Closed 25-26 December, 1 January, Sunday and bank holiday lunch*

Massimo

ITALIAN • ELEGANT XX An opulent, visually impressive restaurant in the luxurious Corinthia hotel. An all-Italian kitchen team bring their own regional influences to the menu, which offers authentic, flavourful Italian dishes including excellent pasta.

Menu £ 30 (dinner) - Carte £ 37/71

Town plan: 31AQ4-x - *Corinthia Hotel, 10 Northumberland Ave. ✉ WC2N 5AE - ⊖ Embankment - ✆ 020 7321 3156 - www.corinthia.com/london - Closed Sunday*

Osteria Dell' Angolo

ITALIAN • NEIGHBOURHOOD XX At lunch, this Italian opposite the Home Office is full of bustle and men in suits; at dinner it's a little more relaxed. Staff are personable and the menu is reassuringly familiar; homemade pasta and seafood dishes are good.

Menu £ 23 (lunch) - Carte £ 26/47

Town plan: 39AP6-n - *47 Marsham St ✉ SW1P 3DR - ⊖ St James's Park - ✆ 020 3268 1077 (booking essential at lunch) - www.osteriadellangolo.co.uk - Closed 1-4 January, 24-28 December, Easter, Saturday lunch, Sunday and bank holidays*

Lorne

MODERN CUISINE • SIMPLE X A small, simply furnished restaurant down a busy side street. The experienced chef understands that less is more and the modern menu is an enticing list of unfussy, well-balanced British and European dishes. Diverse wine list.

Menu £ 22 (lunch) - Carte £ 35/43

Town plan: 38AM7-e - *76 Wilton Rd ✉ SW1V 1DE - ⊖ Victoria - ✆ 020 3327 0210 (booking essential) - www.lornerestaurant.co.uk - Closed 1 week Christmas, Sunday, Monday lunch and bank holiday Mondays*

Olivo

ITALIAN • NEIGHBOURHOOD X A popular, pleasant and relaxed neighbourhood Italian with rough wooden floors, intimate lighting and contemporary styling. Carefully prepared, authentic and tasty dishes, with the robust flavours of Sardinia to the fore.

Menu £ 27 (weekday lunch) - Carte £ 38/50

Town plan: 38AL6-z - *21 Eccleston St ✉ SW1W 9LX - ⊖ Victoria - ✆ 020 7730 2505 (booking essential) - www.olivorestaurants.com - Closed lunch Saturday-Sunday and bank holidays*

Olivocarne

ITALIAN • FASHIONABLE Mauro Sanna seems to have this part of town sewn up! As suggested by its name, this smart, spacious restaurant focuses on meat dishes, with a selection of satisfying Sardinian specialities. Head upstairs first for a cocktail in Joe's Bar.

Menu £ 27 (weekday lunch) – Carte £ 39/53

Town plan: 38AK7-d – *61 Elizabeth St ✉ SW1W 9PP – ⊖ Sloane Square – ✆ 020 7730 7997 – www.olivorestaurants.com*

Olivomare

SEAFOOD • DESIGN Expect understated and stylish piscatorial decoration and seafood with a Sardinian base. Fortnightly changing menu, with high quality produce, much of which is available in the deli next door.

Carte £ 36/49

Town plan: 38AL6-b – *10 Lower Belgrave St ✉ SW1W 0LJ – ⊖ Victoria – ✆ 020 7730 9022 – www.olivorestaurants.com – Closed bank holidays*

The Other Naughty Piglet Ⓝ

MODERN CUISINE • SIMPLE A light, spacious restaurant with friendly staff and a relaxed atmosphere, set on the first floor of The Other Palace theatre. Eclectic modern small plates are designed for sharing and accompanied by an interesting list of natural wines.

Carte £ 25/32

Town plan: 38AM5-t – *The Other Palace, 12 Palace St ✉ SW1E 5JA – ⊖ Victoria – ✆ 020 7592 0322 (booking essential) – www.theothernaughtypiglet.co.uk – Closed Christmas, Sunday and lunch Monday*

The Orange

MODERN CUISINE • FRIENDLY The old Orange Brewery is as charming a pub as its stucco-fronted façade suggests. Try the fun bar or book a table in the more sedate upstairs room. The menu has a Mediterranean bias; spelt or wheat-based pizzas are a speciality. Bedrooms are stylish and comfortable.

Carte £ 31/41

4 rooms – †£ 205/240 ††£ 205/240

Town plan: 38AK7-k – *37 Pimlico Rd ✉ SW1W 8NE – ⊖ Sloane Square. – ✆ 020 7881 9844 – www.theorange.co.uk*

Corinthia

GRAND LUXURY • ELEGANT The restored Victorian splendour of this grand, luxurious hotel cannot fail to impress. Tasteful and immaculately finished bedrooms are some of the largest in town; suites come with butlers. The stunning spa is over four floors. Dine on creative British dishes in elegant Northall; opulent Massimo serves seasonal Italian fare.

294 rooms – †£ 570/1026 ††£ 570/1026 – 23 suites

Town plan: 31AQ4-x – *Whitehall Pl. ✉ SW1A 2BD – ⊖ Embankment – ✆ 020 7930 8181 – www.corinthia.com*

Massimo – See restaurant listing

Goring

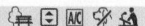

LUXURY • ELEGANT Under the stewardship of the founder's great grandson, this landmark hotel has been restored and renovated while maintaining its traditional atmosphere and pervading sense of Britishness. Expect first class service and immaculate, very comfortable bedrooms, many of which overlook the garden.

69 rooms – †£ 360/615 ††£ 410/710 – 8 suites

Town plan: 38AL6-a – *15 Beeston Pl ✉ SW1W 0JW – ⊖ Victoria – ✆ 020 7396 9000 – www.thegoring.com*

✿ **Dining Room at The Goring** – See restaurant listing

St James' Court

LUXURY • CLASSIC Built in 1897 as serviced accommodation for visiting aristocrats. Behind the impressive Edwardian façade lies an equally elegant interior. The quietest bedrooms overlook a courtyard. Relaxed, bright Bistro 51 comes with an international menu; Bank offers brasserie classics in a conservatory.

318 rooms – £ 315/505 £ 315/505 – £ 20 – 20 suites

Town plan: 39AN5-6-e – *45 Buckingham Gate ✉ SW1E 6BS – ⊖ St James's Park – ✆ 020 7834 6655 – www.tajhotels.com/stjamescourt*

Quilon – See restaurant listing

Artist Residence

TOWNHOUSE • PERSONALISED A converted pub made into a comfortable, quirky townhouse hotel, with stylish bedrooms featuring mini Smeg fridges, retro telephones, reclaimed furniture and pop art. Cool bar and sitting room beneath the busy Cambridge Street Kitchen.

10 rooms – £ 235/450 £ 235/450 – £ 15

Town plan: 38AL7-r – *52 Cambridge St ✉ SW1V 4QQ – ⊖ Victoria – ✆ 020 7931 8946 – www.artistresidencelondon.co.uk*

Lord Milner

TOWNHOUSE • CLASSIC A four storey terraced house, with individually decorated bedrooms, three with four-poster beds and all with smart marble bathrooms. Garden Suite is the best room; it has its own patio. Breakfast served in your bedroom.

11 rooms – £ 110/160 £ 145/290 – £ 17

Town plan: 38AL6-k – *111 Ebury St ✉ SW1W 9QU – ⊖ Victoria – ✆ 020 7881 9880 – www.lordmilner.com*

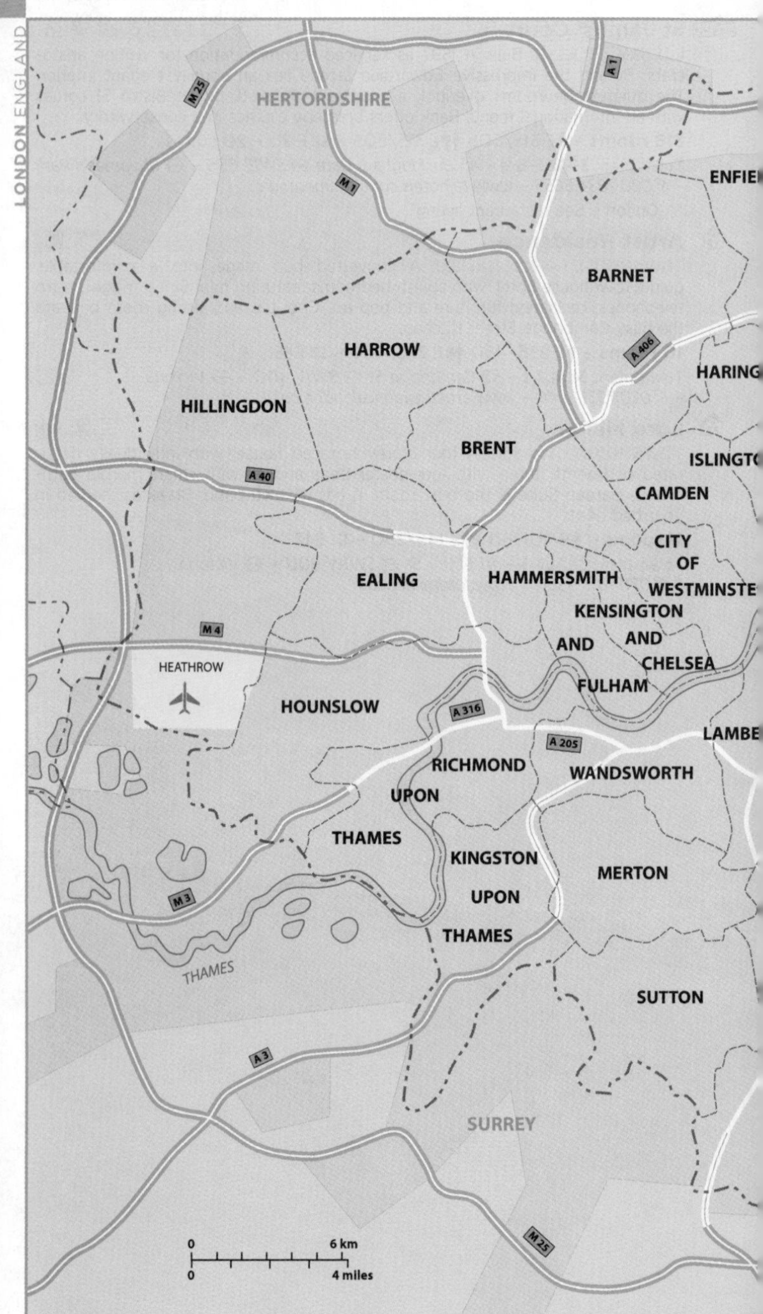

HERTORDSHIRE
M 25
M 1
A 1
ENFIE
BARNET
A 406
HARING
HARROW
HILLINGDON
BRENT
ISLINGTO
A 40
CAMDEN
CITY
OF
WESTMINSTE
EALING
HAMMERSMITH
KENSINGTON
AND
AND
CHELSEA
FULHAM
M 4
HEATHROW
HOUNSLOW
A 316
LAMBE
A 205
RICHMOND
UPON
THAMES
WANDSWORTH
KINGSTON
UPON
THAMES
MERTON
M 3
THAMES
SUTTON
A 3
SURREY
M 25
0
6 km
0
4 miles

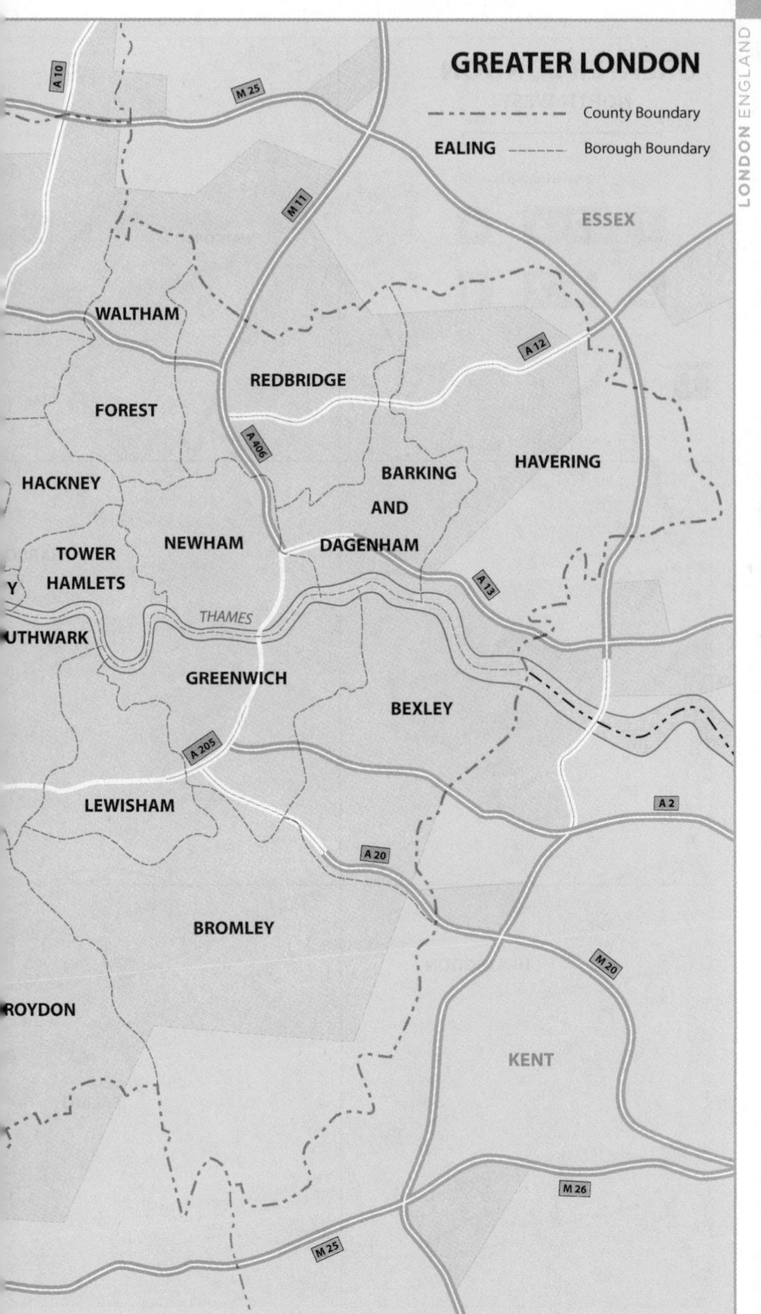
GREATER LONDON
County Boundary
EALING
Borough Boundary
ESSEX
A 10
M 25
M 11
A 12
A 406
A 13
A 205
A 20
A 2
M 20
M 26
M 25
WALTHAM
FOREST
REDBRIDGE
HAVERING
BARKING
AND
DAGENHAM
HACKNEY
NEWHAM
TOWER
HAMLETS
THAMES
UTHWARK
GREENWICH
BEXLEY
LEWISHAM
BROMLEY
ROYDON
KENT

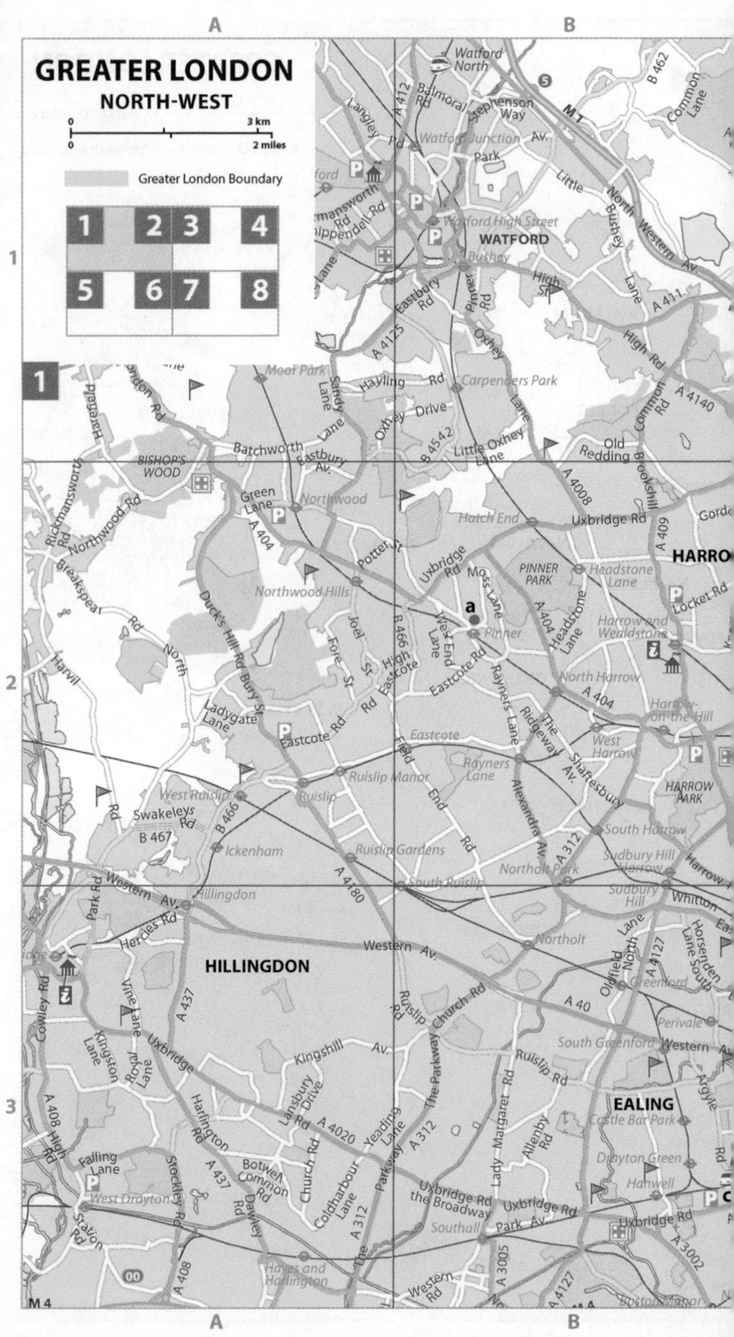
GREATER LONDON
NORTH-WEST
0 3 km
0 2 miles
Greater London Boundary
1 2 3 4
5 6 7 8
A
B
1
2
3
Watford North
Watford Junction
Watford High Street
WATFORD
Bushey
Moor Park
Carpenders Park
Hatch End
Northwood
Northwood Hills
BISHOP'S WOOD
PINNER PARK
Pinner
Headstone Lane
HARROW
Harrow and Wealdstone
North Harrow
Harrow-on-the-Hill
West Harrow
HARROW PARK
Eastcote
Rayners Lane
Ruislip Manor
Ruislip
West Ruislip
Ickenham
Ruislip Gardens
South Ruislip
Northolt Park
South Harrow
Sudbury Hill Harrow
Sudbury Hill
Hillingdon
Northolt
HILLINGDON
Greenford
Perivale
South Greenford
EALING
Castle Bar Park
Drayton Green
Hanwell
West Drayton
Southall
Hayes and Harlington
Boston Manor
M 1
M 4
A 412
A 4125
A 4008
A 404
A 409
A 4140
A 411
B 462
B 4542
B 466
B 467
A 4180
A 312
A 40
A 4127
A 437
A 4020
A 408
A 3005
A 3002
Uxbridge Rd
Western Av.
Ruislip Rd
Eastcote Rd
Field End Rd
Alexandra Av.
Rayners Lane
The Ridgeway
Shaftesbury Av.
Uxbridge Rd the Broadway
Park Av.
Western Rd
Dawley Rd
Station Rd
Stockley Rd
Botwell Common Rd
Harlington Rd
Church Rd
Coldharbour Lane
The Parkway
Yeading Lane
Lansbury Drive
Kingshill Av.
Ruislip Church Rd
Lady Margaret Rd
Allenby Rd
Falling Lane
A 408 High Rd
Cowley Rd
Kingston Lane
Royal Lane
Vine Lane
Hercies Rd
Park Rd
Swakeleys Rd
Ladygate Lane
Duck's Hill Rd
Bury St
Joel St
Fore St
High St
Potter St
Moss Lane
West End Lane
Green Lane
Batchworth Lane
Eastbury Av.
Hayling Rd
Sandy Lane
Oxhey Drive
Oxhey Lane
Little Oxhey Lane
Old Redding
Common Rd
Brookshill
High Rd
Bushey Lane
North Western Av.
Little Park
Stephenson Way
Balmoral Rd
Langley Rd
Rickmansworth Rd
Chippendell Rd
Eastbury Rd
Pinner Rd
High St
Common Lane
Harefield
Northwood Rd
Rickmansworth Rd
Breakspear Rd North
Harvil Rd
Headstone Lane
Locker Rd
Oldfield North Lane
Horsenden Lane South
Whitton
Argyle Rd
Gordon
a

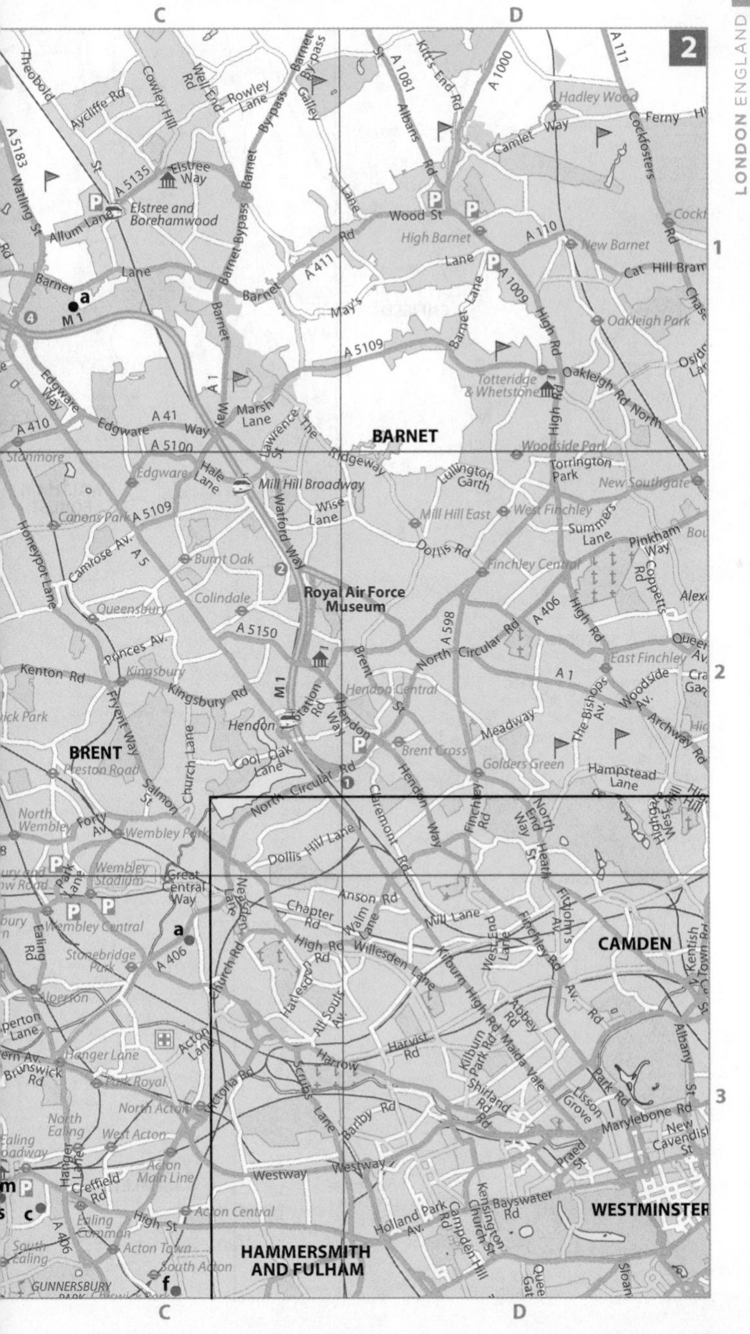
2
BARNET
BRENT
CAMDEN
WESTMINSTER
HAMMERSMITH AND FULHAM
Royal Air Force Museum
Elstree and Borehamwood
High Barnet
New Barnet
Oakleigh Park
Totteridge & Whetstone
Woodside Park
West Finchley
Mill Hill East
Finchley Central
East Finchley
Mill Hill Broadway
Edgware
Burnt Oak
Colindale
Hendon Central
Brent Cross
Golders Green
Wembley Park
Wembley Stadium
Wembley Central
North Acton
West Acton
Acton Central
Acton Town
South Acton

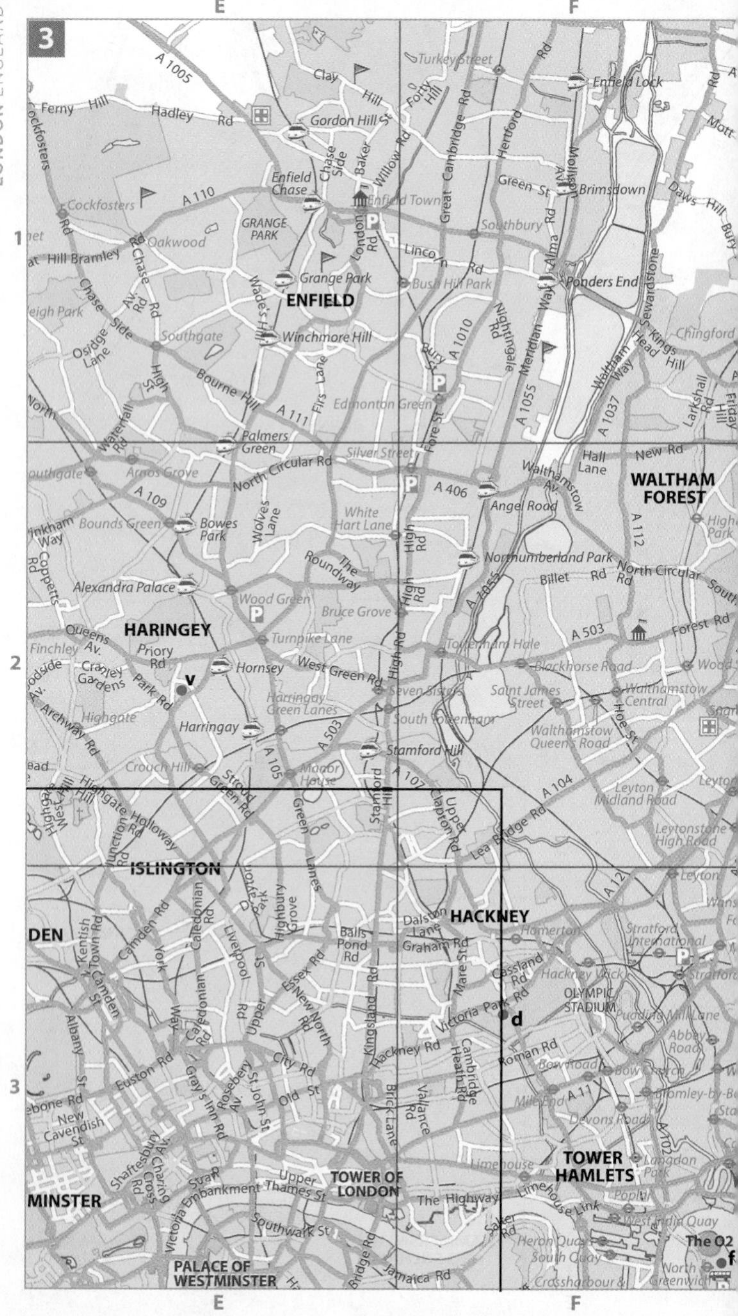

E
F
3
1
2
3
ENFIELD
HARINGEY
WALTHAM FOREST
ISLINGTON
HACKNEY
TOWER HAMLETS
TOWER OF LONDON
PALACE OF WESTMINSTER
OLYMPIC STADIUM
The O2

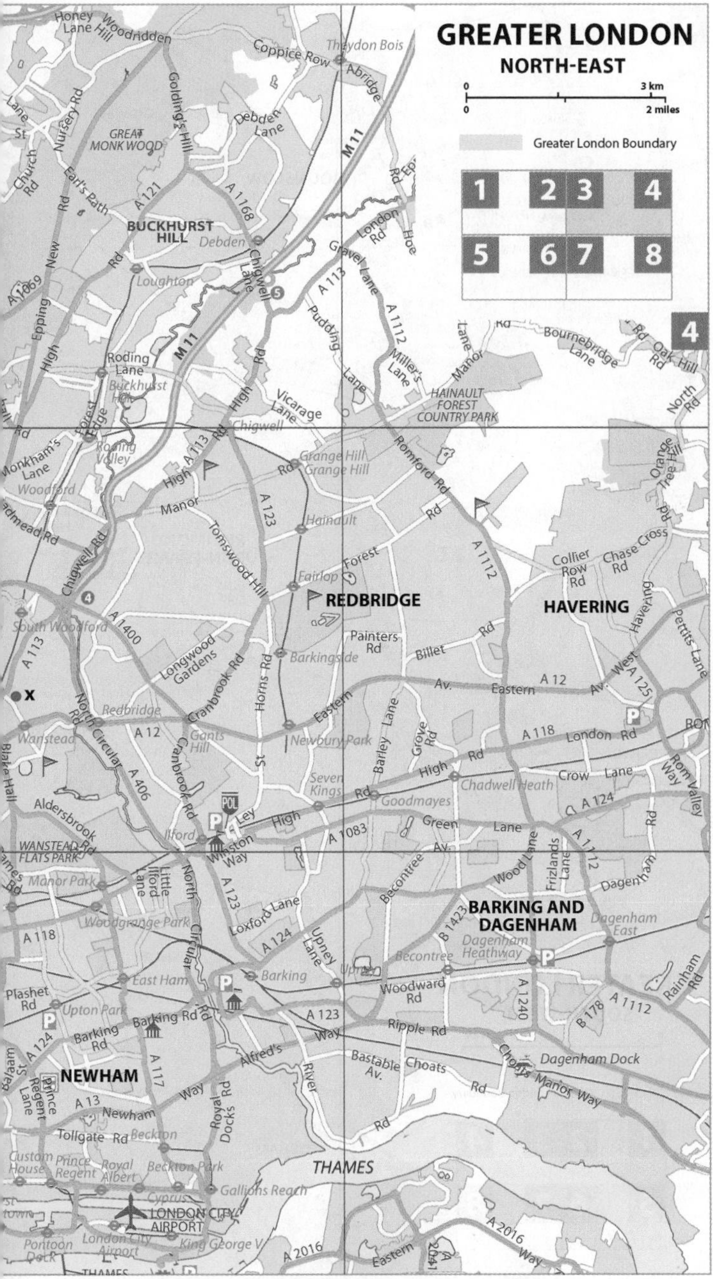

GREATER LONDON
NORTH-EAST

0 3 km
0 2 miles

Greater London Boundary

1 2 3 4
5 6 7 8

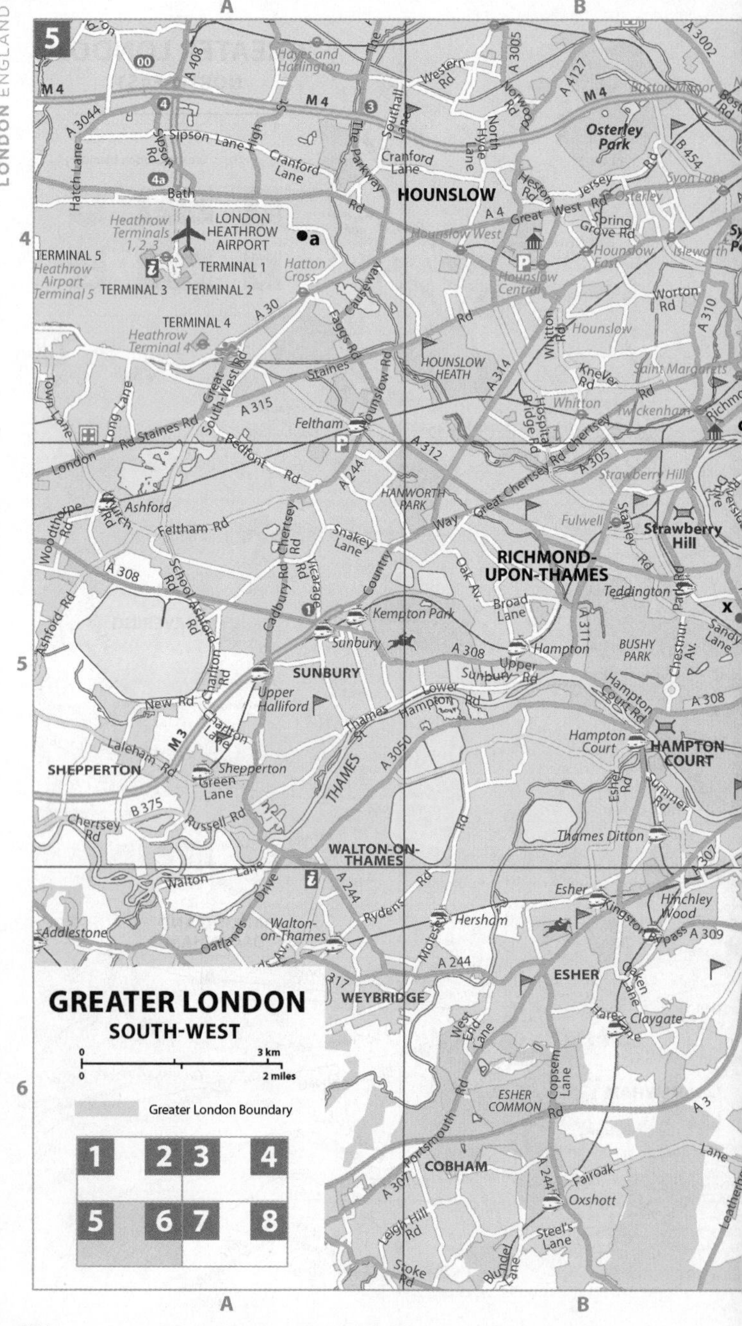
5
GREATER LONDON
SOUTH-WEST
0 3 km
0 2 miles
Greater London Boundary
HOUNSLOW
LONDON HEATHROW AIRPORT
RICHMOND-UPON-THAMES
SUNBURY
SHEPPERTON
WALTON-ON-THAMES
HAMPTON COURT
WEYBRIDGE
ESHER
COBHAM

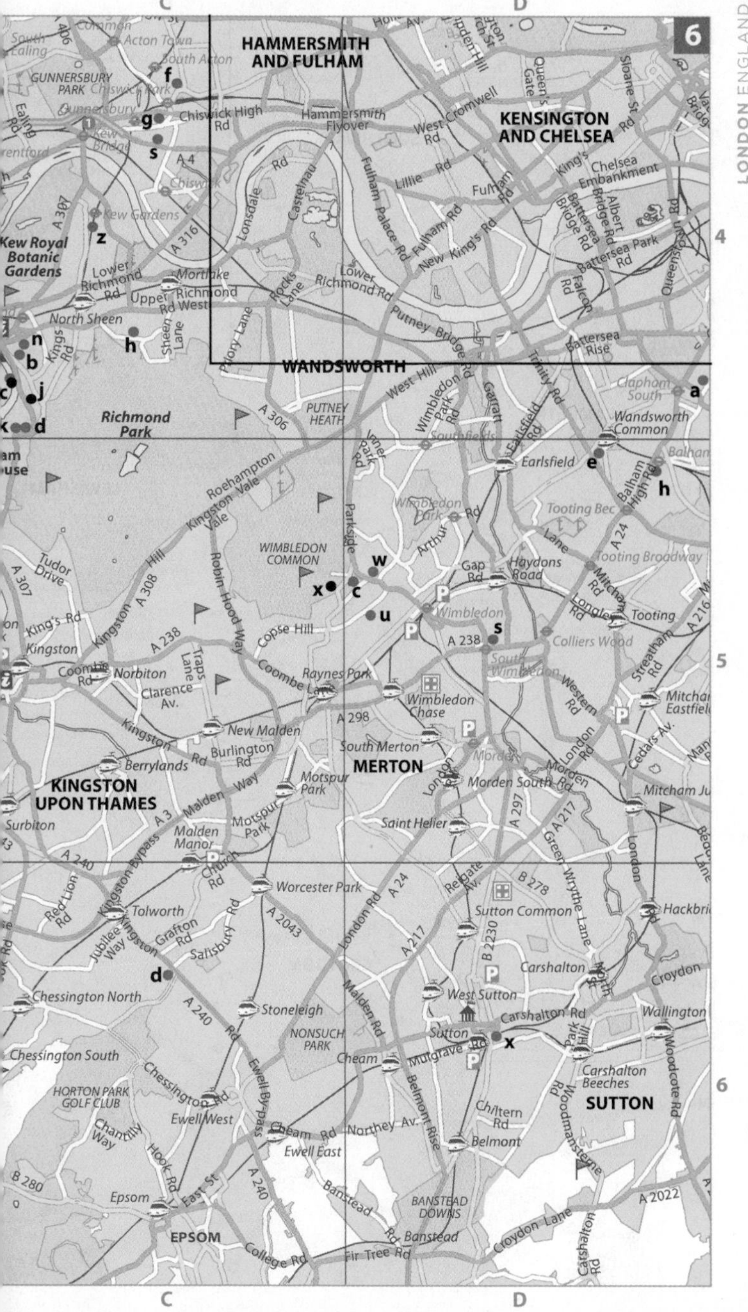
C
D
6
HAMMERSMITH AND FULHAM
KENSINGTON AND CHELSEA
WANDSWORTH
Kew Royal Botanic Gardens
Richmond Park
WIMBLEDON COMMON
PUTNEY HEATH
MERTON
KINGSTON UPON THAMES
SUTTON
EPSOM
NONSUCH PARK
HORTON PARK GOLF CLUB
BANSTEAD DOWNS
4
5
6

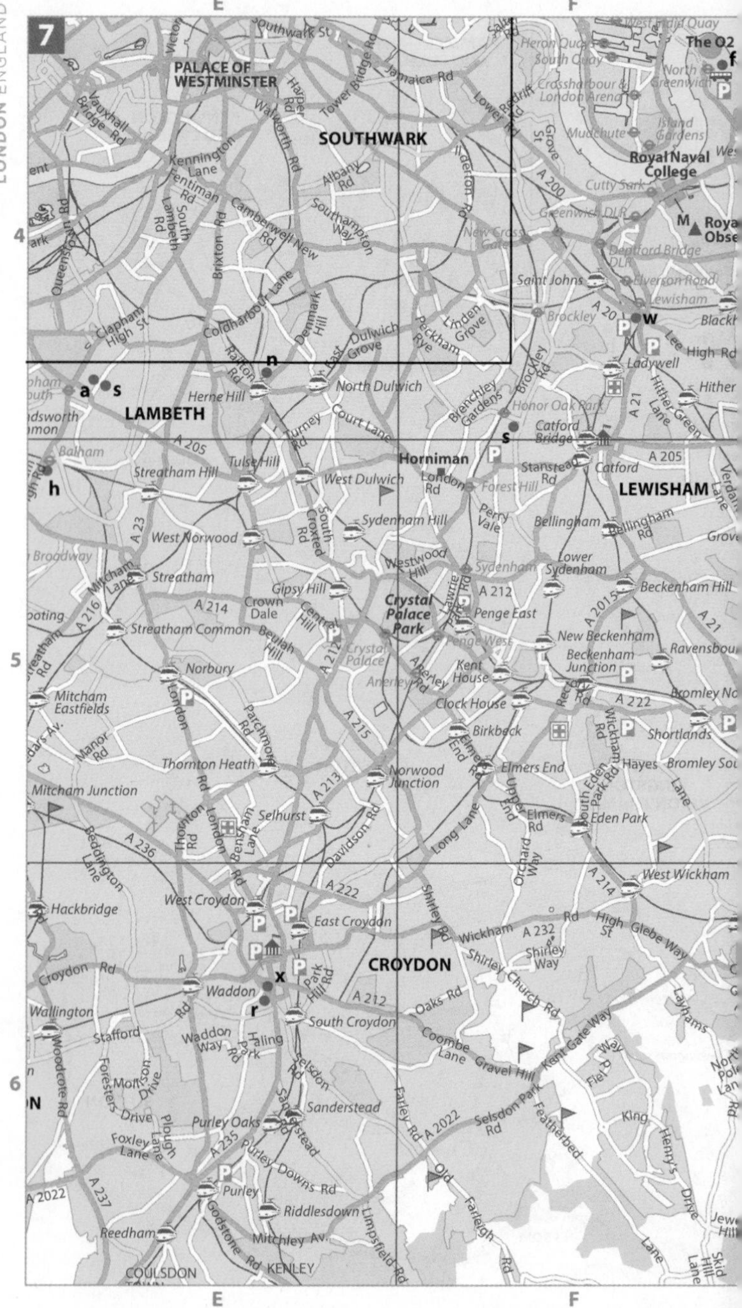
7
E
F
PALACE OF WESTMINSTER
SOUTHWARK
LAMBETH
LEWISHAM
CROYDON
The O2
Royal Naval College
Horniman
Crystal Palace Park
Heron Quay
South Quay
North Greenwich
Crossharbour & London Arena
Mudchute
Island Gardens
Cutty Sark
Greenwich DLR
New Cross Gate
Deptford Bridge DLR
Saint Johns
Elverson Road
Lewisham
Brockley
Ladywell
Hither Green
Honor Oak Park
Catford Bridge
Catford
Forest Hill
Bellingham
Lower Sydenham
Sydenham
Beckenham Hill
Penge East
Penge West
New Beckenham
Beckenham Junction
Ravensbourne
Kent House
Clock House
Birkbeck
Elmers End
Shortlands
Hayes
Eden Park
West Wickham
Herne Hill
North Dulwich
Tulse Hill
West Dulwich
Sydenham Hill
Streatham Hill
West Norwood
Streatham
Gipsy Hill
Crystal Palace
Anerley
Streatham Common
Norbury
Mitcham Eastfields
Mitcham Junction
Thornton Heath
Norwood Junction
Selhurst
West Croydon
East Croydon
Hackbridge
Waddon
Wallington
South Croydon
Sanderstead
Purley Oaks
Purley
Riddlesdown
Reedham
Balham
Broadway
Tooting
COULSDON
KENLEY
Southwark St
Jamaica Rd
Tower Bridge Rd
Harper Rd
Walworth Rd
Albany Rd
Southampton Way
Camberwell New Rd
Kennington Lane
Fentiman Rd
South Lambeth Rd
Brixton Rd
Vauxhall Bridge Rd
Queenstown Rd
Clapham High St
Coldharbour Lane
Denmark Hill
Railton Rd
East Dulwich Grove
Peckham Rye
Linden Grove
Lower Rd
Redriff Rd
Grove St
Ilderton Rd
A 200
A 20
Lee High Rd
Brockley Rd
Brenchley Gardens
A 21
Hither Green Lane
A 205
Stanstead Rd
London Rd
Perry Vale
Bellingham Rd
Verdant Lane
Court Lane
Turney Rd
South Croxted Rd
Westwood Hill
Lawrie Park Rd
A 212
A 2015
A 23
A 214
Crown Dale
Central Hill
Beulah Hill
A 216
Mitcham Lane
Streatham Rd
London Rd
Parchmore Rd
A 215
Anerley Rd
Elmers End Rd
Upper Elmers End Rd
Recreation Rd
A 222
Wickham Rd
South Eden Park Rd
Bromley South
Bromley North
Manor Rd
Cedars Av.
Thornton Rd
Bensham Lane
A 213
Davidson Rd
Long Lane
Orchard Way
A 236
Beddington Lane
Shirley Rd
A 214
Wickham Rd
A 232
High St
Glebe Way
Shirley Way
Shirley Church Rd
Croydon Rd
Park Hill Rd
Oaks Rd
Coombe Lane
Gravel Hill
Kent Gate Way
Fleet Way
Layhams
Stafford Rd
Waddon Way
Haling Park Rd
Selsdon Rd
Sanderstead Rd
Farley Rd
A 2022
Selsdon Park Rd
Featherbed
King Henry's Drive
Woodcote Rd
Foresters Drive
Mollison Drive
Plough Lane
Foxley Lane
A 235
Purley Downs Rd
A 237
Godstone Rd
Mitchley Av.
Limpsfield Rd
Old Farleigh Rd
Jewel Hill
Skid Hill Lane
4
5
6
a
s
n
h
s
w
f
x
r
M

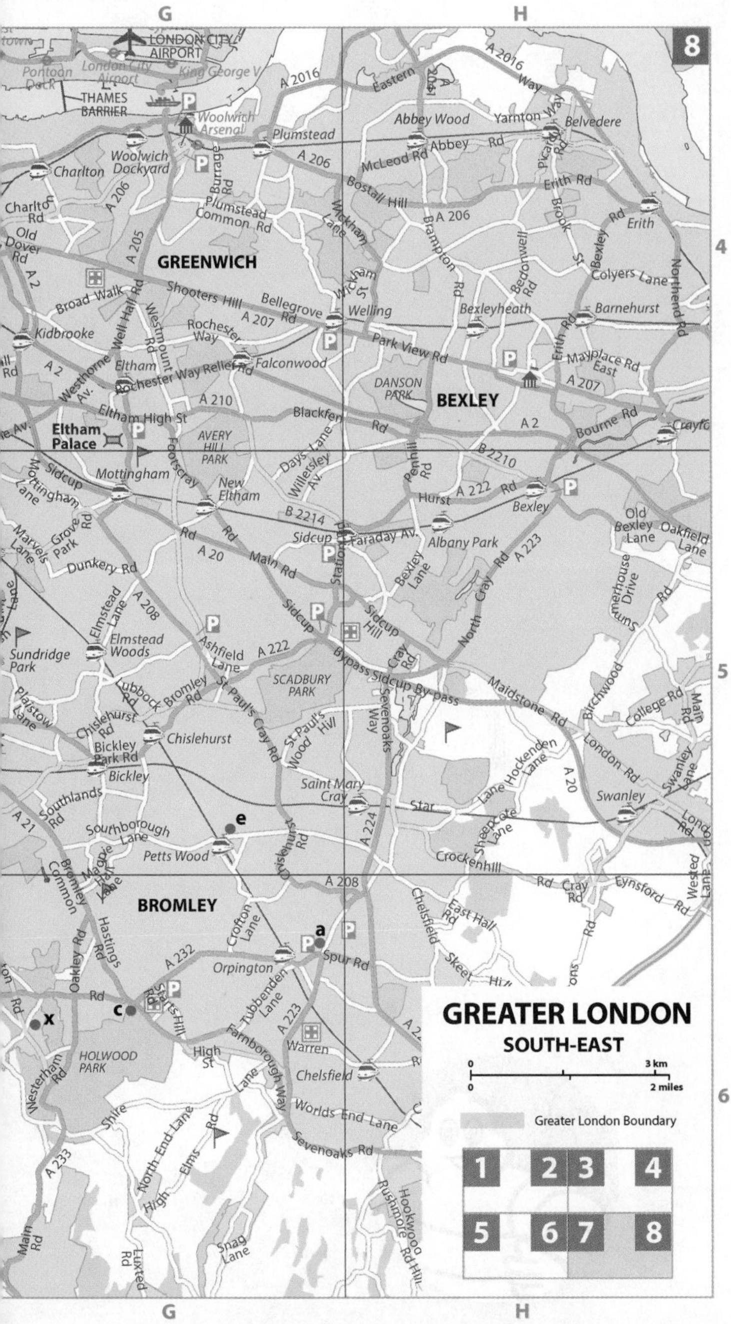

G H

8

GREATER LONDON

SOUTH-EAST

0 3 km
0 2 miles

Greater London Boundary

1 2 3 4
5 6 7 8

LONDON CITY AIRPORT
Pontoon Dock
London City Airport
King George V
THAMES BARRIER
Woolwich Arsenal
Woolwich Dockyard
Charlton
Plumstead
Abbey Wood
Belvedere
Erith
GREENWICH
BEXLEY
BROMLEY
Kidbrooke
Eltham
Eltham Palace
Falconwood
Welling
Bexleyheath
Barnehurst
DANSON PARK
AVERY HILL PARK
Mottingham
New Eltham
Sidcup
Albany Park
Bexley
Old Bexley Lane
Elmstead Woods
Sundridge Park
SCADBURY PARK
Chislehurst
Bickley
Saint Mary Cray
Swanley
Petts Wood
Orpington
HOLWOOD PARK
Chelsfield
Warren
Crockenhill
A 2016
A 206
A 205
A 207
A 2
A 210
A 20
A 208
A 222
A 223
A 224
A 232
A 233
A 21
B 2210
B 2214
Shooters Hill
Bellegrove Rd
Rochester Way
Rochester Way Relief Rd
Eltham High St
Blackfen Rd
Sidcup By-pass
Maidstone Rd
London Rd
Main Rd
Sevenoaks Way
Sevenoaks Rd
Worlds End Lane
Farnborough Way
Spur Rd

4
5
6

G H

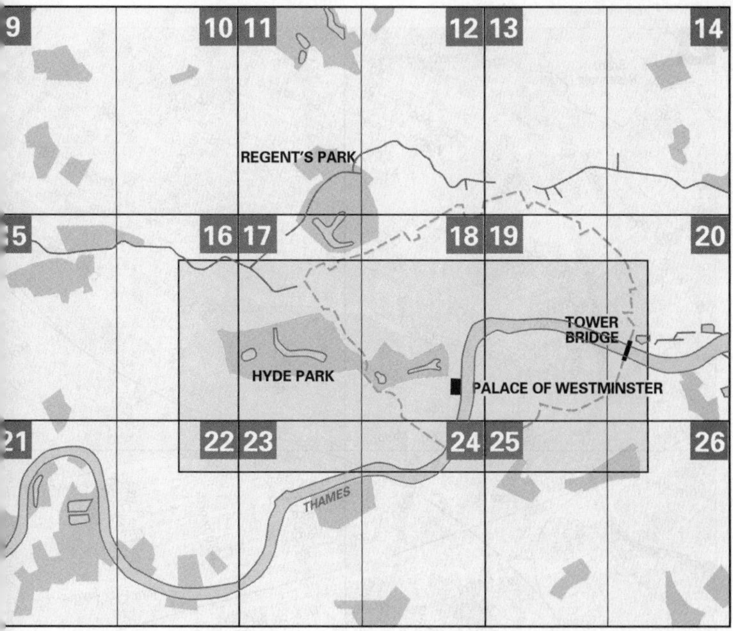

9
10 11
12 13
14
REGENT'S PARK
15
16 17
18 19
20
TOWER BRIDGE
HYDE PARK
PALACE OF WESTMINSTER
21
22 23
24 25
26
THAMES

27
28 29
30 31
32 33
34
THAMES
TOWER BRIDGE
HYDE PARK
35
36 37
38 39
40 41
42
PALACE OF WESTMINSTER

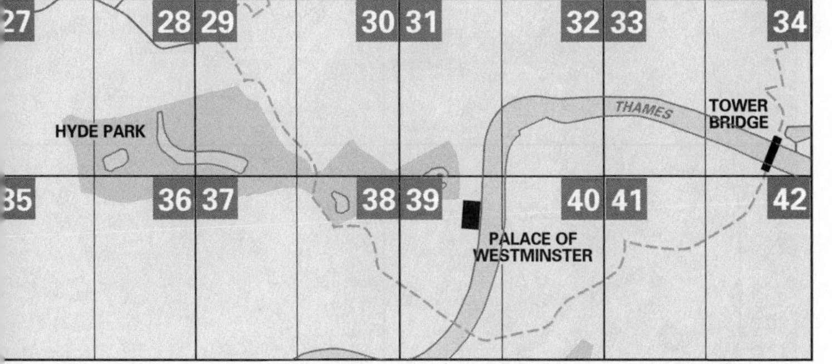

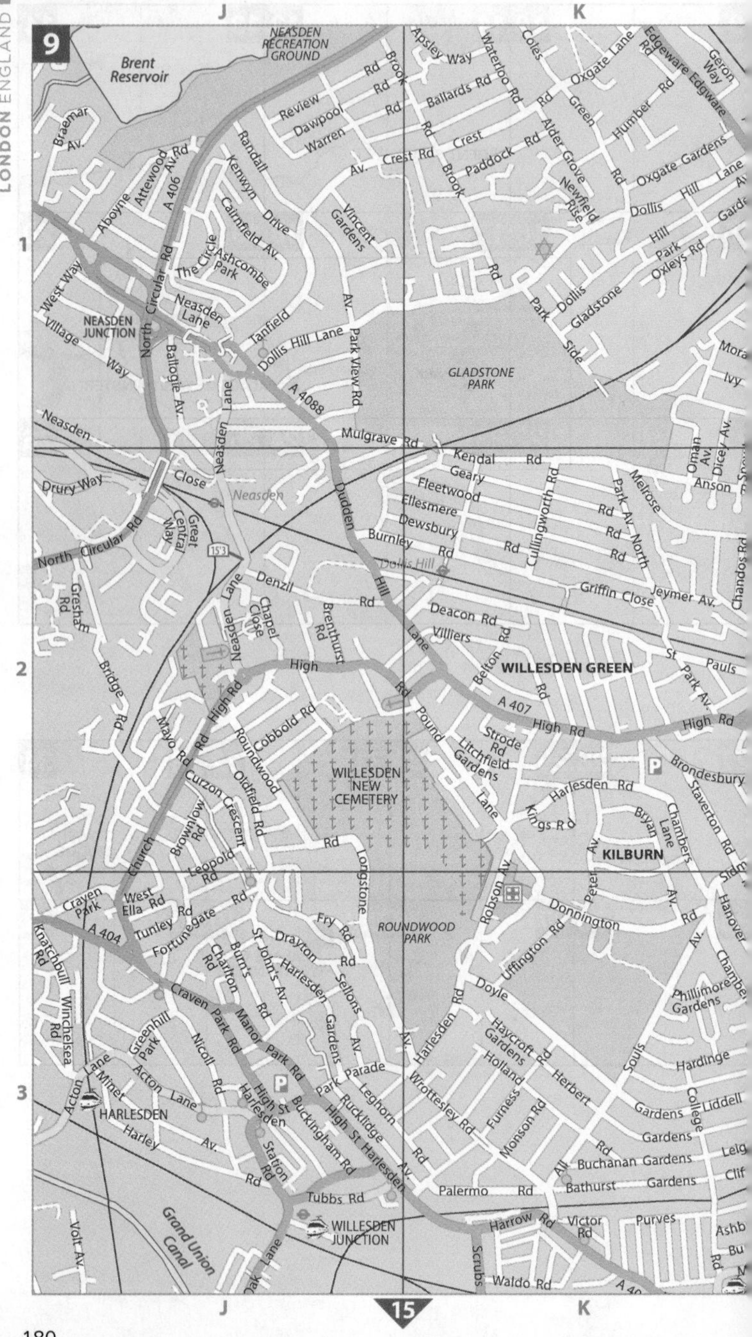
9
J
K
1
2
3
Brent Reservoir
NEASDEN RECREATION GROUND
NEASDEN JUNCTION
GLADSTONE PARK
Neasden
Dollis Hill
WILLESDEN GREEN
WILLESDEN NEW CEMETERY
KILBURN
ROUNDWOOD PARK
HARLESDEN
WILLESDEN JUNCTION
Grand Union Canal
North Circular Rd
A 406
A 4088
A 407
A 404
Dudden Hill Lane
High Rd
Church Rd
Harlesden Rd
Harrow Rd
Mulgrave Rd
Kendal Rd
Dollis Hill Lane
Park View Rd
Crest Rd
Brook Rd
Oxgate Lane
Edgeware Rd
Willesden Lane
Chambers Lane
Acton Lane
Craven Park Rd
Manor Park Rd
High St Harlesden
Tubbs Rd
Station Rd
Old Oak Lane
Scrubs Lane
Waldo Rd
Palermo Rd
Donnington Rd
Longstone Av.
Roundwood Rd
Neasden Lane
Drury Way
Great Central Way
Denzil Rd
Brenthurst Rd
Villiers Rd
Deacon Rd
Griffin Close
Jeymer Av.
St Pauls Av.
Brondesbury Park
15

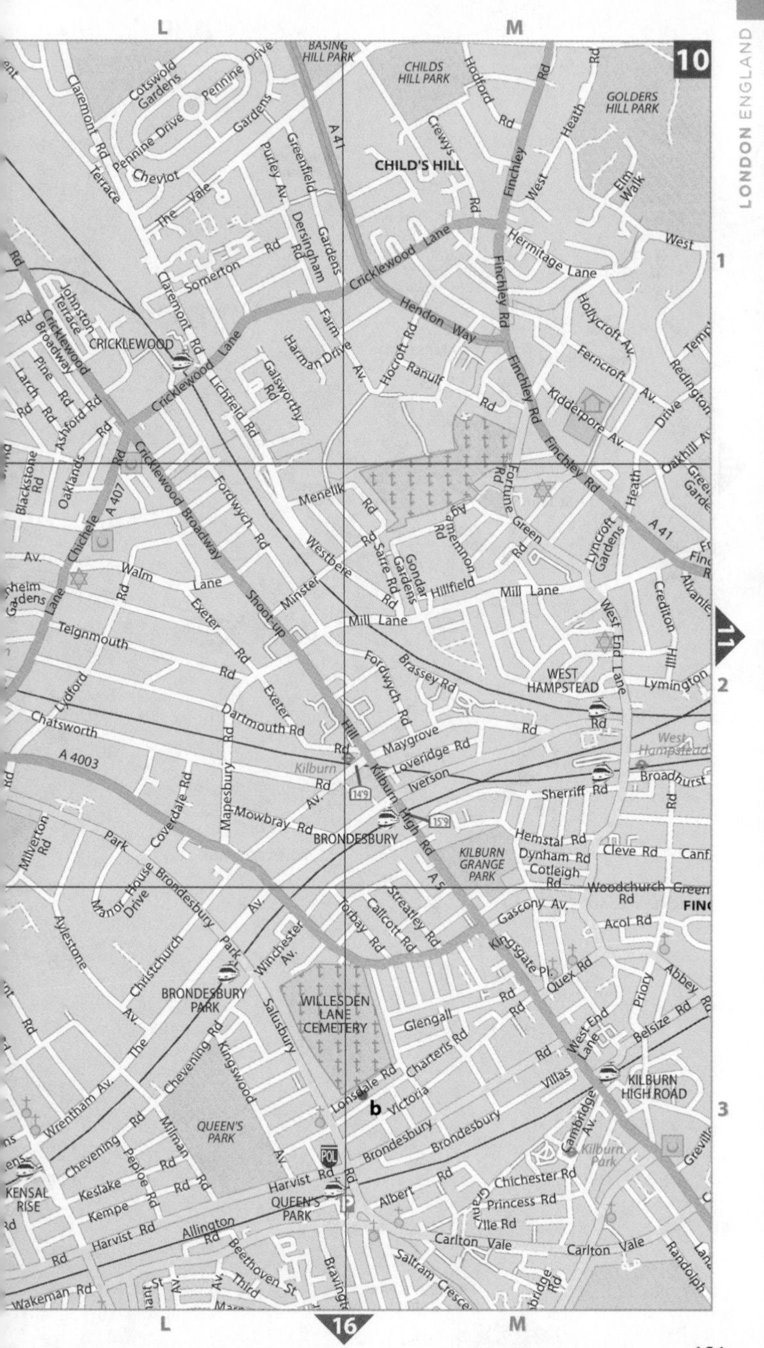
L
M
10
BASING HILL PARK
CHILDS HILL PARK
GOLDERS HILL PARK
CHILD'S HILL
CRICKLEWOOD
WEST HAMPSTEAD
BRONDESBURY
KILBURN GRANGE PARK
BRONDESBURY PARK
WILLESDEN LANE CEMETERY
QUEEN'S PARK
KILBURN HIGH ROAD
KENSAL RISE
Kilburn
Kilburn Park
West Hampstead
A 41
A 407
A 4003
A 5
Cricklewood Lane
Hendon Way
Finchley Rd
Mill Lane
Shoot-up Hill
Kilburn High Rd
Brondesbury Park
Chatsworth Rd
Carlton Vale
11
1
2
3
16

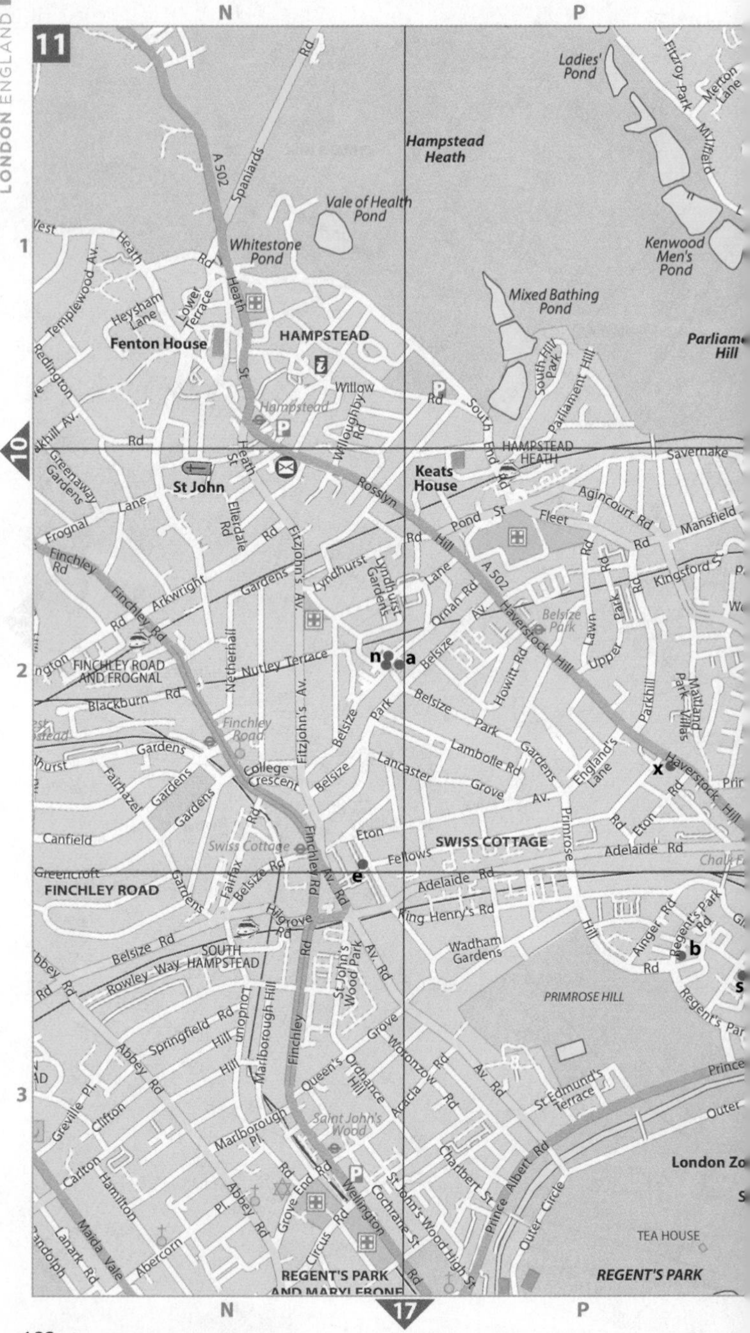

N
P
11
10
17
1
2
3
Hampstead Heath
Ladies' Pond
Vale of Health Pond
Whitestone Pond
Kenwood Men's Pond
Mixed Bathing Pond
Parliament Hill
HAMPSTEAD
Fenton House
St John
Keats House
HAMPSTEAD HEATH
Hampstead
FINCHLEY ROAD AND FROGNAL
Finchley Road
Swiss Cottage
SWISS COTTAGE
FINCHLEY ROAD
SOUTH HAMPSTEAD
PRIMROSE HILL
Saint John's Wood
London Zoo
TEA HOUSE
REGENT'S PARK
REGENT'S PARK AND MARYLEBONE
Belsize Park
A 502
Spaniards Rd
Heath St
Rosslyn Hill
Haverstock Hill
Fitzjohn's Av.
Finchley Rd
Frognal Lane
Arkwright Rd
Nutley Terrace
Belsize Park Gardens
Lambolle Rd
Lancaster Grove
Eton Av.
Adelaide Rd
King Henry's Rd
Wadham Gardens
Fellows Rd
Belsize Rd
Rowley Way
Abbey Rd
Springfield Rd
Marlborough Hill
Finchley Rd
Queen's Grove
Ordnance Hill
Woronzow Rd
Acacia Rd
Avenue Rd
St Edmund's Terrace
Prince Albert Rd
Outer Circle
Wellington Rd
St John's Wood High St
Grove End Rd
Circus Rd
Abercorn Pl.
Maida Vale
Lanark Rd
Hamilton
Carlton
Clifton
Greville Pl.
Canfield
Greencroft
Fairhazel Gardens
College Crescent
Netherhall
Ellerdale Rd
Lyndhurst Gardens
Lyndhurst
Willoughby Rd
Willow Rd
South End Rd
Pond St
Fleet Rd
Agincourt Rd
Mansfield
Kingsford St
Savernake
Parliament Hill
South Hill Park
Fitzroy Park
Merton Lane
Millfield
Templewood Av.
Heysham Lane
Lower Terrace
Redington
Greenaway Gardens
Blackburn Rd
Howitt Rd
Upper Park Rd
Lawn Rd
Parkhill
Maitland Park Villas
England's Lane
Primrose Hill
Ainger Rd
Regent's Park Rd
Ornan Rd
n
a
e
x
b
s

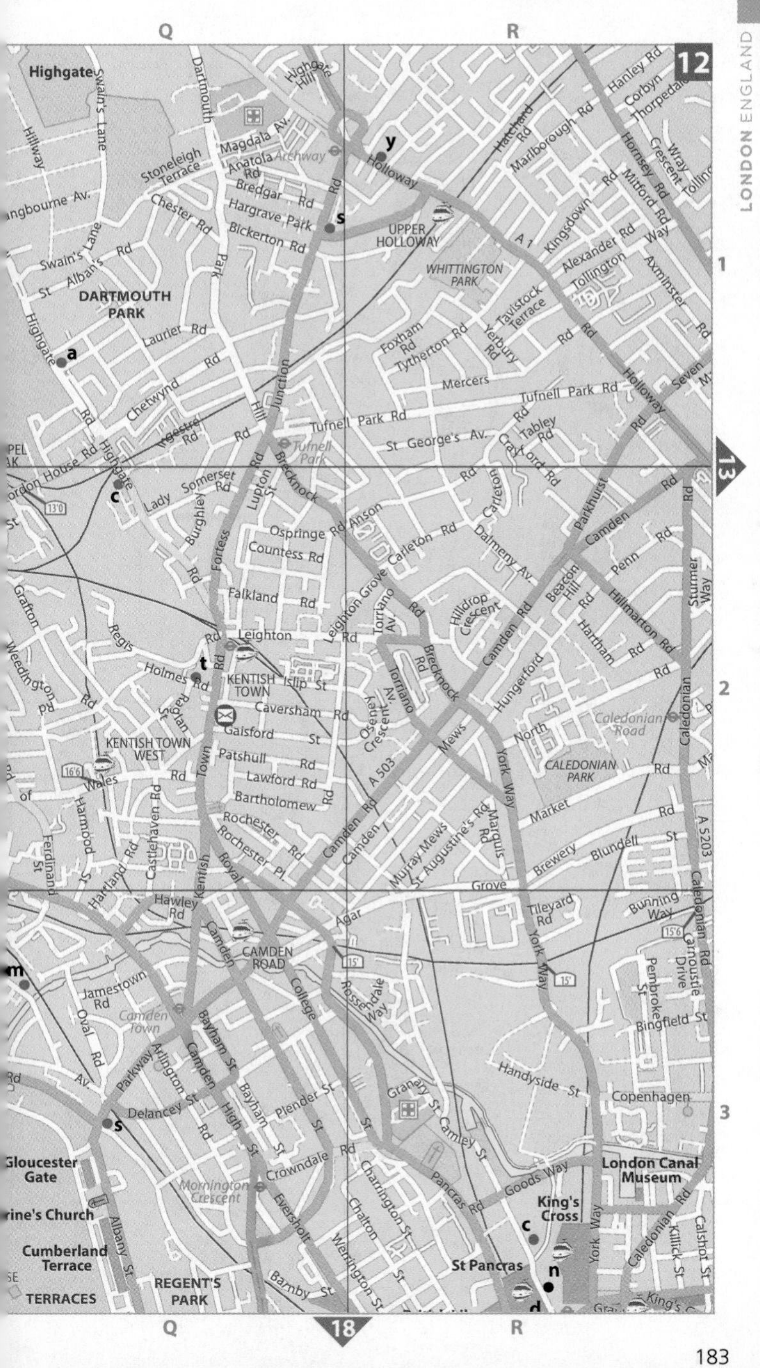
Q
R
12
Highgate
DARTMOUTH PARK
UPPER HOLLOWAY
WHITTINGTON PARK
KENTISH TOWN
KENTISH TOWN WEST
CALEDONIAN PARK
CAMDEN ROAD
London Canal Museum
King's Cross
St Pancras
Gloucester Gate
Cumberland Terrace
TERRACES
REGENT'S PARK
Archway
Tufnell Park
Caledonian Road
Camden Town
Mornington Crescent
1
2
3
13
18
Q
R

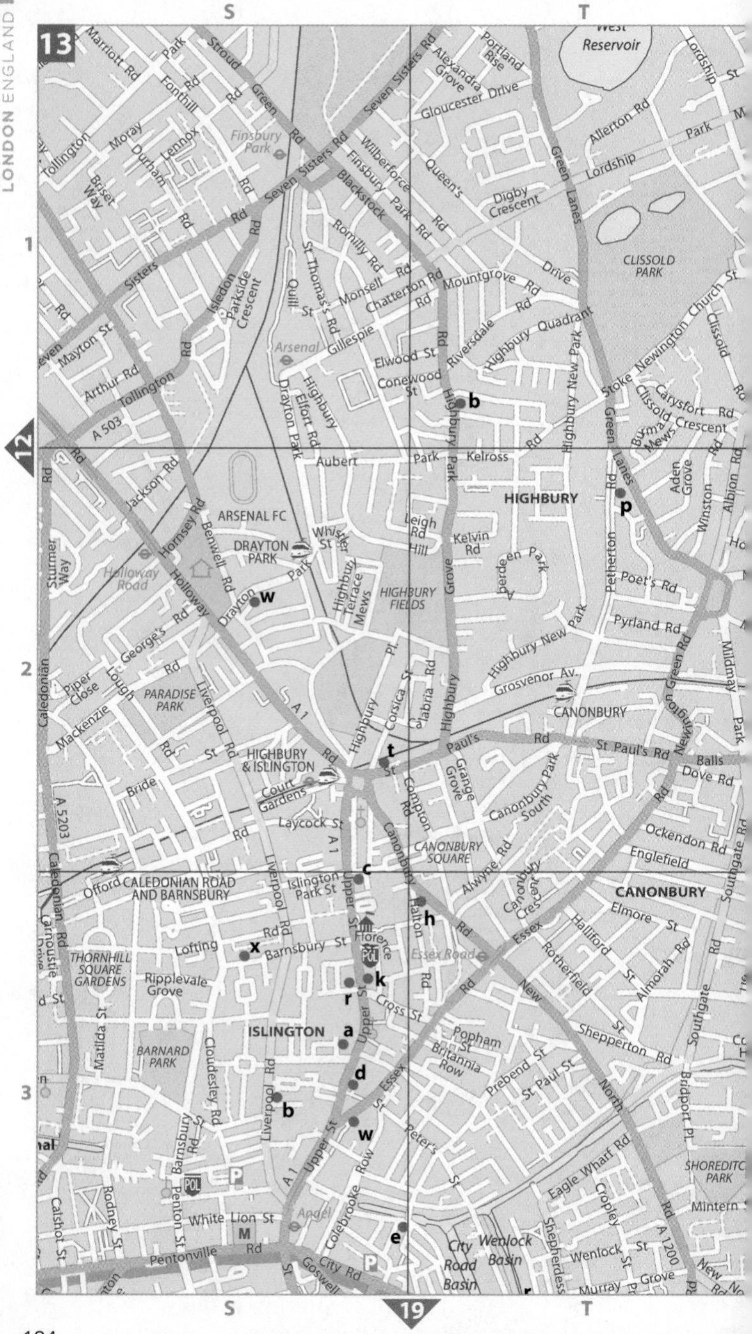

13

S T

West Reservoir
Finsbury Park
Arsenal
CLISSOLD PARK
HIGHBURY
ARSENAL FC
DRAYTON PARK
Holloway Road
HIGHBURY FIELDS
CANONBURY
PARADISE PARK
HIGHBURY & ISLINGTON
CANONBURY SQUARE
CALEDONIAN ROAD AND BARNSBURY
CANONBURY
THORNHILL SQUARE GARDENS
Essex Road
ISLINGTON
BARNARD PARK
Angel
SHOREDITCH PARK
City Road Basin
Wenlock Basin

12
19

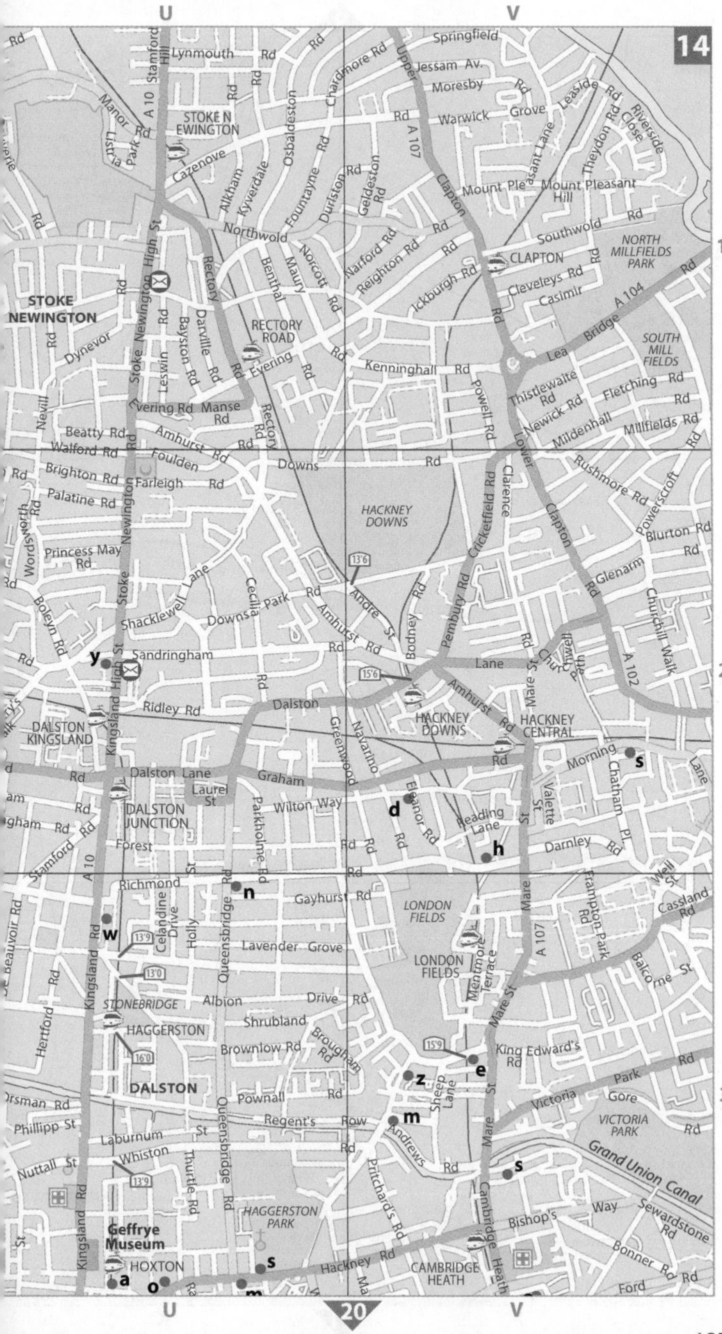

U V

14

Lynmouth Rd
Springfield
Upper Clapton Rd
Jessam Av.
Moresby Rd
Stamford Hill
A 10
Manor Rd
Lordship Park
STOKE NEWINGTON
Cazenove Rd
Chardmore Rd
Osbaldeston Rd
Warwick Grove
Leaside Rd
Theydon Rd
Riverside Close
A 107
Alkham Rd
Kyverdale Rd
Fountayne Rd
Durlston Rd
Geldeston Rd
Mount Pleasant Lane
Mount Pleasant Hill
Clapton
Northwold Rd
Southwold Rd
NORTH MILLFIELDS PARK
Narford Rd
Reighton Rd
CLAPTON
Stoke Newington High St
Rectory Rd
Benthal Rd
Maury Rd
Norcott Rd
Ickburgh Rd
Cleveleys Rd
Casimir Rd
STOKE NEWINGTON
Leswin Rd
Bayston Rd
Darville Rd
RECTORY ROAD
A 104
Lea Bridge Rd
SOUTH MILL FIELDS
Dynevor Rd
Evering Rd
Kenninghall Rd
Powell Rd
Thistlewaite Rd
Fletching Rd
Newick Rd
Mildenhall Rd
Millfields Rd
Nevill Rd
Manse Rd
Beatty Rd
Walford Rd
Amhurst Rd
Downs Rd
Lower Clapton Rd
Foulden Rd
Brighton Rd
Farleigh Rd
Palatine Rd
Wordsworth Rd
Clarence Rd
Rushmore Rd
Powerscroft Rd
Cricketfield Rd
HACKNEY DOWNS
Blurton Rd
Princess May Rd
Glenarm Rd
13'6
Cecilia Rd
Shacklewell Lane
Downs Park Rd
Andre St
Boleyn Rd
Bodney Rd
Pembury Rd
Churchill Walk
Churchwell Path
Sandringham Rd
y
Lane
A 102
15'6
Mare St
Ridley Rd
Dalston Lane
DALSTON KINGSLAND
Kingsland High St
HACKNEY DOWNS
HACKNEY CENTRAL
Greenwood Rd
Navarino Rd
Graham Rd
Morning Lane
Chatham Pl
s
Laurel St
Eleanor Rd
Valette St
Reading Lane
Wilton Way
Parkholme Rd
d
DALSTON JUNCTION
Forest Rd
Darnley Rd
h
Stamford Rd
Well St
Richmond Rd
n
Gayhurst Rd
LONDON FIELDS
Frampton Park Rd
Cassland Rd
De Beauvoir Rd
w
Celandine Drive
Holly St
Queensbridge Rd
Lavender Grove
13'9
13'0
LONDON FIELDS
Mentmore Terrace
Balcorne St
Albion Drive
STONEBRIDGE
Shrubland Rd
HAGGERSTON
Broughham Rd
Hertford Rd
Brownlow Rd
16'0
15'9
King Edward's Rd
e
z
Sheep Lane
Victoria Park Rd
Gore Rd
DALSTON
Pownall Rd
Orsman Rd
Phillipp St
Regent's Row
m
VICTORIA PARK
Laburnum St
Whiston Rd
Andrews Rd
s
Grand Union Canal
Nuttall St
Thurtle Rd
13'9
HAGGERSTON PARK
Pritchard's Rd
Cambridge Heath Rd
Bishop's Way
Sewardstone Rd
Geffrye Museum
HOXTON
s
Hackney Rd
CAMBRIDGE HEATH
Bonner Rd
a
o
m
Ford Rd

U 20 V

1
2
3

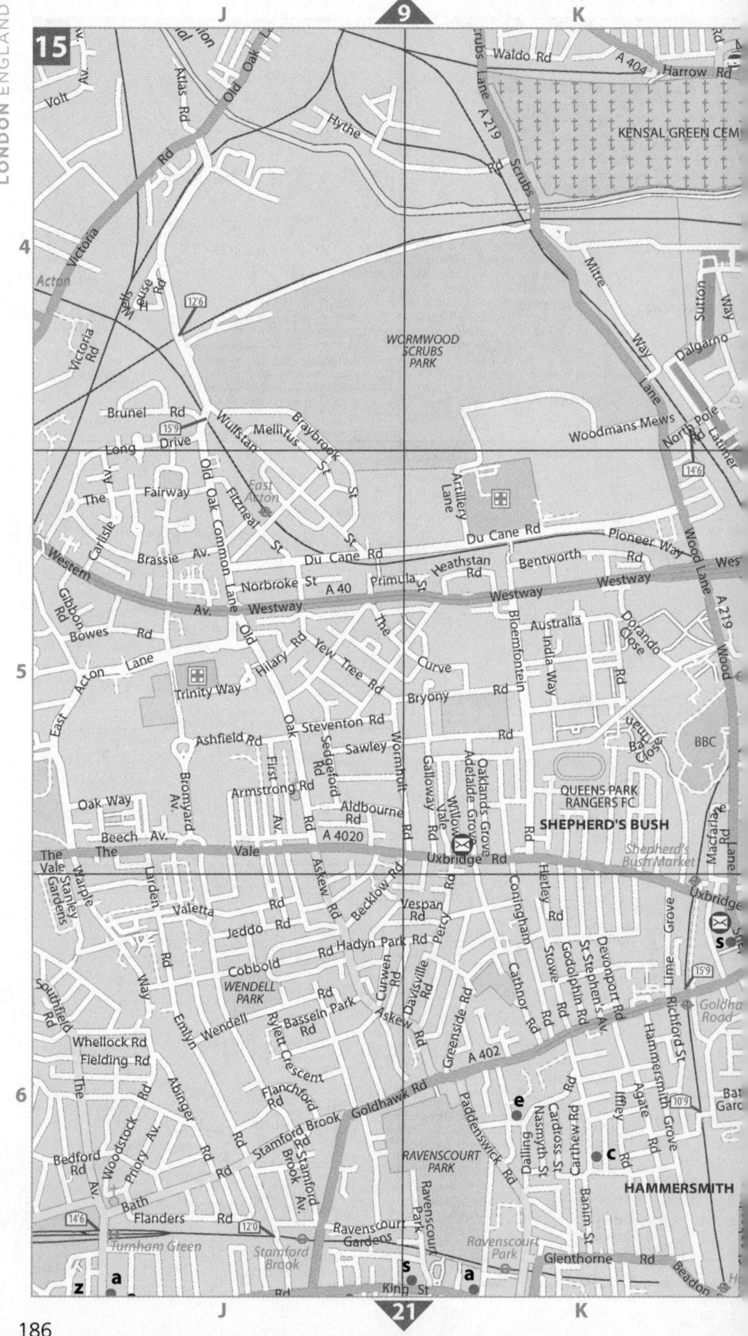
15
J
9
K
4
5
6
21
Waldo Rd
A 404
Harrow Rd
KENSAL GREEN CEM
Scrubs Lane A 219
Hythe
Old Oak
Victoria Rd
Atlas Rd
Volt Av.
Acton
WORMWOOD SCRUBS PARK
Mitre Way
Sutton Way
Dalgarno
Wood Lane
Woodmans Mews
North Pole Rd
Latimer
Brunel Rd
Long Drive
Wulfstan
Mellitus
Braybrook St
East Acton
The Fairway
Carlisle Av.
Old Oak Common Lane
Fitzneal St
Artillery Lane
Du Cane Rd
Pioneer Way
Brassie Av.
Western Av.
Norbroke St
A 40
Primula St
Heathstan Rd
Bentworth Rd
Westway
Gibbon Rd
Bowes Rd
Hilary Rd
Yew Tree Rd
The Curve
Bloemfontein
Australia
India Way
Dorando Close
East Acton Lane
Trinity Way
Bryony Rd
Steventon Rd
Ashfield Rd
Sawley Rd
Sedgeford Rd
BBC
First Av.
Armstrong Rd
Bromyard Av.
Wormholt Rd
Galloway Rd
Willow Vale
Adelaide Grove
Oaklands Grove
QUEENS PARK RANGERS FC
SHEPHERD'S BUSH
Oak Way
Aldbourne Rd
Beech Av.
A 4020
The Vale
Uxbridge Rd
Shepherd's Bush Market
Macfarlane Rd
Stanley Gardens
Larden Rd
Askew Rd
Becklow Rd
Vespan Rd
Percy Rd
Coningham
Hetley Rd
Valetta Rd
Jeddo Rd
Hadyn Park Rd
Cobbold Rd
WENDELL PARK
Curwen Rd
Davisville Rd
Cathnor Rd
Stowe Rd
Godolphin Rd
St Stephen's Av.
Devonport Rd
Lime Grove
Southfield Rd
Emlyn
Wendell
Bassein Park Rd
Rylett Crescent
Greenside Rd
A 402
Richford St
Hammersmith Grove
Goldhawk Road
Whellock Rd
Fielding Rd
Flanchford Rd
Goldhawk Rd
Abinger Rd
Woodstock Rd
Priory Av.
Stamford Brook Rd
Paddenswick Rd
Dalling Rd
Nasmyth St
Cardross St
Carthew Rd
Iffley Rd
Agate Rd
Bedford Rd
Bath Rd
RAVENSCOURT PARK
HAMMERSMITH
Flanders Rd
Ravenscourt Gardens
Ravenscourt Park
Banim St
Turnham Green
Stamford Brook
Glenthorne Rd
Beadon
King St

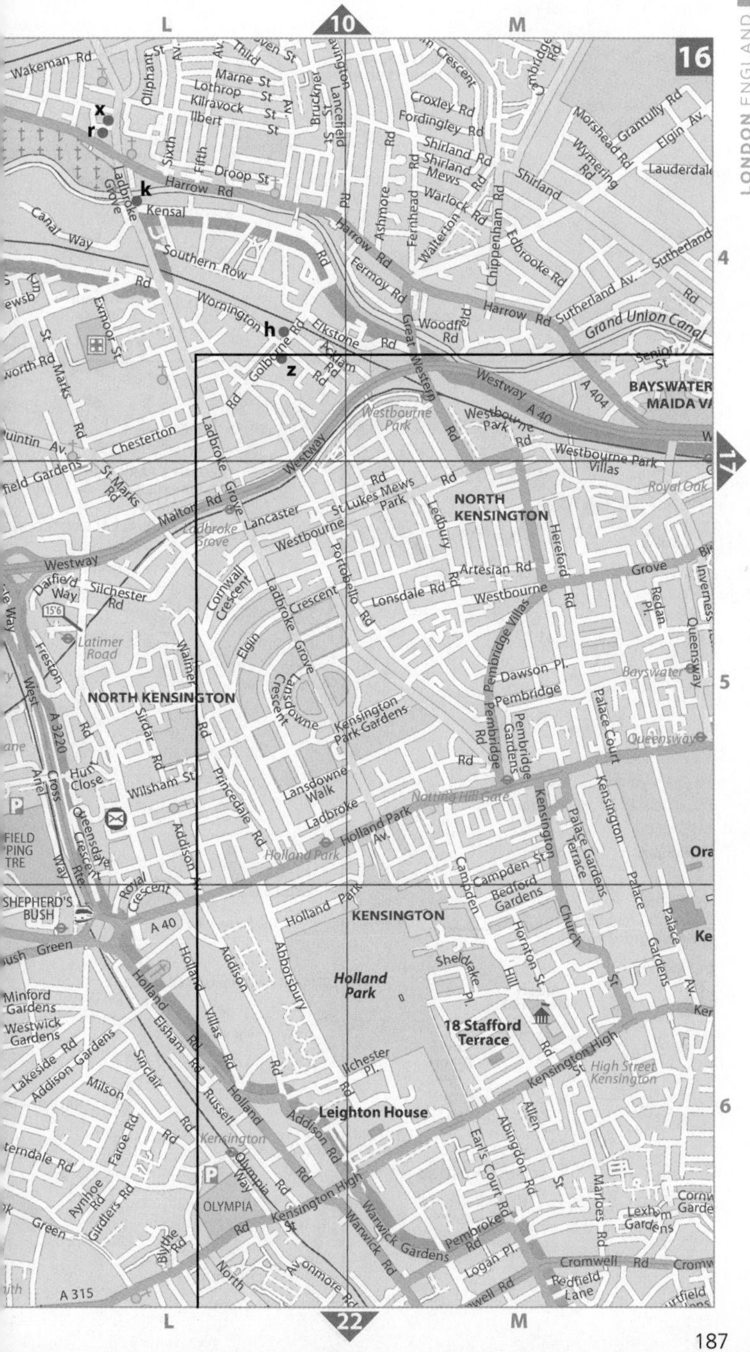

L
10
M
16

Wakeman Rd
Oliphant St
Marne St
Lothrop St
Kilravock St
Ilbert St
Bruckner St
Lancefield St
Croxley Rd
Fordingley Rd
Shirland Rd
Shirland Mews
Warlock Rd
Morshead Rd
Grantully Rd
Elgin Av.
Wymering Rd
Lauderdale
Sixth
Fifth
Droop St
Harrow Rd
Ladbroke Grove
Kensal
Canal Way
Southern Row
Ashmore Rd
Fernhead Rd
Walterton Rd
Chippenham Rd
Edbrooke Rd
Shirland
Fermoy Rd
Sutherland Av.
Grand Union Canal
Wornington Rd
Golborne Rd
Elkstone Rd
Acklam Rd
Great Western Rd
Woodfield Rd
Exmoor St
St Marks Rd
Senior St
Westway A 40
A 404
BAYSWATER
MAIDA VALE
Westbourne Park
Westbourne Park Rd
Westbourne Park Villas
Royal Oak
Chesterton Rd
Quintin Av.
St Marks Rd
Malton Rd
Lancaster Rd
St Lukes Mews
Westbourne Park Rd
Ledbury Rd
NORTH KENSINGTON
Ladbroke Grove
Westway
Darfield Way
Silchester Rd
Cornwall Crescent
Portobello Rd
Artesian Rd
Hereford Rd
Westbourne Grove
Lonsdale Rd
Ladbroke Crescent
Inverness Ter.
Redan Pl.
Queensway
Latimer Road
Freston Rd
West Cross Rte
Walmer Rd
Elgin Crescent
Lansdowne Crescent
Pembridge Villas
Dawson Pl.
Pembridge Rd
Bayswater
NORTH KENSINGTON
A 3220
Sirdar Rd
Kensington Park Gardens
Pembridge Gardens
Palace Court
Queensway
Hunt Close
Wilsham St
Princedale Rd
Lansdowne Walk
Ladbroke Rd
Notting Hill Gate
Kensington Church St
Kensington Palace Gardens
Addison Rd
Queensdale Crescent
Holland Park Av.
Holland Park
Palace Gardens Terrace
Campden Hill Rd
Campden St
Bedford Gardens
Royal Crescent
SHEPHERD'S BUSH
A 40
Holland Park
KENSINGTON
Shepherd's Bush Green
Holland Rd
Addison Rd
Abbotsbury Rd
Holland Park
Sheldrake Pl.
Hornton St
Palace Gardens Ter.
Minford Gardens
Westwick Gardens
Holland Villas Rd
18 Stafford Terrace
Lakeside Rd
Addison Gardens
Sinclair Rd
Elsham Rd
Ilchester Pl.
Kensington High St
High Street Kensington
Milson Rd
Russell Rd
Leighton House
Allen St
Abingdon Rd
Faroe Rd
Kensington (Olympia)
Olympia Way
Addison Rd
Earl's Court Rd
Marloes Rd
Aynhoe Rd
Girdlers Rd
OLYMPIA
Kensington High St
Warwick Gardens
Warwick Rd
Pembroke Rd
Lexham Gardens
Blythe Rd
North End Rd
Avonmore Rd
Logan Pl.
Cromwell Rd
Redfield Lane
A 315

4
5
6

L
22
M

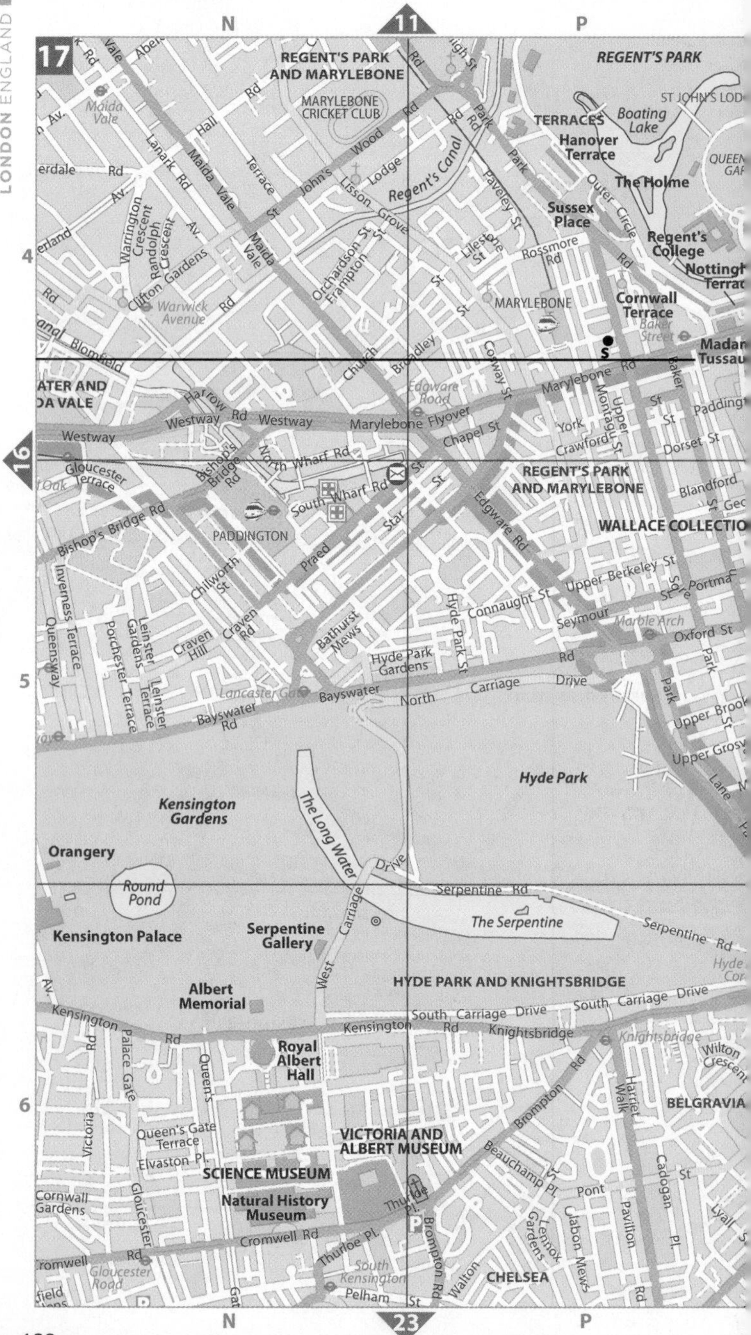

17

N P

11
16
23

4
5
6

REGENT'S PARK AND MARYLEBONE
MARYLEBONE CRICKET CLUB
REGENT'S PARK
Boating Lake
ST JOHN'S LODGE
TERRACES
Hanover Terrace
The Holme
Sussex Place
Regent's College
Cornwall Terrace
Nottingham Terrace
Madame Tussauds
MARYLEBONE
Baker Street
Maida Vale
Warwick Avenue
Regent's Canal
Edgware Road
Marylebone Flyover
Westway
PADDINGTON AND MAIDA VALE
PADDINGTON
REGENT'S PARK AND MARYLEBONE
WALLACE COLLECTION
Marble Arch
Lancaster Gate
Bayswater Rd
North Carriage Drive
Hyde Park
Kensington Gardens
The Long Water
Orangery
Round Pond
Kensington Palace
Serpentine Gallery
The Serpentine
Serpentine Rd
Albert Memorial
HYDE PARK AND KNIGHTSBRIDGE
South Carriage Drive
Kensington Rd
Knightsbridge
Royal Albert Hall
BELGRAVIA
VICTORIA AND ALBERT MUSEUM
SCIENCE MUSEUM
Natural History Museum
Cromwell Rd
Gloucester Road
South Kensington
Brompton Rd
CHELSEA

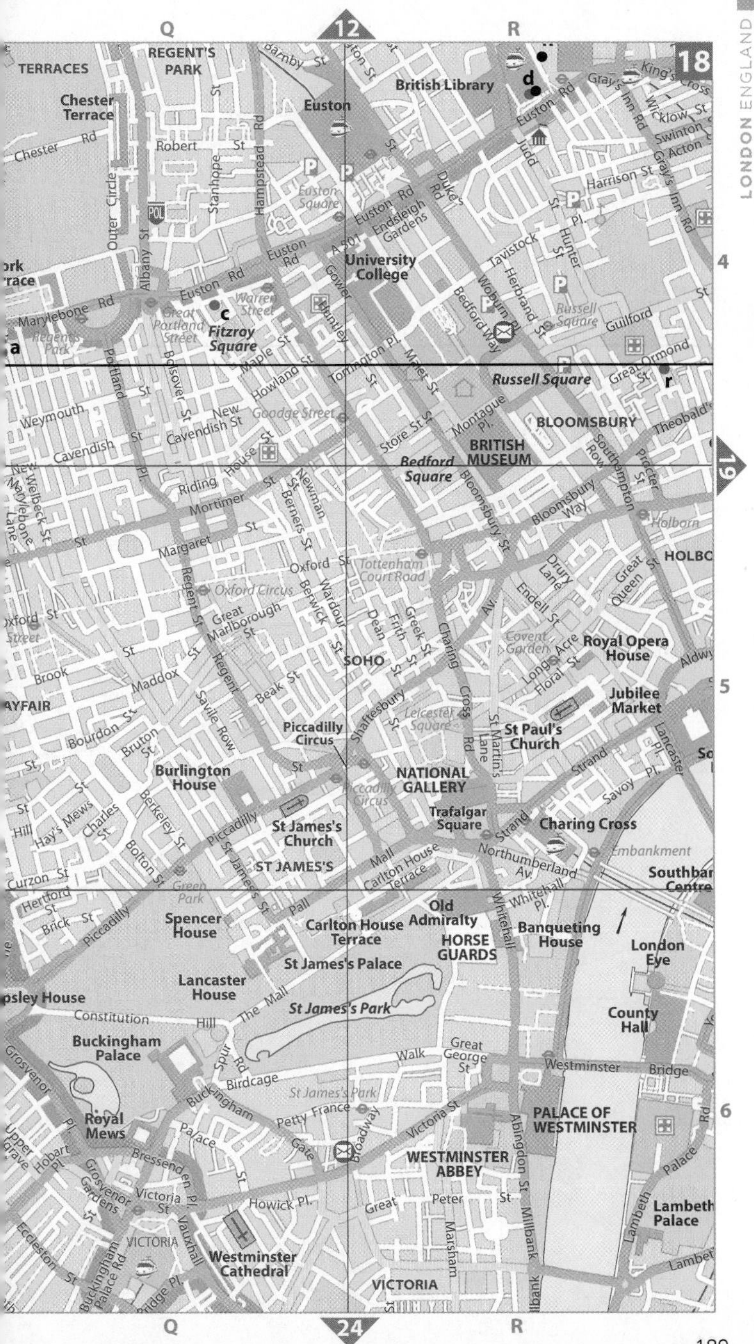

Q
R
12
18
19
24
4
5
6
REGENT'S PARK
TERRACES
Chester Terrace
British Library
Euston
University College
Fitzroy Square
Russell Square
BLOOMSBURY
BRITISH MUSEUM
Bedford Square
HOLBORN
SOHO
Royal Opera House
Jubilee Market
MAYFAIR
Piccadilly Circus
St Paul's Church
Burlington House
NATIONAL GALLERY
Trafalgar Square
Charing Cross
St James's Church
ST JAMES'S
Southbank Centre
Spencer House
Carlton House Terrace
Old Admiralty
HORSE GUARDS
Banqueting House
London Eye
St James's Palace
Lancaster House
Apsley House
St James's Park
County Hall
Buckingham Palace
PALACE OF WESTMINSTER
Royal Mews
WESTMINSTER ABBEY
Lambeth Palace
VICTORIA
Westminster Cathedral

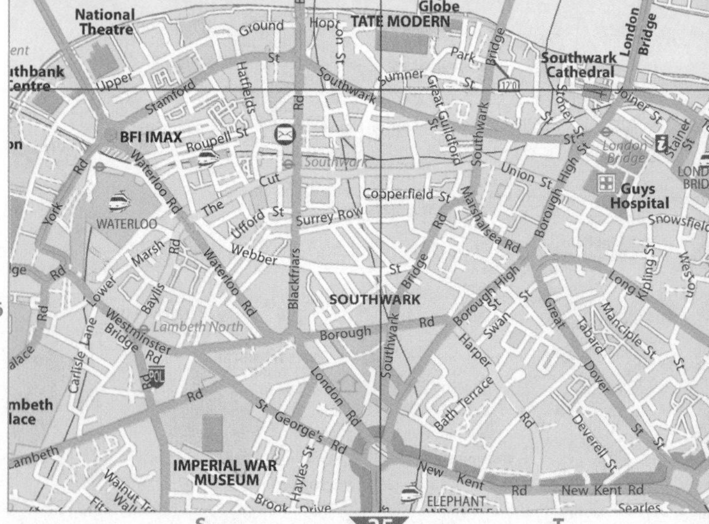
19
S
13
T
City Rd
Goswell Rd
St John St
Road Basin
Murray Grove
Provost St
New North Rd
Bevenden St
Haberdasher St
Chart St
Penton Rise
King's Cross Rd
Cubitt St
Acton St
Amwell St
Spencer St
Moreland St
Central St
A 501
East Rd
Bath St
Old St
Old Street
Percival St
Lever St
Margery St
Calthorpe St
Farringdon Rd
FINSBURY
Pear Tree St
Bastwick St
A 5201
Bunhill Row
Whitecross St
Golden Lane
Great Sutton St
Mount Pleasant
Rosebery Av
Tabernacle St
Paul St
Worship St
Clerkenwell Rd
Charterhouse
Turnmill St
FARRINGDON
Barbican
Beech St
Chiswell St
Moor Lane
A 501
Wilson St
Sun St
Leather Lane
Gray's Inn Rd
Gray's Inn
Greville St
Charterhouse St
St Bartholomew the Great
Museum of London
Chancery Lane
High Holborn
Snow Hill
London Wall
Moorgate
A 1211
Staple Inn
Holborn Viaduct
HOLBORN
New Fetter Lane
Fetter Lane
Chancery Lane
Lincoln's Inn
Carey St
King Edward St
Guildhall
Gresham St
St Paul's
ST PAUL'S CATHEDRAL
Royal Exchange
Fleet St
Ludgate Hill
Farringdon St
Aldwych
St Bride's
St Paul's Church Yard
Mansion House
Bow Lane
Bank
Cornhill
Strand
Tudor St
Blackfriars
Queen Victoria St
Temple
Cannon Street
Upper Thames St
The Monument
Somerset House
Blackfriars Bridge
Lower Thames St
Shakespeare's Globe
National Theatre
Ground
Hopton St
TATE MODERN
Park St
Southwark Bridge Rd
Southwark Cathedral
London Bridge
Southbank Centre
Upper Ground
Stamford St
Hatfields
Sumner St
Great Guildford St
Stoney St
Joiner St
Stainer St
BFI IMAX
Roupell St
Southwark
Southwark St
London Bridge
LONDON BRIDGE
Waterloo Rd
The Cut
Union St
Borough High St
Guys Hospital
WATERLOO
Copperfield St
Marshalsea Rd
Snowsfields
York Rd
Ufford St
Surrey Row
Webber St
Kipling St
Weston St
Lower Marsh
Baylis Rd
Long Lane
SOUTHWARK
Great Dover St
Westminster Bridge Rd
Lambeth North
Borough Rd
Swan St
Tabard St
Mancipie St
Carlisle Lane
Harper Rd
London Rd
Southwark Bridge Rd
Bath Terrace
Deverell St
St George's Rd
Lambeth Rd
IMPERIAL WAR MUSEUM
Hayles St
New Kent Rd
Walnut Tree Walk
Brook Drive
ELEPHANT AND CASTLE
Searles Rd
S
25
T
18
4
5
6

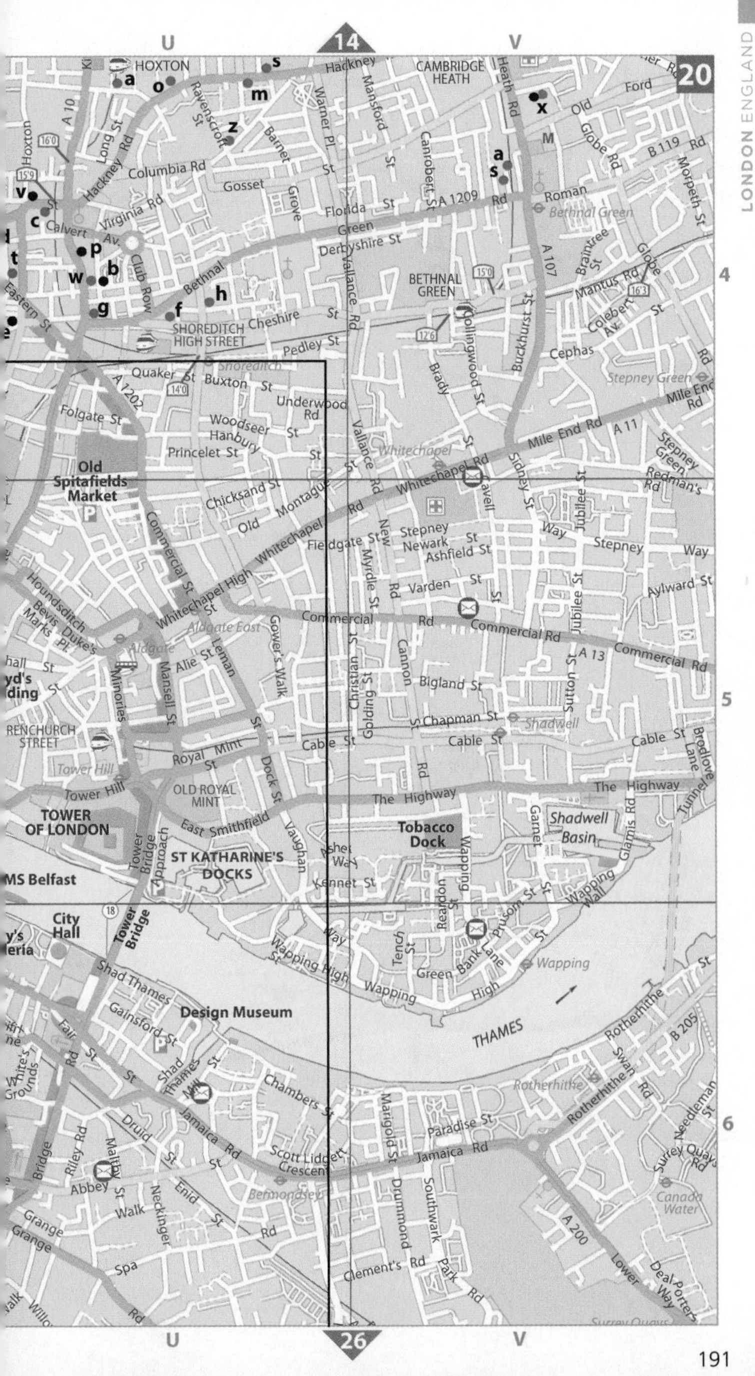
HOXTON
CAMBRIDGE HEATH
BETHNAL GREEN
SHOREDITCH HIGH STREET
Old Spitafields Market
TOWER OF LONDON
OLD ROYAL MINT
ST KATHARINE'S DOCKS
Tobacco Dock
Shadwell Basin
City Hall
Design Museum
THAMES
Whitechapel Rd
Commercial Rd
The Highway
Mile End Rd
Jamaica Rd
Tower Bridge

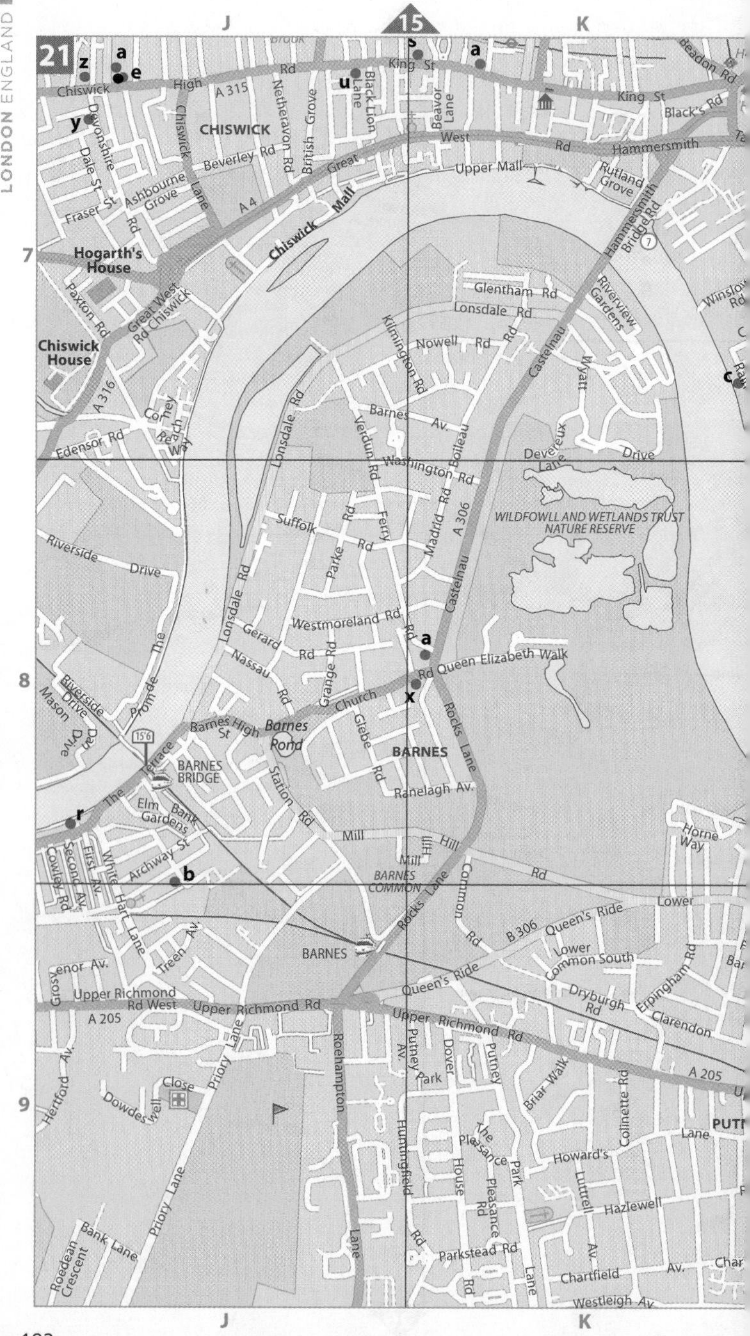
21
15
J
K
7
8
9
CHISWICK
Hogarth's House
Chiswick House
Chiswick High Rd
King St
Chiswick Mall
Great West Rd
Upper Mall
Hammersmith Bridge Rd
Castelnau
WILDFOWL AND WETLANDS TRUST NATURE RESERVE
Queen Elizabeth Walk
Barnes Pond
BARNES
BARNES BRIDGE
BARNES COMMON
BARNES
Upper Richmond Rd
Rocks Lane
Roehampton Lane
Priory Lane
A 315
A 4
A 316
A 306
A 205
B 306
PUTNEY

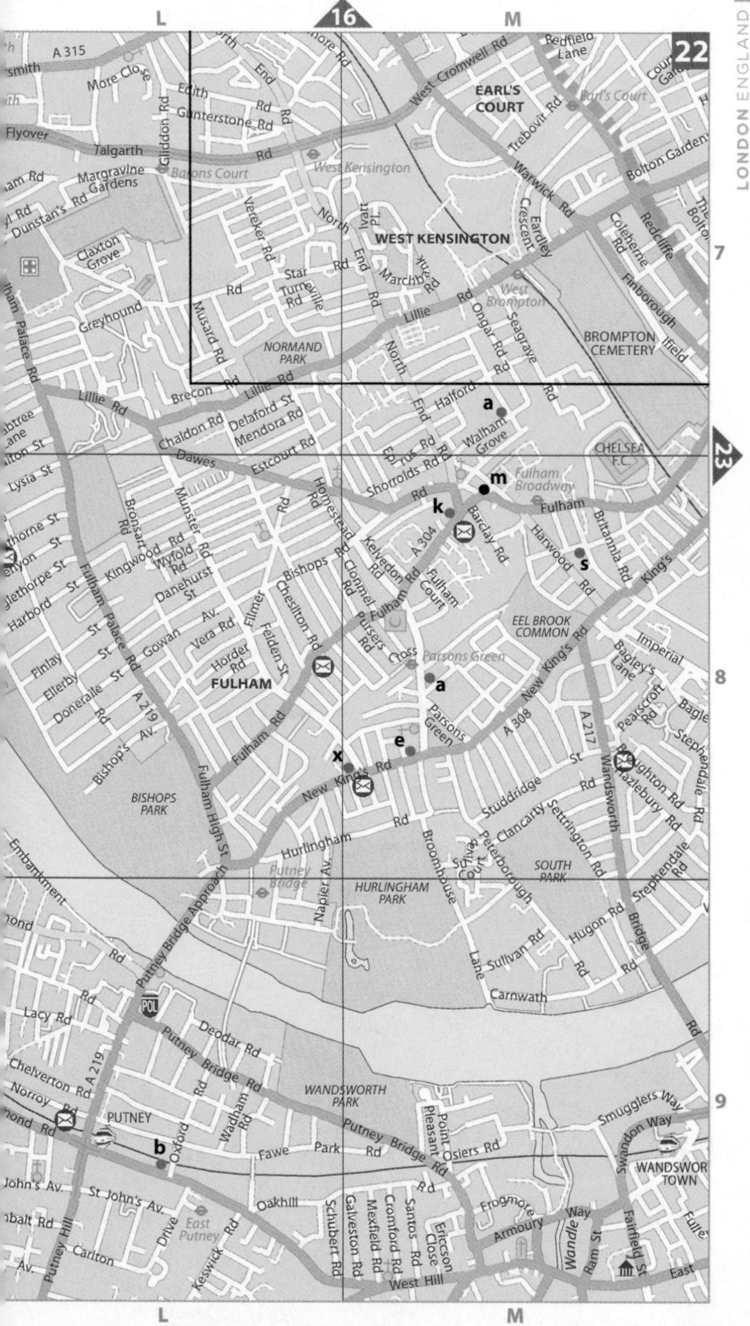

L
16
M
22
7
8
9
23
EARL'S COURT
WEST KENSINGTON
BROMPTON CEMETERY
CHELSEA F.C.
NORMAND PARK
FULHAM
EEL BROOK COMMON
BISHOPS PARK
SOUTH PARK
HURLINGHAM PARK
WANDSWORTH PARK
PUTNEY
WANDSWORTH TOWN
Barons Court
West Kensington
Earl's Court
West Brompton
Fulham Broadway
Parsons Green
Putney Bridge
East Putney
A 315
A 304
A 308
A 217
A 219
West Cromwell Rd
Talgarth Rd
Lillie Rd
North End Rd
Fulham Rd
Fulham Palace Rd
New King's Rd
Fulham High St
Putney Bridge Approach
Putney Bridge Rd
Wandsworth Bridge Rd
Hurlingham Rd
Putney Hill
West Hill
L
M

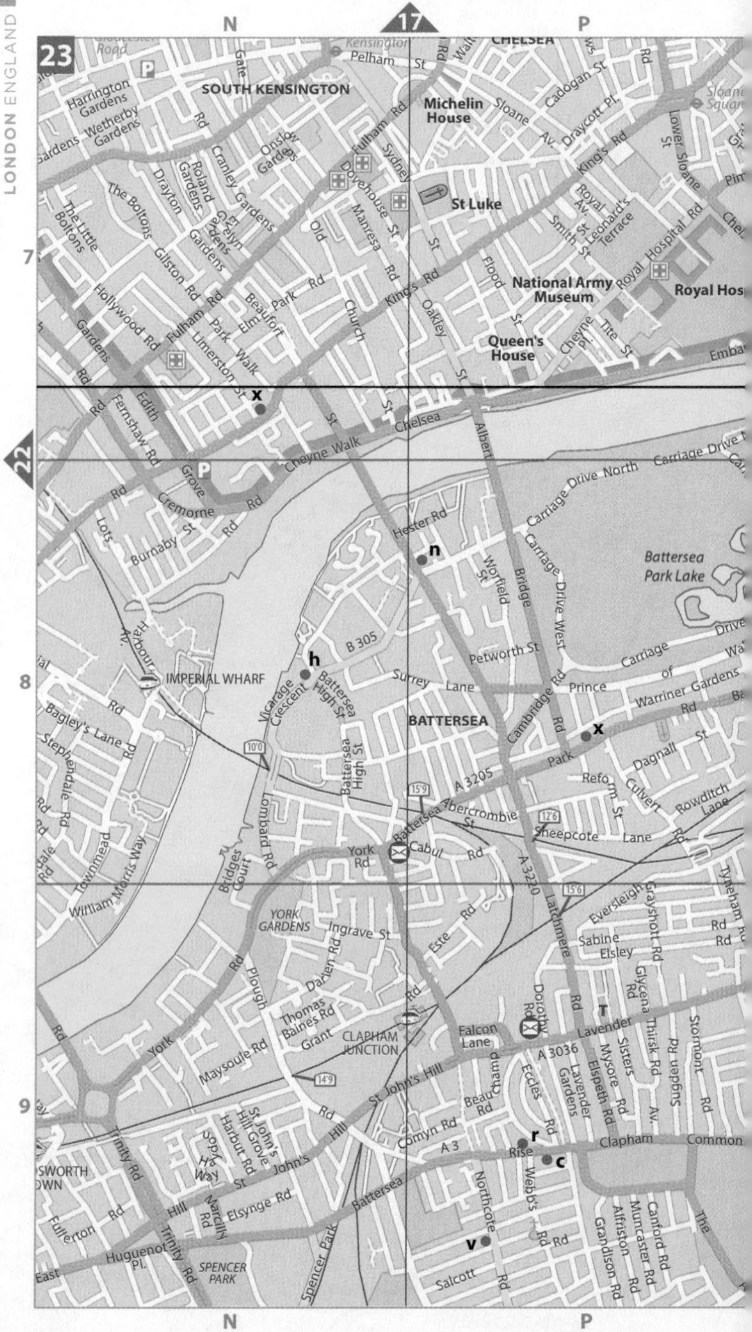

23

N P

17

22

7 8 9

SOUTH KENSINGTON
CHELSEA
Michelin House
St Luke
National Army Museum
Royal Hos
Queen's House
BATTERSEA
IMPERIAL WHARF
CLAPHAM JUNCTION
YORK GARDENS
SPENCER PARK
Battersea Park Lake

Gloucester Road
Kensington
Pelham St
Sloane Square
Harrington Gardens
Wetherby Gardens
Gardens
Onslow Gardens
Fulham Rd
Sydney St
Sloane Av.
Cadogan St
Draycott Pl.
King's Rd
Lower Sloane St
Pimlico
Chelsea
Royal Av.
St Leonard's Terrace
Smith St
Royal Hospital Rd
Roland Gardens
Cranley Gardens
Drayton Gardens
The Boltons
The Little Boltons
Gilston Rd
Evelyn Gardens
Dovehouse St
Manresa Rd
Old Church St
Oakley St
Flood St
Tite St
Cheyne Pl.
Embankment
Hollywood Rd
Fulham Rd
Park Walk
Limerston St
Elm Park Rd
Beaufort St
Edith Grove
Fernshaw Rd
Gardens
Cheyne Walk
Chelsea
Albert Bridge Rd
Cremorne Rd
Lots Rd
Burnaby St
Carriage Drive North
Carriage Drive
Carriage Drive West
Hester Rd
Worfield St
Harbour Av.
B 305
Petworth St
Surrey Lane
Prince of Wales Drive
Warriner Gardens
Cambridge Rd
Park Rd
Vicarage Crescent
Battersea High St
Bagley's Lane
Stephendale Rd
Rd
Dagnall St
Reform St
Culvert Rd
Rowditch Lane
A 3205
Battersea Abercrombie St
Sheepcote Lane
Lombard Rd
Bridges Court
Townmead Rd
William Morris Way
York Rd
Cabul Rd
A 3220
Latchmere Rd
Eversleigh Rd
Grayshott Rd
Tyneham Rd
Sabine Rd
Elsley Rd
Ingrave St
Este Rd
Darien Rd
Plough Rd
Thomas Baines Rd
Grant Rd
Maysoule Rd
Falcon Lane
Dorothy Rd
Lavender Hill
A 3036
Glycena Rd
Thirsk Rd
Stormont Rd
Sisters Av.
Mysore Rd
Elspeth Rd
Lavender Gardens
Eccles Rd
Chatham Rd
Beauchamp Rd
St John's Hill
St John's Hill Grove
Harbut Rd
Comyn Rd
A 3
Rise
Webb's Rd
Clapham Common
Alfriston Rd
Muncaster Rd
Canford Rd
Grandison Rd
Northcote Rd
Salcott Rd
Wandsworth Common
Fullerton Rd
Trinity Rd
Marcilly Rd
Elsynge Rd
Battersea Rise
Spencer Park
Huguenot Pl.
East Hill
Ha Way
St John's Rd

10'0 15'9 12'6 15'6 14'9

x n h x r c v T

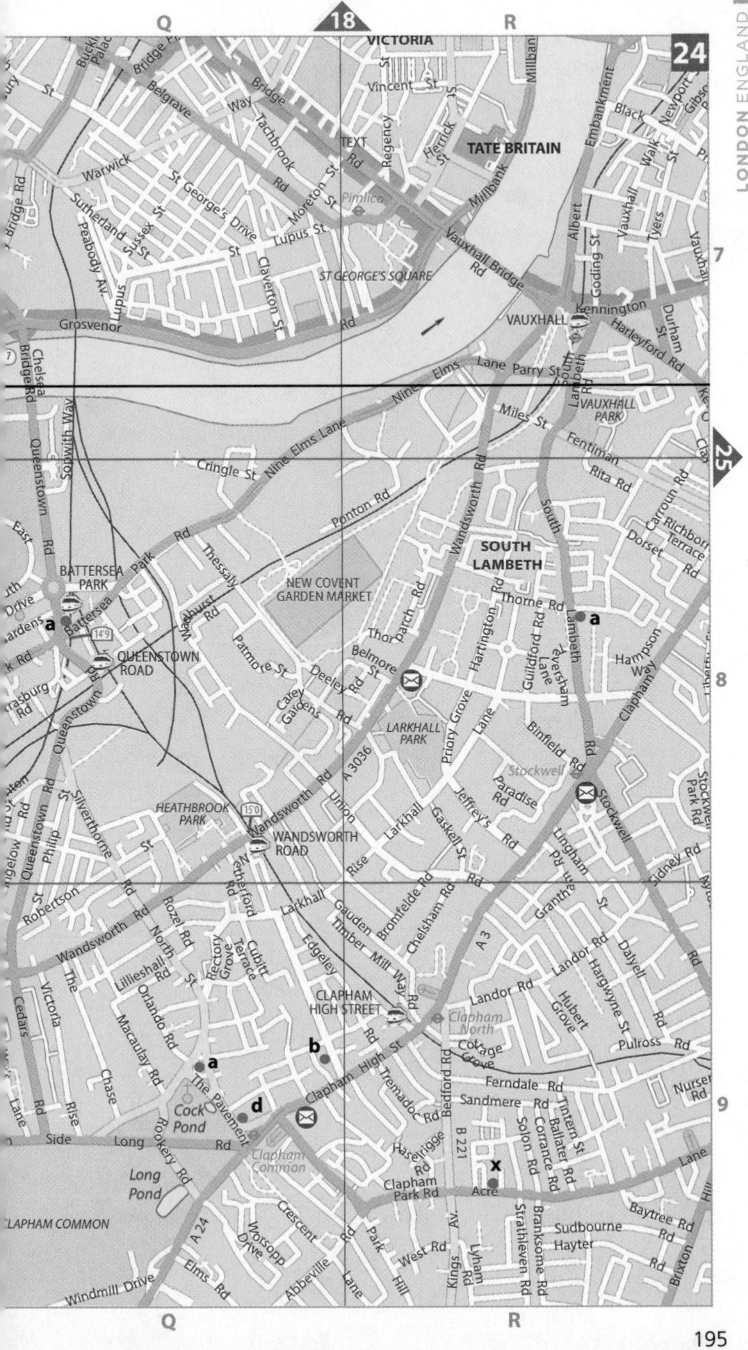

18

24

25

Q R

VICTORIA

TATE BRITAIN

Pimlico

ST GEORGE'S SQUARE

VAUXHALL

VAUXHALL PARK

BATTERSEA PARK

QUEENSTOWN ROAD

NEW COVENT GARDEN MARKET

SOUTH LAMBETH

LARKHALL PARK

Stockwell

HEATHBROOK PARK

WANDSWORTH ROAD

CLAPHAM HIGH STREET

Clapham North

Cock Pond

Clapham Common

Long Pond

CLAPHAM COMMON

Belgrave Rd
Warwick Way
St George's Drive
Lupus St
Grosvenor Rd
Millbank
Vauxhall Bridge Rd
Albert Embankment
Kennington Lane
Harleyford Rd
Nine Elms Lane
Parry St
South Lambeth Rd
Miles St
Fentiman Rd
Rita Rd
Cringle St
Ponton Rd
Queenstown Rd
Battersea Park Rd
Thessaly Rd
Wandsworth Rd
Thorne Rd
Hartington Rd
Guildford Rd
Binfield Rd
Clapham Rd
Hampson Way
Larkhall Rise
Union Rd
Jeffrey's Rd
Paradise Rd
Stockwell Rd
Silverthorne Rd
Robertson St
Lingham St
Landor Rd
Pulross Rd
Ferndale Rd
Sandmere Rd
Bedford Rd
Clapham High St
Clapham Park Rd
Acre Lane
Tremadoc Rd
The Pavement
Long Rd
Rookery Rd
Windmill Drive
Elms Rd
Abbeville Rd
Park Hill
Kings Av.
Strathleven Rd
Branksome Rd
Sudbourne Rd
Hayter Rd
Baytree Rd
Brixton Hill

7

8

9

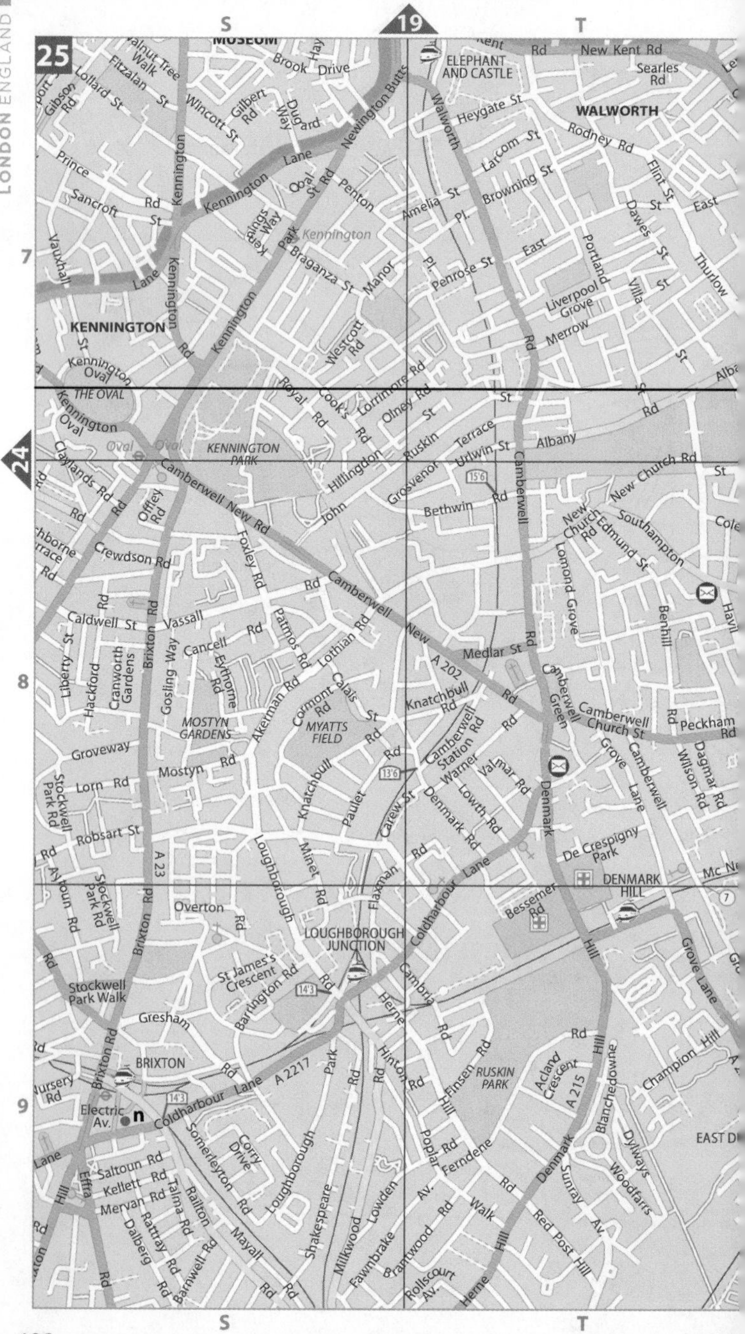

25
S
19
T
MUSEUM
ELEPHANT AND CASTLE
WALWORTH
New Kent Rd
Searles Rd
Kennington
KENNINGTON
THE OVAL
Oval
KENNINGTON PARK
24
Camberwell New Rd
MOSTYN GARDENS
MYATTS FIELD
A 202
A 23
LOUGHBOROUGH JUNCTION
DENMARK HILL
Coldharbour Lane
A 2217
BRIXTON
RUSKIN PARK
A 215
Denmark Hill
Champion Hill
Electric Av.
7
8
9
S
T

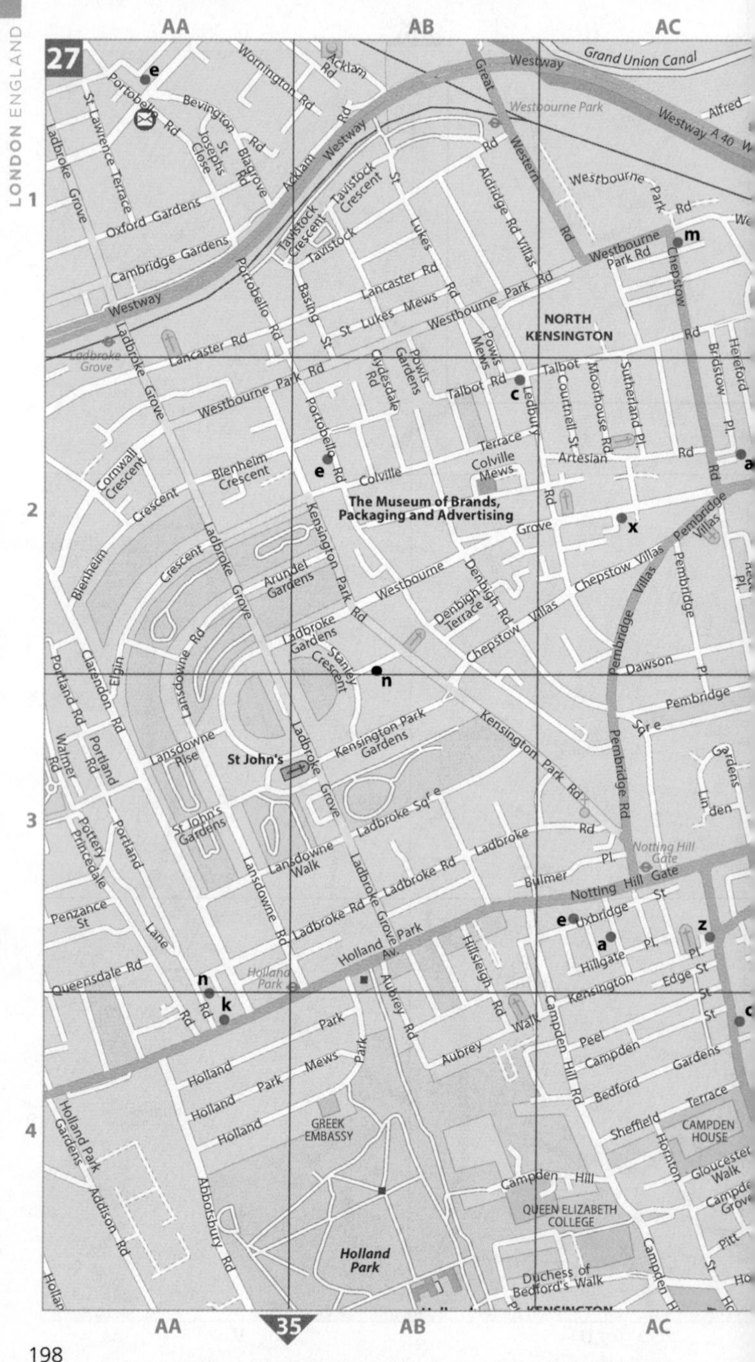
AA
AB
AC
27
1
2
3
4
35
Grand Union Canal
Westway
Westway A 40
Westbourne Park
Westbourne Park Rd
Great Western Rd
NORTH KENSINGTON
The Museum of Brands, Packaging and Advertising
St John's
Ladbroke Grove
Notting Hill Gate
Holland Park
GREEK EMBASSY
CAMPDEN HOUSE
QUEEN ELIZABETH COLLEGE
Portobello Rd
Wornington Rd
Acklam Rd
Bevington Rd
St Lawrence Terrace
Oxford Gardens
Cambridge Gardens
Lancaster Rd
St Lukes Mews
Talbot Rd
Ledbury Rd
Colville Terrace
Colville Mews
Kensington Park Rd
Westbourne Grove
Chepstow Villas
Pembridge Villas
Pembridge Rd
Pembridge Sq
Blenheim Crescent
Elgin Crescent
Lansdowne Rd
Lansdowne Rise
Ladbroke Sq
Ladbroke Rd
Kensington Park Gardens
Holland Park Av.
Queensdale Rd
Pottery Lane
Campden Hill Rd
Holland Park Gardens
Addison Rd
Abbotsbury Rd
Duchess of Bedford's Walk
Kensington Church St

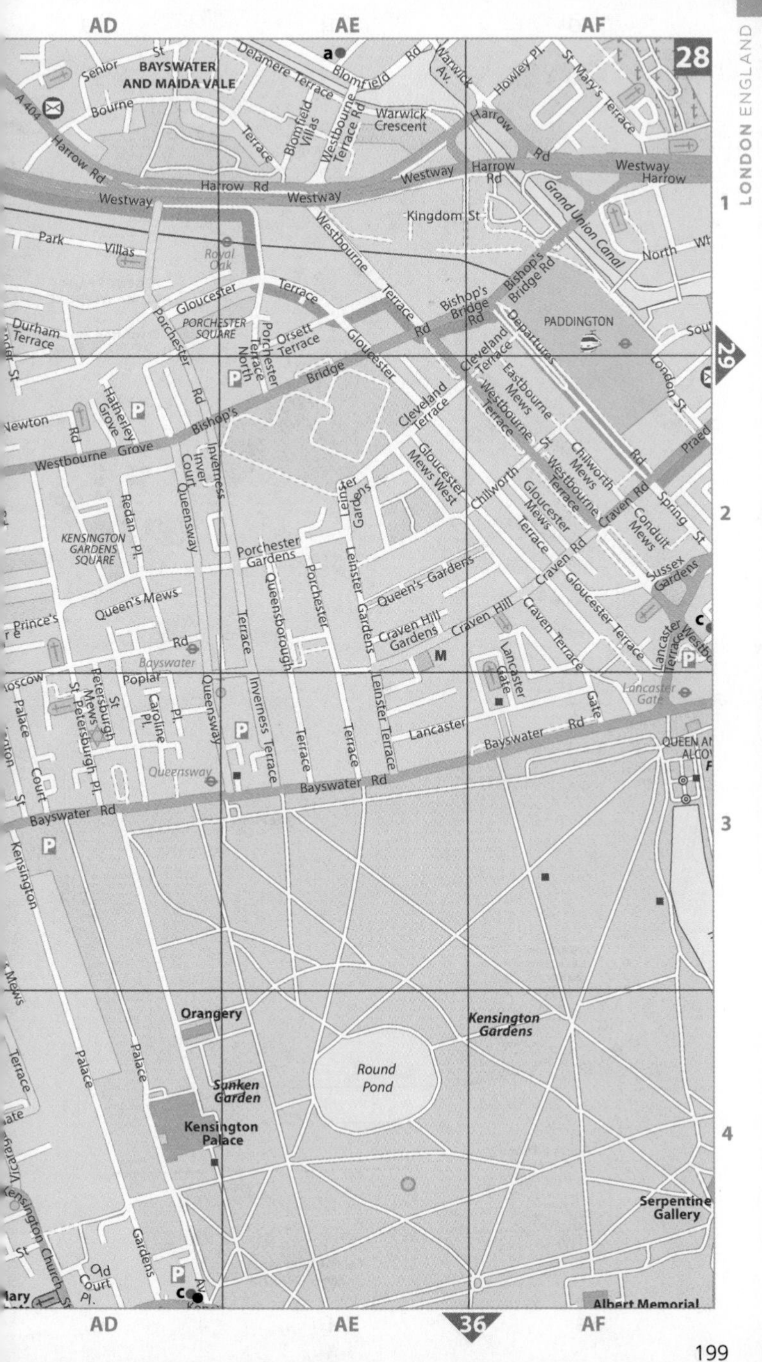
AD
AE
AF
28
29
36
1
2
3
4
BAYSWATER AND MAIDA VALE
Senior St
Bourne Terrace
A 404
Harrow Rd
Westway
Delamere Terrace
Blomfield Rd
Blomfield Villas
Westbourne Terrace Rd
Warwick Crescent
Warwick Av.
Howley Pl.
St Mary's Terrace
Harrow Rd
Westway Harrow
Grand Union Canal
Kingdom St
North Wharf
Park Villas
Royal Oak
Gloucester Terrace
Westbourne Terrace
Bishop's Bridge Rd
PADDINGTON
Departures
Durham Terrace
Porchester Rd
PORCHESTER SQUARE
Porchester Terrace North
Orsett Terrace
Cleveland Terrace
Eastbourne Mews
London St
Praed St
Newton Rd
Hatherley Grove
Westbourne Grove
Inver Court
Inverness Terrace
Queensway
Leinster Gardens
Gloucester Mews West
Chilworth St
Chilworth Mews
Westbourne Terrace
Gloucester Mews
Craven Rd
Conduit Mews
Spring St
Sussex Gardens
KENSINGTON GARDENS SQUARE
Redan Pl.
Porchester Gardens
Queensborough Terrace
Porchester Terrace
Leinster Gardens
Queen's Gardens
Gloucester Terrace
Queen's Mews
Prince's Sq
Craven Hill Gardens
Craven Hill
Craven Terrace
Lancaster Terrace
Westbourne St
Bayswater
M
Lancaster Gate
Moscow Rd
Poplar Pl.
St Petersburgh Mews
St Petersburgh Pl.
Caroline Pl.
Queensway
Inverness Terrace
Leinster Terrace
Lancaster Gate
Bayswater Rd
QUEEN ANNE'S ALCOVE
Palace Court
Kensington Palace Gardens
Orangery
Kensington Gardens
Round Pond
Sunken Garden
Kensington Palace
Serpentine Gallery
Palace Gardens Terrace
Vicarage Gate
Kensington Church St
Gardens
Old Court Pl.
Albert Memorial
a
c
P

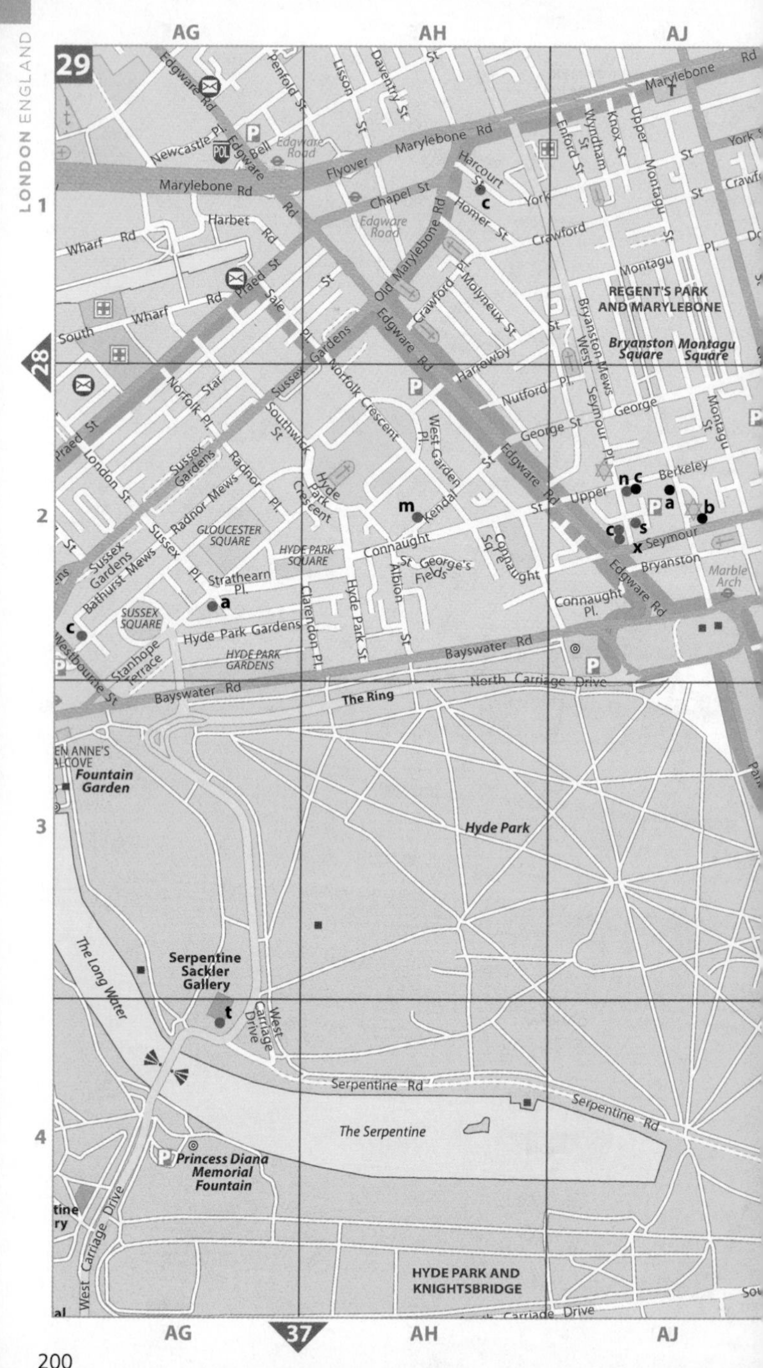
29
28
37
AG
AH
AJ
1
2
3
4
REGENT'S PARK AND MARYLEBONE
Bryanston Square
Montagu Square
GLOUCESTER SQUARE
HYDE PARK SQUARE
SUSSEX SQUARE
HYDE PARK GARDENS
St George's Fields
Edgware Road
Marble Arch
The Ring
Fountain Garden
Hyde Park
Serpentine Sackler Gallery
The Long Water
The Serpentine
Princess Diana Memorial Fountain
HYDE PARK AND KNIGHTSBRIDGE
Marylebone Rd
Edgware Rd
Praed St
Sussex Gardens
Bayswater Rd
North Carriage Drive
Serpentine Rd
West Carriage Drive
Connaught St
Seymour St
George St
Hyde Park Gardens
Old Marylebone Rd
Chapel St
Crawford St
Harrowby St
Nutford Pl.
Upper Berkeley St
Bryanston St
Connaught Pl.
Westbourne St
Stanhope Terrace
Strathearn Pl.
Norfolk Crescent
Southwick St
Hyde Park Crescent
Kendal St
West Garden Pl.
Clarendon Pl.
Hyde Park St
Albion St
Connaught Sq.
Radnor Pl.
Radnor Mews
Bathurst Mews
Sussex Pl.
Norfolk Pl.
London St
Star St
Sale Pl.
Wharf Rd
South Wharf Rd
Harbet Rd
Newcastle Pl.
Bell St
Penfold St
Lisson St
Daventry St
Harcourt St
Homer St
York St
Enford St
Wyndham St
Knox St
Upper Montagu St
Montagu Pl.
Bryanston Mews West
Seymour Pl.
Molyneux St
Montagu St
Flyover

AK
AL
AM
30
31
38
1
2
3
4
WALLACE COLLECTION
MANCHESTER SQUARE
PORTMAN SQUARE
All Souls Church
CAVENDISH SQUARE
St Peter
Oxford Circus
Liberty
HANNOVER SQUARE
Bond Street
MAYFAIR
Grosvenor Square
Immaculate Conception
Berkeley Square
Grosvenor Chapel
Burlington House
Burlington Arcade
Curzon Street
Green Park
Spencer House
Lancaster House
Apsley House
Devonshire St
Weymouth St
Cavendish Pl.
Wigmore St
Oxford St
Regent St
Portland Pl
Harley St
Wimpole St
Welbeck St
Marylebone Lane
Baker St
Duke St
North Audley St
South Audley St
Park Lane
Piccadilly
St James's Street
Old Bond St
New Bond St
Brook St
Grosvenor St
Mount St
Hay's Mews
Charles St
Half Moon St
Dover St
Albemarle St
Savile Row
Carnaby St
Great Portland St
Mortimer St
Margaret St
Great Castle St
Maddox St
Bruton St
Hertford St
Piccadilly
Cleveland Row

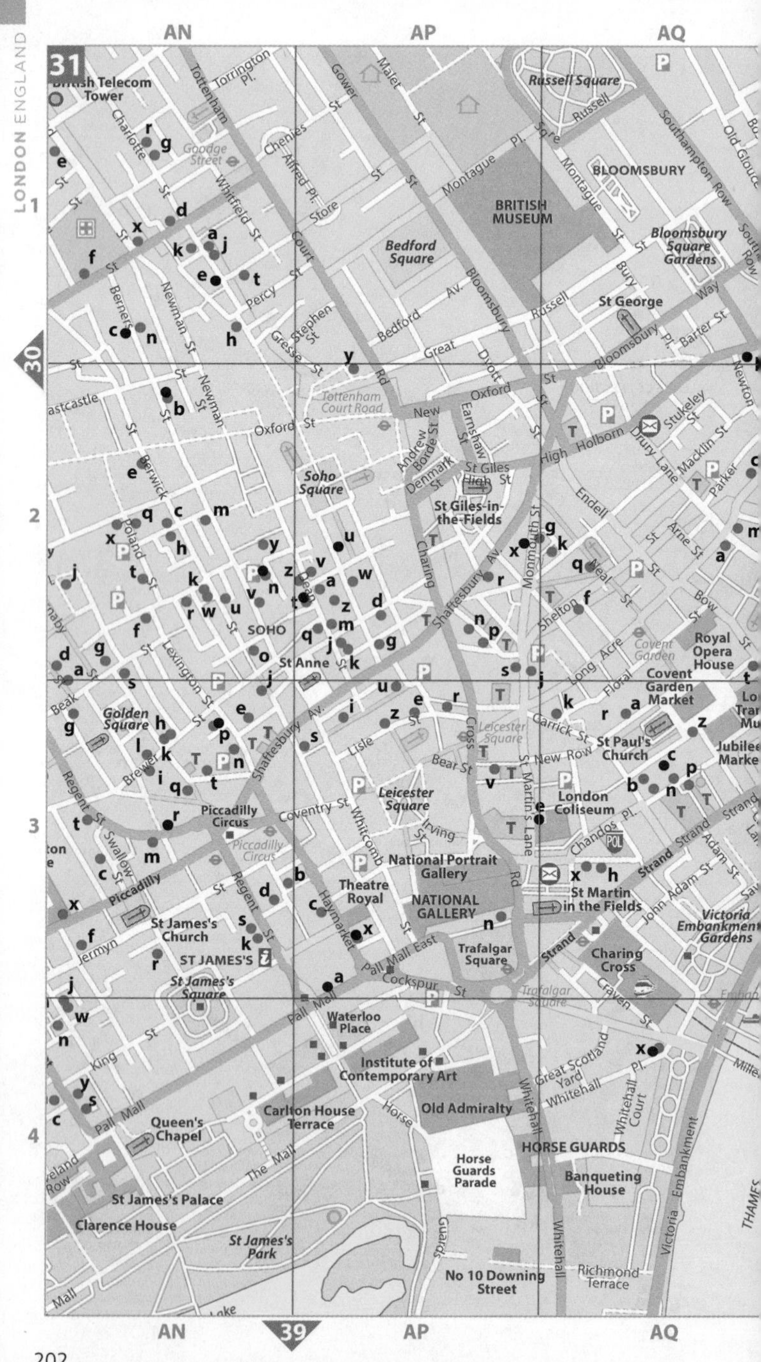
AN
AP
AQ
31
British Telecom Tower
Russell Square
BLOOMSBURY
BRITISH MUSEUM
Bedford Square
Bloomsbury Square Gardens
St George
Tottenham Court Road
Oxford St
Soho Square
St Giles-in-the-Fields
SOHO
St Anne
Royal Opera House
Covent Garden Market
Golden Square
St Paul's Church
Jubilee Market
Leicester Square
London Coliseum
Piccadilly Circus
National Portrait Gallery
Theatre Royal
NATIONAL GALLERY
St Martin in the Fields
St James's Church
ST JAMES'S
Trafalgar Square
Charing Cross
Victoria Embankment Gardens
St James's Square
Waterloo Place
Institute of Contemporary Art
Carlton House Terrace
Old Admiralty
Queen's Chapel
HORSE GUARDS
Horse Guards Parade
Banqueting House
St James's Palace
Clarence House
St James's Park
No 10 Downing Street
Richmond Terrace
30
39
1
2
3
4

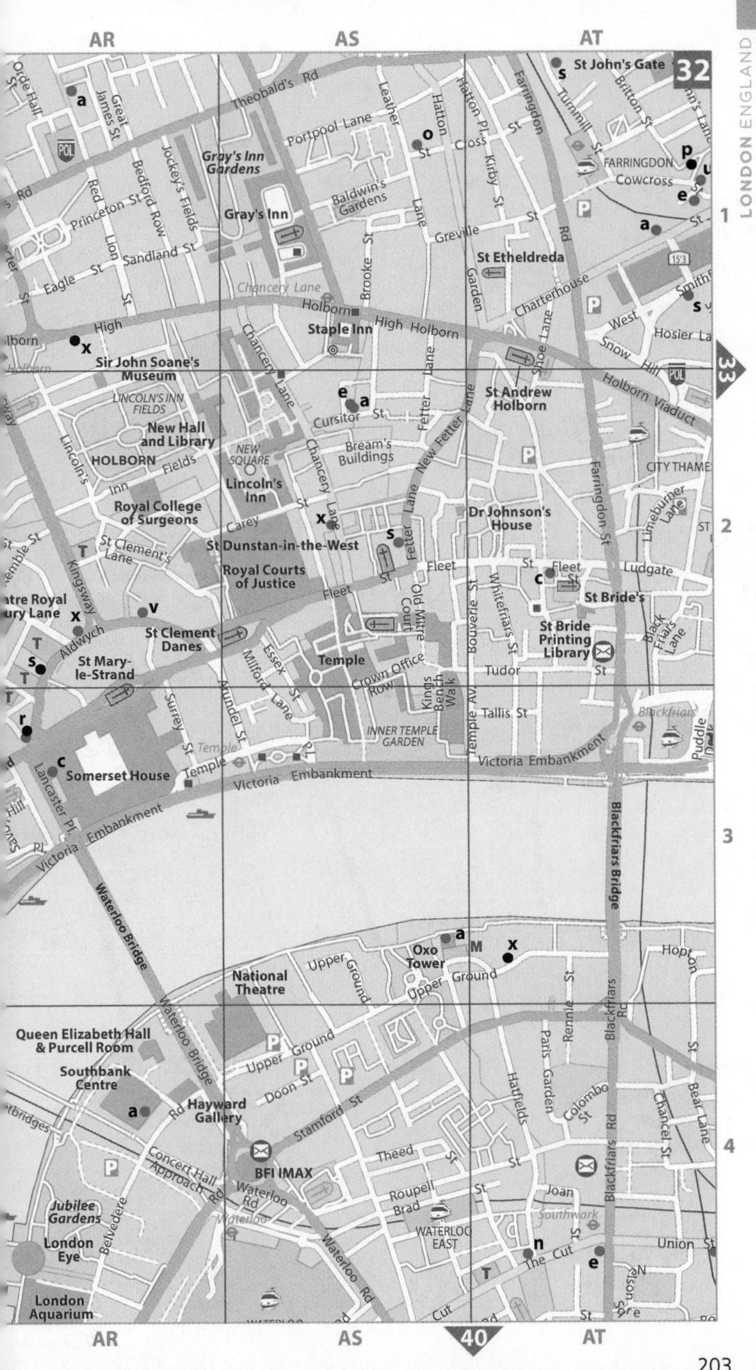
AR
AS
AT
32
33
40
1
2
3
4
St John's Gate
Theobald's Rd
Portpool Lane
Leather Lane
Hatton Garden
Hatton Pl.
Kirby St
Farringdon Rd
Turnmill St
Britton St
Cowcross St
FARRINGDON
Orde Hall St
Great James St
Red Lion St
Bedford Row
Jockey's Fields
Gray's Inn Gardens
Gray's Inn
Princeton St
Sandland St
Eagle St
Baldwin's Gardens
Brooke St
Greville St
St Cross St
St Etheldreda
Charterhouse St
Chancery Lane
Holborn
High Holborn
Staple Inn
West Smithfield
Hosier La
Snow Hill
Holborn Viaduct
Sir John Soane's Museum
LINCOLN'S INN FIELDS
New Hall and Library
HOLBORN
Lincoln's Inn Fields
NEW SQUARE
Lincoln's Inn
Cursitor St
Bream's Buildings
Fetter Lane
New Fetter Lane
Shoe Lane
St Andrew Holborn
Farringdon St
CITY THAMES
Limeburner Lane
Royal College of Surgeons
Carey St
Dr Johnson's House
St Clement's Lane
St Dunstan-in-the-West
Royal Courts of Justice
Fleet St
Ludgate
St Bride's
Kingsway
Aldwych
St Clement Danes
St Mary-le-Strand
Milford Lane
Essex St
Temple
Old Mitre Court
Bouverie St
Whitefriars St
St Bride Printing Library
Black Friars Lane
Crown Office Row
Kings Bench Walk
Tudor St
Tallis St
Temple Av
INNER TEMPLE GARDEN
Blackfriars
Puddle Dock
Surrey St
Arundel St
Temple Pl.
Victoria Embankment
Somerset House
Lancaster Pl.
Waterloo Bridge
Blackfriars Bridge
Oxo Tower
Upper Ground
National Theatre
Hopton St
Blackfriars Rd
Rennie St
Paris Garden
Queen Elizabeth Hall & Purcell Room
Southbank Centre
Hayward Gallery
Doon St
Stamford St
Hatfields
Colombo St
Chancel St
Bear Lane
Concert Hall Approach
BFI IMAX
Theed St
Roupell St
Brad St
Joan St
Waterloo Rd
Waterloo
WATERLOO EAST
Southwark
Jubilee Gardens
London Eye
Belvedere Rd
London Aquarium
The Cut
Union St
Nelson Sq
Theatre Royal Drury Lane

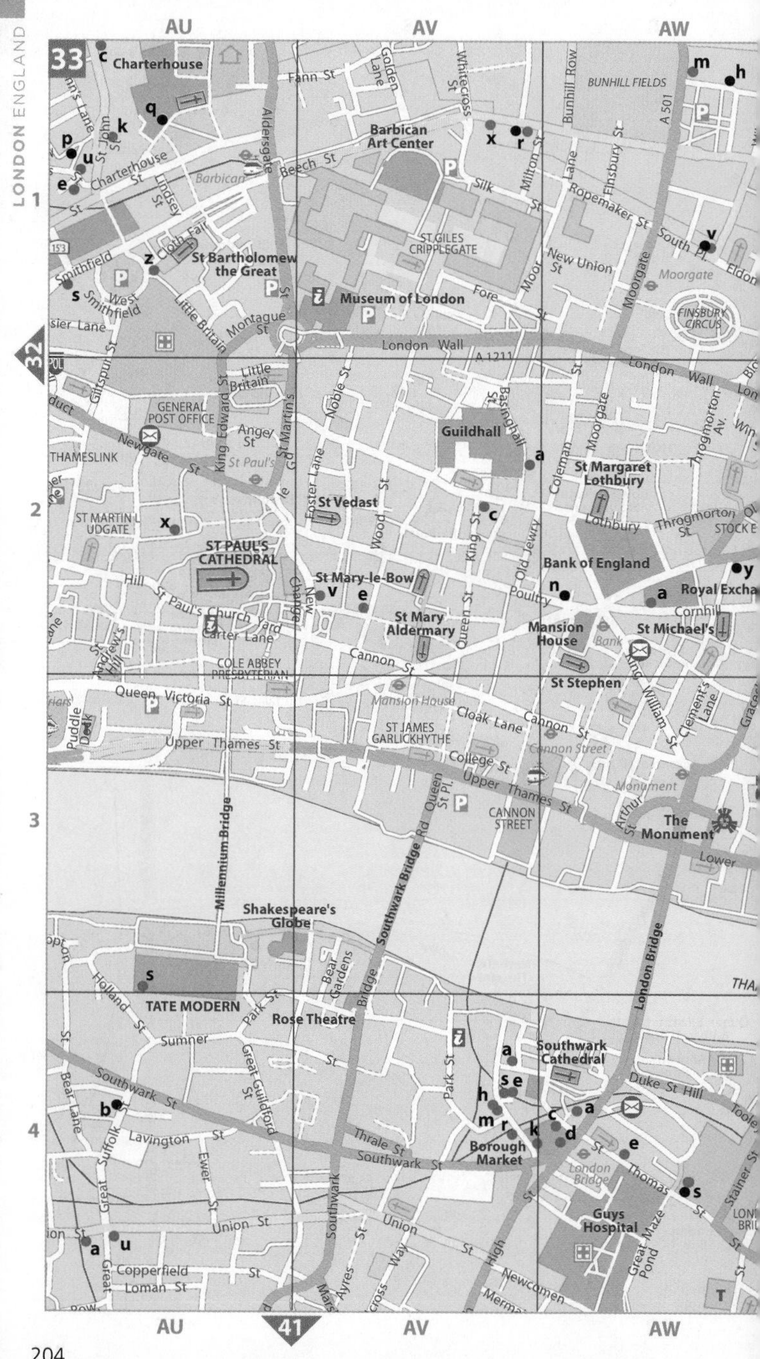
AU
AV
AW
33
Charterhouse
Barbican Art Center
BUNHILL FIELDS
St Bartholomew the Great
ST GILES CRIPPLEGATE
Museum of London
Moorgate
FINSBURY CIRCUS
London Wall
GENERAL POST OFFICE
Guildhall
THAMESLINK
St Margaret Lothbury
St Vedast
ST MARTIN LUDGATE
ST PAUL'S CATHEDRAL
Bank of England
St Mary-le-Bow
Royal Exchange
St Mary Aldermary
Mansion House
St Michael's
COLE ABBEY PRESBYTERIAN
St Stephen
Queen Victoria St
ST JAMES GARLICKHYTHE
Cannon St
Upper Thames St
CANNON STREET
The Monument
Millennium Bridge
Southwark Bridge
London Bridge
Shakespeare's Globe
TATE MODERN
Rose Theatre
Southwark Cathedral
Borough Market
Southwark St
Guys Hospital
Union St
32
41
1
2
3
4

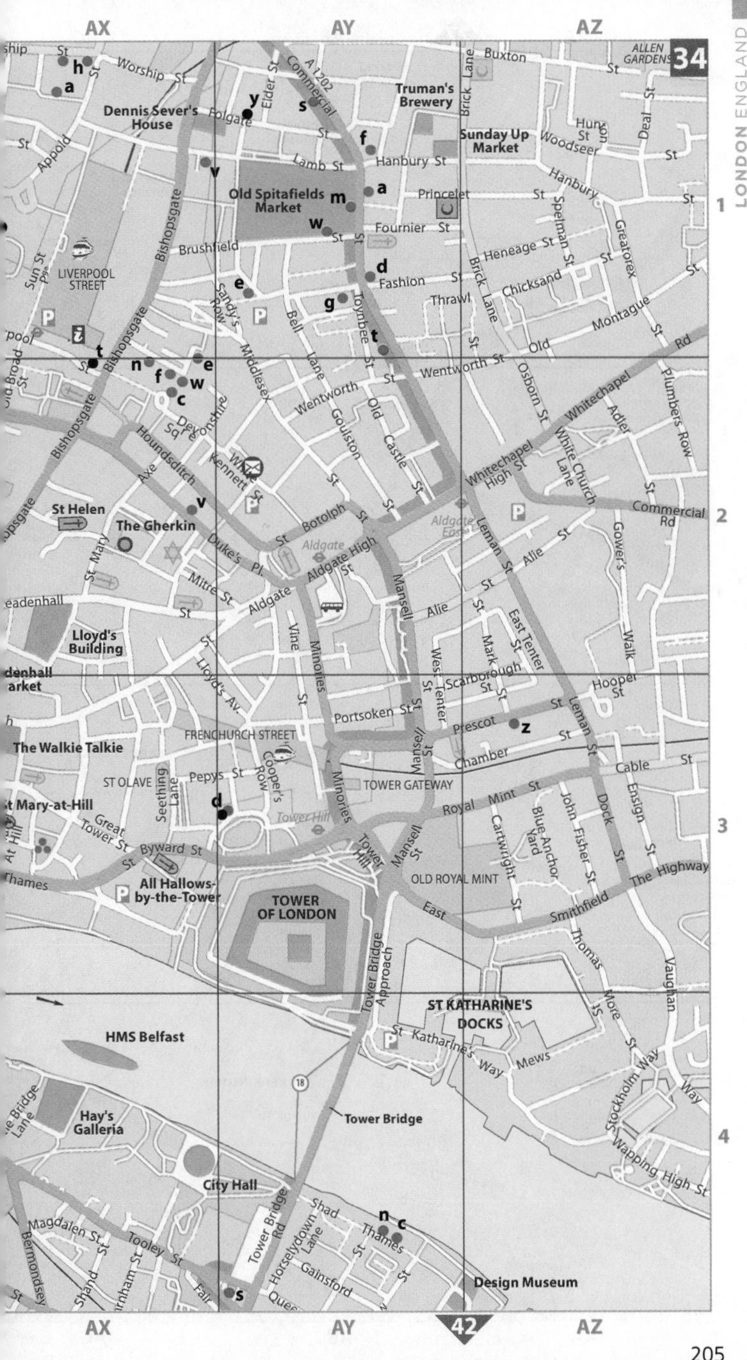
AX
AY
AZ
34
42
1
2
3
4
ALLEN GARDENS
Truman's Brewery
Dennis Sever's House
Sunday Up Market
Old Spitafields Market
LIVERPOOL STREET
St Helen
The Gherkin
Lloyd's Building
The Walkie Talkie
FRENCHURCH STREET
ST OLAVE
TOWER GATEWAY
St Mary-at-Hill
All Hallows-by-the-Tower
TOWER OF LONDON
OLD ROYAL MINT
ST KATHARINE'S DOCKS
HMS Belfast
Hay's Galleria
Tower Bridge
City Hall
Design Museum
Aldgate
Aldgate East
Tower Hill
Worship St
Folgate
Commercial St
A1202
Elder St
Lamb St
Hanbury St
Princelet St
Fournier St
Brushfield St
Bishopsgate
Fashion St
Thrawl
Brick Lane
Heneage St
Chicksand
Spelman St
Greatorex
Montague
Old Montague St
Wentworth St
Whitechapel Rd
Plumbers Row
Adler
Osborn St
Whitechapel High St
White Church Lane
Commercial Rd
Gower's Walk
Middlesex St
Bell Lane
Goulston St
Old Castle St
Toynbee St
Sandy's Row
Devonshire Sq
Houndsditch
White Kennett St
Botolph St
Aldgate High St
Duke's Pl.
Mitre St
St Mary Axe
Leadenhall St
Leman St
Alie St
Mansell St
Vine St
Minories
East Tenter St
Mark St
West Tenter St
Scarborough St
Hooper St
Portsoken St
Prescot St
Chamber St
Cable St
Ensign St
Royal Mint St
Blue Anchor Yard
John Fisher St
Cartwright St
Dock St
The Highway
East Smithfield
Thomas More St
Vaughan Way
Lloyd's Av.
Pepys St
Cooper's Row
Seething Lane
Great Tower St
Byward St
Thames
Tower Bridge Approach
St Katharine's Way
Mews
Stockholm Way
Wapping High St
Tower Bridge Rd
Tooley St
Magdalen St
Bermondsey St
Shad Thames
Horselydown Lane
Gainsford St
Buxton St
Deal St
Woodseer St
Hunton St
Appold St
Sun St Pas
Old Broad St
Duke's Pl.
Bridge Lane

35

AA 27 AB AC

Holland Park
Holland House
KENSINGTON
18 Stafford Terrace
Leighton House
EDWARDES SQUARE
OLYMPIA
EARL'S COURT
NEVERN SQUARE
WEST KENSINGTON
NORMAND PARK
Kensington
West Kensington
West Brompton

5 6 7 8

AA AB AC

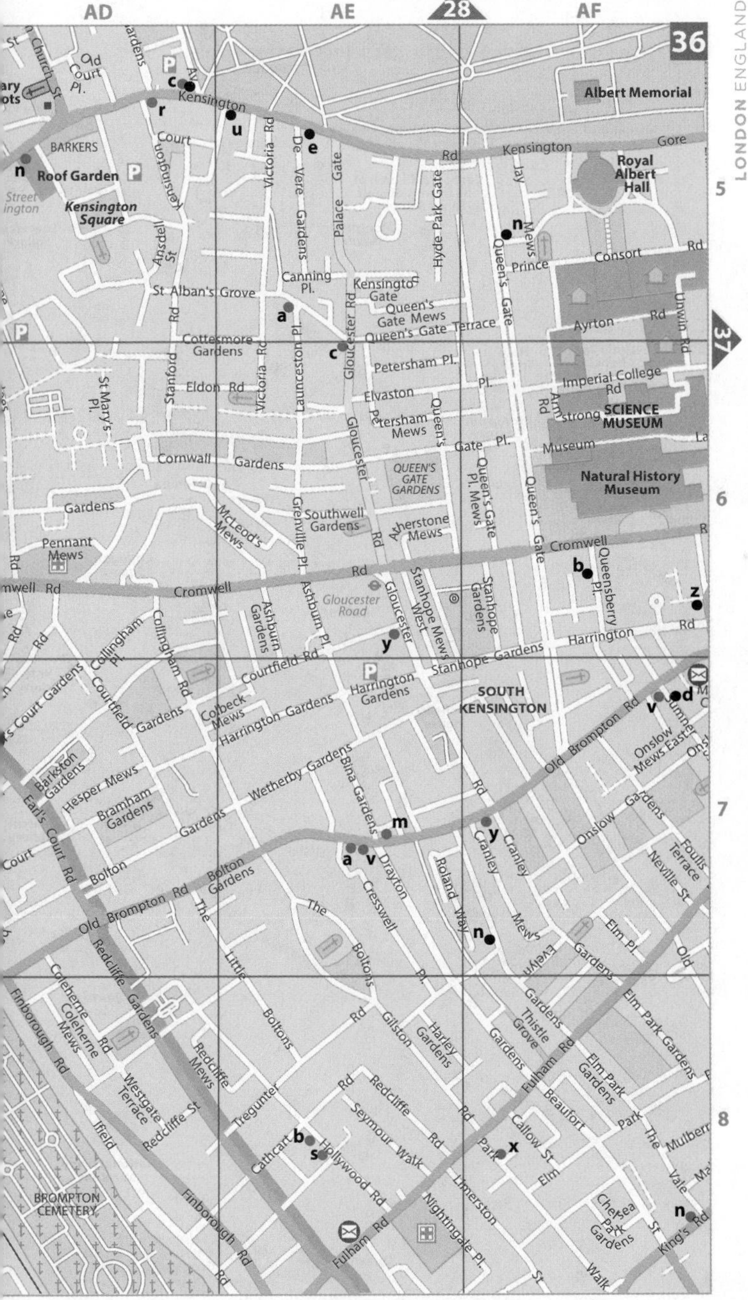
AD
AE
AF
28
36
37
5
6
7
8
Albert Memorial
Royal Albert Hall
Kensington
Gore
Roof Garden
Kensington Square
BARKERS
Queen's Gate
Prince Consort Rd
Imperial College Rd
SCIENCE MUSEUM
Natural History Museum
Cromwell Rd
Gloucester Road
QUEEN'S GATE GARDENS
SOUTH KENSINGTON
Old Brompton Rd
Harrington Gardens
Courtfield Rd
Earl's Court Rd
Redcliffe Gardens
Fulham Rd
The Boltons
Onslow Gardens
Elm Park Gardens
King's Rd
BROMPTON CEMETERY
Finborough Rd
Cathcart
Hollywood Rd
Drayton
Cranley
Evelyn Gardens
Cresswell

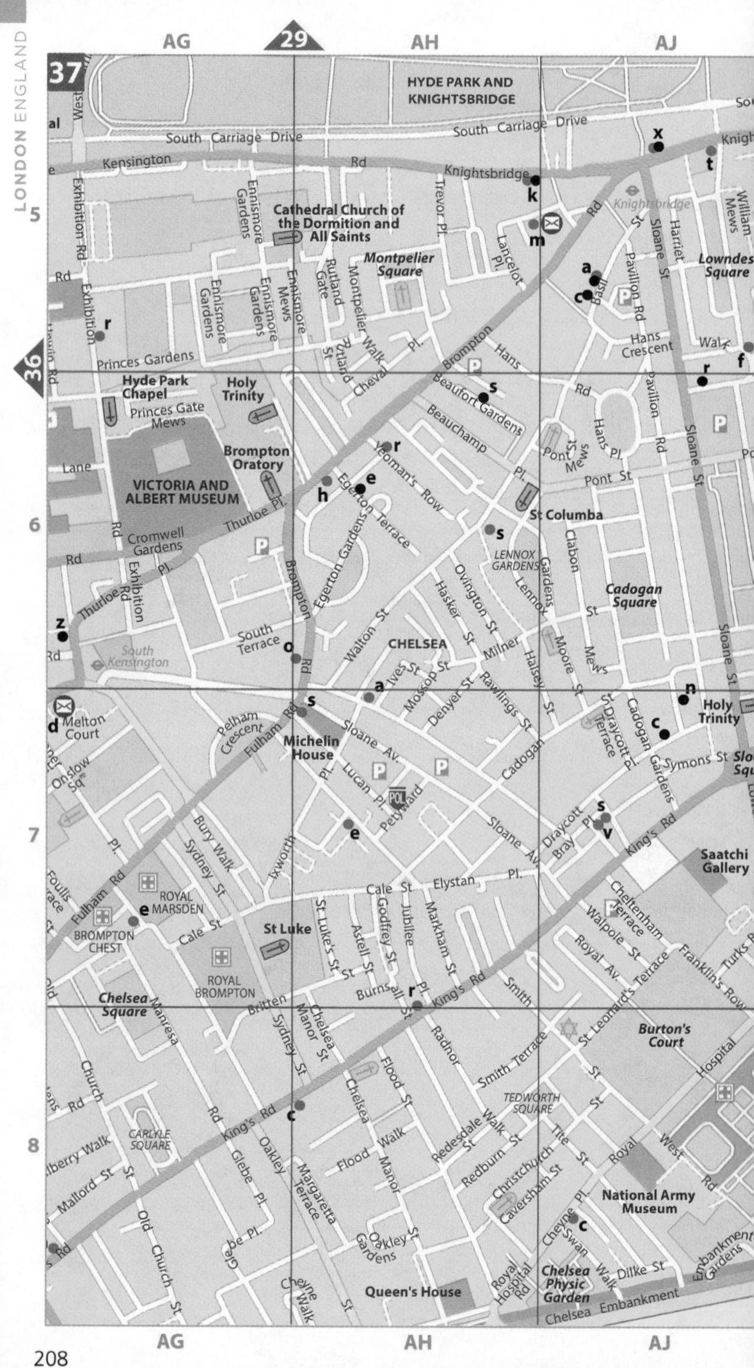
AG
29
AH
AJ
37
HYDE PARK AND KNIGHTSBRIDGE
South Carriage Drive
Kensington Rd
Knightsbridge
Exhibition Rd
Ennismore Gardens
Cathedral Church of the Dormition and All Saints
Montpelier Square
Trevor Pl.
Lancelot Pl.
Knightsbridge
Sloane St
Harriet
William Mews
Lowndes Square
Basil
Pavilion Rd
Hans Crescent
Ennismore Mews
Rutland Gate
Montpelier St
Montpelier Walk
Cheval Pl.
Brompton Rd
Hans Rd
Princes Gardens
36
Hyde Park Chapel
Holy Trinity
Princes Gate Mews
Beaufort Gardens
Beauchamp Pl.
Hans Pl.
Pont St Mews
Pont St
Brompton Oratory
VICTORIA AND ALBERT MUSEUM
Yeoman's Row
Egerton Terrace
Egerton Gardens
St Columba
Lane
Thurloe Pl.
Cromwell Gardens
LENNOX GARDENS
Lennox Gardens
Clabon Mews
Cadogan Square
Walton St
Ovington St
Hasker St
Milner St
Halsey St
Moore St
South Terrace
South Kensington
CHELSEA
Ives St
Mossop St
Denyer St
Rawlings St
Draycott Terrace
Cadogan Gardens
Holy Trinity
Melton Court
Pelham Crescent
Fulham Rd
Michelin House
Sloane Av.
Lucan Pl.
Petyward
Cadogan
Symons St
Onslow Sq
Bury Walk
Sydney St
Ixworth
Draycott Pl.
Bray Pl.
King's Rd
Saatchi Gallery
ROYAL MARSDEN
Cale St
Elystan Pl.
BROMPTON CHEST
St Luke
St Luke's St
Astell St
Godfrey St
Jubilee Pl.
Markham St
Cheltenham Terrace
Walpole St
Royal Av.
Franklin's Row
Turks
ROYAL BROMPTON
Chelsea Square
Manresa
Britten
Chelsea Manor St
Burnsall St
Smith St
St Leonard's Terrace
Burton's Court
Radnor
Smith Terrace
Hospital
Church
Flood St
TEDWORTH SQUARE
Redesdale St
Tite St
CARLYLE SQUARE
Mallord St
Old Church St
Glebe Pl.
Oakley
Margaretta Terrace
Flood Walk
Manor
Redburn St
Christchurch
Caversham St
Royal
West Rd
National Army Museum
Oakley Gardens
Oakley St
Cheyne Walk
Queen's House
Royal Hospital Rd
Cheyne Pl.
Swan Walk
Dilke St
Embankment Gardens
Chelsea Physic Garden
Chelsea Embankment
5
6
7
8
AG
AH
AJ

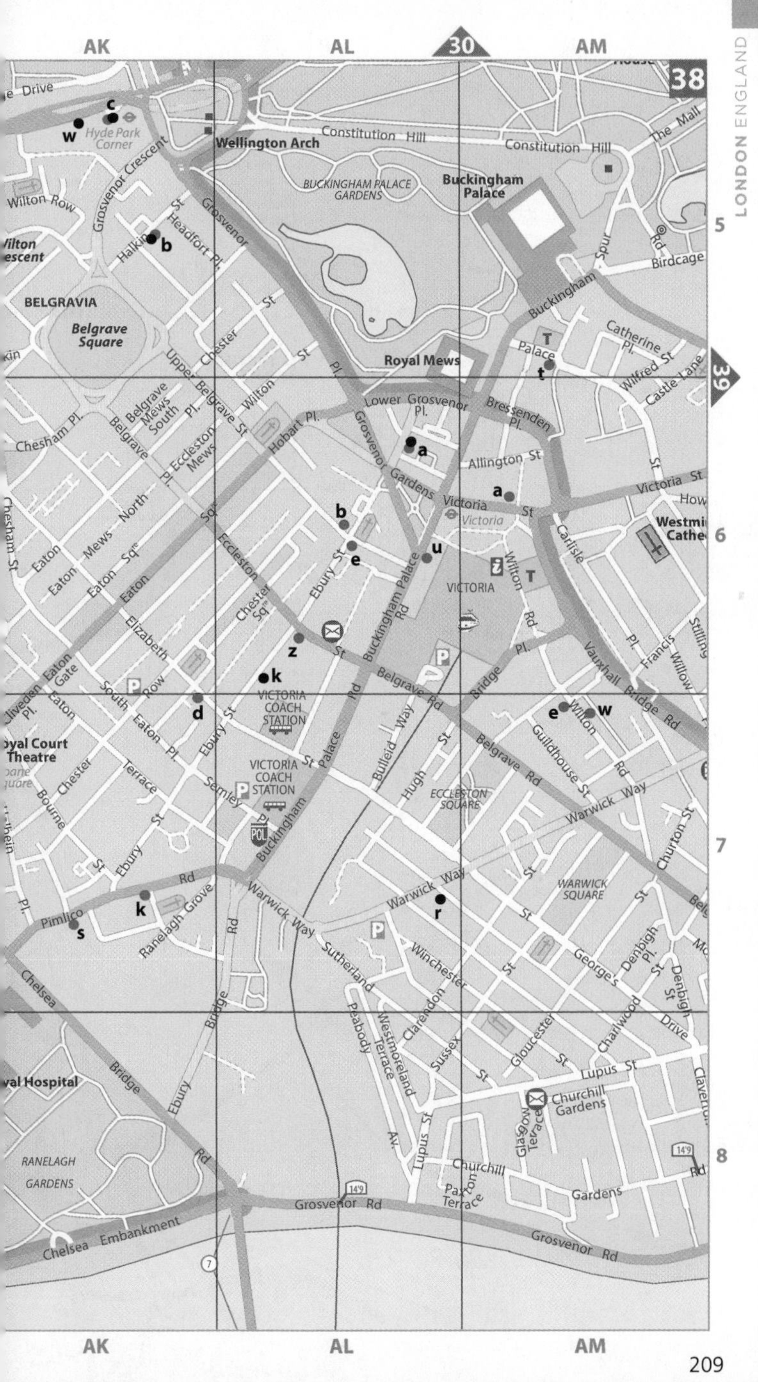
AK
AL
AM
30
38
39
5
6
7
8
Hyde Park Corner
Wellington Arch
Constitution Hill
The Mall
BUCKINGHAM PALACE GARDENS
Buckingham Palace
Grosvenor Crescent
Wilton Row
Halkin St
Headfort Pl.
Grosvenor Pl.
Birdcage
Spur Rd
BELGRAVIA
Belgrave Square
Upper Belgrave St
Chester St
Wilton St
Buckingham Palace Rd
Catherine Pl.
Wilfred St
Castle Lane
Royal Mews
Lower Grosvenor Pl.
Bressenden Pl.
Belgrave Mews South
Belgrave Pl.
Eccleston Mews
Hobart Pl.
Chesham Pl.
Chesham St
Allington St
Grosvenor Gardens
Victoria St
Victoria
VICTORIA
Westminster Cathedral
Eaton Mews North
Eaton Sq.
Eccleston Sq.
Ebury St
Carlisle Pl.
Wilton Rd
Elizabeth St
Chester Sq.
Belgrave Rd
Bridge Pl.
Vauxhall Bridge Rd
Francis St
Willow Pl.
Stillington St
Eaton Gate
South Eaton Pl.
Cliveden Pl.
Royal Court Theatre
VICTORIA COACH STATION
Bulleid Way
Hugh St
Guildhouse St
Chester Row
Eaton Terrace
Semley Pl.
Bourne St
ECCLESTON SQUARE
Warwick Way
Churton St
Ebury Bridge Rd
Ranelagh Grove
Pimlico Rd
WARWICK SQUARE
St George's Dr
Denbigh Pl.
Denbigh St
Chelsea Bridge Rd
Sutherland St
Winchester St
Peabody Av.
Westmoreland Terrace
Clarendon St
Sussex St
Gloucester St
Charlwood St
Lupus St
Claverton St
Royal Hospital
Churchill Gardens
Glasgow Terrace
RANELAGH GARDENS
Paxton Terrace
Churchill Gardens Rd
Grosvenor Rd
Chelsea Embankment

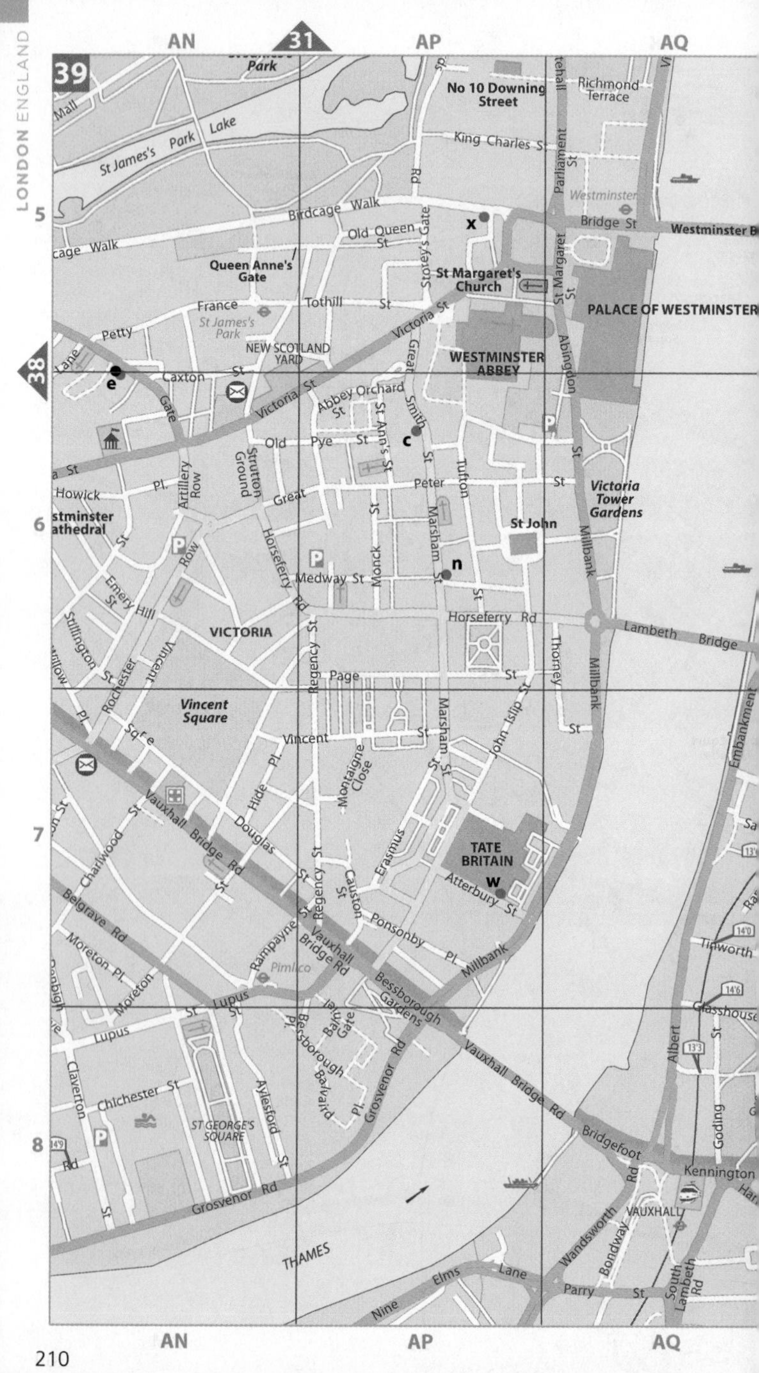
AN
31
AP
AQ
39
38
5
6
7
8
No 10 Downing Street
Richmond Terrace
King Charles St
St James's Park Lake
Birdcage Walk
Old Queen St
Queen Anne's Gate
St Margaret's Church
Westminster
Bridge St
Westminster B
PALACE OF WESTMINSTER
WESTMINSTER ABBEY
NEW SCOTLAND YARD
Tothill St
Victoria St
Caxton St
Petty France
St James's Park
Abbey Orchard St
Great Smith St
Old Pye St
St Ann's St
Tufton St
Peter St
Great Peter St
Howick Pl
Artillery Row
Strutton Ground
Westminster Cathedral
Victoria Tower Gardens
St John
Millbank
Marsham St
Horseferry Rd
Medway St
Monck St
Lambeth Bridge
Thorney St
VICTORIA
Emery Hill St
Stillington St
Rochester Row
Vincent Sq
Vincent St
Regency St
Page St
Vincent Square
John Islip St
Montaigne Close
Hide Pl
Douglas St
Vauxhall Bridge Rd
Charlwood St
Belgrave Rd
Moreton Pl
Moreton St
TATE BRITAIN
Atterbury St
Erasmus St
Causton St
Ponsonby Pl
Rampayne St
Pimlico
Bessborough Gardens
Bessborough Pl
Balvaird Pl
Grosvenor Rd
Lupus St
Claverton St
Chichester St
ST GEORGE'S SQUARE
Aylesford St
THAMES
Nine Elms Lane
Wandsworth Rd
Bondway
VAUXHALL
Parry St
South Lambeth Rd
Kennington La
Bridgefoot
Goding St
Albert Embankment
Tinworth St
Glasshouse St
e
c
n
x
w

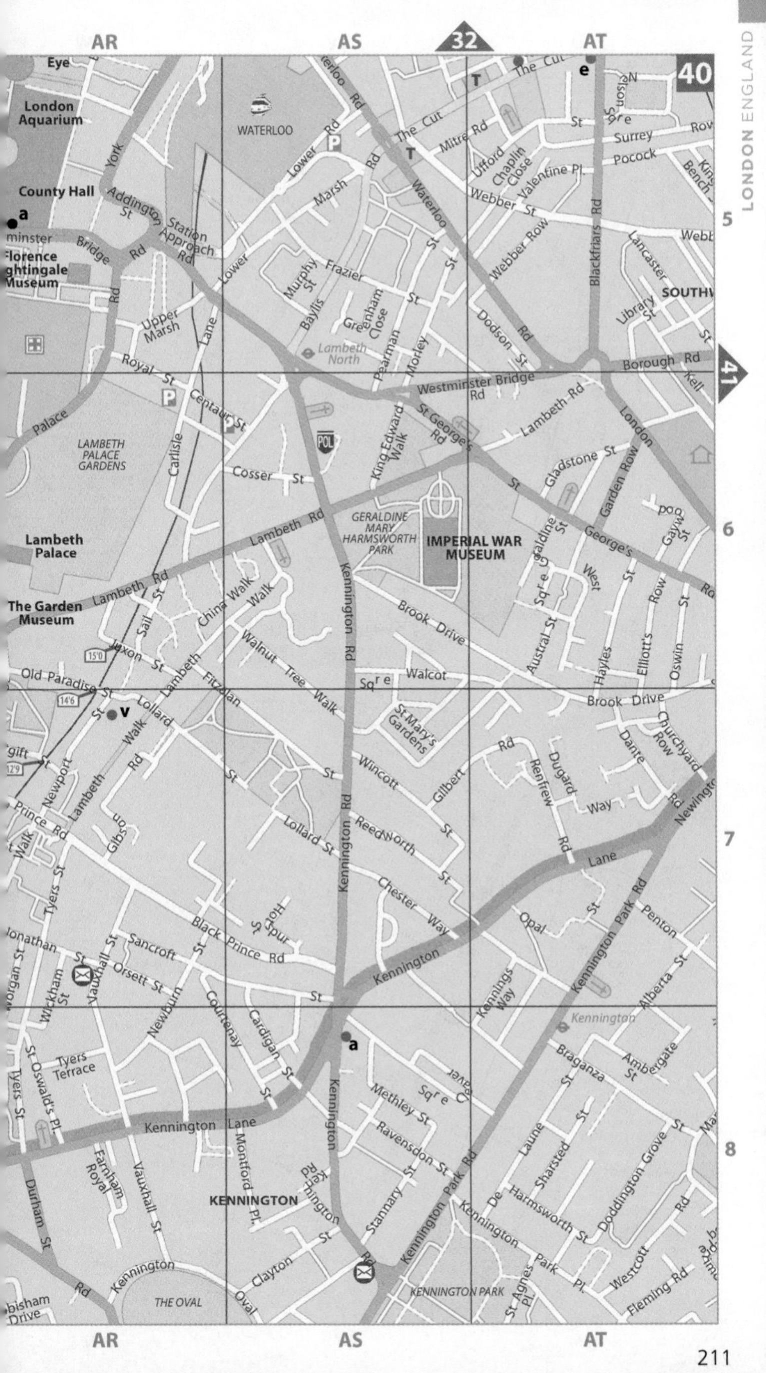
AR
AS
32
AT
40
41
5
6
7
8
Eye
London Aquarium
County Hall
Florence Nightingale Museum
WATERLOO
Lower Marsh
The Cut
Mitre Rd
Ufford
Chaplin Close
Valentine Pl.
Surrey
Pocock
Webber St
Webber Row
Blackfriars Rd
Lancaster
Library St
Waterloo Rd
York Rd
Addington St
Station Approach Rd
Westminster Bridge Rd
Upper Marsh
Lower Lane
Murphy St
Frazier St
Baylis
Greenham Close
Pearman
Morley
Lambeth North
Dodson St
Borough Rd
Royal St
Centaur St
Palace
LAMBETH PALACE GARDENS
Carlisle
Cosser St
King Edward Walk
St George's Rd
Lambeth Rd
London Rd
Gladstone St
Garden Row
GERALDINE MARY HARMSWORTH PARK
IMPERIAL WAR MUSEUM
Geraldine St
West Sq
Lambeth Palace
The Garden Museum
China Walk
Kennington Rd
Brook Drive
Austral St
Hayles
Elliott's Row
Oswin
Jaxon St
Old Paradise St
Walnut Tree Walk
Walcot Sq
Fitzalan
Lollard St
St Mary's Gardens
Dante
Churchyard Row
Wincott
Gilbert Rd
Renfrew Rd
Dugard Way
Newington
Newport
Lambeth Walk
Prince Rd
Gibson
Reedworth St
Lane
Tyers St
Chester Way
Opal
Penton
Kennington Park Rd
Jonathan St
Sancroft St
Black Prince Rd
Hotspur St
Orsett St
Kennington Lane
Alberta St
Kennings Way
Kennington
Vauxhall St
Wickham St
Newburn
Courtenay
Cardigan St
Braganza St
Ambergate St
Tyers Terrace
St Oswald's Pl.
Methley St
Cleaver Sq
Ravensdon St
De Laune St
Sharsted St
Doddington Grove
Farnham Royal
Montford Pl.
KENNINGTON
Stannary St
Harmsworth St
Durham St
Clayton St
Kennington Park Pl.
Westcott
Fleming Rd
Kennington Rd
THE OVAL
KENNINGTON PARK
St Agnes Pl.
Oval

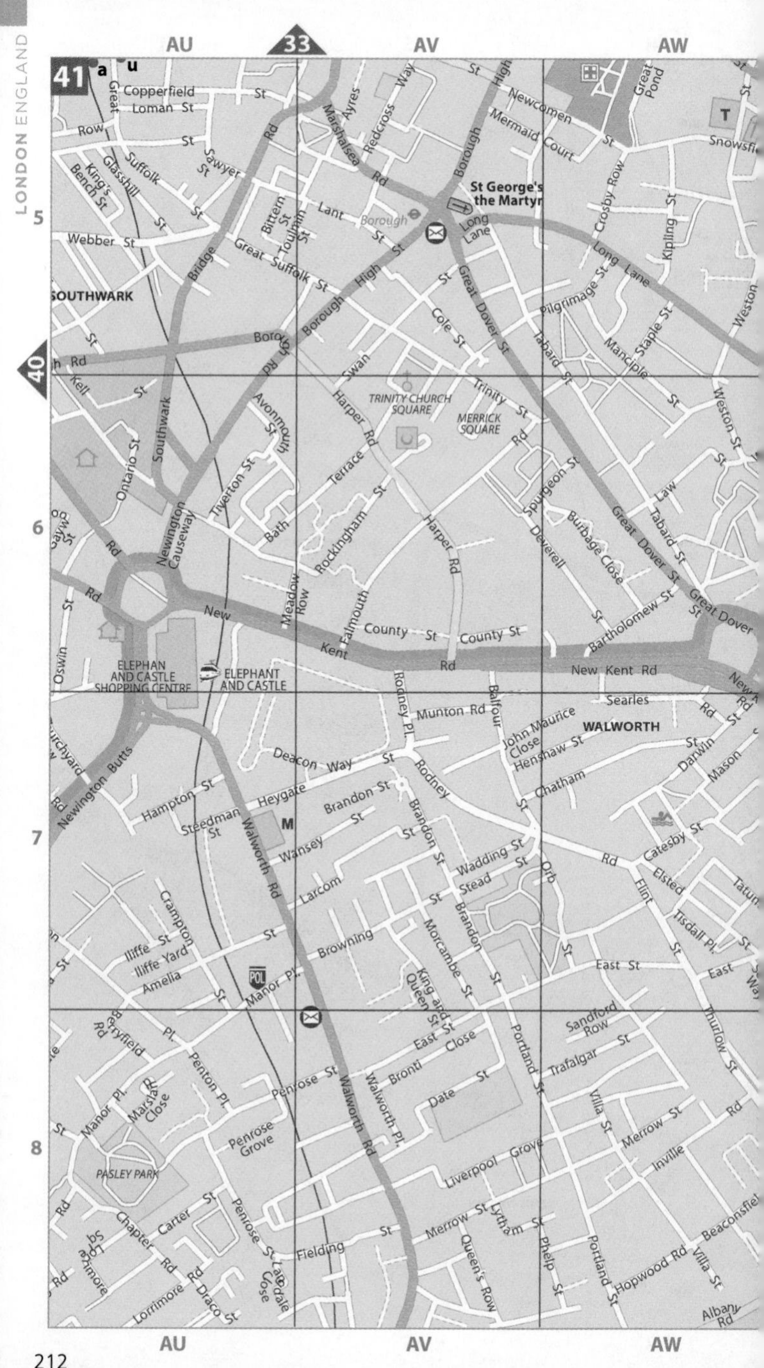
AU
33
AV
AW
41
5
6
7
8
40
SOUTHWARK
WALWORTH
St George's the Martyr
TRINITY CHURCH SQUARE
MERRICK SQUARE
ELEPHAN AND CASTLE SHOPPING CENTRE
ELEPHANT AND CASTLE
PASLEY PARK
Borough
Copperfield St
Loman St
Great Suffolk St
Webber St
Southwark Bridge Rd
Borough High St
Marshalsea Rd
Long Lane
Great Dover St
Newcomen St
Mermaid Court
Crosby Row
Kipling St
Pilgrimage St
Tabard St
Staple St
Manciple St
Weston St
Harper Rd
Trinity St
Newington Causeway
New Kent Rd
County St
Falmouth Rd
Rockingham St
Deverell St
Burbage Close
Bartholomew St
Munton Rd
Rodney Pl.
Rodney Rd
Balfour St
Searles Rd
Heygate St
Deacon Way
Walworth Rd
Brandon St
Wansey St
Larcom St
Browning St
Morecambe St
East St
Portland St
Thurlow St
Penrose St
Penrose Grove
Merrow St
Liverpool Grove
Trafalgar St
Villa St
Hopwood Rd
Fielding St
Lorrimore Rd
Chapter Rd
Newington Butts
AU
AV
AW

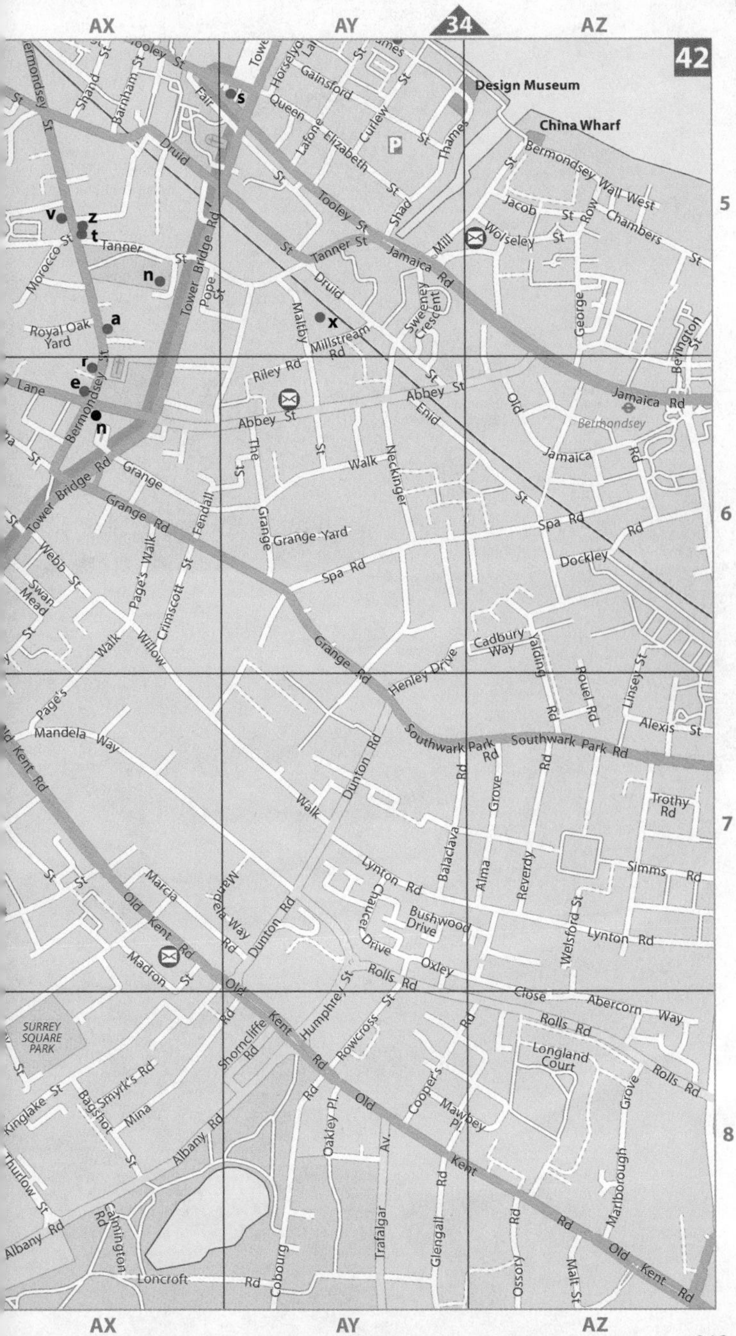

AX AY 34 AZ

42

Design Museum

China Wharf

5 6 7 8

AX AY AZ

ENGLAND

A vision of England sweeps across historic buildings and rolling landscapes, but from the rugged splendour of Cornwall's cliffs to pounding Northumbrian shores, this image seeks parity with a newer picture of Albion: refined cities whose industrial past has been reshaped by a shiny, interactive reality. The country's bones and bumps are a reassuring constant: the windswept moors of the south west and the craggy peaks of the Pennines, the summery orchards of the Kentish Weald, the constancy of East Anglian skies and the mirrored calm of Cumbria's lakes.

Renewed interest in all things regional means restaurants are increasingly looking to serve dishes rooted in their locality. Think Melton Mowbray pie in Leicestershire or Lancashire hotpot in the north west – and what better place to eat cheese than where it was made? Seafood is an important part of the English diet: try shrimps from Morecambe Bay, oysters from Whitstable, crab from Cromer and fish from Brixham. Sunday pub roasts are another quintessential part of English life – and a trip to the South West wouldn't be complete without a cream tea.

- Michelin Road maps
  n° 502, 503, 504 and 713
- Michelin Green Guide:
  Great Britain

1 Cornwall, Devon, Isles of Scilly

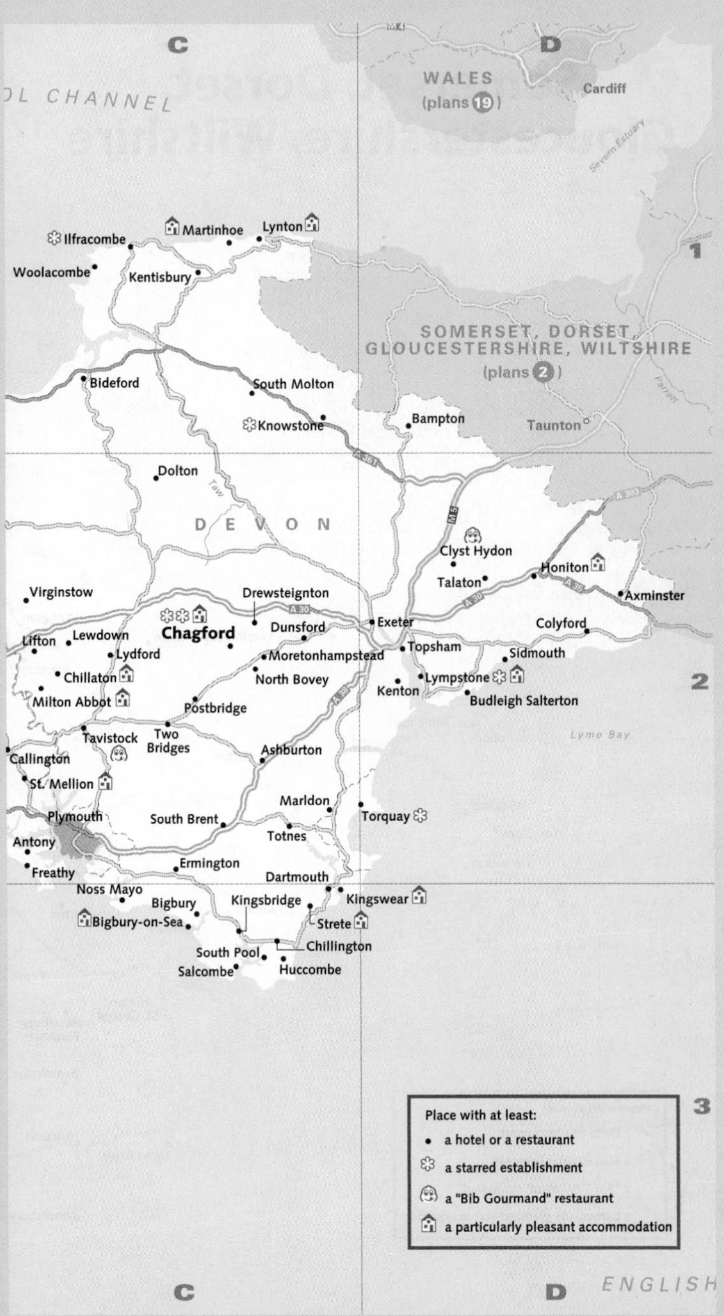
C
D
WALES
(plans 19)
Cardiff
Severn Estuary
BRISTOL CHANNEL
1
Ilfracombe
Martinhoe
Lynton
Woolacombe
Kentisbury
SOMERSET, DORSET, GLOUCESTERSHIRE, WILTSHIRE
(plans 2)
Bideford
South Molton
Knowstone
Bampton
Taunton
Parrett
A 361
Dolton
Taw
DEVON
M 5
A 303
Clyst Hydon
Honiton
Talaton
A 35
Axminster
Virginstow
Drewsteignton
A 30
Chagford
Exeter
Colyford
Lifton
Lewdown
Dunsford
Lydford
Moretonhampstead
Topsham
Sidmouth
Chillaton
North Bovey
Lympstone
Kenton
2
Milton Abbot
Postbridge
A 38
Budleigh Salterton
Tavistock
Two Bridges
Lyme Bay
Callington
Ashburton
St. Mellion
Marldon
Plymouth
South Brent
Torquay
Antony
Totnes
Freathy
Ermington
Dartmouth
Noss Mayo
Bigbury
Kingsbridge
Kingswear
Bigbury-on-Sea
Strete
Chillington
South Pool
Salcombe
Huccombe
3
Place with at least:
a hotel or a restaurant
a starred establishment
a "Bib Gourmand" restaurant
a particularly pleasant accommodation
ENGLISH

2 Somerset, Dorset, Gloucestershire, Wiltshire

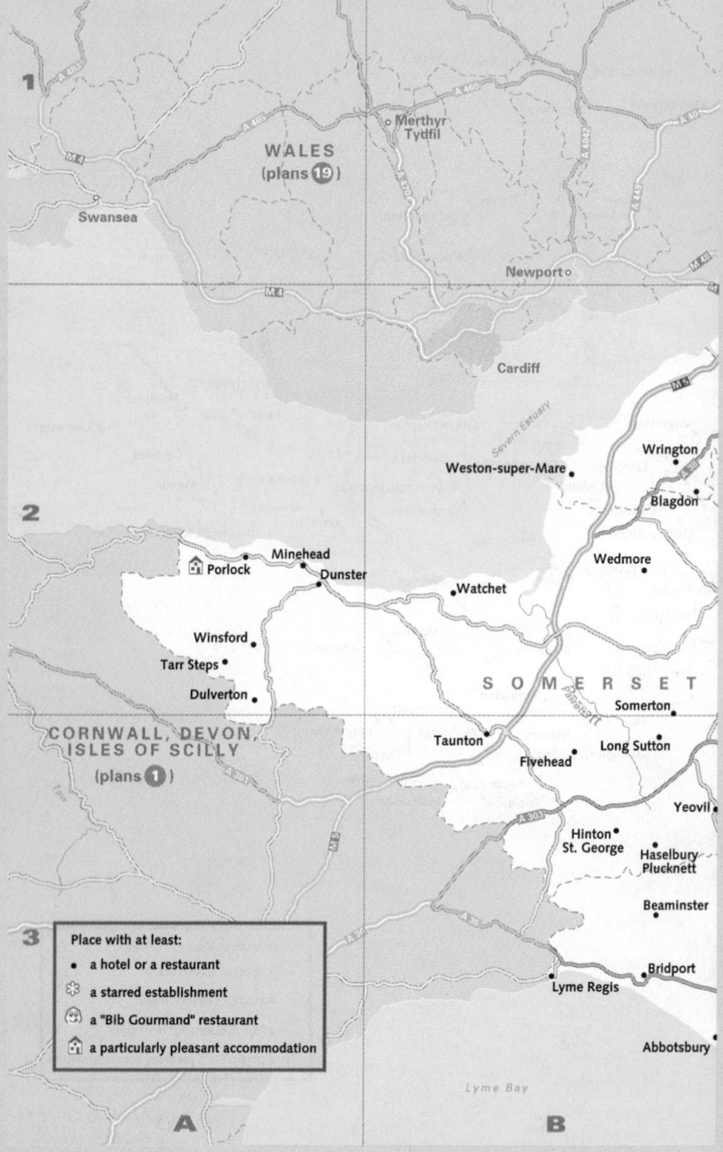

A
B
1
2
3
Merthyr Tydfil
WALES
(plans 19)
Swansea
Newport
Cardiff
Severn Estuary
Weston-super-Mare
Wrington
Blagdon
Porlock
Minehead
Dunster
Watchet
Wedmore
Winsford
Tarr Steps
Dulverton
SOMERSET
Somerton
Taunton
Long Sutton
Fivehead
CORNWALL, DEVON, ISLES OF SCILLY
(plans 1)
Yeovil
Hinton St. George
Haselbury Plucknett
Beaminster
Lyme Regis
Bridport
Abbotsbury
Lyme Bay
Place with at least:
a hotel or a restaurant
a starred establishment
a "Bib Gourmand" restaurant
a particularly pleasant accommodation

C
D
HEREFORDSHIRE, WORCESTERSHIRE, SHROPSHIRE, STAFFORDSHIRE, WARWICKSHIRE
(plans 10)
Chipping Campden
Tewkesbury
Moreton-in-Marsh
Winchcombe
Stow-on-the-Wold
Cheltenham
Lower Slaughter
GLOUCESTERSHIRE
Bourton-on-the-Water
1
Cowley
Arlingham
Northleach
Clearwell
Painswick
Bibury
Barnsley
Stroud
Southrop
Cirencester
Fairford
Nailsworth
Tetbury
Ewen
Thornbury
Westonbirt
Cricklade
OXFORDSHIRE, BUCKINGHAMSHIRE
Malmesbury
(plans 6)
Bristol
Foxham
Castle Combe
Long Ashton
Colerne
Calne
Ramsbury
Marlborough
Chew Magna
Bath
Upper South Wraxall
Hunstrete
Holt
Little Bedwyn
Newbury
Bradford-on-Avon
Devizes
2
Ston Easton
WILTSHIRE
Chilcompton
Edington
East Chisenbury
Holcombe
Mells
Wells
Frome
Warminster
Shrewton
Bruton
HAMPSHIRE, ISLE OF WIGHT, SURREY, WEST SUSSEX
Lovington
Fonthill Bishop
Teffont Evias
Tisbury
Salisbury
Corton Denham
West Hatch
(plans 4)
Rimpton
Shaftesbury
Donhead-St-Andrew
Trent
Sherborne
Fontmell Magna
Tollard Royal
Nomansland
Cranborne
DORSET
Evershot
Blandford Forum
Southampton
Cerne Abbas
Wimborne Minster
3
Maiden Newton
Bournemouth
Christchurch
Highcliffe
Poole
Dorchester
Wareham
Isle of Wight
Studland
Corfe Castle
C
D

Channel Islands 3

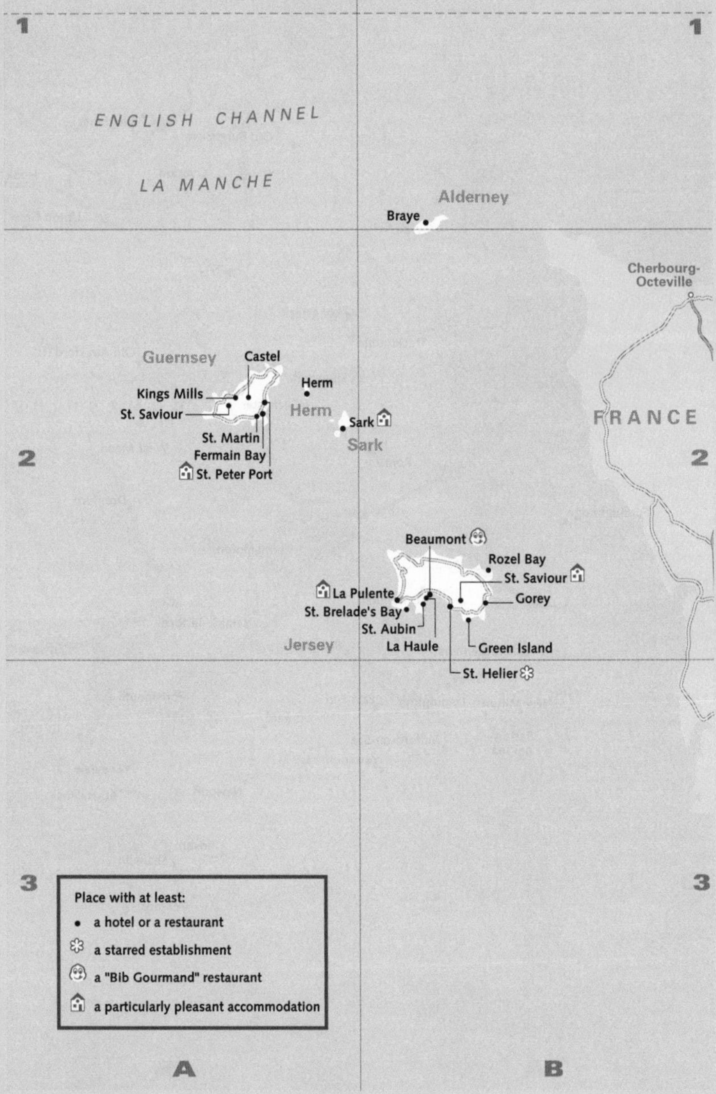

A
B
1
1
ENGLISH CHANNEL
LA MANCHE
Alderney
Braye
Cherbourg-Octeville
Guernsey
Castel
Herm
Kings Mills
St. Saviour
Herm
Sark
Sark
FRANCE
St. Martin
Fermain Bay
St. Peter Port
2
2
Beaumont
Rozel Bay
St. Saviour
La Pulente
Gorey
St. Brelade's Bay
St. Aubin
Jersey
La Haule
Green Island
St. Helier
3
3
Place with at least:
a hotel or a restaurant
a starred establishment
a "Bib Gourmand" restaurant
a particularly pleasant accommodation
A
B

4 Hampshire, Isle of Wight, Surrey, West Sussex

A
B
1
2
3
Reading
M4
Newbury
SOMERSET, DORSET, GLOUCESTERSHIRE, WILTSHIRE (plans 2)
A 339
Baughurst
Old Burghclere
A 34
Overton
Hook
Upton Grey
A 303
Longstock
Stockbridge
M 3
Old Alresford
Salisbury
Sparsholt
Winchester
HAMPSHIRE
West Meon
Romsey
A 36
Droxford
Fordingbridge
M 27
Southampton
A 31
Lyndhurst
Hamble-le-Rice
Brockenhurst
Beaulieu
Emsworth
Sway
New Milton
Lymington
East End
Portsmouth
Hayling Island
Gurnard
Barton-on-Sea
Milford-on-Sea
Bournemouth
Yarmouth
Seaview
Newport
St. Helens
Godshill
Shanklin
Isle of Wight
Ventnor

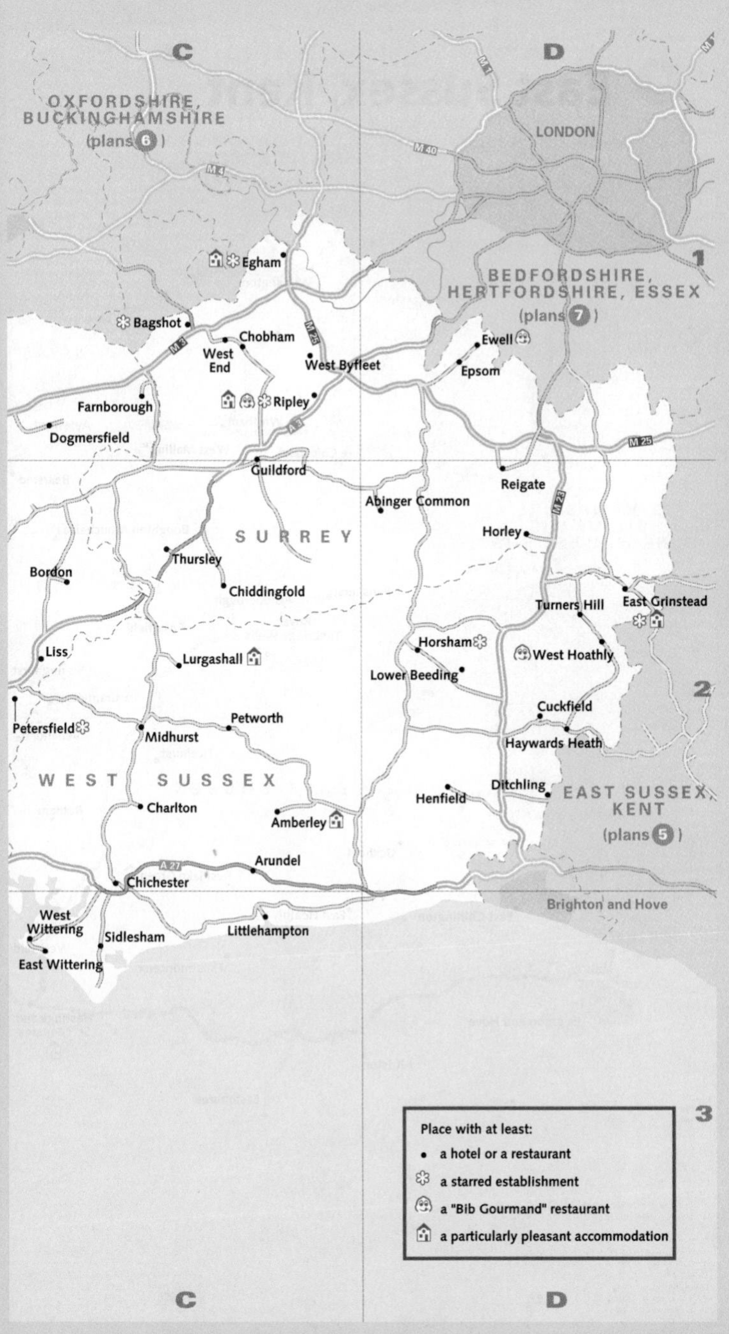

C
D
OXFORDSHIRE, BUCKINGHAMSHIRE
(plans 6)
LONDON
M 40
M 4
M 1
1
Egham
BEDFORDSHIRE, HERTFORDSHIRE, ESSEX
(plans 7)
Bagshot
Chobham
M 25
Ewell
M 3
West End
West Byfleet
Epsom
Ripley
Farnborough
A 3
Dogmersfield
M 25
Guildford
Reigate
Abinger Common
M 23
SURREY
Horley
Thursley
Bordon
Chiddingfold
Turners Hill
East Grinstead
Horsham
West Hoathly
Liss
Lurgashall
Lower Beeding
2
Cuckfield
Petworth
Petersfield
Midhurst
Haywards Heath
WEST SUSSEX
Ditchling
Henfield
EAST SUSSEX, KENT
Charlton
Amberley
(plans 5)
A 27
Arundel
Chichester
Brighton and Hove
West Wittering
Sidlesham
Littlehampton
East Wittering
3
Place with at least:
a hotel or a restaurant
a starred establishment
a "Bib Gourmand" restaurant
a particularly pleasant accommodation
C
D

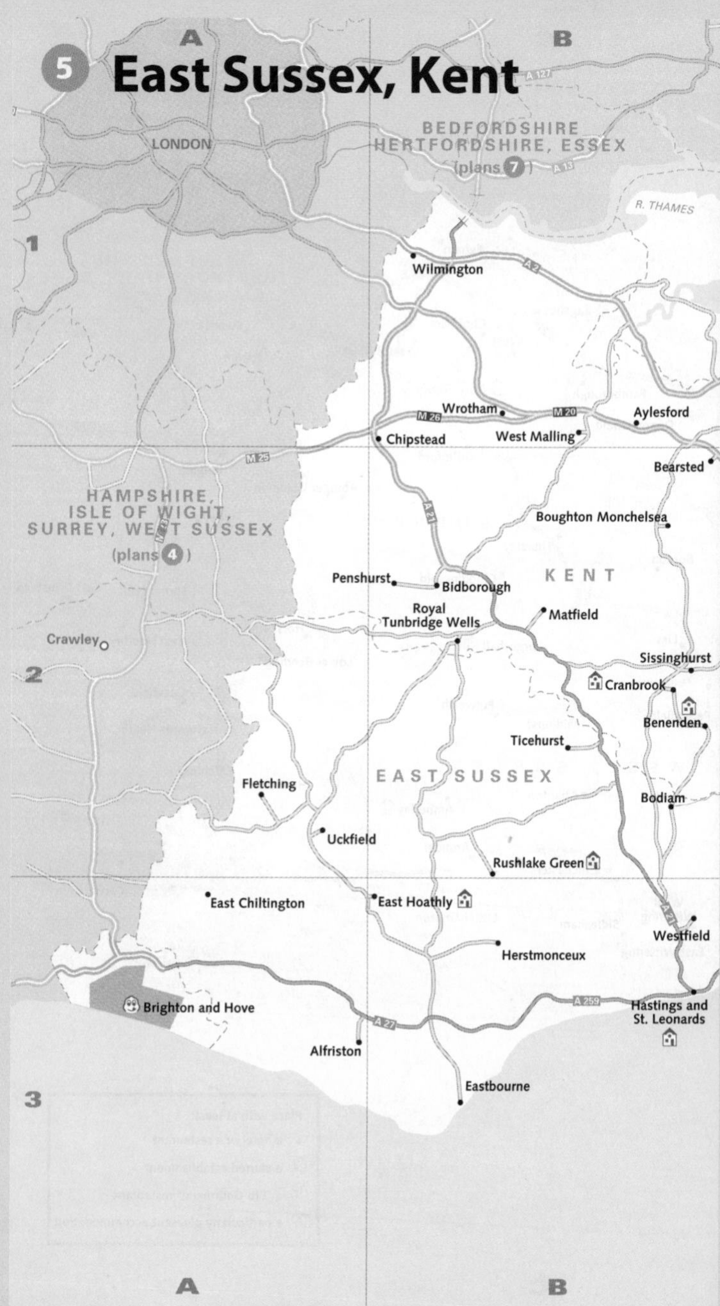

A
B
5
East Sussex, Kent
A 127
LONDON
BEDFORDSHIRE
HERTFORDSHIRE, ESSEX
(plans 7)
A 13
R. THAMES
1
Wilmington
A 2
Wrotham
M 26
M 20
Aylesford
Chipstead
West Malling
M 25
Bearsted
HAMPSHIRE,
ISLE OF WIGHT,
SURREY, WEST SUSSEX
(plans 4)
A 21
Boughton Monchelsea
Penshurst
Bidborough
KENT
Royal
Tunbridge Wells
Matfield
Crawley
2
Sissinghurst
Cranbrook
Benenden
Ticehurst
EAST SUSSEX
Fletching
Bodiam
Uckfield
Rushlake Green
East Chiltington
East Hoathly
Westfield
Herstmonceux
Brighton and Hove
A 259
Hastings and
St. Leonards
A 27
Alfriston
Eastbourne
3
A
B

C
D
BEDFORDSHIRE
HERTFORDSHIRE, ESSEX
(plans 7)
Southend-
on-Sea
1
2
3
Margate
Whitstable
Seasalter
Broadstairs
A 299
Minster
Faversham
Milstead
M 2
Doddington
Ickham
Canterbury
Hollingbourne
Leeds
Stalisfield
KENT
A 2
A 256
Deal
Crundale
Egerton
Wye
Alkham
Ashford
Biddenden
M 20
Tenterden
Folkestone
A 259
New Romney
Rye
Place with at least:
• a hotel or a restaurant
a starred establishment
a "Bib Gourmand" restaurant
a particularly pleasant accommodation
C
D

6 Oxfordshire, Buckinghamshire

A
B
A
B
1
2
3
HEREFORDSHIRE, WORCESTERSHIRE, SHROPSHIRE, STAFFORDSHIRE, WARWICKSHIRE
(plans 10)
SOMERSET, DORSET, GLOUCESTERSHIRE, WILTSHIRE
(plans 2)
HAMPSHIRE, ISLE OF WIGHT, SURREY, WEST SUSSEX
(plans 4)
OXFORDSHIRE
Thames
Sibford Gower
Great Tew
Chipping Norton
Hethe
Churchill
Kingham
Church Enstone
Wootton
Woodstock
Hampton Poyle
Murcott
Burford
Minster Lovell
South Leigh
Oxford
Filkins
Clanfield
Northmoor
Kelmscott
Fyfield
Abingdon
Stadhampton
Faringdon
Little Coxwell
Sutton Courtenay
Berrick Salome
Sparsholt
East Hendred
Swindon
Goring
Yattendon
Stanford Dingley
Newbury
A 46
A 34
A 40
M 40
M 4
M 4
A 339
Place with at least:
• a hotel or a restaurant
a starred establishment
a "Bib Gourmand" restaurant
a particularly pleasant accommodation

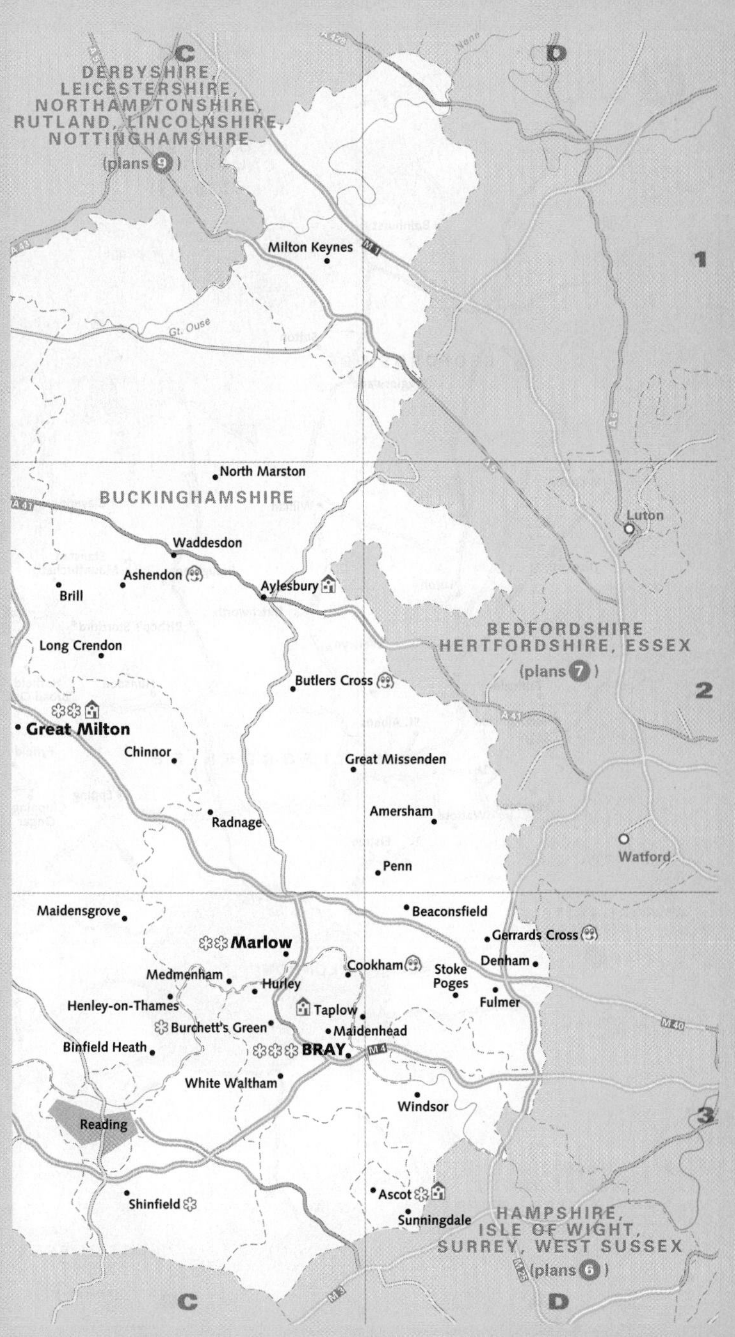
C
D
DERBYSHIRE, LEICESTERSHIRE, NORTHAMPTONSHIRE, RUTLAND, LINCOLNSHIRE, NOTTINGHAMSHIRE
(plans 9)
Milton Keynes
M 1
1
Gt. Ouse
North Marston
BUCKINGHAMSHIRE
A 41
Luton
Waddesdon
Ashendon
Brill
Aylesbury
A 5
A 6
BEDFORDSHIRE
HERTFORDSHIRE, ESSEX
(plans 7)
Long Crendon
Butlers Cross
2
Great Milton
Chinnor
Great Missenden
Amersham
Radnage
Watford
Penn
Maidensgrove
Beaconsfield
Gerrards Cross
Marlow
Cookham
Stoke Poges
Denham
Medmenham
Hurley
Fulmer
Henley-on-Thames
Taplow
Burchett's Green
Maidenhead
M 40
Binfield Heath
BRAY
M 4
White Waltham
Windsor
3
Reading
Shinfield
Ascot
Sunningdale
HAMPSHIRE, ISLE OF WIGHT, SURREY, WEST SUSSEX
(plans 6)
M 25
M 3
C
D

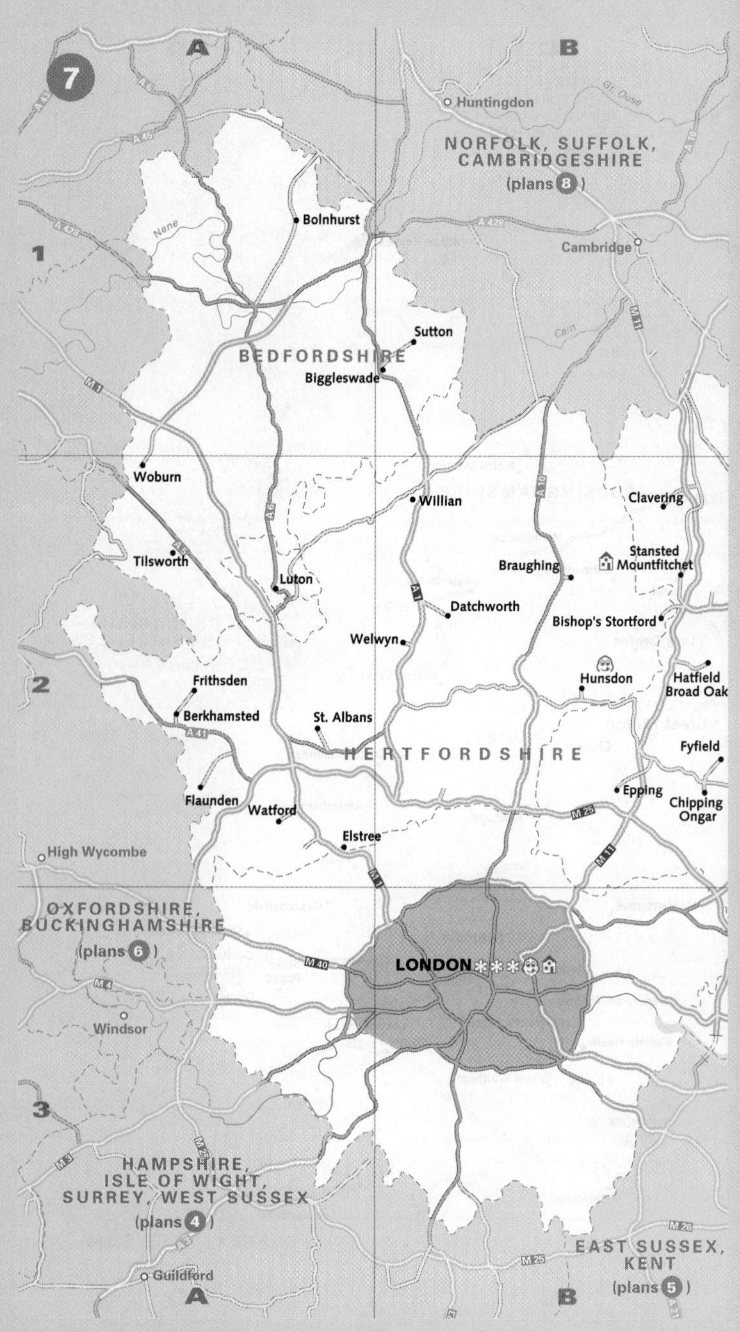
7
A
B
Huntingdon
Gt. Ouse
NORFOLK, SUFFOLK, CAMBRIDGESHIRE
(plans 8)
Bolnhurst
Nene
A 428
Cambridge
1
Sutton
Cam
BEDFORDSHIRE
Biggleswade
M 1
M 11
Woburn
Willian
Clavering
A 10
A 6
A 5
Tilsworth
Stansted Mountfitchet
Braughing
Luton
A 1
Datchworth
Bishop's Stortford
Welwyn
Hunsdon
2
Frithsden
Hatfield Broad Oak
Berkhamsted
St. Albans
A 41
HERTFORDSHIRE
Fyfield
Flaunden
Epping
Watford
Chipping Ongar
M 25
Elstree
High Wycombe
OXFORDSHIRE, BUCKINGHAMSHIRE
(plans 6)
M 40
LONDON ***
M 4
Windsor
3
M 3
M 23
HAMPSHIRE, ISLE OF WIGHT, SURREY, WEST SUSSEX
(plans 4)
A 3
M 26
M 25
EAST SUSSEX, KENT
(plans 5)
Guildford
A
B

Bedfordshire, Hertfordshire, Essex

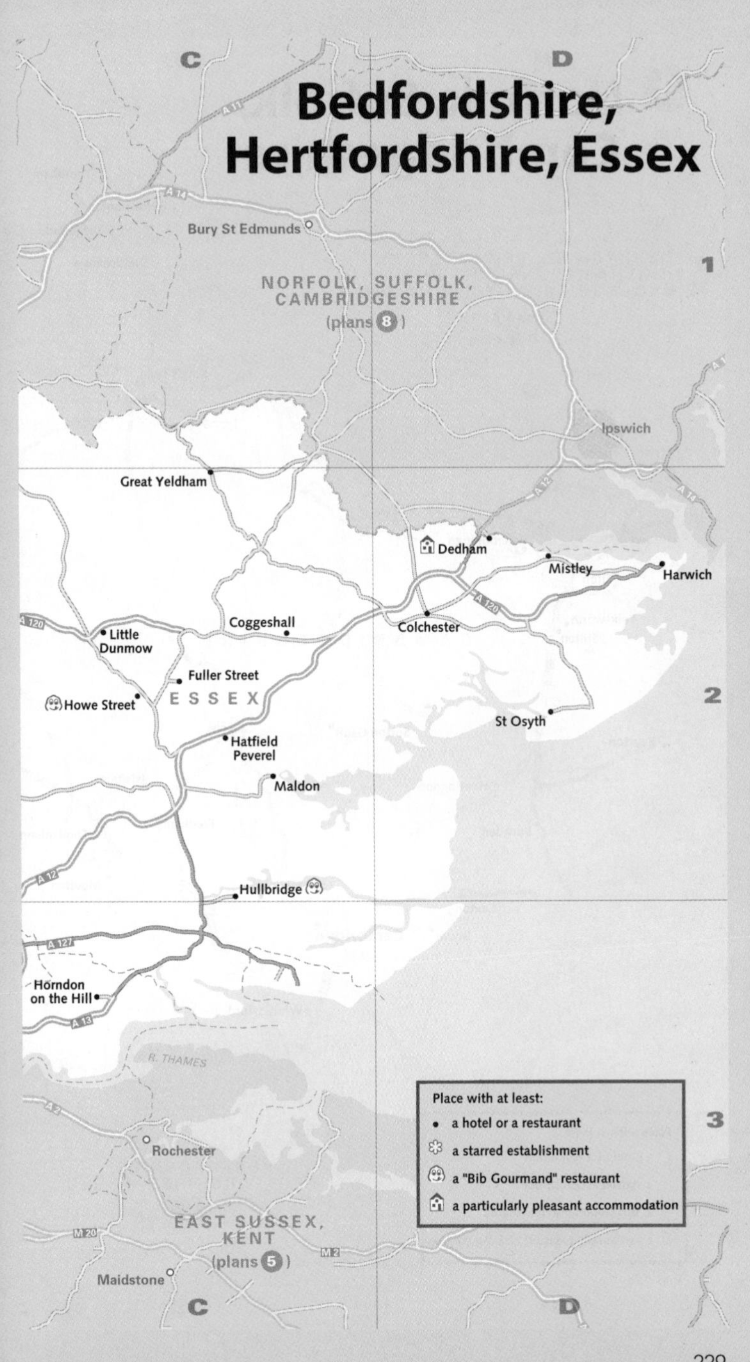

8 Norfolk, Suffolk, Cambridgeshire

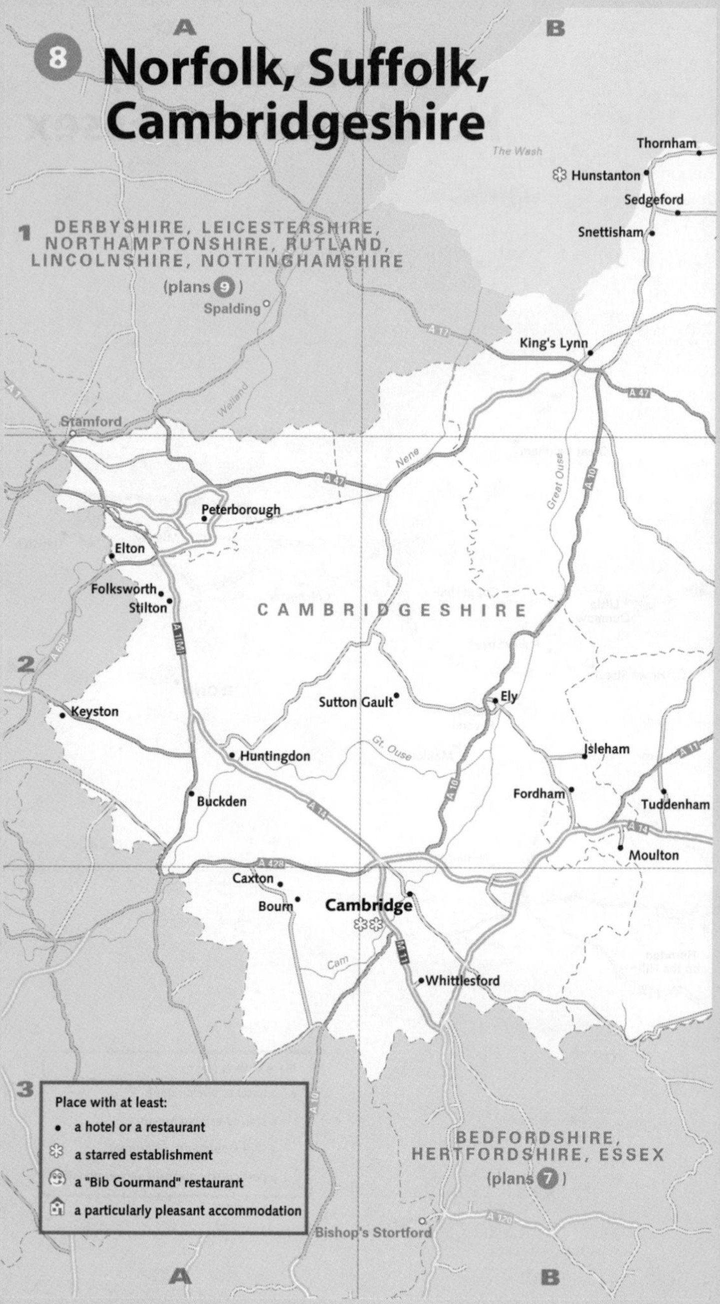

A B

1 DERBYSHIRE, LEICESTERSHIRE, NORTHAMPTONSHIRE, RUTLAND, LINCOLNSHIRE, NOTTINGHAMSHIRE
(plans 9)

Spalding

The Wash

Thornham
Hunstanton
Sedgeford
Snettisham
King's Lynn
Stamford
Peterborough
Elton
Folksworth
Stilton

CAMBRIDGESHIRE

2
Keyston
Sutton Gault
Ely
Huntingdon
Isleham
Fordham
Tuddenham
Buckden
Moulton
Caxton
Bourn
Cambridge
Whittlesford

3
Place with at least:
- a hotel or a restaurant
- a starred establishment
- a "Bib Gourmand" restaurant
- a particularly pleasant accommodation

BEDFORDSHIRE, HERTFORDSHIRE, ESSEX
(plans 7)

Bishop's Stortford

A B

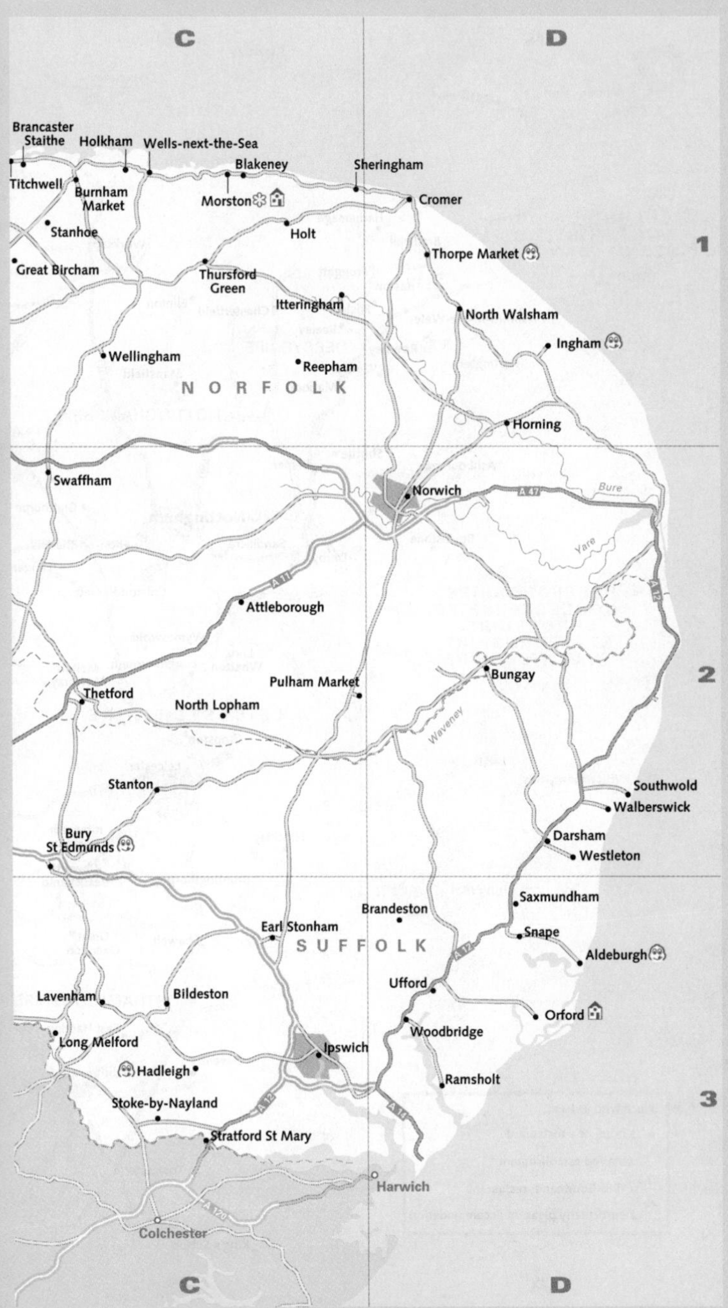
C
D
1
2
3
Brancaster Staithe
Holkham
Wells-next-the-Sea
Blakeney
Sheringham
Titchwell
Burnham Market
Morston
Cromer
Holt
Stanhoe
Thorpe Market
Great Bircham
Thursford Green
Itteringham
North Walsham
Ingham
Wellingham
Reepham
NORFOLK
Horning
Swaffham
Norwich
A 47
Bure
Yare
A 11
A 12
Attleborough
Bungay
Pulham Market
Thetford
North Lopham
Waveney
Southwold
Stanton
Walberswick
Darsham
Bury St Edmunds
Westleton
Saxmundham
Brandeston
Earl Stonham
Snape
SUFFOLK
A 12
Aldeburgh
Ufford
Lavenham
Bildeston
Orford
Woodbridge
Long Melford
Ipswich
Hadleigh
Ramsholt
A 12
A 14
Stoke-by-Nayland
Stratford St Mary
Harwich
A 120
Colchester
C
D

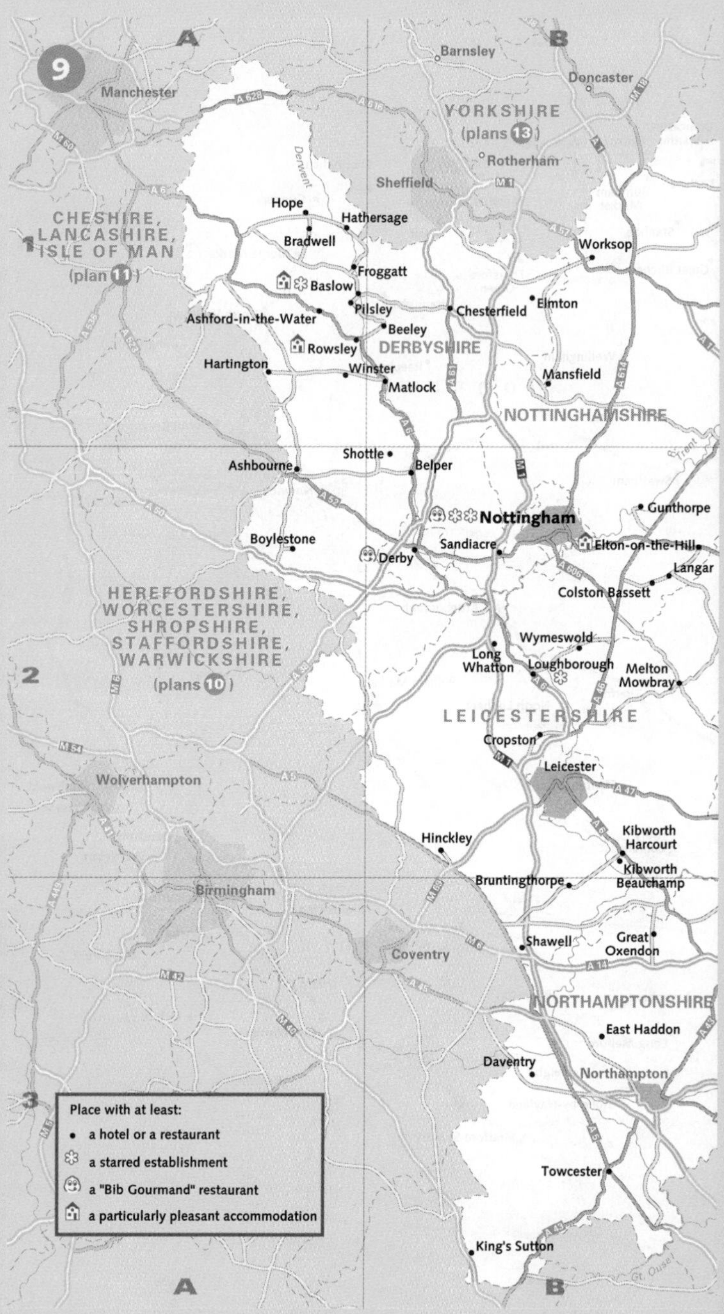
9
Manchester
Barnsley
Doncaster
YORKSHIRE
(plans 13)
Rotherham
Sheffield
CHESHIRE,
LANCASHIRE,
ISLE OF MAN
(plan 11)
Hope
Hathersage
Bradwell
Worksop
Froggatt
Baslow
Pilsley
Chesterfield
Elmton
Ashford-in-the-Water
Beeley
Rowsley
DERBYSHIRE
Hartington
Winster
Matlock
Mansfield
NOTTINGHAMSHIRE
Shottle
Ashbourne
Belper
Gunthorpe
Nottingham
Boylestone
Sandiacre
Elton-on-the-Hill
Derby
Langar
Colston Bassett
HEREFORDSHIRE,
WORCESTERSHIRE,
SHROPSHIRE,
STAFFORDSHIRE,
WARWICKSHIRE
(plans 10)
Wymeswold
Long Whatton
Loughborough
Melton Mowbray
LEICESTERSHIRE
Cropston
Leicester
Wolverhampton
Hinckley
Kibworth Harcourt
Kibworth Beauchamp
Bruntingthorpe
Birmingham
Shawell
Great Oxendon
Coventry
NORTHAMPTONSHIRE
East Haddon
Daventry
Northampton
Towcester
King's Sutton
A
B
1
2
3
Place with at least:
a hotel or a restaurant
a starred establishment
a "Bib Gourmand" restaurant
a particularly pleasant accommodation

Derbyshire, Leicestershire, Northamptonshire, Rutland, Lincolnshire, Nottinghamshire

10 Herefordshire, Worcestershire, Shropshire, Staffordshire, Warwickshire

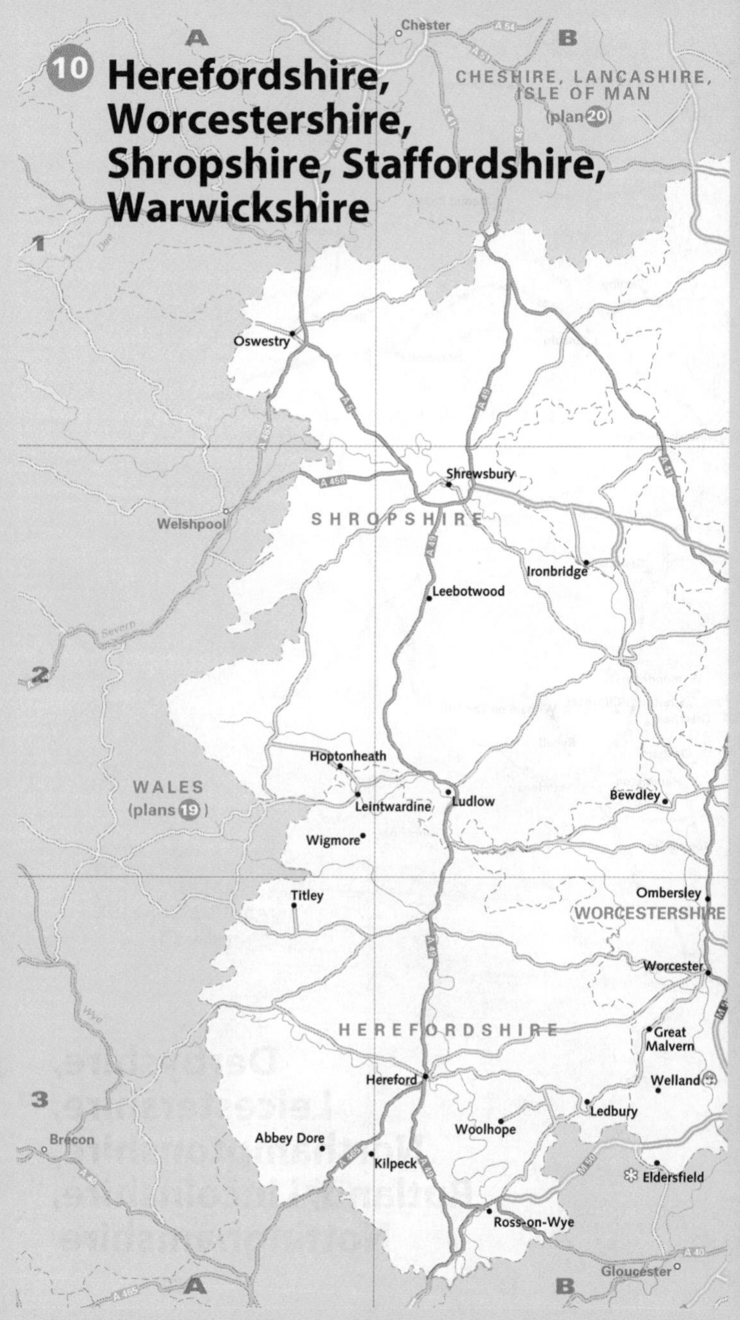

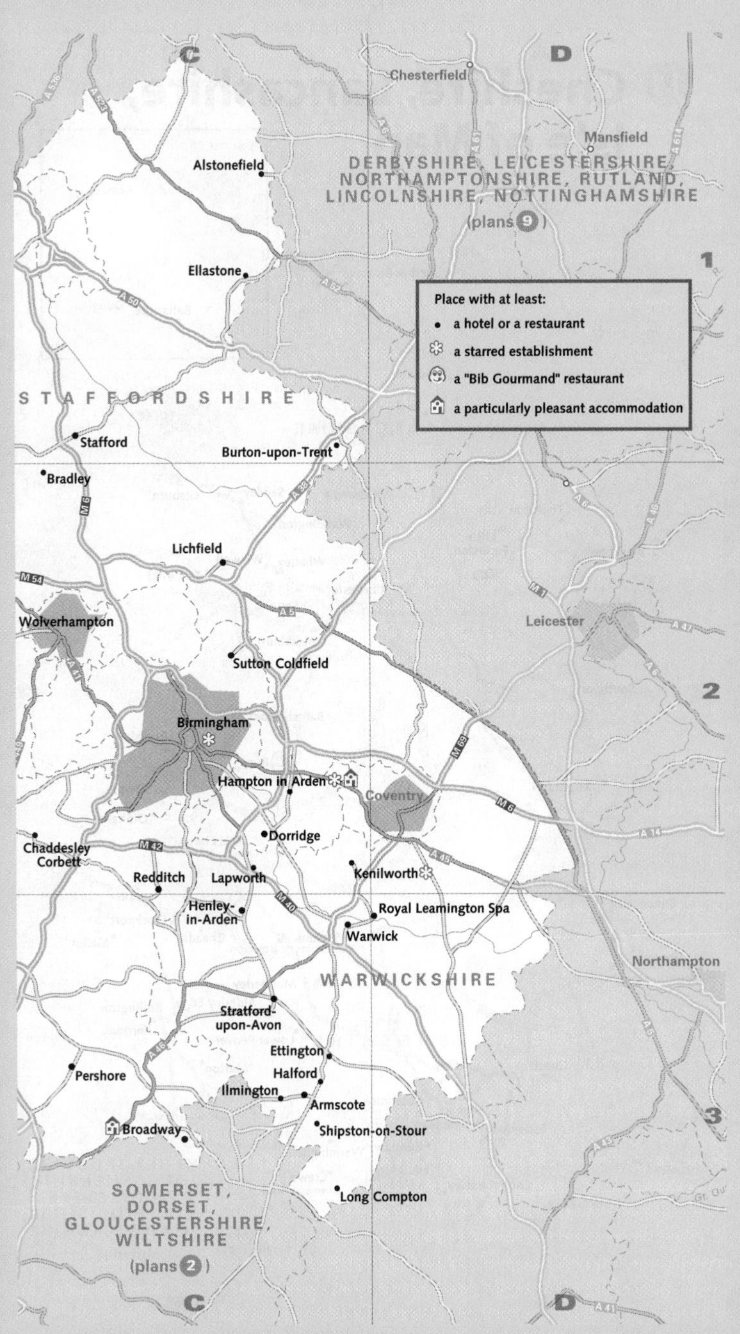
C
D
Chesterfield
Mansfield
DERBYSHIRE, LEICESTERSHIRE,
NORTHAMPTONSHIRE, RUTLAND,
LINCOLNSHIRE, NOTTINGHAMSHIRE
(plans 9)
1
Place with at least:
a hotel or a restaurant
a starred establishment
a "Bib Gourmand" restaurant
a particularly pleasant accommodation
Alstonefield
Ellastone
STAFFORDSHIRE
Stafford
Burton-upon-Trent
Bradley
Lichfield
Wolverhampton
Sutton Coldfield
Leicester
2
Birmingham
Hampton in Arden
Coventry
Dorridge
Chaddesley Corbett
Redditch
Lapworth
Kenilworth
Henley-in-Arden
Royal Leamington Spa
Warwick
Northampton
WARWICKSHIRE
Stratford-upon-Avon
Ettington
Pershore
Halford
Ilmington
Armscote
3
Broadway
Shipston-on-Stour
Long Compton
SOMERSET,
DORSET,
GLOUCESTERSHIRE,
WILTSHIRE
(plans 2)
C
D

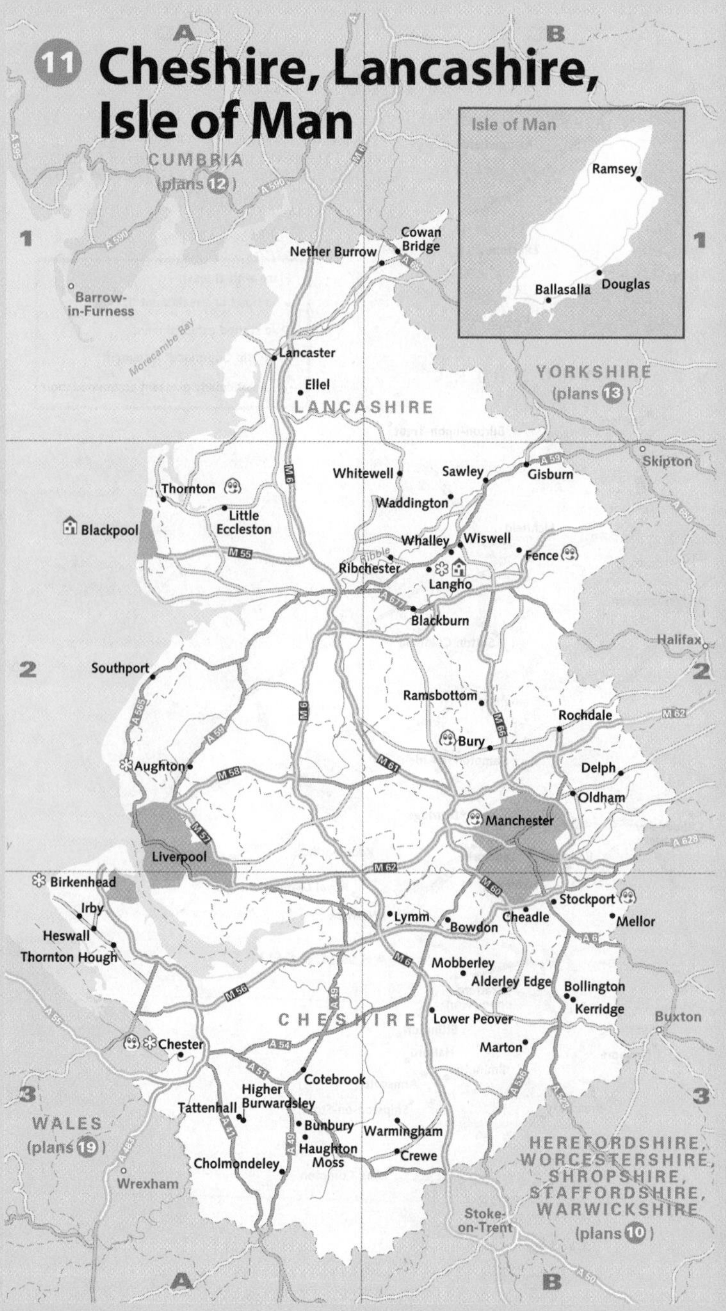
11 Cheshire, Lancashire, Isle of Man
A
B
CUMBRIA
(plans 12)
Isle of Man
Ramsey
Ballasalla
Douglas
1
Cowan Bridge
Nether Burrow
Barrow-in-Furness
Morecambe Bay
Lancaster
Ellel
LANCASHIRE
YORKSHIRE
(plans 13)
Skipton
Whitewell
Sawley
Gisburn
Thornton
Waddington
Little Eccleston
Blackpool
Whalley
Wiswell
Fence
Ribble
Ribchester
Langho
Blackburn
Halifax
2
Southport
Ramsbottom
Rochdale
Bury
Aughton
Delph
Oldham
Manchester
Liverpool
Birkenhead
Stockport
Irby
Heswall
Thornton Hough
Lymm
Bowdon
Cheadle
Mellor
Mobberley
Alderley Edge
Bollington
Kerridge
CHESHIRE
Lower Peover
Buxton
Chester
Marton
Cotebrook
3
Higher Burwardsley
Tattenhall
WALES
(plans 19)
Bunbury
Warmingham
Haughton Moss
Crewe
Cholmondeley
Wrexham
HEREFORDSHIRE, WORCESTERSHIRE, SHROPSHIRE, STAFFORDSHIRE, WARWICKSHIRE
(plans 10)
Stoke-on-Trent
A 595
A 590
M 6
A 65
A 59
A 680
M 55
A 671
A 565
M 65
M 62
M 58
M 61
M 57
A 628
M 60
A 6
M 56
A 49
A 54
A 51
A 41
A 536
A 523
A 483
A 50
A 55

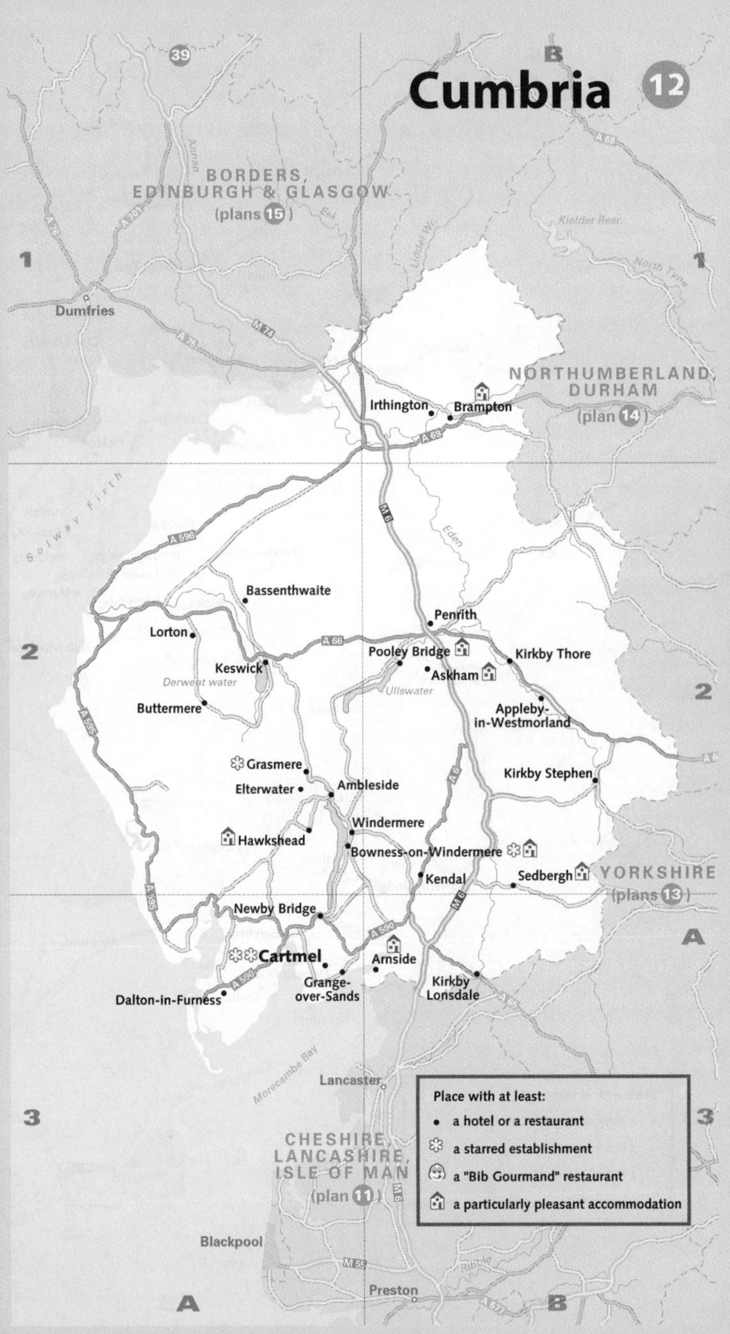

Cumbria 12
BORDERS, EDINBURGH & GLASGOW (plans 15)
NORTHUMBERLAND, DURHAM (plan 14)
YORKSHIRE (plans 13)
CHESHIRE, LANCASHIRE, ISLE OF MAN (plan 11)
Dumfries
Irthington
Brampton
Bassenthwaite
Penrith
Lorton
Pooley Bridge
Kirkby Thore
Keswick
Askham
Derwent water
Ullswater
Buttermere
Appleby-in-Westmorland
Grasmere
Kirkby Stephen
Elterwater
Ambleside
Windermere
Hawkshead
Bowness-on-Windermere
Kendal
Sedbergh
Newby Bridge
Cartmel
Arnside
Grange-over-Sands
Kirkby Lonsdale
Dalton-in-Furness
Lancaster
Blackpool
Preston
Solway Firth
Morecambe Bay
Place with at least:
a hotel or a restaurant
a starred establishment
a "Bib Gourmand" restaurant
a particularly pleasant accommodation

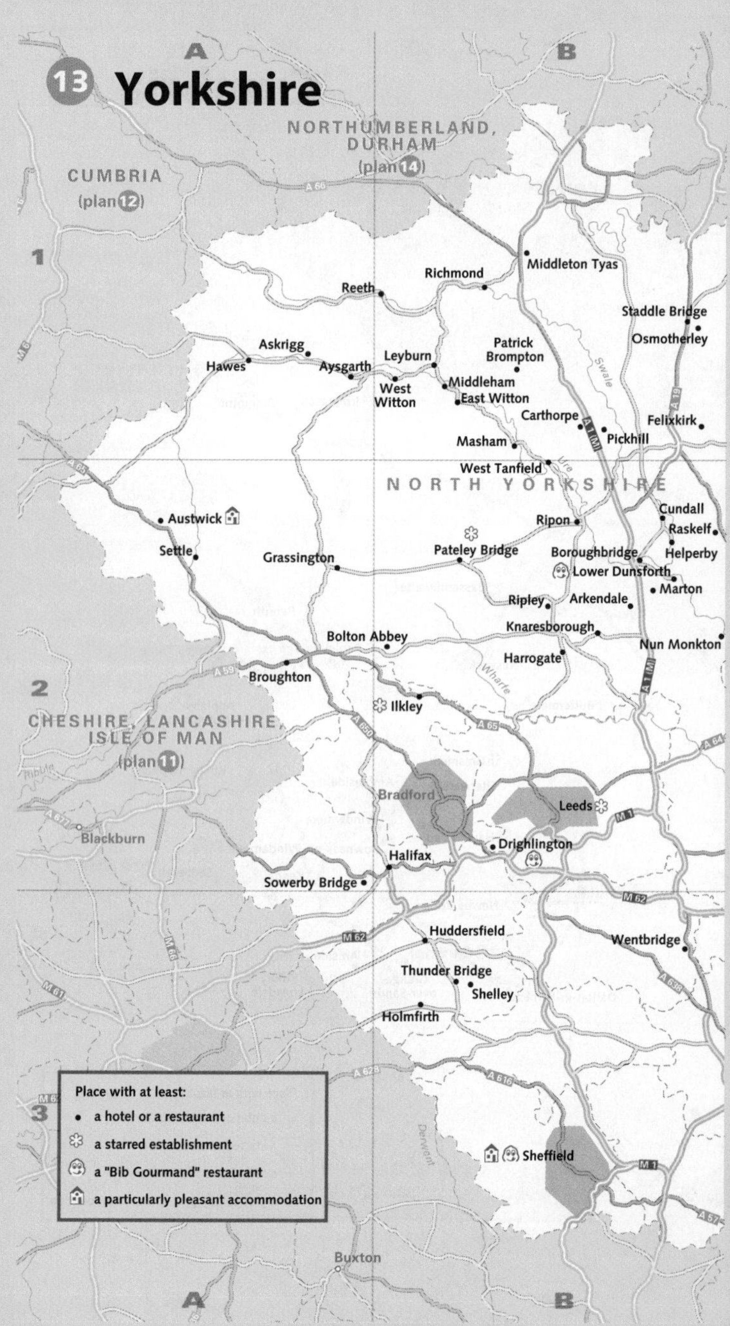

13 Yorkshire
A
B
NORTHUMBERLAND, DURHAM (plan 14)
CUMBRIA (plan 12)
1
Middleton Tyas
Richmond
Reeth
Staddle Bridge
Osmotherley
Askrigg
Hawes
Aysgarth
Leyburn
Patrick Brompton
West Witton
Middleham
East Witton
Carthorpe
Pickhill
Felixkirk
Masham
West Tanfield
NORTH YORKSHIRE
Austwick
Settle
Ripon
Cundall
Raskelf
Grassington
Pateley Bridge
Boroughbridge
Helperby
Lower Dunsforth
Marton
Ripley
Arkendale
Knaresborough
Bolton Abbey
Nun Monkton
Harrogate
Broughton
2
Ilkley
CHESHIRE, LANCASHIRE, ISLE OF MAN (plan 11)
Bradford
Leeds
Blackburn
Drighlington
Halifax
Sowerby Bridge
Huddersfield
Wentbridge
Thunder Bridge
Shelley
Holmfirth
3
Sheffield
Buxton
Place with at least:
a hotel or a restaurant
a starred establishment
a "Bib Gourmand" restaurant
a particularly pleasant accommodation

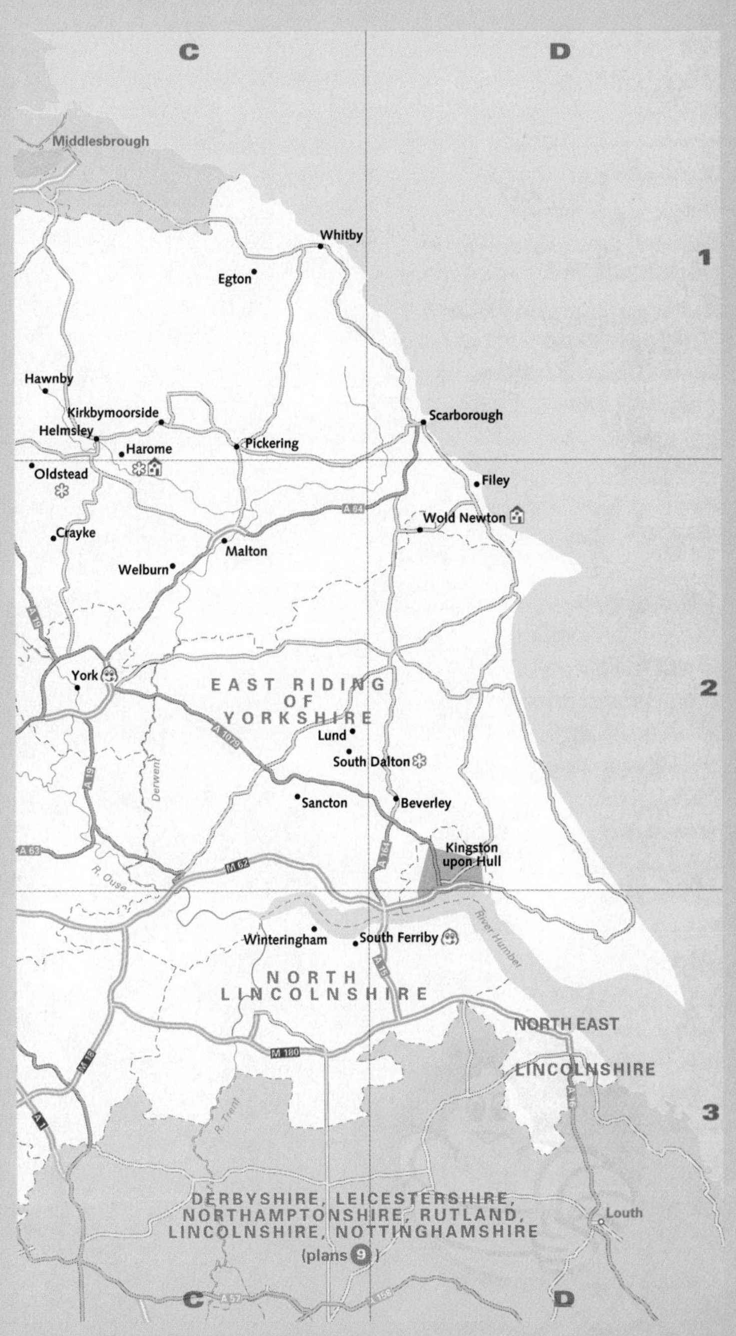
C
D
Middlesbrough
Whitby
1
Egton
Hawnby
Kirkbymoorside
Helmsley
Pickering
Harome
Scarborough
Oldstead
Filey
Wold Newton
A 64
Crayke
Malton
Welburn
A 19
York
2
EAST RIDING OF YORKSHIRE
A 1079
Lund
South Dalton
Derwent
A 19
Sancton
Beverley
A 63
Kingston upon Hull
A 164
M 62
R. Ouse
River Humber
Winteringham
South Ferriby
A 15
NORTH LINCOLNSHIRE
NORTH EAST LINCOLNSHIRE
M 180
M 18
A 16
3
A 1
R. Trent
DERBYSHIRE, LEICESTERSHIRE, NORTHAMPTONSHIRE, RUTLAND, LINCOLNSHIRE, NOTTINGHAMSHIRE
Louth
(plans 9)
C
A 57
A 158
D

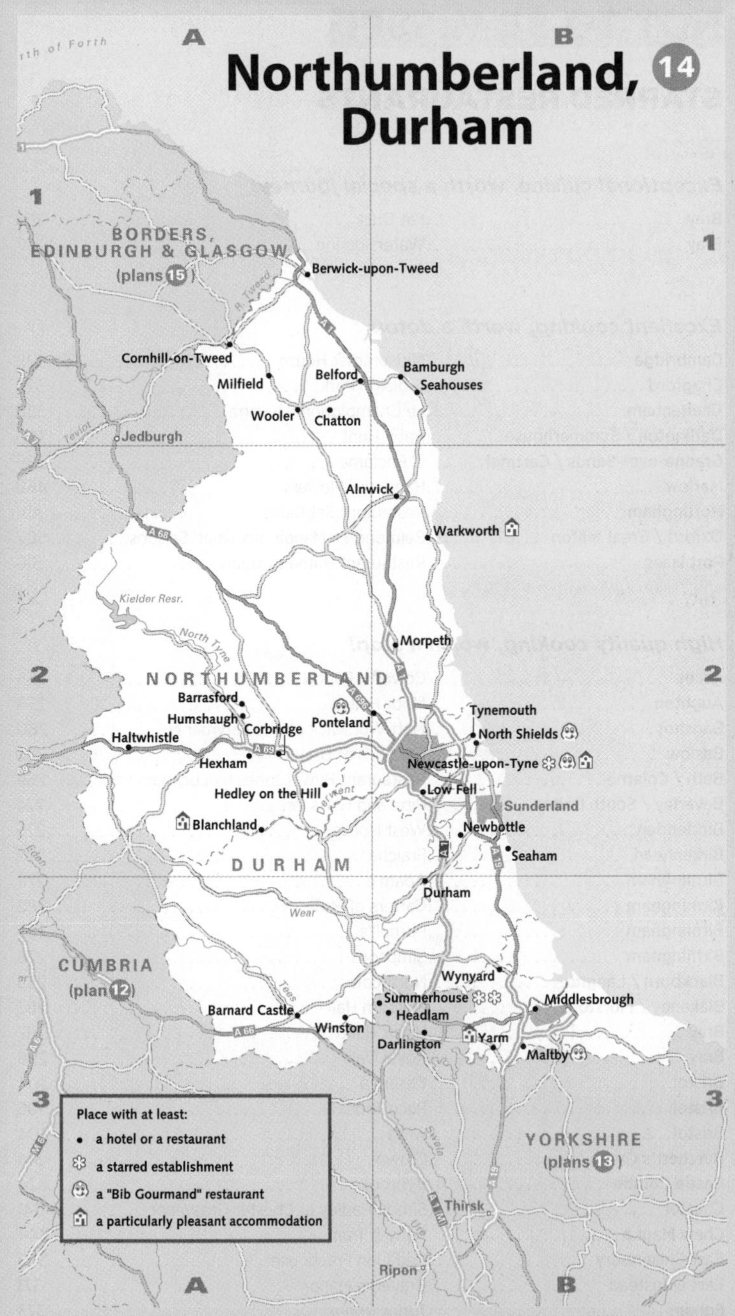
A
B
Northumberland, Durham 14
1
2
3
BORDERS, EDINBURGH & GLASGOW (plans 15)
Berwick-upon-Tweed
Cornhill-on-Tweed
Milfield
Belford
Bamburgh
Seahouses
Wooler
Chatton
Jedburgh
Alnwick
Warkworth
Kielder Resr.
Morpeth
NORTHUMBERLAND
Barrasford
Humshaugh
Corbridge
Ponteland
Tynemouth
North Shields
Haltwhistle
Hexham
Newcastle-upon-Tyne
Low Fell
Hedley on the Hill
Sunderland
Blanchland
Newbottle
Seaham
DURHAM
Durham
CUMBRIA (plan 12)
Wynyard
Summerhouse
Middlesbrough
Barnard Castle
Headlam
Winston
Darlington
Yarm
Maltby
YORKSHIRE (plans 13)
Thirsk
Ripon
Place with at least:
a hotel or a restaurant
a starred establishment
a "Bib Gourmand" restaurant
a particularly pleasant accommodation

NOT TO BE MISSED

STARRED RESTAURANTS

Exceptional cuisine, worth a special journey!

Town	Restaurant	Page
Bray	Fat Duck	297
Bray	Waterside Inn	297

Excellent cooking, worth a detour!

Town	Restaurant	Page
Cambridge	Midsummer House	319
Chagford	Gidleigh Park	325
Cheltenham	Le Champignon Sauvage	336
Darlington / Summerhouse	Raby Hunt	360
Grange-over-Sands / Cartmel	L' Enclume	389
Marlow	Hand and Flowers	469
Nottingham	Restaurant Sat Bains	491
Oxford / Great Milton	Belmond Le Manoir aux Quat' Saisons	502
Port Isaac	Restaurant Nathan Outlaw	516

High quality cooking, worth a stop!

Town	Restaurant	Page
Ascot	Coworth Park **N**	255
Aughton	Moor Hall **N**	258
Bagshot	Matt Worswick at The Latymer **N**	260
Baslow	Fischer's at Baslow Hall	262
Bath / Colerne	Restaurant Hywel Jones by Lucknam Park	269
Beverley / South Dalton	Pipe and Glass Inn	274
Biddenden	West House	275
Birkenhead	Fraiche	277
Birmingham	Adam's	278
Birmingham	Carters of Moseley	282
Birmingham	Purnell's	282
Birmingham	Simpsons	278
Blackburn / Langho	Northcote	285
Blakeney / Morston	Morston Hall	287
Bray	Hinds Head	297
Bray	Royal Oak	298
Bristol	Casamia	304
Bristol	Paco Tapas **N**	305
Bristol	wilks	304
Burchett's Green	Crown	314
Castle Combe	Bybrook	324
Chester	Simon Radley at Chester Grosvenor	341
Chew Magna	Pony & Trap	344
East Chisenbury	Red Lion Freehouse	370
East Grinstead	Gravetye Manor	371
Egham	Tudor Room	373

Michelin

BIB GOURMAND RESTAURANTS

Good quality, good value cooking

Restaurant Nathan Outlaw, Port Isaac

OUR TOP PICKS

Boutique boltholes by the sea

Name	Location	Page
Driftwood	(Portscatho)	518
Hell Bay	(Scilly (Isles of)/Bryher)	541
Hotel Tresanton	(St Mawes)	537
Old Quay House	(Fowey)	386
Padstow Townhouse	(Padstow)	504
Pig on the Beach	(Studland)	563
Rocksalt	(Folkestone)	384
La Sablonnerie	(Channel Islands/Sark)	334
Seafood	(Padstow)	504

Charming chocolate box pubs

Name	Location	Page
Beckford Arms	(Tisbury)	572
Drunken Duck Inn	(Ambleside)	252
Feathered Nest	(Stow-on-the-Wold/Nether Westcote)	560
Masons Arms	(Knowstone)	430
Olive Branch & Beech House	(Clipsham)	353
Punch Bowl Inn	(Kendal/Crosthwaite)	423
Star Inn	(Helmsley/Harome)	405
Talbot Inn	(Mells)	472
Village Pub	(Cirencester/Barnsley)	351
The Wild Rabbit	(Kingham)	426

Bunch of Grapes

Regional stand-outs

Something a little different

Iconic country houses

The ultimate in luxury

ABBEY DORE

Herefordshire - Regional map n° **10**-A3

Toi et Moi

CLASSIC FRENCH • RURAL It's not just the views that set this charming little hillside restaurant apart. The spacious, Scandinavian lodge style building is simply but stylishly furnished, the atmosphere is delightfully relaxed and the monthly French menu is refreshingly honest. Cooking is precise and flavours are pronounced.

Menu £ 35/45

Holling Grange ✉ HR2 0JJ - Northwest : 1.5 mi on Ewyas Harold Common rd - ✆ 01981 240244 (booking essential) - www.toietmoi.co.uk - Closed January-mid March, Sunday-Wednesday, lunch Thursday and Saturday

ABBOTSBURY

Dorset - Pop. 481 - Regional map n° **2**-B3

Abbey House

HISTORIC • COSY A characterful guesthouse-cum-tea-shop in a stunning location, with the ruins of an 11C abbey and a Benedictine watermill in its grounds. Well-kept, classical bedrooms have feature beds and one has its bathroom in an old monk's cell.

5 rooms - †£ 90/140 ††£ 90/150

Church St ✉ DT3 4JJ - ✆ 01305 871330 - www.theabbeyhouse.co.uk

ABBOTS RIPTON - Cambridgeshire ➜ See Huntingdon

ABINGDON

Oxfordshire - Pop. 38 262 - Regional map n° **6**-B2

Rafters

FAMILY • MODERN A modest-looking house which belies its modern interior. Scandic-style bedrooms come with striking bathrooms and plenty of extra touches; the best boasts a small 'Zen Garden'. Local produce features at breakfast.

4 rooms - †£ 60/114 ††£ 115/139

Abingdon Rd, Marcham ✉ OX13 6NU - West : 3 mi on A 415 - ✆ 01865 391298 - www.bnb-rafters.co.uk - Closed 2 weeks Christmas and New Year

ABINGER COMMON

Surrey - Regional map n° **4**-D2

Abinger Hatch

TRADITIONAL BRITISH • RUSTIC 18C pub in a charming hamlet - with its low beams, cosy corners and log fires it oozes country gentility. It's open throughout the day, offering snacks, sharing boards and comfort dishes; come summer, the outside kitchen is a hit.

Carte £ 23/30

Abinger Ln ✉ RH5 6HZ - ✆ 01306 730737 - www.theabingerhatch.com - Closed 25 December

ALDEBURGH

Suffolk - Pop. 2 341 - Regional map n° **8**-D3

Lighthouse

MEDITERRANEAN CUISINE • BISTRO Popular, long-standing, split-level eatery with bright yellow décor, amiable service and a laid-back feel. Menus change constantly, featuring fish from the boats 200m away and local, seasonal meats and vegetables. Cooking is rustic and flavoursome, and dishes arrive generously proportioned.

Menu £ 15 (lunch and early dinner) - Carte £ 20/36

77 High St ✉ IP15 5AU - ✆ 01728 453377 (booking essential) - www.lighthouserestaurant.co.uk - Closed 26 December and lunch 1 January

Sea Spice

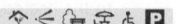

INDIAN • ELEGANT XX Hidden in a hotel is this dark, moody restaurant with period lighting and contrastingly bright, patterned crockery. Freshly ground spices and local fish, meat and game feature; try the muntjac vindaloo and the delicious rasmalai.

Menu £ 15/25 – Carte £ 22/46

White Lion Hotel, Market Cross Pl ✉ IP15 5BJ
– ✆ 01728 452720 – www.seaspice.co.uk – Closed Monday

Aldeburgh Market

SEAFOOD • BISTRO X Set in a shop brimming with local veg and fresh seafood; the best tables are in the bay window, with views across the street. Well-priced, flavoursome cooking and friendly service. Arrive early to try one of the tasty breakfasts.

Carte £ 16/31

170-172 High St ✉ IP15 5EY
– ✆ 01728 452520 – www.thealdeburghmarket.co.uk – lunch only – Closed 25 December

Wentworth

TRADITIONAL • PERSONALISED The friendly, engaging team know all the regulars at this family-run seaside hotel. The conservatory and large front terrace are popular spots. Extremely comfortable bedrooms come with a copy of locally set 'Orlando the Marmalade Cat'. The formal dining room serves a traditional daily menu.

35 rooms (dinner included) – †£ 83/124 ††£ 135/303

Wentworth Rd ✉ IP15 5BD
– ✆ 01728 452312 – www.wentworth-aldeburgh.com

Brudenell

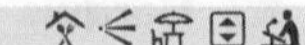

FAMILY • MODERN Contemporary hotel right on the beachfront, with a relaxed ambience and superb sea views; take it all in from the large terrace. New England style bedrooms come with modern bathrooms and up-to-date facilities. The informal, split-level bar-cum-restaurant offers an accessible menu of modern classics.

44 rooms – †£ 109/151 ††£ 150/262

The Parade ✉ IP15 5BU
– ✆ 01728 551636 – www.brudenellhotel.co.uk

ALDERLEY EDGE

Cheshire East – Pop. 5 280 – Regional map n° **11**-B3

Alderley

MODERN BRITISH • ELEGANT XX Set in a gothic style building in the grounds of a country house, this formal conservatory restaurant has a long-standing reputation. Modern British dishes feature some interesting twists; the wine list offers a good range of bordeaux.

Carte £ 46/51

Alderley Edge Hotel, Macclesfield Rd ✉ SK9 7BJ
– ✆ 01625 583033 – www.alderleyedgehotel.com – Closed Sunday dinner to non residents

The Brasserie

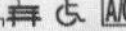

TRADITIONAL BRITISH • BRASSERIE X An informal French-style brasserie with mirrored walls and leather banquettes, set within a country house hotel. Retro British dishes like prawn and crayfish cocktail, scampi in a basket and jam roly poly are given a modern twist.

Carte £ 27/38

Alderley Edge Hotel, Macclesfield Rd ✉ SK9 7BJ
– ✆ 01625 583033 – www.alderleyedgehotel.com – Closed Sunday

Alderley Edge

BUSINESS • CLASSIC This well-run, early Victorian country house sits in an affluent village. Compact guest areas are smartly furnished. Bedrooms in the main house have the most character; those at the back are smaller but look out over the gardens.

50 rooms – £ 110/140 £ 120/160 – 1 suite

Macclesfield Rd ✉ SK9 7BJ – ☎ 01625 583033 – www.alderleyedgehotel.com

The Brasserie • **Alderley** – See restaurant listing

ALFRISTON

East Sussex – ✉ Polegate – Pop. 829 – Regional map n° **5**-A3

Wingrove House

MODERN BRITISH • BRASSERIE XX This imposing colonial-style building conceals a spacious brasserie and a comfy lounge. It's personally run and has a relaxed, informal feel. Menus change seasonally and offer appealing, unfussy dishes with a modern British style. Bedrooms are stylish and understated; two have access to the heated balcony.

Menu £ 25/35

12 rooms – £ 100/180 £ 125/200

High St ✉ BN26 5TD – ☎ 01323 870276 – www.wingrovehousealfriston.com – dinner only and lunch Saturday and Sunday – Closed 25 December

ALKHAM

Kent – Pop. 351 – Regional map n° **5**-D2

Marquis

MODERN CUISINE • DESIGN XX Fashionable former pub with a smart bar, a stylish dining room and a relaxed atmosphere. Accomplished cooking features classic combinations with original touches and modern presentation. The lunch menu is good value and they even have their own sparkling wine! Chic, sexy bedrooms boast luxurious bathrooms.

Menu £ 20 (lunch) – Carte £ 35/44

10 rooms – £ 129/149 £ 159/189

Alkham Valley Rd ✉ CT15 7DF – ☎ 01304 873410 – www.themarquisatalkham.co.uk

Alkham Court

FAMILY • RURAL Set on a hill, surrounded by mature grounds, is this delightful guesthouse with a hot tub and sauna. Homely, well-equipped bedrooms come with complimentary sherry and stylish bathrooms. The large conservatory has lovely country views.

4 rooms – £ 80/100 £ 140/170

Meggett Ln ✉ CT15 7DG – Southwest : 1 mi by Alkham Valley Rd – ☎ 01303 892056 – www.alkhamcourt.co.uk

ALNWICK

Northumberland – Pop. 8 116 – Regional map n° **14**-B2

Greycroft

TOWNHOUSE • PERSONALISED 19C house near the Castle, run by welcoming owners with good local knowledge. Bedrooms are well-equipped and have homely touches; the conservatory breakfast room overlooks a lovely walled garden.

6 rooms – £ 65/85 £ 95/135

Croft Pl ✉ NE66 1XU – via Prudhoe St – ☎ 01665 602127 – www.greycroftalnwick.co.uk – Closed mid December-mid January

West Acre House

TOWNHOUSE • PERSONALISED Proudly run Edwardian villa with a beautifully maintained 1 acre garden. Well-proportioned rooms come with bold wallpapers, Arts and Crafts features and a keen eye for detail; choose a Georgian, Edwardian, Oriental or Parisian theme.

4 rooms – †£ 100/130 ††£ 100/130

West Acres ✉ NE66 2QA – East : 0.5 mi by A 1068
– ✆ 01665 510374 – www.westacrehouse.co.uk

ALSTONEFIELD

Staffordshire – Pop. 274 – Regional map n° **10**-C1

The George

TRADITIONAL CUISINE • PUB Simply furnished, 18C pub on the village green, with a roaring fire and a relaxed, cosy atmosphere; it has been in the same family for three generations. Daily changing menus offer well-priced, down-to-earth dishes.

Carte £ 23/49

✉ DE6 2FX – ✆ 01335 310205 – www.thegeorgeatalstonefield.com – Closed 25 December

AMBERLEY

West Sussex – ✉ Arundel – Pop. 586 – Regional map n° **4**-C2

Queen's Room

MODERN BRITISH • ELEGANT XXX Within the walls of a stunning 12C castle is this elegant dining room with a barrel-vaulted ceiling, lancet windows and an open fire. Ambitious modern dishes arrive artfully presented. Henry VIII's wives all visited, hence its name.

Menu £ 35/68

Amberley Castle Hotel, ✉ BN18 9LT – Southwest : 0.5 mi on B 2139
– ✆ 01798 831992 (booking essential) – www.amberleycastle.co.uk

Amberley Castle

LUXURY • HISTORIC Stunning 12C castle displaying original stonework, battlements and evidence of a moat. The charming grounds consist of lovely gardens, lakes and a croquet lawn, and are matched inside by a characterful array of rooms. Sumptuous bedrooms have a palpable sense of history; those in the main castle are the best.

19 rooms – †£ 175/300 ††£ 175/660 – 6 suites

✉ BN18 9LT
– ✆ 01798 831992 – www.amberleycastle.co.uk

Queen's Room – See restaurant listing

AMBLESIDE

Cumbria – Pop. 2 529 – Regional map n° **12**-A2

The Samling

MODERN CUISINE • DESIGN XXX A stunning glass and slate restaurant with wonderful lake and country views; start with drinks on the terrace or in the stylish lounge. Eye-catching modern dishes have playful elements and showcase garden ingredients.

Menu £ 45/80 – tasting menu only

The Samling Hotel, Ambleside Rd ✉ LA23 1LR – South : 1.5 mi on A 591
– ✆ 015394 31922 (booking essential) – www.thesamlinghotel.co.uk

Lake Road Kitchen

SCANDINAVIAN • NEIGHBOURHOOD The passionate chef-owner of this small restaurant used to work in Copenhagen and the concise daily menu features some excellent Nordic-inspired combinations. Well-crafted modern dishes use top Scandic and locally foraged produce.

Menu £ 65 – tasting menu only

Lake Rd ✉ LA22 0AD – ✆ 015394 22012 – www.lakeroadkitchen.co.uk – dinner only – Closed Monday and Tuesday

Old Stamp House

MODERN CUISINE • INTIMATE Named after William Wordsworth, the 'Distributor of Stamps' for Westmorland from 1813-1843. A stone floor and exposed beams set the scene for an intimate dining experience. Cooking is modern, complex and champions Cumbrian produce.

Menu £ 20 (lunch) – Carte £ 36/52

Church St ✉ LA22 0BU – ✆ 015394 32775 – www.oldstamphouse.com – Closed Christmas, 3-25 January, Sunday and Monday

Drunken Duck Inn

TRADITIONAL BRITISH • RURAL Attractive pub in the heart of the beautiful Lakeland countryside, with a characterful, fire-lit bar and two more formal dining rooms. Simple lunches are followed by elaborate dinners with prices to match; cooking is generous and service, attentive. Ales are brewed on-site. Boutique, country house bedrooms – some with patios – have large squashy beds and country views.

Menu £ 38 (dinner) – Carte lunch approx. £ 19

13 rooms – †£ 94/244 ††£ 125/325

Barngates ✉ LA22 0NG – Southwest : 3 mi by A 593 and B 5286 on Tarn Hows rd – ✆ 015394 36347 (booking essential at dinner) – www.drunkenduckinn.co.uk – Closed 25 December

The Samling

COUNTRY HOUSE • CONTEMPORARY A former farmhouse and outbuildings perched on the hillside; the outdoor hot tub is the perfect spot to take in the stunning lake and fell views. Both the guest areas and the bedrooms have a stylish, contemporary look.

11 rooms – †£ 350/420 ††£ 350/420 – 2 suites

Ambleside Rd ✉ LA23 1LR – South : 1.5 mi on A 591 – ✆ 015394 31922 – www.thesamlinghotel.co.uk

The Samling – See restaurant listing

Nanny Brow

COUNTRY HOUSE • HISTORIC Charming Arts and Crafts house with views of the River Brathay and the Langdale Fells. Spacious, antique-furnished bedrooms sit above an elegant lounge. Original stained glass, wood panelling and impressive fireplaces feature.

14 rooms – †£ 145/280 ††£ 160/295

Clappersgate ✉ LA22 9NF – Southwest : 1.25 mi on A 593 – ✆ 015394 33232 – www.nannybrow.co.uk – Closed 25-26 December

Riverside

TRADITIONAL • COSY A homely slate house in a peaceful riverside location; run by delightful owners. The steep, mature garden is filled with rhododendrons. Bedroom 2 has a four-poster, a whirlpool bath and water views. Breakfast is locally sourced.

6 rooms – †£ 106/126 ††£ 116/136

Under Loughrigg ✉ LA22 9LJ – West : 1 mi by A 591 and A 593 – ✆ 015394 32395 – www.riverside-at-ambleside.co.uk – Closed 7 December-24 January

AMERSHAM (Old Town)

Buckinghamshire – Pop. 23 086 – Regional map n° **6**-D2

Artichoke

MODERN BRITISH · ELEGANT XX 16C red-brick house in a picturesque town. A narrow beamed room with polished tables leads through to a Scandic-style extension with a semi-open kitchen and glass screens etched with branches. Modern dishes are nicely presented.

Menu £ 28 (weekday lunch)/48 – Carte lunch £ 43/49

9 Market Sq ✉ HP7 0DF
– ✆ 01494 726611 (booking essential at dinner) – www.artichokerestaurant.co.uk – Closed 2 weeks Christmas-New Year, 2 weeks late August, 1 week Easter, Sunday and Monday

Hawkyns N

MODERN BRITISH · DESIGN XX Set within a 16C red-brick coaching inn, in the heart of a picturesque town, this heavily timbered restaurant has a warm, welcoming feel. Original modern dishes are artistically presented; the Green Egg is used to good effect.

Menu £ 32 (lunch) – Carte £ 31/52

Crown Inn, 16 High St ✉ HP7 0DH
– ✆ 01494 721541 (bookings advisable at dinner) – www.hawkynsrestaurant.co.uk – Closed Sunday dinner and Monday

Gilbey's

TRADITIONAL BRITISH · COSY X Set within a 17C former school, a long-standing neighbourhood restaurant which comprises three rustic rooms and a delightful terrace. It's rooted in tradition, from the furnishings to the food; go for the steak.

Menu £ 15 (weekdays)/29 – Carte £ 34/58

1 Market Sq ✉ HP7 0DF
– ✆ 01494 727242 (booking essential) – www.gilbeygroup.com – Closed 23-30 December

AMPLEFORTH – North Yorkshire → See Helmsley

ANTONY

Cornwall – Regional map n° **1**-C2

Carew Arms N

MODERN CUISINE · FRIENDLY A friendly little pub with a bright interior; they also operate the village shop from the next room. Pop in for a local beer and a scotch egg, a pub favourite or something more interesting like scallops with chorizo and apple jam.

Carte £ 23/37

Antony Hill ✉ PL11 3AB
– ✆ 01752 814440 – www.carewarms.com – Closed 25 December and Monday

APPLEBY-IN-WESTMORLAND

Cumbria – Pop. 2 862 – Regional map n° **12**-B2

Tufton Arms

TRADITIONAL · CLASSIC 16C coaching inn, in an old market town; a popular place for fishing and shooting parties. Guest areas include two traditional lounges and a bar; chic bedrooms are a complete contrast with their bold, contemporary furnishings. The classical, cane-furnished restaurant offers an easy-going menu.

22 rooms – †£ 85/145 ††£ 140/210

Market Sq ✉ CA16 6XA
– ✆ 017683 51593 – www.tuftonarmshotel.co.uk – Closed 24-27 December

ARKENDALE

North Yorkshire – Regional map n° **13**-B2

Blue Bell

TRADITIONAL BRITISH • COSY This might be a modern dining pub but it still has plenty of character, courtesy of hops hanging over the bar, sofas set in front of a wood burning stove and locals hanging out with their dogs. When it comes to the food, everything is homemade. Upstairs are four smart bedrooms with super king sized beds.

Carte £ 23/31

4 rooms – †£ 70/130 ††£ 80/140

Moor Ln ✉ HG5 0QT – ✆ 01423 369242 – www.thebluebellatarkendale.co.uk

ARLINGHAM

Gloucestershire – Pop. 459 – Regional map n° **2**-C1

Old Passage Inn

SEAFOOD • FRIENDLY XX Sit out on the terrace or beside the window, surrounded by colourful art, and watch the famous Severn bore travel up the estuary. Extensive seafood menus offer everything from a fish pie to a fruits de mer platter or lobster direct from their saltwater tank. Simply furnished modern bedrooms share the view.

Menu £ 16 (weekday lunch) – Carte £ 38/61

2 rooms – †£ 80/120 ††£ 110/140

Passage Rd ✉ GL2 7JR – West : 0.75 mi – ✆ 01452 740547 – www.theoldpassage.com – Closed 25-27 December, Sunday dinner, Monday and dinner Tuesday-Wednesday January-March

ARMSCOTE

Warwickshire – Regional map n° **10**-C3

Fuzzy Duck

TRADITIONAL CUISINE • PUB Siblings Adrian and Tania – also owners of toiletries company Baylis & Harding – took this place from boarded up boozer to welcoming, fashionably attired dining pub. Seasonal British dishes use great quality local and sustainable ingredients. Stylish boutique bedrooms complete the picture.

Menu £ 20 (weekday lunch) – Carte £ 24/43

4 rooms – †£ 110/160 ††£ 110/160

Ilmington Rd ✉ CV37 8DD – ✆ 01608 682635 (booking advisable) – www.fuzzyduckarmscote.com – Closed 26 December, Sunday dinner and Monday

ARNSIDE

Cumbria – Pop. 2 334 – Regional map n° **12**-A3

Number 43

TRADITIONAL • GRAND LUXURY Stylishly converted Victorian townhouse boasting superb views over the estuary and fells. Contemporary bedrooms have smart bathrooms, quality furnishings, good facilities and plenty of extras. The comfortable open-plan lounge and dining room offers light meat and cheese sharing platters in the evening. Start the day with breakfast on the glass-enclosed terrace.

6 rooms – †£ 90/145 ††£ 135/185

43 The Promenade ✉ LA5 0AA – ✆ 01524 762761 – www.no43.org.uk

ARUNDEL

West Sussex – Pop. 3 285 – Regional map n° **4**-C2

Parsons Table

MODERN BRITISH • FRIENDLY XX Tucked away in a little courtyard is this lovely restaurant with a fresh modern feel. Flavoursome dishes have a hint of modernity and are as seasonal and local as the quality of the produce will allow. Service comes with a smile.

Menu £ 18 (lunch) – Carte £ 30/38

2 & 8 Castle Mews, Tarrant St ✉ BN18 9DG – ✆ 01903 883477 – www.theparsonstable.co.uk – Closed 1 week February, 1 week late August, 24-28 December, Sunday and Monday

Town House

MODERN CUISINE • ELEGANT XX If you're a fan of Renaissance architecture, head for this early 17C townhouse, where you'll find a gilt walnut panelled ceiling which was originally installed in the Medici Palace in Florence. Confidently executed, tried-and-tested dishes have a classic base. Bedrooms include a family room in the old attic.

Menu £ 18/30

5 rooms – †£ 75/110 ††£ 110/150

65 High St ✉ BN18 9AJ – ✆ 01903 883847 – www.thetownhouse.co.uk – Closed 2 weeks Easter, 2 weeks October-November, 25-26 December, 1-2 January, Sunday and Monday

at Burpham Northeast: 3 mi by A27 ✉ Arundel

The George at Burpham

MODERN BRITISH • RUSTIC A local consortium headed by three local businessmen saved this pub from closure and it's since been given a smart new look, to which beams, fires and a smugglers' wheel add character. The seasonal menu is full of tasty, popular classics.

Carte £ 30/40

Main St ✉ BN18 9RR – ✆ 01903 883131 – www.georgeatburpham.co.uk – Closed 25 December and dinner Sunday-Monday in winter

ASCOT

Windsor and Maidenhead – Pop. 15 761 – Regional map n° **6**-D3

Coworth Park

MODERN CUISINE • ELEGANT XXXX An elegant, intimate restaurant in a beautiful house, with a striking copper chandelier to match the autumnal colours, and a lovely terrace overlooking manicured gardens. The assured, technically skilled cooking is modern yet respectful of classic combinations and display real depth and finesse.

→ Marinated langoustines with pork belly, fermented cabbage and apple. Lamb with sweetbreads, artichoke and asparagus. Almond mousse with Granny Smith and calvados

Menu £ 35/70

Coworth Park Hotel, London Rd ✉ SL5 7SE – East : 2.75 mi on A 329 – ✆ 01344 876600 (booking essential) – www.dorchestercollection.com – dinner only and lunch Friday-Sunday – Closed Sunday dinner, Monday and Tuesday

Ascot Grill

MEATS AND GRILLS • FASHIONABLE XX Neighbourhood restaurant with a slick, minimalistic interior featuring leather, silk and velvet; full-length windows open onto a pleasant pavement terrace. Wide-ranging modern grill menu offers steak and seafood. Good value lunches.

Carte £ 21/50

6 Hermitage Par, High St ✉ SL5 7HE – ✆ 01344 622285 – www.ascotgrill.co.uk – Closed first week January, Sunday dinner and Monday

Coworth Park

COUNTRY HOUSE • GRAND LUXURY A luxurious 18C property set in 246 acres, with stylish, contemporary guest areas and beautiful bedrooms featuring bespoke furniture, marble bathrooms and excellent facilities; those in main house are the largest. Dine in the elegant restaurant or more causal brasserie, overlooking their championship polo fields. The superb spa has a 'living roof' of herbs and flowers.

70 rooms – £ 354/1077 £ 354/1077 – 21 suites

London Rd ✉ SL5 7SE – East : 2.75 mi on A 329 – ✆ 01344 876600 – www.dorchestercollection.com

Coworth Park – See restaurant listing

ASHBOURNE

Derbyshire – Pop. 8 377 – Regional map n° **9**-A2

Callow Hall

TRADITIONAL • PERSONALISED Traditional Victorian country house in 30 acres of gardens, fields and woodland. Individually styled bedrooms boast original features, spacious bathrooms, and traditional fabrics and furnishings. Seasonal menus showcase local produce in classically based dishes with the occasional modern touch.

16 rooms – £ 115/160 £ 115/160 – 1 suite

Mapleton Rd ✉ DE6 2AA – West : 0.75 mi by Union St (off Market Pl) – ✆ 01335 300900 – www.callowhall.co.uk

at Shirley Southeast: 5 mi by A515 and off A52

Saracen's Head

TRADITIONAL BRITISH • RUSTIC A rustic, open-plan dining pub opposite the village church, in a remote, picturesque village. Menus are chalked on blackboards above the open fire and offer an eclectic mix of generously portioned pub and restaurant-style classics.

Carte £ 21/38

Church Ln ✉ DE6 3AS – ✆ 01335 360330 – www.saracens-head-shirley.co.uk

ASHBURTON

Devon – Pop. 3 346 – Regional map n° **1**-C2

Agaric 

TOWNHOUSE • THEMED Friendly owners welcome you to this rustic guesthouse on the main street with its comfortable, simply furnished bedrooms. The single is decorated in a Chinese style, while the best is Havana with its four-poster bed and roll top bath.

4 rooms – £ 58/90 £ 120/140

36 North St ✉ TQ13 7QD – ✆ 01364 654478 – www.agaricrestaurant.co.uk – Closed Christmas

ASHENDON

Buckinghamshire – Regional map n° **6**-C2

The Hundred of Ashendon

REGIONAL CUISINE • FRIENDLY In Saxon times, shires were divided into 'hundreds' for military and judicial purposes. This charming 17C inn keeps the concept alive by sourcing its produce from within its 'hundred'. Great value dishes arrive in hearty portions, packed full of flavour – and influences from Matt's time at St John are clear to see. Modest bedrooms are continually being upgraded.

Menu £ 15 (weekday lunch) – Carte £ 24/36

5 rooms – £ 55/85 £ 70/105

Lower End ✉ HP18 0HE – ✆ 01296 651296 – www.thehundred.co.uk – Closed 25 December, Sunday dinner and Monday

ASHFORD

Kent – Pop. 67 528 – Regional map n° **5**-C2

Eastwell Manor

LUXURY • HISTORIC Impressive manor house with Tudor origins, surrounded by beautifully manicured gardens and extensive parkland. Rebuilt in 1926 following a fire but some superb plaster ceilings and stone fireplaces remain. Characterful guest areas and luxurious bedrooms. Sizeable spa and golf course. Choice of wood-panelled restaurant complete with pianist or more casual brasserie and terrace.

42 rooms – £ 99/450 £ 99/450 – 20 suites

Eastwell Park, Boughton Lees ✉ TN25 4HR – North : 3 mi by A 28 on A 251 – ✆ 01233 213000 – www.eastwellmanor.co.uk

ASHFORD-IN-THE-WATER

Derbyshire – Regional map n° **9**-A1

Riverside House

TRADITIONAL • COSY Charming former hunting lodge with gardens running down to the river. Comfy, individually styled bedrooms are named after flowers and birds: one is a four-poster and some have French doors opening onto garden terraces. Classical dining takes place over four different rooms. It has a homely feel throughout.

14 rooms – £ 120/155 £ 145/195

Fennel St ✉ DE45 1QF – ✆ 01629 814275 – www.riversidehousehotel.co.uk

ASKHAM – Cumbria ➜ See Penrith

ASKRIGG

North Yorkshire – ✉ Leyburn – Pop. 1 002 – Regional map n° **13**-A1

Yorebridge House

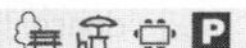

MODERN BRITISH • INTIMATE XX Romantic restaurant set within an old schoolmaster's house and offering lovely countryside views. Concise menus evolve with the seasons and feature locally sourced produce; dishes are modern, flavoursome and attractively presented.

Menu £ 60

Yorebridge House Hotel, Bainbridge ✉ DL8 3EE – West : 1.25 mi – ✆ 01969 652060 (bookings essential for non-residents) – www.yorebridgehouse.com – dinner only

Yorebridge House

COUNTRY HOUSE • CONTEMPORARY Stylish former schoolmaster's house in a lovely Dales setting, with a snug bar and great country views. Bold modern bedrooms are themed around the owner's travels; those in the old schoolhouse have riverside patios and hot tubs.

12 rooms – £ 195/230 £ 220/410

Bainbridge ✉ DL8 3EE – West : 1.25 mi – ✆ 01969 652060 – www.yorebridgehouse.com

Yorebridge House – See restaurant listing

ATTLEBOROUGH

Norfolk – Pop. 10 549 – Regional map n° **8**-C2

Mulberry Tree

MODERN CUISINE • BRASSERIE X A casual, contemporary bar-cum-restaurant in an imposing Victorian property. The bar menu is popular at lunchtime, while the modern à la carte offers attractively presented, globally-influenced dishes. In summer, head through to the pleasant garden and terrace. Bedrooms are stylish and very comfortable.

Carte £ 24/41

7 rooms – £ 85 £ 120

Station Rd ✉ NR17 2AS – ✆ 01953 452124 – www.mulberrytree.co.uk – Closed 24-27 December and Sunday

AUGHTON

Lancashire – Pop. 8 342 – Regional map n° **11**-A2

Moor Hall (Mark Birchall)

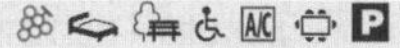

MODERN BRITISH • DESIGN XXX Set in charming grounds; a 16C house with stylish, spacious bedrooms. Cosy wood-panelled lounges contrast with an ultra-modern glass-fronted restaurant and an impressive open kitchen. The experienced chef brings his knowledge together in a style of his own: vibrant dishes stay true to the classic flavours of the region whilst skilfully combining modern techniques.

➜ Aged beef in charcoal with barbecued celeriac, mustard and shallot. Turbot with mussel cream and sea vegetables. Honey beer, bramley apple, aged caramel and marigold.

Menu £ 35/95

7 rooms – †£ 195/350 ††£ 195/350

Prescot Rd ✉ L39 6RT – On B 5197
– ✆ 01695 572511 (booking essential) – www.moorhall.com – Closed first 2 weeks August, 2 weeks January, Monday and Tuesday

AUSTWICK

North Yorkshire – Pop. 463 – Regional map n° **13**-A2

Traddock

COUNTRY HOUSE • PERSONALISED Unusually named after a horse trading paddock; a Georgian country house with Victorian additions – once a private residence. Inside it's traditional with bright, airy lounges and bedrooms boasting feature beds and country views. The formal dining room serves local produce in updated versions of old classics.

12 rooms – †£ 99/170 ††£ 99/260

✉ LA2 8BY – ✆ 015242 51224 – www.thetraddock.co.uk

Austwick Hall

HISTORIC BUILDING • PERSONALISED Set in a delightful village on the edge of the Dales and surrounded by tiered gardens, is this characterful house built in 1590 for the Master of the Mint. The flagged hall has an impressive stained glass window framed by two columns and antiques abound. Nothing is too much trouble for the friendly owners.

4 rooms – †£ 110/140 ††£ 125/155

Townhead Lane ✉ LA2 8BS – ✆ 015242 51794 – www.austwickhall.co.uk

AXMINSTER

Devon – Pop. 5 761 – Regional map n° **1**-D2

River Cottage Canteen

REGIONAL CUISINE • RUSTIC X Busy restaurant, deli and coffee shop owned by Hugh Fearnley-Whittingstall. The slightly stark rear room was once a dance hall. Menus change twice-daily and offer gutsy, flavoursome country dishes which showcase local produce.

Carte £ 26/38

Trinity Sq ✉ EX13 5AN – ✆ 01297 631715 – www.rivercottage.net – Closed 25 December, Sunday-Monday dinner and Tuesday November-April

AYLESBURY

Buckinghamshire – Pop. 71 977 – Regional map n° **6**-C2

Hartwell House

HISTORIC · CLASSIC An impressive palatial house set in 90 acres of parkland: the erstwhile residence of Louis XVIII, exiled King of France, and now owned by the National Trust. It boasts ornate furnishings, luxurious lounges, an intimate spa and magnificent antique-filled bedrooms. The formal restaurant offers traditional country house cooking and afternoon tea is a speciality.

48 rooms – £ 230/660 £ 310/720 – 10 suites

Oxford Rd ✉ HP17 8NR – Southwest : 2 mi on A 418
– ✆ 01296 747444 – www.hartwell-house.com

AYLESFORD

Kent – Regional map n° **5**-B1

Hengist

MODERN BRITISH · FASHIONABLE XX Sit either on the rustic ground floor or on the boldly decorated first floor of this characterful 16C timbered house. Good-sized menus offer ambitious modern British dishes. In summer, find a spot on the terrace beside the stream.

Menu £ 15 (weekday lunch) – Carte £ 26/48

7-9 High St ✉ ME20 7AX
– ✆ 01622 885800 – www.hengistrestaurant.co.uk – Closed 26 December

AYOT GREEN – Hertfordshire ➜ See Welwyn

AYSGARTH

North Yorkshire – Regional map n° **13**-A1

Aysgarth Falls

MODERN BRITISH · INN Just up the road from the waterfalls, you'll find this homely roadside inn with three terraces. Menus evolve constantly and offer a mix of pub classics, homemade pizzas and more ambitious dishes; specials are often based around east coast fish. Contemporary bedrooms have views of the surrounding Dales.

Carte £ 21/41

13 rooms – £ 85/135 £ 85/135

✉ DL8 3SR
– ✆ 01969 663775 – www.aysgarthfallshotel.com – Restricted opening in January

Stow House

COUNTRY HOUSE · PERSONALISED A Gothic-style residence built in 1876 for the Rev Stow, which sits in an enviable position looking down the valley. The owners have an extensive art collection and the smart retro bedrooms are named after pictures on their walls.

7 rooms – £ 100/165 £ 110/175

✉ DL8 3SR – East : 0.5 mi on A 684
– ✆ 01969 663635 – www.stowhouse.co.uk

Prices quoted after the symbol refer to the lowest rate for a single room in low season, followed by the highest rate in high season. The same principle applies to the symbol for a double room.

BABBACOMBE - Torbay → See Torquay

BAGSHOT
Surrey - Pop. 5 430 - Regional map n° **4**-C1

✿ **Matt Worswick at The Latymer**

MODERN CUISINE • CLASSIC DÉCOR XXX Traditional dark wood panels and beams are offset by colourful, boldly printed fabrics, which give this formal hotel dining room an elegant, contemporary feel. Choose between two set menus of deceptively simple-looking dishes, which have superb depth and show a great understanding of complimentary flavours.

→ Smoked eel with pickled turnip, compressed apple and dashi. Loin of venison with roasted heart and chanterelle mushrooms. Passion fruit cream, mango gel and coconut ice cream.

Menu £ 70/100 - tasting menu only

Pennyhill Park Hotel, London Rd ✉ GU19 5EU - Southwest : 1 mi on A 30 - ✆ 01276 471774 - www.exclusivehotels.co.uk - dinner only and lunch Thursday-Friday - Closed 3 weeks January and Monday-Tuesday

Pennyhill Park 

LUXURY • CLASSIC An impressive 19C manor house set in 123 acres and boasting one of Europe's best spas. Both the guest areas and the bedrooms are spacious, with period furnishings and modern touches; feature bathrooms come with rain showers or glass baths. Dine in the elegant restaurant or stylish brasserie.

123 rooms - †£ 255/455 ††£ 255/455 - ☕ £ 21 - 11 suites

London Rd ✉ GU19 5EU - ✆ 01276 471774 - www.exclusivehotels.co.uk

✿ **Matt Worswick at The Latymer** - See restaurant listing

BALLASALLA → See Man (Isle of)

BAMBURGH
Northumberland - Pop. 279 - Regional map n° **14**-B1

Potted Lobster Ⓝ 

SEAFOOD • FRIENDLY X A sweet, homely bistro hung with dramatic local seascapes; sit outside for a view of the majestic castle. Classic dishes come in large portions. Check the blackboard for the latest catch; the squid and oysters are must-tries.

Carte £ 25/40

3 Lucker Rd ✉ NE69 7BS - ✆ 01668 214088 - www.thepottedlobsterbamburgh.co.uk - Restricted opening in winter

Lord Crewe Arms 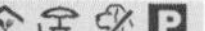

INN • COSY Smart 17C former coaching inn, privately owned and superbly set in the shadow of a famous Norman castle. Comfy, cosy bedrooms have a modern feel, yet are in keeping with the age of the building. Characterful stone-walled bar and New England style restaurant serve brasserie dishes. Efficient service.

7 rooms ☕ - †£ 80 ††£ 105/135

Front St ✉ NE69 7BL - ✆ 01668 214243 - www.lord-crewe.co.uk - Closed 25 December

at Waren Mill West: 2.75 mi on B1342 ✉ Belford

 **Waren House** 

FAMILY • CLASSIC Personally run, antique-furnished country house set in beautiful, tranquil gardens. Bedrooms - some named after the owners' family members - mix classic and modern styles: some have four-posters and coastal views. Formal dining room boasts an ornate ceiling; traditional menus showcase local ingredients.

15 rooms ☕ - †£ 60/100 ††£ 100/160 - 2 suites

✉ NE70 7EE - ✆ 01668 214581 - www.warenhousehotel.co.uk

BAMPTON
Devon - Pop. 1 260 - Regional map n° **1**-D1

Swan

TRADITIONAL BRITISH • INN The Swan dates back to 1450, when it provided accommodation for craftsmen working on the village church. Its original inglenook fireplace and bread oven remain but the open-plan layout gives it an up-to-date feel. Unfussy pub classics arrive neatly presented. Smart, modern bedrooms are found on the 2nd floor.

Carte £ 24/38

3 rooms – £ 75/100 £ 85/105

Station Rd ✉ EX16 9NG

– ✆ 01398 332248 – www.theswan.co – Closed 25 December

BARNARD CASTLE

Durham – Pop. 7 040 – Regional map n° **14**-A3

at Greta Bridge Southeast: 4.5 mi off A66✉ Barnard Castle

Gilroy's

MODERN CUISINE • CLASSIC DÉCOR XX Smart hotel dining room with a lovely parquet floor, wood-panelling and bold splashes of colour here and there. Dishes are modern, attractively presented and employ some complex techniques. Start with a drink by the fire in the cosy lounge.

Menu £ 35

Morritt Hotel, ✉ DL12 9SE

– ✆ 01833 627232 – www.themorritt.co.uk – dinner only

Morritt

INN • PERSONALISED Attractive 19C inn on the site of an old Roman fort. The characterful interior cleverly blends the old and the new, with antiques and feature bedsteads offset by contemporary décor. The superb spa has a car garage theme. All-day snacks are served in the bar-bistro and there's a modern menu in the restaurant.

26 rooms – £ 65/110 £ 75/179 – 1 suite

✉ DL12 9SE

– ✆ 01833 627232 – www.themorritt.co.uk

Gilroy's – See restaurant listing

at Hutton Magna Southeast: 7.25 mi by A66

Oak Tree Inn

TRADITIONAL BRITISH • COSY Small but charming whitewashed pub with six tables flanked by green settles and a bench table for drinkers. It's run by a husband and wife team; he cooks, while she serves. Cooking is hearty and flavoursome with a rustic British style.

Carte £ 34/47

✉ DL11 7HH

– ✆ 01833 627371 (booking essential) – www.theoaktreehutton.co.uk – dinner only – Closed 24-27 and 31 December, 1-2 January and Monday

at Romaldkirk Northwest: 6 mi by A67 on B6277✉ Barnard Castle

Rose and Crown

TRADITIONAL BRITISH • INN A delightful Georgian inn overlooking three village greens, with a wonderfully characterful bar and a smart dining room. Menus focus on pub classics and showcase local produce. Well-equipped bedrooms are spread between the main building, the courtyard and the "Monk's House".

Carte £ 25/42 **s**

14 rooms – £ 100/165 £ 115/180

✉ DL12 9EB

– ✆ 01833 650213 – www.rose-and-crown.co.uk – Closed Christmas

BARNSLEY - Gloucestershire → See Cirencester

BARRASFORD

Northumberland – Regional map n° **14**-A2

Barrasford Arms

BRITISH TRADITIONAL • PUB Personally run 19C stone inn, close to Kielder Water and Hadrian's Wall. It has a traditional, homely atmosphere and the cosy fire is a huge draw. Pub classics are the focus at lunch, followed by more refined dishes at dinner, and many come for the local game. Bedrooms are comfortable and sensibly priced.

Menu £ 19/28 – Carte £ 24/32

7 rooms – £ 67 £ 87

NE48 4AA – 01434 681237 – www.barrasfordarms.co.uk
– Closed 25-26 December, Sunday dinner, Monday lunch and bank holidays

BARTON-ON-SEA

Hampshire – Regional map n° **4**-A3

Pebble Beach

SEAFOOD • FASHIONABLE XX Head for the terrace of this split-level restaurant for impressive views to the Isle of Wight. Inside, the open kitchen takes pride of place and the fish tank gives a clue as to the menu. Assured classic cooking comes from an experienced chef. Bedrooms are smart and well-kept; the Penthouse has the views.

Menu £ 25 – Carte £ 30/72

4 rooms – £ 80/110 £ 80/110

Marine Dr BH25 7DZ – 01425 627777 – www.pebblebeach-uk.com

BARWICK - Somerset → See Yeovil

BASLOW

Derbyshire – Pop. 1 178 – Regional map n° **9**-A1

Fischer's at Baslow Hall

MODERN CUISINE • ELEGANT XXX A fine Edwardian manor house with a country house feel, impressive formal grounds and a walled vegetable garden. The two dining rooms, with their ornate ceilings, offer a mix of classic and original modern dishes, prepared using skilful techniques; sit at the 'Kitchen Tasting Bench' to be part of the action. Bedrooms are charming – the garden rooms are the largest.

→ Pan-fried scallops with cauliflower, black pudding and Granny Smith apple. Roast loin of veal with crispy egg yolk, artichokes, leeks and truffle. Rhubarb crumble soufflé with vanilla ice cream and rhubarb schnapps.

Menu £ 30/78

11 rooms – £ 155/195 £ 230/295 – 1 suite

Calver Rd DE45 1RR – on A 623 – 01246 583259 (booking essential)
– www.fischers-baslowhall.co.uk – Closed 25-26 December

The Gallery

MODERN BRITISH • ELEGANT XXX A striking modern restaurant in an elegant hotel – sit below antique oil paintings looking out over the grounds. Well-presented, contemporary British dishes use estate produce; for a ringside seat book the chef's table.

Menu £ 50

Cavendish Hotel, Church Ln DE45 1SP – on A 619 – 01246 582311 (bookings advisable at dinner) – www.cavendish-hotel.net

Rowley's

TRADITIONAL CUISINE • BRASSERIE Stone-built former blacksmith's; now a contemporary bar-restaurant with a small terrace and friendly service. Dine in the buzzy ground floor bar or more intimate upstairs rooms. Hearty, satisfying dishes have classic French roots.

Menu £ 21/31 – Carte £ 27/39

Church St ✉ DE45 1RY – ✆ 01246 583880 (booking advisable) – www.rowleysrestaurant.co.uk – Closed 25 December and Sunday dinner

Cavendish

TRADITIONAL • PERSONALISED Set on the edge of the Chatsworth Estate is this fine stone building with superb parkland views. Delightful bedrooms are full of period charm and many are styled by national designers and the Duchess of Devonshire herself. Enjoy drinks in the plush bar-cum-sitting room or afternoon tea in the Garden Room.

24 rooms – †£ 165/340 ††£ 215/340 – ☕ £ 20 – 1 suite

Church Ln ✉ DE45 1SP – on A 619 – ✆ 01246 582311 – www.cavendish-hotel.net

The Gallery – See restaurant listing

Heathy Lea

COUNTRY HOUSE • PERSONALISED 17C farmhouse owned by the Chatsworth Estate – which has access to the grounds through its garden gate. Cosy, comfortable bedrooms have views over the farmland. The estate farm shop provides much of the produce used at breakfast.

3 rooms ☕ – †£ 60/120 ††£ 90/120

✉ DE45 1PQ – East : 0.75 mi on A 619 – ✆ 01246 583842 – www.heathylea.co.uk – Closed Christmas

BASSENTHWAITE

Cumbria – Pop. 433 – Regional map n° **12**-A2

Bistro at the Distillery

MODERN BRITISH • BISTRO Smart modern bistro in a former cattle shed; the other farm buildings now house a shop and a working gin, vodka and whisky distillery. Extensive lunches are followed by afternoon teas, with more ambitious dishes appearing at dinner.

Menu £ 21 (weekday lunch) – Carte £ 28/49

Bassenthwaite Lake ✉ CA13 9SJ – West : 2.75 mi by A 591 on B 5291 – ✆ 017687 88850 (booking advisable) – www.bistroatthedistillery.com – Closed 25 December

Pheasant

INN • CLASSIC Characterful 16C coaching inn with comfy lounges and welcoming open fires. Bedrooms are spacious and retain a classic look appropriate to the building's age; some have lovely country outlooks. Have drinks amongst polished brass in the bar then make for the rustic oak-furnished bistro or more formal restaurant.

15 rooms ☕ – †£ 115/135 ††£ 130/210

✉ CA13 9YE – Southwest : 3.25 mi by B 5291 on Wythop Mill Rd – ✆ 017687 76234 – www.the-pheasant.co.uk – Closed 25 December

I. Dagnall/age fotostock

GOOD TIPS!

Known for its Georgian architecture and its Roman Baths, this city is one in which to relax and rejuvenate, so keep a look out for the spa symbol when choosing a hotel. Locally produced Bath Buns are the star of the show at afternoon tea in the **Royal Crescent** hotel, in the centre of the famous terrace designed by John Wood the Younger.

BATH

Bath and North East Somerset – Pop. 94 782 – Regional map n° **2**-C2

Restaurants

Dower House

MODERN CUISINE • ELEGANT XXX Across the garden of a smart hotel is this elegant restaurant with gold and blue hues and a feature wall of hand-stitched silk. Dishes are modern and very visual; desserts are a highlight. 'Wine walls' display their finest bottles.

Carte £ 54/60

Town plan: C1-a – *Royal Crescent Hotel, 16 Royal Cres ✉ BA1 2LS – ✆ 01225 823333 – www.royalcrescent.co.uk – dinner only*

Menu Gordon Jones

MODERN CUISINE • SIMPLE XX Tiny restaurant comprising 8 tables and an open kitchen. Daily tasting menus showcase some unusual British ingredients such as beef tendons or rabbit kidneys. Complex modern dishes have interesting texture and flavour combinations.

Menu £ 45/55 – tasting menu only

Town plan: A2-e – *2 Wellsway ✉ BA2 3AQ – ✆ 01225 480871 (booking essential at dinner) – www.menugordonjones.co.uk – Closed 2 weeks January, 1-7 June, 1-14 September, 1-7 November, Christmas-New Year, Sunday and Monday*

Olive Tree

MODERN CUISINE • INTIMATE XX A stylish, well-run restaurant in the basement of a boutique hotel, with a small bar and three dining rooms – all on different levels. Refined, classic dishes focus on natural flavours and are delivered in a modern style.

Menu £ 32/68

Town plan: C1-x – *Queensberry Hotel, Russel St ✉ BA1 2QF – ✆ 01225 447928 – www.olivetreebath.co.uk – dinner only and lunch Friday-Sunday – Closed 1 week January, 2 weeks July-August and 1 week November*

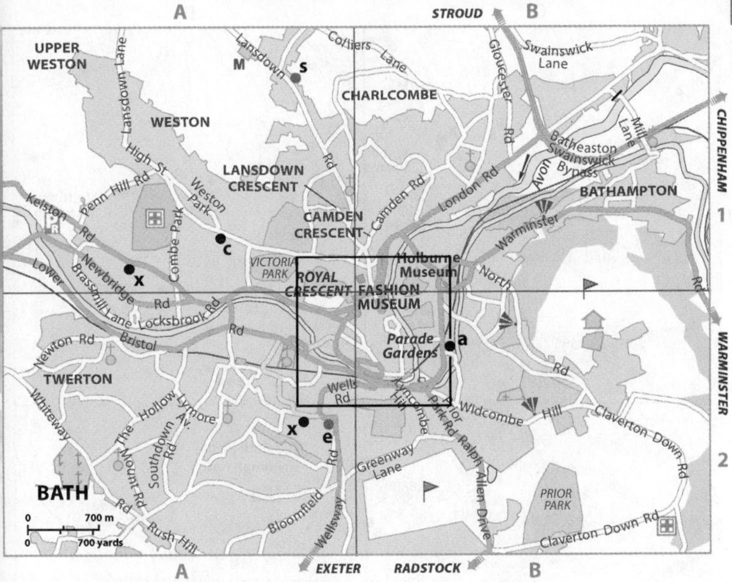

A
B
STROUD
UPPER WESTON
WESTON
CHARLCOMBE
LANSDOWN CRESCENT
CAMDEN CRESCENT
BATHAMPTON
VICTORIA PARK
ROYAL CRESCENT
FASHION MUSEUM
Holburne Museum
Parade Gardens
TWERTON
PRIOR PARK
BATH
0 700 m
0 700 yards
CHIPPENHAM
WARMINSTER
EXETER
RADSTOCK
1
2
Lansdown Lane
Lansdown
Colliers Lane
Gloucester Rd
Swainswick Lane
Mill Lane
Batheaston Swainswick Bypass
Avon
London Rd
Camden Rd
Warminster
North Rd
Kelston Rd
Penn Hill Rd
High St
Weston Park
Combe Park
Newbridge Rd
Lower Brassmill Lane
Locksbrook Rd
Bristol Rd
Newton Rd
Whiteway
The Hollow
Lymore Av.
Southdown Rd
The Mount Rd
Rush Hill
Wells Rd
Lyncombe Hill
Prior Park Rd
Widcombe Hill
Claverton Down Rd
Ralph Allen Drive
Greenway Lane
Bloomfield Rd
Wellsway
M
s
c
x
a
e

Acorn Ⓝ

VEGETARIAN • INTIMATE A sweet, intimate, split-level restaurant set within one of Bath's oldest buildings. Modern vegetarian dishes are full of colour and show a great understanding of flavours. Wines are carefully chosen to match the food.

Menu £ 23/34

Town plan: D2-a – *2 North Parade Passage ✉ BA1 1NX – ✆ 01225 446059 – www.acornvegetariankitchen.co.uk – Closed Christmas*

Circus

TRADITIONAL BRITISH • NEIGHBOURHOOD The small pavement terrace of this neighbourhood bistro is the perfect spot for people-watching in the historic heart of the city. Unfussy dishes use West Country produce and have a Mediterranean bias. Wines come from small growers.

Carte £ 21/37

Town plan: C1-c – *34 Brock St ✉ BA1 2LN – ✆ 01225 466020 (bookings advisable at dinner) – www.thecircusrestaurant.co.uk – Closed 23 December-14 January and Sunday*

Henry's

MODERN BRITISH • NEIGHBOURHOOD A laid-back bistro in a pretty pedestrianised street. It's simple yet appealing, with wooden furnishings and pictures of local scenes. Original modern dishes include some interesting vegetarian options.

Menu £ 18 (weekday lunch) – Carte £ 30/39

Town plan: C1-n – *4 Saville Row ✉ BA1 2QP – ✆ 01225 780055 – www.henrysrestaurantbath.com – Closed first week January, last 2 weeks July, 25-26 December, Sunday and Monday*

Chequers

TRADITIONAL CUISINE • NEIGHBOURHOOD Simply furnished pub set in a smart residential street, amid elegant Georgian terraces. Cooking is sophisticated and presentation, elaborate. The homemade bread is a highlight and creative desserts offer something a little different.

Carte £ 26/46

Town plan: C1-s – *50 Rivers St ✉ BA1 2QA – ✆ 01225 360017 – www.thechequersbath.com – Closed 25 December*

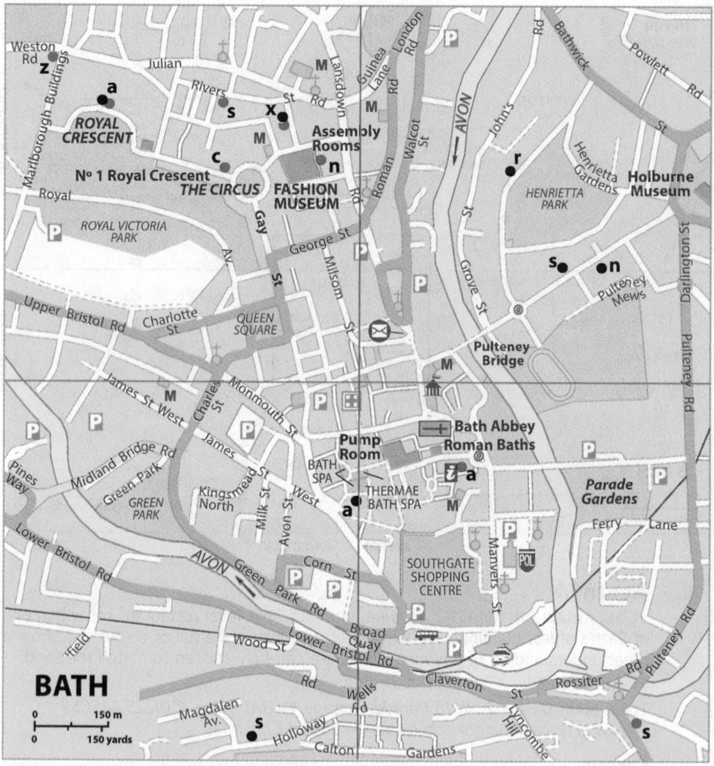

Hare & Hounds

TRADITIONAL CUISINE • PUB A huge pub, more suited to a celebration with friends than a romantic dinner for two. Its hillside location affords superb views and its gardens and terrace come into their own in summer. Menus offer modern versions of classic dishes.

Carte £ 25/41

Town plan: A1-s – *Lansdown Rd ✉ BA1 5TJ – North : 1.5 mi on Lansdown Rd – ✆ 01225 482682 – www.hareandhoundsbath.com*

Marlborough Tavern

TRADITIONAL BRITISH • NEIGHBOURHOOD 18C pub on the edge of Victoria Park, close to the Royal Crescent. Chic, fashionable interior with boldly patterned wallpapers and contemporary art. Carefully sourced ingredients feature in pub classics and interesting specials.

Carte £ 26/44

Town plan: C1-z – *35 Marlborough Buildings ✉ BA1 2LY – ✆ 01225 423731 – www.marlborough-tavern.com – Closed dinner 25-26 December*

Don't confuse the classification X with the Stars ✿!
The number of X denotes levels of comfort and service, while Stars are awarded solely for the cooking.

White Hart

TRADITIONAL CUISINE • SIMPLE Appealing pub on the south east edge of the city centre, with a local following and a neighbourhood feel. Generous portions of hearty cooking; smaller tapas plates are also popular.

Menu £ 15 (weekday lunch) – Carte £ 29/36

Town plan: D2-s – *Widcombe Hill ✉ BA2 6AA – ✆ 01225 338053 (booking essential at dinner) – www.whitehartbath.co.uk – Closed 25-26 December, 1 January, Sunday dinner and bank holidays*

Hotels

Royal Crescent

HISTORIC • ELEGANT Smartly refurbished Grade I listed building at the centre of a magnificent sweeping terrace. Ornate plasterwork, pastel shades and gilt-framed portraits evoke feelings of the Georgian era; bedrooms are plush and luxurious and come with marble-walled bathrooms. The lovely spa is in an old gothic chapel.

45 rooms – †£ 330/610 ††£ 330/610 – 12 suites

Town plan: C1-a – *16 Royal Cres ✉ BA1 2LS – ✆ 01225 823333 – www.royalcrescent.co.uk*

Dower House – See restaurant listing

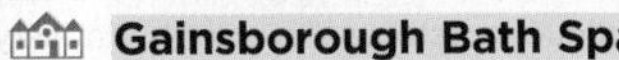

Gainsborough Bath Spa

THERMAL SPA • ELEGANT Set within two Grade II listed buildings, this hotel comes with an impressive state-of-the-art spa whose three thermal pools tap into the city's original springs. Bedrooms are elegantly understated and three have thermal water supplied directly to their baths. Enjoy afternoon tea in the Canvas Room and innovative, dramatically presented dishes in the restaurant.

99 rooms – †£ 242/495 ††£ 242/495 – £ 25

Town plan: C2-a – *Beau St ✉ BA1 1QY – ✆ 01225 358888 – www.thegainsboroughbathspa.co.uk*

Bath Priory

COUNTRY HOUSE • ELEGANT Two adjoining Georgian houses with formal gardens, an outdoor pool and an intimate spa. Country house guest areas are filled with antiques and oil paintings and luxurious bedrooms blend the traditional with the modern. Dine in the elegant restaurant, the more informal Pantry or out on the terrace.

33 rooms – †£ 155/795 ††£ 155/795 – £ 20 – 6 suites

Town plan: A1-c – *Weston Rd ✉ BA1 2XT – ✆ 01225 331922 – www.thebathpriory.co.uk*

Queensberry

TOWNHOUSE • CLASSIC A series of Georgian townhouses in one of the oldest parts of the city, run by a friendly team. Guest areas include a charming wood-panelled lounge and a chic bar with an extensive array of unusual spirits. Funky, individually designed bedrooms boast designer touches and a host of extras.

29 rooms – †£ 95/450 ††£ 95/450 – £ 13

Town plan: C1-x – *Russel St ✉ BA1 2QF – ✆ 01225 447928 – www.thequeensberry.co.uk*

Olive Tree – See restaurant listing

Dukes

TOWNHOUSE • CLASSIC Two Grade I listed Palladian-style townhouses, built in 1789, with a friendly, informal feel. Bedrooms are named after famous Dukes and have period themes. If you've skipped dinner, they offer a late night cheeseboard and port.

17 rooms – †£ 90/195 ††£ 90/195 – 4 suites

Town plan: D1-n – *Great Pulteney St ✉ BA2 4DN – ✆ 01225 787960 – www.dukesbath.co.uk – Closed 23-28 December*

No.15 Great Pulteney Ⓝ

TOWNHOUSE • ELEGANT Behind the Georgian façade there's a dramatic fusion of the elegant and the contemporary. Chic, restful bedrooms have top quality bedding and bespoke furnishings. Café No.15 serves light lunches and dinner Wednesday-Saturday, while the cocktail elegant bar is so popular you have to book at weekends.

40 rooms – †£ 110/530 ††£ 110/595 – ☕£ 20

Town plan: D1-s – *13-15 Great Pulteney St* ✉ *BA2 4BS*
– *☎ 01225 807015* – *www.no15greatpulteney.co.uk*

Apsley House

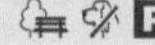

TOWNHOUSE • PERSONALISED Substantial 18C house built for the Duke of Wellington and still retaining many grand features. High-ceilinged guest areas have large fireplaces and chandeliers. Luxuriously appointed bedrooms display a subtle contemporary style.

12 rooms ☕ – †£ 90/220 ††£ 105/220

Town plan: A1-x – *141 Newbridge Hill* ✉ *BA1 3PT*
– *☎ 01225 336966* – *www.apsley-house.co.uk*
– *Closed 24-26 December*

Grays

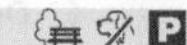

TOWNHOUSE • PERSONALISED This boutique guesthouse is run by a very hands-on family team. The ground floor bedrooms are largest, while those at the top have a cosy feel. The décor is light and modern, featuring family antiques and good attention to detail.

12 rooms ☕ – †£ 90/185 ††£ 110/205

Town plan: A2-x – *9 Upper Oldfield Pk* ✉ *BA2 3JX*
– *☎ 01225 403020* – *www.graysbath.co.uk*
– *Closed 24-26 December*

Paradise House

TOWNHOUSE • CLASSIC Elegant 18C house with award-winning gardens, set on Beechen Cliff, overlooking the city. The interior is charming and homely, with a cosy, classical lounge and bedrooms ranging from traditional four-posters to more modern styles.

12 rooms ☕ – †£ 89/205 ††£ 95/230

Town plan: C2-s – *86-88 Holloway* ✉ *BA2 4PX*
– *☎ 01225 317723* – *www.paradise-house.co.uk*
– *Closed 24-25 December*

Villa at Henrietta Park

TOWNHOUSE • CONTEMPORARY A smart Victorian house in an attractive residential area, set overlooking a park. The modern interior features two impressive staircases, and the stylish, airy bedrooms come with shuttered windows and feature wallpapers.

21 rooms – †£ 105/495 ††£ 105/495 – ☕£ 13

Town plan: D1-r – *Henrietta Rd* ✉ *BA2 6LX*
– *☎ 01225 466329* – *www.villahenriettapark.co.uk*

Brindleys

TOWNHOUSE • DESIGN Victorian house tucked away in a residential street and concealing a surprisingly chic interior. Cosy lounge and neatly laid breakfast room. Tastefully decorated bedrooms in colour themes ranging from lavender to monochrome.

6 rooms ☕ – †£ 75/180 ††£ 75/200

Town plan: B2-a – *14 Pulteney Gdns* ✉ *BA2 4HG*
– *☎ 01225 310444* – *www.brindleysbath.co.uk*
– *Closed Christmas*

at Colerne Northeast: 6.5 mi by A4 ✉ Chippenham

✿ Restaurant Hywel Jones by Lucknam Park

MODERN BRITISH • ELEGANT XXXX An aperitif in the library of this impressive mansion is a fine prelude to a formal dinner in the opulent dining room. Service is professional and the kitchen, knowledgeable. Classical menus display modern European influences, with dishes expertly crafted from top quality produce - some from the estate.

→ Dressed white crab, Exmoor caviar, violet artichoke, sesame and lemon. Brecon lamb, pea, asparagus and morels. Banana parfait with rum and raisin sponge, banana and passion fruit sorbet.

Menu £ 87 (weekdays)/110

Lucknam Park Hotel, ✉ SN14 8AZ - North : 0.5 mi on Marshfield rd - ☎ 01225 742777 (booking essential) - www.lucknampark.co.uk - dinner only and Sunday lunch - Closed Monday and Tuesday

Brasserie

INTERNATIONAL • FASHIONABLE XX A stylish brasserie in a beautiful courtyard within Lucknam Park's state-of-the-art spa. There's a spacious bar-lounge and an airy dining room with full-length windows. Precise, modern cooking arrives in well-judged combinations and many healthy options are available. Dine on the charming terrace in summer.

Menu £ 27 (lunch) - Carte £ 25/54

Lucknam Park Hotel, ✉ SN14 8AZ - North : 0.5 mi on Marshfield rd - ☎ 01225 742777 - www.lucknampark.co.uk

Lucknam Park

GRAND LUXURY • CLASSIC A grand Palladian mansion with a mile-long tree-lined drive, rich, elegant décor, luxurious furnishings and sumptuous fabrics. Bedrooms are classically furnished and extremely comfortable. Top class facilities include an impressive spa and well-being centre, a renowned equestrian centre and a cookery school.

42 rooms - †£ 305/625 ††£ 305/625 - ☕ £ 29 - 5 suites

✉ SN14 8AZ - North : 0.5 mi on Marshfield rd - ☎ 01225 742777 - www.lucknampark.co.uk

✿ **Restaurant Hywel Jones by Lucknam Park** • **Brasserie** - See restaurant listing

at Monkton Combe Southeast: 4.5 mi by A36 ✉ Bath

Wheelwrights Arms

TRADITIONAL CUISINE • PUB This charming inn is tucked away in a beautiful valley and, apart from the sound of birdsong, peace and quiet reigns. Cooking is traditional, although you'll find the occasional modern twist, and the blackboard specials are worth a look. There's a sunny terrace and bedrooms are warm and welcoming.

Menu £ 13 (weekday lunch) - Carte £ 25/37 **s**

7 rooms ☕ - †£ 85 ††£ 125/155

Church Ln ✉ BA2 7HB - ☎ 01225 722287 - www.wheelwrightsarms.co.uk - Closed dinner 25-26 December and 1 January

at Combe Hay Southwest: 5 mi by A367 ✉ Bath

Wheatsheaf

MODERN BRITISH • COSY It began life as a farmhouse in 1576 but now boasts modern styling, typified by pink flock wallpaper and vivid art, and a relaxed atmosphere, helped on its way by open fires and the pub's resident spaniels. Flavourful, seasonal food is presented in a contemporary style. Bedrooms have a spacious, modern feel.

Menu £ 24 - Carte £ 31/49

3 rooms ☕ - †£ 100/150 ††£ 120/150

✉ BA2 7EG - ☎ 01225 833504 - www.wheatsheafcombehay.com - Closed 10 days January, Sunday dinner and Monday

BAUGHURST

Hampshire – Regional map n° **4**-B1

Wellington Arms

TRADITIONAL CUISINE • PUB At this smart cream pub they have their own herb and vegetable beds, keep sheep, pigs, chickens and bees, and source the rest of their meats from within 20 miles. Menus feature 6 dishes per course – supplemented by a selection of specials – and cooking is generous and satisfying. Smart, rustic bedrooms come with slate floors, sheepskin rugs and big, comfy beds.

Menu £ 19 (weekday lunch) – Carte £ 22/45

4 rooms – £ 110/200 £ 110/200

Baughurst Rd RG26 5LP – Southwest : 0.5 mi – 0118 982 0110 (booking essential) – www.thewellingtonarms.com – Closed Sunday dinner

BEACONSFIELD

Buckinghamshire – Pop. 13 797 – Regional map n° **6**-D3

No 5 London End

MODERN BRITISH • BISTRO A welcoming, modern bistro with a faux-distressed interior and a mix of banquettes and burnished leather seats. Creative menus are highly seasonal and textures and flavours are well thought out; the set lunch is great value.

Menu £ 19 (lunch) – Carte £ 29/37

London End HP9 2HN – 01494 355500 – www.no5londonend.co.uk – Closed 25 December and Sunday dinner

Crazy Bear

LUXURY • DESIGN A unique hotel with sumptuous, over-the-top styling. Moody, masculine bedrooms blend original features with rich fabrics and idiosyncratic furnishings (some slightly less flamboyant bedrooms are located over the road). The lavishly styled 'English' restaurant uses produce from their farm shop, while sexy, extravagant 'Thai' serves Asian cuisine.

49 rooms – £ 290/490 £ 290/490

75 Wycombe End HP9 1LX – 01494 673086 – www.crazybeargroup.co.uk

at Seer Green Northeast: 2.5 mi by A355

Jolly Cricketers

TRADITIONAL BRITISH • PUB Charming Victorian pub filled with a host of cricketing memorabilia; even the menu is divided into 'Openers', 'Main Play' and 'Sticky Wicket'. Cooking pleasingly balances the classics with more modern choices. Staff are welcoming.

Carte £ 26/44

24 Chalfont Rd HP9 2YG – 01494 676308 (booking advisable) – www.thejollycricketers.co.uk – Closed Sunday dinner

BEAMINSTER

Dorset – Pop. 2 957 – Regional map n° **2**-B3

Beaminster Brasserie

MODERN CUISINE • BRASSERIE Start with a fireside drink in the bar of this charming hotel, then head for the Georgian dining room, the conservatory or the covered terrace. Menus showcase local produce and dishes are fresh, vibrant and attractively presented.

Menu £ 30 (weekday lunch) – Carte £ 33/45

Bridge House Hotel, 3 Prout Bridge DT8 3AY – 01308 862200 – www.bridge-house.co.uk

Brassica

MEDITERRANEAN CUISINE • BISTRO Two pretty little 16C houses on the small town square: one is a homeware shop and the other a laid-back restaurant. Tasty, rustic cooking is full of flavour; influences are Mediterranean, with a particular focus on Spain and Italy.

Menu £ 19 (lunch) – Carte £ 22/37

3-4 The Square ✉ DT8 3AS
– ✆ 01308 538100 (booking essential) – www.brassicarestaurant.co.uk – Closed 25-26 December, Sunday dinner, Monday and Tuesday

Bridge House

HISTORIC BUILDING • CONTEMPORARY Hugely characterful 13C priests' house. Relax by an inglenook fireplace in one of the traditional flag-floored lounges. Bedrooms in the main house are spacious and have original features; those in the 'CoachHouse' are more modern.

13 rooms – †£ 85/269 ††£ 99/269

3 Prout Bridge ✉ DT8 3AY
– ✆ 01308 862200 – www.bridge-house.co.uk

Beaminster Brasserie – See restaurant listing

BEARSTED

Kent – Regional map n° **5**-B2

Fish On The Green

SEAFOOD • NEIGHBOURHOOD Tucked away on a corner of the Green is this simply decorated restaurant with a pleasant terrace. Professional cooking focuses on fresh, tasty local seafood. The lunch menu is good value and service is polite and knowledgeable.

Menu £ 23 (lunch) – Carte £ 33/53

Church Ln, Bearsted Grn ✉ ME14 4EJ
– ✆ 01622 738300 (booking essential) – www.fishonthegreen.com – Closed 25 December-mid January, Sunday dinner and Monday

BEAULIEU

Hampshire – ✉ Brockenhurst – Pop. 726 – Regional map n° **4**-B2

The Terrace

MODERN BRITISH • TRADITIONAL DÉCOR This elegant dining room is found at the heart of an alluring 18C inn; sit on the terrace for views across the lovely gardens. Classically based dishes have a modern touch; fish is from the Solent and game from the New Forest.

Menu £ 30/70

Montagu Arms Hotel, Palace Ln ✉ SO42 7ZL
– ✆ 01590 612324 – www.montaguarmshotel.co.uk – Closed Monday and lunch Tuesday

Montagu Arms

INN • CLASSIC With its characterful parquet floors and wood panelling, this 18C inn has a timeless elegance. Traditional country house bedrooms marry antique furniture with modern facilities, and the conservatory and terrace overlook the lovely gardens. Dine on updated classics in the dining room or pub classics in Monty's.

22 rooms – †£ 139/244 ††£ 159/369 – 4 suites

Palace Ln ✉ SO42 7ZL
– ✆ 01590 612324 – www.montaguarmshotel.co.uk

The Terrace – See restaurant listing

BEAUMONT - Saint Peter → See Channel Islands (Jersey)

BEELEY

Derbyshire - Pop. 165 - Regional map n° **9**-B1

Devonshire Arms

TRADITIONAL BRITISH • INN Stone inn with a hugely characterful low-beamed bar and a bright modern brasserie extension with views of the village and stream. Have afternoon tea or choose from the lengthy classically based main menu; estate game is a speciality. Bedrooms in the inn and next door are cosy; those opposite are more modern.

Carte £ 25/40

14 rooms - †£ 89/279 ††£ 99/299

Devonshire Sq ✉ DE4 2NR - ✆ 01629 733259 (booking advisable) - www.devonshirebeeley.co.uk

BELCHFORD

Lincolnshire - ✉ Horncastle - Regional map n° **9**-C1

Blue Bell Inn

TRADITIONAL CUISINE • PUB Welcoming pub in a tiny hamlet in the Lincolnshire Wolds. A traditional bar with a copper-topped counter leads to a bright red dining room. Menus cover all bases, offering honest, home-cooked dishes which are big on flavour.

Carte £ 20/36

1 Main Rd ✉ LN9 6LQ - ✆ 01507 533602 - www.bluebellbelchford.co.uk - Closed 8-22 January

BELFORD

Northumberland - Pop. 1 258 - Regional map n° **14**-A1

Market Cross

TOWNHOUSE • PERSONALISED 200 year old stone townhouse, set close to the medieval cross in the market square and run by friendly, welcoming owners. Bright modern bedrooms come in neutral hues and feature complimentary sherry and Lindisfarne Mead. Local produce features at breakfast and dinner is served by arrangement.

4 rooms - †£ 60/100 ††£ 80/110

1 Church St ✉ NE70 7LS - ✆ 01668 213013 - www.marketcrossbelford.co.uk - Closed 21-28 December

BELPER

Derbyshire - Pop. 23 417 - Regional map n° **9**-B2

Chevin Green Farm

FAMILY • PERSONALISED Chevin Green has been in the family since 1929, when it was a working farm; the outbuildings are now homes, and the residents' families supply fresh produce to the farmhouse. The delightful owners have a passion for tea, so you'll find a great selection, alongside tea-themed artwork, ornaments and furnishings.

4 rooms - †£ 75/90 ††£ 99/125

Chevin Rd ✉ DE56 2UN - West : 2 mi by A 517 and Farnah Green Rd - ✆ 01773 822328 - www.chevingreenfarm.com

BENENDEN

Kent - Pop. 787 - Regional map n° **5**-B2

Ramsden Farm

FAMILY • PERSONALISED Attractive clapboard house with a refreshingly relaxed air and modern styling. Bedrooms are spacious, with a slight New England look, and the luxurious bathrooms have underfloor heating. Have breakfast in the country kitchen or out on the terrace and take in lovely garden and countryside views.

3 rooms – £ 95/120 £ 95/120

Dingleden Ln ✉ TN17 4JT – Southeast : 1 mi by B 2086 – ✆ 01580 240203 – www.ramsdenfarmhouse.co.uk

BEPTON

- West Sussex ➜ See Midhurst

BERKHAMSTED

Hertfordshire – Pop. 20 641 – Regional map n° **7**-A2

The Gatsby

MODERN BRITISH • HISTORIC XX Charming cinema built in 1938 and sympathetically converted to incorporate a trendy art deco bar and glamorous restaurant. Dine among elegant columns and ornate plasterwork. Menus offer detailed, classically based dishes with modern twists.

Menu £ 15 (lunch and early dinner) – Carte £ 32/49

97 High St ✉ HP4 2DG – ✆ 01442 870403 – www.thegatsby.net – Closed 25-26 December

BERRICK SALOME

Oxfordshire – Pop. 326 – Regional map n° **6**-B2

Chequers

TRADITIONAL BRITISH • FRIENDLY Delightful 17C pub with a spacious garden and a warm, welcoming interior with fresh flowers and candles on the tables and warming open fires. Hearty menus list British classics and at lunchtime they offer a good value 2 course menu.

Menu £ 13 (weekday lunch) – Carte £ 25/43

✉ OX10 6JN – ✆ 01865 891118 – www.chequersberricksalome.co.uk – Closed 25 December, Sunday dinner and Tuesday

BERWICK-UPON-TWEED

Northumberland – Pop. 13 265 – Regional map n° **14**-A1

Granary

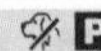

TOWNHOUSE • PERSONALISED Discreet Georgian house on a side street near the river. Guest areas are on the first floor; breakfast features organic and Fairtrade produce. The 2nd floor bedrooms are bright and modern with eye-catching art and thoughtful extras.

3 rooms – £ 90/96 £ 108/138

11 Bridge St ✉ TD15 1ES – ✆ 01289 304403 – www.granaryguesthouse.co.uk

BEVERLEY

East Riding of Yorkshire – ✉ Kingston-Upon-Hull – Pop. 30 587 – Regional map n° **13**-D2

Westwood

MODERN BRITISH • BRASSERIE XX The twins who own this smart modern brasserie clearly share the same vision. Appealing menus offer unfussy, recognisable dishes and the meats cooked 'a la plancha' are a hit. It sits in the wing of an impressive Georgian courthouse.

Menu £ 20 (weekdays) – Carte £ 27/50

New Walk ✉ HU17 7AE – ✆ 01482 881999 (booking advisable) – www.thewestwood.co.uk – Closed 27 December-15 January, Sunday dinner and Monday

Whites 

CREATIVE • NEIGHBOURHOOD XX An enthusiastic chef-owner runs this small restaurant beside the old city walls. Ambitious modern cooking is delivered in 4 and 9 course surprise menus. Black furnishings and eye-catching art stand out against plain walls. Two of the simple bedrooms overlook the North Bar and breakfast is served in your room.

Menu £ 25/50 – surprise menu only

4 rooms – †£ 80 ††£ 95

12a North Bar Without ✉ HU17 7AB – ✆ 01482 866121 (booking advisable) – www.whitesrestaurant.co.uk – dinner only and Saturday lunch – Closed 1 week Christmas, 1 week August, Sunday and Monday

at Tickton Northeast: 3.5 mi by A1035 ✉ Kingston-Upon-Hull

Tickton Grange 

COUNTRY HOUSE • CLASSIC A warm, welcoming, family-run hotel in an extended Georgian house – a popular wedding venue. Bedrooms are stylish and up-to-date, and the spacious sitting room looks out over the immaculately kept gardens. Ambitious, modern cooking is served in the contemporary restaurant.

21 rooms – †£ 98/160 ††£ 130/200

✉ HU17 9SH – on A 1035 – ✆ 01964 543666 – www.ticktongrange.co.uk

at South Dalton Northwest: 5 mi by A164 and B1248 ✉ Beverley

Pipe and Glass Inn (James Mackenzie) 

MODERN BRITISH • FRIENDLY Warm, bustling and inviting pub; very personally run by its experienced owners. Dishes are generously proportioned, carefully executed and flavourful, with judicious use of local, seasonal and traceable produce. Luxurious designer bedrooms boast the latest mod cons and have their own patios overlooking the estate woodland; breakfast is served in your room.

→ Salt beef hash with rhubarb ketchup and crispy pickled onion rings. Wild turbot with asparagus, mushrooms, langoustines and seaweed-buttered potato. Buttermilk pudding with blood orange granita, citrus and pumpkin seed flapjack.

Carte £ 27/60

5 rooms – †£ 195/250 ††£ 195/250

West End ✉ HU17 7PN – ✆ 01430 810246 – www.pipeandglass.co.uk – Closed 2 weeks January, Sunday dinner and Monday except bank holidays

BEWDLEY

Worcestershire – Pop. 8 571 – Regional map n° **10**-B2

Kateshill House 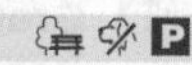

TOWNHOUSE • PERSONALISED This elegant Georgian manor house is surrounded by beautiful gardens; where you'll find a tree from the reign of King Henry VIII. Sumptuous, contemporary furnishings provide a subtle contrast to the house's original features.

8 rooms – †£ 75/85 ††£ 90/140

Redhill ✉ DY12 2DR – South : 0.25 mi on B 4194 – ✆ 01299 401563 – www.kateshillhouse.co.uk

BIBURY

Gloucestershire – ✉ Cirencester – Pop. 570 – Regional map n° **2**-D1

Swan 

INN • PERSONALISED Set in a delightful village, this ivy-clad coaching inn has a trout stream running through the garden and a cosy, characterful interior. Bedrooms mix cottagey character with contemporary touches; the best are in the annexes. The brasserie has an unusual log wall and opens onto a lovely flag-stoned courtyard.

22 rooms – †£ 110/250 ††£ 110/380 – 4 suites

✉ GL7 5NW – ✆ 01285 740695 – www.cotswold-inns-hotels.co.uk/swan

Cotteswold House

FAMILY • PERSONALISED This pleasant guesthouse is set just outside picturesque Bibury and provides an ideal base for exploring the area. The Victorian façade conceals traditional, spotlessly kept bedrooms and the friendly owner offers a warm welcome.

3 rooms – £ 65 £ 90

Arlington GL7 5ND – on B 4425
– 01285 740609 – www.cotteswoldhouse.net

BIDBOROUGH

Kent – Regional map n° **5**-B2

Kentish Hare

MODERN CUISINE • PUB Saved from development by local residents Lord and Lady Mills of Olympic Committee fame and run by the Tanner brothers, this smart pub features a hare theme, quirky wallpaper and an open kitchen. Tasty steaks from the green egg grill.

Menu £ 18 (weekdays) – Carte £ 26/49

95 Bidborough Ridge TN3 0XB
– 01892 525709 – www.thekentishhare.com – Closed Sunday dinner and Monday except bank holidays

BIDDENDEN

Kent – Pop. 1 303 – Regional map n° **5**-C2

West House (Graham Garrett)

MODERN BRITISH • RUSTIC Two 16C weavers' cottages at the heart of a picturesque village; the heavily timbered interior hung with modern art is a mirror of the food, where classically based dishes are given a modern twist. Cooking is assured and everything is on the plate for a reason. Service is refreshingly unpretentious.
→ Crispy chicken wings with parmesan sauce, roast onion, dandelion and bacon. Barbecued turbot with potato purée, sea purslane and parsley. Amador chocolate crémeux, feuilletine crisp, mascarpone and kaffir lime ice cream.

Menu £ 25/60

28 High St TN27 8AH
– 01580 291341 (booking advisable) – www.thewesthouserestaurant.co.uk
– Closed Christmas, Saturday lunch, Sunday dinner and Monday

The Three Chimneys

CLASSIC CUISINE • PUB A delightful pub which dates back to 1420 and boasts dimly lit, low-beamed rooms, an old world feel and a charming terrace and garden. Dishes are mainly British based and there are some tempting local wines, ciders and ales on offer too. Bedrooms are at the end of the garden and open onto a private terrace.

Carte £ 25/38

5 rooms – £ 90 £ 130/150

Hareplain Rd TN27 8LW – West : 1.5 mi by A 262
– 01580 291472 (booking essential) – www.thethreechimneys.co.uk

Barclay Farmhouse

TRADITIONAL • CLASSIC A converted farmhouse and barn in an acre of neatly kept gardens, complete with a duck pond. Comfortable bedrooms feature French oak furniture and characterful beams; extra touches include chocolate truffles on your pillow.

3 rooms – £ 70/75 £ 90/95

Woolpack Corner TN27 8BQ – South : 0.5 mi by A 262 on Benenden rd
– 01580 292626 – www.barclayfarmhouse.co.uk

BIDEFORD

Devon – Pop. 18 029 – Regional map n° **1**-C1

Yeoldon House

COUNTRY HOUSE • PERSONALISED A delightfully run 19C house featuring original stained glass and wood-panelling. It's set in a peaceful riverbank location and the landscaped gardens offer lovely walks. Some of the cosy bedrooms have balconies with river views.

10 rooms – £ 115/130 £ 130/145

Durrant Ln, Northam ✉ EX39 2RL – North : 1.5 mi by B 3235 off A 386 – ✆ 01237 474400 – www.yeoldonhouse.co.uk – Closed Christmas and February

BIGBURY

Devon – Regional map n° **1**-C3

Oyster Shack

SEAFOOD • NEIGHBOURHOOD X Former oyster farm with a small oyster bar and lounge, and a large terrace. The brightly decorated room is hung with fishing nets and centred around a large fish tank. Cooking is fresh and unfussy, focusing on shellfish and the daily catch.

Carte £ 20/54

Milburn Orchard Farm, Stakes Hill ✉ TQ7 4BE – East : 1 mi by Easton rd on Tidal rd – ✆ 01548 810876 (booking essential) – www.oystershack.co.uk – Closed 3-31 January and Sunday dinner in winter

BIGBURY-ON-SEA

Devon – ✉ Kingsbridge – Pop. 220 – Regional map n° **1**-C3

Burgh Island

HISTORIC • ART DÉCO Grade II listed house on its own island, accessed using the hotel's Land Rover (or tractor at high tide!). It has classic art deco styling throughout, from the guest areas to the individually designed bedrooms; some rooms have small balconies and most have excellent bay views. 1930s themed 'black tie' dinners take place in the ballroom; there's live music Weds and Sat.

25 rooms (dinner included) – £ 320/680 £ 420/680 – 12 suites

✉ TQ7 4BG – South : 0.5 mi by hotel transport – ✆ 01548 810514 – www.burghisland.com – Closed 2-17 January

Henley

TRADITIONAL • PERSONALISED Not only is this extended cottage very personally run by its welcoming owners but it also affords superb views over Burgh Island and towards Bolt Tail. Charming bedrooms mix antique and modern furnishings and all share the wonderful view. Home-cooked meals are taken in the wicker-furnished conservatory.

5 rooms – £ 95 £ 127/160

Folly Hill ✉ TQ7 4AR – ✆ 01548 810240 – www.thehenleyhotel.co.uk – Closed November-mid March

BIGGLESWADE

Bedfordshire – Pop. 15 383 – Regional map n° **7**-B1

Croft Kitchen

MODERN BRITISH • FRIENDLY XX Two enthusiastic brothers, of Indian and Scottish descent, run this simple little restaurant – one cooks and one serves. Creative modern dishes are attractively presented and subtle Indian spicing adds another dimension to the cooking.

Menu £ 28/45

28 Palace St ✉ SG18 8DP – ✆ 01767 601502 – www.thecroftbiggleswade.com – dinner only and Saturday lunch – Closed Sunday-Wednesday

BILDESTON

Suffolk – Regional map n° **8**-C3

Bildeston Crown

MODERN BRITISH • INTIMATE Sit in the bar or one of several dining rooms in this historic inn, where you'll find thick walls, heavy beams and vast open fires. Choose from the 'Classic' or more complex 'Select' menu which, in season, has game at its heart.

Menu £ 15 (weekday lunch) – Carte £ 30/60

Bildeston Crown Hotel, 104 High St IP7 7EB – 01449 740510 (booking essential) – www.thebildestoncrown.co.uk – Closed dinner 25-26 December, 1 January and Sunday

Bildeston Crown

INN • CONTEMPORARY A hugely characterful 15C wool merchant's with a lovely rear courtyard. The stylish interior has warm colours and open fires. Luxurious bedrooms vary from florally feminine to bright and bold – all have designer furnishings.

12 rooms – £ 80/150 £ 90/150

104 High St IP7 7EB – 01449 740510 – www.thebildestoncrown.com

Bildeston Crown – See restaurant listing

BINFIELD HEATH

Oxfordshire – Pop. 709 – Regional map n° **6**-C3

Bottle & Glass Inn

MODERN BRITISH • PUB This pretty thatched pub sits in a lovely rural spot. The original part is the most characterful, while the restaurant is more up-to-date. Modern British cooking is refined but unfussy and has an appealing simplicity.

Menu £ 19 (weekday lunch) – Carte £ 31/37

Bones Ln RG9 4JT – North : 0.5 mi by Arch Hill and Common Ln. – 01491 412625 – www.bottleandglassinn.com – Closed 25-26 December, Sunday dinner and Monday

BIRKENHEAD

Merseyside – Pop. 142 968 – Regional map n° **11**-A3

Fraiche (Marc Wilkinson)

CREATIVE • INTIMATE Enter into the cosy bar, where seasonal images are projected onto the wall, then head through to the boldly decorated restaurant which seats just 10 diners. Cooking is innovative and presentation is key – both the colours of the ingredients and the shape and style of the crockery play their part.

→ Slow-roasted carrot with smoked yoghurt and parsley granita. Quail with charred cabbage and confit morels. Blood orange textures, pistachio parfait and roasted white chocolate.

Menu £ 88 – tasting menu only

11 Rose Mount, Oxton CH43 5SG – Southwest : 2.25 mi by A 552 and B 5151 – 0151 652 2914 (booking essential) – www.restaurantfraiche.com – dinner only and Sunday lunch – Closed 25 December, 1-7 September, Sunday dinner, Monday and Tuesday

GOOD TIPS!

Known as a city of cars, canals and chocolate, the 'Second City of the Kingdom' is also a centre for culinary excellence, boasting four Michelin-starred restaurants. 21C Brum is a major convention and retail destination, and redevelopment continues apace; hotels like **Malmaison** and **Hotel Indigo** provide luxury accommodation for its many visitors.

BIRMINGHAM

West Midlands – Pop. 1 085 810 – Regional map n° **10**-C2

Restaurants

✿ Simpsons (Andreas Antona & Luke Tipping)

MODERN CUISINE • FASHIONABLE XXX Behind the walls of this suburban Georgian house is a sleek dining room and three contemporary bedrooms. Cooking has a clean, Scandic style and the visually appealing dishes are packed with flavour. Lunch sees a 2-choice set price menu; dinner a 4-course set price menu and a tasting option – some courses are served by the chefs. Desserts are satisfyingly traditional.

→ Cured salmon with prawns, cucumber, buttermilk and dill. Roasted lamb chump, black garlic and sheep's curd. Speculoos biscuit with caramelised white chocolate and coffee granité.

Menu £ 35/90

3 rooms – †£ 110 ††£ 110

Town plan: A2-e – *20 Highfield Rd, Edgbaston ✉ B15 3DU – ✆ 0121 454 3434 – www.simpsonsrestaurant.co.uk – Closed 25 December, Sunday dinner and Monday*

✿ Adam's (Adam Stokes)

MODERN CUISINE • ELEGANT XXX Enjoy a drink in the smart cocktail bar then move on to the bright, elegant restaurant with a subtle retro feel. Choose from a concise set menu or an 8 course tasting menu: top notch produce is used in carefully prepared dishes which have wonderfully bold complementary flavours and contrasting textures.

→ Veal sweetbread with roasted cauliflower, air-dried ham and raisins. Goosnargh chicken with asparagus, morels and haggis. 63% dark chocolate with salted milk and blood orange.

Menu £ 38/60

Town plan: E2-c – *New Oxford House, 16 Waterloo St ✉ B2 5UG – ✆ 0121 643 3745 (booking essential) – www.adamsrestaurant.co.uk – Closed 2 weeks summer, Christmas-New Year, Sunday and Monday*

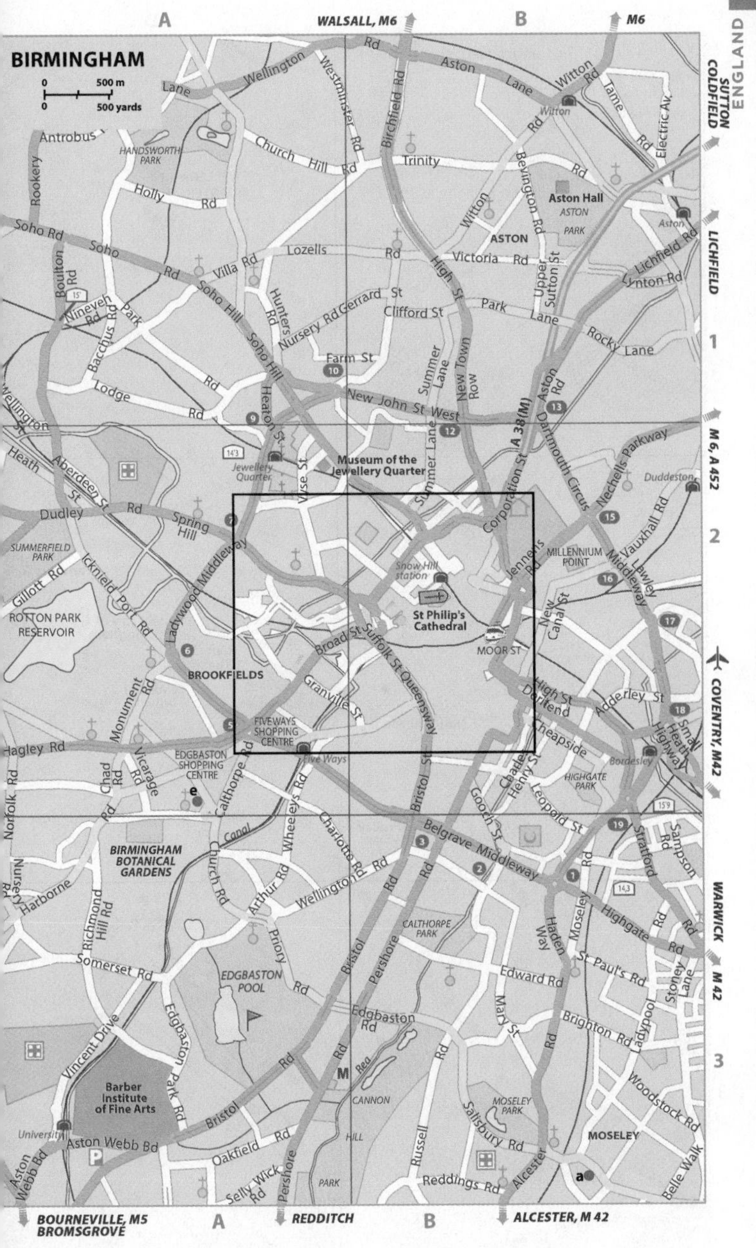
BIRMINGHAM
0 500 m
0 500 yards
WALSALL, M6
M6
SUTTON COLDFIELD
LICHFIELD
M 6, A 452
COVENTRY, M42
WARWICK
M 42
BOURNEVILLE, M5
BROMSGROVE
REDDITCH
ALCESTER, M 42
Aston Hall
ASTON
Museum of the Jewellery Quarter
St Philip's Cathedral
BROOKFIELDS
BIRMINGHAM BOTANICAL GARDENS
EDGBASTON POOL
Barber Institute of Fine Arts
MOSELEY
MILLENNIUM POINT
ROTTON PARK RESERVOIR
FIVEWAYS SHOPPING CENTRE
EDGBASTON SHOPPING CENTRE

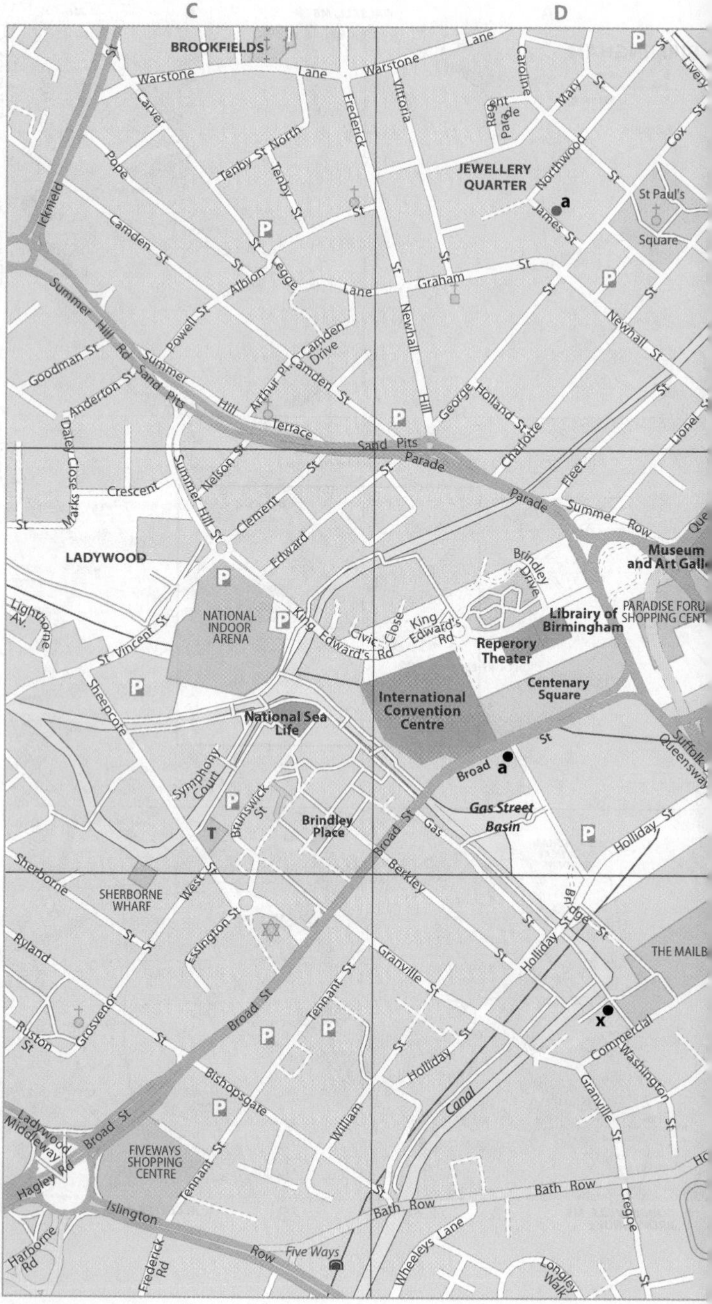

C
D
BROOKFIELDS
JEWELLERY QUARTER
St Paul's Square
LADYWOOD
NATIONAL INDOOR ARENA
Museum and Art Gall
PARADISE FORU SHOPPING CENT
Library of Birmingham
Reperory Theater
Centenary Square
International Convention Centre
National Sea Life
Brindley Place
Gas Street Basin
SHERBORNE WHARF
THE MAILB
FIVEWAYS SHOPPING CENTRE
Five Ways
1
2
3
a
a
x

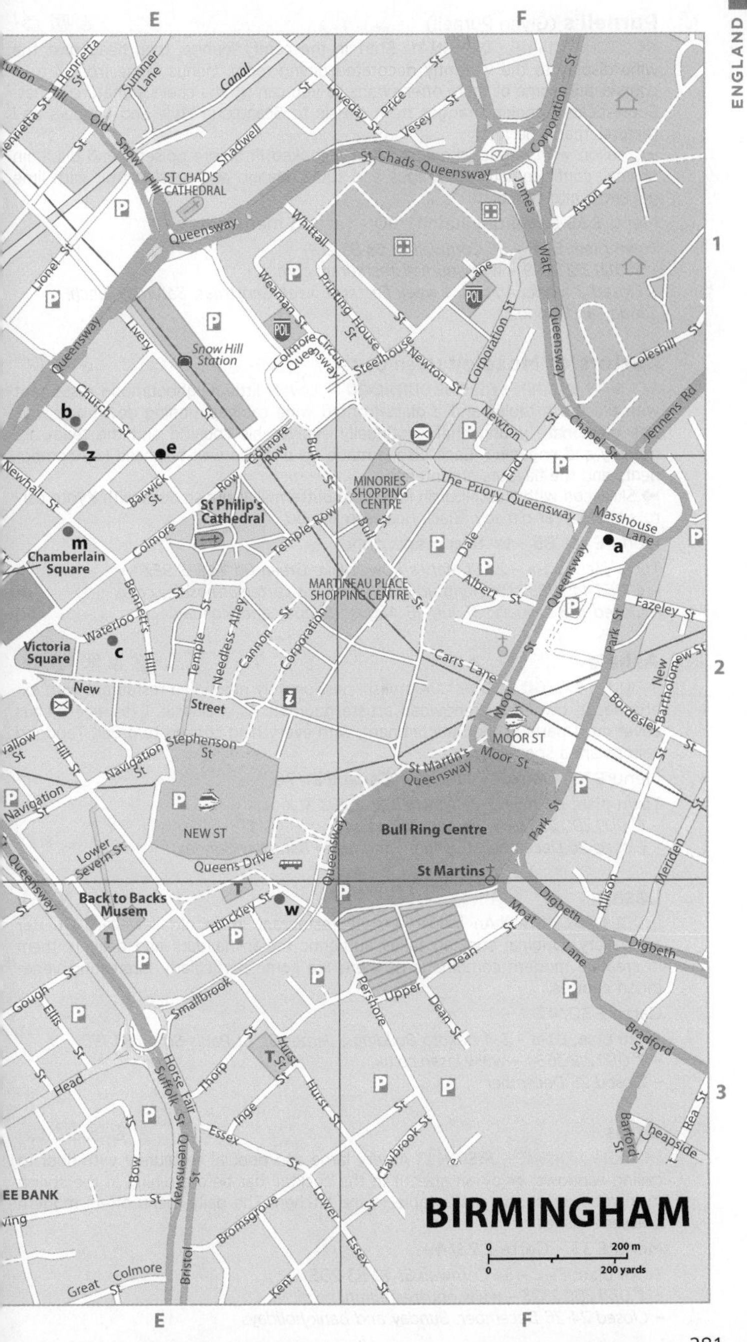
BIRMINGHAM
St Chad's Cathedral
Snow Hill Station
St Philip's Cathedral
Minories Shopping Centre
Martineau Place Shopping Centre
Chamberlain Square
Victoria Square
Back to Backs Museum
New St
Moor St
Bull Ring Centre
St Martins
Queensway
New Street
Corporation St
Colmore Row
Digbeth
0 200 m
0 200 yards

Purnell's (Glynn Purnell)

MODERN CUISINE • DESIGN XXX Start in the comfy lounge, then head past the wine display to the vibrantly decorated dining room. Menus range from 3 to 9 courses and some of them offer swaps so you can try the chef's signature dishes. Sophisticated cooking ranges from classic to Scandic in style and flavours and textures marry perfectly.

→ Scallop with mussel chowder, potato cooked in beurre noisette and dill. Loin of veal, confit tomato, asparagus and squid. Mango and passion fruit with lime gel and white chocolate.

Menu £ 35 (weekday lunch)/90 – tasting menu only

Town plan: E1-b – *55 Cornwall St ✉ B3 2DH*
– *0121 212 9799 – www.purnellsrestaurant.com*
– *Closed 2 weeks August, 1 week Easter, 1 week Christmas, Saturday lunch, Sunday and Monday*

Carters of Moseley (Brad Carter)

MODERN BRITISH • NEIGHBOURHOOD XX Lovely little neighbourhood restaurant with black ash tables and a glass-fronted wine cabinet running down one wall. The passionate young chef continually evolves his cooking and the team are friendly and engaging. Each dish is made up of three well-balanced key components and the flavours are intense.

→ Skrei cod with Musselburgh leeks and buttermilk. Cornish duck with Kyoto carrots and 5 year old soy. Black rice with kombu.

Menu £ 40/85 – tasting menu only

Town plan: B3-a – *2c St Mary's Row, Wake Green Rd ✉ B13 9EZ*
– *0121 449 8885 (booking advisable) – www.cartersofmoseley.co.uk*
– *Closed 1-18 January, 31 July-16 August, Sunday and Monday*

Asha's

INDIAN • EXOTIC DÉCOR XX A stylish, passionately run Indian restaurant with exotic décor; owned by renowned artiste/gourmet Asha Bhosle. Extensive menus cover most parts of the Subcontinent, with everything cooked to order. Tandoori kebabs are a speciality.

Menu £ 18 (weekday lunch) – Carte £ 21/76

Town plan: E2-m – *12-22 Newhall St ✉ B3 3LX*
– *0121 200 2767 – www.ashasuk.co.uk*
– *Closed 26 December, 1 January and lunch Saturday-Sunday*

Lasan

INDIAN • DESIGN XX An industrial-style restaurant in an old Jewellery Quarter art gallery. Original cooking takes authentic Indian flavours and delivers them in creative modern combinations; there are some particularly interesting vegetarian choices.

Carte £ 30/47

Town plan: D1-a – *3-4 Dakota Buildings, James St, St Pauls Sq ✉ B3 1SD*
– *0121 212 3664 – www.lasan.co.uk*
– *Closed 25 December*

Opus

MODERN CUISINE • DESIGN XX A very large and popular restaurant with floor to ceiling windows; enjoy an aperitif in the cocktail bar before dining in the stylish main room or at the chef's table in the kitchen. The daily menu offers modern brasserie dishes.

Menu £ 33 – Carte £ 23/49

Town plan: E1-z – *54 Cornwall St ✉ B3 2DE*
– *0121 200 2323 – www.opusrestaurant.co.uk*
– *Closed 24-26 December, Sunday and bank holidays*

Turners at 69

MODERN BRITISH • NEIGHBOURHOOD XX A cosy, elegant restaurant in a suburban parade; its walls covered in mirrors etched with the chef's name, which reflect the chandeliers. Classically based, seasonal cooking allows good ingredients to speak for themselves.

Menu £ 25 (lunch) – Carte £ 38/57

69 High St, Harborne ✉ B17 9NS – Southwest : 4 mi by A 456 and Norfolk Rd – ✆ 0121 426 4440 (booking essential) – www.turnersat69.co.uk – Closed lunch Monday and Friday, Saturday lunch May-September, Sunday dinner, Tuesday-Wednesday and bank holidays

The Wilderness (N)

MODERN BRITISH • SIMPLE X A small, casual restaurant located in the avant-garde Birmingham Open Media gallery. The enthusiastic team serve artfully presented set menus which marry just a few local and home-grown ingredients in playful combinations.

Menu £ 35/70 – tasting menu only

Town plan: E3-w – *1 Dudley St ✉ B5 4EG – ✆ 0121 643 2673 (booking advisable) – www.wearethewilderness.co.uk – Closed Sunday-Tuesday*

Hotels

Hyatt Regency

BUSINESS • CONTEMPORARY An eye-catching, mirror-fronted, tower block hotel in a prime city centre location, with a covered link to the International Convention Centre. Spacious bedrooms have floor to ceiling windows and an excellent level of facilities. Aria restaurant, in the atrium, offers modern European menus.

319 rooms – †£ 114/220 ††£ 146/220 – ☕ £ 19 – 11 suites

Town plan: D2-a – *2 Bridge St ✉ B1 2JZ – ✆ 0121 643 1234 – www.birmingham.regency.hyatt.com*

Hotel Du Vin

BUSINESS • DESIGN A characterful former eye hospital with a relaxed, shabby-chic style. Bright bedrooms are named after wine companies and estates; one suite boasts an 8 foot bed, two roll-top baths and a gym. Kick-back in the small cellar pub or comfy champagne bar; the classical bistro has a lively buzz and a French menu.

66 rooms ☕ – †£ 99/250 ††£ 99/350

Town plan: E1-e – *25 Church St ✉ B3 2NR – ✆ 0121 794 3005 – www.hotelduvin.com*

Hotel La Tour

BUSINESS • MODERN A striking modern building with spacious, stylish guest areas. With their media hubs and TV recording facilities, bedrooms are ideal for business travellers; Superiors come with baths which have TVs mounted above them. The informal chophouse serves an extensive menu of hearty, unfussy classics and steaks.

174 rooms – †£ 98/245 ††£ 98/328 – ☕ £ 18

Town plan: F2-a – *Albert St ✉ B5 5JE – ✆ 0121 718 8000 – www.hotel-latour.co.uk – Closed 23-30 December*

Malmaison

BUSINESS • MODERN A stylish hotel with dark, moody décor, set on the site of the old Royal Mail sorting office, next to designer clothing and homeware shops. Bedrooms are spacious and stylish; the Penny Black suite has a mini-cinema and a steam room. Dine from an accessible British menu in the bright, bustling brasserie.

192 rooms – †£ 89/179 ††£ 99/189 – ☕ £ 17 – 1 suite

Town plan: E2-e – *Mailbox, 1 Wharfside St ✉ B1 1RD – ✆ 0121 246 5000 – www.malmaison.com*

Hotel Indigo

BUSINESS · DESIGN Stylish hotel located on the top three floors of the eye-catching 'Cube' building. Both the appealingly styled guest areas and vividly decorated bedrooms come with floor to ceiling windows. A smart steakhouse serves classic dishes and boasts a champagne bar, a terrace and a view from every table.

52 rooms - †£ 99/200 ††£ 140/210 - ☕ £ 16

Town plan: D3-x - *The Cube* ✉ *B1 1PR*
- *✆ 0121 643 2010* - *www.hotelindigobirmingham.com*

at National Exhibition Centre Southeast : 9.5 mi on A 45 ✉ Birmingham

Andy Waters

TRADITIONAL BRITISH · CHIC XX Unusually set in a shopping centre, beside the cinema, is this comfy, formal restaurant run by an experienced chef – ask for one of the booths. Traditional cooking is given a personal touch; the 2 course lunch menu is good value.

Menu £ 22/38

Floor One, Resorts World, Pendigo Way ✉ *B40 1PU*
- *✆ 020 1273 1238* - *www.watersrestaurant.co.uk*
- *Closed 25 December*

BISHOP'S STORTFORD

Hertfordshire – Pop. 37 838 – Regional map n° **7**-B2

Lemon Tree

TRADITIONAL CUISINE · FRIENDLY XX Wattle and daub walls, exposed timbers and wood-panelling give these adjoining 16 and 17C houses a characterful feel. Choose something from the Classics Menu or a more globally influenced dish from the à la carte.

Carte £ 23/45

14-16 Water Ln ✉ *CM23 2JZ*
- *✆ 01279 757788* - *www.lemontree.co.uk*
- *Closed 25-27 December, 1-2 January, bank holidays, dinner Sunday and Monday*

Water Lane

INTERNATIONAL · BISTRO X An atmospheric restaurant set over two floors, with a busy cellar bar below. Menus offer a range of classic British, American and Asian dishes, from bubble and squeak to Bourbon-glazed ribs to curries.

Carte £ 25/32

31 Water Ln ✉ *CM23 2JZ*
- *✆ 01279 211888* - *www.waterlane.co*

BLACKBURN

Blackburn with Darwen – Pop. 117 963 – Regional map n° **11**-B2

Clog & Billycock

TRADITIONAL BRITISH · PUB This modern pub is named after a former landlord's favourite attire. Lancashire classics sit beside international dishes and steaks matured in a Himalayan salt-aging chamber are a feature. Alongside cocktails, they offer over 40 gins.

Menu £ 14 (weekdays) – Carte £ 21/39

Billinge End Rd, Pleasington ✉ *BB2 6QB* - *West : 2 mi by A 677*
- *✆ 01254 201163* - *www.theclogandbillycock.com*

at Langho North: 4.5 mi on A666✉ Whalley

✿ Northcote (Nigel Haworth)

MODERN BRITISH · ELEGANT XXX An elegant restaurant set within an impressive Victorian house. Refined, sophisticated cooking shows real depth of flavour and a lightness of touch. Produce is either biodynamic or organic, with as much as possible coming from the kitchen garden. Watch the chefs close-up from the glass-walled kitchen table.

→ Celeriac and chestnut ravioli with pearl vegetables and celeriac consommé. Norfolk quail with smoked Jerusalem artichoke and pickled onions. Valrhona chocolate cylinder with smoked nuts and salted organic sheep's milk ice cream.

Menu £ 34 (lunch) – Carte £ 51/87

Northcote Hotel, Northcote Rd ✉ BB6 8BE – North : 0.5 mi on A 59 at junction with A 666 – ✆ 01254 240555 (booking essential) – www.northcote.com

Northcote

COUNTRY HOUSE · ELEGANT This well-run Victorian house sits on the edge of the Ribble Valley. Individually designed bedrooms are spacious, stylish and sophisticated – all have queen or king-sized beds and some have garden terraces. Enjoy afternoon tea beside the fire in the lounge, followed by drinks in the bright, glitzy bar.

26 rooms – †£ 230/575 ††£ 270/615 – 1 suite

Northcote Rd ✉ BB6 8BE – North : 0.5 mi on A 59 at junction with A 666 – ✆ 01254 240555 – www.northcote.com

✿ **Northcote** – See restaurant listing

at Mellor Northwest: 3.25 mi by A677✉ Blackburn

Stanley House

LUXURY · DESIGN Attractive part-17C manor house boasting superb country views and a smart spa with four types of sauna. Bedrooms in the main house are elegant and feature original beams and mullioned windows; the 'Woodland Rooms' are more contemporary. Stylish 'Grill on the Hill' offers modern favourites and views over the garden towards the coast; 'Mr Fred's' serves simpler fare.

30 rooms – †£ 155/250 ††£ 190/275

✉ BB2 7NP – Southwest : 0.75 mi by A 677 and Further Ln – ✆ 01254 769200 – www.stanleyhouse.co.uk

BLACKPOOL

Blackpool – Pop. 147 663 – Regional map n° **11**-A2

Number One St Lukes

TOWNHOUSE · DESIGN A boutique guesthouse set close to the promenade and the Pleasure Beach and run by a very charming owner. Bedrooms are named after the town's piers: 'North' has an African feel and 'Central' has a white half-tester and a more feminine touch. There's also an outdoor hot tub and a mini pitch and putt green!

3 rooms – †£ 80/135 ††£ 100/135

1 St Lukes Rd ✉ FY4 2EL – ✆ 01253 343901 – www.numberoneblackpool.com

at Thornton Northeast: 5.5 mi by A584 -(BY)- on B5412✉ Blackpool

Twelve

MODERN BRITISH · DESIGN XX This passionately run cocktail bar and restaurant sits beside one of Europe's tallest working windmills. Dine in the main room, on the mezzanine or in the bar, surrounded by brick walls, reclaimed wood and graffiti art. Hearty, wholesome cooking has a refined edge; the à la carte menu is the most innovative.

Menu £ 27 – Carte £ 24/44

Marsh Mill, Fleetwood Rd North ✉ FY5 4JZ – ✆ 01253 821212 – www.twelve-restaurant.co.uk – dinner only and Sunday lunch – Closed first 2 weeks January and Monday

BLAGDON

North Somerset – Pop. 1 001 – Regional map n° **2**-B2

Seymour Arms

MODERN BRITISH • INN Set in a small village in the Mendip Hills, overlooking a Lake. Hole up beside the wood-burning stove with a pint of locally brewed ale. The regularly changing menus are refreshingly concise and the unfussy, confidently prepared dishes have a modern British style. Up-to-date bedrooms are simply furnished.

Carte £ 21/34

5 rooms – †£ 86/90 ††£ 95/120

Bath Rd ✉ BS40 7TH – On A 368 – ✆ 01761 462279 – www.theseymourarmsblagdon.co.uk – Closed Monday lunch

BLAKENEY

Norfolk – ✉ Holt – Pop. 801 – Regional map n° **8**-C1

Wiveton Farm Café

REGIONAL CUISINE • FRIENDLY An extension of a farm shop, set down a dusty track and run by a smiley young team. Light breakfasts and tasty, salad-based lunches; weekends see 'Norfolk' tapas in the evenings. Take in glorious farm and sea views from the terrace.

Carte £ 22/33

✉ NR25 7TE – West : 0.5 mi on A 149 – ✆ 01263 740515 – www.wivetonhall.co.uk – lunch only and dinner Thursday-Saturday – Closed November-March

White Horse

TRADITIONAL CUISINE • INN A brick and flint pub near the harbour; if the sun's shining, find a spot on the suntrap terrace. Inside it's bright and airy with pastel colours and modern art. The menu champions local produce in tried-and-tested combinations, with seafood a feature in summer. Smart bedrooms are named after nautical knots.

Carte £ 25/37

9 rooms – †£ 99 ††£ 114/144

4 High St ✉ NR25 7AL – ✆ 01263 740574 (booking advisable) – www.blakeneywhitehorse.co.uk

Blakeney

FAMILY • CONTEMPORARY Traditional hotel in a great quayside location, affording views over the estuary and the salt marshes. It has various comfy lounges and a bar with subtle modern touches. Some of the individually designed bedrooms have balconies or sea views. The formal dining room offers a good outlook and a wide-ranging menu.

64 rooms – †£ 93/350 ††£ 186/350

The Quay ✉ NR25 7NE – ✆ 01263 740797 – www.blakeneyhotel.co.uk

at Cley next the Sea East: 1.5 mi on A149 ✉ Holt

Cley Windmill

HISTORIC • COSY With its views over the marshes and river, this restored 18C windmill is a birdwatcher's paradise. Snug, characterful bedrooms are split between the mill, the stables and the boatshed. The flagstoned dining room offers a set menu of homemade country dishes and the tea room opens in the summer months.

9 rooms – †£ 159/199 ††£ 179/225

The Quay ✉ NR25 7RP – ✆ 01263 740209 – www.cleywindmill.co.uk

at Wiveton South: 1 mi by A149 on Wiveton Rd

Wiveton Bell

TRADITIONAL BRITISH • FASHIONABLE Modernised pub featuring beams, stripped floors and wood-burning stoves; with picnic tables out the front and a beautifully landscaped rear terrace. Seasonal menu offers pub classics, carefully crafted from quality local ingredients. Stylish, cosy bedrooms have smart bathrooms; continental breakfasts.

Carte £ 24/37

6 rooms – £ 100/170 £ 100/170

Blakeney Rd ✉ NR25 7TL – ✆ 01263 740101 (booking essential) – www.wivetonbell.com

at Morston West: 1.5 mi on A149 ✉ Holt

Morston Hall (Galton Blackiston)

MODERN BRITISH • ELEGANT XX Set in an attractive country house surrounded by landscaped gardens: choose between a traditionally furnished room or a beautiful conservatory. The set 7 course daily menu (served at 8pm), offers well-balanced seasonal dishes. Cooking is classically based, sophisticated and exhibits a delicate, modern touch.

→ Miso-glazed chicken wing with confit egg yolk and cauliflower purée. Huntsham Farm suckling pig with burnt apple purée and sauce Robert. Sharrington raspberry soufflé with tonka bean ice cream and raspberry and mint sauce.

Menu £ 75 – tasting menu only

Morston Hall Hotel, The Street ✉ NR25 7AA – ✆ 01263 741041 (booking essential) – www.morstonhall.com – dinner only and Sunday lunch – Closed 1-27 January and 24-26 December

Morston Hall

LUXURY • CLASSIC Attractive, personally run country house with manicured gardens, set in a small coastal hamlet. Comfy guest areas feature antiques and paintings. Bedrooms are split between the main house and an annexe – the latter are larger and have subtle contemporary touches. Service is keen and friendly.

13 rooms (dinner included) – £ 275/305 £ 390/410

The Street ✉ NR25 7AA – ✆ 01263 741041 – www.morstonhall.com – Closed 1-27 January and 24-26 December

Morston Hall – See restaurant listing

BLANCHLAND

Northumberland – Regional map n° **14**-A2

Bishop's Dining Room

TRADITIONAL BRITISH • RUSTIC X A bright, hunting-themed restaurant in a characterful hotel; the monks from the neighbouring abbey once dined here. Menus offer robust, flavoursome British dishes which feature kitchen garden, home-smoked and spit-roast produce.

Carte £ 19/38

Lord Crewe Arms Hotel, The Square ✉ DH8 9SP – ✆ 01434 677100 – www.lordcrewearmsblanchland.co.uk

Lord Crewe Arms

TRADITIONAL • CONTEMPORARY A 12C abbot's priory, which has also spent time as a hunting lodge and a lead miners' hostelry. Its hugely characterful guest areas don't disappoint and the delightful garden offers commanding country views. Bespoke-furnished bedrooms have a modern country charm; many are located around the village square.

21 rooms – £ 123/197 £ 138/212 – 2 suites

The Square ✉ DH8 9SP – ✆ 01434 675469 – www.lordcrewearmsblanchland.co.uk

Bishop's Dining Room – See restaurant listing

BLANDFORD FORUM

Dorset - Pop. 11 694 - Regional map n° **2**-C3

at Farnham Northeast: 7.5 mi by A354 ✉ Blandford Forum

Farnham Farm House

FAMILY • COSY Welcoming farmhouse on a 300 acre working farm, complete with a swimming pool and a holistic therapy centre. Homely, immaculately kept bedrooms have country views. Enjoy tea and cake on arrival; the eggs are from their own hens.

3 rooms - †£ 80/90 ††£ 90/100

✉ DT11 8DG - North : 1 mi by Shaftesbury rd - ✆ 01725 516254 - www.farnhamfarmhouse.co.uk - Closed 25-26 December

BLEDINGTON - Gloucestershire ➜ See Stow-on-the-Wold

BODIAM

East Sussex - Regional map n° **5**-B2

Curlew

MODERN BRITISH • DESIGN XX Contemporary restaurant behind a white clapboard pub façade, with funky cow print wallpaper and a Scandinavian feel. Menus are modern, the wine list promotes organic and biodynamic wines, and service is smooth and professional.

Menu £ 20 (weekdays) - Carte £ 30/50

Junction Rd ✉ TN32 5UY - Northwest : 1.5 mi at junction with B 2244 - ✆ 01580 861394 - www.thecurlewrestaurant.co.uk - Closed 26 December, 1 January and Monday

BODMIN

Cornwall - Pop. 14 614 - Regional map n° **1**-B2

Bokiddick Farm

TRADITIONAL • PERSONALISED A traditional farmhouse on a 180 acre working dairy farm - a warm welcome is guaranteed and they serve cream teas on arrival. Homely, spotlessly kept bedrooms come with super king sized beds and country views; the largest rooms are in the old barn. Hearty breakfasts are taken overlooking the garden.

3 rooms - †£ 60/65 ††£ 90/95

Lanivet ✉ PL30 5HP - South : 5 mi by A 30 following signs for Lanhydrock and Bokiddick - ✆ 01208 831481 - www.bokiddickfarm.co.uk - Closed Christmas

BOLLINGTON

Cheshire East - ✉ Cheshire - Pop. 7 373 - Regional map n° **11**-B3

Tapa Ⓝ

MODERN CUISINE • RUSTIC X As its name suggests, this appealing restaurant serves small plates designed for sharing. Interesting cooking uses a diverse range of ingredients and has global influences; the fish dishes are usually a highlight.

Menu £ 18

22 High St ✉ SK10 5PH - ✆ 01625 575058 (booking advisable) - www.tapawinebar.co.uk - dinner only - Closed 25-26 December and 1 January

BOLNHURST

Bedford - Regional map n° **7**-A1

Plough at Bolnhurst

MODERN BRITISH • INN Charming whitewashed pub with a rustic bar, a modern restaurant, a lovely garden and a bustling atmosphere. Menus change with the seasons but always feature 28-day aged Aberdeenshire steaks, dishes containing Mediterranean ingredients like Sicilian black olives, and a great selection of wines and cheeses.

Menu £ 25 (weekdays) – Carte £ 32/51

Kimbolton Rd ✉ MK44 2EX – South : 0.5 mi on B 660
– ☎ 01234 376274 – www.bolnhurst.com
– Closed 2 weeks January, Sunday dinner and Monday

BOLTON ABBEY

North Yorkshire – ✉ Skipton – Pop. 117 – Regional map n° **13**-B2

The Burlington

MODERN BRITISH • ELEGANT XXX An antique-filled hotel dining room hung with impressive oils; sit in the conservatory overlooking the Italian garden. Elaborate modern dishes utilise fine ingredients, with many coming from the kitchen garden and estate.

Menu £ 70

Devonshire Arms Hotel & Spa, ✉ BD23 6AJ
– ☎ 01756 710441 – www.thedevonshirearms.co.uk
– dinner only – Closed Monday

Brasserie

TRADITIONAL BRITISH • RUSTIC X Relaxed hotel brasserie with an attractive wine cellar; set opposite the kitchen garden. Sit on stripy banquettes in the bar or red velour chairs in the dining room. The extensive menu offers satisfying brasserie classics.

Carte £ 27/54

Devonshire Arms Hotel & Spa, ✉ BD23 6AJ – ☎ 01756 718105
– www.devonshirebrasserie.co.uk

Devonshire Arms H. & Spa

LUXURY • CONTEMPORARY A charming coaching inn and spa on the Duke and Duchess of Devonshire's 30,000 acre estate in the Yorkshire Dales. Comfy lounges display part of the owners' vast art collection and dogs are welcome. Bedrooms in the wing are bright, modern and compact; those in the inn are traditional.

40 rooms – †£ 139/250 ††£ 158/468 – 2 suites

✉ BD23 6AJ
– ☎ 01756 710441 – www.thedevonshirearms.co.uk

The Burlington • **Brasserie** – See restaurant listing

BORDON

Hampshire – Pop. 16 035 – Regional map n° **4**-C2

Groomes

COUNTRY HOUSE • CONTEMPORARY A part 17C former farmhouse set in 185 acres, which has been made 'green' by the installation of biomass boilers and solar panels. Spacious, modern bedrooms come with roll-top baths; it even has its own games room. Dining takes place at two communal tables – local produce features in dishes cooked on the Aga.

6 rooms – †£ 90/150 ††£ 130/160

Frith End ✉ GU35 0QR – North : 2.75 mi by A 325 on Frith End Sand Pit rd
– ☎ 01420 489858 – www.groomes.co.uk

BOROUGHBRIDGE

North Yorkshire – Pop. 3 610 – Regional map n° **13**-B2

thediningroom

MODERN BRITISH • INTIMATE XX Characterful bow-fronted cottage concealing an opulent bar-lounge and an intimate beamed dining room. Wide-ranging menus offer boldly flavoured, Mediterranean-influenced dishes and chargrilled meats. In summer, head for the terrace.

Menu £ 23 (weekdays) – Carte £ 27/49

20 St James's Sq ✉ YO51 9AR – ✆ 01423 326426 – www.thediningroomonline.co.uk – dinner only and Sunday lunch – Closed 26 December, 1 January, Sunday dinner and Monday

Grantham Arms

TRADITIONAL BRITISH • INN A proper roadside inn where the locals come to watch the latest sporting events. The all-encompassing menu ranges from pie and mash to pan-roasted duck. If gin's your thing, this is the place for you – there are over 30 varieties. Smart bedrooms come with contemporary oak furnishings and Egyptian cotton linen.

Menu £ 17 (weekday lunch) – Carte £ 23/38

7 rooms – †£ 45/100 ††£ 55/110

Milby ✉ YO51 9BW – North : 0.25 mi on B 6265 – ✆ 01423 323980 – www.granthamarms.co.uk

at Roecliffe West: 1 mi

Crown Inn

REGIONAL CUISINE • INN 14C inn in a delightful position by the village green. Menus offer pub classics alongside more ambitious dishes; if you can't decide on a dessert, try them all with the assiette of puddings. Well-appointed bedrooms come with feature beds, roll-top baths and plenty of extra touches.

Carte £ 26/44

4 rooms – †£ 80/100 ††£ 85/120

✉ YO51 9LY – ✆ 01423 322300 – www.crowninnroecliffe.co.uk

at Lower Dunsforth Southeast : 4.25 mi by B 6265

The Dunsforth

MODERN BRITISH • PUB You can tailor your experience at this contemporary pub: if you like things lively, sit in its fire-lit front rooms; for a more intimate meal head for the smart restaurant. Menus offer admirable choice and value for money, and seasonality and freshness are key. Most dishes come with a modern twist.

Menu £ 20 (lunch and early dinner) – Carte £ 23/38

Mary Ln ✉ YO26 9SA – ✆ 01423 320700 – www.thedunsforth.co.uk – Closed Sunday dinner and Monday-Tuesday

BOSCASTLE

Cornwall – Regional map n° **1**-B2

Boscastle House

FAMILY • PERSONALISED Modern styling in a detached Victorian house with a calm, relaxing air. Bedrooms are light and spacious, with roll-top baths and walk-in showers. Hearty breakfasts feature home-baked muffins and banana bread. Tea and cake on arrival.

6 rooms – †£ 88 ††£ 115/140

Tintagel Rd ✉ PL35 0AS – South : 0.75 mi on B 3263 – ✆ 01840 250654 – www.boscastlehouse.com – Closed November-February

Old Rectory

COUNTRY HOUSE • ROMANTIC A lovely house with a Victorian walled garden; Thomas Hardy once stayed here. Bedrooms are characterful: one has a wood stove; another, a whirlpool bath. Breakfast includes bacon and sausages from the owner's pigs. Dinner is by arrangement.

4 rooms - £ 60/105 £ 75/115

St Juliot ✉ PL35 0BT - Northeast : 2.5 mi by B 3263 - ☎ 01840 250225 - www.stjuliot.com - Closed Christmas

BOUGHTON MONCHELSEA

Kent - Pop. 2 863 - Regional map n° **5**-B2

Mulberry Tree

MODERN BRITISH • FRIENDLY XX This rurally located restaurant has lovely gardens, a large paved terrace and a surprisingly stylish interior. Modern British menus feature confidently prepared, imaginatively presented dishes and ingredients are well-sourced.

Menu £ 25 (weekdays) - Carte £ 31/44

Hermitage Ln. ✉ ME17 4DA - South : 1.5 mi by Park Lane and East Hall Hill - ☎ 01622 749082 - www.themulberrytreekent.co.uk - Closed first 2 weeks January, Sunday dinner and Monday

BOURN

Cambridgeshire - Pop. 669 - Regional map n° **8**-A3

Willow Tree

MODERN BRITISH • CONTEMPORARY DÉCOR X Named after the vast tree in the garden, this quirky restaurant comes complete with gilt mirrors, chandeliers, Louis XV style furniture, a heated terrace and even a tepee. Contemporary European dishes include some small plates.

Carte £ 19/49

29 High St ✉ CB23 2SQ - ☎ 01954 719775 - www.thewillowtreebourn.com

BOURNEMOUTH

Bournemouth - Pop. 187 503 - Regional map n° **2**-D3

Arbor

MODERN CUISINE • CONTEMPORARY DÉCOR XX Located in an eco-friendly hotel, Arbor comes complete with a feature tree, FSC timbered floors, low energy induction cookers and honey bees on the roof. Modern menus display innovative touches and produce is local and sustainable.

Menu £ 20 (lunch) - Carte £ 23/40

Town plan: C2-n - *Green House Hotel, 4 Grove Rd ✉ BH1 3AX - ☎ 01202 498900 - www.arbor-restaurant.co.uk*

Neo

MODERN BRITISH • BRASSERIE XX Have a cocktail on the ground floor of this unusual round building then head up to the restaurant for views of the gardens and pier. Appetising dishes change with the seasons; the Josper-grilled meats and Dorset lobster are hits.

Menu £ 19 (lunch and early dinner) - Carte £ 28/49

Town plan: B2-c - *Hermitage Hotel, Exeter Rd ✉ BH2 5AH - ☎ 01202 203610 - www.neorestaurant.co.uk*

Green House

BUSINESS • DESIGN Bright, eco-friendly hotel set in a small Grade II listed property. Furnishings are reclaimed and wallpapers are printed using vegetable ink. They generate their own electricity and even use old cooking oil to power their car!

32 rooms - £ 99/160 £ 99/160

Town plan: C2-n - *4 Grove Rd ✉ BH1 3AX - ☎ 01202 498900 - www.thegreenhousehotel.com*

Arbor - See restaurant listing

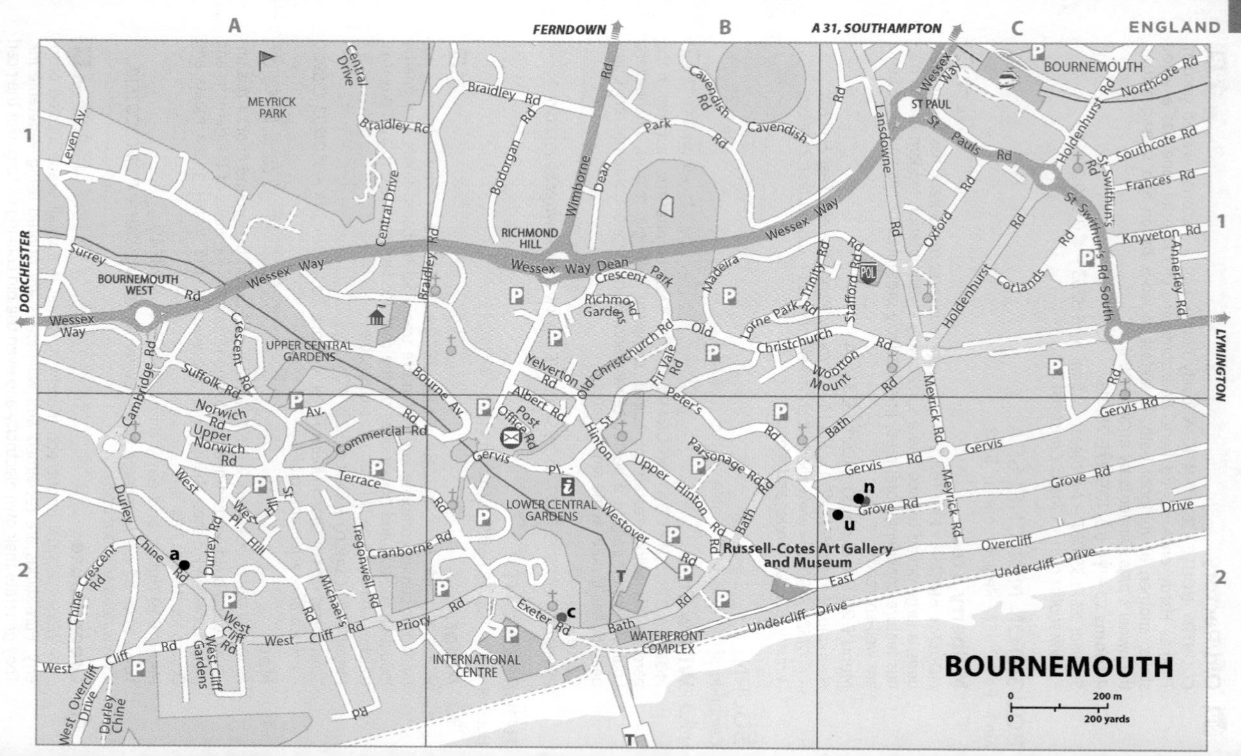
BOURNEMOUTH
0
200 m
0
200 yards
FERNDOWN
A 31, SOUTHAMPTON
DORCHESTER
LYMINGTON
A
B
C
1
2
Russell-Cotes Art Gallery and Museum
MEYRICK PARK
RICHMOND HILL
LOWER CENTRAL GARDENS
UPPER CENTRAL GARDENS
INTERNATIONAL CENTRE
WATERFRONT COMPLEX
West Cliff Gardens
BOURNEMOUTH WEST
BOURNEMOUTH
ST PAUL
Wessex Way
Lansdowne Rd
Holdenhurst Rd
St Swithun's Rd
St Swithun's Rd South
St Pauls Rd
Oxford Rd
Meyrick Rd
Gervis Rd
Grove Rd
Bath Rd
Christchurch Rd
Old Christchurch Rd
Madeira Rd
Cavendish Rd
Park Rd
Dean Park Crescent
Wimborne Rd
Richmond Gardens
Yelverton Rd
Albert Rd
Post Office Rd
Bourne Av.
Braidley Rd
Bodorgan Rd
Central Drive
Commercial Rd
Terrace Rd
Cranborne Rd
Tregonwell Rd
St Michael's Rd
West Hill Rd
West Hill Pl.
Priory Rd
Exeter Rd
Westover Rd
Upper Hinton Rd
Hinton Rd
St Peter's Rd
Parsonage Rd
Gervis Pl.
Undercliff Drive
Overcliff Drive
East Overcliff Drive
West Cliff Rd
West Cliff Rd
Durley Chine Rd
Durley Rd
Chine Crescent Rd
Cambridge Rd
Suffolk Rd
Crescent Rd
Norwich Rd
Upper Norwich Rd
Surrey Rd
Leven Av.
West Overcliff Drive
Durley Chine
Annerley Rd
Knyveton Rd
Frances Rd
Southcote Rd
Northcote Rd
Trinity Rd
Stafford Rd
Lorne Park Rd
Wootton Mount
Fir Vale Rd
Cotlands
a
c
n
u

Miramar

TRADITIONAL • CLASSIC Late Edwardian villa intended as a summer residence for the Austrian ambassador – until WW1 intervened. Close to town yet boasting peaceful, award-winning gardens and superb sea views. Large, classical bedrooms; some with balconies. Traditional dinner menu and snacks in the bar or on the terrace.

43 rooms – £ 50/145 £ 100/280

Town plan: C2-u – *19 Grove Rd, East Overcliff ✉ BH1 3AL – ✆ 01202 556581 – www.miramar-bournemouth.com*

Chocolate

TOWNHOUSE • PERSONALISED A unique, chocolate-themed hotel, owned by a chocolatier who runs regular workshops. Contemporary bedrooms come in browns and creams. The small lounge-bar features an automatic cocktail machine – they even serve 'choctails'.

15 rooms – £ 69/129 £ 79/189

Town plan: A2-a – *5 Durley Rd ✉ BH2 5JQ – ✆ 01202 556857 – www.thechocolateboutiquehotel.co.uk*

at Southbourne East : 3.75 mi. by A 35 on B 3059

Roots

MODERN BRITISH • NEIGHBOURHOOD In a parade of shops, behind frosted glass, is this bright, modern restaurant with 9 tables and a jovial, laid-back feel. Dishes are attractively prepared and delicately constructed; choose between 2 tasting menus at dinner.

Menu £ 23/46

141 Belle Vue Rd ✉ BH6 3EN – ✆ 01202 430005 (booking essential) – www.restaurantroots.co.uk – Closed 2 weeks July-August, 23 December-mid January, Sunday dinner, Wednesday-Thursday lunch, Monday and Tuesday

Cliff House

TOWNHOUSE • PERSONALISED A smartly refurbished 120 year old house which retains some of its original Victorian features. Comfortable bedrooms feature Smart TVs and coffee machines. The elegant, modern lounge-bar leads onto a landscaped garden and terrace.

14 rooms – £ 55/70 £ 100/140

13 Belle Vue Rd ✉ BH6 3DA – ✆ 01202 424701 – www.cliffhouse-hotel.com – Closed January

BOURTON-ON-THE-WATER

Gloucestershire – Pop. 3 296 – Regional map n° **2**-D1

Coombe House

TRADITIONAL • PERSONALISED A spacious 1920s house in a delightful village. The breakfast room boasts full-length leaded windows and overlooks the attractive garden, and the first floor terrace is perfect for sunny days. Homely bedrooms offer good comforts.

4 rooms – £ 80/100 £ 90/110

Rissington Rd ✉ GL54 2DT – ✆ 01451 821966 – www.coombehouse.net – Closed 24 December-5 January

at Lower Slaughter Northwest: 1.75 mi by A429 ✉ Cheltenham

Slaughters Manor House

MODERN CUISINE • CHIC An elegant dining room in a bright, airy extension of a fine manor house hotel, overlooking its lovely gardens. Immaculately laid tables have beautiful floral displays. Menus offer accomplished modern dishes with a classical base.

Menu £ 30/68

Slaughters Manor House Hotel, ✉ GL54 2HP – ✆ 01451 820456 – www.slaughtersmanor.co.uk

Slaughters Manor House

LUXURY • CLASSIC A beautiful part-17C manor house built from warm Cotswold stone and surrounded by delightful grounds. Elegant bedrooms are split between the house and the stables: the former are individually styled, while the latter are more up-to-date – and two have private hot tubs. Guest areas are modern and stylish.

19 rooms – £ 210/510 £ 250/550

GL54 2HP – 01451 820456 – www.slaughtersmanor.co.uk

Slaughters Manor House – See restaurant listing

Slaughters Country Inn

INN • CONTEMPORARY Originally a crammer school for Eton College, this stone-built manor house is a good choice for families – and they welcome dogs too! It's relaxed and understated, with modern styling; the cosy bedrooms have feature walls and up-to-date facilities. The pub and restaurant serve British classics.

31 rooms – £ 105/360 £ 125/380 – 7 suites

GL54 2HS – 01451 822143 – www.theslaughtersinn.co.uk

at Upper Slaughter Northwest: 2.5 mi by A429 Bourton-On-The-Water

Lords of the Manor

LUXURY • CLASSIC A charming 17C rectory in a pretty Cotswold village, with beautiful gardens, a superb outlook and a real sense of tranquility. Country house style bedrooms have subtle contemporary touches. Enjoy an aperitif on one of two luxurious sitting rooms then dine from a concise modern menu in the traditional dining room.

24 rooms – £ 150/510 £ 150/510 – 2 suites

GL54 2JD – 01451 820243 – www.lordsofthemanor.com

BOWDON

Greater Manchester – Greater Manchester – Pop. 6 079 – Regional map n° **11**-B3

Borage

MODERN CUISINE • NEIGHBOURHOOD XX An airy neighbourhood restaurant in a pleasant village. Well-presented, colourful European dishes showcase Polish ingredients and are full of flavour. The homemade breads are a highlight, as is the chocolate mousse.

Menu £ 17 (lunch) – Carte £ 24/28

7 Vale View, Vicarage Ln WA14 3BD – 0161 929 4775 – www.boragebowdon.co.uk – Closed Monday, Tuesday and 24 December

BOWNESS-ON-WINDERMERE – Cumbria → See Windermere

BOYLESTONE

Derbyshire – Regional map n° **9**-A2

Lighthouse

MODERN BRITISH • DESIGN XX It may not be near the coast, but the Lighthouse does attract your attention. The self-taught chef prepares ambitious, complex dishes with good combinations of flavours and textures; the tasting menu, in particular, is a hit.

Menu £ 55

New Rd DE6 5AA – behind Rose & Crown public house – 01335 330658 – www.the-lighthouse-restaurant.co.uk – dinner only – Closed Sunday-Tuesday

BRADFORD-ON-AVON

Wiltshire – Pop. 9 149 – Regional map n° **2**-C2

ENGLAND

Weaving Shed

MODERN CUISINE • BRASSERIE Cast iron pillars and exposed lightbulbs give a nod to this old mill's weaving days. Well-spaced tables look out over a riverside terrace and you are encouraged to talk to the chefs in the open kitchen. Dishes are modern and appealing.

Carte £ 25/40

3 Bridge Yard, Kingston Mills ✉ BA15 1EJ – ✆ 01225 866519 – www.weaving-shed.co.uk – Closed 25-26 December and Sunday dinner in winter

Bunch of Grapes

FRENCH • PUB A collaboration between 5 friends who love the food and wine of South West France. Rustic cooking focuses on the wood-fired Bertha oven and wines are imported directly from France. The place has an appealingly bijou, brocante feel.

Menu £ 18/25 – Carte £ 23/40

14 Silver St ✉ BA15 1JY – ✆ 01225 938088 – www.thebunchofgrapes.com – Closed 25-26 December

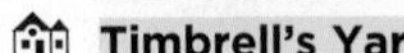

Timbrell's Yard

INN • CONTEMPORARY This Grade II listed riverside inn was once part of the old dye works. Bedrooms come in muted tones and feature reclaimed furnishings, quirky contemporary art and vintage touches; ask for a duplex room with river and church views. Enjoy appealing modern day classics in the rustic bar or restaurant.

17 rooms – †£ 85/145 ††£ 85/145

49 St Margaret's St ✉ BA15 1DE – ✆ 01225 869492 – www.timbrellsyard.com

Woolley Grange

COUNTRY HOUSE • CLASSIC Fine Jacobean manor house that's geared towards families, with a crèche, a kids' club, a games room and outdoor activities. For adults, there's a chic spa and some lovely country views. Smart bedrooms come in many styles. Accomplished, classical cooking is served in the restaurant and more relaxed orangery.

25 rooms – †£ 120/360 ††£ 120/360 – 6 suites

Woolley Green ✉ BA15 1TX – Northeast : 0.75 mi by B 3107 on Woolley St – ✆ 01225 864705 – www.woolleygrangehotel.co.uk

BRADLEY

Staffordshire – Pop. 513 – Regional map n° **10**-C2

The Red Lion

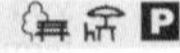

TRADITIONAL CUISINE • PUB An airy bar and conservatory opens onto a dining room hung with photos of the pub through the ages. Menus offer plenty of choice, with hearty, flavoursome dishes ranging from whole roast witch sole to curried chicken Kiev.

Menu £ 15 (weekday lunch) – Carte £ 22/40

Smithy Ln ✉ ST18 9DZ – ✆ 01785 780297 – www.redlionbradley.co.uk – Closed 25 December

BRADWELL

Derbyshire – Pop. 1 416 – Regional map n° **9**-A1

Samuel Fox Country Inn

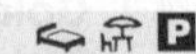

MODERN BRITISH • PUB An attractive, light-stone pub with smart, cosy bedrooms and a dramatic, hilly backdrop: named after the inventor of the steel-ribbed umbrella, who was born in the village. Flavourful classic dishes have modern touches and make good use of seasonal local produce. Popular 7 course tasting menu.

Menu £ 35/49

4 rooms – †£ 80/115 ††£ 100/140

Stretfield Rd ✉ S33 9JT – ✆ 01433 621562 – www.samuelfox.co.uk – dinner only and Sunday lunch – Closed 2-18 January, Sunday dinner, Monday and Tuesday

BRAITHWAITE - Cumbria ➜ See Keswick

BRAMPFORD SPEKE - Devon ➜ See Exeter

BRAMPTON

Cumbria – Pop. 4 229 – Regional map n° **12**-B1

Farlam Hall

TRADITIONAL · PERSONALISED A well-run, family-owned country house, whose origins can be traced back to the 1600s. Bedrooms are furnished with antiques but also have modern touches like Bose radios. The sumptuous dining room has a traditional daily menu and romantic views across a lake, while afternoon tea is served in the curio-filled lounges, overlooking the immaculate ornamental gardens.

12 rooms (dinner included) – †£ 118/148 ††£ 216/276

✉ *CA8 2NG – Southeast : 2.75 mi on A 689 – ✆ 016977 46234 – www.farlamhall.co.uk – Closed 7-26 January and 25-30 December*

BRANCASTER STAITHE

Norfolk – Regional map n° **8**-C1

White Horse

CLASSIC CUISINE · PUB The rear views over the marshes and Scolt Head Island really make this pub. Choose from old favourites, tapas-style dishes and a few more ambitious offerings on the bar menu; or seasonally changing dishes supplemented by daily specials on the à la carte. Smart, New England style bedrooms – some with terraces.

Carte £ 27/38

15 rooms – †£ 110/150 ††£ 110/150

✉ *PE31 8BY – ✆ 01485 210262 (booking essential) – www.whitehorsebrancaster.co.uk*

BRANDESTON

Suffolk – Pop. 296 – Regional map n° **8**-D3

The Queen

TRADITIONAL BRITISH · RUSTIC A rustic, shabby-chic pub with snug corners. Veg comes from the huge kitchen garden and whole beasts are brought in from a farm nearby. Puddings are delightful, there's an amazing array of cheeses and it's worth getting up early for breakfast. If you're a fan of glamping, they have some lovely shepherd's huts.

Carte £ 21/35

The Street ✉ IP13 7AD – ✆ 01728 685307 – www.thequeenatbrandeston.co.uk – Closed 8-23 January and Monday

BRAUGHING

Hertfordshire – Pop. 854 – Regional map n° **7**-B2

Golden Fleece

TRADITIONAL BRITISH · INN A proudly run pub with striking 17C features, a spacious garden and a pretty terrace overlooking the village. Comforting dishes include gluten and dairy free options and are followed by satisfying puddings.

Carte £ 21/39

20 Green End ✉ SG11 2PG – ✆ 01920 823555 – www.goldenfleecebraughing.co.uk – Closed 25-26 December and Sunday dinner

BRAY

Windsor and Maidenhead – Pop. 8 121 – Regional map n° **6**-C3

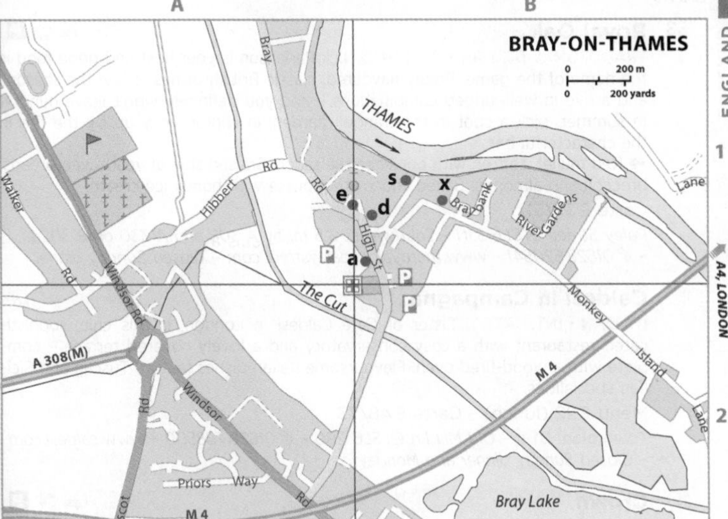

✿✿✿ Waterside Inn (Alain Roux)

CLASSIC FRENCH · ELEGANT XxxX An illustrious restaurant in a glorious spot on a bank of the Thames, with a relaxed dining room and a delightful terrace ideal for aperitifs. Service is charming and expertly structured. Carefully considered French menus reflect the seasons and use top quality luxury ingredients in perfectly judged, sophisticated combinations. Bedrooms are chic and sumptuous.

→ Tronçonnettes de homard poêlées minute au porto blanc. Filets de lapereau grillés sur un fondant de céleri-rave, sauce à l'armagnac et aux marrons glacés. Soufflé chaud aux mirabelles.

Menu £ 64 (weekday lunch)/168 – Carte £ 125/174

11 rooms – †£ 260/570 ††£ 260/570 – 2 suites

Town plan: B1-s – *Ferry Rd ✉ SL6 2AT – ☎ 01628 620691 (booking essential) – www.waterside-inn.co.uk – Closed 26 December-1 February and Monday-Tuesday*

✿✿✿ Fat Duck (Heston Blumenthal)

CREATIVE · MINIMALIST XxX Heston Blumenthal takes you on a theatrical, multi-sensory journey informed by a narrative which evokes memories of childhood. Cooking is inventive, playful and perfectly judged, and no matter how elaborate the presentation, it is never at the expense of flavour. The experience is made all the more enjoyable by the delightful staff.

→ Hot and cold tea. Duck à l'orange. Botrytis cinerea.

Menu £ 265 – tasting menu only

Town plan: B1-d – *High St ✉ SL6 2AQ – ☎ 01628 580333 (booking essential) – www.thefatduck.co.uk – Closed 2 weeks Christmas-New Year, Sunday and Monday*

✿ Hinds Head

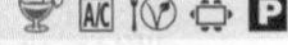

TRADITIONAL BRITISH · HISTORIC X Start with a cocktail in The Royal Lounge – surrounded by unusual taxidermy – before heading for the characterful 15C restaurant. Monthly changing 3, 4 and 6 course set menus celebrate traditional British dishes but Heston Blumenthal's creative influences can also be seen in the sophisticated cooking.

→ Scallops Waldorf with pickled shallots and walnut dressing. Roast duck, asparagus, wild garlic and celeriac. White chocolate and lemon cheesecake with biscuit ice cream.

Menu £ 25/58 – tasting menu only

Town plan: B1-e – *High St ✉ SL6 2AB – ☎ 01628 626151 (booking essential) – www.hindsheadbray.com – Closed 25 December and Sunday dinner*

Royal Oak

TRADITIONAL BRITISH • DESIGN Nick Parkinson is your host and good food is the name of the game. Boldly flavoured, classic British dishes follow the seasons and arrive in well-judged combinations – and you definitely won't leave hungry! In summer, pick a spot in the tranquil garden; in winter, cosy up by the fire in the characterful bar.

→ Red mullet, saffron with bouillabaisse sauce. Braised shin of veal, sweetbreads, broccoli and almonds. Baked chocolate mousse with honey ice cream.

Carte £ 32/51

Paley Street ✉ SL6 3JN – Southwest : 3.5 mi by A 308 and A 330 on B 3024 – ✆ 01628 620541 – www.theroyaloakpaleystreet.com – Closed Sunday dinner

Caldesi in Campagna

ITALIAN • INTIMATE XX Sister of Café Caldesi in London, is this chic, sophisticated restaurant with a cosy conservatory and a lovely covered terrace – complete with a wood-fired oven. Flavoursome Italian dishes feature Tuscan and Sicilian specialities.

Menu £ 22 (lunch) – Carte £ 48/73

Town plan: B1-x – *Old Mill Ln ✉ SL6 2BG – ✆ 01628 788500 – www.caldesi.com – Closed Sunday dinner and Monday*

Crown

TRADITIONAL BRITISH • PUB Charmingly restored 16C building; formerly two cottages and a bike shop! Drinkers mingle with diners, and dark columns, low beams and roaring fires create a cosy atmosphere. Carefully prepared British dishes are robust and flavoursome.

Carte £ 29/47

Town plan: B1-a – *High St ✉ SL6 2AH – ✆ 01628 621936 – www.thecrownatbray.com*

BRAYE

→ See Channel Islands (Alderney)

BRIDPORT

Dorset – Pop. 13 737 – Regional map n° **2**-B3

Riverside

SEAFOOD • BISTRO X Since 1964, this restaurant has offered unfussy seafood dishes crafted from local produce – much of it landed just 100m away. It sits beside the river on its own little island and is accessed via a bridge. Go for the daily specials.

Menu £ 17 (lunch) – Carte £ 30/67

West Bay ✉ DT6 4EZ – South : 1.75 mi by B 3157 – ✆ 01308 422011 (booking essential) – www.thefishrestaurant-westbay.co.uk – Closed January-mid February, Sunday dinner in winter and Monday except bank holidays

at Burton Bradstock Southeast: 2 mi by B3157

Seaside Boarding House

TRADITIONAL BRITISH • CONTEMPORARY DÉCOR XX Stunningly located on the clifftop, this old hotel has been given a fresh new look. The bright, airy restaurant has a subtle maritime theme and there's a lovely terrace with sea views. Menus offer everything from a croque monsieur to lemon sole with samphire. Classically understated bedrooms come with claw-foot baths and there's a pleasant bar and library for residents.

Menu £ 18 (weekday lunch) – Carte £ 22/41

8 rooms – †£ 175 ††£ 195

Cliff Rd ✉ DT6 4RB – Southeast : 0.5 mi – ✆ 01308 897205 – www.theseasideboardinghouse.com

Michelin

GOOD TIPS!

The jewel of the south coast is a city that knows how to have a good time, with plenty of cool, quirky hotels and restaurants. Enjoy vistas out over the Channel from your bedroom at **Drakes** or **A Room with a View**. **Terre à Terre** is a vegetarian's dream; pescatarians should book a table at **Little Fish Market**, while carnivores can head for **Coal Shed**.

BRIGHTON AND HOVE

Brighton and Hove – Pop. 229 700 – Regional map n° **5**-A3

Restaurants

64°

MODERN BRITISH • SIMPLE X If you like things fun and fuss-free, then this intimate modern restaurant is the place for you! Menus are divided into four – 'Meat', 'Fish', 'Veg' and 'Dessert' – and each section also has four choices. Cooking is simple but well-textured and flavoursome; most of the dining takes place at the counter.

Carte £ 21/38

Town plan: B2-c – *53 Meeting House Ln. ✉ BN1 1HB – ✆ 01273 770115 (booking essential) – www.64degrees.co.uk – Closed 25-26 December*

Chilli Pickle

INDIAN • BISTRO X Simple restaurant with a relaxed, buzzy vibe and friendly, welcoming service. The passionate chef uses good quality ingredients to create oft-changing menus of thoughtfully prepared, authentic Indian dishes with delicate spicing. Beside the terrace they also have a cart selling street food style snacks.

Menu £ 25 (dinner) – Carte £ 22/34

Town plan: C2-z – *17 Jubilee St ✉ BN1 1GE – ✆ 01273 900383 – www.thechillipickle.com – Closed 25-26 December*

Pike & Pine (N)

MODERN BRITISH • FASHIONABLE XX A smart, light-filled restaurant filled with plants and trees; sit on comfy banquettes and watch the chefs in action. Punchy, eye-catching dishes blend classic and modern techniques – some have playful touches.

Menu £ 45/75

Town plan: C2-a – *1D St James's ✉ BN2 1RE – ✆ 01273 686668 (booking essential) – www.pikeandpine.co.uk – dinner only – Closed 25 December, Monday and Tuesday*

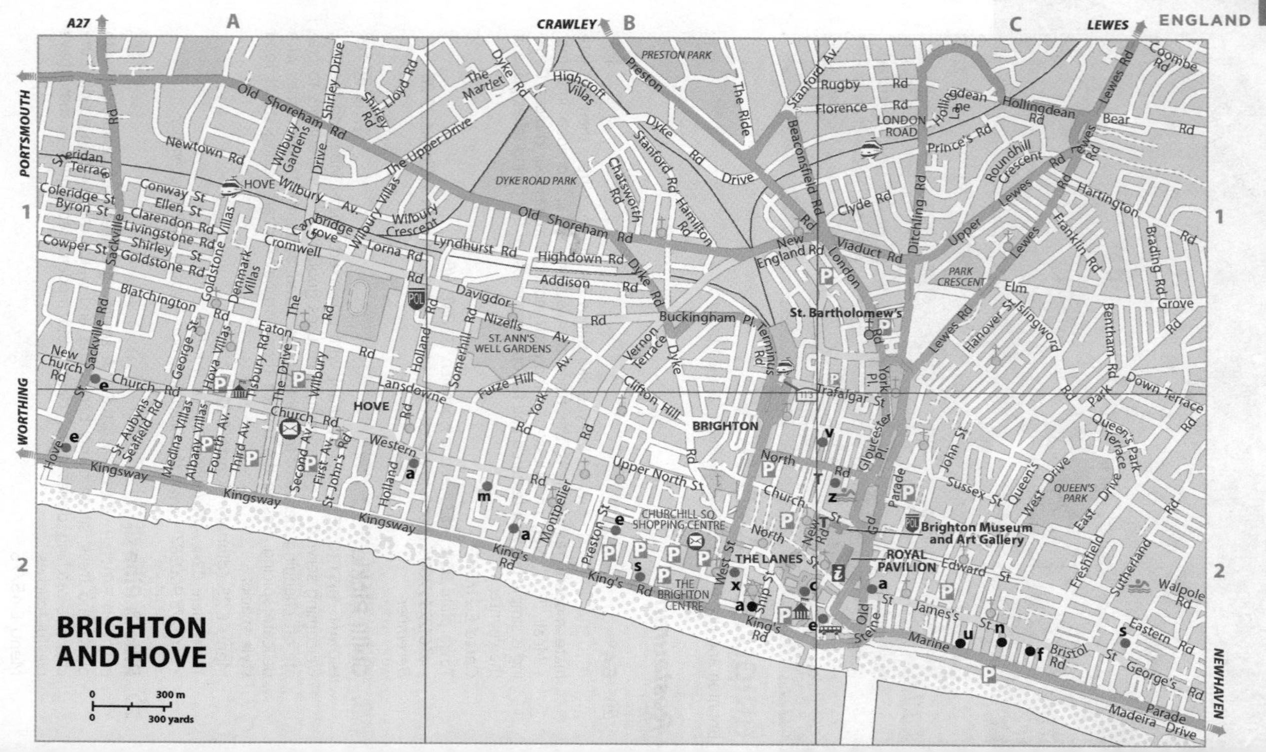
BRIGHTON AND HOVE
0 300 m
0 300 yards
A27
CRAWLEY
LEWES
PORTSMOUTH
WORTHING
NEWHAVEN
A
B
C
1
2
BRIGHTON
HOVE
ROYAL PAVILION
Brighton Museum and Art Gallery
THE LANES
CHURCHILL SQ. SHOPPING CENTRE
THE BRIGHTON CENTRE
QUEEN'S PARK
PARK CRESCENT
PRESTON PARK
DYKE ROAD PARK
ST. ANN'S WELL GARDENS
LONDON ROAD
St. Bartholomew's
York Pl.
Lewes Rd
Ditchling Rd
Preston
Dyke Rd
Old Shoreham Rd
Beaconsfield Rd
New England Rd
Terminus Rd
West St
North St
Church St
Western Rd
King's Rd
Kingsway
Marine Parade
Madeira Drive
Old Steine
Parade
Edward St
St James's St
Eastern Rd
Sackville Rd
Church Rd
The Drive
Holland Rd
Montpelier Rd
Upper North St
Clifton Hill
Buckingham Pl.
Vernon Terrace
Highcroft Villas
The Upper Drive
Shirley Drive
Lloyd Rd
Shirley Rd
Newtown Rd
Goldstone Villas
Denmark Villas
First Av.
Second Av.
Third Av.
Fourth Av.
Hove St
Queen's Park Terrace
Freshfield Rd
Sutherland Rd
Bentham Rd
Brading Rd
Franklin Rd
Hollingdean Rd
Hollingdean Lane
Bear Rd
Coombe Rd
Hartington Rd
Stanford Rd
Stanford Av.
The Ride
The Martlet
Chatsworth Rd
Highdown Rd
Addison Rd
Somerhill Rd
Lansdowne Rd
Wilbury Villas
Wilbury Gardens
Wilbury Crescent
Wilbury Av.
Cambridge Grove
Cromwell Rd
Lorna Rd
Lyndhurst Rd
Blatchington Rd
George St
Medina Villas
Albany Villas
Tisbury Rd
St John's Rd
Trafalgar St
Gloucester Pl.
John St
Sussex St
Queen's West Drive
East Drive
Elm Grove
Islingword Rd
Hanover St
Walpole Rd
Bristol Rd
Upper Lewes Rd
Roundhill Crescent
Prince's Rd
Viaduct Rd
Clyde Rd
Florence Rd
Rugby Rd
Dyke Rd Drive
Hamilton Rd
Davigdor Rd
Nizells Av.
Furze Hill
York Av.
Hove Villas
Eaton Rd
Conway St
Ellen St
Clarendon Rd
Livingstone Rd
Shirley St
Goldstone Rd
St Aubyns
Seafield Rd
New Church Rd
Coleridge St
Byron St
Cowper St
Sheridan Terrace
Preston St
Ship St
New Rd
St George's Rd
Down Terrace
Park Rd

Salt Room

SEAFOOD • FASHIONABLE XX This city hotspot has a lovely 'rustic-meets-industrial' style and has views from many of its tables and the terrace. Menus focus on seafood, with some fish cooked whole on the Josper grill. Service is attentive and personable.

Menu £ 15 (lunch) - Carte £ 27/48

Town plan: B2-s - *106 Kings Rd ✉ BN1 2FY - ☎ 01273 929488 - www.saltroom-restaurant.co.uk - Closed 25-26 December*

Coal Shed

MEATS AND GRILLS • NEIGHBOURHOOD X A keenly run, rustic steakhouse hidden away in the Brighton Lanes district. Cooking centres around the charcoal oven; they specialise in 35-day matured organic steaks but there's also a tasty selection of fresh fish dishes to try.

Menu £ 15 (lunch and early dinner) - Carte £ 26/47

Town plan: B2-x - *8 Boyces St ✉ BN1 1AN - ☎ 01273 322998 - www.coalshed-restaurant.co.uk - Closed 25-26 December*

Etch by Steven Edwards

MODERN BRITISH • NEIGHBOURHOOD X This compact restaurant is a hit with the locals. Ask to sit in one of the bay window booths then choose between two weekly set menus - go for 6 courses at lunch or 8 courses at dinner. Cooking captures flavours to the full.

Menu £ 40/60 - tasting menu only

Town plan: A1-e - *216 Church Rd, Hove ✉ BN3 2DJ - ☎ 01273 227485 (booking essential) - www.etchfood.co.uk - dinner only and Saturday lunch - Closed last week December, first week January and Sunday-Tuesday*

Gingerman

MODERN CUISINE • NEIGHBOURHOOD X There's a smart Scandic feel to the decoration and an intimacy to the atmosphere at this long-standing neighbourhood restaurant. Lunch is fairly classical while dinner features more elaborate, innovative combinations.

Menu £ 20 (weekdays)/38

Town plan: B2-a - *21a Norfolk Sq ✉ BN1 2PD - ☎ 01273 326688 (booking essential) - www.gingermanrestaurants.com - Closed 2 weeks winter, 25 December and Monday*

Little Fish Market

SEAFOOD • SIMPLE X Fish is the focus at this simple restaurant, set in a converted fishmonger's opposite the old Victorian fish market. The owner cooks alone and his set 5 course menu offers refined, interesting modern seafood dishes.

Menu £ 55 - tasting menu only

Town plan: B2-m - *10 Upper Market St, Hove ✉ BN3 1AS - ☎ 01273 722213 (booking essential) - www.thelittlefishmarket.co.uk - dinner only and Saturday lunch - Closed 1 week April, 2 weeks September, 1 week December, Sunday and Monday*

Market

MODERN CUISINE • TAPAS BAR X Bright green glazed tiles, a large counter and cheery hands-on service from the owners give this intimate space a vibrant feel. Cooking is equally colourful with punchy flavours; choose 4-5 small plates or one of the daily specials.

Menu £ 12 (weekday lunch) - Carte £ 20/31

Town plan: A2-a - *42 Western Rd, Hove ✉ BN3 1JD - ☎ 01273 823707 (booking advisable) - www.market-restaurantbar.co.uk - Closed 25-26 December and 1 January*

Silo

MODERN CUISINE • RUSTIC The UK's first zero-waste restaurant: furnishings are made from reclaimed materials, plates are recycled from carrier bags, drinks are served in jam jars and food waste is composted and distributed back to suppliers. Choose a set menu – Plant, Dairy, Meat or Fish – or mix and match dishes as you please.

Menu £ 25/28 – Carte £ 30/46

Town plan: C2-v – *39 Upper Gardner St ✉ BN1 4AN – ✆ 01273 674259 (booking essential at dinner) – www.silobrighton.com – lunch only and dinner Thursday-Saturday*

The Set

MODERN BRITISH • RUSTIC Two communal tables make up the café, while the counter and tables behind form the restaurant. Exposed wood, brick and iron set the scene. Modern tasting plates reflect the seasons; the three restaurant menus comprise 4 set courses.

Menu £ 34/40 – Carte £ 16/20

Town plan: B2-e – *Artist Residence Hotel, 33 Regency Sq ✉ BN1 2GG – ✆ 01273 855572 (booking essential) – www.thesetrestaurant.com*

Terre à Terre

VEGETARIAN • NEIGHBOURHOOD Relaxed, friendly restaurant decorated in warm burgundy colours. Appealing menu of generous, tasty, original vegetarian dishes which include items from Japan, China and South America. Mini épicerie sells wine, pasta and chutney.

Menu £ 33 – Carte £ 33/46

Town plan: C2-e – *71 East St ✉ BN1 1HQ – ✆ 01273 729051 (booking essential) – www.terreaterre.co.uk – Closed 25-26 December and Monday in winter*

Ginger Dog

MODERN BRITISH • PUB A charming Victorian pub with a pleasingly shabby-chic feel. Ornately carved woodwork sits comfortably alongside more recent additions like bowler hat lampshades. Cooking has a modern British style and uses the latest techniques.

Menu £ 18 (weekdays) – Carte £ 25/43

Town plan: C2-s – *12 College Pl ✉ BN2 1HN – ✆ 01273 620990 – www.gingermanrestaurants.com – Closed 25 December*

Ginger Pig

TRADITIONAL BRITISH • PUB A striking mock-Tudor building with a beautiful antique revolving door and a charming wooden bar counter. The original, highly seasonal menu has a distinct European accent and gives the odd nod to North Africa. Modern, loft-style bedrooms have Hyponos beds – BBQs and picnic hampers are available to borrow.

Menu £ 15 (weekdays) – Carte £ 27/44

11 rooms – †£ 80/160 ††£ 80/160 – ☕ £ 11

Town plan: A2-e – *3 Hove St, Hove ✉ BN3 2TR – ✆ 01273 736123 – www.gingermanrestaurants.com – Closed 25 December*

Hotels

Hotel du Vin

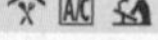

BUSINESS • PERSONALISED Made up of various different buildings; the oldest being a former wine merchant's. Kick-back in the cavernous, gothic-style bar-lounge or out on the terrace. Bedrooms are richly decorated and have superb monsoon showers. The relaxed brasserie, with its hidden courtyard, serves French bistro classics.

49 rooms ☕ – †£ 155/455 ††£ 155/455

Town plan: B2-a – *2-6 Ship St ✉ BN1 1AD – ✆ 01273 718588 – www.hotelduvin.com*

Drakes

TOWNHOUSE • DESIGN A pair of 18C townhouses on the promenade, with a smart cocktail bar. Chic, well-equipped bedrooms have wooden feature walls and sea or city views – one even has a bath in the bay window! Minimum 2 night stay at weekends.

20 rooms – †£ 120/160 ††£ 120/360 – ☕£ 15

Town plan: C2-u – *43-44 Marine Par ✉ BN2 1PE – ☎ 01273 696934 – www.drakesofbrighton.com*

A Room with a View

TOWNHOUSE • PERSONALISED Snuggle into a Hungarian goose down duvet and, if your room is at the front of this Regency townhouse, enjoy the views out over the Channel. All have Nespresso machines and a soft drink mini-bar; Room 10 has a roof terrace.

10 rooms ☕ – †£ 70/250 ††£ 150/250

Town plan: C2-u – *41 Marine Par. ✉ BN2 1PE – ☎ 01273 682885 – www.aroomwithaviewbrighton.com*

Fab Guest

TOWNHOUSE • DESIGN Don't be fooled by the classic Georgian exterior; inside it's stylish and modern, with minimalist bedrooms displaying a mix of antiques and bespoke furnishings by local artists. There's no reception and no keys – just access codes.

14 rooms ☕ – †£ 59/149 ††£ 89/249

Town plan: C2-f – *9 Charlotte St ✉ BN2 1AG – ☎ 01273 625505 – www.fabguest.co.uk – Closed Christmas*

Kemp Townhouse

TOWNHOUSE • MODERN A boutique townhouse with a basement breakfast room turned bar-lounge which opens onto a courtyard terrace. Stylish bedrooms have compact wet rooms; those at the front are larger and more comfortable and two have four-poster beds.

11 rooms ☕ – †£ 75/95 ††£ 125/145

Town plan: C2-n – *21 Atlingworth St ✉ BN2 1PL – ☎ 01273 681400 – www.kemptownhouse.com – Closed 24-26 December*

BRILL

Buckinghamshire – Pop. 1 141 – Regional map n° **6**-C2

The Pointer

TRADITIONAL BRITISH • INN Sit in one of two beamed dining rooms or beside the fire in one of the smaller rooms and take time to read the menu, which explains what they are currently growing in the gardens and using in the cooking. Rare breed meats come from their 240 acre farm; take something home from the adjoining butcher's shop. Stylish, contemporary bedrooms are in the cottage opposite.

Menu £ 18 (weekday lunch) – Carte £ 30/67

4 rooms ☕ – †£ 140/170 ††£ 140/170

27 Church St ✉ HP18 9RT – ☎ 01844 238339 – www.thepointerbrill.co.uk – Closed first week January and Monday

Michelin

GOOD TIPS!

The unofficial capital of the West Country has a vibrant cultural and recreational scene, yet retains the friendly feel of a smaller town. For a home from home feel, stay at boutique townhouse **Number 38 Clifton** with its city views. Michelin Starred **Casamia** – meaning 'My House' – showcases the innovative seasonal cooking of Peter Sanchez-Iglesias.

BRISTOL

City of Bristol – Pop. 535 907 – Regional map n° **2**-C2

Restaurants

✿ Casamia (Peter Sanchez-Iglesias)

CREATIVE • DESIGN XX Casamia sits in an impressive listed Victorian hospital overlooking Bathurst Basin. You enter through double glass doors, under an arch and through into a pared down, Scandic-style room. The team are charming and the passionate chefs personally deliver the skilfully prepared, highly creative, seasonal dishes.

➜ Beetroot risotto. Brown trout with crab. Passion fruit and tarragon.

Menu £ 98 – tasting menu only

Town plan: C2-e – *The General, Lower Guinea St ✉ BS1 6SY*
– *✆ 0117 959 2884 (booking essential) – www.casamiarestaurant.co.uk*
– *dinner only and lunch Friday-Saturday*
– *Closed 1-7 January, 29 May-2 June, 28 August-1 September, 23-27 October, 25-31 December and Sunday- Tuesday*

✿ wilks (James Wilkins)

MODERN BRITISH • FRIENDLY XX Vibrant modern art hangs on grey walls at this appealing neighbourhood restaurant. The experienced chef is well-travelled and skilfully balances different textures with flavours from around the globe. French and British ingredients jostle with one another on the menu and all of the fish is wild.

➜ Hand-dived scallops with smoked duck ham and tarragon gnocchi. Wild turbot, white asparagus, monk's beard and sea urchin. Muscovado meringue with marinated pineapple, rhum baba and piña colada sorbet.

Menu £ 29 (weekday lunch) – Carte £ 50/62

Town plan: A1-d – *1 Chandos Rd ✉ BS6 6PG*
– *✆ 0117 973 7999 (booking essential) – www.wilksrestaurant.co.uk*
– *Closed 24 December-17January, 30 July-22 August, Monday, Tuesday and lunch Wednesday*

The symbol ❀ denotes a particularly interesting wine list.

Paco Tapas

SPANISH • TAPAS BAR X This buzzy tapas bar is the sister to Casamia. Sit on the terrace for nibbles accompanied by one of their fine Spanish wines or head for the 8-seater counter set around the large open grill. Authentic, skilfully prepared dishes are packed with flavour; try the "Chef's Menu" for a best-of-the-best tour of Spain.

→ Red mullet with saffron rice. Cocido Andaluz. Crema Catalana.

Menu £ 50 - Carte £ 28/45

Town plan: C2-t - *The General, Lower Guinea St ✉ BS1 6SY - ✆ 0117 925 7021 (booking essential) - www.pacotapas.co.uk - Closed Sunday dinner, Monday, Tuesday and Wednesday-Thursday lunch*

No Man's Grace

MODERN BRITISH • NEIGHBOURHOOD X Simple neighbourhood restaurant run by an experienced young chef. Boldly flavoured small plates feature just 3 or 4 ingredients and have a classic heart and a modern touch. For something sweeter, pay a visit to the dessert bar, where every dish is matched with a dessert wine and a cocktail.

Menu £ 16 (weekday lunch) - Carte £ 28/43

Town plan: AB1-w - *6 Chandos Rd ✉ BS6 6PE - ✆ 0117 974 4077 - www.nomansgrace.com - dinner only and lunch Friday-Sunday - Closed 24 December-2 January, Sunday dinner, Monday and Tuesday*

Second Floor at Harvey Nichols

MODERN CUISINE • DESIGN XXX A spacious and elegant light-filled restaurant with stylish gold décor. Good value lunch menu and concise à la carte offering original, modern dishes. Chic lounge bar for cocktails and light bites. Attentive service.

Menu £ 22 (lunch) - Carte £ 32/43

Town plan: D1-a - *27 Philadelphia St, Quakers Friars, Cabot Circus ✉ BS1 3BZ - ✆ 0117 916 8898 - www.harveynichols.com - Closed 25 December, 1 January, Easter, Sunday and Monday*

Spiny Lobster

SEAFOOD • BRASSERIE XX The Spiny Lobster brings a taste of the sea to the city. Enter through the fishmonger's to view the daily catch on a marble slab on your way to the leather-furnished dining room. Simply prepared dishes are cooked in the Josper oven.

Menu £ 18 (lunch and early dinner) - Carte £ 25/54

Town plan: A1-c - *128 Whiteladies Rd ✉ BS8 2RS - ✆ 0117 973 7384 - www.thespinylobster.co.uk - Closed dinner 24 December-4 January, Sunday and Monday*

Adelina Yard

MODERN CUISINE • INTIMATE X The experienced chef-owners named their first restaurant after their old home. Well-presented, well-balanced modern dishes are brought to the tables by the chefs. Sit at the far end of the simple L-shaped room, overlooking the quay.

Menu £ 17 (weekday lunch) - Carte £ 34/47

Town plan: C2-c - *3 Queen Quay, Welsh Back ✉ BS1 4SL - ✆ 0117 911 2112 (booking advisable) - www.adelinayard.com - Closed 24 December-9 January, Sunday and Monday*

Bell's Diner & Bar Rooms

MEDITERRANEAN CUISINE • BISTRO X A bustling city institution with a bohemian feel, which retains evidence of its old grocer's shop days. Flavoursome Mediterranean cooking shows a good understanding of ingredients; try the charcoal-grilled chicken oyster pinchos.

Carte £ 22/40

Town plan: B1-e - *1-3 York Rd, Montpelier ✉ BS6 5QB - ✆ 0117 924 0357 (bookings advisable at dinner) - www.bellsdiner.com - Closed 24-26 December, 1 January, Monday and Tuesday lunch, Wednesday and Thursday lunch October-April*

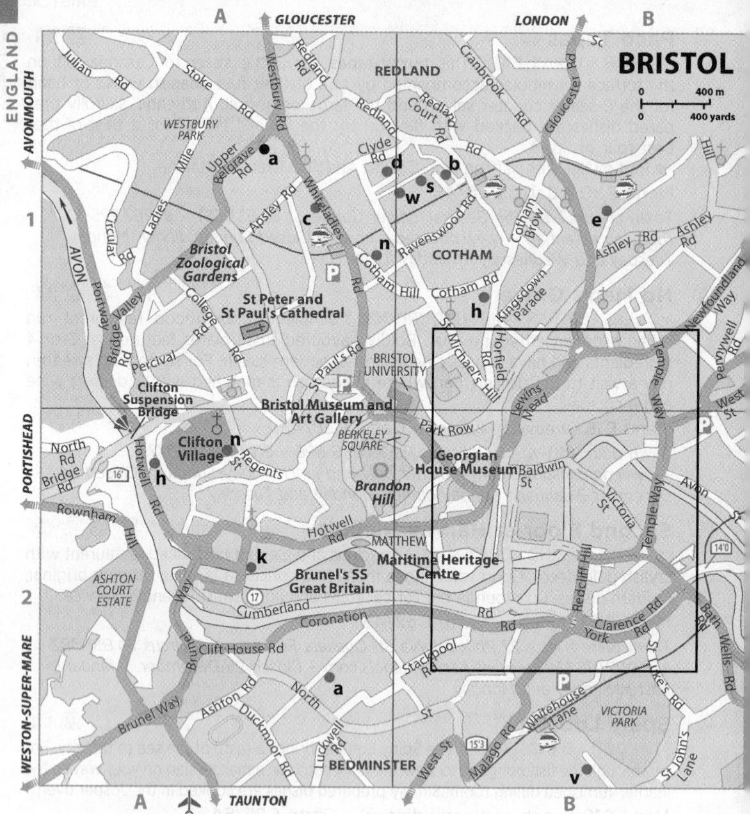

Bellita

MEDITERRANEAN CUISINE • TAPAS BAR X Bellita will put a smile on your face with its bright décor and unpretentious atmosphere. The menu is all about sharing, with vibrant small plates inspired by the Med, the Middle East and North Africa. Try the 8 year old Galician beef.

Carte £ 15/37

Town plan: A1-n – *34 Cotham Hill ✉ BS6 6LA*
– *☎ 0117 923 8755 – www.bellita.co.uk*
– *dinner only and lunch Thursday-Saturday – Closed 24-26 December and Sunday*

Birch

TRADITIONAL BRITISH • SIMPLE X Simple neighbourhood restaurant on a long, terraced street. Chef Sam's time at St John shows in his concise menu of rustic British dishes, which use lesser-known produce and are packed with flavour. Service is charming and attentive.

Carte £ 22/34

Town plan: A2-a – *47 Raleigh Rd ✉ BS3 1QS*
– *☎ 0117 902 8326 (booking essential) – www.birchbristol.co*
– *dinner only and Saturday lunch – Closed 3 weeks August, 2 weeks Christmas-New Year and Sunday-Tuesday*

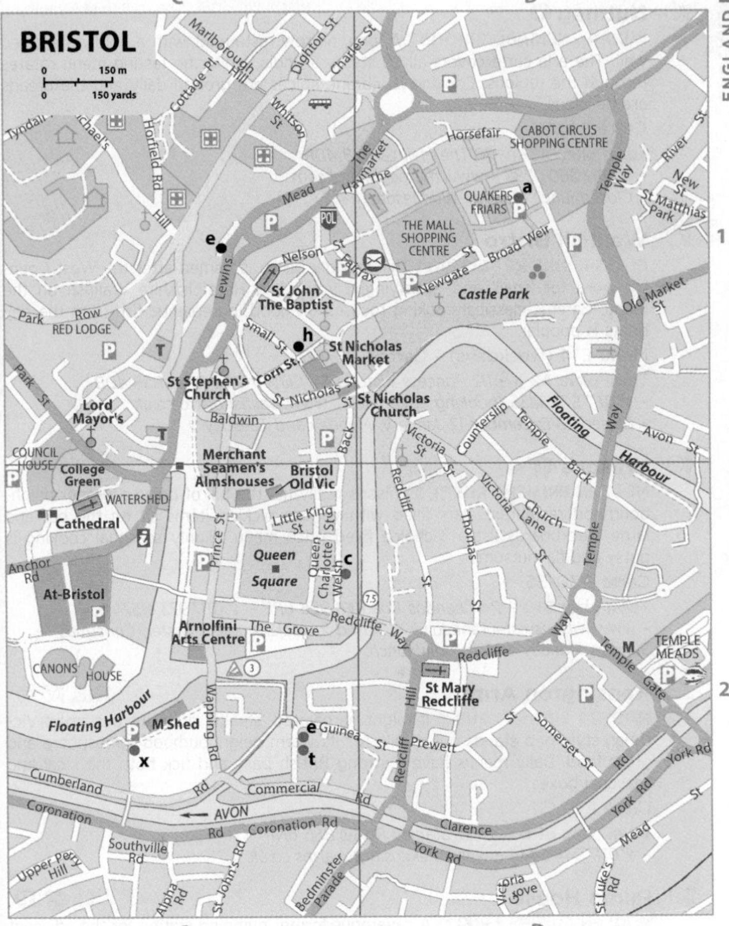

BOX-E

MODERN BRITISH • SIMPLE Wapping Wharf is home to Cargo, a retail yard made of converted shipping containers, and on the first floor is intimate BOX-E, a compact restaurant clad in chipboard. Dishes are modern and colourful; the panna cotta is a must.

Carte £ 24/31

Town plan: C2-x – *Unit 10, Cargo 1, Wapping Wharf ✉ BS1 6WP – www.boxebristol.com – Closed Sunday-Tuesday lunch*

Bulrush

MODERN BRITISH • BISTRO On looks alone, you might pass it by, but its simplicity is part of its charm. A whitewashed wall divides the room and service is engaging. Modern British dishes are boldly flavoured with the odd Asian touch.

Menu £ 19 (weekday lunch) – Carte £ 29/41

Town plan: B1-h – *21 Cotham Rd South ✉ BS6 5TZ – ✆ 0117 329 0990 (booking essential) – www.bulrushrestaurant.co.uk – Closed 2 weeks January, 1 week May, 2 weeks August, Sunday, Monday and lunch Tuesday-Wednesday*

Nutmeg

INDIAN • NEIGHBOURHOOD A long, narrow restaurant with a boldly stencilled wall. The à la carte covers all 29 states of India, while the tasting menu rotates through the regions. Cooking is vibrant, spices are ground daily and the breads are delicious.

Carte £ 14/31

Town plan: A2-n – *10 The Mall ✉ BS8 4DR – ✆ 0117 360 0288 – www.nutmegbristol.com – Closed lunch Monday-Wednesday*

Wallfish Bistro

CLASSIC CUISINE • BISTRO This friendly bistro is named after the West Country word for 'snail' and, satisfyingly, you'll find Herefordshire Wallfish on the menu. Careful, classical cooking focuses on good ingredients; fish from the day boats is popular.

Menu £ 14 (weekdays) – Carte £ 26/56

Town plan: A2-h – *112 Princess Victoria St, Clifton Village ✉ BS8 4DB – ✆ 0117 973 5435 (booking advisable) – www.wallfishbistro.co.uk – Closed 23 December-12 January, Monday and Tuesday*

Wilsons

MODERN BRITISH • RUSTIC Wilsons really fits the bill of being a proper neighbourhood restaurant. Jars filled with various pickled items sit on the bar and large blackboards list a 3-choice fixed price menu. Highly seasonal cooking is gutsy and flavoursome.

Carte £ 30/35

Town plan: B1-s – *24 Chandos Road ✉ BS6 6PF – ✆ 0117 973 4157 – www.wilsonsrestaurant.co.uk – Closed 2 weeks August, Easter, Christmas, Sunday, Monday and Tuesday lunch.*

Kensington Arms

MODERN BRITISH • PUB It might be painted 'stealth' grey but this smart Victorian-style pub stands out a mile for its warm neighbourhood atmosphere and great food. Daily menus have a strong British base and tick both the local and seasonal boxes.

Carte £ 22/37

Town plan: B1-b – *35-37 Stanley Rd ✉ BS6 6NP – ✆ 0117 944 6444 – www.thekensingtonarms.co.uk*

Pump House

MODERN CUISINE • PUB A cavernous former pumping station for the adjacent docks; now a rustic pub with a smart mezzanine restaurant. Modern classics change with seasons; Thurs-Sat there's also a more refined tasting menu. Watch the boats from the terrace.

Carte £ 28/41

Town plan: A2-k – *Merchants Rd ✉ BS8 4PZ – ✆ 0117 927 2229 – www.the-pumphouse.com – Closed 25 December*

Victoria Park

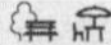

MODERN BRITISH • NEIGHBOURHOOD This neighbourhood pub is named after the nearby park and its jewel in the crown is its spacious terrace and tiered gardens which offer lovely views over the rooftops. Menus list a great mix of dishes that you'll know and love.

Carte £ 20/31

Town plan: B2-v – *66 Raymend Rd ✉ BS3 4QW – ✆ 0117 330 6043 – www.thevictoriapark.co.uk – Closed 26 December*

Hotels

Bristol Harbour

HISTORIC BUILDING • ELEGANT Located within two listed 1840s banks with stunning facades. Bedrooms are spacious and modern, the ballroom is an impressive space and the old vault now hides a delightful spa. The 'Gold Bar' comprises 4 intimate, ornately decorated rooms, while the large, bustling brasserie specialises in seafood.

42 rooms – £ 125/180 £ 135/310

Town plan: C1-h – *55 Corn St ✉ BS1 1HT*
– *☎ 0117 203 4456 – www.bristol-harbour-hotel.co.uk*

Hotel du Vin

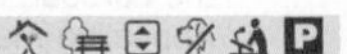

BUSINESS • DESIGN Characterful 18C former sugar refinery with classical Hotel du Vin styling and a wine-theme running throughout. Dark-hued bedrooms and duplex suites boast Egyptian cotton linen – one room has twin roll-top baths. Cosy lounge-bar; French brasserie with a pleasant courtyard terrace for bistro classics.

40 rooms – £ 129/215 £ 139/225

Town plan: C1-e – *The Sugar House ✉ BS1 2NU*
– *☎ 0117 403 2979 – www.hotelduvin.com*

Berwick Lodge

COUNTRY HOUSE • PERSONALISED A popular wedding and events venue, run by gregarious, hands-on owners. It's surrounded by 18 acres of grounds and offers views over Avonmouth and the Severn Bridge. Inside, original features combine with Eastern furnishings and mosaic tiles. The intimate restaurant has fine chandeliers and a modern menu.

14 rooms – £ 85/99 £ 125/200

Berwick Dr ✉ BS10 7TD – Northwest : 5 mi by A 4018
– *☎ 0117 958 1590 – www.berwicklodge.co.uk*

Number 38 Clifton

TOWNHOUSE • PERSONALISED Built in 1820, this substantial townhouse overlooks both the city and the Clifton Downs. Boutique bedrooms have coloured wood-panelled walls, Roberts radios and smart bathrooms with underfloor heating; the most luxurious are the loft suites, complete with copper baths. The rear terrace makes a great suntrap.

9 rooms – £ 115/200 £ 130/235

Town plan: A1-a – *38 Upper Belgrave Rd ✉ BS8 2XN*
– *☎ 0117 946 6905 – www.number38clifton.com*

Is breakfast included? If it is, the cup symbol appears after the number of rooms.

at Long Ashton Southwest: 2.5 mi by A370 off B3128

Bird in Hand

TRADITIONAL BRITISH • COSY Tiny country pub with three small but smartly decorated rooms. Quirky touches include an antelope's head and a wall covered in pages from Mrs Beeton's Book of Household Management. Menus offer tasty, carefully cooked British dishes which let local and foraged ingredients speak for themselves.

Carte £ 25/31

17 Weston Rd ✉ BS41 9LA
– *☎ 01275 395222 (booking essential at dinner) – www.bird-in-hand.co.uk*

BROADSTAIRS

Kent – Pop. 23 632 – Regional map n° **5**-D1

Albariño

SPANISH • TAPAS BAR Run by a husband and wife team and named after her favourite wine. Freshly prepared, full-flavoured tapas dishes; 3 per person will suffice – let the chef choose. Counter seating for 7. Good views of the Channel.

Carte £ 12/31

29 Albion St CT10 1LX – 01843 600991 – www.albarinorestaurant.co.uk – dinner only and Saturday lunch – Closed 25-26 December, 1 January and Sunday

Stark

MODERN BRITISH • SIMPLE Their slogan 'Good food, laid bare', sums up this bijou restaurant, where ladders and rope lights hang beside rustic wood-panelled walls. The modern 6 course tasting menu is highly seasonal and dishes are beautifully presented.

Menu £ 45 – tasting menu only

1 Oscar Rd CT10 1QJ – 01843 579786 (booking essential) – www.starkfood.co.uk – dinner only – Closed 24-26 December and Sunday-Tuesday

Wyatt & Jones

MODERN BRITISH • BISTRO Follow the narrow road under the arch, towards the harbour; here you'll find 3 old fishermen's cottages with pleasant sea views. Appealing menus keep things regional, with local lobsters a speciality; start with some tempting nibbles.

Carte £ 24/39

23-27 Harbour St CT10 1EU – 01843 865126 – www.wyattandjones.co.uk – Closed 25-26 December, Monday except bank holiday and Tuesday

Belvidere Place

TOWNHOUSE • PERSONALISED Centrally located Georgian house with a charming owner, green credentials and an eclectic, individual style. Bohemian, shabby-chic lounge boasts a retro football table. Spacious bedrooms mix modern facilities with older antique furnishings.

5 rooms – £ 140/160 £ 160/200

Belvedere Rd CT10 1PF – 01843 579850 – www.belvidereplace.co.uk – Closed 25-26 December

BROADWAY

Worcestershire – Pop. 2 496 – Regional map n° **10**-C3

Buckland Manor

MODERN BRITISH • INTIMATE A formal restaurant set within a country house hotel. The elegant room has wood-clad walls hung with oil paintings and offers views over the gardens and there are cosy lounges in which to begin and end your meal. Time-honoured dishes have clean flavours and are brought up-to-date in their presentation.

Menu £ 30/70

Buckland Manor Hotel, Buckland WR12 7LY – Southwest : 2.25 mi by B 4632 – 01386 852626 (booking essential) – www.bucklandmanor.com

Russell's

MODERN BRITISH • FASHIONABLE An attractive Cotswold stone house in the centre of the village, with a smart brasserie-style interior and both a front and rear terrace. Choose from a constantly evolving selection of modern British dishes. Service is relaxed and friendly and bedrooms are stylish – there's even a spacious suite!

Menu £ 16 (weekdays) – Carte £ 28/54

7 rooms – £ 130/300 £ 130/300

20 High St WR12 7DT – 01386 853555 – www.russellsofbroadway.co.uk – Closed Sunday dinner and bank holidays

Buckland Manor

HISTORIC • CLASSIC With its 13C origins, beautiful gardens and peaceful setting, this is one of England's most charming country houses. The elegant interior comprises tastefully appointed country house bedrooms and traditionally furnished guest areas featuring parquet floors, wood panelling and big open fires.

15 rooms – £ 195/655 £ 215/675

Buckland ✉ WR12 7LY – Southwest : 2.25 mi by B 4632 – 01386 852626 – www.bucklandmanor.com

Buckland Manor – See restaurant listing

Dormy House

LUXURY • CONTEMPORARY Behind the original farmhouse façade you'll find a modern interior and a luxurious spa. The odd beam and fireplace remain but bold contemporary fabrics and designer furnishings now feature too; wood and stone play a big part and the atmosphere is laid-back. The Potting Shed has an informal bistro feel and the stylish Garden Room offers a more sophisticated alternative.

38 rooms – £ 265/295 £ 265/500 – 9 suites

Willersey Hill ✉ WR12 7LF – East : 4 mi by A 44 – 01386 852711 – www.dormyhouse.co.uk

The Fish

TRADITIONAL • PERSONALISED Up until the 16C the Benedictine monks kept their fish stocks in the local hillside caves – hence its name. Guest areas are set in a wood-clad building and include a British brasserie specialising in meats and grills. Scandinavian-style bedrooms are set in various outbuildings and have lovely country views.

68 rooms – £ 95/105 £ 125/450 – 3 suites

Farncombe Estate ✉ WR12 7LJ – East : 4 mi by A 44 – 01386 858000 – www.thefishhotel.co.uk

Foxhill Manor

COUNTRY HOUSE • DESIGN Once home to Henry Maudslay, who died in the Dam Busters raid; a Grade II listed Arts and Crafts house, where guests are made to feel as if they're staying in a private home. Striking bedrooms have first class facilities – 'Oak' has his and hers baths with a view. Modern 4 course menus are discussed with the chef; after dinner, relax on bean bags in front of the 74" TV.

8 rooms – £ 299/680 £ 299/680 – 2 suites

Farncombe Estate ✉ WR12 7LJ – East : 3.75 mi by A 44 – 01386 852711 – www.foxhillmanor.com

East House

HISTORIC • PERSONALISED Beautifully furnished, 18C former farmhouse in lovely mature gardens, with wood-burning stoves and a welcoming feel. Sumptuous beamed bedrooms mix antique furniture with modern technology; superb bathrooms have underfloor heating. The Jacobean Suite is the biggest room, with a four-poster and garden views.

4 rooms – £ 185/225 £ 185/225

162 High St ✉ WR12 7AJ – 01386 853789 – www.easthouseuk.com

Mill Hay House

HISTORIC • ELEGANT This lovely 17C house, tucked away on the edge of the village, comes with beautiful gardens overlooking a lake. With just three individually furnished bedrooms, the atmosphere is intimate, and guests are treated as family friends.

3 rooms – £ 175/225 £ 195/245

Snowshill Rd ✉ WR12 7JS – South : 0.5 mi – 01386 852498 – www.millhay.co.uk – Closed Christmas-New Year

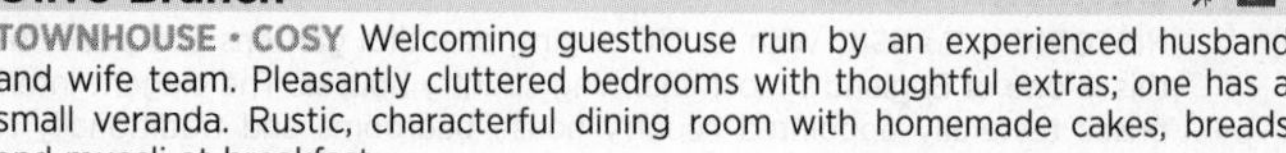

Olive Branch

TOWNHOUSE • COSY Welcoming guesthouse run by an experienced husband and wife team. Pleasantly cluttered bedrooms with thoughtful extras; one has a small veranda. Rustic, characterful dining room with homemade cakes, breads and muesli at breakfast.

8 rooms ☕ - 🚹£ 80/105 🚹🚹£ 108/138

78 High St ✉ WR12 7AJ - ✆ 01386 853440 - www.theolivebranch-broadway.com

Windrush House

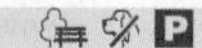

FAMILY • COSY Welcoming guesthouse in a pretty village. Individually decorated bedrooms have bold feature walls: some use Laura Ashley designs and have wrought iron beds; four-poster 'Snowshill' is the best. Homemade jams feature at breakfast.

5 rooms ☕ - 🚹£ 75/95 🚹🚹£ 85/105

Station Rd ✉ WR12 7DE - ✆ 01386 853577 - www.windrushhouse.com

BROCKENHURST

Hampshire – Pop. 3 552 – Regional map n° **4**-A2

The Pig

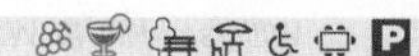

TRADITIONAL BRITISH • BRASSERIE X A delightful conservatory with plants dotted about, an eclectic collection of old tables and chairs, and a bustling atmosphere. The forager and kitchen gardener supply what's best and any ingredients they can't get themselves are sourced from within 25 miles. Cooking is unfussy, wholesome and British-based.

Carte £ 24/43

The Pig Hotel, Beaulieu Rd ✉ SO42 7QL - East : 1 mi on B 3055 - ✆ 01590 622354 - www.thepighotel.com

The Pig

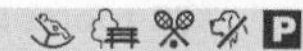

COUNTRY HOUSE • PERSONALISED This smart manor house hotel follows a philosophy of removing barriers and bringing nature indoors. Characterful bedrooms are divided between the house and a stable block, and boast distressed wood floors, chunky furnishings and large squashy beds. The comfy lounges and dining room have a shabby-chic style.

31 rooms - 🚹£ 155/420 🚹🚹£ 155/420 - ☕ £ 15

Beaulieu Rd ✉ SO42 7QL - East : 1 mi on B 3055 - ✆ 01590 622354 - www.thepighotel.com

The Pig – See restaurant listing

Cloud

TRADITIONAL • COSY Well-kept hotel made up of four cottages, set on the edge of a pretty New Forest village. It has a homely feel, from the cosy lounges to the immaculately kept bedrooms; a collection of photos in the bar attest to the owner's past as a tiller girl. The restaurant and conservatory offer traditional menus.

18 rooms ☕ - 🚹£ 97/105 🚹🚹£ 140/190

Meerut Rd ✉ SO42 7TD - ✆ 01590 622165 - www.cloudhotel.co.uk - Closed 23 December-13 January

Daisybank Cottage

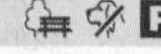

LUXURY • PERSONALISED A charming Arts and Crafts house built in 1902. Modern bedrooms come with seating areas; one room opens onto an internal courtyard and another, onto a terrace. Aga-cooked breakfasts come in English, Irish and American versions.

7 rooms ☕ - 🚹£ 95/130 🚹🚹£ 110/150

Sway Rd ✉ SO42 7SG - South : 0.5 mi on B 3055 - ✆ 01590 622086 - www.bedandbreakfast-newforest.co.uk

BROMESWELL - Suffolk → See Woodbridge

BROUGHTON

North Yorkshire – Regional map n° **13**-A2

Bull

REGIONAL CUISINE • PUB The big, solid-looking Bull is part of the Ribble Valley Inns group. Expect real ales and local meats and cheeses, as well as traditional British dishes, rediscovered classics and the sort of puddings that make you feel patriotic.

Carte £ 22/35

BD23 3AE – 01756 792065 – www.thebullatbroughton.com

BRUNTINGTHORPE

Leicestershire – Regional map n° **9**-B3

The Joiners

TRADITIONAL BRITISH • RUSTIC Beams and a tiled floor bring 17C character to this dining pub but designer wallpaper and fresh flower displays give it a chic overall feel. There's plenty of choice on the menus, with the likes of pork rillettes or pot-roast pheasant.

Menu £ 16 (weekday lunch) – Carte £ 27/34

Church Walk LE17 5QH – 0116 247 8258 (booking essential) – www.thejoinersarms.co.uk – Closed Sunday dinner and Monday

BRUTON

Somerset – Pop. 2 984 – Regional map n° **2**-C2

Roth Bar & Grill

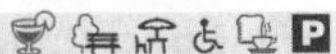

TRADITIONAL BRITISH • DESIGN The converted outbuildings of a working farm now house this charming restaurant with its striking modern art exhibitions. Beef, pork and lamb from the farm are aged in their salting room. Be sure to try the caramelised lemonade.

Carte £ 20/53

Durslade Farm, Dropping Ln BA10 0NL – Southeast : 0.5 mi on B 3081 – 01749 814700 (booking advisable) – www.rothbarandgrill.co.uk – lunch only and dinner Friday-Saturday – Closed first week January, 25-27 December and Monday except bank holidays

At The Chapel

MEDITERRANEAN CUISINE • DESIGN Stylish, informal restaurant in a former 18C chapel, with a bakery to one side and a wine shop to the other. Daily menus offer rustic, Mediterranean-influenced dishes; specialities include wood-fired breads, pizzas and cakes. The chic club lounge and cocktail bar opens at weekends. Bedrooms are luxurious.

Carte £ 20/59

8 rooms – †£ 150 ††£ 250

High St BA10 0AE – 01749 814070 (booking advisable) – www.atthechapel.co.uk – Closed 25 December

BRYHER

→ See Scilly (Isles of)

BUCKDEN

Cambridgeshire – Pop. 2 385 – Regional map n° **8**-A2

George

HISTORIC • PERSONALISED Delightfully restored part black and white, part red-brick coaching inn. Original flag floors mix with modern furnishings, creating a stylish, understated feel. The simple yet tastefully decorated bedrooms are named after famous 'Georges'. Classic brasserie dishes feature in the restaurant.

12 rooms – †£ 95/150 ††£ 120/150

High St PE19 5XA – 01480 812300 – www.thegeorgebuckden.com

ENGLAND

BUDE

Cornwall – Pop. 5 091 – Regional map n° **1**-B2

 **Beach** 

BOUTIQUE HOTEL • CONTEMPORARY Spacious New England style hotel with views over the Atlantic Ocean and a pleasingly laid-back feel. Contemporary bedrooms have limed oak furnishings and all the latest mod cons; 'Deluxe' boast roll-top baths and either a terrace or a balcony. The smart brasserie offers a menu of classic dishes and grills.

16 rooms – †£ 138/238 ††£ 138/238 – £ 25

Summerleaze Cres. ✉ EX23 8HL – ✆ 01288 389800 – www.thebeachatbude.co.uk – Closed 24-26 December

BUDLEIGH SALTERTON

Devon – Pop. 5 185 – Regional map n° **1**-D2

 **Heath Close** 

FAMILY • PERSONALISED Smart detached house with a lovely rear garden. The open-plan lounge and dining room are stylish and modern. Good-sized bedrooms display personal touches and bathrooms have underfloor heating. The welcoming owners offer tea and cake on arrival and traditional home-cooked dinners on a Saturday.

5 rooms – †£ 75 ††£ 95/105

3 Lansdowne Rd ✉ EX9 6AH – West : 1 mi by B 3178 – ✆ 01395 444337 – www.heathclose.com – Closed Sunday

Long Range 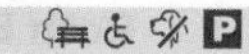

FAMILY • PERSONALISED Spotlessly kept guesthouse with a large garden, set on a quiet street. Choice of two lounges; one in a conservatory and complete with a small bar. Unfussy, brightly coloured bedrooms have good facilities; those to the rear can see the sea.

9 rooms – †£ 78/82 ††£ 110/148

5 Vales Rd ✉ EX9 6HS – by Raleigh Rd – ✆ 01395 443321 – www.thelongrangehotel.co.uk – Restricted opening in winter

BUNGAY

Suffolk – Pop. 5 127 – Regional map n° **8**-D2

Castle Inn

REGIONAL CUISINE • PUB Sky-blue pub, formerly known as The White Lion, with an open-plan dining area and an intimate rear bar. Fresh, simple and seasonal country based cooking; the Innkeeper's platter of local produce is a perennial favourite. Tasty homemade cakes and cookies on display. Homely, comfortable bedrooms.

Carte £ 21/33

4 rooms – †£ 70/80 ††£ 95/100

35 Earsham St ✉ NR35 1AF – ✆ 01986 892283 – www.thecastleinn.net – Closed 25 December, Monday October-March and dinner Sunday and Tuesday

BURCHETT'S GREEN

Windsor and Maidenhead – Regional map n° **6**-C3

Crown (Simon Bonwick) 

REGIONAL CUISINE • RUSTIC The Crown is very personally and passionately run by the Bonwick family and comes with a small bar and two intimate, open-fired dining rooms. The refined, deftly prepared dishes – six per course – are decided upon daily; the options are diverse and appealing, with flavours clearly defined.

➜ Salcombe crab with apple, passion fruit and cashew. Salt marsh lamb rump with garlic and thyme sauce. Raspberry bavarois.

Carte £ 24/43

✉ SL6 6QZ – ✆ 01628 824079 – www.thecrownburchettsgreen.com – Closed Monday, Sunday April-September and Tuesday October-March.

BURFORD

Oxfordshire – Pop. 1 171 – Regional map n° **6**-A2

Lamb Inn

TRADITIONAL BRITISH • COSY This charming 15C inn is a place of two halves: the cosy, antique-furnished bar serves old favourites, while the more romantic, crisply-laid candlelit restaurant offers skilfully prepared, creative modern dishes. The garden is a must in warmer weather and the bijoux country bedrooms offer plenty of extras.

Carte £ 28/51

17 rooms – †£ 110/200 ††£ 120/210

Sheep St ✉ OX18 4LR – ✆ 01993 823155 – www.cotswold-inns-hotels.co.uk/the-lamb-inn

Burford House

TRADITIONAL • PERSONALISED The welcome is warm at this delightful part-timbered 17C house, where spacious, comfy bedrooms – including 3 four-posters – mix traditional styling with contemporary touches. Cosy sitting rooms and a lovely terrace for afternoon tea.

6 rooms – †£ 110/180 ††£ 125/180

99 High St ✉ OX18 4QA – ✆ 01993 823151 – www.burford-house.co.uk

at Swinbrook East: 2.75 mi by A40 ✉ Burford

Swan Inn

MODERN BRITISH • PUB Wisteria-clad, honey-coloured pub on the riverbank, boasting a lovely garden filled with fruit trees. The charming interior displays an open oak frame and exposed stone walls hung with old lithographs and handmade walking sticks. The daily menu showcases the latest local produce and features modern takes on older recipes. Well-appointed bedrooms have a luxurious feel.

Carte £ 28/42

11 rooms – †£ 100/125 ††£ 125/200

✉ OX18 4DY – ✆ 01993 823339 – www.theswanswinbrook.co.uk – Closed 25-26 December

at Shilton Southeast : 2.5 mi by A40 off B4020

Rose & Crown

TRADITIONAL CUISINE • RUSTIC Charming Cotswold stone pub with flickering fires, exposed beams and a welcoming owner. Meats are from local farms and game, from nearby shoots. Gutsy country cooking is full of flavour and reasonably priced; Sunday lunch is popular.

Carte £ 21/35

✉ OX18 4AB – ✆ 01993 842280 – www.shiltonroseandcrown.com – Closed 25 December

BURNHAM MARKET

Norfolk – Pop. 877 – Regional map n° **8**-C1

Hoste

INN • PERSONALISED Personally and passionately run is this greatly extended former inn at the heart of a picturesque village. Stylish, luxurious bedrooms in the main building and two annexes; smart beauty and wellness spa in the wing. The extensive restaurant comprises an appealing bar, four dining rooms and a courtyard garden.

62 rooms – †£ 165/260 ††£ 195/330

The Green ✉ PE31 8HD – ✆ 01328 738777 – www.thehoste.com

BURPHAM – West Sussex → See Arundel

BURTON BRADSTOCK → See Bridport

BURTON-UPON-TRENT

Staffordshire – Pop. 72 299 – Regional map n° **10**-C1

99 Station Street

TRADITIONAL BRITISH • NEIGHBOURHOOD X Amongst the vast brewing towers is this bright, boldly decorated neighbourhood restaurant, run by two experienced locals. They make everything on the premises daily and showcase regional ingredients; try the mature rare breed meats.

Menu £ 13 (weekday lunch) – Carte £ 25/36

99 Station St ✉ DE14 1BT – ☎ 01283 516859 – www.99stationstreet.com – Closed Sunday dinner-Wednesday lunch

BURY

Greater Manchester – Pop. 77 211 – Regional map n° **11**-B2

Waggon

TRADITIONAL BRITISH • NEIGHBOURHOOD X Both the building and the décor may be unassuming and understated but the focus at the Waggon is where it matters – on the food. Classical dishes change with the seasons and the experienced chef clearly knows how to get the best out of his ingredients. The midweek 'Market' menu offers excellent value.

Menu £ 17 (weekdays) – Carte £ 22/39

131 Bury and Rochdale Old Rd, Birtle ✉ BL9 6UE – East : 2 mi on B 6222 – ☎ 01706 622955 – www.thewaggonatbirtle.co.uk – dinner only and lunch Thursday, Friday and Sunday – Closed 2 weeks summer, first week January, Monday and Tuesday

Bird at Birtle

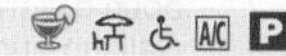

TRADITIONAL BRITISH • BISTRO X A very popular restaurant in a modernised pub. Start with a cocktail on a comfy sofa or out on the terrace then head upstairs to the stylish dining room with its balcony and fell views. Classic dishes are given a modern touch.

Carte £ 24/37

293 Bury and Rochdale Old Rd, Birtle ✉ OL10 4BQ – East : 2.25 mi on B 6222 – ☎ 01706 540500 – www.thebirdatbirtle.co.uk

BURY ST EDMUNDS

Suffolk – Pop. 41 113 – Regional map n° **8**-C2

Pea Porridge

MODERN BRITISH • BISTRO X A charming former bakery in two 19C cottages, with its original bread oven still in situ. Tasty country cooking is led by the seasons and has a Mediterranean bias; many dishes are cooked in the wood-fired oven. It has a stylish, rustic look and a homely feel – its name is a reference to the old town green.

Menu £ 26 (lunch) – Carte dinner £ 25/34

28-29 Cannon St ✉ IP33 1JR – ☎ 01284 700200 (booking advisable) – www.peaporridge.co.uk – Closed first week January, 2 weeks summer, last week December, Sunday-Monday and lunch Tuesday-Wednesday

Maison Bleue

SEAFOOD • NEIGHBOURHOOD XX Passionately run neighbourhood restaurant in a converted 17C house, with a smart blue canopy, wooden panelling and impressive fish sculptures. Menus focus on seafood; cooking is modern in style but with classic influences and Gallic and Asian touches; you must try the excellent French cheeses.

Menu £ 20 (weekdays)/37 – Carte £ 37/54

30-31 Churchgate St ✉ IP33 1RG – ☎ 01284 760623 – www.maisonbleue.co.uk – Closed 23 December-16 January, first 2 weeks September Sunday and Monday

1921

MODERN CUISINE • INTIMATE XX A fine period house located at 19-21 Angel Hill; its smart, modern facelift complements the original beams and red-brick inglenook fireplace. Cooking displays a modern flair and features some interesting combinations.

Menu £ 18 (lunch) – Carte £ 31/51

19-21 Angel Hill ✉ IP33 1UZ
– ✆ 01284 704870 – www.nineteen-twentyone.co.uk – Closed 2 weeks Christmas-New Year and Sunday

Eaterie

TRADITIONAL BRITISH • BRASSERIE X An airy two-roomed bistro set within an attractive 15C coaching inn where Dickens once stayed. There's an impressive modern chandelier and a display of the owner's contemporary art. Tasty British brasserie dishes use local produce.

Menu £ 19 (lunch and early dinner) – Carte dinner £ 22/49

Angel Hotel, 3 Angel Hill ✉ IP33 1LT
– ✆ 01284 714000 – www.theangel.co.uk

Angel

HISTORIC • PERSONALISED The creeper-clad Georgian façade hides a surprisingly stylish hotel. Relax in the atmospheric bar or smart lounges. Individually designed bedrooms offer either classic four-poster luxury or come with funky décor and iPod docks.

74 rooms – £ 132/340 £ 132/340

3 Angel Hill ✉ IP33 1LT
– ✆ 01284 714000 – www.theangel.co.uk

Eaterie – See restaurant listing

Northgate

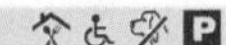

TOWNHOUSE • CONTEMPORARY Stylish, elegantly understated bedrooms give this fine period townhouse a luxurious feel. Try something from the extensive cocktail list in the cosy bar or head through to the pleasant terrace. The two dining rooms have impressive ceilings and serve flavoursome modern dishes; there's also a chef's table.

9 rooms – £ 115/130 £ 130/195

Northgate St ✉ IP33 1HP
– ✆ 01284 339604 – www.thenorthgate.com

at Ixworth Northeast: 7 mi by A143 ✉ Bury St Edmunds

Theobalds

TRADITIONAL BRITISH • NEIGHBOURHOOD XX Part-16C cottage in a charming village, with a cosy, fire-lit lounge and a beamed dining room. Professionally run by a husband and wife and a jolly chef. Monthly changing menus offer heart-warming, well-presented, traditional dishes.

Menu £ 29/33

68 High St ✉ IP31 2HJ
– ✆ 01359 231707 – www.theobaldsrestaurant.co.uk
– dinner only and lunch Friday and Sunday – Closed 1 week spring, 1 week autumn, Sunday dinner and Monday

at Horringer Southwest: 3 mi on A143 ✉ Bury St Edmunds

Ickworth

HISTORIC • CLASSIC This family-orientated hotel occupies the east wing of a grand 200 year old mansion set in 1,800 acres: former home of the 7th Marquess of Bristol and now owned by the National Trust. It features huge art-filled lounges, antique-furnished bedrooms and luxurious suites. Dine in the formal restaurant or in the impressive orangery, which serves relaxed meals and high teas.

39 rooms – £ 175/275 £ 225/500 – 12 suites

✉ IP29 5QE
– ✆ 01284 735350 – www.ickworthhotel.co.uk

BUTLERS CROSS
Buckinghamshire – Regional map n° **6**-C2

Russell Arms
TRADITIONAL BRITISH • INN You'll find walkers relaxing at the tables to the side and a large terrace to the rear. Daily coffee mornings are followed by a great value lunchtime 'plat du jour' and on Fridays they host children's tea parties. The chef knows how to get the best out of his ingredients and dishes are packed with flavour.

Carte £ 25/33

2 Chalkshire Rd ✉ HP17 0TS – ✆ 01296 624411 – www.therussellarms.co.uk – Closed 25-26 December and Monday

BUTTERMERE
Cumbria – Pop. 139 – Regional map n° **12**-A2

Wood House

TRADITIONAL • CLASSIC Charming part-16C house with Victorian additions and lovely gardens, in a wonderfully serene lakeside setting. Welcoming owners, stunning views and no TVs to disturb the peace! Classical lounge and cosy dining room with a communal antique table, silver cutlery and cut crystal glassware.

3 rooms – †£ 90 ††£ 130

✉ CA13 9XA – Northwest : 0.5 mi on B 5289 – ✆ 017687 70208 – www.woodhousebuttermere.uk – Closed November-February

CALLINGTON
Cornwall – Pop. 4 698 – Regional map n° **1**-C2

Langmans
MODERN BRITISH • INTIMATE XX Langmans is run by a husband and wife and dining here is an all-night affair. Pre-dinner drinks with your fellow guests are followed by a tasting menu in the formal dining room; cooking is refined and they have a great cheese selection.

Menu £ 48 – tasting menu only

3 Church St ✉ PL17 7RE – ✆ 01579 384933 (booking essential) – www.langmansrestaurant.co.uk – dinner only – Closed Sunday-Wednesday

Cadson Manor

COUNTRY HOUSE • PERSONALISED Welcoming guesthouse on a 600 year old working farm, with views over an iron age settlement. Cosy, individually furnished bedrooms feature antiques, fresh flowers and a decanter of sherry. Rayburn-cooked breakfasts include weekly specials.

3 rooms – †£ 85 ††£ 120/125

✉ PL17 7HW – Southwest : 2.75 mi by A 390 – ✆ 01579 383969 – www.cadsonmanor.co.uk – Closed Christmas

CALNE
Wiltshire – Pop. 17 274 – Regional map n° **2**-C2

at Compton Bassett Northeast: 4.5 mi by A4

White Horse Inn

MODERN BRITISH • FRIENDLY The White Horse dates back over a century: the cosy bar is where you'll find the regulars, while most diners head for the rustic room next door. For traditionalists there are pub classics; for those with more adventurous tastes there's the à la carte. Beyond the large garden are 8 snug bedrooms.

Menu £ 25 (weekday lunch) – Carte £ 24/46

8 rooms – †£ 75/85 ††£ 85/115

✉ SN11 8RG – ✆ 01249 813118 – www.whitehorse-comptonbassett.co.uk – Closed 25 December, Sunday dinner and Monday

CAMBER – East Sussex ➔ See Rye

Midsummerhouse

GOOD TIPS!

This thriving city has stood on the banks of the River Cam since Roman times, with the world-famous university appearing relatively recently in the 13C. Where better to celebrate obtaining a first-class degree than Michelin Two-Starred Midsummer House? Wherever you find students, you'll also find pubs; try Pint Shop for gutsy, satisfying fare.

CAMBRIDGE

Cambridgeshire – Pop. 123 867 – Regional map n° **8**-B3

Restaurants

✿✿ Midsummer House (Daniel Clifford)

MODERN CUISINE • ELEGANT XXX A stylish restaurant in an idyllic location on Midsummer Common; enjoy an aperitif in the first floor lounge overlooking the River Cam. Set 7 or 10 course menus (with 5 courses also available at lunch). Creative, highly accomplished cooking showcases top quality produce and flavours are well-balanced, with the main ingredient of each dish allowed to shine.

→ Cornish crab with avocado and sorrel. Roast Anjou pigeon, crispy leg, wild garlic and mushrooms. Aerated pear, blueberry and white chocolate.

Menu £ 57/120

Town plan: B1-a – *Midsummer Common ✉ CB4 1HA*
– ✆ 01223 369299 – www.midsummerhouse.co.uk
– Closed 2 weeks December, Sunday, Monday and lunch Tuesday

Alimentum

BRITISH MODERN • MINIMALIST XX Alimentum is unusually located on the ground floor of a suburban apartment block but, inside, has a smart, modern feel. Combinations are original and flavours are clearly defined. Ask for a table by the kitchen window.

Menu £ 35 (lunch and early dinner)/70

152-154 Hills Rd ✉ CB2 8PB – Southeast : 1.5 mi by Regent St on Hills Rd
– ✆ 01223 413000 – www.restaurantalimentum.co.uk
– Closed 24-30 December and bank holiday Mondays

If you want the special atmosphere of a pub, look for the symbol.

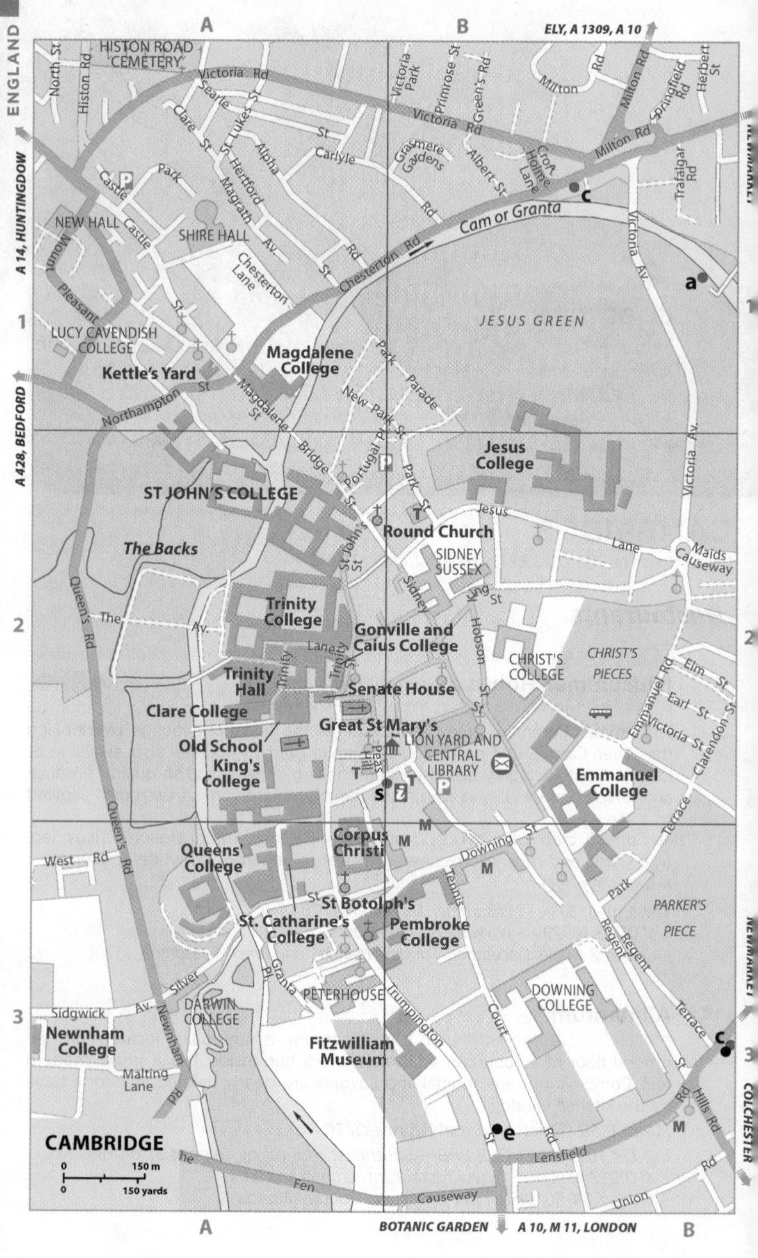
CAMBRIDGE
ELY, A 1309, A 10
A 14, HUNTINGDOW
A 428, BEDFORD
BOTANIC GARDEN
A 10, M 11, LONDON
COLCHESTER
NEWMARKET
HISTON ROAD CEMETERY
NEW HALL
SHIRE HALL
LUCY CAVENDISH COLLEGE
Kettle's Yard
Magdalene College
JESUS GREEN
Cam or Granta
Jesus College
ST JOHN'S COLLEGE
Round Church
SIDNEY SUSSEX
The Backs
Trinity College
Gonville and Caius College
Trinity Hall
Senate House
Clare College
Great St Mary's
Old School
LION YARD AND CENTRAL LIBRARY
King's College
CHRIST'S COLLEGE
CHRIST'S PIECES
Emmanuel College
Corpus Christi
Queens' College
St Botolph's
St. Catharine's College
Pembroke College
PARKER'S PIECE
PETERHOUSE
DARWIN COLLEGE
DOWNING COLLEGE
Newnham College
Fitzwilliam Museum
0 150 m
0 150 yards

Cotto

MODERN CUISINE • INTIMATE XX A stylish, sophisticated hotel restaurant set in a modern glass extension. The experienced chef skilfully prepares a wide range of dishes which are made up of many different components; the chocolate desserts are a highlight.

Menu £ 70

Town plan: B3-c - *Gonville Hotel, Gonville Pl. ✉ CB1 1LY - ☎ 01223 302010 (booking essential) - www.cottocambridge.co.uk - dinner only - Closed 2 weeks August, Easter, Sunday and Monday*

Navadhanya

INDIAN • CONTEMPORARY DÉCOR XX This former pub is home to a well-regarded restaurant with white décor and a contemporary look. Dishes take their influences from around India and exhibit a modern style, while at the same time respecting tradition.

Carte £ 20/49

73 Newmarket Rd ✉ CB5 8EG - East : 0.75 mi on A 1134 - ☎ 01223 300583 - www.navadhanya.co.uk - dinner only - Closed Monday

Restaurant 22

FRENCH • NEIGHBOURHOOD XX A converted Victorian townhouse with a formal dining room; personally run, with ten tables set with flowers and candles. Monthly changing, four course menu of classically based, flavourful cooking with Italian influences.

Menu £ 41

Town plan: B1-c - *22 Chesterton Rd ✉ CB4 3AX - ☎ 01223 351880 (booking essential) - www.restaurant22.co.uk - dinner only - Closed 24 December-2 January, Sunday and Monday*

Pint Shop

BRITISH TRADITIONAL • PUB 'MEAT. BEER. BREAD.' is written on the window - and that pretty much sums this place up. Cooking is gutsy and satisfying and the charcoal grill takes centre stage. To accompany are 10 keg beers, 6 cask beers and over 70 different gins.

Menu £ 13 (lunch and early dinner) - Carte £ 21/39

Town plan: B2-s - *10 Peas Hill ✉ CB2 3NP - ☎ 01223 352293 - www.pintshop.co.uk - Closed 25-26 December and 1 January*

Hotels

Hotel du Vin

TOWNHOUSE • DESIGN Stylish hotel set over a row of 16C and 17C ex-university owned buildings. Original quarry tiled floors and wood-panelled walls feature, along with plenty of passages, nooks and crannies. Chic, modern bedrooms include one with its own cinema. The appealing bistro has a Gallic-led menu.

41 rooms - †£ 140/360 ††£ 140/360 - ☕ £ 17

Town plan: B3-e - *15-19 Trumpington St ✉ CB2 1QA - ☎ 01223 227330 - www.hotelduvin.com*

Tamburlaine

BUSINESS • CONTEMPORARY This modern business hotel is named after Christopher Marlowe's play and is well-located for those travelling by train. Bedrooms are spacious, light and well-equipped, and make good use of different textures in their furnishings. The pretty restaurant has a botanical theme and a laid-back feel.

155 rooms - †£ 200/340 ††£ 200/340 - ☕ £ 10 - 2 suites

27-29 Station Rd ✉ CB1 2FB - Southeast : 0.75 mi by Regent St off Hills Rd - ☎ 01223 792888 - www.thetamburlaine.co.uk

Gonville

BUSINESS • CONTEMPORARY A well-located hotel with the city's main attractions just a stroll away across the common. Bedrooms have smart black and red colour schemes and come with iPads; the rear rooms are quieter. Enjoy a cocktail in the chic bar followed by a casual meal in the brasserie or dinner in the sophisticated restaurant.

84 rooms – £ 99 £ 99/250

Town plan: B3-c – *Gonville Pl ✉ CB1 1LY – ✆ 01223 366611 – www.gonvillehotel.co.uk*

Cotto – See restaurant listing

at Horningsea Northeast: 4 mi by A1303 and B1047 ✉ Cambridge

Crown & Punchbowl

MODERN BRITISH • PUB Watch your head on the beams as you enter the bar, then take you pick from several different seating areas. Start with rustic bread and zingy olive oil then move on to modern seasonal dishes or one of the wide-ranging specials chalked on the fish board. Cosy, welcoming bedrooms are named after local writers.

Menu £ 16 (weekdays) – Carte £ 25/36

5 rooms – £ 90/130 £ 90/130 – £ 10

High St ✉ CB25 9JG – ✆ 01223 860643 – www.cambscuisine.com

at Madingley West: 4.5 mi by A1303 ✉ Cambridge

Three Horseshoes

TRADITIONAL CUISINE • PUB This charming thatched pub sits within an equally beautiful village. Dine in the cosy bar, the more formal conservatory or the lovely garden. An interesting wine list complements a mix of unfussy British and Italian dishes.

Menu £ 22 (weekdays) – Carte £ 28/46

High St ✉ CB23 8AB – ✆ 01954 210221 – www.threehorseshoesmadingley.com – Closed Sunday dinner November-February

CAMELFORD

Cornwall – Pop. 2 335 – Regional map n° **1**-B2

Pendragon Country House

COUNTRY HOUSE • COSY This former vicarage is run by an extremely enthusiastic couple and offers views across the fields to the church it once served. There's always a jigsaw on the go in the period furnished drawing room and Cornish artwork features throughout. Home-baked breads, homemade cake and local produce feature.

7 rooms – £ 65/75 £ 95/150

Davidstow ✉ PL32 9XR – Northeast : 3.5 mi by A 39 on A 395 – ✆ 01840 261131 – www.pendragoncountryhouse.com – Closed 23-27 December

CANTERBURY

Kent – Pop. 54 880 – Regional map n° **5**-D2

Ambrette

INDIAN • TRENDY This modern restaurant is hidden away, just off the main street. A striking tiled floor leads through to a spacious, moodily lit room. Local ingredients – some foraged from the woods – feature in deftly spiced Anglo-Indian dishes.

Menu £ 25 (lunch) – Carte £ 34/54

14-15 Beer Cart Ln ✉ CT1 2NY – ✆ 01227 200777 – www.theambrette.co.uk

County

MODERN BRITISH • DESIGN XX Spacious, modern restaurant divided in two by a smart, glass-walled wine cellar. Accomplished, contemporary cooking is stylishly presented, with classic combinations of ingredients interpreted in a modern fashion. Private chef's table.

Menu £ 28 (lunch and early dinner) – Carte £ 34/55

Abode Canterbury Hotel, High St ✉ CT1 2RX – ✆ 01227 826684 – www.abodecanterbury.co.uk – Closed Monday and Tuesday lunch

Corner House

MODERN BRITISH • BISTRO X A characterful former pub on the edge of the city; reputedly Charles Dickens' local, with underground passages leading to the cathedral. Appealing modern British dishes make good use of Kentish produce and everything is made on-site. Bedrooms are comfy – the rate includes a continental breakfast in your room.

Menu £ 15 (weekday lunch) – Carte £ 29/37

3 rooms – †£ 79/150 ††£ 79/150

1 Dover St ✉ CT1 3HD – ✆ 01227 780793 – www.cornerhouserestaurants.co.uk

Deesons

TRADITIONAL BRITISH • TRADITIONAL DÉCOR X Charming building in the shadow of the cathedral, with a dark, rustic interior decked out with old wood furnishings. Hearty British cooking uses ingredients from the owner's smallholding; at lunch they also serve small plates.

Menu £ 15 (weekdays) – Carte £ 29/40

25-26 Sun St ✉ CT1 2HX – ✆ 01227 767854 – www.deesonsrestaurant.co.uk – Closed Tuesday, lunch Wednesday and 25-26 December

The Goods Shed

TRADITIONAL BRITISH • RUSTIC X Daily farmers' market and food hall in an early Victorian locomotive shed, selling an excellent variety of organic, free range and homemade produce. Hearty, rustic, daily changing dishes are served at scrubbed wooden tables.

Carte £ 27/41

Station Rd West, St Dunstans ✉ CT2 8AN – ✆ 01227 459153 – www.thegoodsshed.net – Closed 25-26 December, 1-2 January, Sunday dinner and Monday

Abode Canterbury

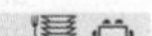

HISTORIC BUILDING • PERSONALISED Centrally located former coaching inn; heavily beamed, yet with a stylish, boutique feel. Comfy champagne bar and atmospheric first floor lounge. Contemporary bedrooms come in 4 categories: 'Enviable' and 'Fabulous' are the most luxurious.

72 rooms – †£ 89/349 ††£ 89/349 – £ 15 – 1 suite

30-33 High St ✉ CT1 2RX – ✆ 01227 766266 – www.abodecanterbury.co.uk

County – See restaurant listing

CARBIS BAY

– Cornwall → See St Ives

CARTHORPE

North Yorkshire – Regional map n° **13**-B1

Fox and Hounds

TRADITIONAL BRITISH • PUB This traditional country pub has an open-fired bar packed with memorabilia and a bright dining room with an old forge on display. Good-sized menu offers unfussy home-cooked dishes. Local organic and homemade products are for sale.

Carte £ 22/50

✉ DL8 2LG – ✆ 01845 567433 – www.foxandhoundscarthorpe.co.uk – Closed first 2 weeks January, 25 December and Monday

CARTMEL - Cumbria ➔ See Grange-over-Sands

CASTLE COMBE

Wiltshire - Pop. 347 - Regional map n° **2**-C2

Bybrook

MODERN BRITISH • ELEGANT XXX Spacious dining room within a charming 14C manor house. Large, well-spaced oak tables are immaculately laid. Menus offer refined, carefully prepared dishes with a classical base and modern overtones. Local and kitchen garden produce plays a pivotal role, with cooking following the seasons.

➔ Fillet of mackerel with crab, mooli, avocado and raisin. Loin and faggot of fallow deer, parsnip purée, sprouts and sloe sauce. Amalfi lemon tart with raspberries, basil and raspberry sorbet.

Menu £ 66

Manor House Hotel and Golf Club, ✉ SN14 7HR - ✆ 01249 782206 - www.exclusive.co.uk - dinner only and Sunday lunch

Manor House H. and Golf Club

LUXURY • ELEGANT Fine period manor house in 365 acres of formal gardens and parkland. The interior exudes immense charm, with characterful oak panelling and a host of open-fired lounges. Luxurious bedrooms are split between the main house and mews cottages. Book ahead for one of the event days.

50 rooms - †£ 215/455 ††£ 215/455 - 8 suites

✉ SN14 7HR - ✆ 01249 782206 - www.exclusive.co.uk

Bybrook - See restaurant listing

Castle Inn

HISTORIC • COSY Delightful 12C former inn set in a charming village, with two small, cosy lounges and a pubby dining room where rustic features blend with contemporary touches. Dishes range from old favourites to more sophisticated choices. Bedrooms mix old beams with modern furnishings; some have four-posters.

12 rooms - †£ 65/235 ††£ 145/235

✉ SN14 7HN - ✆ 01249 783030 - www.thecastleinn.co.uk - Closed 25 December

CATEL/CASTEL ➔ See Channel Islands (Guernsey)

CAXTON

Cambridgeshire - Pop. 572 - Regional map n° **8**-A3

No 77

THAI • CONTEMPORARY DÉCOR X The cream and blue exterior leads to a rustic interior with a copper bar and blue velvet cushioned chairs from an old cinema. An extensive list of dishes includes Kantok sharing platters and there are Thai cocktails to match.

Carte £ 17/28

77 Ermine St ✉ CB23 3PQ - ✆ 01954 269577 - www.77cambridge.com - Closed Tuesday lunch and Monday

CERNE ABBAS

Dorset - Pop. 784 - Regional map n° **2**-C3

New Inn

TRADITIONAL BRITISH • FRIENDLY This delightful village is home to the famous Chalk Giant, as well as this 16C part-flint inn. It's a charming place with a relaxed ambience and menus which mix the modern and the traditional. Spacious, stylish bedrooms are split between the pub and the courtyard and some are duplex suites.

Carte £ 21/47

12 rooms - †£ 90/105 ††£ 100/140 - 2 suites

14 Long St ✉ DT2 7JF - ✆ 01300 341274 - www.thenewinncerneabbas.co.uk - Closed 25 December

CHADDESLEY CORBETT

Worcestershire – Pop. 1 440 – Regional map n° **10**-C2

Brockencote Hall

COUNTRY HOUSE · CONTEMPORARY Follow the long drive, past a lake and grazing cattle, to this 19C mansion with the feel of a French château. Period features blend well with contemporary country house furnishings and bold colour schemes, and bedrooms are spacious and well-equipped. The elegant restaurant overlooks the gardens.

21 rooms – £ 165/365 £ 185/385

DY10 4PY – On A 448 – 01562 777876 – www.brockencotehall.com

CHAGFORD

Devon – Pop. 1 020 – Regional map n° **1**-C2

Gidleigh Park

CREATIVE · ELEGANT XXXX Within a grand Edwardian house you'll find these three intimate dining rooms. Innovative modern cooking combines French, local and kitchen garden produce in well-considered combinations. Preparation is skilful, there's an Asian influence and the chef's personality really shines through.

→ Pipers Farm chicken with garlic panna cotta, frozen lovage and tapioca. Lemon sole with miso potatoes, seaweed, kohlrabi and mussels. Amalfi lemon with pistachio, olive oil and crème fraîche.

Menu £ 60/145

Gidleigh Park Hotel, TQ13 8HH – Northwest : 2 mi by Gidleigh Rd – 01647 432367 (booking essential) – www.gidleigh.co.uk – Closed 3-15 January

Gidleigh Park

LUXURY · ELEGANT An impressive, timbered Arts and Crafts house with lovely tiered gardens and Teign Valley views. Luxurious sitting and drawing rooms have a classic country house feel but a contemporary edge; wonderfully comfortable bedrooms echo this, with their appealing mix of styles. Service is superb.

24 rooms – £ 350/1085 £ 350/1085 – 1 suite

TQ13 8HH – Northwest : 2 mi by Gidleigh Rd – 01647 432367 – www.gidleigh.co.uk – Closed 3-15 January

Gidleigh Park – See restaurant listing

at Sandypark Northeast: 2.25 mi on A382 Chagford

Mill End

TRADITIONAL · PERSONALISED Whitewashed former mill off a quiet country road: once home to Frank Whittle, inventor of the jet engine. Comfy, cosy lounges with beams and open fires. Contemporary bedrooms have bold feature walls and colourful throws. Bright dining room offers classical dishes prepared using local produce.

15 rooms – £ 75/195 £ 125/210 – 1 suite

TQ13 8JN – On A 382 – 01647 432282 – www.millendhotel.com – Closed 5-21 January

Michelin

CHANNEL ISLANDS

Regional map n° **3**-B2

ALDERNEY

Alderney – Pop. 2 400 – Regional map n° **3**-B1

Braye

 **Braye Beach**

COUNTRY HOUSE • MODERN Stylish hotel on Braye beach, just a stone's throw from the harbour. The vaulted basement houses two lounges and a 19-seater cinema; above is a modern bar with a delightful terrace. Bedrooms are beech-furnished, and some have balconies and bay views. The formal restaurant showcases local island seafood.

27 rooms – †£ 95/155 ††£ 105/175

Braye St. ✉ GY9 3XT – ☎ 01481 824300 – www.brayebeach.com

GUERNSEY

Guernsey – Pop. 58 867 – Regional map n° **3**-A2

Castel

 **Cobo Bay**

FAMILY • MODERN Modern hotel set on the peaceful side of the island and well run by the 3rd generation of the family. Bright, stylish bedrooms come with fresh fruit, irons, safes and bathrobes – some have large balconies overlooking the sandy bay. Smart dining room; sit on the spacious terrace for lovely sunset views.

34 rooms – †£ 59/219 ††£ 99/219

Cobo Coast Rd ✉ GY5 7HB
– ☎ 01481 257102 – www.cobobayhotel.com
– Closed 1 January-21 March

Fermain Bay

 **Fermain Valley**

COUNTRY HOUSE • MODERN Stylish hotel with beautiful gardens, hidden in a picturesque valley and affording pleasant bay views through the trees. Well-equipped bedrooms are widely dispersed; the 'Gold' rooms have balconies. Dine with a view in Ocean or from a steakhouse menu – accompanied by cocktails – in contemporary Rock Garden.

45 rooms – †£ 115/145 ††£ 130/195

Fermain Ln ✉ GY1 1ZZ
– ☎ 01481 235666 – www.fermainvalley.com

Kings Mills

Fleur du Jardin

TRADITIONAL CUISINE • INN An attractive inn with a stylish terrace, lovely landscaped gardens and several charming, rustic rooms. The main menu offers pub classics such as homemade burgers while more ambitious specials could include tasty island seafood. Stylish bedrooms have a New England theme and there's even a heated outdoor pool.

Menu £ 13 (lunch and early dinner) - Carte £ 22/42

13 rooms - †£ 62/92 ††£ 84/120

Grand Moulins ✉ GY5 7JT - ✆ 01481 257996 - www.fleurdujardin.com - Closed dinner 25 December and 1 January

St Martin

Auberge

TRADITIONAL CUISINE • FASHIONABLE XX Long-standing restaurant in a great location. Simple interior with a bar and well-spaced tables; concertina doors open onto a lovely terrace, which offers views across to the other islands. Classical menu features plenty of island seafood.

Menu £ 14 (lunch and early dinner) - Carte £ 27/63

Jerbourg Rd ✉ GY4 6BH - ✆ 01481 238485 (booking essential) - www.theauberge.gg - Closed 25-26 December and 1 January

St Peter Port

Le Nautique

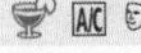

CLASSIC CUISINE • MEDITERRANEAN DÉCOR XX An old sailmaker's warehouse on the quayside, with a stylish nautical interior and a pleasant marina view - ask for a window seat. The large menu offers classic dishes and the fish specials are worth considering.

Menu £ 18 (weekday lunch) - Carte £ 28/61

Town plan: A1-u - *Quay Steps ✉ GY1 2LE - ✆ 01481 721714 - www.lenautiquerestaurant.co.uk - Closed Saturday lunch and Sunday*

The Hook (N)

MEATS AND GRILLS • FASHIONABLE X Start with a cocktail on the 3rd floor then head for the sushi bar or the buzzy restaurant with harbour views. Dishes arrive in satisfying portions - steaks are a speciality, with larger 'sharing' cuts featured on the blackboard.

Menu £ 19 (lunch and early dinner) - Carte £ 28/45

Town plan: A1-h - *North Plantation (1st floor) ✉ GY1 2LQ - ✆ 01481 701373 - www.thehook.gg - Closed Sunday lunch January-April and Sunday dinner*

Red

MEATS AND GRILLS • FASHIONABLE X Popular harbourfront restaurant run by an experienced owner; the first floor cocktail lounge is a real hit. Its name refers to 'red' wines and 'red' meat, with the large menu focusing on top quality chargrilled Scottish steaks.

Menu £ 20 (weekday lunch) - Carte £ 20/43

Town plan: A1-r - *61 Le Poulet ✉ GY1 1WL - ✆ 01481 700299 (booking essential) - www.red.gg - Closed 25 December, Saturday lunch and Sunday*

Slaughterhouse (N)

TRADITIONAL BRITISH • FASHIONABLE X Old meat hooks hanging from the ceiling of this chic, buzzy bar and brasserie, hint at its past as the island's former slaughterhouse. Dine on the mezzanine for the best views. Extensive menus list fresh, tasty dishes.

Carte £ 25/46

Town plan: A2-s - *Castle Pier ✉ GY1 1AU - ✆ 01481 712123 - www.slaughterhouse.gg*

ST PETER PORT

L'ANCRESE, ST-SAMPSON · ST MARTIN · CÖBO BAY, SAUMAREZ PARK, PARISH CHURCH · LITTLE CHAPEL, GERMAN UNDERGROUND HOSPITAL

Beau Sejour Centre · Cambridge Park · QE II Marina · East Breakwater · Guernsey Museum and Gallery · Candie Gardens · Victoria Tower · Monument Gardens · Guernsey Tapestry · Royal Court House · St-Peter's Church · Market Halls · Hauteville House · Harbour · Albert Pier · Castle Pier · Castle Emplacement · Castle Cornet and museums

Old Government House H. & Spa

HISTORIC BUILDING · CLASSIC Fine, classically furnished 18C building, with many of its original features restored, including a glorious ballroom. Individually styled bedrooms have padded walls, modern bathrooms and a personal touch. Relax in the well-equipped spa or outdoor pool. Authentic Indian cooking in The Curry Room. The smart yet informal brasserie has a delightful terrace.

62 rooms – £ 187/220 £ 187/290 – 1 suite

Town plan: A1-a – *St Ann's Pl* ✉ *GY1 2NU* – *✆ 01481 724921* – *www.theoghhotel.com*

Duke of Richmond

BUSINESS · CONTEMPORARY Contemporary hotel with a bright reception area and a stylish lounge ideal for afternoon tea. Smart, modern bedrooms; some with balconies. Relax in the secluded pool or on the patio overlooking the 19C Candie Gardens. A chic bar with leopard print furnishings leads to the restaurant and terrace.

73 rooms – £ 90/150 £ 158/250 – 1 suite

Town plan: A1-s – *Cambridge Pk.* ✉ *GY1 1UY* – *✆ 01481 726221* – *www.dukeofrichmond.com*

Duke of Normandie

BUSINESS • MODERN A former German HQ during the WW2 invasions; superbly located in the centre of town. Brightly coloured designer bedrooms have a cosy feel and some are set in the courtyard. The characterful bar is decorated with historical island memorabilia and offers traditional pub dishes.

37 rooms - £ 49/89 £ 80/159

Town plan: A1-c - *Lefebvre St ✉ GY1 2JP - ✆ 01481 721431 - www.dukeofnormandie.com*

La Frégate

HISTORIC BUILDING • CONTEMPORARY Greatly extended 18C property offering stunning panoramic views across the harbour and out towards the island of Herm. Bedrooms have a clean contemporary style; go for one with a balcony or terrace. Extensive menus feature modern international dishes. Breakfast on the terrace is hard to beat.

22 rooms - £ 100/110 £ 205/260 - 1 suite

Town plan: A1-b - *Beauregard Ln, Les Cotils ✉ GY1 1UT - ✆ 01481 724624 - www.lafregatehotel.com*

Ziggurat (N)

TOWNHOUSE • MEDITERRANEAN A relaxed, boutique townhouse with a slightly bohemian style. The North African décor focuses on warm colours and ornate furnishings and the restaurant has a North African menu to match. A lovely terrace overlooks the harbour and the castle, and luxury sheds in the garden are great for small gatherings.

14 rooms - £ 90/120 £ 120/150

Town plan: A2-x - *5 Constitution Steps ✉ GY1 2PN - ✆ 01481 723008 - www.hotelziggurat.com - Restricted opening January*

St Saviour

Farmhouse

TRADITIONAL • MODERN Former farm restyled in a boutique vein. Stylish, sumptuous bedrooms come with hi-tech amenities and the bathrooms have heated floors. The pleasant garden features a pool, a terrace and a kitchen garden. Contemporary cooking has an international edge and uses the island's finest produce in eclectic ways.

14 rooms - £ 99/170 £ 170/270

Route des Bas Courtils ✉ GY7 9YF - ✆ 01481 264181 - www.thefarmhouse.gg

HERM

Herm - Pop. 60 - Regional map n° **3**-A2

White House

COUNTRY HOUSE • TRADITIONAL The only hotel on this tranquil, car-free island. The lounge offers bay views and the vast tropical gardens come with tennis courts and a pool. Airy bedrooms are split between the house and various cottages. Enjoy classically prepared local produce in the Conservatory or more modern fare in the Ship Inn.

40 rooms (dinner included) - £ 85/150 £ 170/300

✉ GY1 3HR - ✆ 01481 750075 - www.herm.com - Closed October-March

JERSEY

C.I. - Pop. 85 150 - Regional map n° **3**-B2

Beaumont

Mark Jordan at the Beach

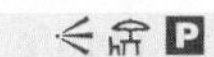

MEDITERRANEAN CUISINE • NEIGHBOURHOOD XX Modern brasserie with a small lounge and bar; a paved terrace with bay views; and a dining room with heavy wood tables, modern seashore paintings and animal ornaments. Menus showcase island produce and fish from local waters. Cooking is refined but hearty, mixing tasty brasserie and restaurant style dishes.

Menu £ 25 (weekdays)/28 - Carte £ 30/59

La Plage, La Route de la Haule ✉ JE3 7YD - ✆ 01534 780180 - www.markjordanatthebeach.com - Closed 5-20 November and Monday in winter

Gorey

Sumas

MODERN CUISINE • TRENDY XX A well-known restaurant in a whitewashed house, with a smart heated terrace affording lovely harbour views. Modern European dishes feature island produce. The monthly changing lunch and midweek dinner menus represent good value.

Menu £ 20 (weekdays) - Carte £ 25/46

Gorey Hill ✉ JE3 6ET - ✆ 01534 853291 (booking essential)
- www.sumasrestaurant.com - Closed 21 December-19 January and Sunday dinner

Walker's

TRADITIONAL CUISINE • TRADITIONAL DÉCOR XX Formal hotel restaurant with a modern lounge, harbour views and local artwork on display. Good value menus offer well-prepared, unashamedly traditional dishes in tried-and-tested combinations and feature the odd personal twist.

Menu £ 25 - Carte £ 33/65

Moorings Hotel, Gorey Pier ✉ JE3 6EW - ✆ 01534 853633
- www.themooringshotel.com - dinner only and Sunday lunch - Closed lunch Easter-September

Bass and Lobster

TRADITIONAL CUISINE • BISTRO X This simply furnished 'Foodhouse' sits close to the beach. Menus offer plenty of choice and you can watch fresh seafood, meats and vegetables from around the island being prepared through the kitchen window.

Menu £ 17/24 - Carte £ 26/43

Gorey Coast Rd ✉ JE3 6EU - ✆ 01534 859590 - www.bassandlobster.com
- Closed 26 December and Monday

Moorings

TRADITIONAL • PERSONALISED Keenly run hotel below the ramparts of Mont Orgueil castle, overlooking the harbour. Leather-furnished first floor lounge. Modern bedrooms in cream, brown and purple colour schemes; some have small balconies. Formal restaurant or casual bistro and terrace for comfort dishes and seafood specials.

15 rooms - £ 70/110 £ 140/170

Gorey Pier ✉ JE3 6EW - ✆ 01534 853633 - www.themooringshotel.com

Walker's - See restaurant listing

Green Island

Green Island

MEDITERRANEAN CUISINE • FRIENDLY X Friendly, personally run restaurant with a terrace and beachside kiosk; the southernmost restaurant in the British Isles. Mediterranean-influenced dishes and seafood specials showcase island produce. Flavours are bold and perfectly judged.

Menu £ 19 (lunch) - Carte £ 33/48

St Clement ✉ JE2 6LS - ✆ 01534 857787 (booking essential)
- www.greenisland.je - Closed 31 December-early February, Sunday dinner and Monday

La Haule

La Haule Manor

TOWNHOUSE • ELEGANT Attractive Georgian house overlooking the fort and bay, with a lovely terrace, a good-sized pool and neat lawned gardens. Stylish guest areas and spacious bedrooms mix modern and antique furnishings; those in the wing are the largest.

16 rooms - £ 81/217 £ 107/217

St Aubin's Bay ✉ JE3 8BS - ✆ 01534 741426 - www.lahaulemanor.com

La Pulente

Ocean

MODERN CUISINE • LUXURY XxX A charming hotel dining room with modern art on display and a fresh, understated feel. Service is smooth and professional and the atmosphere is friendly and relaxed. Well-crafted dishes make good use of island ingredients.

Menu £ 28/85

Atlantic Hotel, Le Mont de la Pulente ✉ JE3 8HE - on B 35 - ✆ 01534 744101 (booking essential) - www.theatlantichotel.com - Closed 3 January-1 February

Atlantic

LUXURY • CONTEMPORARY Set in a superb spot overlooking St Ouen's Bay, this understatedly elegant hotel strikes the perfect balance with its service, which is polished and professional yet warm and welcoming. Stone and wood feature in the laid-back guest areas and many bedrooms look out over the lovely pool and terrace to the sea.

50 rooms - £ 130/310 £ 150/330 - 1 suite

Le Mont de la Pulente ✉ JE3 8HE - on B 35 - ✆ 01534 744101 - www.theatlantichotel.com - Closed 3 January-2 February

Ocean - See restaurant listing

Rozel Bay

Rozel

TRADITIONAL CUISINE • PUB A cosy pub in small coastal hamlet. The upstairs dining room has distant sea views but, come summer, the terraced garden is the place to be. Cooking is traditional and homely and ales are from the island's Liberation Brewery.

Carte £ 27/39

Rozel Valley ✉ JE3 6AJ - ✆ 01534 863438 - www.rozelpubanddining.co.uk

Chateau La Chaire

HISTORIC • CLASSIC An attractive, traditionally styled 19C house surrounded by peaceful gardens and mature woodland. Bedrooms are well-equipped - the 1st floor rooms are the largest and some also have balconies. The formal restaurant leads through to a conservatory and terrace and offers classic dishes with a twist.

13 rooms - £ 125/185 £ 145/325 - 1 suite

Rozel Valley ✉ JE3 6AJ - ✆ 01534 863354 - www.chateau-la-chaire.co.uk

St Aubin

Panorama

TRADITIONAL • PERSONALISED An immaculately-kept house with Georgian origins, colourful gardens and stunning views over the fort and bay. It's run by welcoming owners and has a traditional feel. Over 1,400 teapots are displayed about the place.

14 rooms - £ 55/135 £ 110/190

La Rue du Crocquet ✉ JE3 8BZ - ✆ 01534 742429 - www.panoramajersey.com - Closed November-early April

St Brelade's Bay

Oyster Box

SEAFOOD • BRASSERIE X Glass-fronted eatery with pleasant heated terrace, set on the promenade and affording superb views over St Brelade's Bay. Stylish, airy interior hung with sail cloths and fishermen's floats. Laid-back, friendly service. Accessible seasonal menu features plenty of fish and shellfish; oysters are a speciality.

Carte £ 22/51

La Route de la Baie ✉ JE3 8EF - ✆ 01534 850888 (booking advisable) - www.oysterbox.co.uk - Closed 25-26 December, 1 January, dinner Sunday-Monday October-April and Monday lunch

L'Horizon Beach H & Spa

LUXURY • SEASIDE Long-standing hotel located right on the beachfront and boasting stunning views over the bay. Luxurious interior with extensive guest areas and subtle modern styling. Choose a deluxe bedroom, as they come with balconies and sea views. Stylish, formal restaurant; modern British menus focus on local seafood.

106 rooms - £85/210 £160/315 - 6 suites

La Route de la Baie ✉ JE3 8EF
- ✆ 01534 743101 - www.handpickedhotels.co.uk

St Brelade's Bay

FAMILY • SEASIDE Smart seafront hotel with charming tropical gardens and panoramic bay views. Modern guest areas, an excellent leisure club and contemporary bedrooms fit well alongside original parquet floors and ornate plaster ceilings. The formal restaurant offers impressive sea views and a classic menu.

74 rooms - £100/150 £150/300 - 5 suites

La Route de la Baie ✉ JE3 8EF
- ✆ 01534 746141 - www.stbreladesbayhotel.com

St Helier

Bohemia

MODERN CUISINE • FASHIONABLE XXX Marble-fronted hotel restaurant with a chic cocktail bar and an intimate dining room. The emphasis is on tasting menus, with both pescatarian and vegetarian options available. Cooking is modern, vibrant and has a lightness of touch; original texture and flavour combinations feature.

→ Crab tart and custard with mango & coriander. Lamb loin and braised neck with artichoke, goat's cheese, morels and wild garlic. Popcorn parfait with caramel and lime.

Menu £28/65

Town plan: B2-e - *Club Hotel & Spa, Green St ✉ JE2 4UH*
- ✆ 01534 880588 (booking advisable) - www.bohemiajersey.com - Closed 24-30 December, Sunday and bank holidays

Ormer by Shaun Rankin

MODERN CUISINE • DESIGN XX This elegant restaurant features bold blue banquettes and yellow leather chairs, and is named after a rare shellfish found in local waters. Cooking is refined and assured and uses only the very best seasonal island produce. Inside, it's intimate yet buzzy, and there's a pavement terrace for warmer days.

→ Pancetta-wrapped loin of rabbit with baby gem, morels and truffle sauce. Lobster with kohlrabi, grapefruit and gin & vanilla beurre blanc. Strawberry baked Alaska with yoghurt and strawberry sorbet.

Menu £27 (weekday lunch) - Carte £51/63

Town plan: B1-2-c - *7-11 Don St ✉ JE2 4SP*
- ✆ 01534 725100 (booking advisable) - www.ormerjersey.com - Closed 25 December, 1 January, Sunday and bank holidays

Banjo

INTERNATIONAL • BRASSERIE X Substantial former gentlemen's club with an ornate façade; the banjo belonging to the owner's great grandfather is displayed in a glass-fronted wine cellar. The appealing, wide-ranging menu features everything from brasserie classics to sushi. Stylish bedrooms have Nespresso machines and Bose sound systems.

Carte £21/51

4 rooms - £80/180 £80/180 - £10

Town plan: B1-a - *8 Beresford St ✉ JE2 4WN*
- ✆ 01534 850890 - www.banjojersey.com - Closed 25-26 December and Sunday

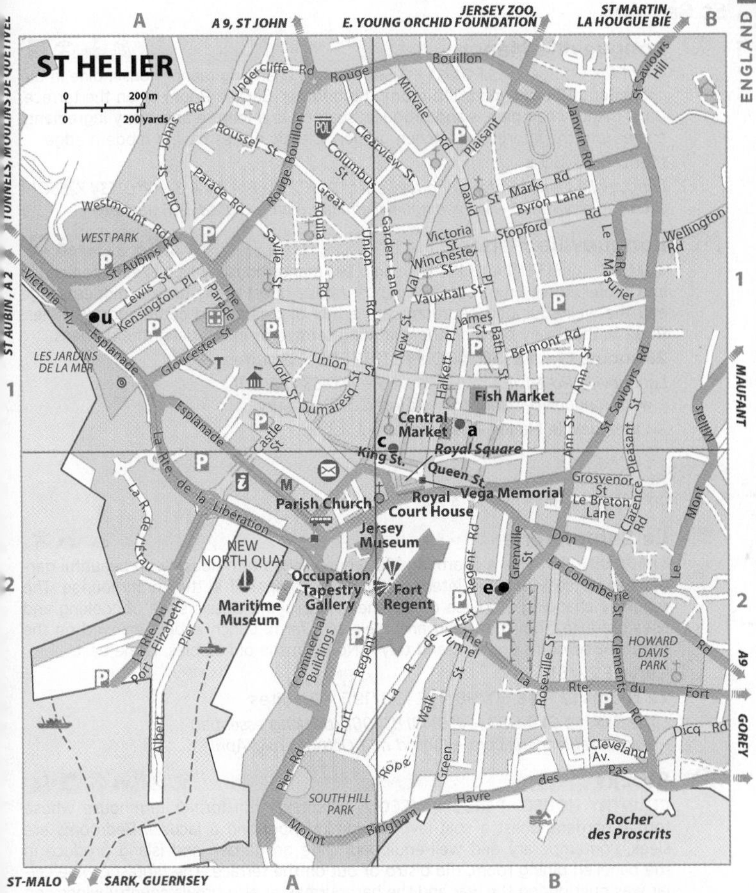

ST HELIER

Grand Jersey

LUXURY • MODERN Welcoming hotel with a large terrace overlooking the bay. The stylish interior incorporates a chic champagne bar, a well-equipped spa and a corporate cinema. Contemporary bedrooms come in bold colours; some have balconies and sea views. Watch TV footage from the kitchen in intimate Tassili; Victoria's serves brasserie dishes.

123 rooms – †£ 89/200 ††£ 100/250

Town plan: A1-u – *The Esplanade ✉ JE2 3QA – ✆ 01534 722301 – www.handpickedhotels.co.uk*

Club Hotel & Spa

BUSINESS • MODERN Modern hotel with stylish guest areas, an honesty bar and a split-level breakfast room. Contemporary bedrooms have floor to ceiling windows and good facilities. Relax in the smart spa or on the terrace beside the small outdoor pool.

46 rooms – †£ 99/245 ††£ 99/245 – 4 suites

Town plan: B2-e – *Green St ✉ JE2 4UH – ✆ 01534 876500 – www.theclubjersey.com – Closed 24-30 December*

✿ **Bohemia** – See restaurant listing

St Saviour

Longueville Manor

MODERN CUISINE • ELEGANT XXX Set within a charming manor house; dine in the characterful 15C oak-panelled room, the brighter Garden Room or on the terrace. Daily menus champion island produce; seafood is a feature and many ingredients come from the impressive kitchen garden. Classic dishes have a modern edge.

Menu £ 25/60 **s**

Longueville Manor Hotel, Longueville Rd ✉ JE2 7WF - on A 3 - ☏ 01534 725501 (booking advisable) - www.longuevillemanor.com - Closed 3-31 January

Longueville Manor

LUXURY • CONTEMPORARY An iconic 13C manor house, which is very personally and professionally run. Comfy, country house guest areas have a modern edge and the well-equipped bedrooms are a mix of classic and contemporary styles. Relax in the lovely pool, on the charming terrace or in the delightful gardens.

28 rooms - £ 150/400 £ 195/595 - 2 suites

Longueville Rd ✉ JE2 7WF - on A 3 - ☏ 01534 725501 - www.longuevillemanor.com - Closed 3-31 January

Longueville Manor - See restaurant listing

SARK

Sark - Pop. 550 - Regional map n° **3**-A2

La Sablonnerie

SEAFOOD • COSY XX A charming 16C whitewashed farmhouse with beautiful gardens and a cosy beamed interior; start with an aperitif in the comfy lounge. The regularly changing 5 course dinner menu displays a classic style of cooking and uses produce from the island and their own farm. Lunch is best enjoyed on the terrace. Bedrooms are neat and tidy - No.14, in the old stables, is the best.

Carte £ 27/51

22 rooms - £ 50/98 £ 100/195 - 2 suites

Little Sark ✉ GY9 OSD - ☏ 01481 832061 (booking essential) - www.lasablonnerie.com - Closed mid October-mid April

Stocks

COUNTRY HOUSE • PERSONALISED A personally run former farmhouse whose formal gardens boast a split-level swimming pool and a jacuzzi. Bedrooms are sleek, contemporary and well-equipped. Dine on garden and island produce in the panelled dining room, the bistro or out on the terrace. The fantastic wine cellar was built during the war and the harbourmaster also brews country wines and liqueurs here.

23 rooms - £ 243/263 £ 273/295 - 5 suites

✉ GY10 1SD - ☏ 01481 832001 - www.stockshotel.com - Closed January-February

CHARLTON

West Sussex - Regional map n° **4**-C2

Fox Goes Free

TRADITIONAL CUISINE • RUSTIC Charming 17C flint pub with a superb garden and terrace and a lovely outlook. Original features include exposed stone walls, low beamed ceilings and brick floors. Dishes range from simple pub classics to more substantial local offerings; some are to share. Clean, unfussy bedrooms; a few with low beamed ceilings.

Carte £ 21/44

5 rooms - £ 73/165 £ 98/190

✉ PO18 OHU - ☏ 01243 811461 - www.thefoxgoesfree.com - Closed dinner 25 December

CHARWELTON - Northamptonshire ➔ See Daventry

CHATTON

Northumberland - Pop. 438 - Regional map n° **14**-A1

Chatton Park House

TRADITIONAL · PERSONALISED Charming 1730s house in 6 acres of formal gardens. It has a smart parquet-floored hallway, a huge open-fired sitting room and spacious bedrooms which blend modern décor and original features. Excellent breakfasts use local produce.

5 rooms – £ 130/235 £ 145/250

NE66 5RA - East : 1 mi on B 6348 - 01688 215507 - www.chattonpark.com - Closed November-March

CHEADLE

Greater Manchester - Regional map n° **11**-B3

Oddfellows on the Park

HISTORIC BUILDING · PERSONALISED Set close to Manchester Airport, in the middle of a park; a Victorian mansion which blends original features with modern furnishings. Opt for a suite in the tower above the front door; the Douglas tartan is a nod to house's original owners. Modern British dishes are served in the stunningly restored ballroom.

22 rooms – £ 155/210 £ 155/395 – £ 20

Bruntwood Hall, Bruntwood Park SK8 1RS - South : 1.25 mi by A 560 and Wilmslow Rd off Cheadle Rd - 0161 697 3066 - www.oddfellowsonthepark.com

CHELMONDISTON - Suffolk ➔ See Ipswich

Le Champignon Sauvage

GOOD TIPS!

This pretty spa town on the edge of the Cotswolds is renowned for its splendid Regency architecture, two examples being the elegant, Grade II listed **Malmaison** hotel and the chic, centrally located **Hotel du Vin**. The grounds of the magnificent, part-15C **Ellenborough Park** hotel stretch down to Cheltenham's famous racecourse, home of the Gold Cup.

CHELTENHAM

Gloucestershire – Pop. 116 447 – Regional map n° **2**-C1

Restaurants

✿✿ Le Champignon Sauvage (David Everitt-Matthias) A/C

MODERN CUISINE • INTIMATE XXX The chef has cooked here proudly and passionately for 30 years, creating dishes with classic French roots and a personal touch. Visually impressive and boldly flavoured, they often feature foraged ingredients such as dandelion or burdock. Come at lunch or midweek to take advantage of the good value set menus.

➜ Scallop and salsify with milk crumbs, cured jowl, onion dashi and leek purée. Lamb with sweetbreads, artichoke and burdock. Acorn delice with mocha sorbet and beurre noisette purée.

Menu £ 34/67

Town plan: A2-a – *24-28 Suffolk Rd ✉ GL50 2AQ – ✆ 01242 573449 – www.lechampignonsauvage.co.uk – Closed 3 weeks June, 10 days Christmas, Sunday and Monday*

⑩ The Beaufort

MODERN CUISINE • INTIMATE XXX With its Tudor stone fireplaces, original oak wood panelling and stained glass windows, this characterful hotel restaurant lends itself to sophisticated dining. Cooking is modern and accomplished and relies on local ingredients.

Menu £ 55 **s**

Ellenborough Park Hotel, Southam Rd ✉ GL52 3NJ – Northeast : 2.75 mi on B 4632 – ✆ 01242 545454 – www.ellenboroughpark.com – dinner only and Sunday lunch – Closed Sunday dinner and Monday

⑩ Lumière A/C

MODERN CUISINE • INTIMATE XXX Friendly, personally run restaurant; its unassuming exterior concealing a long, stylish room decorated with mirrors. Seasonal dishes are modern and intricate with the occasional playful twist – desserts are often the highlight.

Menu £ 35/65

Town plan: AB1-z – *Clarence Par ✉ GL50 3PA – ✆ 01242 222200 (booking essential) – www.lumiere.cc – dinner only and lunch Friday-Saturday – Closed 2 weeks January, 2 weeks summer and Sunday-Tuesday*

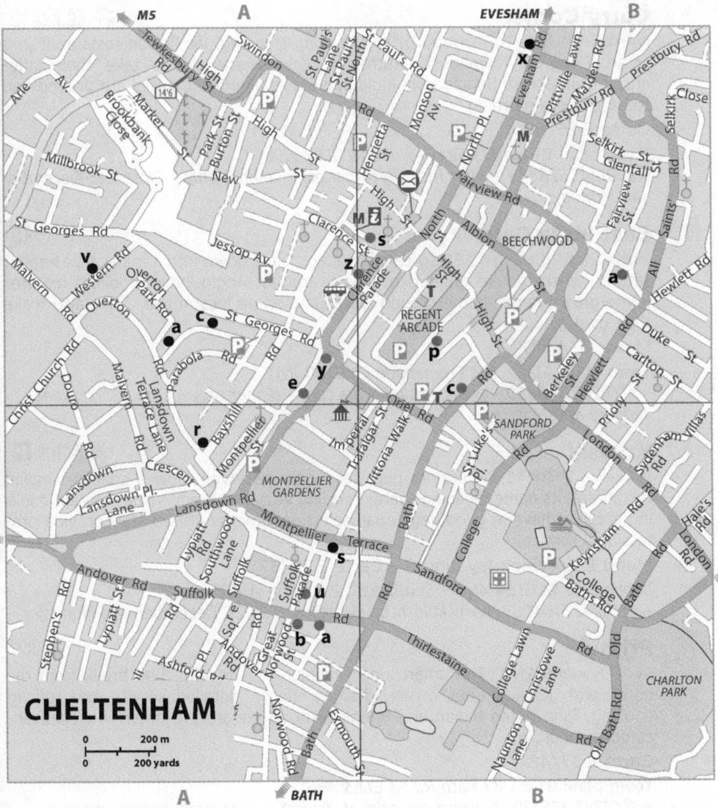

Daffodil

MODERN BRITISH • BRASSERIE XX A delightful 1920s art deco cinema: the tables are in the old stalls, the kitchens are in the screen area and the stylish lounge is up on the balcony. A slick team serve classic brasserie dishes include steaks from the Josper grill. Buy something to take home from their deli – they even sell live lobsters!

Carte £ 30/52

Town plan: A2-u – *18-20 Suffolk Par ✉ GL50 2AE – ✆ 01242 700055 – www.thedaffodil.com – Closed 25-26 December, Sunday and lunch Monday-Thursday*

Bhoomi

INDIAN • ROMANTIC XX Its name means 'earth' in the Keralan dialect and the cooking focuses on southeast India. The preparation and presentation may have been subtly modernised but the essence of each dish remains. The room has a plush, luxurious feel.

Menu £ 28/45 – Carte £ 31/39

Town plan: A2-b – *52 Suffolk Rd ✉ GL50 2AQ – ✆ 01242 222010 – www.bhoomi.co.uk – Closed 25 December-9 January, Easter Sunday, Monday and lunch Tuesday-Thursday*

Curry Corner

BANGLADESHI • NEIGHBOURHOOD XX Long-standing, family-run restaurant in a smart Regency townhouse. Authentic, flavoursome dishes take their influences from across Bangladesh, India and Persia. Imported spices are ground and roasted every morning.

Carte £ 26/42

Town plan: B1-a – *133 Fairview Rd ✉ GL52 2EX – ✆ 01242 528449 – www.thecurrycorner.com – dinner only – Closed 25 December and Monday*

East India Cafe Ⓝ

INDIAN • FRIENDLY XX Steep candlelit steps leads down into a magical basement setting, where you're greeted by lovely aromas. Anglo-Indian cooking features home-grown herbs, home-ground spices and prime local meats. They also make their own gin.

Menu £ 34/50

Town plan: A1-y – *103 Promenade ✉ GL50 1NW – ✆ 01242 300850 – www.eastindiacafe.com – dinner only – Closed first week January and Monday*

Koloshi

INDIAN • INTIMATE XX Former pub, set by the reservoir; now a spacious Indian restaurant, its name meaning 'water carrying vessel' in Hindi. Visual, vibrant cooking is full of flavour; good vegetarian selection. Smartly attired staff provide professional service.

Menu £ 10 (weekday lunch) – Carte £ 20/37

London Rd ✉ GL54 4HG – Southeast : 2.5 mi on A 40 – ✆ 01242 516400 – www.koloshi.co.uk – Closed 25-26 December and Monday

Prithvi

INDIAN • DESIGN XX This smart Indian restaurant is a refreshing break from the norm, with its ambitious owner, designer décor, detailed service and refined cooking. Reinvented Indian and Bangladeshi dishes are presented in a sophisticated manner.

Carte £ 37/48

Town plan: B1-c – *37 Bath Rd ✉ GL53 7HG – ✆ 01242 226229 (booking essential at dinner) – www.prithvirestaurant.com – dinner only and lunch Saturday-Sunday – Closed 23 December-6 January, 18-24 June, Sunday dinner and Monday*

White Spoon

MODERN BRITISH • ELEGANT XX Hidden away in the town centre, down a tiny passageway, is this impressive Regency building with lovely views of Cheltenham Minster. The passionate, knowledgeable chef-owner is an advocate of modern techniques and natural flavours.

Menu £ 12 (weekday lunch) – Carte £ 33/44

Town plan: B1-s – *8 Well Walk ✉ GL50 3JX – ✆ 01242 228555 – www.thewhitespoon.co.uk – Closed Sunday dinner, Monday and Tuesday*

No. 131

MEATS AND GRILLS • BISTRO X The columned exterior of this fine 1820s building overlooks an attractive park. Inside, original features remain but it now has a cool, contemporary style, with impressive modern artwork featuring throughout. The menu lists well-prepared, unfussy classics, with steaks cooked on the Josper grill a feature at dinner. Bedrooms are individually and tastefully furnished.

Carte £ 29/56

11 rooms – †£ 120/410 ††£ 120/410

Town plan: A1-e – *131 Promenade ✉ GL50 1NW – ✆ 01242 822939 (booking essential) – www.no131.com*

Purslane

MODERN BRITISH • INTIMATE A stylishly minimalistic neighbourhood restaurant with relaxed, efficient service. Fresh seafood from Cornwall and Scotland is combined with good quality, locally sourced ingredients to produce interesting, original dishes.

Menu £17 (lunch and early dinner)/38

Town plan: B1-p – *16 Rodney Rd ✉ GL50 1JJ – ✆ 01242 321639 – www.purslane-restaurant.co.uk – Closed 2 weeks January, 2 weeks August, Sunday and Monday*

Royal Oak

TRADITIONAL BRITISH • RUSTIC This was once owned by batting legend Tom Graveney, hence the 'Pavilion' function room. Lunch offers tasty, satisfying dishes like kedgeree, while dinner steps things up a level. Sit in the cosy bar, dark wood dining room or heated garden.

Carte £26/37

The Burgage, Prestbury ✉ GL52 3DL – Northeast : 2 mi by A 435, off B 4075 – ✆ 01242 522344 – www.royal-oak-prestbury.co.uk – Closed 25 December

Hotels

Ellenborough Park

LUXURY • ELEGANT Part-15C timbered manor house, with stone annexes, an understated Indian-themed spa and large grounds stretching down to the racecourse. Beautifully furnished guest areas have an elegant, classical style. Nina Campbell designed bedrooms have superb bathrooms, the latest mod cons and plenty of extras. Dine in the sophisticated restaurant or informal brasserie.

61 rooms – †£147/285 ††£147/744

Southam Rd ✉ GL52 3NJ – Northeast : 2.75 mi on B 4632 – ✆ 01242 545454 – www.ellenboroughpark.com

The Beaufort – See restaurant listing

Hotel du Vin

TOWNHOUSE • THEMED Attractive Regency house in an affluent residential area. Inside it's chic and laid-back, with a leather-furnished bar and a comfy lounge. Some of the individually designed, well-equipped, wine-themed bedrooms have baths in the room. The French bistro features an eye-catching wine glass chandelier.

49 rooms – †£122/257 ††£122/257 – 1 suite

Town plan: A1-c – *Parabola Rd ✉ GL50 3AQ – ✆ 01242 588450 – www.hotelduvin.com*

Malmaison

TOWNHOUSE • MODERN Chic Regency townhouse, where stylish modern guest areas are hung with an impressive collection of contemporary art. Light wood furnished bedrooms come with Nespresso machines, complimentary mini bars and in-room info on an iPod touch. Dine on British dishes at marble-topped tables or on one of two terraces.

61 rooms – †£145/525 ††£145/525 – £15

Town plan: A2-r – *Bayshill Rd ✉ GL50 3AS – ✆ 01242 527788 – www.malmaison.com*

No 38 The Park

TOWNHOUSE • DESIGN Behind the attractive Georgian façade is a very original, tastefully designed hotel with a relaxed atmosphere and supremely comfortable furnishings. Bedrooms come with coffee machines and vast walk-in showers or feature baths.

13 rooms – †£110/315 ††£120/325

Town plan: B1-x – *38 Eversham Rd ✉ GL52 2AH – ✆ 01242 248656 – www.no38thepark.com*

Beaumont House

TOWNHOUSE • CONTEMPORARY Your hosts here are warm and welcoming, just like the hotel. The lounge and breakfast room are comfortably and classically furnished, while the bedrooms are more contemporary; there are two themed rooms – Africa and Asia.

16 rooms – £ 75/250 £ 115/250

56 Shurdington Rd ✉ GL53 0JE – South : 1.5 mi on A 46
– ✆ 01242 223311 – www.bhhotel.co.uk

Wyastone Townhouse

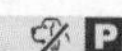

TOWNHOUSE • CONTEMPORARY Nothing is too much trouble for the charming young owner of this attractive townhouse. Inside, contemporary décor blends with period features. Bedrooms – split between the house and the courtyard – are surprisingly spacious.

16 rooms – £ 65/98 £ 110/165

Town plan: A1-a – *Parabola Rd ✉ GL50 3BG*
– ✆ 01242 245549 – www.wyastonehotel.co.uk – Closed 23 December-1 January

Butlers

TOWNHOUSE • PERSONALISED The bedrooms of this tastefully furnished Victorian townhouse are named after famous butlers – a theme which continues in the classical lounge and breakfast room. There's also an interesting collection of hats about the place!

9 rooms – £ 75/135 £ 80/180

Town plan: A1-v – *Western Rd ✉ GL50 3RN*
– ✆ 01242 570771 – www.butlers-hotel.co.uk

Detmore House

COUNTRY HOUSE • CONTEMPORARY Peace and tranquility reign at this 1840s country house, which is accessed via a private drive and offers pleasant rural views. Bedrooms are modern and comfortable – 'Oak' is the best. Breakfast is served at a fine oak table.

4 rooms – £ 75/95 £ 95/110

London Rd, Charlton Kings ✉ GL52 6UT – Southeast : 2.5 mi by A 40
– ✆ 01242 582868 – www.detmorehouse.com – Closed Christmas and New Year

at Shurdington Southwest: 3.75 mi on A46 ✉ Cheltenham

Greenway

COUNTRY HOUSE • CLASSIC 16C ivy-clad manor house, set in 8 acres of peaceful grounds and offering pleasant views over the hills. Comfy drawing rooms and well-equipped bedrooms have a pleasant country house style. Enjoy a laid-back brasserie-style lunch on the terrace of the lovely spa. The oak-panelled restaurant offers classic dishes with modern overtones and overlooks the lily pond.

21 rooms – £ 110/390 £ 135/420 – 1 suite

✉ GL51 4UG
– ✆ 01242 862352 – www.thegreenwayhotelandspa.com

at Piff's Elm Northwest: 4 mi on A4019

Gloucester Old Spot

TRADITIONAL BRITISH • RUSTIC Cosy, relaxing inn with a snug, quarry-tiled bar, a baronial dining room and open fires aplenty. Menus offer tasty, seasonal dishes, with rare breed pork a speciality. Nursery puddings. Cheery, welcoming staff.

Menu £ 14 (weekday lunch) – Carte £ 27/38

Tewkesbury Rd ✉ GL51 9SY
– ✆ 01242 680321 – www.thegloucesteroldspot.co.uk – Closed 25-26 December

B. Kadic/age fotostock

GOOD TIPS!

There is evidence of Chester's Roman origins all around the city; not least, its two miles of ancient walls. It is also known for its black & white half-timbered buildings, like the Grade II listed **Chester Grosvenor** hotel – home to Simon Radley's Michelin Starred restaurant. Carnivores will appreciate the quality of the meat on offer **Upstairs at the Grill**.

CHESTER

Cheshire West and Chester – Pop. 86 011 – Regional map n° **11**-A3

Restaurants

Simon Radley at Chester Grosvenor

MODERN CUISINE • LUXURY XXXX Elegant restaurant with a fresh, classic feel, a stylish cocktail lounge and an impressive wine cellar. Confident cooking shows respect for ingredients, bringing together clean, clear flavours in sophisticated dishes that display interesting, innovative touches. Formal and detailed service.

→ Hot and cold king scallop with lacquered pork ribs and sweet lychee. Butter-poached Black Leg chicken with lobster and summer truffle. Iced nectar, fruit candy, goat's curd and almond turrón.

Menu £ 69/99

Town plan: B2-a – *Chester Grosvenor Hotel, Eastgate ✉ CH1 1LT – ✆ 01244 324024 – www.chestergrosvenor.com – dinner only – Closed 1 January-13 February, 25 December, Sunday and Monday*

Joseph Benjamin

MODERN CUISINE • BISTRO X This personally and passionately run bistro is named after its owners, Joe and Ben. The light, simple décor mirrors the style of cooking and the monthly menu offers tasty, well-judged dishes. They serve breakfast, lunch, coffee and homemade pastries and, from Thursday to Saturday, intimate candlelit dinners.

Carte £ 20/34

Town plan: A1-u – *134-140 Northgate St ✉ CH1 2HT – ✆ 01244 344295 (booking essential) – www.josephbenjamin.co.uk – lunch only and dinner Thursday-Saturday – Closed 25 December-1 January and Monday*

La Brasserie

INTERNATIONAL • BRASSERIE XX Parisian-style brasserie with a hand-painted glass skylight, mirrors, brass rails and colourful light fittings; sit on a leather banquette or in a booth. Refined British, French and Mediterranean dishes are cooked on the Josper grill.

Menu £ 25 (weekdays) – Carte £ 31/57

Town plan: B2-a – *Chester Grosvenor Hotel, Eastgate ✉ CH1 1LT – ✆ 01244 324024 – www.chestergrosvenor.com – Closed 1 January-13 February and 25 December*

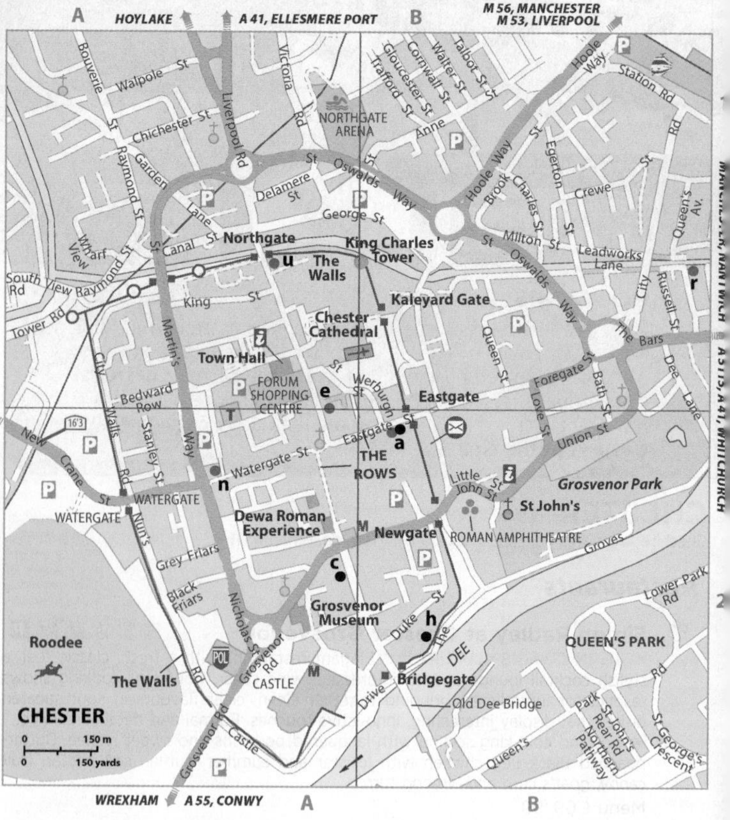

CHESTER

Upstairs at the Grill

MEATS AND GRILLS • BISTRO XX Smart restaurant offering prime quality steaks – including porterhouse and bone-in fillet or rib-eye; the 5 week dry-aged cuts are from premium Welsh beef. Eat in the moody cocktail bar or downstairs amongst the cow paraphernalia.

Carte £ 22/51

Town plan: A2-n – *70 Watergate St* ✉ *CH1 2LA*
– *✆ 01244 344883 – www.upstairsatthegrill.co.uk*
– *dinner only and lunch Thursday-Sunday – Closed 25 December and 1 January*

Artichoke

MODERN CUISINE • BISTRO X Sit outside beside the canal towpath or inside the Victorian mill building, where you'll find original beams, bare brick walls and a contemporary cocktail bar. Cooking ranges from homemade cakes to seasonal 3 course meals.

Carte £ 23/34

Town plan: B1-r – *The Steam Mill, Steam Mill St* ✉ *CH3 5AN*
– *✆ 01244 329229 – www.artichokechester.co.uk*
– *Closed 25-26 December*

Chef's Table

MODERN BRITISH • SIMPLE A cosy city centre bistro with a loyal following and a pleasingly laid-back vibe. Menus change daily, depending on the latest produce available. Colourful, artfully presented dishes are made up of many ingredients.

Menu £18 (lunch) – Carte £28/41

Town plan: A1-2-e – *4 Music Hall Passage ✉ CH1 2EU – ✆ 01244 403040 (booking essential) – www.chefstablechester.co.uk – Closed Monday lunch*

Porta

SPANISH • TAPAS BAR Close to the city wall, behind a narrow terrace, is this cosy, characterful little tapas bar. It has no phone number or reservation system, but it does offer generous, tasty dishes which are served by a friendly young team.

Carte £10/20

Town plan: A1-u – *140 Northgate St ✉ CH1 2HT (bookings not accepted) – www.portatapas.co.uk – dinner only – Closed 25 December-1 January*

Sticky Walnut

MODERN BRITISH • SIMPLE Run by a confident young team, a quirky, slightly bohemian restaurant in a residential parade of shops. Concise menus feature quality ingredients in a mix of British, French and Italian dishes; the breads and pastas are all homemade.

Menu £16 (weekday lunch) – Carte £23/38

11 Charles St ✉ CH2 3AZ – Northeast : 1 mi by Hoole Way (A 56) off Faulkner St – ✆ 01244 400400 (booking essential at dinner) – www.stickywalnut.com – Closed 25-26 December

Hotels

Chester Grosvenor

GRAND LUXURY • CLASSIC 19C hotel with a grand, black and white timbered façade, a stunning Rococo chocolate shop and a buzzy lounge serving all-day snacks. Stylish bedrooms blend traditional furnishings and modern fabrics; luxurious, marble-floored bathrooms.

80 rooms – £129/425 £139/425 – 6 suites

Town plan: B2-a – *Eastgate ✉ CH1 1LT – ✆ 01244 324024 – www.chestergrosvenor.com – Closed 25 December*

Simon Radley at Chester Grosvenor • **La Brasserie** – See restaurant listing

Oddfellows

TOWNHOUSE • DESIGN It was originally an Oddfellows Hall built in 1676 to help the poor but its name also suits its unique, quirky styling. Well-equipped, contemporary bedrooms include some duplex suites: some have circular beds and others, double roll-top baths. The garden-themed restaurant serves unfussy Mediterranean dishes.

22 rooms – £99/150 £150/280

Town plan: A2-c – *20 Lower Bridge St ✉ CH1 1RS – ✆ 01244 345454 – www.oddfellowschester.com – Closed 25 December*

Edgar House

TOWNHOUSE • ELEGANT A charming 17C house by the city walls, in the historic heart of Chester. The delightful garden overlooks the River Dee and the bright, modern bedrooms have raised-up beds so you can see the water. An honesty bar is housed in an old telephone box and the rustic dining room offers a traditional menu.

7 rooms – £199/279 £199/279

Town plan: B2-h – *22 City Walls ✉ CH1 1SB – ✆ 01244 347007 – www.edgarhouse.co.uk*

CHESTERFIELD

Derbyshire – Pop. 88 483 – Regional map n° **9**-B1

Cocina

MEDITERRANEAN CUISINE • BRASSERIE XX Stylish hotel restaurant with a well-stocked cocktail bar. Mediterranean menus have a strong Spanish influence; try the tapas or the mature steaks from the Josper oven. Organic rare breed beef comes from the owners' 350 acre farm.

Menu £ 24 (early dinner) – Carte £ 27/48

Casa Hotel, Lockoford Ln ✉ S41 7JB – North : 1 mi off A 61 – ✆ 01246 245999 – www.casahotels.com – dinner only and Sunday lunch

Casa

BUSINESS • MODERN Modern hotel with 11 state-of-the-art meeting rooms and a smart bar with a heated terrace. Sizeable bedrooms are furnished in autumnal colours and come with useful extras; some of the suites have balconies and outdoor hot tubs.

100 rooms – †£ 95/150 ††£ 110/165

Lockoford Ln ✉ S41 7JB – North : 1 mi off A 61 – ✆ 01246 245999 – www.casahotels.com

Cocina – See restaurant listing

CHEW MAGNA

Bath and North East Somerset – Pop. 1 149 – Regional map n° **2**-C2

Pony & Trap (Josh Eggleton)

MODERN BRITISH • COSY Sit in the characterful front bar, the rustic rear room or out on the terrace – the latter two afford wonderful country views. The daily menu sees herbs and fruits from the garden come together with West Country meats and fish. Precisely prepared dishes range from appealing snacks to more refined main courses.

→ Beetroot, apple and ewe's curd. Hake with mushrooms, chicken wing and tarragon. Sticky ale pudding with candied walnut and stout ice cream.

Carte £ 33/48

Knowle Hill, New Town ✉ BS40 8TQ – South : 1.25 mi on Bishop Sutton rd – ✆ 01275 332627 (booking essential) – www.theponyandtrap.co.uk – Closed 25 December, dinner 26 and 31 December, 1 January and bank holidays

Salt & Malt

SEAFOOD • FRIENDLY X Smart lakeside eatery with lovely views over the water. They're open all day for breakfast, coffee and cakes, light lunches and cream teas. The evening menu steps things up a gear; fish and chips is the thing to go for.

Carte £ 16/36

Walley Ln, Chew Stoke ✉ BS40 8TF – South : 1.25 mi by Bishop Sutton rd and Denny Rd – ✆ 01275 333345 – www.saltmalt.com – Closed Sunday dinner and dinner Monday-Tuesday in winter

CHICHESTER

West Sussex – Pop. 28 657 – Regional map n° **4**-C2

Chichester Harbour

BUSINESS • MODERN Grade II listed former home to one of Nelson's men. Some impressive Georgian features remain, including a cantilevered wrought iron staircase. Stylish, up-to-date bedrooms and a spacious, contemporary bar. Airy brasserie offers a modern European menu, with meat and game from the nearby estate.

37 rooms – †£ 90/140 ††£ 130/350

57 North St ✉ PO19 1NH – ✆ 01243 778000 – www.chichester-harbour-hotel.co.uk

at Mid Lavant North: 2 mi on A286

Earl of March

TRADITIONAL CUISINE • PUB This 18C inn offers the perfect blend of contemporary styling and relaxed country character. Good quality seasonal produce is showcased in British-based dishes. Find a spot on the terrace to take in the amazing South Downs views.

Menu £ 25 (lunch and early dinner) – Carte £ 32/44

✉ PO18 0BQ

– ✆ 01243 533993 – www.theearlofmarch.com

Rooks Hill

COUNTRY HOUSE • PERSONALISED Grade II listed house with a pleasant view across to the Goodwood estate. Relax on the charming courtyard terrace or next to the wood burner in the cosy sitting room. Individually decorated bedrooms have contemporary touches.

4 rooms – †£ 105/125 ††£ 125/175

Lavant Rd ✉ PO18 0BQ

– ✆ 01243 528400 – www.rookshill.co.uk

at Tangmere East: 2 mi by A27 ✉ Chichester

Cassons

MODERN CUISINE • RUSTIC XX Passionately run restaurant with exposed brick, wooden beams and a rustic feel. Boldly flavoured dishes are generously proportioned. Cooking is classically based but employs modern techniques. The regular gourmet evenings are a hit.

Menu £ 39

Arundel Rd ✉ PO18 0DU – Northwest : 0.25 mi off A 27 (westbound)

– ✆ 01243 773294 – www.cassonsrestaurant.co.uk

– dinner only and Sunday lunch – Closed 25-30 December and Sunday dinner

at West Ashling Northwest: 4.5 mi by B2178 and B2146

Richmond Arms

INTERNATIONAL • RUSTIC Appealing, laid-back country pub opposite a duck pond in a lovely little village. The menu offers an appealing mix, from freshly sliced hams and local steaks to game from the family estate in Anglesey; many meats are cooked on the rotisserie or the Japanese robata grill. Two luxurious bedrooms are above.

Carte £ 23/45

2 rooms – †£ 125/135 ††£ 125/135

Mill Rd ✉ PO18 8EA

– ✆ 01243 572046 – www.therichmondarms.co.uk

– Closed Sunday dinner, Monday and Tuesday

at Funtington Northwest: 4.75 mi by B2178 on B2146 ✉ Chichester

Hallidays

CLASSIC CUISINE • INTIMATE XX Characterful thatched cottage comprising a series of interconnecting rooms with low beams. The chef knows a thing or two about sourcing good ingredients and his menu changes regularly. Cooking is skilful and classically based.

Menu £ 18/38

Watery Ln ✉ PO18 9LF

– ✆ 01243 575331 – www.hallidays.info.co.uk

– Closed 2 weeks August, 1 week March, 1 week Christmas-New Year, Saturday lunch, Sunday dinner, Monday and Tuesday

CHIDDINGFOLD

Surrey – Pop. 2 211 – Regional map n° **4**-C2

Swan Inn

MODERN CUISINE • INN It might be over 200 years old but the Swan has a modern feel and its 11 comfy bedrooms are equally stylish. The extensive menu changes a little each day and offers a mix of pub and restaurant style dishes. Unsurprisingly, on sunny days, the stepped rear terrace is a popular spot.

Carte £ 29/43

11 rooms – £ 109/205 £ 119/215

Petworth Rd ✉ GU8 4TY – ✆ 01428 684688 – www.theswaninnchiddingfold.com

CHILCOMPTON

Somerset – Pop. 2 062 – Regional map n° **2**-C2

Redan Inn

MODERN BRITISH • PUB This smartly refurbished pub displays an impressive selection of old curios. The concise weekly menu offers an enticing mix of accomplished dishes. They cure their own meats, make their own sausages and use apples from the garden for their chutney. Service is relaxed and engaging and bedrooms are stylish.

Menu £ 15 (weekday lunch) – Carte £ 27/42

8 rooms – £ 95/160 £ 100/170

Fry's Well ✉ BA3 4HA – ✆ 01761 258560 – www.theredaninn.co.uk

CHILLATON

- Devon → See Tavistock

CHILLINGTON

Devon – Regional map n° **1**-C3

whitehouse

COUNTRY HOUSE • CONTEMPORARY Attractive Georgian house run in a relaxed manner. Stylish bedrooms are boldly decorated and feature a mix of modern and retro furnishings; all have heavy handmade beds and smart bathrooms. The breakfast room overlooks the gardens.

6 rooms – £ 170/210 £ 190/230

✉ TQ7 2JX – ✆ 01548 581196 – www.whitehousedevon.com

CHINNOR

Oxfordshire – Pop. 5 473 – Regional map n° **6**-C2

at Sprigg's Alley

Southeast: 2.5 mi by Bledlow Ridge rd ✉ Chinnor

Sir Charles Napier

MODERN BRITISH • COSY Enjoy an aperitif in the delightful garden or beside the log fire in this quirky restaurant, where animal sculptures peer out from every corner. British cooking is modern yet unfussy and the wine list is a labour of love.

Menu £ 20 (weekdays) – Carte £ 39/57

Sprigs Holly ✉ OX39 4BX – ✆ 01494 483011 (booking advisable) – www.sircharlesnapier.co.uk – Closed 24-26 December, Sunday dinner and Monday except bank holidays

CHIPPING CAMPDEN

Gloucestershire – Pop. 2 037 – Regional map n° **2**-D1

Kings

MODERN CUISINE • RUSTIC An appealing, rustic restaurant in a stylish boutique townhouse. Exposed stone walls, wooden beams and a large inglenook fireplace feature. Modern British menus use top quality ingredients and dishes are refined and flavoursome.

Carte £ 22/42

Kings Hotel, The Square ✉ GL55 6AW – ✆ 01386 840256 – www.kingscampden.co.uk

Cotswold House H. and Spa

TOWNHOUSE • CONTEMPORARY A set of stylish Regency townhouses with lovely gardens, boldly decorated lounges hung with eclectic modern art, and a beautiful staircase winding upwards towards luxurious modern bedrooms. Relax in the spa our outdoor hot tub then enjoy sophisticated modern dishes amongst Regency columns.

28 rooms – £ 125/245 £ 135/255 – 3 suites

The Square ✉ GL55 6AN
– ✆ 01386 840330 – www.cotswoldhouse.com

Kings

TOWNHOUSE • CLASSIC Beautiful Cotswold stone townhouse with a stylish boutique interior. Bedrooms in the main house mix antiques with modern facilities – some boast sleigh beds; rooms in the cottage at the end of the garden are more up-to-date.

18 rooms – £ 120/325 £ 130/325

The Square ✉ GL55 6AW
– ✆ 01386 840256 – www.kingscampden.co.uk

Kings – See restaurant listing

at Ebrington East: 2 mi by B4035

Ebrington Arms

MODERN CUISINE • COSY Set in a charming chocolate box village, a proper village local with a beamed, flag-floored bar at its hub. Choose from pub classics on the blackboard or more elaborate dishes on the à la carte. Be sure to try one of the ales brewed to their own recipe. Bedrooms have country views and thoughtful extras.

Carte £ 26/41

5 rooms – £ 90/150 £ 99/150

✉ GL55 6NH
– ✆ 01386 593223 – www.theebringtonarms.co.uk – Closed 25 December

at Paxford Southeast : 3 mi by B 4035

Churchill Arms

TRADITIONAL BRITISH • COSY This charming 17C inn sits in a residential spot in a delightful Cotswold village and the intimate bar is hung with photos of local scenes taken by the owner himself. A bewildering array of menus offers everything from unfussy classics to more modern dishes. Bedrooms are comfy and well-appointed.

Menu £ 20 (lunch) – Carte £ 27/39

4 rooms – £ 90 £ 100/120

✉ GL55 6XH
– ✆ 01386 593159 – www.churchillarms.co.uk – Closed Sunday dinner and Monday

CHIPPING NORTON

Oxfordshire – Pop. 5 719 – Regional map n° **6**-A1

Wild Thyme

TRADITIONAL BRITISH • COSY A cosy, keenly run restaurant with rustic tables; No. 10, in the window, is the best. Wholesome regional British cooking has Mediterranean influences, with tasty homemade breads and game in season. Simply appointed bedrooms; the friendly owners go out of their way to ensure their guests' comfort.

Menu £ 23 (weekdays)/40

3 rooms – £ 75/95 £ 85/105

10 New St ✉ OX7 5LJ
– ✆ 01608 645060 (booking advisable) – www.wildthymerestaurant.co.uk – dinner only and lunch Thursday-Saturday – Closed first week January, Sunday and Monday

CHIPPING ONGAR

Essex – Pop. 6 093 – Regional map n° **7**-B2

Smith's

SEAFOOD • BRASSERIE XX Long-standing, locally acclaimed seafood restaurant with a buzzy atmosphere. The à la carte and extensive daily set menu offer dishes ranging from Cornish squid to Scottish smoked salmon. Lobster, cooked several ways, is a speciality.

Menu £ 22/30 – Carte £ 29/63

Fyfield Rd ✉ CM5 0AL – ✆ 01277 365578 (booking essential) – www.smithsrestaurants.com – Closed 25-26 December, 1 January and Monday lunch

CHIPSTEAD

Kent – Regional map n° **5**-B1

George & Dragon

MODERN BRITISH • PUB Superbly set, 450 year old inn with a beamed bar and a wonky-floored upstairs dining room. Delightful garden with terrace and children's play area. The menu is a roll call of seasonal English classics; herbs and salad are home-grown.

Carte £ 19/38

39 High St ✉ TN13 2RW – ✆ 01732 779019 – www.georgeanddragonchipstead.com

CHOBHAM

Surrey – Pop. 2 771 – Regional map n° **4**-C1

Stovell's

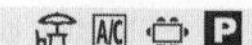

MODERN BRITISH • INTIMATE XXX The owner of this characterful 16C farmhouse has put Chobham firmly on the culinary map. Creative, often intricate dishes use top quality ingredients. Highlights include the bespoke tasting menu and dishes from the wood-fired grill.

Menu £ 25/45

125 Windsor Rd ✉ GU24 8QS – North : 0.75 mi on B 383 – ✆ 01276 858000 (booking essential) – www.stovells.com – Closed 1-10 January, Sunday and Monday

CHOLMONDELEY

Cheshire East – Regional map n° **11**-A3

Cholmondeley Arms

TRADITIONAL BRITISH • RUSTIC The eponymous estate's old schoolhouse, with high, vaulted ceilings, large windows and roaring fires. Modern pub favourites might include calves' liver or homemade lamb faggots. Gin lovers will be in clover with more than 200 from which to choose. The 6 comfy bedrooms are in the Old Headmaster's House.

Carte £ 20/37

6 rooms – †£ 75/85 ††£ 95/110

Wrenbury Rd ✉ SY14 8HN – ✆ 01829 720300 – www.cholmondeleyarms.co.uk

CHRISTCHURCH

Dorset – Pop. 54 210 – Regional map n° **2**-D3

Jetty

MODERN BRITISH • DESIGN XX Set within the grounds of the Christchurch Harbour hotel, this contemporary, eco-friendly restaurant offers fantastic water views. Appealing menus reflect what's available locally, with fish from nearby waters and game from the forest.

Menu £ 25 (weekdays) – Carte £ 32/65

Christchurch Harbour Hotel, 95 Mudeford ✉ BH23 3NT – East : 2 mi by B 3059 – ✆ 01202 400950 – www.thejetty.co.uk

Splinters

CLASSIC CUISINE • BISTRO XX A very traditional family-run restaurant, named after the splinters the carpenters got when building the booths! Choose from several cosy, characterful rooms. Cooking is wholesome and classical with rich, tasty sauces a feature.

Menu £15 (lunch) – Carte £24/50

12 Church St ✉ BH23 1BW
– ✆ 01202 483454 – www.splinters.uk.com – Closed Sunday and Monday

Kings Arms

TRADITIONAL BRITISH • BRASSERIE X Smart hotel brasserie offering gutsy cooking. The £15 weekly menu is made up of produce sourced from within 15 miles; Friday is 'Fizz 'n' Chips' night and they also offer afternoon tea. Start with a cocktail in the stylish bar.

Menu £15 (lunch and early dinner) – Carte £21/40

Kings Arms Hotel, 18 Castle St ✉ BH23 1DT
– ✆ 01202 588933 – www.thekings-christchurch.co.uk

Captain's Club

BUSINESS • CONTEMPORARY Striking modern building with art deco and nautical influences, set in a lovely riverside spot – floor to ceiling windows offer fantastic views. Bedrooms are sleek and contemporary; some are three-roomed suites. The restaurant offers all-day menus. Relax in the stylish spa or out on the water in their boat.

29 rooms – £189/299 £189/299 – 12 suites

Wick Ferry, Wick Ln ✉ BH23 1HU
– ✆ 01202 475111 – www.captainsclubhotel.com

Christchurch Harbour

BUSINESS • CONTEMPORARY Don't be fooled by the unassuming exterior; inside is a cool, chic hotel with a smart basement spa – its waterside location reflected in the modern, nautical-inspired décor. Some bedrooms have waterfront terraces or balconies. Both of the restaurants open onto delightful terraces with far-reaching views.

64 rooms – £75/179 £110/179

95 Mudeford ✉ BH23 3NT – East : 2 mi by B 3059
– ✆ 01202 483434 – www.christchurch-harbour-hotel.co.uk

Jetty – See restaurant listing

Kings Arms

TOWNHOUSE • PERSONALISED This lovingly restored Georgian inn stands opposite the bowling green and castle ruins, and has been given a smart modern makeover. Guest areas have a chic yet characterful feel and the boutique-style bedrooms are well-appointed.

20 rooms – £105/125 £125/185

18 Castle St ✉ BH23 1DT
– ✆ 01202 588933 – www.thekings-christchurch.co.uk

Kings Arms – See restaurant listing

Druid House

FAMILY • PERSONALISED Hidden behind an unassuming exterior, a bright, well-kept house that's passionately run and great value for money. Bedrooms are bright and modern; some of those in the newer wing open out onto a small terrace. Excellent breakfasts include a buffet and hot specials such as muffins with poached eggs and bacon.

11 rooms – £98/165 £98/165

26 Sopers Ln ✉ BH23 1JE
– ✆ 01202 485615 – www.druid-house.co.uk

CHURCHILL

Oxfordshire – Pop. 502 – Regional map n° **6**-A1

Chequers

TRADITIONAL CUISINE • PUB Welcoming limestone pub in the heart of the village; it's a vital part of the community and the owners have got the formula just right. The bar is stocked with local ales; gutsy, traditional dishes include steaks cooked on the Josper grill.

Menu £ 13 (weekday lunch) – Carte £ 23/36

Church Rd ✉ OX7 6NJ – 01608 659393 – www.thechequerschurchill.com – Closed 25 December

CHURCH ENSTONE

Oxfordshire – Regional map n° **6**-B1

Crown Inn

TRADITIONAL BRITISH • PUB 17C inn set among pretty stone houses in a picturesque village. Sit in the slate-floored conservatory, the beamed dining room or the rustic bar. Meat, fruit and veg come from local farms; seafood is a speciality, as is the steak pie.

Menu £ 16 (weekday lunch) – Carte £ 20/33

Mill Ln ✉ OX7 4NN – 01608 677262 – www.crowninnenstone.co.uk – Closed 25-26 December, 1 January and Sunday dinner

CIRENCESTER

Gloucestershire – Pop. 16 325 – Regional map n° **2**-D1

Made by Bob

MEDITERRANEAN CUISINE • FASHIONABLE The name says it all: Bob makes most of the products himself – be it for the informal eatery or the crammed deli – and the rest of the ingredients are organic and locally sourced. Service is bright and breezy, and the flexible daily menus are appealing. If you can't find a seat, they also do takeaway.

Carte £ 20/39

The Corn Hall, 26 Market Pl ✉ GL7 2NY – 01285 641818 (bookings not accepted) – www.foodmadebybob.com – Closed 25-26 December, 1 January, Sunday and dinner Monday-Tuesday and Saturday

The Coterie N

MODERN BRITISH • COSY Inside a 300 year old house is this cosy little restaurant with a beamed ceiling and exposed brick walls. The young chef cooks alone and his parents deliver his appealing seasonal dishes. Cooking is honest and flavoursome.

Carte £ 31/42

50 Cricklade St ✉ GL7 1JN – 01285 658971 – www.thecoterie.co.uk – Closed 24 December-late January, Sunday dinner, Monday and Tuesday

Jesse's Bistro

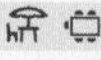

TRADITIONAL CUISINE • COSY This rustic bistro is hidden away in a little courtyard behind the Jesse Smith butcher's shop. Local meat and veg feature alongside Cornish fish and good use is made of the wood-fired oven. Beams and flagstones give it a cosy feel.

Menu £ 20 (weekday lunch) – Carte £ 29/50

14 Blackjack St ✉ GL7 2AA – 01285 641497 – www.jessesbistro.co.uk – Closed Sunday dinner and Monday

Kings Head

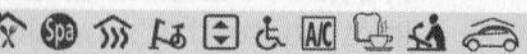

HISTORIC • DESIGN A former coaching inn built from local stone, set overlooking the Market Place. Original features attest to its age but it's now a stylish, modern hotel offering spacious bedrooms with all the latest mod cons. The popular restaurant offers hearty classics and Cotswold beef cooked on the Robata grill.

45 rooms – †£ 140/289 ††£ 140/289 – ☕ £ 18

24 Market Pl ✉ GL7 2NR – 01285 700900 – www.kingshead-hotel.co.uk

No 12

TOWNHOUSE · PERSONALISED This 16C townhouse provides plenty of contrasts: its Georgian façade hides a modern interior and the large bedrooms blend stylish furnishings with original features. In summer, breakfast on organic products in the delightful garden.

4 rooms – £ 100 £ 130/150

12 Park St GL7 2BW – 01285 640232 – www.no12cirencester.co.uk

Old Brewhouse

TOWNHOUSE · PERSONALISED 17C former brewhouse in busy central spot, with a characterful cluttered interior and two stone-walled breakfast rooms. Choose between cottage-style bedrooms – most with wrought iron beds – or more modern rooms set around a small courtyard.

9 rooms – £ 90/95 £ 99/110

7 London Rd GL7 2PU – 01285 656099 – www.theoldbrewhouse.com – Closed 24 December-2 January

at Barnsley Northeast: 4 mi by A429 on B4425 Cirencester

The Potager

MEDITERRANEAN CUISINE · FASHIONABLE XX Understated hotel restaurant with a pleasant garden outlook and a laid-back feel. Influencing more than just the name, the kitchen gardens inform what's on the menu each day. Unfussy cooking has Mediterranean overtones; don't miss the freshly baked breads with herb-infused oils and salsa verde.

Menu £ 29 (lunch) – Carte dinner £ 19/53

Barnsley House Hotel, GL7 5EE – 01285 740000 – www.barnsleyhouse.com

Village Pub

TRADITIONAL BRITISH · DESIGN With an interior straight out of any country homes magazine, this place has the cosy, open-fired, village pub vibe down to a tee. It has four intimate rooms and a carefully manicured terrace. Appealing modern British dishes and irresistible nibbles feature locally sourced meats, charcuterie from Highgrove and comforting desserts. Bedrooms are tastefully styled.

Carte £ 27/42

6 rooms – £ 94/144 £ 94/144

GL7 5EF – 01285 740421 (booking essential) – www.thevillagepub.co.uk

Barnsley House

HISTORIC · PERSONALISED 17C Cotswold manor house with a wonderfully relaxed vibe, set in the midst of beautiful gardens styled by Rosemary Verey. A very stylish interior blends original features with modern touches, from the open-fired lounges to the chic bedrooms; there's also a spa and even a cinema in the grounds.

18 rooms – £ 210/506 £ 229/524 – 8 suites

GL7 5EE – 01285 740000 – www.barnsleyhouse.com

The Potager – See restaurant listing

at Sapperton West: 5 mi by A419 Cirencester

The Bell

TRADITIONAL CUISINE · RUSTIC Charming and characterful Cotswold pub with flagged floors, exposed stone, an abundance of beams and warming log fires. Menus offer the expected burger or fish and chips, as well as dishes which show off more of the chef's skills.

Carte £ 23/49

GL7 6LE – 01285 760298 – www.bellsapperton.co.uk – Closed 25 December and Sunday dinner

CLANFIELD

Oxfordshire – Pop. 1 709 – Regional map n° **6**-A2

Cotswold Plough

TRADITIONAL BRITISH • FRIENDLY XX Set within a 16C hotel, a lovely three-roomed restaurant with relaxed service, a gin pantry and a comfortingly traditional feel. Classic menus provide plenty of appeal and all wines are available by the glass or carafe.

Carte £ 25/45

Cotswold Plough Hotel, Bourton Rd ✉ OX18 2RB – on A 4095 – ✆ 01367 810222 – www.cotswoldploughhotel.com – Closed 24-27 December

Cotswold Plough

TRADITIONAL • CLASSIC Charming 16C wool merchant's house in the heart of a pretty village, with an antique-furnished lounge and a characterful bar boasting two open fires and over 500 types of gin. Bedrooms in the main house are cosy with mullioned windows; those in the extension are more spacious.

11 rooms – †£ 89/120 ††£ 115/175

Bourton Rd ✉ OX18 2RB – on A 4095 – ✆ 01367 810222 – www.cotswoldploughhotel.com – Closed 24-27 December

Cotswold Plough – See restaurant listing

CLAVERING

Essex – Pop. 882 – Regional map n° **7**-B2

Cricketers

MEDITERRANEAN CUISINE • INN A characterful pub set close to the cricket pitch in a sleepy village. Bread is baked daily, specials are chalked on a board above the fire and the cooking mixes British and Italian influences. The owners' son, Jamie Oliver, supplies fruit, veg and herbs from his organic garden. Bedrooms are welcoming.

Carte £ 23/43

20 rooms – †£ 70/100 ††£ 95/135

✉ CB11 4QT – ✆ 01799 550442 – www.thecricketers.co.uk – Closed 25-26 December

CLEARWELL

Gloucestershire – Regional map n° **2**-C1

Tudor Farmhouse

COUNTRY HOUSE • CONTEMPORARY A group of converted farm buildings in the heart of the Forest of Dean. Two cosy dining rooms serving carefully prepared, interesting dishes are found in the old farmhouse and, above them, characterful bedrooms with old beams and wonky floors. More modern bedrooms are housed in two of the outbuildings.

20 rooms – †£ 130/250 ††£ 130/250 – 5 suites

High St ✉ GL16 8JS – ✆ 01594 833046 – www.tudorfarmhousehotel.co.uk

CLEESTANTON – Shropshire → See Ludlow

CLEY-NEXT-THE-SEA – Norfolk → See Blakeney

CLIFTON – Cumbria → See Penrith

CLIPSHAM

Rutland – Pop. 120 – Regional map n° **9**-C2

Olive Branch & Beech House

TRADITIONAL BRITISH • PUB Characterful village pub made up of a series of small rooms which feature open fires and exposed beams. The selection of rustic British dishes changes daily, reflecting the seasons and keeping things fiercely local. These are accompanied by real ales, homemade lemonade and vodka made from hedgerow berries. Bedrooms are cosy and thoughtfully finished.

Menu £17/35 - Carte £26/48

6 rooms - £115/200 £135/205

Main St ✉ LE15 7SH - ✆ 01780 410355 (booking essential) - www.theolivebranchpub.com

CLOVELLY

Devon - Pop. 439 - Regional map n° **1**-B1

Red Lion

TRADITIONAL • COSY Traditional inn set in a wonderful location under the cliffs, right on the harbourfront. Good-sized, comfortable bedrooms all have sea views; the newest and largest rooms are in the converted sail loft. Enjoy classic dishes and a superb vista in the dining room; lighter snacks are served in the bar.

17 rooms - £130/165 £130/165

The Quay ✉ EX39 5TF - ✆ 01237 431237 - www.stayatclovelly.co.uk/red-lion

CLYST HYDON

Devon - Regional map n° **1**-D2

Five Bells Inn

TRADITIONAL BRITISH • PUB Pretty, thatched, Grade II listed pub, deep in the Devon countryside. Experienced chef uses the finest local ingredients in well-balanced dishes with real clarity of flavour. Blackboard of pub favourites and a more creative à la carte. Set lunch menu is excellent value for money. Smooth, friendly service.

Menu £16/28 (weekdays) - Carte £24/39

✉ EX15 2NT - West : 0.5 mi on Clyst St Lawrence rd - ✆ 01884 277288 (bookings advisable at dinner) - www.fivebells.uk.com

COGGESHALL

Essex - Pop. 3 919 - Regional map n° **7**-C2

Ranfield's Brasserie

INTERNATIONAL • BRASSERIE XX A cosy country restaurant in a 16C building on the market square. Globally-influenced dishes are made up of lots of different ingredients. Service is warm and welcoming and it has a loyal local following.

Menu £18/21 (weekdays) - Carte £30/50

4-6 Stoneham St ✉ CO6 1TT - ✆ 01376 561453 - www.ranfieldsbrasserie.co.uk - Closed Monday

COLCHESTER

Essex - Pop. 119 441 - Regional map n° **7**-D2

Memoirs

MODERN BRITISH • ELEGANT XX The town's old Victorian library is a grand, impressive place, with high beamed ceilings, wood-panelled walls and a big stone tablet depicting the Great Exhibition of 1853 - and the menu of classics is equally large. Alternatively, you can dine more informally in the next door former prison cells.

Menu £19/22 (weekdays) - Carte £26/35

65 West Stockwell St ✉ CO1 1HE - ✆ 01206 562400 - www.memoirscolchester.co.uk - Closed Sunday

Church Street Tavern

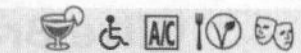

TRADITIONAL BRITISH • BRASSERIE Modern brasserie run in a relaxed, efficient manner. The trendy, shabby-chic bar serves cocktails and light bites. The upstairs restaurant offers British classics with Mediterranean influences; the early evening menu is great value.

Menu £ 20 (lunch and early dinner) – Carte £ 25/39

3 Church St ✉ CO1 1NF – ✆ 01206 564325 – www.churchstreettavern.co.uk – Closed 25-26 December, first week January, Sunday dinner, Monday and Tuesday

Greyfriars

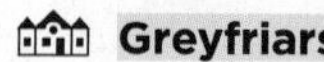

HISTORIC • ELEGANT It took five years to convert this former monastery into the fine hotel that it is today. Stunning public areas include beautiful rooms hung with Murano chandeliers, and the bedrooms are a curious mix of the simple and the ostentatious. Dine on complex dishes in the old chapel, under stained glass windows.

26 rooms – †£ 115 ††£ 135/340 – 17 suites

High St ✉ CO1 1UG – ✆ 01206 575913 – www.greyfriarscolchester.co.uk

COLERNE – Wiltshire → See Bath

COLSTON BASSETT

Nottinghamshire – Pop. 239 – Regional map n° **9**-B2

The Martins Arms

TRADITIONAL CUISINE • TRADITIONAL DÉCOR Creeper-clad pub in a charming village, with a cosy fire-lit bar and period furnished dining rooms. The menu has a meaty, masculine base, with a mix of classical and more modern dishes – and plenty of local game in season.

Menu £ 22 (weekday lunch) – Carte £ 34/60

School Ln ✉ NG12 3FD – ✆ 01949 81361 – www.themartinsarms.co.uk – Closed dinner 25 December and Sunday dinner

COLYFORD

Devon – Pop. 563 – Regional map n° **1**-D2

Swallows Eaves

TRADITIONAL • PERSONALISED Smart creamwashed house clad with wisteria, located in the heart of a pretty village. Bright bedrooms come with books, wi-fi and views over the gardens or the Axe Valley. Relax in the comfy lounge or out on the terrace. The light, airy restaurant serves traditional dishes of locally sourced produce.

7 rooms – †£ 90/100 ††£ 115/145

Swan Hill Rd ✉ EX24 6QJ – ✆ 01297 553184 – www.swallowseaves.co.uk

COMBE HAY – Bath and North East Somerset → See Bath

COMPTON BASSETT – Wiltshire → See Calne

CONDOVER – Shropshire → See Shrewsbury

COOKHAM

Windsor and Maidenhead – ✉ Maidenhead – Pop. 5 304 – Regional map n° **6**-C3

White Oak

TRADITIONAL BRITISH • FRIENDLY One could argue about whether this is a contemporary pub or a pubby restaurant, as it's set up quite formally, but what is in no doubt is the warmth of the welcome and the affection in which the place is held by its many regulars. Cooking is carefully executed and full of flavour. Great value 'Menu Auberge'.

Menu £ 15 (weekdays) – Carte £ 24/37

Pound Ln ✉ SL6 9QE – ✆ 01628 523043 – www.thewhiteoak.co.uk – Closed Sunday dinner

CORBRIDGE

Northumberland – Pop. 2 946 – Regional map n° **14**-A2

Duke of Wellington

TRADITIONAL BRITISH • DESIGN Smart, modern country-style pub looking out over the Tyne Valley – head for the terrace on sunnier days. Breakfast includes brioche French toast and local eggs Benedict, after which pub classics sit alongside more adventurous dishes. Stylish, luxurious bedrooms have characterful exposed beams.

Menu £ 16 (weekday lunch) – Carte £ 26/40 **s**

7 rooms – †£ 80/110 ††£ 95/140

Newton ✉ NE43 7UL – East : 3.5 mi by A 69 – ✆ 01661 844446 – www.thedukeofwellingtoninn.co.uk

CORFE CASTLE

Dorset – Pop. 1 355 – Regional map n° **2**-C3

Mortons House

FAMILY • PERSONALISED An Elizabethan manor house built in the shape of an "E" to honour the Queen. The castle ruins are close above it and a steam railway runs just below. Bedrooms are classical and well-kept; one has a Victorian bath and four are in an annexe. Have lunch in the bar or lounges and dinner in the panelled restaurant.

21 rooms – †£ 95/140 ††£ 160 – 2 suites

45 East St ✉ BH20 5EE – ✆ 01929 480988 – www.mortonshouse.co.uk

CORNHILL-ON-TWEED

Northumberland – Pop. 347 – Regional map n° **14**-A1

Tillmouth Park

COUNTRY HOUSE • HISTORIC Late Victorian country house set in 15 acres of prime shooting and fishing country. The welcoming interior comes with grand staircases, wood panelling and characterful stained glass. Traditional guest areas have lovely views; the most popular bedrooms boast four-poster beds. Cooking is fittingly classical.

14 rooms – †£ 72/163 ††£ 185/258

✉ TD12 4UU – Northeast : 2.5 mi on A 698 – ✆ 01890 882255 – www.tillmouthpark.co.uk – Closed 1 February-29 March

CORSE LAWN – Worcestershire → See Tewkesbury (Glos.)

CORTON DENHAM

Somerset – ✉ Sherborne – Pop. 210 – Regional map n° **2**-C3

Queens Arms

MODERN BRITISH • PUB This hub-of-the-village pub hosts plenty of events and comes with plush bedrooms. The menu lists food 'metres' and much of the produce is from their smallholding; choose from small plates, pub classics and more elaborate dishes. The bar is topped with tempting treats and they do a great trade in afternoon tea.

Carte £ 27/52

8 rooms – †£ 90/109 ††£ 125/150

✉ DT9 4LR – ✆ 01963 220317 (booking advisable) – www.thequeensarms.com

COTEBROOK

Cheshire West and Chester – Regional map n° **11**-A3

Fox and Barrel

TRADITIONAL BRITISH • PUB Well-run pub with wood-panelled walls, heaving bookshelves and a smart terrace. The constantly evolving menu offers originality and interest, with sensibly priced dishes arriving neatly presented and generously sized.

Carte £ 24/38

Foxbank ✉ CW6 9DZ – ✆ 01829 760529 – www.foxandbarrel.co.uk – Closed dinner 25-26 December and 1 January

COVERACK

Cornwall – Regional map n° **1**-A3

Bay

COUNTRY HOUSE • COSY Imposing, family-run country house located in a pretty fishing village and boasting views over the bay. Homely lounge and bar. Spotless, modern bedrooms with a slight New England edge. Dining room and conservatory offer a classical daily menu and local seafood specials.

14 rooms (dinner included) – £ 104/232 ££ 140/290

North Corner ✉ TR12 6TF – ☎ 01326 280464 – www.thebayhotel.co.uk – Closed November-25 March

COWAN BRIDGE

Lancashire – Regional map n° **11**-B1

Hipping Hall

MODERN CUISINE • ROMANTIC XX A formal, airy hotel restaurant with a superb beamed ceiling, a minstrel's gallery and a medieval feel. Choose between a fixed price menu and a 7 course tasting menu: creative, original dishes come with matching wine pairings.

Menu £ 55/75

Hipping Hall Hotel, on A 65 ✉ LA6 2JJ – ☎ 015242 71187 (booking essential) – www.hippinghall.com – dinner only and lunch Saturday-Sunday

Hipping Hall

COUNTRY HOUSE • PERSONALISED Charming part 15/16C blacksmith's named after the stepping (or 'hipping') stones over the beck by the old washhouse. Sleek white bedrooms in the main house; the best rooms are in two outbuildings and are spacious and contemporary.

15 rooms – £ 152/252 ££ 169/269 – 3 suites

On A 65 ✉ LA6 2JJ – ☎ 015242 71187 – www.hippinghall.com

Hipping Hall – See restaurant listing

COWLEY

Gloucestershire – Regional map n° **2**-C1

Cowley Manor

LUXURY • CONTEMPORARY Impressive Regency house in 55 acres, with beautiful formal gardens, a superb spa, and lake views from some of the bedrooms. Original features and retro furnishings mix with bold colours and modern fittings to create a laid-back, understated vibe. The carved wood panelling in the restaurant is a feature.

30 rooms – £ 200/675 ££ 230/675 – 8 suites

✉ GL53 9NL – ☎ 01242 870900 – www.cowleymanor.com

CRANBORNE

Dorset – Pop. 606 – Regional map n° **2**-D3

10 Castle Street N

HISTORIC BUILDING • ELEGANT A listed Queen Anne house with a lovely terrace looking out over beautiful gardens. The stunning interior has a relaxed, contemporary country house style and bedrooms are supremely comfortable. Laid-back dining features fresh, unfussy flavours. The first floor comprises a residents' and private members' club.

9 rooms – £ 145 ££ 195/350

10 Castle St ✉ BH21 5PZ – ☎ 01725 551133 – www.10castlestreet.com – Closed 25 and 31 December

CRANBROOK

Kent – Pop. 4 225 – Regional map n° **5**-B2

Cloth Hall Oast

HISTORIC • PERSONALISED Superbly restored oast house that was rebuilt in 2001. Antiques, family photos and fine artwork fill the drawing room. Bedrooms are well-equipped but retain some original character; one boasts a splendid four-poster bed. Communal breakfasts at an antique table set below restored rafters in the main hall.

3 rooms ☕ – 🚹£ 65/130 👥£ 95/130

Coursehorn Ln ✉ TN17 3NR – East : 1 mi by Tenterden rd – ✆ 01580 712220 – www.clothhalloast.co.uk – Closed Christmas

CRAYKE

North Yorkshire – Regional map n° **13**-C2

Durham Ox

TRADITIONAL BRITISH • PUB A 300 year old pub in a sleepy hamlet; in summer, head for the lovely courtyard. Menus focus on honest, homely cooking, with everything made on-site; choose a blackboard special – often game or seafood accompanied by something 'wild'. Cosy bedrooms feature original brickwork and quarry tiling.

Menu £ 18 (weekday lunch) – Carte £ 23/52

6 rooms ☕ – 🚹£ 100/120 👥£ 120/150

Westway ✉ YO61 4TE – ✆ 01347 821506 (booking advisable) – www.thedurhamox.com

CREWE

Cheshire East – Pop. 71 722 – Regional map n° **11**-B3

Crewe Hall

BUSINESS • HISTORIC A tree-lined drive leads up to this impressive 19C mansion designed by Edward Barry. Dramatic Jacobean features provide plenty of character in the main house and lovely chapel, while bedrooms and events rooms in the extensions are stylish and contemporary. The modern brasserie offers a menu to match.

117 rooms ☕ – 🚹£ 89/199 👥£ 99/215 – 4 suites

Weston Road ✉ CW1 6UZ – Southeast : 1.75 mi on A 5020 – ✆ 01270 253333 – www.qhotels.co.uk

CRICKLADE

Wiltshire – Regional map n° **2**-D1

Red Lion

TRADITIONAL BRITISH • RUSTIC Traditional 17C pub just off the Thames path with a characterful, low-beamed bar. Classic cooking makes good use of local produce; burgers are a speciality. They smoke some of their own meats and fish and even brew their own ales on-site. Comfortable, well-equipped bedrooms are found in the old stables.

Carte £ 21/36

5 rooms ☕ – 🚹£ 85 👥£ 85

74 High St ✉ SN6 6DD – ✆ 01793 750776 – www.theredlioncricklade.co.uk

CROCKERTON – Wiltshire → See Warminster

CROMER

Norfolk – Pop. 7 949 – Regional map n° **8**-D1

No1 Cromer

FISH AND CHIPS • SIMPLE This is fish and chips with a difference: looking out over the beach and pier and offering everything from fresh fish and battered local sausages to cockle popcorn and mushy pea fritters. Potatoes are from their farm and the varieties change throughout the year. Head up to the bistro for some tasty fish tapas.

Carte £ 18/31

1 New St ✉ NR27 9HP – ✆ 01263 515983 – www.no1cromer.com – Closed 2 weeks January, 1 week November and 24-25 December

CROPSTON

Leicestershire – Regional map n° **9**-B2

 **Horseshoe Cottage Farm** 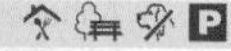

FAMILY • CLASSIC Well-run, extended farmhouse and outbuildings, beside Bradgate Country Park. Traditional bedrooms with beams, exposed stonework and coordinating fabrics. Small breakfast room and a larger, high-ceilinged drawing room, with a solid oak table where communal dinners are served; local and garden produce features.

3 rooms – †£ 65/70 ††£ 100/110

Roecliffe Rd, Hallgates ✉ LE7 7HQ – Northwest : 1 mi on Woodhouse Eaves rd – ✆ 0116 235 0038 – www.horseshoecottagefarm.com

CROSTHWAITE – Cumbria ➜ See Kendal

CRUDWELL – Wiltshire ➜ See Malmesbury

CRUNDALE

Kent – Regional map n° **5**-C2

Compasses Inn

CLASSIC CUISINE • PUB An enthusiastically run 1420s pub. The characterful bar has hop-hung beams and inglenook fireplaces and the large dining room opens onto the garden. The set menu offers comfort dishes while the à la carte shows a little more finesse.

Menu £ 18 (weekday lunch) – Carte £ 28/42

Sole Street ✉ CT4 7ES – Northwest : 1.25 mi – ✆ 01227 700300 – www.thecompassescrundale.co.uk – Closed Sunday dinner and Monday

CUCKFIELD

West Sussex – Pop. 3 500 – Regional map n° **4**-D2

Ockenden Manor

CLASSIC CUISINE • CLASSIC DÉCOR XXX A contemporary orangery-style dining room within a manor house hotel; it opens onto the gardens and affords pleasant views over the South Downs. The passionate chef uses seasonal local produce to create appealing, original menus.

Menu £ 23 (weekday lunch) – Carte £ 55/65

Ockenden Manor Hotel, Ockenden Ln ✉ RH17 5LD – ✆ 01444 416111 (booking essential) – www.ockenden-manor.co.uk

Ockenden Manor 

HISTORIC • CLASSIC Part-Elizabethan manor house in 9 acres of parkland. Kick-back in the cosy panelled bar or beside the grand fireplace in the elegant drawing room. Stay in a characterful period bedroom or one of the modern rooms above the chic spa.

28 rooms – †£ 159/449 ††£ 199/449 – 3 suites

Ockenden Ln ✉ RH17 5LD – ✆ 01444 416111 – www.ockenden-manor.co.uk

Ockenden Manor – See restaurant listing

CUNDALL

North Yorkshire – Regional map n° **13**-B2

Cundall Lodge Farm

COUNTRY HOUSE • RURAL Grade II listed Georgian farmhouse on a working arable farm; its 150 acres include a stretch of the River Swale. Country bedrooms come with homemade shortbread and Roberts radios. The friendly owners have great local knowledge.

3 rooms – †£ 60/75 ††£ 85/100

✉ YO61 2RN – Northwest : 0.5 mi on Asenby rd – ✆ 01423 360203 – www.cundall-lodgefarm.co.uk – Closed Christmas-New Year, late February-mid March

DALTON-IN-FURNESS

Cumbria – Pop. 7 827 – Regional map n° **12**-A3

Clarence House

MODERN BRITISH • TRADITIONAL DÉCOR XX This is a proper country house hotel restaurant with luxurious furnishings and willing service. Dishes are traditionally based but are modern in their execution. They use the finest Cumbrian meats, so steak is always a good bet.

Carte £ 26/50

Clarence House Hotel, Skelgate ✉ LA15 8BQ – ✆ 01229 462508 – www.clarencehouse-hotel.co.uk – Closed 26 December

Clarence House

FAMILY • CLASSIC The majority of guests here are repeat customers – which says a lot about the way the family run it. Relax in the peaceful, mature gardens or in one of the plush sitting rooms. Some bedrooms come with jacuzzis or four-posters.

28 rooms – £ 115/130 £ 140/160

Skelgate ✉ LA15 8BQ – ✆ 01229 462508 – www.clarencehouse-hotel.com – Closed 26 December

Clarence House – See restaurant listing

DARLEY ABBEY – Derby ➜ See Derby

DARLINGTON

Darlington – Pop. 92 363 – Regional map n° **13**-B1

Clow Beck House

FAMILY • COSY A collection of converted farm buildings not far from the River Tees, with welcoming owners and a homely interior. Immaculately kept, tastefully furnished bedrooms come with bathrobes and chocolates; the larger ones have dressing rooms. Dinners are home-cooked, with puzzles supplied while you wait.

13 rooms – £ 90 £ 140

Monk End Farm, Croft-on-Tees ✉ DL2 2SP – South : 5.25 mi by A 167 off Barton rd – ✆ 01325 721075 – www.clowbeckhouse.co.uk – Closed 24 December-3 January

Houndgate Townhouse

TOWNHOUSE • CONTEMPORARY This smart Georgian townhouse – formerly a registry office – is set on a quiet square in the heart of town. Inside, stylish colour schemes and contemporary furnishings create a boutique feel; bedroom Two has a bath in the room. The bistro has comfy booths, a terrace and a menu of modern classics.

8 rooms – £ 80/135 £ 90/145

11 Houndgate ✉ DL1 5RF – ✆ 01325 486011 – www.houndgatetownhouse.co.uk

at Hurworth-on-Tees South: 5.5 mi by A167

The Orangery

MODERN CUISINE • INTIMATE XXX An elegant glass extension in a country house hotel. Set menus include vegetarian, pescatarian and surprise options. Dishes are carefully crafted and eye-catching, with contrasting textures and flavours.

Menu £ 60

Rockcliffe Hall Hotel, ✉ DL2 2DU – ✆ 01325 729999 (booking essential) – www.rockliffehall.com – dinner only – Closed Sunday and Monday

Bay Horse

MODERN CUISINE • PUB A good-looking pub with a smart, elegant feel; the jewel in its crown is a lovely garden and terrace. Appealing modern menus include the likes of rabbit ballotine with creamed polenta and confit rabbit lasagne.

Menu £ 20 (weekday lunch) – Carte £ 35/59

45 The Green ✉ DL2 2AA – ✆ 01325 720663 – www.thebayhorsehurworth.com – Closed 25-26 December

Rockliffe Hall

LUXURY • MODERN An impressive red-brick manor house in 376 acres of grounds, complete with a championship golf course and extensive, state-of-the-art leisure facilities. The original Victorian house has grand guest areas and characterful bedrooms; rooms in the extensions are more modern. Dining options include ambitious restaurant choices, modern brasserie dishes, classics and grills.

61 rooms – †£ 190/270 ††£ 210/540

DL2 2DU – 01325 729999 – www.rockliffehall.com

The Orangery – See restaurant listing

at Summerhouse Northwest: 6.5 mi by A68 on B6279

Raby Hunt (James Close)

MODERN BRITISH • INTIMATE XX A former drovers' inn in a rural hamlet and originally part of the Raby Estate, this was a favourite finishing point for the old hunt. It's now an elegantly decorated family-run restaurant, where a passionate self-taught chef uses first class ingredients to create original dishes which leave you impatient for the next. Contemporary bedrooms are set in the old stables.

→ Artichoke and offal. Razor clam with almond and celeriac. Black olive, chocolate and sheep's yoghurt.

Menu £ 95/100 – tasting menu only

3 rooms – †£ 170 ††£ 170

DL2 3UD – 01325 374237 (booking essential) – www.rabyhuntrestaurant.co.uk – dinner only and Saturday lunch – Closed 1 week spring, 1 week autumn, 25-26 December, 1 January and Sunday-Tuesday

at Headlam Northwest: 8 mi by A67 ✉ Gainford

Headlam Hall (N)

CLASSIC CUISINE • ROMANTIC XX Headlam Hall's restaurant is a bright, airy conservatory with views over the charming gardens. Menus have a traditional bent and feature the likes of locally smoked salmon and homemade ham hock terrine; the panna cotta is a must.

Menu £ 25 (weekday lunch) – Carte £ 31/46

Headlam Hall Hotel, DL2 3HA – 01325 730238 – www.headlamhall.co.uk – Closed 24-27 December

Headlam Hall

FAMILY • HISTORIC A family-run manor house with delightful walled gardens, set in a secluded country spot. Spacious sitting rooms are furnished with antiques and the well-equipped bedrooms are a mix of the traditional and the modern.

38 rooms – †£ 110/200 ††£ 140/230 – 4 suites

DL2 3HA – 01325 730238 – www.headlamhall.co.uk – Closed 24-27 December

Headlam Hall – See restaurant listing

DARSHAM

Suffolk – Regional map n° **8**-D2

Darsham Nurseries Café

INTERNATIONAL • SIMPLE X In 2014, the owners of this nursery opened a smart gift shop and a small café. Expect colourful, richly flavoured small plates of garden produce, with Mediterranean and Middle Eastern leanings. On Sundays they only serve brunch.

Carte £ 14/29

Main Rd IP17 3PW – (on A 12) – 01728 667022 (booking essential) – www.darshamnurseries.co.uk – lunch only and dinner Friday-Saturday – Closed 25 -26 December

DARTMOUTH

Devon – Pop. 6 008 – Regional map n° **1**-C3

Seahorse

SEAFOOD • CHIC XX Smart restaurant in a lovely spot on the embankment; sit outside looking over the estuary or inside, beside the glass-walled kitchen. Seafood orientated menus have a Mediterranean bias; whole fish cooked on the Josper grill are a hit.

Menu £ 20 (lunch and early dinner) – Carte £ 31/58

5 South Embankment ✉ TQ6 9BH – ✆ 01803 835147 (booking essential) – www.seahorserestaurant.co.uk – Closed Monday and Sunday dinner

Rockfish

SEAFOOD • NEIGHBOURHOOD X Buzzy 'beach shack' style eatery run by a chatty team. Good old comfort dishes arrive in paper-lined baskets and rely on sustainable produce. Closely set tables have paper cloths proclaiming 'fish so fresh, tomorrow's are still in the sea'.

Carte £ 20/44

8 South Embankment ✉ TQ6 9BH – ✆ 01803 832800 (bookings not accepted) – www.therockfish.co.uk – Closed 25 December

Dart Marina

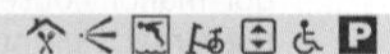

TRADITIONAL • DESIGN Once an old boat works and chandlery, now a relaxed, modern hotel with a small spa and leisure centre. Smart, contemporary bedrooms have lovely outlooks over either the river or marina – many also boast balconies. The stylish, formal restaurant offers up-to-date versions of British classics.

53 rooms – †£ 115/155 ††£ 180/450 – 4 suites

Sandquay Rd ✉ TQ6 9PH – ✆ 01803 832580 – www.dartmarina.com

at Kingswear East: via lower ferry ✉ Dartmouth

Nonsuch House

TOWNHOUSE • CLASSIC Charming Edwardian house run by friendly hands-on owners; boasting lovely views over the castle, town and sea. Bright Mediterranean-style décor blends nicely with original features. Bedrooms are spacious and well-appointed and one has a small balcony. Tea and homemade cake on arrival; local, seasonal cooking and excellent views from the conservatory dining room.

4 rooms – †£ 95/140 ††£ 135/185

Church Hill ✉ TQ6 0BX – from lower ferry take first right onto Church Hill before Steam Packet Inn – ✆ 01803 752829 – www.nonsuch-house.co.uk – Closed January

at Strete Southwest: 4.5 mi on A379 ✉ Dartmouth

Laughing Monk

TRADITIONAL CUISINE • BISTRO X Built in 1839 as the village schoolhouse; the original wooden floor and a huge stone fireplace remain. Tasty, traditional dishes feature meats from nearby farms and seafood from local waters; cooking is unfussy and uses classical pairings.

Carte £ 33/51

Totnes Rd ✉ TQ6 0RN – ✆ 01803 770639 – www.thelaughingmonkdevon.co.uk – dinner only – Closed December, January, Sunday and Monday

Strete Barton House

HISTORIC • PERSONALISED Attractive part-16C manor house in a quiet village, with partial views over the rooftops to the sea. The contemporary interior has a personal style; bedrooms come with bold feature walls and modern facilities. Homemade cake is served on arrival and top quality local ingredients feature at breakfast.

6 rooms – †£ 79/170 ††£ 79/170

Totnes Rd ✉ TQ6 0RU – ✆ 01803 770364 – www.stretebarton.co.uk – Closed 2 weeks January

DATCHWORTH

Hertfordshire – Pop. 1 210 – Regional map n° **7**-B2

Tilbury

MODERN BRITISH • FRIENDLY Charming 18C inn run by two brothers, set just off the village green. Pub classics will please traditionalists, while more creative dishes really showcase the kitchen's skills. There's a great wine and ale selection too.

Carte £ 26/43

1 Watton Rd ✉ SG3 6TB – ✆ 01438 815550 – www.thetilbury.co.uk – Closed Monday and Sunday dinner

DAVENTRY

Northamptonshire – Pop. 23 879 – Regional map n° **9**-B3

Fawsley Hall

COUNTRY HOUSE • PERSONALISED Set in 2,000 peaceful acres, a luxurious Tudor manor house with Georgian and Victorian extensions. Have afternoon tea in the Great Hall or unwind in the exclusive spa. Smart, well-appointed bedrooms vary from wing to wing. Have lunch in the courtyard and dinner in the atmospheric restaurant.

60 rooms – †£ 133/249 ††£ 143/259 – 2 suites

Fawsley ✉ NN11 3BA – South : 6.5 mi by A 45 off A 361 – ✆ 01327 892000 – www.handpicked.co.uk/fawsley

at Staverton Southwest: 2.75 mi by A45 off A425 ✉ Daventry

Colledges House

TRADITIONAL • PERSONALISED Lovely 17C thatched cottage and barn run by a charming owner. The cosy lounge is filled with antiques and curios; the conservatory is a pleasant spot in summer. Bedrooms have floral fabrics and good extras.

4 rooms – †£ 65/70 ††£ 95/99

Oakham Ln ✉ NN11 6JQ – off Glebe Ln – ✆ 01327 702737 – www.colledgeshouse.co.uk

at Charwelton South : 6.25 mi by A 45 on A 361

Fox & Hounds

TRADITIONAL BRITISH • PUB The Fox & Hounds has been a fixture in Charwelton since 1871, so when it closed its doors, the despairing villagers decided to buy it themselves. Menus offer everything from pork faggots to some excellent Indian-spiced dishes.

Menu £ 18 (weekdays) – Carte £ 24/44

Banbury Rd ✉ NN11 3YY – ✆ 01327 260611 – www.foxandhoundscharwelton.co.uk – Closed 2 weeks January and Sunday dinner

DAYLESFORD – Gloucestershire → See Stow-on-the-Wold

DEAL

Kent – Pop. 30 555 – Regional map n° **5**-D2

Frog and Scot

MODERN BRITISH • BISTRO A quirky bistro with yellow canopies and mismatched furnishings; its unusual name refers to its French and Scottish owners. Large blackboard menus list refined, innately simple dishes which let the ingredients do the talking.

Menu £ 15/24 – Carte £ 26/43

86 High St ✉ CT14 6EG – ✆ 01304 379444 – www.frogandscot.co.uk – Closed 25 December, 1 January, Monday-Tuesday and Sunday dinner

Victuals & Co

MODERN BRITISH • BISTRO X You'll find this enthusiastically run restaurant down a narrow passageway – its name a reference to the victuallers who once supplied the local ships. Classic dishes are given modern twists; the set menu represents good value.

Menu £ 25 (lunch) – Carte £ 34/53

St Georges Passage ✉ CT14 6TA – ☎ 01304 374389 – www.victualsandco.com – Closed January-February, Monday-Tuesday except bank holiday Mondays and lunch Wednesday-Friday

Number One

TOWNHOUSE • MODERN Stylish guesthouse near the promenade, run by an enthusiastic owner. Bedrooms have bold wallpapers, fine linen and luxury bathrooms with tower showers. A delightful breakfast room hosts award-winning breakfasts of Kentish produce.

4 rooms ☕ – †£ 72/107 ††£ 82/117

1 Ranelagh Rd ✉ CT14 7BG – ☎ 01304 364459 – www.numberonebandb.co.uk

at Worth Northwest: 5 mi by A258

Solley Farm House

FAMILY • PERSONALISED Attractive 300 year old house overlooking the duck pond and run by a charming owner. In the beamed lounge, a vast inglenook fireplace takes centre stage; colour-themed bedrooms come with great extras. Have breakfast on the terrace.

3 rooms ☕ – †£ 105/115 ††£ 155/165

The Street ✉ CT14 0DG – ☎ 01304 613701 – www.solleyfarmhouse.co.uk

DEDHAM

Essex – ✉ Colchester – Pop. 719 – Regional map n° **7**-D2

Le Talbooth

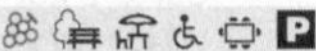

MODERN BRITISH • RUSTIC XXX This superbly characterful property on the riverbank is the restaurant of a charming hotel; if you're staying the night, you can be chauffeured over by Bentley. Inside it has a stylish rustic-chic design and most tables have a river view. Cooking has classic roots and subtle modern touches.

Menu £ 35 (weekday lunch) – Carte £ 46/65

Maison Talbooth Hotel, Gun Hill ✉ CO7 6HN – West : 0.75 mi – ☎ 01206 323150 – www.milsomhotels.com – Closed Sunday dinner October-May

Sun Inn

ITALIAN • INN Characterful yellow inn with an appealing shabby-chic style, located in a picturesque spot in the heart of Constable Country. The monthly menu offers generous Italian-inspired dishes and the well-chosen wine list offers plenty by the glass. Bedrooms are cosy – two have a modern New England style.

Carte £ 23/40

7 rooms ☕ – †£ 90/130 ††£ 145

High St ✉ CO7 6DF – ☎ 01206 323351 – www.thesuninndedham.com – Closed 25-26 December

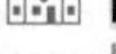

Maison Talbooth

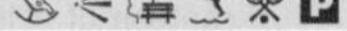

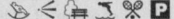

LUXURY • CONTEMPORARY A charming part-Georgian house in rolling countryside, with a modern country house feel and views over the river valley. Luxurious bedrooms boast quality furnishings and come in a mix of classic and contemporary styles. Seek out the tennis court and the year-round heated outdoor pool and hot tub.

12 rooms ☕ – †£ 275/499 ††£ 275/499

Stratford Rd ✉ CO7 6HN – West : 0.5 mi – ☎ 01206 322367 – www.milsomhotels.com

Le Talbooth – See restaurant listing

Milsoms

COUNTRY HOUSE • MODERN A late 19C country house with modern additions, overlooking Dedham Vale; its interior is stylish and contemporary, and its bedrooms are luxurious and well-equipped. The airy bar-restaurant with its covered terrace is a popular spot – it's open all day and offers an appealing menu.

15 rooms – £135/170 £135/170

Stratford Rd ✉ CO7 6HW – West : 0.75 mi – ✆ 01206 322795 – www.milsomhotels.com

DELPH

Greater Manchester – Pop. 2 224 – Regional map n° **11**-B2

Old Bell Inn

TRADITIONAL BRITISH • TRADITIONAL DÉCOR 18C coaching inn set high up on the moors, with a cosy bar, a smart modern brasserie and well-kept bedrooms. Choose from sharing platters, hearty pub favourites, 35 day matured steaks and more modern set menus. Their gin selection features over 600 different types and is the biggest in the world.

Menu £25 (lunch and early dinner) – Carte £23/44

18 rooms – £60/70 £95/125

Huddersfield Rd ✉ OL3 5EG – ✆ 01457 870130 – www.theoldbellinn.co.uk

DENHAM

Buckinghamshire – Pop. 1 432 – Regional map n° **6**-D3

Swan Inn

TRADITIONAL BRITISH • PUB Located in a picture postcard village; a wisteria-clad, red-brick Georgian pub with a pleasant terrace and mature gardens. Menus change with the seasons and offer plenty of interest – the side dishes are appealing and pudding is a must.

Carte £23/46

Village Rd ✉ UB9 5BH – ✆ 01895 832085 (booking essential) – www.swaninndenham.co.uk

DERBY

Derby – Pop. 255 394 – Regional map n° **9**-B2

Ibérico World Tapas

MEDITERRANEAN CUISINE • FRIENDLY It's all in the name: the main concept is Spanish, with plenty of tapas dishes and Spanish classics, but there's also a more global feel, courtesy of Mediterranean-style décor and some dishes with Asian origins. The imported hams are a must-try, and the lunch and early evening menus are excellent value.

Menu £10 (lunch and early dinner) – Carte £13/29

9-11 Bold Ln ✉ DE1 3NT – ✆ 01332 345456 – www.ibericotapas.com – Closed 1-5 January and Sunday

at Darley Abbey North : 2.5 mi off A6 ✉ Derby

Darleys

MODERN CUISINE • FRIENDLY Popular weir-side restaurant, located in the old canteen of a 19C silk mill. Start with drinks in the modern bar-lounge or on the attractive terrace. Good value lunches are followed by more ambitious European dishes in the evening.

Menu £20 (weekday lunch) – Carte £40/46

Darley Abbey Mill ✉ DE22 1DZ – ✆ 01332 364987 (booking advisable) – www.darleys.com – Closed 25 December-10 January, Sunday dinner and bank holidays

DEVIZES

Wiltshire – Pop. 18 064 – Regional map n° **2**-C2

Blounts Court Farm

COUNTRY HOUSE · PERSONALISED Delightfully run farmhouse on a 150 acre working farm; the village cricket team play in one of their fields! The snug interior consists of a cosy lounge and a spacious breakfast room filled with clocks and curios. Warm, well-kept bedrooms show good attention to detail. Pastel artwork and country photos abound.

3 rooms - £ 56/62 £ 90/98

Coxhill Ln, Potterne ✉ SN10 5PH - South : 2.25 mi by A 360 - ✆ 01380 727180 - www.blountscourtfarm.co.uk

at Rowde Northwest: 2 mi by A361 on A342 ✉ Devizes

George & Dragon

SEAFOOD · PUB Rustic and cosy 16C coaching inn with open fires, solid stone floors and wooden beams. The oft-changing menu has a strong emphasis on seafood, with fish delivered daily from Cornwall. Old-world charm meets modern facilities in the individually designed bedrooms.

Carte £ 26/50

3 rooms - £ 75/125 £ 75/125

High St ✉ SN10 2PN - ✆ 01380 723053 - www.thegeorgeanddragonrowde.co.uk - Closed Sunday dinner

DIDSBURY - Greater Manchester ➜ See Manchester

DITCHLING

East Sussex - Pop. 1 476 - Regional map n° **5**-D2

Tovey Lodge

COUNTRY HOUSE · PERSONALISED Well-appointed guesthouse with mature gardens and views over the South Downs. Smart bedrooms have modern facilities; Maple, with its balcony, is the best. Beyond the communal breakfast room you'll find a swimming pool and sauna.

5 rooms - £ 90/160 £ 100/195

Underhill Ln ✉ BN6 8XE - South : 1 mi by B 2112 off Ditchling Beacon rd - ✆ 01273 256156 - www.toveylodge.co.uk - Closed January

DODDINGTON

Kent - Regional map n° **5**-C2

Old Vicarage

FAMILY · CLASSIC Grade II listed former vicarage with 16C origins, where wood and stone blend with modern furnishings. There's an impressive galleried hall and a striking antique breakfast table. Bedrooms feature coffee machines and Bose sound systems.

5 rooms - £ 72/85 £ 95/105

Church Hill ✉ ME9 0BD - ✆ 01795 886136 - www.oldvicaragedoddington.co.uk - Closed 24 December-2 January

DOGMERSFIELD

Hampshire - Regional map n° **4**-C1

Four Seasons

LUXURY · CLASSIC An attractive part-Georgian house in 350 acres of parkland, where you can try your hand at all manner of outdoor pursuits. Luxurious bedrooms are well-equipped and come with marble bathrooms. A superb spa is found in the converted coach house. Seasons, the contemporary restaurant, offers sophisticated modern dishes, while the casual bistro offers steaks and grills.

133 rooms - £ 395/455 £ 395/455 - £ 30 - 21 suites

Dogmersfield Park, Chalky Ln ✉ RG27 8TD - ✆ 01252 853000 - www.fourseasons.com/hampshire

DOLTON

Devon – Pop. 687 – Regional map n° **1**-C2

Rams Head Inn

TRADITIONAL CUISINE • INN The Rams Head has a cosy, characterful feel. Enjoy a drink by the inglenook fireplace in the large beamed bar or head for the traditional dining room. Dishes are a mix of old favourites and more restaurant-style dishes; the daily changing suet pudding is a hit. Simply furnished bedrooms have a modern feel.

Carte £ 22/49

9 rooms – £ 59/75 £ 85/115

South St ✉ EX19 8QS – ✆ 01805 804255 – www.theramsheadinn.co.uk – Closed Monday

DONHEAD-ST-ANDREW

Wiltshire – Regional map n° **2**-C3

The Forester

TRADITIONAL BRITISH • RUSTIC Gloriously rustic, 13C thatched pub, hidden down narrow lanes in a delightful village. Exposed stone walls and vast open fires feature throughout. Seasonal menus showcase well-prepared, flavoursome dishes with a classical country base and a refined edge; they also offer a daily seafood selection.

Menu £ 26 (weekdays) – Carte £ 29/43

Lower St ✉ SP7 9EE – ✆ 01747 828038 – www.theforesterdonheadstandrew.co.uk – Closed Sunday dinner and Monday except bank holidays

DORCHESTER

Dorset – Pop. 19 060 – Regional map n° **2**-C3

Sienna

MODERN CUISINE • COSY XX This unassuming high street restaurant is run by a keen young chef. Terse menu descriptions belie the complexity of the dishes, which are modern and ambitious both in flavour and presentation. It has just five tables, so book ahead.

Carte £ 23/43

36 High West St ✉ DT1 1UP – ✆ 01305 250022 (booking essential) – www.siennadorchester.co.uk – Closed 25-26 December, 1 January and Sunday dinner-Tuesday

Yalbury Cottage

TRADITIONAL BRITISH • RUSTIC XX This very proudly and personally run restaurant is set within an old thatched cottage and has a snug beamed interior. Cooking is traditional, gutsy and flavoursome. Produce is sourced from within 9 miles and the menu evolves as new ingredients become available. Well-kept cottagey bedrooms are located in a wing.

Menu £ 35

8 rooms – £ 75/85 £ 99/125

Lower Bockhampton ✉ DT2 8PZ – East : 3.75 mi by A 35 – ✆ 01305 262382 (booking essential) – www.yalburycottage.com – dinner only and Sunday lunch - Residents only Sunday-Monday dinner – Closed 23 December-18 January

Little Court

TRADITIONAL • CLASSIC Lutyens-style house boasting Edwardian wood and brickwork, leaded windows and mature gardens with a pool and tennis court. Bedrooms display original features and modern furnishings; one has a four-poster bed.

8 rooms – £ 69/99 £ 79/129

5 Westleaze, Charminster ✉ DT2 9PZ – North : 1 mi by B3147, turning right at Loders garage – ✆ 01305 261576 – www.littlecourt.net – Closed 22 December-2 January

Westwood House

TOWNHOUSE • COSY Georgian townhouse built in 1815 by Lord Illchester. Spotlessly kept bedrooms have bold colours, king-sized beds and fridges containing fresh milk. The sunny drawing room opens onto a conservatory where hearty breakfasts are served.

6 rooms – †£ 65/79 ††£ 85/99

29 High St West ✉ DT1 1UP
– ✆ 01305 268018 – www.westwoodhouse.co.uk
– Closed 31 December-5 January

DORRIDGE

West Midlands – ✉ Birmingham – Regional map n° **10**-C2

Forest

MODERN BRITISH • DESIGN XX Surprisingly stylish restaurant located in a 19C hotel opposite the railway station: choose the bar-lounge for unfussy classics or head to the dining room for ambitious dishes with interesting modern twists. Cooking is accomplished and well-judged. Comfortable, contemporary bedrooms complete the picture.

Carte £ 22/33

12 rooms – †£ 105/135 ††£ 120/150

25 Station Approach ✉ B93 8JA
– ✆ 01564 772120 – www.forest-hotel.com
– Closed 25 December and Sunday dinner

DOUGLAS – Douglas ➜ See Man (Isle of)

DREWSTEIGNTON

Devon – Pop. 668 – Regional map n° **1**-C2

Old Inn

MODERN BRITISH • INTIMATE XX Olive green former pub in the centre of a lovely Devonshire village. It has two small, cosy dining rooms and a parquet-floored lounge with modern art for sale on the walls and a wood-burning stove in the large inglenook fireplace. A concise menu offers hearty, classical dishes. Bedrooms are simply furnished.

Menu £ 52

3 rooms – †£ 80 ††£ 100/110

✉ EX6 6QR
– ✆ 01647 281276 (booking essential) – www.old-inn.co.uk
– dinner only and lunch Friday-Saturday – Closed 3 weeks January, 1-7 June and Sunday-Tuesday

DRIGHLINGTON

West Yorkshire – Regional map n° **13**-B2

Prashad

INDIAN VEGETARIAN • NEIGHBOURHOOD XX Stylish former pub with wooden panels from India fronting the bar; head upstairs to admire the huge picture of a Mumbai street scene. Authentic vegetarian dishes range from enticing street food to more original creations, with influences from Southern India and Gujarat; be sure to try the dosas.

Carte £ 25/40

137 Whitehall Rd ✉ BD11 1AT
– ✆ 0113 285 2037 – www.prashad.co.uk
– dinner only and lunch Saturday-Sunday – Closed 25 December

DROXFORD

Hampshire – Pop. 675 – Regional map n° **4**-B2

Bakers Arms

TRADITIONAL BRITISH • PUB A small, cosy pub with wooden beams and an open fire – it also doubles as the village post office and has a loyal local following. Cooking is simple and classical, with the likes of pie of the day and snails in garlic butter.

Carte £ 22/41

High St ✉ SO32 3PA
– ✆ 01489 877533 – www.thebakersarmsdroxford.com
– Closed Sunday dinner

DULVERTON

Somerset – Pop. 1 052 – Regional map n° **2**-A2

Woods

MODERN BRITISH • PUB Former bakery, with a cosy, hugely characterful interior. Tasty, carefully prepared dishes offer more than just the usual pub fare. Provenance is taken seriously, with quality local ingredients including meat from the owner's farm.

Carte £ 22/35

4 Banks Sq ✉ TA22 9BU
– ✆ 01398 324007 (bookings advisable at dinner) – www.woodsdulverton.co.uk
– Closed 25 December, dinner 26 December and 1 January

DUNSFORD

Devon – Regional map n° **1**-C2

Weeke Barton

HISTORIC • CONTEMPORARY The owners of this 15C Devonshire longhouse are friendly and laid-back, and the place itself has a funky yet cosy feel. The interior combines old world character with stylish furnishings, and bedrooms are modern and minimalistic. Rustic, home-cooked dishes feature in the communal dining room.

5 rooms – †£ 100/120 ††£ 110/130

✉ EX6 7HH – Southeast : 1.5 mi by B 3212 and Christow rd, turning right up unmarked road after river bridge
– ✆ 01647 253505 – www.weekebarton.com – Closed Christmas and New Year

DUNSTER

Somerset – Pop. 408 – Regional map n° **2**-A2

Luttrell Arms

HISTORIC • PERSONALISED A stone built 15C inn – once a hostelry for monks – with open fires, period features and a small medieval courtyard. Bedrooms are named after local landmarks: one has an ornate plaster fireplace; another a four-poster and an impressive timbered ceiling. Traditional dishes are served in the formal restaurant.

28 rooms – †£ 95/100 ††£ 130/150

32-36 High St ✉ TA24 6SG
– ✆ 01653 821555 – www.luttrellarms.co.uk

DURHAM

Durham – Pop. 47 785 – Regional map n° **14**-B3

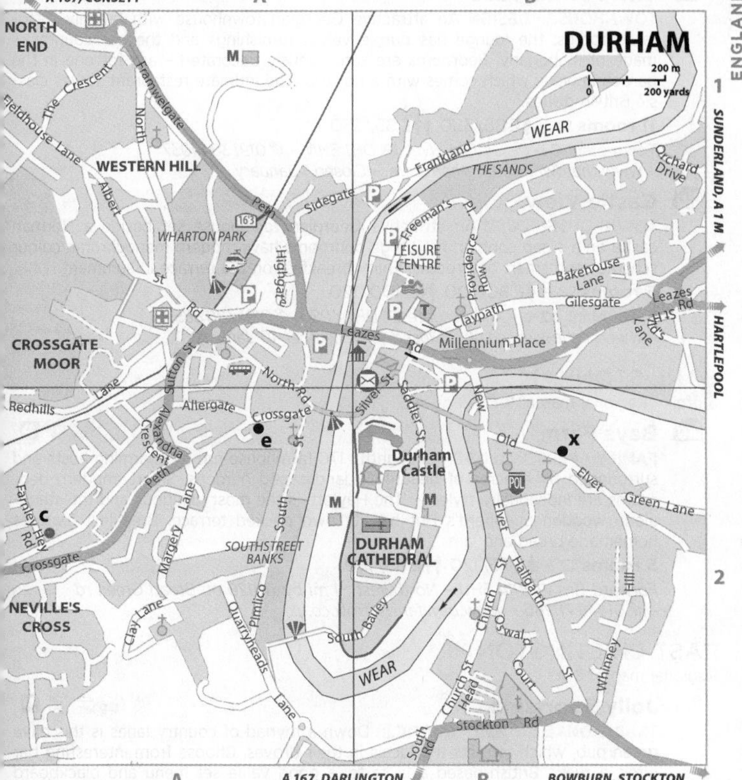

DH1

MODERN CUISINE · INTIMATE XX An intimate restaurant on the lower floor of a large Victorian house overlooking the city. An array of choices mean everything from a weekly market menu to a vegetarian tasting menu; dishes are modern and full of flavour.

Menu £ 45/60

Town plan: A2-c – *The Avenue* ✉ *DH1 4DX*

– ✆ 0191 384 6655 – www.restaurantdh1.co.uk – dinner only – Closed first week January, one week summer, one week autumn, 25-26 December, Sunday and Monday

Finbarr's

MODERN BRITISH · BISTRO XX Finbarr's has relocated to a converted farm building on the edge of the city – it's a place familiar to the owners, who both worked here previously. Menus offer plenty of choice and the hearty brasserie cooking suits the area well.

Menu £ 18/25 (weekdays) – Carte £ 27/58

Aykley Heads House, Aykley Heads ✉ DH1 5TS – Northwest : 1.5 mi by A 691 and B 6532.

– ✆ 0191 307 7033 – www.finbarrsrestaurant.co.uk – Closed first week January, 25-26 December and bank holidays

The Town House

TOWNHOUSE • DESIGN An attractive Georgian townhouse with lavishly decorated rooms: the lounge has purple velvet furnishings and the bar counter is made of mahogany. Bedrooms are sumptuously decorated – ask for one in the garden annexe, which comes with a hot tub. The intimate restaurant serves classic British dishes.

11 rooms – £ 85/350 £ 85/350

Town plan: B2-x – *34 Old Elvet ✉ DH1 3HN – ✆ 0191 384 1037 – www.thetownhousedurham.com – Closed 1 January*

Castle View

TOWNHOUSE • COSY An attractive Georgian townhouse set beside a Norman castle on a steep cobbled hill. Large bedrooms have modern monochrome colour schemes and smart bathrooms. Enjoy breakfast on the terrace in summer.

5 rooms – £ 80/100 £ 100/120

Town plan: A2-e – *4 Crossgate ✉ DH1 4PS – ✆ 0191 386 8852 – www.castle-view.co.uk – Closed 18 December-10 January*

EARL STONHAM

Suffolk – Regional map n° **8**-C3

Bays Farm

FAMILY • PERSONALISED A delightful 17C farmhouse run by charming hosts and surrounded by 4 acres of beautifully landscaped gardens. Smart, modern bedrooms are individually styled – 'The Hayloft' is the most luxurious and the standalone wooden Shepherd's Hut has its own decked terrace. Breakfast features homemade bread and jam.

5 rooms – £ 75/120 £ 85/130

Forward Grn ✉ IP14 5HU – Northwest : 1 mi by A 1120 on Broad Green rd – ✆ 01449 711286 – www.baysfarmsuffolk.co.uk

EAST CHILTINGTON

Regional map n° **8**-A3

Jolly Sportsman

TRADITIONAL BRITISH • RUSTIC Down a myriad of country lanes is this olive green pub, which attracts the locals in their droves. Choose from interesting bar bites, a rustic British-based à la carte, a good value set menu and blackboard specials which come and go.

Menu £ 20 (weekday lunch) – Carte £ 29/45

Chapel Ln ✉ BN7 3BA – ✆ 01273 890400 (booking essential) – www.thejollysportsman.com – Closed 25 December, Sunday dinner and Monday

EAST CHISENBURY

Wiltshire – Regional map n° **2**-D2

Red Lion Freehouse (Guy Manning)

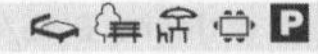

CLASSIC CUISINE • SIMPLE Set on the edge of Salisbury Plain, this charming thatched pub and its pretty garden immediately draw you in. The daily à la carte is a roll-call of carefully prepared classics, which arrive fully garnished and packed with flavour; the midweek lunch is great value. Smart, well-equipped bedrooms are set opposite and have private terraces overlooking the river.

→ Mushroom pappardelle with truffle cream and crisp breadcrumbs. Roasted veal loin with herb spätzle and Roscoff onions. Mango and vanilla terrine with basil granité, vanilla genoise and mango salad.

Menu £ 25 (lunch and early dinner) – Carte £ 35/50

5 rooms – £ 180/230 £ 180/230

✉ SN9 6AQ – ✆ 01980 671124 (booking advisable) – www.redlionfreehouse.com – Closed Sunday dinner except bank holidays, Monday and Tuesday

EAST END

Hampshire – Regional map n° **4**-A3

East End Arms

TRADITIONAL BRITISH • RUSTIC This traditional country pub is owned by John Illsley of Dire Straits and boasts a great display of photos from his personal collection in its shabby bar and pine-furnished dining room. Concise menus feature local produce in satisfying British dishes. Modern cottage-style bedrooms provide a smart contrast.

Carte £ 25/45

5 rooms – £ 85/100 £ 110/130

Lymington Rd ✉ SO41 5SY – ✆ 01590 626223 – www.eastendarms.co.uk – Closed dinner Sunday

EAST GRINSTEAD

West Sussex – Pop. 29 084 – Regional map n° **4**-D2

Gravetye Manor

MODERN BRITISH • TRADITIONAL DÉCOR XXX A charming country house dining room with wood-panelled walls and a cosy feel. Classically based, highly seasonal menus use excellent quality produce from the kitchen garden to create refined, flavourful dishes. The wine list is well-chosen, service is polished and professional, and desserts are a highlight.

➜ Gravetye spring garden salad. Poached loin of rabbit with wild garlic leaves, leg sausage, morels and baby carrots. Roasted acorn burnt cream with fresh thyme, hazelnut granola and parsnip cake.

Menu £ 40/75

Gravetye Manor Hotel, Vowels Ln ✉ RH19 4LJ – ✆ 01342 810567 (booking essential) – www.gravetyemanor.co.uk – Closed 2 January-mid May

Gravetye Manor

LUXURY • CLASSIC A quintessential English country house set in a forest and surrounded by 35 acres of glorious gardens. Ornate Elizabethan ceilings and fireplaces dominate beautifully furnished lounges, which provide the perfect spot for afternoon tea. Bedrooms are luxurious and the service is personalised and detailed. They will close in early 2018 while they create a new restaurant.

17 rooms – £ 170/220 £ 290/595 – 1 suite

Vowels Ln ✉ RH19 4LJ – Southwest : 4.5 mi by B 2110 taking second turn left towards West Hoathly – ✆ 01342 810567 – www.gravetyemanor.co.uk – Closed 2 January-mid May

Gravetye Manor – See restaurant listing

EAST HADDON

Northamptonshire – Regional map n° **9**-B3

Red Lion

TRADITIONAL CUISINE • PUB A thatched, honey-stone inn at the heart of an attractive village, with a pleasing mix of exposed wood, brick and slate, a pretty garden and chic, cosy bedrooms. The seasonal menu offers an eclectic mix of generously proportioned dishes; the scotch egg is a favourite. Service is smiley and enthusiastic.

Carte £ 22/42

7 rooms – £ 80/95 £ 95/110

Main St ✉ NN6 8BU – ✆ 01604 770223 – www.redlioneasthaddon.co.uk – Closed 25 December

EAST HENDRED

Oxfordshire – Regional map n° **6**-B3

Eyston Arms

INTERNATIONAL • PUB A series of cosy, low-beamed rooms centre around an inglenook fireplace at this charming pub, and candles and caricatures of the locals add a modern touch. The menu draws on many cuisines, from Italian to Asian.

Carte £ 25/41

High St ✉ OX12 8JY – ✆ 01235 833320 – www.eystonarms.co.uk – Closed 25 December

EAST HOATHLY

East Sussex – Pop. 893 – Regional map n° **5**-B3

Old Whyly

TRADITIONAL • PERSONALISED Charming red-brick house built in 1760, set in beautiful grounds and very personally run by its delightful owner. Guest areas mix the classic and the contemporary. Bedrooms are individually designed around a subtle theme: choose from Tulip, French or Chinese. The minimalist dining room offers a daily changing 3 course dinner, and homemade yoghurts and jams at breakfast.

4 rooms – £ 90/150 £ 98/150

London Rd ✉ BN8 6EL – Northwest : 0.5 mi, turning right by post box on right and then taking centre drive – ✆ 01825 840216 – www.oldwhyly.co.uk

EAST WITTERING

West Sussex – Pop. 5 647 – Regional map n° **4**-C3

Samphire

TRADITIONAL BRITISH • SIMPLE A brightly decorated bistro with a shabby-chic beach café style, set 100 metres from the sea. Freshly caught seafood comes from the local day boats and meats are from the surrounding countryside. Cooking is unfussy and good value.

Menu £ 16 (lunch) – Carte £ 24/38

57 Shore Rd ✉ PO20 8DY – ✆ 01243 672754 – www.samphireeastwittering.co.uk – Closed 2 weeks January, Christmas and Sunday

EAST WITTON

North Yorkshire – ✉ Leyburn – Regional map n° **13**-B1

Blue Lion

TRADITIONAL CUISINE • INN Characterful country pub with a charming flag-floored bar. Sit at a polished wooden table in the glow of candlelight and enjoy unfussy, hearty, full-flavoured dishes crafted from local produce. Bedrooms in the pub are antique-furnished; those in the old stables are more contemporary.

Menu £ 17 (weekday lunch) – Carte £ 25/56 **s**

15 rooms – £ 94/145 £ 94/145

✉ DL8 4SN – ✆ 01969 624273 (booking essential) – www.thebluelion.co.uk

EASTBOURNE

East Sussex – Pop. 109 185 – Regional map n° **5**-B3

Grand

LUXURY • CLASSIC Built in 1875 and offering all its name promises, the Grand retains many original features including ornate plasterwork, columned corridors and a Great Hall. The delightful gardens feature a superb outdoor pool and sun terrace. Bedrooms are spacious and classical – it's worth paying extra for a sea view. Dine in formal Mirabelle or the more accessible Garden Restaurant.

152 rooms – £ 210/355 £ 240/355 – 13 suites

King Edward's Par. ✉ BN21 4EQ – ✆ 01323 412345 – www.grandeastbourne.com

Ocklynge Manor

HISTORIC • PERSONALISED Sit in the small summerhouse and admire the beautiful mature gardens of this charming, traditional guesthouse. Mabel Lucie Attwell – the illustrator of 'Peter Pan and Wendy' – once lived here. Homemade cake is served on arrival.

3 rooms – £ 60/100 £ 100/130

Mill Rd ✉ BN21 2PG – Northwest : 2 mi by A 259 and A 2270 – ✆ 01323 734121 – www.ocklyngemanor.co.uk

EBRINGTON - Gloucestershire → See Chipping Campden

ECKINGTON - Worcestershire → See Pershore

EDINGTON

Wiltshire - Regional map n° **2**-C2

Three Daggers

MODERN BRITISH • COSY Attractive pub with original wood beams and flagstones, and a large conservatory overlooking the garden. The accessible menu always features a homemade soup and a 'pie of the day', and the Huntsman's and Fisherman's sharing platters are extremely popular. Charming bedrooms feature bespoke oak furnishings.

Carte £ 27/34

3 rooms – £ 90/110 £ 99/165

47 Westbury Rd BA13 4PG – 01380 830940 – www.threedaggers.co.uk

EGERTON

Kent - Regional map n° **5**-C2

The Barrow House

TRADITIONAL BRITISH • PUB This stylishly modernised inn was built in 1576 using timbers from old sailing ships. Wide-ranging menus appeal to all, with flavoursome small plates and satisfying mains. Meats are free-range and all ingredients are sourced from within 20 miles. Bedrooms blend modern décor with heavy beams.

Carte £ 19/39

3 rooms – £ 80/140 £ 80/140

The Street TN21 9DJ – 01233 756599 – www.thebarrowhouse.co.uk – Closed 25 December and Sunday dinner October-Easter

EGHAM

Surrey - Pop. 25 996 - Regional map n° **4**-C1

Tudor Room

MODERN CUISINE • INTIMATE An intimate hotel dining room with mullioned windows, burgundy décor and large tapestries on the walls. The menu might be concise but dishes are interesting, accomplished and full of flavour. Cooking is sophisticated but not over-complicated and the kitchen garden provides many of the ingredients.

→ Anjou pigeon with walnut, pomegranate and celeriac. Wild sea bass with asparagus and clams. Rhubarb, ginger and vanilla Breton.

Menu £ 38/70 – tasting menu only

Great Fosters Hotel, Stroude Rd TW20 9UR – South : 1.25 mi by B 388 – 01784 433822 (booking essential) – www.greatfosters.co.uk – dinner only and lunch Thursday-Friday – Closed Sunday-Tuesday

Great Fosters

BUSINESS • ELEGANT Striking Elizabethan manor built as a hunting lodge for Henry VIII, boasting 50 acres of gardens, a beautiful parterre and an amphitheatre. The charming interior displays characterful original detailing. Bedrooms come with feature beds and a flamboyant touch; those in the annexes are more modern. Dine on steaks from the Josper grill or more formally in the Tudor Room.

43 rooms – £ 180 £ 215/550 – £ 20 – 3 suites

Stroude Rd TW20 9UR – South : 1.25 mi by B 388 – 01784 433822 – www.greatfosters.co.uk

Tudor Room – See restaurant listing

EGTON

North Yorkshire – Regional map n° **13**-C1

Wheatsheaf Inn

TRADITIONAL BRITISH • PUB Family-run, late 17C inn on the edge of the picturesque North Yorkshire Moors. Menu offers a real taste of Yorkshire with fresh, hearty dishes like lambs' kidneys, local steak, Whitby scampi and game sourced from within 2 miles.

Carte £ 22/40

YO21 1TZ – 01947 895271 – www.wheatsheafegton.com – Closed 25 December and Monday

ELDERSFIELD

Worcestershire – Regional map n° **10**-B3

Butchers Arms (James Winter)

MODERN BRITISH • RUSTIC A sweet rural inn with two cosy dining rooms and a small bar, where the beams are fringed with hop bines and villagers meet for a pint at the end of the day. The chef, who cooks alone, has a great appreciation for natural ingredients and knows how to use them to create simple yet wonderfully well-flavoured dishes.

→ Grilled octopus with steamed pork bun, chilli and coriander dressing. Roasted Looe turbot with Evesham asparagus, saffron mayonnaise and crispy potato. Dark chocolate fondant with pistachio ice cream.

Carte £ 43/57

Lime Street GL19 4NX – Southeast : 1 mi – 01452 840381 (booking essential) – www.thebutchersarms.net – dinner only and lunch Friday-Sunday – Closed 1 week early January, 1 week late August, Sunday dinner, Monday and bank holidays

ELLASTONE

Staffordshire – Regional map n° **10**-C1

Duncombe Arms

TRADITIONAL BRITISH • COSY A stylish dining pub owned by the Hon. Johnny Greenall – of the famous brewing family – and his wife, a descendant of the Duncombe family after which the pub is named. There are several cosy rooms to choose from, each with their own identity. Menus mix pub classics with more ambitious restaurant-style dishes.

Carte £ 26/48

Main Road DE6 2GZ – 01335 324275 – www.duncombearms.co.uk – Closed 1 week January

ELLEL

Lancashire – Regional map n° **11**-A1

Bay Horse Inn

REGIONAL CUISINE • PUB Cosy, homely pub in a pleasant rural location, with a characterful interior and an attractive terrace. Seasonal, locally sourced produce is crafted into classic, tried-and-tested dishes. The Lancashire cheeseboard is a speciality.

Menu £ 25 (weekdays) **s** – Carte £ 25/46 **s**

Bay Horse Ln, Bay Horse LA2 0HR – South 1.5 mi by A 6 on Quernmore rd – 01524 791204 – www.bayhorseinn.com – Closed Monday and Tuesday

ELMTON

Derbyshire – Regional map n° **9**-B1

Elm Tree

TRADITIONAL CUISINE • PUB 18C stone pub with a brightly lit bar, characterful beamed rooms, a wood-burning stove and a large garden. The good value menu offers pub classics presented in a modern manner, with most ingredients sourced from within 10 miles.

Menu £ 15 (weekday lunch) – Carte £ 18/36

S80 4LS – 01909 721261 – www.elmtreeelmton.co.uk – Closed Tuesday

ELSTREE

Hertfordshire – Pop. 1 986 – Regional map n° **7**-A2

Laura Ashley-The Manor H. Elstree

HISTORIC • PERSONALISED An eye-catching, timbered Edwardian house which showcases the latest fabrics, furnishings and fittings from the famous company. Well-equipped bedrooms: the largest and most characterful are in the main house. The intimate, formal restaurant offers modern cooking and views over the extensive gardens.

49 rooms – £ 89/129 £ 95/280

Barnet Ln WD6 3RE – 020 8327 4700 – www.lauraashleyhotels.com/elstree

ELTERWATER

Cumbria – Regional map n° **12**-A2

The Eltermere

MODERN BRITISH • CLASSIC DÉCOR XX Take in lovely lake and mountain views from this handsome 17C farmhouse, where you'll find three elegantly furnished dining-cum-sitting rooms, a darkly decorated fire-lit bar and 12 capacious bedrooms. Cooking is fresh, unfussy and appealing, and many of the leaves and berries come from the attractive garden.

Menu £ 30 (dinner) – Carte £ 30/43

12 rooms – £ 135/280 £ 149/295

LA22 9HY – At edge of village on Coniston rd – 015394 37207 – www.eltermere.co.uk – Closed 23-27 December and 2-16 January

ELTON

Cambridgeshire – Regional map n° **8**-A2

Crown Inn

TRADITIONAL BRITISH • PUB 17C honey-stone pub in a delightful country parish, with a thatched roof, a cosy inglenook fireplace in the bar and a laid-back feel. Menus offer homely British dishes which arrive in generous portions. Bedrooms are smart and individually styled – some have feature beds or roll-top baths.

Carte £ 24/37

8 rooms – £ 80 £ 140/160

8 Duck St PE8 6RQ – 01832 280232 – www.crowninnelton.co.uk – Closed Sunday dinner and Monday lunch except bank holidays

ELTON-ON-THE-HILL

Nottinghamshire – Regional map n° **9**-B2

The Grange

FAMILY • COSY What better way to start your holiday than in this charming Georgian farmhouse with a slice of homemade cake? The owners are lovely, the gardens are delightful and the country views are superb. Bedrooms are homely and come with good facilities and thoughtful touches; one is accessed via a spiral staircase.

3 rooms – £ 50/55 £ 85/90

Sutton Ln. NG13 9LA – 07887 952181 – www.thegrangebedandbreakfastnotts.co.uk

ELY

Cambridgeshire – Pop. 19 090 – Regional map n° **8**-B2

 Poets House

BUSINESS • MODERN A series of 19C townhouses set opposite the cathedral. Spacious, boutique bedrooms come with beautiful bathrooms, good extras and a moody feel. The modern bar overlooks the pretty walled garden and also offers afternoon tea. Dine on ambitious dishes, which include plenty of vegetarian options.

21 rooms – †£ 150/270 ††£ 170/320

St Mary's St ✉ CB7 4EY – ✆ 01353 887777 – www.poetshouse.uk.com

EMSWORTH

Hampshire – Pop. 18 777 – Regional map n° **4**-B2

36 on the Quay

MODERN BRITISH • ELEGANT XX Long-standing, intimate restaurant and conservatory bar-lounge in a quayside cottage with pleasant harbour views. Concise menus offer elaborate modern dishes in some unusual combinations and foraged ingredients feature highly. Stylish bedrooms have good comforts; be ready to order breakfast at check-in.

Menu £ 24/58

4 rooms – †£ 75/90 ††£ 100/175

47 South St, The Quay ✉ PO10 7EG – ✆ 01243 375592 (booking advisable) – www.36onthequay.co.uk – Closed 2 weeks January, 1 week May, 1 week October, 24-27 December, Sunday and Monday

Fat Olives

MODERN BRITISH • RUSTIC X This sweet 17C fisherman's cottage sits in a characterful coastal town, in a road leading down to the harbour. It's run by a charming couple and has a rustic modern feel, courtesy of locally crafted tables and upholstered chairs. Classic British dishes have a modern edge and rely on small local suppliers.

Menu £ 21 (lunch) – Carte £ 30/46

30 South St ✉ PO10 7EH – ✆ 01243 377914 (booking essential) – www.fatolives.co.uk – Closed 2 weeks late June, Christmas, New Year, Tuesday after bank holiday, Sunday and Monday

EPPING

Essex – Pop. 10 289 – Regional map n° **7**-B2

Haywards

MODERN CUISINE • INTIMATE XX This proudly run restaurant is the realisation of a couple's dream. A hammerbeam ceiling and cherry wood tables set the scene. Appealing dishes follow the seasons and flavours are well-balanced. Service is extremely welcoming.

Menu £ 31 (weekdays)/45

111 Bell Common ✉ CM16 4DZ – Southwest : 1 mi by B 1393 and Theydon Rd – ✆ 01992 577350 – www.haywardsrestaurant.co.uk – Closed 1-24 January and Sunday dinner-Wednesday lunch

EPSOM

Surrey – Pop. 31 474 – Regional map n° **4**-D1

Le Raj

BANGLADESHI • ELEGANT XXX A local institution run by a larger-than-life owner. It has a comfy bar-lounge and a smart restaurant where wooden panels are picked out with gold leaf. White-gloved waiters serve carefully prepared, authentic Bangladeshi dishes.

Carte £ 28/37

211 Fir Tree Rd, Epsom Downs ✉ KT17 3LB – Southeast : 2 mi by B 289 and B 284 on B 291 – ✆ 01737 371371 – www.lerajrestaurant.co.uk

ERMINGTON

Devon – Regional map n° **1**-C2

Plantation House

MODERN CUISINE • INTIMATE XX Georgian former rectory in a pleasant country spot, with a small drinks terrace, an open-fired lounge and two dining rooms: one formal, with black furnishings; one more relaxed, with polished wood tables. Interesting modern menus feature local produce. Stylish bedrooms come with fresh milk and homemade cake.

Menu £ 40 **s**

8 rooms – £ 90/190 £ 110/230

Totnes Rd ✉ PL21 9NS – Southwest : 0.5 mi on A 3121 – ✆ 01548 831100 (bookings essential for non-residents) – www.plantationhousehotel.co.uk – dinner only

ESHOTT

Northd. → See Morpeth

ETTINGTON

Warwickshire – Pop. 1 039 – Regional map n° **10**-C3

Chequers Inn

TRADITIONAL CUISINE • PUB Chandeliers, brushed velvet furniture and chequered tables make this pub a little different. Internationally influenced menus list pub favourites and British classics alongside dishes of Mediterranean persuasion.

Carte £ 18/38

91 Banbury Rd ✉ CV37 7SR – ✆ 01789 740387
– www.the-chequers-ettington.co.uk – Closed Sunday dinner and Monday

EVERSHOT

Dorset – ✉ Dorchester – Pop. 225 – Regional map n° **2**-C3

Summer Lodge

LUXURY • ELEGANT An attractive former dower house in mature gardens, featuring a smart wellness centre, a pool and a tennis court. Plush, individually designed bedrooms come with marble bathrooms and country house guest areas display heavy fabrics and antiques – the drawing room was designed by Thomas Hardy. Dine formally from a classic menu, which is accompanied by a superb wine list.

24 rooms – £ 215/760 £ 215/760 – 4 suites

9 Fore St ✉ DT2 0JR – ✆ 01935 482000 – www.summerlodgehotel.com

Acorn Inn

INN • CLASSIC The historic Acorn Inn was mentioned in 'Tess of the d'Urbervilles' and to this day is the hub of the village. Cosy, individually appointed bedrooms have fabric-covered walls – some have four-posters and the attic is perfect for families. Dine in the classic restaurant or the locals bar with its skittle alley.

10 rooms – £ 89/135 £ 99/220

28 Fore St ✉ DT2 0JW – ✆ 01935 83228 – www.acorn-inn.co.uk

Wooden Cabbage

COUNTRY HOUSE • COSY The unusual name comes from the local term for a stunted oak tree. An attractive former gamekeeper's cottage, it sits in a quiet spot and has lovely countryside views from its pretty bedrooms and tropical plant filled orangery.

3 rooms – £ 105 £ 115/125

East Chelborough ✉ DT2 0QA – ✆ 01935 83362 – www.woodencabbage.co.uk

EWELL

Surrey – ✉ Surrey – Regional map n° **4**-D1

See Greater London Plan 6

Dastaan

INDIAN • NEIGHBOURHOOD Two friends who worked in London's Gymkhana own this simple restaurant in a parade of shops. Its name means 'story' – their story – and they even made the tables and benches themselves! Great value cooking is mainly northern Indian and ranges from street food and classics to some more unusual choices.

Carte £ 20/29

Town plan: C6-d – *447 Kingston Rd ✉ KT19 0DB – ✆ 020 8786 8999 – www.dastaan.co.uk – dinner only and lunch Saturday-Sunday – Closed Monday*

EWEN

Gloucestershire – Pop. 257 – Regional map n° **2**-C1

Wild Duck

TRADITIONAL CUISINE • RUSTIC The Wild Duck is a charming place, both inside and out. Snack on charcuterie sliced on the ornate slicer behind the bar, choose a healthy option such as soy-glazed mackerel or really push the boat out with the duck for two to share.

Menu £ 15 (weekday lunch) – Carte £ 27/42

Drakes Island ✉ GL7 6BY – ✆ 01285 770310 – www.thewildduckewen.com

EXETER

Devon – Pop. 113 507 – Regional map n° **1**-D2

Southernhay House

TOWNHOUSE • CONTEMPORARY Attractive Georgian townhouse with original ceiling roses and ornate coving. Smart, compact guest areas include a stylish lounge and a bar with bright blue furniture. Warmly decorated bedrooms have sumptuous beds, luxurious fabrics and chic bathrooms. The small dining room offers British-based menus.

10 rooms – †£ 100/170 ††£ 100/260 – ☕ £ 12

Town plan: B2-x – *36 Southernhay East ✉ EX1 1NX – ✆ 01392 435324 – www.southernhayhouse.com*

at Brampford Speke North: 5 mi by A377

Lazy Toad Inn

REGIONAL CUISINE • COSY In winter, sit under a lovely oak-beamed ceiling beside an inviting log fire; in summer, head for the beautiful walled garden or charming cobbled courtyard. Hearty British dishes showcase produce from the garden and polytunnel.

Menu £ 20 (weekdays) – Carte £ 19/37

✉ EX5 5DP – ✆ 01392 841591 – www.thelazytoad.com – Closed 1 week January, Sunday dinner and Monday

FAIRFORD

Gloucestershire – Pop. 2 960 – Regional map n° **2**-D1

The Bull

TRADITIONAL CUISINE • INN The 14C Bull sits in the marketplace of an attractive little town and is a hit with fisherman courtesy of its mile of fishing rights. The main bar is characterful and cosy, while the two smaller dining rooms have a quirky feel. Menus offer plenty of choice, from antipasti, pizza and pasta to hearty British dishes. Bedrooms come with exposed timbers and designer touches.

Menu £ 17 (weekday lunch) – Carte £ 30/40

21 rooms – †£ 75 ††£ 100/220

✉ GL7 4AA – ✆ 01285 712535 – www.thebullhotelfairford.co.uk

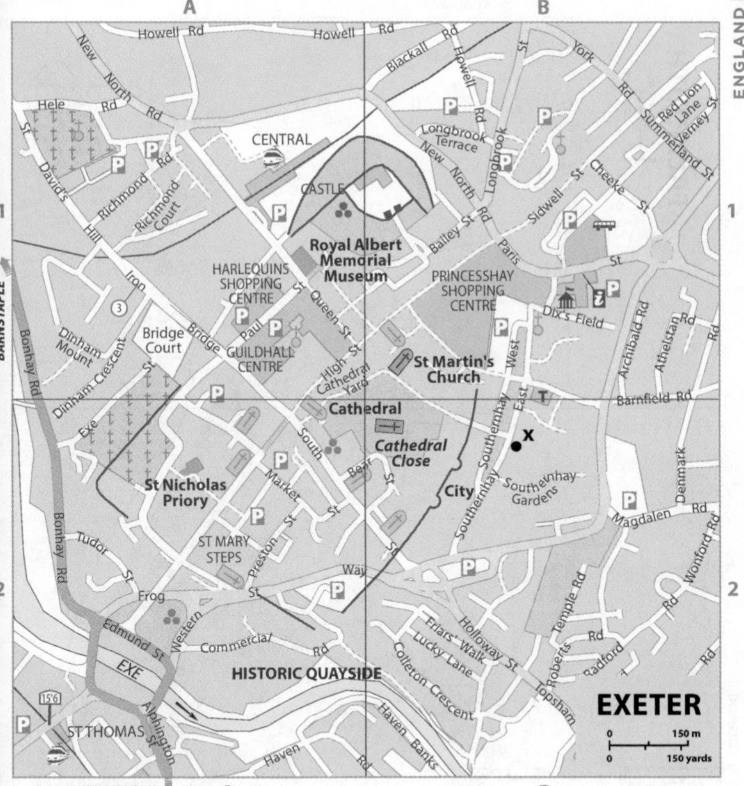

FALMOUTH

Cornwall – Pop. 22 686 – Regional map n° **1**-A3

Oliver's

TRADITIONAL CUISINE • NEIGHBOURHOOD Although it's just a few paces from the water, Oliver's is known more for its game than anything else. Good value lunches are followed by more ambitious dinners. It's a simple place, run with plenty of passion, and a hit with the locals.

Menu £ 23 (lunch) – Carte dinner £ 28/34

Town plan: B1-s – *33 High St ✉ TR11 2AD – ✆ 01326 218138 – www.oliversfalmouth.com – Closed 10 December-7 January, Sunday, Monday and bank holidays*

Rick Stein's Fish

A/C

SEAFOOD • BRASSERIE With their own special beef dripping batter and fish chilli burgers to takeaway, this is more than your usual fish 'n' chips. Head inside and, alongside your favourites, you'll find the likes of dressed crab, fruits de mer and cod curry.

Menu £ 12 (lunch and early dinner) – Carte £ 23/44

Town plan: B2-a – *Discovery Quay ✉ TR11 3XA – ✆ 01841 532700 (booking advisable) – www.rickstein.com – Closed 25-26 December*

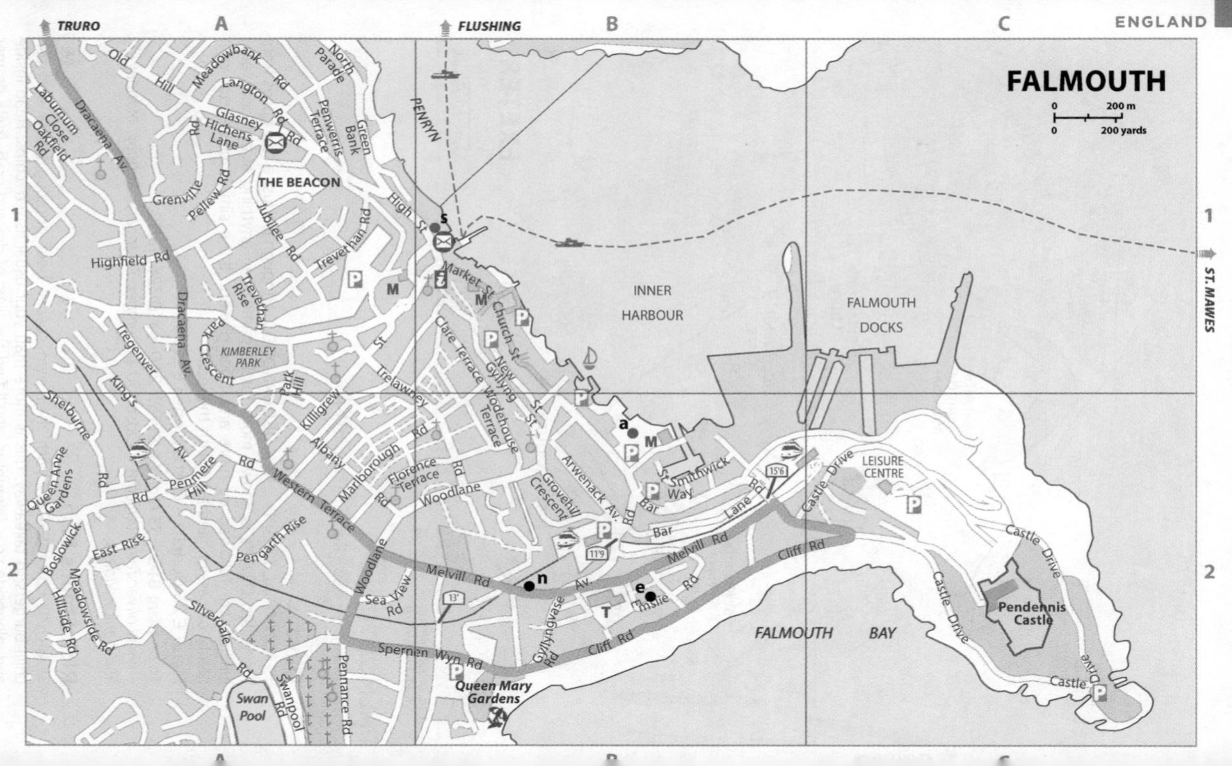
FALMOUTH
0 200 m
0 200 yards
TRURO
FLUSHING
ST. MAWES
A
B
C
1
2
PENRYN
INNER HARBOUR
FALMOUTH DOCKS
LEISURE CENTRE
Pendennis Castle
Castle Drive
FALMOUTH BAY
Cliff Rd
Melvill Rd
Lane Rd
Bar Rd
Bar Way
St Smithwick
Arwenack Av.
Grovehill Crescent
Gyllyngvase Rd
Av.
Queen Mary Gardens
Spernen Wyn Rd
Pennance Rd
Swanpool Rd
Swan Pool
Silverdale Rd
Sea View Rd
Woodlane
Western Terrace
Marlborough Rd
Florence Terrace
Woodlane Rd
Albany Rd
Killigrew St
Trelawney Rd
Clare Terrace
Wodehouse Terrace
New Gyllyng St
Church St
Market St
High St
Trevethan Rd
Green Bank
North Parade
Penwerris Terrace
THE BEACON
Jubilee Rd
Trevethan Rise
KIMBERLEY PARK
Park Hill
Park Crescent
Dracaena Av.
Pengarth Rise
Penmere Hill
Av.
Tregenver Rd
King's
Highfield Rd
Grenville
Pellew Rd
Hichens Lane
Glasney Rd
Langton Rd
Meadowbank Rd
Old Hill
Laburnum Close
Oakfield Rd
Shelburne Rd
Queen Anne Gardens
Boslowick Rd
East Rise
Meadowside Rd
Hillside Rd
s
a
e
n
M
T
P

Chelsea House

TOWNHOUSE • PERSONALISED An imposing Edwardian house in a quiet residential street close to the beaches. It's a trendy spot where retro furnishings fuse with vibrant fabrics to create a modish, boutique feel. Bedrooms on the top floors have good sea views.

9 rooms – £ 78/95 £ 95/168

Town plan: B2-e – *2 Emslie Rd ✉ TR11 4BG*
– 01326 212230 – www.chelseahousehotel.com
– Closed 3-31 January

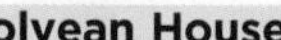

Dolvean House

TOWNHOUSE • CLASSIC Victorian house built in 1870; its homely lounge has lots of local guide books and magazines. Neat breakfast room. Good-sized bedrooms with thoughtful touches; Room 9, with a big bay window, is the best.

10 rooms – £ 50/60 £ 95/110

Town plan: B2-n – *50 Melvill Rd ✉ TR11 4DQ*
– 01326 313658 – www.dolvean.co.uk
– Closed first 2 weeks November and 22-28 December

at Maenporth Beach South: 3.75 mi by Pennance Rd

Cove

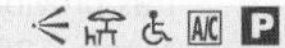

MODERN CUISINE • ROMANTIC A bright, stylish restaurant in a smart glass-fronted building overlooking the beach, the cove and St Anthony's Head. The modern dining room leads through to a lovely split-level terrace with a retractable roof. Menus are contemporary, with a strong seafood base and some Asian influences.

Menu £ 21 – Carte £ 25/38

Maenporth Beach ✉ TR11 5HN
– 01326 251136 – www.thecovemaenporth.co.uk
– Closed 25 December

FARINGDON

Oxfordshire – Pop. 7 121 – Regional map n° **6**-A2

Restaurant 56

MODERN CUISINE • ELEGANT Georgian manor house in the grounds of a corporate hotel – its wood-panelling and red fabrics give it a smart, formal feel. Attractive dishes are crafted from good quality produce; cooking is classically based with a modern edge.

Menu £ 55

Sudbury House Hotel, 56 London St ✉ SN7 7AA
– 01367 245389 (booking advisable) – www.restaurant56.co.uk
– dinner only – Closed 2-16 January, Sunday and Monday

Sudbury House

BUSINESS • FUNCTIONAL Corporate hotel in 9 acres of grounds, not far from the Folly Tower. The eight meeting rooms include a 100-seater tiered lecture theatre. Bedrooms are modern and functional with smart bathrooms. Have snacks in the bar, wood-fired specialities in relaxed Magnolia or more elaborate dishes in Restaurant 56.

50 rooms – £ 124/450 £ 144/470 – £ 13

56 London St. ✉ SN7 7AA
– 01367 241272 – www.sudburyhouse.co.uk
– Closed 2-16 January

Restaurant 56 – See restaurant listing

FARNBOROUGH

Hampshire - Pop. 65 034 - Regional map n° **4**-C1

Aviator

BUSINESS • MODERN Eye-catching modern hotel overlooking Farnborough Airport with a striking circular atrium, a stylish cocktail bar and an American burger joint. Sleek, good-sized bedrooms feature light wood and modern facilities. The contemporary restaurant serves modern British dishes and steaks from the Josper grill.

169 rooms - £ 125/250 £ 125/250 - £ 15

55 Farnborough Rd ✉ GU14 6EL - Southwest : 1 mi on A 325 - ✆ 01252 555890 - www.aviatorbytag.com

FARNHAM - Dorset → See Blandford Forum

FAVERSHAM

Kent - Pop. 19 829 - Regional map n° **5**-C1

Read's

TRADITIONAL CUISINE • ELEGANT XXX An elegant Georgian manor house in landscaped grounds, with traditional country house styling, antique furnishings and lovely oil paintings. Classically based dishes have subtle modern touches and make use of seasonal produce from the walled kitchen garden and the nearby quay. Comfortable bedrooms are full of period charm and thoughtful extras provide a sense of luxury.

Menu £ 28/65

6 rooms - £ 180/210 £ 195/210

Macknade Manor, Canterbury Rd ✉ ME13 8XE - East : 1 mi on A 2 - ✆ 01795 535344 - www.reads.com - Closed 2 weeks early September, 1 week early January, 25-26 December, Sunday and Monday

FELIXKIRK

North Yorkshire - Regional map n° **13**-B1

Carpenter's Arms

TRADITIONAL BRITISH • PUB A proper village pub with 18C origins, set in a village mentioned in the Domesday Book. Choose from blackboard specials or a wide-ranging menu of seasonal dishes, and be sure to save room for pudding. Stylishly appointed, well-equipped bedrooms overlook the Vale of Mowbray - as does the lovely terrace.

Menu £ 18 (weekday lunch) - Carte £ 25/41

10 rooms - £ 110/180 £ 120/190

✉ YO7 2DP - ✆ 01845 537369 - www.thecarpentersarmsfelixkirk.com

FENCE

Lancashire - Pop. 1 459 - Regional map n° **11**-B2

White Swan

MODERN BRITISH • SIMPLE Traditional pub owned by Timothy Taylor's brewery: you're guaranteed a perfect pint here - and the food is just as good. Concise menus offer a daily selection of well-crafted dishes; on Friday and Saturday there's also a tasting menu. The cheeseboard with homemade crackers and truffle honey is a hit.

Menu £ 28 - Carte £ 30/44

300 Wheatley Lane Rd ✉ BB12 9QA - ✆ 01282 611773 - www.whiteswanatfence.co.uk - Closed Monday

FERMAIN BAY → See Channel Islands (Guernsey)

FERRENSBY - North Yorkshire → See Knaresborough

FILEY

North Yorkshire - Pop. 6 530 - Regional map n° **13**-D2

All Seasons

TOWNHOUSE • PERSONALISED This unassuming Victorian terraced house – just a stone's throw from the sea – conceals a smart, stylish interior, where no detail is forgotten. The cosy lounge is filled with magazines and local info, and bedrooms are bright, comfy and immaculately kept. You are welcomed with homemade cake and brownies.

6 rooms – £ 65/110 £ 85/120

11 Rutland St ✉ YO14 9JA
– ✆ 01723 515321 – www.allseasonsfiley.co.uk
– Closed 24-26 December

FILKINS

Oxfordshire – Pop. 434 – Regional map n° **6**-A2

Five Alls

TRADITIONAL BRITISH • PUB Like its curious logo, this pub has it all: an open-fired bar where they serve snacks and takeaway burgers, a locals bar stocked with fine ales, three antique-furnished dining rooms, and a lovely terrace and garden. The menu is satisfyingly traditional and bedrooms are modern and cosy.

Menu £ 26 (weekdays) – Carte £ 21/44

9 rooms – £ 95/180 £ 95/180

✉ GL7 3JQ
– ✆ 01367 860875 – www.thefiveallsfilkins.co.uk
– Closed 25 December and Sunday dinner

FIVEHEAD

Somerset – Pop. 609 – Regional map n° **2**-B3

Langford Fivehead

MODERN CUISINE • INTIMATE XX A beautiful, personally run country house with 13C origins, set in 7 acres of well-tended gardens – with its antique panelling, old stone fireplaces and mullioned windows, it conveys a real sense of history. Well-balanced modern menus are highly seasonal and feature lots of kitchen garden ingredients. Bedrooms are tastefully furnished and many have four-poster beds.

Menu £ 33/39

6 rooms – £ 105/210 £ 120/225

Lower Swell ✉ TA3 6PH – East : 0.5 mi by Westport rd on Swell rd
– ✆ 01460 282020 (booking essential) – www.langfordfivehead.co.uk
– dinner only and lunch Wednesday-Friday
– Closed 1-15 January, 22 July-6 August, 25-26 December, Sunday and Monday

FLAUNDEN

Hertfordshire – Pop. 5 468 – Regional map n° **7**-A2

Bricklayers Arms

TRADITIONAL CUISINE • INN Smart pub tucked away in a small hamlet, serving hearty, French-inspired dishes and old-school puddings. The wine list is a labour of love and features some boutique Australian wines. Sunday lunch is a real family affair.

Menu £ 22 (weekdays) – Carte £ 24/45

Hogpits Bottom ✉ HP3 0PH
– ✆ 01442 833322 – www.bricklayersarms.com
– Closed 25 December

FLETCHING

East Sussex – Pop. 301 – Regional map n° **5**-A2

Griffin Inn

TRADITIONAL BRITISH • CLASSIC DÉCOR Hugely characterful coaching inn, under the same ownership for over 30 years. There's a sizeable garden and a terrace with a wood-burning oven for summer BBQs. Menus feature British classics and some Mediterranean influences. Individually decorated bedrooms are accessed via narrow, sloping corridors.

Carte £ 26/46

13 rooms – £ 70/80 £ 90/160

TN22 3SS – 01825 722890 – www.thegriffininn.co.uk – Closed 25 December

FOLKESTONE

Kent – Pop. 51 337 – Regional map n° **5**-D2

Rocksalt

SEAFOOD • DESIGN XX Set within a stylish harbourfront eco-building affording lovely sea views. Smart cantilevered dining room with full-length windows opening onto a terrace; semi open air bar upstairs. Menus mix seafood and local meats; veg is from their farm. Nearby, bedrooms boast antique beds, Egyptian cotton linen and wet rooms.

Menu £ 25 (weekday lunch) – Carte £ 31/56

4 rooms – £ 85/115 £ 85/115

4-5 Fish Market CT19 6AA – 01303 212070 – www.rocksaltfolkestone.co.uk – Closed Sunday dinner

10 to12 Folkestone

TOWNHOUSE • MODERN Classic Victorian end-of-terrace house, close to the seafront. It's run by friendly owners and is the perfect place to stop before getting the ferry. Bedrooms are particularly spacious and are appointed in a simple, modern manner.

10 rooms – £ 100/120 £ 110/130

10-12 Langhorne Gdns CT20 2EA – 01303 210127 – www.10to12folkestone.co.uk – Closed 1 week Christmas

FOLKSWORTH

Cambridgeshire – Pop. 881 – Regional map n° **8**-A2

The Fox at Folksworth N

MODERN CUISINE • CONTEMPORARY DÉCOR The Fox's dining room is hung with chandeliers and its light, bright bar is filled with designer furniture and has sliding doors which open onto a huge terrace. Dine on pub favourites or more creative modern dishes.

Carte £ 20/38

34 Manor Rd PE7 3SU – 01733 242867 – www.clarkespeterborough.co.uk – Closed Sunday dinner

FONTHILL BISHOP

Wiltshire – Regional map n° **2**-C2

Riverbarn

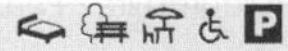

MODERN CUISINE • SIMPLE X Two riverside cottages in a characterful village. Dining takes place in a series of beamed, low-ceilinged rooms adorned with copper pans and prints. Two brothers create carefully prepared, flavoursome dishes, which their parents bring to the table. Simple, comfortable bedrooms are found in the old barn.

Menu £ 20 (lunch) – Carte £ 30/47

4 rooms – £ 75/125 £ 90/195

SP3 5SF – 01747 820232 (bookings advisable at dinner) – www.theriverbarn.org.uk – lunch only and dinner Thursday-Saturday – Closed 22 December-mid January, except 25 December and Monday

FONTMELL MAGNA

Dorset - Pop. 333 - Regional map n° **2**-C3

Fontmell

MODERN CUISINE • PUB Stylish, modern pub with a simple front bar; the smart dining room straddles the brook, so keep an eye out for otters. Daily menus offer an eclectic mix of carefully executed dishes, from Mediterranean to Thai. Bedrooms are named after butterflies; Mallyshag is particularly spacious, with a roll-top bath.

Carte £ 22/50

6 rooms - £ 75/165 £ 85/175

SP7 0PA - 01747 811441 - www.thefontmell.com - Closed 1-15 January

FORDHAM

Cambridgeshire - Regional map n° **8**-B2

White Pheasant

MODERN CUISINE • SIMPLE An enthusiastic chef-owner runs this cosy former pub in the centre of the village. Cooking is all-encompassing, including everything from well-presented classics to creative modern dishes.

Carte £ 28/51

21 Market St CB7 5LQ - 01638 720414 - www.whitepheasant.com - Closed first week January, Sunday dinner and Monday

FORDINGBRIDGE

Hampshire - Pop. 4 474 - Regional map n° **4**-A2

Three Lions

FAMILY • COSY A former farmhouse and pub in a small hamlet. Homely bedrooms are split between this and various outbuildings; those in the garden are the largest and come with French windows and outdoor seating. Blackboard menus offer classically inspired Anglo-French dishes crafted from local, seasonal produce.

7 rooms - £ 79 £ 125

Stuckton Rd, Stuckton SP6 2HF - Southeast : 1 mi by B 3078 - 01425 652489 - www.thethreelionsrestaurant.co.uk - Closed last 2 weeks February

FOWEY

Cornwall - Pop. 2 131 - Regional map n° **1**-B2

Q

MODERN CUISINE • INTIMATE Ask for a window seat or head to the terrific waterside terrace of this romantic hotel restaurant. Dinner is the main event, with modern takes on old classics: presentation is colourful and provenance is key.

Menu £ 29/40

Old Quay House Hotel, 28 Fore St PL23 1AQ - 01726 833302 - www.theoldquayhouse.com - Closed lunch October-April except 24 December-2 January

The Globe 

TRADITIONAL BRITISH • COSY A 400 year old posting house run by lifelong friends and refurbished by local craftsmen. The food keeps things pleasingly regional too, with bread from the adjacent bakery, fish from the nearby harbour, meats from a local farm and beer from St Austell. Bedrooms are comfy and cosy.

Menu £ 20 (weekday lunch) - Carte £ 27/44

4 rooms - £ 50/120 £ 50/150

19 Fore St PL23 1AQ - 01726 337076 - www.theglobefowey.co.uk - Closed 2 January-9 February

Fowey Hall

COUNTRY HOUSE · PERSONALISED A striking 19C manor house with an ornate lounge and a mix of traditional and modern bedrooms. It's set high above the village and has lovely views. Families are well-catered for and an informal feel pervades. There's an oak-panelled restaurant reserved for adults and a conservatory for those with children.

36 rooms – †£ 190/690 ††£ 190/690

Hanson Dr ✉ PL23 1ET – West : 0.5 mi off A 3082 – ✆ 01726 833866 – www.foweyhallhotel.co.uk

Old Quay House

TOWNHOUSE · CONTEMPORARY A 19C seamen's mission in a pretty harbour village; now a boutique hotel with a laid-back feel and a lovely riverside terrace. Bedrooms have an understated modern style; most have balconies and water views.

11 rooms – †£ 165/205 ††£ 195/340

28 Fore St ✉ PL23 1AQ – ✆ 01726 833302 – www.theoldquayhouse.com

Q – See restaurant listing

at Golant North: 3 mi by B3269 ✉ Fowey

Cormorant

COUNTRY HOUSE · PERSONALISED Well-run hotel in a superb waterside position. At only one room deep, all of its bedrooms overlook the estuary; the superior rooms boast balconies. Appealing seasonal menus feature local meats and seafood dishes. Light lunches offered in the formal restaurant or on the terrace.

14 rooms – †£ 85/195 ††£ 85/215

✉ PL23 1LL – ✆ 01726 833426 – www.cormoranthotel.co.uk

FOXHAM

Wiltshire – Regional map n° **2**-C2

Foxham Inn

CLASSIC CUISINE · SIMPLE Family-run pub in a sleepy Wiltshire village. A semi-covered terrace overlooks the fields and inside there's a cosy bar and a light, airy restaurant in a conservatory extension. Dishes are uniformly priced, and everything from the condiments to the ice creams is homemade. Bedrooms are warm and homely.

Carte £ 28/43

2 rooms – †£ 75 ††£ 90

✉ SN15 4NQ – ✆ 01249 740665 (booking advisable) – www.thefoxhaminn.co.uk – Closed 2 weeks early January, Sunday dinner and Monday

FREATHY

Cornwall – Regional map n° **1**-C2

The View

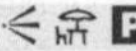

MODERN BRITISH · SIMPLE Charming and informal converted café perched on a cliff, with coastal views. Relaxed daytime vibe; more atmospheric in the evening. Assured, confident, generous cooking and friendly service. Plenty of seafood and tasty homemade bread.

Menu £ 15 (lunch) – Carte £ 33/42

✉ PL10 1JY – East : 1 mi – ✆ 01752 822345 – www.theview-restaurant.co.uk – Closed 1-14 February, Monday and Tuesday

FRILSHAM – West Berkshire → See Yattendon

FRITHSDEN

Hertfordshire – Regional map n° **7**-A2

Alford Arms

TRADITIONAL BRITISH • INN Attractive Victorian pub beside the village green. The traditional British menu follows the seasons closely, with salads and fish featuring in the summer and game and comfort dishes in the winter; go for one of the tempting specials.

Carte £ 22/41

HP1 3DD – 01442 864480 – www.alfordarmsfrithsden.co.uk – Closed 25-26 December

FROGGATT

Derbyshire – Regional map n° **9**-A1

Chequers Inn

TRADITIONAL BRITISH • PUB Traditional 16C inn built right into the stone boulders of Froggatt Edge and boasting a direct path up to the peak. Cooking is unfussy, tasty and largely classical, with more imaginative specials on the blackboard. Comfortable bedrooms; Number One, to the rear, is the quietest.

Carte £ 26/38

7 rooms – †£ 125/135 ††£ 125/135

Hope Valley S32 3ZJ – On A 625 – 01433 630231 – www.chequers-froggatt.com – Closed 25 December

FROME

Somerset – Pop. 26 203 – Regional map n° **2**-C2

Babington House

LUXURY • TRENDY Behind this country house's classic Georgian façade is a cool, fashionable hotel with bold colour schemes, modern understated bedrooms and a bohemian feel. Unwind in the luxurious lounges or in the beautiful spa with its superb fitness area and pool. The Orangery offers an accessible menu of Italian-influenced dishes which showcase ingredients from the walled garden.

32 rooms – †£ 245/370 ††£ 395/495 – £ 17 – 11 suites

Babington BA11 3RW – Northwest : 6.5 mi by A 362 on Vobster rd – 01373 812266 – www.babingtonhouse.co.uk

FULLER STREET

Essex – Pop. 50 – Regional map n° **7**-C2

Square & Compasses

TRADITIONAL BRITISH • PUB A hugely characterful pub hidden down rural lanes: run with a passion by its welcoming owners. One menu lists classic dishes; the other features more adventurous choices, including fish caught off the Essex coast and local game in season.

Carte £ 19/33

CM3 2BB – 01245 361477 – www.thesquareandcompasses.co.uk

FULMER

Buckinghamshire – Pop. 230 – Regional map n° **6**-D3

Black Horse

TRADITIONAL BRITISH • PUB Whitewashed village pub with thick walls, cosy alcoves, a wood-burning stove and a gem of a garden for sunny days. The stylish, formal dining area is hung with delightful portraits. Dishes include sharing boards, small plates and grills. Uniquely styled bedrooms have spacious, modern bathrooms.

Carte £ 24/44

2 rooms – †£ 120/150 ††£ 120/150

Windmill Rd SL3 6HD – 01753 663183 – www.theblackhorsefulmer.co.uk – Closed 25 December and Sunday dinner

FUNTINGTON - West Sussex ➔ See Chichester

See Chichester

FYFIELD

Oxfordshire - Regional map n° **6**-B2

White Hart

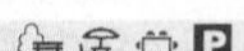

TRADITIONAL BRITISH • PUB An intriguing 15C chantry house with a cosy open-fired bar, a minstrels' gallery and an impressive three-storey high vaulted dining room; not forgetting a pleasant terrace. The diverse range of dishes is guided by produce from the vegetable plot. Save room for one of the excellent desserts.

Menu £ 17 (weekday lunch) - Carte £ 26/53

Main Rd ✉ OX13 5LW - ✆ 01865 390585 - www.whitehart-fyfield.com - Closed Monday except bank holidays and Sunday lunch

FYFIELD

Essex - Pop. 737 - Regional map n° **7**-B2

Queens Head

MODERN CUISINE • PUB Characterful village pub with a pretty rear garden leading down to the river. The inviting interior features original 16C beams and fireplaces. Menus change regularly and offer a good choice of classics and blackboard specials.

Menu £ 17 (weekdays) - Carte £ 31/45

Queen St ✉ CM5 0RY - ✆ 01277 899231 - www.thequeensheadfyfield.co.uk - Closed 26 December and Mondays

GERRARDS CROSS

Buckinghamshire - Pop. 20 633 - Regional map n° **6**-D3

Three Oaks

MODERN BRITISH • PUB An appealing, well-run pub in a rural location, comprising several different areas: dine in the brighter room overlooking the terrace and pretty garden. Cooking is tasty, satisfying and seasonal, and they offer particularly good value set lunch and dinner menus. The bright young staff are eager to please.

Menu £ 19 (weekdays) - Carte £ 24/37

Austenwood Ln ✉ SL9 8NL - Northwest : 0.75 mi by A 413 on Gold Hill rd - ✆ 01753 899016 (booking advisable) - www.thethreeoaksgx.co.uk - Closed Sunday dinner

GISBURN

Lancashire - Regional map n° **11**-B2

La Locanda

ITALIAN • NEIGHBOURHOOD A charming low-beamed, flag-floored restaurant run by a keen couple: a little corner of Italy in Lancashire. Extensive menu of hearty homemade dishes; try the tasty pastas. Top quality local and imported produce; well-chosen wine list.

Carte £ 21/35

Main St ✉ BB7 4HH - ✆ 01200 445303 - www.lalocanda.co.uk - Closed 25 December, 1 January and lunch Monday-Wednesday

Park House

TOWNHOUSE • CLASSIC Imposing Victorian house with a classical open-fired drawing room and a small library leading to a hidden stepped garden. Bedrooms mix antique and more modern furnishings. Good breakfast selection; tea and homemade cake served on arrival.

6 rooms - †£ 55/110 ††£ 65/125

13 Church View ✉ BB7 4HG - ✆ 01200 445269 - www.parkhousegisburn.co.uk - Closed 26 November-14 February

GLINTON - Peterborough → See Peterborough

GODSHILL - Isle of Wight → See Wight (Isle of)

GOLANT Cornwall → See Fowey

GOREY → See Channel Islands (Jersey)

GORING

Oxfordshire – Pop. 4 193 – Regional map n° **6**-B3

Miller of Mansfield

MODERN BRITISH · FRIENDLY Large 18C inn close to the Thames; sit in the cosy bar rooms, the dining room or out on the terrace. Dishes range from homemade sausage rolls to poached lobster salad; the homemade bread and desserts are a highlight. Bedrooms blend modern furnishings with original features.

Menu £ 18 (lunch) – Carte £ 30/46

13 rooms – †£ 90/180 ††£ 90/180

High St ✉ RG8 9AW

– ✆ 01491 872829 – www.millerofmansfield.com

GRANGE-OVER-SANDS

Cumbria – Pop. 4 788 – Regional map n° **12**-A3

Clare House 

FAMILY · PERSONALISED Family-run Victorian house set in lovely gardens, overlooking Morecambe Bay. Two classical sitting rooms. Stylish, boldly coloured bedrooms in the main house and smaller, simpler rooms with balconies in the wing. The smart, modern dining room offers traditional daily menus.

18 rooms (dinner included) – †£ 76/133 ††£ 152/180

Park Rd ✉ LA11 7HQ

– ✆ 015395 33026 – www.clarehousehotel.co.uk – Closed mid December-mid March

at Cartmel Northwest: 3 mi ✉ Grange-Over-Sands

✿✿ L'Enclume (Simon Rogan)

CREATIVE · HISTORIC XXX Set in the centre of a sleepy Lakeland village, this characterful old smithy is a destination in itself. Produce from their farm – including some unusual vegetables and leaves – guides the well-balanced, perfectly paced set menu. Confidently prepared, innovative dishes are full of interest, and flavours are understated and harmonious. Bedrooms are spread about the village.

→ Artichoke with stout and Ragstone. Turbot marinated in fermented rice bran, kale shoots and shrimp cream. Pear, sweet cheese and hazelnut.

Menu £ 55/145 – tasting menu only

16 rooms – †£ 130/175 ††£ 180/435

Cavendish St ✉ LA11 6PZ

– ✆ 015395 36362 (booking essential) – www.lenclume.co.uk – Closed 2 weeks January and Monday

Rogan & Company

MODERN BRITISH · NEIGHBOURHOOD X The informal cousin to L'Enclume, set in a converted cottage by a lovely stream. The rustic, open-plan interior has dark wood beams and you can watch the chefs at the kitchen pass. Modern dishes rely on local, seasonal produce.

Menu £ 26 (lunch) – Carte £ 33/49

The Square ✉ LA11 6QD

– ✆ 015395 35917 – www.roganandcompany.co.uk – Closed 2 weeks January

GRANTHAM

Lincolnshire - Pop. 41 998 - Regional map n° **9**-C2

Harry's Place

TRADITIONAL BRITISH • COSY XX Long-standing, intimate restaurant in a former farmhouse: it consists of just 3 tables and is personally run by a dedicated and delightful husband and wife team. Warm, welcoming feel, with fresh flowers, candles and antiques. Classically based menus offer 2 choices per course. Good cheese selection.

Carte £ 59/73

17 High St, Great Gonerby ✉ NG31 8JS - Northwest : 2 mi on B 1174 - ✆ 01476 561780 (booking essential) - Closed 2 weeks August, Christmas-New Year, Sunday and Monday

at Hough-on-the-Hill North: 6.75 mi by A607 ✉ Grantham

Brownlow Arms

MODERN BRITISH • INN XX Characterful former shooting lodge for the nearby Belton Estate, with wood-panelled walls and large open fireplaces. Lengthy menu and specials list offer classically based dishes with modern presentation. Lovely terrace and friendly service. Delightful bedrooms are furnished with contemporary fabrics and period pieces.

Carte £ 28/48

5 rooms - †£ 75 ††£ 120

High Rd ✉ NG32 2AZ - ✆ 01400 250234 - www.thebrownlowarms.com - Closed 25-26 December, 1 January, Sunday dinner-Tuesday lunch and bank holidays

GRASMERE

Cumbria - Regional map n° **12**-A2

Forest Side

MODERN BRITISH • CHIC XX Sit in deep leather armchairs and take in the view over the 48 acre hotel grounds. With produce originating from the walled garden and foraged from the surrounding area, their strapline 'inspired by the Cumbrian landscape' is spot on. Scandic-style dishes are creative and modern with a deceptive simplicity.

→ Duck heart salad. Line-caught halibut. Scorched pear.

Menu £ 35/85

Forest Side Hotel, Keswick Rd ✉ LA22 9RN - On A 591 - ✆ 015394 35250 (booking advisable) - www.theforestside.com - Closed lunch Monday and Tuesday

Dining Room

MODERN CUISINE • CHIC XX Split-roomed hotel restaurant in a Victorian house, with a pleasant conservatory overlooking the garden. The concise daily menu features interesting modern dishes crafted from seasonal Lakeland produce; everything is made in-house.

Menu £ 28 (lunch) - Carte £ 36/50

Oak Bank Hotel, Broadgate ✉ LA22 9TA - ✆ 015394 35217 (booking essential) - www.lakedistricthotel.co.uk - Closed 2-18 January and 16-26 December

Rothay Garden

COUNTRY HOUSE • CONTEMPORARY Slate-built Lakeland house with modern extensions, which include a spa and a copper-roofed conservatory restaurant with a lovely outlook and a classically based menu. Bedrooms are stylish and contemporary - many have king-sized beds and some have balconies or patios; the Loft Suites are the best.

30 rooms - †£ 115/195 ††£ 160/310

Broadgate ✉ LA22 9RJ - ✆ 015394 35334 - www.rothaygarden.com

Forest Side

COUNTRY HOUSE • ELEGANT Enjoy afternoon tea in the elegant fire-lit lounge while admiring the view over the deer-filled grounds towards the mountains. Both the guest areas and bedrooms have a modern country house style and there's a laid back feel throughout.

20 rooms – †£ 189/329 ††£ 209/349

Keswick Rd ✉ LA22 9RN – On A 591 – ✆ 015394 35250 – www.theforestside.com

✿ **Forest Side** – See restaurant listing

Grasmere

TRADITIONAL • PERSONALISED This welcoming Victorian country house sits close to the village centre and comes with original features and traditional décor. The bright bedrooms are named after writers and are immaculately kept. The dining room overlooks the garden and the River Rothay which meanders through it.

11 rooms – †£ 66/72 ††£ 122/134

Broadgate ✉ LA22 9TA – ✆ 015394 35277 – www.grasmerehotel.co.uk – Restricted opening in winter

Moss Grove Organic

COUNTRY HOUSE • MODERN Laid-back house with a stylish interior featuring many reclaimed furnishings. Funky bedrooms boast large beds, Bose sound systems and whirlpool baths. Organic breakfasts include tasty veggie options; help yourself from the kitchen.

11 rooms – †£ 79/164 ††£ 94/265

✉ LA22 9SW – ✆ 015394 35251 – www.mossgrove.com – Closed 24-25 December

Oak Bank

TRADITIONAL • PERSONALISED Passionately run Victorian house with a pretty rear garden. Relax beside the converted range in the sitting room or next to the open fire in the lounge-bar. Modern bedrooms have comfortable beds, bold fabrics and bright colours.

13 rooms – †£ 80/135 ††£ 98/189

Broadgate ✉ LA22 9TA – ✆ 015394 35217 – www.lakedistricthotel.co.uk – Closed 2-18 January and 16-26 December

Dining Room – See restaurant listing

GRASSINGTON

North Yorkshire – ✉ Skipton – Pop. 1 126 – Regional map n° **13**-A2

Grassington House

MODERN BRITISH • BRASSERIE XX Georgian house with a large bar-lounge, two dining rooms and delightful service. Classical menus display Mediterranean touches and include their home-bred pork. Smart, modern bedrooms; No.6 has a roll-top bath in the room. Home-cured bacon or sausages are offered at breakfast and they host regular wine dinners.

Menu £ 18 (lunch and early dinner) – Carte £ 25/55

9 rooms – †£ 108/150 ††£ 125/235

5 The Square ✉ BD23 5AQ – ✆ 01756 752406 – www.grassingtonhouse.co.uk – Closed 25 December

GREAT BIRCHAM

Norfolk – Regional map n° **8**-C1

King's Head

INN • PERSONALISED This family run inn dates from the Edwardian era and is well-located for the north Norfolk coast and the Sandringham Estate. Individually decorated bedrooms are contemporary in style. Enjoy a pub classic and a G&T from the 'gin wall' in the cosy bar or choose from more modern dishes in the restaurant.

12 rooms – †£ 75/155 ††£ 75/175

✉ PE31 6RJ – ✆ 01485 578265 – www.thekingsheadcountryhotel.com

GREAT LIMBER

Lincolnshire – Pop. 271 – Regional map n° **9**-C1

New Inn

MODERN CUISINE • INN Smart modern pub with a stylish terrace. The bar is a hit with the locals, while the lounge is the perfect spot for a fireside G&T before dinner in the contemporary restaurant. Carefully prepared, sophisticated dishes have a modern touch. Smart bedrooms exceed expectations; some are in a barn conversion.

Carte £ 26/41

10 rooms – †£ 89 ††£ 99/135

2 High St ⊠ DN37 8JL – ✆ 01469 569998 – www.thenewinngreatlimber.co.uk – Closed Sunday dinner and Monday lunch

GREAT MALVERN

Worcestershire – Pop. 36 770 – Regional map n° **10**-B3

L' Amuse Bouche

TRADITIONAL CUISINE • CONTEMPORARY DÉCOR XX Start with an aperitif in the stylish bar or traditional lounge of this Gothic hotel, then head for the contemporary dining room overlooking the gardens. Boldly flavoured, classically based dishes have a subtle modern touch.

Carte £ 32/46

Cotford Hotel, 51 Graham Rd ⊠ WR14 2HU – ✆ 01684 572427 – www.cotfordhotel.co.uk – dinner only and Sunday lunch

Cotford

TOWNHOUSE • CONTEMPORARY The owners of this 1851 Gothic-style house (built for the Bishop of Worcester), put a lot of effort into getting things right. It mixes the traditional and the contemporary and has stylish bedrooms and a chic black and pink bar.

15 rooms – †£ 75/95 ††£ 140/155

51 Graham Rd ⊠ WR14 2HU – ✆ 01684 572427 – www.cotfordhotel.co.uk

L' Amuse Bouche – See restaurant listing

at Welland Southeast: 5 mi on B4208

The Inn at Welland

TRADITIONAL BRITISH • CONTEMPORARY DÉCOR The owners have turned this pub from wreck to "by 'eck!" Inside it's light, open and stylish, with charming features and designer touches; outside there's a landscaped garden and a smart decked terrace. Pub classics sit alongside more adventurous dishes – all tasty, generous of portion and sensibly priced.

Carte £ 25/44

Hook Bank ⊠ WR13 6LN – East : 1 mi on A 4104 – ✆ 01684 592317 – www.theinnatwelland.co.uk – Closed 25-26 December, 31 December-2 January, Sunday dinner and Monday

GREAT MILTON – Oxfordshire → See Oxford

GREAT MISSENDEN

Buckinghamshire – Pop. 7 980 – Regional map n° **6**-C2

Nags Head

TRADITIONAL BRITISH • PUB Traditional 15C inn whose features include original oak beams, thick brick walls and an inglenook fireplace. Gallic charm mixes with British classics on the interesting menus and service is keen and cheerful. Bedrooms are stylish and modern (Number One is the best), and breakfasts are tasty.

Carte £ 27/51

6 rooms – †£ 85/115 ††£ 95/135

London Rd ⊠ HP16 0DG – Southeast : 1.5 mi by A 413 and Holmer Green rd. – ✆ 01494 862200 – www.nagsheadbucks.com – Closed 25 December

GREAT OXENDON

Northamptonshire – Regional map n° **9**-B3

The George

MODERN BRITISH · FASHIONABLE XX An experienced chef has transformed this roadside inn by creating a modern country house lounge and a lovely New England style dining room complete with glass doors opening onto the pretty terrace and garden. Classically based British dishes have an unfussy modern style. Bedrooms are bright and contemporary.

Carte £ 22/35

7 rooms – £ 75 £ 120

Harborough Rd ✉ LE16 8NA
– ✆ 01858 452286 – www.thegeorgegreatoxendon.co.uk – Closed Christmas

GREAT TEW

Oxfordshire – Pop. 145 – Regional map n° **6**-B1

Soho Farmhouse

RESORT · DESIGN Set in 100 acres of rolling countryside, this exclusive resort offers everything you could want. Luxurious self-contained cabins are dotted about the estate and come with wellies and bikes. There's a range of different restaurants and breakfast is transported on a milk float and cooked outside your door. Unwind in the stunning spa or the outside pool set within a lake.

44 rooms – £ 350 £ 350 – £ 13 – 18 suites

✉ OX7 4JS – South 0.75 mi by New Rd and Ledwell Ln. – ✆ 01608 691000
– www.sohofarmhouse.com

GREAT YELDHAM

Essex – Pop. 1 844 – Regional map n° **7**-C2

White Hart

MODERN BRITISH · ROMANTIC XX Charming 16C house with a characterful interior. The open-fired bar with its wonky floors and exposed beams serves unfussy favourites, while the elegant restaurant (open later in the week) offers a refined modern menu of skilfully prepared dishes. Bedrooms are stylish and comfortable.

Carte £ 30/49

13 rooms – £ 70/90 £ 90/180

Poole St ✉ CO9 4HJ – ✆ 01787 237250 (booking advisable)
– www.whitehartyeldham.co.uk – Closed 1-18 January, dinner 25-26 December, Monday, Tuesday and lunch Wednesday

GREEN ISLAND → See Channel Islands (Jersey)

GREETHAM

Rutland – Regional map n° **9**-C2

Wheatsheaf Inn

TRADITIONAL BRITISH · FAMILY The aroma of fresh bread greets you at this simple, family-friendly country pub. Cooking is unfussy and traditional; cheaper cuts keep prices sensible and desserts are a must. It's run by a charming couple.

Carte £ 23/34

1 Stretton Rd ✉ LE15 7NP – ✆ 01572 812325 – www.wheatsheaf-greetham.co.uk
– Closed first 2 weeks January, Sunday dinner and Monday except bank holidays

GRETA BRIDGE - Durham ➔ See Barnard Castle

GRIMSTON - Norfolk ➔ See King's Lynn

GROUVILLE ➔ See Channel Islands (Jersey)

GUILDFORD

Surrey - Pop. 77 057 - Regional map n° **4**-C1

at Shere East: 6.75 mi by A246 off A25 ✉ Guildford

Kinghams

MODERN BRITISH • RUSTIC XX Characterful 17C creeper-clad cottage with a cosy low-beamed interior and a pleasant terrace. Cooking has a classic foundation, with plenty of fish specials and game in season. The good value 2 course menu includes a side dish too.

Menu £ 19 (weekdays) - Carte £ 32/40

Gomshall Ln ✉ GU5 9HE - ✆ 01483 202168 - www.kinghams-restaurant.co.uk - Closed 25 December-5 January, Sunday dinner and Monday

GULWORTHY - Devon ➔ See Tavistock

GUNTHORPE

Nottinghamshire - Pop. 646 - Regional map n° **9**-B2

Tom Brown's Brasserie

MODERN CUISINE • BRASSERIE X Stylish modern restaurant in an old Victorian schoolhouse beside the river. Tables are spread over several different areas - including a mezzanine - and the team are friendly and efficient. Dishes are fresh, tasty and well-presented.

Menu £ 19 (lunch and early dinner) - Carte £ 26/50

The Old School House, Trentside ✉ NG14 7FB - ✆ 0115 966 3642 - www.tombrowns.co.uk - Closed dinner 25-26 December and 1 January

GURNARD ➔ See Wight (Isle of)

HADLEIGH

Suffolk - Pop. 8 150 - Regional map n° **8**-C3

Hadleigh Ram

MODERN CUISINE • RUSTIC Smart, modern pub with a formal feel. Brunch is served from 10am-2pm, while the extensive à la carte covers everything from interesting bar snacks and sharing boards to Shetland mussels several ways and 21 day dry-aged local steaks. Fish dishes are a strength and desserts keep things pleasingly traditional.

Menu £ 17/24 (weekdays) - Carte £ 24/37

5 Market Pl ✉ IP7 5DL - ✆ 01473 822880 - www.thehadleighram.co.uk - Closed Sunday dinner

Edge Hall

TOWNHOUSE • CLASSIC A lovely Queen Anne style house with a Georgian brick façade, dating from 1453 and supposedly the oldest house in town. Bedrooms are spacious and furnished with antiques. The breakfast room overlooks the delightful garden.

6 rooms - †£ 55/70 ††£ 100/150

2 High St ✉ IP7 5AP - ✆ 01473 822458 - www.edgehall.co.uk - Closed 23-29 December

HALFORD

Warwickshire – Pop. 301 – Regional map n° **10**-C3

Old Manor House

COUNTRY HOUSE • HISTORIC Characterful part-timbered house in a pleasant spot next to the River Stour. Well-appointed drawing room with garden views and an antique-furnished breakfast room with a large inglenook. Appealing period style bedrooms have rich fabrics.

3 rooms – £ 65/85 £ 100/110

Queens St ✉ CV36 5BT
– ✆ 01789 740264 – www.oldmanor-halford.co.uk

HALIFAX

West Yorkshire – Pop. 88 134 – Regional map n° **13**-B2

Ricci's Tapas & Cicchetti

MEDITERRANEAN CUISINE • FASHIONABLE Buzzy restaurant on the Dean Clough mill complex. Sit on the spacious terrace, at a wooden table or on white leather stools at the wood and metal bar. The Spanish and Italian small plates are perfect for sharing.

Carte £ 13/28

F Mill, Ground Floor, Dean Clough, (Gate 9) ✉ HX3 5AX
– ✆ 01422 740001 – www.riccistapasandcicchetti.co.uk – Closed 25 December-1 January

Shibden Mill Inn

MODERN BRITISH • COSY A former corn mill set in a tranquil, deep-sided valley, with beamed ceilings, welcoming fires and lots of cosy corners. Menus offer plenty of choice, with pub favourites alongside more ambitious dishes. Well-drilled staff. Comfy, individually furnished bedrooms; choose Room 14 if it's luxury you're after.

Menu £ 15 (lunch and early dinner) **s** – Carte £ 26/39 **s**

11 rooms – £ 90/170 £ 95/230

Shibden Mill Fold ✉ HX3 7UL
– ✆ 01422 365840 – www.shibdenmillinn.com – Closed 25-26 December and 1 January

Holdsworth House

HISTORIC • COSY Attractive 17C property with beautiful gardens and a parterre within its old stone walls. Characterful rooms feature original wood panelling and mullioned windows; bedrooms are contemporary. The three-roomed restaurant offers a mix of homely classics and more refined dishes – all use local produce.

38 rooms – £ 85/150 £ 95/170

Holdsworth Rd ✉ HX2 9TG – North : 3 mi by A 629 and Shay Ln
– ✆ 01422 240024 – www.holdsworthhouse.co.uk

HALTWHISTLE

Northumberland – Pop. 3 791 – Regional map n° **14**-A2

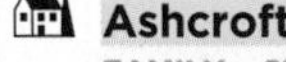

Ashcroft

FAMILY • CLASSIC A family-run early Victorian vicarage, with beautiful award-winning gardens. The spacious interior retains many of its original features and smoothly blends the classic with the contemporary. Some of the bedrooms have roof terraces.

9 rooms – £ 72/90 £ 84/110

Lantys Lonnen ✉ NE49 0DA
– ✆ 01434 320213 – www.ashcroftguesthouse.co.uk – Closed 25 December

HAMBLE-LE-RICE

Hampshire - Pop. 4 695 - Regional map n° **4**-B2

Bugle

TRADITIONAL BRITISH · PUB Set in a charming spot in a quaint little village, this Grade II listed building has views over the river and is popular with the sailing community. Choose from small plates, pub classics or more interesting dishes on the main menu.

Menu £ 18 (weekday lunch) - Carte £ 22/41 **s**

High St ✉ SO31 4HA - ✆ 023 8045 3000 (booking advisable) - www.idealcollection.co.uk/buglehamble - Closed 25 December

HAMBLETON - Rutland ➜ See Oakham

HAMPTON IN ARDEN

West Midlands - Pop. 1 678 - Regional map n° **10**-C2

Peel's

CREATIVE BRITISH · ELEGANT XXX This elegant dining room is situated within an impressive manor house and features beautiful plasterwork, oak panelling and hand-painted Chinoiserie wallpaper. Modern dishes come from a confident kitchen and feature refined, original combinations with some playful elements. Service is pitched perfectly.

➜ Asparagus with chicken, burrata and egg yolk. Monkfish with kohlrabi, miso and coriander. Blood orange with white chocolate 'Aero' and star anise.

Menu £ 50/85

Hampton Manor Hotel, Shadowbrook Ln ✉ B92 0DQ - ✆ 01675 446080 (booking essential) - www.hamptonmanor.com - dinner only - Closed Sunday and Monday

Hampton Manor

HISTORIC · GRAND LUXURY An early Victorian Gothic-style manor house set in 45 acres of mature grounds - it was built for Sir Robert Peel's son. Contemporary décor blends with characterful original plasterwork and wood panelling in various lounges and drawing rooms. Spacious bedrooms have a smart modern style and superb bathrooms.

15 rooms - †£ 160/350 ††£ 160/350 - ☕ £ 15 - 3 suites

Shadowbrook Ln ✉ B92 0DQ - ✆ 01675 446080 - www.hamptonmanor.com

Peel's - See restaurant listing

HAMPTON POYLE

Oxfordshire - Pop. 106 - Regional map n° **6**-B2

Bell at Hampton Poyle

MEDITERRANEAN CUISINE · PUB Passionately run pub with several comfy lounge areas and a chic restaurant. The open kitchen adds a buzz and the pizza oven and glass meat ageing fridge draw your eye. The menu covers many bases and has strong Mediterranean undertones. Stylish bedrooms are located above the bar and in a cottage.

Menu £ 10 (weekdays) - Carte £ 21/45

9 rooms ☕ - †£ 95/130 ††£ 120/175

11 Oxford Rd ✉ OX5 2QD - ✆ 01865 376242 - www.thebellathamptonpoyle.co.uk

HAROME - North Yorkshire ➜ See Helmsley

HARROGATE

North Yorkshire - Pop. 73 576 - Regional map n° **13**-B2

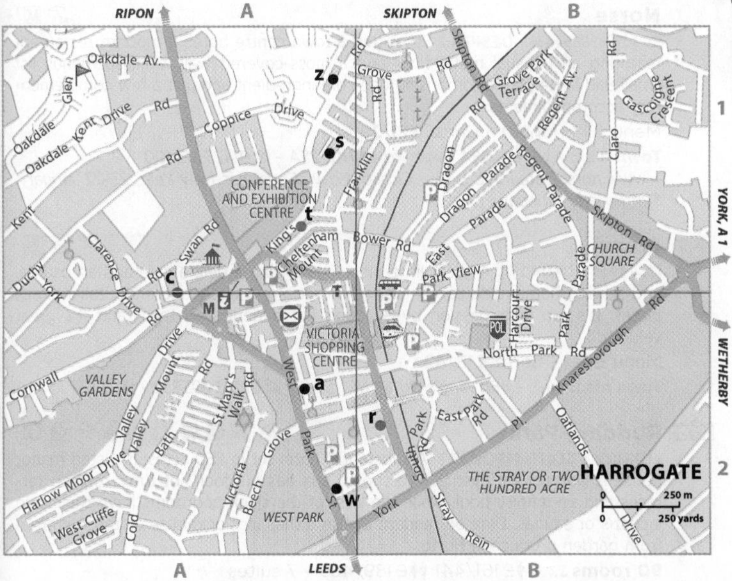

Horto

MODERN BRITISH • DESIGN XX This smart restaurant is set in Rudding Park's spa and has full-length windows overlooking the grounds. Choose between a concise fixed price menu and a tasting menu; much of the produce is picked from the garden each morning.

Menu £ 54/64

Rudding Park Hotel, Rudding Park, Follifoot ✉ HG3 1JH – Southeast : 3.75 mi by A 661
– ✆ 01423 871350 (booking essential) – www.ruddingpark.co.uk
– dinner only

Orchid

ASIAN • FASHIONABLE XX Below the chic cocktail bar is a spacious room with etched glass screens, Asian artefacts and a TV screening live kitchen action. The extensive pan-Asian menu indicates the dishes' origins and spiciness; Sunday lunch is a buffet.

Menu £ 15 (weekday lunch) – Carte £ 20/38

Town plan: A1-2-c – *28 Swan Rd ✉ HG1 2SE*
– ✆ 01423 560425 – www.orchidrestaurant.co.uk
– Closed 25-26 December and Saturday lunch

Restaurant 92

MODERN BRITISH • FASHIONABLE XX A large bay-windowed Victorian property in the town centre plays host to this modern restaurant with eye-catching chandeliers and marble-topped sewing machine tables. Ambitious dishes feature many different ingredients.

Menu £ 27 (lunch and early dinner) – Carte £ 35/51

Town plan: B2-r – *92-94 Station Par ✉ HG1 1HQ*
– ✆ 01423 503027 – www.restaurant92.co.uk
– Closed 1-17 January, Sunday dinner, Monday and Tuesday

Norse

SCANDINAVIAN • DESIGN Set within a town centre hotel; a modern restaurant featuring an unusual metal floor and a moss-covered wall. Concise menus list small and large plates comprising one core ingredient and just a few complementary accompaniments.

Menu £ 18 (lunch) - Carte £ 21/29

Town plan: A1-2-c - *28A Swan Rd ✉ HG1 2SA - ✆ 01423 313400 - www.norserestaurant.co.uk - Closed 4 days Christmas-New Year, 23-27 January, Sunday and Monday*

Stuzzi

ITALIAN • TRENDY A great little place comprising a deli, a café and an osteria, and serving homemade cakes, topped focaccia and fresh, authentic Italian small plates. It's run with passion by a young but experienced team and it's great value too.

Menu £ 30 - Carte £ 18/42

Town plan: A1-t - *46b King's Rd ✉ HG1 5JW - ✆ 01423 705852*

Rudding Park

LUXURY • CONTEMPORARY A substantial hotel set in 250 acres; its listed manor house is popular for events. The superb spa has outdoor hot tubs, rooftop terraces and an infinity pool, while the best of the sleek bedrooms have their own jacuzzis or saunas. Dine on modern British dishes in Clockhouse or those crafted from garden produce in Horto.

90 rooms - †£ 161/441 ††£ 189/469 - 7 suites

Rudding Park, Follifoot ✉ HG3 1JH - Southeast : 3.75 mi by A 661 - ✆ 01423 871350 - www.ruddingpark.com

Horto - See restaurant listing

Hotel du Vin

TOWNHOUSE • DESIGN Smart hotel with a small basement spa, set in a terrace of Georgian houses overlooking the green. Inside it has a stylish, boutique-style feel; the attic rooms boast huge bathrooms with 'his and hers' roll-top baths. Have a drink at the smart zinc bar before dinner in the chic French bistro or the courtyard.

49 rooms - †£ 110/360 ††£ 110/360 - £ 17

Town plan: A2-a - *Prospect Pl ✉ HG1 1LB - ✆ 01423 856800 - www.hotelduvin.com*

West Park

INN • CONTEMPORARY It might still look like a pub but once inside you'll find a stylish, contemporary hotel. Bedrooms have the latest mod cons, including coffee machines; the suites overlook the park and have small balconies. The lively open-plan bar and modern restaurant serve an extensive list of brasserie favourites.

25 rooms - †£ 125/200 ††£ 145/225 - 2 suites

Town plan: A2-w - *19 West Park Rd ✉ HG1 1BJ - ✆ 01423 524471 - www.thewestparkhotel.com*

Ascot House

TOWNHOUSE • COSY A family-run Victorian property - once home to W H Baxter, inventor of the 'knapping' machine (used in road-making). Original features include ornate plasterwork, coving and an impressive stained glass window; floral fabrics and king-sized beds feature. The traditional restaurant has a classic menu to match.

19 rooms - †£ 59/109 ††£ 79/150

Town plan: A1-z - *53 King's Rd ✉ HG1 5HJ - ✆ 01423 531005 - www.ascothouse.com*

Brookfield House

TOWNHOUSE • CONTEMPORARY A well-run, three-storey Victorian townhouse on a quiet street. Modern bedrooms come in light hues: the first floor rooms are bright and airy, while the top floor rooms are cosy and intimate – all have fridges and ironing boards.

6 rooms – £ 75/95 £ 85/105

Town plan: A1-s – *5 Alexandra Rd ✉ HG1 5JS – ✆ 01423 506646 – www.brookfieldhousehotel.co.uk – Closed 2 weeks Christmas-New Year*

at Kettlesing West: 6.5 mi by A 59 ✉ Harrogate

Cold Cotes

TRADITIONAL • COSY A remote former farmhouse bordered by colourful gardens. Bedrooms are in the outbuildings: those in the barn are suites with lounges and private terraces. Local produce features at breakfast – try the bacon and onion relish sandwich.

7 rooms – £ 79/99 £ 89/109

Cold Cotes Rd, Felliscliffe ✉ HG3 2LW – West : 1 mi by A 59 – ✆ 01423 770937 – www.coldcotes.com – Closed February

HARTINGTON

Derbyshire – ✉ Buxton – Pop. 1 604 – Regional map n° **9**-A1

Biggin Hall

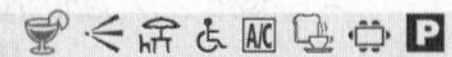

TRADITIONAL • COSY Characterful house with traditional, rustic appeal. Many guests follow the Tissington and High Peak Trails: bike storage and picnics are offered. Classical, low-beamed bedrooms in the main house; brighter rooms in the barns. Pleasant garden views and homely cooking in the dining room .

21 rooms – £ 70/130 £ 90/140

Biggin ✉ SK17 0DH – Southeast : 2 mi by B 5054 – ✆ 01298 84451 – www.bigginhall.co.uk

HARWICH

Essex – Pop. 19 738 – Regional map n° **7**-D2

The Pier

SEAFOOD • CONTEMPORARY DÉCOR XX This stylish 1st floor hotel brasserie boasts a terrific balcony with North Sea views. Seafood forms the foundation of the menu, with much landed locally. The chic bar has an impressive gin library.

Carte £ 27/60 **s**

The Pier Hotel, The Quay ✉ CO12 3HH – ✆ 01255 241212 – www.milsomhotels.com

The Pier

TOWNHOUSE • CONTEMPORARY A striking Victorian hotel by the quayside, built for rail travellers waiting to board their cruise liners and ideal if you're catching the ferry. Some of the stylish New England style bedrooms have views of the port. Dine on seafood dishes or Nordic-inspired snacks overlooking the pier.

14 rooms – £ 135/220 £ 135/220

The Quay ✉ CO12 3HH – ✆ 01255 241212 – www.milsomhotels.com

The Pier – See restaurant listing

HASELBURY PLUCKNETT

Somerset – Pop. 744 – Regional map n° **2**-B3

White Horse

MEDITERRANEAN CUISINE • PUB Traditional village pub with dried hops hung on exposed beams, a mix of wood and flagged floors, and a fire at either end. Most produce comes from within 50 miles; alongside British classics, you'll find Gallic and Mediterranean dishes.

Menu £ 17 – Carte £ 24/41

North St ✉ TA18 7RJ – ✆ 01460 78873 – www.thewhitehorsehaselbury.co.uk – Closed Sunday dinner, Monday and Tuesday

HASTINGS and ST LEONARDS

East Sussex – Pop. 91 053 – Regional map n° **5**-B3

Old Custom House

SEAFOOD • SIMPLE Built in 1725, this former Customs House is as small as they come. It's been designed to resemble the old net huts and the wooden blocks on the ceiling are from the old pier. The all-day menu offers small plates and a few main courses.

Carte £ 22/39

Town plan: C2-c – *19 East Par ✉ TN34 3AL*
– *☎ 01424 447724 (bookings not accepted)*
– *www.theoldcustomhousehastings.co.uk*
– *Closed Monday except bank holidays*

St Clements

MODERN CUISINE • BISTRO Pleasant neighbourhood restaurant decorated with local art. The lunch and midweek menus represent good value. Tasty modern European cooking is unfussy with a rustic edge and fish from the Hastings day boats plays a key role.

Menu £ 18/28 – Carte £ 28/46

Town plan: A2-a – *3 Mercatoria, St Leonards on Sea ✉ TN38 0EB*
– *☎ 01424 200355 – www.stclementsrestaurant.co.uk*
– *Closed 25-26 December, 1 January, Sunday dinner and Monday*

Webbe's Rock-a-Nore

SEAFOOD • BRASSERIE Bustling family-friendly restaurant on the promenade, boasting a large terrace overlooking the Stade. Sit at the marble-topped horseshoe counter to watch the chefs prepare small plates and classic dishes based on the latest catch.

Carte £ 23/38

Town plan: C2-x – *1 Rock-a-Nore ✉ TN34 3DW*
– *☎ 01424 721650 – www.webbesrestaurants.co.uk*
– *Closed 2-17 January*

Zanzibar

TOWNHOUSE • DESIGN An enthusiastically run Victorian seafront property with a stylish boutique interior. The chic restaurant faces the sea and leads through to a delightful tiered terrace. Bedrooms are named and themed after places the owner has visited on his travels; 'Japan' has an authentic small, square spa bath in the room.

8 rooms – †£ 99/199 ††£ 99/349

Town plan: A2-c – *9 Eversfield Pl ✉ TN37 6BY*
– *☎ 01424 460109 – www.zanzibarhotel.co.uk*

Old Rectory

TOWNHOUSE • ELEGANT A delightful Georgian house with beautiful tiered gardens, set next to the church at the bottom of the hill, just a short walk from the sea. No expense has been spared inside, with hand-painted feature walls, bespoke designer furnishings and luxurious styling. They smoke the fish and cure the bacon on-site.

8 rooms – †£ 90/115 ††£ 110/165

Town plan: C1-r – *Harold Rd, Old Town ✉ TN35 5ND*
– *☎ 01424 422410 – www.theoldrectoryhastings.co.uk*
– *Closed 2 weeks January and 1 week Christmas*

Large towns and cities have detailed maps showing restaurant and hotel locations. Use the coordinates (eg.6CX-u) to find them.

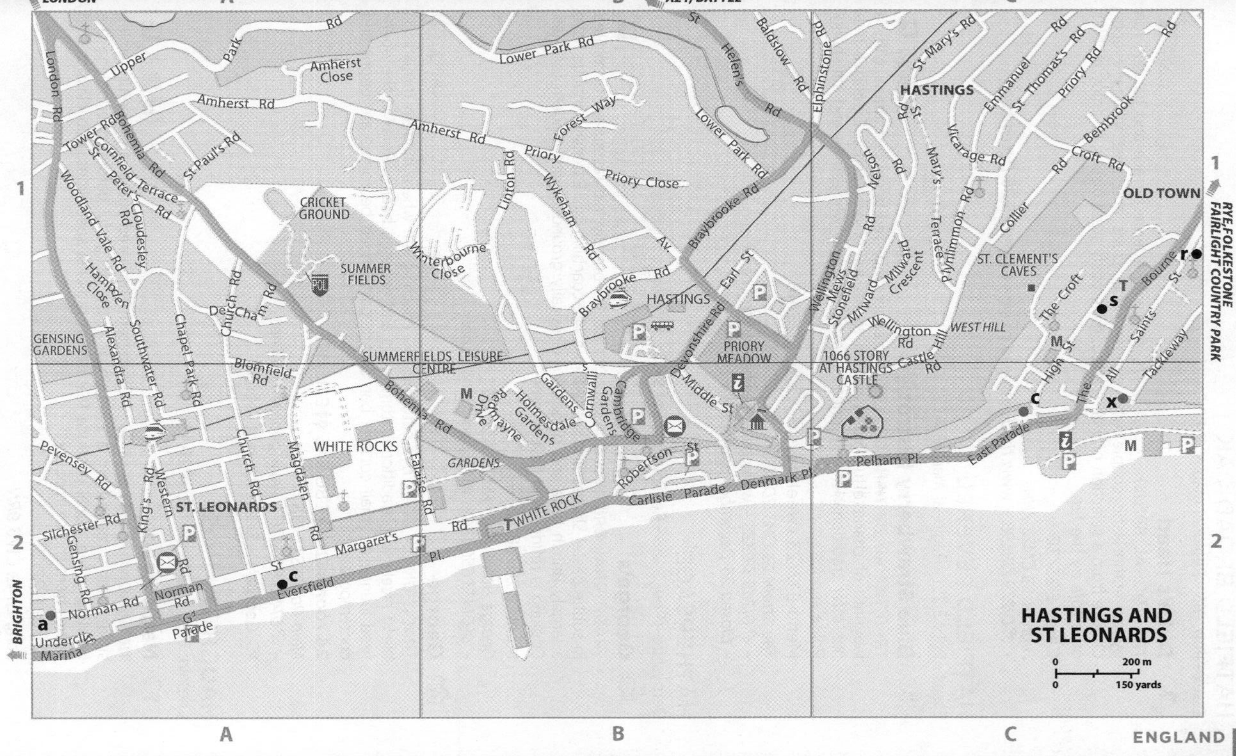

LONDON
HASTINGS AND ST LEONARDS
0 200 m
0 150 yards
RYE, FOLKESTONE
FAIRLIGHT COUNTRY PARK
BRIGHTON
OLD TOWN
HASTINGS
ST. CLEMENT'S CAVES
WEST HILL
1066 STORY AT HASTINGS CASTLE
PRIORY MEADOW
SUMMERFIELDS LEISURE CENTRE
SUMMER FIELDS
CRICKET GROUND
WHITE ROCKS
WHITE ROCK
GARDENS
GENSING GARDENS
ST. LEONARDS
Tackleway
All Saints' St
Bourne St
The Croft
High St
East Parade
Pelham Pl.
Denmark Pl.
Carlisle Parade
Robertson St
Middle St
Cambridge Gardens
Devonshire Rd
Earl St
Wellington Mews
Stonefield Rd
Milward Rd
Milward Crescent
Wellington Rd
Castle Hill Rd
Plynlimmon Rd
Collier Rd
Croft Rd
Bembrook Rd
Priory Rd
St Thomas's Rd
Emmanuel Rd
Vicarage Rd
St Mary's Terrace
St Mary's Rd
Nelson Rd
Elphinstone Rd
Baldslow Rd
St Helen's Rd
Lower Park Rd
Braybrooke Rd
Priory Close
Forest Way
Priory Av.
Wykeham Rd
Linton Rd
Amherst Rd
Amherst Close
Upper Park Rd
Winterbourne Close
Cornwallis Gardens
Holmesdale Gardens
Redmayne Drive
Bohemia Rd
Falaise Rd
Magdalen Rd
Eversfield Pl.
St Margaret's Rd
Church Rd
Blomfield Rd
De Cham Rd
St Paul's Rd
Chapel Park Rd
Southwater Rd
Alexandra Rd
Hampden Close
Woodland Vale Rd
Cloudesley Rd
St Peter's Rd
Cornfield Terrace
Tower Rd
London Rd
Western Rd
King's Rd
Norman Rd
Pevensey Rd
Silchester Rd
Gensing Rd
Undercliff
Marina
G' Parade
ENGLAND

HATFIELD BROAD OAK

Essex – Pop. 916 – Regional map n° **7**-B2

Duke's Head

TRADITIONAL BRITISH • COSY 17C pub with a large terrace and garden, run by an enthusiastic couple who support local clubs and host village events. Choose from a selection of well-crafted, generously sized dishes, or enjoy nibbles on a sofa by the fire.

Carte £ 23/36

High St ✉ CM22 7HH
– ✆ 01279 718598 – www.thedukeshead.co.uk – Closed 25-26 December

HATFIELD PEVEREL

Essex – Pop. 3 251 – Regional map n° **7**-C2

Blue Strawberry Bistrot

TRADITIONAL BRITISH • COSY XX A creeper-clad, red-brick restaurant with a labyrinth of characterful, old-fashioned rooms full of ornaments. Extensive menus offer traditional, keenly priced cooking which is wholesome and satisfying. Polite service.

Menu £ 17/23 (weekdays) – Carte £ 25/45

The Street ✉ CM3 2DW
– ✆ 01245 381333 – www.bluestrawberrybistrot.co.uk
– Closed 26 December and Sunday dinner

HATHERSAGE

Derbyshire – Pop. 2 018 – Regional map n° **9**-A1

George's

TRADITIONAL BRITISH • CLASSIC DÉCOR XX Formally laid restaurant decorated in subtle pastel shades and set within a 14C coaching inn. Extensive menus have a largely British base and dishes are classically grounded with modern touches. Cooking is refined and flavoursome.

Menu £ 20/38

George Hotel, Main Rd ✉ S32 1BB
– ✆ 01433 650436 – www.george-hotel.net

George

TRADITIONAL • COSY Eye-catching 14C coaching inn where modern furnishings blend nicely with traditional stone walls and exposed beams. Relax in the open-fired lounge or small cocktail bar. Smart, pastel-hued bedrooms are bright and contemporary.

24 rooms – † £ 80/145 †† £ 115/185

Main Rd ✉ S32 1BB
– ✆ 01433 650436 – www.george-hotel.net

George's – See restaurant listing

HAUGHTON MOSS

Cheshire East – Regional map n° **11**-A3

Nag's Head

TRADITIONAL BRITISH • PUB Characterful timbered pub in a peaceful hamlet; sit at a table made from a shotgun or in the delightful garden overlooking the bowling green. Local produce features in regional specialities, pub classics and dishes from the charcoal grill.

Carte £ 22/36

Long Ln ✉ CW6 9RN
– ✆ 01829 260265 – www.nagsheadhaughton.co.uk

HAWES

North Yorkshire – Pop. 887 – Regional map n° **13**-A1

Stone House

COUNTRY HOUSE • COSY Characterful stone house built in 1908. Guest areas include a pleasant drawing room with an oak-panelled fireplace and a small billiard-room-cum-library. Bedrooms vary in size and décor; some have conservatories and are ideal for those with dogs. The traditional beamed dining room offers a classical menu.

24 rooms – £ 80/190 £ 149/211

Sedbusk ✉ DL8 3PT – North : 1 mi by Muker rd – ☎ 01969 667571 – www.stonehousehotel.co.uk – Closed January and mid-week December

HAWKSHEAD

Cumbria – ✉ Ambleside – Pop. 570 – Regional map n° **12**-A2

West Vale

TRADITIONAL • PERSONALISED A welcoming slate house boasting lovely views over Grizedale Forest and The Old Man of Coniston. Relax in one of two comfy lounges and enjoy hearty breakfasts in the smart country house style dining room. Good-sized bedrooms have a warm, boutique style; ask for one on the top floor.

7 rooms – £ 90/105 £ 90/170

Far Sawrey ✉ LA22 0LQ – Southeast : 2 mi on B 5285 – ☎ 015394 42817 – www.westvalecountryhouse.co.uk – Closed 25-26 December and restricted opening 3 January-4 February

HAWNBY

North Yorkshire – ✉ Helmsley – Regional map n° **13**-C1

Laskill Country House

TRADITIONAL • PERSONALISED A delightful stone house draped with wisteria. It's remotely set and very personally run, with a welcoming house party atmosphere. There's a cosy open-fired lounge and a communal dining room where they serve meat from the family farm. Simple bedrooms have country views and there's even a hot tub in the garden.

3 rooms – £ 50/70 £ 100/130

Easterside, Laskill ✉ YO62 5NB – Northeast : 2.25 mi by Osmotherley rd – ☎ 01439 798265 – www.laskillcountryhouse.co.uk – Closed 24-25 December

HAYDON BRIDGE – Northumberland

➔ See Hexham

HAYWARDS HEATH

West Sussex – Pop. 33 845 – Regional map n° **4**-D2

Jeremy's at Borde Hill

MODERN CUISINE • FRIENDLY XX Converted stable block with exposed rafters, contemporary sculptures, vivid artwork and delightful views towards the Victorian walled garden. Interesting, modern European dishes and a good value 'menu of the day'. Regular gourmet nights.

Menu £ 22 (weekdays) – Carte £ 32/47

Borde Hill Gdns ✉ RH16 1XP – North : 1.75 mi by B 2028 and Balcombe Rd on Borde Hill Ln. – ☎ 01444 441102 – www.jeremysrestaurant.co.uk – Closed 2-15 January, Monday except bank holidays and Sunday dinner

HEADLAM – Durham

➔ See Darlington

HEATHROW AIRPORT – Greater London

➔ See London

HEDLEY ON THE HILL

Northumberland – Regional map n° **14**-A2

Feathers Inn

TRADITIONAL BRITISH • PUB Traditional stone inn set on a steep hill in the heart of a rural village. Daily changing menu of hearty British classics, cooked using carefully sourced regional produce, with meat and game to the fore. Relaxed, friendly atmosphere.

Carte £19/32

NE43 7SW – 01661 843607 – www.thefeathers.net – Closed first 2 weeks January, Sunday dinner, Monday except bank holidays and lunch Tuesday-Wednesday

HELMSLEY

North Yorkshire – Pop. 1 515 – Regional map n° **13**-C1

Gallery

MODERN BRITISH • BRASSERIE XX Bright, modern restaurant within a historic 15C coaching inn; its walls are filled with artwork for sale and at dinner, the plate becomes the canvas. Attractive, modern dishes have a classical base; the tasting menu is a highlight.

Carte £37/55

Black Swan Hotel, Market Pl YO62 5BJ – 01439 770466 – www.blackswan-helmsley.co.uk – dinner only and Sunday lunch

The Weathervane

MODERN CUISINE • BRASSERIE XX Modern hotel restaurant with a pleasingly laid-back style. In summer, have lunch in the garden or on the poolside terrace. Dishes feature the latest local produce and cooking is refined and accurate; the tasting menu is worth a try.

Menu £48 – bar lunch Monday-Saturday

Feversham Arms Hotel, 1-8 High St YO62 5AG – 01439 770766 – www.fevershamarmshotel.com

Black Swan

HISTORIC • PERSONALISED Set overlooking the historic marketplace, The Black Swan is one of the country's best known coaching inns. The charming interior features beamed lounges, a modern bar and a tea shop. Bedrooms are a mix of characterful and contemporary. On Friday and Saturday nights, dinner is included in the rate.

45 rooms – £140/169 £155/184 – 1 suite

Market Pl YO62 5BJ – 01439 770466 – www.blackswan-helmsley.co.uk

Gallery – See restaurant listing

Feversham Arms H. & Verbena Spa

TRADITIONAL • CONTEMPORARY 19C former coaching inn with a lovely stone façade. Relax on the terrace beside the outdoor pool; the spa is superb and boasts a salt vapour room and an ice cave. Be sure to book one of the stylish newer bedrooms; many have stoves or fires.

33 rooms – £110/420 £120/430 – 21 suites

1-8 High St YO62 5AG – 01439 770766 – www.fevershamarmshotel.com

The Weathervane – See restaurant listing

at Wombleton East: 4 mi by A170

Plough Inn

TRADITIONAL CUISINE • PUB 16C inn, popular with locals, serving tasty traditional dishes, including game in season. Prices are laudably low and service, friendly and relaxed. Sit in the hugely characterful restaurant, which is kept cosy by wood burners.

Carte £25/37

Main St YO62 7RW – 01751 431356 – www.theploughinnatwombleton.co.uk – Closed 25 December and Monday lunch

at Harome Southeast: 2.75 mi by A170 ✉ York

✿ Star Inn (Andrew Pern)

MODERN BRITISH • INN 14C thatched pub with a delightful terrace, a low-ceilinged bar and a brasserie-like restaurant with a chef's table. Dishes have assured flavours and a skilled, classical style; they use the very best of local produce, including veg from the kitchen garden and meats from their own pigs and chickens. → Black pudding and foie gras with apple & vanilla chutney. Roe deer with smoked sweet potato, coffee bean and game tea. Yorkshire rhubarb and custard.

Menu £ 25 (weekdays) - Carte £ 36/61

High St ✉ YO62 5JE - ✆ 01439 770397 (booking essential) - www.thestaratharome.co.uk - Closed Monday lunch except bank holidays

Pheasant

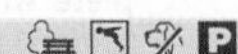

MODERN BRITISH • ELEGANT XX Elegant hotel dining room with both classical and contemporary touches - along with a less formal conservatory and a lovely terrace overlooking the village duck pond. Appealing menus of seasonal dishes with a classical base and a modern touch. Skilful, knowledgeable cooking; smooth, assured service.

Menu £ 33 (lunch) - Carte £ 38/61

Pheasant Hotel, Mill St ✉ YO62 5JG - ✆ 01439 771241 - www.thepheasanthotel.com

Pheasant

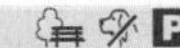

TRADITIONAL • PERSONALISED An attractive hotel in a picturesque hamlet, with a delightful duck pond and a mill stream close by. Beautiful, very comfortable lounges and spacious, well-furnished bedrooms; Rudland - running the width of the building and with views of the pond - is one of the best. Pleasant service. Excellent breakfasts.

16 rooms - †£ 95/240 ††£ 180/270

Mill St ✉ YO62 5JG - ✆ 01439 771241 - www.thepheasanthotel.com

Pheasant - See restaurant listing

Cross House Lodge

COUNTRY HOUSE • DESIGN These sympathetically converted farm buildings have a rustic ski-chalet style and ultra-stylish, individually decorated bedrooms; one boasts a snooker table; another, a bed suspended on ropes. Relax in the open-plan, split-level lounge; excellent breakfasts are taken in the dramatic beamed 'Wheelhouse'.

9 rooms - †£ 150/260 ††£ 150/260

High St ✉ YO62 5JE - ✆ 01439 770397 - www.thestaratharome.co.uk

✿ **Star Inn** - See restaurant listing

at Ampleforth Southwest: 4.5 mi by A170 off B1257 ✉ Helmsley

Shallowdale House

TRADITIONAL • CLASSIC A remotely set, personally run house with a well-tended garden and stunning views of the Howardian Hills. Charming, antique-furnished interior, with an open-fired sitting room and good-sized bedrooms decorated in bright, Mediterranean tones. Four course set menu of home-cooked fare.

3 rooms - †£ 105/120 ††£ 125/160

✉ YO62 4DY - West : 0.5 mi - ✆ 01439 788325 - www.shallowdalehouse.co.uk - Closed Christmas-New Year

at Scawton West : 5 mi. by B 1257 ✉ Helmsley

The Hare Inn

MODERN CUISINE • COSY XX Exposed bricks and wooden beams give this passionately run, part-13C inn a characterful pubby feel but, despite its appearance, this is a restaurant through and through. The self-taught chef offers 2 set menus of creative, accomplished dishes which are attractively presented and full of flavour.

Menu £ 55 (weekdays)/70 - tasting menu only

✉ YO7 2HG - ✆ 01845 597769 (booking essential) - www.thehare-inn.com - dinner only - Closed 2-27 January, 1 week June, 1 week November and Sunday-Tuesday

HELPERBY

North Yorkshire – Regional map n° **13**-B2

Oak Tree Inn

TRADITIONAL BRITISH • INN A pub of two halves, with a large bar, a tap room and two snugs in the main building, and a smart dining room in the old hay barn. Cooking is based around the Bertha charcoal oven, with steaks, chops, poultry and fish to the fore. Chic modern bedrooms come with 'Yorkie' bars and spa baths.

Menu £ 18 (weekday lunch) – Carte £ 22/42

6 rooms – £ 90/120 £ 100/160

Raskelf Rd ✉ YO61 2PH – ✆ 01423 789189 – www.theoaktreehelperby.com

HELSTON

Cornwall – Pop. 11 311 – Regional map n° **1**-A3

Nansloe Manor Ⓝ

TRADITIONAL • ELEGANT An immaculately kept Georgian manor house complete with a charming orchard and a Mediterranean walled garden. The elegant, understated interior features furnishings and art from the Loire Valley and stylish bedrooms have excellent comforts. Modern British menus display Mediterranean influences.

15 rooms – £ 117/153 £ 130/285

Meneage Rd ✉ TR13 OSB – South : 1.5 mi on A 394 – ✆ 01326 558400 – www.nansloe-manor.co.uk – Closed first 2 weeks January

at Trelowarren Southeast: 4 mi by A394 and A3083 on B3293 ✉ Helston

New Yard

MODERN BRITISH • RUSTIC Converted 17C stable building adjoining a craft gallery. Spacious, rustic room with timbered walls and doors opening onto the terrace. Seasonal menu uses quality Cornish produce; breads and ice creams are homemade. Friendly service.

Menu £ 24 – Carte £ 28/45

Trelowarren Estate ✉ TR12 6AF – ✆ 01326 221595 (bookings advisable at dinner) – www.trelowarren.com – Closed 3 weeks January, Monday and Tuesday October-Easter

HEMINGFORD GREY – Cambridgeshire ➜ See Huntingdon

HENFIELD

West Sussex – Pop. 4 527 – Regional map n° **4**-D2

Ginger Fox

CLASSIC CUISINE • PUB Spot the fox running across the thatched roof and you know you're in the right place. Monthly changing menu offers good value, flavourful dishes, with a popular vegetarian tasting plate. Desserts are a highlight, so save space.

Menu £ 17 (weekday lunch) – Carte £ 27/43

Muddleswood Rd, Albourne ✉ BN6 9EA – Southwest : 3 mi on A 281 – ✆ 01273 857888 – www.gingermanrestaurants.com – Closed 25 December

HENLEY – West Sussex ➜ See Midhurst

HENLEY-IN-ARDEN

Warwickshire – Pop. 2 846 – Regional map n° **10**-C3

Cheal's of Henley

MODERN CUISINE • ELEGANT XX A 400 year old house on the high street, which has been smartly refurbished yet retains plenty of character – it's owned by a local couple and run by their son. Complex modern cooking relies on classic flavour combinations.

Menu £ 30/50

65 High St ✉ B95 5BX
– ✆ 01564 793856 – www.chealsofhenley.co.uk
– Closed 2 weeks August, 1 week October, 1 week Easter, 25-26 December, 1 January, Sunday dinner, Monday and Tuesday

Bluebell Ⓝ

MODERN BRITISH • NEIGHBOURHOOD This early 16C pub in a busy market town is run by a brother and sister: he cooks and she looks after the service. Modern dishes have bold, distinctive flavours – the Aubrey Allen steaks are popular and desserts are a highlight.

Menu £ 19 (weekday lunch) – Carte £ 24/34

93 High St ✉ B95 5AT
– ✆ 01564 793049 – www.thebluebell-henley.co.uk

HENLEY-ON-THAMES

Oxfordshire – Pop. 11 494 – Regional map n° **6**-C3

Shaun Dickens at The Boathouse

MODERN BRITISH • FRIENDLY XX This modern restaurant is sure to please with its floor to ceiling glass doors and decked terrace overlooking the Thames. The young chef-owner offers an array of menus; attractively presented dishes centre around local ingredients.

Menu £ 26 (lunch) – Carte £ 39/49

Station Rd ✉ RG9 1AZ
– ✆ 01491 577937 – www.shaundickens.co.uk – Closed 25-26 December, Monday and Tuesday

Luscombes at The Golden Ball

TRADITIONAL CUISINE • FRIENDLY X A pretty former pub – now a cosy restaurant popular with the locals. Appealing menus offer well-executed modern classics; the afternoon tea with homemade preserves is a hit. Service is friendly and attentive.

Menu £ 17 (weekday lunch) – Carte £ 32/43

Lower Assendon ✉ RG9 6AH – Northwest : 1.5 mi by A 4130 on B 480
– ✆ 01491 574157 – www.luscombes.co.uk – Closed Sunday dinner and Monday

Three Tuns

TRADITIONAL BRITISH • PUB Pretty town centre pub with a lively bar and two homely dining rooms. Traditional, seasonal dishes are well-presented, satisfying and full of flavour. Breads are homemade and the meats come from the neighbouring butcher's.

Menu £ 13 (weekday lunch) – Carte £ 25/41

5 Market Pl ✉ RG9 2AA
– ✆ 01491 410138 – www.threetunshenley.co.uk – Closed 25 December and Sunday dinner

Hotel du Vin

BUSINESS • MODERN Characterful 1857 building that was formerly the Brakspear Brewery. Stylish bedrooms include airy doubles and duplex suites: one features two roll-top tubs and a great view of the church; others boast heated balconies and outdoor baths. Choose from a list of brasserie classics and over 400 wines in the bistro.

43 rooms – †£ 130/300 ††£ 130/300 – ☕ £ 17 – 2 suites

New St. ✉ RG9 2BP
– ✆ 01491 848400 – www.hotelduvin.com

at Shiplake South: 2 mi on A4155

Orwells

MODERN BRITISH • RUSTIC XX This 18C building may look like a rural inn but inside it has a modern, formal feel. Creative cooking uses top quality produce and flavours are pronounced. It's named after George Orwell, who spent his childhood in the area.

Menu £ 30/35 (weekdays) – Carte £ 44/61

Shiplake Row ✉ RG9 4DP – West 0.5 mi on Binfield Heath rd. – ✆ 0118 940 3673 – www.orwellsatshiplake.co.uk – Closed first 2 weeks January, first 2 weeks September, 1 week June, Sunday dinner, Tuesday and Monday except bank holidays

HEREFORD

Herefordshire – Pop. 60 415 – Regional map n° **10**-B3

Castle House

MODERN CUISINE • ELEGANT XX This elegant restaurant looks out over the hotel gardens and across the old moat of Hereford Castle. Classic dishes are reinvented in a modern manner and ingredients from Herefordshire feature highly. Menus offer plenty of choice.

Carte £ 22/48

Castle House Hotel, Castle St ✉ HR1 2NW – ✆ 01432 356321 – www.castlehse.co.uk

Castle House

TOWNHOUSE • CONTEMPORARY This elegant Georgian house sits close to the cathedral. An impressive staircase leads to warmly furnished bedrooms of various sizes; some overlook the old castle moat. More contemporary rooms can be found in nearby 'Number 25'.

24 rooms – †£ 120/150 ††£ 150/250

Castle St ✉ HR1 2NW – ✆ 01432 356321 – www.castlehse.co.uk

Castle House – See restaurant listing

Somerville House

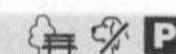

TOWNHOUSE • CLASSIC A Victorian villa with cathedral views and an enclosed garden; home-grown apples, plums and pears are used to make the breakfast preserves. Bedrooms on the first floor are the most spacious; all have mini-bars and good facilities.

12 rooms – †£ 65/95 ††£ 85/125

12 Bodenham Rd ✉ HR1 2TS – Northeast : 0.75 mi by A 465 and Southbank Rd. – ✆ 01432 273991 – www.somervillehouse.net

HERSTMONCEUX

East Sussex – Pop. 1 130 – Regional map n° **5**-B3

Sundial

CLASSIC FRENCH • TRADITIONAL DÉCOR XX With its original leaded windows and beamed ceiling, this characterful 16C cottage is a real hit with the locals. Service is structured and the room is formally laid. Rich, classic French dishes use luxurious seasonal ingredients.

Menu £ 30/45

Gardner St ✉ BN27 4LA – ✆ 01323 832217 – www.sundialrestaurant.co.uk – Closed Sunday dinner and Monday

at Wartling Southeast: 3.75 mi by A271 on Wartling rd ✉ Herstmonceux

Wartling Place

COUNTRY HOUSE • CLASSIC A charming part-Georgian house with a homely feel, set in three acres of mature grounds and run by a delightful owner. Two of the bedrooms have four-poster beds; DAB radios and iPod docks provide a contrast to the antique furniture.

4 rooms – †£ 100/125 ††£ 135/165

✉ BN27 1RY

– ✆ 01323 832590 – www.wartlingplace.co.uk

HESWALL

Mersey. – Pop. 29 977 – Regional map n° **11**-A3

Burnt Truffle

MODERN BRITISH • BISTRO X A friendly team run this sweet modern bistro. Menus offer a good range of original dishes with global influences. Start with the sourdough bread with truffle and walnut butter and be sure to save room for the delicious desserts.

Menu £ 18 (lunch and early dinner) – Carte dinner £ 24/44

106 Telegraph Rd ✉ CH60 0AQ

– ✆ 0151 342 1111 – www.burnttruffle.net – Closed 25-26 December and Monday

HETHE

Oxfordshire – Regional map n° **6**-B1

Muddy Duck

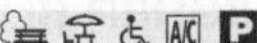

MODERN CUISINE • FRIENDLY An unpretentious local with a happy feel and ultra-smiley staff, this modernised mellow stone pub stays true to its traditional roots. Choose pub staples or more adventurous choices, with dishes from the wood-fired oven in summer.

Carte £ 24/57

Main St ✉ OX27 8ES

– ✆ 01869 278099 – www.themuddyduckpub.co.uk – Closed 25 December and Sunday dinner

HEXHAM

Northumberland – Pop. 11 388 – Regional map n° **14**-A2

Bouchon

CLASSIC FRENCH • INTIMATE XX Well-run French restaurant with a simply styled ground floor room and a more romantic first floor with opulent purple furnishings. Excellent value set price lunch menu and more ambitious à la carte. Classic French dishes use local produce.

Menu £ 16/20 (weekdays) – Carte £ 24/41

4-6 Gilesgate ✉ NE46 3NJ

– ✆ 01434 609943 – www.bouchonbistrot.co.uk – Closed 24-26 December and Sunday

Rat Inn

TRADITIONAL BRITISH • PUB Traditional 18C drovers' inn with wooden beams, an open range and a multi-level garden boasting arbours and Tyne Valley views. The daily changing blackboard menu showcases interesting dishes; the rib of beef for two is a must.

Menu £ 20 (weekdays) – Carte £ 23/43

Anick ✉ NE46 4LN – Northeast : 1.75 mi by A 6079

– ✆ 01434 602814 – www.theratinn.com – Closed 25 December, Monday except bank holidays and Sunday dinner

at Haydon Bridge West: 7.5 mi on A69 ✉ Hexham

Langley Castle

HISTORIC BUILDING • CLASSIC Impressive 14C castle in 12 acres; its charming guest areas feature stone walls, tapestries and heraldic shields. Characterful bedrooms, some with four-posters; Castle View rooms are more uniform in style. Modern, international menus in the romantic dining room or in the glass cube overlooking the gardens.

27 rooms – £ 135/225 £ 165/285

Langley-on-Tyne ✉ NE47 5LU – South : 2 mi by Alston rd on A 686 – ✆ 01434 688888 – www.langleycastle.com

HIGHCLIFFE

Dorset – Regional map n° **2**-D3

Lord Bute

BUSINESS • PERSONALISED Some of the suites in this elegant hotel stand where the original 18C entrance lodges to Highcliffe Castle (home of Lord Bute), were once located. Bedrooms are well-appointed and decorated in a contemporary style. The smart restaurant and courtyard offer classical menus and host jazz and cabaret evenings.

13 rooms – £ 130/155 £ 130/155 – 2 suites

179-185 Lymington Rd ✉ BH23 4JS – ✆ 01425 278884 – www.lordbute.co.uk

HIGHER BURWARDSLEY

Cheshire West and Chester – Regional map n° **11**-A3

Pheasant Inn

TRADITIONAL BRITISH • PUB Well-run, modern pub set atop a sandstone escarpment, with views across the Cheshire Plains. The menu focuses on simple pub classics, with no-nonsense cooking and clear, gutsy flavours. Spacious, beamed bedrooms in the main building; more modern rooms with views in the barn. Staff are keen to please.

Carte £ 23/43

12 rooms – £ 115/190 £ 125/200

✉ CH3 9PF – ✆ 01829 770434 – www.thepheasantinn.co.uk

HINCKLEY

Leicestershire – Pop. 45 249 – Regional map n° **9**-B2

34 Windsor St

MODERN CUISINE • FASHIONABLE XX This stylish modern restaurant is well-run by an experienced, hands-on owner. It has a relaxed feel and a smart chill-out terrace to the rear. Cooking is also contemporary; the 8 course tasting menu shows the kitchen's ambition.

Carte £ 28/43

34 Windsor St, Burbage ✉ LE10 2EF – Southeast : 2.25 mi by B 4669 off B 578 – ✆ 01455 234342 – www.34windsorst.com – Closed 27-28 December, 1-3 January, Sunday dinner, Monday and Tuesday

HINTLESHAM – Suffolk → See Ipswich

HINTON ST GEORGE

Somerset – Regional map n° **2**-B3

Lord Poulett Arms

MODERN BRITISH • RURAL Characterful pub with open fires and beams fringed with hop bines; outside it's just as charming, with a lavender-framed terrace, a boules pitch and a secret garden. Creative cooking has a British base but also displays a wide range of influences. Stylish bedrooms come with feature beds and Roberts radios.

Menu £ 16 (lunch and early dinner) – Carte £ 24/41

4 rooms – £ 60/85 £ 85/115

High St ✉ TA17 8SE – ✆ 01460 73149 – www.lordpoulettarms.com – Closed 25-26 December and 1 January

HOLCOMBE

Somerset – Regional map n° **2**-C2

Holcombe Inn

MODERN BRITISH • RUSTIC Charming 17C inn set in the heart of the Somerset countryside, with a lovely south-facing garden and a peaceful air. Menus offer quite a range of dishes, from good old pub classics to more sophisticated offerings. Bedrooms are luxuriously appointed; some boast views over Downside Abbey.

Carte £ 25/49

10 rooms – £ 75/125 £ 100/145

Stratton Rd ✉ BA3 5EB – West : 0.25 mi on Stratton-on-the-Fosse rd – ✆ 01761 232478 – www.holcombeinn.co.uk

HOLKHAM

Norfolk – Regional map n° **8**-C1

INN • COSY An extended flint inn with a relaxed, modern style, large lawned gardens and pleasant country views, set close to the beach at the gates of Holkham Hall. Stylish bedrooms – some in 'Ancient House' across the road. Dine on traditional British dishes overlooking the marshes of the adjacent nature reserve.

20 rooms – £ 125/155 £ 150/240

Park Rd ✉ NR23 1RG – ✆ 01328 711008 – www.holkham.co.uk/victoria

HOLLINGBOURNE

Kent – Regional map n° **5**-C2

The Windmill

TRADITIONAL BRITISH • PUB With its giant inglenook fireplace and low-slung beams, the Windmill is as characterful as they come. You'll find tempting bar snacks, sharing roasts on Sundays and, alongside the hearty British classics, some more refined dishes too.

Menu £ 15 (weekday lunch) – Carte £ 26/47

32 Eyhorne St ✉ ME17 1TR – ✆ 01622 889000 – www.thewindmillbyrichardphillips.co.uk

HOLMFIRTH

West Yorkshire – Pop. 21 706 – Regional map n° **13**-B3

Sunnybank

TOWNHOUSE • ELEGANT Attractive Victorian house with lovely gardens and great views; hidden up a narrow road in the village where 'Last of the Summer Wine' was filmed. Cosy bedrooms have a personal touch. Look out for the original stained glass window.

6 rooms – £ 75/110 £ 85/120

78 Upperthong Ln ✉ HD9 3BQ – Northwest : 0.5 mi by A 6024 – ✆ 01484 684065 – www.sunnybankguesthouse.co.uk

HOLT
Wiltshire – Pop. 1 532 – Regional map n° **2**-C2

Tollgate Inn
TRADITIONAL CUISINE • PUB If there was an award for the most welcoming pub, then this village inn would surely be the winner. The attentive staff pitch things just right, from the cheery hello to the charming personal touches in the cosy bedrooms. Cooking keeps things simple – as befits a pub – with hearty, flavoursome dishes.

Carte £ 23/33

5 rooms – £ 50/120 £ 60/120

Ham Grn BA14 6PX – 01225 782326 – www.tollgateinn.co.uk – Closed 25 December and Sunday dinner

HOLT
Norfolk – Pop. 3 550 – Regional map n° **8**-C1

Byfords
TOWNHOUSE • MODERN Grade II listed, 15C flint house. Stunning bedrooms come with feature beds, underfloor heating and plenty of extras. Numerous characterful rooms incorporate a deli, a café and a restaurant. Light meals are served during the day and more substantial dishes in the evening; it's a real hit with the locals.

17 rooms – £ 135/185 £ 165/215

Shirehall Plain NR25 6BG – 01263 711400 – www.byfords.org.uk

HONITON
Devon – Pop. 11 483 – Regional map n° **1**-D2

The Pig
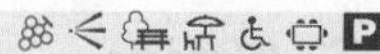

TRADITIONAL BRITISH • RUSTIC A bubbly team welcome you to the Pig hotel's laid-back restaurant. The '25 mile' menu showcases produce from the beautiful kitchen gardens and local suppliers. Appealing, classical dishes have an unfussy style and rely on fresh, natural flavours to do the talking. A comprehensive range of wines accompanies.

Carte £ 30/47

The Pig Hotel, Gittisham EX14 3AD – Southwest : 5 mi by A 30 and B 3177 – 01404 540400 (booking essential) – www.thepighotel.com

Holt
REGIONAL CUISINE • PUB A rustic, family-run pub, where their passion for food is almost palpable. The regularly changing menu features regional and homemade produce, with meats and fish smoked and cured on-site; ales are from their nearby family brewery.

Carte £ 29/38

178 High St EX14 1LA – 01404 47707 – www.theholt-honiton.com – Closed 25-26 December, 1 January, Sunday and Monday

The Pig

COUNTRY HOUSE • CONTEMPORARY A hugely impressive Elizabethan mansion at the end of a winding drive. Its traditional interior has been stylishly redesigned (the historic entrance hall is now a bar) and service is relaxed. Bedrooms in the house boast wonderful country views; those in the old stables still have their original partitions.

30 rooms – £ 145/460 £ 145/460 – £ 15

Gittisham EX14 3AD – Southwest : 5 mi by A 30 and B 3177 – 01404 540400 – www.thepighotel.com

The Pig – See restaurant listing

HOOK
Hampshire – Pop. 7 934 – Regional map n° **4**-B1

Tylney Hall

LUXURY • CLASSIC Impressively restored 19C mansion full of period grandeur. Bedrooms are split between the main house and courtyard: the former are traditionally furnished with period features; the latter benefit from views over the delightful gardens, designed by Jekyll. The formal panelled restaurant offers classic dishes.

112 rooms – †£ 230/520 ††£ 250/540 – 20 suites

Rotherwick ✉ RG27 9AZ – Northwest : 2.5 mi by A 30 and Newnham Rd on Ridge Ln – ✆ 01256 764881 – www.tylneyhall.com

HOPE

Derbyshire – ✉ Sheffield – Regional map n° **9**-A1

Losehill House

TRADITIONAL • PERSONALISED Peacefully located former walkers' hostel affording wonderful views up to Win Hill; in summer it's a popular wedding venue. It has an airy open-plan lounge-bar and bright modern bedrooms. Unwind in the spa or in the hot tub on the terrace. The formally laid restaurant offers classic dishes with a modern edge.

23 rooms – †£ 145/225 ††£ 195/295

Lose Hill Ln, Edale Rd ✉ S33 6AF – North : 1 mi by Edale Rd – ✆ 01433 621219 – www.losehillhouse.co.uk

Underleigh House

TRADITIONAL • PERSONALISED Former Derbyshire longhouse and shippon with far-reaching views; the gregarious owner offers a friendly welcome. Traditional bedrooms, some opening onto the garden. Communal breakfasts include homemade preserves, bread and muesli.

4 rooms – †£ 75/105 ††£ 95/125

Losehill Ln, Hope Valley ✉ S33 6AF – North : 1 mi by Edale Rd – ✆ 01433 621372 – www.underleighhouse.co.uk – Closed Christmas-New Year and January

HOPTON HEATH

Shropshire – Regional map n° **10**-A2

Hopton House

COUNTRY HOUSE • PERSONALISED Take in views over the Shropshire Hills from this charming guesthouse. Spacious open-plan bedrooms boast super king sized beds, Smart TVs, silent fridges and double-ended baths. A freshly baked cake is a pleasing extra.

2 rooms – †£ 90/130 ††£ 125/130

✉ SY7 0QD – On Clun rd – ✆ 01547 530885 – www.shropshirebreakfast.co.uk

HORLEY

Surrey – Pop. 22 693 – Regional map n° **4**-D2

Mulberry

MODERN BRITISH • CHIC XX Smart hotel dining room set within a Part-Elizabethan manor house. Well-presented dishes have a classical heart but are given personal twists by the experienced team. They use many herbs, fruits and vegetables from the gardens.

Menu £ 50

Langshott Manor Hotel, Langshott ✉ RH6 9LN – North : 0.5 mi by A 23 turning right at Chequers Hotel onto Ladbroke Rd – ✆ 01293 786680 – www.langshottmanor.com – dinner only and Sunday lunch

Langshott Manor

HISTORIC • PERSONALISED Characterful 16C manor house set amidst roses, vines and ponds. The traditional exterior contrasts with contemporary furnishings and many of the bedrooms have fireplaces, four-posters or balconies. Afternoon tea is a feature.

22 rooms – †£ 99/309 ††£ 99/309 – ☕£ 17 – 1 suite

Langshott ✉ RH6 9LN – North : 0.5 mi by A 23 turning right at Chequers Hotel onto Ladbroke Rd – ✆ 01293 786680 – www.alexanderhotels.com

Mulberry – See restaurant listing

HORNCASTLE

Lincolnshire – Pop. 6 815 – Regional map n° **9**-C1

Magpies

TRADITIONAL BRITISH • FAMILY XX Three adjoining 18C cottages; now a cosy, family-run restaurant which hosts regular gourmet and wine dinners. Hearty, classically based dishes are attractively presented; don't miss the tasty homemade canapés and breads. Modern bedrooms have bold floral feature walls and impressive bathrooms.

Menu £ 26/49

3 rooms ☕ – †£ 70/85 ††£ 110/130

71-75 East St ✉ LN9 6AA – ✆ 01507 527004 – www.magpiesrestaurant.co.uk – Closed 26-30 December, 1-5 January, Saturday lunch, Monday and Tuesday

HORNDON ON THE HILL

Thurrock – Pop. 1 596 – Regional map n° **7**-C3

Bell Inn

TRADITIONAL BRITISH • INN The Bell was built in the first half of the 15C and positively oozes history; keep an eye out for the hot cross bun collection! Cooking has a pleasingly classical edge and a modern touch. Two neighbouring Georgian buildings house contemporary bedrooms and the Ostlers restaurant (open Fri and Sat nights).

Carte £ 21/51

26 rooms – †£ 70/140 ††£ 75/145 – ☕£ 9

High Rd ✉ SS17 8LD – ✆ 01375 642463 – www.bell-inn.co.uk – Closed 25-26 December

HORNING

Norfolk – Pop. 1 098 – Regional map n° **8**-D1

Bure River Cottage

SEAFOOD • FRIENDLY X Friendly restaurant tucked away in a lovely riverside village that's famed for its boating. Informal, L-shaped room with modern tables and chairs. Blackboard menu features fresh, carefully cooked fish and shellfish; much from Lowestoft.

Carte £ 24/46

27 Lower St ✉ NR12 8AA – ✆ 01692 631421 (booking advisable) – www.burerivercottagerestaurant.co.uk – dinner only – Closed 25 December-13 February, Sunday and Monday

HORNINGSEA – Cambridgeshire ➜ See Cambridge

HORRINGER – Suffolk ➜ See Bury St Edmunds

HORSHAM

West Sussex – Pop. 48 041 – Regional map n° **4**-D2

Restaurant Tristan (Tristan Mason)

MODERN BRITISH • RUSTIC A characterful beamed dining room on the first floor of a 16C town centre property. Carefully crafted, creative dishes are delivered with a modern touch; ingredients are excellent and flavours, distinct and well-matched. Service is enthusiastic and friendly and the atmosphere, refreshingly relaxed.

→ Duck egg with morels and wild garlic. Lamb, kid and goat. Granny Smith apple with fennel and tonka bean.

Menu £ 25/45

3 Stans Way, East St ✉ RH12 1HU – ✆ 01403 255688 – www.restauranttristan.co.uk – Closed 25 December,1 January, Sunday and Monday

at Rowhook Northwest: 4 mi by A264 and A281 off A29 ✉ Horsham

Chequers Inn

TRADITIONAL BRITISH • COSY Part-15C inn with a charming open-fired, stone-floored bar and an unusual dining room extension. The chef-owner grows, forages for or shoots the majority of his produce. Classical menus.

Carte £ 25/39

✉ RH12 3PY – ✆ 01403 790480 – www.thechequersrowhook.com – Closed 25 December and Sunday dinner

HOUGH-ON-THE-HILL – Lincolnshire → See Grantham

HOWE STREET

Essex – Regional map n° **7**-C2

Green Man (N)

TRADITIONAL BRITISH • FRIENDLY The Galvin brothers couldn't resist buying this pub in their native county. The original 14C building offers all the rustic charm you'd expect and they've added a beautiful, modern barn extension. Classic British dishes are carefully cooked and full of flavour; flatbreads from the wood oven are a speciality.

Menu £ 16 (weekday lunch) – Carte £ 25/44

Main Rd ✉ CM3 1BG – ✆ 01245 408820 – www.galvingreenman.com

HUCCOMBE

Devon – Regional map n° **1**-C3

Huccombe House

FAMILY • PERSONALISED Converted Victorian school – the owner herself once went to school here! Pleasant lounge with high beamed ceilings and huge windows affording countryside views. Large bedrooms with sleigh beds made up with Egyptian cotton linen. Aga-cooked breakfasts at the communal table or on the patio.

3 rooms – †£ 80 ††£ 95

✉ TQ7 2EP – ✆ 01548 580669 – www.southdevonbandb.co.uk

HUDDERSFIELD

West Yorkshire – Pop. 162 949 – Regional map n° **13**-B3

Eric's

MODERN CUISINE • NEIGHBOURHOOD Contemporary neighbourhood restaurant offering appealing, boldly flavoured dishes. The lunch and early evening menu is great value and on selected Saturdays they host brunch or afternoon tea.

Menu £ 20/25 – Carte £ 32/58

73-75 Lidget St, Lindley ✉ HD3 3JP – Northwest : 3.25 mi by A 629 and Birchencliffe Hill Rd. – ✆ 01484 646416 (booking advisable) – www.ericsrestaurant.co.uk – Closed Monday except December and Sunday dinner

HULLBRIDGE

Essex - Pop. 6 097 - Regional map n° **7**-C2_3

Anchor

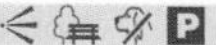

MODERN CUISINE • BRASSERIE X A large, busy, open-plan restaurant with a sleek bar and a superb terrace; sit here or in the Orangery for views of the River Crouch. The à la carte offers a wide range of tasty dishes and there's an excellent value weekday set menu too. Service is friendly and the summer barbecues are a hit.

Menu £ 18 (weekdays) - Carte £ 25/41

Ferry Rd ✉ SS5 6ND
- ✆ 01702 230777 - www.theanchorhullbridge.co.uk - Closed 25 December

HUMSHAUGH

Northumberland - Regional map n° **14**-A2

Carraw

FAMILY • PERSONALISED A converted stone farmhouse and barn built on the foundations of Hadrian's Wall. Stay here in beamed bedrooms or in the more modern lodge which has a delightful lounge with full-length windows and panoramic country views.

9 rooms ☕ - 🚹£ 55/69 🚹🚹£ 60/115

Carraw Farm, Military Rd ✉ NE46 4DB - West : 5 mi on B 6318
- ✆ 01434 689857 - www.carraw.co.uk

HUNSDON

Hertfordshire - Regional map n° **7**-B2

Fox & Hounds

TRADITIONAL BRITISH • PUB 🍺 A welcoming high street pub with contemporary styling. The chef's ethos is to let good quality ingredients speak for themselves. Alongside homemade pasta dishes you'll find meats cooked on the Josper grill and plenty of local game. Flavours are pronounced, combinations are classical and portions are hearty.

Menu £ 20 (weekdays) - Carte £ 20/38

2 High St ✉ SG12 8NH
- ✆ 01279 843999 - www.foxandhounds-hunsdon.co.uk - Closed 25-26 December, Sunday dinner and Monday

HUNSTANTON

Norfolk - Pop. 8 704 - Regional map n° **8**-B1

✿ **The Neptune** (Kevin Mangeolles) ⟳ P

MODERN CUISINE • FRIENDLY XX Very personally run, attractive, red-brick former pub. New England style interior with a rattan-furnished bar and large nautical photographs in the dining room. The constantly evolving menu relies on the latest local produce to arrive at the door. Presentation is modern; service is relaxed and efficient. Comfy bedrooms have Nespresso machines and thoughtful extras.

→ Brancaster lobster with star anise mousse, pea purée and poached tail. Loin of hare with celeriac tart, wild mushrooms and bitter chocolate sauce. Colombian white chocolate mousse with poached Yorkshire rhubarb.

Menu £ 60

4 rooms ☕ - 🚹£ 120/150 🚹🚹£ 160/190

85 Old Hunstanton Rd, Old Hunstanton ✉ PE36 6HZ - Northeast : 1.5 mi on A 149
- ✆ 01485 532122 - www.theneptune.co.uk
- dinner only and Sunday lunch - Closed 3 weeks January, 1 week May, 1 week November and Monday

Lodge

FAMILY • PERSONALISED After a day at the beach head for this laid-back hotel and one of its modern, well-equipped bedrooms; go for a suite for views over the rooftops to the sea. Dine in the smart, cosy bar or head through to the more formal, intimate dining room; the menu offers a mix of pub classics and Italian-based dishes.

16 rooms – £ 75/85 £ 120/130

Old Hunstanton Rd ✉ PE36 6HX – Northeast : 1.5 mi on A 149 – 01485 532896 – www.thelodgehunstanton.co.uk

No. 33

LUXURY • DESIGN A Victorian house with an unusual façade, set in a peaceful street. Designer touches feature throughout, from the cosy open-fired lounge to the boutique bedrooms with their creative feature walls; some even have baths in the room.

5 rooms – £ 90/150 £ 90/150

33 Northgate ✉ PE36 6AP – 01485 524352 – www.33hunstanton.co.uk

HUNSTRETE

Bath and North East Somerset – Regional map n° **2**-C2

The Pig

TRADITIONAL CUISINE • BRASSERIE XX This rustic hotel conservatory takes things back to nature with pots of fresh herbs placed on wooden tables and chimney pots filled with flowering shrubs. The extremely knowledgeable team serve dishes which showcase ingredients from their extensive gardens, along with produce sourced from within 25 miles.

Carte £ 24/43

The Pig Hotel, Hunstrete House ✉ BS39 4NS – 01761 490490 (booking essential) – www.thepighotel.com

The Pig

COUNTRY HOUSE • PERSONALISED Nestled in the Mendip Hills, with deer roaming around the parkland, this Grade II listed house is all about getting back to nature. It has a relaxed, friendly atmosphere and extremely comfortable bedrooms which feature handmade beds and fine linens; some are in converted sheds in the walled vegetable garden.

29 rooms – £ 155/315 £ 155/315 – £ 15

Hunstrete House ✉ BS39 4NS – 01761 490490 – www.thepighotel.com

The Pig – See restaurant listing

HUNTINGDON

Cambridgeshire – Pop. 23 937 – Regional map n° **8**-A2

Old Bridge

TOWNHOUSE • CONTEMPORARY Attractive 18C former bank next to the River Ouse; its bright, contemporary décor cleverly blended with the property's original features. Individually styled, up-to-date bedrooms; some with four-poster beds. Cosy oak-panelled bar, conservatory restaurant with a lovely terrace and a superbly stocked wine shop.

24 rooms – £ 95/135 £ 129/230

1 High St ✉ PE29 3TQ – 01480 424300 – www.huntsbridge.com

Abbots Ripton North: 6.5 mi by B1514 and A141 on B1090

Abbot's Elm

TRADITIONAL BRITISH • INN A modern reconstruction of an attractive 17C pub, with a spacious open-plan layout, homely touches and a vaulted, oak-beamed roof. Extensive menus offer hearty, flavoursome cooking; the wine list is a labour of love and the cosy, comfy bedrooms come with fluffy bathrobes and complimentary mineral water.

Carte £ 17/43

4 rooms – †£ 65/70 ††£ 80/90

Moat Lane ✉ PE28 2PA – ✆ 01487 773773 – www.theabbotselm.co.uk – Closed 1-14 January, Sunday dinner and Monday

at Hemingford Grey Southeast: 5 mi by A1198 off A14 ✉ Huntingdon

The Cock

TRADITIONAL CUISINE • PUB A homely country pub with a split-level bar and a spacious dining room; run by an experienced team. Tried-and-tested British cooking includes good value lunches and a repertoire of over 100 sausages.

Menu £ 16 (weekday lunch) – Carte £ 24/36

47 High St ✉ PE28 9BJ – ✆ 01480 463609 – www.cambscuisine.com

HURLEY

Windsor and Maidenhead – Pop. 1 712 – Regional map n° **6**-C3

Hurley House N

MODERN BRITISH • PUB Hurley House is a stylish place: outside you'll find a charming canopied terrace with patio heaters and its own bar, while inside smart furnishings sit amongst exposed bricks, beams and flagstones. Well-sourced ingredients underpin modern British dishes, which confidently blend contrasting tastes and textures. Well-appointed bedrooms pay great attention to detail.

Menu £ 29 (weekday lunch) – Carte £ 34/55

10 rooms – †£ 160/285 ††£ 170/295

Henley Rd ✉ SL6 5LH – East : 1 mi on A 4130 – ✆ 01628 568500 – www.hurleyhouse.co.uk – Closed Sunday dinner

HURWORTH-ON-TEES – Darlington → See Darlington

HUTTON MAGNA – Durham → See Barnard Castle

ICKHAM

Kent – Regional map n° **5**-D2

Duke William

MODERN BRITISH • PUB The smart exterior has more of a city than a country look but inside it has a good old neighbourhood vibe. Keenly priced menus list time-honoured classics everyone knows and loves. Cosy up on fur throw covered benches by the fire, then stay the night in one of the smart yet casual bedrooms.

Carte £ 22/46

4 rooms – †£ 90/110 ††£ 90/110

The Street ✉ CT3 1QP – ✆ 01227 721308 – www.thedukewilliamickham.com

ILFRACOMBE

Devon – Pop. 11 184 – Regional map n° **1**-C1

Thomas Carr @ The Olive Room

SEAFOOD • RUSTIC X A simple, homely restaurant set in a 19C townhouse and run by an experienced local chef. Ultra-fresh seafood is the focus, with dishes only confirmed once the day boat deliveries come in. Cooking is creative, with distinct flavours, and each dish comprises just 4 or 5 complementary ingredients. Bedrooms have a pleasant period feel and some have great views over the town.
→ Mackerel, leek and potato terrine with curried shrimp, celeriac and apple. Hake with bacon, lentils, Jerusalem artichoke, hazelnuts and scallops. Passion fruit parfait with doughnuts, meringue and frozen yoghurt.

Menu £ 48

5 rooms – †£ 55/90 ††£ 75/120

56 Fore St ✉ EX34 9DJ – ✆ 01271 867831 (booking essential) – www.thomascarrchef.co.uk – dinner only and lunch Friday-Saturday – Closed January, Sunday and Monday

Quay

MODERN BRITISH • DESIGN XX Long-standing restaurant on the harbourside; one of the first floor rooms overlooks the sea. It's owned by local lad Damien Hirst, who designed everything from the uniform to the crockery. Menus focus on local fish and Devon beef.

Carte £ 24/44

11 The Quay ✉ EX34 9EQ – ✆ 01271 868090 – www.11thequay.co.uk – Closed 2 weeks January

La Gendarmerie

MODERN CUISINE • RUSTIC X Once a police station, now a simple little restaurant with exposed stone walls and an intimate feel; personally run by a husband and wife team. Concise, daily changing menu showcases market produce in precise, skilfully executed combinations.

Menu £ 39

63 Fore St ✉ EX34 9ED – ✆ 01271 865984 (booking advisable) – www.lagendarmerie.co.uk – dinner only – Closed November-December, Sunday-Wednesday

Westwood

FAMILY • DESIGN Perched on the hillside overlooking the rooftops, this appealingly styled Victorian house offers warm décor and an eclectic mix of modern and retro furniture. Spacious bedrooms boast bold feature wallpaper; those to the front are the best.

5 rooms – †£ 80/115 ††£ 85/125

Torrs Pk ✉ EX34 8AZ – ✆ 01271 867443 – www.west-wood.co.uk

ILKLEY

West Yorkshire – Pop. 14 809 – Regional map n° 13-B2

Box Tree

MODERN BRITISH • ELEGANT XXX An iconic Yorkshire restaurant established back in 1962. It's set in two charming sandstone cottages and has a plush, antique-furnished lounge and two luxurious dining rooms. Cooking is refined and skilful, with a classical French base, and dishes are light and delicate. Only the best ingredients are used.
→ Hand-dived scallop with celeriac purée, truffle, Granny Smith apple and smoked eel. Mignon of veal 'ossobuco' with crispy sweetbreads, soubise, asparagus and Madeira. Apricot soufflé with bitter chocolate sauce.

Menu £ 38/80

37 Church St ✉ LS29 9DR – on A 65 – ✆ 01943 608484 – www.theboxtree.co.uk – dinner only and lunch Friday-Sunday – Closed 26-30 December, 1-7 January, Sunday dinner, Monday and Tuesday

ILMINGTON

Warwickshire – Pop. 712 – Regional map n° **19**-C3

Howard Arms

MODERN BRITISH • PUB Built from golden stone quarried in the village itself, The Howard Arms really is part of the local community. Hearty flavours are the order of the day and pub favourites are listed alongside more global dishes. Bedroom styles vary between the pub and the extension: 'Village' overlooks the village green.

Carte £ 22/45

8 rooms – †£ 88/120 ††£ 110/150

Lower Green ✉ CV36 4LT – ✆ 01608 682226 – www.howardarms.com

INGHAM

Norfolk – Pop. 376 – Regional map n° **8**-D1

Ingham Swan

MODERN BRITISH • PUB An attractive thatched pub with flint walls and exposed wooden beams. There's an array of menus – including a good value 'menu du jour' – all of which feature produce from their farm; eye-catching dishes are made up of many different elements. Bedrooms come with muted colour schemes and designer furnishings.

Menu £ 18/28 (weekdays) **s** – Carte £ 32/46 **s**

4 rooms – †£ 160/205 ††£ 160/205

Sea Palling Rd ✉ NR12 9AB – ✆ 01692 581099 (booking essential at dinner) – www.theinghamswan.co.uk – Closed 25-26 December

IPSWICH

Suffolk – Pop. 144 957 – Regional map n° **8**-C3

Trongs

CHINESE • FRIENDLY XX Loyal locals are always a good sign, and this sweet little restaurant has plenty. One brother cooks and the other looks after the service. Authentic dishes include spicy Hunanese specialities – ask and they will adjust the heat.

Carte £ 17/35

23 St Nicholas St ✉ IP1 1TW – ✆ 01473 256833 – dinner only – Closed 3 weeks August and Sunday

Eaterie

MODERN CUISINE • BRASSERIE X Modern hotel brasserie in an old salt warehouse, with a zinc-topped bar, gold pillars, modern art and padded booths. Tasty brasserie dishes and numerous specials focus largely on seafood. Eat on the terrace, overlooking the marina.

Menu £ 18 (lunch) – Carte dinner £ 25/40

Salthouse Harbour Hotel, 1 Neptune Quay ✉ IP4 1AX – ✆ 01473 226789 (bookings advisable at dinner) – www.salthouseharbour.co.uk

Salthouse Harbour

BUSINESS • PERSONALISED Stylish former salt warehouse – its trendy lobby-lounge boasts floor to ceiling windows and great marina views. Modern boutique bedrooms have well-appointed bathrooms; some feature chaise longues, copper slipper baths or balconies.

70 rooms – †£ 135/185 ††£ 160/250 – £ 14

1 Neptune Quay ✉ IP4 1AX – ✆ 01473 226789 – www.salthouseharbour.co.uk

Eaterie – See restaurant listing

Kesgrave Hall

HISTORIC • MODERN An impressive house built in 1812, with a delightful terrace overlooking large lawned gardens to a 38 acre wood. Stylish lounges have a relaxed, urban-chic feel. Luxurious bedrooms boast quality furnishings, modern facilities and stylish bathrooms. The busy brasserie offers a European menu.

23 rooms - £ 125/325 £ 125/325

Hall Rd, Kesgrave ✉ IP5 2PU - East : 4.75 mi by A 1214 on Bealings rd
- ✆ 01473 333471 - www.kesgravehall.com

at Chelmondiston Southeast : 6 mi by A 137 on B 1456

Red Lion

TRADITIONAL CUISINE • BISTRO X Smartly refurbished former pub with a few comfy chairs in the bar and two dining rooms furnished with dark wood tables and Lloyd Loom chairs. Menus offer a broad range of dishes and daily specials. The bubbly owner leads the service.

Carte £ 23/39

Main St ✉ IP9 1DX
- ✆ 01473 780400 - www.chelmondistonredlion.co.uk - Closed Sunday and Monday

at Hintlesham West: 5 mi by A1214 on A1071 ✉ Ipswich

Hintlesham Hall

COUNTRY HOUSE • CLASSIC Impressive Georgian manor house with 16C roots; the original ornate plasterwork and gold leaf inlaid cornicing remain. Bedrooms in the main house are grand; the courtyard rooms are more modern and some have terraces. Dine in the impressive 'Salon' or wood-panelled 'Parlour'; fresh herbs come from the garden.

32 rooms - £ 95/160 £ 195/225 - £ 13 - 1 suite

✉ IP8 3NS - West : 0.25 mi on A 1071
- ✆ 01473 652334 - www.hintleshamhall.com

IRBY

Merseyside - Regional map n° **11**-A3

Da Piero

ITALIAN • FAMILY XX The passionate owners of Da Piero extend a very warm welcome to one and all. The wide-ranging menu takes its influences from Sicily, where the chef grew up, and from Northern Italy, the birthplace of his mother. Portions are hearty.

Menu £ 19 (early dinner) - Carte £ 20/40

5-7 Mill Hill Rd ✉ CH61 4UB
- ✆ 0151 648 7373 (booking essential) - www.dapiero.co.uk - dinner only - Closed 1 week January, Sunday and Monday

IRONBRIDGE

Telford and Wrekin - Pop. 1 560 - Regional map n° **10**-B2

Library House

TOWNHOUSE • PERSONALISED Attractive former library, just a stone's throw from the famous bridge. It has a farmhouse-style breakfast room and a homely lounge where books sit on the old library shelves. Tastefully furnished bedrooms are named after poets.

3 rooms - £ 75/90 £ 100/125

11 Severn Bank ✉ TF8 7AN
- ✆ 01952 432299 - www.libraryhouse.com

IRTHINGTON

Cumbria – Regional map n° **12**-B1

Golden Fleece

TRADITIONAL BRITISH • COSY Find a spot beside the wood-burning stove and choose from a list of tasty pub classics, juicy mature steaks and proper pub puddings, and be sure to try something from the selection of local ales too. Comfy, cosy bedrooms are named after the words Cumbrian shepherds once used to count their sheep.

Carte £ 22/45

8 rooms – †£ 75/85 ††£ 85/120

Ruleholme ✉ CA6 4NF – Southeast : 1.5 mi off A 689 – ✆ 01228 573686 – www.thegoldenfleececumbria.co.uk – Closed 25 December and 1 January

ISLEHAM

Cambridgeshire – Pop. 2 228 – Regional map n° **8**-B2

Merry Monk

TRADITIONAL BRITISH • NEIGHBOURHOOD Originally 17C cottages, with time spent as a pub, this is now a quirky, rustic restaurant with beamed ceilings and farmhouse kitchen style décor. Hearty, flavoursome dishes use local produce and are given a personal twist by the chef.

Carte £ 23/47

30 West St ✉ CB7 5SB – ✆ 01638 780900 – www.merry-monk.co.uk – Closed 25-26 December

ISLE OF MAN → See Man (Isle of)

ITTERINGHAM

Norfolk – ✉ Aylsham – Regional map n° **8**-C1

Walpole Arms

MODERN BRITISH • PUB Pretty 18C pub in a sleepy village, with a surprisingly modern yet sympathetically designed interior. Refined dishes champion local ingredients and feature produce from their own farm; rare breed beef is a speciality.

Carte £ 21/42

The Common ✉ NR11 7AR – ✆ 01263 587258 – www.thewalpolearms.co.uk – Closed 25 December and Sunday dinner in winter

IXWORTH – Suffolk → See Bury St Edmunds

KELMSCOTT

Oxfordshire – Regional map n° **6**-A2

Plough

TRADITIONAL CUISINE • RURAL The 16C Plough has all the character you would expect of a pub its age, with rough stone walls, open fires and a cottage-style garden. Traditional menus list dishes you'll know and love, from buck rarebit to devilled lambs' kidneys.

Carte £ 25/35

8 rooms – †£ 100/120 ††£ 110/130

✉ GL7 3HG – ✆ 01367 253543 – www.theploughinnkelmscott.com – Closed dinner Sunday and Monday

KENDAL

Cumbria – Pop. 28 586 – Regional map n° **12**-B2

at Crosthwaite West: 5.25 mi by All Hallows Ln✉ Kendal

Punch Bowl Inn

TRADITIONAL BRITISH • INN Charming 17C inn set in the picturesque Lyth Valley, boasting antiques, cosy fires and exposed wood beams; dine either in the rustic bar or the more formal restaurant. Cooking has a classical base but also features some modern touches; dishes display a degree of complexity that you wouldn't usually find in a pub. Luxury bedrooms boast quality linens and roll-top baths.

Carte £ 28/48

9 rooms – £ 95/310 £ 110/310

✉ LA8 8HR – ✆ 015395 68237 – www.the-punchbowl.co.uk

KENILWORTH

Warwickshire – Pop. 22 413 – Regional map n° **10**-C2

Cross at Kenilworth (Adam Bennett)

CLASSIC CUISINE • ELEGANT Smartly furnished pub with eager, welcoming staff. Skilfully executed, classical cooking uses prime seasonal ingredients, and dishes not only look impressive but taste good too. Sit in the back room to watch the kitchen team in action. The bright, airy room next door used to be a classroom.

→ Crispy duck egg with Wye Valley asparagus, beer-cured ham and chicken jus. Wiltshire pork belly with crispy pig's head, salted plum purée and Yukon Gold mash. Rhubarb and gingerbread crumble soufflé with ginger ice cream.

Menu £ 25 (lunch) – Carte £ 43/60

16 New St ✉ CV8 2EZ – ✆ 01926 853840 – www.thecrosskenilworth.co.uk – Closed 25-26 December, 1 January, Sunday dinner and bank holidays

KENTISBURY

Devon – Regional map n° **1**-C1

Coach House by Michael Caines

MODERN CUISINE • DESIGN XX This smart hotel restaurant has a lovely walnut and marble bar counter, a funky lounge under the eaves and an elegant dining room featuring plush blue velvet booths. Flavoursome modern dishes use local meats and south coast fish.

Menu £ 20/52

Kentisbury Grange Hotel, ✉ EX31 4NL – Southeast : 1 mi by B 3229 on A39 – ✆ 01271 882295 – www.kentisburygrange.co.uk

Kentisbury Grange

COUNTRY HOUSE • DESIGN This Victorian country house may have a Grade II listing but it's been smartly decked out with designer fabrics and furnishings in the colours of its original stained glass windows. Go for one of the chic, detached Garden Suites.

16 rooms – £ 110/260 £ 110/260

✉ EX31 4NL – Southeast : 1 mi by B 3229 on A39 – ✆ 01271 882295 – www.kentisburygrange.co.uk

Coach House by Michael Caines – See restaurant listing

KENTON

Devon – Regional map n° **1**-D2

Rodean

TRADITIONAL BRITISH • NEIGHBOURHOOD XX Family-run restaurant – once a butcher's shop – overlooking a tiny village green. There's a small bar-lounge and two beamed dining rooms with dark wood panelling. Constantly evolving menus have a classical base and a modern edge.

Menu £ 24 – Carte £ 30/50

The Triangle ✉ EX6 8LS – ✆ 01626 890195 (booking advisable) – www.rodeanrestaurant.co.uk – dinner only and Sunday lunch – Closed Sunday dinner and Monday

KERRIDGE

Cheshire East – Regional map n° **11**-B3

Lord Clyde

MODERN CUISINE • PUB This keenly run village pub started life in 1843 as two weavers' cottages and has a pleasingly simple, rustic feel. Cooking is contrastingly modern: seasonal dishes are well-presented and the tasting menu is a popular choice.

Menu £ 20 (lunch and early dinner) – Carte £ 24/38

36 Clarke Ln ✉ SK10 5AH – ✆ 01625 562123 – www.thelordclyde.co.uk – Closed Monday

KESWICK

Cumbria – Pop. 4 984 – Regional map n° **12**-A2

Brossen

STEAKHOUSE • FRIENDLY XX Meaning 'stuffed' in Cumbrian, Brossen is a sleek, Scandic-style steakhouse in a smartly refurbished coaching inn. Local steaks are the focus, although there are plenty of other choices too, from rotisserie chicken to venison.

Carte £ 26/49

Inn on the Square Hotel, Market Sq ✉ CA12 5JF – ✆ 017687 73333 – www.innonthesquare.co.uk

Morrel's

MODERN BRITISH • BRASSERIE XX Popular local eatery with scrubbed wood flooring, etched glass dividers and a buzzy atmosphere. Seasonally changing dishes have subtle Mediterranean influences; some come in two sizes. Good value menus.

Menu £ 22 (weekdays) – Carte £ 23/40

34 Lake Rd ✉ CA12 5DQ – ✆ 017687 72666 – www.morrels.co.uk – dinner only – Closed 4-17 January, 24-26 December and Monday

Inn on the Square

TOWNHOUSE • CONTEMPORARY This classic 19C coaching inn stands proudly on the square. Inside it's surprisingly modern, with bright, bold furnishings, a cocktail bar and a cosy pub. Bedrooms have top facilities and locally made beds; some have sheep murals!

34 rooms – †£ 148 ††£ 296

Market Sq ✉ CA12 5JF – ✆ 017687 73333 – www.innonthesquare.co.uk

Brossen – See restaurant listing

Howe Keld 

FAMILY • CONTEMPORARY These two strikingly decorated slate cottages stand in the centre of town but if you have a room with a view down the valley, you'll find that hard to believe. Breakfast is a must and comes with a Swiss accent.

12 rooms – †£ 70/90 ††£ 115/135

5-7 The Heads ✉ CA12 5ES – ✆ 017687 72417 – www.howekeld.co.uk – Closed January-mid February

at Braithwaite West: 2 mi by A66 on B5292✉ Keswick

Cottage in the Wood 

MODERN BRITISH • ROMANTIC XX A keenly run restaurant in a superb forest setting, with a lovely terrace and great views over the fells and valley below; watch the birds and squirrels as you eat. Ambitious dishes feature many ingredients foraged from the surrounding forest. Bedrooms are contemporary – some have whirlpool baths.

Menu £ 45/55 **s**

10 rooms – †£ 96/120 ††£ 120/220

Magic Hill, Whinlatter Forest ✉ CA12 5TW – Northwest : 1.75 mi on B 5292 – ✆ 017687 78409 (bookings essential for non-residents) – www.thecottageinthewood.co.uk – Closed 2-25 January, Sunday and Monday

KETTERING

Northamptonshire – Pop. 56 226 – Regional map n° **9**-C3

at Rushton Northwest : 3.5 mi by A 14 and Rushton Rd

Tresham

MODERN CUISINE • ELEGANT XXX Named after the man who built the magnificent mansion in which this grand restaurant resides. Sit under an ornate plaster ceiling, surrounded by wood-panelled walls. Cooking is modern and elaborate.

Menu £ 55

Rushton Hall Hotel, ✉ NN14 1RR – ✆ 01536 713001 – www.rushtonhall.com – dinner only

Rushton Hall

COUNTRY HOUSE • HISTORIC An imposing 15C house with stunning architecture, set in 28 acres of countryside. The Grand Hall features huge stained glass windows and an impressive fireplace. Luxurious bedrooms are classically furnished.

50 rooms – £ 150/380 £ 170/400 – 3 suites

✉ NN14 1RR – ✆ 01536 713001 – www.rushtonhall.com

Tresham – See restaurant listing

KETTLESING – North Yorkshire ➔ See Harrogate

KEYSTON

Cambridgeshire – ✉ Huntingdon – Pop. 257 – Regional map n° **8**-A2

Pheasant

TRADITIONAL BRITISH • PUB Hidden away in a sleepy hamlet is this big pub with enormous character; think exposed beams, hunting scenes and John Bull wallpaper. The wide-ranging menu includes a section of classics and there's an excellent value set menu. Staff are warm and attentive and there's a delightful rear terrace too.

Menu £ 20 (lunch and early dinner) – Carte £ 24/42

Village Loop Rd ✉ PE28 0RE – ✆ 01832 710241 (booking essential) – www.thepheasant-keyston.co.uk – Closed 2-15 January, Sunday dinner and Monday

KIBWORTH BEAUCHAMP

Leicestershire – Pop. 3 550 – Regional map n° **9**-B2

Lighthouse

SEAFOOD • NEIGHBOURHOOD X With its array of nautical knick-knacks, the Lighthouse is a fitting name. The flexible menu has a seafood emphasis and offers many dishes in two different sizes; the 'Nibbles' are a popular choice.

Menu £ 15 (weekdays) – Carte £ 20/38

9 Station St ✉ LE8 0LN – ✆ 0116 279 6260 (booking essential) – www.lighthousekibworth.co.uk – dinner only – Closed Sunday, Monday and bank holidays

KIBWORTH HARCOURT

Leicestershire – Pop. 5 433 – Regional map n° **9**-B2

Boboli

ITALIAN • NEIGHBOURHOOD X Buzzy, laid-back Italian restaurant with a sunny terrace; formerly a pub, it has a central bar and a rustic feel. Choose from an extensive selection of boldly flavoured seasonal dishes and satisfyingly affordable wines.

Menu £ 15 (weekday lunch) – Carte £ 18/43

88 Main St ✉ LE8 0NQ – ✆ 0116 279 3303 – www.bobolirestaurant.co.uk – Closed 25-26 December and 1 January

KILPECK

Herefordshire – Regional map n° **10**-A3

Kilpeck Inn

TRADITIONAL CUISINE • PUB A popular pub which narrowly escaped being turned into private housing thanks to the villagers' valiantly fought 'Save Our Pub' campaign. Its spacious interior and bedrooms are smart, modern and characterful, with impressive green credentials. Menus offer locally sourced meats and old fashioned puddings.

Carte £ 24/40

4 rooms – £ 70/100 £ 80/110

HR2 9DN – 01981 570464 – www.kilpeckinn.com – Closed 25 December, Monday lunch except bank holidays and Sunday dinner

KINGHAM

Oxfordshire – Pop. 547 – Regional map n° **6**-A1

The Wild Rabbit

MODERN BRITISH • ELEGANT Just down the road from the Daylesford Farm Shop is the Bamford family's lovely stone pub with a subtle leporine theme. Well-judged, flavoursome modern dishes have plenty of appeal – aside from the 40-day matured charcoal-grilled steak, this is restaurant-style food. Bedrooms are delightfully understated.

Carte £ 41/61

15 rooms – £ 160/420 £ 175/420

Church St OX7 6YA – 01608 658389 (booking advisable) – www.thewildrabbit.co.uk – Closed 1-4 January

Kingham Plough

MODERN BRITISH • PUB A rustic, laid-back pub located on the green of an unspoilt Cotswold village and run by an experienced chef-owner and a friendly team. The bar menu offers tasty classics, while the à la carte evolves as new ingredients arrive. Comfy bedrooms await: numbers 6 and 7 are the best.

Carte £ 34/48

6 rooms – £ 110/150 £ 145/195

The Green OX7 6YD – 01608 658327 – www.thekinghamplough.co.uk – Closed 25 December

KING'S LYNN

Norfolk – Pop. 46 093 – Regional map n° **8**-B1

Bank House

MODERN CUISINE • BRASSERIE This Georgian townhouse was also once a bank. Dine in the contemporary former kitchen, the billiard room or the old banking hall, from a menu of British classics and Mediterranean-inspired fare. Colourful dishes burst with flavour.

Carte £ 22/35

Bank House Hotel, King's Staithe Sq PE30 1RD – 01553 660492 – www.thebankhouse.co.uk

Market Bistro

MODERN BRITISH • BISTRO 17C beams and a fireplace remain but this relaxed bistro is more up-to-date than its exterior suggests. Fresh, unfussy cooking uses passionately sourced local produce and modern techniques. The chef's wife looks after the service.

Menu £ 17 (weekday lunch) – Carte £ 25/43

11 Saturday Market Pl PE30 5DQ – 01553 771483 – www.marketbistro.co.uk – Closed 26 December, 1 and 7-14 January, Sunday, Monday and lunch Tuesday

Bank House

TOWNHOUSE • COSY A charming Grade II Georgian townhouse on the quayside; it was once a wine merchant's house and later the place where Barclays Bank was founded. Cosy bedrooms mix modern fabrics with antique furnishings; bathrooms are luxurious.

12 rooms – £ 85/120 £ 115/220

King's Staithe Sq ✉ PE30 1RD
– ✆ 01553 660492 – www.thebankhouse.co.uk

Bank House – See restaurant listing

at Grimston East: 6.25 mi by A148

Congham Hall

MODERN CUISINE • INTIMATE XXX Start with a drink in the elegant hotel bar, then head for the spacious dining room with its super terrace and garden views. Appealing menus have something to please everyone, from good old classics to more modern fare.

Menu £ 18 (weekday lunch) – Carte £ 29/41

Congham Hall Hotel, Lynn Rd. ✉ PE32 1AH
– ✆ 01485 600250 – www.conghamhallhotel.co.uk

Congham Hall

COUNTRY HOUSE • ELEGANT Part-Georgian country house in 30 acres of peaceful grounds. Guest areas include a snug bar and a spacious drawing room with a subtle modern style. Opt for a lovely Garden Room by the spa, overlooking the flower or herb gardens.

26 rooms – £ 135/399 £ 135/399 – £ 15 – 2 suites

Lynn Rd. ✉ PE32 1AH
– ✆ 01485 600250 – www.conghamhallhotel.co.uk

Congham Hall – See restaurant listing

KINGS MILLS → See Channel Islands (Guernsey)

KING'S SUTTON

Northamptonshire – Pop. 2 069 – Regional map n° **9**-B3

White Horse

MODERN BRITISH • PUB Pretty sandstone pub run by a keen young couple. The self-taught chef makes everything from scratch and always tries to exceed his guests' expectations. Produce is fresh and local and follows a 'when it's gone, it's gone' approach.

Menu £ 12 (lunch) – Carte £ 24/40

2 The Square ✉ OX17 3RF
– ✆ 01295 812440 – www.whitehorseks.co.uk – Closed 27-30 December, Sunday dinner and Monday-Tuesday

KINGSBRIDGE

Devon – Pop. 6 116 – Regional map n° **1**-C3

Buckland-Tout-Saints

HISTORIC • CLASSIC Appealing Queen Anne mansion set in large, peaceful grounds. Traditional, antique-furnished interior with wood-panelling in many rooms. Bedrooms vary in shape and size; some have a classic country house feel and others are more contemporary. Choice of two dining rooms offering accomplished dishes.

16 rooms – £ 79/189 £ 141/243 – 2 suites

Goveton ✉ TQ7 2DS – Northeast : 3 mi by A 381
– ✆ 01548 853055 – www.tout-saints.co.uk

KINGSTON-UPON-HULL

Kingston upon Hull – Pop. 284 321 – Regional map n° **13**-D2

1884 Dock Street Kitchen

MODERN CUISINE • FASHIONABLE XX A red-brick former ropery by the marina; built in 1884, it's now a stylish brasserie with a smart bar, an open kitchen and a buzzy feel. Elaborate modern dishes feature many different ingredients.

Menu £ 20 (weekdays) – Carte £ 35/55

Humber Dock St, Hull Marina ✉ HU1 1TB
– ✆ 01482 222260 – www.1884dockstreetkitchen.co.uk
– Closed 2-5 January, Sunday dinner and Monday lunch

Tapasya

INDIAN • DESIGN XX White banquettes set under chandeliers, a glass wine cellar, and a wall of water behind the bar set the scene for some sophisticated cooking. Carefully spiced dishes use good ingredients and are presented in a modern manner.

Carte £ 18/35

590-582 Beverley High Rd ✉ HU6 7LH – North : 1.5 mi on A 1079
– ✆ 01482 242606 – www.tapasyarestaurants.co.uk

KINGSWEAR

Devon → See Dartmouth

KIRKBY LONSDALE

Cumbria – Pop. 1 843 – Regional map n° **12**-B3

Sun Inn

TRADITIONAL BRITISH • PUB 17C inn with a characterful beamed bar and a smartly furnished restaurant which comes into its own in the evening. Menus are concise; bar snacks are served throughout the day and dinner is a serious affair. Smart modern bedrooms boast quality linens and thoughtful extras – the breakfasts are delicious.

Menu £ 28 (dinner) – Carte lunch £ 17/32

11 rooms – †£ 75/180 ††£ 99/190

6 Market St ✉ LA6 2AU
– ✆ 015242 71965 – www.sun-inn.info – Closed Monday lunch

Royal 

TRADITIONAL • CONTEMPORARY Well-run Georgian hotel overlooking a characterful town square. The décor is a mix of modern and shabby-chic, and the owner has a keen eye for detail. Bedrooms are spacious; some have free-standing baths in the room. Snug, open-fired lounge and an all-day brasserie serving classics and wood-fired pizzas.

14 rooms – †£ 80/160 ††£ 95/230

Main St ✉ LA6 2AE
– ✆ 015242 71966 – www.royalhotelkirkbylonsdale.co.uk

Plato's 

TOWNHOUSE • PERSONALISED Georgian-style townhouse once home to Plato Harrison wine merchants. Tastefully decorated bedrooms blend modern furnishings with period charm and come with thoughtful extras. The all-day coffee-shop-cum-café offers an extensive range of modern, international dishes ranging from tapas to tasting boards.

9 rooms – †£ 72/112 ††£ 78/162

2 Mill Brow ✉ LA6 2AT
– ✆ 015242 74180 – www.platoskirkbylonsdale.co.uk

at Lupton Northwest: 4.75 mi on A65

Plough

TRADITIONAL BRITISH • PUB A homely former coaching inn with exposed beams and open fires, set on the main road from the Lake District to North Yorkshire. Sit in the shabby-chic bar or smarter pink-hued restaurant and choose from an appealing list of traditionally-based dishes. Smart, individually styled bedrooms boast roll-top baths.

Carte £ 24/34

6 rooms – £ 85/195 £ 85/195

Cow Brow LA6 1PJ – 015395 67700 – www.theploughatlupton.co.uk

KIRKBY STEPHEN

Cumbria – Pop. 1 522 – Regional map n° **12**-B2

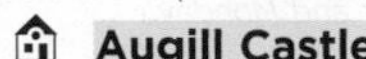

Augill Castle

FAMILY • CLASSIC A carefully restored, castellated country house filled with period furniture and antiques. It has three interconnecting sitting rooms with vast open fires and a dining room with an ornate plaster ceiling; traditional dishes are taken at a communal table. Many bedrooms have four-poster beds or roll-top baths.

15 rooms – £ 160 £ 160/320

CA17 4DE – Northeast : 4.25 mi by A 685 – 017683 41937 – www.stayinacastle.com

KIRKBY THORE

Cumbria – Pop. 758 – Regional map n° **12**-B2

Bridge

TRADITIONAL CUISINE • BISTRO A remodelled roadside pub with a bright extension and a bistro feel, which is keenly run by a husband and wife team. Cooking has a likeable simplicity, with the odd Asian touch, and there's a tempting display of cakes on the counter.

Menu £ 14 (weekday lunch) – Carte £ 21/39

CA10 1UZ – on A66 – 017683 62766 – www.thebridgebistro.co.uk – Closed Sunday dinner

KIRKBYMOORSIDE

North Yorkshire – Pop. 2 751 – Regional map n° **13**-C1

Cornmill

HISTORIC • TRADITIONAL Charming 18C cornmill with a pleasant courtyard and gardens; look for the mill race running beneath the glass panel in the characterful breakfast room. The cosy lounge and elegant bedrooms are set in the old farmhouse and stables.

5 rooms – £ 65/110 £ 85/110

Kirby Mills YO62 6NP – East : 0.5 mi by A 170 – 01751 432000 – www.kirbymills.co.uk

KNARESBOROUGH

North Yorkshire – Pop. 15 484 – Regional map n° **13**-B2

at Ferrensby Northeast: 3 mi on A6055

General Tarleton

TRADITIONAL BRITISH • INN XX Characterful 18C coaching inn with low beams and exposed stone walls; most sit in the main room but there's also a glass-roofed courtyard and a large terrace for warmer days. Hearty dishes champion Yorkshire produce. Bedrooms feature solid oak furnishings and come with home-baked biscuits.

Menu £ 15 (lunch and early dinner) – Carte £ 26/44

13 rooms – £ 75/85 £ 129/150

Boroughbridge Rd HG5 0PZ – 01423 340284 – www.generaltarleton.co.uk

KNOWSTONE

Devon – ✉ South Molton – Regional map n° **1**-C1

 **Masons Arms** (Mark Dodson) 

CLASSIC FRENCH • PUB This pretty 13C inn sits in a secluded village. Dine in the cosy bar or take in delightful country views from beneath a Grecian ceiling mural in the bright rear dining room. Cooking is refined, ingredients are top class and flavours are pronounced and assured. Charming service is a perfect match for the food.

➜ Arrancini with beetroot '3 ways'. Fillet of halibut with sage crust and chive sauce. Trio of raspberry desserts.

Menu £ 25 (lunch) – Carte £ 42/51

✉ EX36 4RY – ✆ 01398 341231 (booking essential) – www.masonsarmsdevon.co.uk – Closed first week January, 1 week mid-February, 10 days August-September, Sunday dinner and Monday

LA HAULE ➜ See Channel Islands (Jersey)

LA PULENTE ➜ See Channel Islands (Jersey)

LANCASTER

Lancashire – Pop. 48 085 – Regional map n° **11**-A1

Ashton 

TRADITIONAL • MODERN Georgian house surrounded by lawned gardens; stylishly decorated and personally run by a friendly owner. Good-sized boldly coloured bedrooms feature a blend of modern and antique furniture. Meat, fish or cheese dinner platters by arrangement.

5 rooms – †£ 105/135 ††£ 135/185

Wyresdale Rd ✉ LA1 3JJ – Southeast : 1.25 mi by A 6 on Clitheroe rd – ✆ 01524 68460 – www.theashtonlancaster.com

LANGAR

Nottinghamshire – Regional map n° **9**-B2

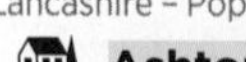

Langar Hall

COUNTRY HOUSE • QUIRKY Characterful Georgian manor surrounded by over 20 acres of pastoral land and ponds; its antique-furnished bedrooms named after those who've featured in the house's history. Dine by candlelight in the elegant, pillared dining room; classically based cooking features veg from the kitchen garden and local game.

12 rooms – †£ 100/160 ††£ 125/225 – 1 suite

✉ NG13 9HG – ✆ 01949 860559 – www.langarhall.co.uk

LANGHO – Lancashire ➜ See Blackburn

LANGTHWAITE – North Yorkshire ➜ See Reeth

LAPWORTH

Warwickshire – Pop. 2 100 – Regional map n° **10**-C2

 **Boot Inn** 

TRADITIONAL BRITISH • PUB A big, buzzy pub boasting a large terrace, a traditional quarry-floored bar and a modern restaurant. Dishes range from sandwiches, picnic boards and sharing plates to more sophisticated specials. You can eat in a tepee in the summer!

Menu £ 15 (lunch and early dinner) – Carte £ 24/44

Old Warwick Rd ✉ B94 6JU – ✆ 01564 782464 (booking essential) – www.bootinnlapworth.co.uk

LAVENHAM

Suffolk – ✉ Sudbury – Pop. 1 413 – Regional map n° **8**-C3

Great House

CLASSIC FRENCH • ELEGANT XXX Passionately run restaurant on the main square of an attractive town; its impressive Georgian façade concealing a timbered house with 14C origins. Choose between two dining rooms and a smart enclosed terrace. Concise menus offer ambitious dishes with worldwide influences and a French heart. Stylish, contemporary décor blends well with the old beams in the bedrooms.

Menu £ 25/37 – Carte £ 43/54

5 rooms – †£ 95/215 ††£ 125/215 – ☕ £ 12

Market Pl ✉ CO10 9QZ
– ✆ 01787 247431 – www.greathouse.co.uk
– Closed 3 weeks January, 2 weeks summer, Sunday dinner, Monday and lunch Tuesday

Brasserie

MODERN CUISINE • RUSTIC XX Smart restaurant offering a classic bistro menu. Modern furnishings blend with the more traditional elements of the historic inn in which it resides. In winter, sit by the fire; in summer, sit on the terrace overlooking the gardens.

Menu £ 24/60

The Swan at Lavenham Hotel, High St ✉ CO10 9QA
– ✆ 01787 247477 – www.theswanatlavenham.co.uk

The Swan at Lavenham H & Spa

HISTORIC • PERSONALISED A characterful 15C coaching inn with several delightful lounges, a hugely atmospheric bar and a smart spa with a terrace. Beamed bedrooms have a subtle contemporary style. Dine on classics in the smart brasserie or on more modern dishes beneath a minstrels' gallery – with piano accompaniment at weekends.

45 rooms ☕ – †£ 98 ††£ 180/360 – 1 suite

High St ✉ CO10 9QA
– ✆ 01787 247477 – www.theswanatlavenham.co.uk

Brasserie – See restaurant listing

at Preston St Mary Northeast 2.75 mi by A 1141

Six Bells

TRADITIONAL CUISINE • PUB An attractive brick and timber pub in a small hamlet. Heavy timbers are hung with tankards, open fires punctuate brick walls and a hunting theme runs throughout. Restaurant-style dishes are carefully and confidently prepared.

Menu £ 17 (weekday lunch) – Carte £ 24/33

The Street ✉ CO10 9NG
– ✆ 01787 247440 – www.thesixbellspreston.com – Closed Monday and Tuesday

LEDBURY

Herefordshire – Pop. 8 862 – Regional map n° **10**-B3

Verzon

MODERN BRITISH • CHIC XX A smartly restored Georgian manor house with a laid-back vibe. The chic restaurant offers a menu of precisely prepared, classic British dishes. It's owned by the local Chase Distillery, so the gins and vodkas are well worth a try. Most of the seductively styled bedrooms have a country view.

Carte £ 27/51

8 rooms ☕ – †£ 80/95 ††£ 100/250

Hereford Rd ✉ HR8 2PZ – Northwest: 3.25 mi on A 438
– ✆ 01531 670381 – www.verzonhouse.com
– Closed Sunday dinner and Monday

LEEBOTWOOD

Shropshire – Regional map n° **10**-B2

The Pound Inn

TRADITIONAL CUISINE • NEIGHBOURHOOD It might have been modernised inside but there's still plenty of character to be found, courtesy of flagged floors, a large inglenook fireplace and a wooden bar. Choose from a small list of classics or some more ambitious options.

Carte £ 24/31

SY6 6ND – 01694 751477 – www.thepound.org.uk – Closed first 2 weeks November, Sunday dinner, Monday and Tuesday

LEEDS

Kent – Regional map n° **5**-C2

Leeds Castle

HISTORIC BUILDING • PERSONALISED This unique accommodation is found in the grounds of 900 year old Leeds Castle. Stay in smart, modern bedrooms in the 1920s stable block or in a more historic room in the Maiden's Tower (an old Tudor bakehouse beside the castle). The timbered café morphs into a candlelit restaurant in the evening.

22 rooms – †£ 85/100 ††£ 120/170

Broomfield Gate ME17 1PL – Southeast: 3 mi by A 20 – 01622 767823 – www.leeds-castle.co.uk – Closed 24-26 December

R. Harding/hemis.fr

GOOD TIPS!

This former mill town is now known as the 'Knightsbridge of the North', so it comes as no surprise to find restaurants located in retail spaces: from **Crafthouse** in the Trinity shopping centre to the brasserie on the **Fourth Floor at Harvey Nichols** and Michelin Starred **The Man Behind the Curtain** in a basement in Vicar Lane.

LEEDS

West Yorkshire – Pop. 751 485 – Regional map n° **13**-B2

Restaurants

✿ The Man Behind the Curtain (Michael O'Hare)

MODERN CUISINE • FASHIONABLE XX A uniquely styled restaurant comprising black marble, polished concrete and bold modern art. Accomplished, highly skilled cooking showcases some very original, creative combinations and the artful presentation is equally striking. Choose 10 courses at lunch or 14 at dinner from a 'collection' of 30 dishes.

➜ Raw Denia prawn; roasted head. Ox cheek with foie gras, puffed wild rice, black truffle and spinach. Praline and passion fruit.

Menu £ 60/90 – surprise menu only

Town plan: B2-c – *68-78 Vicar Ln ✉ LS1 7JH – ✆ 0113 243 2376 (booking essential) – www.themanbehindthecurtain.co.uk – dinner only and lunch Thursday-Saturday – Closed 23 December-4 January and Sunday-Monday*

Brasserie Forty 4

CLASSIC CUISINE • BRASSERIE XX A bright, stylish bar and brasserie sit within this 18C warehouse. Classic dishes have French foundations and fine Yorkshire ingredients underpin the menu. Pick a table overlooking the canal or head for the small terrace.

Carte £ 25/34

Town plan: B2-z – *44 The Calls ✉ LS2 7EW – ✆ 0113 234 3232 – www.brasserie44.com – Closed 3 days Christmas*

Crafthouse

MODERN CUISINE • DESIGN XX A bright, chic restaurant in the Trinity shopping centre, with great rooftop views and a wraparound terrace. Creative, elaborate dishes showcase a huge array of ingredients. The open kitchen and marble counter take centre stage. Start with a cocktail in all-day Angelica.

Menu £ 19 (weekday lunch) – Carte £ 28/60

Town plan: A2-a – *Trinity Leeds (5th Floor), 70 Boar Ln ✉ LS1 6HW – ✆ 0113 897 0444 – www.crafthouse-restaurant.co.uk – Closed 25 December and 1 January*

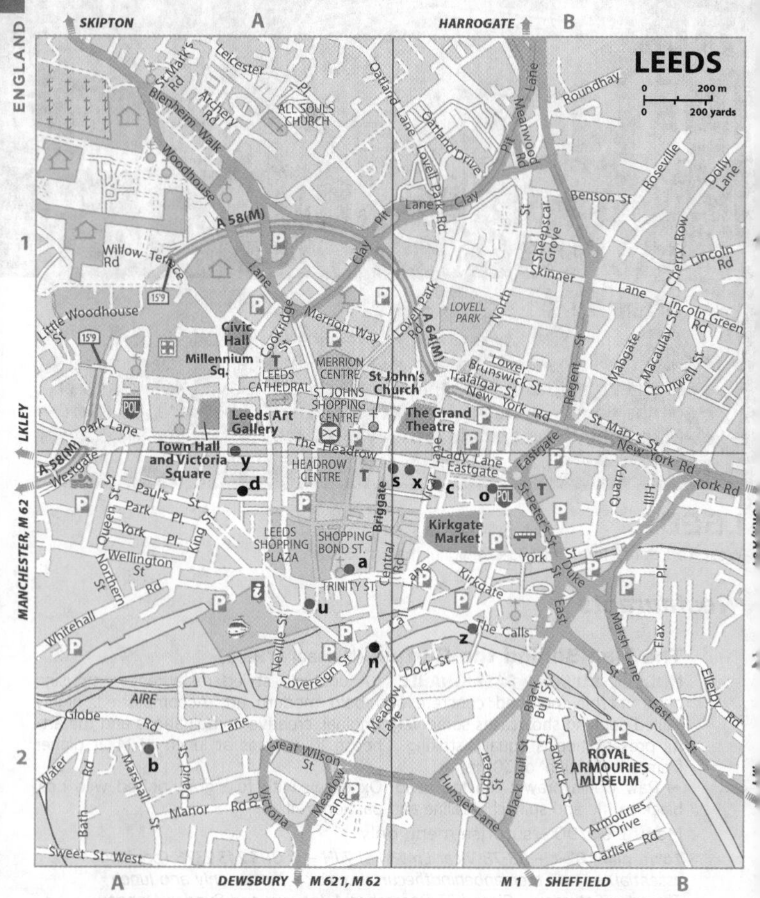

Fourth Floor at Harvey Nichols

MODERN BRITISH • BRASSERIE XX Set at the top of a famous department store; the airy open-plan bar and dining room are divided by metal fretwork screens, and full length windows and a terrace provide rooftop views. Cooking is modern and globally influenced.

Menu £ 22 (lunch and early dinner) – Carte £ 24/51

Town plan: AB2-s – *107-111 Briggate ✉ LS1 6AZ – ✆ 0113 204 8000 (booking essential at lunch) – www.harveynichols.com – Closed 25 December, 1 January, Easter Sunday and dinner Sunday-Monday*

Issho (N)

JAPANESE • FASHIONABLE XX This chic eatery in Victoria Gate serves modern Japanese cooking in a stylish setting, including sushi, tempura and dishes from the robata grill. Enjoy cocktails in the bar and city skyline views from the roof-top terrace.

Menu £ 25 (early dinner) – Carte £ 22/57

Town plan: B2-o – *Victoria Gate ✉ LS2 7JL – ✆ 0113 426 5000 – www.issho-restaurant.com – Closed Sunday dinner and Monday*

Stockdales of Yorkshire

MEATS AND GRILLS • CLASSIC DÉCOR Here, it's is all about showcasing the county's best ingredients in attractively presented dishes, with Josper-cooked beef – including Yorkshire Wagyu – a speciality. Sit in the comfy lounge-bar or attractive basement restaurant.

Menu £ 23 (weekday lunch) – Carte £ 26/67

Town plan: A1-2-y – *8 South Par ✉ LS1 5QX – ✆ 0113 204 2460 – www.stockdales-restaurant.com – Closed 24-26 December, 1 January and Sunday dinner*

Bundobust

INDIAN VEGETARIAN • EXOTIC DÉCOR The simplicity is part of the fun: order at the bar, grab a paper plate and some plastic cutlery, find a space on the communal benches and get stuck in! Authentic vegetarian street food includes delicious masala dosas and okra fries.

Carte £ 12/18

Town plan: A2-u – *6 Mill Hill ✉ LS1 5DQ – ✆ 0113 243 1248 – www.bundobust.com – Closed 25-26 December and 1 January*

Foundry

TRADITIONAL CUISINE • WINE BAR Simply styled bistro-cum-wine bar on the site of the legendary steel foundry, with a vaulted ceiling, ornate bar and laid-back feel. Wine box ends and 'squashed' bottles feature. Classic dishes include plenty of specials.

Menu £ 13 (weekday lunch) – Carte £ 22/40

Town plan: A2-b – *1 Saw Mill Yard, The Round Foundry ✉ LS11 5WH – ✆ 0113 245 0390 – www.thefoundrywinebar.co.uk – Closed first week January, last week August, 25-26 December, Saturday lunch, Sunday and Monday*

Ox Club

BARBECUE • SIMPLE A former mill houses this multi-floor venue comprising a beer hall, cocktail bar, event space and restaurant. The latter boasts a wood-fired grill imported from the USA; rustic, smoky-flavoured dishes showcase Yorkshire ingredients.

Menu £ 17 (early dinner) – Carte £ 20/30

Town plan: B2-x – *Bramleys Yard, The Headrow ✉ LS1 6PU – ✆ 07470 359961 – www.oxclub.co.uk – dinner only and lunch Saturday-Sunday – Closed 25-26 December, 1 January, Sunday dinner and Monday*

Tharavadu

INDIAN • EXOTIC DÉCOR A simple-looking restaurant with seascape murals. The extensive menu offers superbly spiced, colourful Keralan specialities and refined street food – the dosas are a hit. Service is friendly and dishes arrive swiftly.

Carte £ 19/33

Town plan: A2-u – *7-8 Mill Hill ✉ LS1 5DQ – ✆ 0113 244 0500 (booking essential) – www.tharavadurestaurants.com – Closed 23-26 December and Sunday*

Hotels

Dakota Deluxe

BUSINESS • MODERN Its location in the heart of the business district and its stylish, well-equipped bedrooms make this design hotel ideal for business travellers. It's tucked away in a pedestrianised square and its dark, intimate décor provides a calming influence. The bar is a popular spot, as is the seductive restaurant.

84 rooms – †£ 115/275 ††£ 115/275 – 1 suite

Town plan: A2-d – *8 Russell St ✉ LS1 5RN – ✆ 0113 322 6261 – www.leeds.dakotahotels.co.uk*

Malmaison

BUSINESS • DESIGN A chic boutique hotel in the former offices of the city's tram and bus department. Generously sized bedrooms have warm colour schemes and good comforts; for special occasions book the stylish suite. Smart, intimate guest areas include a relaxing bar and a modern take on a brasserie.

100 rooms – †£ 85/175 ††£ 85/175 – ☕ £ 14 – 1 suite

Town plan: A2-n – *1 Swinegate* ✉ *LS1 4AG*
– *✆ 0113 426 0047 – www.malmaison.com*

LEICESTER

Leicester – Pop. 443 760 – Regional map n° **9**-B2

Hotel Maiyango

BUSINESS • MODERN Privately owned city centre hotel in a 150 year old shoe factory. The interior is stylish and the trendy bar boasts a terrace overlooking the rooftops. Spacious, individually designed bedrooms have bespoke wood furnishings and a colonial feel. The oriental restaurant serves global dishes with Indian spicing.

14 rooms – †£ 79/149 ††£ 79/149 – ☕ £ 10 – 1 suite

Town plan: A1-a – *13-21 St Nicholas Pl* ✉ *LE1 4LD*
– *✆ 0116 251 8898 – www.maiyango.com*
– *Closed 25-26 December*

LEINTWARDINE

Herefordshire – ✉ Craven Arms – Regional map n° **10**-A2

The Lion

TRADITIONAL BRITISH • CLASSIC DÉCOR 18C inn on the banks of the River Teme, next to an attractive medieval bridge. It's relaxed and stylish with a proper bar and a slightly smarter dining room with river views. Dishes are nicely presented and local produce plays a big part. Smart bedrooms have up-to-date facilities; some have river views.

Carte £ 23/38

8 rooms ☕ – †£ 75/95 ††£ 100/120

✉ *SY7 0JZ*
– *✆ 01547 540203 – www.thelionleintwardine.co.uk*
– *Closed 25 December*

LEWANNICK

Cornwall – Regional map n° **1**-B2

Coombeshead Farm

COUNTRY HOUSE • PERSONALISED Set on a working farm, in 66 acres of meadows and woodland, this former farmhouse offers accommodation and communal dining for just 12 guests. Menus offer a mix of small and large sharing dishes; the owners' aim is to bring diners closer to where raw ingredients are produced. They also run cookery workshops.

6 rooms ☕ – †£ 55/120 ††£ 120/185

✉ *PL15 7QQ – Southeast 0.7mi by Callington/ North Hill rd and Trelaske rd on Congdons Shop rd*
– *✆ 01566 782009 – www.coombesheadfarm.co.uk – Closed January*

LEWDOWN

Devon – Regional map n° **1**-C2

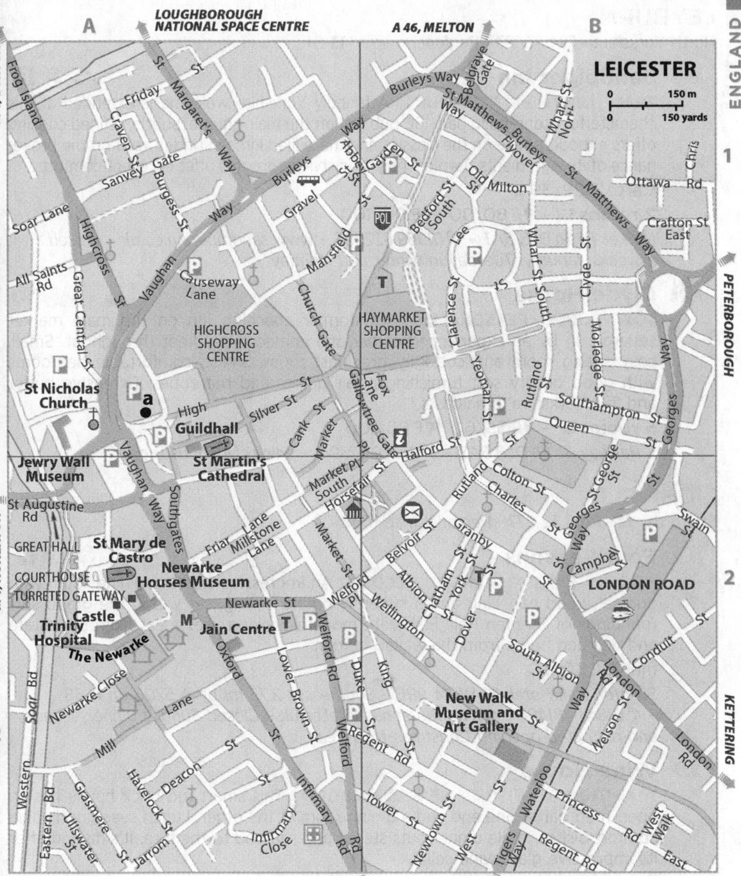

Lewtrenchard Manor

MODERN BRITISH • INTIMATE XX Intimate wood-panelled dining room in a Jacobean manor house. Cooking is contrastingly modern yet refreshingly unadorned; flavoursome garden produce features. For a more unique experience book 'Purple Carrot' (the chef's table).

Menu £ 50 (dinner) – Carte £ 27/40

Lewtrenchard Manor Hotel, ✉ EX20 4PN – South : 0.75 mi by Lewtrenchard rd – ✆ 01566 783222 (booking essential) – www.lewtrenchard.co.uk

Lewtrenchard Manor

HISTORIC • ELEGANT Hugely impressive Grade II listed Jacobean manor house in mature grounds. The characterful antique-furnished interior features huge fireplaces, ornate oak panelling, intricately designed ceilings and mullioned windows. Bedrooms are spacious and well-equipped; those in the coach house are the most modern.

14 rooms – †£ 145/235 ††£ 180/280 – 1 suite

✉ EX20 4PN – South : 0.75 mi by Lewtrenchard rd – ✆ 01566 783222 – www.lewtrenchard.co.uk

Lewtrenchard Manor – See restaurant listing

LEYBURN

North Yorkshire – Pop. 2 183 – Regional map n° **13**-B1

Sandpiper Inn

TRADITIONAL BRITISH • PUB A friendly Yorkshire welcome is extended at this characterful, stone-built, part-16C pub just off the main square. Subtle, refined cooking offers a modern take on the classics and the skilled kitchen prides itself on the provenance of its ingredients. Two country-chic style bedrooms offer excellent comforts.

Carte £ 29/39 **s**

2 rooms – †£ 80/90 ††£ 90/100

Market Pl ✉ DL8 5AT – ☎ 01969 622206 – www.sandpiperinn.co.uk – Closed 2 weeks January, Tuesday in winter and Monday

Clyde House

TOWNHOUSE • PERSONALISED 18C former coaching inn on the main market square, run by an experienced owner and immaculately kept throughout. Small, cosy sitting room and cottagey breakfast room. Smart, comfortable bedrooms with good quality soft furnishings, hair dryers and bathrobes. Extensive buffet and 'full Yorkshire' breakfasts.

5 rooms – †£ 55/60 ††£ 85/100

5 Railway St ✉ DL8 5AY – ☎ 01969 623941 – www.clydehouse.com

LICHFIELD

Staffordshire – Pop. 32 877 – Regional map n° **10**-C2

Four Seasons

MODERN BRITISH • CLASSIC DÉCOR XX An impressive classical dining room with original wood panelling and a superbly ornate ceiling, set within the grand surroundings of Swinfen Hall. Elaborate modern cooking uses meat from the estate and veg and herbs from the walled garden.

Menu £ 30/60

Swinfen Hall Hotel, ✉ WS14 9RE – Southeast : 2.75 mi by A 5206 on A 38 – ☎ 01543 481494 – www.swinfenhallhotel.co.uk – Closed Sunday dinner, Monday and restricted opening Christmas-New Year

Wine House

TRADITIONAL CUISINE • NEIGHBOURHOOD X This smart red-brick house has an open-fired bar at one end and a dining room at the other. Lunch sees good value comfort dishes, while dinner puts steaks and seafood to the fore. It's named after its impressive glass wine cellar.

Carte £ 23/47

27 Bird St ✉ WS13 6PW – ☎ 01543 419999 – www.thewinehouselichfield.co.uk – Closed Sunday dinner

The Boat Inn N

MODERN BRITISH • PUB This old roadside hostelry was once backed by a canal and its walls are filled with black and white photos of the area's locks. Colourful, eye-catching dishes are modern, refined and allow local ingredients to shine.

Carte £ 19/37

Walsall Rd ✉ WS14 0BU – Southwest : 4 mi on A 461 – ☎ 01543 361692 – www.theboatinnlichfield.com – Closed Monday

Swinfen Hall

COUNTRY HOUSE • HISTORIC Grade II listed Georgian mansion with an impressive façade, set in 100 acres. Original features abound, including a stucco ceiling in the magnificent foyer. Individually styled bedrooms; extras include fruit and freshly baked shortbread.

17 rooms – †£ 160/340 ††£ 180/360 – 1 suite

✉ WS14 9RE – Southeast : 2.75 mi by A 5206 on A 38 – ☎ 01543 481494 – www.swinfenhallhotel.co.uk – Restricted opening Christmas-New Year

Four Seasons – See restaurant listing

Netherstowe House

COUNTRY HOUSE · CLASSIC Extensively restored 19C country house, professionally run by a family team. Period lounges and luxurious bedrooms come with antique furnishings and original fireplaces; modern apartments complete with kitchenettes are located in the grounds. The elegant formal restaurant offers ambitious modern cooking.

24 rooms – £ 89/195 £ 105/195 – 10 suites

Netherstowe Ln ✉ WS13 6AY – Northeast : 1.75 mi following signs for A 51 and A 38, off Eastern Ave – ✆ 01543 254270 – www.netherstowehouse.com

St Johns House

TOWNHOUSE · CONTEMPORARY Impressive Regency townhouse fronted by large columns. Enter through a beautiful tiled hallway into a contemporary drawing room with ornate cornicing and chandeliers. Individually styled bedrooms have a modern, understated feel.

12 rooms – £ 75 £ 120/250

28 St John St ✉ WS13 6PB
– ✆ 01543 252080 – www.stjohnshouse.co.uk – Closed 25-30 December

at Wall South: 2.75 mi by A5127

The Trooper

TRADITIONAL CUISINE · FRIENDLY Feast like a Roman general after battle on mature steaks including Wagyu fillet and 24oz rib-eye on the bone. Pizzas are cooked to order in a wood-fired oven and there's a huge selection of pub classics and sharing boards too

Carte £ 22/45

Watling St ✉ WS14 0AN
– ✆ 01543 480413 – www.thetrooperwall.co.uk

LICKFOLD – West Sussex ➜ See Petworth

LIFTON

Devon – Pop. 1 180 – Regional map n° **1**-C2

Arundell Arms

TRADITIONAL · COSY Family-run roadside coaching inn with cosy, traditional bedrooms and access to 20 miles of private fishing on the River Tamar and its tributaries. The characterful lounge and bar serve a brasserie menu, while the restaurant – which overlooks the terrace and gardens – offers classical fare.

25 rooms – £ 115/120 £ 160/180

Fore St ✉ PL16 0AA
– ✆ 01566 784666 – www.arundellarms.com

LINCOLN

Lincolnshire – Pop. 100 160 – Regional map n° **9**-C1

Jews House

MODERN CUISINE · COSY XX At the bottom of a steep cobbled hill is this cosy stone house dating from 1150; reputedly Europe's oldest surviving dwelling. Bold, ambitious dishes display an eclectic mix of influences – the tasting menu is a hit. Service is charming.

Menu £ 22 (lunch) – Carte £ 32/42

Town plan: B1-v – *15 The Strait ✉ LN2 1JD*
– ✆ 01522 524851 – www.jewshouserestaurant.co.uk – Closed 2 weeks January, 2 weeks July, 1 week November, Sunday, Monday and lunch Tuesday

LINCOLN

A B

1

2

Museum of Lincolnshire Life
Newport Arch
The Lawn
LIQUORICE PARK
Castle
Castle Hill
Exchequer Gate
LINCOLN CATHEDRAL
Norman House
Vicar's Court
Bishop's Palace
The Collection - Usher Gallery
Jew's House
Danes Terrace
CITY AND COUNTY MUSEUM
Stonebow and Guildhall
High Bridge
Brayford Pool
Witham
LINCOLN CENTRAL

A15, A46, A158
WORKSOP
A 1434, A 15
SLEAFORD, NEWARK
A 1434

0 100 m
0 100 yards

Bronze Pig

MODERN BRITISH • DESIGN This former pop-up, run by an Irishman and a Sicilian, has taken root. It's split over 4 rooms and is decorated with country scenes and colourful chairs. The modern menu offers 5 choices per course and reflects what's in season.

Carte £ 38/60

Town plan: A1-r – *4 Burton Rd ✉ LN1 3LB*
– *✆ 01522 524817 – www.thebronzepig.co.uk – dinner only and Sunday lunch*
– *Closed Sunday dinner, Monday and Tuesday*

Take note of the classification: you should not expect the same level of service in a X or ⌂ as in a XXXXX or ⌂⌂⌂⌂⌂.

Wig & Mitre

TRADITIONAL BRITISH • PUB Well-established pub with a cosy bar, period dining rooms and an airy beamed restaurant. Menus offer classical dishes with the odd Mediterranean or Asian influence, alongside daily specials, hearty breakfasts and over 20 wines by the glass.

Menu £ 15 (weekdays) – Carte £ 20/55

Town plan: B1-r – *30-32 Steep Hill ✉ LN2 1LU*
– *✆ 01522 535190* – *www.wigandmitre.com* – *Closed 25 December*

Symbols shown in red 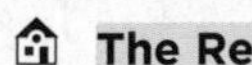 indicate particularly charming establishments.

The Rest

TOWNHOUSE • CONTEMPORARY With direct access to the bedrooms from the street, guests can come and go freely at this laid-back hotel. Breakfast is served in the coffee shop-cum-bar. Chic bedrooms feature bespoke furnishings and bathrooms with heated floors.

10 rooms – †£ 89/160 ††£ 89/160

Town plan: B1-t – *55A Steep Hill ✉ LN2 1LR*
– *✆ 01522 247888* – *www.theresthotellincoln.co.uk*

St Clements Lodge

TOWNHOUSE • PERSONALISED Cosy, Edwardian-style house close to the cathedral and castle (where you can view the Magna Carta). Cheerful owners offer good old-fashioned hospitality. Spacious, well-equipped bedrooms have pine furnishings and a homely feel.

3 rooms – †£ 70 ††£ 85/90

Town plan: B1-u – *21 Langworthgate ✉ LN2 4AD*
– *✆ 01522 521532* – *www.stclementslodge.co.uk*

LISKEARD

Cornwall – Pop. 9 237 – Regional map n° **1**-B2

Pencubitt Country House

TRADITIONAL • PERSONALISED Sympathetically restored Victorian property with delightful views over the gardens and countryside – take it all in from the veranda or from the balcony in bedroom 3. Look out too for the original windows and staircase in the lovely hall. They offer home-cooked dinners, cream teas and picnics by arrangement.

9 rooms – †£ 59/69 ††£ 69/119

Station Rd ✉ PL14 4EB – South : 0.5 mi by B 3254 on Lamellion rd
– *✆ 01579 342694* – *www.pencubitt.com*
– *Closed January and February*

LISS

Hampshire – Pop. 6 248 – Regional map n° **4**-C2

Madhuban

INDIAN • FRIENDLY XX Smartly furnished restaurant owned by three enthusiastic brothers. The focus is on fresh north Indian dishes; most of which can be prepared to the desired heat – the menu provides a useful glossary of terms. They also sell their sauces.

Carte £ 15/27

94 Station Rd ✉ GU33 7AQ
– *✆ 01730 893363* – *www.madhubanrestaurant.co.uk*
– *Closed 25-26 December and Friday lunch*

LITTLE BEDWYN - Wiltshire → See Marlborough

LITTLE COXWELL

Oxfordshire - Pop. 132 - Regional map n° **6**-A2

Eagle Tavern

TRADITIONAL BRITISH • TRADITIONAL DÉCOR This welcoming pub was built in 1901 for the farmers of this sleepy hamlet and, although it might look a little different now, a convivial atmosphere still reigns. The self-taught chef cooks the kind of food he likes to eat, including dishes from his homeland, Slovakia. Spacious bedrooms are spotlessly kept.

Menu £ 16 (weekday lunch) - Carte £ 23/38

6 rooms - £ 60/80 £ 70/100

SN7 7LW
- 01367 241879 - www.eagletavern.co.uk
- Closed Sunday dinner and Monday

LITTLE DUNMOW

Essex - Pop. 2 190 - Regional map n° **7**-C2

Flitch of Bacon

MODERN BRITISH • INTIMATE XX This is a place where the serving team are confident and the chef is experienced. An extensive range of modern dishes are allied with the odd pub classic: good ingredients are used in accomplished ways, flavour combinations are great and presentation is top notch. Contemporary bedrooms are boldly decorated.

Menu £ 20/55

3 rooms - £ 150/305 £ 150/305

The Street CM6 3HT - 01371 821660 (booking essential)
- www.flitchofbacon.co.uk - Closed Sunday dinner-Wednesday lunch

LITTLE ECCLESTON

Lancashire - Regional map n° **11**-A2

Cartford Inn

TRADITIONAL CUISINE • PUB The Cartford Inn stands next to small toll bridge on the River Wyre and comes complete with a deli and farm shop. Cooking is gutsy and satisfying and many of the tried-and-tested classics come with a twist. The owner played a big part in the interior design, particularly the bold, boutique bedrooms.

Carte £ 24/40

17 rooms - £ 80/150 £ 130/280

Cartford Ln PR3 0YP - 01995 670166 - www.thecartfordinn.co.uk - Closed 25 December and Monday lunch except bank holidays

LITTLE MARLOW - Buckinghamshire → See Marlow

LITTLEHAMPTON

West Sussex - Pop. 55 706 - Regional map n° **4**-C3

Bailiffscourt H. & Spa

COUNTRY HOUSE • HISTORIC Charming, reconstructed medieval manor in immaculately kept gardens. Bedrooms are split between the main house and the outbuildings; the newer rooms are in the grounds and are more suited to families. Beautiful spa facility. Classic country house cooking served in the formal dining room.

39 rooms - £ 235/335 £ 265/385

Climping St, Climping BN17 5RW - West : 2.75 mi by A 259 - 01903 723511
- www.hshotels.co.uk

LITTLETON - Hants. → See Winchester

LIVERPOOL

Merseyside – Pop. 552 267 – Regional map n° **11**-A3

The Art School

MODERN BRITISH • ELEGANT XXX Bright red chairs contrast with crisp white tablecloths at this elegant restaurant, where a huge glass roof floods the room with light. The experienced local chef carefully prepares a bewildering array of colourful modern dishes.

Menu £ 30/69

Town plan: D2-s – *1 Sugnall St ✉ L7 7DX – ✆ 0151 230 8600 – www.theartschoolrestaurant.co.uk – Closed 25-26 December, 1-7 January, 1-7 August, Sunday and Monday*

Panoramic 34

MODERN BRITISH • FASHIONABLE XXX On the 34th floor of the city's highest skyscraper you'll find this elegant restaurant with under-lit tables and fabulous 360° views. Ambitious dishes arrive swiftly and are attractively presented; the lunch menu offers good value.

Menu £ 27 (lunch) – Carte £ 34/49

Town plan: A1-r – *West Tower (34th floor), Brook St ✉ L3 9PJ – ✆ 0151 236 5534 – www.panoramic34.com – Closed 25-26 December, 1 January and Monday*

60 Hope Street

REGIONAL CUISINE • BRASSERIE XX An attractive Grade II listed Georgian house concealing a well-established modern brasserie with battleship grey walls and a smart basement wine bar. Menus feature interesting regional dishes; the set selection provides good value.

Menu £ 25 (lunch and early dinner) – Carte £ 35/57

Town plan: C3-x – *60 Hope St ✉ L1 9BZ – ✆ 0151 707 6060 – www.60hopestreet.com – Closed 26 December*

Etsu

JAPANESE • FRIENDLY X Behind a rather ordinary looking exterior lies a vibrant little restaurant. The three chefs have over 60 years' experience between them and carefully create authentic Japanese dishes which are great value – the sushi is a highlight.

Carte £ 18/32

Town plan: A2-a – *Beetham Plaza, 25 The Strand ✉ L2 0XJ – (Off Brunswick St) – ✆ 0151 236 7530 (booking essential) – www.etsu-restaurant.co.uk – Closed Monday and lunch Wednesday, Saturday and Sunday*

Neon Jamón

SPANISH • TAPAS BAR X In the bustling Penny Lane, you'll find this equally buzzy, industrial-style tapas bar. Service is friendly and obliging, and dishes are carefully prepared and full of flavour. Sit in the livelier downstairs room.

Carte £ 19/36

12 Smithdown Pl ✉ L15 9EH – Southeast : 3.5 mi by Upper Parliament St (A 562) – ✆ 0151 734 3840 (bookings not accepted) – www.neonjamon.com – Closed 25 December

Spire

MODERN BRITISH • BISTRO X Simple neighbourhood restaurant set in the Penny Lane area of the city. Good value, understated menus offer regional and modern European dishes. Flavoursome cooking and friendly service.

Menu £ 18/19 – Carte £ 25/43

1 Church Rd ✉ L15 9EA – Southeast : 3.5 mi by Upper Parliament St (A 562) – ✆ 0151 734 5040 – www.spirerestaurant.co.uk – Closed 25-26 December, 1-7 January, Sunday and lunch Saturday and Monday

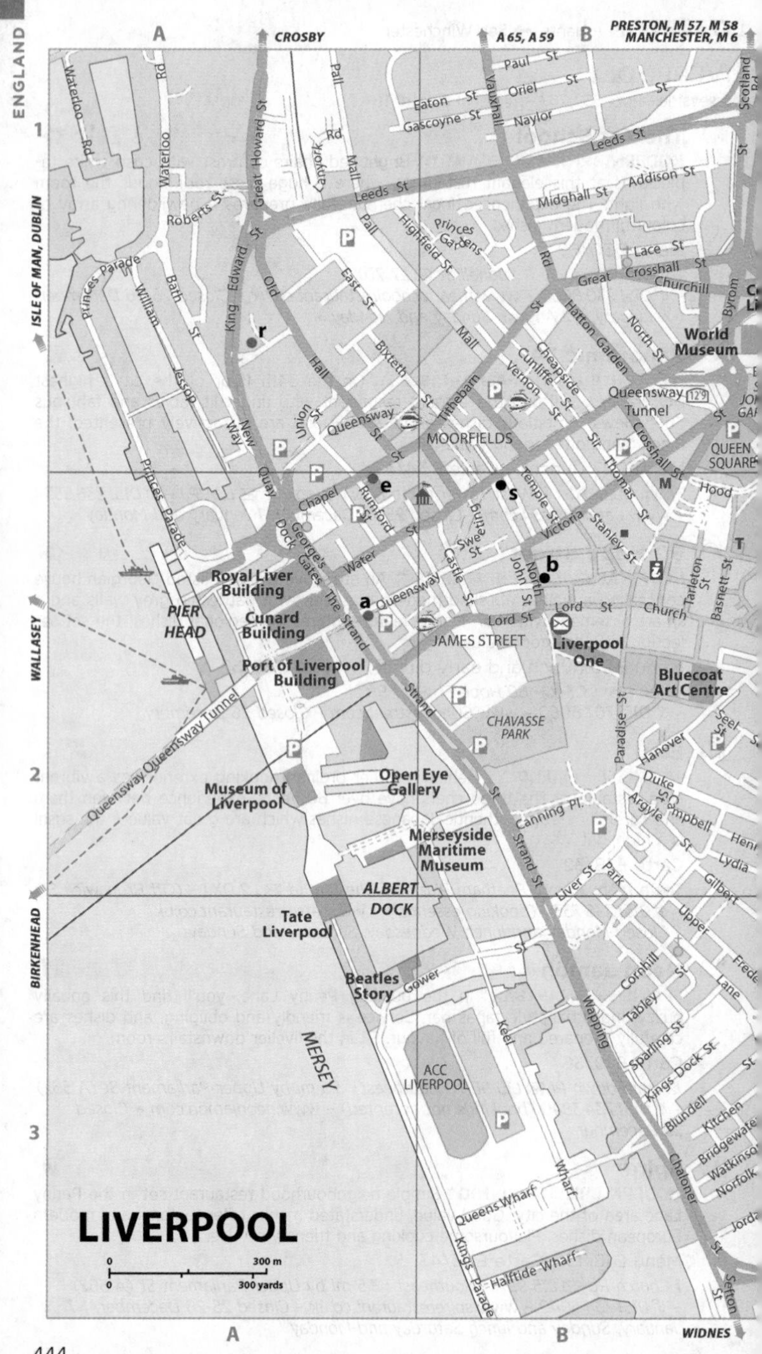
LIVERPOOL
CROSBY
A 65, A 59
PRESTON, M 57, M 58
MANCHESTER, M 6
ISLE OF MAN, DUBLIN
WALLASEY
BIRKENHEAD
WIDNES
World Museum
Royal Liver Building
Cunard Building
Port of Liverpool Building
PIER HEAD
Museum of Liverpool
Open Eye Gallery
Merseyside Maritime Museum
ALBERT DOCK
Tate Liverpool
Beatles Story
Liverpool One
Bluecoat Art Centre
CHAVASSE PARK
MOORFIELDS
JAMES STREET
QUEEN SQUARE
ACC LIVERPOOL
MERSEY
Queensway Tunnel
300 m
300 yards

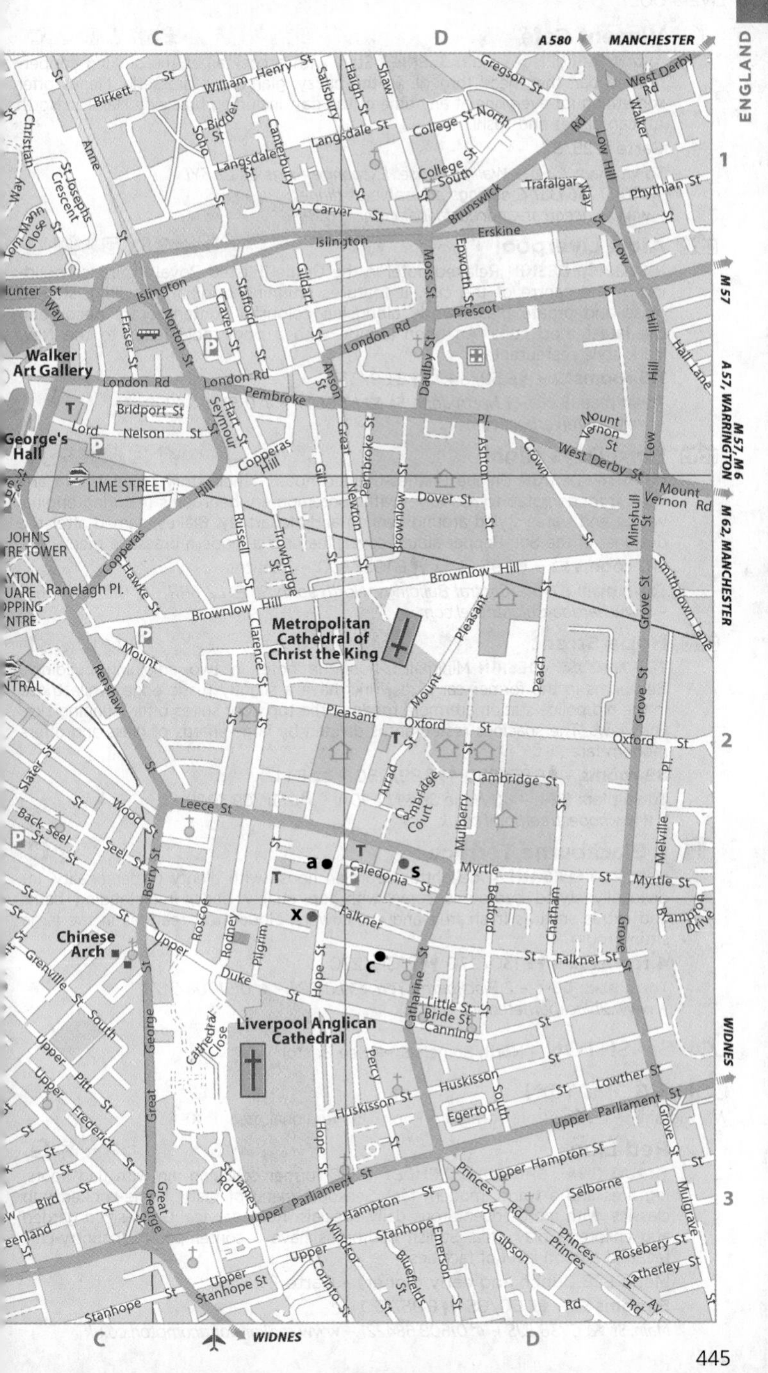
C
D
A 580
MANCHESTER
M 57
A 57, WARRINGTON
M 57, M 6
M 62, MANCHESTER
WIDNES
1
2
3
Walker Art Gallery
George's Hall
LIME STREET
Metropolitan Cathedral of Christ the King
Liverpool Anglican Cathedral
Chinese Arch
Islington
London Rd
Pembroke Pl.
West Derby St
Mount Vernon Rd
Brownlow Hill
Mount Pleasant
Oxford St
Leece St
Myrtle St
Falkner St
Upper Parliament St
Great George St
Hope St
Catharine St
Grove St
Low Hill
Erskine St
Prescot St
Caledonia St
Duke St
Upper Duke St
a
s
x
c

Vincent Café

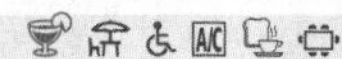

ASIAN INFLUENCES • BRASSERIE Start with a cocktail at the striking copper-fronted bar, then head through to the buzzy, glamorous brasserie. Menus offer something for everyone at any time of the day, including brasserie classics, North African dishes and sushi.

Carte £ 25/57

Town plan: A2-e – *Walker House, Exchange Flags* ✉ *L2 3YL* – *✆ 0151 236 1331 (bookings advisable at dinner)* – *www.vincentcafeandcocktailbar.com*

Aloft Liverpool

HISTORIC • DESIGN Relaxed hotel in the Grade II listed Royal Insurance building in the centre of the city. It features stunning original panelling, stained glass and ornate plasterwork, alongside colourful contemporary décor and the latest mod cons. An open lounge with a pool table leads to the New York style restaurant.

116 rooms – †£ 59/349 ††£ 69/359

Town plan: B2-s – *1 North John St* ✉ *L2 5QW* – *✆ 0151 294 4050* – *www.aloftliverpool.com*

Hard Days Night

LUXURY • DESIGN Unique Beatles-themed hotel – their story recounted in artwork from doorstep to rooftop – with contemporary bedrooms featuring original works, and suites styled around Lennon and McCartney. Blakes, named after the designer of the Sgt. Pepper album cover, features a modern brasserie menu.

110 rooms – †£ 95/320 ††£ 105/330 – 2 suites

Town plan: B2-b – *Central Buildings, North John St* ✉ *L2 6RR* – *✆ 0151 236 1964* – *www.harddaysnighthotel.com*

Hope Street

TOWNHOUSE • DESIGN Minimalist boutique hotel in two adjoining buildings. Bedrooms in the former carriage works have a slightly rustic edge, while those in the old police station are more modern; the top floor suites offer stunning skyline views. The spacious restaurant is divided by large shards of glass and offers modern fare.

89 rooms – †£ 89/250 ††£ 89/250 – £ 14

Town plan: C2-a – *40 Hope St* ✉ *L1 9DA* – *✆ 0151 709 3000* – *www.hopestreethotel.co.uk*

2 Blackburne Terrace

LUXURY • ELEGANT A delightful Georgian house with plenty of personality. Individually styled bedrooms come with top quality beds, free-standing baths and extras such as fresh fruit and cut flowers. Modern art features in the large sitting room.

4 rooms – †£ 130/270 ††£ 130/270

Town plan: D3-c – *2 Blackburne Terr* ✉ *L8 7PJ* – *✆ 0151 708 5474* – *www.2blackburneterrace.com*

LONG ASHTON – North Somerset ➜ See Bristol

LONG COMPTON

Warwickshire – ✉ Shipston-On-Stour – Pop. 705 – Regional map n° **10**-C3

Red Lion

TRADITIONAL BRITISH • FRIENDLY 18C former coaching inn with flag floors, log fires and a warm, modern feel. Seasonal menu of tasty, home-cooked pub classics, with more adventurous daily specials. Keen service. Good-sized garden and children's play area. Stylish bedrooms have a contemporary, country-chic feel and a good level of facilities.

Menu £ 18 (lunch and early dinner) – Carte £ 26/34

5 rooms – †£ 60/65 ††£ 95/150

Main St ✉ *CV36 5JS* – *✆ 01608 684221* – *www.redlion-longcompton.co.uk*

LONG CRENDON

Buckinghamshire – ✉ Aylesbury – Pop. 2 335 – Regional map n° **6**-C2

Mole & Chicken

TRADITIONAL BRITISH • RURAL A charming pub built in 1831 as part of a local farm workers' estate, with low wonky ceilings, open fires and a large garden offering commanding country views. The menu features classic British dishes and heartwarming puddings. Staff are friendly and there are five cosy bedrooms in the adjoining house.

Menu £ 18 (lunch) – Carte £ 27/43

5 rooms – £ 85/95 £ 110/125

Easington ✉ HP18 8EY – North 0.5 mi by Dorton rd – ✆ 01844 208387 – www.themoleandchicken.co.uk – Closed 25 December

LONG MELFORD

Suffolk – Pop. 2 898 – Regional map n° **8**-C3

Scutchers

TRADITIONAL CUISINE • RUSTIC XX This converted medieval hall house is now a smart, personally run restaurant. Cooking is skilful, classical and full of flavour; everything from the bread to the sorbet is homemade. The wine list features some top class producers.

Carte £ 35/56

Westgate St ✉ CO10 9DP – on A 1092 – ✆ 01787 310200 – www.scutchers.com – Closed 2 weeks Christmas and Sunday-Wednesday

Swan

MODERN CUISINE • PUB Smart double-fronted pub in a characterful old wool town. The appealing menu provides plenty of choice, ranging from refined French classics to dishes with an Asian bent. From the flavoursome cooking to the eye-catching décor and stylish bedrooms, this is a place where you can really see that they care.

Carte £ 31/47

7 rooms – £ 95/120 £ 155/210

Hall St ✉ CO10 9JQ – ✆ 01787 464545 – www.longmelfordswan.co.uk

LONG ROCK

Cornwall – Pop. 570 – Regional map n° **1**-B2

Mexico Inn

TRADITIONAL BRITISH • FRIENDLY This roadside inn is run by an experienced local couple. It has a touch of the shabby-chic about it, with a wood-burner in the bar and a sunnier room to the rear; there's a lovely suntrap terrace too. Cooking is gutsy and flavourful.

Menu £ 22 (lunch and early dinner) – Carte £ 20/40

4 Riverside ✉ TR20 8JD – ✆ 01736 710625 – www.themexicoinn.com – Closed 1 week late January-early February and Sunday dinner

LONG SUTTON

Somerset – ✉ Langport – Regional map n° **2**-B3

Devonshire Arms

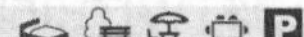

REGIONAL CUISINE • INN A striking Grade II listed former hunting lodge overlooking the village green. Wing-back chairs sit by an open fire and blue panelled walls are broken up by bold wallpaper. Appealing menus follow the seasons: stick with British classics or choose something Mediterranean. Bedrooms are modern and well-furnished.

Carte £ 26/40

9 rooms – £ 90/150 £ 100/155

✉ TA10 9LP – ✆ 01458 241271 – www.thedevonshirearms.com – Closed 25-26 December

LONG WHATTON

Leicestershire – Pop. 1 124 – Regional map n° **9**-B2

Royal Oak

TRADITIONAL BRITISH • PUB Smartly modernised pub in a sleepy village. Menus offer plenty of choice, from updated pub favourites to ambitious main courses, many with Mediterranean influences. Most people eat in the cosy dining room but there's also a beamed bar. Bedrooms are smart, modern and well-equipped.

Menu £ 14 (lunch and early dinner) – Carte £ 24/39

12 rooms – †£ 69/89 ††£ 79/109

The Green ✉ LE12 5BD – ✆ 01509 843694 – www.theroyaloaklongwhatton.co.uk

LONGHORSLEY – Northumberland ➜ See Morpeth

LONGSTOCK

Hampshire – ✉ Stockbridge – Regional map n° **4**-B2

Peat Spade Inn

TRADITIONAL BRITISH • COSY An attractive 19C inn in the heart of the Test Valley, with fishing rights on the nearby river. Menus mix pub classics with more interesting dishes. In the evening, find a spot on the lovely terrace and cosy up beside the fire-pit. Charming bedrooms are split between the inn and an old barn.

Menu £ 15 (lunch and early dinner) – Carte £ 22/45

8 rooms – †£ 99/189 ††£ 99/189

Village Street ✉ SO20 6DR – ✆ 01264 810612 – www.peatspadeinn.co.uk

LOOE

Cornwall – Pop. 5 112 – Regional map n° **1**-B2

Beach House

FAMILY • PERSONALISED A personally run, detached house in a fantastic spot on the edge of town, looking out to sea. Bedrooms are immaculately kept; Fistral, with its balcony, is the best. The breakfast room is on the first floor and offers super views.

5 rooms – †£ 75/110 ††£ 80/130

Marine Dr, Hannafore ✉ PL13 2DH – Southwest : 0.75 mi by Quay Rd – ✆ 01503 262598 – www.thebeachhouselooe.co.uk – Closed Christmas

LORTON

Cumbria – Regional map n° **12**-A2

New House Farm

TRADITIONAL • COSY Part-17C former farmhouse with several beamed, open-fired lounges, a hot tub boasting fell views and a tea room in the old cow byres. Richly furnished bedrooms have king or super king sized beds and some feature double jacuzzis.

5 rooms – †£ 60 ††£ 120/180

✉ CA13 9UU – South : 1.25 mi on B 5289 – ✆ 07841 159818 – www.newhouse-farm.co.uk

LOSTWITHIEL

Cornwall – Pop. 2 659 – Regional map n° **1**-B2

Asquiths

MODERN CUISINE • INTIMATE XX Smartly converted shop with exposed stone walls hung with modern Cornish art, funky lampshades and contemporary styling. Confidently executed dishes feature some original flavour combinations. The atmosphere is relaxed and intimate.

Carte £ 26/35

19 North St ✉ PL22 0EF – ✆ 01208 871714 – www.asquithsrestaurant.co.uk – dinner only – Closed first 2 weeks January, Sunday and Monday

LOUGHBOROUGH

Leicestershire – Pop. 59 932 – Regional map n° **9**-B2

✿ John's House (John Duffin)

MODERN CUISINE • RUSTIC XX A 16C farmhouse where the eponymous and talented John was born and now cooks; his family also own the surrounding farm with its shop, café, petting farm and motor museum. Produce from the surrounding fields is used to create original, interesting dishes which show a real understanding of textures and flavours.

➜ Tom's potatoes, crispy chicken skin, truffle and wild garlic. Lightly salted cod with brawn, passion fruit and curry spices. Sea buckthorn sorbet, meringue, liquorice and mint.

Menu £ 28/47

Stonehurst Farm, 141 Loughborough Rd, Mountsorrel ✉ LE12 7AR – Southeast : 4.5 mi by A 6 – ✆ 01509 415569 (booking essential) – www.johnshouse.co.uk – Closed Sunday and Monday

Blacksmiths Arms

TRADITIONAL CUISINE • FRIENDLY X A former pub and, before that, a 1753 blacksmith's forge; now a stylish eatery with a sunny terrace, friendly service and a laid-back feel. Menus include all the favourites and cooking is fresh and tasty.

Carte £ 20/42

2-4 Church Ln, off North St, Barrow-upon-Soar ✉ LE12 8PP – Southeast : 3 mi by A 6 – ✆ 01509 413100 – www.blacksmiths1753.co.uk – Closed Sunday dinner and Monday

LOUTH

Lincolnshire – Pop. 16 419 – Regional map n° **9**-D1

14 Upgate

MODERN CUISINE • INTIMATE XX This elegant townhouse conversion seats 12 diners at 6 polished tables. The modern tasting menu changes weekly and presents some unusual twists and turns along the way. Start with a drink in the first floor sitting room.

Menu £ 25/45 – tasting menu only

14 Upgate ✉ LN11 9ET – ✆ 01507 610610 – www.14upgate.co.uk – dinner only – Closed 25 December-1 February and Sunday-Tuesday

Brackenborough

BUSINESS • PERSONALISED Contemporary hotel with a relaxed feel and a warm, personal style. Spacious, individually designed bedrooms have bold feature walls, Egyptian cotton linen and the latest mod cons; executive rooms come with jacuzzi baths. The bistro and conservatory lounge-bar serve grills and classics with a modern twist.

24 rooms – †£ 103 ††£ 118/130

Cordeaux Corner, Brackenborough ✉ LN11 0SZ – North : 2 mi by A 16 – ✆ 01507 609169 – www.oakridgehotels.co.uk

LOVINGTON

Somerset – Regional map n° **2**-C2

Pilgrims

MODERN BRITISH • RUSTIC X Cosy, hugely characterful restaurant with low-beamed ceilings, flagged floors and a roaring fire; run by a passionate husband and wife team. Well-prepared, classical dishes are made with quality local produce. Comfortable, contemporary bedrooms, luxurious bathrooms and substantial breakfasts.

Carte £ 26/47

5 rooms – †£ 70/130 ††£ 100/130

✉ BA7 7PT – ✆ 01963 240597 – www.pilgrimsrestaurant.co.uk – dinner only and lunch Friday-Saturday – Closed Sunday and Monday

LOW FELL

Tyne and Wear – Regional map n° **14**-B2

Eslington Villa

TRADITIONAL CUISINE • BISTRO XX This bright, airy hotel dining room feels like a conservatory and offers pleasant views over the tiered gardens. Menus are based on dishes people know and love and come with a few unusual twists along the way. Service is chatty.

Menu £ 18/21 – Carte £ 31/42

Eslington Villa Hotel, 8 Station Rd ✉ NE9 6DR – West : 0.75 mi by Belle Vue Bank, turning left at T junction, right at roundabout then taking first turn right – ✆ 0191 487 6017 – www.eslingtonvilla.co.uk – Closed 25-26 December and 1 January

Eslington Villa

TRADITIONAL • PERSONALISED This Victorian villa has been keenly run by the same family since 1987. Bedrooms come in various shapes and sizes and most have feature walls and colourful fabrics. The large lawned garden is a lovely place to relax in summer.

18 rooms – †£ 80/90 ††£ 95/125

8 Station Rd ✉ NE9 6DR – West : 0.75 mi by Belle Vue Bank, turning left at T junction, right at roundabout then taking first turn right – ✆ 0191 487 6017 – www.eslingtonvilla.co.uk – Closed 25-26 December and 1 January

Eslington Villa – See restaurant listing

LOWER BEEDING

West Sussex – Regional map n° **4**-D2

Camellia

MODERN CUISINE • ELEGANT XX Named after the tree at the front of the house, Camellia occupies three wood-panelled rooms with grand fireplaces and chandeliers. Refined dishes are light but boldly flavoured and showcase garden produce.

Menu £ 28 (lunch) – Carte £ 38/68

South Lodge Hotel, Brighton Rd ✉ RH13 6PS – South : 1.5 mi by B 2110 on A 281 – ✆ 01403 891711 – www.southlodgehotel.co.uk – Closed Monday and Tuesday

Crabtree

TRADITIONAL CUISINE • PUB A family-run affair with a cosy, lived-in feel, warming fires and cheery, helpful staff. Traditional English dishes come with a touch of refinement and plenty of flavour, and the wine list is well-priced and full of helpful information.

Menu £ 16 (weekdays) – Carte £ 25/42

Brighton Rd ✉ RH13 6PT – South : 1.5 mi by B 2110 on A 281 – ✆ 01403 892666 – www.crabtreesussex.com – Closed Sunday dinner

South Lodge

LUXURY • HISTORIC Intricate carved fireplaces and ornate ceilings are proudly displayed in this Victorian mansion, which affords superb South Downs views from its 93 acres. Bedrooms are beautifully appointed – some are traditional, while others are more modern. Dine in the grand restaurant or in the kitchen itself.

85 rooms – †£ 195/355 ††£ 195/355 – 4 suites

Brighton Rd ✉ RH13 6PS – South : 1.5 mi by B 2110 on A 281 – ✆ 01403 891711 – www.southlodgehotel.co.uk – Closed 1-14 January

Camellia – See restaurant listing

LOWER DUNSFORTH – North Yorkshire ➜ See Boroughbridge

LOWER ODDINGTON – Gloucestershire ➜ See Stow-on-the-Wold

LOWER PEOVER

Cheshire East – ✉ Cheshire – Regional map n° **11**-B3

Bells of Peover

MEDITERRANEAN CUISINE • PUB 16C coaching inn set down a narrow cobbled lane; its regulars once included Generals Eisenhower and Patton. It has a cosy bar, three tastefully decorated dining rooms and a smart terrace. Italian, Greek and Turkish dishes feature.

Carte £ 24/40

The Cobbles ✉ WA16 9PZ – ✆ 01565 722269 – www.thebellsofpeover.com

LOWER SLAUGHTER – Gloucestershire ➜ See Bourton-on-the-Water

LUDLOW

Shropshire – Pop. 10 515 – Regional map n° **10**-B2

Forelles

MODERN CUISINE • INTIMATE XX Appealing conservatory restaurant named after the pear tree outside, with lovely views over the hotel gardens. Attractively presented dishes use local produce and modern techniques, and feature good flavour and texture combinations.

Menu £ 50

Fishmore Hall Hotel, Fishmore Rd ✉ SY8 3DP – North : 1.5 mi by B 4361 and Kidderminster rd on Fishmore Rd – ✆ 01584 875148 – www.fishmorehall.co.uk – Closed Sunday and Monday

Mortimers

MODERN BRITISH • ELEGANT XX A local forest gives this 16C townhouse restaurant its name. It has plenty of character, courtesy of exposed stone, sloping floors and lovely wood panelling. Concise set menus offer classically rooted dishes with a personal touch.

Menu £ 23/60

Town plan: B1-s – *17 Corve St ✉ SY8 1DA – ✆ 01584 872325 – www.mortimersludlow.co.uk – Closed 29 January-10 February, 1-12 October, Sunday and Monday*

Old Downton Lodge

MODERN CUISINE • RURAL XX Set on a 5,500 acre estate, these supremely characterful farm buildings date from medieval to Georgian times. Dining takes place in the 13C stone and timber barn and cooking is contemporary and original with a Scandic style. Bedrooms combine period features with modern amenities.

Menu £ 60/75 – tasting menu only

10 rooms – †£ 135/300 ††£ 135/300

Downton on the Rock ✉ SY8 2HU – West : 7.5 mi by A 49, off A 4113 – ✆ 01568 771826 (booking essential) – www.olddowntonlodge.com – dinner only – Closed 23-27 December, Sunday and Monday

French Pantry

FRENCH • COSY X Pretty little café-cum-bistro on a paved side street, selling produce and wines imported from Parisian markets. Authentic Gallic dishes are crafted from local and French ingredients. Cooking is rustic, hearty and full of flavour.

Menu £ 26 (dinner) – Carte lunch £ 24/33

Town plan: B2-r – *15 Tower St. ✉ SY8 1RL – ✆ 01584 879133 (booking essential) – www.thefrenchpantry.co.uk – Closed 1-5 January and Sunday*

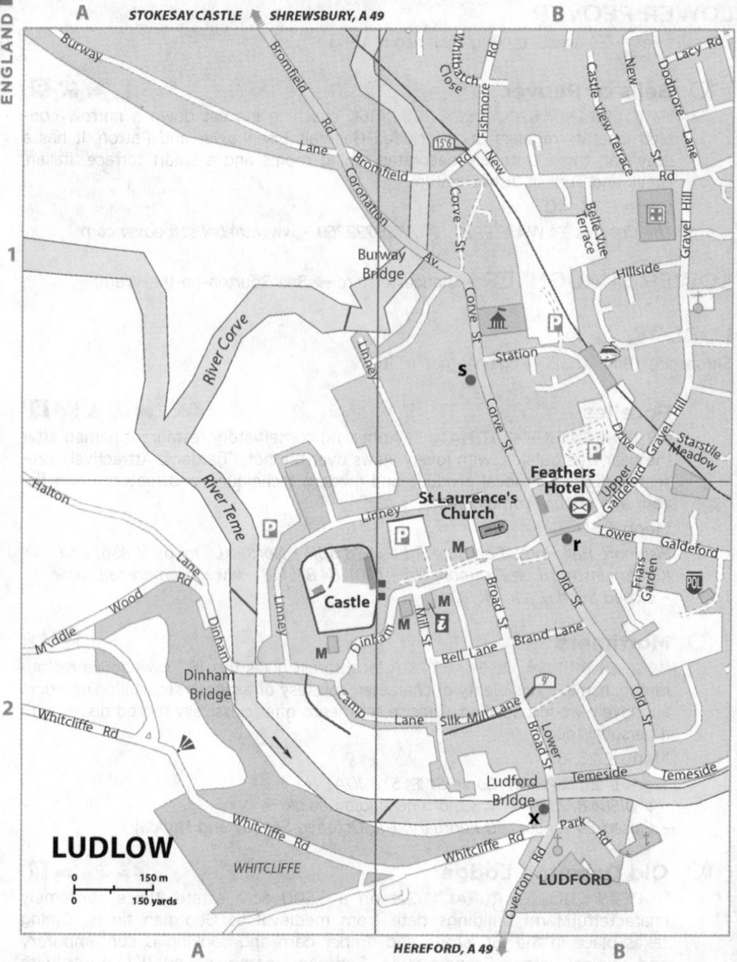

A STOKESAY CASTLE SHREWSBURY, A 49 B

LUDLOW

Burway
Bromfield Rd
Lane
Bromfield Rd
Coronation Av.
Whitbatch Close
Fishmore Rd
New Rd
Corve St
Castle View Terrace
New St
Dodmore Lane
Lacy Rd
Belle Vue Terrace
Gravel Hill
Hillside
Burway Bridge
River Corve
Linney
Station
Drive
Upper Galdeford
Gravel Hill
Starstile Meadow
Feathers Hotel
St Laurence's Church
Lower Galdeford
Friars Garden
Halton
River Teme
Lane Rd
Wood
Middle
Dinham
Castle
Mill St
Broad St
Old St
Brand Lane
Bell Lane
Dinham Bridge
Camp Lane
Silk Mill Lane
Lower Broad St
Whitcliffe Rd
Temeside
Ludford Bridge
Park Rd
Whitcliffe Rd
Overton Rd
WHITCLIFFE
LUDFORD
0 150 m
0 150 yards
A HEREFORD, A 49 B

Charlton Arms

TRADITIONAL BRITISH • RUSTIC Claude Bosi is arguably the man who put Ludlow on the map and this pub in a commanding position on the banks of the River Teme is owned by his brother Cedric and Cedric's wife, Amy. Menus have something for everyone and dishes are good value and full of flavour. Up-to-date bedrooms; most have river outlooks.

Carte £ 22/38

9 rooms – †£ 90/100 ††£ 100/160

Town plan: B2-x – *Ludford Bridge* ✉ *SY8 1PJ*
– *01584 872813*
– *www.thecharltonarms.co.uk*
– *Closed 25-26 December*

Fishmore Hall

COUNTRY HOUSE • DESIGN Whitewashed Georgian mansion in half an acre of mature gardens, just out of town. Original features mix with modern fittings to create a boutique country house feel. Smart bedrooms have bold wallpapers, stylish bathrooms and good views.

15 rooms – £ 135/275 £ 175/275

Fishmore Rd ✉ SY8 3DP – North : 1.5 mi by B 4361 and Kidderminster rd on Fishmore Rd – ✆ 01584 875148 – www.fishmorehall.co.uk

Forelles – See restaurant listing

Overton Grange

TRADITIONAL • CLASSIC Well-maintained Edwardian country house where subtle modern touches sit alongside original features. Well-equipped bedrooms and smart bathrooms. Good-sized pool, sauna and 2 treatment rooms. Dining rooms offer immaculately laid tables and countryside views; cooking has a refined French base.

14 rooms – £ 99/199 £ 119/239

Old Hereford Rd ✉ SY8 4AD – South : 1.75 mi on B 4361 – ✆ 01584 873500 – www.overtongrangehotel.com – Closed 28 December-9 January

at Cleestanton Northeast: 5.5 mi by A4117 and B4364

Timberstone

COUNTRY HOUSE • PERSONALISED This pair of cosy 17C cottages offer a wonderfully peaceful atmosphere and lovely rural views. Beamed bedrooms come with stylish modern bathrooms; one room even has its own balcony. Dine around the large farmhouse table – there's always a good selection, which includes many organic or home-grown options.

4 rooms – £ 65/100 £ 65/100

✉ SY8 3EL – ✆ 01584 823519 – www.timberstoneludlow.co.uk

LUND

East Riding of Yorkshire – Regional map n° **13**-C2

Wellington Inn

TRADITIONAL BRITISH • FRIENDLY A well-run pub with a beamed bar for daytime dining and a rustic brasserie and linen-laid restaurant for the evening. Generously portioned dishes are imaginative, flavoursome and showcase top ingredients.

Carte £ 31/42

19 The Green ✉ YO25 9TE – ✆ 01377 217294 – www.thewellingtoninn.co.uk – Closed 25 December, 1 January, Sunday dinner and Monday

LUPTON

- Cumbria → See Kirkby Lonsdale

LURGASHALL

West Sussex – Regional map n° **4**-C2

Noah's Ark Inn

TRADITIONAL CUISINE • COSY A quintessentially English pub in a picturesque village green location; its garden overlooks the cricket pitch. The gloriously rustic interior features a bar, a baronial-style room with cosy sofas and 'The Restaurant' with its large inglenook fireplace. Generous dishes keep things in the traditional vein.

Carte £ 25/38

The Green ✉ GU28 9ET – ✆ 01428 707346 – www.noahsarkinn.co.uk

Barn at Roundhurst

HISTORIC • ELEGANT Beautifully restored mid-17C threshing barn, on a 250 acre working farm in the South Downs. Characterful bedrooms – in the old outbuildings – are designed by the owner and come with homemade biscuits and luxurious bathrooms. The spacious lounge features fresh flowers, sculptures and modern art. Meals use eggs and meats from the farm, along with other local ingredients.

6 rooms – £ 98/200 £ 98/240

Lower Roundhurst Farm, Jobson's Ln ✉ GU27 3BY – Northwest : 3 mi by Haslemere rd – ✆ 01428 642535 – www.thebarnatroundhurst.com – Closed 22-26 December

LUTON

Luton – Pop. 211 228 – Regional map n° **7**-A2

Luton Hoo

GRAND LUXURY • HISTORIC Stunning 18C house in over 1,000 acres of gardens; some designed by Capability Brown. The main mansion boasts an impressive hallway, numerous beautifully furnished drawing rooms and luxurious bedrooms. The marble-filled Wernher restaurant offers sophisticated classic cuisine. The old stable block houses the smart spa and casual, contemporary brasserie.

228 rooms – £ 180/300 £ 200/320 – 23 suites

The Mansion House ✉ LU1 3TQ – Southeast : 2.5 mi by A 505 on A 1081 – ✆ 01582 734437 – www.lutonhoo.com

LYDDINGTON – Rutland ➜ See Uppingham

LYDFORD

Devon – ✉ Okehampton – Pop. 1 734 – Regional map n° **1**-C2

Dartmoor Inn

MODERN BRITISH • PUB Rustic pub with a shabby-chic style. Low ceilings add a cosy feel, while artwork provides a modern touch. Classic dishes are satisfying and full of flavour and there is an emphasis on local produce; Devon Ruby Red beef and dishes from the charcoal grill are the specialities. Spacious, elegant bedrooms.

Carte £ 23/38

3 rooms – £ 65/100 £ 100/140

Moorside ✉ EX20 4AY – East : 1 mi on A 386 – ✆ 01822 820221 – www.dartmoorinn.com – Closed Sunday dinner and Monday

LYME REGIS

Dorset – Pop. 4 712 – Regional map n° **2**-B3

HIX Oyster & Fish House

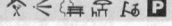

SEAFOOD • SIMPLE Modern, Scandic-style restaurant with a chef's table, a terrace and breathtaking views over Lyme Bay and the Cobb. Menus focus on the latest catch brought in by the day boats and dishes have a likeable simplicity. Service is charming and efficient and there's a relaxed, buzzy vibe to the place.

Menu £ 18 (weekdays) – Carte £ 23/47

Lister Gdns, Cobb Rd ✉ DT7 3JP – ✆ 01297 446910 (booking essential) – www.hixoysterandfishhouse.co.uk – Closed 25-26 December and Monday-Tuesday November-March except half-term holidays

Alexandra

BOUTIQUE HOTEL • CONTEMPORARY 18C dower house with superb views over the Cobb and out to sea. There's a small terrace and a lookout tower (for hire) in the lovely gardens. The lounges and bedrooms are contemporary; No.12 has a large bay window to take in the views. Modern menus are served in the formal restaurant and conservatory.

25 rooms – £ 95 £ 180/330

Pound St ✉ DT7 3HZ – ✆ 01297 442010 – www.hotelalexandra.co.uk – Closed 3-29 January

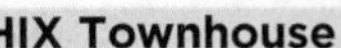

HIX Townhouse

TOWNHOUSE · QUIRKY Georgian townhouse with stylishly understated bedrooms designed around various themes, including hunting and sailing; two rooms have lounges and two have terraces. There's a communal kitchen and breakfast is delivered in a hamper.

8 rooms - £ 110/125 £ 120/135

1 Pound St ✉ DT7 3HZ - ☎ 01297 442499 - www.hixtownhouse.co.uk - Closed January

LYMINGTON

Hampshire - Pop. 15 218 - Regional map n° **4**-A3

Elderflower

MODERN CUISINE · FAMILY XX Their motto is 'quintessentially British, with a sprinkling of French', and that's just what you'll find at this proudly run restaurant. Cooking is playful and imaginative - as well as an à la carte they also serve small plates. Bedrooms are simply appointed and the quay is just a stone's throw away.

Carte £ 38/47

2 rooms - £ 95 £ 100

4-5 Quay St ✉ SO41 3AS - ☎ 01590 676908 (bookings advisable at dinner) - www.elderflowerrestaurant.co.uk - Closed Sunday dinner and Monday

Stanwell House

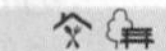

TOWNHOUSE · PERSONALISED An attractive 18C house. Tastefully designed bedrooms are comfy and well-equipped: those in the original house are the most characterful; those in the extension are more contemporary. Dine on modern British dishes in the formal bistro; the restaurant offers small plates of New Forest produce. The trendy wine bar is themed around Sir Ben Ainslie, who once lived here.

29 rooms - £ 135/195 £ 135/195 - 7 suites

14-15 High St ✉ SO41 9AA - ☎ 01590 677123 - www.stanwellhouse.com

LYMM

Warrington - Pop. 11 608 - Regional map n° **11**-B3

Church Green

MODERN BRITISH · PUB A double-fronted pub beside Lymm Dam, with an attractive decked terrace and a kitchen garden. Choose from an extensive list of small plates, an appealing set selection or a grill menu where you choose a cut, then add sauce and extras.

Menu £ 30 (weekdays) - Carte £ 28/58

Higher Ln ✉ WA13 0AP - on A 56 - ☎ 01925 752068 (booking essential) - www.thechurchgreen.co.uk - Closed 25 December

LYMPSTONE

Devon - Pop. 1 763 - Regional map n° **1**-D2

Lympstone Manor (Michael Caines)

MODERN CUISINE · ELEGANT XXX This elegant restaurant sits within a luxurious country house hotel. At lunch dine in the Berry Head room; for dinner choose the intimate booths of the Powderham room. Accomplished modern cooking is superbly balanced and packed with flavour - the 8 course tasting menu best demonstrates the team's abilities.

→ Tartlet of quail with onion confit, black truffle and smoked bacon. Boudin of John Dory and langoustine with pork belly, apple and ginger purée. Poached rhubarb with hibiscus, lemon sponge, lemon curd and rhubarb sorbet.

Menu £ 55/115

Lympstone Manor Hotel, Courtlands Ln. ✉ EX8 3NZ - Southeast : 1.75 mi by A 376 - ☎ 01395 202040 (booking essential) - www.lympstonemanor.co.uk

Lymptone Manor

COUNTRY HOUSE • ELEGANT A tastefully restored Georgian country house set in peaceful grounds which stretch down to the estuary – the pretty veranda is the perfect spot to admire the view. Luxurious bedrooms are beautifully furnished and have a stylish, modern feel; opt for a Garden Room with a fire and hot tub on the terrace.

21 rooms – £ 220/1025 £ 245/1050

Courtlands Ln. ✉ EX8 3NZ – Southeast : 1.75 mi by A 376 – ✆ 01395 202040 – www.lympstonemanor.co.uk

Lympstone Manor – See restaurant listing

LYNDHURST

Hampshire – Pop. 2 347 – Regional map n° **4**-A2

Hartnett Holder & Co

ITALIAN • ELEGANT XX Elegant restaurant in an impressive Georgian mansion, offering a relaxed, clubby feel and views over the delightful grounds. The main menu lists Italian favourites like pizzetta, pastas and risottos as well as authentic fish and meat dishes. The sharing menu offers the likes of whole duck 'family-style'.

Menu £ 20 (weekday lunch) – Carte £ 41/68

Lime Wood Hotel, Beaulieu Rd ✉ SO43 7FZ – Southeast : 1 mi by A 35 on B 3056 – ✆ 023 8028 7177 – www.limewood.co.uk

Lime Wood

LUXURY • ELEGANT Impressive Georgian mansion with a stunning spa topped by a herb garden roof. Stylish guest lounges have quality fabrics and furnishings; one is set around a courtyard and features a retractable glass roof. Beautifully furnished bedrooms boast luxurious marble-tiled bathrooms, and many have New Forest views.

33 rooms – £ 330/510 £ 330/510 – £ 25 – 14 suites

Beaulieu Rd ✉ SO43 7FZ – Southeast : 1 mi by A 35 on B 3056 – ✆ 023 8028 7177 – www.limewoodhotel.co.uk

Hartnett Holder & Co – See restaurant listing

LYNMOUTH – Devon ➔ See Lynton

LYNTON

Devon – Pop. 1 157 – Regional map n° **1**-C1

Hewitt's - Villa Spaldi

HISTORIC • CLASSIC Splendid cliffside Arts and Crafts house in mature gardens. Antique-furnished bedrooms have up-to-date facilities, sea views and smart modern bathrooms. Informal weekday meals in wood-panelled bar; fine dining on Friday and Saturday evenings. High tea, with its homemade scones and excellent tea selection, is a must and the terrace is a delightful spot for breakfast.

8 rooms – £ 80/180 £ 90/210 – £ 15

North Walk ✉ EX35 6HJ – ✆ 01598 752293 – www.hewittshotel.com – Closed October-March

Castle Hill

FAMILY • PERSONALISED Stone-built house on the main street of this popular tourist village. Spacious, simply decorated bedrooms; 3 of the 7 have their own sitting area. Lounge with plenty of local info and a large fish tank. Friendly owners.

7 rooms – £ 50/75 £ 75/95

Castle Hill ✉ EX35 6JA – ✆ 01598 752291 – www.castlehillguesthousedevon.co.uk

at Lynmouth East: 1 mi

Shelley's

TRADITIONAL · COSY A bright, keenly run hotel overlooking the sea; the eponymous poet honeymooned here in 1812. Traditionally styled guest areas include a homely lounge and a formally laid breakfast room with coastal views. Good-sized bedrooms.

11 rooms – £ 80/130 £ 80/130

8 Watersmeet Rd ✉ EX35 6EP – ✆ 01598 753219 – www.shelleyshotel.co.uk – Closed November-February

at Martinhoe West: 4.25 mi via Coast rd (toll) ✉ Barnstaple

Old Rectory

TRADITIONAL · ELEGANT Built in the 19C for a rector of Martinhoe's 11C church, this quiet country retreat is in a charming spot, with a well-tended 3 acre garden and a cascading brook. Fresh, bright bedrooms are modern, yet retain period touches: Heddon and Paddock are two of the best. Comfortable dining room; simple home-cooking.

11 rooms (dinner included) – £ 165/260 £ 205/275

✉ EX31 4QT – ✆ 01598 763368 – www.oldrectoryhotel.co.uk – Closed November-March

MADINGLEY – Cambridgeshire → See Cambridge

MAENPORTH BEACH – Cornwall → See Falmouth

MAIDEN NEWTON

Dorset – Pop. 1 268 – Regional map n° **2**-C3

Le Petit Canard

TRADITIONAL BRITISH · COSY XX This double-fronted former shop has a welcoming feel, with its cosy beamed interior and flickering candlelight. Run by a husband and wife team, it offers a seasonal menu of classic dishes; tasty duck and homemade bread feature.

Menu £ 35

Dorchester Rd ✉ DT2 0BE – ✆ 01300 320536 – www.le-petit-canard.co.uk – dinner only and Sunday lunch – Closed 2 weeks January, 1 week May, 1 week September, Sunday dinner, alternate Sunday lunch and Monday

MAIDENCOMBE – Torbay → See Torquay

MAIDENHEAD

Windsor and Maidenhead – Pop. 63 580 – Regional map n° **6**-C3

Boulters Riverside Brasserie

MODERN BRITISH · BRASSERIE XX Stylish modern eatery beside a lock, on a small island in the Thames. Full-length windows open onto the terrace; superb river views. Menu offers dishes ranging from fish and chips to roast partridge, with mature steaks and lighter salads.

Menu £ 20 (lunch) – Carte £ 20/37

Boulters Lock Island ✉ SL6 8PE – Northeast : 2.25 mi by A 4094 – ✆ 01628 621291 – www.boultersrestaurant.co.uk – Closed 27-30 December and Sunday dinner

Fredrick's

BUSINESS · CLASSIC It's hard to imagine that this smart red-brick hotel – with its stylish spa – was once an inn. It's classically styled, with a marble reception, a clubby bar and a formal restaurant serving modern French dishes. Bedrooms have panelled walls and bespoke wooden furnishings, and most overlook the gardens.

37 rooms – £ 119/189 £ 129/199 – 1 suite

Shoppenhangers Rd ✉ SL6 2PZ – ✆ 01628 581000 – www.fredricks-hotel.co.uk

MAIDENSGROVE

Oxfordshire – Pop. 1 572 – Regional map n° **6**-C3

Five Horseshoes

TRADITIONAL BRITISH • NEIGHBOURHOOD This lovely red-brick inn sits in a delightful country setting; if the weather's good, head straight for the terrace. Unfussy, traditional dishes make use of tip-top local ingredients and are packed full of flavour.

Menu £ 16 (weekday lunch) – Carte £ 26/47

RG9 6EX – 01491 641282 – www.thefivehorseshoes.co.uk – Closed Monday except bank holidays

MALDON

Essex – Pop. 21 462 – Regional map n° **7**-C3

Rubino Kitchen

MODERN BRITISH • COSY XX Hidden away on Chigborough Farm is this tiny restaurant, where you can come for a meal at any time of day. Cooking mixes English and Italian influences; at dinner choose 2-5 courses from 9 tasty weekly dishes.

Menu £ 18/30 – Carte lunch £ 21/23

Chigborough Farm, Chigborough Rd, Heybridge CM9 4RE – East : 2.5 mi by B 1022 off B 1026 – 01621 855579 (booking essential) – www.rubinokitchen.co.uk – Closed Sunday dinner, Monday and Tuesday

MALMESBURY

Wiltshire – Pop. 6 318 – Regional map n° **2**-C2

The Dining Room

MODERN CUISINE • ELEGANT XXX This country house hotel's intimate dining room has a serene feel and its neutral décor keeps the focus on the food. Modern cooking has a well-measured playfulness and brings together British, French and Asian flavours in an appealing multi-course set menu; the chefs present and explain the dishes themselves.

→ Egg white with custard, tamari and salmon roe. Aged beef loin with lettuce, pomme purée and glazed tendon. Chocolate and caramel with crème fraîche.

Menu £ 99 **s** – tasting menu only

Whatley Manor Hotel, Easton Grey SN16 0RB – West : 2.25 mi on B 4040 – 01666 822888 (booking essential) – www.whatleymanor.com – dinner only – Closed Monday and Tuesday

Grey's Brasserie

MODERN BRITISH • BRASSERIE XX The more casual alternative to Whatley Manor's 'Dining Room' is this unfussy brasserie. Salad and vegetables from the kitchen garden feature in dishes such as smoked mussels on toast, omelette Arnold Bennett and cottage pie.

Menu £ 25 (weekday lunch) – Carte £ 31/40 **s**

Whatley Manor Hotel, Easton Grey SN16 0RB – West : 2.25 mi on B 4040 – 01666 822888 – www.whatleymanor.com

Whatley Manor

LUXURY • CONTEMPORARY A charming Cotswold stone house in 12 acres of formal gardens. Guest areas include a delightful wood-panelled sitting room, a stunning spa, a top class business centre and a cinema. Luxurious, individually decorated bedrooms have sumptuous bathrooms and a contemporary feel.

23 rooms – †£ 350/895 ††£ 350/895 – 8 suites

Easton Grey SN16 0RB – West : 2.25 mi on B 4040 – 01666 822888 – www.whatleymanor.com

The Dining Room • **Grey's Brasserie** – See restaurant listing

at Crudwell North: 4 mi on A429 ✉ Malmesbury

Potting Shed Pub

REGIONAL CUISINE • COSY Spacious, light-filled pub with contemporary décor, exposed beams and a relaxing feel. Monthly changing menus offer wholesome, satisfying dishes, with vegetables and herbs from their garden.

Carte £ 23/35

The Street ✉ SN16 9EW – ✆ 01666 577833 – www.thepottingshedpub.com – Closed dinner 25 December

The Rectory

COUNTRY HOUSE • CONTEMPORARY Classical 18C former rectory with high ceilings, period features and a laid-back feel. Stylish fabrics and contemporary furnishings in the lounge and bar. Bedrooms boast bold feature walls, iPod docks, Roberts radios and some antiques. Oak-panelled dining room offers carefully cooked modern dishes.

12 rooms – †£ 95/205 ††£ 105/205

✉ SN16 9EP – ✆ 01666 577194 – www.therectoryhotel.com

MALTBY

Stockton-on-Tees – Regional map n° **14**-B3

Chadwicks Inn

MODERN CUISINE • COSY This 19C pub was a favourite haunt of the Spitfire pilots before their missions. The à la carte features ambitious, intricate dishes and is supplemented by a simpler early evening bistro menu and a good value set selection. The live acoustic sessions and wine tasting evenings are popular.

Menu £ 17 (weekday lunch)/28 – Carte £ 32/42

High Ln ✉ TS8 0BG – ✆ 01642 590300 (booking advisable) – www.chadwicksinnmaltby.co.uk – Closed 26 December, 1 January and Monday except bank holidays

MALTON

North Yorkshire – Pop. 4 888 – Regional map n° **13**-C2

Wentworth

MODERN BRITISH • CLASSIC DÉCOR XX Grand country house restaurant with an elegant chandelier, heavy drapes and fine paintings. Good quality local and estate ingredients feature in carefully prepared, classically-based dishes. Service is amiable, from a charming team.

Carte £ 38/49 – set menu only on Saturday evenings

Talbot Hotel, Yorkersgate ✉ YO17 7AJ – ✆ 01653 639096 (booking advisable) – www.talbotmalton.co.uk – dinner only and Sunday lunch

New Malton

TRADITIONAL BRITISH • PUB 18C stone pub with open fires, reclaimed furniture and photos of old town scenes. A good-sized menu offers hearty pub classics with the odd more adventurous dish thrown in; cooking is unfussy and flavoursome with an appealing Northern bias.

Carte £ 20/35

2-4 Market Pl ✉ YO17 7LX – ✆ 01653 693998 – www.thenewmalton.co.uk – Closed 25-26 December and 1 January

Talbot

HISTORIC • CLASSIC Early 17C hunting lodge owned by the Fitzwilliam Estate, featuring an impressive wooden staircase and country house style rooms filled with family artefacts. Traditional bedrooms have smart marble bathrooms. Dine in the grand restaurant or in the rustic modern brasserie in the glass-enclosed courtyard.

26 rooms – †£ 150/330 ††£ 150/330

Yorkersgate ✉ YO17 7AJ – ✆ 01653 639096 – www.talbotmalton.co.uk

Wentworth – See restaurant listing

MAN (Isle of)

I.O.M. - Pop. 80 058 - Regional map n° **11**-B1

Ballasalla

Abbey

MODERN BRITISH · FRIENDLY X An appealing former pub that was once a judge's house and a jam factory. Inside it's a cosy mix of the old and new; outside, a delightful terrace overlooks the abbey gardens. Careful modern British cooking showcases homemade produce.

Menu £ 20 (lunch) - Carte £ 20/49

Rushen Abbey, Mill Rd ✉ IM9 3DB - ✆ 01624 822393 - www.theabbey.im

Douglas

Macfarlane's

MODERN BRITISH · COSY XX Small restaurant in the heart of town, run by a personable couple. Sit in high-sided booths or on tall banquettes. Unfussy menus rely on fresh local produce; the blackboard specials have fresh fish and shellfish to the fore.

Menu £ 15 (weekday lunch) - Carte £ 29/47

24 Duke St ✉ IM1 2AY - ✆ 01624 624777 (booking essential) - www.macfarlanes.im - dinner only and lunch Thursday-Friday - Closed first 2 weeks January, 2 weeks July, 20 August-5 September, Saturday lunch, Sunday and Monday

Portofino

INTERNATIONAL · DESIGN XX This proudly run restaurant is on the ground floor of a chic apartment block on the harbour's edge. Menus offer classical international dishes with lots of Italian choices and verbally presented specials. Tables are smartly laid.

Menu £ 24 (weekdays) - Carte £ 23/53

Quay West ✉ IM1 5AG - ✆ 01624 617755 - www.portofino.im - Closed 25 December, Saturday lunch and Sunday

Tanroagan

SEAFOOD · BISTRO X Friendly restaurant off the quayside, with seafaring décor and a cosy feel. Fish from the island's day boats are simply cooked, making the most of their natural flavours. Portions are hearty; bread, desserts and ice creams are homemade.

Carte £ 24/54

9 Ridgeway St ✉ IM1 1EW - ✆ 01624 612355 - www.tanroagan.co.uk - Closed 25-26 December and Sunday

Claremont

BUSINESS · FUNCTIONAL Smart, modern hotel made up of several Victorian seaside properties. Bedrooms have good quality dark wood furnishings, Hungarian duck feather pillows, superb wet rooms, and state-of-the-art TV and audio equipment. The large brasserie-style restaurant serves modern dishes, which are presented by a cheery team.

56 rooms - †£ 90/190 ††£ 120/250

18-22 Loch Promenade ✉ IM1 2LX - ✆ 01624 617068 - www.claremont.im

Regency

TRADITIONAL · PERSONALISED Restored Victorian townhouse featuring wood panelling, stained glass and a substantial collection of seascape watercolours. Bedrooms are well-equipped for business travellers and mobile phones and iPads are available on loan.

38 rooms - †£ 85/115 ††£ 140/170 - 5 suites

Queens Promenade ✉ IM2 4NN - ✆ 01624 680680 - www.regency.im

Inglewood

TOWNHOUSE · FUNCTIONAL Modern hotel at the quieter end of the promenade; the front-facing rooms enjoy views over the bay. Spacious bedrooms have chunky, contemporary furnishings, leather armchairs and modern shower rooms. Well-stocked residents' bar.

16 rooms – £ 50/95 £ 75/140

26 Palace Terr, Queens Promenade ✉ IM2 4NF – ✆ 01624 674734 – www.inglewoodhotel-isleofman.com – Closed mid-end October and Christmas-New Year

Ramsey

River House

TRADITIONAL · PERSONALISED Attractive Georgian country house in an idyllic riverside setting; its bright, spacious interior filled with antique furnishings and objets d'art. Traditional bedrooms come with floral fabrics, knick-knacks and large baths.

4 rooms – £ 78 £ 98

✉ IM8 3DA – North : 0.25 mi by A 9 turning left immediately after bridge – ✆ 01624 816412 – www.theriverhouse-iom.com – Closed 16-26 June, 8-30 September and 8-25 November

P. Frilet/hemis.fr

GOOD TIPS!

The Manchester dining scene has exploded in recent years and now offers a vibrancy and diversity unrivalled outside of London. Sample tasty, authentic tapas at **El Gato Negro** in the city centre; try modern Indian cuisine at **Asha's**; or enjoy cocktails and an innovative, 18 course set menu of 'space age Asian food' at **Rabbit in the Moon**.

MANCHESTER

Greater Manchester - Pop. 510 746 - Regional map n° **11**-B2

Restaurants

El Gato Negro

SPANISH • TAPAS BAR X 'The Black Cat' sits in a three storey building in a pedestrianised street. The ground floor bar offers snacks and charcuterie, the first floor houses an industrial-style dining room and the third floor boasts a cocktail bar with a retractable roof. Appealing tapas dishes include meats from the Josper grill.

Carte £ 15/32

Town plan: A2-e - *52 King St ✉ M2 4LY - ✆ 0161 694 8585 (booking essential) - www.elgatonegrotapas.com - Closed 25 December*

Adam Reid at The French

MODERN BRITISH • ELEGANT XXX An intimate hotel restaurant created in the Belle Époque age and now brought up-to-date. Dinner sees a set menu, while lunch is more flexible. Boldly flavoured modern dishes focus on one main ingredient; desserts are playful.

Menu £ 45 (weekday dinner)/85 - Carte lunch £ 22/39

Town plan: A2-x - *Midland Hotel. Peter St. ✉ M60 2DS - ✆ 0161 932 4198 (booking essential) - www.the-french.co.uk - dinner only and lunch Friday-Saturday - Closed first 2 weeks August, 1 week Christmas, Sunday and Monday*

Wings

CHINESE • ELEGANT XXX Well-run restaurant off a busy square. The narrow room features comfy booths, terracotta army replicas, Hong Kong skyline murals and celebrity-signed plates. Extensive menus offer authentic Cantonese dim sum; sea bass is a speciality.

Carte £ 26/88

Town plan: A2-d - *1 Lincoln Sq ✉ M2 5LN - ✆ 0161 834 9000 (booking essential at dinner) - www.wingsrestaurant.co.uk*

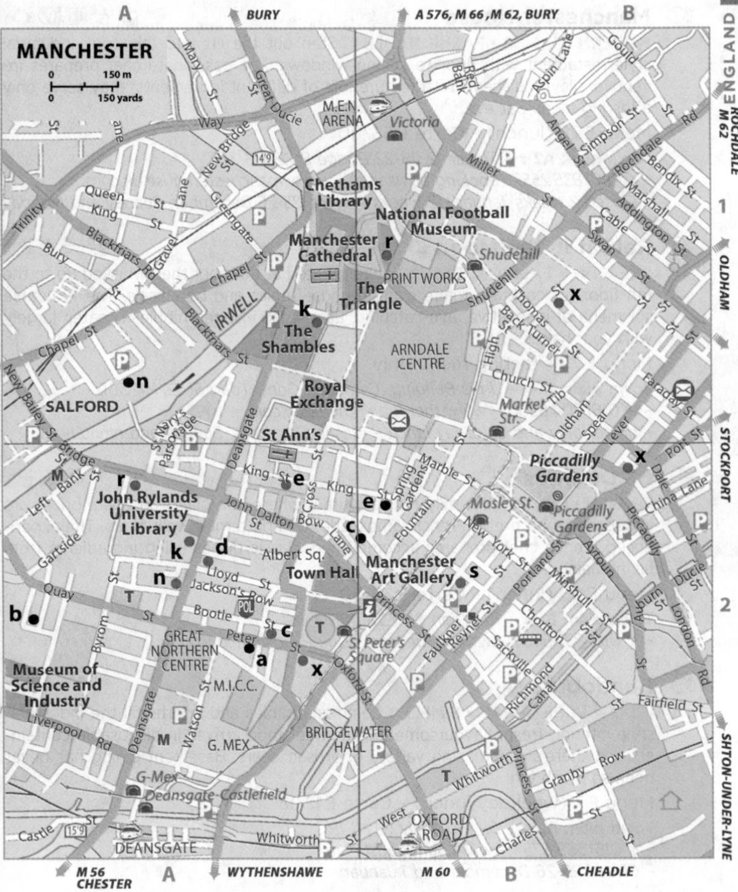

Asha's

INDIAN • ELEGANT XX Start in the intimately lit basement cocktail bar then move up to the exotic, glamorous restaurant. The modern Indian menu offers both 'Classic' and 'Creative' curries; kebabs are a specialty, as is the traditional masala recipe.

Menu £ 17 (weekday lunch) – Carte £ 28/41

Town plan: A2-c – *47 Peter St ✉ M2 3NG – ✆ 0161 832 5309 – www.ashasrestaurant.co.uk*

Australasia

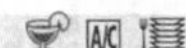

MODERN CUISINE • TRENDY XX Fun, fashionable basement restaurant on the site of the old Manchester Evening News; come for cocktails, small plates, sushi, DJs and a clubby vibe. Vibrant dishes have European, Pacific Rim and Asian influences. Helpful staff.

Menu £ 16 (weekday lunch) – Carte £ 25/78

Town plan: A2-k – *1 The Avenue, Spinningfields ✉ M3 3AP – ✆ 0161 831 0288 – www.australasia.uk.com – Closed 25-26 December and 1 January*

Manchester House

MODERN CUISINE • FASHIONABLE XX Step out the lift into this cool, industrial style restaurant with floor to ceiling windows. The passionate chef prepares inventive, playful dishes which feature lots of different ingredients; they serve only a tasting menu Sat eve.

Menu £ 28 (lunch) – Carte £ 53/80

Town plan: A2-r – *Tower 12, 18-22 Bridge St ✉ M3 3BZ*
– *✆ 0161 835 2557 (booking advisable) – www.manchesterhouse.uk.com*
– *Closed 2 weeks January, 2 weeks August, 25-26 December, Sunday and Monday*

Rabbit in the Moon (N)

CREATIVE • FASHIONABLE XX You're greeted at the door then whisked up to the 6th floor for cocktails made from in-house tonics and botanicals. The 18 course set menu of innovative, eye-catching, East Asian inspired nibbles is eaten largely with your hands.

Menu £ 75 – tasting menu only

Town plan: B1-r – *Urbis Building, Cathedral Gdns, Todd St ✉ M4 3BG*
– *✆ 0161 804 8560 – www.therabbitinthemoon.com*
– *dinner only and Saturday lunch – Closed Christmas, Sunday and Monday*

63 Degrees

FRENCH • BISTRO XX Family-run restaurant where iron pillars and bare bricks are juxtaposed with pretty French lampshades and patterned wallpapers. The experienced French chef prepares accomplished, classic dishes using ingredients from his homeland.

Menu £ 20 (lunch) – Carte £ 29/58

Town plan: B1-x – *104 High St. ✉ M4 1HQ*
– *✆ 0161 832 5438 – www.63degrees.co.uk – Closed Monday*

Bundobust (N)

INDIAN VEGETARIAN • SIMPLE X Communal tables and booths fill the industrial-style interior, fresh, flavoursome Indian street food arrives in disposable containers and there's an amazing variety of artisan beers. Basement dining has never been so much fun!

Menu £ 7 (weekday lunch) – Carte £ 12/18

Town plan: B2-x – *59 Piccadilly ✉ M1 1RG*
– *✆ 0161 359 6757 – www.bundobust.com*
– *Closed 25-26 December and 1 January*

Hawksmoor Manchester

MEATS AND GRILLS • BISTRO X A large former probate office with plenty of charm and character. Have a bespoke beer and snacks at the bar or head through to the high-ceilinged dining room. The bovine-based menu offers steaks for one or to share, from 500g-1kg.

Menu £ 28 – Carte £ 23/59

Town plan: A2-n – *184-186 Deansgate ✉ M3 3WB*
– *✆ 0161 836 6980 – www.thehawksmoor.com*

Second Floor Brasserie at Harvey Nichols

MODERN BRITISH • DESIGN X Take a break from shopping and head for this relaxed restaurant with huge windows overlooking the street below. Choose from small plates, seasonal mains and steaks from the charcoal grill; they also serve brunch and afternoon tea.

Carte £ 20/46

Town plan: A1-k – *21 New Cathedral St ✉ M1 1AD*
– *✆ 0161 828 8898 – www.harveynichols.com*
– *Closed 25 December, 1 January, Easter Sunday and dinner Sunday-Monday*

Yuzu

JAPANESE • SIMPLE Climb the steps to the upper floor of this converted Victorian warehouse, where you'll find an open kitchen, a counter and four communal tables. The Japanese cooking is fresh, authentic and healthy; the dumplings are delicious.

Carte £ 10/21

Town plan: B2-s - *39 Faulkner St ✉ M1 4EE - ✆ 0161 236 4159 (booking advisable) - www.yuzumanchester.co.uk - Closed 2 weeks August, 2 weeks Christmas-New Year, Sunday and Monday*

Hotels

Lowry

LUXURY • DESIGN Modern and hugely spacious, with excellent facilities, an impressive spa and a minimalist feel: art displays and exhibitions feature throughout. Stylish bedrooms with oversized windows; some have river views. The airy first floor restaurant serves a wide-ranging menu.

165 rooms ☕ - †£ 119/699 ††£ 119/699 - 7 suites

Town plan: A1-n - *50 Dearmans Pl, Chapel Wharf, Salford ✉ M3 5LH - ✆ 0161 827 4000 - www.thelowryhotel.com*

Radisson Blu Edwardian

BUSINESS • GRAND LUXURY This 14 floor hotel cleverly incorporates the façade of the former Free Trade Hall and has a great pool and spa. Bedrooms are contemporary – some have part-covered verandas; the Valentino Suite is the best and offers superb views. Sultry 'Opus One' is popular for afternoon tea, cocktails and seasonal modern dinners. Informal 'Steak and Lobster' serves an all-day menu.

263 rooms - †£ 209/334 ††£ 224/349 - ☕ £ 21 - 4 suites

Town plan: A2-a - *Free Trade Hall, Peter St ✉ M2 5GP - ✆ 0161 835 9929 - www.radissonblu-edwardian.com*

Hotel Gotham

LUXURY • ELEGANT This Grade II listed former bank has something of a Manhattan-style exterior, hence its name. Stylish modern bedrooms have black and white prints of Manchester and New York on the walls and some have projected 'wonderwalls' instead of windows. The delightful all-day dining room serves English classics.

60 rooms - †£ 129/695 ††£ 129/695 - ☕ £ 15

Town plan: B2-e - *100 King St ✉ M2 4WU - ✆ 0161 413 0000 - www.hotelgotham.co.uk*

King Street Townhouse

TOWNHOUSE • CONTEMPORARY A boutique townhouse in an impressive Italianate building designed in 1872 by local architect Edward Salomons. Stylish bedrooms have super king sized beds and top quality furnishings. Relax in the infinity plunge pool looking out across the rooftops then sit on bold red banquettes and enjoy bistro classics.

40 rooms - †£ 252/420 ††£ 252/420 - ☕ £ 18

Town plan: B2-c - *10 Booth St ✉ M2 4AW - ✆ 0161 667 0707 - www.kingstreettownhouse.co.uk*

Great John Street

HISTORIC • CONTEMPORARY This stylish, boutique hotel was once a wonderful Victorian schoolhouse; you can hold a meeting in the old Headmaster's study! All of the bedrooms are duplex suites with roll-top baths. Relax on the roof terrace with its cocktail bar and hot-tub. There's no restaurant but they do offer room service.

30 rooms - †£ 120/360 ††£ 140/360 - ☕ £ 18

Town plan: A2-b - *Great John St ✉ M3 4FD - ✆ 0161 831 3211 - www.greatjohnstreet.co.uk*

at Didsbury South: 5.5 mi by A5103 on A5145 ✉ Manchester

Hispi

MODERN BRITISH • NEIGHBOURHOOD With its bright green façade, this simple yet stylish neighbourhood restaurant certainly stands out. Good value dishes are a pleasing mix of the classic and the modern and the concise wine list features some lesser-known producers.

Menu £ 16 (weekday lunch)/18 – Carte £ 25/46

1c School Ln ✉ M20 6RD – ✆ 0161 445 3996 – www.hispi.net – Closed 25-26 December

Didsbury House

LUXURY • PERSONALISED A whitewashed Victorian villa with original features and a boutique feel – look out for the impressive stained glass window. Stylish, well-appointed bedrooms include duplex suites. There's no designated restaurant area but you can dine from an accessible menu in the bar and lounges or in your room. They also own similarly styled Eleven Didsbury Park, just down the road.

27 rooms – †£ 90/174 ††£ 90/174 – ☕ £ 16 – 2 suites

Didsbury Pk ✉ M20 5LJ – South : 1.5 mi on A 5145 – ✆ 0161 448 2200 – www.didsburyhouse.com

MANSFIELD

Nottinghamshire – Pop. 77 551 – Regional map n° **9**-B1

No.4 Wood Street

TRADITIONAL BRITISH • RUSTIC Modern restaurant on the first floor of a converted warehouse. Exposed stone walls and chunky wood furniture give it a rustic feel. Classical cooking has clearly defined flavours. Start with a speciality gin in the spacious lounge.

Menu £ 11 (lunch) – Carte £ 22/37

4 Wood St ✉ NG18 1QA – ✆ 01623 424824 (booking advisable) – www.4woodstreet.co.uk – Closed 1-9 January, Sunday dinner, Monday and Tuesday

MARAZION

Cornwall – Pop. 1 294 – Regional map n° **1**-A3

Ben's Cornish Kitchen

MODERN CUISINE • SIMPLE Rustic family-run eatery; sit upstairs for views over the rooftops to St Michael's Mount. Unfussy lunches are followed by sophisticated dinners, which feature some interesting flavour combinations. They offer 25 wines by the glass.

Menu £ 18/33

West End ✉ TR17 0EL – ✆ 01736 719200 – www.benscornishkitchen.com – Closed 25-26 December, 1 January, Sunday and Monday

Mount Haven

COUNTRY HOUSE • PERSONALISED A small, stylish hotel overlooking St Michael's Mount, with a spacious bar, a chic lounge and a lovely terrace. Contemporary bedrooms offer good amenities and most have a balcony and a view. The bright, attractive dining room offers elaborate modern dishes with ambitious flavour combinations.

19 rooms ☕ – †£ 90/170 ††£ 120/280

Turnpike Rd ✉ TR17 0DQ – East : 0.25 mi – ✆ 01736 719937 – www.mounthaven.co.uk – Closed 6 January-1 March

at Perranuthnoe Southeast: 1.75 mi by A394 ✉ Penzance

Victoria Inn

CLASSIC CUISINE • PUB A well-established, bright pink pub, in a small village close to the sea; the owner is a local returned home. Menus stick mainly to the classics and fish, landed at nearby Newlyn, is in abundance. Be sure to save room for one of the tasty puddings! Cosy, unfussy bedrooms have a seaside feel.

Carte £ 25/39

2 rooms – †£ 95 ††£ 95

✉ TR20 9NP – ✆ 01736 710309 – www.victoriainn-penzance.co.uk – Closed 25 December and 1 January

Ednovean Farm

FAMILY • PERSONALISED 17C granite barn in a tranquil spot overlooking the bay and surrounded by 22 acres of sub-tropical gardens and paddocks. Individually styled bedrooms feature local toiletries; the Blue Room has a French bed, a roll-top bath and a terrace. Complimentary sherry is left in the hall. Have a range-cooked breakfast at the oak table or a continental selection in bed.

3 rooms – †£ 90/140 ††£ 110/140

✉ TR20 9LZ – ✆ 01736 711883 – www.ednoveanfarm.co.uk – Closed Christmas

MARGATE

Kent – Pop. 61 223 – Regional map n° **5**-D1

Ambrette Margate

INDIAN • COSY Quirky restaurant with modest surroundings. The concise menu showcases Kentish produce in an original modern style; freshly prepared dishes offer well-balanced flavours and subtle Indian spicing – you won't find any curries here!

Menu £ 22 (lunch) – Carte £ 31/49

44 King St ✉ CT9 1QE – ✆ 01843 231504 – www.theambrette.co.uk – Closed Monday in winter

Sands

BOUTIQUE HOTEL • PERSONALISED Set between the high street and the sea – a smartly refurbished hotel, with extremely stylish bedrooms. Have a cocktail in the white leather furnished lounge-bar overlooking the beach before watching the sun go down from the roof terrace. The brasserie serves modern British dishes and also shares the view.

20 rooms – †£ 130/210 ††£ 130/210

16 Marine Dr ✉ CT9 1DH – (entrance on High St) – ✆ 01843 228228 – www.sandshotelmargate.co.uk

Crescent Victoria

TOWNHOUSE • PERSONALISED A classic Georgian terraced house with pleasant views over the Winter Gardens and Margate Sands. Most of the bedrooms share the outlook; all are boldly decorated and come with quality linens and very comfortable beds.

14 rooms – †£ 60/120 ††£ 90/280

25-26 Ford Cres ✉ CT9 1HX – ✆ 01843 230375 – www.crescentvictoria.co.uk

Reading Rooms

TOWNHOUSE • PERSONALISED Passionately run guesthouse with original plaster walls and worn woodwork. Three bedrooms – one per floor – boast distressed furniture, super-comfy beds, huge bathrooms and Square views. Extensive breakfasts are served in your room.

3 rooms – †£ 95/160 ††£ 160/190

31 Hawley Sq ✉ CT9 1PH – ✆ 01843 225166 – www.thereadingroomsmargate.co.uk

MARKET RASEN

Lincolnshire - Pop. 4 773 - Regional map n° **9**-C1

Advocate Arms

TRADITIONAL BRITISH • INN Former hotel close to the market square, with an original revolving door and a smart, modern interior divided by etched glass walls. Lunch sticks to good old pub classics and at dinner, mature local steaks are a speciality; they also serve breakfast and afternoon tea. Bedrooms are spacious and well-equipped.

Menu £ 19 (weekday lunch) - Carte £ 21/47

10 rooms - †£ 60/140 ††£ 60/140 - ☕ £ 8

2 Queen St ✉ LN8 3EH - ✆ 01673 842364 - www.advocatearms.co.uk - Closed Sunday dinner

MARLBOROUGH

Wiltshire - Pop. 8 092 - Regional map n° **2**-D2

Rick Stein

SEAFOOD • ELEGANT An attractive double-fronted townhouse where 5 charming rooms spread over 2 floors make you feel like you're dining privately. The daily menu offers the best value; for those pushing the boat out, try the turbot on the bone.

Menu £ 25 (weekday lunch) - Carte £ 23/51

Lloran House, 42a High St ✉ SN8 1HQ - ✆ 01672 233333 - www.rickstein.com - Closed 25 December

at Little Bedwyn East: 9.5 mi by A4 ✉ Marlborough

Harrow at Little Bedwyn (Roger Jones)

MODERN CUISINE • INTIMATE A red-brick former pub off the beaten track, with an intimate, understated style; look out for the wine bottle capsule pictures. Assured cooking has a classical base but there are plenty of modern elements too. The comprehensive wine list champions the New World and they offer wine pairings with every menu.

➜ Diver-caught scallop with mango chutney, curry jam and bhaji. New season hogget with Isle of Wight tomatoes, minted couscous and asparagus. Blackberry soufflé with blackberry parfait and vanilla crème.

Menu £ 40/70

✉ SN8 3JP - ✆ 01672 870871 - www.theharrowatlittlebedwyn.com - Closed 25 December-4 January and Sunday-Tuesday

at West Overton West: 4 mi on A4

Bell

MODERN BRITISH • PUB A simple, friendly pub, rescued from oblivion by a local couple, who hired an experienced pair to run it. The menu mixes pub classics with Mediterranean-influenced dishes; presentation is modern but not at the expense of flavour.

Carte £ 24/51

Bath Rd ✉ SN8 1QD - ✆ 01672 861099 - www.thebellwestoverton.co.uk - Closed Sunday dinner and Monday except bank holidays

MARLDON

Devon - Pop. 1 906 - Regional map n° **1**-C2

Church House Inn

TRADITIONAL BRITISH • PUB A charming, well-run inn with wooden beams, open fires and eye-catching Strawberry Gothic windows. Several blackboards offer a range of classically based dishes with Mediterranean influences, including tapas and sharing plates.

Carte £ 25/37

Village Rd ✉ TQ3 1SL - ✆ 01803 558279 - www.churchhousemarldon.com - Closed 25 December and dinner 26 December

MARLOW

Buckinghamshire - Pop. 14 823 - Regional map n° **6**-C3

✿✿ Hand and Flowers (Tom Kerridge)

MODERN BRITISH • FRIENDLY A destination dining pub with a smart, rustic feel courtesy of low beams, flagged floors and nooks and crannies. Refined pub food is elevated to new heights and isn't afraid to push the boundaries. Sourcing of ingredients is given due reverence, execution is confident and presentation is first-rate; desserts are a highlight. Luxurious bedrooms are situated close by.

→ Salt-baked swede and haggis tart with crispy lamb, 'Chantilly de chèvre' and raw mushroom. Slow-cooked duck breast 'à l'orange' with duck sausage, trompette and rillette tart. Banana soufflé with pistachio crumble.

Menu £ 25 (weekday lunch) - Carte £ 54/72

8 rooms - †£ 195/275 ††£ 195/275

126 West St. ✉ SL7 2BP

- ✆ 01628 482277 (booking essential) - www.thehandandflowers.co.uk - Closed 24-26 December, dinner 1 January and Sunday dinner

✿ The Coach

MODERN BRITISH • FRIENDLY Tom Kerridge's second pub is a pleasingly unpretentious kind of a place, with studded red leather chairs and a comfortingly traditional air. The menu of small plates is headed 'Meat', 'No Meat' and 'Sweet', allowing you to compose your meal however you wish. Dishes are refined, detailed and packed with flavour.

→ Potted Loch Duart salmon with cucumber chutney. Venison chilli with chocolate and toasted rice cream. Banana custard with dates and honeycomb.

Carte £ 18/38

3 West St ✉ SL7 2LS

- ✆ 01628 481704 (bookings not accepted) - www.thecoachmarlow.co.uk - Closed 25 December

Sindhu

INDIAN • INTIMATE XX Traditional stained glass and dark wood blend with bold modern fabrics in this glitzy waterside restaurant within a smart hotel. Authentic South Indian cooking is confidently spiced and features specialities from the tandoor oven.

Menu £ 20 (weekday lunch) - Carte £ 22/35

Compleat Angler Hotel, Marlow Bridge, Bisham Rd ✉ SL7 1RG

- ✆ 01628 405405 - www.sindhurestaurant.co.uk

Vanilla Pod

FRENCH • INTIMATE XX An intimate, well-established restaurant in T. S. Eliot's former home, featuring a plush interior and smartly laid tables. The chef works alone, cooking ambitious dishes with classical French foundations and original touches.

Menu £ 20/45 **s**

31 West St ✉ SL7 2LS

- ✆ 01628 898101 (booking essential) - www.thevanillapod.co.uk - Closed 24 December-8 January, 14-18 April, 29 May- 6 June, 28 August-5 September, Sunday, Monday and bank holidays

Royal Oak

MODERN BRITISH • PUB Part-17C, country-chic pub with a herb garden, a petanque pitch and a pleasant terrace. Set close to the M40 and M4, it's an ideal London getaway. Cooking is British-led; wash down an ox cheek pasty with a pint of local Rebellion ale.

Carte £ 22/44

Frieth Rd, Bovingdon Green ✉ SL7 2JF - West : 1.25 mi by A 4155

- ✆ 01628 488611 - www.royaloakmarlow.co.uk - Closed 25-26 December

Compleat Angler

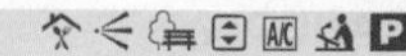

TRADITIONAL • CLASSIC Well-kept hotel in an idyllic spot on the Thames, with views of the weir and the chain bridge. Comfy, corporate-style bedrooms blend classic furnishings with contemporary fabrics: some have balconies – go for a Feature Room. The restaurants offer modern British and South Indian cooking overlooking the river.

64 rooms – †£ 150/290 ††£ 165/350 – 3 suites

Marlow Bridge, Bisham Rd ✉ SL7 1RG – ✆ 0344 879 9128
– www.macdonald-hotels.co.uk/compleatangler

Sindhu – See restaurant listing

at Little Marlow East: 3 mi on A4155

Queens Head

TRADITIONAL BRITISH • FRIENDLY Tucked away down a lane, a truly charming 16C pub with a picture-postcard look. Hearty, flavoursome cooking offers something for everyone, from a fig and mozzarella salad at lunchtime to rump of lamb with ratatouille.

Carte £ 24/38

Pound Ln ✉ SL7 3SR – ✆ 01628 482927 – www.marlowslittlesecret.co.uk – Closed 25-26 December

MARTINHOE – Devon ➔ See Lynton

MARTON

Cheshire East – Regional map n° **11**-B3

La Popote

CLASSIC FRENCH • BISTRO With its French-themed prints and bistro feel, this is the perfect destination for Francophiles; ask for a table overlooking the garden or head for the terrace. The menu is a roll-call of tasty Gallic classics; lunch is good value.

Menu £ 18 (weekday lunch) – Carte £ 26/49

✉ SK11 9HF – ✆ 01260 224785 (booking essential) – www.la-popote.co.uk – Closed Sunday dinner, Monday and Tuesday

MARTON CUM GRAFTON

North Yorkshire – Regional map n° **13**-B2

Punch Bowl Inn

TRADITIONAL BRITISH • RUSTIC A delightful crescent-shaped, part-14C inn, comprising several little rooms and a lovely terrace. The all-encompassing menu includes a seafood platter and a Yorkshire board, along with excellent fish and chips and rib-eye steak.

Menu £ 18 (weekday lunch) – Carte £ 24/45

✉ YO51 9QY – ✆ 01423 322519 – www.thepunchbowlmartoncumgrafton.com

MASHAM

North Yorkshire – ✉ Ripon – Pop. 1 205 – Regional map n° **13**-B1

Samuels

MODERN BRITISH • ELEGANT Set within a castle, a beautiful rococo-style dining room with an ornate gilt ceiling and park views. Well-spaced tables are adorned with lilies. Complex modern cooking uses produce from the huge kitchen gardens and local suppliers.

Menu £ 58

Swinton Park Hotel, Swinton ✉ HG4 4JH – Southwest : 1 mi – ✆ 01765 680900 (booking essential) – www.swintonpark.com – dinner only and lunch Saturday-Sunday

Vennell's

TRADITIONAL BRITISH • INTIMATE XX This personally run restaurant has purple walls, boldly patterned chairs and a striking feature wall – at weekends, sit downstairs surrounded by local art. Seasonal menus offer 4 choices per course and cooking has a modern edge.

Menu £ 36 **s**

7 Silver St ✉ HG4 4DX – ✆ 01765 689000 (booking essential) – www.vennellsrestaurant.co.uk – dinner only and Sunday lunch – Closed first 2 weeks January, 1 week Easter, 1 week August, Sunday dinner and Monday

Swinton Park

HISTORIC • CLASSIC A 17C castle with Georgian and Victorian additions, set on a 22,000 acre estate; try your hand at shooting, riding or falconry or relax in the state-of-the-art spa. The grand interior features open fires, ornate plasterwork, oil portraits and antiques. Dine in the relaxed brasserie or impressive dining room.

32 rooms – †£ 155/345 ††£ 155/345 – 6 suites

Swinton ✉ HG4 4JH – Southwest : 1 mi – ✆ 01765 680900 – www.swintonestate.com

Samuels – See restaurant listing

MATFIELD

Kent – Regional map n° **5**-B2

Wheelwrights Arms

TRADITIONAL BRITISH • RUSTIC 17C former Kentish farmhouse: outside it's all clapboard and colourful flower baskets; inside it's rustic with low beamed ceilings crammed with hanging hops. Expect an abundance of local, seasonal produce in classic dishes.

Carte £ 22/46

The Green ✉ TN12 7JX – ✆ 01892 722129 – www.thewheelwrightsarmsfreehouse.co.uk – Closed Sunday dinner and Monday

MATLOCK

Derbyshire – Pop. 14 956 – Regional map n° **9**-B1

Stones

MODERN BRITISH • NEIGHBOURHOOD XX Negotiate the steep steps down to this small riverside restaurant and head for the front room with its floor to ceiling windows. Unfussy, modern British dishes are attractively presented and display the odd Mediterranean touch.

Menu £ 22/36

1C Dale Rd ✉ DE4 3LT – ✆ 01629 56061 (booking advisable) – www.stones-restaurant.co.uk – Closed 25 December-5 January, Sunday, Monday and lunch Tuesday

MAWGAN PORTH – Cornwall → See Newquay

MEDMENHAM

Buckinghamshire – Regional map n° **6**-C3

Dog & Badger (N)

MODERN BRITISH • DESIGN XX This former pub dates from 1390 yet it's anything but old-fashioned, with its striking Riva speedboat inspired bar and a chic restaurant where rustic timbers blend with colourful furnishings. Well-presented classics are given a modern flourish and some Asian touches. Stylish bedrooms are well-equipped.

Menu £ 18 (weekday lunch) – Carte £ 30/49

6 rooms – †£ 195/250 ††£ 195/250

Henley Rd ✉ SL7 2HE – ✆ 01491 579944 – www.thedogandbadger.com – Closed 25-26 December and Sunday dinner

MELLOR - Lancashire → See Blackburn

MELLOR

Greater Manchester - Regional map n° **11**-B3

Oddfellows

TRADITIONAL BRITISH • PUB Oddies – as it is known locally – has a light, uncluttered feel, with wood-burning stoves adding an element of cosiness. The appealing, daily changing menu offers tasty, locally sourced 'British food with a modern twist'.

Carte £ 20/38

Moor End Rd ✉ SK6 5PT - ✆ 0161 449 7826 - www.oddfellowsmellor.com - Closed Monday except bank holidays

MELLS

Somerset - Pop. 2 222 - Regional map n° **2**-C2

Talbot Inn

MODERN BRITISH • RUSTIC Characterful 15C coaching inn with a cobbled courtyard, a cosy sitting room with an open fire, a snug bar offering real ales and an elegant Grill Room to keep carnivores happy at weekends. Delightful bedrooms are well-priced and understated in style. Food is seasonal, modern and full of flavour; and staff may be casually attired, but their manner is anything but.

Carte £ 23/34

8 rooms - †£ 100/160 ††£ 100/160

Selwood St ✉ BA11 3PN - ✆ 01373 812254 - www.talbotinn.com

MELTON MOWBRAY

Leicestershire - Pop. 27 158 - Regional map n° **9**-B2

Stapleford Park

COUNTRY HOUSE • PERSONALISED Beautiful stately home in 500 acres of landscaped grounds, with grand drawing rooms, exceedingly comfortable bedrooms and an ornate rococo dining room. British designers have styled the rooms in keeping with their original features; look out for the impressive Grinling Gibbons wood carvings.

55 rooms - †£ 140/268 ††£ 160/288 - 3 suites

✉ LE14 2EF - East : 5 mi by B 676 on Stapleford rd - ✆ 01572 787000 - www.staplefordpark.com

MEVAGISSEY

Cornwall - Pop. 2 117 - Regional map n° **1**-B3

Trevalsa Court

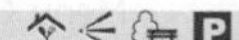

HISTORIC • PERSONALISED Charming Arts and Crafts style house which combines dark wood panelling and stone fireplaces with bright modern art and bold soft furnishings. Most of the well-appointed bedrooms have coastal views. The oak-panelled dining room looks onto the lovely terrace and garden, and dishes showcase local produce.

14 rooms - †£ 70/120 ††£ 125/290

School Hill ✉ PL26 6TH - East : 0.5 mi - ✆ 01726 842468 - www.trevalsa-hotel.co.uk - Closed January and December

Pebble House

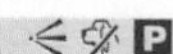

TOWNHOUSE • PERSONALISED This impressive three-storey property looks out over the bay to Chapel Point and all but one of its stylish, luxurious bedrooms share the view. Guests are welcomed with champagne and in summer they serve afternoon tea on the terrace. Breakfasts are extensive and the keen owners are very hands-on.

6 rooms - †£ 135/220 ††£ 135/220

Polkirt Hill ✉ PL26 6UX - South : 0.5 mi on Porthmellon rd - ✆ 01726 844466 - www.pebblehousecornwall.co.uk - Closed early November-mid February except New Year

MID LAVANT - West Sussex ➔ See Chichester

MIDDLEHAM

North Yorkshire - Pop. 754 - Regional map n° **13**-B1

The Saddle Room

TRADITIONAL BRITISH • RUSTIC Located within an area of parkland close to the 'Forbidden Corner', is this converted stable decked out with equine paraphernalia - ask for a table in a stall! Unfussy menus offer the usual pub favourites alongside more interesting dishes like sticky pig cheeks. Stylish bedrooms are named after racehorses.

Carte £ 25/50

9 rooms - ♦£ 70 ♦♦£ 130

Tupgill Park, Coverdale ✉ DL8 4TJ - Southwest : 2.5 mi by Coverham rd - ☎ 01969 640596 - www.thesaddleroom.co.uk - Closed Sunday dinner

MIDDLESBROUGH

Middlesbrough - Pop. 174 700 - Regional map n° **14**-B3

Brasserie Hudson Quay

ITALIAN • BRASSERIE X Set in the shadows of Middlesbrough Football Stadium; be sure to find a window seat or a spot on the terrace so you can look out over Hudson Quay's old docks. Mediterranean menus have a Tuscan bias.

Menu £ 12 (weekday lunch) - Carte £ 21/49

Windward Way ✉ TS2 1QG - ☎ 01642 261166 - www.brasseriehudsonquay.com - Closed Monday

MIDDLETON TYAS

North Yorkshire - Pop. 581 - Regional map n° **13**-B1

The Coach House at Middleton Lodge

MODERN BRITISH • DESIGN XX A stylishly converted coach house to the Georgian mansion where the owner grew up. The dining area is in the former stables and the bar is where the coaches once parked. Concise, constantly evolving menus feature produce from within 40 miles. Contemporary bedrooms come with roll-top baths and Roberts radios.

Menu £ 15 (weekday lunch) - Carte £ 20/44

15 rooms - ♦£ 120/170 ♦♦£ 140/190

Kneeton Ln ✉ DL10 6NJ - Northwest : 1 mi on Barton rd - ☎ 01325 377977 - www.middletonlodge.co.uk/coachhouse - Closed dinner 24-25 December, 26 December, lunch 31 December, 2 January, Monday and Tuesday

MIDHURST

West Sussex - Pop. 4 914 - Regional map n° **4**-C2

Spread Eagle

HISTORIC • TRADITIONAL Part-15C coaching inn retaining plenty of its original character and decked out with antiques, tapestries and gleaming brass - although there's also a modern, well-equipped spa. Bedrooms are traditional. Dine next to an inglenook fireplace under wooden beams and look out for the Christmas puddings too!

39 rooms - ♦£ 99/339 ♦♦£ 119/359 - 3 suites

South St ✉ GU29 9NH - ☎ 01730 816911 - www.hshotels.co.uk

Church House

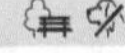

TOWNHOUSE • PERSONALISED An enthusiastically run townhouse; the main part dates from 1383 and features low beams and oak pillars. Bedrooms are quirky and luxurious; the best are 'Silver', with its slipper bath and 'Gaudi', with its vaulted ceiling and sleigh bed.

5 rooms - ♦£ 80/100 ♦♦£ 150/170

Church Hill ✉ GU29 9NX - ☎ 01730 812990 - www.churchhousemidhurst.com - Closed Christmas

at Henley North: 4.5 mi by A286

Duke of Cumberland Arms

TRADITIONAL BRITISH • COSY A hidden gem, nestled in pretty tiered gardens with trickling streams, trout ponds and splendid South Downs views. Sit in the cosy bar or more modern dining area which opens onto a terrace. Appealing menus offer carefully prepared seasonal dishes: lunch sees pub classics and dinner shifts things up a gear.

Carte £ 31/55

✉ GU27 3HQ – ✆ 01428 652280 – www.dukeofcumberland.com – Closed 25-26 December and dinner Sunday-Monday

at Bepton Southwest: 2.5 mi by A286 on Bepton rd✉ Midhurst

Park House

COUNTRY HOUSE • CONTEMPORARY Family-run country house with a light modern style and smart spa and leisure facilities. Spacious, homely bedrooms are split between this and South Downs Cottage; they come in neutral hues and most have views of the well-tended gardens and golf course. The stylish conservatory restaurant serves modern menus.

21 rooms – †£ 135/430 ††£ 135/430 – 1 suite

✉ GU29 0JB – ✆ 01730 819000 – www.parkhousehotel.com – Closed 24-26 December

MILFIELD

Northumberland – Regional map n° **14**-A1

Red Lion Inn

TRADITIONAL BRITISH • NEIGHBOURHOOD This former coaching inn really is the heart of the village. It has a traditional look and feel, matched by a classical menu which makes good use of the larders of Scotland and England – and you definitely won't leave hungry! Bedrooms are homely; most are in wooden lodges.

Menu £ 11 (weekday lunch) – Carte £ 18/34

6 rooms – †£ 45/50 ††£ 85/90

Main Rd ✉ NE71 6JD – ✆ 01668 216224 (booking advisable) – www.redlionmilfield.co.uk – Closed 25-26 December

MILFORD-ON-SEA

Hampshire – ✉ Lymington – Pop. 4 348 – Regional map n° **4**-A3

Verveine

SEAFOOD • FRIENDLY Behind this attractive-looking fishmonger's is a bright and airy New England style restaurant with an open kitchen. Breads are baked twice-daily, veg is from the raised beds and smoking takes place on-site. The focus is on wonderfully fresh fish and cooking is original with the odd playful twist.

Menu £ 19 (lunch) – Carte £ 41/56

98 High St ✉ SO41 0QE – ✆ 01590 642176 – www.verveine.co.uk – Closed Sunday and Monday

MILSTEAD

Kent – Pop. 264 – Regional map n° **5**-C1

Red Lion

CLASSIC FRENCH • PUB Simple, cosy country pub, personally run by an experienced couple. Ever-changing blackboard menu offers French-influenced country cooking. Dishes are honest, wholesome and richly flavoured.

Carte £ 24/41

Rawling St ✉ ME9 0RT – ✆ 01795 830279 (booking advisable) – www.theredlionmilstead.co.uk – Closed Sunday and Monday

MILTON ABBOT - Devon ➔ See Tavistock

MILTON KEYNES

Milton Keynes - Pop. 171 750 - Regional map n° **6**-C1

Brasserie Blanc

CLASSIC FRENCH • BRASSERIE XX This buzzy brasserie sits within a striking building and its open kitchen dominates the room. Well-presented French dishes are full of flavour; there's a good value fixed price menu and the soufflé is well worth the wait.

Menu £ 15 (lunch and early dinner) - Carte £ 24/40

Chelsea House, 301 Avebury Blvd ✉ MK9 2GA - ✆ 01908 546590 (booking essential) - www.brasserieblanc.com

MINEHEAD

Somerset - Pop. 11 981 - Regional map n° **2**-A2

Channel House

TRADITIONAL • CLASSIC Passionately run, detached Edwardian house in an elevated position, with the sea just visible through its mature gardens. Comfy lounge and a cosy bar. Immaculately kept bedrooms have a modern edge; Rooms 7 and 8 are the most comfortable. Traditional, daily changing dinner menu and comprehensive breakfasts.

8 rooms (dinner included) - †£ 105 ††£ 170

Church Path ✉ TA24 5QG - off Northfield Dr - ✆ 01643 703229 - www.channelhouse.co.uk - Closed November-February

MINSTER

Kent - Regional map n° **5**-D1

Corner House

TRADITIONAL BRITISH • NEIGHBOURHOOD X Pass the stone bar inset with a cart wheel, and the small lounge and terrace, to the characterful dining room with its low beamed ceiling and quarry tiled floor. Classic recipes use good quality produce; the dishes for two are a hit. Bedrooms have smart feature walls and modern facilities.

Menu £ 18 (weekday lunch) - Carte £ 29/38

2 rooms - †£ 70/110 ††£ 70/110

42 Station Rd ✉ CT12 4BZ - ✆ 01843 823000 - www.cornerhouserestaurants.co.uk - Closed dinner Sunday, Monday and lunch Tuesday

MINSTER LOVELL

Oxfordshire - Pop. 1 236 - Regional map n° **6**-A2

Old Swan

TRADITIONAL CUISINE • INN A quintessential country inn set in a lovely riverside village. Dine in the charming garden or in one of the open-fired front rooms with their beams and flagged floors. Menus blend hearty pub favourites with more restaurant-style dishes. Characterful bedrooms have a romantic feel.

Carte £ 25/43

16 rooms - †£ 115/415 ††£ 125/425

✉ OX29 0RN - ✆ 01993 774441 - www.oldswanminstermill.co.uk

Minster Mill

HISTORIC BUILDING • ELEGANT Charming 17C Cotswold stone mill on the riverbank, with admirable eco-credentials and a modern mini-spa. The open-fired lounge has a minstrels' gallery. Well-appointed bedrooms come with robes and sloe gin and the best boast riverside terraces. Meals are at the Old Swan, their sister pub.

36 rooms - †£ 115/415 ††£ 125/425

✉ OX29 0RN - ✆ 01993 774441 - www.oldswanminstermill.co.uk

MISTLEY

Essex – Pop. 1 696 – Regional map n° **7**-D2

Mistley Thorn

SEAFOOD • FRIENDLY An appealing bistro with a homeware shop and cookery school. The focus is on sourcing local, seasonal ingredients and then showing them off. Local seafood is to the fore and most of the fish and meat is grilled over wood. Bedrooms are stylishly understated; some have river views.

Menu £ 17 (weekday lunch) – Carte £ 24/41

12 rooms – †£ 85/95 ††£ 100/150

High St ✉ CO11 1HE – ✆ 01206 392821 – www.mistleythorn.co.uk – Closed 25 December

MITTON – Lancashire

→ See Whalley

MOBBERLEY

Cheshire East – Pop. 2 034 – Regional map n° **11**-B3

Church Inn

TRADITIONAL CUISINE • COSY 18C brick pub beside the bowling green, offering lovely views of the 12C church from its terrace. Regularly changing menus reflect the seasons, with light dishes in summer and hearty stews in winter. Hand-pumped local beers feature.

Carte £ 27/48

Church Ln ✉ WA16 7RD – ✆ 01565 873178 – www.churchinnmobberley.co.uk

MONKTON COMBE – Bath and North East Somerset

→ See Bath

MORETONHAMPSTEAD

Devon – ✉ Newton Abbot – Pop. 1 339 – Regional map n° **1**-C2

The Horse

MEDITERRANEAN CUISINE • PUB Pub with rustic, flag-floored rooms and a sunny, Mediterranean-style courtyard. Tasty, unfussy dishes offer more than a hint of Italy. Thin crust pizzas are baked in a custom-built oven.

Carte £ 21/40

7 George St ✉ TQ13 8PG – ✆ 01647 440242 – www.thehorsedartmoor.co.uk – Closed 25 December and Monday lunch

MORETON-IN-MARSH

Gloucestershire – Pop. 3 493 – Regional map n° **2**-D1

Mulberry

MODERN BRITISH • DESIGN Formal restaurant with an enclosed walled garden, set within a part-16C manor house. Cooking is modern and adventurous and features some challenging combinations – choose between a 4 course set menu and an 8 course tasting menu.

Menu £ 43

Manor House Hotel, High St ✉ GL56 0LJ – ✆ 01608 650501 – www.cotswold-inns-hotels.co.uk – dinner only and Sunday lunch

Manor House

INN • ELEGANT Part-16C manor house with a smart interior which mixes old beams and inglenook fireplaces with modern fabrics and contemporary art. Chic, stylish bedrooms boast bold décor and feature walls; those in the main house are the most characterful. Dine in the sophisticated restaurant or classical brasserie.

35 rooms – †£ 100/120 ††£ 140/350 – 1 suite

High St ✉ GL56 0LJ – ✆ 01608 650501 – www.cotswold-inns-hotels.co.uk

Mulberry – See restaurant listing

Old School

COUNTRY HOUSE • PERSONALISED Change pace at this laid-back, stone-built former school, where you can relax in the gardens over a game of boules or croquet. The impressive upstairs lounge features an exposed A-frame ceiling and original ecclesiastical-style windows; bright, modern bedrooms offer a high level of facilities.

4 rooms - £ 110/130 £ 130/150

Little Compton ✉ GL56 0SL - East : 3.75 mi on A 44 - ✆ 01608 674588 - www.theoldschoolbedandbreakfast.com

MORPETH

Northumberland – Pop. 14 403 – Regional map n° **14**-B2

at Eshott North: 8.5 mi by A1 ✉ Morpeth

Eshott Hall

COUNTRY HOUSE • CLASSIC Attractive Georgian manor house in a quiet, rural location – yet only 5min from the A1. Classically stylish guest areas. Smart, modern bedrooms boast warm fabrics, antique furniture and good facilities. Formal dining room offers contemporary menus; local produce includes fruit and veg from the kitchen garden.

17 rooms - £ 70/140 £ 155/320

✉ NE65 9EN - ✆ 01670 787454 - www.eshotthall.co.uk

at Longhorsley Northwest: 6.5 mi by A192 on A697 ✉ Morpeth

Thistleyhaugh Farm

FAMILY • COSY Attractive Georgian farmhouse, set off the beaten track on a 750 acre organic farm, with the River Coquet flowing through its grounds. Cosy, open-fired lounge and antique-filled dining room. Spacious, comfortable bedrooms – most have luxurious bathrooms with feature baths. Communal dinners; home-cooking features beef and lamb from the farm. Charming owners.

4 rooms - £ 70/90 £ 100

✉ NE65 8RG - Northwest : 3.75 mi by A 697 and Todburn rd taking first right turn - ✆ 01665 570098 - www.thistleyhaugh.co.uk - Closed Christmas-1 February

MORSTON - Norfolk → See Blakeney

MOULTON

Suffolk – Regional map n° **8**-B2

Packhorse Inn

MODERN CUISINE • PUB A smart modern pub in a pretty village, named after the 15C flint bridge which spans the river. Cooking keeps things classical, with the focus firmly on the ingredients' natural flavours; for dessert, the assiettes are a good way to go. Bedrooms are ultra-stylish with quality furnishings and roll-top baths.

Menu £ 18 (weekday lunch) - Carte £ 28/44

8 rooms - £ 100 £ 100/225

Bridge St ✉ CB8 8SP - ✆ 01638 751818 - www.thepackhorseinn.com

MOUSEHOLE

Cornwall – ✉ Penzance – Regional map n° **1**-A3

Old Coastguard

MEDITERRANEAN CUISINE • BISTRO X Old coastguard's cottage in a small fishing village, with a laid-back, open-plan interior, a sub-tropical garden and views towards St Clement's Isle. Well-presented brasserie dishes display a Mediterranean edge; great wine selection. Individually styled bedrooms – some with balconies, most with sea views.

Menu £ 18 - Carte £ 24/38 **s**

14 rooms - £ 140/225 £ 140/225

The Parade ✉ TR19 6PR - ✆ 01736 731222 - www.oldcoastguardhotel.co.uk - Closed 25 December and early January

2 Fore Street

SEAFOOD • FRIENDLY X Friendly café-cum-bistro with a delightful courtyard terrace and garden. All-day menus offer everything from coffee and cake to a full meal, with brunch a feature at weekends. Tasty, unfussy dishes are guided by the day's catch.

Carte £ 28/38

2 Fore St ✉ TR19 6PF – ✆ 01736 731164 (booking essential at dinner) – www.2forestreet.co.uk – Closed January and Monday in winter

MULLION

Cornwall – ✉ Helston – Pop. 1 955 – Regional map n° **1**-A3

Polurrian Bay

HISTORIC BUILDING • CONTEMPORARY Imposing Victorian hotel with 12 acres of grounds, set in a commanding clifftop position. The spacious modern interior is geared towards families, with a crèche, a games room and a cinema. Most of the bright bedrooms boast views across Mount's Bay. Unfussy menus showcase seasonal, local produce.

41 rooms – †£ 130/660 ††£ 130/660

✉ TR12 7EN – ✆ 01326 240421 – www.polurrianhotel.com

MURCOTT

Oxfordshire – ✉ Kidlington – Pop. 1 293 – Regional map n° **6**-B2

Nut Tree (Mike North)

TRADITIONAL BRITISH • RUSTIC With its 15C origins and smartly thatched roof it looks like a typical English pub but this is no ordinary village local. Menus comprise mainly of satisfying, full-flavoured restaurant-style dishes; for a quick snack try the Bar & Garden menu or for the full experience, go for the 7 course tasting menu.

→ Salad of Cornish lobster with crème fraiche and red pepper ketchup. Ballotine of Cotswold White chicken with potato purée, asparagus and morel jus. Glazed lemon tart with poached Nut Tree rhubarb.

Carte £ 28/61

Main St ✉ OX5 2RE – ✆ 01865 331253 – www.nuttreeinn.co.uk – Closed 26 December-10 January, Sunday dinner and Monday

NAILSWORTH

Gloucestershire – Pop. 7 728 – Regional map n° **2**-C1

Wild Garlic

MODERN BRITISH • INTIMATE XX This attractive little restaurant offers something for everyone. One room is a rustic tapas bar with a south-facing terrace and a menu of Spanish favourites; the second is a modern restaurant serving a concise à la carte and a biweekly tasting menu. Three stylish, well-equipped bedrooms complete the picture.

Carte £ 22/45

5 rooms – †£ 80/160 ††£ 85/160

3 Cossack Sq ✉ GL6 0DB – ✆ 01453 832615 – www.wild-garlic.co.uk – Closed first week January and Sunday dinner-Tuesday

NATIONAL EXHIBITION CENTRE – W. Mids. → See Birmingham

NETHER BURROW

Lancashire – ✉ Kirkby Lonsdale – Regional map n° **11**-B1

Highwayman

REGIONAL CUISINE • PUB Sizeable 18C coaching inn with an open-fired bar and a lovely terrace. A rustic, no-nonsense approach to food makes for well-crafted, flavourful dishes. Produce is local and seasonal, with Lancashire hotpot a perennial favourite.

Carte £ 21/40

LA6 2RJ – 015242 73338 – www.highwaymaninn.co.uk

NETHER WESTCOTE - Gloucestershire

→ See Stow-on-the-Wold

NETLEY MARSH - Hampshire

→ See Southampton

NEW MILTON

Hampshire – Pop. 19 969 – Regional map n° **4**-A3

The Kitchen (N)

MODERN BRITISH • FASHIONABLE A striking new build with an impressive kitchen garden and a greenhouse beside it; set at the entrance of the Chewton Glen hotel. Brasserie dishes showcase local and garden produce. The glass-fronted cookery school is popular.

Carte £ 26/43

Chewton Glen Hotel, Christchurch Rd BH25 6QS – West : 2 mi by A 337 and Ringwood Rd on Chewton Farm Rd – 01425 282212 – www.chewtonglen.com/the-kitchen – Closed Sunday dinner

Chewton Glen

GRAND LUXURY • CLASSIC A professionally run country house with an impressive spa, set in 130 acres of New Forest parkland – try a host of outdoor pursuits, including croquet, archery and clay pigeon shooting. Luxurious bedrooms range from classic to contemporary; opt for one with a balcony or terrace, or try a unique Treehouse suite. Dine in the traditional restaurant or modern brasserie.

70 rooms – †£ 370/725 ††£ 370/725 – 15 suites

Christchurch Rd BH25 6QS – West : 2 mi by A 337 and Ringwood Rd on Chewton Farm Rd – 01425 275341 – www.chewtonglen.com

The Kitchen – See restaurant listing

NEW ROMNEY

Kent – Regional map n° **5**-C2

Romney Bay House

HISTORIC • ART DÉCO Built by Sir Clough Williams-Ellis in the 1920s for actress Hedda Hopper, and accessed via a private coast road. It has an open-fired drawing room with an honesty bar, 10 homely bedrooms and a first floor lounge with a telescope and lovely sea views. The conservatory dining room offers a seafood-based menu.

10 rooms – †£ 75/95 ††£ 95/164

Coast Rd, Littlestone TN28 8QY – East : 2.25 mi by B 2071 – 01797 364747 – www.romneybayhousehotel.co.uk – Closed 1 week Christmas and first week January

NEWARK-ON-TRENT

Nottinghamshire – Pop. 37 084 – Regional map n° **9**-C1

Grange

TOWNHOUSE • PERSONALISED Personally run hotel with a small terrace and award-winning gardens. The main house has mock Tudor gables, a Victorian-style bar and lounge, and a smart restaurant decorated with antique plates and cutlery. Individually styled bedrooms are split between this and a second house, and offer good comforts.

10 rooms – †£ 80/100 ††£ 100/140

73 London Rd NG24 1RZ – South : 0.5 mi on Grantham rd (B 6326) – 01636 703399 – www.grangenewark.co.uk – Closed 22 December-6 January

at Norwell North: 7.25 mi by A1

Willoughby House

HISTORIC • PERSONALISED A three-storey farmhouse and converted stables, with a chic, stylish interior, a small open-fired lounge and a deep red breakfast room. Bedrooms feature good quality furnishings and antiques, along with contemporary art

4 rooms – £ 80 ££ 120/125

Main St ✉ NG23 6JN
– ✆ 01636 636266 – www.willoughbyhousebandb.co.uk

NEWBOTTLE

Tyne and Wear – Regional map n° **14**-B2

Hideaway at Herrington Hill

FAMILY • REGIONAL The charming owners really look after their guests at this spacious former shooting lodge, built in 1838 for the Earl of Durham. Bedrooms blend period features and modern amenities. The Garden Room is largest, with views of the grounds.

5 rooms – £ 85/110 ££ 85/180

High Ln ✉ DH4 4NH – West : 1 mile
– ✆ 07730 957795 – www.hideawayatherringtonhill.com – Closed 23 December-2 January

NEWBURY

West Berkshire – Pop. 38 762 – Regional map n° **6**-B3

Woodspeen (John Campbell)

MODERN CUISINE • FASHIONABLE Despite being set in an old pub, this smart neighbourhood eatery has more of a bistro feel, courtesy of its Scandic styling and bright, modern thatched extension. Mouth-watering seasonal dishes feature local and garden produce; flavour is paramount and dishes have a comforting, modern classic style.

→ Crab ravioli with artichoke and shellfish bisque. Lamb rump and belly with roasted onions and balsamic mint dressing. Chocolate brownie and maple vinegar ice cream.

Menu £ 29 (lunch and early dinner) – Carte £ 38/58

Lambourn Rd, Bagnor ✉ RG20 8BN – Northwest : 2 mi by A 4 and Station Rd - signed Watermill Theatre
– ✆ 01635 265070 – www.thewoodspeen.com – Closed Sunday dinner and Monday

The Vineyard

MODERN CUISINE • ELEGANT Smart hotel restaurant split over two levels. Accomplished dishes are attractively presented; choose between a set and two tasting menus. They offer over 100 wines by the glass – some from their own Californian vineyard.

Menu £ 29/89

Vineyard Hotel, Stockcross ✉ RG20 8JU – Northwest : 2 mi by A 4 on B 4000
– ✆ 01635 528770 – www.the-vineyard.co.uk

The Newbury

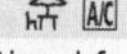

TRADITIONAL BRITISH • SIMPLE A relaxed, trendy pub behind a traditional façade. There's an experienced team in charge and a lively buzz when it's busy. Dishes range from pub classics to more adventurous offerings; head upstairs for pizza fresh from the oven.

Carte £ 27/60

137 Bartholomew St ✉ RG14 5HB
– ✆ 01635 49000 – www.thenewburypub.co.uk

The Vineyard

BUSINESS • CLASSIC Extended former hunting lodge with over 1,000 pieces of art and a striking fire and water feature. Some bedrooms have a country house style, while others are more contemporary; all boast smart marble bathrooms. The owner also has a vineyard in California, hence the stunning wine vault and the wine-themed bar.

49 rooms – £ 275/660 £ 275/660 – £ 21 – 32 suites

Stockcross RG20 8JU – Northwest : 2 mi by A 4 on B 4000 – 01635 528770 – www.the-vineyard.co.uk

The Vineyard – See restaurant listing

Donnington Valley H. & Spa

BUSINESS • FUNCTIONAL Modern business-orientated hotel on the outskirts of town; its large grounds include a golf course. Guest areas are spacious and stylishly furnished and there's a well-equipped gym and spa. Smart bedrooms offer a high level of facilities. The restaurant has an unusual pyramid roof and offers modern fare.

111 rooms – £ 105/265 £ 105/325

Old Oxford Rd, Donnington RG14 3AG – North : 1.75 mi by A 4 off B 4494 – 01635 551199 – www.donningtonvalley.co.uk

NEWBY BRIDGE

Cumbria – Regional map n° **12**-A3

Lakeside

TRADITIONAL • CLASSIC Superbly situated hotel on the water's edge. Extremely comfy guest areas have a traditional style. Bedrooms are smart and modern – some have four-poster beds and great views. Relax in the spa and leisure club, then dine in the stylish modern brasserie or more traditional dining room; and be sure to find time for afternoon tea in the conservatory, overlooking the lake.

74 rooms – £ 140/170 £ 180/220 – 7 suites

Lakeside LA12 8AT – Northeast : 1 mi on Hawkshead rd – 015395 30001 – www.lakesidehotel.co.uk – Closed 3-20 January

Knoll

TRADITIONAL • GRAND LUXURY Keenly run, slate-built Edwardian house opposite the lake, with a smart interior that blends classic and modern styles. Comfy, leather-furnished lounge. Good-sized bedrooms with bold décor and modern bathrooms; 'The Retreat' has a private entrance and hot tub. Simple dining room displays heart-themed art.

9 rooms – £ 75/95 £ 90/220

Lakeside LA12 8AU – Northeast : 1.25 mi on Hawkshead rd – 015395 31347 – www.theknoll-lakeside.co.uk – Closed 22-27, 31 December and 1 January

NEWCASTLE UPON TYNE

Tyne and Wear – Pop. 268 064 – Regional map n° **14**-B2

House of Tides (Kenny Atkinson)

MODERN CUISINE • INTIMATE XX A characterful 16C merchant's house on the quayside. Flagged floors, cast iron pillars and exposed bricks feature in the bar, while the upstairs restaurant boasts carved beams and a stone fireplace. Tasting menus list accomplished, creative dishes which are well-balanced and attractively presented.

→ Lindisfarne oyster, cucumber, ginger and caviar. Sea bass, chicken wings and artichoke. Dark chocolate with hazelnut and gold leaf.

Menu £ 60/75 – tasting menu only

Town plan: B3-h – *28-30 The Close NE1 3RF – 0191 230 3720 (booking essential) – www.houseoftides.co.uk – Closed 2 weeks Christmas-New Year, Sunday, Monday and lunch Tuesday-Thursday*

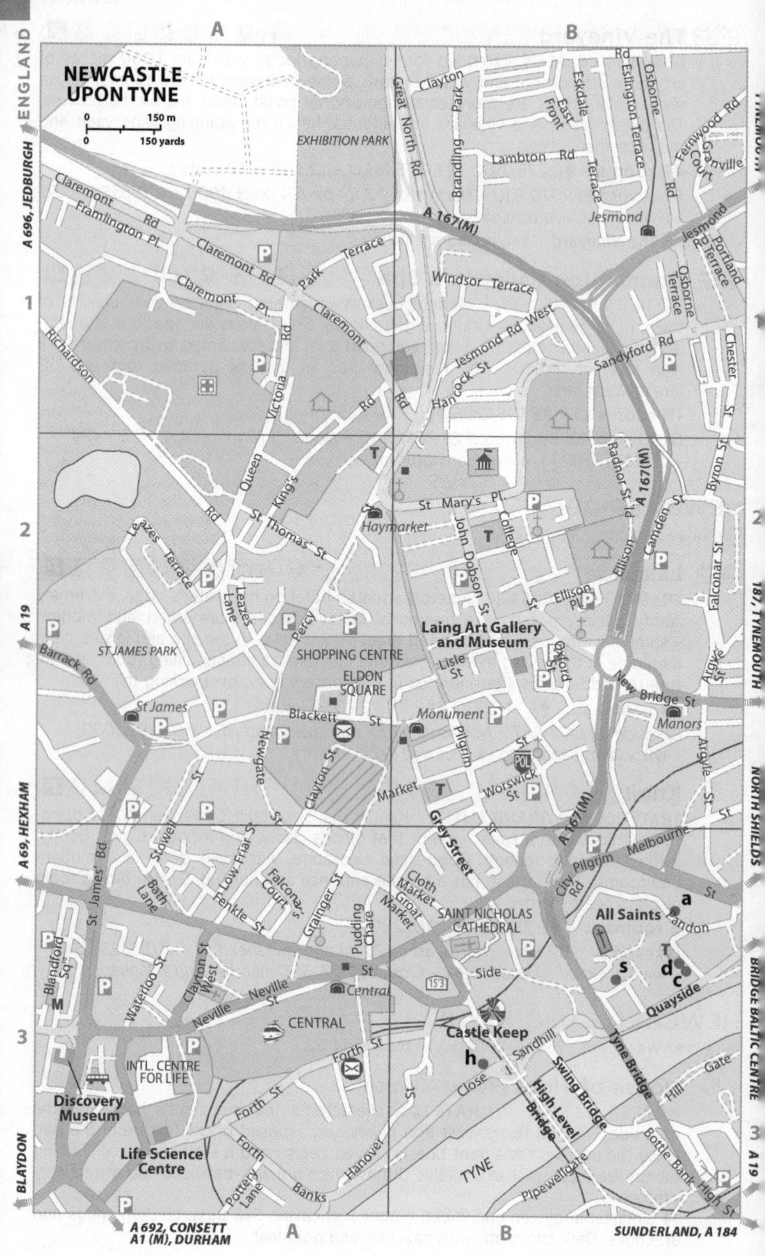
NEWCASTLE UPON TYNE
0 150 m
0 150 yards
A
B
1
2
3
EXHIBITION PARK
A 696, JEDBURGH
A 19
A 69, HEXHAM
BLAYDON
A 692, CONSETT
A1 (M), DURHAM
SUNDERLAND, A 184
A 19
BRIDGE BALTIC CENTRE
NORTH SHIELDS
187, TYNEMOUTH
Claremont Rd
Framlington Pl.
Claremont Rd
Claremont Pl.
Park Terrace
Claremont Rd
Richardson Rd
Victoria
Queen Victoria Rd
King's Rd
St Thomas' St
Leazes Terrace
Leazes Lane
Percy St
Barrack Rd
ST JAMES PARK
St James
SHOPPING CENTRE
ELDON SQUARE
Blackett St
Newgate St
Clayton St
Haymarket
Great North Rd
Clayton Rd
Brandling Park
Lambton Rd
Eskdale Terrace
East Front
Eslington Terrace
Osborne Rd
Jesmond
Fernwood Rd
Granville Court
A 167(M)
Windsor Terrace
Jesmond Rd West
Hancock St
Sandyford Rd
Jesmond Rd
Portland Terrace
Osborne Terrace
Chester St
Byron St
Radnor St
A 167(M)
Camden St
Ellison Pl.
Falconar St
St Mary's Pl
College St
John Dobson St
Ellison Pl
Laing Art Gallery and Museum
Lisle St
Oxford St
New Bridge St
Argyle St
Manors
Monument
Pilgrim St
Market St
Worswick St
Grey Street
A 167(M)
City Rd
Pilgrim St
Melbourne St
All Saints
Pandon
Quayside
Tyne Bridge
Swing Bridge
High Level Bridge
Sandhill
Castle Keep
Close
Side
SAINT NICHOLAS CATHEDRAL
Cloth Market
Groat Market
Pudding Chare
Grainger St
Falconar's Court
Low Friar St
Fenkle St
Stowell St
Bath Lane
St James' Bd
Blandford Sq
Waterloo St
Clayton St West
Neville St
Central
CENTRAL
Forth St
Forth Banks
Pottery Lane
Hanover St
INTL. CENTRE FOR LIFE
Discovery Museum
Life Science Centre
TYNE
Pipewellgate
Hill Gate
Bottle Bank
High St
a
s
d
c
h

Broad Chare

TRADITIONAL BRITISH • PUB Sit in the snug ground floor bar or more comfortable upstairs dining room of this quayside pub. Choose from a snack menu of 'Geordie Tapas', an appealing 'on toast' selection, hearty daily specials and tasty nursery puddings. They also offer over 40 ales, including some which are custom-made for the pub.

Carte £ 21/42

Town plan: B3-c – *25 Broad Chare ✉ NE1 3DQ – ✆ 0191 211 2144 (booking advisable) – www.thebroadchare.co.uk – Closed 25-26 December, 1 January and Sunday dinner*

Jesmond Dene House

MODERN BRITISH • DESIGN XXX Smart, understated restaurant on the ground floor of an Arts and Crafts house hotel in a tranquil city dene. Sit in the bright extension for views over the gardens. Classic dishes may have a French heart but are crafted from local produce.

Menu £ 22 (weekday lunch) **s** – Carte £ 33/55

Jesmond Dene House Hotel, Jesmond Dene Rd ✉ NE2 2EY – Northeast : 1.5 mi by B 1318 off A 189 – ✆ 0191 212 3000 – www.jesmonddenehouse.co.uk

Dobson & Parnell

MODERN CUISINE • DESIGN XX An iconic address in the city, this elegant restaurant is named after Victorian architects John Dobson and William Parnell. Cooking has a Nordic style, with plenty of drying, pickling and curing. Dishes are colourful and satisfying.

Menu £ 21/25 – Carte £ 28/54

Town plan: B3-s – *21 Queen St ✉ NE1 3UG – ✆ 0191 221 0904 – www.dobsonandparnell.co.uk – Closed Sunday dinner and Monday*

Peace & Loaf

MODERN CUISINE • NEIGHBOURHOOD XX Found in a smart suburban parade, this fashionable restaurant and bar is set over three levels and has a lively atmosphere. Attractively presented modern dishes are ambitious, complex and employ many different cooking techniques.

Menu £ 22 (lunch and early dinner) – Carte £ 35/60

217 Jesmond Rd, Jesmond ✉ NE2 1LA – Northeast : 1.5 mi by A 1058 – ✆ 0191 281 5222 – www.peaceandloaf.co.uk – Closed 25-26 December, 1 January and Sunday dinner

21

MODERN BRITISH • BRASSERIE XX Start with a gin from the large selection behind the zinc-topped counter then head through to the smart red and black brasserie. Menus offer a comprehensive array of confidently cooked classics; the 'menu du jour' is good value.

Menu £ 19 (lunch) – Carte £ 30/59

Town plan: B3-a – *Trinity Gardens ✉ NE1 2HH – ✆ 0191 222 0755 – www.21newcastle.co.uk – Closed 25-26 December and 1 January*

Bistro Forty Six

MODERN BRITISH • NEIGHBOURHOOD X A refreshingly honest bistro with a homely interior. The self-taught chef hunts and forages, using the local larder to full effect. Passionately seasonal dishes will appeal to one and all; check the blackboard for the daily specials.

Menu £ 17 (dinner) – Carte £ 23/33

46 Brentwood Ave, Jesmond ✉ NE2 3DH – Northeast :1.25 mi by B 1318 and Forsyth Rd – ✆ 0191 281 8081 – www.bistrofortysix.co.uk – Closed Sunday dinner, Monday and lunch Tuesday-Wednesday

Caffé Vivo

ITALIAN • BRASSERIE In a converted quayside warehouse – also home to a theatre. Zinc ducting and steel pillars give it an industrial feel, while hams, salamis and oils add a touch of the Mediterranean. Simple, satisfying cooking of classic Italian dishes.

Menu £ 18 (weekdays) – Carte £ 24/46

Town plan: B3-d – *29 Broad Chare ✉ NE1 3DQ – ✆ 0191 232 1331 – www.caffevivo.co.uk – Closed Sunday, Monday and bank holidays*

The Patricia

MODERN BRITISH • NEIGHBOURHOOD This simply furnished suburban bistro is named after the owner's grandmother. Well-priced small plates feature throughout the day and are supplemented by more substantial dishes at night. The wine list is good value.

Carte £ 29/49

139 Jesmond Rd, Jesmond ✉ NE2 1JY – Northeast : 1.5 mi by A 1058 – ✆ 0191 281 4443 (booking essential) – www.the-patricia.com – Closed Sunday, Monday and Tuesday lunch

Jesmond Dene House

LUXURY • MODERN Stone-built Arts and Crafts house in a peaceful city dene; originally owned by the Armstrong family. Characterful guest areas with wood panelling, local art and striking original fireplaces. Individually furnished bedrooms have bold feature walls, modern facilities and smart bathrooms with underfloor heating.

40 rooms – †£ 125/315 ††£ 135/330

Jesmond Dene Rd ✉ NE2 2EY – Northeast : 1.5 mi by B 1318 off A 189 – ✆ 0191 212 3000 – www.jesmonddenehouse.co.uk

Jesmond Dene House – See restaurant listing

Hotel du Vin

BUSINESS • CONTEMPORARY Extended red-brick building overlooking the river – formerly home to the Tyne Tees Steam Shipping Company. Characterful lounge with gas fire and zinc-topped bar. Chic, stylish, wine-themed bedrooms; some boast feature baths or terraces. Classical brasserie features a glass-fronted wine tasting room.

42 rooms – †£ 100/200 ††£ 100/200 – £ 17

Allan House, City Rd ✉ NE1 2BE – East : 0.75 mi on A 186 – ✆ 0191 229 2200 – www.hotelduvin.com/newcastle

The Townhouse

TOWNHOUSE • CONTEMPORARY End of terrace Victorian house in a residential area. All-day café serves breakfast, snacks, cakes and the like. Smart, stylish bedrooms offer bold, contemporary décor and extra touches such as iPod docks; Room 10 has a bath in the bedroom.

10 rooms – †£ 95/120 ††£ 95/120

1 West Ave, Gosforth ✉ NE3 4ES – North : 2.5 mi by B 1318 – ✆ 0191 285 6812

at Ponteland Northwest: 8.25 mi by A167 on A696 ✉ Newcastle Upon Tyne

Haveli

INDIAN • FASHIONABLE Haveli means 'grand house' and this neighbourhood restaurant is certainly very smart. Influences come from all over India; try one of the chef's signature curries. Staff combine personality with professionalism.

Menu £ 20 (early dinner) – Carte £ 19/34

3-5 Broadway, Darras Hall ✉ NE20 9PW – Southwest : 1.5 mi by B 6323 off Darras Hall Estate rd – ✆ 01661 872727 – www.haveliponteland.com – dinner only – Closed 25 December and Monday except bank holidays

NEWLYN

Cornwall – Pop. 3 536 – Regional map n° **1**-A3

Tolcarne Inn

SEAFOOD • TRADITIONAL DÉCOR An unassuming, family-run pub behind the sea wall. Inside it's narrow and cosy, with 18C beams, a wood-burning stove and a long bar. The experienced chef offers appealing, flavoursome dishes which centre around fresh, locally landed fish and shellfish – go for the turbot if it's on the menu.

Carte £ 23/41

Tolcarne Pl ✉ TR18 5PR
– ✆ 01736 363074 – www.tolcarneinn.co.uk – Closed 25-26 December

NEWPORT – Isle of Wight ➜ See Wight (Isle of)

NEWQUAY

Cornwall – Pop. 20 189 – Regional map n° **1**-A2

at Watergate Bay Northeast: 3 mi by A3059 on B3276 ✉ Newquay

Fifteen Cornwall

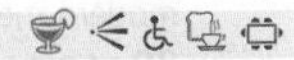

ITALIAN • TRENDY XX Lively beachfront restaurant with fabulous bay views; a social enterprise where the profits go to their registered charity, who train disengaged adults to become chefs. Unfussy Italian menus have a Cornish twist and feature homemade pastas and steaks from the Josper grill. They open for breakfast too.

Menu £ 32 (lunch) – Carte dinner £ 39/48

On The Beach ✉ TR8 4AA
– ✆ 01637 861000 (booking essential) – www.fifteencornwall.co.uk – Closed 2 weeks in January

Zacry's

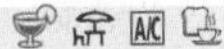

MODERN BRITISH • CHIC XX Set within a seaside hotel, a lively brasserie with a modish feel. There's lots of choice on the menu, which draws on the chef's love of American and fusion cuisine; cooking is full of flavour and the charcoal oven plays a key role.

Menu £ 38

Watergate Bay Hotel, On The Beach ✉ TQ8 4AA
– ✆ 01637 861231 – www.zacrys.com – dinner only

Watergate Bay

FAMILY • CONTEMPORARY A long-standing seaside hotel where fresh, contemporary bedrooms range from standards to family suites; some have freestanding baths with sea outlooks. The beautiful infinity pool and hot tub share the view and there's direct beach access, beach changing rooms and even a surfboard store. Dine in the bar, the laid-back sandy-floored café or the smart modern brasserie.

71 rooms ☕ – 🚹£ 131/334 🚹🚹£ 175/445

On The Beach ✉ TR8 4AA
– ✆ 01637 860543 – www.watergatebay.co.uk

Zacry's – See restaurant listing

at Mawgan Porth Northeast: 6 mi by A3059 on B3276

Scarlet

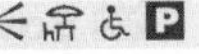

MODERN BRITISH • DESIGN XX Contemporary hotel restaurant with huge windows offering stunning coastal views; start with a drink on the lovely terrace or in the chic bar. Concise daily menus promote small local suppliers; cooking is light, modern and seasonal.

Menu £ 24/46

Scarlet Hotel, Tredragon Rd ✉ TR8 4DQ
– ✆ 01637 861800 (bookings essential for non-residents) – www.scarlethotel.co.uk – Closed 3-31 January

 **Scarlet**

LUXURY · MODERN Eco-centric, adults only hotel set high on a cliff and boasting stunning coastal views. Modern bar and lounges, and a great spa offering extensive treatments. Bedrooms range from 'Just Right' to 'Indulgent' and have unusual open-plan bathrooms and a cool, Scandic style – every room has a terrace and sea view.

37 rooms – £ 190/440 £ 210/460

Tredragon Rd ✉ TR8 4DQ – ✆ 01637 861800 – www.scarlethotel.co.uk – Closed 3-31 January

Scarlet – See restaurant listing

Bedruthan

FAMILY · CONTEMPORARY Unassuming hotel set in an elevated position overlooking the shore and boasting direct access to the beach. The interior is surprisingly contemporary and bedrooms are bright. Facilities and activities are family-orientated but the cocktail bar and lounge are set aside for adults. Interesting modern menus in Herring and accessible, family-focused dining in Wild Café.

89 rooms – £ 99/129 £ 135/225 – 10 suites

✉ TR8 4BU – Northeast : 0.5 mi on B 3276 – ✆ 01637 860860 – www.bedruthan.com – Closed 2 January-2 February

NEWTON-ON-OUSE – North Yorkshire → See York

Dawnay Arms

MODERN BRITISH · PUB A handsome pub with stone floors, low beams, open fires and all manner of bric-a-brac – its delightful dining room has views over the garden and down to the river. Gutsy, well executed British dishes include plenty of local game.

Menu £ 14 (lunch and early dinner) – Carte £ 21/52

✉ YO30 2BR – ✆ 01347 848345 – www.thedawnayatnewton.co.uk – Closed Sunday dinner and Monday except bank holidays

NOMANSLAND

Hampshire – Regional map n° **4**-D3

Les Mirabelles

CLASSIC FRENCH · FRIENDLY XX This bright, modern restaurant overlooks the common and is enthusiastically run by a welcoming Frenchman. The well-balanced menu features unfussy, classic Gallic dishes and the superb wine selection lists over 3,000 bins!

Menu £ 20 (weekdays) – Carte £ 31/48

Forest Edge Rd ✉ SP5 2BN – ✆ 01794 390205 – www.lesmirabelles.co.uk – Closed 22 December-13 January, 1 week May, 1 week September, Sunday and Monday

NORTH BOVEY

Devon – ✉ Newton Abbot – Pop. 254 – Regional map n° **1**-C2

Bovey Castle

HISTORIC · CLASSIC An impressive manor house on an extensive country estate, beautifully set within Dartmoor National Park. It has a relaxed, homely feel; bedrooms have contemporary touches but still retain their classic edge. The restaurant has a modern menu of local seasonal produce and the brasserie offers British classics.

64 rooms – £ 199/519 £ 224/576 – 4 suites

✉ TQ13 8RE – Northwest : 2 mi by Postbridge rd, bearing left at fork just out of village – ✆ 01647 445000 – www.boveycastle.com

Gate House

HISTORIC • COSY Charming 15C medieval hall house in the heart of an attractive village, boasting a characterful thatched roof, a large oak door and a lovely country garden with a small pool. Homely lounge, cosy low-beamed breakfast room and simple, spotlessly kept bedrooms, some with moor views. Charming owners.

3 rooms – £ 55 £ 90

TQ13 8RB – just off village green, past "Ring of Bells" public house – 01647 440479 – www.gatehouseondartmoor.com – Closed 24-26 December

NORTH LOPHAM

Norfolk – Regional map n° **8**-C2

Church Farm House

FAMILY • PERSONALISED Characterful thatched farmhouse in the shadow of the village church, with lovely gardens and a terrace for summer breakfasts. The comfy conservatory and spacious beamed lounge are filled with antiques and musical curios; bedrooms are traditional. The charming owners prepare homely meals of local produce.

3 rooms – £ 55/75 £ 110

Church Rd IP22 2LP – 01379 687270 – www.churchfarmhouse.org – Closed January-mid February

NORTH MARSTON

Buckinghamshire – Pop. 781 – Regional map n° **6**-C2

The Pilgrim

MODERN CUISINE • FRIENDLY A friendly community pub filled with heavy timbers; find a spot by the wood-burning stove in the cosy bar-lounge. Proper home-cooking relies on local, sustainable produce. Every Tuesday the menu changes for 'Village Night'.

Carte £ 21/30

25 High St MK18 3PD – 01296 670969 – www.thepilgrimpub.co.uk – Closed Sunday dinner, Monday and Tuesday lunch

NORTH SHIELDS

Tyne and Wear – Pop. 39 042 – Regional map n° **14**-B2

River Cafe on the Tyne

TRADITIONAL BRITISH • BISTRO Laid-back restaurant run by a friendly local team, set above a pub in the North Shields fish quay. The daily changing à la carte offers unfussy, bistro-style dishes of fresh local produce, including fish from the market on the quayside. The 3 course set lunch and early dinner menu is a steal.

Menu £ 8 (lunch and early dinner) – Carte £ 19/34

51 Bell St, Fish Quay NE30 1HF – 0191 296 6168 (booking advisable) – www.rivercafeonthetyne.co.uk – Closed 25-26 December, 1-2 January, Monday, Sunday dinner and Tuesday lunch

Staith House

TRADITIONAL BRITISH • PUB A stone's throw from market stalls overflowing with crab, lobster and Craster kippers, is this smart quayside pub. Photos of the old docks line the walls of numerous dining areas and it has a pleasingly cluttered feel. Daily changing dishes showcase Northumberland's latest yield; the fish is smoked on-site.

Carte £ 23/39

57 Low Lights NE30 1JA – 0191 270 8441 (booking essential at dinner) – www.thestaithhouse.co.uk – Closed 25-26 December and 1-2 January

Irvins Brasserie

CLASSIC CUISINE • BRASSERIE X A busy, informal restaurant with a Spanish deli, set in an old industrial building on the historic fish quay. The experienced chef has worked in a wide variety of places, so his menus are appealing and eclectic with personal twists.

Menu £ 16 (weekday lunch) – Carte £ 21/44

The Richard Irvin Building, Union Quay ✉ NE30 1HJ – ✆ 0191 296 3238 – www.irvinsnewcastle.co.uk – Closed Monday and Tuesday

NORTH WALSHAM

Norfolk – Pop. 12 463 – Regional map n° **8**-D1

Beechwood

TOWNHOUSE • CLASSIC A red-brick, creeper-clad, part-Georgian property with classical furnishings and bright, eye-catching colour schemes. Period bedrooms vary in size and comfort – many have feature beds and the best have terraces onto the lovely gardens. A '10 Mile Menu' offers local ingredients in modern Mediterranean dishes.

18 rooms – †£ 90 ††£ 130/175

20 Cromer Rd ✉ NR28 0HD – ✆ 01692 403231 – www.beechwood-hotel.co.uk

NORTHLEACH

Gloucestershire – Pop. 1 854 – Regional map n° **2**-D1

Wheatsheaf Inn

TRADITIONAL BRITISH • INN Smart 17C coaching inn with a pretty tiered terrace and two traditional dining rooms, one either side of the stone-floored, open-fired bar. The same menu is available throughout, offering classical dishes and something to suit every taste. Stylish, contemporary bedrooms have quirky touches and feature interesting French flea market finds; some have baths in the rooms.

Menu £ 13 (weekday lunch) – Carte £ 25/41

14 rooms – †£ 110/310 ††£ 110/310

West End ✉ GL50 3EZ – ✆ 01451 860244 – www.cotswoldswheatsheaf.com

NORTHMOOR

Oxfordshire – Regional map n° **6**-B2

Red Lion

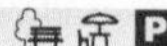

TRADITIONAL BRITISH • FRIENDLY Extremely welcoming pub owned by the villagers and run by an experienced young couple and a friendly team. Low beams, open fires and fresh flowers abound and the menu is a great mix of pub classics and more modern daily specials.

Carte £ 24/34

Standlake Rd ✉ OX29 5SX – ✆ 01865 300301 – www.theredlionnorthmoor.com – Closed Sunday dinner and Monday

NORWELL – Nottinghamshire ➜ See Newark-on-Trent

NORWICH

Norfolk – Pop. 186 682 – Regional map n° **8**-D2

Bishop's

TRADITIONAL BRITISH • ROMANTIC XX Intimate restaurant of only eight tables, in a 15C building with a country-chic décor of floral prints, oval mirrors, crystal chandeliers and silk curtains. Simply presented, traditional dishes. Efficient service.

Menu £ 15/35

Town plan: A1-a – *8-10 St Andrew's Hill ✉ NR2 1AD – ✆ 01603 767321 (booking essential) – www.bishopsrestaurant.co.uk – Closed Sunday and Monday*

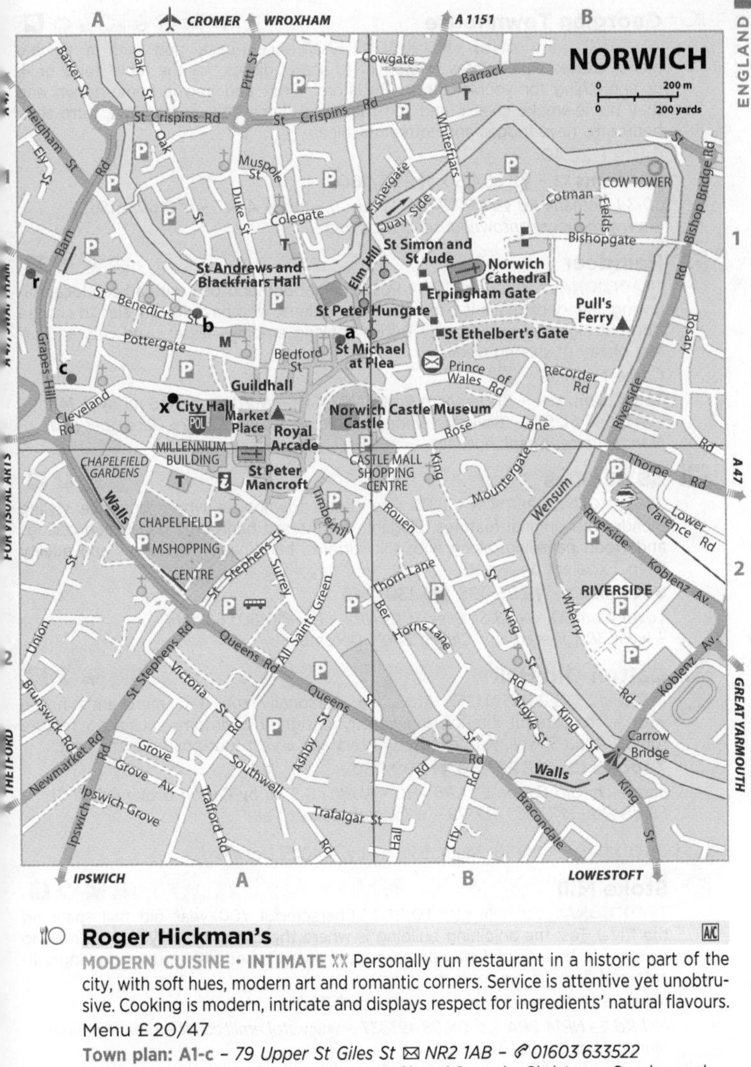

NORWICH

0 200 m
0 200 yards

A CROMER WROXHAM A 1151 B

A 47 GREAT YARMOUTH

IPSWICH A B LOWESTOFT

THETFORD

St Crispins Rd
Cowgate
Barrack St
Whitefriars
Colegate
Quay Side
St Simon and St Jude
Norwich Cathedral
Erpingham Gate
COW TOWER
Bishopgate
Pull's Ferry
St Andrews and Blackfriars Hall
St Benedicts St
St Peter Hungate
St Ethelbert's Gate
Pottergate
Bedford St
St Michael at Plea
Prince of Wales Rd
Recorder Rd
Guildhall
City Hall
Market Place
Royal Arcade
Norwich Castle Museum
Castle
Rose Lane
MILLENNIUM BUILDING
CHAPELFIELD GARDENS
St Peter Mancroft
CASTLE MALL SHOPPING CENTRE
CHAPELFIELD SHOPPING CENTRE
Walls
Thorpe Rd
Riverside
Lower Clarence Rd
Koblenz Av.
RIVERSIDE
Wensum
Mountergate
King St
Rouen Rd
Thorn Lane
Ber St
Horns Lane
St Stephens St
Surrey St
All Saints Green
Queens Rd
Victoria St
Grove Rd
Grove Av.
Ipswich Grove
Ipswich Rd
Newmarket Rd
Brunswick Rd
Union St
Southwell Rd
Trafford Rd
Trafalgar St
Hall Rd
City Rd
Bracondale
Carrow Bridge
Argyle St
Wherry Rd
Grapes Hill
Cleveland Rd
Heigham St
Barn Rd
Barker St
Oak St
Pitt St
Duke St
Muspole St
Elm Hill
Fishergate
Cotman Fields
Bishop Bridge Rd
Rosary Rd
Timberhill

Roger Hickman's

MODERN CUISINE • INTIMATE XX Personally run restaurant in a historic part of the city, with soft hues, modern art and romantic corners. Service is attentive yet unobtrusive. Cooking is modern, intricate and displays respect for ingredients' natural flavours.

Menu £ 20/47

Town plan: A1-c – *79 Upper St Giles St ✉ NR2 1AB – ✆ 01603 633522 – www.rogerhickmansrestaurant.com – Closed 2 weeks Christmas, Sunday and Monday*

Benedicts

MODERN CUISINE • BISTRO X A huge window lets in lots of light and white wood panelling keep things suitably down-to-earth. Tried-and-tested combinations are given subtle modern touches and show respect for good quality Norfolk ingredients.

Menu £ 20/37

Town plan: A1-b – *9 St Benedicts Street ✉ NR2 4PE – ✆ 01603 926080 – www.restaurantbenedicts.com – Closed 24 December-7 January, Sunday and Monday*

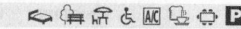

ENGLAND

Georgian Townhouse

TRADITIONAL CUISINE • NEIGHBOURHOOD Laid-back pub with a flexible menu: choose small plates to start or to share; dishes 'for the table' for 2 or 4; or something for yourself 'from the store'. Fruit and veg is home-grown and they home-smoke cheese and spit-roast and flame-grill meats. Bold, retro-style bedrooms have fridges and coffee machines.

Carte £ 21/40

22 rooms – £ 85/150 £ 95/160

30-34 Unthank Rd ✉ NR2 2RB – West : 0.5 mi by A 147 – ✆ 01603 615655 – www.thegeorgiantownhousenorwich.com

Reindeer

TRADITIONAL CUISINE • PUB Rustic neighbourhood pub with a keen local following. Plenty of space is kept aside for drinkers, who have 10 real ales to choose from. Straightforward, proudly British cooking employs lesser-used cuts and offers plenty of sharing dishes.

Carte £ 20/32

Town plan: A1-r – *10 Dereham Rd ✉ NR2 4AY – Northwest : 0.5 mi by A 147 – ✆ 01603 612995 – www.thereindeerpub.co.uk – Closed 25-26 December and Monday except bank holidays*

38 St Giles

TOWNHOUSE • PERSONALISED City centre townhouse where boutique styling blends with original features. Elegant, uncluttered bedrooms boast high ceilings and wood panelling, along with silk curtains, handmade mattresses and quality linen. Excellent breakfasts.

8 rooms – £ 95/195 £ 130/245

Town plan: A1-x – *38 St Giles St ✉ NR2 1LL – ✆ 01603 662944 – www.38stgiles.co.uk – Closed 24-27 December*

Catton Old Hall

HISTORIC • PERSONALISED Attractive, personally run, 17C merchant's house with a characterful interior. Individually designed bedrooms include 5 feature rooms; Anna Sewell, with exposed rafters and a vast four-poster, is the best.

7 rooms – £ 99/150 £ 99/150

Lodge Ln, Old Catton ✉ NR6 7HG – North : 3.5 mi by Catton Grove Rd off St Faiths Rd – ✆ 01603 419379 – www.catton-hall.co.uk

at Stoke Holy Cross South: 5.75 mi by A140 ✉ Norwich

Stoke Mill

TRADITIONAL CUISINE • HISTORIC XX Characterful 700 year old mill spanning the River Tas; the adjoining building is where the Colman family started making mustard in 1814. Confidently prepared, classically based dishes use good ingredients and flavours are distinct.

Menu £ 19 (weekday lunch) – Carte £ 32/52

Mill Rd ✉ NR14 8PA – ✆ 01508 493337 – www.stokemill.co.uk – Closed Sunday dinner, Monday and Tuesday

Wildebeest

MODERN BRITISH • PUB A smart dining pub run by one of the locals. Comfy leather chairs are set at chunky tree trunk tables. Cooking is modern and refined and the colourful dishes blend many different ingredients to create pleasing contrasts of flavour.

Menu £ 28 – Carte £ 30/45

82-86 Norwich Rd ✉ NR14 8QJ – ✆ 01508 492497 (booking essential) – www.thewildebeest.co.uk – Closed 25-26 December

NOSS MAYO

Devon – Regional map n° **1**-C3

Ship Inn

TRADITIONAL BRITISH • PUB Large, busy, well-run pub with characterful, nautical décor and wonderful waterside views from its peaceful spot on the Yealm Estuary. Appealing menu of unfussy pub classics. Bright, friendly service. Keep an eye on the tide!

Carte £ 22/33

PL8 1EW

– 01752 872387 – www.nossmayo.com

– Closed 25 December

NOTTINGHAM

Nottingham – Pop. 289 301 – Regional map n° **9**-B2

Restaurant Sat Bains

CREATIVE • INTIMATE Set beneath a flyover on the city's edge; a modern restaurant with an urban kitchen garden and smart bedrooms. 7 courses lunches are served at the chef's table and in the kitchen, while the main room comes alive at night. Cooking is highly technical, with good balance and a delicate style. Dishes incorporate the five tastes, and presentation is detailed and creative.

→ Scallop 'black'. Lavinton lamb '3 ways'. Condensed milk ice cream with tomato and extra virgin olive oil.

Menu £ 95/130 – tasting menu only

7 rooms – £ 140/290 £ 140/290 – 2 suites

Trentside, Lenton Ln NG7 2SA – Southwest : 3.5 mi by A 6005 (Castle Bd.) and A 52

– 0115 986 6566 (booking essential) – www.restaurantsatbains.com

– Closed 3 weeks late December-early January, 2 weeks August, 1 week April and Sunday-Tuesday

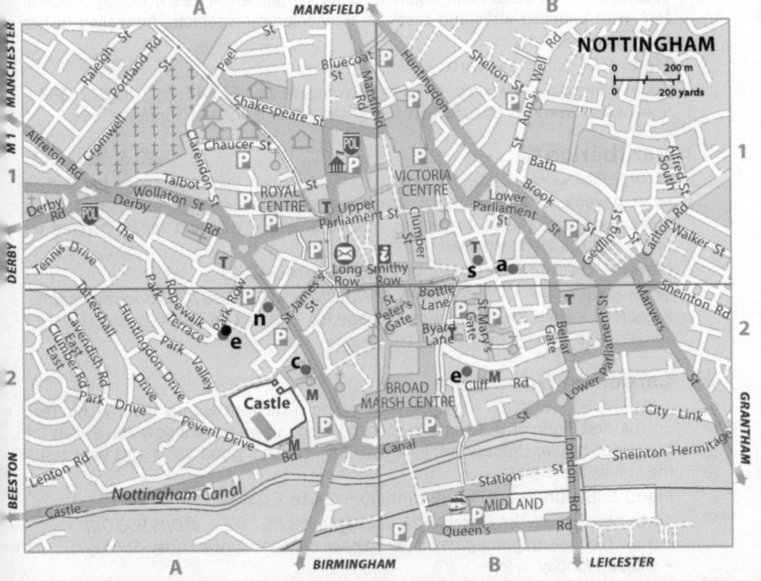

Ibérico World Tapas

MEDITERRANEAN CUISINE • FASHIONABLE Lively, well-run restaurant hidden away in the basement of the former city jail and law courts, with a vaulted ceiling, colourful Moorish tiles and ornate fretwork. Tapas menu with 'Spanish' and 'World' sections; skilful cooking is full of flavour. Friendly staff offer good recommendations.

Menu £ 13 (weekdays) **s** – Carte £ 13/29 **s**

Town plan: B2-e – *The Shire Hall, High Pavement ✉ NG1 1HN – ✆ 0115 941 0410 (booking essential at dinner) – www.ibericotapas.com – Closed 1-5 January and Sunday*

Hart's

MODERN BRITISH • FASHIONABLE Contemporary restaurant in the A&E department of the old city hospital; ask to sit in one of the central booths. British brasserie dishes feature on the daily menu and cooking is flavourful and well-priced. Lighter snacks are also served.

Menu £ 19 (lunch)/28 (weekday dinner) – Carte £ 32/49

Town plan: A2-e – *Hart's Hotel, Standard Ct., Park Row ✉ NG1 6GN – ✆ 0115 988 1900 – www.hartsnottingham.co.uk – Closed 1 January and dinner 25-26 December*

MemSaab

INDIAN • EXOTIC DÉCOR Professionally run restaurant with eye-catching artwork and a wooden 'Gateway of India'. Original, authentic cooking has a distinct North Indian influence. Spicing is well-judged and dishes from the charcoal grill are a highlight.

Carte £ 20/39

Town plan: A2-n – *12-14 Maid Marian Way ✉ NG1 6HS – ✆ 0115 957 0009 – www.mem-saab.co.uk – dinner only – Closed 25 December*

World Service

INTERNATIONAL • CHIC Hidden in the extension of a Georgian property and accessed via an Indonesian-inspired courtyard garden. It has a clubby, colonial feel, with panelled walls and cases of archaeological artefacts. Appealing dishes have global influences.

Menu £ 17 (lunch) – Carte £ 26/50

Town plan: A2-c – *Newdigate House, Castlegate ✉ NG1 6AF – ✆ 0115 847 5587 – www.worldservicerestaurant.com – Closed 1-5 January and Sunday dinner*

Bar Ibérico N

MEDITERRANEAN CUISINE • TAPAS BAR A buzzy, laid-back tapas bar with a large pavement terrace. The wide-ranging menu is designed for sharing, from charcuterie and cheese to pintxos from the Josper grill and tapas inspired by Spain and the Mediterranean.

Menu £ 10 (lunch and early dinner) – Carte £ 12/21

Town plan: B1-s – *17-19 Carlton St ✉ NG1 1NL – ✆ 0115 988 1133 (bookings not accepted) – www.ibericotapas.com/baribérico – Closed 25-26 December, 1 January and Sunday dinner*

Larder on Goosegate

TRADITIONAL BRITISH • RUSTIC Appealing restaurant with a shabby-chic feel, on the first floor of a listed Victorian building; sit in the window for a view of the street below. Unfussy dishes are skilfully cooked, good value and very tasty; the steaks are a hit.

Menu £ 18 (lunch and early dinner) – Carte £ 24/38

Town plan: B1-a – *1st Floor, 16-22 Goosegate ✉ NG1 1FE – ✆ 0115 950 0111 – www.thelarderongoosegate.co.uk – dinner only and lunch Friday-Sunday – Closed Monday*

Lime

INDIAN • NEIGHBOURHOOD Bright, modern Indian restaurant away from the city centre; personally run by the cheery owner. Flavoursome food with distinctive spicing. Non-alcoholic bar, and no corkage fee if you bring your own wine or beer.

Carte £15/30

4-6 Upminster Dr, Nuthall ✉ NG16 1PT - Northwest : 4.5 mi by Alfreton Rd, A 610 and A 6002 - ✆ 0115 975 0005 - www.lime-restaurant.co.uk - dinner only - Closed 25 December

Hart's

BUSINESS • DESIGN Sophisticated, boutique-style hotel built on the ramparts of a medieval castle. Compact bedrooms have modern bathrooms and a high level of facilities; some open onto garden terraces. The small bar-lounge doubles as a breakfast room.

32 rooms - †£134/274 ††£134/274 - ☕ £15 - 2 suites

Town plan: A2-e - *Standard Hill, Park Row ✉ NG1 6FN - ✆ 0115 988 1900 - www.hartsnottingham.co.uk*

Hart's - See restaurant listing

at West Bridgford Southeast: 1.75 mi by A60 ✉ Nottingham

escabeche

MEDITERRANEAN CUISINE • FRIENDLY Informal, modern, Mediterranean-inspired restaurant with a sunny front terrace. The broad main menu lists vibrant, well-presented tapas dishes, offering a great variety of flavours. Excellent value set menu.

Menu £11 (lunch and early dinner) **s** - Carte £15/23

27 Bridgford Rd ✉ NG2 6AU - ✆ 0115 981 7010 - www.escabeche.co.uk - Closed 25-26 December and 1 January

at Plumtree Southeast: 5.75 mi by A60 off A606 ✉ Nottingham

Perkins

MODERN BRITISH • FRIENDLY Formerly a Victorian railway station, now a bright family-run brasserie; find a spot in the conservatory overlooking the railway line. Menus evolve daily and the modern British cooking features home-smoked fish, game and cheeses.

Menu £14/19 (weekdays) - Carte £22/38

Old Railway Station, Station Rd ✉ NG12 5NA - ✆ 0115 937 3695 (booking advisable) - www.perkinsrestaurant.co.uk - Closed Sunday dinner

at Ruddington South : 5.5 mi on A 60 ✉ Nottinghamshire

Ruddington Arms

TRADITIONAL CUISINE • NEIGHBOURHOOD This dramatically refurbished, faux-industrial style pub is found in a sleepy village. Flavoursome dishes cater for one and all, with everything from pub classics to more adventurous offerings. Tasty marmalades and chutneys are for sale.

Carte £23/36

56 Wilford Rd ✉ NG11 6EQ - ✆ 0115 984 1628 - www.theruddingtonarms.com

NUN MONKTON

North Yorkshire - Regional map n° **13**-B2

Alice Hawthorn Inn

MODERN CUISINE • PUB This smart, stylish pub sits on a picturesque village green complete with a duck pond, grazing cattle and the country's tallest maypole. Well-presented dishes have classical roots and showcase local and garden produce.

Carte £24/46

The Green ✉ YO26 8EW - ✆ 01423 330303 - www.thealicehawthorn.com - Closed Monday except bank holidays and Tuesday

OAKHAM

Rutland - Pop. 10 922 - Regional map n° **9**-C2

at Hambleton East: 3 mi by A606 ⊠ Oakham

Hambleton Hall

CLASSIC CUISINE • COUNTRY HOUSE XXX A traditional dining room in a lovely Victorian manor house, boasting superb views over Rutland Water. Accomplished cooking marries together a host of top quality seasonal ingredients. Gallic dishes are classically based but display the occasional modern touch; the delicious bread is from their artisan bakery.

→ Lasagne of morel mushrooms with chicken mousse and wild garlic. Merryfield Farm duck with blood orange, beetroot and sesame. Dark chocolate with fennel, olive and orange.

Menu £ 39 (weekday lunch)/73

Hambleton Hall Hotel, ⊠ LE15 8TH - ✆ 01572 756991 - www.hambletonhall.com

Finch's Arms

TRADITIONAL BRITISH • PUB A pretty stone inn with a homely bar, two contrastingly stylish dining rooms and a delightful terrace overlooking Rutland Water. Assured, seasonal dishes rely on local produce; desserts are satisfyingly old school and afternoon tea is also an option. Modern bedrooms complete the picture.

Menu £ 14 (weekday lunch) - Carte £ 25/45

10 rooms - †£ 85 ††£ 100/130

Oakham Rd ⊠ LE15 8TL - ✆ 01572 756575 - www.finchsarms.co.uk

Hambleton Hall

LUXURY • CLASSIC Beautiful Victorian manor house in a peaceful location, with mature grounds sloping down to Rutland Water. Classical country house drawing rooms boast heavy drapes, open fires and antiques. Good-sized bedrooms are designed by the owner herself and come with a host of thoughtful extras. Service is engaging.

16 rooms - †£ 200/220 ††£ 290/600 - 1 suite

⊠ LE15 8TH - ✆ 01572 756991 - www.hambletonhall.com

Hambleton Hall - See restaurant listing

OLD ALRESFORD

Hampshire - Pop. 577 - Regional map n° **4**-B2

Pulpo Negro

SPANISH • TAPAS BAR X A characterful, well run restaurant in an old townhouse in the heart of the town; its name translates as the Black Octopus. Stylish interior with exposed brick, rough floorboards, an open kitchen and a relaxed atmosphere. Tasty authentic Spanish tapas is accompanied by a good choice of Spanish wines.

Carte £ 14/34

28 Broad St ⊠ SO24 9AQ - ✆ 01962 732262 (booking essential) - www.pulponegro.co.uk - Closed 25-26 December, 1 January, Sunday, Monday and bank holidays

OLD BURGHCLERE

Hampshire - ⊠ Newbury - Regional map n° **4**-B1

Dew Pond

CLASSIC FRENCH • COSY XX A part-16C farmhouse with well-tended gardens leading down to a dew pond. The longstanding restaurant is family owned and run and serves classic French cooking; enjoy an aperitif on the terrace, overlooking the real Watership Down.

Menu £ 36

⊠ RG20 9LH - ✆ 01635 278408 - www.dewpond.co.uk - dinner only - Closed 2 weeks Christmas-New Year, Sunday and Monday

OLDHAM

Greater Manchester – Pop. 96 555 – Regional map n° **11**-B2

Dining Room

MODERN BRITISH • DESIGN XX Tucked away to the back of a pub, this small but stylish restaurant is a destination in its own right. Refined modern dishes are skilfully prepared and have Mediterranean influences; the 7 course tasting menu is a good option.

Carte £ 31/49

White Hart Inn, 51 Stockport Rd, Lydgate ✉ OL4 4JJ – East : 3 mi by A 669 on A 6050 – ✆ 01457 872566 (booking advisable) – www.thewhitehart.co.uk – dinner only and Sunday lunch – Closed 1 January, 26 December, Sunday dinner and Monday

White Hart Inn

MODERN BRITISH • CLASSIC DÉCOR The original part of this stone-built inn dates from 1788 but there's always something new going on here. With its formal restaurant, private dining room, large function room and smart bedrooms, it can be a busy place. The menu offers a good range of refined pub classics, many with a Mediterranean slant.

Menu £ 20 (lunch and early dinner) – Carte £ 27/49

16 rooms – †£ 135/145 ††£ 175/185

51 Stockport Rd, Lydgate ✉ OL4 4JJ – East : 3 mi by A 669 on A 6050 – ✆ 01457 872566 – www.thewhitehart.co.uk – Closed 1 January and 26 December

Dining Room – See restaurant listing

OLDSTEAD

North Yorkshire – Regional map n° **13**-C2

Black Swan (Tommy Banks)

MODERN BRITISH • FAMILY XX The Black Swan is owned by a family who've farmed in the area for generations. Enjoy an aperitif in the characterful bar, then head upstairs to the restaurant. Modern menus are driven by meats from their farm and produce grown in the garden; cooking is highly skilled and dishes are carefully presented. Antique-furnished bedrooms have smart bathrooms and private patios.

→ Cod cheek with broccoli and onion. Scallop cured with rhubarb. Sheep's milk with Douglas fir oil.

Menu £ 95 – tasting menu only

9 rooms – †£ 140/270 ††£ 140/270

✉ YO61 4BL – ✆ 01347 868387 (bookings essential for non-residents) – www.blackswanoldstead.co.uk – dinner only and Saturday lunch – Closed Sunday

OMBERSLEY

Worcestershire – Pop. 623 – Regional map n° **10**-B3

Venture In

TRADITIONAL BRITISH • COSY XX A hugely characterful black and white timbered house with 15C origins and a large inglenook fireplace in the bar. Cooking is classically based but has modern overtones and there's always a good choice of specials available.

Menu £ 30/46

Main St ✉ WR9 0EW – ✆ 01905 620552 – www.theventurein.co.uk – Closed 2 weeks August, 1 week March, 1 week June, 1 week Christmas, Monday and dinner Sunday

ORFORD

Suffolk – ✉ Woodbridge – Pop. 1 153 – Regional map n° **8**-D3

🍴 Crown and Castle

MODERN CUISINE • CONTEMPORARY DÉCOR XX A relaxed hotel restaurant decorated with eclectic art. Cooking mixes British and Italian traditions; try the lunchtime cicchetti or the cooked-to-order steak and kidney pie. Fish is landed at the nearby quay and service is efficient.

Carte £ 30/45

Crown and Castle Hotel, ✉ IP12 2LJ – ✆ 01394 450205 (booking essential at dinner) – www.crownandcastle.co.uk

Crown and Castle

HISTORIC • PERSONALISED It is thought that the original 12C inn which stood on this site was built into the walls of neighbouring Orford Castle. The latest incarnation, a Tudor-style house, is run in a relaxed yet professional manner. Most of the well-furnished bedrooms are in chalets – many have terraces and distant sea views.

21 rooms – 🚹£ 112/210 🚻£ 140/250 – 1 suite

✉ IP12 2LJ – ✆ 01394 450205 – www.crownandcastle.co.uk

🍴 **Crown and Castle** – See restaurant listing

OSMOTHERLEY

North Yorkshire – ✉ Northallerton – Pop. 668 – Regional map n° **13**-B1

🍴 Golden Lion

TRADITIONAL BRITISH • PUB 18C stone inn set in a historic village in the North York Moors; make for the atmospheric bar which offers over 80 different whiskies. Cooking is traditional and satisfying, with filling dishes on the main menu and more ambitious weekly specials. Modern bedrooms have heavy oak furnishings and good facilities.

Carte £ 24/40

7 rooms – 🚹£ 75 🚻£ 95

6 West End ✉ DL6 3AA – ✆ 01609 883526 – www.goldenlionosmotherley.co.uk – Closed 25 December and lunch Monday-Tuesday

OSWESTRY

Shropshire – Pop. 16 660 – Regional map n° **10**-A1

🍴 Sebastians

TRADITIONAL CUISINE • COSY XX Housed in three characterful 17C cottages, Sebastians is a long-standing restaurant with an open fire, lots of beams and bags of charm. Cooking uses good ingredients and is classically based, and you'll be well looked after by the team. Many of the cosy, characterful bedrooms are set around a courtyard.

Menu £ 45

6 rooms – 🚹£ 75 🚻£ 85 – £ 12

45 Willow St ✉ SY11 1AQ – ✆ 01691 655444 – www.sebastians-hotel.co.uk – dinner only – Closed 25-26 December, 1 January, Sunday-Tuesday and bank holidays except Good Friday

🍴 Townhouse

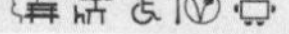

MODERN BRITISH • FASHIONABLE XX Contemporary restaurant in a Georgian townhouse. There's a flamboyant cocktail bar, a sunny terrace and an airy dining room featuring glitzy chandeliers. Classical cooking has a modern edge and dishes are attractively presented.

Menu £ 15 – Carte £ 20/31

35 Willow St ✉ SY11 1AQ – ✆ 01691 659499 – www.townhouseoswestry.com – Closed Sunday dinner

at Rhydycroesau West: 3.5 mi on B4580 ✉ Oswestry

Pen-Y-Dyffryn

TRADITIONAL · COSY An early Victorian rectory in a peaceful countryside setting, with a pretty garden and a lovely outlook. Classical lounges feature antique furnishings and roaring fires. Bedrooms have subtle modern touches and the Coach House rooms come with private terraces. Daily menus use local and organic produce.

12 rooms - £ 89/99 £ 188/272

✉ SY10 7JD - ✆ 01691 653700 - www.peny.co.uk - Closed 14 December-15 January

OVERTON

Hampshire - Pop. 3 318 - Regional map n° **4**-B1

White Hart

TRADITIONAL CUISINE · RUSTIC The lounge has retained its original stone fireplace and the dining room its characterful wood panelling and parquet floor but there's also a more modern extension, an attractive terrace and 12 cosy boutique-style bedrooms. Menus offer something for one and all, from the traditional to the more adventurous.

Carte £ 22/35

12 rooms - £ 80/120 £ 90/130

London Rd ✉ RG25 3NW - ✆ 01256 771431 - www.whitehartoverton.co.uk

M. Carassale/

GOOD TIPS!

England's oldest university city has a rich architectural heritage and this is reflected in our hotel selection, with **Malmaison**, for example, offering the opportunity to sleep in a former prison cell. A global restaurant scene sees British, Italian, Spanish and Thai restaurants all featured, with a couple of Bib Gourmands and plenty of pubs too.

OXFORD

Oxfordshire - Pop. 159 994 - Regional map n° **6**-B2

Restaurants

Oli's Thai

THAI • FRIENDLY X This lovely little restaurant is set off the beaten track, in an up-and-coming residential area. Start with a drink on the patio then make for the cool, relaxed restaurant; if you haven't booked, try for a seat at the counter. The concise menu offers fresh, meticulously prepared, vibrantly flavoured dishes.

Carte £ 18/25

Town plan: B2-r - *38 Magdalen Rd* ✉ *OX4 1RB*
- ✆ 01865 790223 (booking essential) - www.olisthai.com - Closed Tuesday dinner, Sunday and Monday

Magdalen Arms

TRADITIONAL BRITISH • PUB Buzzy battleship-grey pub boasting quirky old standard lamps, an eclectic collection of 1920s posters, board games and a bar billiards table. The experienced chef uses local ingredients to create flavoursome, good value dishes. Be sure to try the delicious fresh juices and homemade lemonade.

Carte £ 22/40

Town plan: B2-s - *243 Iffley Rd* ✉ *OX4 1SJ*
- ✆ 01865 243159 - www.magdalenarms.co.uk - Closed 24-26 December, 1 January, Monday lunch and bank holidays

Oxford Kitchen

MODERN BRITISH • MINIMALIST XX Bright, modern neighbourhood restaurant hidden in a parade of shops in trendy Summertown. Menus list appealing, original dishes with a modern British base and cooking is refined and flavoursome. Come at the weekend for brunch.

Menu £ 25 (weekday lunch)/40

Town plan: A1-e - *215 Banbury Rd, Summertown* ✉ *OX2 7HQ*
- ✆ 01865 511149 - www.theoxfordkitchen.co.uk - Closed 2-16 January, Sunday dinner and Monday

Quod

INTERNATIONAL • BRASSERIE XX Buzzy brasserie in an old banking hall (now a stylish hotel). It's open from early 'til late and has a lovely terrace to the rear. Modern menus offer a mix of Italian and European dishes, along with twice-daily blackboard specials.

Menu £ 13 (lunch and early dinner) – Carte £ 24/48

Town plan: D2-s – *Old Bank Hotel, 92-94 High St ✉ OX1 4BJ – ✆ 01865 799599 – www.quod.co.uk*

Arbequina

SPANISH • NEIGHBOURHOOD X A simply furnished, bohemian tapas bar: sit downstairs by the vintage stainless steel counter or upstairs in the bay window. The concise menu offers tasty, authentic, filling tapas dishes; 3 plus dessert is about right.

Carte £ 14/31

Town plan: B2-a – *74 Cowley Rd ✉ OX4 1JB – ✆ 01865 792777 (bookings advisable at dinner) – www.arbequina.co.uk – dinner only and Thursday-Saturday lunch – Closed Christmas-New Year and Sunday*

Branca

ITALIAN • BISTRO X Bustling restaurant with a spacious, modern interior and French doors opening onto a courtyard terrace. The menu is a roll call of Italian classics; portions are generous and lunch deals, good value. Friendly young staff; adjoining deli.

Menu £ 15 (lunch and early dinner) – Carte £ 21/38

Town plan: C1-a – *111 Walton St ✉ OX2 6AJ – ✆ 01865 556111 – www.branca.co.uk*

The Anchor

TRADITIONAL BRITISH • PUB Not your typical pub, with subtle art deco styling and black and white dining room floor tiles. The main menu offers largely British classics with some Mediterranean influences as well as morning coffee and cakes and weekend brunches.

Carte £ 22/42

Town plan: A1-u – *2 Hayfield Rd ✉ OX2 6TT – ✆ 01865 510282 – www.theanchoroxford.com – Closed 25 December*

Black Boy

INTERNATIONAL • NEIGHBOURHOOD A relaxed neighbourhood pub that's a real social hub. Dine in the white wood-panelled bar or the formal restaurant with its funky wallpaper. Classically based dishes are full of flavour and the home-baked bread is hard to resist. Boutique bedrooms feature bathrobes, fresh fruit and locally made furnishings.

Carte £ 24/40

5 rooms – †£ 140/280 ††£ 140/280

Town plan: B1-v – *91 Old High St, Headington ✉ OX3 9HT – ✆ 01865 741137 – www.theblackboy.uk.com – Closed 26 December and 1 January*

Pint Shop

TRADITIONAL BRITISH • PUB Plate glass windows bearing the words 'MEAT', 'BREAD' and 'BEER' say it all. Interesting, gutsy British cooking uses the charcoal grill to good effect. The large bar offers 18 keg beers, 3 cask beers, 80 whiskies and 120 gins.

Menu £ 13 (weekday lunch) – Carte £ 21/39

Town plan: C2-n – *27-29 George St ✉ OX1 2AU – ✆ 01865 251194 – www.pintshop.co.uk – Closed 25-26 December and 1 January*

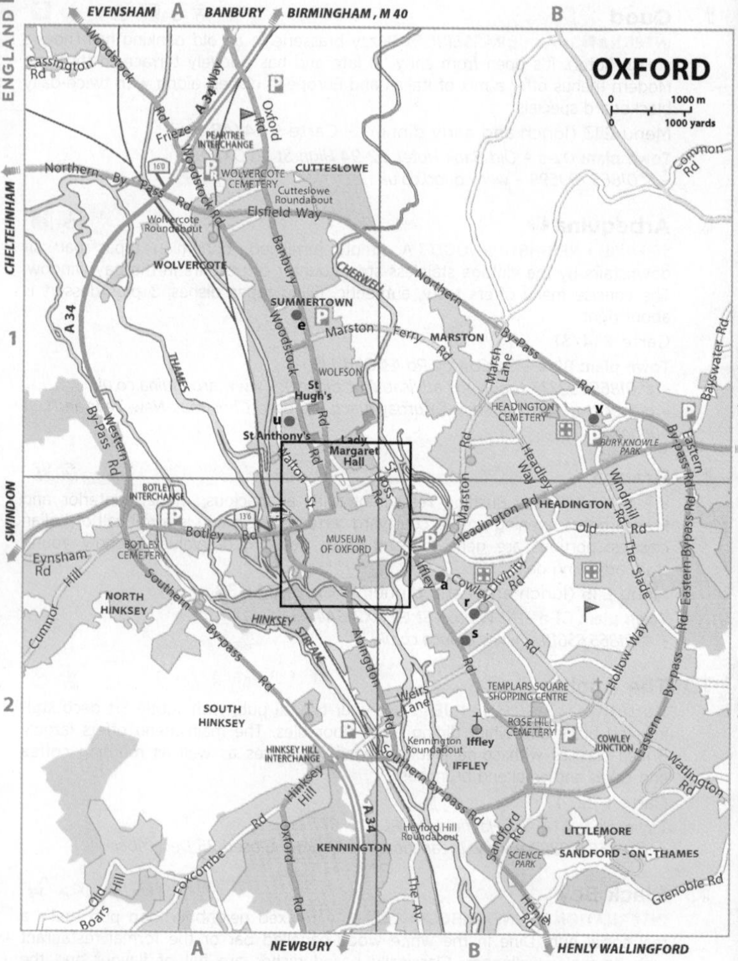

EVENSHAM A BANBURY BIRMINGHAM, M 40 B

OXFORD

0 1000 m
0 1000 yards

CHELTENHAM
SWINDON
LONDON, M 40
1
2

Cassington Rd
Woodstock Rd
A 34 Way
Oxford Rd
Frieze Way
PEARTREE INTERCHANGE
Northern By-Pass Rd
WOLVERCOTE CEMETERY
CUTTESLOWE
Cutteslowe Roundabout
Elsfield Way
Wolvercote Roundabout
WOLVERCOTE
A 34
CHERWELL
Northern By-Pass Rd
Common Rd
SUMMERTOWN
e
Banbury Rd
Marston Ferry Rd
MARSTON
Marsh Lane
Bayswater Rd
THAMES
WOLFSON
St Hugh's
u
St Anthony's
Lady Margaret Hall
HEADINGTON CEMETERY
v
BURY KNOWLE PARK
Eastern By-pass Rd
Western By-Pass Rd
Walton St
St Cross Rd
Marston Rd
Headley Way
Windmill Rd
BOTLEY INTERCHANGE
Botley Rd
MUSEUM OF OXFORD
Headington Rd
HEADINGTON
Old Rd
Eynsham Rd
BOTLEY CEMETERY
Iffley Rd
a
Cowley Rd
Divinity Rd
The Slade
Cumnor Hill
NORTH HINKSEY
Southern By-pass Rd
r
s
HINKSEY STREAM
Abingdon Rd
Hollow Way
Eastern By-pass Rd
Weirs Lane
TEMPLARS SQUARE SHOPPING CENTRE
SOUTH HINKSEY
ROSE HILL CEMETERY
Kennington Roundabout
Iffley
COWLEY JUNCTION
HINKSEY HILL INTERCHANGE
IFFLEY
Southern By-pass Rd
Watlington Rd
Hinksey Hill
A 34
Hevford Hill Roundabout
Sandford Rd
LITTLEMORE
Foxcombe Rd
Oxford Rd
KENNINGTON
SCIENCE PARK
SANDFORD - ON - THAMES
The Av.
Grenoble Rd
Old Boars Hill
Henley Rd

A NEWBURY B HENLY WALLINGFORD

Hotels

Randolph

HISTORIC · CLASSIC This grand old lady exudes immense charm and character, and comes complete with an intricate wrought iron staircase and plush modern bedrooms. Have a cocktail in the magnificent bar or afternoon tea in the drawing room beneath Sir Osbert Lancaster oils. The impressive formal dining room offers classic menus.

151 rooms – £ 200/350 £ 260/400 – 9 suites

Town plan: C1-n – *Beaumont St.* ✉ *OX1 2LN* – *0344 879 9132*
– *www.macdonaldhotels.co.uk/randolph* – *Restricted opening at Christmas*

On a budget? Take advantage of lunchtime prices.

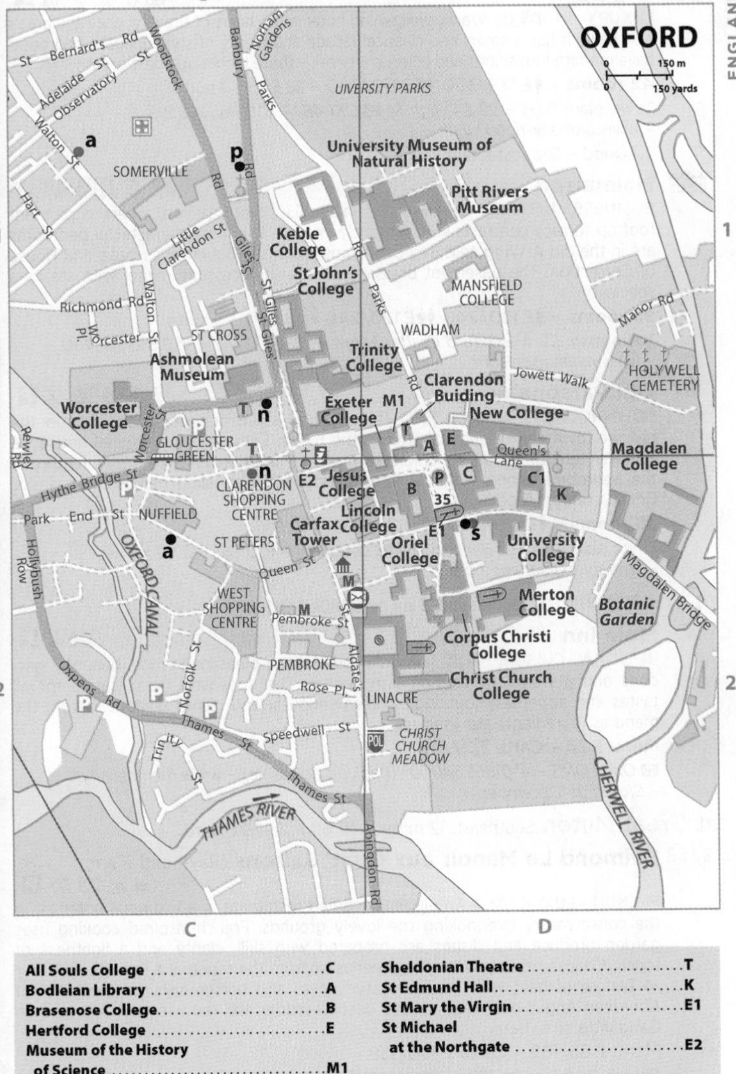

All Souls College	**C**	**Sheldonian Theatre**	**T**
Bodleian Library	**A**	**St Edmund Hall**	**K**
Brasenose College	**B**	**St Mary the Virgin**	**E1**
Hertford College	**E**	**St Michael at the Northgate**	**E2**
Museum of the History of Science	**M1**		
Queen's College (The)	**C1**	**Radcliffe Square**	**35**
Radcliffe Camera	**P**		

Old Bank

LUXURY • MODERN Warm, welcoming hotel in the heart of the city: once the area's first bank. It has a smart neo-classical façade and plenty of style. Elegant bedrooms have modern furnishings and eclectic artwork – those higher up boast great views.

42 rooms – †£ 179/360 ††£ 179/360 – ☕ £ 15 – 1 suite

Town plan: D2-s – *92-94 High St ✉ OX1 4BJ – ✆ 01865 799599 – www.oldbank-hotel.co.uk*

Quod – See restaurant listing

Malmaison

BUSINESS • HISTORIC Unique hotel in the 13C castle prison, where a pleasant rooftop terrace contrasts with a moody interior. The most characterful bedrooms are in the old A Wing cells; feature rooms are in the Governor's House and House of Correction. The basement brasserie serves an accessible menu, with steaks a speciality.

95 rooms – †£ 120/240 ††£ 120/240 – ☕ £ 14 – 3 suites

Town plan: C2-a – *Oxford Castle, 3 New Rd ✉ OX1 1AY – ✆ 01865 268400 – www.malmaison.com*

Old Parsonage

TOWNHOUSE • PERSONALISED This ivy-clad sandstone parsonage sits in the historic town centre and dates from the 1660s. Enter into the original house via a pretty terrace; inside it's chic and modern – bold greys and purples feature in the bedrooms, along with the latest mod cons. Appealing menus offer classic British comfort food.

35 rooms – †£ 179/360 ††£ 179/360 – ☕ £ 15

Town plan: C1-p – *1 Banbury Rd ✉ OX2 6NN – ✆ 01865 310210 – www.oldparsonage-hotel.co.uk*

at Toot Baldon Southeast: 5.5 mi by B480 ✉ Oxford

Mole Inn

REGIONAL CUISINE • PUB Popular pub with a pleasant terrace, beautiful gardens and a warm, welcoming atmosphere. The appealing menu caters for all tastes and appetites; sourcing is taken seriously and dishes disappear from the menu as ingredients are used up.

Menu £ 24 – Carte £ 27/42

✉ OX44 9NG – ✆ 01865 340001 (booking advisable) – www.themoleinn.com – Closed 25 December

at Great Milton Southeast: 12 mi by A40 off A329 ✉ Oxford

Belmond Le Manoir aux Quat' Saisons (Raymond Blanc)

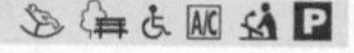

FRENCH • LUXURY XXXX An elegant beamed restaurant in a luxurious hotel; sit in the conservatory overlooking the lovely grounds. French-inspired cooking uses garden produce and dishes are prepared with skill, clarity and a lightness of touch. Choose one of two tasting menus or from the monthly à la carte.

➜ Tartare of beef with garden oyster leaves and horseradish. Roasted fillet of Aberdeen Angus beef with braised Jacob's ladder and red wine jus. A theme on Gariguette strawberry.

Menu £ 85/162 – Carte £ 130/138

Church Rd ✉ OX44 7PD – ✆ 01844 278881 (booking essential) – www.belmond.com/lemanoir

Belmond Le Manoir aux Quat' Saisons

GRAND LUXURY • PERSONALISED A majestic, part-15C country house offering the ultimate in guest services. Bedrooms are extremely comfortable – those in the Garden Wing are the most luxurious. Relax by an open fire in the sumptuous sitting rooms or out on the delightful terrace overlooking the gardens.

32 rooms ☕ – †£ 595/1050 ††£ 595/1050 – 14 suites

Church Rd ✉ OX44 7PD – ✆ 01844 278881 – www.belmond.com/lemanoir

Belmond Le Manoir aux Quat' Saisons – See restaurant listing

PADSTOW

Cornwall – Pop. 2 449 – Regional map n° **1**-B2

✿ Paul Ainsworth at No.6

MODERN CUISINE • INTIMATE X A delightful Georgian townhouse on a harbour back-water, with a clubby lounge and a funky dining room. Original modern cooking uses first class ingredients, flavours are clearly defined and there are lots of Cornish references. Service is friendly and enthusiastic and diners are encouraged to talk to the chefs.

→ Crispy Porthilly oysters with cured pork, green apple and fennel. Lamb with salt-baked celeriac, red garlic and hogget pudding. 'A trifle Cornish' with strawberry, hibiscus and saffron.

Menu £ 26 (lunch) – Carte £ 55/68

Town plan: A1-n – *6 Middle St ✉ PL28 8AP – ✆ 01841 532093 – www.paul-ainsworth.co.uk – Closed 23-26 December, Sunday and Monday*

Rick Stein's Café

INTERNATIONAL • BISTRO X A deceptively large café hidden behind a tiny shop front on a side street. The concise, seasonally changing menu offers tasty, unfussy dishes which display influences from Thailand, Morocco and the Med. The home-made bread is worth a try, as are the great value set menus. Bedrooms are comfy and simply furnished; have breakfast in the café or the small courtyard garden.

Menu £ 24 – Carte £ 25/36

3 rooms – †£ 113/165 ††£ 113/165

Town plan: A1-p – *10 Middle St ✉ PL28 8AP – ✆ 01841 532700 (booking essential at dinner) – www.rickstein.com – Closed 24-26 December and 1 May*

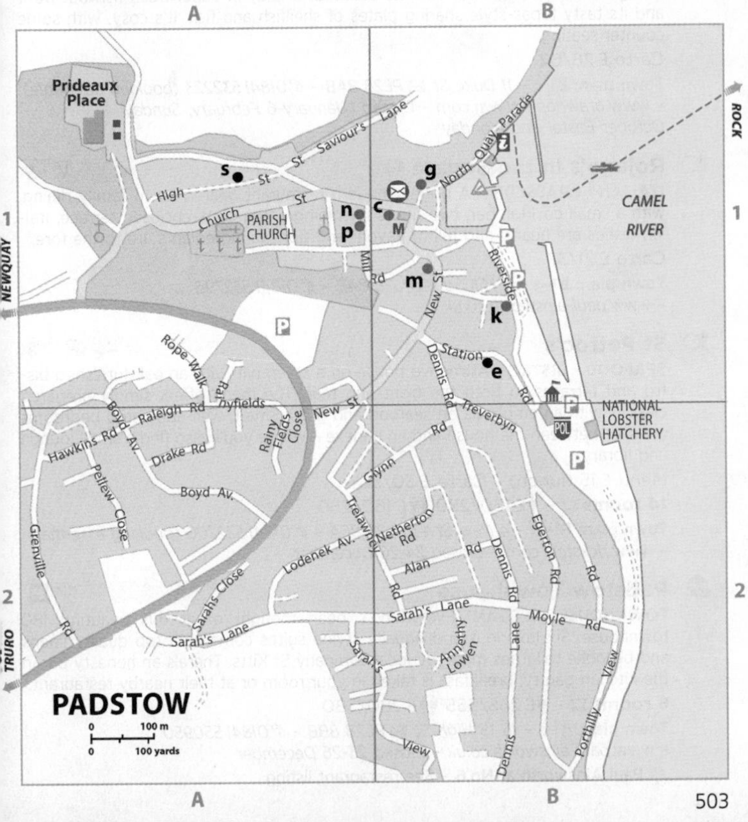

PADSTOW

Seafood

SEAFOOD • ROMANTIC XXX Stylish, laid-back, local institution – dominated by a large pewter-topped bar. Daily menus showcase fresh fish and shellfish. Classic dishes sit alongside those influenced by Rick Stein's travels; perhaps Singapore chilli crab or Madras fish curry. New England style bedrooms boast good quality furnishings; some have terraces or balconies and estuary views.

Carte £ 42/91

22 rooms – †£ 165/300 ††£ 165/300

Town plan: B1-k – *Riverside PL28 8BY – 01841 532700 (booking essential) – www.rickstein.com – Closed 25-26 December*

Appleton's at the Vineyard

MEDITERRANEAN CUISINE • FRIENDLY X An enterprising couple bought this old mill and planted over 11,000 vines. Enjoy their homemade wines, ciders and apple juices while sitting on the terrace, gazing down the valley and dining on fresh, unfussy Italian-influenced dishes.

Carte £ 33/46

Trevibban Mill, Dark Ln PL27 7SE – South : 3.5 mi by A 389 off B 3274 – 01841 541413 – www.trevibbanmill.com – Closed January, Monday, Tuesday and dinner Sunday-Wednesday

Prawn on the Lawn

SEAFOOD • TAPAS BAR X If you like seafood then you'll love this modern fishmongers-cum-seafood bar with its beautiful display of super-fresh fish out front and its tasty tapas-style sharing plates of shellfish and fish. It's cosy, with some counter seating.

Carte £ 26/62

Town plan: B1-c – *11 Duke St PL28 8AB – 01841 532223 (booking advisable) – www.prawnonthelawn.com – Closed 1 January-6 February, Sunday October-Easter and Monday*

Rojano's in the Square N

ITALIAN • BRASSERIE X A bright, modern restaurant geared up to family dining, with a small cocktail bar, two floors for dining and a glass-enclosed terrace. Italian dishes are hearty and full of flavour and Cornish ingredients are to the fore.

Carte £ 21/37

Town plan: B1-g – *9 Mill Sq PL28 8AE – 01841 532796 – www.paul-ainsworth.co.uk*

St Petroc's

SEAFOOD • BISTRO X Attractive house on a steep hill, with an oak-furnished bistro and terraces to both the front and rear. The menu offers simply prepared classics with an emphasis on seafood and grills. Smart, well-appointed bedrooms are split between the house and an annexe – where you'll also find a small lounge and library.

Menu £ 15 (lunch) – Carte £ 30/56

14 rooms – †£ 160/250 ††£ 160/250

Town plan: B1-m – *4 New St PL28 8EA – 01841 532700 (booking essential) – www.rickstein.com – Closed 24-26 December*

Padstow Townhouse

TOWNHOUSE • ELEGANT Everything's been thought of at this beautiful 18C townhouse. Six luxurious, individually styled suites come with top quality linens and bespoke toiletries made by local company St Kitts. There's an honesty bar in the kitchen pantry; breakfast is taken in your room or at their nearby restaurant.

6 rooms – †£ 255/355 ††£ 280/380

Town plan: A1-s – *16-18 High St PL28 8BB – 01841 550950 – www.paul-ainsworth.co.uk – Closed 23-26 December*

Paul Ainsworth at No.6 – See restaurant listing

Treverbyn House

TOWNHOUSE • PERSONALISED Charming Edwardian house built for a wine merchant and run by a delightful owner. Comfy bedrooms feature interesting furniture from local sale rooms; one has a huge roll-top bath and all have harbour views – the Turret Room is the best. Have breakfast in your bedroom, the dining room or the garden.

3 rooms – £100 £130

Town plan: B1-e – *Station Rd PL28 8DA – 01841 532855 – www.treverbynhouse.com – Closed November-March*

PAINSWICK

Gloucestershire – Pop. 1 762 – Regional map n° **2**-C1

The Painswick

MODERN BRITISH • BRASSERIE XX Pass the hams hanging on the walls and the coffee tables by the wood-burning oven (where the bread is cooked), into the bright parquet-floored dining room with blue leather chairs. Unfussy modern cooking follows the seasons; the charcuterie board is worth a try. Dine on the terrace to enjoy Slad Valley views.

Carte £ 33/46

The Painswick Hotel, Kemps Ln GL6 6YB – 01452 813688 – www.thepainswick.co.uk

The Painswick

HISTORIC • PERSONALISED A wonderful Regency house in the heart of a delightful village. A lovely inner hall leads to a relaxed, stylish sitting room but the jewel in the crown is the magnificent wisteria-clad stone terrace with valley views – the perfect spot for afternoon tea. Immaculate bedrooms have an understated designer feel.

16 rooms – £129/179 £129/179 – £16 – 1 suite

Kemps Ln GL6 6YB – 01452 813688 – www.thepainswick.co.uk

The Painswick – See restaurant listing

PATELEY BRIDGE

North Yorkshire – Harrogate – Pop. 1 432 – Regional map n° **13**-B2

Yorke Arms (Frances Atkins)

MODERN CUISINE • FRIENDLY XXX This charming 17C inn sits on the green of a small hamlet and, despite its polished stone floors, exposed beams and antique furnishings, has a subtle modern feel. Fiercely seasonal cooking showcases excellent ingredients in boldly flavoured, classical combinations which are given a contemporary touch. Bedrooms range from small and cosy to stylishly luxurious duplex rooms.

→ Rabbit, leek and morels. Roast brill with lovage and native lobster. Dark chocolate, lemon ginger and salted milk ice cream.

Menu £ 45 (weekday lunch) – Carte £ 49/65

15 rooms (dinner included) – £250/275 £345/430 – 4 suites

Ramsgill-in-Nidderdale HG3 5RL – Northwest : 5 mi by Low Wath Rd – 01423 755243 – www.yorke-arms.co.uk – Closed Sunday and Monday except bank holidays

PATRICK BROMPTON

North Yorkshire – Bedale – Regional map n° **13**-B1

Elmfield House

TRADITIONAL • COSY Spacious former gamekeeper's house in a peaceful farmland setting, complete with a fishing lake and a 14 acre forest. Guests are welcomed into the conservatory-cum-breakfast-room with homemade cake. Bedrooms are warm and welcoming.

4 rooms – £65/85 £80/100

Arrathorne DL8 1NE – Northwest : 2.25 mi by A 684 on Richmond rd – 01677 450558 – www.elmfieldhouse.co.uk

PENN

Buckinghamshire – Pop. 3 779 – Regional map n° **6**-D2

Old Queens Head

TRADITIONAL BRITISH • PUB A characterful country pub purchased in 1666 by one of the King's physicians. Sit on the paved terrace, in the lively bar or in the characterful dining room. Choose from 'small' or 'big' plates – many have influences from the Med.

Carte £ 23/46

Hammersley Ln ✉ HP10 8EY – ✆ 01494 813371 – www.oldqueensheadpenn.co.uk

PENRITH

Cumbria – Pop. 15 181 – Regional map n° **12**-B2

Four&Twenty

MODERN BRITISH • FRIENDLY Come at lunch for a good value menu; come at dinner for a more substantial à la carte. Well-executed, unfussy cooking is a mix of traditional and modern British. The bright, capacious room is simply furnished – it used to be a bank.

Menu £ 16 (lunch) – Carte £ 24/35

42 King St ✉ CA11 7AY – ✆ 01768 210231 – www.fourandtwentypenrith.co.uk – Closed Sunday and Monday

Brooklands

TRADITIONAL • PERSONALISED This Victorian terraced house is located close to the town centre and is run by warm, welcoming owners. It has a traditional, antique-furnished hall and a smart breakfast room with marble-topped tables. Homely bedrooms come with fridges and robes; one has a locally crafted four-poster bed.

6 rooms – †£ 45/75 ††£ 85/95

2 Portland Pl ✉ CA11 7QN – ✆ 01768 863395 – www.brooklandsguesthouse.com – Closed Christmas and New Year

at Temple Sowerby East: 6.75 mi by A66 ✉ Penrith

Temple Sowerby House

COUNTRY HOUSE • CLASSIC An attractive, enthusiastically run, red-brick Georgian mansion with spacious, classically styled guest areas. Traditional country house bedrooms boast antique furnishings and contemporary facilities. Ambitious, modern menus of local, seasonal produce are served overlooking the enclosed lawned gardens.

12 rooms – †£ 110/130 ††£ 150/180

✉ CA10 1RZ – ✆ 017683 61578 – www.templesowerby.com – Closed Christmas

at Clifton Southeast: 3 mi on A6

George and Dragon

TRADITIONAL CUISINE • INN Whitewashed coaching inn with a characterful 18C bar and modern, brasserie-style restaurant. Appealing dishes feature vegetables from the garden, game from the moors and organic meats from the Lowther Estate farms. Modern bedrooms showcase furniture and paintings from the family's collection.

Menu £ 23 (weekdays) – Carte £ 28/40

11 rooms – †£ 85/119 ††£ 100/160

✉ CA10 2ER – ✆ 01768 865381 – www.georgeanddragonclifton.co.uk – Closed 26 December

at Askham South: 6 mi by A6

Askham Hall

MODERN BRITISH • INTIMATE XX Relax by the fire then head to the modish country house restaurant with its unique tiled floor and elegant private room. Concise menus showcase meats from their farm and veg from their superb kitchen garden.

Menu £ 50/65

CA10 2PF - 01931 712350 (booking essential) - www.askhamhall.co.uk - dinner only - Closed 3 January-mid February, Christmas, Sunday and Monday

Askham Hall

COUNTRY HOUSE • CONTEMPORARY At the edge of the Lowther Estate you'll find this fine, family-run castle dating from the 1300s and surrounded by beautiful gardens. It's been stylishly yet sympathetically refurbished and its spacious rooms are full of original features and old family furnishings. Go for one of the bedrooms with a view.

15 rooms - £ 138/308 £ 150/320

CA10 2PF - 01931 712350 - www.askhamhall.co.uk - Closed 3 January-mid February and Christmas

Askham Hall - See restaurant listing

PENSHURST

Kent - Pop. 708 - Regional map n° **5**-B2

Leicester Arms

TRADITIONAL BRITISH • INN Sympathetically refurbished 16C former coaching inn offering an evolving menu of rustic and satisfying pub classics. Sit in the garden room: a large bright space with a lovely rural view. Bedrooms are furnished in a contemporary style; ask for Room 8, which is the biggest, with the best outlook.

Carte £ 23/53

13 rooms - £ 69/89 £ 99/139

High St TN11 8BT - 01892 871617 - www.theleicesterarmshotel.com

PENZANCE

Cornwall - Pop. 16 336 - Regional map n° **1**-A3

Harris's

TRADITIONAL CUISINE • CLASSIC DÉCOR XX Long-standing, split-level restaurant with a spiral staircase and an unusual Welsh black metal plate ceiling; run by a keen husband and wife. Classical cooking uses seasonal Cornish produce; try the steamed lobster when it's in season.

Carte £ 33/45

Town plan: B1-a - *46 New St TR18 2LZ - 01736 364408 - www.harrissrestaurant.co.uk - Closed 3 weeks winter, 25-26 December, Sunday and Monday*

Shore

SEAFOOD • INTIMATE XX The name refers to the cooking rather than the location of this small bistro. The experienced chef works alone: his produce is ethically sourced and many of his precisely prepared dishes have Mediterranean or Asian influences.

Menu £ 19 (lunch) - Carte £ 32/39

Town plan: B1-s - *13-14 Alverton St TR18 2QP - 01736 362444 (booking essential at lunch) - www.theshorerestaurant.uk - Closed 2 weeks January, Sunday and Monday*

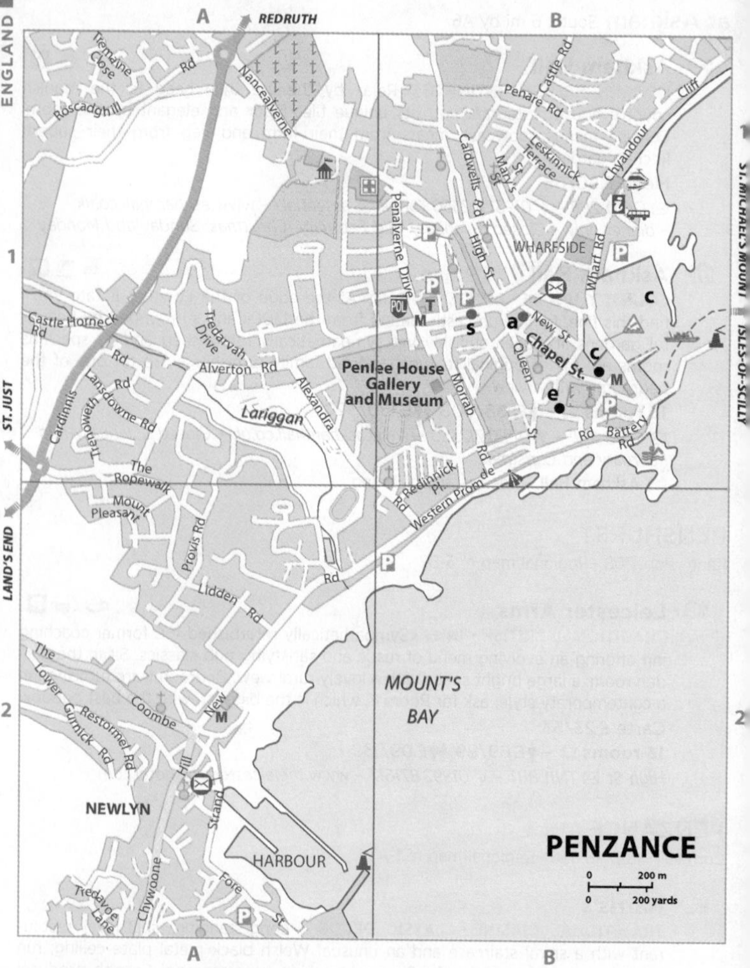

PENZANCE

0 200 m
0 200 yards

Chapel House

TOWNHOUSE · CONTEMPORARY A smartly refurbished 18C house with a pretty walled garden. Sumptuous lounges are filled with modern art and there's a fabulous basement dining room where they serve breakfast and pre-booked weekend meals. Bedrooms have a cool, understated elegance and sea views: all feature fresh flowers and hand-crafted oak furnishings and one has a bathroom with a retractable roof!

6 rooms ☕ – 🚹£ 125/145 🚹🚹£ 150/190

Town plan: B1-c – *Chapel St* ✉ *TR18 4AQ* – ✆ *01736 362024*
– *www.chapelhouse.pz.co.uk*

The symbol 🐌 guarantees a peaceful night's sleep.

Chy-An-Mor

TOWNHOUSE · PERSONALISED This fine Georgian townhouse overlooks the promenade; fittingly, its name means 'House of the Sea'. Bedrooms have lovely soft furnishings - two have 6ft cast iron beds. In the evening, twinkling garden lights welcome you home and at breakfast they offer homemade muffins, Scotch pancakes and granola sundaes.

9 rooms - £ 48 £ 85/98

Town plan: B1-e - *15 Regent Terr ✉ TR18 4DW - ✆ 01736 363441 - www.chyanmor.co.uk - Closed November-March*

PERRANUTHNOE - Cornwall ➜ See Marazion

PERSHORE

Worcestershire - Pop. 7 125 - Regional map n° **10**-C3

Belle House

TRADITIONAL BRITISH · TRADITIONAL DÉCOR XX A pleasantly restored Georgian house in the centre of town, offering classically based cooking with modern touches; be sure to try the homemade bread. The well-stocked 'traiteur' selling freshly prepared takeaway dishes is a hit.

Menu £ 27/37 **s**

Bridge St ✉ WR10 1AJ - ✆ 01386 555055 - www.belle-house.co.uk - Closed first 2 weeks January, 25-30 December, Sunday, Monday and Tuesday

Barn

TRADITIONAL · COSY A hugely characterful series of hillside outbuildings, run by a charming owner. There's a homely beamed lounge and three warmly decorated bedrooms; one even boasts a sauna. The apple juice comes from the fruit trees in the garden.

3 rooms - £ 65/75 £ 95

Pensham Hill House, Pensham ✉ WR10 3HA - Southeast : 1 mi by B 4084 - ✆ 01386 555270 - www.pensham-barn.co.uk

at Eckington Southwest: 4 mi by A4104 on B4080

Eckington Manor

MODERN CUISINE · DESIGN XX You'll find this proudly run 13C manor house and its characterful, converted barns on a 300 acre farm. In the restaurant, a husband and wife duo offer a constantly evolving set priced menu of refined, classical dishes which feature plenty of farm produce. For those who want to get involved there's a cookery school, along with stylish bedrooms for those wishing to stay.

Menu £ 48

17 rooms - £ 119/169 £ 129/249

Manor Farm, Hammock Rd ✉ WR10 3BH - (via Drakes Bridge Rd) - ✆ 01386 751600 - www.eckingtonmanor.co.uk - dinner only and Sunday lunch - Closed 25-26 December, 2-16 January, Sunday dinner, Monday and Tuesday

PETERBOROUGH

Peterborough - Pop. 161 707 - Regional map n° **8**-A2

Prévost

CREATIVE BRITISH · DESIGN XX Enter via an alleyway into a bright, spacious room, where local artists' work is displayed on the walls and the tables overlook a small kitchen garden. Choose from 3 set menus, where attractive dishes have a creative Scandic style.

Menu £ 33/75 - tasting menu only

20 Priestgate ✉ PE1 1JA - ✆ 01733 313623 (booking essential) - www.prevostpeterborough.co.uk - Closed last 2 weeks August, 1-14 January, 25 December and Sunday-Tuesday

Beehive

TRADITIONAL BRITISH • PUB Set just off the ring road, with a smart, modern interior, a zinc-topped bar and a mix of seating from high stools to armchairs. From sharing boards to 28-day aged steaks, dishes are well-presented, flavoursome and satisfying.

Menu £ 17 (weekday dinner) – Carte £ 21/40

62 Albert Pl ✉ PE1 1DD – ✆ 01733 310600 – www.beehivepub.co.uk – Closed 1 January and Sunday dinner

at Glinton North: 5 mi off A15

Blue Bell

TRADITIONAL BRITISH • PUB Characterful 18C pub in a pretty village. A colourful flower display greets you and there's a terrace and garden hidden at the back. Menus offer plenty of choice, including satisfying classics and tasty desserts.

Menu £ 14 (weekday lunch) – Carte £ 23/39

10 High St ✉ PE6 7LS – ✆ 01733 252285 – www.thebluebellglinton.co.uk – Closed Sunday dinner

PETERSFIELD

Hampshire – Pop. 14 974 – Regional map n° **4**-C2

JSW (Jake Watkins)

MODERN BRITISH • INTIMATE XXX A smart former inn on the main road through this busy town; it dates from the 17C and features heavy beams and a modern rustic style. The confident chef delivers well-judged, classical cooking with recognisable combinations of ingredients and a touch of originality. An impressive, well-priced wine list accompanies. Simply furnished bedrooms; continental breakfast.

→ Watermelon gazpacho with crab mayonnaise. Chicken with girolles, wild garlic and asparagus. Strawberry and elderflower cheesecake.

Menu £ 45/55 **s**

4 rooms – †£ 95/115 ††£ 125/145

20 Dragon St ✉ GU31 4JJ – ✆ 01730 262030 (booking essential) – www.jswrestaurant.com – Closed 2 weeks April, 2 weeks August, Sunday dinner, Monday, Tuesday and lunch Wedesday

PETWORTH

West Sussex – Pop. 2 544 – Regional map n° **4**-C2

Leconfield

MODERN BRITISH • CONTEMPORARY DÉCOR XX Beside the Hungry Guest Bakery is their tastefully furnished restaurant with a cobbled walled courtyard. Modern dishes are made up of many different elements and provide a great range of flavours; desserts are a highlight.

Menu £ 27 (weekday lunch) – Carte £ 34/48

New St ✉ GU28 0AS – ✆ 01798 345111 – www.theleconfield.co.uk – Closed 25 December, Sunday dinner, Monday and lunch Tuesday

Old Railway Station

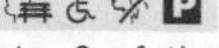

HISTORIC • PERSONALISED The perfect place for train enthusiasts: 8 of the 10 bedrooms are sited in wonderfully restored, genuine Pullman carriages which display impressive marquetry. They are sited at what was the platform; check in at the ticket booth.

10 rooms – †£ 82/120 ††£ 110/198

✉ GU28 0JF – South : 1.5 mi by A 285 – ✆ 01798 342346 – www.old-station.co.uk – Closed 23-26 December

at Tillington West: 1 mi on A272

Horse Guards Inn

REGIONAL CUISINE • RUSTIC In the heart of a quiet village sits this charming mid-17C inn, with views over the valley from its lavender-filled garden. Cooking mixes the rustic and the more elaborate and local seafood stands out. Service is chatty and willing. Bedrooms are charmingly understated; families can book the cottage next door.

Carte £ 23/38

3 rooms – £ 100/130 £ 110/150

Upperton Rd ✉ GU28 9AF – ✆ 01798 342332 – www.thehorseguardsinn.co.uk – Closed 25-26 December

at Lickfold Northwest : 6 mi by A 272✉ Petworth

Lickfold Inn

MODERN BRITISH • COSY XX A pretty Grade II listed brick and timber pub with a characterful lounge-bar serving small plates and a formal first floor restaurant. Terse descriptions hide the true complexities of the innovative dishes, which echo the seasons and are given a touch of theatre. Staff are friendly and eager to please.

Menu £ 24 (lunch) – Carte £ 35/53

Highstead Ln ✉ GU28 9EY – ✆ 01789 532535 (booking essential) – www.thelickfoldinn.co.uk – Closed 2 weeks January, Sunday dinner, Monday except bank holidays and Tuesday

PICKERING

North Yorkshire – Pop. 6 588 – Regional map n° **13**-C1

White Swan Inn

HISTORIC • COSY Characterful 17C coaching inn – its cosy bar and lounge decorated in modern hues. Bedrooms are appealing and come with smart bathrooms; those in the outbuildings have heated stone floors and one even has a bath in the lounge. The brasserie-style restaurant specialises in meats and grills.

21 rooms – £ 129/139 £ 159/169 – 2 suites

Market Pl ✉ YO18 7AA – ✆ 01751 472288 – www.white-swan.co.uk

17 Burgate

TOWNHOUSE • PERSONALISED The stained glass window on the stairway of this classic Georgian townhouse is a talking point and the garden behind is a pleasant place to relax. Bedrooms are spacious and individually styled. Local ingredients feature at breakfast.

3 rooms – £ 85/115 £ 90/115

17 Burgate ✉ YO18 7AU – ✆ 01751 473463 – www.17burgate.co.uk – Restricted opening in spring and winter

at Sinnington Northwest: 4 mi by A170✉ York

Fox and Hounds

TRADITIONAL BRITISH • PUB It's always a good sign if a pub has regulars and this pretty, traditional 18C inn has plenty. What keeps them coming back is the generously proportioned, hearty Yorkshire cooking: pub classics, slow braises and plenty of game in season. Stay the night in one of the homely, individually decorated bedrooms.

Carte £ 25/50

10 rooms – £ 59/84 £ 70/170

Main St ✉ YO62 6SQ – ✆ 01751 431577 – www.thefoxandhoundsinn.co.uk – Closed 25-27 December

PICKHILL

North Yorkshire – ✉ Thirsk – Pop. 401 – Regional map n° **13**-B1

Nags Head Country Inn

TRADITIONAL CUISINE • PUB Quirky pub with a rustic open-fired bar filled with over 700 framed ties and a dining room with booths and hunting prints. Blackboard menus list plenty of classics, accompanied by seasonal vegetables and a jug of gravy; the owner is an avid shooter, so game season is a good time to visit. Bedrooms are cosy.

Carte £ 15/41

7 rooms – †£ 60/80 ††£ 80/120

✉ YO7 4JG
– ☎ 01845 567391 – www.nagsheadpickhill.co.uk – Closed 25 December

PIFF'S ELM – Gloucestershire ➔ See Cheltenham

PILSLEY

Derbyshire – Regional map n° **9**-A1

Devonshire Arms

TRADITIONAL BRITISH • INN Traditional pub dishes get a makeover on the menu sourced from the Chatsworth Estate; servings are generous and dishes, satisfyingly filling. The stylish, contemporary bedrooms were designed by the Duchess of Devonshire. Stock up in the nearby Chatsworth Farm shop before going home.

Carte £ 21/36

13 rooms – †£ 80/250 ††£ 94/264

✉ DE45 1UL
– ☎ 01246 583258 (booking advisable) – www.devonshirepilsley.co.uk

PLUMTREE – Nottinghamshire ➔ See Nottingham

PLYMOUTH

Plymouth – Pop. 234 982 – Regional map n° **1**-C2

Barbican Kitchen

INTERNATIONAL • DESIGN XX An informal eatery in the Plymouth Gin Distillery (where gin was once distilled for the Navy). Brasserie menus offer a good choice of simply cooked dishes, with classic comfort food to the fore; vegetarians are well catered for.

Menu £ 17 (lunch and early dinner) – Carte £ 24/49 **s**

Town plan: C1-u – *Black Friars Distillery, 60 Southside St ✉ PL1 2LQ*
– ☎ 01752 604448 (booking advisable) – www.barbicankitchen.com – Closed 25-26 December, dinner 31 December and Sunday

Greedy Goose

MODERN BRITISH • ELEGANT XX Smart restaurant housed in a delightful building dating from 1482 and named after the children's book 'Chocolate Mousse for Greedy Goose'. Cooking is modern and flavoursome and the local beef is superb. Sit in the 'quad' in summer.

Menu £ 13 (lunch and early dinner) – Carte £ 26/59

Town plan: B1-n – *Prysten House, Finewell St ✉ PL1 2AE*
– ☎ 01752 252001 – www.thegreedygoose.co.uk – Closed Christmas and Monday

Rockfish 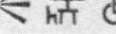

SEAFOOD • RUSTIC X This buzzy quayside shack is ideal for those in 'holiday mode'. The rustic interior features reclaimed wood, hull-shaped banquettes and seaside snaps. Simply prepared seafood sits on greaseproof paper, atop stainless steel plates.

Carte £ 20/44

Town plan: C2-r – *Sutton Harbour, Cox Side, 3 Rope Walk ✉ PL4 OLB*
– ☎ 01752 255974 – www.therockfish.co.uk – Closed 25 December

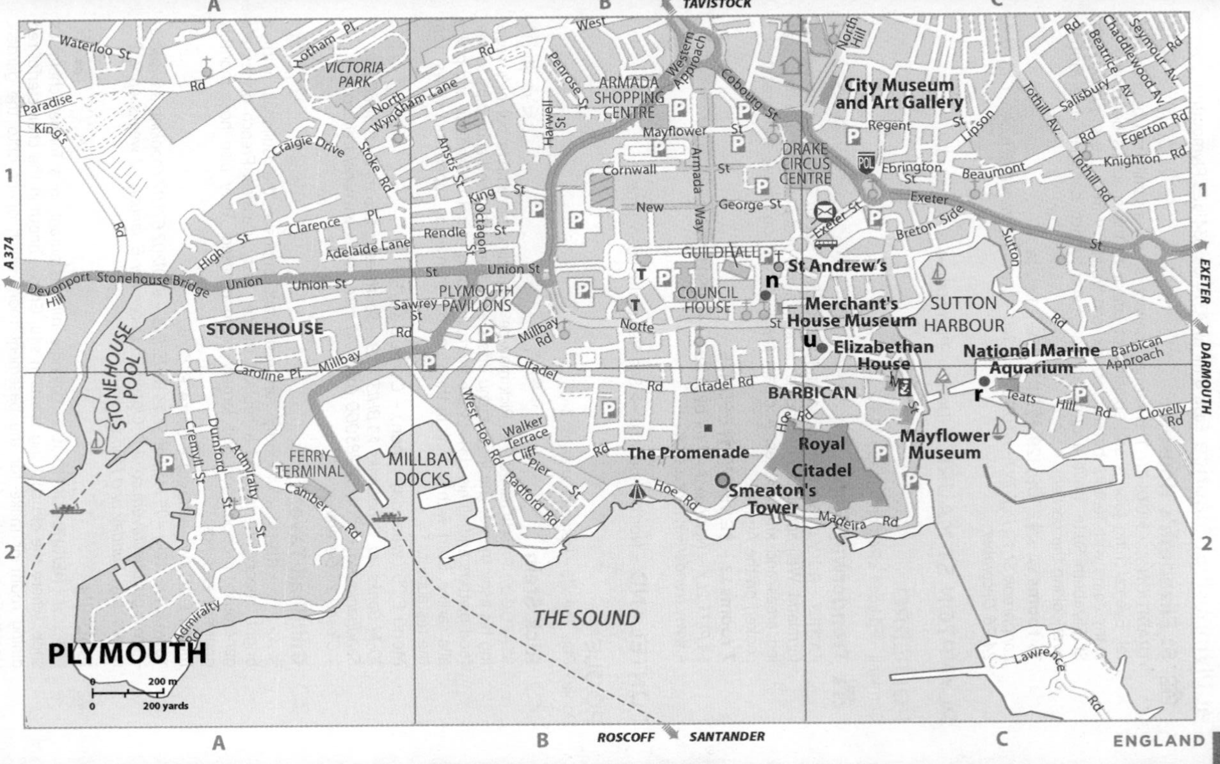
PLYMOUTH
0
200 m
0
200 yards
TAVISTOCK
EXETER
DARMOUTH
ROSCOFF
SANTANDER
A 374
A
B
C
1
2
City Museum and Art Gallery
St Andrew's
Merchant's House Museum
Elizabethan House
National Marine Aquarium
Mayflower Museum
Royal Citadel
Smeaton's Tower
The Promenade
BARBICAN
SUTTON HARBOUR
STONEHOUSE
STONEHOUSE POOL
THE SOUND
VICTORIA PARK
ARMADA SHOPPING CENTRE
DRAKE CIRCUS CENTRE
GUILDHALL
COUNCIL HOUSE
PLYMOUTH PAVILIONS
FERRY TERMINAL
MILLBAY DOCKS
Waterloo St
Paradise
King's
Hotham Pl.
North
Wyndham Lane
Craigie Drive
Stoke Rd
Clarence Pl.
Adelaide Lane
High St
Devonport Hill
Stonehouse Bridge
Union St
Anstis St
King St
Octagon St
Rendle St
Harwell St
Penrose St
West
Western Approach
Cobourg St
Mayflower St
Armada Way
Cornwall St
New St
George St
Regent St
Ebrington St
Exeter St
Breton Side
Sutton Rd
North Hill
Lipson
Beaumont
Tothill Av.
Tothill Rd
Salisbury Rd
Beatrice Av.
Chaddlewood Av.
Seymour Av.
Egerton Rd
Knighton Rd
Sawrey St
Millbay Rd
Notte St
Caroline Pl.
Citadel Rd
Hoe Rd
Madeira Rd
West Hoe Rd
Walker Terrace
Cliff
Pier St
Radford Rd
Cremyll St
Durnford St
Admiralty St
Admiralty Rd
Camber Rd
Barbican Approach
Teats Hill Rd
Clovelly Rd
Lawrence Rd
ENGLAND

at Plympton St Maurice East: 6 mi by A374 on B3416✉ Plymouth

St Elizabeth's House

TRADITIONAL · MODERN This former convent is now a family-run boutique hotel. Eye-catching fabrics add splashes of colour to the spacious bedrooms and many come with feature bathrooms; you can watch TV from the spa bath in the St Elizabeth Suite. Have a drink at the pewter-topped bar then dine formally overlooking the gardens.

15 rooms – †£ 109/129 ††£ 119/259 – 1 suite

Longbrook St ✉ PL7 1NJ – ✆ 01752 344840 – www.stelizabeths.co.uk – Closed 24-26 December

PLYMPTON ST MAURICE Devon – Plymouth ➔ See Plymouth

POLPERRO

Cornwall – ✉ Looe – Regional map n° **1**-B2

Trenderway Farm

FAMILY · RURAL 16C farmhouse and outbuildings set in 206 acres of working farmland. Well-appointed bedrooms come in a mix of styles and some have seating areas and kitchenettes. A cream tea is served on arrival and breakfast is cooked on the Aga.

7 rooms – †£ 95/175 ††£ 95/175

✉ PL13 2LY – Northeast : 2 mi by A 387 – ✆ 01503 272214 – www.trenderwayfarm.co.uk

PONTELAND – Northumberland ➔ See Newcastle upon Tyne

POOLE

Poole – Pop. 154 718 – Regional map n° **2**-C3

Rick Stein

SEAFOOD · FASHIONABLE XX Rick may be expanding his empire but he's keeping his fishy theme. The large menu offers everything from cod and chips to seafood platters and all his classics are there, including turbot hollandaise and plaice alla carlina. Start with a drink in the sleek bar then enjoy superb sea views from the restaurant.

Menu £ 25 (weekday lunch) – Carte £ 30/58

10-14 Banks Rd, Sandbanks ✉ BH13 7QB – Southeast : 4.75 mi by B 3068 and Sandbanks Rd – ✆ 01202 283000 (booking essential) – www.rickstein.com – Closed 25 December

Guildhall Tavern

SEAFOOD · BISTRO XX Proudly run restaurant opposite the Guildhall, with a bright, cheery interior and a nautical theme. Tasty, classical French dishes are generously proportioned and largely seafood-based. They also host monthly gourmet evenings.

Menu £ 26 (weekdays) – Carte £ 27/62

Town plan: A2-x – *15 Market St ✉ BH15 1NB – ✆ 01202 671717 (booking advisable) – www.guildhalltavern.co.uk – Closed 25 December-6 January, 2 weeks April, 2 weeks July, Sunday and Monday*

Isabel's

FRENCH · NEIGHBOURHOOD XX Lovingly run restaurant in a former chemist's shop, where the old shelving is still in situ. Grab a booth in the characterful red dining room or make for the basement room which opens onto the garden. Hearty French dishes feature.

Menu £ 25/36 – Carte £ 30/43

32 Station Rd, Lower Parkstone ✉ BH14 8UD – East : 2 mi by B 3069 off A 35 – ✆ 01202 747885 (booking essential) – www.isabelsrestaurant.co.uk – Closed Monday, Sunday dinner and lunch Tuesday-Wednesday

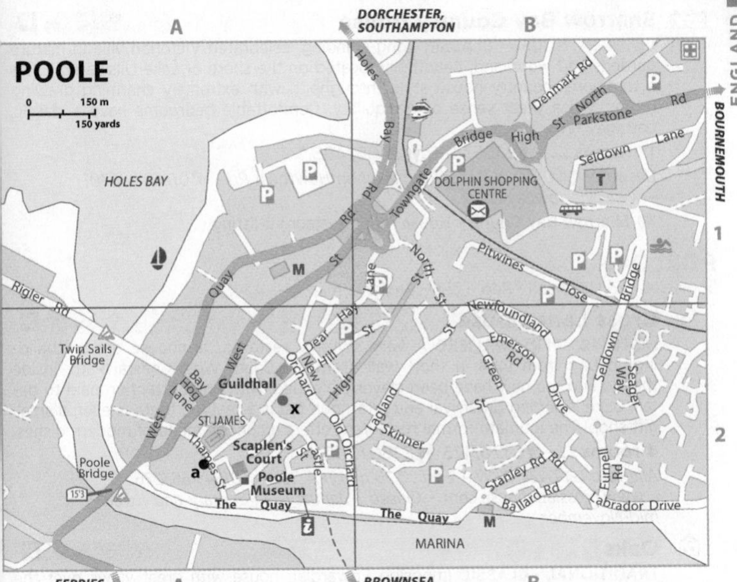

Hotel du Vin

TOWNHOUSE • MODERN A strikingly extended Queen Anne property in the old town. Smart guest areas have eye-catching wine-themed murals; stylish, modern bedrooms are named after wine or champagne houses – one boasts an 8ft bed and twin roll-top baths. Local produce features in classic French dishes and there's a 300 bin wine list.

38 rooms – £ 109/159 £ 109/199

Town plan: A2-a – *7-11 Thames St.* ✉ *BH15 1JN* – *✆ 01305 819027 – www.hotelduvin.com*

Harbour Heights

HISTORIC • CONTEMPORARY 1920s whitewashed hotel, perched on the hillside, overlooking Poole Bay and Brownsea Island; the modern lounge-bar boasts a superb three-tiered terrace which makes the most of the view. Contemporary bedrooms come with good mod cons and smart bathrooms. The open-plan restaurant serves a modern menu.

38 rooms – £ 84/269 £ 94/354

73 Haven Rd, Sandbanks ✉ *BH13 7LW – Southeast : 3 mi by A 35 and B 3369 – ✆ 01202 707272 – www.fjbhotels.co.uk*

POOLEY BRIDGE

Cumbria – Regional map n° **12**-B2

Sharrow Bay Country House

CLASSIC CUISINE • ELEGANT XXX Two delightful dining rooms in a beautifully located, traditional country house; 'Lakeside' has superb views over Lake Ullswater. Service is formal and dishes are as classic as they come; don't miss the 'icky sticky toffee pudding'.

Menu £ 25/68

Sharrow Bay Country House Hotel, Ullswater ✉ *CA10 2LZ – South : 2 mi on Howtown Rd – ✆ 017684 86301 (booking essential) – www.sharrowbay.co.uk*

Sharrow Bay Country House

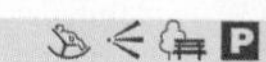

COUNTRY HOUSE • CLASSIC Long-standing, celebrated Victorian villa in mature gardens and woodland; beautifully located on the shore of Lake Ullswater. It has a traditional country house style throughout, with extremely charming drawing rooms and a great sense of tranquillity. Comfortable bedrooms have a classic, cottagey feel.

17 rooms – £ 165/485 £ 165/485

Ullswater ✉ CA10 2LZ – South : 2 mi on Howtown Rd – ✆ 017684 86301 – www.sharrowbay.co.uk

Sharrow Bay Country House – See restaurant listing

PORLOCK

Somerset – ✉ Minehead – Pop. 1 395 – Regional map n° **2**-A2

Cross Lane House

HISTORIC • PERSONALISED A very stylishly restored farmhouse and outbuildings dating from 1484; a short walk from the South West Coastal Path. Inside the old and the new have been cleverly blended, with great attention paid to detail. Cake is served on arrival and afternoon tea is a feature; there is even a small gift shop! The intimate formal restaurant offers a concise menu of modern dishes.

4 rooms – £ 120/175 £ 150/200

Allerford ✉ TA24 8HW – East : 1.25 mi on A 39 – ✆ 01643 863276 – www.crosslanehouse.com – Closed 3 January-12 February and 1 week mid-November

Oaks

TRADITIONAL • CLASSIC Imposing Edwardian house with great views over the weir and bay; the builder quarried the stone used to build it himself. The antique-filled entrance hall boasts a beautiful parquet floor and the large bedrooms come with fresh fruit and smart bathrooms. The dining room offers a classical daily menu and views from every table; cake is served on arrival in the snug lounge.

7 rooms – £ 120/130 £ 160/180

✉ TA24 8ES – ✆ 01643 862265 – www.oakshotel.co.uk – Closed November-March

PORT ISAAC

Cornwall – Regional map n° **1**-B2

Restaurant Nathan Outlaw (Nathan Outlaw)

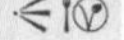

SEAFOOD • INTIMATE XX A smart yet casual restaurant in a great headland location – the views from the first floor dining room are stunning. No-choice set menus focus on ultra-fresh fish and shellfish landed at the nearby harbour. Classical combinations are very carefully crafted, keeping the focus firmly on the main ingredient.

➔ Crab with St Enodoc asparagus. Turbot, smoked mushroom and bacon. Banana, chocolate, peanut and lime.

Menu £ 62/125 – tasting menu only

6 New Rd ✉ PL29 3SB – ✆ 01208 880896 (booking essential) – www.nathan-outlaw.com – dinner only and lunch Friday-Saturday – Closed January and Sunday-Tuesday

Outlaw's Fish Kitchen

SEAFOOD • INTIMATE X This intimate 15C building has low ceilings and wonky walls and is found in the heart of this famous harbourside fishing village. The day boats guide the menu, which offers a delicious mix of old favourites and appealing small plates – 3 or 4 dishes should suffice. Cornish gins, beers and wines also feature.

➔ Fennel-cured salmon with radish and salad cream. Baked hake with leeks, bacon and seaweed butter. Vanilla mousse, almonds and blood orange.

Menu £ 45 (dinner) – Carte £ 30/40

1 Middle St ✉ PL29 3RH – ✆ 01208 881183 (booking essential at dinner) – www.outlaws.co.uk/fishkitchen – Closed January, Monday October-May and Sunday

PORTHLEVEN

Cornwall – Pop. 3 059 – Regional map n° **1**-A3

Kota

ASIAN INFLUENCES • RUSTIC XX Welcoming harbourside granary with thick stone walls, a tiled floor and an array of wood furnishings; its name means 'shellfish' in Maori. Menus mix unfussy and more elaborate dishes and display subtle Asian influences courtesy of the owner's Chinese and Malaysian background. Many of the ingredients are foraged. Bedrooms are simply furnished – one overlooks the harbour.

Menu £ 25 – Carte £ 24/43

2 rooms – †£ 60/95 ††£ 75/110

Harbour Head ✉ TR13 9JA – ✆ 01326 562407 – www.kotarestaurant.co.uk – dinner only and lunch Friday-Saturday – Closed January, 25-26 December, Sunday and Monday

Square

MODERN CUISINE • SIMPLE X Small harbourside bistro: in summer, bag a table on the terrace; in winter, cosy up and watch the waves crash on the harbour wall. Coffee and cakes are followed by snacks and sharing platters, with more structure at dinner. Well-prepared modern classics have punchy flavours; go for the freshly landed seafood.

Menu £ 17 (lunch) – Carte £ 27/35

7 Fore St ✉ TR13 9HQ – ✆ 01326 573911 – www.thesquareatporthleven.co.uk – Closed Sunday in winter

Rick Stein

SEAFOOD • FASHIONABLE XX This old harbourside clay store has been transformed into a smart restaurant with floor to ceiling windows and a first floor terrace. Top quality seafood small plates are inspired by Rick Stein's travels and sharing is encouraged.

Menu £ 22 (lunch) – Carte £ 24/39

Mount Pleasant Rd ✉ TR13 9JS – ✆ 01326 565636 – www.rickstein.com – Closed 25 December, Sunday dinner and Monday in winter

PORTLOE

Cornwall – Regional map n° **1**-B3

Lugger

INN • PERSONALISED This 17C smugglers' inn sits in a picturesque fishing village and affords dramatic views over the rugged bay. It's snug and cosy throughout, with open fires, low ceilings and friendly, personal service. Have a drink on the terrace and dinner in the elegant dining room, which serves seafood fresh from the bay.

24 rooms – †£ 150/320 ††£ 155/325

✉ TR2 5RD – ✆ 01872 501322 – www.luggerhotel.co.uk

PORTSCATHO

Cornwall – ✉ Truro – Regional map n° **1**-B3

Driftwood

MODERN CUISINE • DESIGN XX Bright, New England style restaurant in an attractive house, in a peaceful clifftop setting; it's delightfully run by a friendly, efficient team and boasts superb views out to sea. Unfussy, modern, seasonally pertinent dishes display technical adroitness and feature excellent flavour and texture combinations.

➜ Cuttlefish, cauliflower and samphire. Beef fillet with braised neck and red wine jus. Thunder and lightning tart.

Menu £ 65

Driftwood Hotel, Rosevine ✉ TR2 5EW – North : 2 mi by A 3078 – ✆ 01872 580644 (booking essential) – www.driftwoodhotel.co.uk – dinner only – Closed 11 December-1 February

 **Driftwood** 

COUNTRY HOUSE · PERSONALISED Charming clifftop hotel looking out over mature grounds, which stretch down to the shore and a private beach. Stylish, contemporary guest areas are decorated with pieces of driftwood. Smart bedrooms – in the main house and annexed cottages – have a good level of modern facilities; some have decked terraces.

15 rooms – £169/244 £215/275

Rosevine ✉ TR2 5EW – North : 2 mi by A 3078 – ✆ 01872 580644 – www.driftwoodhotel.co.uk – Closed 11 December-1 February

✿ **Driftwood** – See restaurant listing

 **Rosevine** 

COUNTRY HOUSE · ELEGANT Dramatically refurbished country house overlooking the sea, with modern guest areas and stylish bedrooms featuring kitchenettes. They cater strongly for families: children have their own lounge, they offer family high tea and the large grounds have a pool and play area. The all-day brasserie uses local produce.

15 rooms – £109/399 £139/429

Rosevine ✉ TR2 5EW – North : 2 mi by A 3078 – ✆ 01872 580206 – www.rosevine.co.uk

PORTSMOUTH and SOUTHSEA

Portsmouth – Pop. 238 137 – Regional map n° **4**-B3

Restaurant 27 

MODERN BRITISH · NEIGHBOURHOOD XX This elegant restaurant is professionally and passionately run. Attractively presented, contemporary dishes have a slight Scandic style; they only serve tasting menus, supplemented by a set priced Sunday lunch.

Menu £ 45/55 – tasting menu only

27a South Par, Southsea ✉ PO5 2JF – ✆ 023 9287 6272 (booking advisable) – www.restaurant27.com – dinner only and Sunday lunch – Closed 25-26 December, Sunday dinner, Monday and Tuesday

Clarence 

TOWNHOUSE · PERSONALISED Immaculately kept, bay windowed house, just a short walk from the sea. Bedrooms come in various sizes and feature contemporary décor, superb modern bathrooms and pleasing extra touches; some have a TV inset in the bathroom wall.

8 rooms – £95/165 £115/245

Clarence Rd, Southsea ✉ PO5 2LQ – ✆ 023 9200 9777 – www.theclarencehotel.co.uk

POSTBRIDGE

Devon – Regional map n° **1**-C2

 **Lydgate House** 

TRADITIONAL · COSY Personally run whitewashed house, set in a secluded spot high on the moors and accessed via a narrow track. Homely, cosy lounge and conservatory restaurant offering home-cooked local produce. Bedrooms are named after birds; many offer lovely views over the 36 acre grounds and the East Dart River.

7 rooms – £50/61 £95/132

✉ PL20 6TJ – ✆ 01822 880209 – www.lydgatehouse.co.uk – Closed January

PULHAM MARKET

Norfolk – ✉ Diss – Pop. 722 – Regional map n° **8**-C2

Old Bakery

TOWNHOUSE · CLASSIC Pretty 16C former bakery just off the green. The characterful interior features exposed beams and inglenooks. There's a homely lounge and breakfast room and good-sized bedrooms with modern facilities. Don't miss the 'Baker's Breakfast'.

5 rooms – †£ 65/90 ††£ 85/105

Church Walk ✉ IP21 4SL
– ✆ 01379 676492 – www.theoldbakery.net – Closed Christmas-New Year

PAXFORD – Gloucestershire ➜ See Chipping Camden

RADNAGE

Buckinghamshire – Regional map n° **6**-C2

The Mash Inn

MODERN BRITISH · INN Characterful 18C pub with flagged floors, exposed timbers, hand-crafted oak tables, and great country views from the terrace. Top quality local and garden ingredients lead the handwritten daily menu and the bespoke wood-fired chargrill is used to great effect. Bedrooms are modern and simply furnished.

Menu £ 19 (lunch) – Carte £ 31/48

4 rooms – †£ 100/130 ††£ 100/130

Horseshoe Rd, Bennett End ✉ HP14 4EB – North : 1.25 mi by Town End rd
– ✆ 01494 482440 (booking advisable) – www.themashinn.com
– Closed Sunday dinner, Monday and Tuesday

RAMSBOTTOM

Greater Manchester – Pop. 17 872 – Regional map n° **11**-B2

Levanter

SPANISH · TAPAS BAR Joe has a passion for all things Spanish – he's even a trained flamenco guitarist – so, unsurprisingly, his sweet little tapas bar has an authentic feel. The menu is dictated by market produce; be sure to try some of the freshly sliced Iberico ham. He also owns the nearby Basque-style Baratxuri pintxo bar.

Carte £ 20/25

10 Square St ✉ BL0 9BE
– ✆ 01706 551530 (bookings not accepted) – www.levanterfinefoods.co.uk
– Closed Monday, Tuesday and lunch Wednesday

RAMSBURY

Wiltshire – Pop. 1 540 – Regional map n° **2**-D2

Bell

MODERN CUISINE · INN Charming 16C pub with stylish, well-appointed bedrooms. Dine on pub favourites among hop-covered beams in the open-fired bar or sit on smart tartan banquettes in the crisply laid dining room and choose from more ambitious, accomplished dishes. You'll find the locals at the back in 'Café Bella'.

Carte £ 28/52

9 rooms – †£ 110/120 ††£ 130/160

The Square ✉ SN8 2PE
– ✆ 01672 520230 – www.ramsbury.com – Closed 25 December

RAMSEY - Ramsey ➔ See Man (Isle of)

RAMSHOLT
Suffolk – Regional map n° **8**-D3

Ramsholt Arms

TRADITIONAL BRITISH • SIMPLE Honest, well-priced pub food and Suffolk ales in a great location. This striking inn is set against the spectacular backdrop of the River Deben; particularly magnificent at sunset and on summer days. Plenty of room on the terrace.

Carte £ 20/31

Dock Rd ✉ IP12 3AB – ✆ 01394 411209 – www.theramsholtarms.com – Closed weekdays January-mid February and Monday-Wednesday dinner October-April

RASKELF
North Yorkshire – Pop. 519 – Regional map n° **13**-B2

Rascills

TRADITIONAL BRITISH • FRIENDLY XX Experienced husband and wife team, Richard and Lindsey, run this welcoming restaurant with pride. It's set on a working farm in a charming village and has a welcoming feel. Dishes are honest, unfussy and prepared with care.

Menu £ 39 (dinner) – Carte lunch £ 31/50

Village Farm, Howker Ln ✉ YO61 3LF – ✆ 01347 822031 – www.rascillsrestaurant.vpweb.co.uk – Closed first 10 day January, Sunday-Tuesday and Wednesday dinner

READING
Reading – Pop. 218 705 – Regional map n° **6**-C3

Forbury's

MODERN CUISINE • FASHIONABLE XX In a city centre square near the law courts, with a pleasant terrace, a leather-furnished bar-lounge and a smart, spacious dining room decorated with wine paraphernalia. Menus offer French-inspired dishes. Popular monthly wine events.

Menu £ 26/28 (weekday dinner) – Carte £ 31/57

1 Forbury Sq ✉ RG1 3BB – ✆ 0118 957 4044 – www.forburys.co.uk – Closed 1-5 January and Sunday

London Street Brasserie

TRADITIONAL CUISINE • BRASSERIE X Bright, 200 year old building which was once a post office; the two decked terraces and some of the first floor tables overlook the River Kennet. The extensive menu offers something for everyone and dishes are stout and satisfying.

Menu £ 17 (lunch and early dinner) – Carte £ 34/56

2-4 London St ✉ RG1 4PN – ✆ 0118 950 5036 (booking essential) – www.londonstbrasserie.co.uk – Closed 25 December

The Forbury

TOWNHOUSE • DESIGN An impressive former civic hall overlooking Forbury Square Gardens; now a smart townhouse hotel where contemporary designs meet with original features. Luxurious bedrooms come with Nespresso machines, fridges and Bang & Olufsen electronics. The chic basement bar and restaurant offer modern menus.

23 rooms – †£ 174/298 ††£ 174/298

26 Forbury ✉ RG1 3EJ – ✆ 0118 952 7770 – www.roseatehotels.com

Holiday Inn

BUSINESS • MODERN Conveniently located for the M4, with spacious open-plan guest areas, smart function facilities and a well-equipped leisure club. Stylish, uniform bedrooms come with good facilities and compact, up-to-date bathrooms. Have snacks in the comfy lounge or classic dishes in the formal split-level restaurant.

174 rooms – †£ 63/199 ††£ 63/199 – ☕£ 15

Wharfedale Rd, Winnersh Triangle ✉ RG41 5TS – Southeast : 4.5 mi by A 4 and A 3290 off Winnerish rd – ✆ 0118 944 0444 – www.hireadinghotel.com

at Sonning-on-Thames Northeast: 4.25 mi by A4 on B4446

French Horn

TRADITIONAL BRITISH • ELEGANT XXX Beautifully located, 200 year old coaching inn, set on a bank of the Thames fringed by weeping willows; on sunny days head for the splendid terrace. The formal dining room has delightful views over the river and gardens and offers a classical menu of dishes from yesteryear – a gueridon trolley adds to the theatre. The cosy bedrooms are also traditionally appointed.

Menu £ 31 (weekdays) – Carte £ 45/80 **s**

21 rooms ☕ – †£ 170/225 ††£ 185/235 – 4 suites

✉ RG4 6TN – ✆ 0118 969 2204 – www.thefrenchhorn.co.uk – Closed 2-5 January and dinner 25 December and 1 January

at Shinfield South: 4.25 mi on A327 ✉ Reading

L'Ortolan

FRENCH • INTIMATE XXX Beautiful, red-brick former vicarage with stylish, modern décor, several private dining rooms and a conservatory-lounge overlooking a lovely garden. Cooking is confident and passionate, with well-crafted, classically based dishes showing flair, originality and some playful, artistic touches.

→ Goose liver terrine with blood orange and honey. Poached guinea fowl breast with asparagus and wild garlic. Strawberry parfait, Gariguette strawberries and champagne.

Menu £ 32/65

Church Ln ✉ RG2 9BY – ✆ 0118 988 8500 – www.lortolan.com – Closed 25 December-4 January, Sunday and Monday

REDDITCH

Worcestershire – Pop. 81 919 – Regional map n° **10**-C2

Old Rectory House

TRADITIONAL • PERSONALISED A part-Elizabethan, part-Georgian former rectory set in well-tended gardens. Guest areas have a cosy, country house feel. Bedrooms are split between the house and stables; the latter, with their exposed beams, are the most characterful. Dine in the bright conservatory restaurant overlooking the garden.

10 rooms ☕ – †£ 85/120 ††£ 85/149

Ipsley Ln, Ipsley ✉ B98 0AP – Southeast : 2.5 mi by A 4023 off B 4497 – ✆ 01527 523000 – www.oldrectoryhouse.co.uk – Closed 25 December

REEPHAM

Norfolk – Pop. 2 405 – Regional map n° **8**-C1

Dial House

TRADITIONAL CUISINE • SIMPLE X An attractive Georgian house in a pretty village; all of its furniture, fabrics and antiques are for sale. Dine in the endearing Garden Room or in the Aga Room, where you can watch them making pancakes. Cooking is simple, fresh and tasty. Charming bedrooms are named after places from the Grand Tour.

Carte £ 27/36

8 rooms ☕ – †£ 100/160 ††£ 200/275

7 Market Pl ✉ NR10 4JJ – ✆ 01603 879900 – www.thedialhouse.org.uk

REETH

North Yorkshire – Pop. 724 – Regional map n° **13**-B1

 **Burgoyne** 

TRADITIONAL • CLASSIC A late Georgian house with a cosy, comforting feel, set in a lovely spot overlooking the village green and the Yorkshire Dales. The two lounges are filled with antiques and vases of flowers. Bedrooms are individually styled and traditionally appointed. The elegant dining room offers an all-encompassing menu.

10 rooms – †£ 70/120 ††£ 100/210

On The Green ✉ DL11 6SN – ✆ 01748 884292 – www.theburgoyne.co.uk – Closed 23-27 December and restricted opening in January

at Langthwaite Northwest: 3.25 mi on Langthwaite rd ✉ Reeth

Charles Bathurst Inn 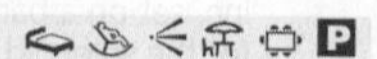

TRADITIONAL CUISINE • PUB Characterful 18C hostelry, set in a peaceful hillside village and offering commanding rural views. Lunchtime sees hearty British pub classics, while more elaborate dishes follow in the evening, with plenty of fish and game in season. Local beers include Black Sheep Ale. Bedrooms are spacious and comfortable.

Carte £ 22/49

19 rooms – †£ 75/135 ††£ 95/140

✉ DL11 6EN – ✆ 0333 700 0779 – www.cbinn.co.uk – Closed 25 December

REIGATE

Surrey – Pop. 22 123 – Regional map n° **4**-D2

Tony Tobin @ The Dining Room

CLASSIC CUISINE • ELEGANT XX Chic, contemporary restaurant with a comfortable atmosphere and professional staff. Cooking demonstrates the chef's classical background whilst also incorporating some international influences. Most plump for the 5 course tasting menu.

Menu £ 28/49

59a High St (1st Floor) ✉ RH2 9AE – ✆ 01737 226650 – www.tonytobinrestaurants.co.uk – Closed 23 December-4 January, Saturday lunch, Sunday dinner and bank holidays

Barbe 

CLASSIC FRENCH • NEIGHBOURHOOD X A long-standing French bistro with a cheery owner and a huge local following. Two main dining areas are strewn with Gallic memorabilia. Simply laid, tightly packed tables. Classical, bi-monthly menu.

Menu £ 23/36

71 Bell St ✉ RH2 7AN – ✆ 01737 241966 – www.labarbe.co.uk – Closed 26-28 December, 1 January, Saturday lunch, Sunday dinner and bank holiday Mondays

RHYDYCROESAU – Shropshire → See Oswestry

RIBCHESTER

Lancashire – Pop. 888 – Regional map n° **11**-B2

Angels 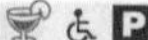

MODERN CUISINE • INTIMATE XXX Smartly converted roadside pub with a cocktail bar and comfy lounge seating. Two formally dressed dining rooms offer a comfortable, intimate dining experience. Classic dishes with a modern edge are tasty, well-balanced and good value.

Menu £ 23 (weekdays) – Carte £ 36/50

Fleet Street Ln ✉ PR3 3ZA – Northwest : 1.5 mi by B 6245 (Longridge Rd) – ✆ 01254 820212 – www.angelsribchester.co.uk – dinner only and Sunday lunch – Closed Monday

RICHMOND

North Yorkshire – Pop. 8 413 – Regional map n° **13**-B1

Frenchgate

MODERN CUISINE • INTIMATE XX Part-dating from the 17C, with two open-fired lounges filled with vivid art, a simply furnished dining room and a lovely terrace and walled garden. Modern, ambitious dishes. Immaculately kept, well-equipped bedrooms; breakfast features local bacon and sausages, and preserves made from berries picked nearby.

Menu £ 29/39

9 rooms – £ 70/198 £ 118/250

59-61 Frenchgate DL10 7AE – 01748 822087 – www.thefrenchgate.co.uk

Easby Hall

COUNTRY HOUSE • PERSONALISED The views of the church, the abbey ruins and the hills are as stunning as this part-18C hall itself. There are two gardens, an orchard, a kitchen garden and a paddock – and even stables for your horse! Inside it's elegant and luxurious. Tea and scones or cocktails are served on arrival, depending on the time.

3 rooms – £ 150 £ 180

Easby DL10 7EU – Southeast : 2.5 mi by A 6108 off B 6271 – 01748 826066 – www.easbyhall.com

at Whashton Northwest : 4.5 mi by A 6108 off Ravensworth rd

Hack & Spade

INN • PERSONALISED The unusual name is a reference to the copper and lead mines that used to operate in the area. Extremely spacious bedrooms are tastefully done out with traditional furnishings and modern comforts. The beamed, open-fired restaurant has a homely feel; a short menu of home-cooked favourites is served Thurs-Sat.

5 rooms – £ 120/140 £ 120/140

DL11 7JL – 01748 823721 – www.hackandspade.com – Closed January and 24-26 and 31 December

RIMPTON

Somerset – Pop. 235 – Regional map n° **2**-C3

White Post

CLASSIC CUISINE • PUB On the Dorset/Somerset border, with stunning views of the West Country. Plenty of pub classics alongside more imaginative creations and quirky touches like piggy nibbles and the Sunday roast board: surely every carnivore's dream dish? Bedrooms are simply furnished: ask for Dorset, which has the best views.

Carte £ 23/42

3 rooms – £ 80 £ 95

BA22 8AR – 01935 851525 – www.thewhitepost.com – Closed Sunday dinner and Monday

RIPLEY

North Yorkshire – Harrogate – Pop. 193 – Regional map n° **13**-B2

Boar's Head

INN • COSY 18C creeper-clad coaching inn, set in an estate-owned village and reputedly furnished from the nearby castle's attics. Family portraits and knick-knacks fill the lounges. Comfy bedrooms are found in the inn, the courtyard and an adjacent house. The all-encompassing menu is served in various different rooms.

25 rooms (dinner included) – £ 106/140 £ 161/201

HG3 3AY – 01423 771888 – www.boarsheadripley.co.uk

RIPLEY
Surrey – Pop. 2 041 – Regional map n° **4**-C1

Clock House

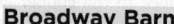

MODERN CUISINE • INTIMATE A beautiful Georgian building with a double-sided clock above the door. The panelled bar leads to an elegant timbered dining room overlooking a delightful garden. Creative cooking has a refined, understated style and displays plenty of finesse. Bold flavours come together in well-balanced combinations.

➜ Seared & cured scallop with apple and ginger. Beef with sweetbreads, brassicas, morels and mustard. Rhubarb with buckwheat and sorrel.

Menu £ 30/70

High St ✉ GU23 6AQ – ✆ 01483 224777 – www.theclockhouserestaurant.co.uk – Closed 2 weeks August, 1 week Easter, Christmas, 1 week January, Sunday, Monday and Tuesday

Anchor

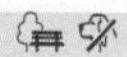

CLASSIC CUISINE • CONTEMPORARY DÉCOR A smart yet rustic pub with a 400 year history, polished slate floors and on-trend grey walls. Despite its name, it's nowhere near the water, but it is close to a famous cycle route, which explains the bicycle-themed interior. Restaurant-style dishes are carefully executed and bursting with flavour.

Menu £ 18 (weekday lunch) – Carte £ 25/47

High St ✉ GU23 6AE – ✆ 01483 211866 – www.ripleyanchor.co.uk – Closed 25 December and Monday except bank holidays

Broadway Barn

TOWNHOUSE • DESIGN This charming double-fronted house spent time as an antiques shop before being converted into a guesthouse. The large open-fired lounge leads to a conservatory breakfast room which overlooks a well-tended garden. Bedrooms display good attention to detail and come with thoughtful extras.

4 rooms – †£ 120 ††£ 120

High St ✉ GU23 6AQ – ✆ 01483 223200 – www.broadwaybarn.com

RIPON
North Yorkshire – Pop. 16 363 – Regional map n° **13**-B2

Bay Tree Farm

TRADITIONAL • COSY 18C sandstone barn on a working beef farm, with a smartly furnished farmhouse interior and country views. The open-fired lounge is hung with farm implements and opens onto the garden. The welcoming owners always make time to talk.

6 rooms – †£ 60/80 ††£ 90/110

Aldfield ✉ HG4 3BE – Southwest : 3.75 mi by B6265 – ✆ 01765 620394 – www.baytreefarm.co.uk

ROCHDALE
Greater Manchester – Pop. 107 926 – Regional map n° **11**-B2

Nutters

MODERN BRITISH • FRIENDLY Enthusiastically run restaurant in a beautiful old manor house – a popular spot for afternoon tea. Appealing menus list modern British dishes with international influences. Can't decide? Go for the 6 course 'Surprise' menu.

Menu £ 17 (weekday lunch) – Carte £ 31/45

Edenfield Rd, Norden ✉ OL12 7TT – West : 3.5 mi on A 680 – ✆ 01706 650167 – www.nuttersrestaurant.com – Closed 27-28 December, 2-3 January and Monday

The Peacock Room

MODERN CUISINE • CHIC XX A winding drive leads up to this Victorian house; bypass the pub and head for the cocktail bar. The restaurant boasts a mirrored-ceiling and two striking chandeliers. Constantly evolving modern menus rely on classic combinations.

Carte £ 29/44

Crimble Hall, Crimble Ln, Bamford ✉ OL11 4AD – West : 2 mi on B 6222 – ✆ 01706 368591 – www.thepeacockroom.com – Closed Monday, Tuesday and lunch Saturday

ROCK

Cornwall – ✉ Wadebridge – Pop. 4 593 – Regional map n° **1**-B2

Dining Room

MODERN BRITISH • NEIGHBOURHOOD XX Immaculately kept, understated restaurant with modern seascapes on the walls; run by a friendly, family-led team. Flavoursome, classically based cooking features local seasonal produce. Everything is homemade, including the butter.

Carte £ 41/53

Pavilion Buildings, Rock Rd ✉ PL27 6JS – ✆ 01208 862622 (booking essential) – www.thediningroomrock.co.uk – dinner only – Closed 6 weeks January-February, Sunday in winter, Monday except bank holidays and Tuesday

St Enodoc

MODERN CUISINE • FRIENDLY X Enjoy great views over the estuary from the floor to ceiling windows of the brasserie or out on the terrace. Cooking is unfussy and full of flavour, with the occasional Spanish touch. Try the fresh shellfish from nearby Porthilly.

Menu £ 28/38

St Enodoc Hotel, ✉ PL27 6LA – ✆ 01208 863394 – www.enodoc-hotel.co.uk – Closed 17 December-25 January

Mariners

TRADITIONAL CUISINE • PUB Two of Cornwall's top ambassadors – Sharp's Brewery and Nathan Outlaw – have come together to run this pub. Satisfying dishes feature local seafood and top quality meats. Sit on the terrace for stunning views of the Camel Estuary.

Carte £ 27/44

Slipway ✉ PL27 6LD – ✆ 01208 863679 – www.themarinersrock.com – Closed 5-21 January and 25 December

St Enodoc

FAMILY • PERSONALISED Beautifully located hotel boasting stunning bay views. There's a strong New England feel throughout, courtesy of striped sofas and pastel coloured woodwork. Most of the contemporary, well-appointed bedrooms have a sea outlook.

20 rooms – †£ 170/495 ††£ 170/495

✉ PL27 6LA – ✆ 01208 863394 – www.enodoc-hotel.co.uk – Closed 17 December-25 January

St Enodoc – See restaurant listing

ROECLIFFE – North Yorkshire → See Boroughbridge

ROMALDKIRK – Durham → See Barnard Castle

ROMSEY

Hampshire - Pop. 16 998 - Regional map n° **4**-A2

Three Tuns

TRADITIONAL BRITISH • PUB Cosy 300 year old pub off the market square. Original features include oak beams and a central bar which divides the place in two - head left if you want to dine. Classic pub dishes are generously proportioned and full of flavour.

Carte £ 16/33

58 Middlebridge St ✉ SO51 8HL
- ✆ 01794 512639 - www.the3tunsromsey.co.uk - Closed Christmas, Easter - Saturday lunch and Sunday dinner

White Horse

INN • CONTEMPORARY Smartly refurbished coaching inn; one of only 12 in the country to have continuously served as a hotel since the 14C - maybe even earlier! Guest areas feature beams, exposed brick and inglenook fireplaces. Well-equipped modern bedrooms include two duplex suites. The extensive brasserie menu suits all tastes.

29 rooms - £ 95/105 £ 145/235

Market Pl ✉ SO51 8ZJ
- ✆ 01794 512431 - www.thewhitehorseromsey.co.uk

ROSS-ON-WYE

Herefordshire - Pop. 10 582 - Regional map n° **10**-B3

Wilton Court

HISTORIC • COSY An attractive part-Elizabethan house just out of town, on the banks of the River Wye. Comfortable bedrooms have a subtle modern style - those to the front have river views. Tasty breakfasts feature homemade preserves. For dinner there's a choice of two different rooms; classic menus utilise local produce.

11 rooms - £ 100/165 £ 125/185

Wilton Ln, Wilton ✉ HR9 6AQ - West : 0.75 mi by B 4260
- ✆ 01989 562569 - www.wiltoncourthotel.com - Closed 2-22 January

Bridge House

TOWNHOUSE • ELEGANT You get a lot more than you bargained for at this 18C townhouse: original features combine with chic, stylish furnishings; there's a superb view of the town and the River Wye; and the ruins of Castle Wilton border the grounds.

8 rooms - £ 80/95 £ 95/130

Wilton ✉ HR9 6AA - West : 0.75 mi by B 4260
- ✆ 01989 562655 - www.bridgehouserossonwye.co.uk - Closed 15 December-31 January, minimum 2 nights stay at weekends

at Upton Bishop Northeast: 3 mi by A40 on B4221

Moody Cow

TRADITIONAL BRITISH • FRIENDLY A traditional country pub serving classic dishes to match the surroundings. What the food may lack in originality, it makes up for with quality ingredients, careful cooking and distinct flavours. Friendly owners run the place with a passion.

Menu £ 30 (weekday lunch) - Carte £ 28/42

✉ HR9 7TT
- ✆ 01989 780470 - www.moodycowpub.co.uk - Closed 1-14 January, Sunday dinner, Monday and Tuesday in winter

at Walford South: 3 mi on B4234

Mill Race

TRADITIONAL BRITISH • PUB It might not look like a village pub but there's definitely an atmosphere of relaxed contentment. Simple cooking uses produce from their estate and farm and lets ingredients speak for themselves; try the steaks from the charcoal oven.

Carte £ 23/35

HR9 5QS – 01989 562891 – www.millrace.info

ROWDE – Wiltshire → See Devizes

ROWHOOK – West Sussex → See Horsham

ROWSLEY

Derbyshire – Matlock – Pop. 451 – Regional map n° **9**-A1

Peacock

MODERN CUISINE • CHIC XX Elegant hotel restaurant where old mullioned stone windows, oak Mousey Thompson furnishings and antique oil paintings are juxtaposed with modern lighting and contemporary art. Classic dishes at lunch are followed by more complex, elaborate combinations comprising lots of ingredients in the evening.

Carte £ 43/66

Peacock Hotel, Bakewell Rd DE4 2EB – 01629 733518 – www.thepeacockatrowsley.com – Closed first 2 weeks January, 24-26 December and Sunday dinner

Peacock

TRADITIONAL • PERSONALISED Characterful 17C Dower House of the Duchess of Rutland, with gardens leading down to the river. There's a snug open-fired sitting room and a characterful bar with stone walls, wood-panelling and a large peacock mural. Bedrooms mix antique furnishings with modern facilities and service is top notch.

15 rooms – †£ 145/165 ††£ 270/330

Bakewell Rd DE4 2EB – 01629 733518 – www.thepeacockatrowsley.com – Closed first 2 weeks January

Peacock – See restaurant listing

East Lodge

TRADITIONAL • PERSONALISED 17C hunting lodge surrounded by 10 acres of landscaped gardens dotted with ponds. Guest areas are elegant and well-appointed. Many of the bedrooms have great views; the two 'Luxury' rooms come with four-poster beds and TVs in the bathrooms. The formal dining room boasts a delightful chef's table.

12 rooms – †£ 105/295 ††£ 105/295

Main St DE4 2EF – 01629 734474 – www.eastlodge.com

ROYAL LEAMINGTON SPA

Warwickshire – Pop. 55 733 – Regional map n° **10**-D3

Brasserie at Mallory

MODERN CUISINE • BRASSERIE XX The bar-lounge has striking black art deco features and the conservatory dining room looks out over the pretty walled garden of this charming country house. Wide-ranging modern menus follow the seasons.

Carte £ 27/53

Mallory Court Hotel, Harbury Ln, Bishop's Tachbrook CV33 9QB – South : 2.25 mi by B 4087 (Tachbrook Rd) – 01926 453939 (booking essential) – www.mallory.co.uk – Closed Sunday dinner

Restaurant 23

MODERN CUISINE • CHIC XX Behind the smart Regency façade lies a chic cocktail bar and a stylish restaurant with doors leading out to a balcony. Attractively presented dishes arrive in original combinations. Afternoon tea is an event in itself.

Menu £ 25 (lunch and early dinner) - Carte dinner £ 42/63

34 Hamilton Terr ✉ CV32 4LY - ✆ 01926 422422 (booking advisable) - www.restaurant23.co.uk - Closed 1-17 January, 14-30 August, 25-26 December, 1 January, Sunday dinner, Monday and Tuesday

Oscar's

CLASSIC FRENCH • BISTRO X Friendly French bistro with two rustic rooms downstairs and a third above. There's a buzzy atmosphere, especially on the good value 'Auberge' nights, and the classic Gallic dishes are truly satisfying.

Menu £ 22 (lunch) - Carte dinner £ 30/44

39 Chandos St ✉ CV32 4RL - ✆ 01926 452807 (booking essential) - www.oscarsfrenchbistro.co.uk - Closed Sunday and Monday

Mallory Court

COUNTRY HOUSE • PERSONALISED A part-Edwardian house in Lutyens' style, with lovely gardens, a smart spa and classical lounges displaying fine antiques. Fresh flowers feature in the bedrooms: those in the main house are characterful, those in Orchard House are contemporary and those in the Knight's Suite have a more corporate feel. Dine from modern menus in the elegant dining room or brasserie.

43 rooms - †£ 139/450 ††£ 165/495

Harbury Ln, Bishop's Tachbrook ✉ CV33 9QB - South : 2.25 mi by B 4087 (Tachbrook Rd) - ✆ 01926 330214 - www.mallory.co.uk

Brasserie at Mallory - See restaurant listing

ROYAL TUNBRIDGE WELLS

Kent - Pop. 57 772 - Regional map n° **5**-B2

Thackeray's

MODERN BRITISH • INTIMATE XXX A softly illuminated clapboard house; the oldest in town and once home to the eponymous author. Classic dishes have modern elements and feature lots of different ingredients. The moody first floor private rooms showcase local art.

Menu £ 18/55

85 London Rd ✉ TN1 1EA - ✆ 01892 511921 - www.thackerays-restaurant.co.uk - Closed Sunday dinner and Monday

The Warren (N)

MODERN BRITISH • INTIMATE XX This large, multi-roomed restaurant is set above the High Street shops and its eclectic décor includes gold walls, brightly coloured linen and objets d'art. Well-judged modern cooking showcases meats from their 650 acre estate.

Menu £ 20 (lunch) - Carte £ 32/48

1st Floor, 5a High St ✉ TN1 1UL - ✆ 01892 328191 - www.thewarren.restaurant - Closed 26 December, first week January, Sunday dinner and Monday

The Old Fishmarket (N)

SEAFOOD • SIMPLE X This small black and white building in The Pantiles was once the town's fish market, so it's fitting that it's now an intimate seafood restaurant. The menu focuses on oysters, fruits de mer platters and the daily catch.

Menu £ 12 (weekday lunch) - Carte £ 30/62

19 The Upper Pantiles ✉ TN2 5TN - ✆ 01892 511422 (booking essential) - www.sankeys.co.uk - Closed 25-26 December, 1 January, Sunday October-March and Monday

The Beacon

MODERN CUISINE • PUB The Beacon is stunningly built into a stone escarpment and has fantastic views over the town. It's set over three levels and its original decorative features include carved wood and stained glass. Classic pub dishes are driven by the latest seasonal ingredients and have bold flavours and a comforting feel.

Menu £18 (weekdays)/27

Tea Garden Ln ✉ TN3 9JH
– ✆ 01892 524252 – www.the-beacon.co.uk – Closed Sunday dinner and Monday

Black Pig

MODERN BRITISH • FRIENDLY The black façade may feel quite austere but inside it's quite the opposite, courtesy of a friendly team, a laid-back vibe and rustic shabby-chic styling. Dishes are gutsy and full-flavoured and there's even a 'PIG Heaven' section.

Carte £26/34

18 Grove Hill Rd ✉ TN1 1RZ
– ✆ 01892 523030 – www.theblackpig.net – Closed 26 December and 1 January

Hotel du Vin

TOWNHOUSE • PERSONALISED Attractive Georgian property in the town centre, boasting southerly views over Calverley Park. It's wine-themed throughout, with a well-stocked clubby bar, two comfy lounges and contemporary bedrooms; some have emperor-sized beds and baths in the rooms. The rustic bistro and terrace serve French cuisine.

34 rooms – †£124/274 ††£124/274 – ☕ £17

Crescent Rd ✉ TN1 2LY
– ✆ 01892 320749 – www.hotelduvin.com

One Warwick Park (N)

BOUTIQUE HOTEL • DESIGN A smart, centrally located hotel comprising a townhouse, an old brewhouse and a former school. Crisply decorated bedrooms have dark wood furnishings, silver fabrics and state-of-the-art bathrooms. Sleek guest areas include an underground art gallery. The stylish restaurant offers an ambitious Italian menu.

39 rooms ☕ – †£85/300 ††£95/300

1 Warwick Pk ✉ TN2 5TA
– ✆ 01892 520587 – www.onewarwickpark.co.uk

Danehurst

TRADITIONAL • PERSONALISED Attractive Edwardian house with a pleasant terrace and koi carp pond; set in a peaceful residential area. Furnishings are top quality and show good attention to detail. The charming owners make the tasty bread and jam for breakfast.

4 rooms ☕ – †£129/179 ††£135/189

41 Lower Green Rd, Rusthall ✉ TN4 8TW – West : 1.75 mi by A 264
– ✆ 01892 527739 – www.danehurst.net – Closed 20 December-2 January

at Southborough North : 2 m. on A 26

The Twenty Six

MODERN CUISINE • BISTRO A homely, rustic restaurant overlooking the village green – it has 26 seats, 26 light bulbs hanging from the ceiling and 26 stars fixed to the window! Satisfying, seasonal modern dishes; you'll wish you could try everything on the menu.

Menu £27

15a Church Rd ✉ TN4 0RX
– ✆ 01892 544607 – www.thetwenty-six.co.uk – dinner only and lunch Saturday
– Closed Sunday and Monday

at Speldhurst Northwest: 3.5 mi by A26

George & Dragon

TRADITIONAL BRITISH • PUB Hugely characterful Wealden Hall house dating back to 1212 and boasting an impressive beamed ceiling and an unusual Queen's post. Generous cooking uses local, organic produce, offering pub classics alongside more elaborate dishes.

Carte £ 25/47

Speldhurst Hill ✉ TN3 0NN – ✆ 01892 863125 – www.speldhurst.com – Closed Sunday dinner

ROZEL BAY → See Channel Islands (Jersey)

RUDDINGTON – Nottinghamshire → See Nottingham

RUSHLAKE GREEN

East Sussex – ✉ Heathfield – Regional map n° **5**-B2

Stone House

HISTORIC • PERSONALISED Beautiful gardens lead up to this charming part-15C house, set in 1,000 acres of tranquil grounds. It's been in the family for 500 years and is very personally run. The traditional country house interior features original staircases, wood-panelling and antiques; some of the individually decorated bedrooms have four-poster beds. Classic menus use kitchen garden produce.

7 rooms – £ 160/170 £ 170/315 – 1 suite

✉ TN21 9QJ – (Northeast corner of the green) – ✆ 01435 830553 – www.stonehousesussex.co.uk – Closed 23 December-3 January and 15 February-10 March

RUSHTON – Northamptonshire → See Kettering

RYE

East Sussex – Pop. 3 708 – Regional map n° **5**-C2

Tuscan Rye

ITALIAN • RUSTIC Centrally located, with dark wood tables, studded leather chairs, Italian memorabilia and even a stuffed wild boar. Rustic, classical cooking with everything homemade. The olive oil comes from the family farm in Tuscany.

Carte £ 25/40

8 Lion St ✉ TN31 7LB – ✆ 01797 223269 (booking advisable) – www.tuscankitchenrye.co.uk – dinner only and Sunday lunch – Closed Monday and Tuesday

Webbe's at The Fish Café

SEAFOOD • BISTRO Relaxed café in a former antiques warehouse and teddy bear factory, with terracotta-coloured brick walls, a small counter and a cookery school above. Extensive menus offer simply prepared seafood from the Rye and Hastings day boats.

Carte £ 23/38

17 Tower St. ✉ TN31 7AT – ✆ 01797 222226 – www.webbesrestaurants.co.uk – Closed 2-17 January

George in Rye

INN • DESIGN A deceptively large, centrally located coaching inn offering an attractive blend of the old and the new. Stylish bedrooms have bold modern colour schemes and good facilities. There's a characterful beamed bar, a cosy wood-panelled lounge and a smart restaurant. Steaks are the highlight of the grill menu.

34 rooms – £ 125/325 £ 125/325

98 High St. ✉ TN31 7JT – ✆ 01797 222114 – www.thegeorgeinrye.com

Mermaid Inn

INN • HISTORIC One of England's oldest coaching inns, which offers immense charm and character, from its heavy beams and carved wooden fireplaces to its tapestries, false stairways and priests' holes. Formal dining features mainly local fish and game. The owner has been looking after guests here for over three decades.

31 rooms – £ 90/130 £ 150/220

Mermaid St. ✉ TN31 7EY – ✆ 01797 223065 – www.mermaidinn.com

Jeake's House

TOWNHOUSE • PERSONALISED Three 17C houses joined together over time, set down a cobbled lane. A former wool store and Quaker meeting place, it is set apart by its substantial charm. Characterful beamed rooms are warmly decorated and filled with antiques.

11 rooms – £ 120 £ 120/150

Mermaid St. ✉ TN31 7ET – ✆ 01797 222828 – www.jeakeshouse.com

Willow Tree House

TOWNHOUSE • COSY 300 year old boathouse on the main road into town. Comfy bedrooms are decorated in warm colours and are tastefully furnished; those at the top have exposed beams. Substantial breakfasts are served in a conservatory-style room.

6 rooms – £ 95/110 £ 95/140

113 Winchelsea Rd. ✉ TN31 7EL – South : 0.5 mi on A 259 – ✆ 01797 227820 – www.willow-tree-house.com – Closed 3-11 September and 22-27 December

at Camber Southeast: 4.25 mi by A259 ✉ Rye

Gallivant

MODERN BRITISH • BISTRO X Informal hotel bistro with distressed wood furniture, white and blue hues and a pleasant covered terrace. Appealing all-day menus keep local seafood to the fore; refreshingly, the good value two-choice set menu is always available.

Menu £ 16 (weekday lunch) – Carte £ 25/46

Gallivant Hotel, New Lydd Rd. ✉ TN31 7RB – ✆ 01797 225057 – www.thegallivant.co.uk

Gallivant

BOUTIQUE HOTEL • SEASIDE Laid-back hotel opposite Camber Sands, run by a friendly team. Relax by the fire in the New England style lounge. Bedrooms come in blues and whites, with distressed wood furniture and modern facilities; some have decked terraces.

20 rooms – £ 95/275 £ 95/275 – £ 12

New Lydd Rd. ✉ TN31 7RB – ✆ 01797 225057 – www.thegallivant.co.uk

Gallivant – See restaurant listing

RYHALL

Rutland – Pop. 1 459 – Regional map n° **9**-C2

Wicked Witch

CLASSIC CUISINE • NEIGHBOURHOOD XX A smart former pub with dark wood panelling, purple walls and a relaxed formality; one owner cooks and the other serves. Seasonal menus have a classic base but combinations are original and there's a real emphasis on presentation.

Menu £ 18/30

Bridge St ✉ PE9 4HH – ✆ 01780 763649 – www.thewickedwitchexperience.co.uk – Closed Sunday dinner and Monday

ST ALBANS

Hertfordshire – Pop. 82 146 – Regional map n° **7**-A2

Galvin at Centurion Club

FRENCH • FASHIONABLE XX A stylish golf clubhouse provides the setting for this comfy bar, lounge and restaurant. Carefully prepared modern classics look to France for their foundation. The fixed price lunch and dinner menu offers good value.

Menu £ 20/26 – Carte £ 33/58

Hemel Hempstead Rd ✉ HP3 8LA – West : 3.75 mi by A 5183 on A 4147 – ☎ 01442 510520 – www.galvinatcenturionclub.co.uk

THOMPSON St Albans

MODERN CUISINE • INTIMATE XX Come on a Sunday for 'lobster and steak' night or any day of the week for refined, tasty dishes with a modern edge. Three contemporary dining rooms feature bold artwork from the local gallery. Try the lesser-known wines by the glass.

Menu £ 15 (weekday lunch)/35 – Carte £ 46/60

2 Hatfield Rd ✉ AL1 3RP – ☎ 01727 730777 – www.thompsonstalbans.co.uk – Closed 2-12 January, Sunday dinner, Monday and lunch Tuesday

St Michael's Manor

HISTORIC BUILDING • CONTEMPORARY A part-16C William and Mary manor house with well-kept gardens and lake views. Characterful guest areas display contemporary touches. Bedrooms are well-appointed; those located in the Garden Wing are the most contemporary and some have terraces. The orangery restaurant offers a modern menu.

30 rooms – †£ 110/115 ††£ 150/340 – 1 suite

St Michael's Village, Fishpool St ✉ AL3 4RY – ☎ 01727 864444 – www.stmichaelsmanor.com

ST AUBIN

→ See Channel Islands (Jersey)

ST AUSTELL

Cornwall – Pop. 23 864 – Regional map n° **1**-B2

Anchorage House

FAMILY • PERSONALISED A contemporary guesthouse run by lovely owners – one is an ex-Canadian Naval Commander! Charming, antique-filled bedrooms boast modern fabrics, state-of-the-art bathrooms and plenty of extras. There's a lovely indoor pool with a sauna and a hot tub, along with a chill-out lounge, and afternoon tea is a hit.

5 rooms – †£ 75/110 ††£ 125/155

Nettles Corner, Boscundle ✉ PL25 3RH – East : 2.75 mi by A 390 – ☎ 01726 814071 – www.anchoragehouse.co.uk – Closed 15 November-15 March

ST BRELADE'S BAY

→ See Channel Islands (Jersey)

ST EWE

Cornwall – Regional map n° **1**-B3

Lower Barns

FAMILY • ELEGANT The gregarious owner extends a warm welcome at this stylishly converted 18C granite barn (formerly part of the Heligan Estate). Quirky, vibrantly decorated bedrooms are spread about the place and a hot tub on the decking overlooks the garden. Home-cooked dinners are served in the 'shack'.

6 rooms – †£ 85/95 ††£ 115/225

Bosue ✉ PL26 6ET – North : 1.25 mi by Crosswyn rd, St Austell rd and signed off St Mawes rd – ☎ 01726 844881 – www.lowerbarns.co.uk

ST HELENS → See Wight (Isle of)

ST HELIER → See Channel Islands (Jersey)

ST IVES

Cornwall - Pop. 9 966 - Regional map n° **1**-A3

Black Rock

REGIONAL CUISINE • NEIGHBOURHOOD X A relaxed, modern bistro with a semi-open kitchen and contemporary art. The regularly changing menu places its emphasis on local seafood and the owner is a third generation fisherman so has lots of local contacts. Cooking is gutsy and big on flavour; come before 7pm for a good value 3 course selection.

Menu £ 20 (early dinner) - Carte £ 21/38

Town plan: A1-v - *Market Pl ✉ TR26 1RZ - ✆ 01736 791911 (booking advisable) - www.theblackrockstives.co.uk - dinner only - Closed November-February and Sunday*

Alba

MODERN BRITISH • ROMANTIC XX A former lifeboat station in a great harbourside location. Dishes are European in base with a modern slant - go for one of the fish specials. The ground floor cocktail bar offers small plates and a good range of wines by the glass.

Menu £ 24 - Carte £ 34/48

Town plan: A1-d - *Old Lifeboat House, The Wharf ✉ TR26 1LF - ✆ 01736 797222 - www.alba-stives.co.uk - dinner only - Closed 25-26 December*

Porthgwidden Beach Café

MODERN CUISINE • NEIGHBOURHOOD X Tucked away by the beach, this super-friendly all-day café offers fantastic views over the bay to the lighthouse. The appealing menu comprises unfussy Mediterranean-influenced dishes, including plenty of seafood from St Ives, Looe and Mevagissey; be sure to have the Penang curry if it's on the specials list.

Carte £ 23/34

Town plan: B1-b - *The Island ✉ TR26 1PL - ✆ 01736 796791 (booking essential) - www.porthgwiddencafe.co.uk - Closed 7-20 and 25 December, Sunday dinner, Monday and Tuesday-Wednesday dinner except Easter-October*

Porthminster Beach Café

SEAFOOD • FASHIONABLE X Charming 1930s beach house in a superb location overlooking Porthminster Sands. It's hung with Cornish artwork, has a nautical style and leads out onto a large heated terrace. The seasonal seafood menu offers unfussy, vibrantly flavoured dishes with Asian influences. Service is relaxed and friendly.

Carte £ 28/57

Town plan: B2-p - *Porthminster Beach ✉ TR26 2EB - ✆ 01736 795352 (booking advisable) - www.porthminstercafe.co.uk - Closed 1-13 January*

Porthmeor Café Bar

MODERN CUISINE • NEIGHBOURHOOD X A popular beachfront café where you can sit inside, on the terrace or in heated pods. They offer breakfast, cakes, Mediterranean small plates and a few more substantial dishes too. Every table has a great view, especially at sunset.

Carte £ 21/32

Town plan: A1-z - *Porthmeor Beach ✉ TR26 1JZ - ✆ 01736 793366 (booking essential at dinner) - www.porthmeor-beach.co.uk - Closed November-March*

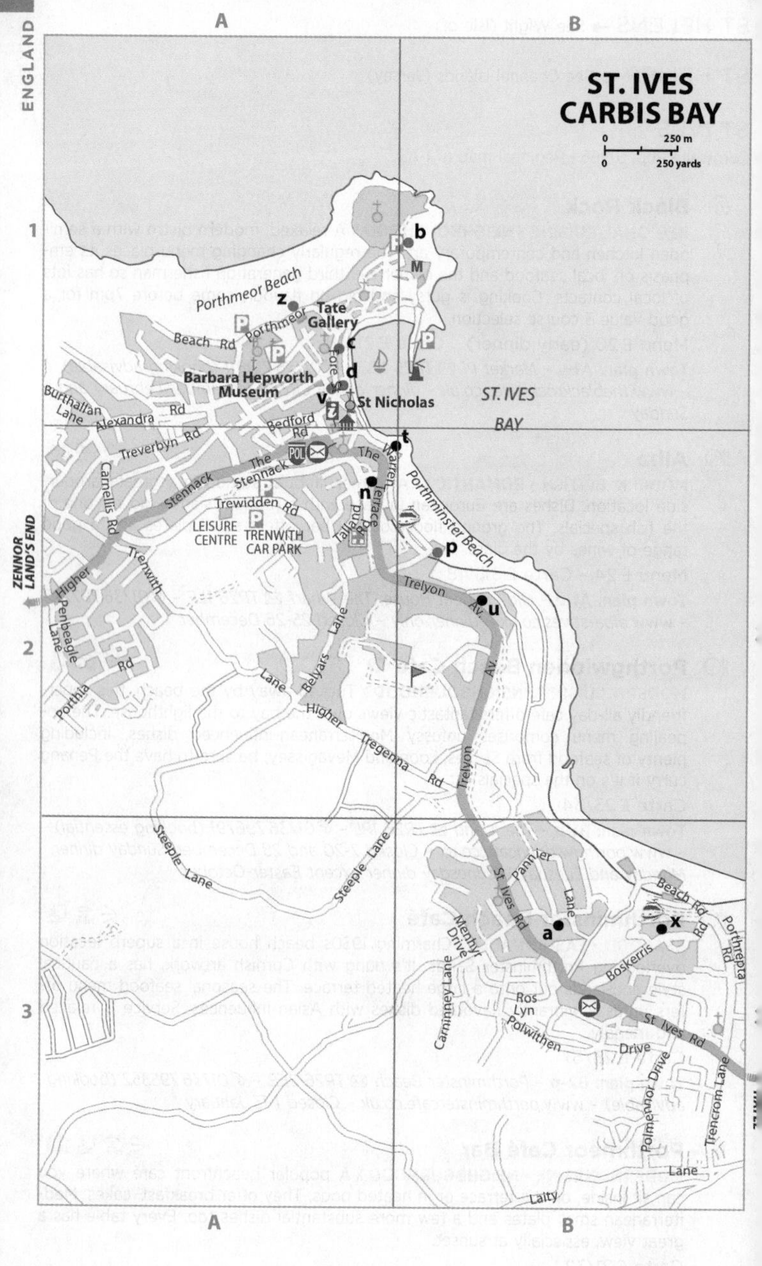
ST. IVES
CARBIS BAY
0
250 m
0
250 yards
A
B
1
2
3
Porthmeor Beach
Tate Gallery
Porthmeor
Beach Rd
Barbara Hepworth Museum
St Nicholas
ST. IVES BAY
Fore St
Burthallan Lane
Alexandra Rd
Bedford Rd
Treverbyn Rd
The Stennack
Stennack
The Warren
Terrace
Porthminster Beach
Trewidden Rd
Carnellis Rd
LEISURE CENTRE
TRENWITH CAR PARK
Talland Rd
ZENNOR LAND'S END
Higher
Trenwith
Trelyon Av.
Penbeagle Lane
Rd
Porthia
Lane
Belyars Lane
Higher Tregenna Rd
Trelyon Av.
Steeple Lane
Steeple Lane
Pannier Lane
St Ives Rd
Menthyr Drive
Beach Rd
Porthrepta Rd
Boskerris Rd
Carninney Lane
Ros Lyn
Polwithen
Drive
St Ives Rd
Polmennor Drive
Trencrom Lane
Lane
Lalty
POL
b
M
z
c
d
v
t
n
p
u
a
x

Porthminster Kitchen

MODERN CUISINE • NEIGHBOURHOOD Follow the narrow staircase up to this contemporary bistro and you'll be rewarded with glorious harbour views from both the restaurant and terrace. The all-day menu offers light, fresh, global cuisine with a focus on local seafood.

Carte £ 15/34

Town plan: A1-c – *The Wharf ✉ TR26 1LG – ✆ 01736 799874 – www.porthminster.kitchen*

Blue Hayes

HISTORIC • PERSONALISED Built in 1922 for Professor Whitnall, a surgeon friend of Edward III. Comfy bedrooms: one with French doors onto a roof terrace; another with a four-poster and a balcony. Single course dinner available. Breakfast on the terrace in summer.

6 rooms – †£ 130/150 ††£ 230/280

Town plan: B2-u – *Trelyon Ave ✉ TR26 2AD – ✆ 01736 797129 – www.bluehayes.co.uk – Closed November-February*

No 27

HISTORIC • PERSONALISED Unusually for St Ives, this stylishly restored Georgian house has its own car park... even more unusually, it also owns the beach beneath it! Bedrooms are modern and appealing. Take in a view of the bay from the airy breakfast room.

9 rooms – †£ 110/165 ††£ 110/165

Town plan: A2-n – *27 The Terrace ✉ TR26 2BP – ✆ 01736 797450 – www.27theterrace.co.uk – Closed January and Christmas*

Trevose Harbour House

TOWNHOUSE • CONTEMPORARY The experienced owners have decorated this stylish townhouse themselves, so you'll find lots of personal touches alongside an unusual mix of designer and upcycled furnishings. Breakfast features local produce and is a real highlight. They have 3 parking spaces reserved at the nearby station.

6 rooms – †£ 110/265 ††£ 160/275

Town plan: AB2-t – *22 The Warren ✉ TR26 2EA – ✆ 01736 793267 – www.trevosehouse.co.uk – Closed mid December-March*

at Carbis Bay South: 1.75 mi on A3074 ✉ St Ives

Boskerris

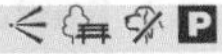

FAMILY • CONTEMPORARY A passionately run hotel with a light and airy feel. The French-style lounge-bar leads out onto a huge terrace with panoramic views of Carbis Bay. Uncluttered bedrooms come in cool modern designs and some have baths for two.

15 rooms – †£ 117/218 ††£ 155/290

Town plan: B3-x – *Boskerris Rd ✉ TR26 2NQ – ✆ 01736 795295 – www.boskerrishotel.co.uk – Closed mid-November-March*

Beachcroft

LUXURY • PERSONALISED Set in an elevated position, with stunning views across the bay. Contemporary interior with subtle 1920s touches. Comfy, understated bedrooms have bespoke furnishings and luxurious bathrooms. Have your breakfast on the delightful terrace.

5 rooms – †£ 150/210 ††£ 150/210

Town plan: B3-a – *Valley Rd ✉ TR26 2QS – ✆ 01736 794442 – www.beachcroftstives.co.uk – Closed November-March except New Year*

ST KEVERNE

Cornwall – Pop. 939 – Regional map n° **1**-A3

Greenhouse

REGIONAL CUISINE • RUSTIC X Simple eatery in a sleepy little village, where they sell their own bread and meringues. Daily blackboard menus are centred around local, organic and gluten free produce. Cooking is unfussy and flavoursome and seafood is a feature.

Carte £ 24/31

6 High St. ✉ TR12 6NN – ☎ 01326 280800 (booking advisable) – www.tgor.co.uk – dinner only and occasional Sunday lunch – Closed January

Old Temperance House

TOWNHOUSE • CONTEMPORARY This pretty pink-washed cottage framed by olive trees was once a 15C temperance house. The interior is contemporary and immaculately kept. Bright bedrooms are named after alcoholic drinks and display thoughtful touches. Fresh fruit and produce from the local butcher features at breakfast.

4 rooms – †£ 75/90 ††£ 75/90

The Square ✉ TR12 6NA – ☎ 01326 280986 – www.oldtemperancehouse.co.uk

ST KEW

Cornwall – Regional map n° **1**-B2

St Kew Inn

TRADITIONAL BRITISH • PUB A characterful country pub with a lovely garden and patio heaters, set in a quintessentially English location. Menus offer a wide range of appealing, good value dishes. Be sure to order a beer from the wooden casks behind the bar.

Carte £ 25/33

✉ PL30 3HB – ☎ 01208 841259 – www.stkewinn.co.uk – Closed 25-26 December

ST MARTIN

→ See Channel Islands (Guernsey)

ST MARY'S

→ See Scilly (Isles of)

ST MAWES

Cornwall – ✉ Truro – Regional map n° **1**-B3

Restaurant Tresanton

MODERN BRITISH • FASHIONABLE XX Take in superb bay views from this bright hotel restaurant, which has attractive mosaic flooring and a nautical theme. Daily menus offer unfussy dishes crafted from quality local produce and seafood is a feature. The large terrace is a popular spot, especially when they're hosting their summer BBQs.

Menu £ 25 (lunch) – Carte £ 34/74

Hotel Tresanton, 27 Lower Castle Rd ✉ TR2 5DR – ☎ 01326 270055 (booking essential) – www.tresanton.com

Watch House

MEDITERRANEAN CUISINE • SIMPLE X Old Customs and Excise watch house on the quayside, with a nautically styled interior, friendly service and harbour views. Light lunches and substantial dinners; unfussy cooking follows a Mediterranean theme – try the tasty fish specials.

Carte £ 24/44

1 The Square ✉ TR2 5DJ – ☎ 01326 270038 (booking advisable) – www.watchhousestmawes.co.uk – Closed 25-26 December, 4 January-9 February, Sunday dinner-Tuesday except March-October

Hotel Tresanton

TOWNHOUSE • GRAND LUXURY Set in a collection of old fishermen's cottages and a former yacht club. Elegant, nautically themed guest areas include an intimate bar and a movie room. Understated bedrooms – some in cottages – have a high level of facilities and superb sea views. The lovely split-level terrace shares the outlook.

30 rooms – £ 215/425 £ 215/425 – 4 suites

27 Lower Castle Rd TR2 5DR – 01326 270055 – www.tresanton.com

Restaurant Tresanton – See restaurant listing

Idle Rocks

BOUTIQUE HOTEL • PERSONALISED Boutique hotel on the water's edge, with fabulous views over the harbour and the estuary. The décor is personalised and local art is displayed throughout. Cosy, contemporary bedrooms have pleasing subtle touches and are well-equipped. The relaxed restaurant has bay views, a modern menu and a superb terrace.

19 rooms – £ 200/395 £ 200/395

Harbourside TR2 5AN – 01326 270270 – www.idlerocks.com – Closed 2 weeks January

St Mawes

BOUTIQUE HOTEL • CONTEMPORARY A smart refurbishment has revived this classic harbourside hotel, leaving it with a cool and trendy vibe. Bedrooms are understated and immaculately kept and the restful lounge boasts squashy sofas and opens onto a small balcony. The lively front restaurant serves fresh seafood and wood-fired pizzas.

7 rooms – £ 140/290 £ 140/290

Harbourside TR2 5DN – 01326 270170 – www.stmaweshotel.com

ST MELLION

Cornwall – Regional map n° **1**-C2

Pentillie Castle

COUNTRY HOUSE • HISTORIC A 17C house which was later transformed into a castle, set in 2,000 acres of stunning grounds overlooking the river. Spacious, elegant bedrooms have antique furnishings, luxurious bathrooms and offer some great views. Guest areas have a classical feel. It's a popular haunt for shooting parties in the winter.

9 rooms – £ 105/235 £ 125/250

PL12 6QD – Southeast : 1 mi by A 388 on Cargreen rd – 01579 350044 – www.pentillie.co.uk

ST OSYTH

Essex – Pop. 2 118 – Regional map n° **7**-D2

Park Hall

HISTORIC • PERSONALISED Charming 14C former monastery with a homely feel, surrounded by 400 acres of arable farmland. The characterful Garden Suites come with many extras. Seek out the hidden seating areas in the large grounds.

5 rooms – £ 90 £ 140/195

Bypass Rd CO16 8HG – East : 1.5 mi on B 1027 – 01255 820922 – www.romanticbreaksfortwo.com

ST PETER PORT → See Channel Islands (Guernsey)

ST SAVIOUR → See Channel Islands (Jersey)

ST SAVIOUR → See Channel Islands (Guernsey)

ST TUDY

Cornwall – Pop. 604 – Regional map n° **1**-B2

St Tudy Inn

TRADITIONAL BRITISH • FRIENDLY A lovingly restored pub in a pretty village – inside there's a labyrinth of cosy rooms with fresh flowers, open fires and rustic, modish overtones. Beautifully presented dishes are unfussy, seasonal and satisfying; meats are from Launceston and seafood is from Padstow. The chef is passionate, service is friendly and unfussy modern bedrooms complete the picture.

Carte £ 26/37

4 rooms – †£ 135/155 ††£ 135/155

Churchtown ✉ PL30 3NN – ✆ 01208 850656 – www.sttudyinn.com – Closed lunch 25-26 December

SALCOMBE

Devon – Pop. 1 893 – Regional map n° **1**-C3

Beachside

SEAFOOD • FASHIONABLE XX Large, airy hotel restaurant with full-length windows opening onto a delightful decked terrace overlooking the bay. Modern, daily changing menus offer a good mix of unfussy, flavoursome dishes, with plenty of fresh seafood options.

Menu £ 27/45

South Sands Hotel, Bolt Head ✉ TQ8 8LL – Southwest : 1.25 mi – ✆ 01548 845900 (booking advisable) – www.southsands.com

Salcombe Harbour

LUXURY • CONTEMPORARY Take in views of the estuary from this contemporary seaside hotel, with its sleek, nautical edge. Stylish bedrooms come with Nespresso machines and tablets; many also have balconies. For relaxation there's a chic spa and even a cinema! The restaurant offers modern menus, with local seafood a feature.

50 rooms – †£ 195/395 ††£ 195/475 – 1 suite

Cliff Rd ✉ TQ8 8JH – ✆ 01548 844444 – www.salcombe-harbour-hotel.co.uk

South Sands

FAMILY • DESIGN Stylish hotel by the water's edge, with a subtle New England theme running throughout and South Sands views. Small, modern bar and lounges. Smart bedrooms have heavy wood furnishings and good facilities; opt for one with a balcony.

27 rooms – †£ 200/595 ††£ 215/595 – 5 suites

Bolt Head ✉ TQ8 8LL – Southwest : 1.25 mi – ✆ 01548 845900 – www.southsands.com

Beachside – See restaurant listing

at Soar Mill Cove Southwest: 4.25 mi by A381✉ Salcombe

Soar Mill Cove

FAMILY • PERSONALISED Family-run hotel built from local slate and stone; delightfully set above a secluded cove. Relax in the modern lounge or smart bar. Spacious bedrooms come in bright, contemporary styles; half have private patios and sea views. Blue-hued restaurant offers a modern menu and a lovely outlook from every table.

22 rooms – †£ 149/171 ††£ 199/229

✉ TQ7 3DS – ✆ 01548 561566 – www.soarmillcove.co.uk – Closed 28 December-10 February

SALISBURY

Wiltshire – Pop. 44 748 – Regional map n° **2**-D3

Anokaa

INDIAN • DESIGN XX A smart Indian restaurant that's a little different, with colour-changing lights and interesting water features. Originality is also expressed in the extensive menu: expect dishes like spiced crushed scallops or duck jaalsha.

Menu £ 17 (lunch and early dinner) – Carte £ 22/64

60 Fisherton St ✉ SP2 7RB – ✆ 01722 414142 – www.anokaa.com

at Teffont Evias West: 10.25 mi by A36 and A30 on B3089 ✉ Salisbury

Howard's House

COUNTRY HOUSE • COSY This charming Grade II listed dower house stands in a beautiful English village; the eponymous 'Howard' was a tenant here for 20yrs. Bright, airy bedrooms have an understated feel and offer village or garden views. The dining room has a sophisticated menu and its French windows open onto a sheltered terrace. Good old-fashioned hospitality is provided by a family team.

9 rooms – £ 120 £ 190/225

✉ SP3 5RJ – ✆ 01722 716392 – www.howardshousehotel.co.uk – Closed 23-26 December

SANCTON

East Riding of Yorkshire – Pop. 286 – Regional map n° **13**-C2

Star

MODERN CUISINE • FRIENDLY Personally run pub in a small village, with a cosy bar, two smart dining rooms and a smiley team. The bar menu offers hearty, boldly flavoured dishes, while the à la carte has some imaginative twists.

Menu £ 17 (weekday lunch) – Carte £ 28/51

King St ✉ YO43 4QP – ✆ 01430 827269 – www.thestaratsancton.co.uk – Closed Monday

SANDIACRE

Derbyshire – Pop. 9 600 – Regional map n° **9**-B2

La Rock

MODERN BRITISH • RUSTIC XX Charming, personally run restaurant with an airy feel – it was once a butcher's. Exposed brick walls and antler chandeliers feature. Cooking combines classical flavours with modern techniques; home-grown fruits are well utilised.

Menu £ 29 (lunch) – Carte £ 36/52

4 Bridge St ✉ NG10 5QT – ✆ 0115 939 9833 – www.larockrestaurant.co.uk – Closed 24 December-mid January, Monday, Tuesday and lunch Wednesday

SANDSEND – North Yorkshire → See Whitby

SANDYPARK – Devon → See Chagford

SAPPERTON – Gloucestershire → See Cirencester

SAWLEY

Lancashire – Pop. 237 – Regional map n° **11**-B2

Spread Eagle

TRADITIONAL CUISINE • TRADITIONAL DÉCOR Very much at the heart of the community is this stylish, characterful pub with lovely river views. Cooking is gutsy and flavourful with pub favourites available in two sizes, classic main courses, and platters and tapas-style nibbles perfect for sharing. Comfortable bedrooms have smart, modern bathrooms.

Carte £ 24/35

7 rooms – £ 65/85 £ 105/155

✉ BB7 4NH – ✆ 01200 441202 – www.spreadeaglesawley.co.uk

SAXILBY

Lincolnshire – Pop. 3 992 – Regional map n° **9**-C1

 **Canal View** 

FAMILY • HOMELY Guests are welcomed to this pleasant guesthouse with a cup of tea and a slice of homemade cake. Neat bedrooms come with fridges, goose feather duvets and Egyptian cotton linen. As the name suggests, it has a view over the canal.

3 rooms ☕ – 👤£ 50/55 👥£ 70/79

Lincoln Rd ✉ LN1 2NF – on A 57 – ✆ 01522 704475 – www.canal-view.co.uk

SAXMUNDHAM

Suffolk – Pop. 2 712 – Regional map n° **8**-D3

The Bell at Sax' Ⓝ 

TRADITIONAL BRITISH • TRADITIONAL DÉCOR The Bell sits at the centre of the community: it's a favourite haunt of the Rotary Club and the market takes place next door. It's comfy and cosy inside, from the well-kept bedrooms to the homely dining rooms. The experienced chef has a great understanding of flavours and his dishes are carefully priced.

Carte £ 21/33

10 rooms ☕ – 👤£ 80/100 👥£ 100/125

31 High St ✉ IP17 1AF – ✆ 01728 602331 – www.thebellatsax.co.uk

SCARBOROUGH

North Yorkshire – Pop. 61 749 – Regional map n° **13**-D1

Jeremy's 

MODERN BRITISH • NEIGHBOURHOOD This smart, buzzy bistro started life as a 1930s butcher's shop, and the original tiles on the walls and floors still remain. Flavoursome, classically based dishes have Asian touches and come courtesy of an assured, confident chef.

Carte £ 28/50

33 Victoria Park Ave ✉ YO12 7TR – ✆ 01723 363871 (booking essential) – www.jeremys.co – dinner only and Sunday lunch – Closed first week January, 1 week May, 1 week October, Sunday dinner, Tuesday except mid July-August and Monday

Crown Spa 

TRADITIONAL • SEASIDE 19C landmark hotel, in a prime position on the headland of a Victorian seaside town. Contemporary guest areas, superb leisure facilities and state-of-the-art meeting rooms. Smart bedrooms feature bespoke furnishings and the latest mod cons. Informal, bistro-style dining is split over four different rooms.

115 rooms – 👤£ 48/250 👥£ 59/250 – ☕ £ 10 – 2 suites

8-10 Esplanade ✉ YO11 2AG – ✆ 01723 357400 – www.crownspahotel.com

 **Ox Pasture Hall** 

TRADITIONAL • COSY This charming creeper-clad farmhouse in set in 17 acres of landscaped grounds and is a popular venue for weddings. Guest areas are stylish and contemporary. Bedrooms are well-equipped – those in the courtyard wing are the most modern and afford the best views. Dine from a modern menu in the formal restaurant or choose from hearty, unfussy dishes in the bistro.

32 rooms ☕ – 👤£ 95/150 👥£ 115/350

Lady Edith's Dr, Raincliffe Woods ✉ YO12 5TD – West : 3.25 mi by A 171 following signs for Raincliffe Woods – ✆ 01723 365295 – www.oxpasturehallhotel.com

Alexander

TOWNHOUSE • COSY 1930s red-brick house at the popular North Beach end of town. The well-kept lounge and cocktail bar are traditional styled; bedrooms are more contemporary and have a clean, uncluttered style – extras include robes, biscuits and seaside rock. The linen-laid dining room offers a 3 choice set menu; local seafood is a highlight. Homemade shortbread is served on arrival.

8 rooms – †£ 60/120 ††£ 80/120

33 Burniston Rd ✉ YO12 6PG – ✆ 01723 363178
– www.alexanderhotelscarborough.co.uk – Closed mid October-mid March

SCAWTON – North Yorkshire → See Helmsley

SCILLY (Isles of)

Cornwall – Regional map n° **1**-A3

Bryher

Cornwall – Pop. 78

Hell Bay

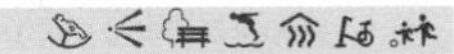

MODERN CUISINE • FRIENDLY XX Hotel restaurant with a relaxed 'boat house' feel. Light, Mediterranean-influenced lunches in the bar, courtyard or terrace. Dinner steps things up a gear, with unfussy, modern dishes displaying fresh ingredients and clear flavours.

Menu £ 48 (dinner) – Carte lunch £ 28/45

Hell Bay Hotel, ✉ TR23 0PR – ✆ 01720 422947 (booking essential)
– www.hellbay.co.uk – Closed November-February

Hell Bay

BOUTIQUE HOTEL • PERSONALISED Several charming, New England style buildings arranged around a central courtyard, with a contemporary, nautical-style interior displaying an impressive collection of modern art. Immaculately kept bedrooms come with plenty of thoughtful extras. The fabulous coastal location allows for far-reaching views.

25 rooms (dinner included) – †£ 118/385 ††£ 190/620 – 14 suites

✉ TR23 0PR – ✆ 01720 422947 – www.hellbay.co.uk – Closed November-February

Hell Bay – See restaurant listing

St Martin's

Cornwall – Pop. 113 – Regional map n° **1**-A3

Karma St Martin's

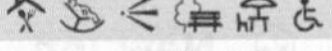

FAMILY • PERSONALISED The owner of Karma Resorts spent time on the Isles of Scilly when he was young and its sandy white beaches and clear blue waters fit the group's ethos perfectly. The hotel resembles a row of cottages and has a bright, calming feel; Indonesian-style furniture is a feature. The modern menu is all-encompassing.

30 rooms – †£ 280/350 ††£ 280/350 – 3 suites

Lower Town ✉ TR25 0QW – ✆ 01720 422368 – www.karmastmartins.com
– Closed November-March

St Mary's

Cornwall – Pop. 1 607

Atlantic

INN • FUNCTIONAL Former Customs Office in a charming bay setting, affording lovely views across the harbour. Bedrooms – accessed through twisty passages – are well-equipped, and many share the view. There's a comfortable lounge and a small bar, along with a wicker-furnished restaurant which offers an accessible menu.

21 rooms – †£ 125/140 ††£ 125/200

Hugh St, Hugh Town ✉ TR21 0PL – ✆ 01720 422417
– www.atlantichotelscilly.co.uk – Closed November-February

Star Castle

HISTORIC BUILDING • TRADITIONAL Elizabethan castle in the shape of an 8-pointed star. Well-appointed, classical bedrooms and brighter garden suites – some with harbour or island views. 17C staircase leads from the stone ramparts to the charming Dungeon bar. Fabulous fireplace and kitchen garden produce in the dining room. Seafood menus in the conservatory.

38 rooms – £ 85/157 £ 160/394 – 4 suites

The Garrison TR21 0JA – 01720 422317 – www.star-castle.co.uk – Closed November-mid February

Evergreen Cottage

FAMILY • COSY 300 year old captain's cottage with colourful window boxes, set in the heart of town. The interior is cosy, with a small, low-ceilinged lounge and breakfast room. The modest oak-furnished bedrooms are compact but spotlessly kept.

5 rooms – £ 40/75 £ 80/88

Parade, Hugh Town TR21 0LP – 01720 422711 – www.evergreencottageguesthouse.co.uk – Closed 1 week February and Christmas-New Year

Tresco

Cornwall – Pop. 167

Ruin Beach Café

MEDITERRANEAN CUISINE • RUSTIC Relaxed beachside restaurant in an old smugglers cottage – part of an aparthotel. The rustic room is decorated with striking Cornish art and opens onto a terrace with superb St Martin views. Colourful Mediterranean dishes have big, bold flavours; seafood and pizzas from the wood-burning oven are a hit.

Carte £ 26/44

Sea Garden Cottages Hotel, Old Grimsby TR24 0QQ – 01720 424849 (booking essential) – www.tresco.co.uk – Closed November-mid March

Sea Garden Cottages

A smart aparthotel divided into New England style 'cottages'. Each has an open-plan kitchen and lounge with a terrace; the first floor bedroom opens onto a balcony offering stunning views over Old Grimsby Quay and Blockhouse Point.

9 rooms – £ 262/337 £ 350/450

Old Grimsby TR24 0QQ – 01720 422849 – www.tresco.co.uk – Closed November-mid March

Ruin Beach Café – See restaurant listing

New Inn

INN • COSY Stone-built inn boasting a large terrace, an appealing outdoor pool and pleasant coastal views. Bedrooms are bright, fresh and very comfy. Regular live music events attract guests from near and far. The hugely characterful bar and restaurant offer accessible menus.

16 rooms – £ 65/110 £ 130/220

New Grimsby TR24 0QQ – 01720 422849 – www.tresco.co.uk – Restricted opening November-February

SEAHAM

Durham – Pop. 22 373 – Regional map n° **14**-B2

Seaham Hall

LUXURY • CONTEMPORARY An imposing part-18C mansion which combines grand original features with striking modern styling. Spacious, contemporary bedrooms have luxurious touches and comfy sitting areas – and many have coastal views. There's also a chic lounge; a grill restaurant with velour booths and a zinc-topped bar; and a stylish Asian restaurant set within the impressively equipped spa.

21 rooms – £ 179/295 £ 179/296 – 5 suites

Lord Byron's Walk SR7 7AG – 0191 516 1400 – www.seaham-hall.com

SEAHOUSES

Northumberland – Pop. 1 959 – Regional map n° **14**-B1

 **St Cuthbert's House** 

HISTORIC • MODERN Former Georgian Presbyterian chapel, with comfortable modern bedrooms, a homely lounge and a wood-furnished breakfast room; large arched windows and many original features remain. The friendly, welcoming owners often host music nights.

6 rooms – †£ 90/135 ††£ 110/135

192 Main St ✉ NE68 7UB – Southwest : 0.5 mi by Beadnell rd on North Sunderland rd – ☎ 01665 720456 – www.stcuthbertshouse.com – Restricted opening in winter

SEASALTER – Kent → See Whitstable

SEAVIEW – Isle of Wight → See Wight (Isle of)

SEDBERGH

Cumbria – Pop. 2 171 – Regional map n° **12**-B2

 **The Malabar** Ⓝ 

FAMILY • PERSONALISED A stylishly converted stone barn surrounded by rolling hills. The hands-on owners provide a warm welcome: Graham previously lived on an Indian tea plantation, so there's always a good choice of teas. Smart bedrooms mix antique furnishings with modern facilities. Cumbrian produce features at breakfast.

6 rooms – †£ 140/220 ††£ 160/240

Garths ✉ LA10 5ED – West : 1.75 mi on A 684 – ☎ 015396 20200 – www.themalabar.co.uk

SEDGEFORD

Norfolk – Pop. 613 – Regional map n° **8**-B1

 **Magazine Wood** 

LUXURY • CONTEMPORARY Stylish guesthouse on a family farm beside the Peddars Way. Luxuriously appointed bedrooms come with dining areas, continental breakfasts and terraces overlooking the fields; you can order a newspaper or a cooked breakfast online.

3 rooms – †£ 105/144 ††£ 105/144

Peddars Way ✉ PE36 5LW – East : 0.75 mi on B 1454 – ☎ 01485 750740 – www.magazinewood.co.uk – Closed Christmas (minimum two night stay at weekends)

SEER GREEN – Buckinghamshire → See Beaconsfield

SENNEN COVE

Cornwall – Pop. 410 – Regional map n° **1**-A3

🍴 **Ben Tunnicliffe Sennen Cove** 

CLASSIC CUISINE • SIMPLE X Just along from Land's End, you'll find this modern timber and glass eatery, superbly located overlooking a lovely sandy cove. Tasty, unfussy dishes showcase fresh local ingredients, including seafood from the nearby day boats.

Carte £ 27/39

Sennen Cove ✉ TR19 7BT – ☎ 01736 871191 (bookings advisable at dinner) – www.benatsennen.com – Closed Monday-Tuesday and dinner Wednesday-Thursday November-April and Sunday dinner

SETTLE

North Yorkshire – Pop. 3 621 – Regional map n° **13**-A2

 Falcon Manor

COUNTRY HOUSE • DESIGN Just out of town is this fine stone manor house with partial Fell views. It's owned by an interior designer, who has added some flamboyant touches to its Gothic Victorian architecture; it's worth paying the extra to stay in the huge Rafters Suite. Dine on modern classics in the snug bar or bright brasserie.

16 rooms – £ 95/225 £ 95/225

Skipton Rd ✉ BD24 9BD – South : 0.25 mi on B 6479 – ✆ 01729 823814 – www.falconmanor.co.uk

SHAFTESBURY

Dorset – Pop. 7 314 – Regional map n° **2**-C3

 Fleur de Lys 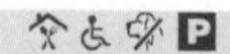

TRADITIONAL • CLASSIC Keenly run, creeper-clad stone house in a lovely market town. Comfortable, well-kept bedrooms are named after grape varieties and each comes with its own laptop. The cosy lounge features a mahogany bar. Dine from traditional menus either in the L-shaped restaurant or on the wood-furnished terrace.

8 rooms – £ 90/160 £ 100/175

Bleke St ✉ SP7 8AW – ✆ 01747 853717 – www.lafleurdelys.co.uk – Closed 2 weeks January

 Retreat 

TRADITIONAL • CLASSIC Pretty Georgian house on a narrow street in a delightful market town; built for a local doctor on the old site of a school for poor boys. Wood-furnished breakfast room and immaculately kept bedrooms with good facilities. Charming owner.

9 rooms – £ 70/75 £ 100/105

47 Bell St ✉ SP7 8AE – ✆ 01747 850372 – www.the-retreat.co.uk – Closed 28 December-31 January

SHANKLIN – Isle of Wight ➔ See Wight (Isle of)

SHAWELL

Leicestershire – Regional map n° **9**-B3

White Swan Ⓝ

MODERN BRITISH • PUB This welcoming village pub consists of a bar and two cosy rooms at the front and a contrastingly smart restaurant extension to the rear. Dishes are modern and sophisticated; come on a Saturday for their champagne breakfast.

Menu £ 29 (weekday lunch) – Carte dinner £ 35/56

Main St ✉ LE17 6AG – ✆ 01788 860357 – www.whiteswanshawell.co.uk – Closed Sunday dinner and Monday

SHEFFIELD

South Yorkshire – Pop. 518 090 – Regional map n° **13**-B3

 Jöro Ⓝ

SCANDINAVIAN • SIMPLE A simple but stylish place housed in the Krynkl shipping container development; book the Chef's Bench to feel part of the action. Daily changing small plates with unusual flavour combinations draw on New Nordic cuisine.

Carte £ 20/38

0.2-0.5 Krynkl, 294 Shalesmoor ✉ S3 8US – ✆ 0114 299 1539 – www.jororestaurant.co.uk – Closed 23-31 December, 16-22 April, 6-20 August, 1 week October, Sunday-Tuesday

Old Vicarage

MODERN CUISINE • FAMILY XX A delightful former vicarage in a semi-rural spot on the city's edge. Two fixed price menus offer sophisticated dishes with assured flavours and subtle modern influences; the 'Prestige' best showcases the chef's abilities.

Menu £ 40/60

Ridgeway Moor ✉ S12 3XW – Southeast : 6.75 mi by A 6135 (signed Hyde Park) and B 6054 on Marsh Lane rd. – ✆ 0114 247 5814 – www.theoldvicarage.co.uk – Closed 26 December-4 January, 24 July-8 August, Easter, Saturday lunch, Sunday and Monday

Rafters

MODERN BRITISH • CLASSIC DÉCOR XX A long-standing city institution; the owners stamped their own identity on it by using Sheffield cutlery and Yorkshire tweed covered chairs. Refined cooking sees well-judged flavour combinations presented in an attractive manner.

Menu £ 48

220 Oakbrook Rd, Nether Green ✉ S11 7ED – West : 2.5 mi by A 57 and Fulwood rd, turning left onto Hangingwater Rd – ✆ 0114 230 4819 – www.raftersrestaurant.co.uk – dinner only and Sunday lunch – Closed 1-9 January, 27 August-4 September, Monday and Tuesday

Kitchen

TRADITIONAL BRITISH • BISTRO X A bright, laid-back 'urban kitchen' in a stylish hotel. It's open for breakfast, coffee and cakes, lunch and dinner, and offers some great salads and small plates, followed by more ambitious modern dishes in the evening.

Menu £ 22 (lunch) – Carte £ 25/44

Brocco on the Park Hotel, 92 Brocco Bank ✉ S11 8RS – Southwest : 2 mi by B 6547 and Clarkehouse Rd – ✆ 0114 266 1233 – www.brocco.co.uk – Closed 25 December

Milestone

MODERN BRITISH • NEIGHBOURHOOD X Spacious 18C former pub set over two floors, in a regenerated area of the city. An array of regularly changing, seasonal menus offer boldly flavoured dishes; presentation mixes the traditional and the modern.

Menu £ 17 (lunch) – Carte £ 24/35

84 Green Ln ✉ S3 8SE – North : 1.25 mi by A 61 off Mowbray St – ✆ 0114 272 8327 – www.the-milestone.co.uk – Closed 25-26 December and 1 January

Nonnas

ITALIAN • NEIGHBOURHOOD X Long-standing Italian restaurant with a lively atmosphere. The extensive menu offers old favourites, from antipasti and sharing dishes to tasty homemade pastas and stews. You can also stop by for coffee and homemade cake in the bar.

Carte £ 23/45

535-541 Ecclesall Rd ✉ S11 8PR – Southwest : 2.25 mi on A 625 – ✆ 0114 268 6166 – www.nonnas.co.uk – Closed 25 December and 1 January

Brocco on the Park

TOWNHOUSE • MODERN Broccos's claim to fame is that Picasso once stayed here! It's a compact place, overlooking a park, and has plenty of style and individuality, albeit set by a roundabout. Bedrooms have a chic modern feel courtesy of light colour schemes, quality furnishings and great attention to detail.

8 rooms – †£ 100/240 ††£ 100/240 – ☕ £ 10

92 Brocco Bank ✉ S11 8RS – Southwest : 2 mi by B 6547 and Clarkehouse Rd – ✆ 0114 266 1233 – www.brocco.co.uk

Kitchen – See restaurant listing

SHELLEY

West Yorkshire – Regional map n° **13**-B3

Three Acres

TRADITIONAL BRITISH • ROMANTIC XX Traditional stone inn on top of the moors, with a maze of charmingly cluttered low-beamed dining rooms. Choose from a large, traditional menu which features steaks, grills and British classics. Bedrooms are warmly decorated; those in the adjacent cottages are the most modern and also the most peaceful.

Carte £ 31/59

17 rooms – £ 50 £ 80/100

Roydhouse ✉ HD8 8LR – Northeast : 1.5 mi on Flockton rd – ✆ 01484 602606 (booking essential) – www.3acres.com – Closed dinner 25-26 December, lunch 31 December and dinner 1 January

SHERBORNE

Dorset – Pop. 9 523 – Regional map n° **2**-C3

The Green

MODERN BRITISH • BISTRO X A pretty Grade II listed stone property at the top of the hill, with an inglenook fireplace and ecclesiastical panelling. Cooking is classical, confident and satisfying; choose from an à la carte or a good value mid-week menu.

Menu £ 22 (weekdays) – Carte £ 29/49

3 The Green ✉ DT9 3HY – ✆ 01935 813821 – www.greenrestaurant.co.uk – Closed 1-16 January, Sunday and Monday

SHERE – Surrey ➜ See Guildford

SHERINGHAM

Norfolk – Pop. 7 367 – Regional map n° **8**-C1

Ashbourne House

TOWNHOUSE • PERSONALISED Well-appointed guesthouse in an elevated position; its large, landscaped garden has access to the clifftop. Two of the homely, comfortable bedrooms have coastal views. Local bacon and sausages feature at breakfast, which is taken beside an impressive fireplace in the wood-panelled breakfast room.

3 rooms – £ 60/90 £ 85/90

1 Nelson Rd ✉ NR26 8BT – ✆ 01263 821555 – www.ashbournehousesheringham.co.uk – Closed 15 December-3 January

SHILTON – Oxfordshire ➜ See Burford

SHINFIELD – Wokingham ➜ See Reading

SHIPLAKE – Oxfordshire ➜ See Henley-on-Thames

SHIPSTON-ON-STOUR

Warwickshire – Pop. 5 038 – Regional map n° **10**-C3

Bower House (N)

MODERN BRITISH • BRASSERIE X This smart brasserie occupies two former shops in the heart of a small but characterful town. Appealing dishes are attractively presented and have a modern edge. Sit in the larger room with its comfy banquettes and copper-topped tables. Spacious bedrooms come with Hungarian-tiled bathrooms.

Menu £ 19 (weekday lunch) – Carte £ 30/36

5 rooms – £ 125/200 £ 125/200

Market Pl ✉ CV36 4AG – ✆ 01608 663333 – www.thebowerhouseshipston.com – Closed dinner 24- lunch 31 December, Sunday dinner and Monday

SHIRLEY - Derbyshire → See Ashbourne

SHOTTLE

Derbyshire - Regional map n° **9**-B2

Dannah Farm Country House

TRADITIONAL · PERSONALISED 18C stone farmhouse on a 154 acre working farm owned by the Chatsworth Estate; its outbuildings converted into spacious, well-equipped bedrooms. Many rooms have spa baths and the Granary and Studio Suites have hot tubs and terraces.

8 rooms - †£ 95/125 ††£ 150/295

Bowmans Ln. ✉ DE56 2DR - North : 0.25 mi by Alport rd - ☎ 01773 550273 - www.dannah.co.uk - Closed 24-26 December

SHREWSBURY

Shropshire - Pop. 71 715 - Regional map n° **10**-B2

Lion and Pheasant

MODERN BRITISH · FASHIONABLE Head through the hotel's café-bar and up the stairs to this cosy beamed restaurant. Carefully prepared dishes rely on quality ingredients and have a subtle modern touch. Another more formally set room is also opened at weekends.

Carte £ 25/42

Lion and Pheasant Hotel, 49-50 Wyle Cop ✉ SY1 1XJ - ☎ 01743 770345 - www.lionandpheasant.co.uk - Closed 25-26 December

Lion and Pheasant

HISTORIC · CONTEMPORARY A collection of adjoining 16C and 18C townhouses on a famous medieval street. Inside it's modern, quirky and understated. Chic bedrooms - designed by the owner's daughter - have a boutique French feel; the rear rooms are quieter.

22 rooms - †£ 99 ††£ 129/225

49-50 Wyle Cop ✉ SY1 1XJ - ☎ 01743 770345 - www.lionandpheasant.co.uk - Closed 25-26 December

Lion and Pheasant - See restaurant listing

at Upton Magna East : 6 mi by A 5064 off B 4380

The Haughmond

TRADITIONAL CUISINE · PUB A stylish dining pub complete with a 'Village Shop', smart modern bedrooms and a recurring stag theme. Lunchtime sees a good value selection of pub classics, the evening menus are more ambitious and at weekends they open Basil's - an 18-seater restaurant offering a sophisticated 5 course set menu.

Menu £ 25 - Carte £ 24/38

5 rooms - †£ 80/100 ††£ 90/120

✉ SY4 4TZ - ☎ 01743 709918 - www.thehaughmond.co.uk - Closed 25 December and 1 January

at Condover South: 5 mi by A49

Grove Farm House

COUNTRY HOUSE · PERSONALISED The friendly owners of this 18C farmhouse have opened up their family home. Bedrooms are pleasantly furnished and come with well-equipped bathrooms and country views. Extensive breakfasts showcase local and homemade choices.

4 rooms - †£ 70/75 ††£ 95/100

✉ SY5 7BH - South : 0.75 mi on Dorrington rd - ☎ 01743 718544 - www.grovefarmhouse.com - Closed Christmas-New Year

SHREWTON

Wiltshire - Pop. 1 723 - Regional map n° **2**-D2

 **Rollestone Manor** 

COUNTRY HOUSE • PERSONALISED Grade II listed house on a part-working farm just outside the village; reputed to once have been the home of Jane Seymour's family. Good-sized, antique-furnished bedrooms offer modern facilities; one even has a bath mounted on top of a plinth in the room. The contemporary restaurant serves modern classics.

7 rooms - †£ 80/125 ††£ 90/125

SP3 4HF - Southeast : 0.5 mi on A 360

- 01980 620216 - www.rollestonemanor.com - Closed 24-26 December

SHURDINGTON - Gloucestershire ➔ See Cheltenham

SIBFORD GOWER

Oxfordshire - Regional map n° **6**-B1

Wykham Arms

TRADITIONAL BRITISH • PUB Set down narrow country lanes, this 17C thatched building is a true village pub. Menus feature local produce and offer everything from light bites to the full 3 courses; there's also a good choice of wines by the glass and carafe.

Carte £ 21/39

Temple Mill Rd OX15 5RX

- 01295 788808 - www.wykhamarms.co.uk - Closed Monday except bank holidays

SIDFORD - Devon ➔ See Sidmouth

SIDLESHAM

West Sussex - Regional map n° **4**-C3

Crab & Lobster

SEAFOOD • PUB This sympathetically modernised inn is superbly located within the striking landscape of Pagham Harbour Nature Reserve. Well-presented, seafood-focused dishes are at the restaurant end of the scale, although lunch also sees sandwiches and salads. Comfortable bedrooms have a modern, minimalist style.

Menu £ 27 (weekday lunch) - Carte £ 31/52

5 rooms - †£ 100/120 ††£ 175/300

Mill Ln PO20 7NB

- 01243 641233 (booking advisable) - www.crab-lobster.co.uk

Landseer House

FAMILY • ELEGANT Tastefully furnished guesthouse, with numerous antiques and pleasant views of the surrounding wetlands. Contemporary bedrooms; go for Room 1 - the most luxurious. Those in the garden have their own terraces and kitchens.

6 rooms - †£ 120/140 ††£ 130/250

Cow Ln PO20 7LN - South : 1.5 mi by B 2145 and Keynor Ln

- 01243 641525 - www.landseerhouse.co.uk - Closed 23-28 December

SIDMOUTH

Devon - Pop. 12 569 - Regional map n° **1**-D2

Riviera

TRADITIONAL • PERSONALISED This characterful Regency hotel stands proudly on the promenade and has been family run for over 40 years. The marble entrance hall leads through to modern guest areas. Classical bedrooms come in blues and golds and many have bay windows and sea views. Menus are traditional and cream teas are a speciality.

26 rooms (dinner included) – £ 112/201 £ 224/450

The Esplanade ✉ EX10 8AY
– ✆ 01395 515201 – www.hotelriviera.co.uk
– Closed 2 January-mid February

at Sidford North: 2 mi

Salty Monk

REGIONAL CUISINE • INTIMATE XX Smart, proudly run restaurant in an old 16C salt house, featuring striking purple woodwork and a pleasant blend of the old and new. The Abbots Den offers a casual brasserie menu, while the Garden Room serves more elaborate modern dishes. Bedrooms have good extras and there's a gym and hot tub in the garden.

Carte £ 28/52

7 rooms – £ 85/125 £ 135/190

Church St ✉ EX10 9QP – on A 3052
– ✆ 01395 513174 (booking essential) – www.saltymonk.com
– dinner only – Closed January, 2 weeks November, Sunday and Monday

SINNINGTON – North Yorkshire → See Pickering

SISSINGHURST

Kent – Pop. 1 068 – Regional map n° **5**-B2

The Milk House

TRADITIONAL BRITISH • PUB Turn right into the bar with its soft sofas, huge fire and appetising grazing menu; turn left into the dining room for a seasonal list of modern British dishes. Pub classics are available in both areas and in the summer they serve wood-fired pizzas in the garden. Bedrooms are smart and contemporary.

Carte £ 20/44

4 rooms – £ 80/140 £ 80/140

The Street ✉ TN17 2JG
– ✆ 01580 720200 – www.themilkhouse.co.uk

SNAPE

Suffolk – Pop. 1 509 – Regional map n° **8**-D3

Crown Inn

REGIONAL CUISINE • PUB The affable owners of this characterful 15C former smugglers' inn grow fruit and vegetables and raise various animals, which provide much of the meat for their constantly evolving menus; the rosettes in the bar come from showing their Gloucester Old Spot pigs. Rustic bedrooms have beams and sloping floors.

Carte £ 19/48

2 rooms – £ 75/90 £ 75/90

Bridge Rd ✉ IP17 1SL
– ✆ 01728 688324 – www.snape-crown.co.uk

SNETTISHAM

Norfolk – Pop. 2 570 – Regional map n° **8**-B1

Rose and Crown

TRADITIONAL CUISINE • PUB 14C pub featuring a warren of rooms with uneven floors and low beamed ceilings. Gutsy cooking uses locally sourced produce, with globally influenced dishes alongside trusty pub classics. Impressive children's adventure fort. Modern bedrooms are decorated in sunny colours, and offer a good level of facilities.

Carte £ 22/37

16 rooms – †£ 100 ††£ 120

Old Church Rd ✉ PE31 7LX – ☎ 01485 541382 – www.roseandcrownsnettisham.co.uk – Closed 25 December

SOAR MILL COVE – Devon → See Salcombe

SOMERTON

Somerset – Pop. 4 133 – Regional map n° **2**-B2

White Hart

MEDITERRANEAN CUISINE • RUSTIC A 16C inn on the village's main market square; its beautiful parquet-floored entrance leads to six characterful rooms, including 'the barn' where you can watch the chefs at work. Seasonal food centres around the wood burning oven. Bedrooms are cosy and modern; Room 3, with a bath centre stage, is the best.

Carte £ 25/32

8 rooms – †£ 75/115 ††£ 75/115

Market Pl ✉ TA11 7LX – ☎ 01458 272273 – www.whitehartsomerton.com

SONNING-ON-THAMES – Wokingham → See Reading

SOUTH BRENT

Devon – Pop. 2 559 – Regional map n° **1**-C2

Glazebrook House

COUNTRY HOUSE • PERSONALISED A stunning 150 year old property set in 4 acres of peaceful grounds. It's been delightfully refurbished and features a lovely teak parquet floor and an eclectic mix of décor. Beautifully appointed, boutique bedrooms are named after characters from 'Alice in Wonderland'. Menus offer seasonal British dishes.

9 rooms – †£ 159/209 ††£ 239/299

✉ TQ10 9JE – Southwest : 0.5 mi by Exeter Rd – ☎ 01364 73322 – www.glazebrookhouse.com – Closed 7-20 January

SOUTH DALTON – East Riding of Yorkshire → See Beverley

SOUTH FERRIBY

North Lincolnshire – Pop. 651 – Regional map n° **13**-C3

Hope & Anchor

TRADITIONAL BRITISH • PUB A rustic, nautically-themed pub with Humber views. Tasty British dishes display touches of originality and showcase fish from Grimsby, fruit and veg from their smallholding and meats from the Lake District – which are aged in a glass-fronted drying cabinet. Bedrooms are modern; some have estuary views.

Carte £ 19/36

5 rooms – †£ 95/115 ††£ 95/115 – £ 10

Sluice Rd ✉ DN18 6JQ – ☎ 01652 635334 (booking advisable) – www.thehopeandanchorpub.co.uk – Closed first week January and Monday except bank holidays

SOUTH MOLTON

Devon – Pop. 5 108 – Regional map n° **1**-C1

Ashley House 

HISTORIC · PERSONALISED You'll be warmly welcomed into this snug guesthouse, set next to the village green. It dates from 1879 and is named after the majestic ash tree out the front. Bedrooms are homely; dramatic photos of the local area hang on the walls.

3 rooms – £ 65/95 £ 75/105

3 Paradise Lawn ✉ EX36 3DJ – ✆ 01769 573444 – www.ashleyhousebedandbreakfast.com

SOUTH POOL

Devon – Regional map n° **1**-C3

Millbrook Inn 

TRADITIONAL CUISINE · PUB A passionately run, appealingly worn pub squeezed in between the houses on a narrow village street. Sit in the cosy low-beamed interior or on one of two terraces. Cooking is traditional and hearty with Mediterranean influences.

Carte £ 24/59

✉ TQ7 2RW – ✆ 01548 531581 – www.millbrookinnsouthpool.co.uk

SOUTH RAUCEBY

Lincolnshire – Pop. 335 – Regional map n° **9**-C2

Bustard Inn

MODERN CUISINE · PUB Grade II listed inn set in a peaceful hamlet, with a light and airy flag-floored bar and a spacious, beamed restaurant. Good value lunch menu and a more ambitious à la carte offering modern English dishes. Satisfying desserts.

Menu £ 15 (weekday lunch) – Carte £ 20/47

44 Main St ✉ NG34 8QG – ✆ 01529 488250 – www.thebustardinn.co.uk – Closed 1 January, Sunday dinner and Monday except bank holidays

SOUTHAMPTON

Southampton – Pop. 253 651 – Regional map n° **4**-B2

Pig in the Wall

TOWNHOUSE · PERSONALISED Delightfully run, early 19C property that's been lovingly restored. The rustic lounge-cum-deli serves superb breakfasts and light meals; for something more substantial they will chauffeur you to their sister restaurant. Smart, boutique bedrooms come with antiques, super-comfy beds and Egyptian cotton linen.

12 rooms – £ 135/190 £ 135/190 – £ 10

8 Western Esplanade ✉ SO14 2AZ – ✆ 023 8063 6900 – www.thepighotel.co.uk

at Netley Marsh West: 6.5 mi by A33 off A336

Restaurant TerraVina 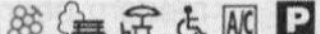

MODERN CUISINE · BRASSERIE XX Modern hotel restaurant with a glass-fronted wine cave and a covered terrace. Lunch sticks to the classics, while dinner introduces more imaginative dishes and a 6 course tasting menu. The sommelier offers some original wine pairings.

Menu £ 22 (weekday lunch) – Carte £ 37/51

Hotel TerraVina, 174 Woodlands Rd ✉ SO40 7GL – ✆ 023 8029 3784 – www.hotelterravina.co.uk

Hotel TerraVina

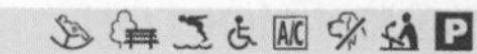

BUSINESS · MODERN Victorian red-brick house with wood-clad extensions, in a peaceful New Forest location. Brown and orange hues create a relaxed Mediterranean feel. Bedrooms have superb bedding, good facilities and thoughtful extras; some have roof terraces.

11 rooms – †£ 155/165 ††£ 165/265

174 Woodlands Rd ✉ SO40 7GL – ✆ 023 8029 3784 – www.hotelterravina.co.uk

Restaurant TerraVina – See restaurant listing

SOUTHBOROUGH - Kent → See Royal Tunbridge Wells

SOUTHBOURNE - Bournemouth → See Bournemouth

SOUTH LEIGH

Oxfordshire – Regional map n° **6**-B2

Mr Hanbury's Mason Arms

MODERN CUISINE · INN This attractive thatched pub might look traditional but inside it's as quirky and idiosyncratic as its name implies. Flagged floors and antique signs are juxtaposed with intriguing modern art. Lunch features bar snacks and classics, while dinner menus are modern and creative. Bedrooms are stylishly furnished.

Carte £ 26/46

5 rooms – †£ 95/320 ††£ 95/320

Station Rd ✉ OX29 6XF – ✆ 01993 656238 – www.hanburysmasonarms.co.uk

SOUTHPORT

Merseyside – Pop. 91 703 – Regional map n° **11**-A2

Bistrot Vérité

CLASSIC FRENCH · FRIENDLY Simple neighbourhood bistro with panelled walls and candles; sit on the red banquette which runs down one side. Gutsy, traditional French cooking, with desserts a speciality. Friendly, efficient service.

Menu £ 17 (lunch) – Carte dinner £ 22/44

7 Liverpool Rd, Birkdale ✉ PR8 4AR – South : 1.5 mi by A 565 – ✆ 01704 564199 (booking essential) – www.bistrotverite.co.uk – Closed 1 week summer, 1 week winter, 25-26 December, 1 January, Sunday, Monday and lunch Tuesday

V-Café

ASIAN INFLUENCES · BRASSERIE Relaxed café in a striking modern hotel, its glass façade overlooking the street. Open all-day and offering everything from sushi at the counter to 3 courses of globally influenced dishes.

Carte £ 24/60

Vincent Hotel, 98 Lord St ✉ PR8 1JR – ✆ 01704 883800 – www.thevincenthotel.com

Vincent

BUSINESS · DESIGN Striking glass, steel and stone hotel beside the gardens and bandstand. Stylish, boutique interior with chic bar, fitness room and spa. Sleek, modern bedrooms come in dark colours, boasting Nespresso machines and deep Japanese soaking tubs.

59 rooms – †£ 96/244 ††£ 96/244 – £ 10 – 2 suites

98 Lord St ✉ PR8 1JR – ✆ 01704 883800 – www.thevincenthotel.com

V-Café – See restaurant listing

SOUTHROP

Gloucestershire – Pop. 245 – Regional map n° **2**-D1

Swan

TRADITIONAL BRITISH • NEIGHBOURHOOD Delightful Virginia creeper clad inn set in a quintessential Cotswold village in the Leach Valley. With its characterful low-beamed rooms and charming service, it's popular with locals and visitors alike. Dishes are mainly British-based and feature garden produce; try the delicious homemade bread.

Menu £ 19 (weekdays) – Carte £ 25/42

GL7 3NU – 01367 850205 – www.theswanatsouthrop.co.uk
– Closed 25 December

SOUTHWOLD

Suffolk – Pop. 1 098 – Regional map n° **8**-D2

Swan

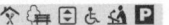

HISTORIC BUILDING • PERSONALISED An attractive 17C coaching inn located in the town centre – it's owned by Adnams and set close to their brewery. The cosy lounge and bar have subtle modern touches, while bedrooms are a mix of the traditional, the boldly coloured and the charming. The grand dining room has a modern European menu.

42 rooms – £ 120/150 £ 185/245 – 2 suites

Market Pl IP18 6EG – 01502 722186 – www.adnams.co.uk

Crown

INN • CONTEMPORARY A few doors down from its sister, the Swan, is this 17C coaching inn with an appealingly relaxed feel. Bedrooms have a modern New England style; those to the rear are the quietest. Have a pint of Adnams in the tiny nautically-themed bar, a stone's throw from their brewery. Daily menus keep things traditional.

14 rooms – £ 99/205 £ 165/255

90 High St IP18 6DP – 01502 722275 – www.adnams.co.uk

SOWERBY BRIDGE

West Yorkshire – Pop. 4 601 – Regional map n° **13**-A2

Gimbals

MODERN CUISINE • BISTRO XX Personally and passionately run restaurant on the high street; look out for the eye-catching illuminated window display. Modern monthly menus have subtle Mediterranean influences and the desserts are a real highlight.

Menu £ 25 (weekdays) – Carte £ 23/39

76 Wharf St HX6 2AF
– 01422 839329 – www.gimbals.co.uk – dinner only – Closed 25-27 December, 1-2 January, Sunday and Monday

SPARKWELL

Devon – Regional map n° **1**-C2

Treby Arms

MODERN CUISINE • RUSTIC A pretty whitewashed inn built by Brunel in the 1950s to serve workers constructing the Royal Albert rail bridge. English ingredients are to the fore and include seafood from the local day boats.

Menu £ 25 (weekday lunch) – Carte £ 38/66

Newtons Row PL7 5DD
– 01752 837363 (booking essential) – www.thetrebyarms.co.uk
– Closed 25-26 December, Monday-Tuesday and bank holidays

SPARSHOLT - Hampshire → See Winchester

SPARSHOLT

Oxfordshire – Regional map n° **6**-A3

Star Inn

MODERN CUISINE • FRIENDLY Have a drink on the squashy sofas by the wood-burning stove at this lovingly restored village inn, then dine overlooking the garden. Carefully prepared, appealing dishes range from the comforting to the adventurous and game features highly. The barn behind houses comfy bedrooms.

Menu £ 22 (lunch) – Carte £ 27/38

8 rooms – †£ 85/95 ††£ 95/135

Watery Ln ✉ OX12 9PL – ✆ 01235 751873 – www.thestarsparsholt.co.uk

SPELDHURST - Kent → See Royal Tunbridge Wells

SPRIGG'S ALLEY - Oxfordshire → See Chinnor

STADDLEBRIDGE

North Yorkshire – Regional map n° **13**-B1

Cleveland Tontine

TRADITIONAL BRITISH • BISTRO XX New life has been breathed into the iconic Cleveland Tontine. Have a drink in the contemporary lounge-bar, then descend to the conservatory or the atmospheric bistro with its quarry tiled floor and listed ceiling. Yorkshire meets France on the appealing menu. Quirky modern bedrooms have bold wallpapers.

Menu £ 19 (lunch and early dinner) – Carte £ 27/53

7 rooms – †£ 79/190 ††£ 99/190

✉ DL6 3JB – On southbound carriageway of A 19 – ✆ 01609 882671 – www.theclevelandtontine.com

STADHAMPTON

Oxfordshire – Pop. 702 – Regional map n° **6**-B2

Thai

THAI • INTIMATE XX Cosy hotel restaurant in an intimate basement room, with ornate silk hangings and 8 tables topped with polished brass. Flavoursome, authentic dishes are skilfully prepared by a Thai chef; the 10 and 12 plate sharing menus are popular.

Menu £ 30 – Carte £ 24/60

Crazy Bear Hotel, Bear Ln ✉ OX44 7UR – Off Wallingford rd – ✆ 01865 890714 (booking essential) – www.crazybeargroup.co.uk – Closed Sunday lunch

Crazy Bear

LUXURY • MODERN Wacky converted pub with a London bus reception, a characterful bar, a smart glasshouse and even a Zen garden. Sumptuous, quirky bedrooms are spread about the place; some have padded walls and infinity baths. Eat in 'Thai' or flamboyant 'English', with its mirrored walls and classic British and French dishes.

18 rooms – †£ 199/399 ††£ 199/399

Bear Ln ✉ OX44 7UR – Off Wallingford rd – ✆ 01865 890714 – www.crazybeargroup.co.uk

Thai – See restaurant listing

STAFFORD

Staffordshire – Pop. 68 472 – Regional map n° **10**-C1

Moat House

MODERN BRITISH • FRIENDLY XX Head to this attractive hotel restaurant for views over the leafy garden to the barges gliding by on the canal. Cooking is modern British and dishes are accomplished and well-judged; the tasting menu is a hit with the regulars.

Menu £ 21 (lunch and early dinner) – Carte £ 32/49

Moat House Hotel, Lower Penkridge Rd, Acton Trussell ✉ ST17 0RJ – South: 3.75 mi by A 449
– ✆ 01785 712217 – www.moathouse.co.uk – Closed 25 December

Moat House

BUSINESS • CLASSIC The original 15C farmhouse is now a pub and the sympathetically added extensions house characterful wood-panelled lounges, attractively furnished modern bedrooms and an orangery restaurant. There's a duck pond to the front and a canal to the rear. It's been owned and run by the same family for many years.

41 rooms – †£ 125 ††£ 145 – 1 suite

Lower Penkridge Rd, Acton Trussell ✉ ST17 0RJ – South : 3.75 mi by A 449
– ✆ 01785 712217 – www.moathouse.co.uk – Closed 25 December

Moat House – See restaurant listing

The Swan

INN • CONTEMPORARY This 17C coaching inn is found among some impressive old buildings, including a neighbouring Jacobean townhouse. Inside it's stylish and contemporary with up-to-date bedrooms. The brasserie offers a large menu of modern classics and there's also a coffee shop and two bars which share a pleasant terrace.

31 rooms – †£ 75/100 ††£ 80/120

46 Greengate St ✉ ST16 2JA
– ✆ 01785 258142 – www.theswanstafford.co.uk – Closed 24-25 December

STALISFIELD

Kent – Regional map n° **5**-C2

Plough Inn

TRADITIONAL BRITISH • RUSTIC Rurally set, 15C pub with thick walls, exposed beams, farming implements and hop bines. The usual suspects on the bar snack menu; more ambitious dishes on the à la carte. Nursery puddings and an impressive range of Kentish real ales.

Menu £ 16 (weekday lunch) – Carte £ 24/34

✉ ME13 0HY
– ✆ 01795 890256 – www.theploughinnstalisfield.co.uk – Closed Sunday dinner and Monday

STAMFORD

Lincolnshire – Pop. 22 574 – Regional map n° **9**-C2

The Oak Panelled Restaurant

TRADITIONAL BRITISH • INN XXX Smart dress is required in this lovely oak-panelled dining room, which is found at the heart of an equally charming 16C coaching inn. Classical menus are largely British based with a few international influences. Alongside their speciality beef carving trolley, there are also 'cheese' and 'sweet' trolleys.

Menu £ 29 (weekday lunch) – Carte £ 36/84

George of Stamford Hotel, 71 St Martins ✉ PE9 2LB
– ✆ 01780 750750 – www.georgehotelofstamford.com

Zada

TURKISH • NEIGHBOURHOOD Its name means 'fortunate' and the locals are lucky to have it in town. Turkish rugs hang on exposed stone walls and fresh bread is made behind the counter. The menu features all the favourites, from hummus and kebabs to baklava.

Carte £ 18/32

13 St Mary's Hill ✉ PE9 2DP – ✆ 01780 766848 – www.zadarestaurant.co.uk – dinner only and lunch Saturday-Sunday – Closed 25 December

Bull & Swan

TRADITIONAL BRITISH • INN A stone-built medieval hall house which was converted into an inn during the 1600s and later taken over by a former coachman to the Earl of Exeter in 1739. Dishes range from sharing slates to regional classics and local steaks. Like the characterful beamed bar, bedrooms have a traditional feel.

Carte £ 28/36

9 rooms – †£ 90/160 ††£ 100/180

St Martins ✉ PE9 2LJ – ✆ 01780 766412 – www.thebullandswan.co.uk

George of Stamford

INN • COSY This characterful coaching inn dates back over 500 years and, despite its bedrooms having a surprisingly contemporary feel, it still offers good old-fashioned hospitality. There are plenty of places to relax, with various bars, lounges and a walled garden. Dine in the laid-back Garden Room or the more formal restaurant – both spill out into the lovely courtyard in summer.

45 rooms – †£ 130/180 ††£ 215/360 – 1 suite

71 St Martins ✉ PE9 2LB – ✆ 01780 750750 – www.georgehotelofstamford.com

The Oak Panelled Restaurant – See restaurant listing

Crown

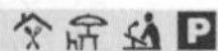

HISTORIC • PERSONALISED Former coaching inn set in a historic market town. Bedrooms in the main house have a funky, boutique style; those in the townhouse and cottage are larger with a more classical feel. Dine in the modern cocktail bar, in one of the cosy lounges, in the quieter rear dining room or out on the large terrace.

28 rooms – †£ 90/120 ††£ 110/175

All Saints Pl. ✉ PE9 2AG – ✆ 01780 763136 – www.kneadpubs.co.uk

William Cecil

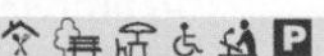

COUNTRY HOUSE • HISTORIC This 17C stone rectory is named after the 1st Baron Burghley and is where they filmed Pride and Prejudice. Inside it's shabby-chic, with Colonial-style bedrooms featuring wood carvings and pastoral scene wallpaper. The restaurant has intimate, Regency-style booths; be sure to have afternoon tea on the terrace.

27 rooms – †£ 85/190 ††£ 95/190 – 1 suite

High St, St Martins ✉ PE9 2LJ – ✆ 01780 750070 – www.thewilliamcecil.co.uk

STANFORD DINGLEY

West Berkshire – Pop. 179 – Regional map n° **6**-B3

Bull Inn

TRADITIONAL BRITISH • RUSTIC Locals and their dogs gather in the rustic bar of this beamed 15C inn, while the garden plays host to alfresco diners, chickens and the annual village dog show. The experienced chef-owner offers a wide range of tasty dishes; 'beer tapas' allows you to sample local ales and bedrooms are cosy and great value.

Carte £ 28/44

5 rooms – †£ 55/70 ††£ 55/80 – £ 12

Cock Ln ✉ RG7 6LS – ✆ 0118 974 4582 – www.thebullinnstanforddingley.co.uk

STANHOE

Norfolk – Pop. 289 – Regional map n° **8**-C1

Duck Inn

TRADITIONAL CUISINE • INN Fairy lights decorate the picket fence and ducks waddle over from the pond round the corner. Enjoy Elgood's ales and bar bites in the buzzy slate-floored bar or go for fresh fish dishes or thick, juicy local steaks in one of three relaxed, rustic dining rooms. Bedrooms are cosy and well-kept.

Carte £ 23/48

2 rooms – £ 90/110 £ 135/165

Burnham Rd ✉ PE31 8QD – ✆ 01485 518330 – www.duckinn.co.uk – Closed 25 December

STANSTED MOUNTFITCHET

Essex – Pop. 6 669 – Regional map n° **7**-B2

Linden House

TOWNHOUSE • ROMANTIC This part-timbered former antique shop is now a smart hotel. Bedrooms have a pleasing mix of classic and modern elements and most come with a bath in the room. The bar has a shabby-chic, masculine feel and the rustic restaurant offers a menu of classic dishes given a modern twist.

9 rooms – £ 80/125 £ 80/125 – £ 10

1-3 Silver St ✉ CM24 8HA – ✆ 01279 813003 – www.lindenhousestansted.co.uk

Chimneys

TOWNHOUSE • COSY Charming 17C house with low-beamed ceilings and cosy guest areas. Pine-furnished bedrooms have a modern cottagey style and come with homely touches. Tasty breakfasts include Manx kippers and smoked haddock with poached eggs.

3 rooms – £ 59/72 £ 85

44 Lower St ✉ CM24 8LR – on B 1351 – ✆ 01279 813388 – www.chimneysguesthouse.co.uk

STANTON

Suffolk – Pop. 2 073 – Regional map n° **8**-C2

Leaping Hare

MODERN BRITISH • BISTRO This beautiful 17C timber-framed barn sits at the centre of a 7 acre vineyard. Carefully judged cooking relies on well-sourced, seasonal ingredients; many from their own farm. Sit on the lovely terrace and try the interesting all-day light bites or choose something from the more substantial daily menu.

Menu £ 19 (weekdays) – Carte £ 26/39

Wyken Vineyards ✉ IP31 2DW – South : 1.25 mi by Wyken Rd – ✆ 01359 250287 (booking essential) – www.wykenvineyards.co.uk – lunch only and dinner Friday-Saturday – Closed 25 December-5 January

STAVERTON – Northamptonshire → See Daventry

STILTON

Cambridgeshire – ✉ Peterborough – Pop. 2 455 – Regional map n° **8**-A2

Bell Inn

INN • COSY This historic coaching inn on the Great North Road is where the first stilton cheese was sold. Most of the bedrooms have a traditional feel and two have four-posters and jacuzzi baths. The characterful lounge and bar feature exposed brick and beams, and the Galleried Restaurant offers a modern menu.

22 rooms – £ 88 £ 113/148

Great North Rd ✉ PE7 3RA – ✆ 01733 241066 – www.thebellstilton.co.uk – Closed 25 December

STOCKBRIDGE

Hampshire – Pop. 570 – Regional map n° **4**-B2

Greyhound on the Test

MODERN BRITISH • PUB Mustard-coloured pub with over a mile of River Test fishing rights to the rear. Low beams and wood burning stoves abound and elegant décor gives it a French bistro feel. The appealing range of dishes includes modern small plates, a selection 'on toast' and a classical daily menu; the chef will also cook your catch. Homely bedrooms have large showers and quality bedding.

Menu £ 20 (weekday lunch) – Carte £ 22/42

10 rooms – £ 90/150 £ 145/220

31 High St SO20 6EY – 01264 810833 (booking advisable) – www.thegreyhoundonthetest.co.uk – Closed 25-26 December

STOCKPORT

Greater Manchester – Pop. 105 878 – Regional map n° **11**-B3

brassicagrill

MODERN BRITISH • NEIGHBOURHOOD The walls of this neighbourhood restaurant are filled with old lithographs of brassica plants and tea lights twinkle on the tables in the evening. Cooking is honest, flavoursome and good value; be sure to try the 'stout' ice cream. The team have worked together for many years and it shows.

Menu £ 17 – Carte £ 18/42

27 Shaw Rd SK4 4AG – Northwest : 2.5 mi by A 6 off B 5169 – 0161 442 6730 – www.brassicagrill.com – Closed 25-26 December, 1 January, Monday and Sunday dinner

Where The Light Gets In

MODERN BRITISH • RUSTIC This large, loft-style restaurant is located on the top floor of a Victorian coffee warehouse and its open kitchen forms part of the room. The surprise menu is formed from whatever they have foraged that day and beasts are brought in whole and fully utilised. Matching wine flights focus on natural wines.

Menu £ 75 – surprise menu only

7 Rostron Brow SK1 7JY – 0161 477 5744 (booking essential) – www.wtlgi.co – dinner only – Closed last week August, first week September, 1 week Easter, Christmas-New Year and Sunday-Tuesday

STOKE BY NAYLAND

Suffolk – Regional map n° **8**-C3

Crown

REGIONAL CUISINE • PUB Smart, relaxed pub in a great spot overlooking the Box and Stour river valleys. Globally influenced menus feature produce from local farms and estates, with seafood from the east coast. Well-priced wine list with over 25 wines by the glass. Large, luxurious, superbly equipped bedrooms with king or super king sized beds; some have French windows and terraces.

Carte £ 20/42

11 rooms – £ 95/140 £ 145/265

CO6 4SE – 01206 262001 – www.crowninn.net – Closed 25-26 December

STOKE HOLY CROSS – Norfolk → See Norwich

STOKE POGES

Buckinghamshire – Pop. 3 962 – Regional map n° **6**-D3

Humphry's

MODERN BRITISH • ELEGANT XXXX Impressive hotel dining room named after 18C landscape gardener Humphry Repton, who designed the surrounding gardens; the lake and parkland views are superb. Classically based dishes are presented in a modern style. Service is professional.

Menu £ 68

Stoke Park Hotel, Park Rd ✉ SL2 4PG – ✆ 01753 717171 (booking essential) – www.humphrysrestaurant.co.uk – dinner only and Sunday lunch – Closed 3-6 January, 25-26 December, Monday and Tuesday

Stoke Park

LUXURY • CLASSIC Grade I listed Palladian property – once home to the Penn family, who created England's first country club. Extensive sporting activities, impressive spa and characterful guest areas. Mix of chic and luxurious 'Feature' bedrooms.

49 rooms – †£ 190/330 ††£ 190/380 – ☕ £ 25 – 1 suite

Park Rd ✉ SL2 4PG – Southwest : 0.75 mi on B 416 – ✆ 01753 717171 – www.stokepark.com – Closed 3-6 January and 25-26 December

Humphry's – See restaurant listing

Stoke Place

HISTORIC • MODERN A 17C Queen Anne mansion set by a large lake and surrounded by delightful gardens and parkland. Quirky guest areas feature bold wallpapers and original furnishings and the uniquely styled bedrooms are spread about the house and the grounds. Modern menus use herbs, veg and fruit from the kitchen garden.

39 rooms – †£ 95/200 ††£ 95/330 – ☕ £ 16

Stoke Green ✉ SL2 4HT – South : 0.5 mi by B 416 – ✆ 01753 534790 – www.stokeplace.co.uk

STON EASTON

Somerset – Pop. 579 – Regional map n° **2**-C2

Ston Easton Park

GRAND LUXURY • ELEGANT Striking Palladian mansion in 36 acres of delightful grounds. Fine rooms of epic proportions are filled with antiques, curios and impressive flower arrangements. Many of the bedrooms have coronet or four-poster beds; three are set in a cottage. Classic menus showcase produce from the Victorian kitchen garden.

23 rooms ☕ – †£ 125/200 ††£ 175/300 – 2 suites

✉ BA3 4DF – ✆ 01761 241631 – www.stoneaston.co.uk

STOW-ON-THE-WOLD

Gloucestershire – Pop. 2 042 – Regional map n° **2**-D1

Old Butchers

CLASSIC CUISINE • FRIENDLY XX An old butcher's shop with quirky décor, colourful chairs and ice bucket and colander lampshades. The menu offers plenty of choice from old favourites to dishes with a Mediterranean slant. The 'bin end' wine list is worth a look.

Carte £ 27/56

7 Park St ✉ GL54 1AQ – ✆ 01451 831700 – www.theoldbutchers.com – Closed 25-26 December

Number Four at Stow

BUSINESS • CONTEMPORARY Contemporary, open-plan hotel; so named as it's the fourth this experienced family own. The comfy lounge boasts bold brushed velvet seating, while the bright, compact bedrooms feature smart leather headboards, cream furniture and modern facilities. The comfortable brasserie offers a classical menu.

18 rooms ☕ – †£ 105/150 ††£ 130/175 – 3 suites

Fosseway ✉ GL54 1JX – South : 1.25 mi by A 429 on A 424 – ✆ 01451 830297 – www.hotelnumberfour.co.uk – Closed 23 December-27 January

Number Nine

FAMILY • COSY Expect a warm welcome at this ivy-clad, 18C stone house, close to the historic town square. The cosy lounge and breakfast room boast exposed stone walls, open fireplaces and dark wood beams. A winding staircase leads up to the pleasant wood-furnished bedrooms, which come with plenty of extras.

3 rooms – £ 50/60 £ 85

9 Park St GL54 1AQ – 01451 870333 – www.number-nine.info

at Lower Oddington East: 3 mi by A436 Stow-On-The-Wold

Fox Inn

TRADITIONAL BRITISH • PUB Creeper-clad, quintessentially English pub at the heart of a peaceful Cotswold village, with beamed ceilings, solid stone walls, flagged floors and plenty of cosy nooks and crannies. The menu focuses on carefully prepared, tasty British classics and the comfortable bedrooms are individually furnished.

Menu £ 20 (weekday lunch) – Carte £ 25/41

3 rooms – £ 95/125 £ 95/125

GL56 0UR – 01451 870555 (booking essential) – Closed 25 December

at Daylesford East: 3.5 mi by A436 Stow-On-The-Wold

Café at Daylesford Organic

MODERN BRITISH • FASHIONABLE Stylish café attached to a farm shop; its rustic interior boasting an open charcoal grill and a wood-fired oven. Throughout the day, tuck into light dishes and small plates; at night, candle-lit suppers step things up a gear. Everything is organic, with much of the produce coming from the farm.

Carte £ 24/44

GL56 0YG – 01608 731700 (bookings not accepted) – www.daylesford.com – lunch only and dinner Friday-Saturday – Closed 25-26 December

at Bledington Southeast: 4 mi by A436 on B4450

Kings Head Inn

TRADITIONAL BRITISH • INN Charming 16C former cider house on a picturesque village green, bisected by a stream filled with bobbing ducks. Appealing bar snacks include pheasant in a basket; pub classics and some interesting modern dishes on the à la carte. Large bar with a vast inglenook fireplace. Cosy bedrooms.

Carte £ 26/41

12 rooms – £ 75/100 £ 100/135

The Green OX7 6XQ – 01608 658365 – www.kingsheadinn.net – Closed 25-26 December

at Nether Westcote Southeast: 4.75 mi by A429 and A424

Feathered Nest

MODERN CUISINE • INN Smart pub with a laid-back bar, a rustic snug, a casual conservatory and a formal dining room. Sit on quirky horse saddle stools and sample unfussy dishes from the daily blackboard or head through to elegant antique tables for more complex offerings; the wine list features over 200 bins. Comfy bedrooms boast antiques, quality linens and roll-top baths. The views are superb.

Menu £ 29 (weekday lunch)/68

4 rooms – £ 245/295 £ 245/295

OX7 6SD – 01993 833030 – www.thefeatherednestinn.co.uk – Closed 1 week January, 1 week October, 25 December, Sunday dinner and Monday

STRATFORD ST MARY

Suffolk – Pop. 701 – Regional map n° **8**-C3

Swan

CLASSIC CUISINE • PUB A homely 16C coaching inn overlooking the river, with characterful low beams, whitewashed walls and open fires. The short menu changes daily and uses local ingredients in time-honoured ways. Each dish is matched to a wine and an ale.

Carte £ 23/40

Lower St ✉ CO7 6JR – ✆ 01206 321244 – www.stratfordswan.com – Closed Monday and Tuesday

STRATFORD-UPON-AVON

Warwickshire – Pop. 27 830 – Regional map n° **10**-C3

No 9 Church St.

MODERN BRITISH • BISTRO XX A friendly, cosy restaurant in a 400 year old townhouse a little off the main streets. The experienced chef-owner offers flavoursome British cooking with an original modern twist. Dishes are attractive and use lots of ingredients.

Menu £ 20 (lunch and early dinner) – Carte dinner £ 26/47 **s**

Town plan: A2-a – *9 Church St ✉ CV37 6HB – ✆ 01789 415522 – www.no9churchst.com – Closed 25 December-3 January, Sunday, Monday and bank holidays*

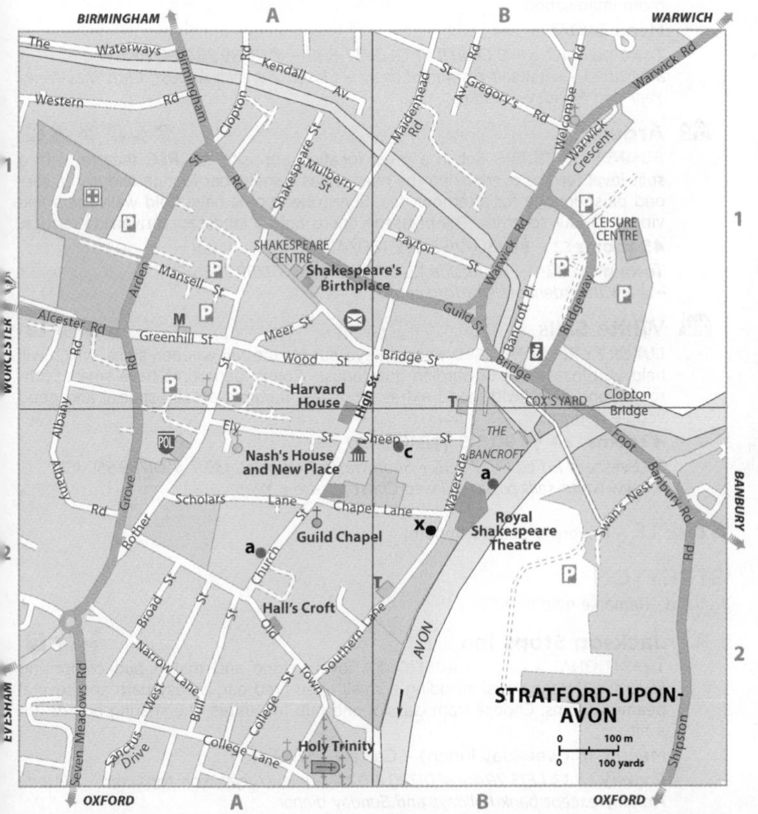

ENGLAND

Lambs

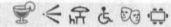

TRADITIONAL CUISINE • RUSTIC Attractive 16C house with an interesting history; dine on one of several intimate levels, surrounded by characterful beams and original features. The classic bistro menu lists simply, carefully prepared favourites and daily fish specials.

Menu £ 19 (lunch and early dinner) – Carte £ 25/38

Town plan: B2-c – *12 Sheep St ✉ CV37 6EF – ☎ 01789 292554 – www.lambsrestaurant.co.uk – Closed 25-26 December and lunch Monday except bank holidays*

Rooftop

MODERN BRITISH • DESIGN Set atop the RSC Theatre; a curvaceous restaurant with a superb terrace and lovely views from its window tables. Come for a light lunch, afternoon tea, cocktails and snacks, or the pre-theatre set menu.

Menu £ 21 (dinner) – Carte £ 24/35

Town plan: B2-a – *Royal Shakespeare Theatre, Waterside ✉ CV37 6BB – ☎ 01789 403449 (bookings advisable at dinner) – www.rsc.org.uk/eat – Closed 25 December and Sunday dinner*

Salt N

MODERN BRITISH • RUSTIC An intimate restaurant with whitewashed walls and flagged floors; the simple look is in perfect harmony with the purity of the cooking. The fixed price menus offer hearty dishes, while the tasting menus show more imagination.

Menu £ 20/37

Town plan: A2-a – *8 Church St ✉ CV37 6HB – ☎ 01789 263566 (booking advisable) – www.salt-restaurant.co.uk – Closed 2 weeks August, Christmas-New Year and Monday-Tuesday*

Arden

BUSINESS • MODERN Set in a great location opposite the RSC theatre, with a split-level terrace overlooking the river. It has a smart bar-lounge and also a second plush lounge for afternoon tea. Stylish bedrooms have bold wallpapers and vibrant colour schemes. The brasserie opens onto a landscaped riverside terrace.

45 rooms – †£ 130/263 ††£ 160/425

Town plan: B2-x – *Waterside ✉ CV37 6BA – ☎ 01789 298682 – www.theardenhotelstratford.com*

White Sails

LUXURY • PERSONALISED Keep an eye out for the tall wooden signs, which will help you locate this Edwardian guesthouse. Comfy bedrooms have smart bathrooms and come with good extras. Breakfast features a daily special and good veggie options.

4 rooms – †£ 90/115 ††£ 105/130

85 Evesham Rd ✉ CV37 9BE – Southwest : 1 mi on B 439 – ☎ 01789 550469 – www.white-sails.co.uk – Closed Christmas-New Year

STRETE – Devon ➜ See Dartmouth

STRETTON

Rutland – Regional map n° **9**-C2

Jackson Stops Inn

TRADITIONAL BRITISH • RUSTIC A lovely stone and thatch pub comprising several different areas, including a small open-fired bar, a cosy barn and several beamed rooms. Choose from classics and pub favourites; the sharing boards are a hit.

Menu £ 16 (weekday lunch) – Carte £ 25/39

Rookery La ✉ LE15 7RA – ☎ 01780 410237 – www.thejacksonstops.com – Closed Monday except bank holidays and Sunday dinner

STROUD

Gloucestershire - Pop. 32 670 - Regional map n° **2**-C1

Bell Inn

MODERN BRITISH • INN This Grade II listed stone inn dates back to the 16C and its delightful terrace and conservatory afford great countryside views. Interesting modern dishes showcase produce from the chef-owner's allotment and there's a great vegetarian selection. Make a night of it by staying in one of the homely bedrooms.

Carte £ 22/31

2 rooms - £ 80/115 £ 85/120 - £ 12

Bell Ln, Selsley ✉ GL5 5LY - Southwest : 2 mi by A 419 and on B 4048 - ✆ 01453 753801 - www.thebellinnselsley.com - Closed Sunday dinner

Bisley House

TRADITIONAL CUISINE • FRIENDLY Stroud's oldest pub has been given a new lease of life and now sports a bright, modern look, with tiled floors, white walls - and not a beam or a horse brass in sight! The menu changes almost daily and cooking is simple, fresh and tasty.

Carte £ 19/34

Middle St ✉ GL5 1DZ - ✆ 01453 751328 - www.bisleyhousecafe.co.uk - Closed Monday

The Bear of Rodborough

INN • TRADITIONAL There's plenty of character to this 17C coaching inn, which stands on Rodborough Common and affords pleasant country views. The cosy beamed lounge and bar provide an atmospheric setting for a casual meal, while the more formal library offers modern cuisine. Bedrooms are stylish and contemporary.

45 rooms - £ 85/160 £ 95/200

Rodborough Common ✉ GL5 5DE - Southeast : 2 mi by A 419 on Butterow Hill rd - ✆ 01453 878522 - www.cotswold-inns-hotels.co.uk

STUDLAND

Dorset - Pop. 299 - Regional map n° **2**-C3

Pig on the Beach

REGIONAL CUISINE • FRIENDLY Set within a large, plant-filled conservatory in a delightful country house; a rustic, shabby-chic restaurant where the wonderful kitchen garden informs the menu and additional produce comes from within 25 miles. Cooking is light and fresh and is accompanied by superb views over the lawns to Studland Bay.

Carte £ 24/45

The Pig on the Beach Hotel, Manor Rd ✉ BH19 3AU - ✆ 01929 450288 - www.thepighotel.com

Shell Bay

SEAFOOD • BISTRO Simply furnished seafood restaurant with a decked terrace; superbly set on the waterfront and boasting views over the water to Brownsea Island - all tables have a view. The daily menu mixes the classical with the more adventurous.

Menu £ 24 - Carte £ 20/52

Ferry Rd ✉ BH19 3BA - North : 3 mi or via car ferry from Sandbanks - ✆ 01929 450363 (booking essential) - www.shellbay.net - Closed November-February

Pig on the Beach

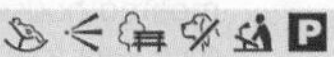

COUNTRY HOUSE • GRAND LUXURY Delightful country house with commanding coastal views and lovely gardens leading down to the sea. It has a relaxed, shabby-chic style and the furnishings are a pleasing mix of the old and the new. For something a little different, stay in an old gardener's bothy or dovecote. Staff are extremely welcoming.

23 rooms - £ 135/330 £ 135/330 - £ 15

Manor Rd ✉ BH19 3AU - ✆ 01929 450288 - www.thepighotel.com

Pig on the Beach - See restaurant listing

SUMMERHOUSE - Darlington → See Darlington

See Darlington

SUNNINGDALE

Windsor and Maidenhead – Regional map n° **6**-D3

Bluebells

MODERN CUISINE • INTIMATE XXX The smart façade of this professionally run restaurant is matched by a sophisticated interior, where white leather furnishings stand out against dark green walls. Beautifully presented dishes are crafted using modern techniques.

Menu £ 26/37

Shrubbs Hill, London Rd ✉ SL5 0LE – Northeast : 0.75 mi on A 30 – ✆ 01344 622722 – www.bluebells-restaurant.com – Closed 1-12 January, 25-26 December, Sunday dinner, Monday and Tuesday

SUTTON

Central Bedfordshire – Pop. 299 – Regional map n° **7**-B1

John O'Gaunt Inn

TRADITIONAL CUISINE • COSY Well-run by experienced owners, this is a cosy, honest village inn with a fire-warmed bar, a smart dining room and delightful gardens overlooking wheat fields. The tried-and-tested menu includes some tasty 'Crumps Butchers' steaks.

Carte £ 25/42

30 High St ✉ SG19 2NE – ✆ 01767 260377 – www.johnogauntsutton.co.uk – Closed Monday except bank holidays and Sunday dinner

SUTTON GAULT

Cambridgeshire – Regional map n° **8**-B2

Anchor Inn

MODERN CUISINE • RUSTIC A pretty little cottage built in 1650; its history can be felt in its 3 cosy, rustic dining rooms. You'll find the odd pub classic but in the main cooking has more of a restaurant style, with some ambitious modern dishes thrown in.

Menu £ 15 (weekday lunch) – Carte dinner £ 25/49

4 rooms – †£ 59/112 ††£ 79/155

✉ CB6 2BD – ✆ 01353 778537 – www.anchor-inn-restaurant.co.uk – Closed 25-26 December

SUTTON COLDFIELD

West Midlands – Pop. 109 015 – Regional map n° **10**-C2

New Hall

HISTORIC • ELEGANT Despite its name, this is one of the oldest inhabited moated houses in England, dating back to the 13C. Mature, topiary-filled grounds give way to a characterful interior of wood panelling and stained glass. Bedrooms are luxurious. A mix of classic and modern dishes are offered in the restaurant.

60 rooms – †£ 115/199 ††£ 115/199 – 5 suites

Walmley Rd ✉ B76 1QX – Southeast : 2.5 mi by A 5127 off Wylde Green Rd – ✆ 0121 378 2442 – www.handpickedhotels.co.uk/newhall

SUTTON COURTENAY

Oxfordshire – Pop. 2 421 – Regional map n° **6**-B2

Fish

TRADITIONAL CUISINE • FRIENDLY You'll receive a warm Gallic welcome at this French-orientated pub. The best places to sit are the bright conservatory and under the pergola in the lovely garden. Menus blend classic French and British dishes; go for the former.

Menu £ 19 (weekdays) – Carte £ 27/48

4 Appleford Rd ✉ OX14 4NQ – ☎ 01235 848242 – www.thefishatsuttoncourtenay.co.uk – Closed January, Monday except bank holidays and Sunday dinner

SWAFFHAM

Norfolk – Pop. 6 734 – Regional map n° **8**-C2

Strattons

TOWNHOUSE • PERSONALISED Laid-back, eco-friendly hotel in an eye-catching 17C villa with Victorian additions. Quirky, individually styled bedrooms are spread about the place: some are duplex; some have terraces or courtyards. The rustic basement restaurant serves modern British dishes; on quieter days, breakfast is taken in their deli.

14 rooms – †£ 94/225 ††£ 99/275

4 Ash Cl ✉ PE37 7NH – ☎ 01760 723845 – www.strattonshotel.com – Closed 21-27 December

SWAY

Hampshire – Pop. 2 294 – Regional map n° **4**-A3

Manor at Sway

FAMILY • PERSONALISED The Manor is set in the centre of a busy New Forest village and comes with a delightful rear garden where a mature Cedar of Lebanon takes centre stage. Inside it's bold and bright, with cosy modern bedrooms and Hypnos beds. The showy dining room has flock wallpaper, black tables and a French-inspired menu.

15 rooms – †£ 90/150 ††£ 130/220

Station Rd ✉ SO41 1QE – ☎ 01590 682754 – www.themanoratsway.com

SWINBROOK – Oxfordshire → See Burford

TALATON

Devon – Regional map n° **1**-D2

Larkbeare Grange

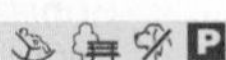

FAMILY • PERSONALISED A friendly, experienced couple run this well-kept house. Start the day with homemade yoghurt and preserves, and end it beside the wood-burner in the cosy lounge. Bedrooms feature stripped pine furnishings and floral fabrics.

4 rooms – †£ 87/125 ††£ 115/195

Larkbeare ✉ EX5 2RY – South : 1.5 mi by Fairmile rd – ☎ 01404 822069 – www.larkbeare.net

TANGMERE – West Sussex → See Chichester

TAPLOW

Buckinghamshire – Pop. 518 – Regional map n° **6**-C3

André Garrett at Cliveden House

MODERN CUISINE • LUXURY XXX A grand hotel dining room with views over the parterre garden. Classic recipes are brought up-to-date in refined, well-presented dishes where local and seasonal produce feature highly. These are accompanied by a superb wine list.

Menu £ 33/55 – Carte £ 55/82

Cliveden House, ✉ SL6 0JF – North : 2 mi by Berry Hill – ☎ 01628 607100 – www.clivedenhouse.co.uk

Astor Grill

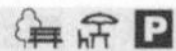

TRADITIONAL BRITISH • BISTRO Set in the former stable wing: a small hotel restaurant complete with its old horse rail, an equestrian theme and a delightful terrace. The menu is a roll-call of English classics, with grills a specialty; be sure to try the trifle.

Carte £ 29/60

Cliveden House, ✉ SL6 0JF – North : 2 mi by Berry Hill – ✆ 01628 607107 – www.clivedenhouse.co.uk

Cliveden House

HISTORIC • CLASSIC Stunning Grade I listed, 19C stately home in a superb location, boasting views over the formal parterre and National Trust gardens towards the Thames. The opulent interior boasts sumptuous antique-filled lounges and luxuriously appointed bedrooms. Unwind in the smart spa then take a picnic or afternoon tea hamper and kick-back in style on one of their vintage launches.

47 rooms – †£ 495/750 ††£ 495/750 – 6 suites

✉ SL6 0JF – North : 2 mi by Berry Hill – ✆ 01628 668561 – www.clivedenhouse.co.uk

André Garrett at Cliveden House • Astor Grill – See restaurant listing

TARR STEPS

Somerset – Regional map n° **2**-A2

Tarr Farm Inn

TRADITIONAL BRITISH • RUSTIC Cosy beamed pub in an idyllic riverside spot, overlooking a 1000 BC, stone-slab clapper bridge. If it's sunny, head for the garden for afternoon tea; if not, make for the narrow bar or cosy restaurant for everything from potted shrimps to Devon Ruby steak. Bedrooms are comfy and well-equipped.

Carte £ 23/41

9 rooms – †£ 75/90 ††£ 100/150

✉ TA22 9PY – ✆ 01643 851507 – www.tarrfarm.co.uk – Closed 1-13 February

TATTENHALL

Cheshire West and Chester – Pop. 1 950 – Regional map n° **11**-A3

Allium by Mark Ellis (N)

MODERN BRITISH • DESIGN You can't miss the bow-fronted façade of this former village shop, where you can come for everything from a light lunch or afternoon tea to a tasting menu and cocktails. Some dishes have a playful element and you can even cook your own steak on a lava stone at your table. Bedrooms are fresh and modern.

Carte £ 25/43

5 rooms – †£ 65/110 ††£ 65/110

Lynedale House, High St ✉ CH3 9PX – ✆ 01829 771477 – www.theallium.co.uk – Closed Monday and Tuesday

TAUNTON

Somerset – Pop. 60 479 – Regional map n° **2**-B3

Castle Bow

MODERN CUISINE • FRIENDLY Elegant, art deco style restaurant in the old snooker room of a Norman castle. Regularly changing menus showcase top quality regional produce. Well-balanced dishes are classically based yet refined, and feature some playful modern touches.

Carte £ 31/48

Castle Hotel, Castle Grn ✉ TA1 1NF – ✆ 01823 328328 (booking advisable) – www.castlebow.com – dinner only – Closed January, Sunday, Monday and Tuesday

Mint and Mustard

INDIAN • FASHIONABLE XX Smart glass doors lead to a teak-furnished lounge and a contemporary, split-level restaurant in shades of green and mustard. Highly original, modern dishes with Keralan influences; the lunchtime thalis offer great value for money.

Carte £ 18/33

10 Station Rd ✉ TA1 1NH – ✆ 01823 330770 – www.mintandmustard.com – Closed 25-26 December

Willow Tree

MODERN CUISINE • INTIMATE XX Intimate restaurant in a 17C townhouse, featuring exposed beams and a large inglenook fireplace. Daily menus evolve with the seasons and blend a robust classical base with artful, innovative ideas. Service is friendly and efficient.

Menu £ 28/33

3 Tower Ln ✉ TA1 4AR – ✆ 01823 352835 (booking essential) – www.thewillowtreerestaurant.com – dinner only – Closed January, August, Sunday, Monday and Thursday

Augustus

MODERN BRITISH • BISTRO X A simple little bistro run by an experienced chef and featuring a conservatory terrace with a retractable roof. Good-sized menu of hearty, unfussy dishes which mix French, British and some Asian influences. Bright and breezy service.

Carte £ 24/43

3 The Courtyard, St James St. ✉ TA1 1JR – ✆ 01823 324354 (booking essential) – www.augustustaunton.co.uk – Closed 23 December-2 January, Sunday and Monday

Castle

HISTORIC BUILDING • CLASSIC Part-12C, wisteria-clad Norman castle with impressive gardens, a keep and two wells. It's been run by the Chapman family for three generations and retains a fittingly traditional style. Well-kept, individually decorated bedrooms. Castle Bow serves modern dishes; relaxed Brazz offers brasserie classics.

44 rooms – †£ 99/125 ††£ 125/225

Castle Green ✉ TA1 1NF – ✆ 01823 272671 – www.the-castle-hotel.com

Castle Bow – See restaurant listing

TAVISTOCK

Devon – Pop. 12 280 – Regional map n° **1**-C2

Cornish Arms

TRADITIONAL CUISINE • COSY It might have been refurbished but the Cornish Arms is still a pleasingly traditional pub and its quarry-tiled bar is invariably filled with regulars playing darts and watching football. The ambitious, talented chef prepares a range of tasty classic and modern dishes, and attractive, sophisticated desserts.

Menu £ 20 (weekday lunch) – Carte £ 22/41

15 West St ✉ PL19 8AN – ✆ 01822 612145 – www.thecornisharmstavistock.co.uk – Closed dinner 24 December

Rockmount

TOWNHOUSE • CONTEMPORARY 1920s house with a contrastingly contemporary interior, set beside the Tavistock viaduct and overlooking the town's rooftops. Individually furnished bedrooms are compact but come with plenty of extras. Breakfast is brought to your room.

6 rooms – †£ 45/110 ††£ 55/130

Drake Rd ✉ PL19 0AX – ✆ 07445 009880 – www.rockmountbandb.co.uk

Tavistock House

TOWNHOUSE • CONTEMPORARY This attractive 1820s townhouse has been carefully restored by its passionate owners and, whilst some original features remain, it now has a stylish boutique appearance. There's an honesty bar in the chic lounge and light snacks are offered at lunch and dinner.

6 rooms - £ 85/139 £ 99/139

50 Plymouth Rd ✉ PL19 8BU - ✆ 01822 481627 - www.tavistockhousehotel.co.uk

at Gulworthy West: 3 mi on A390 ✉ Tavistock

Horn of Plenty

MODERN CUISINE • ELEGANT XX Extremely friendly restaurant in an attractive creeper-clad country house, which offers lovely moor and valley views; ask for a window table. The modern menu has wide-ranging influences – the tasting menu best showcases the chef's talent. Bedrooms are bright and modern and many have balconies or terraces.

Menu £ 20/65

16 rooms - £ 110/255 £ 120/265

Gulworthy ✉ PL19 8JD - Northwest : 1 mi by B 3362 - ✆ 01822 832528 - www.thehornofplenty.co.uk

at Milton Abbot Northwest: 6 mi on B3362 ✉ Tavistock

Restaurant Endsleigh

MODERN CUISINE • INTIMATE XX Elegant, wood-panelled restaurant in a peacefully located hotel; ask for a window table for superb countryside views. Classic cooking with a modern edge; dishes are neatly presented and flavoursome, with local produce to the fore. Attentive service, with a pleasant degree of informality.

Menu £ 22/47 - Carte £ 29/48

Hotel Endsleigh, ✉ PL19 0PQ - Southwest : 1 mi - ✆ 01822 870000 (bookings essential for non-residents) - www.hotelendsleigh.com

Hotel Endsleigh

HISTORIC • CLASSIC Restored Regency lodge in an idyllic rural setting; spacious guest areas offer wonderful countryside views and have a warm, classical style with a contemporary edge. Comfortable, antique-furnished bedrooms boast an understated elegance; choose one overlooking the magnificent gardens.

17 rooms - £ 171/405 £ 190/450 - 5 suites

✉ PL19 0PQ - Southwest : 1 mi - ✆ 01822 870000 - www.hotelendsleigh.com

Restaurant Endsleigh – See restaurant listing

at Chillaton Northwest: 6.25 mi by Chillaton rd ✉ Tavistock

Tor Cottage

TRADITIONAL • CLASSIC Remotely set cottage in 28 hillside acres, with peaceful gardens and a lovely outdoor pool. Bedrooms, most in converted outhouses, boast small kitchenettes and wood burning stoves. Breakfast is taken on the terrace or in the conservatory. Charming owner.

5 rooms - £ 98 £ 150/170

✉ PL16 0JE - Southwest : 0.75 mi by Tavistock rd, turning right at bridle path - ✆ 01822 860248 - www.torcottage.co.uk - Closed mid-December-1 February (minimum 2 night stay)

TEFFONT EVIAS - Wiltshire → See Salisbury

TEMPLE SOWERBY - Cumbria → See Penrith

TENTERDEN

Kent – Pop. 7 118 – Regional map n° **5**-C2

Swan Wine Kitchen

MODERN BRITISH • FRIENDLY XX This rustic modern restaurant sits above the shop in the Chapel Down vineyard and boasts a cosy lounge and a lovely rooftop terrace with views over the vines; naturally, wines from the vineyard feature. Refined cooking is full of flavour and relies on just a few ingredients to do the talking.

Menu £ 28

Chapel Down Winery, Small Hythe Rd ✉ TN30 7NG
- ✆ 01580 761616 - www.swanchapeldown.co.uk - Closed dinner Sunday-Wednesday

TETBURY

Gloucestershire - Pop. 5 250 - Regional map n° **2**-C1

Gumstool Inn

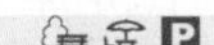

TRADITIONAL CUISINE • CONTEMPORARY DÉCOR Set in the grounds of Calcot Manor; an attractive outbuilding with a contemporary 'Country Living' style. A flexible menu offers snacks, two sizes of starter and hearty British main courses - the open fire with a chargrill is a feature.

Carte £ 21/41

Calcot Manor Hotel, Calcot ✉ GL8 8YJ - West : 3.5 mi on A 4135
- ✆ 01666 890391 - www.calcot.co

Calcot Manor

FAMILY • CONTEMPORARY Impressive collection of converted farm buildings in a peaceful country setting, comprising ancient barns, old stables and a characterful farmhouse. Comfy lounges and stylish bedrooms have good mod cons; the outbuildings house a crèche, conference rooms and a superb spa complex. The laid-back conservatory offers classical dishes and there's a popular pub in the grounds.

35 rooms - †£ 209/354 ††£ 209/354 - 1 suite

Calcot ✉ GL8 8YJ - West : 3.5 mi on A 4135
- ✆ 01666 890391 - www.calcot.co

Gumstool Inn - See restaurant listing

The Close

TOWNHOUSE • CONTEMPORARY The rear garden and courtyard of this 16C townhouse provide the perfect spot on a warm summer's day. Bold colours and contemporary furnishings blend well with the building's period features; look out for the superb cupola ceiling in the bar. Choose from a list of classics in the brasserie or a selection of refined, modern dishes in the more sophisticated restaurant.

18 rooms - †£ 110/150 ††£ 180/220

Long St ✉ GL8 8AQ
- ✆ 01666 502272 - www.cotswold-inns-hotels.co.uk

TEWKESBURY

Gloucestershire - Pop. 19 778 - Regional map n° **2**-C1

at Corse Lawn Southwest: 6 mi by A38 and A438 on B4211 ✉ Gloucester

Corse Lawn House

COUNTRY HOUSE • CLASSIC Elegant Grade II listed Queen Anne house, just off the village green and fronted by a pond. The traditionally appointed interior features open fires and antiques; some of the spacious bedrooms have four-poster or half-tester beds. Dine from classical menus in the formal restaurant or characterful bistro-bar.

18 rooms - †£ 75/100 ††£ 120/160 - 3 suites

✉ GL19 4LZ
- ✆ 01452 780771 - www.corselawn.com - Closed 24-26 December

THETFORD

Norfolk – Pop. 24 833 – Regional map n° **8**-C2

The Mulberry

MEDITERRANEAN CUISINE • NEIGHBOURHOOD A bell tinkles as you enter this delightful stone property and the charming owner welcomes you in. The dining room leads through to a conservatory and a walled garden complete with a mulberry tree. Cooking is gutsy and boldly flavoured.

Carte £ 25/38

11 Raymond St ✉ IP24 2EA – ✆ 01842 824122 (booking advisable) – www.mulberrythetford.co.uk – dinner only – Closed 6-20 August, 26-29 December, Sunday and Monday

THORNBURY

South Gloucestershire – ✉ Bristol – Pop. 11 687 – Regional map n° **2**-C1

Thornbury Castle

MODERN CUISINE • ELEGANT Sited in a tower within the main 16C part of Thornbury Castle; a small, partly wood-panelled, circular room decorated in deep red, with coats of arms and an impressive fireplace. Elegantly laid tables; elaborate, modern dishes.

Menu £ 27 (weekdays)/50 – Carte £ 50/65

Thornbury Castle Hotel, Castle St ✉ BS35 1HH – ✆ 01454 281182 – www.thornburycastle.co.uk

Romy's Kitchen

INDIAN • SIMPLE In the centre of a medieval market town, in a listed stone building which was once part of the castle, is this sweet, friendly restaurant. The bubbly chef-owner freshly prepares everything from the naan to the chai-spiced ice cream.

Carte £ 17/32

2 Castle St ✉ BS35 1HB – ✆ 01454 416728 – www.romyskitchen.co.uk – Closed Sunday and Monday

Thornbury Castle

HISTORIC • CLASSIC Impressive 16C castle with a long and illustrious history; Henry VIII stayed here on his honeymoon with Anne Boleyn! Characterful, baronial style bedrooms feature mullioned windows, wall tapestries, beams and huge fireplaces.

27 rooms – †£ 255 ††£ 295/565 – 4 suites

Castle St ✉ BS35 1HH – ✆ 01454 281182 – www.thornburycastle.co.uk

Thornbury Castle – See restaurant listing

THORNHAM

Norfolk – Regional map n° **8**-B1

Chequers Inn

TRADITIONAL CUISINE • FASHIONABLE Sit on the terrace or hire a wooden pavilion and take in the view. Cooking makes use of the local bounty; alongside the main menu there's tapas, such as tempura mussels, and pizzas which are stone-baked using local ingredients.

Carte £ 26/38

11 rooms – †£ 120/195 ††£ 120/195

High St ✉ PE36 6LY – ✆ 01485 512229 – www.chequersinnthornham.com

THORNTON – Lancashire → See Blackpool

THORNTON HOUGH

Merseyside – Regional map n° **11**-A3

Thornton Hall

BUSINESS • CONTEMPORARY A substantial manor house which has been added to over the years. Stained glass, carved wood reliefs and an oak-panelled restaurant with a ceiling crafted from wood, leather and mother of pearl contrast with an impressive spa. The luxurious bedrooms are also a mix of the classic and contemporary.

62 rooms - £ 89/299 £ 89/299 - £ 16 - 1 suite

Neston Rd ✉ CH63 1JF - On B 5136 - ☎ 0151 336 3938 - www.thorntonhallhotel.com

THORPE MARKET

Norfolk - ✉ North Walsham - Regional map n° **8**-D1

Gunton Arms

MODERN BRITISH • INN Charming pub overlooking the 1,000 acre Gunton Estate deer park. Enjoy a tasty homemade snack over a game of pool or darts in the bar or make for a gnarled wood table by the fireplace in the flag-floored Elk Room. Dishes are fiercely seasonal; some - such as the Aberdeen Angus steaks - are cooked over the fire. Well-equipped bedrooms have a stylish, country house feel.

Carte £ 19/42

16 rooms - £ 85/310 £ 95/320

Gunton Park ✉ NR11 8TZ - South : 1 mi on A 149 - ☎ 01263 832010 (booking advisable) - www.theguntonarms.co.uk - Closed 25 December and dinner 1 January

THUNDER BRIDGE

West Yorkshire - Regional map n° **13**-B3

Woodman Inn

MODERN CUISINE • INN Set in a lovely wooded spot in a South Pennine valley. The low-beamed bar buzzes with a mix of drinkers and diners, and there's an upstairs restaurant and a small garden over the road. Sophisticated restaurant-style dishes arrive elaborately presented. Smart, modern country bedrooms include a three-level suite.

Carte £ 28/49

19 rooms - £ 59/99 £ 79/119

✉ HD8 0PX - ☎ 01484 605778 - www.woodman-inn.com

THURSFORD GREEN

Norfolk - Regional map n° **8**-C1

Holly Lodge

TRADITIONAL • COSY Remotely set 18C house surrounded by delightful gardens. Bedrooms are located in the old stable block and boast exposed beams, feature beds and numerous extra touches. Communal breakfasts in the smart conservatory use local and homemade produce; home-cooked dinners are from a daily changing set menu.

3 rooms - £ 80/110 £ 100/130

The Street ✉ NR21 0AS - ☎ 01328 878465 - www.hollylodgeguesthouse.co.uk - Restricted opening January-March

THURSLEY

Surrey - Regional map n° **4**-C2

Three Horseshoes

TRADITIONAL CUISINE • CLASSIC DÉCOR There's no doubting this pub is at the heart of the community - the locals clubbed together to save it from developers. Hearty meals are high on flavour yet low on price. Real fires and fresh flowers give it a homely feel.

Carte £ 23/43

Dye House Rd ✉ GU8 6QD - ☎ 01252 703268 - www.threehorseshoesthursley.com - Closed Sunday dinner

TICEHURST

East Sussex – ✉ Wadhurst – Pop. 1 705 – Regional map n° **5**-B2

Bell

TRADITIONAL BRITISH • INN With top hats as lampshades, tubas in the loos and a dining room called 'The Stable with a Table', quirky is this 16C coaching inn's middle name. Seasonal menus offer proper pub food, and the rustic bedrooms – many with their own silver birch tree – share the pub's idiosyncratic charm.

Carte £ 25/42

11 rooms – †£ 75/295 ††£ 85/295

High St ✉ TN5 7AS – ✆ 01580 200300 (booking advisable) – www.thebellinticehurst.com

TICKTON – East Riding of Yorkshire

→ See Beverley

TILLINGTON – West Sussex

→ See Petworth

TILSWORTH

Central Bedfordshire – Pop. 331 – Regional map n° **7**-A2

The Anchor

MODERN CUISINE • CONTEMPORARY DÉCOR It's miles from the sea but The Anchor has an appealing nautical theme. The food is also something a little different: cooking is sophisticated, flavours are well balanced and straightforward dishes are elevated to another level.

Menu £ 15 – Carte £ 31/40

1 Dunstable Rd ✉ LU7 9PU – ✆ 01525 211404 – www.anchortilsworth.co.uk – Closed Sunday dinner-Wednesday lunch

TISBURY

Wiltshire – Pop. 2 178 – Regional map n° **2**-C3

Beckford Arms

TRADITIONAL CUISINE • FRIENDLY Charming 18C inn with a beamed dining room, a rustic bar and a lovely country house sitting room – where films are screened on Sundays. There's a delightful terrace and garden with hammocks, a petanque pitch and even a dog bath. Tasty, unfussy classics and country-style dishes. Tasteful bedrooms provide thoughtful comforts. Smart duplex suites, a 3min drive away.

Carte £ 25/37

10 rooms – †£ 95/130 ††£ 95/130

Fonthill Gifford ✉ SP3 6PX – Northwest : 2 mi by Greenwich Rd – ✆ 01747 870385 (booking essential) – www.beckfordarms.com – Closed 25 December

TITCHWELL

Norfolk – Pop. 99 – Regional map n° **8**-C1

The Conservatory

MODERN CUISINE • FASHIONABLE XX An appealing hotel restaurant offering plenty of choice. The trendy 'Eating Rooms' area offers sea views and comfort food. The smart 'Conservatory' area offers two more ambitious, accomplished menus of interesting modern dishes.

Menu £ 33 (dinner) – Carte £ 24/47 **s**

Titchwell Manor Hotel, ✉ PE31 8BB – ✆ 01485 210221 – www.titchwellmanor.com

Titchwell Manor

COUNTRY HOUSE • GRAND LUXURY This attractive brick farmhouse has a stylish interior, where bare floorboards and seaside photos feature. Bedrooms in the grounds are modern, colourful and originally styled; those in the main house are slightly more conservative.

26 rooms ☕ - 🚹£ 75/200 🚹🚹£ 100/260

✉ PE31 8BB - ✆ 01485 210221 - www.titchwellmanor.com

🍴 **The Conservatory** - See restaurant listing

Briarfields

FAMILY • MODERN In winter, sink into a sofa by the cosy fire; in summer, relax in the secluded courtyard beside the pond or on the deck overlooking the salt marshes and the sea. Bedrooms are modern and immaculately kept; some open onto the garden.

23 rooms ☕ - 🚹£ 80/85 🚹🚹£ 115/140

Main Street ✉ PE31 8BB - ✆ 01485 210742 - www.briarfieldshotelnorfolk.co.uk

TITLEY

Herefordshire - ✉ Kington - Regional map n° **10**-A3

Stagg Inn

MODERN BRITISH • PUB Deep in rural Herefordshire, at the meeting point of two drover's roads, sits this characterful, part-medieval, part-Victorian pub. Seasonal menus offer tried-and-tested combinations; be sure to save room for one of the generous desserts. The cosy pub bedrooms can be noisy; opt for one in the former vicarage.

Carte £ 27/46

6 rooms ☕ - 🚹£ 80/120 🚹🚹£ 100/140

✉ HR5 3RL - ✆ 01544 230221 (booking essential) - www.thestagg.co.uk - Closed 29 January-9 February, 27 June-4 July, 1-17 November, 25-27 December, Monday and Tuesday

TOLLARD ROYAL

Wiltshire - Regional map n° **2**-C3

King John Inn

REGIONAL CUISINE • PUB Modern black and white hunting photos line the walls and provide a clue both to the cooking and the clientele. The short daily menu is printed on brown paper and lists the origin of ingredients; start with the tasty homemade bread.

Menu £ 20 (weekday lunch) - Carte £ 28/51

8 rooms ☕ - 🚹£ 89/149 🚹🚹£ 109/189

✉ SP5 5PS - ✆ 01725 516207 - www.kingjohninn.co.uk - Closed 25 December

TOOT BALDON - Oxfordshire → See Oxford

TOPSHAM

Devon - ✉ Exeter - Pop. 3 730 - Regional map n° **1**-D2

Salutation Inn

MODERN CUISINE • DESIGN XX 1720s coaching inn with a surprisingly contemporary interior. The glass-covered courtyard serves breakfast, light lunch and afternoon tea, while the stylish dining room offers nicely balanced weekly 4, 6 and 8 course menus of well-judged modern cooking. Bedrooms are similarly up-to-date and understated.

Menu £ 43/85 (dinner) - Carte lunch £ 22/31

6 rooms ☕ - 🚹£ 115/205 🚹🚹£ 135/285

68 Fore St ✉ EX3 0HL - ✆ 01392 873060 (booking essential at dinner) - www.salutationtopsham.co.uk - Closed 26 December and 1 January

TORQUAY

Torbay – Pop. 49 094 – Regional map n° 1-C-D2

✿ The Elephant (Simon Hulstone)

MODERN BRITISH • FRIENDLY XX For over 10 years the dedicated chef-owner has proudly run this bright, modern restaurant, which sits in a Georgian terrace overlooking the harbour. Menus offer well-judged, beautifully presented dishes with no unnecessary elaboration. Ingredients are top notch – most come from their 96 acre farm near Brixham.

→ Brixham crab with dashi jelly, crispy chicken skin and lemon thyme. Loin of Exmoor venison with celeriac, ceps and apple sauerkraut. Poached rhubarb with lemon crème, white chocolate and champagne.

Menu £ 20 (lunch) – Carte £ 30/49

Town plan: B2-e – *3-4 Beacon Terr ✉ TQ1 2BH*
– ✆ 01803 200044 – www.elephantrestaurant.co.uk – Closed 1-19 January, Sunday and Monday

Orange Tree

CLASSIC FRENCH • NEIGHBOURHOOD XX A homely, split-level restaurant set down a narrow town centre backstreet. The seasonally evolving menu is made up of classically based, French-influenced dishes, which are carefully prepared and rely on fresh, local produce.

Menu £ 48 – Carte £ 27/46

Town plan: B2-u – *14-16 Parkhill Rd ✉ TQ1 2AL*
– ✆ 01803 213936 (booking essential) – www.orangetreerestaurant.co.uk – dinner only – Closed 2 weeks January, 2 weeks October-November, Sunday and Monday

Harbour Kitchen 

SEAFOOD • BISTRO X A laid-back eatery on the harbourside; sit on the pavement terrace or at high communal tables for cocktails and snacks or head for the first floor for a more intimate atmosphere. Regularly changing menus keep their focus on seafood.

Carte £ 25/42

Town plan: B2-k – *16 Victoria Par ✉ TQ1 2BB*
– ✆ 01803 211075 – www.harbourkitchen.co.uk – Closed lunch October-April except December

Number 7

SEAFOOD • BISTRO X Personally run bistro in a terrace of Regency houses. The walls are covered with fish-related photos and artefacts, as well as extensive blackboard menus of seafood fresh from the Brixham day boats; the simplest dishes are the best.

Carte £ 23/45

Town plan: B2-e – *7 Beacon Terr. ✉ TQ1 2BH*
– ✆ 01803 295055 (booking advisable) – www.no7-fish.com – dinner only and lunch Wednesday-Saturday – Closed 2 weeks February, 1 week November, Christmas-New Year, Monday November-May and Sunday October-June

On the Rocks 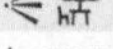

MODERN BRITISH • BISTRO X Two local lads opened this lovely restaurant overlooking Torbay. It's modern and laid-back, with a split-level room and furniture made from reclaimed scaffold boards. Appealing menus champion produce from the bay and the fields above.

Carte £ 22/49

Town plan: B1-r – *1 Abbey Cres. ✉ TQ2 5HB*
– ✆ 01803 203666 (bookings advisable at dinner)
– www.ontherocks-torquay.co.uk – Closed 26 December, 1 January and weekday lunches October-March

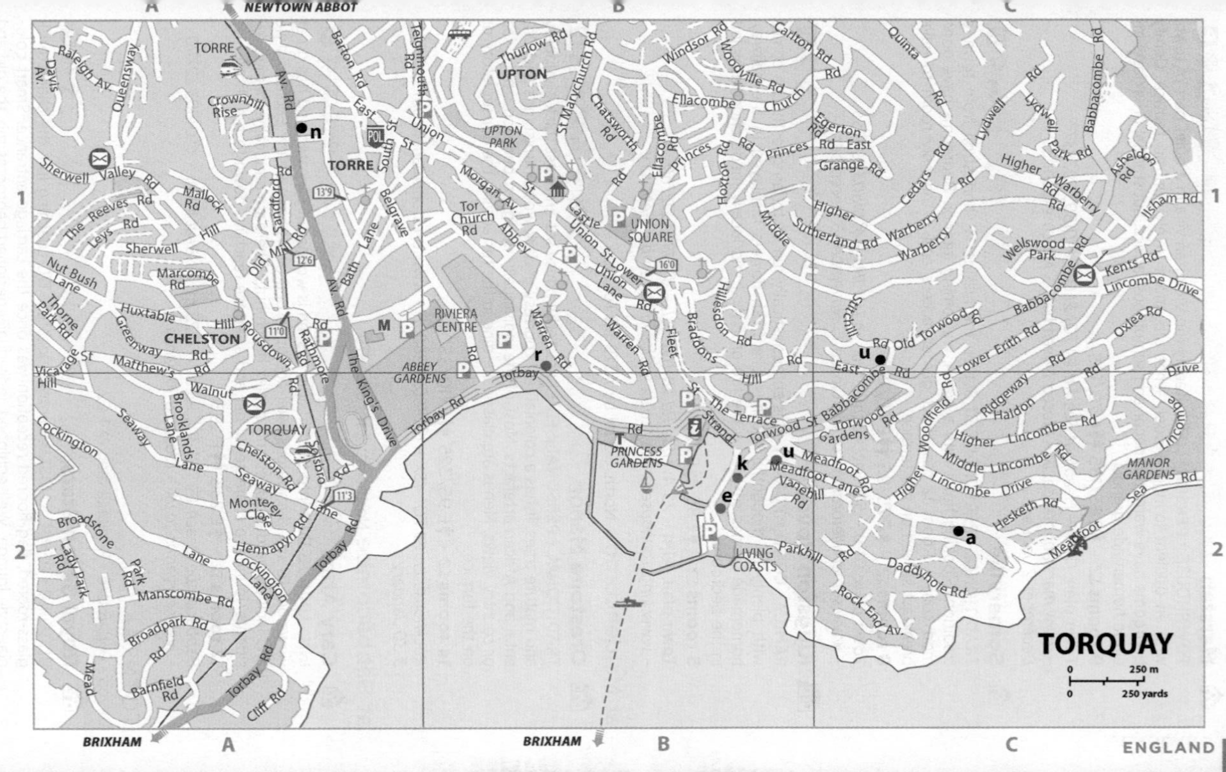
TORQUAY
0 250 m
0 250 yards
NEWTOWN ABBOT
BRIXHAM
BRIXHAM
A
B
C
1
2
TORRE
TORRE
UPTON
UPTON PARK
CHELSTON
TORQUAY
UNION SQUARE
RIVIERA CENTRE
ABBEY GARDENS
PRINCESS GARDENS
LIVING COASTS
MANOR GARDENS
Wellswood Park
The King's Drive
Torbay Rd
Babbacombe Rd
Lincombe Drive
Meadfoot Rd
Meadfoot Lane
Meadfoot Sea Rd
Daddyhole Rd
Rock End Av.
Parkhill Rd
Vanehill Rd
Torwood St
Torwood Gardens Rd
Strand
The Terrace
Fleet St
Braddons Hill Rd East
Hillesdon Rd
Warren Rd
Abbey Rd
Union St
Lower Union Lane
Castle Rd
St Marychurch Rd
Chatsworth Rd
Ellacombe Rd
Ellacombe Church Rd
Princes Rd
Princes Rd East
Hoxton Rd
Woodville Rd
Windsor Rd
Carlton Rd
Thurlow Rd
Teignmouth Rd
Tor Church Rd
Morgan Av.
Belgrave Rd
Bath Lane
Avenue Rd
Sandford Rd
Old Mill Rd
Rathmore Rd
Rousdown Rd
Chelston Rd
Seaway Lane
Seaway Rd
Walnut Rd
Brooklands Lane
Cockington Lane
Cockington
Sherwell Valley Rd
Sherwell Hill
Queensway
Raleigh Av.
Davis Av.
Mallock Rd
Marcombe Rd
Huxtable Hill
Greenway Rd
St Matthew's Rd
Vicarage Hill
Thorne Park Rd
Nut Bush Lane
The Reeves Rd
Leys Rd
Broadpark Rd
Barnfield Rd
Manscombe Rd
Lady Park Rd
Broadstone Park Rd
Mead
Cliff Rd
Hennapyn Rd
Monterey Close
Solsbro Rd
Crownhill Rise
Barton Rd
East St
South St
Higher Woodfield Rd
Middle Lincombe Rd
Higher Lincombe Rd
Hesketh Rd
Haldon Rd
Ridgeway Rd
Lower Erith Rd
Old Torwood Rd
Stitchill Rd
East Rd
Oxlea Rd
Lincombe Drive
Kents Rd
Ilsham Rd
Asheldon Rd
Lydwell Rd
Lydwell Park Rd
Higher Warberry Rd
Warberry Rd
Middle Warberry Rd
Quinta Rd
Cedars Rd
Egerton Rd
Grange Rd
Higher Sutherland Rd
M
T
a
e
k
n
r
u
u

Marstan

TOWNHOUSE · PERSONALISED Keenly run Victorian villa in a quiet part of town, with an opulent lounge, a pool, a hot tub and a lovely suntrap terrace. Comfy bedrooms have warm red décor and sumptuous fabrics. Substantial breakfasts include homemade granola.

9 rooms - £ 65/155 £ 79/165

Town plan: C2-a - *Meadfoot Sea Rd ✉ TQ1 2LQ - ✆ 01803 292837 - www.marstanhotel.co.uk - Closed November-15 March except 30 December-2 January*

Somerville

TRADITIONAL · PERSONALISED Set on the hillside, a short stroll from town, a traditional-looking hotel with a warm, welcoming interior. Bedrooms have good mod cons – Room 12 has direct garden access and is the only room to have breakfast served on the terrace.

8 rooms - £ 75/95 £ 80/150

Town plan: C1-u - *515 Babbacombe Rd. ✉ TQ1 1HJ - ✆ 01803 294755 - www.somervilletorquay.co.uk - Closed 15 November-8 December*

Kingston House

FAMILY · CONTEMPORARY This enthusiastically run Victorian guesthouse comes with plenty of thoughtful touches, like fresh flowers displayed in the hallway, homemade scones served by the fire on arrival and locally made chocolates left in the bedrooms.

5 rooms - £ 85 £ 85/105

Town plan: A1-n - *75 Avenue Rd ✉ TQ2 5LL - ✆ 01803 212760 - www.kingstonhousetorquay.co.uk - Closed December-February*

at Maidencombe North: 3.5 mi by A379 ✉ Torquay

Orestone Manor

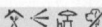

TRADITIONAL · PERSONALISED Characterful house set amongst thick shrubbery and mature trees. It has a colonial feel courtesy of dark wood furnishings and Oriental and African artefacts. Most of the individually designed bedrooms have sea or country views. Menus are classical – dine in the restaurant, the conservatory or on the terrace.

14 rooms - £ 95/325 £ 110/350

Rockhouse Ln ✉ TQ1 4SX - ✆ 01803 328098 - www.orestonemanor.com - Closed 3-30 January

at Babbacombe Northeast: 2 mi on A379

Cary Arms

INN · UNIQUE Built into the cliffside, this inn is wonderfully located and has great views out to sea. Sumptuous, well-equipped bedrooms have a New England style and include garden suites and duplex beach huts. There's a nautically-themed residents' lounge, a characterful bar and a terrace reaching down to the shore.

12 rooms - £ 236 £ 295

Babbacombe Beach ✉ TQ1 3LX - East : 0.25 mi by Beach Rd. - ✆ 01803 327110 - www.caryarms.co.uk - Closed 8-16 January

TOTNES

Devon – Pop. 8 076 – Regional map n° **1**-C2

Royal Seven Stars

HISTORIC · PERSONALISED Centrally located, 17C coaching inn; the characterful glass-roofed, flag-floored reception was once the carriage entrance. Smart colonial-style lounge. Well-equipped, individually designed bedrooms mix the old and the new; some have jacuzzi baths. Snacks in the bars or on the terrace; brasserie dishes in TQ9.

21 rooms - £ 90/120 £ 125/179

The Plains ✉ TQ9 5DD - ✆ 01803 862125 - www.royalsevenstars.co.uk

TOWCESTER

Northamptonshire – Pop. 9 057 – Regional map n° **9**-B3

Vine House

MODERN CUISINE • INTIMATE XX A pair of pretty stone cottages in a tranquil village: dating from the 17C and home to a passionately run restaurant. The daily changing fixed price menu comprises accomplished modern dishes made using good quality ingredients. Cosy beamed bedrooms are named after grape vines.

Menu £ 33

6 rooms – †£ 69 ††£ 95/105

100 High St, Paulerspury ✉ NN12 7NA – Southeast : 4 mi by A 5 – ☎ 01327 811267 (booking advisable) – www.vinehousehotel.com – dinner only – Closed 1 week January and Sunday

TREGONY

Cornwall – Pop. 768 – Regional map n° **1**-B3

Hay Barton

COUNTRY HOUSE • COSY The owner has lived in this warm, cosy farmhouse since the 1960s and still keeps some cattle. Country-style bedrooms come with Roberts radios and plenty to read; two have antique bath tubs. Cornish produce features at breakfast.

3 rooms – †£ 70/80 ††£ 90/100

✉ TR2 5TF – South : 1 mi on A 3078 – ☎ 01872 530288 – www.haybarton.com

TRELOWARREN – Cornwall → See Helston

TRENT

Dorset – Regional map n° **2**-C3

Rose & Crown

MODERN CUISINE • RUSTIC Sit in the characterful 'Buffs Bar' or the bright conservatory of this part-thatched 14C pub. Tasty country cooking is the order of the day – bypass the pub classics and go for the likes of pig's head with apple purée or calves' liver with sage fritters. Bedrooms come with patios overlooking the countryside.

Carte £ 25/40

3 rooms – †£ 75/100 ††£ 85/120

✉ DT9 4SL – ☎ 01935 850776 – www.theroseandcrowntrent.co.uk – Closed 25-26 December

TRESCO → See Scilly (Isles of)

TRURO

Cornwall – Pop. 20 332 – Regional map n° **1**-B3

Tabb's

MODERN BRITISH • NEIGHBOURHOOD XX A series of lilac-painted rooms with matching chairs, in a small former pub. The appealing menu lists refined, classically based dishes where good quality produce shines through. Tasty tapas-style lunches offer three dishes for £ 12.

Carte £ 29/39

85 Kenwyn St ✉ TR1 3BZ – ☎ 01872 262110 (booking essential at lunch) – www.tabbs.co.uk – Closed 1 week January, 1 week October, Saturday lunch, Sunday dinner and Monday

Mannings

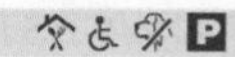

BUSINESS • MODERN Imposing hotel located in the city centre, close to the cathedral. Boutique bedrooms are bright, modern and stylish; spacious apartment-style rooms – in the neighbouring mews – boast over-sized beds and galley kitchens. There's a chic cocktail bar and a stylish restaurant offering an eclectic all-day menu.

43 rooms – £ 65/115 £ 105/135

Lemon St ✉ TR1 2QB – ✆ 01872 270345 – www.manningshotels.co.uk – Closed Christmas

TUDDENHAM

Suffolk – Pop. 400 – Regional map n° **8**-B2

Tuddenham Mill

CREATIVE BRITISH • INTIMATE XX Delightful 18C watermill overlooking the mill-pond; the old workings are still in situ in the stylish bar and there's a beamed restaurant with black furnishings above. Cooking features quality seasonal produce in unusual, innovative combinations. Some of the trendy bedrooms are in attractive outbuildings.

Menu £ 18 (weekday lunch) – Carte dinner £ 35/50

20 rooms – £ 145/395 £ 145/395

High St ✉ IP28 6SQ – ✆ 01638 713552 – www.tuddenhammill.co.uk

TURNERS HILL

West Sussex – Pop. 885 – Regional map n° **4**-D2

AG's

MODERN CUISINE • CHIC XXX Have drinks in the champagne bar before dinner by the marble fireplace in the formal restaurant of this fabulous 18C country house. Cooking follows the seasons and presentation and flavour combinations are modern and original.

Menu £ 60

Alexander House Hotel, East St ✉ RH10 4QD – East : 1 mi on B 2110 – ✆ 01342 714914 (booking essential) – www.alexanderhouse.co.uk – dinner only and Sunday lunch

Alexander House

COUNTRY HOUSE • ELEGANT A stunning 18C country house in extensive grounds – once owned by Percy Shelley's family. The superb spa has 21 treatment rooms and a Grecian pool. Spacious bedrooms are well-equipped; the contemporary Cedar Lodge Suites have mood lighting and either a balcony or terrace. Dine in the brasserie or formal AG's.

58 rooms – £ 194/744 £ 209/759 – 3 suites

East St ✉ RH10 4QD – East : 1 mi on B 2110 – ✆ 01342 714914 – www.alexanderhouse.co.uk

AG's – See restaurant listing

TWO BRIDGES

Devon – ✉ Yelverton – Regional map n° **1**-C2

Prince Hall

TRADITIONAL • COSY Remote former hunting lodge with a welcoming, shabby-chic interior and wide-ranging views. Dogs are welcome throughout, except in the bright restaurant, where you'll find vibrantly flavoured dishes with Mediterranean influences. Homely bedrooms display subtle modern touches; some overlook the moor.

9 rooms – £ 99 £ 160/190

✉ PL20 6SA – East : 1 mi on B 3357 – ✆ 01822 890403 – www.princehall.co.uk

TYNEMOUTH

Tyne and Wear – Pop. 67 519 – Regional map n° **14**-B2

Grand

TRADITIONAL · CLASSIC A Victorian hotel with superb sea views: the Duchess of Northumberland's one-time holiday home. Original features include an impressive staircase. Bedrooms are either spacious and traditional or smaller and more modern – Room 222 has a four-poster and jacuzzi. The brasserie serves a modern menu.

46 rooms – †£ 86/139 ††£ 99/160

14 Grand Par. ✉ NE30 4ER – ✆ 0191 293 6666 – www.grandhotel-uk.com

Martineau

TOWNHOUSE · COSY Attractive 18C red-brick house named after Harriet Martineau. Cosy, individually furnished bedrooms come with thoughtful extras; two offer pleasant Tyne views. Superb communal breakfasts or a pre-ordered hamper in your room.

4 rooms – †£ 80 ††£ 100

57 Front St ✉ NE30 4BX – ✆ 0191 257 9038 – www.martineau-house.co.uk – Closed 23-29 December

UCKFIELD

East Sussex – Pop. 15 213 – Regional map n° **5**-A2

Horsted Place

HISTORIC · CLASSIC Impressive country house in Victorian Gothic style. The tiled entrance hall leads to an impressive main gallery, where ornate sitting rooms are furnished with fine antiques. Individually styled bedrooms are well-equipped; most have great views over the parkland. The formal dining room offers a classical menu.

17 rooms – †£ 145/190 ††£ 145/375 – 5 suites

Little Horsted ✉ TN22 5TS – South : 2.5 mi by B 2102 and A 22 on A 26 – ✆ 01825 750581 – www.horstedplace.co.uk – Closed first week January

UFFORD

Suffolk – Regional map n° **8**-D3

Ufford Crown

TRADITIONAL BRITISH · FRIENDLY A welcoming former coaching inn run by an enthusiastic husband and wife team. The daily menu of hearty, honest cooking includes a great grill section and some Mediterranean-inspired dishes. Portions are generous and service is keen.

Carte £ 21/41

High St ✉ IP13 6EL – ✆ 01394 461030 – www.theuffordcrown.com – Closed Tuesday

UPPER SLAUGHTER – Gloucestershire → See Bourton-on-the-Water

UPPER SOUTH WRAXALL

Wiltshire – Regional map n° **2**-C2

Longs Arms

TRADITIONAL BRITISH · PUB Handsome, bay-windowed, Bath stone pub opposite a medieval church in a sleepy village. Traditional British dishes are full-flavoured, hearty and satisfying; everything is homemade and they smoke their own meats and fish. Dine in the characterful area in front of the bar. Warm, friendly service.

Carte £ 19/42

✉ BA15 2SB – ✆ 01225 864450 (booking essential) – www.thelongsarms.com – Closed 3 weeks January,1 week September, Sunday dinner, Monday and Tuesday

UPPINGHAM

Rutland – Pop. 4 745 – Regional map n° **9**-C2

Lake Isle

CLASSIC CUISINE • FRIENDLY XX Characterful 18C town centre property accessed via a narrow passageway and very personally run by experienced owners. It has a cosy lounge and a heavy wood-furnished dining room. Light lunches are followed by much more elaborate modern dinners. Bedrooms come with good extras and some have whirlpool baths.

Carte £ 26/48

12 rooms – †£ 75/90 ††£ 90/125

16 High St East ✉ LE15 9PZ – ✆ 01572 822951 – www.lakeisle.co.uk – Closed Sunday dinner and Monday lunch

at Lyddington South: 2 mi by A6003✉ Uppingham

Old White Hart

TRADITIONAL CUISINE • PUB Sit in low-beamed bar or the larger dining room and conservatory. Well-hung steaks and homemade sausages are a feature, however, fish isn't overlooked, with the chef visiting Birmingham market twice a week. Prices are reasonable, especially from Monday-Thursday, and you can book for a game of petanque too. Bedrooms are smart and modern; some are in roadside cottages.

Carte £ 12/32

14 rooms – †£ 75/85 ††£ 100/110

51 Main St ✉ LE15 9LR – ✆ 01572 821703 – www.oldwhitehart.co.uk – Closed 25 December and Sunday dinner in winter

UPTON BISHOP – Herefordshire → See Ross-on-Wye

UPTON GREY

Hampshire – Pop. 449 – Regional map n° **4**-B1

Hoddington Arms

TRADITIONAL BRITISH • RUSTIC Sit in the lovely garden, the smart cabana or the characterful, laid-back pub – the restored barn area is particularly atmospheric. Lunch offers pub classics while dinner sees the likes of venison scotch egg or braised lamb shoulder.

Menu £ 22 (weekday lunch) – Carte £ 24/41

Bidden Rd ✉ RG25 2RL – ✆ 01256 862371 – www.hoddingtonarms.co.uk – Closed 26 December, 1 January and Sunday dinner

UPTON MAGNA – Shropshire → See Shrewsbury

VENTNOR – Isle of Wight → See Wight (Isle of)

VERYAN

Cornwall – ✉ Truro – Pop. 877 – Regional map n° **1**-B3

Nare

COUNTRY HOUSE • CLASSIC Personally run, classic country house with a stunning bay outlook; take it in from the pool or hot tub. Most bedrooms have views and some have patios or balconies. Have afternoon tea in the drawing room followed by canapés in the bar, then choose from either a traditional daily menu in the dining room or more modern fare in Quarterdeck.

37 rooms – †£ 150/290 ††£ 290/835 – 7 suites

Carne Beach ✉ TR2 5PF – Southwest : 1.25 mi – ✆ 01872 501111 – www.narehotel.co.uk

VIRGINSTOW

Devon – Regional map n° **1**-C2

Percy's

TRADITIONAL • COSY Stone house in 130 acres of fields and woodland. The owners grow veg, breed racehorses, rear pigs and sheep, and sell wool, skins and produce. Spacious, comfy bedrooms in the former barn – some have jacuzzi baths. Set menu of traditional dishes in the formal dining room; ingredients are from the estate.

7 rooms – £ 90/180 £ 140/230

Coombeshead Estate ✉ EX21 5EA – Southwest : 1.75 mi on Tower Hill rd – ✆ 01409 211236 – www.percys.co.uk

WADDESDON

Buckinghamshire – ✉ Aylesbury – Pop. 1 797 – Regional map n° **6**-C2

Five Arrows

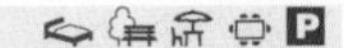

TRADITIONAL BRITISH • INN XX A half-timbered house on the Rothschild Estate, with Elizabethan chimney stacks, attractive gabling and mullioned windows (its name is derived from the Rothschild family emblem). Contemporary country house bedrooms are split between the main house and the courtyard. Local game is a highlight in the restaurant.

Menu £ 18 (weekday lunch)/22 – Carte £ 30/42

16 rooms – £ 95/105 £ 145/165

High St ✉ HP18 0JE – ✆ 01296 651727 – www.fivearrowshotel.co.uk

WADDINGTON

Lancashire – Pop. 3 992 – Regional map n° **11**-B2

Higher Buck

TRADITIONAL CUISINE • FRIENDLY A smartly refurbished pub with pastel-painted wood panelling and modern furnishings, in a lovely Ribble Valley village. Bag a spot at one of the U-shaped banquettes or on the sunny terrace overlooking the Square and dine on reassuringly robust, seasonal dishes. Service is friendly and stylish bedrooms await.

Carte £ 24/42

7 rooms – £ 65/125 £ 95/125

The Square ✉ BB7 3HZ – ✆ 01200 423226 – www.higherbuck.com – Closed 25 December

WADEBRIDGE

Cornwall – Pop. 6 599 – Regional map n° **1**-B2

Ship Inn

TRADITIONAL CUISINE • COSY This 16C inn is one of the oldest public houses in town and has a real community feel. The menu offers something for everyone, mixing pub classics with more modern dishes. Choose a seat in one of the three cosy, low-beamed rooms.

Carte £ 23/34

Gonvena Hill ✉ PL27 6DF – ✆ 01208 813845 – www.shipinnwadebridge.com – Closed Sunday dinner in winter

Trewornan Manor

COUNTRY HOUSE • ELEGANT Stunning Grade II listed 13C manor house set in 25 acres beside the River Amble, with over 8 acres of delightfully manicured gardens. Sumptuous, ultra-chic bedrooms all have views of the grounds. Welcoming young owners offer cream tea by the fire in the restful sitting room and fresh home-cooked breakfasts.

5 rooms – £ 115/190 £ 125/210

Trewornan Bridge, St Minver ✉ PL27 6EX – North : 1.75 mi on B3314 (Rock rd) – ✆ 01208 812359 – www.trewornanmanor.co.uk

WALBERSWICK

Suffolk – Pop. 380 – Regional map n° **8**-D2

Anchor

TRADITIONAL CUISINE • PUB A welcoming pub in an Arts and Crafts building; its sizeable garden features a wood-fired oven and leads down to the beach. Dishes are prepared with real care and global flavours punctuate the menu. If you're staying the night, choose a wood-clad chalet in the garden; breakfasts are impressive.

Carte £ 25/38

10 rooms – £ 105/125 £ 125/165

Main St IP18 6UA – 01502 722112 – www.anchoratwalberswick.com – Closed 25 December

WALFORD – Herefordshire → See Ross-on-Wye

WALL – Staffordshire → See Lichfield

WAREHAM

Dorset – Pop. 5 496 – Regional map n° **2**-C3

Priory

HISTORIC BUILDING • CLASSIC Delightfully located part-16C priory, which is proudly and personally run. Have afternoon tea on the terrace, overlooking the beautifully manicured gardens and on towards the river – here, peace and tranquility reign. The country house inspired bedrooms are charming; those in the 'Boathouse' are the most luxurious. Dress smartly for dinner in the formal candlelit cellar.

17 rooms – £ 176/304 £ 220/380 – 2 suites

Church Grn BH20 4ND – 01929 551666 – www.theprioryhotel.co.uk

Gold Court House

HISTORIC BUILDING • CLASSIC Charmingly run Georgian house in a small square off the high street; which stands on the foundations of a 13C goldsmith's house. It has a fire-lit lounge, a lovely breakfast room with garden views and traditional, restful bedrooms.

3 rooms – £ 70 £ 85

St John's Hill BH20 4LZ – 01929 553320 – www.goldcourthouse.co.uk – Closed 25 December-2 January

WAREN MILL – Northumberland → See Bamburgh

WARKWORTH

Northumberland – Regional map n° **14**-B2

Roxbro House

TOWNHOUSE • GRAND LUXURY 'Elegant' and 'opulent' are suitable adjectives to describe these two houses in the shadow of Warkworth Castle, where boutique bedrooms mix modern facilities with antique furniture. Choose between two comfy lounges – one with an honesty bar; tasty breakfasts are served in a conservatory-style room.

6 rooms – £ 85/105 £ 105/160

5 Castle Terr NE65 0UP – 01665 711416 – www.roxbrohouse.co.uk – Closed 24-28 December

WARMINGHAM

Cheshire East – Regional map n° **11**-B3

Bear's Paw

TRADITIONAL BRITISH • INN Handsome 19C inn with a spacious, wood-panelled bar and a huge array of local ales. The menu will please all appetites, with everything from nibbles, salads and deli boards to European dishes, pub favourites and steaks you can cook yourself on a hot stone. Stylish, good value bedrooms.

Carte £ 23/46

17 rooms - †£ 105/165 ††£ 115/175

School Ln ✉ CW11 3QN - ✆ 01270 526317 - www.thebearspaw.co.uk

WARMINSTER

Wiltshire - Pop. 17 490 - Regional map n° **2**-C2

Weymouth Arms

TRADITIONAL BRITISH • NEIGHBOURHOOD Grade II listed building with plenty of history. It's immensely characterful, with wood panelling, antiques and lithographs, as well as two fireplaces originally intended for nearby Longleat House. Cooking is fresh and fittingly traditional. Cosy bedrooms have charming original fittings.

Carte £ 25/43

6 rooms - †£ 85/120 ††£ 95/120

12 Emwell St ✉ BA12 8JA - ✆ 01985 216995 - www.weymoutharms.co.uk - Closed Monday-Wednesday lunch

at Crockerton South: 2 mi by A350

Bath Arms

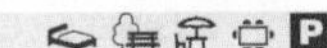

TRADITIONAL BRITISH • RUSTIC This down-to-earth pub was once part of the Longleat Estate. The daily menu features snacks, grills and classic pub dishes, along with a selection of specials; try the legendary sticky beef with braised red cabbage. The two ultra-spacious, contemporary bedrooms are amusingly named 'Left' and 'Right'.

Carte £ 21/33

2 rooms - †£ 80/110 ††£ 80/110

Clay St ✉ BA12 8AJ - On Shearwater rd - ✆ 01985 212262 - www.batharmscrockerton.co.uk - Closed Sunday dinner in winter

WARTLING - East Sussex → See Herstmonceux

WARWICK

Warwickshire - Pop. 31 345 - Regional map n° **10**-C3

Tailors

MODERN CUISINE • INTIMATE As well as a tailor's, this intimate restaurant was once a fishmonger's, a butcher's and a casino! It's run by two ambitious chefs, who offer good value modern lunches, and elaborate dinners which feature unusual flavour combinations.

Menu £ 20/40

22 Market Pl ✉ CV34 4SL - ✆ 01926 410590 - www.tailorsrestaurant.co.uk - Closed Christmas, Sunday and Monday

WATCHET

Somerset - Pop. 3 581 - Regional map n° **2**-B2

Swain House

TOWNHOUSE • PERSONALISED In the characterful high street of this coastal town, you'll find this super smart guesthouse with spacious bedrooms and a sleek yet cosy feel. Parts of famous paintings make up feature walls and all have roll-top baths and rain showers.

4 rooms - †£ 115/135 ††£ 115/135

48 Swain St ✉ TA23 0AG - ✆ 01984 631038 - www.swain-house.com

WATERGATE BAY - Cornwall → See Newquay

→ See Newquay

WATFORD

Hertfordshire - Pop. 131 982 - Regional map n° **7**-A2

Colette's

MODERN CUISINE • DESIGN XXX A sleek, contemporary hotel restaurant with high ceilings and large windows overlooking the grounds. Complex modern dishes feature imaginative combinations; choose from a 3 course fixed price menu or a 5 course set menu.

Menu £ 65

Grove Hotel, Chandler's Cross ✉ WD3 4TG - Northwest : 2 mi on A 411 - ✆ 01923 296015 - www.thegrove.co.uk - dinner only and Sunday lunch - Closed Sunday dinner except bank holidays and Monday

Stables

INTERNATIONAL • RUSTIC X Informal New England style restaurant in the clubhouse of an impressive Grade II listed country house. It boasts its own sports bar, has pleasant views over the golf course and offers a gutsy British menu with plenty of grills.

Menu £ 26 - Carte £ 32/40

Grove Hotel, Chandler's Cross ✉ WD3 4TG - Northwest : 2 mi on A 411 - ✆ 01923 296010 - www.thegrove.co.uk

Grove

BUSINESS • GRAND LUXURY An impressive Grade II listed country house in 300 acres, with elegant lounges and smart, contemporary bedrooms - some with balconies. There's a superb spa and an outdoor pool, as well as tennis, croquet, golf and volleyball facilities. Enjoy fine dining in Colette's, casual meals in Stables or buffets in Glasshouse.

214 rooms - £ 315/650 £ 350/650 - 6 suites

Chandler's Cross ✉ WD3 4TG - Northwest : 2 mi on A 411 - ✆ 01923 807807 - www.thegrove.co.uk

Colette's • **Stables** - See restaurant listing

WEDMORE

Somerset - Pop. 1 409 - Regional map n° **2**-B2

Swan

TRADITIONAL BRITISH • INN Spacious 18C coaching inn with a buzzy bar, a comfy restaurant and an open-plan kitchen with an appealing display of freshly baked breads linking the two. Good quality British ingredients match the seasons and daily changing dishes are unfussy and flavoursome. Stylish bedrooms complete the picture.

Carte £ 25/31

7 rooms - £ 75/135 £ 75/135

Cheddar Rd ✉ BS28 4EQ - ✆ 01934 710337 (booking essential) - www.theswanwedmore.com

WELBURN

North Yorkshire - Regional map n° **13**-C2

Crown and Cushion

CLASSIC CUISINE • FRIENDLY Well run 18C pub two miles from Castle Howard. The menu champions local meats and the kitchen's pride and joy is its charcoal-fired rotisserie. Dishes are hearty, sandwiches are doorstops, and puddings are of the nursery variety.

Menu £ 18 (weekday lunch) - Carte £ 24/43

✉ YO60 7DZ - ✆ 01653 618777 - www.thecrownandcushionwelburn.com

WELLAND - Worcestershire → See Great Malvern

WELLINGHAM

Norfolk – Regional map n° **8**-C1

Manor House Farm

WORKING FARM · CLASSIC Attractive, wisteria-clad farmhouse with large gardens, set by a church in a beautifully peaceful spot. Spacious, airy bedrooms are located in the former stables. Home-grown and home-reared produce is served at breakfast.

5 rooms – †£ 70/80 ††£ 120/130

✉ PE32 2TH

– ✆ 01328 838227 – www.manor-house-farm.co.uk – Closed Christmas

WELLS

Somerset – Pop. 10 536 – Regional map n° **2**-C2

Swan

INN · ELEGANT 15C former coaching inn with a good outlook onto the famous cathedral; its charming interior has subtle contemporary touches, particularly in the lounge and bar. Comfortable, stylish, well-equipped bedrooms and an opulent 'Cathedral Suite'. The formal, wood-panelled restaurant serves classic dishes.

48 rooms – †£ 85/115 ††£ 120/450 – 1 suite

11 Sadler St ✉ BA5 2RX

– ✆ 01749 836300 – www.swanhotelwells.co.uk

Beryl

COUNTRY HOUSE · CLASSIC A fine 19C country house in 13 acres of mature gardens, complete with a pond and a swimming pool. The delightful drawing rooms are packed with antiques and curios from the owner's travels. Go for one of the four-poster bedrooms.

13 rooms – †£ 80/95 ††£ 110/160

✉ BA5 3JP – East : 1.25 mi by B 3139 off Hawkers Lane

– ✆ 01749 678738 – www.beryl-wells.co.uk – Closed 23-30 December

Stoberry House

TRADITIONAL · PERSONALISED 18C coach house with a delightful walled garden, overlooking Glastonbury Tor. Large lounge with a baby grand piano and antique furniture. Breakfast is an event, with 7 homemade breads, a porridge menu and lots of cooked dishes. Immaculately kept bedrooms come with fresh flowers, chocolates and a pillow menu.

5 rooms – †£ 75/95 ††£ 105/155

Stoberry Park ✉ BA5 3LD – Northeast : 0.5 mi by A 39 on College Rd

– ✆ 01749 672906 – www.stoberryhouse.co.uk – Closed Christmas and New Year.

WELLS-NEXT-THE-SEA

Norfolk – Pop. 2 165 – Regional map n° **8**-C1

Crown

INN · MODERN Characterful 16C former coaching inn located in the centre of town, overlooking the green. Individually styled bedrooms blend classical furniture with more modern décor and facilities. Dine from an accessible menu in the charming bar, orangery or dining room.

20 rooms – †£ 80/240 ††£ 100/260

The Buttlands ✉ NR23 1EX

– ✆ 01328 710209 – www.flyingkiwiinns.co.uk

ENGLAND

at Wighton Southeast: 2.5 mi by A149

 **Meadowview** 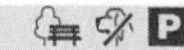

FAMILY · MODERN Set in the centre of a peaceful village, this smart, modern guesthouse is the perfect place to unwind, as its neat garden boasts a hot tub and a comfy seating area overlooking a meadow. Breakfast is cooked on the Aga in the country kitchen.

5 rooms – £ 115/125 £ 115/125

53 High St ✉ NR23 1PF – ✆ 01328 821527 – www.meadow-view.net

WELWYN

Hertfordshire – Pop. 3 497 – Regional map n° **7**-B2

 **Tewin Bury Farm** 

BUSINESS · RURAL A collection of converted farm buildings set on a 400 acre working farm next to a nature reserve. Comfy oak-furnished bedrooms are located in various wings and the function room is in an impressive tithe barn beside the old mill race. In the old chicken shed, menus mix classic dishes with the more adventurous.

36 rooms – £ 99/146 £ 99/146

✉ AL6 0JB – Southeast : 3.5 mi by A 1000 on B 1000 – ✆ 01438 717793 – www.tewinbury.co.uk

at Ayot Green Southwest: 2.5 mi by B 197

Waggoners 

FRENCH · PUB A popular 17C Gallic-themed pub. Join local drinkers in the cosy bar for dishes such as crispy monkfish cheeks; the restaurant offers more ambitious modern fare, including the likes of beef short rib with treacle-cured bacon.

Menu £ 10 (weekday lunch) – Carte £ 27/46

Brickwall Cl ✉ AL6 9AA – ✆ 01707 324241 – www.thewaggoners.co.uk – Closed Sunday dinner

WENTBRIDGE

West Yorkshire – ✉ Pontefract – Regional map n° **13**-B3

 **Wentbridge House** 

INN · CONTEMPORARY An attractive, creeper-clad Georgian coaching inn on the Great North Road; its pretty grounds make it a popular place for weddings. Bedrooms are spacious and modern, with good facilities – the two four-poster rooms have an elegant feel and some outside can accommodate dogs. Dine from a mix of classics and elaborate modern dishes in the brasserie or formal restaurant.

41 rooms – £ 90/130 £ 120/160

Old Great North Rd. ✉ WF8 3JJ – ✆ 01977 620444 – www.wentbridgehouse.co.uk

WEST ASHLING – West Sussex → See Chicester

WEST BRIDGFORD – Nottinghamshire → See Nottingham

WEST BYFLEET

Surrey – Regional map n° **4**-C1

London House 

MODERN BRITISH · FASHIONABLE XX A pleasant neighbourhood restaurant in a busy parade of shops; where white walls are hung with modern art. Colourful modern dishes take their influences from Britain and the Med. Top quality ingredients include local rare breed pork.

Menu £ 39 (dinner) – Carte lunch £ 20/25

30 Station Approach ✉ KT14 6NF – ✆ 01932 482026 – www.restaurantlondonhouse.co.uk – Closed first 2 weeks August, first week January, Sunday dinner, Monday and lunch Tuesday and Saturday

WEST END

Surrey – ✉ Guildford – Pop. 4 135 – Regional map n° **4**-C1

The Inn West End

TRADITIONAL CUISINE • PUB A lively atmosphere and genuine hospitality are two reasons why this pub is always busy. There's something for everyone on the menu, which fuses pub classics with more modern dishes; portions are generous and flavours robust. The wine shop specialises in Europe. Chic bedrooms complete the picture.

Menu £ 13 (weekday lunch) – Carte £ 25/46

12 rooms – †£ 90/150 ††£ 100/160

42 Guildford Rd ✉ GU24 9PW – on A 322
– ✆ 01276 858652 – www.the-inn.co.uk

WEST HATCH

Wiltshire – Regional map n° **2**-C3

Pythouse Kitchen Garden

TRADITIONAL BRITISH • SIMPLE Simple, rustic café in a former potting shed, serving breakfast, coffee, lunch and afternoon tea; order in the well-stocked shop. Tasty, unfussy cooking uses seasonal produce from the charming 18C walled garden. Save room for some cake!

Carte £ 27/44

✉ SP3 6PA
– ✆ 01747 870444 (booking advisable) – www.pythousekitchengarden.co.uk
– lunch only and dinner Friday-Saturday – Closed 25-26 December and 1 January

WEST HOATHLY

West Sussex – Pop. 709 – Regional map n° **4**-D2

Cat Inn

TRADITIONAL BRITISH • COSY Popular with the locals and very much a village pub, with beamed ceilings, pewter tankards, open fires and plenty of cosy corners. Carefully executed, good value cooking focuses on tasty pub classics like locally smoked ham, egg and chips or steak, mushroom and ale pie. Service is friendly and efficient – and four tastefully decorated bedrooms complete the picture.

Carte £ 23/37

4 rooms – †£ 95/145 ††£ 125/175

North Ln. ✉ RH19 4PP
– ✆ 01342 810369 – www.catinn.co.uk – Closed 25 December and dinner 26 December and 1 January

WEST MALLING

Kent – Pop. 2 266 – Regional map n° **5**-B1

Swan

MODERN CUISINE • FASHIONABLE An informal 15C coaching inn where original beams blend with stylish furnishings and there are smart bars both upstairs and downstairs. Modern European menus offer flavoursome combinations (side dishes are required); brunch is a hit.

Menu £ 18 (weekdays) – Carte £ 27/35

35 Swan St. ✉ ME19 6JU
– ✆ 01732 521910 (booking essential) – www.theswanwestmalling.co.uk – Closed 1 January

WEST MEON

Hampshire – Regional map n° **4**-B2

Thomas Lord

TRADITIONAL CUISINE • PUB This smart, early 19C pub is named after the founder of Lord's Cricket Ground and decorated with cricketing memorabilia. The atmosphere is warm and welcoming and the menu perfectly balances the classics with some more adventurous offerings. The lovely garden is home to a wood-burning stove, as well as to 4 delightful wooden lodges for those who wish to stay.

Carte £ 26/48

4 rooms – †£ 85/280 ††£ 85/280

High St ✉ GU32 1LN – ✆ 01730 829244 – www.thethomaslord.co.uk – Closed 25 December

WEST OVERTON – Wiltshire → See Marlborough

WEST TANFIELD

North Yorkshire – ✉ Ripon – Pop. 293 – Regional map n° **13**-B2

Old Coach House

TOWNHOUSE • MODERN Smart 18C coach house nestled between the Dales and the Moors. Bedrooms differ in size but all have a bright modern style and are furnished by local craftsmen. The breakfast room overlooks the fountain in the courtyard garden.

8 rooms – †£ 75/105 ††£ 85/115

2 Stable Cottage, North Stainley ✉ HG4 3HT – Southeast : 1 mi on A 6108 – ✆ 07912 632296 – www.oldcoachhouse.info

WEST WITTERING

West Sussex – Pop. 875 – Regional map n° **4**-C3

Beach House

TRADITIONAL CUISINE • FRIENDLY It might be 10 minutes' from the beach but the Beach House definitely has a seaside feel, with its large veranda, shuttered windows and scrubbed wooden tables. Tasty breakfasts, coffee and cakes morph into fresh, bistro-style dishes later in the day. Bedrooms are bright and modern with a New England style.

Carte £ 18/42

7 rooms – †£ 85/90 ††£ 120/130

Rookwood Rd ✉ PO20 8LT – ✆ 01243 514800 (booking advisable) – www.beachhse.co.uk – Closed Monday-Wednesday in winter

WEST WITTON

North Yorkshire – ✉ Leyburn – Regional map n° **13**-B1

Wensleydale Heifer

TRADITIONAL • PERSONALISED Pretty, whitewashed former pub on the main street of the village. Quirky, themed bedrooms boast quality linen and the latest mod cons. Characterful lounge has a roaring fire. Dine in the fish bar or at clothed tables in the beamed restaurant; cooking has a strong seafood base.

13 rooms – †£ 90 ††£ 120/190

✉ DL8 4LS – ✆ 01969 622322 – www.wensleydaleheifer.co.uk

WESTONBIRT

Gloucestershire – Regional map n° **2**-C1

Hare & Hounds

COUNTRY HOUSE • CONTEMPORARY Attractive former farmhouse with lovely gardens, set between Highgrove House and the National Arboretum. The country house style interior features several lounges and a small library; bedrooms blend modern fabrics with period furniture - half are located in the old outbuildings. Formal Beaufort offers classical dishes with a modern edge, while Jack Hare's serves a pub-style menu and real ales.

42 rooms - £ 140/210 £ 140/335 - 3 suites

GL8 8QL - on A 433 - 01666 881000 - www.cotswold-inns-hotels.co.uk

WESTFIELD

East Sussex - Pop. 1 509 - Regional map n° **5**-B3

Wild Mushroom

CLASSIC FRENCH • ELEGANT XX Keenly run restaurant in an old 17C farmhouse, with a contemporary brown and green theme and an intimate conservatory lounge-bar. Classic French menus continually evolve and feature well-presented, tried-and-tested combinations.

Menu £ 23 (weekday lunch) - Carte £ 23/38

Woodgate House, Westfield Ln. TN35 4SB - Southwest : 0.5 mi on A 28 - 01424 751137 (booking essential) - www.webbesrestaurants.co.uk - Closed 2-17 January, 30-October-9 November, 25-27 December, Sunday dinner, Monday and Tuesday

WESTLETON

Suffolk - Saxmundham - Pop. 349 - Regional map n° **8**-D2

Westleton Crown

MODERN BRITISH • PUB Good-looking, 17C former coaching inn with an appealing terrace and garden, set in a pretty little village. Welcoming beamed bar with open fires; more modern conservatory. Seasonal menu, with special diets well-catered for. Uncluttered bedrooms are named after birds found on the adjacent RSPB nature reserve.

Carte £ 26/40

34 rooms - £ 100/110 £ 110/225

The Street IP17 3AD - 01728 648777 - www.westletoncrown.co.uk

WESTON-SUPER-MARE

North Somerset - Pop. 83 641 - Regional map n° **2**-B2

Duets

TRADITIONAL BRITISH • NEIGHBOURHOOD XX A husband and wife team duet here, with him in the kitchen and her out front; there's also always a duet dish to share. Carefully prepared classical dishes follow the seasons. It's more modern inside than the exterior suggests.

Menu £ 19 (weekday lunch)/33

103 Upper Bristol Rd. BS22 8ND - Northeast : 1.75 mi by Bristol Rd Lower - 01934 413428 (booking essential at lunch) - www.duets.co.uk - Closed 1 week spring, 1 week summer, 1 week winter, Sunday dinner, Monday and Tuesday

Cove

TRADITIONAL BRITISH • BRASSERIE X Every table at Cove has views over the bay to Knightstone Island but, when the weather's good, the terrace is definitely the place to be. Pop in for coffee and cake or visit on a Friday for grill and fish night.

Carte £ 19/33

Birnbeck Rd BS23 2BX - Northwest : 1.5 mi by A 370 and Knightstone Rd - 01934 418217 - www.the-cove.co.uk - Closed 25 December

WHALLEY

Lancashire - ✉ Blackburn - Pop. 3 230 - Regional map n° **11**-B2

at Mitton Northwest: 2.5 mi on B6246✉ Whalley

Three Fishes

REGIONAL CUISINE • PUB 'Regional' and 'local' are the buzzwords at this behemoth of a country pub. Expect shrimps from Morecambe Bay, Ribble Valley beef and Fleetwood fish, with specialities like hotpot and cheese soufflé firmly rooted in the region.

Carte £ 21/35

Mitton Rd ✉ BB7 9PQ - ✆ 01254 826888 - www.thethreefishes.com

WHASHTON - N. Yorks. → See Richmond

WHITBY

North Yorkshire - Pop. 13 213 - Regional map n° **13**-C1

The Star Inn The Harbour

MODERN BRITISH • BRASSERIE Andrew Pern has fulfilled a dream by opening this modern brasserie by the harbour in his home town. The extensive menu offers classic British brasserie dishes from the 'Harbourside', the 'Countryside' and the 'Ice Cream Parlour'.

Carte £ 24/43

1 Langborne Rd ✉ YO21 1YN - ✆ 01947 821900 (booking advisable) - www.starinntheharbour.co.uk - Closed Sunday dinner

Raithwaite Hall

LUXURY • CONTEMPORARY Modern resort hotel with a smart spa, set in 80 acres of delightful parkland. Stylish bedrooms are spread about the place: some are in a modern mock-castle, some are in cottages and others are in a house overlooking the lake. Brace serves a modern menu, while informal Hunters offers brasserie-style dishes.

81 rooms - †£ 125/425 ††£ 135/425

Sandsend Rd ✉ YO21 3ST - West : 2 mi on A 197 - ✆ 01947 661661 - www.raithwaiteestate.com

Dillons of Whitby

TOWNHOUSE • DESIGN Charming Victorian townhouse built for a sea captain, set opposite the beautiful Pannett Park. Immaculately kept bedrooms are individually themed and feature Egyptian cotton linens. Extensive breakfasts are something of an event.

5 rooms - †£ 75/125 ††£ 85/145

14 Chubb Hill Rd ✉ YO21 1JU - ✆ 01947 600290 - www.dillonsofwhitby.co.uk - Closed 3-21 January

at Sandsend Northwest: 3 mi on A174✉ Whitby

Estbek House

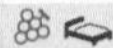

SEAFOOD • FRIENDLY Personally run Regency house close to the beach, with a lovely front terrace and an elegant dining room. The basement bar overlooks the kitchen and doubles as a breakfast room. Menus offer unfussy dishes of sustainable wild fish from local waters. Smart bedrooms come with stylish bathrooms.

Carte £ 32/58

5 rooms - †£ 125/150 ††£ 150/200

East Row ✉ YO21 3SU - ✆ 01947 893424 - www.estbekhouse.co.uk - dinner only - Closed January-9 February

WHITE WALTHAM

Windsor and Maidenhead - Pop. 349 - Regional map n° **6**-C3

Beehive

CLASSIC CUISINE • PUB A traditional English pub overlooking the cricket pitch, where you'll find local drinkers in the bar and a comfy, light-filled dining room. Eye-catching daily dishes are full of flavour and exhibit a staunch sense of Britishness.

Menu £ 20 (weekday lunch) – Carte £ 29/47

Waltham Rd ✉ SL6 3SH – ✆ 01628 822877 – www.thebeehivewhitewaltham.com – Closed 25-26 December and Sunday dinner

WHITEWELL

Lancashire – ✉ Clitheroe – Pop. 5 617 – Regional map n° **11**-B2

Inn at Whitewell

TRADITIONAL BRITISH • CLASSIC DÉCOR XX 14C inn in the heart of the Trough of Bowland. Antique furniture and a valley view make the bar the most atmospheric place to sit. For a more formal meal, head to the smart dining room. Classic menus of wholesome, regionally inspired dishes.

Carte £ 28/41

Inn at Whitewell, Forest of Bowland ✉ BB7 3AT – ✆ 01200 448222 – www.innatwhitewell.com

Inn at Whitewell

INN • PERSONALISED 14C creeper-clad inn, high on the banks of the river, with stunning valley views. Spacious bedrooms are split between the inn and a nearby coach house – some are traditional, with four-posters and antique baths; others more contemporary.

23 rooms – †£ 97/214 ††£ 134/265

Forest of Bowland ✉ BB7 3AT – ✆ 01200 448222 – www.innatwhitewell.com

Inn at Whitewell – See restaurant listing

WHITSTABLE

Kent – Pop. 32 100 – Regional map n° **5**-C1

East Coast Dining Room

MODERN CUISINE • NEIGHBOURHOOD XX Find a spot on the terrace or head inside, where you'll find reupholstered chairs from the 1960s and '70s. Concise, modern menus offer fresh, flavoursome dishes with a subtle Asian slant; the fish dishes are always a popular choice.

Menu £ 13 (weekday lunch) – Carte £ 28/37

101 Tankerton Rd ✉ CT5 2AJ – East : 1 mi on B 2205 – ✆ 01227 281180 – www.eastcoastdiningroom.co.uk – Closed 25 December, 1 January, Sunday dinner, Monday and Tuesday

JoJo's

MEDITERRANEAN CUISINE • BISTRO X A buzzy bar and restaurant offering good views over the Thames Estuary; it's unusually converted from an old supermarket. The self-taught chef offers a large menu of meze, sharing boards and Mediterranean dishes – the hummus is hit.

Carte £ 20/35

2 Herne Bay Rd ✉ CT5 2LQ – East : 1.75 mi by B 2205 – ✆ 01227 274591 – www.jojosrestaurant.co.uk – Closed Sunday dinner-Wednesday

Whitstable Oyster Company

SEAFOOD • RUSTIC X An old seafront oyster warehouse with a rustic interior and a great informal atmosphere. Blackboards list simply prepared seafood dishes; from Sept-Dec try oysters from their own beds – the lower staircase leads to the seedling pool.

Carte £ 23/74

Royal Native Oyster Stores, Horsebridge ✉ CT5 1BU – ✆ 01227 276856 (booking essential) – www.whitstableoystercompany.com – Closed 25-26 December and dinner Monday-Wednesday November-January

Crescent Turner

COUNTRY HOUSE • ELEGANT Smart rural retreat named after the artist, who painted the local landscapes. Their strapline is 'British, Boutique and Unique' and with its bold furnishings, it's exactly that. Take in sea views from the terrace, have a drink in the inviting lounge or make for the conservatory for a modern British dish.

17 rooms – £ 69/89 £ 99/220

Wraik Hill ✉ CT5 3BY – Southwest : 2.75 mi by B 2205 off A 290 – ✆ 01227 263506 – www.crescentturner.co.uk

at Seasalter Southwest: 2 mi by B2205 ✉ Whitstable

The Sportsman (Steve Harris)

MODERN BRITISH • PUB An unassuming-looking pub serving excellent food: dishes feature four or five complementary ingredients and are carefully prepared; flavours are well-judged and presentation is original. The full tasting menu must be booked in advance but the 5 course option can be ordered on arrival.

➜ Slip sole grilled in seaweed butter. Roast rack of lamb with mint sauce. Bramley apple soufflé with salted caramel ice cream.

Menu £ 50/70 – Carte £ 41/48

Faversham Rd ✉ CT5 4BP – Southwest : 2 mi following coast rd – ✆ 01227 273370 (booking advisable) – www.thesportsmanseasalter.co.uk – Closed 25-26 December, 1 January, Sunday dinner and Monday

WHITTLESFORD

Cambridgeshire – Regional map n° **8**-B3

Tickell Arms

MODERN BRITISH • PUB Sit in the orangery-style extension overlooking the pond. Fish is delivered 6 days a week, on Tuesdays you can select your own cut for Steak Night, and on Sundays they leave fresh roasties on the bar.

Menu £ 22 (weekdays) – Carte £ 24/42

1 North Rd ✉ CB22 4NZ – ✆ 01223 833025 – www.cambscuisine.com

WIGHT (Isle of)

Isle of Wight – Pop. 138 500 – Regional map n° **4**-A/B 3

Godshill

Taverners

TRADITIONAL BRITISH • PUB Passionately run roadside pub with its own deli selling homemade produce. The main menu lists pub classics like burgers and pies but the more ambitious daily blackboard specials are the ones to go for. Ingredients are local and home-grown.

Carte £ 21/28

High St ✉ PO38 3HZ – ✆ 01983 840707 – www.thetavernersgodshill.co.uk – Closed first 3 weeks January

Gurnard

Little Gloster

TRADITIONAL CUISINE • RUSTIC Set in a great spot among the beach huts, with lovely views over The Solent. Have a cocktail on the terrace then head inside to the tables by the kitchen or the relaxed, shabby chic dining room. Unfussy, flavoursome cooking uses island produce. Stylish bedrooms have a fresh nautical theme and superb views.

Carte £ 19/68

3 rooms – £ 95/175 £ 115/245

31 Marsh Rd ✉ PO31 8JQ – ✆ 01983 298776 – www.thelittlegloster.com – Closed January-mid February, Christmas, dinner Sunday and Monday-Wednesday in winter

Newport

Regional map n° **6**-B3

Thompson's

MODERN BRITISH · TRENDY A stylish yet relaxed restaurant in the centre of town; try to book one of the three tables in front of the open kitchen. Original cooking makes good use of island ingredients and exhibits some interesting flavour combinations.

Menu £ 16 (lunch) - Carte £ 34/54

11 Town Ln ✉ PO30 1JU
- ✆ 01983 526118 - www.robertthompson.co.uk - Closed 25-29 December, 2 weeks February, 1 week September, 2 weeks November, Sunday and Monday

St Helens

Dans Kitchen

TRADITIONAL CUISINE · FRIENDLY Old corner shop in a lovely location overlooking the village green. Simple wood furnishings, scatter cushions and nautical pictures feature. Traditional, hearty dishes showcase island produce; blackboard specials include the daily catch.

Menu £ 20 (lunch) - Carte £ 27/47

Lower Green Rd ✉ PO33 1TS
- ✆ 01983 872303 - www.danskitcheniow.co.uk - Closed 3 weeks January, 1 week June, 1 week October, Sunday dinner, Monday and lunch Tuesday

Seaview

Seaview

MODERN BRITISH · CLASSIC DÉCOR The seafaring décor gives a clue as to the focus at this boldly decorated hotel restaurant. Classically based seafood dishes are well-prepared and come in a choice of two sizes. The 'Naval Mess' and 'Pump Room' provide simpler alternatives and the crab ramekin has become something of an institution.

Menu £ 28 (dinner) - Carte lunch £ 19/34

Seaview Hotel, High St ✉ PO34 5EX
- ✆ 01983 612711 (booking essential) - www.seaviewhotel.co.uk - Closed 24-27 December and Sunday dinner October-May

Seaview

TRADITIONAL · QUIRKY A long-standing seaside hotel with a laid-back feel - its interesting interior filled with nautical charts, maritime photos and model ships. Bright, comfy bedrooms come in various styles; some are in annexes and several are suites.

29 rooms - †£ 95/185 ††£ 95/185 - 6 suites

High St ✉ PO34 5EX
- ✆ 01983 612711 - www.seaviewhotel.co.uk - Closed 24-27 December

Seaview - See restaurant listing

Shanklin

Rylstone Manor

COUNTRY HOUSE · CLASSIC This attractive part-Victorian house sits in the town's historic gardens and was originally a gift from the Queen to one of her physicians. The classical interior has a warm, cosy feel and is furnished with antiques. Carefully prepared dishes are served in the formally laid dining room.

9 rooms - †£ 75/120 ††£ 140/170

Rylstone Gdns ✉ PO37 6RG
- ✆ 01983 862806 - www.rylstonemanor.co.uk - Closed 6 November-6 February

Ventnor

Royal Hotel
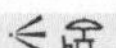

CLASSIC CUISINE • ELEGANT XX An elegant hotel plays host to this grand dining room hung with portraits and chandeliers. Sophisticated dinners offer old favourites alongside some more modern dishes. Good value light lunches are served in the bar.

Menu £ 31 – Carte £ 28/40

Royal Hotel, Belgrave Rd ✉ PO38 1JJ
– ✆ 01983 852186 – www.royalhoteliow.co.uk – dinner only and Sunday lunch

Ale and Oyster

TRADITIONAL BRITISH • BISTRO X This relaxed little bistro sits in a super spot on the esplanade, looking out to sea, and is run by a friendly, experienced team. Enjoy a light lunch on the terrace or come in the evening for the likes of local lobster linguine.

Carte £ 39/51

The Esplanade ✉ PO38 1JX
– ✆ 01983 857025 – www.thealeandoyster.co.uk – Closed 3 weeks January, 1 week November, Monday and Tuesday

Royal
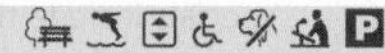

TRADITIONAL • CLASSIC A sympathetically restored Victorian house with mature lawned gardens and a heated outdoor pool. The interior has a bygone elegance with hints of modernity. Traditional bedrooms have good facilities and some offer lovely sea views.

51 rooms (dinner included) – †£ 100/180 ††£ 195/295

Belgrave Rd ✉ PO38 1JJ
– ✆ 01983 852186 – www.royalhoteliow.co.uk

Royal Hotel – See restaurant listing

Hillside

COUNTRY HOUSE • UNIQUE Set high above the town, this wonderful thatched Georgian house has a beautiful terrace and superb sea views. The Danish owner has fused period furnishings with clean-lined Scandinavian styling, and displays over 350 pieces of CoBrA and Scandinavian art. Everything is immaculate and the linens are top quality. Frequently changing menus use local and garden produce.

14 rooms – †£ 78/93 ††£ 156/206

151 Mitchell Ave ✉ PO38 1DR
– ✆ 01983 852271 – www.hillsideventnor.co.uk

Yarmouth

Isla's

MODERN CUISINE • DESIGN XXX At the heart of an old inn you'll find this stylishly understated restaurant with large linen-laid tables and detailed service. The three no-choice set menus change with the seasons – cooking is precise, modern and sophisticated.

Menu £ 45/75 – tasting menu only

The George Hotel, Quay St ✉ PO41 0PE
– ✆ 01983 760331 (booking essential) – www.thegeorge.co.uk – dinner only – Closed Tuesday in Winter, Sunday and Monday

Isla's Conservatory
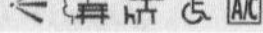

TRADITIONAL BRITISH • BRASSERIE X Hidden at the back of the George hotel is this modern conservatory with a lovely garden leading down to the water's edge. Flexible brasserie-style menus offer tasty nibbles and a choice of dish size; ingredients are local and organic.

Carte £ 29/45

The George Hotel, Quay St ✉ PO41 0PE
– ✆ 01983 760331 – www.thegeorge.co.uk

The George

INN • CLASSIC Set in the shadow of the castle, this cosy 17C inn blends subtle modern touches with characterful period features. Bedrooms vary in shape and style: some are wood-panelled; some have luxurious bathrooms; some open onto the garden or have spacious balconies – and many have excellent Solent views.

17 rooms – £ 125/360 £ 135/385

Quay St PO41 0PE – 01983 760331 – www.thegeorge.co.uk

Isla's • **Isla's Conservatory** – See restaurant listing

WIGHTON – Norfolk → See Wells-Next-The-Sea

WIGMORE

Herefordshire – Regional map n° **10**-A2

The Oak Wigmore

MODERN BRITISH • CONTEMPORARY DÉCOR The charming, hands-on owner spent 3 years transforming this 250 year old pub and its outbuildings into the smart, contemporary inn you see before you today. The experienced local chef really knows how to get the best out of his ingredients. Simple, comfortable bedrooms complete the picture.

Carte £ 26/42

2 rooms – £ 90/95 £ 100/110

Ford St HR6 9UJ – 01568 770424 – www.theoakwigmore.com – Closed Sunday dinner, Monday and Tuesday

WILLIAN

Hertfordshire – Pop. 326 – Regional map n° **7**-B2

Fox

MODERN BRITISH • FRIENDLY The Fox is set in the heart of the village and also plays host to the local Post Office and general store. Monthly menus present carefully constructed, classic dishes which keep natural flavours to the fore. There's a sheltered terrace for warmer days and very comfy, contemporary country bedrooms await.

Carte £ 24/37

8 rooms – £ 75/110 £ 75/110

SG6 2AE – 01462 480233 – www.foxatwillian.co.uk

WILMINGTON

Regional map n° **5**-B1

Rowhill Grange

COUNTRY HOUSE • MODERN An early 19C house set in 15 acres of pretty gardens, with smart modern bedrooms in dark, bold hues. The fantastic spa has 9 treatment rooms, a large gym and a superb swimming pool, along with a separate infinity pool with a waterfall. RG's serves fresh seasonal dishes – try the grills.

38 rooms – £ 115/465 £ 115/465 – £ 16

DA2 7QH – Southwest : 2 mi on Hextable rd (B 258) – 01322 615136 – www.rowhillgrange.com

WIMBORNE MINSTER

Dorset – Pop. 15 174 – Regional map n° **2**-C3

Tickled Pig

MODERN BRITISH • BISTRO Charmingly run restaurant in the heart of a pretty market town, with a modern country interior, a deli, a lovely terrace and a laid-back feel. Daily brown paper menus feature home-grown veg and home-reared pork; their mantra is 'taking food back to its roots'. Cooking is vibrant, flavourful and unfussy.

Menu £ 20 – Carte £ 26/35

26 West Borough BH21 1NF – 01202 886778 – www.thetickledpig.co.uk – Closed 25-26 December, Sunday and Monday

WINCHCOMBE

Gloucestershire – Pop. 4 538 – Regional map n° **2**-D1

5 North St

MODERN BRITISH • COSY XX This long-standing neighbourhood restaurant, run by a husband and wife, is a hit with the locals; it might be small inside but it's big on character. Concise menus feature regional ingredients in classic combinations.

Menu £ 32/52

5 North St ✉ GL54 5LH – ✆ 01242 604566 – www.5northstreetrestaurant.co.uk – Closed 2 weeks January, 1 week August, Monday, Tuesday lunch and Sunday dinner

Wesley House

TRADITIONAL CUISINE • RUSTIC XX Characterful 15C house with lots of beams, a cosy open-fired bar and a smart rear dining room and conservatory. Cooking is classical and flavourful, and service is relaxed and cheery; simpler meals are served in their next door wine bar. The cosy bedrooms have a comfortingly traditional feel.

Menu £ 20 (weekday lunch) – Carte £ 28/68

5 rooms – †£ 65/85 ††£ 95/110

High St ✉ GL54 5LJ – ✆ 01242 602366 – www.wesleyhouse.co.uk – Closed 26 December, Sunday dinner and Monday

WINCHESTER

Hampshire – Pop. 45 184 – Regional map n° **4**-B2

Black Rat

MODERN CUISINE • RUSTIC X You can't help but love this rustic candlelit restaurant with its quirky, bohemian-style interior and lovely heated huts on the terrace. Refined, original cooking arrives in hearty portions and the flavours really pack a punch. A small bar offers cocktails and a selection of over 30 different gins.

→ Beef carpaccio with octopus, white onion ice cream, cornichons and shallots. Veal loin and sweetbreads with artichoke and bone marrow, pommes Anna and pine nut pesto. Beetroot meringue with goat's cheese, pistachio sponge and blood orange.

Menu £ 29 (lunch) – Carte £ 38/50

Town plan: B2-a – *88 Chesil St. ✉ SO23 0HX – ✆ 01962 844465 – www.theblackrat.co.uk – dinner only and lunch Saturday-Sunday – Closed 2 weeks December-January*

Chesil Rectory

MODERN CUISINE • HISTORIC XX This double-gabled wattle and daub house dates from the 15C and its characterful interior takes in heavily beamed ceilings and a large inglenook fireplace. Appealing menus offer classic British dishes with the odd Mediterranean touch.

Menu £ 22 (lunch and early dinner) – Carte £ 26/41

Town plan: B2-r – *Chesil St. ✉ SO23 0HU – ✆ 01962 851555 – www.chesilrectory.co.uk – Closed 25 December*

Rick Stein

SEAFOOD • ELEGANT XX Winchester's high street was the location of the first outpost of the Stein empire outside Cornwall: a smart restaurant with a large open kitchen. Simply cooked fish and seafood dishes have some Asian influences; good value set lunch.

Menu £ 20 (lunch) – Carte £ 29/65

Town plan: B2-e – *7-8 High St ✉ SO23 9JX – ✆ 01962 353535 – www.rickstein.com – Closed 25 December*

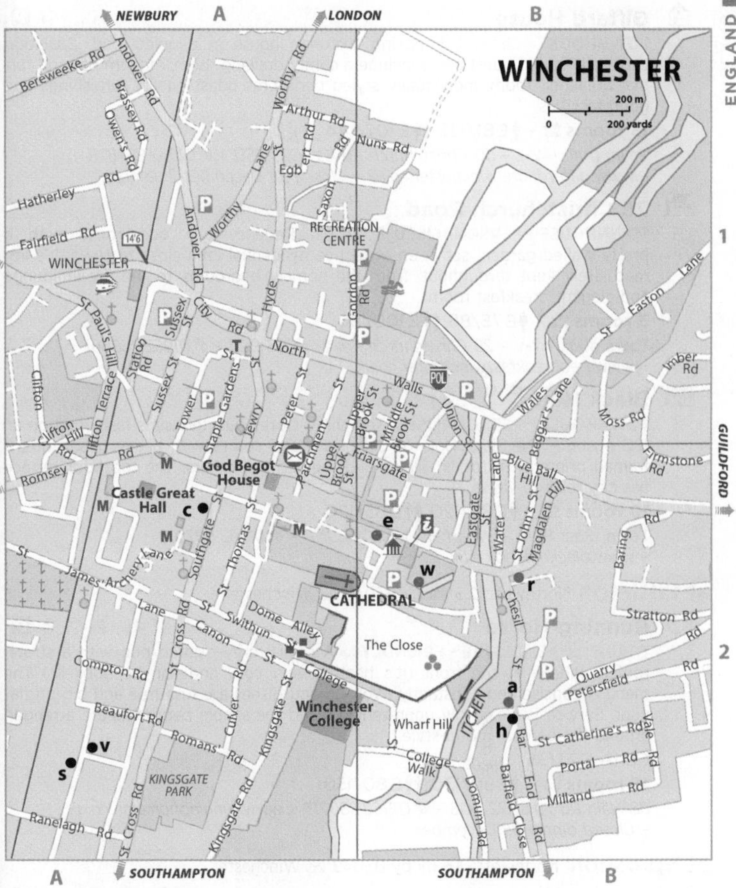

River Cottage Canteen

TRADITIONAL BRITISH • RUSTIC A delightful restaurant set within a 200 year old silk mill in the Abbey Gardens. The lower floor has an open kitchen and the upper floor has exposed timbers and rope lights. Seasonal regional produce is at the core of the menu and dishes are hearty and rustic; the small plates and sharing boards are popular.

Carte £ 22/43

Town plan: B2-w – *Abbey Mill, Abbey Mill Gardens ✉ SO23 9GH*
– *☎ 01962 457747 (booking essential) – www.rivercottage.net – Closed 25 December, Sunday dinner*

Hotel du Vin

TOWNHOUSE • CONTEMPORARY Attractive Georgian house dating from 1715, and the first ever Hotel du Vin. Wine-themed bedrooms, split between the house and garden, are stylish and well-equipped; some have baths in the room. The characterful split-level bistro offers unfussy French cooking and – as hoped – an excellent wine selection.

24 rooms – †£ 162/252 ††£ 162/252

Town plan: A2-c – *14 Southgate St ✉ SO23 9EF*
– *☎ 01962 841414 – www.hotelduvin.com*

Giffard House

TOWNHOUSE · CLASSIC Imposing Victorian house in a quiet road. Spacious, classically styled guest areas include a comfy drawing room, modern bar and formal breakfast room. Individually styled bedrooms boast quality furnishings and good facilities.

13 rooms – †£ 81/132 ††£ 107/144

Town plan: A2-s – *50 Christchurch Rd ✉ SO23 9SU – ✆ 01962 852628 – www.giffardhotelwinchester.co.uk – Closed 24 December-2 January*

29 Christchurch Road

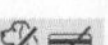

TOWNHOUSE · PERSONALISED Spacious, Regency-style guesthouse with a pretty walled garden, set in an attractive residential area close to town. It's immaculately kept throughout, from the homely bedrooms to the fire-lit lounge and elegant breakfast room.

3 rooms – †£ 75/85 ††£ 100/110

Town plan: A2-v – *29 Christchurch Rd. ✉ SO23 9SU – ✆ 01962 868661 – www.bedbreakfastwinchester.co.uk*

Black Hole

TOWNHOUSE · PERSONALISED This three-storey guesthouse is fashioned on an 18C prison – the Black Hole of Calcutta – and comes with heavy prison doors, framed prints of history's villains and themed wallpapers. The top floor terrace has city rooftop views.

10 rooms – †£ 85/120 ††£ 85/120

Town plan: B2-h – *Wharf Hill ✉ SO23 9NP – ✆ 01962 807010 – www.blackholebb.co.uk*

at Littleton Northwest: 2.5 mi by B3049 ✉ Winchester

Running Horse

TRADITIONAL CUISINE · FRIENDLY A smart, grey-painted pub with a straw-roofed cabana at the front (it's heated, very cosy and can be booked!) The menu is concise and constantly evolving and dishes are fuss-free and big on flavour. Service is pleasingly unpretentious and the simple bedrooms are arranged around the garden, motel-style.

Carte £ 23/35

15 rooms – †£ 80/130 ††£ 80/130

88 Main Rd ✉ SO22 6QS – ✆ 01962 880218 – www.runninghorseinn.co.uk – Closed dinner 25 December

at Sparsholt Northwest: 3.5 mi by B3049 ✉ Winchester

Avenue

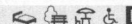

CREATIVE · CHIC XXX  Formal dining room within an impressive 17C country house; named after the mile-long avenue of lime trees it overlooks. Cooking is modern, original and creative and uses lots of produce from the kitchen garden; try the tasting menu.

Menu £ 33 (weekday lunch)/58

Lainston House Hotel, Woodman Ln ✉ SO21 2LT – ✆ 01962 776088 – www.lainstonhouse.com – Closed Monday, Tuesday and lunch Saturday

Lainston House

COUNTRY HOUSE · CONTEMPORARY Impressive 17C William and Mary manor house with attractive gardens and a striking avenue of lime trees. Clubby wood-panelled bar and modern drawing room; bedrooms are spacious and contemporary. Relax over a game of tennis, croquet or boules – or brush up on your culinary skills at the cookery school.

50 rooms – †£ 175/275 ††£ 225/275 – 3 suites

Woodman Ln ✉ SO21 2LT – ✆ 01962 776088 – www.lainstonhouse.com

Avenue – See restaurant listing

WINDERMERE

Cumbria – Pop. 5 243 – Regional map nº **12**-A2

Holbeck Ghyll

MODERN BRITISH • CLASSIC DÉCOR XX A three-roomed restaurant in a traditional stone Arts and Crafts house; its elegant oak-panelled front room offers superb views over Lake Windermere and the mountains. Concise, fixed price menus utilise good quality local ingredients in modern dishes; at dinner there's also an 8 course tasting menu.

Menu £ 45/68

Holbeck Ghyll Hotel, Holbeck Ln ✉ LA23 1LU – Northwest : 3.25 mi by A 591 – ✆ 015394 32375 (booking advisable) – www.holbeckghyll.com – Closed first 2 weeks January

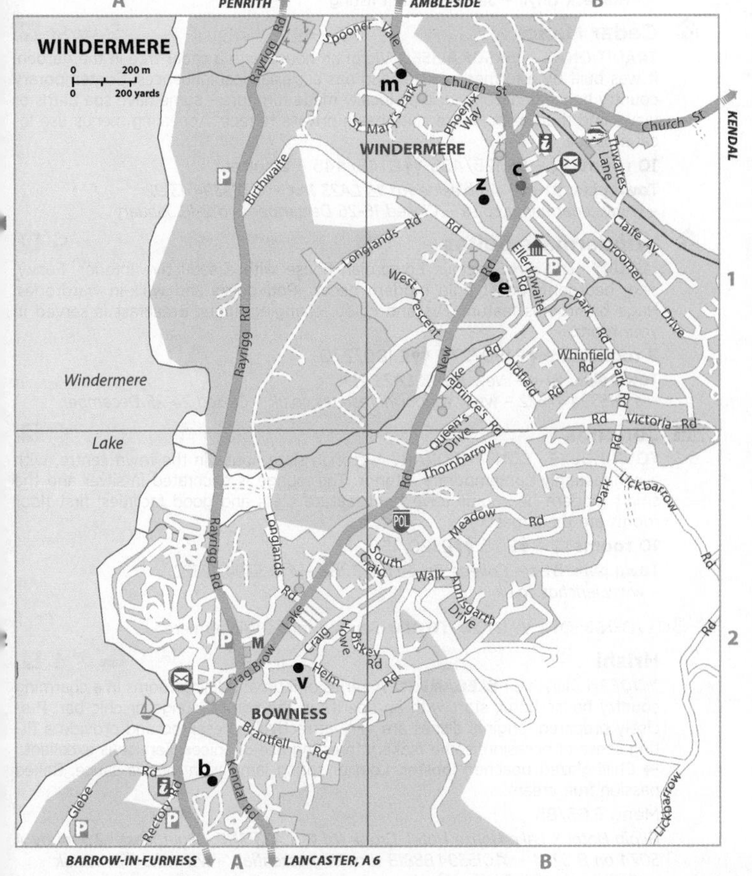

Francine's

TRADITIONAL BRITISH • NEIGHBOURHOOD ☓ Intimate neighbourhood restaurant with a homely feel; local art hangs on the walls and the service is friendly. Wide-ranging menus offer straightforward classical cooking with French influences; the chef is passionate about game.

Menu £ 17 – Carte £ 23/36

Town plan: C1-c – *27 Main Rd ✉ LA23 1DX – ✆ 015394 44088 – www.francinesrestaurantwindermere.co.uk – dinner only – Closed last 2 weeks January, first week December, 25-26 December, 1 January and Monday*

Holbeck Ghyll

TRADITIONAL • CLASSIC A charming Arts and Crafts house boasting stunning views over the lake and mountains. Well-equipped bedrooms are spread about the place and range from classical to contemporary; Miss Potter, complete with a hot tub, is the best.

31 rooms – £ 235/350 £ 320/550 – 4 suites

Holbeck Ln ✉ LA23 1LU – Northwest : 3.25 mi by A 591 – ✆ 015394 32375 – www.holbeckghyll.com – Closed first 2 weeks January

Holbeck Ghyll – See restaurant listing

Cedar Manor

TRADITIONAL • PERSONALISED Victorian house with a cedar tree in the garden; it was built by a former minister and has ecclesiastical influences. Contemporary country house bedrooms display locally made furniture – some have spa baths or views and the Coach House suite has a private terrace. Appealing menus use local produce.

10 rooms – £ 125/425 £ 145/445 – 2 suites

Town plan: B1-m – *Ambleside Rd ✉ LA23 1AX – ✆ 015394 43192 – www.cedarmanor.co.uk – Closed 16-26 December and 2-18 January*

Windermere Suites

LUXURY • DESIGN Spacious Edwardian house with a seductive interior. Funky, sexy bedrooms boast bold modern décor, iPod docks and walk-in wardrobes. Huge bathrooms feature TVs and colour-changing lights. Breakfast is served in your room.

8 rooms – £ 150/270 £ 180/270

Town plan: B1-e – *New Rd ✉ LA23 2LA – ✆ 015394 47672 – www.windermeresuites.co.uk – Closed 24-25 December*

Jerichos

TOWNHOUSE • CONTEMPORARY Victorian slate house in the town centre, with a contrastingly contemporary interior. The lounge is decorated in silver and the smart modern bedrooms have bold feature walls and good facilities; first floor rooms are the largest.

10 rooms – £ 75 £ 120/150

Town plan: B1-z – *College Rd ✉ LA23 1BX – ✆ 015394 42522 – www.jerichos.co.uk*

at Bowness-on-Windermere South: 1 mi ✉ Windermere

Hrishi

MODERN CUISINE • ELEGANT ☓☓☓ A series of intimate dining rooms in a charming country house hotel; start with an aperitif in the comfy lounge or chic bar. Precisely prepared, original dishes are very attractively presented and provide a fitting sense of occasion; some make interesting use of spices. Service is excellent.

→ Chilli-glazed poached lobster. Loin of spring lamb with masala sauce. Baked passion fruit cream.

Menu £ 65/85

Gilpin Hotel & Lake House Hotel, Crook Rd ✉ LA23 3NE – Southeast : 2.5 mi by A 5074 on B 5284 – ✆ 015394 88818 (booking essential) – www.thegilpin.co.uk – dinner only and Sunday lunch

Linthwaite House

MODERN CUISINE • ROMANTIC XXX Contemporary country house restaurant – sit in the intimate Mirror Room or the airy former billiard room. Seasonally evolving menus showcase Lakeland produce; deceptively simple modern cooking is packed with flavour.

Menu £ 25/58

Linthwaite House Hotel, Crook Rd ✉ LA23 3JA – South : 0.75 mi by A 5074 on B 5284 – ✆ 015394 88600 – www.linthwaitehouse.com

Gilpin Spice

ASIAN • EXOTIC DÉCOR XX Cumbria was a key player in the spice trade and this slate-built restaurant in the grounds of Gilpin Hotel is inspired by that history. Extensive menus follow the Silk Road from Cumbria to Asia and dishes are designed for sharing. Enter the colourful rooms via wooden walkways built over stone-filled pools.

Menu £ 35 – Carte £ 17/36

Gilpin Hotel & Lake House Hotel, Crook Rd ✉ LA23 3NE – Southeast : 2.5 mi by A 5074 on B 5284 – ✆ 015394 88818 – www.gilpinspice.co.uk

Gilpin Hotel & Lake House

LUXURY • PERSONALISED A delightful country house hotel run by a charming, experienced family. Bedrooms range from contemporary country doubles to spacious garden suites with outdoor hot tubs. There are even more peaceful, luxurious suites a mile down the road beside a tarn – stay here for exclusive use of the smart spa.

31 rooms (dinner included) – †£ 205/605 ††£ 265/605

Crook Rd ✉ LA23 3NE – Southeast : 2.5 mi by A 5074 on B 5284 – ✆ 015394 88818 (booking essential) – www.thegilpin.co.uk

Hrishi • **Gilpin Spice** – See restaurant listing

Linthwaite House

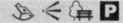

TRADITIONAL • CONTEMPORARY Set in a peaceful spot overlooking the lake and fells and surrounded by 14 acres of beautiful grounds. Guest areas are cosy and stylish and the service is polished and personable. Some of the smart modern bedrooms come with terraces and hot tubs and number 31 has a retractable glass roof. As we go to print, a major refurbishment is underway.

40 rooms – †£ 150/240 ††£ 170/250

Crook Rd ✉ LA23 3JA – South : 0.75 mi by A 5074 on B 5284 – ✆ 015394 88600 – www.linthwaitehouse.com

Linthwaite House – See restaurant listing

Laura Ashley-Belsfield

COUNTRY HOUSE • GRAND LUXURY A Victorian mansion built in Italianate style, perched overlooking Lake Windermere. An eye-catching glass and steel reception opens into four elegant lounges, where contemporary décor marries with original features. Every piece of furniture, every fabric and every ornament is made by Laura Ashley. Dine from classic menus in the all-day brasserie or formal restaurant.

62 rooms – †£ 170/270 ††£ 180/280 – 6 suites

Town plan: A2-b – *Kendal Rd ✉ LA23 3EL – ✆ 015394 42448 – www.lauraashleyhotels.com/thebelsfield*

Lindeth Howe

TRADITIONAL • CLASSIC An attractive country house once bought by Beatrix Potter for her mother. It has a clubby bar, a homely lounge and pleasant views from the drawing room. Bedrooms are traditional: the top floor rooms have the best views, while the suites are more contemporary. The classical restaurant offers a modern menu.

35 rooms – †£ 95/125 ††£ 180/360 – 2 suites

Lindeth Dr. Longtail Hill ✉ LA23 3JF – South : 1.25 mi by A 5074 on B 5284 – ✆ 015394 45759 – www.lindeth-howe.co.uk – Closed 2-14 January

Storrs Hall

HISTORIC • CLASSIC The gardens of this striking part-Georgian country house sweep down to the lake shore and their private jetty. The décor combines the old and the new, while a striking cupola adds a touch of grandeur – as does the polished dark wood and stained glass bar. Dine in the elegant dining room or bright conservatory.

30 rooms – £ 145/215 £ 155/225 – 1 suite

LA23 3LG – South : 2 mi on A 592 – 015394 47111 – www.storrshall.com

Ryebeck

FAMILY • ELEGANT Have afternoon tea on the terrace, looking over the gardens and down to the famous lake. Some of the bright, airy bedrooms share the view and some have patios or Juliet balconies. Kick-back in one of the cosy lounges then head to the dining room for tasty Cumbrian produce in a mix of classic and Asian dishes.

24 rooms – £ 95/185 £ 125/235

Lyth Valley Rd LA23 3JP – South : 0.75 mi on A 5074 – 015394 88195 – www.ryebeck.com – Closed 1 week in January

Angel Inn

INN • MODERN A cosy creamwashed inn just off the main street, with a large open-fired lounge and comfortable, contemporary bedrooms – two are in an annexed 18C cottage with lake views. Dine on classic pub dishes or sharing plates in the welcoming bar or minimalistic dining room, or head for the terraced garden in summer.

13 rooms – £ 99/110 £ 99/180

Town plan: A2-v – *Helm Rd LA23 3BU – 015394 44080 – www.theangelinnbowness.com – Closed 24-25 December*

at Winster South: 4 mi on A5074 Windermere

Brown Horse Inn

TRADITIONAL BRITISH • PUB Shabby-chic coaching inn with a lovely split-level terrace. Seasonal menus feature unfussy, generous dishes and more adventurous specials. Much of the produce is from their fields out the back and they brew their own beers too. Bedrooms are a mix of classic and boutique styles; some have terraces.

Carte £ 22/39

9 rooms – £ 55/110 £ 80/150

LA23 3NR – On A 5074 – 015394 43443 – www.thebrownhorseinn.co.uk

WINDSOR

Windsor and Maidenhead – Pop. 31 225 – Regional map n° **6**-D3

Gilbey's

TRADITIONAL CUISINE • BISTRO Opened by the Gilbey family in 1975, as the first wine bar outside London. It's relaxed and friendly, with an airy conservatory and terrace. Carefully cooked French and British dishes are accompanied by an interesting wine selection.

Menu £ 20 (weekday lunch)/29 – Carte £ 29/53

Town plan: B1-s – *82-83 High St SL4 6AF – 01753 854921 – www.gilbeygroup.com – Closed 23-29 December and Monday lunch*

Greene Oak

MODERN CUISINE • DESIGN The Greene Oak's modern, open-plan bar has a laid-back feel and its large terrace is a real suntrap. Menus mix pub classics with more interesting dishes – start with some 'Tasters' and finish with mini 'Jam Jar' desserts.

Carte £ 24/47

Oakley Green SL4 5UW – West : 3 mi by A 308 on B 3024 – 01753 864294 – www.thegreeneoak.co.uk – Closed Sunday dinner

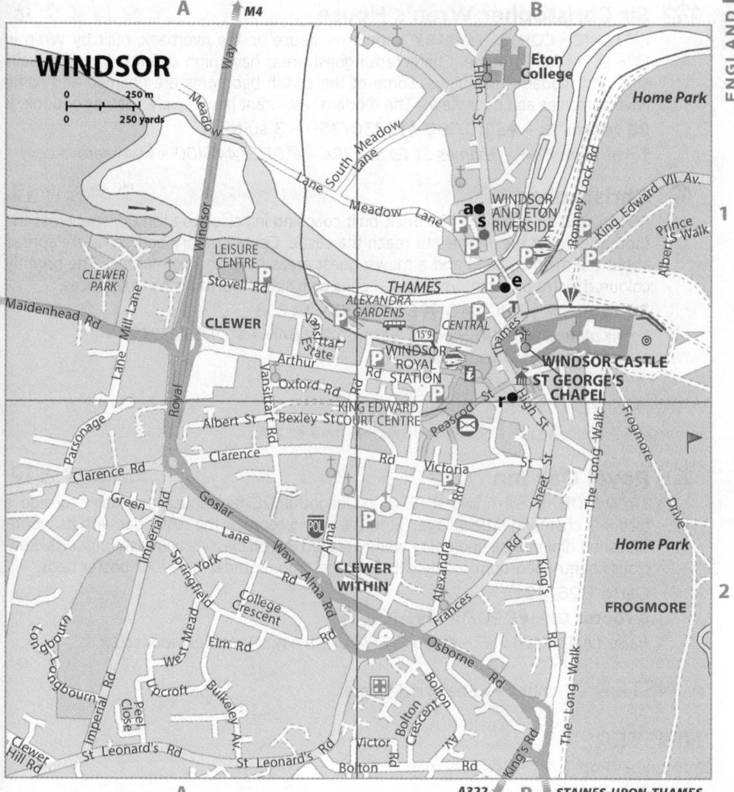

Oxford Blue

MODERN CUISINE • INTIMATE With its contemporary look and smart landscaped grounds, you'd be forgiven for thinking this 100 year old pub is a new-build. Accomplished French dishes offer far more than their descriptions reveal and flavours are intense.

Menu £ 25 (weekday lunch) – Carte £ 33/56

10 Crimp Hill, Old Windsor ✉ SL4 2QY – Southeast : 2.75 mi by A 308 off B 3021 – ✆ 01753 861954 – www.oxfordbluepub.co.uk – Closed 23-29 December, 24 July-2 August, Sunday dinner, Monday and Tuesday

Macdonald Windsor

BUSINESS • DESIGN Set in a former department store opposite the Guildhall. Pass through attractive open-plan guest areas up to contemporary bedrooms with a high level of facilities and bold masculine hues; two have balconies overlooking the castle. The modern brasserie specialises in mature Scottish beef from the Josper grill.

120 rooms – †£ 165/450 ††£ 180/450 – ☕ £ 20

Town plan: B1-2-r – *23 High St. ✉ SL4 1LH – ✆ 01753 483100 – www.macdonald-hotels.co.uk/windsor*

Sir Christopher Wren's House

HISTORIC · CONTEMPORARY Impressive house on the riverbank, built by Wren in 1676 as his family home. Characterful guest areas have high ceilings, panelled walls and bold modern furnishings. Some of the stylish bedrooms are beamed and some have balconies and river views. The modern restaurant has a lovely Thames outlook.

98 rooms – £ 110/190 £ 130/350 – 3 suites

Town plan: B1-e – *Thames St ✉ SL4 1PX – ✆ 01753 442400 – www.sarova.com*

Christopher

INN · CONTEMPORARY 18C brick-built coaching inn close to Eton College; cross the footbridge over the Thames to reach the castle. Contemporary bedrooms are spread about the main building and a mews; guest areas have an informal feel. The brightly coloured bistro offers international menus with subtle North African influences.

34 rooms – £ 110/140 £ 130/170 – £ 18

Town plan: B1-a – *110 High St, Eton ✉ SL4 6AN – ✆ 01753 852359 – www.thechristopher.co.uk*

WINSFORD

Somerset – ✉ Minehead – Pop. 270 – Regional map n° **2**-A2

Royal Oak Inn

TRADITIONAL BRITISH · RUSTIC Delightful 12C farmhouse and dairy, beside a ford in a charming little village. Sit in the dining room or the rustic bar with its wood-furnished dining area and enjoy well-executed British classics and tasty desserts. Spacious country bedrooms come with huge bathrooms; most have four-poster beds.

Carte £ 26/42

8 rooms – £ 90/110 £ 100/150

Halse Ln ✉ TA24 7JE – ✆ 01643 851455 – www.royaloakexmoor.co.uk

WINSTER – Cumbria → See Windermere

WINSTER

Derbyshire – Pop. 1 787 – Regional map n° **9**-A1

Old Shoulder of Mutton

LUXURY · TRADITIONAL This old village pub closed in 1916 but its name and character have been kept and it's been transformed into a stylish, cosy guesthouse. Beams and handmade furniture abound and local produce features at breakfast. (Min 2 nights stay).

3 rooms – £ 110/145 £ 125/150

West Bank ✉ DE4 2DQ – ✆ 01629 650005 – www.oldshoulderofmutton.co.uk – Closed December-February

WINSTON

Durham – Regional map n° **14**-A3

Bridgewater Arms

SEAFOOD · COSY This traditional pub spent the first hundred years of its life as a school; look out for the copperplate alphabet. The chef is known for his seafood and dishes are unashamedly classic, accurately executed and extremely satisfying.

Carte £ 25/67

✉ DL2 3RN – ✆ 01325 730302 – www.thebridgewaterarms.com – Closed 25-26 December, 1 January, Sunday and Monday

WINTERINGHAM

North Lincolnshire – ✉ Scunthorpe – Pop. 1 000 – Regional map n° **13**-C3

Winteringham Fields

MODERN CUISINE • INTIMATE XXX A characterful 16C house in a remote location, featuring an elegant dining room and several private rooms. The chef adopts a modern approach to cooking and many ingredients come from their smallholding. The 'Menu Surprise' consists of 7 or 9 courses and there's also a 4 course set priced menu at lunch. Bedrooms mix classic character with modern comforts.

Menu £ 45/85

15 rooms – †£ 140/160 ††£ 180/220

1 Silver St ✉ DN15 9ND – ✆ 01724 733096 (booking essential) – www.winteringhamfields.co.uk – Closed 3 weeks August, Christmas, 1 week January, Sunday and Monday

WISWELL

Lancashire – Regional map n° **11**-B2

Freemasons

MODERN BRITISH • PUB A delightful pub hidden away on a narrow lane. The antique-furnished upstairs has an elegant feel, while downstairs, with its flagged floors, low beams and open fires is more rustic. The interesting menu features modern versions of traditional pub dishes and cooking is refined and skilful.

Menu £ 25 (lunch and early dinner) – Carte £ 44/69

8 Vicarage Fold ✉ BB7 9DF – ✆ 01254 822218 – www.freemasonsatwiswell.com – Closed 2-14 January and Monday-Tuesday except bank holidays

WITHAM ON THE HILL

Lincolnshire – Pop. 260 – Regional map n° **9**-C2

Six Bells

TRADITIONAL CUISINE • FRIENDLY This pub's spacious courtyard is an obvious draw and the bright, stylish interior keeps things cheery whatever the weather. Choose hand-crafted pizzas cooked in the wood-burning oven in the bar or something more sophisticated from the main menu. Bedrooms are very stylishly appointed; Hayloft is the best.

Menu £ 14 (weekday lunch) – Carte £ 24/37

5 rooms – †£ 65/130 ††£ 80/150

✉ PE10 0JH – ✆ 01778 590360 – www.sixbellswitham.co.uk – Closed 25-31 December and 1-2 January

WIVETON – Norfolk → See Blakeney

WOBURN

✉ Milton Keynes – Pop. 1 534 – Regional map n° **7**-A2

Paris House

CREATIVE • INTIMATE XX A beautiful mock-Tudor house, built in Paris and reassembled in this idyllic location; enjoy an aperitif on the terrace while watching the deer. Cooking is a mix of Asian dishes and British classics given ambitious modern makeovers.

Menu £ 43/109

Woburn Park ✉ MK17 9QP – Southeast : 2.25 mi on A 4012 – ✆ 01525 290692 (booking essential) – www.parishouse.co.uk – Closed 24 December-3 January and Sunday dinner-Tuesday

The Woburn

HISTORIC • CONTEMPORARY The Woburn Estate comprises a 3,000 acre deer park, an abbey and this 18C coaching inn. Charming guest areas include a cosy bar and brasserie-style Olivier's. This is where afternoon tea was popularised in the 1840s. The best of the bedrooms are the themed suites and those in the 300yr old beamed Cottages.

55 rooms – †£ 155/310 ††£ 187/310 – 10 suites

1 George St ✉ MK17 9PX – ✆ 01525 290441 – www.thewoburnhotel.co.uk

WOLD NEWTON

East Riding of Yorkshire – Regional map n° **13**-D2

Wold Cottage

COUNTRY HOUSE • CONTEMPORARY A fine Georgian manor house in 300 acres of tranquil farmland, which guests are encouraged to explore. Enjoy cakes by the fire on arrival and feast on local produce at breakfast. Sizeable bedrooms boast luxurious soft furnishings and antiques and some have feature beds; the courtyard rooms are simpler.

6 rooms – £ 70/90 £ 110/140

YO25 3HL – South : 0.5 mi on Thwing rd – 01262 470696 – www.woldcottage.com

WOLVERHAMPTON

West Midlands – Pop. 210 319 – Regional map n° **10**-C2

Bilash

INDIAN • FAMILY XX This smart contemporary restaurant is well-established and has several generations of the same family involved. Appealing, original menus offer South Indian and Bangladeshi dishes, crafted only from local and home-made produce.

Menu £ 13 (lunch) – Carte £ 23/42

No 2 Cheapside WV1 1TU – 01902 427762 – www.thebilash.co.uk – Closed 25-27 December, 1 January and Sunday

WOMBLETON – North Yorkshire → See Helmsley

WOODBRIDGE

Suffolk – Pop. 11 341 – Regional map n° **8**-D3

Riverside

MODERN CUISINE • BISTRO X A restaurant, cinema and theatre in one – where many menus include entrance to a film. It's light and airy, with full-length windows, a terrace and a marble counter topped with fresh bread. At lunch they serve mix and match tapas boards.

Menu £ 18/35 – Carte £ 25/48

Quayside IP12 1BH – 01394 382174 (booking advisable) – www.theriverside.co.uk – Closed 25-26 December, 1 January and Sunday dinner

Crown

TRADITIONAL CUISINE • PUB A contemporary dining pub in the centre of town – a glass-roofed, granite-floored bar sits at its centre, with four smart dining areas arranged around it. Seasonal menus offer well-presented modern classics and plenty of shellfish. Service is polite and friendly and bedrooms are minimalistic and very cosy.

Carte £ 26/45

10 rooms – £ 130/200 £ 130/200

Thoroughfare IP12 1AD – 01394 384242 – www.thecrownatwoodbridge.co.uk

Turk's Head N

MODERN BRITISH • FAMILY Charming pub with a petanque pitch, lovely gardens and a great terrace with country views. As well as pub classics, the Indian chef creates interesting, cleverly spiced dishes such as paneer steak with curry butter.

Carte £ 25/42

Low Rd, Hasketon IP13 6JGB – Northwest : 2 mi by Burkitt Rd, B 1079 and Shrubbery Rd. – 01394 610343 – www.theturksheadhasketon.co.uk

Seckford Hall

HISTORIC · DESIGN This part-Tudor country house in attractive gardens was reputedly once visited by Elizabeth I – she would hardly recognise it now, with its bold champagne bar, stylish sitting rooms and creatively designed modern bedrooms. The linen-laid restaurant offers a seasonal menu of modern classics.

32 rooms – £ 85/150 £ 95/395 – 7 suites

IP13 6NU – Southwest : 1.25 mi by A 12 – 01394 385678 – www.seckford.co.uk

at Bromeswell Northeast: 2.5 mi by B1438 off A1152

Unruly Pig

MODERN CUISINE · PUB This cosy open-fired pub is far from unruly, with its wooden panelling and interesting art. The Mediterranean-inspired cooking offers plenty of choice, the set menus are good value and there's usually a daily main course for £ 10.

Menu £ 15 (weekdays) – Carte £ 28/38

Orford Rd IP12 2PU – 01394 460310 (booking advisable) – www.theunrulypig.co.uk – Closed Sunday dinner and Monday

WOODSTOCK

Oxfordshire – Pop. 2 389 – Regional map n° **6**-B2

Kitchen by Dominic Chapman N

MODERN CUISINE · INTIMATE This two-roomed hotel restaurant juxtaposes the old and new, with wood-panelling, bold fabrics and contemporary artwork. Concise menus are highly seasonal and dishes are unfussy with a classic British base.

Menu £ 20 (lunch) – Carte dinner £ 26/45

Feathers Hotel, Market St OX20 1SX – 01993 812291 (booking essential) – www.feathers.co.uk

Crown

MEDITERRANEAN CUISINE · FRIENDLY It might have 18C origins but the Crown is not your typical coaching inn, with its bright, almost greenhouse-style dining room complete with an attractive Belgian tiled floor. Fresh, light cooking takes its influences from the Med and makes good use of the wood-fired oven. Bedrooms are beautifully appointed.

Carte £ 24/35

5 rooms – £ 150/250 £ 150/250

31 High St OX20 1TE – 01993 813339 – www.thecrownwoodstock.com

Feathers

TOWNHOUSE · ELEGANT It might date from the 17C but this townhouse has a stylish modern interior. Bedrooms blend bold fabrics and wallpapers with antique furnishings. The bar offers over 400 gins and the courtyard terrace is a great spot for lunch.

21 rooms – £ 99/349 £ 99/349 – 5 suites

Market St OX20 1SX – 01993 812291 – www.feathers.co.uk

Kitchen by Dominic Chapman – See restaurant listing

WOOLACOMBE

Devon – Pop. 840 – Regional map n° **1**-C1

Noel Corston

MODERN BRITISH · INTIMATE A rustic restaurant consisting of just 10 seats set around an open kitchen counter. Choose 7 or 9 courses from the daily set menu and go for the wine pairings. Skilful modern cooking uses seasonal Devonshire produce.

Menu £ 75 (weekdays)/95 – tasting menu only

South St EX34 7BB – 01271 871187 (booking essential) – www.noelcorston.com – dinner only – Closed October-Easter and Sunday-Tuesday

WOOLER

Northumberland – Pop. 1 983 – Regional map n° **14**-A1

Firwood

TRADITIONAL • COSY Bay-windowed dower house in a peaceful setting, with a beautiful tiled hall, a comfy lounge and lovely countryside views. Spacious bedrooms are furnished in a simple period style. The friendly owners are a font of local knowledge.

3 rooms – £ 60/90 £ 60/90

Middleton Hall ✉ NE71 6RD – South : 1.75 mi by Earle rd on Middleton Hall rd – ✆ 01668 283699 – www.firwoodhouse.co.uk – Closed 1 December-13 February

WOOLHOPE

Herefordshire – Regional map n° **10**-B3

Butchers Arms

TRADITIONAL CUISINE • RUSTIC Unfussy, classical cooking, with game in season, plenty of offal, tasty home-baked bread and hearty, reasonably priced dishes. The décor is traditional too, with a welcoming log fire, wattle walls and low-slung beams.

Carte £ 27/36

✉ HR1 4RF

– ✆ 01432 860281 – www.butchersarmswoolhope.com – Closed Sunday dinner in winter and Monday except bank holidays

WOOTTON

Oxfordshire – Regional map n° **6**-B2

Killingworth Castle

TRADITIONAL BRITISH • RUSTIC A welcoming roadside inn dating from the 16C, set just outside the village centre. The chatty staff know what they're doing and food is great value, especially the dish of the day. Interesting menus champion local produce; here they bake their own breads, butcher their own meats and brew their own beers. Retire to one of the spacious bedrooms feeling suitably fortified.

Carte £ 25/42

8 rooms – £ 90/140 £ 99/150

Glympton Rd ✉ OX20 1EJ

– ✆ 01993 811401 – www.thekillingworthcastle.com – Closed 25 December

WORCESTER

Worcestershire – Pop. 100 153 – Regional map n° **10**-B3

Old Rectifying House

TRADITIONAL BRITISH • PUB You'll find shabby-chic décor, easy-going staff and a cocktail list in this striking mock-Tudor building overlooking Worcester Bridge and the River Severn. Most dishes have a British slant, but there's the odd international influence too.

Carte £ 24/38

North Par. ✉ WR1 3NN

– ✆ 01905 619622 – www.theoldrec.co.uk – Closed Monday except bank holidays and 25 December

WORKSOP

Nottinghamshire – Pop. 41 820 – Regional map n° **9**-B1

Browns

TRADITIONAL • COSY Cross the ford to this keenly run, cosy cottage, which dates back to 1730. Lovely garden with mature fruit trees. Bedrooms are in the old cow shed; all have four-posters and open onto a large decked terrace. Appealing breakfast menu.

3 rooms - †£ 59/69 ††£ 91/102

Old Orchard Cottage, Holbeck Ln, Holbeck. ✉ S80 3NF - Southwest : 4.5 mi by A 60 - ✆ 01909 720659 - www.brownsholbeck.co.uk - Closed 24 December-2 January

WORTH - Kent ➜ See Deal

WRINGTON

North Somerset - Pop. 1 918 - Regional map n° **2**-B2

The Ethicurean

MODERN BRITISH • SIMPLE Two rustic, informal glasshouses in a beautifully restored Victorian walled garden; fresh produce leads the daily menu and they strive to be 'ethical' and 'epicurean'. They serve everything from coffee and cake to 5 set courses.

Menu £ 28/46 (dinner) - Carte lunch £ 27/52

Barley Wood Walled Garden, Long Ln ✉ BS40 5SA - East : 1.25 mi by School Rd on Redhill rd - ✆ 01934 863713 (booking essential) - www.theethicurean.com - Closed Sunday dinner and Monday in winter

WROTHAM

Kent - Pop. 1 767 - Regional map n° **5**-B1

The Bull

TRADITIONAL BRITISH • RUSTIC This 14C inn might look a little plain but give it a chance and it will grow on you. The restaurant offers a traditional à la carte but most come for the Bull Pit menu, which is served in the bar and courtyard and features a host of meats cooked on the American-style BBQ. Bedrooms are smart and up-to-date.

Menu £ 23 (lunch) - Carte £ 29/38

11 rooms - †£ 69/139 ††£ 79/159 - £ 8

Bull Ln. ✉ TN15 7RF - ✆ 01732 789800 - www.thebullhotel.com - Closed 1 January

WYE

Kent - ✉ Ashford - Pop. 2 066 - Regional map n° **5**-C2

Wife of Bath

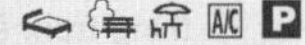

SPANISH • DESIGN An attractive red-brick house plays host to this understated restaurant where a Spanish tiled floor marries with a wooden bar counter and old timbers. The menu champions northern Spain, with colourful, vibrant dishes including sharing plates and a small range of tapas. Stylish bedrooms come with lots of extras.

Menu £ 16 (weekday lunch) - Carte £ 27/44

5 rooms - †£ 105/140 ††£ 105/140

4 Upper Bridge St ✉ TN25 5AF - ✆ 01233 812232 (bookings advisable at dinner) - www.thewifeofbath.com

WYMESWOLD

Leicestershire - Regional map n° **9**-B2

Hammer & Pincers

MODERN BRITISH • ELEGANT Formerly the village forge (the old water pump can still be seen at the back), then a pub, and now a stylish, intimate restaurant. Modern menus have classic British roots; the 7 and 10 course grazing menus are the most creative.

Menu £ 23 (weekdays) - Carte dinner £ 31/49

5 East Rd ✉ LE12 6ST - ✆ 01509 880735 - www.hammerandpincers.co.uk - Closed 25 December, Sunday dinner and Monday

WYMONDHAM

Leicestershire – Pop. 600 – Regional map n° **9**-C2

Berkeley Arms

TRADITIONAL BRITISH • PUB Attractive 16C village pub run by an experienced local couple; turn left for the low-beamed bar or right for the dining room. Appealing, gutsy dishes rely on seasonal local produce and are constantly evolving; alongside British favourites you'll find the likes of mallard with poached pears. Service is relaxed.

Menu £ 16/23 – Carte £ 25/34

59 Main St ✉ LE14 2AG – ✆ 01572 787587 (booking essential) – www.theberkeleyarms.co.uk – Closed first 2 weeks January, 2 weeks summer, Sunday dinner and Monday

WYNYARD

Stockton-on-Tees – Regional map n° **14**-B3

Wynyard Hall

COUNTRY HOUSE • ELEGANT An impressive Georgian mansion built for the Marquis of Londonderry; its smart spa overlooks a lake. Bedrooms in the main house are traditional, while those in the lodges are more modern. Classic guest areas feature stained glass, open fires and antiques. The formal dining room offers modern classics.

24 rooms – †£ 135/200 ††£ 135/200 – 3 suites

✉ TS22 5NF – ✆ 01740 644811 – www.wynyardhall.co.uk

YARM

Stockton-on-Tees – Pop. 19 184 – Regional map n° **14**-B3

Judges Country House

MODERN CUISINE • TRADITIONAL DÉCOR XXX A formal two-roomed restaurant in a traditional country house hotel; the conservatory extension has a lovely outlook over the lawns. Modern, well-prepared dishes are straightforward yet full of flavour.

Menu £ 25 – Carte £ 29/57

Judges Country House, Kirklevington Hall, Kirklevington ✉ TS15 9LW – South : 1.5 mi on A 67 – ✆ 01642 789000 – www.judgeshotel.co.uk

Muse

INTERNATIONAL • BRASSERIE X A smart continental café with a bright modern interior and a popular pavement terrace. Extensive international menus list everything from a bacon sandwich to salads, pastas and grills; they also offer a good value set price menu.

Menu £ 14 (lunch and early dinner) – Carte £ 22/49

104b High St ✉ TS15 9AU – ✆ 01642 788558 (booking advisable) – www.museyarm.com – Closed 25 December, 1 January and Sunday dinner

Judges Country House

COUNTRY HOUSE • CLASSIC A charming Victorian judge's house with a welcoming atmosphere, filled with wood panelling, antiques and ornaments and set within impressive grounds. Traditional country house bedrooms come with a high level of facilities, bright modern bathrooms and extra touches such as fresh fruit and flowers.

21 rooms – †£ 145/205 ††£ 145/225

Kirklevington Hall, Kirklevington ✉ TS15 9LW – South : 1.5 mi on A 67 – ✆ 01642 789000 – www.judgeshotel.co.uk

Judges Country House – See restaurant listing

YARMOUTH – Isle of Wight → See Wight (Isle of)

YATTENDON

West Berkshire – ✉ Newbury – Pop. 288 – Regional map n° **6**-B3

Royal Oak

TRADITIONAL BRITISH • INN A red-brick pub bursting with country charm, set in a picture postcard village; you'll find a heavily beamed bar with a roaring fire at its hub. Menus offer honest British dishes and traditional puddings. Country house style bedrooms are named after guns and even have their own gun cabinets.

Menu £ 15 (weekday lunch) - Carte £ 30/47

10 rooms - £ 99/140 £ 99/140

The Square ✉ RG18 0UF - ✆ 01635 201325 (booking advisable) - www.royaloakyattendon.co.uk

at Frilsham South: 1 mi by Frilsham rd on Bucklebury rd✉ Yattendon

Pot Kiln

TRADITIONAL BRITISH • COSY Head for the cosy bar and order a pint of Brick Kiln beer then follow the delicious aromas through to the dining area, where flavoursome British dishes arrive in gutsy portions. On summer Sundays they fire up the outdoor pizza oven.

Carte £ 30/41

✉ RG18 0XX - ✆ 01635 201366 - www.potkiln.org - Closed 25 December

YEOVIL

Somerset – Pop. 45 784 – Regional map n° **2**-B3

at Barwick South: 2 mi by A30 off A37✉ Yeovil

Little Barwick House

MODERN BRITISH • INTIMATE XX Attractive Georgian dower house on the outskirts of town, run by a hospitable husband and wife team. Relax on deep sofas before heading into the elegant dining room with its huge window and heavy drapes. Cooking is classical, satisfying and full of flavour – a carefully chosen wine list accompanies. Charming, comfortably furnished bedrooms, each with its own character.

Menu £ 30/50

7 rooms - £ 85/105 £ 121/190

✉ BA22 9TD - ✆ 01935 423902 (booking essential) - www.littlebarwickhouse.co.uk - Closed 26 December-27 January, dinner Sunday, Monday and lunch Tuesday

GOOD TIPS!

In the tourist capital of the North, every cobbled twist and turn reveals another historic building. A stone's throw from the magnificent York Minster cathedral is the **Judge's Lodging**; once a doctor's house and now a characterful hotel. Follow the ancient city walls to the Museum Gardens and the **Star Inn The City**, where chargrilled meats are a highlight.

YORK

York – Pop. 198 900 – Regional map n° **13**-C2

Restaurants

Skosh

MODERN BRITISH • FASHIONABLE X A glass-fronted former shop in a Grade II listed building close to 12C Micklegate Bar. Both the décor and the cooking are bright and colourful; sit at the counter to really be a part of what's going on. Constantly evolving small plates keep Yorkshire produce at their heart and display some Asian influences.

Carte £ 16/33

Town plan: A2-s – *98 Micklegate ✉ YO1 6JX – ✆ 01904 634849 (booking essential at dinner) – www.skoshyork.co.uk – Closed 2 weeks January, 1 week May, 1 week September, Sunday dinner, Monday and Tuesday*

Arras

MODERN CUISINE • DESIGN XX A red-brick former coach house with a bright, contemporary interior. Well-priced modern menus offer creative cooking. The bar boasts an unusual white-fronted counter and there's a lovely enclosed terrace hidden to the rear.

Menu £ 24/45

Town plan: B1-x – *The Old Coach House, Peasholme Grn ✉ YO1 7PW – ✆ 01904 633737 – www.arrasrestaurant.co.uk – Closed Christmas-mid January, Sunday dinner, Monday and Tuesday*

Melton's

MODERN BRITISH • NEIGHBOURHOOD XX A cosy-looking shop conversion in the suburbs. The walls are covered in murals of ingredients and happy diners, which is fitting as local produce features highly and the restaurant is well-regarded. Cooking is fresh and flavoursome.

Menu £ 26 (lunch and early dinner) – Carte £ 32/44

Town plan: A2-c – *7 Scarcroft Rd ✉ YO23 1ND – ✆ 01904 634341 (booking essential) – www.meltonsrestaurant.co.uk – Closed 3 weeks Christmas, Sunday and Monday*

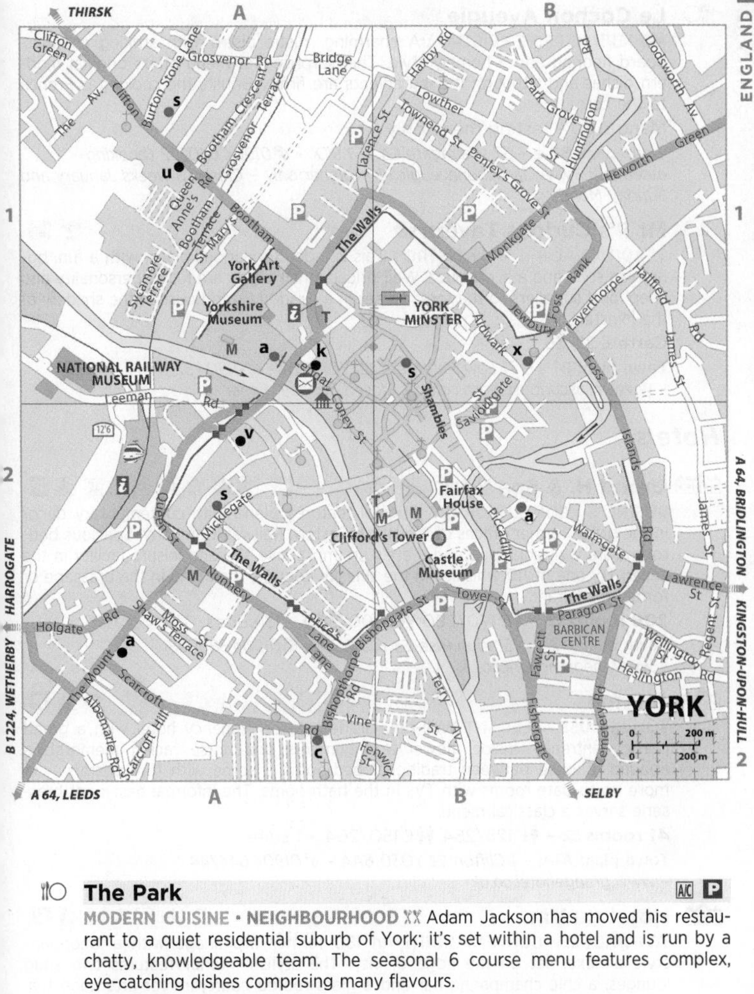

The Park

MODERN CUISINE • NEIGHBOURHOOD XX Adam Jackson has moved his restaurant to a quiet residential suburb of York; it's set within a hotel and is run by a chatty, knowledgeable team. The seasonal 6 course menu features complex, eye-catching dishes comprising many flavours.

Menu £ 60 – tasting menu only

Town plan: A1-s – *Marmadukes Hotel, 4-5 St Peters Grove, Bootham ✉ YO30 6AQ*
– ✆ 01904 540903 – www.theparkrestaurant.co.uk
– dinner only – Closed 2 weeks January, 2 weeks summer, 24-26 December, Sunday and Monday

Star Inn The City

MODERN BRITISH • DESIGN XX A buzzy all-day brasserie set in an old brick engine house, in a delightful riverside spot beside the Museum Gardens. Well-judged dishes are modern yet gutsy and showcase top Yorkshire produce – the chargrilled meats are a highlight.

Menu £ 22 (lunch and early dinner) – Carte £ 27/57

Town plan: A1-a – *Lendal Engine House, Museum St ✉ YO1 7DR*
– ✆ 01904 619208 – www.starinnthecity.co.uk

Le Cochon Aveugle

MODERN CUISINE • BISTRO A charming, rustic bistro with striking chequer-board flooring and a homely style. The 'surprise' set menu offers original modern dishes and although the ingredients are firmly British, the cooking is French to the core.

Menu £ 60 – tasting menu only

Town plan: B2-a – *37 Walmgate ✉ YO1 9TX – ✆ 01904 640222 (booking essential) – www.lecochonaveugle.uk – dinner only – Closed 3 weeks January and Sunday-Monday*

Mr P's Curious Tavern

TRADITIONAL BRITISH • BISTRO This is indeed a curious place, with a fun, bohemian style and a lively buzz. Well-priced small plates are full of personality and keep local suppliers to the fore. It's set in a Grade I listed house in the shadow of the Minster.

Carte £ 22/35

Town plan: B1-s – *71 Low Petergate ✉ YO1 7HY – ✆ 01904 521177 – www.mrpscurioustavern.co.uk – Closed Sunday dinner*

Hotels

Grand H. & Spa York

BUSINESS • CONTEMPORARY Original features blend with contemporary décor in the grand former offices of the North Eastern Railway Company. Spacious bedrooms are well-equipped and there's an impressive spa and leisure facility in the cellar. Try one of 110 whiskies in the Whisky Lounge, then dine in the brasserie or formal restaurant.

208 rooms – †£ 170/280 ††£ 190/320 – 13 suites

Town plan: A2-v – *Station Rise ✉ YO1 6GD – ✆ 01904 380038 – www.thegrandyork.co.uk*

Grange

TOWNHOUSE • ELEGANT Well-run, Grade II listed Regency hotel with a grand portico entrance. Inside, flower arrangements and horse racing memorabilia abound. Choose between traditional bedrooms – some with four-posters – or more up-to-date rooms with TVs in the bathrooms. The informal basement brasserie serves a classical menu.

41 rooms – †£ 125/254 ††£ 150/264 – 1 suite

Town plan: A1-u – *1 Clifton ✉ YO30 6AA – ✆ 01904 644744 – www.grangehotel.co.uk*

Hotel du Vin

TOWNHOUSE • CONTEMPORARY An 18C former orphanage with a Georgian-style annexe, set on the edge of city. The stylish interior features two snug lounges, a chic champagne bar and a glass-roofed courtyard for afternoon tea. Well-equipped bedrooms are wine-themed and they offer an imaginative wine list in the popular French bistro.

44 rooms – †£ 112/302 ††£ 112/302

Town plan: A2-a – *89 The Mount ✉ YO24 1AX – ✆ 01904 557350 – www.hotelduvin.com*

Middlethorpe Hall

HISTORIC • CLASSIC A William and Mary House dating from 1699, set in 20 acres of impressive parkland. The elegant sitting room has French-style furnishings, oil paintings and flower displays. Antique-filled bedrooms are split between the house and the courtyard. Classic cooking uses luxury ingredients and kitchen garden produce.

29 rooms – †£ 129/143 ††£ 199/287 – 9 suites

Bishopthorpe Rd ✉ YO23 2GB – South : 1.75 mi – ✆ 01904 641241 – www.middlethorpe.com

Judge's Lodging

HISTORIC • CONTEMPORARY Built for a doctor in 1706 and later used by judges sitting at the nearby court. Rooms in the main building have high ceilings and antique furnishings; the terrace rooms are more modern with smart shower rooms. It also has a wonderfully characterful barrel-ceilinged bar and a stylish brasserie and terrace.

23 rooms – £ 110/144 £ 110/195

Town plan: A1-k – 9 Lendal ✉ YO1 8AQ – West : 1 mi by A 59 – ☎ 01904 638733 – www.judgeslodgingyork.co.uk

Bishops

TRADITIONAL • PERSONALISED This centrally located Victorian guesthouse is run by a welcoming couple (he was once a professional footballer for Sunderland). Well-kept bedrooms vary in shape and size; some have four-posters. Local produce is served at breakfast.

10 rooms – £ 50/60 £ 70/160

135 Holgate Rd ✉ YO24 4DF – Southwest : 1 mi on A 59 – ☎ 01904 628000 – www.bishopsyork.co.uk – Closed 1 week Christmas

ZENNOR

Cornwall – Regional map n° **1**-A3

Gurnard's Head

REGIONAL CUISINE • INN Surrounded by nothing but fields and livestock; a dog-friendly pub with shabby-chic décor, blazing fires and a relaxed, cosy feel. Menus rely on regional and foraged produce and the wine list offers some interesting choices by the glass. Compact bedrooms feature good quality linen and colourful throws.

Menu £ 21 (weekday lunch)/27 – Carte £ 32/34

7 rooms – £ 120/185 £ 170/235

Treen ✉ TR26 3DE – West : 1.5 mi on B 3306 – ☎ 01736 796928 (booking advisable) – www.gurnardshead.co.uk – Closed 24-25 December and 4 days early December

SCOTLAND

Scotland may be small, but its variety is immense. The vivacity of Glasgow can seem a thousand miles from the vast peatland wilderness of Caithness; the arty vibe of Georgian Edinburgh a world away from the remote and tranquil Ardnamurchan peninsula. Wide golden sands trim the Atlantic at South Harris, and the coastline of the Highlands boasts empty islands and turquoise waters. Meantime, Fife's coast draws golf fans to St Andrews and the more secretive delights of East Neuk, an area of fishing villages and stone harbours. Wherever you travel, a sense of a dramatic history prevails in the shape of castles, cathedrals and rugged lochside monuments to the heroes of old.

Food and drink embraces the traditional too, typified by Speyside's famous Malt Whisky Trail. And what better than Highland game, fresh fish from the Tweed or haggis, neeps and tatties to complement a grand Scottish hike? The country's glorious natural larder yields such jewels as Spring lamb from the Borders, Perthshire venison, fresh fish and shellfish from the Western Highlands and Aberdeen Angus beef.

- Michelin Road maps n° 501, 502 and 713
- Michelin Green Guide: Great Britain

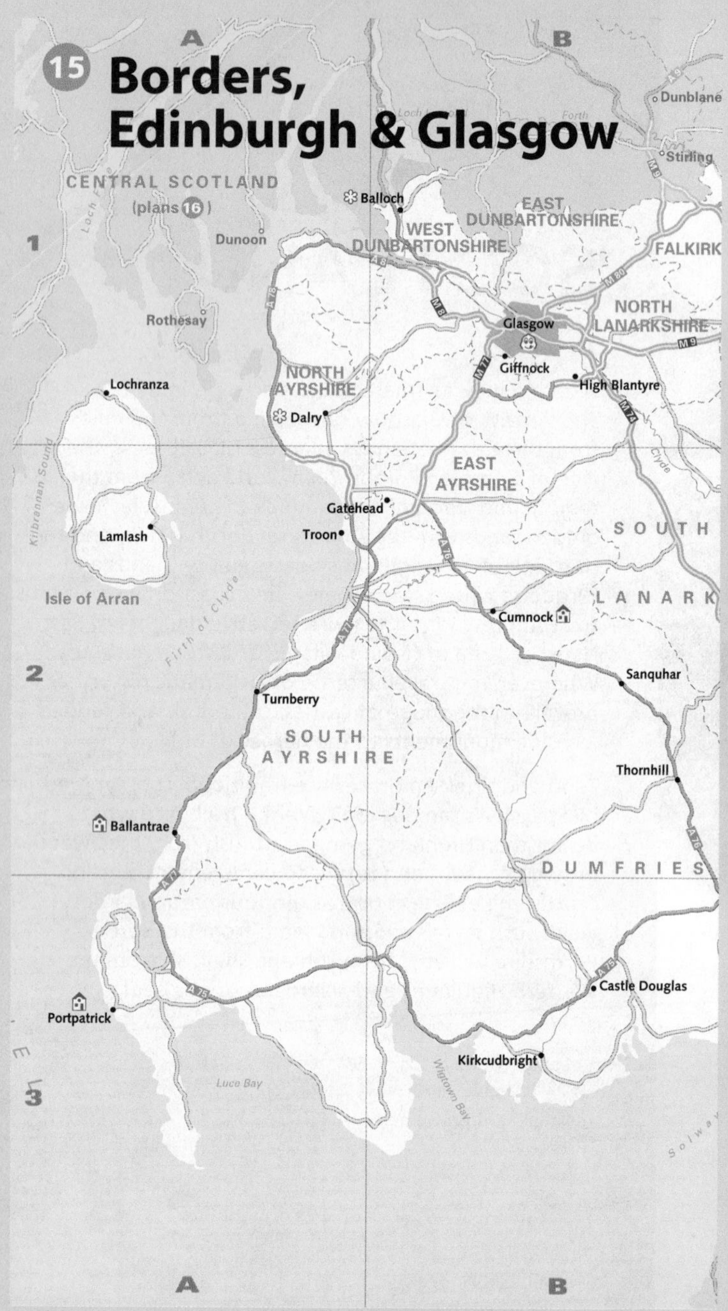
15
Borders, Edinburgh & Glasgow
CENTRAL SCOTLAND
(plans 16)
A
B
1
2
3
Dunblane
Stirling
Balloch
Dunoon
EAST DUNBARTONSHIRE
WEST DUNBARTONSHIRE
FALKIRK
NORTH LANARKSHIRE
Rothesay
Glasgow
Giffnock
High Blantyre
Lochranza
NORTH AYRSHIRE
Dalry
EAST AYRSHIRE
Gatehead
Troon
Lamlash
Isle of Arran
SOUTH
LANARK
Cumnock
Sanquhar
Turnberry
SOUTH AYRSHIRE
Thornhill
Ballantrae
DUMFRIES
Castle Douglas
Portpatrick
Kirkcudbright
Luce Bay
Wigtown Bay
Firth of Clyde
Kilbrennan Sound
Loch Fyne
Clyde
A 78
A 8
M 8
M 77
M 74
M 80
M 9
A 76
A 77
A 75
A 9

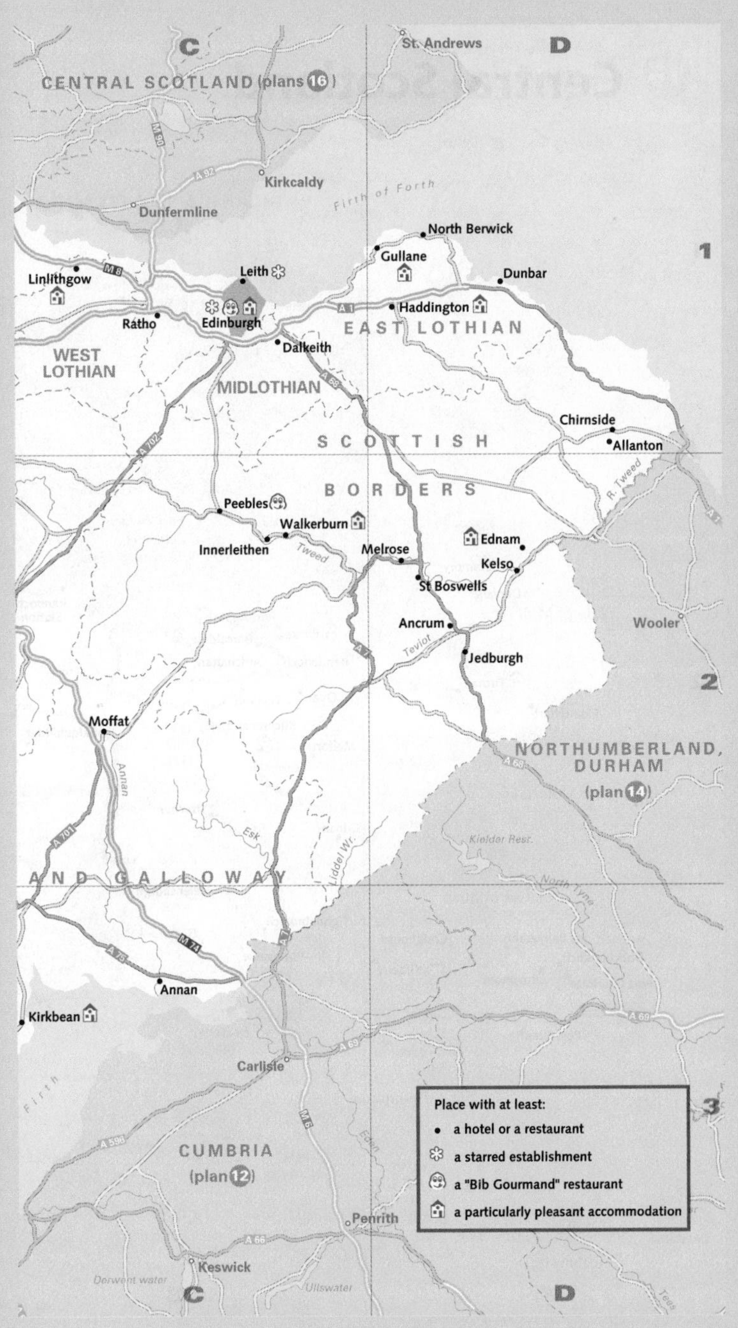

C
D
St. Andrews
CENTRAL SCOTLAND (plans 16)
Kirkcaldy
Firth of Forth
Dunfermline
North Berwick
Gullane
1
Dunbar
Linlithgow
Leith
Edinburgh
Ratho
Haddington
EAST LOTHIAN
Dalkeith
WEST LOTHIAN
MIDLOTHIAN
Chirnside
Allanton
SCOTTISH
BORDERS
R. Tweed
Peebles
Walkerburn
Innerleithen
Tweed
Melrose
Ednam
Kelso
St Boswells
Wooler
Ancrum
Teviot
Jedburgh
2
Moffat
NORTHUMBERLAND, DURHAM
(plan 14)
Annan
Esk
Kielder Rest.
Liddel Wr.
North Tyne
AND GALLOWAY
Annan
Kirkbean
Carlisle
Firth
Place with at least:
a hotel or a restaurant
a starred establishment
a "Bib Gourmand" restaurant
a particularly pleasant accommodation
3
CUMBRIA
(plan 12)
Eden
Penrith
Keswick
Derwent water
Ullswater
C
D
Tees

16 Central Scotland

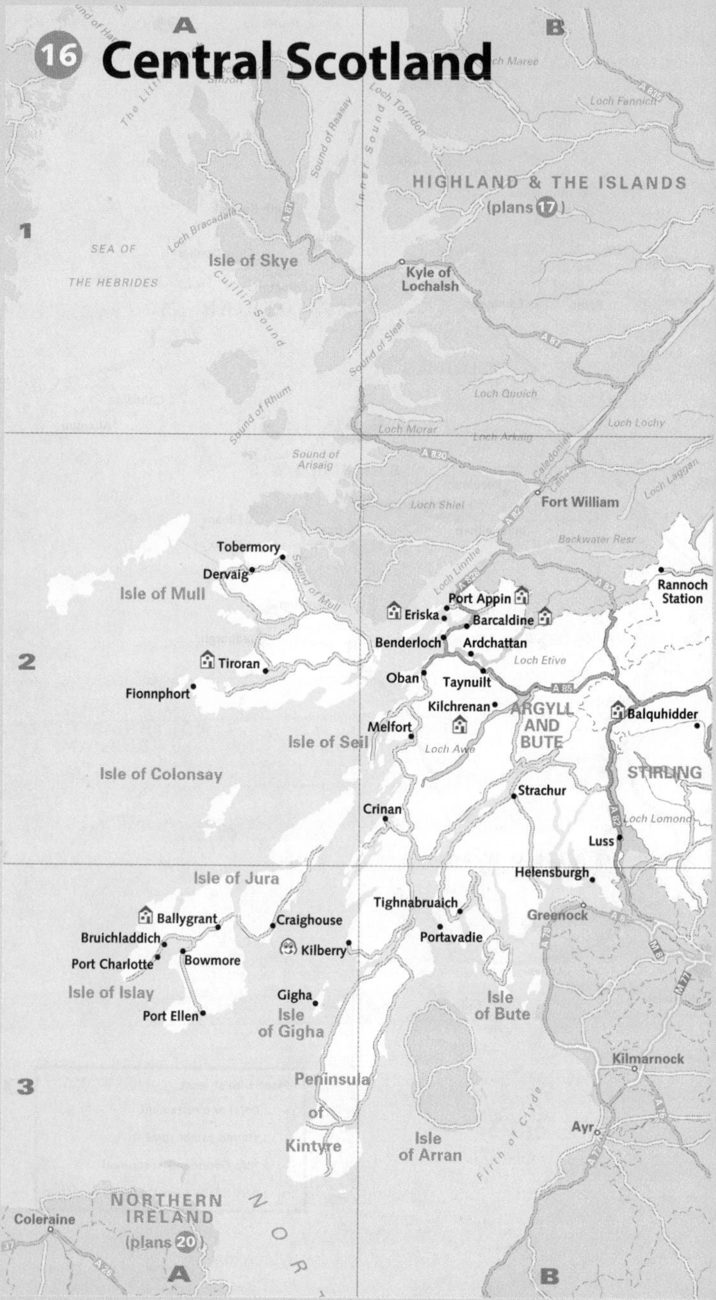

A
B
1
2
3
HIGHLAND & THE ISLANDS
(plans 17)
SEA OF
THE HEBRIDES
Isle of Skye
Kyle of
Lochalsh
Loch Torridon
Inner Sound
Sound of Raasay
Loch Fannich
Loch Bracadale
Cuillin Sound
Sound of Sleat
Sound of Rhum
Loch Quoich
Loch Lochy
Loch Morar
Loch Arkaig
Sound of
Arisaig
Caledonian Canal
Loch Laggan
Fort William
Loch Shiel
Blackwater Resr
Loch Linnhe
Tobermory
Dervaig
Sound of Mull
Isle of Mull
Rannoch
Station
Port Appin
Eriska
Barcaldine
Benderloch
Ardchattan
Loch Etive
Tiroran
Fionnphort
Oban
Taynuilt
Kilchrenan
ARGYLL
AND
BUTE
Balquhidder
Melfort
Isle of Seil
Loch Awe
STIRLING
Isle of Colonsay
Strachur
Crinan
Loch Lomond
Luss
Helensburgh
Isle of Jura
Tighnabruaich
Greenock
Ballygrant
Craighouse
Portavadie
Bruichladdich
Kilberry
Port Charlotte
Bowmore
Isle of Islay
Gigha
Isle
of Gigha
Isle
of Bute
Port Ellen
Kilmarnock
Peninsula
of
Kintyre
Isle
of Arran
Firth of Clyde
Ayr
NORTHERN
IRELAND
(plans 20)
Coleraine
A 87
A 830
A 82
A 828
A 85
A 835
A 8
M 8
M 77
A 78
A 77
A 76
A 26

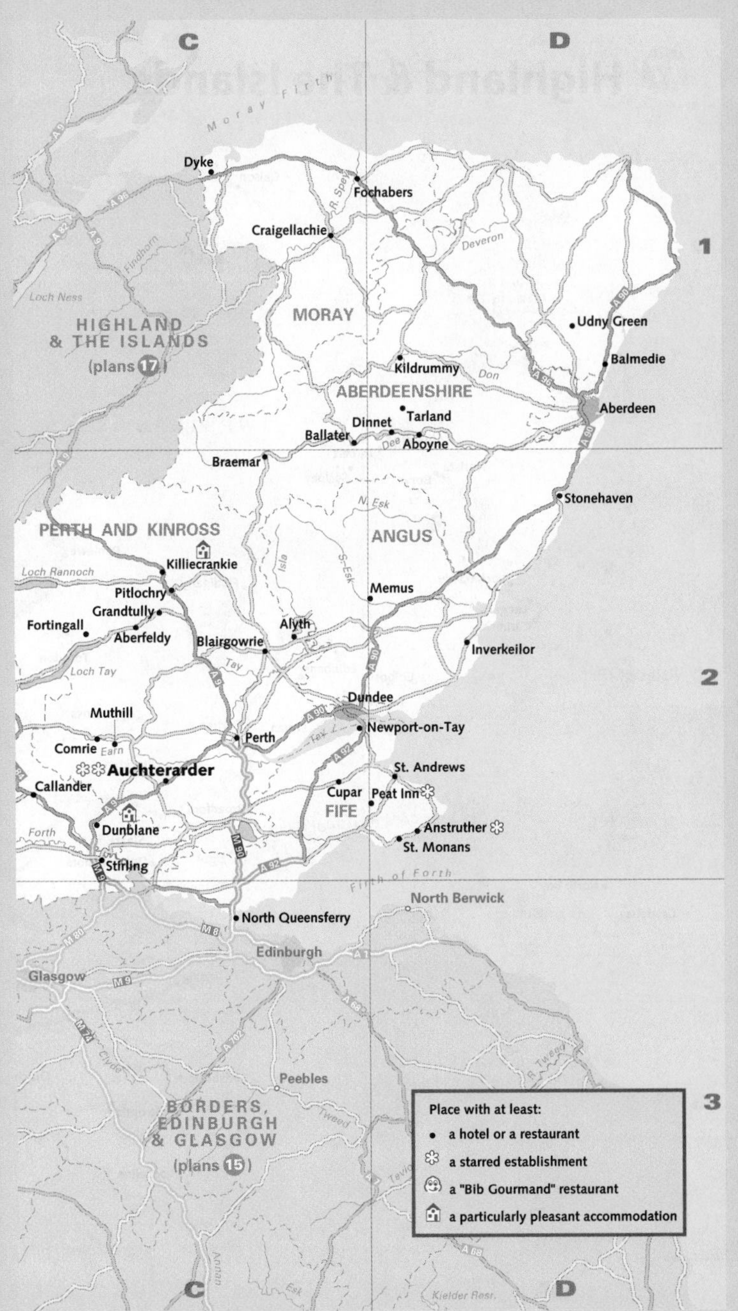
C
D
Moray Firth
Dyke
Fochabers
Craigellachie
Loch Ness
HIGHLAND
& THE ISLANDS
(plans 17)
MORAY
Udny Green
Balmedie
Kildrummy
ABERDEENSHIRE
Aberdeen
Tarland
Dinnet
Ballater
Aboyne
Braemar
Stonehaven
PERTH AND KINROSS
ANGUS
Killiecrankie
Loch Rannoch
Pitlochry
Memus
Grandtully
Fortingall
Aberfeldy
Alyth
Blairgowrie
Inverkeilor
Loch Tay
Muthill
Dundee
Perth
Newport-on-Tay
Comrie
Auchterarder
St. Andrews
Callander
Cupar
Peat Inn
FIFE
Dunblane
Anstruther
St. Monans
Stirling
Firth of Forth
North Berwick
North Queensferry
Edinburgh
Glasgow
Peebles
BORDERS,
EDINBURGH
& GLASGOW
(plans 15)
Place with at least:
a hotel or a restaurant
a starred establishment
a "Bib Gourmand" restaurant
a particularly pleasant accommodation
1
2
3

17 Highland & The Islands

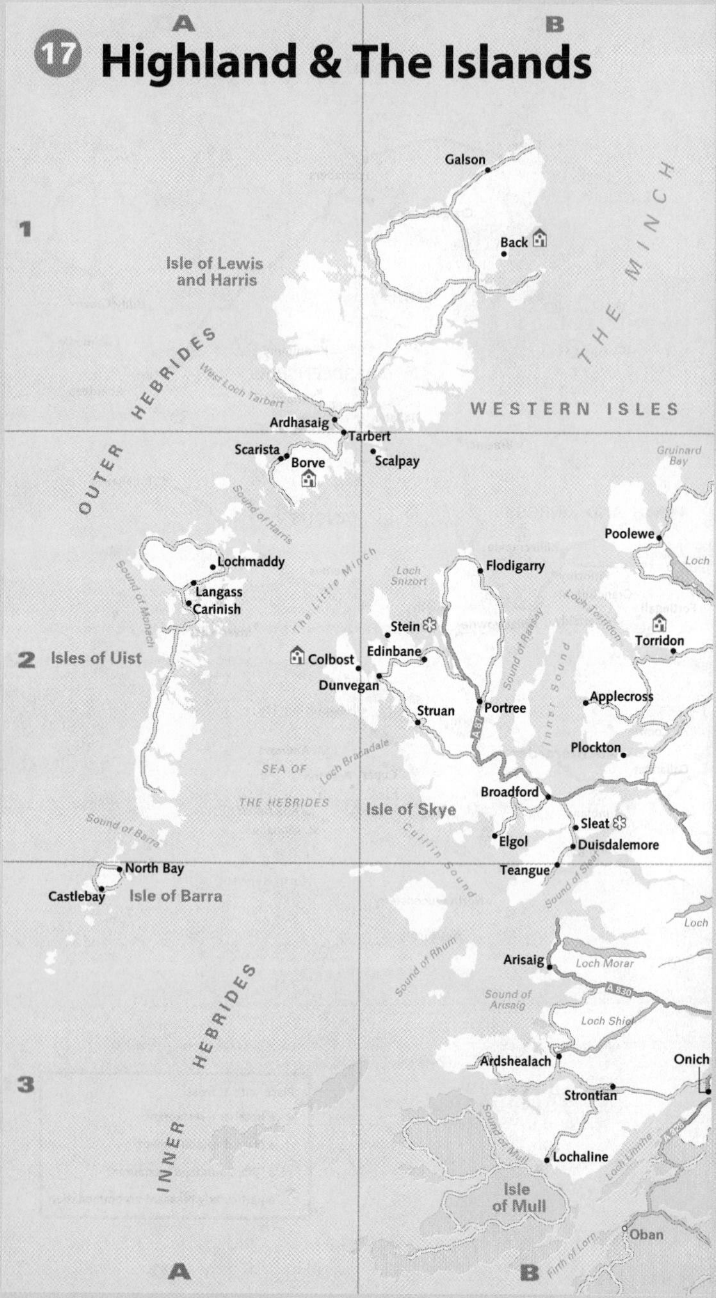

A B

1 2 3

Galson
Back
Isle of Lewis and Harris
THE MINCH
OUTER HEBRIDES
West Loch Tarbert
WESTERN ISLES
Ardhasaig
Tarbert
Scarista
Borve
Scalpay
Gruinard Bay
Sound of Harris
Poolewe
Loch
Lochmaddy
Langass
Carinish
Sound of Monach
The Little Minch
Loch Snizort
Flodigarry
Loch Torridon
Stein
Torridon
Isles of Uist
Colbost
Edinbane
Dunvegan
Sound of Raasay
Inner Sound
Applecross
Struan
Portree
A 87
Plockton
Loch Bracadale
SEA OF THE HEBRIDES
Broadford
Isle of Skye
Sleat
Sound of Barra
Cuillin Sound
Elgol
Duisdalemore
Teangue
North Bay
Castlebay
Isle of Barra
Sound of Sleat
Loch
Sound of Rhum
Arisaig
Loch Morar
A 830
Sound of Arisaig
INNER HEBRIDES
Loch Shiel
Ardshealach
Onich
Strontian
Sound of Mull
A 828
Lochaline
Loch Linnhe
Isle of Mull
Oban
Firth of Lorn

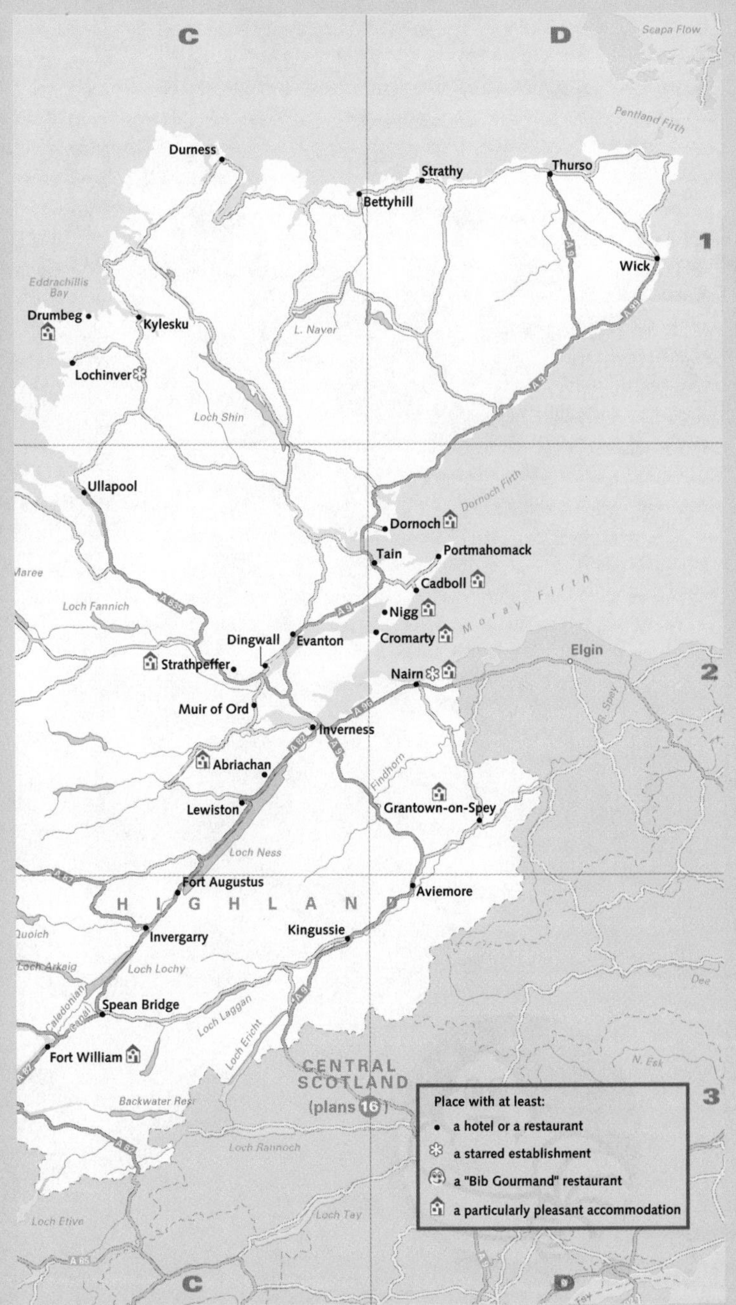

C
D
Scapa Flow
Pentland Firth
Durness
Strathy
Thurso
Bettyhill
1
Wick
Eddrachillis Bay
Drumbeg
Kylesku
L. Naver
Lochinver
Loch Shin
Ullapool
Dornoch Firth
Dornoch
Tain
Portmahomack
Maree
Cadboll
Moray Firth
Loch Fannich
Nigg
Dingwall
Evanton
Cromarty
Elgin
Strathpeffer
Nairn
2
Muir of Ord
Inverness
Abriachan
Findhorn
Grantown-on-Spey
Lewiston
Loch Ness
Fort Augustus
Aviemore
HIGHLAND
Kingussie
Invergarry
Quoich
Loch Arkaig
Loch Lochy
Dee
Caledonian Canal
Spean Bridge
Loch Laggan
Loch Ericht
Fort William
CENTRAL SCOTLAND
(plans 16)
N. Esk
3
Backwater Res
Loch Rannoch
Loch Etive
Loch Tay
C
D
Place with at least:
a hotel or a restaurant
a starred establishment
a "Bib Gourmand" restaurant
a particularly pleasant accommodation

Shetland & Orkney 18

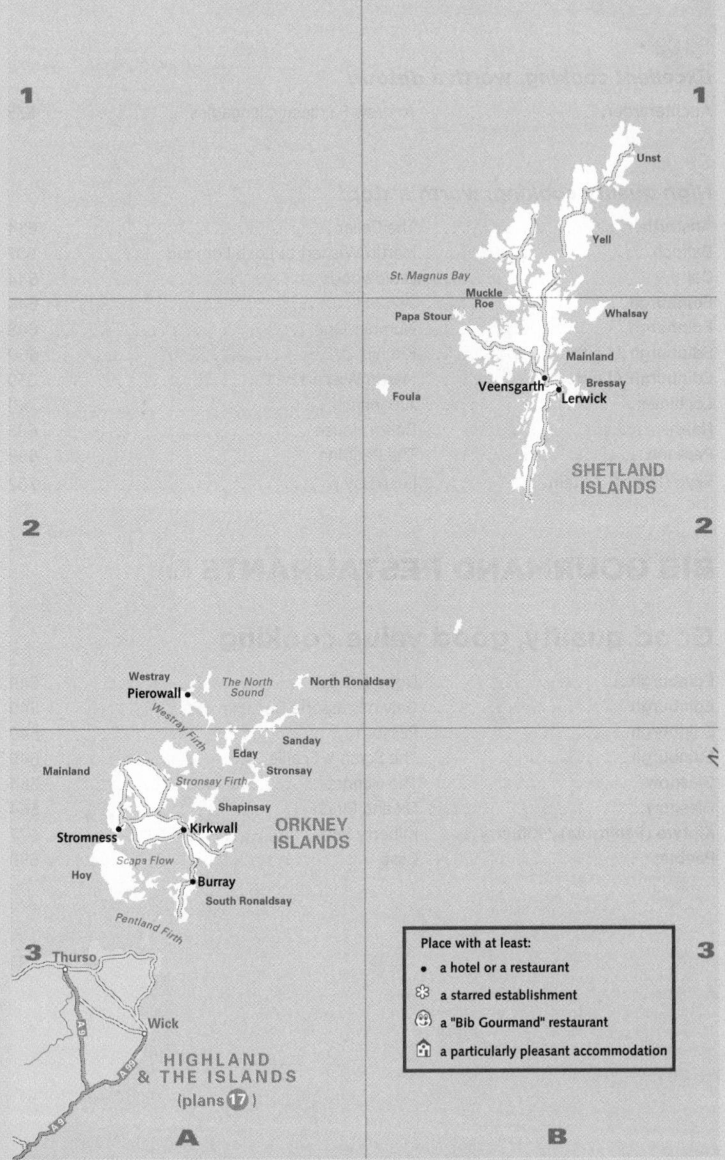

A
B
1
1
Unst
Yell
St. Magnus Bay
Muckle Roe
Papa Stour
Whalsay
Mainland
Veensgarth
Bressay
Foula
Lerwick
SHETLAND ISLANDS
2
2
Westray
Pierowall
The North Sound
North Ronaldsay
Westray Firth
Sanday
Eday
Mainland
Stronsay
Stronsay Firth
Shapinsay
Kirkwall
ORKNEY ISLANDS
Stromness
Scapa Flow
Hoy
Burray
South Ronaldsay
Pentland Firth
3
Thurso
Wick
A 9
A 99
HIGHLAND & THE ISLANDS
(plans 17)
A
B
3
Place with at least:
a hotel or a restaurant
a starred establishment
a "Bib Gourmand" restaurant
a particularly pleasant accommodation

NOT TO BE MISSED

STARRED RESTAURANTS

Excellent cooking, worth a detour!

High quality cooking, worth a stop!

BIB GOURMAND RESTAURANTS

Good quality, good value cooking

Michelin

ABERDEEN

Aberdeen City - Pop. 195 021 - Regional map n° **16**-D1

Fusion

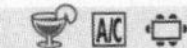

MODERN CUISINE • FASHIONABLE XX Modernised granite townhouse featuring a plush high-ceilinged bar with dark grey furniture and a more intimate mezzanine restaurant. The concise set menu lists well-presented modern dishes which are full of flavour.

Menu £ 25/30

Town plan: C1-c - *10 North Silver St ✉ AB10 1RL - ✆ 01224 652959 - www.fusionbarbistro.com - dinner only and Saturday lunch - Closed 1-5 January, Sunday and Monday*

IX ⓝ

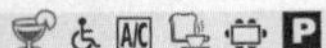

MODERN BRITISH • DESIGN XX Pass through The Chester Hotel's moody cocktail bar and up to the chic split-level restaurant. Creative cooking champions Scottish produce, with Aberdeenshire steaks from the Josper grill a highlight. Brunch is served on Sundays.

Carte £ 43/85

Town plan: A2-v - *The Chester Hotel, 59-63 Queens Rd ✉ AB15 4YP - ✆ 01224 327777 - www.chester-hotel.com - dinner only - Closed Sunday*

Silver Darling

SEAFOOD • FRIENDLY XX Attractively set at the port entrance, on the top floor of the castellated former customs house. Floor to ceiling windows make the most of the superb view. Neatly presented dishes showcase excellent quality seafood.

Menu £ 26 (weekday lunch) - Carte £ 31/56

Pocra Quay, North Pier ✉ AB11 5DQ - Southeast : 1.5 mi by Milner St, St Clement St and York St - ✆ 01224 576229 - www.thesilverdarling.co.uk - Closed 2 weeks Christmas-New Year and Sunday lunch

Moonfish Cafe ⓝ

MODERN BRITISH • BISTRO X A high ceiling and mirrored walls give this former toy shop an airy feel. Concise menus change every 6 weeks and the 2 course lunch is a bargain. Descriptions are terse, presentation is colourful and flavours are well-defined.

Menu £ 14/38 - Carte £ 20/39

Town plan: C1-e - *9 Correction Wynd ✉ AB10 1HP - ✆ 01224 644166 (bookings advisable at dinner) - www.moonfishcafe.co.uk - Closed first 2 weeks January, 24-26 December, Sunday and Monday*

Yatai

JAPANESE • SIMPLE X An atmospheric, laid-back Japanese izakaya. The ground floor has a wooden counter and a robata grill; upstairs is airy and intimate. Menus offer tasty, authentic dishes - the sushi, sashimi and maki are highlights.

Carte £ 18/30

Town plan: C2-x - *53 Langstane Pl ✉ AB11 6EN - ✆ 01224 592355 (booking advisable) - www.yatai.co.uk - dinner only - Closed Sunday-Monday*

Yorokobi by CJ

JAPANESE • INTIMATE X Its name means 'joyous bliss'; C is for chef and J is for Jang, who takes on that role. Good value Japanese and Korean dishes are flavourful and authentic; try one of the sizzling platters or a Korean pot dish.

Carte £ 19/46

Town plan: B2-a - *51 Huntly St ✉ AB10 1TH - ✆ 01224 566002 (booking advisable) - www.yorokobibycj.co.uk - dinner only and lunch Friday-Saturday - Closed 2 weeks summer, 2 weeks Christmas-New Year, Sunday and Monday*

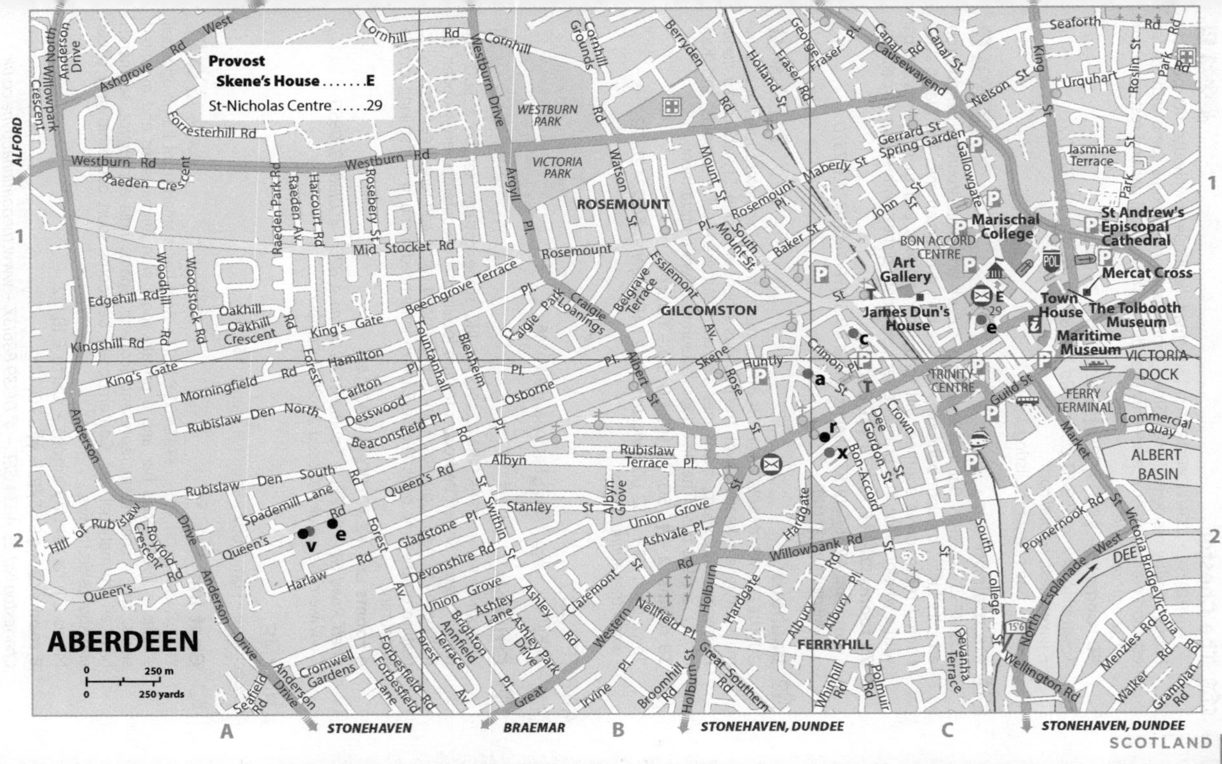
ABERDEEN
0 250 m
0 250 yards
Provost
Skene's House .... E
St-Nicholas Centre 29
Marischal College
St Andrew's Episcopal Cathedral
Mercat Cross
Town House
The Tolbooth Museum
Maritime Museum
Art Gallery
James Dun's House
BON ACCORD CENTRE
TRINITY CENTRE
FERRY TERMINAL
VICTORIA DOCK
ALBERT BASIN
Commercial Quay
GILCOMSTON
ROSEMOUNT
FERRYHILL
WESTBURN PARK
VICTORIA PARK
ALFORD
STONEHAVEN
BRAEMAR
STONEHAVEN, DUNDEE
STONEHAVEN, DUNDEE

The Chester

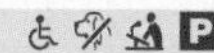

TOWNHOUSE · CONTEMPORARY This smart boutique townhouse fits perfectly in this wealthy residential area. Sleek, contemporary bedrooms come with the latest mod cons and show a keen eye for detail. The cocktail bar and restaurant are set over three levels.

50 rooms - £ 109/185 £ 129/205 - 2 suites

Town plan: A2-v - *59-63 Queens Rd ✉ AB15 4YP - 01224 327777 - www.chester-hotel.com*

IX - See restaurant listing

Malmaison

BUSINESS · DESIGN Set in a smart city suburb and built around a period property; its funky, modern bedrooms are the height of urban chic. The black, slate-floored reception is adorned with bagpipes and kilts and there's a stylish bar with a whisky cellar. The brasserie serves modern dishes, with steaks a speciality.

79 rooms - £ 79/179 £ 89/179

Town plan: A2-e - *49-53 Queens Rd ✉ AB15 4YP - 01224 327370 - www.malmaison.com*

bauhaus

BUSINESS · MINIMALIST Set just off the main street, this hotel's functional, minimalist style is in keeping with the Bauhaus school of design. Stylish, colour-coded bedrooms have sharp, clean lines and an uncluttered feel - 'Gropius' and 'Kandinsky' are the best. The first floor restaurant offers a pizza menu.

39 rooms - £ 50/75 £ 60/90 - 1 suite

Town plan: C2-r - *52-60 Langstane Pl. ✉ AB11 6EN - 01224 212122 - www.thebauhaus.co.uk*

ABERFELDY

Perth and Kinross - Pop. 1 986 - Regional map n° **16**-C2

Errichel (N)

WORKING FARM · PERSONALISED An 18C stone cottage set on a 500 acre working farm. Stylish bedrooms feature locally made, contemporary wooden furnishings with Asian touches. They rear Shetland cattle and rare breed pigs, which feature on the ambitious Middle-Eastern influenced menu in the striking circular restaurant.

4 rooms - £ 70/110 £ 90/140

Crieff Road ✉ PH15 2EL - Southeast : 2 mi on A 826 - 01887 820850 - www.errichel.co.uk - Closed 24-26 December

ABOYNE

Aberdeenshire - Pop. 2 602 - Regional map n° **16**-D1

Boat Inn

TRADITIONAL CUISINE · FRIENDLY The Boat has a smart front bar in eggshell shades, a lively locals bar and a private room with animal skins and mounted skulls. The kitchen team represent Scotland, Spain, India and Egypt, so menus have an international feel. Contemporary bedrooms sport battleship grey décor and sheepskin throws.

Menu £ 11 (weekday lunch) - Carte £ 18/32

8 rooms - £ 65/105 £ 70/120

Charleston Rd ✉ AB34 5EL - 01339 886137 - www.theboatinnaboyne.co.uk - Closed 25-26 December and 1 January

ABRIACHAN

Highland - Pop. 120 - Regional map n° **17**-C2

Loch Ness Lodge

LUXURY • CONTEMPORARY Passionately run modern country house, set in 18 acres of immaculately kept grounds overlooking Loch Ness. A classic-contemporary style features throughout. Spacious bedrooms have a high level of facilities and come with extras such as sherry and Penhaligon's toiletries. Afternoon tea is served on arrival.

6 rooms – £ 95/270 £ 175/335

Brachla ✉ IV3 8LA – on A 82 – ✆ 01456 459469 – www.loch-ness-lodge.com – Closed November-March

ALLANTON

The Scottish Borders – Regional map n° **15**-D1

Allanton Inn

MODERN BRITISH • FRIENDLY Striking stone inn in a conservation village. It's warm and welcoming, with a contemporary open-plan interior and bright, simply furnished bedrooms. Thoughtfully prepared modern dishes are crafted from local farm meats and Eyemouth fish, and the regional cheeses are a hit, as is the pretty garden.

Carte £ 23/39

6 rooms – £ 65/95 £ 75/110

✉ TD11 3JZ – ✆ 01890 818260 – www.allantoninn.co.uk

ALYTH

Perth and Kinross – Pop. 2 403 – Regional map n° **16**-C2

Tigh Na Leigh

LUXURY • MODERN An imposing Victorian house run in a relaxed yet professional manner. The interior is surprisingly modern – guest areas are inviting and contemporary bedrooms boast feature beds and great bathrooms with spa baths. The kitchen garden informs the unfussy modern menu; enjoy the lovely garden view while dining.

5 rooms – £ 55/100 £ 94/133

22-24 Airlie St ✉ PH11 8AJ – ✆ 01828 632372 – www.tighnaleigh.co.uk – Closed December-January

ANCRUM

The Scottish Borders – Regional map n° **15**-D2

Ancrum Cross Keys

TRADITIONAL BRITISH • PUB Set beside the River Ale and run by the owner of the nearby Born in the Borders Brewery. It's not all about the beer here though, as the cooking is fittingly satisfying too, with local produce used in hearty dishes.

Carte £ 22/32

The Green ✉ TD8 6XH – ✆ 01835 830242 – www.ancrumcrosskeys.com – dinner only and lunch Saturday-Sunday – Closed Monday and Tuesday

ANNAN

Dumfries and Galloway – Pop. 8 960 – Regional map n° **15**-C3

Del Amitri (N)

MODERN BRITISH • BRASSERIE X Set within a coastal hotel, a cleanly decorated restaurant with views out over the Solway Firth. The extensive menu has a Scottish bias and focuses on classically based dishes which have a modern edge.

Carte £ 23/32

Powfoot Hotel, Links Ave, Powfoot ✉ DG12 5PN – Southwest : 4 mi by B 721 and B 724 – ✆ 01461 700300 – www.delamitrirestaurant.co.uk – dinner only and Sunday lunch – Closed 26 December

ANSTRUTHER

Fife – Pop. 3 446 – Regional map n° **16**-D2

The Cellar (Billy Boyter)

MODERN CUISINE • RUSTIC XX Previously a smokehouse and a cooperage – now an iconic restaurant with exposed beams, stone walls and a cosy, characterful feel; pleasingly run by a local lad. Delicious, deftly prepared dishes are light, well-balanced and have subtle modern influences. Service is friendly and the atmosphere is relaxed.

➜ Crab with cured cod, smoked shrimp jelly and cucumber juice. Lamb, goat's curd, hay-baked kohlrabi and wild garlic. Crowdie cheesecake mousse with white chocolate 'Aero' and tarragon & yogurt sorbet.

Menu £ 35/60

24 East Green ✉ KY10 3AA – ✆ 01333 310378 (booking essential) – www.thecellaranstruther.co.uk – Closed first 3 weeks January, 10 days May, 10 days September, 24-26 December, lunch Wednesday-Thursday October-March and Monday-Tuesday

APPLECROSS

Highland – Regional map n° **17**-B2

Applecross Walled Garden

TRADITIONAL CUISINE • FRIENDLY X Set in an old potting shed in a 17C walled garden – where much of the produce is grown. In the daytime come for home-made cake, local langoustines or fresh crab lasagne; at night come for boldly flavoured, original dishes.

Carte £ 19/40

✉ IV54 8ND – North : 0.5 mi – ✆ 01520 744440 – www.applecrossgarden.co.uk – Closed November-February

Applecross Inn

SEAFOOD • INN Unpretentious inn with friendly service and a bustling atmosphere; take the scenic route over the hair-raising, single-track Bealach na Ba, with its stunning views and hairpin bends to reach it. Dine on the freshest of seafood, often caught within sight of the door. Simple bedrooms have marvellous sea views.

Carte £ 18/45

7 rooms – †£ 85/100 ††£ 130/150

Shore St ✉ IV54 8LR – ✆ 01520 744262 (booking essential) – www.applecross.uk.com/inn – Closed 25 December and 1 January

ARDCHATTAN

Argyll and Bute – Regional map n° **16**-B2

Blarcreen House

Friendly Victorian former farmhouse set in a tranquil location down a single track and boasting superb views over Loch Etive. Homely lounge and comfy bedrooms: two with four-posters and double-aspects; all with robes, fridges and fresh milk. Lovely dining room offers a daily menu of home-cooked dishes.

3 rooms – †£ 100/140 ††£ 120/140

✉ PA37 1RG – East : 1 mi past Ardchattan Priory and gardens on Bonawe rd – ✆ 01631 750272 – www.blarcreenhouse.com – Closed Christmas and New Year

ARDHASAIG – Western Isles ➜ See Lewis and Harris (Isle of)

ARDSHEALACH

Highland – Regional map n° **17**-B3

Ardshealach Lodge

TRADITIONAL · PERSONALISED Smart Victorian former hunting lodge in 22 acres of grounds; in a fabulous location on the Ardnamurchan Peninsula overlooking Loch Sheil. Traditional bedrooms; ask for one at the front. Wide range of classic dishes served in the restaurant, with fruit, veg and herbs from the garden. Non-resident diners welcome.

3 rooms ☕ – 🚹£ 50 🚹🚹£ 100

✉ *PH36 4JL – On A 861 – ✆ 01967 431399 – www.ardshealach-lodge.co.uk*

ARISAIG

Highland – Regional map n° **17**-B3

Arisaig House

COUNTRY HOUSE · PERSONALISED Attractive Victorian country house surrounded by mature grounds which lead down to the sea. Bedrooms retain their traditional feel and the building's original features are enhanced by a fine collection of artwork. Classic menus use ingredients from the kitchen garden, nearby estates and local waters.

14 rooms ☕ – 🚹£ 120/130 🚹🚹£ 175/235

Beasdale ✉ PH39 4NR – East : 2.5 mi by A 830 – ✆ 01687 450730 – www.arisaighouse.co.uk – Closed November-April

ARRAN (Isle of)

North Ayrshire – Pop. 4 629 – Regional map n° **15**-A2

Lamlash

Glenisle

TRADITIONAL · COSY Attractive whitewashed former inn, boasting views over the bay to Holy Island. It has an open-plan bar-lounge and a small snug. Bright, airy bedrooms come in natural hues; one covers the whole top floor and has a roll-top bath. The rustic dining room and terrace offer fresh, simple, homely cooking.

13 rooms ☕ – 🚹£ 98/102 🚹🚹£ 135/241

Shore Rd. ✉ KA27 8LY – ✆ 01770 600559 – www.glenislehotel.com

Lochranza

Apple Lodge

TRADITIONAL · CLASSIC Former manse with attractive gardens, in a quiet hamlet surrounded by mountains. Traditionally decorated, comfortable and personally run, with many regular guests. Bedrooms have pleasant views; Apple Cottage is a self-contained garden suite. 3 course menu of classic, home-cooked dishes served by candlelight.

4 rooms ☕ – 🚹£ 50 🚹🚹£ 78

✉ *KA27 8HJ – ✆ 01770 830229 – www.applelodgearran.co.uk – Closed 15 December-15 January*

AUCHTERARDER

Perth and Kinross – Pop. 4 206 – Regional map n° **16**-C2

✿✿ Andrew Fairlie at Gleneagles

CREATIVE FRENCH · LUXURY XXXX Within the renowned Gleneagles hotel is this sumptuous restaurant hung with a portrait of its eponymous chef. The kitchen garden supplies over 250 varieties of herbs, vegetables and fruit, which are showcased in refined, elegant French dishes which display a lightness of touch. Service is detailed.

→ Home-smoked lobster, lime and herb butter. Roast loin of roe deer with venison tartare, bonbon and port jus. Passion fruit soufflé with piña colada sorbet and rum sauce.

Menu £ 110/155

Gleneagles Hotel, ✉ PH3 1NF – Southwest : 2 mi by A 824 on A 823 – ✆ 01764 694267 – www.andrewfairlie.co.uk – dinner only – Closed 3-26 January, Christmas and Sunday

Gleneagles

GRAND LUXURY • ART DÉCO This iconic resort hotel boasts a world-famous golf course, a state-of-the-art spa, an equestrian centre and even a gun-dog school. Many of the majestic art deco guest areas and bedrooms are being redesigned – all will be elegant and luxurious with top class comforts. Dining options include a laid-back brasserie, a classical restaurant and intimate Andrew Fairlie.

232 rooms – †£ 325/500 ††£ 325/500 – 26 suites

✉ PH3 1NF – Southwest : 2 mi by A 824 on A 823
– ✆ 01764 662231 – www.gleneagles.com

✿✿ **Andrew Fairlie at Gleneagles** – See restaurant listing

AVIEMORE

Highland – Pop. 3 147 – Regional map n° **17**-D3

Old Minister's Guest House

TRADITIONAL • PERSONALISED A 19C stone-built manse with unusual carved wood animals out the front and pretty gardens leading down to the river. The smart lounge has deep sofas and an honesty bar and the stylish bedrooms are spacious and well-appointed.

5 rooms – †£ 120/125 ††£ 145/150

Rothiemurchus ✉ PH22 1QH – Southeast : 1 mi on B 970
– ✆ 01479 812181 – www.theoldministershouse.co.uk

BACK

BACK – Western Isles → See Lewis and Harris (Isle of)

BALLANTRAE

South Ayrshire – ✉ Girvan – Pop. 672 – Regional map n° **15**-A2

Glenapp Castle

HISTORIC BUILDING • CLASSIC A long wooded drive leads to this stunning baronial castle with beautifully manicured gardens and Ailsa Craig views; it's personally run and the service is charming. The grand antique-filled interior has oak-panelled hallways, luxurious, impressively proportioned lounges and handsomely appointed bedrooms. The elegant dining room showcases local and garden ingredients.

18 rooms (dinner included) – †£ 215/345 ††£ 325/575 – 2 suites

✉ KA26 0NZ – South : 1 mi by A 77 taking first right turn after bridge
– ✆ 01465 831212 – www.glenappcastle.com – Closed January

BALLATER

Aberdeenshire – Pop. 1 533 – Regional map n° **16**-C1

Rothesay Rooms (N)

MODERN BRITISH • COSY XX The Prince of Wales' restaurant sits beside the Highgrove shop and has the look of a Baronial dining room, with its green walls, tartan fabrics and antique furnishings. Seasonal dishes are classically executed and full of flavour.

Carte £ 28/45

3 Netherley Pl ✉ AB35 5EQ
– ✆ 01339 753816 (bookings advisable at dinner) – www.rothesay-rooms.co.uk
– Closed 25 December, Sunday dinner-Wednesday lunch

BALLOCH

West Dunbartonshire – Regional map n° **15**-B1

✿ Martin Wishart at Loch Lomond

MODERN CUISINE • ELEGANT XXX Smart restaurant in a resort hotel; ask for a window table for superb loch and mountain views. Seasonal modern menus showcase Scottish ingredients in well-judged, creative combinations. Cooking is accomplished and dishes are attractively presented. The 6 and 8 course tasting menus include vegetarian options.

→ Orkney scallop with asparagus, fennel and smoked egg yolk. Buckwheat-roasted veal sweetbread with preserved lemon, black garlic and jus gras. Coconut poached meringue with mango, Knockraich Farm yoghurt, mint and lime.

Menu £ 80/95

Cameron House Hotel, Loch Lomond ✉ G83 8QZ - Northwest : 1.5 mi by A 811 on A 82 - ✆ 01389 722504 (booking essential) - www.mwlochlomond.co.uk - dinner only and lunch Saturday-Sunday - Closed 2 weeks January, Monday and Tuesday

Cameron House

COUNTRY HOUSE • CONTEMPORARY An extensive Victorian house and lodges set in 250 acres on the shore of Loch Lomond. Excellent leisure facilities include use of a launch and a seaplane. Bedrooms are modern, aside from the Whisky Suites which boast some original decorative features. Dining options include the informal Claret Jug bar, the waterside Boathouse and masculine grill restaurant Camerons.

136 rooms - †£ 155/425 ††£ 165/435 - 12 suites

Loch Lomond ✉ G83 8QZ - Northwest : 1.5 mi by A 811 on A 82 - ✆ 01389 755565 - www.cameronhouse.co.uk

✿ **Martin Wishart at Loch Lomond** - See restaurant listing

BALLYGRANT - Argyll and Bute → See Islay (Isle of)

BALMEDIE

Aberdeenshire - Pop. 2 534 - Regional map n° **16**-D1

Cock and Bull

TRADITIONAL BRITISH • RUSTIC Quirky pub with a profusion of knick-knacks; dine in the cosy open-fired lounge, the formal dining room or the airy conservatory. Menus offer a mix of well-presented pub classics and more modern restaurant-style dishes. Spacious, contemporary bedrooms are located in the next door bungalow.

Carte £ 20/37

6 rooms - †£ 50/110 ††£ 50/110

Ellon Rd, Blairton ✉ AB23 8XY - North : 1 mi on A 90 - ✆ 01358 743249 - www.thecockandbull.co.uk - Closed 26-27 December and 1-2 January

Trump International Golf Links Scotland

LUXURY • MODERN Intimate hotel with a Championship links golf course, set on a 2,200 acre estate. The hotel is split between an 18C stone house and a lodge and features plush fabrics and opulent furnishings. Large bedrooms have arabesque furnishings and offer all you could want. The intimate restaurant serves a modern menu.

16 rooms - †£ 265/365 ††£ 290/390

MacLeod House and Lodge, Menie Estate ✉ AB23 8YE - North : 2 mi on A 90 - ✆ 01358 743300 - www.trumpgolfscotland.com - Closed November-March

BALQUHIDDER

Stirling - Regional map n° **16**-B2

Monachyle Mhor

MODERN CUISINE • INTIMATE XX In a rurally set hotel is this candlelit conservatory restaurant with a warm, relaxing ambience and views of the glen. The set price menu features produce reared on the family farm and grown in the kitchen garden; cooking is modern and accomplished, with lots of natural flavours.

Menu £ 24/65

Monachyle Mhor Hotel, ✉ FK19 8PQ - West : 3.75 mi - ✆ 01877 384622 (booking essential) - www.mhor.net - Closed 5-25 January

🍴 Mhor 84

TRADITIONAL CUISINE • TRADITIONAL DÉCOR ✗ Food is served all day at this laid-back restaurant, where you're greeted by a welcoming team and a display case bursting with cakes from their bakery. Produce from their farm features in hearty, unfussy dishes and things step up a gear on the daily dinner menu. Simple bedrooms boast extremely comfy beds.

Carte £ 24/39

12 rooms – 🚹£ 80 🚻£ 80 – ☕£ 10

Kingshouse ✉ FK19 8NY – East: 2 mi at junction with A 84 – ✆ 01877 384646 – www.mhor.net

Monachyle Mhor

TRADITIONAL • PERSONALISED A former farmhouse set in a beautiful, very remote glen. Contemporary furnishings blend with original features in the reception, lounge and cosy bar. Bedrooms boast slate-tiled bathrooms with underfloor heating; those in the main house afford great views over the Braes of Balquhidder.

18 rooms ☕ – 🚹£ 185/225 🚻£ 195/285

✉ FK19 8PQ – West : 3.75 mi – ✆ 01877 384622 (booking essential) – www.mhor.net – Closed 5-25 January

🍴 **Monachyle Mhor** – See restaurant listing

BARCALDINE

Argyll and Bute – Regional map n° **16**-B2

Ardtorna

LUXURY • CONTEMPORARY An ultra-modern guesthouse in a stunning spot, with lovely views of the lochs and mountains – and amazing sunsets. Immaculate bedrooms have plenty of space in which to relax, perhaps with a complimentary glass of whisky. Home-baked scones are served on arrival. The charming owners also offer archery lessons.

4 rooms ☕ – 🚹£ 100/175 🚻£ 160/190

Mill Farm ✉ PA37 1SE – Southwest : 1.5 mi on A 828 – ✆ 01631 720125 – www.ardtorna.co.uk – Closed mid November-mid March

Barcaldine Castle

HISTORIC BUILDING • PERSONALISED This lochside castle was built in 1609 and is packed with history. Charming bedrooms have period furnishings – one even has a dressing area in a turret. Breakfast is served in the Great Hall, complete with stags' heads and cannons!

6 rooms ☕ – 🚹£ 175/255 🚻£ 200/280

✉ PA37 1SA – West : 3.5 mi by A 828 – ✆ 01631 720598 – www.barcaldinecastle.co.uk – Closed 1 November-15 December and 5 January-7 March

BARRA (Isle of)

Western Isles – ✉ Castlebay – Regional map n° **17**-A3

Castlebay

Castlebay

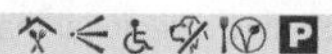

TRADITIONAL • REGIONAL Homely hotel boasting excellent castle and island views – the hub of the island community. Bedrooms are a mix of styles: the newer rooms feature subtle tartan fabrics and 'MacNeil' has harbour views. There's a cosy lounge, a busy locals bar and a linen-clad dining room serving seafood specials.

15 rooms ☕ – 🚹£ 59/70 🚻£ 95/195

✉ HS9 5XD – ✆ 01871 810223 – www.castlebayhotel.com – Closed 22 December-8 January

Grianamul

TRADITIONAL · COSY Pale yellow dormer bungalow at the heart of a small hamlet – a homely place run by caring owners. There's a comfortable lounge and sunny breakfast room where huge, satisfying breakfasts are served. Bedrooms are bright and spacious.

3 rooms – £ 50 £ 80

HS9 5XD – 01871 810416 – www.isleofbarraaccommodation.com – Closed October-March

North Bay

Heathbank

TRADITIONAL · PERSONALISED Former Presbyterian Church, now a smart, modern, well-run hotel that's popular with locals and visitors alike. A bright, airy bar forms the hotel's hub and, along with the dining room, serves straightforward, local seafood orientated menus. Good-sized bedrooms are light, airy and up-to-date.

5 rooms – £ 70/95 £ 110/130

HS9 5YQ – 01871 890266 – www.barrahotel.co.uk

BENDERLOCH

Argyll and Bute – Regional map n° **16**-B2

Hawthorn

MODERN BRITISH · NEIGHBOURHOOD Modern art blends with exposed stone walls at this rustic former croft – look out for the 'Wishing Wall' and leave a coin for luck. Generous, gutsy cooking is full of flavour; local produce includes Argyll meats and Mallaig fish.

Menu £ 15 (lunch and early dinner) – Carte £ 21/44

5 Keils Crofts PA37 1QS – Northwest : 0.5 mi by A 828 on Tralee rd – 01631 720777 (booking advisable) – www.hawthorn-restaurant.co.uk – dinner only and lunch Friday-Sunday – Closed November-April

BETTYHILL

Highland – Regional map n° **17**-C1

Côte du Nord

CREATIVE · INTIMATE Intimate restaurant of just 3 tables; converted from an old school house by a local doctor-cum-self-taught-chef. Modern, innovative cooking; the 10-12 course menu features local and foraged ingredients and salt from evaporated seawater.

Menu £ 39 – tasting menu only

The School House, Kirtomy KW14 7TB – East : 4 mi by A 836 – 01641 521773 (booking essential) – www.cotedunord.co.uk – dinner only – Closed October-March, Sunday-Tuesday and Thursday

BLAIRGOWRIE

Perth and Kinross – Pop. 8 954 – Regional map n° **16**-C2

Kinloch House

TRADITIONAL CUISINE · INTIMATE Formal hotel dining room with twinkling chandeliers and smartly dressed tables. Start with drinks in the clubby bar or cosy, open-fired sitting room. The latest local, seasonal produce informs the daily menu – maybe West Coast crab or Perthshire venison. Dishes are well-crafted, traditional and flavoursome.

Menu £ 26/58

Kinloch House Hotel, PH10 6SG – West : 3 mi on A 923 – 01250 884237 – www.kinlochhouse.com – Closed 14-29 December

Dalmore Inn

TRADITIONAL CUISINE • PUB A traditional-looking pub with a surprisingly stylish interior, where brightly coloured walls are juxtaposed with old stonework. Unfussy, good value cooking is full of flavour; everything is freshly prepared using Scottish produce.

Menu £ 20 (weekdays) - Carte £ 17/43

Perth Rd ✉ PH10 6QB - Southwest : 1.5 mi on A 93 - ☎ 01250 871088 - www.dalmoreinn.com - Closed 25 December and 1-2 January

Kinloch House

FAMILY • PERSONALISED Imposing ivy-clad country house in a tranquil, elevated setting, with beautiful walled gardens to the rear and 25 acres of grounds. Smart oak-panelled hall and a vast array of welcoming guest areas complete with log fires and antiques. Classical bedrooms are well-appointed and immaculately maintained.

15 rooms - single £ 185/340 double £ 185/340 - 1 suite

✉ PH10 6SG - West : 3 mi on A 923 - ☎ 01250 884237 - www.kinlochhouse.com - Closed 14-29 December

Kinloch House - See restaurant listing

BORVE
- Western Isles → See Lewis and Harris (Isle of)

BOWMORE
- Argyll and Bute → See Islay (Isle of)

BRAEMAR

Aberdeenshire - Pop. 500 - Regional map n° **16**-C2

Callater Lodge

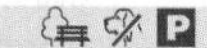

FAMILY • COSY You'll receive a warm welcome from the owners of this Victorian stone hunting lodge, where you can cosy up with tea and cake or a whisky by the open fire, then retire to a bright, modern wood-furnished bedroom.

6 rooms - single £ 55 double £ 85/95

9 Glenshee Rd ✉ AB35 5YQ - ☎ 01339 741275 - www.callaterlodge.co.uk - Closed 1 week Christmas

BROADFORD
- Highland → See Skye (Isle of)

BROUGHTY FERRY
- Dundee City → See Dundee

BRUICHLADDICH
- Argyll and Bute → See Islay (Isle of)

BUNCHREW
- Highland → See Inverness

BURRAY
- Orkney Islands → See Orkney Islands (Mainland)

CADBOLL
- Highland → See Tain

CALLANDER

Stirling - Pop. 3 077 - Regional map n° **16**-C2

Roman Camp

MODERN CUISINE • ELEGANT Start with canapés in the characterful lounge or library of this charming riverside hotel, before dinner in the formal restaurant. Ambitious dishes are well-presented; the tasting menu represents the best value.

Menu £ 30/55 - Carte £ 47/63

Roman Camp Hotel, Main St ✉ FK17 8BG - ☎ 01877 330003 (bookings essential for non-residents) - www.romancamphotel.co.uk

Roman Camp

COUNTRY HOUSE • CLASSIC Pretty pink house – a 17C former hunting lodge – set by the river among well-tended gardens. Traditional bedrooms have a subtle contemporary edge and there's a characterful panelled library and chapel.

15 rooms – †£ 110/165 ††£ 160/290 – 3 suites

Main St ✉ FK17 8BG – ✆ 01877 330003 – www.romancamphotel.co.uk

Roman Camp – See restaurant listing

Westerton

TOWNHOUSE • PERSONALISED Homely stone house run by delightful owners, with a colourful garden sweeping down to the river – take it all in from the terrace. Spotless bedrooms have wrought iron beds and good mod cons; some have mountain views.

3 rooms – †£ 80/130 ††£ 85/135

Leny Rd ✉ FK17 8AJ – ✆ 01877 330147 – www.westertonhouse.co.uk – Closed November-April

CASTLE DOUGLAS

Dumfries and Galloway – Pop. 4 174 – Regional map n° **15**-B3

Douglas House

TOWNHOUSE • PERSONALISED An attractive 19C townhouse run by experienced owners. Comfy, individually decorated bedrooms have a modern edge. The lounge-cum-breakfast-room is light and airy; breakfast offers plenty of choice and features only local produce.

4 rooms – †£ 41 ††£ 78/85

63 Queen St ✉ DG7 1HS – ✆ 01556 503262 – www.douglas-house.com

CASTLEBAY – Western Isles → See Barra (Isle of)

CHIRNSIDE

The Scottish Borders – ✉ Duns – Pop. 1 459 – Regional map n° **15**-D1

Chirnside Hall

COUNTRY HOUSE • CLASSIC Sizeable 1834 country house with a lovely revolving door and beautiful views over the Cheviots. Grand lounges have original cornicing and huge fireplaces. Bedrooms are cosy and classical; some have four-poster beds. Local, seasonal dishes are served in the traditional dining room.

10 rooms – †£ 100/195 ††£ 180/195

✉ TD11 3LD – East : 1.75 mi on A 6105 – ✆ 01890 818219 – www.chirnsidehallhotel.com – Closed March

COLBOST – Highland → See Skye (Isle of)

COMRIE

Perth and Kinross – Pop. 1 927 – Regional map n° **16**-C2

Royal

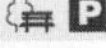

TRADITIONAL CUISINE • COSY XX An intimate dining room and bright conservatory, set within a stylishly decorated coaching inn. Concise menu of classically based dishes with modern touches. Produce is seasonal and locally sourced; the mussels and steaks are superb.

Carte £ 20/37

Royal Hotel, Melville Sq ✉ PH6 2DN – ✆ 01764 679200 – www.royalhotel.co.uk – Closed 25-26 December

Royal

TRADITIONAL · PERSONALISED Charming coaching inn dating back to the 18C and set at the heart of a riverside town. Cosy bar and lovely open-fired library with squashy sofas. Well-appointed bedrooms; some with four-posters and antiques. Relaxed, personable service.

11 rooms – £ 100/120 £ 150/190

Melville Sq ✉ PH6 2DN – ✆ 01764 679200 – www.royalhotel.co.uk – Closed 25-26 December

Royal – See restaurant listing

CRAIGELLACHIE

Moray – Regional map n° **16**-C1

Craigellachie

HISTORIC · PERSONALISED Set in the heart of Speyside, this characterful Victorian hotel is perfectly located for those following the Whisky Trail. Stylish, understated bedrooms have a 'Country Living' style. The bar serves over 700 whiskies and the rustic restaurant serves Scottish pub classics with a modern twist.

26 rooms – £ 125/225 £ 165/225

Victoria St ✉ AB38 9SR – ✆ 01340 881204 – www.craigellachiehotel.co.uk

CRAIGHOUSE – Argyll and Bute

→ See Jura (Isle of)

CRINAN

Argyll and Bute – ✉ Lochgilphead – Regional map n° **16**-B2

Westward

SEAFOOD XX Set within a welcoming, family-run hotel and boasting lovely views out over the Sound of Jura. Concise, seafood-based menus rely on local and island produce; langoustines are landed daily from Loch Crinan, right beside the hotel.

Menu £ 45

Crinan Hotel, ✉ PA31 8SR – ✆ 01546 830261 – www.crinanhotel.com – dinner only – Closed December-February except Christmas and New Year

Crinan

TRADITIONAL · PERSONALISED Built in the 19C to accommodate the Laird of Jura's business associates. Some of the simply furnished bedrooms have balconies and lovely Sound views. The small coffee shop sells homemade cakes, the 3rd floor bar has a superb terrace, and the large wood-panelled bar-restaurant offers an appealing seafood menu.

20 rooms – £ 100/155 £ 110/290

✉ PA31 8SR – ✆ 01546 830261 – www.crinanhotel.com – Closed December-February except Christmas and New Year

Westward – See restaurant listing

CROMARTY

Highland – Pop. 726 – Regional map n° **17**-D2

Sutor Creek Cafe

TRADITIONAL CUISINE · FRIENDLY X A great little eatery hidden away by the harbour in a well-preserved coastal town. Wonderfully seasonal cooking features seafood from the local boats and pizzas from the wood-fired oven. It's run by a friendly, experienced couple.

Carte £ 24/45

21 Bank St ✉ IV11 8YE – ✆ 01381 600855 (booking essential) – www.sutorcreek.co.uk – Closed January and Monday-Wednesday September-April

Factor's House

LUXURY • PERSONALISED This late Georgian house is very passionately run by a charming owner. It sits in a peaceful spot on the edge of an attractive town and offers pleasant sea views from its mature gardens. Bedrooms have a subtle contemporary style and good extras. Breakfast and dinner are taken around a farmhouse table; the latter is four courses and features accomplished home cooking.

3 rooms – £ 105/115 £ 125/140

Denny Rd IV11 8YT – 01381 600394 – www.thefactorshouse.com – Closed 18 December-31 January

CUMNOCK

East Ayrshire – Pop. 9 039 – Regional map n° **15**-B2

Dumfries House Lodge

COUNTRY HOUSE • PERSONALISED Set at the entrance to the 2,000 acre Dumfries Estate is this stylish country house hotel, formerly a factor's house and steading. There are two cosy lounges and a billiard room and some of the furniture is from the original manor house. Bedrooms are designed by the Duchess of Cornwall's sister.

22 rooms – £ 90 £ 130

Dumfries House KA18 2NJ – West : 1.5 mi on A 70 – 01290 429920 – www.dumfrieshouselodge.co.uk – Closed 23-27 December and 31-December-3 January

CUPAR

Fife – Pop. 9 339 – Regional map n° **16**-C2

Ostlers Close

TRADITIONAL CUISINE • INTIMATE XX Cosy, cottagey little restaurant hidden away down a narrow alley. It's been personally run since 1981 and service is warm and chatty. Classic cooking features local ingredients, including mushrooms foraged for by the owner-chef.

Menu £ 33 (weekdays) – Carte £ 34/49

25 Bonnygate KY15 4BU – 01334 655574 – www.ostlersclose.co.uk – dinner only and Saturday lunch – Closed 2 weeks January, 2 weeks April, 25-26 December, 1-2 January, Sunday and Monday

Ferrymuir Stables

LUXURY • CONTEMPORARY The old stables of Ferrymuir House date from 1800 – but you'd never know. The hub of the house is a light, spacious orangery overlooking the stable yard. Modern bedrooms come with designer furnishings, smart wet rooms and Netbooks.

3 rooms – £ 75/80 £ 100/120

Beechgrove Rise KY15 5DT – West : 1 mi by Bonnygate (A91) and West Park Rd off Westfield Rd – 01334 657579 – www.ferrymuirstables.co.uk

DALKEITH

Midlothian – Pop. 12 342 – Regional map n° **15**-C1

Sun Inn

TRADITIONAL CUISINE • PUB A 17C blacksmith's with two open-fired rooms and a rustic modern extension, where bright wallpapers sit beside stone walls. Extensive menus feature top local produce – lunch keeps things simple but appealing, while dinner is more ambitious. Smart bedrooms boast handmade furniture and Egyptian cotton linen.

Menu £ 16 (lunch and early dinner) – Carte £ 20/43

7 rooms – £ 75/125 £ 110/165

Lothian Bridge EH22 4TR – Southwest : 2 mi by A 6094 and B 6392 on A 7 – 0131 663 2456 – www.thesuninnedinburgh.co.uk – Closed 26 December and 1 January

DALRY

North Ayrshire - Regional map n° **15**-A1

Braidwoods (Keith Braidwood)

CLASSIC CUISINE • INTIMATE XX Just 40mins from Glasgow is this whitewashed crofter's cottage surrounded by fields and mountains. It's run in an unassuming manner by Mr and Mrs Braidwood and has a cosy, intimate feel. Menus showcase tried-and-tested classics where the true flavour of each ingredient is allowed to shine.

➜ Arran blue cheese panna cotta with beetroot, apple and toasted hazelnuts. Ayrshire lamb with neck fillet, spinach and wild garlic. Iced heather honey parfait with Tayberry coulis.

Menu £ 30 (weekdays)/55

Drumastle Mill Cottage ✉ KA24 4LN - Southwest : 1.5 mi by A 737 on Saltcoats rd - ✆ 01294 833544 (booking essential) - www.braidwoods.co.uk - Closed 25 December-January, 2 weeks September, Sunday dinner-Tuesday lunch and Sunday May-mid September

DERVAIG - Argyll and Bute ➜ See Mull (Isle of)

DINGWALL

Highland - Pop. 5 491 - Regional map n° **17**-C2

Café India Brasserie

INDIAN • NEIGHBOURHOOD XX Well-run Indian restaurant close to the town centre. Small lounge and several dining areas separated by etched glass screens. Good range of authentic, regional dishes, with tasty Thalis, set menus for 2+ and good value two course lunches.

Menu £ 9 (weekday lunch) - Carte £ 13/32

Lockhart House, Tulloch St ✉ IV15 9JZ - ✆ 01349 862552 - www.cafeindiadingwall.co.uk - Closed 25 December

DINNET

Aberdeenshire - Regional map n° **16**-D1

Glendavan House

FAMILY • CLASSIC Set in 9 lochside acres, this former shooting lodge is somewhere to get away from it all. Two of the three bedrooms are very large suites; all are tastefully furnished with antiques and memorabilia. Delicious communal breakfasts.

3 rooms - £ 108/135 £ 130/170

✉ AB34 5LU - Northwest : 3 mi by A 97 on B 9119 - ✆ 01339 881610 - www.glendavanhouse.com

DORNOCH

Highland - Pop. 1 208 - Regional map n° **17**-D2

Links House

LUXURY • CONTEMPORARY This restored 19C manse sits opposite the first tee of the Royal Dornoch Golf Club. Enjoy a dram from the honesty bar in the pine-panelled library or have tea and cake in the antique-furnished sitting room. Some of the beautifully furnished bedrooms feature bespoke tweed fabrics. The elegant orangery boasts an impressive stone fireplace and an elaborate 4 course menu.

13 rooms - £ 270/370 £ 270/370

Golf Rd ✉ IV25 3LW - ✆ 01862 810279 - www.linkshousedornoch.com - Closed 4 January-20 March and 25-27 December

2 Quail

TOWNHOUSE · PERSONALISED A bijou terraced house built in 1898 for a sea captain. Intimate bedrooms are furnished with antiques – in a Victorian style – and one has a wrought iron bedstead. The small open-fired library-lounge boasts a large array of vintage books. Daily changing set dinners are offered by arrangement.

3 rooms – £ 80/115 £ 90/125

Castle St IV25 3SN – 01862 811811 – www.2quail.com – Closed 2 weeks February-March and Christmas

DRUMBEG

Highland – Regional map n° **17**-C1

Blar na Leisg at Drumbeg House

FAMILY · MODERN This remotely set Edwardian house affords lovely loch views. The large open-fired sitting room is filled with a vast array of books; and impressive modern art and Bauhaus-style furnishings feature throughout. Bedrooms are spacious and luxuriously appointed. Highland beef and game birds are a speciality at dinner, which is served in a smart, contemporary dining room.

5 rooms – £ 90/150 £ 180/190

IV27 4NW – Take first right on entering village from Kylesku direction – 01571 833325 – www.blarnaleisg.com

DUISDALEMORE – Highland → See Skye (Isle of)

DUNBAR

East Lothian – Pop. 8 486 – Regional map n° **15**-D1

Creel

TRADITIONAL CUISINE · BISTRO An unassuming, cosy former pub with wood-panelling on the walls and ceiling. The experienced chef creates good value, full-flavoured dishes using seafood fresh from the adjacent harbour. Service is friendly.

Menu £ 17/29

The Harbour, 25 Lamer St EH42 1HG – 01368 863279 (booking essential) – www.creelrestaurant.co.uk – Closed Sunday dinner-Wednesday lunch

DUNBLANE

Stirling – Pop. 8 811 – Regional map n° **16**-C2

Chez Roux

FRENCH · BRASSERIE Light and spacious conservatory restaurant in a magnificent country house hotel. Smart, yet relaxed, it's a hit with locals and tourists alike thanks to the enthusiastic service and good value, flavoursome cooking. Classic French dishes might include soufflé Suissesse, chateaubriand or tarte au citron.

Menu £ 33 (lunch) – Carte £ 36/52

Cromlix Hotel, Kinbuck FK15 9JT – North : 3.5 mi on B 8033 – 01786 822125 – www.cromlix.com

Cromlix

COUNTRY HOUSE · MODERN This grand house, owned by Sir Andy Murray, has elegant sitting rooms, a whisky room, a chapel and a superb games room, as well as a tennis court in its 30 acre grounds. Luxurious, antique-furnished bedrooms display modern touches while also respecting the house's original style.

16 rooms – £ 275/695 £ 275/695 – 5 suites

Kinbuck FK15 9JT – North : 3.5 mi on B 8033 – 01786 822125 – www.cromlix.com

Chez Roux – See restaurant listing

DUNDEE

Dundee City – Pop. 147 285 – Regional map n° **16**-C2

Castlehill

MODERN CUISINE • INTIMATE XX Both its name and its décor celebrate the city's history. Choose from a set price or tasting menu; at dinner, every dish from the former can be ordered as either a starter or main course. Cooking is complex and elaborate.

Menu £ 18/35

Town plan: B2-c – *22 Exchange St ✉ DD1 3DL – ✆ 01382 220008 – www.castlehillrestaurant.co.uk – Closed Sunday and Monday*

Malmaison

BUSINESS • CONTEMPORARY The best feature of this lovingly restored hotel is the wrought iron cantilevered staircase topped by a domed ceiling. Contemporary bedrooms come in striking bold colours and have a masculine feel. The all-day bar serves cocktails and nibbles and there's a DJ at weekends; the brasserie offers a grill menu.

91 rooms – †£ 67/367 ††£ 79/379

Town plan: B2-s – *44 Whitehall Cres ✉ DD1 4AY – ✆ 01382 339715 – www.malmaison.com*

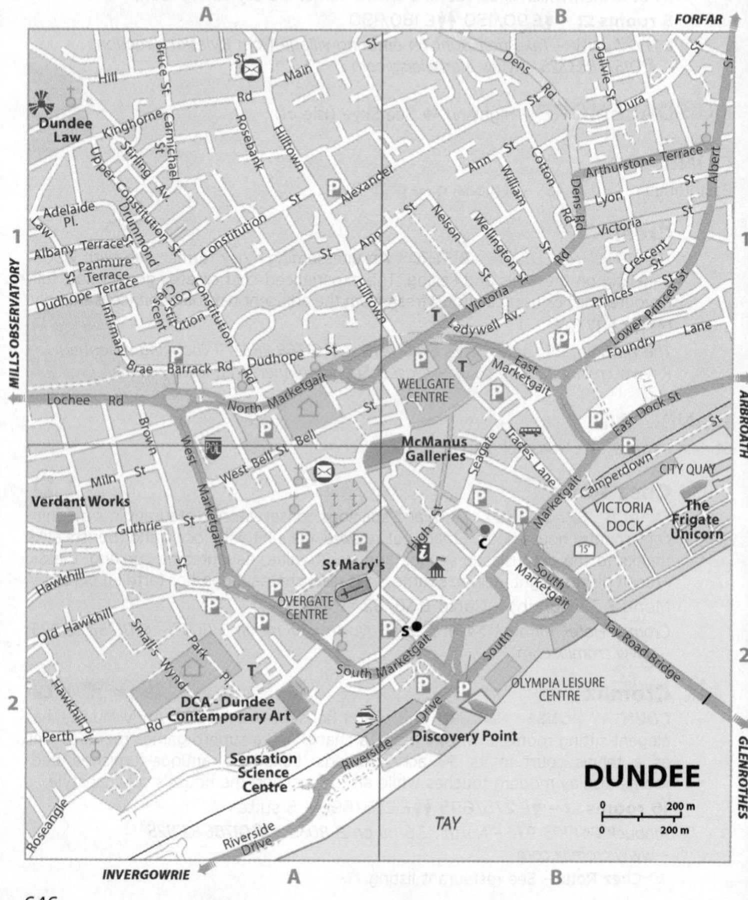

Balmuirfield House 

COUNTRY HOUSE • COSY A double-fronted stone dower house built in 1904; Dighty Water runs past the bottom of the garden. Inside it's spacious and homely, with a cosy open-fired lounge. Two of the bedrooms have four-posters and one has an antique bath.

4 rooms – †£ 55/75 ††£ 85/125

Harestane Rd ✉ DD3 0NU – North : 3.5 mi by A 929, A 90, Claverhouse Rd and Old Glamis Rd – ✆ 01382 819655 – www.balmuirfieldhouse.com

at Broughty Ferry East : 4.5 mi by A 930

Collinsons

CLASSIC CUISINE • FRIENDLY XX You can't miss the name etched in large letters across the floor to ceiling windows of this bright modern restaurant. Cooking is classic to the core, with unfussy, wholesome dishes presented in a refined, eye-catching manner.

Menu £ 22/36

122-124 Brown St ✉ DD5 1EN – ✆ 01382 776000 – www.collinsonsrestaurant.com – Closed 1-10 January, 25-26 December, Sunday and Monday

Tayberry 

MODERN BRITISH • FRIENDLY XX An unassuming roadside property overlooking the mouth of the Tay. The keen young chef offers fresh, tasty cooking with original modern touches and local and foraged ingredients play a key role. Service is engaging and attentive.

Menu £ 18/39

594 Brook St ✉ DD5 2EA – ✆ 01382 698280 – www.tayberryrestaurant.com – Closed 25-28 December, Sunday and Monday

DUNVEGAN – Highland → See Skye (Isle of)

DURNESS

Highland – Regional map n° **17**-C1

Mackay's 

FAMILY • MODERN This smart grey stone house sits at the most north-westerly point of the mainland. It has a light, airy lounge and a cosy open-fired snug. The owner is a textile designer and this shows in the bedrooms, which have a stylish, rustic feel.

7 rooms – †£ 125/149 ††£ 129/169

✉ IV27 4PN – ✆ 01971 511202 – www.visitdurness.com – Closed October-April

DYKE

Moray – Regional map n° **16**-C1

Old Kirk 

HISTORIC • DESIGN A peacefully set, converted 1856 church, surrounded by grain fields. It has an airy interior, a cosy library and a comfortable open-fired lounge with a pretty stained glass window. Charming, individually decorated bedrooms boast original stonework and arched windows; one has a carved four-poster bed.

3 rooms – †£ 85/95 ††£ 85/95

✉ IV36 2TL – Northeast : 0.5 mi – ✆ 01309 641414 – www.oldkirk.co.uk – Closed October-March

EDDLESTON – The Scottish Borders → See Peebles

EDINBANE – Highland → See Skye (Isle of)

P. Hauser/hemis.fr

GOOD TIPS!

A cool, cosmopolitan city with stunning scenery and a colourful history, Scotland's capital is home to Michelin-Starred restaurants as well as busy wine bars and bistros, with global flavours including Korean, Italian and Thai. The famous Royal Mile is the location of the luxurious **G & V** hotel, while the **Sheraton Grand** has views of the iconic castle.

EDINBURGH

City of Edinburgh - Pop. 459 366 - Regional map n° **15**-C1

Restaurants

✿ Number One

MODERN CUISINE • INTIMATE XXXX A stylish, long-standing restaurant with a chic cocktail bar, set in the basement of a grand hotel. Richly upholstered banquettes and red lacquered walls give it a plush, luxurious feel. Cooking is modern and intricate and prime Scottish ingredients are key. Service is professional and has personality.

→ The Balmoral's Tomatin smoked salmon with quail's egg, lemon and caviar. Fillet of Scottish beef with hay-cooked short rib, aubergine and bone marrow fondant. Vanilla soufflé with poached rhubarb and almond ice cream.

Menu £ 75

Town plan: G2-n - *Balmoral Hotel, 1 Princes St ✉ EH2 2EQ*
- *✆ 0131 557 6727 - www.roccofortehotels.com*
- *dinner only - Closed 2 weeks mid-January*

✿ 21212 (Paul Kitching)

CREATIVE • ELEGANT XXX Stunningly refurbished Georgian townhouse designed by William Playfair. The glass-fronted kitchen is the focal point of the stylish, high-ceilinged dining room. Cooking is skilful and innovative and features quirky combinations; '21212' reflects the number of dishes per course at lunch - at dinner it's '31313'. Some of the luxurious bedrooms overlook the Firth of Forth.

→ Crab, celeriac and caviar with scallop. Pintade, pecan and mango with cauli roots. Glazed lemon meringue with marzipan and apple nut crumble.

Menu £ 32/85 **s**

4 rooms ☕ - 🚹£ 95/295 🚹🚹£ 95/295

Town plan: H1-c - *3 Royal Terr ✉ EH7 5AB*
- *✆ 0345 222 1212 (booking essential) - www.21212restaurant.co.uk*
- *Closed 10 days January, 10 days summer, Sunday and Monday*

Galvin Brasserie De Luxe

FRENCH • BRASSERIE XX It's accurately described by its name: a simply styled restaurant which looks like a brasserie of old, but with the addition of a smart shellfish counter and formal service. There's an appealing à la carte and a good value two-choice daily set selection; dishes are refined, flavoursome and of a good size.

Menu £ 23 (lunch and early dinner) – Carte £ 29/65

Town plan: F2-x – *Waldorf Astoria Edinburgh The Caledonian Hotel, Princes St ✉ EH1 2AB*
– ✆ 0131 222 8988 – www.galvinrestaurants.com

Dogs

TRADITIONAL CUISINE • BISTRO X Cosy, slightly bohemian-style eatery on the first floor of a classic Georgian mid-terrace, with two high-ceilinged, shabby chic dining rooms and an appealing bar. Robust, good value comfort food is crafted from local, seasonal produce; dishes such as cock-a-leekie soup and devilled ox livers feature.

Carte £ 12/25

Town plan: F2-c – *110 Hanover St (1st Floor) ✉ EH2 1DR*
– ✆ 0131 220 1208 – www.thedogsonline.co.uk – Closed 25 December and 1 January

Passorn

THAI • FRIENDLY X The staff are super-friendly at this extremely popular neighbourhood restaurant, whose name means 'Angel'. Authentic menus feature Thai classics and old family recipes; the seafood dishes are a highlight and presentation is first class. Spices and other ingredients are flown in from Thailand.

Menu £ 16 (weekday lunch) – Carte £ 24/37

Town plan: F3-e – *23-23a Brougham Pl ✉ EH3 9JU*
– ✆ 0131 229 1537 (booking essential) – www.passornthai.com – Closed 25-26 December, 1-2 January, Sunday and lunch Monday

The Scran & Scallie

TRADITIONAL BRITISH • NEIGHBOURHOOD The more casual venture from Tom Kitchin, located in a smart, village-like suburb. It has a wood-furnished bar and a dining room which blends rustic and contemporary décor. Extensive menus follow a 'Nature to Plate' philosophy and focus on the classical and the local.

Menu £ 15 (weekday lunch) – Carte £ 24/46

Town plan: E1-s – *1 Comely Bank Rd, Stockbridge ✉ EH4 1DT*
– ✆ 0131 332 6281 (booking advisable) – www.scranandscallie.com – Closed 25 December

The Pompadour by Galvin

FRENCH • CHIC XXX A grand hotel restaurant which opened in the 1920s and is modelled on a French salon. Classic Gallic dishes showcase Scottish produce, using techniques introduced by Escoffier, and are executed with a lightness of touch.

Menu £ 35 (early dinner)/65

Town plan: F2-x – *Waldorf Astoria Edinburgh The Caledonian Hotel, Princes St ✉ EH1 2AB*
– ✆ 0131 222 8975 – www.galvinrestaurants.com – dinner only and Saturday lunch – Closed 1-16 January, Monday and Tuesday

Rhubarb

MODERN CUISINE • ELEGANT XX Two sumptuous, richly decorated dining rooms set within a romantic 17C country house; so named as this was the first place in Scotland where rhubarb was grown. The concise menu lists modern dishes with some innovative touches and is accompanied by an interesting wine list, with a great selection by the glass.

Menu £ 25/38 – Carte £ 35/66

Town plan: C3-r – *Prestonfield Hotel, Priestfield Rd ✉ EH16 5UT*
– ✆ 0131 225 1333 – www.prestonfield.com

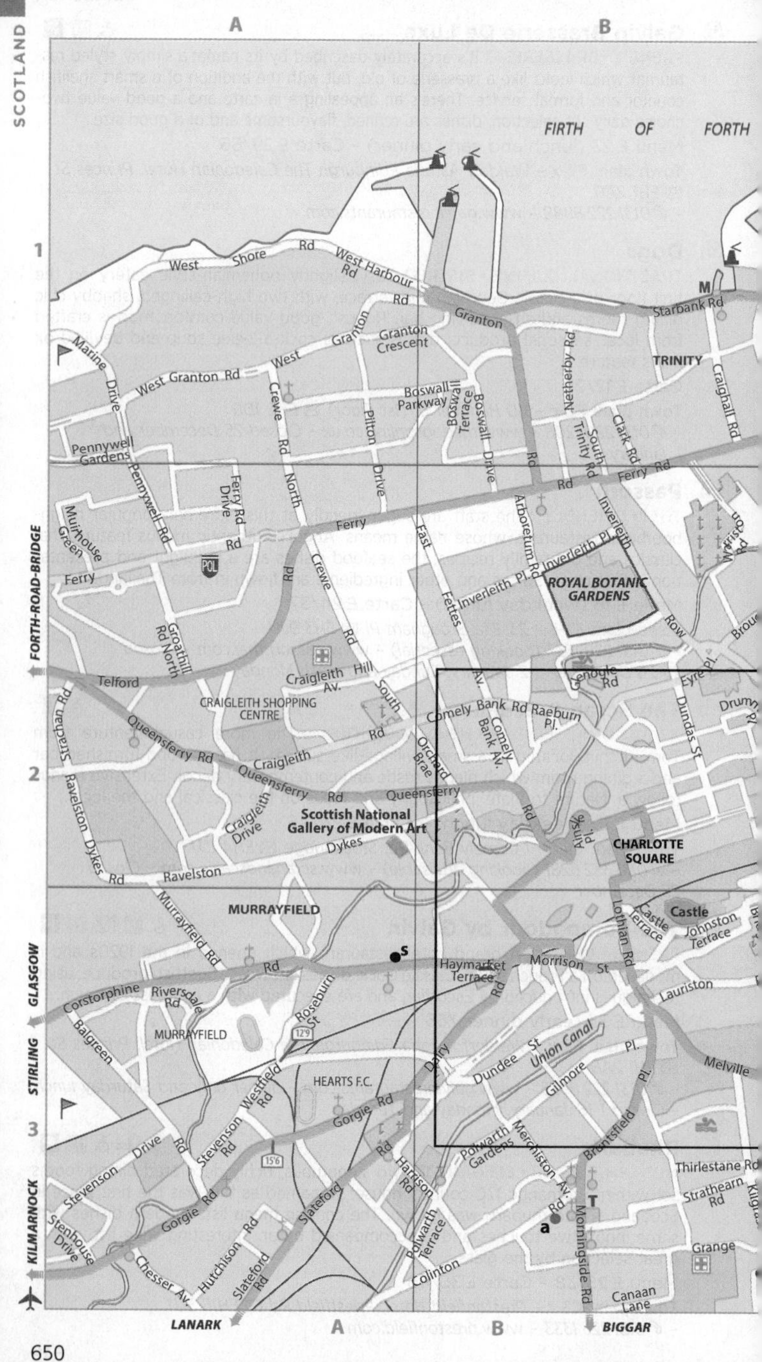
A
B
1
2
3
FIRTH OF FORTH
West Shore Rd
West Harbour Rd
Rd
Granton
Starbank Rd
TRINITY
Marine Drive
West Granton Rd
West Granton
Granton Crescent
Boswall Parkway
Boswall Terrace
Boswall Drive
Netherby Rd
South Trinity Rd
Clark Rd
Craighall Rd
Crewe Rd North
Pilton Drive
Pennywell Gardens
Pennywell Rd
Ferry Rd Drive
Ferry Rd
Muirhouse Green
Ferry
Arboretum Rd
Inverleith Pl.
Inverleith Row
ROYAL BOTANIC GARDENS
East Fettes Av.
Crewe Rd South
Groathill Rd North
Telford
Craigleith Hill Av.
CRAIGLEITH SHOPPING CENTRE
Glenogle Rd
Eyre Pl.
Dundas St
Comely Bank Rd
Comely Bank Av.
Raeburn Pl.
Strachan Rd
Queensferry Rd
Craigleith Rd
Orchard Brae
Ravelston Dykes Rd
Craigleith Drive
Scottish National Gallery of Modern Art
Dykes
Ravelston
Ainslie Pl.
CHARLOTTE SQUARE
MURRAYFIELD
Murrayfield Rd
Castle
Castle Terrace
Johnston Terrace
Lothian Rd
Haymarket Terrace
Morrison St
Lauriston
Corstorphine Rd
Riversdale Rd
Roseburn St
Balgreen
MURRAYFIELD
Dalry Rd
Dundee St
Union Canal
Gilmore Pl.
Melville
HEARTS F.C.
Westfield Rd
Gorgie Rd
Stevenson Drive
Stevenson Rd
Polwarth Gardens
Merchiston Av.
Bruntsfield Pl.
Thirlestane Rd
Strathearn Rd
Harrison Rd
Slateford Rd
Stenhouse Drive
Gorgie Rd
Hutchison Rd
Chesser Av.
Slateford Rd
Polwarth Terrace
Colinton
Morningside Rd
Grange
Canaan Lane
FORTH-ROAD-BRIDGE
GLASGOW
STIRLING
KILMARNOCK
LANARK
BIGGAR
POL
M
T
S
a

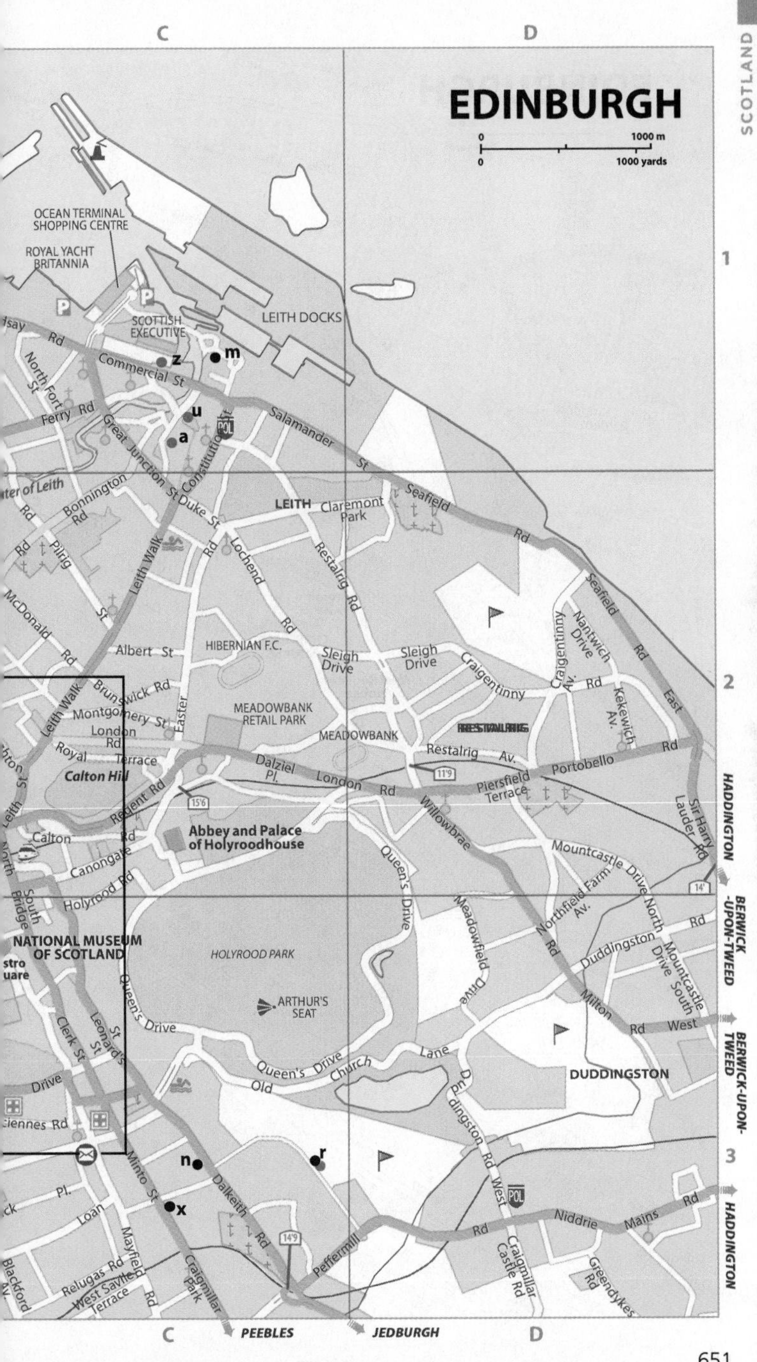
EDINBURGH
0
1000 m
1000 yards
C
D
1
2
3
OCEAN TERMINAL SHOPPING CENTRE
ROYAL YACHT BRITANNIA
SCOTTISH EXECUTIVE
LEITH DOCKS
LEITH
Claremont Park
HIBERNIAN F.C.
MEADOWBANK RETAIL PARK
MEADOWBANK
RESTALRIG
Calton Hill
Abbey and Palace of Holyroodhouse
NATIONAL MUSEUM OF SCOTLAND
HOLYROOD PARK
ARTHUR'S SEAT
DUDDINGSTON
Commercial St
Salamander St
Seafield Rd
Great Junction St
Constitution St
Duke St
Leith Walk
Lochend Rd
Restalrig Rd
Easter Rd
Albert St
Sleigh Drive
Craigentinny Rd
Brunswick Rd
Montgomery St
London Rd
Royal Terrace
Regent Rd
Dalziel Pl.
Restalrig Av.
Portobello Rd
Piersfield Terrace
Willowbrae
Queen's Drive
Mountcastle Drive North
Northfield Farm Av.
Meadowfield Drive
Duddingston Rd
Milton Rd West
Old Church Lane
Duddingston Rd West
Niddrie Mains Rd
Peffermill Rd
Craigmillar Castle Rd
Greendykes Rd
Dalkeith Rd
Minto St
Craigmillar Park
Mayfield Rd
Relugas Rd
West Savile Terrace
Blackford Av.
Canongate
Holyrood Rd
South Bridge
Clerk St
St Leonard's St
Sir Harry Lauder Rd
Seafield Rd East
Ferry Rd
North Fort St
Bonnington Rd
Pilrig St
McDonald Rd
HADDINGTON
BERWICK-UPON-TWEED
PEEBLES
JEDBURGH

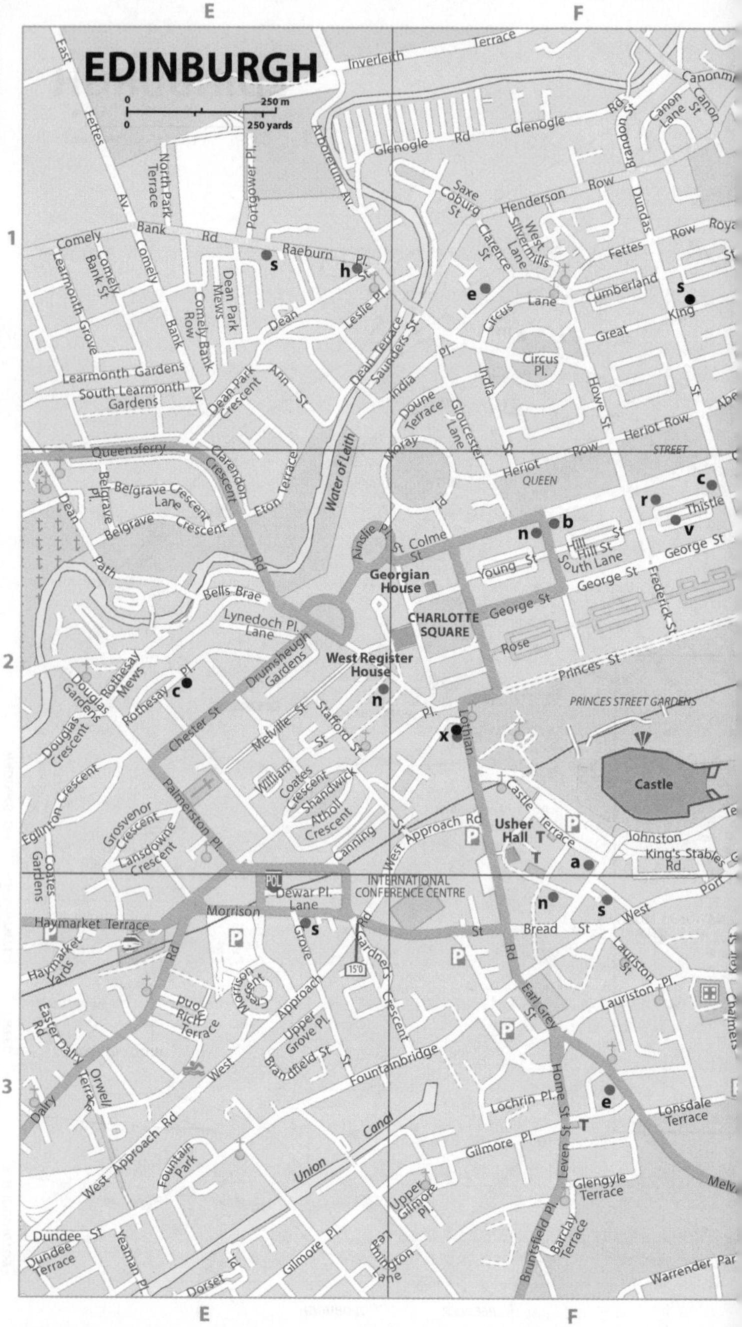
EDINBURGH
0 250 m
0 250 yards
E
F
1
2
3
East Fettes Av.
Inverleith Terrace
Canonmills
Canon Lane
Canon St
Glenogle Rd
Brandon Terrace
North Park Terrace
Portgower Pl.
Arboretum Av.
Saxe Coburg St
Henderson Row
Dundas St
Comely Bank Rd
Raeburn Pl.
Clarence St
West Silvermills Lane
Fettes Row
Royal
Comely Bank St
Learmonth Grove
Comely Bank Row
Dean Park Mews
Leslie Pl.
Dean St
Circus Lane
Cumberland St
King St
Great
Circus Pl.
India Pl.
India St
Saunders St
Dean Terrace
Ann St
Dean Park Crescent
Learmonth Gardens
South Learmonth Gardens
Comely Bank Av.
Doune Terrace
Gloucester Lane
Howe St
Heriot Row
Abercromby
Queensferry Rd
Clarendon Crescent
Eton Terrace
Water of Leith
Moray Pl.
Heriot Row
Queen Street
Belgrave Pl.
Belgrave Crescent Lane
Belgrave Crescent
Dean Path
Ainslie Pl.
St Colme St
Hill St
Hill St South Lane
Thistle
George St
Young St
Georgian House
Charlotte Square
Frederick St
Rose
Bells Brae
Lynedoch Pl. Lane
Drumsheugh Gardens
West Register House
Princes St
Princes Street Gardens
Rothesay Mews
Rothesay Pl.
Douglas Gardens
Douglas Crescent
Chester St
Melville St
Stafford St
Lothian
Castle
William St
Coates Crescent
Shandwick Pl.
Atholl Crescent
Eglinton Crescent
Grosvenor Crescent
Lansdowne Crescent
Palmerston Pl.
Canning St
West Approach Rd
Usher Hall
Castle Terrace
Johnston Terrace
King's Stables Rd
Coates Gardens
International Conference Centre
Dewar Pl. Lane
Morrison St
Haymarket Terrace
Haymarket Yards
Bread St
West Port
Lauriston St
Lauriston Pl.
Chalmers
Grove St
Gardner's Crescent
Earl Grey St
Easter Dalry Rd
Richmond Terrace
Morrison Crescent
Approach
Upper Grove Pl.
Brandfield St
Fountainbridge
Dalry Rd
Orwell Terrace
West Approach Rd
Home St
Lochrin Pl.
Lonsdale Terrace
Union Canal
Fountain Park
Gilmore Pl.
Upper Gilmore Pl.
Leven St
Glengyle Terrace
Melville
Dundee St
Dundee Terrace
Yeaman Pl.
Dorset Pl.
Gilmore Pl.
Leamington Lane
Bruntsfield Pl.
Barclay Terrace
Warrender Park
POL
P
T

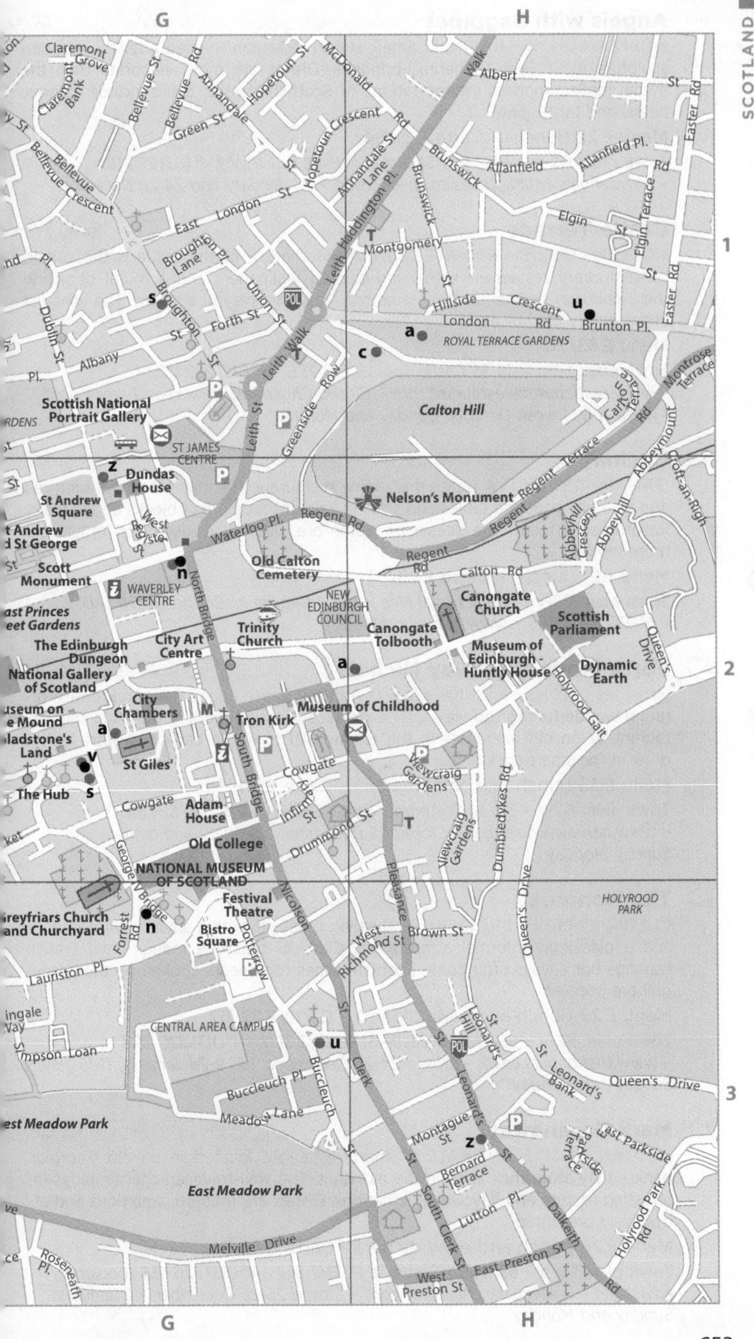
G
H
1
2
3
Claremont Grove
Claremont Bank
Bellevue St
Bellevue Rd
Annandale
Green St
Hopetoun St
McDonald Rd
Hopetoun Crescent
Annandale St Lane
Leith Walk
Albert St
Easter Rd
Brunswick Rd
Allanfield Pl.
Allanfield
Bellevue Crescent
East London St
Leith Haddington Pl.
Brunswick St
Elgin Terrace
Elgin St
Montgomery St
Broughton Pl. Lane
Union St
Broughton St
Forth St
Dublin St
Hillside Crescent
London Rd
Brunton Pl.
ROYAL TERRACE GARDENS
Albany St
Greenside Row
Calton Hill
Carlton Terrace
Montrose Terrace
Scottish National Portrait Gallery
ST JAMES CENTRE
Leith St
Regent Terrace
Abbeymount
Croft-an-Righ
Dundas House
St Andrew Square
Nelson's Monument
Regent Rd
Abbeyhill Crescent
Abbeyhill
Waterloo Pl.
West Register St
St Andrew and St George
Scott Monument
Old Calton Cemetery
Calton Rd
WAVERLEY CENTRE
North Bridge
NEW EDINBURGH COUNCIL
Canongate Church
East Princes Street Gardens
Trinity Church
Canongate Tolbooth
Scottish Parliament
The Edinburgh Dungeon
City Art Centre
Museum of Edinburgh - Huntly House
Dynamic Earth
Queen's Drive
National Gallery of Scotland
Museum on the Mound
City Chambers
Tron Kirk
Museum of Childhood
Holyrood Gait
Gladstone's Land
St Giles'
South Bridge
Cowgate
Viewcraig Gardens
The Hub
Adam House
Infirmary St
Drummond St
Dumbiedykes Rd
Old College
NATIONAL MUSEUM OF SCOTLAND
George IV Bridge
Pleasance
Queen's Drive
HOLYROOD PARK
Greyfriars Church and Churchyard
Festival Theatre
Nicolson St
Forrest Rd
Bistro Square
Potterrow
West Richmond St
Brown St
Lauriston Pl.
CENTRAL AREA CAMPUS
St Leonard's Hill
St Leonard's Bank
Simpson Loan
Buccleuch Pl.
Buccleuch St
Clerk St
St Leonard's St
Queen's Drive
Meadow Lane
East Meadow Park
Montague St
East Parkside
Parkside Terrace
Bernard Terrace
East Meadow Park
Lutton Pl.
Holyrood Park Rd
Melville Drive
South Clerk St
Dalkeith Rd
Roseneath Pl.
East Preston St
West Preston St
G
H

Angels with Bagpipes

MODERN CUISINE • BISTRO XX Small, stylish restaurant named after the wooden sculpture in St Giles Cathedral, opposite. Dishes are more elaborate than the menu implies; modern interpretations of Scottish classics could include 'haggis, neeps and tattiesgine'.

Menu £ 22 (lunch) - Carte £ 31/54

Town plan: G2-a - *343 High St, Royal Mile ✉ EH1 1PW - ✆ 0131 220 1111 - www.angelswithbagpipes.co.uk - Closed 7-23 January and 24-28 December*

Castle Terrace

MODERN CUISINE • INTIMATE XX Set in the shadow of the castle is this bright, contemporary restaurant with hand-painted wallpapers and a mural depicting the Edinburgh skyline. Cooking is ambitious with a playful element. The wine list offers plenty of choice.

Menu £ 33/70

Town plan: F2-a - *33-35 Castle Terr ✉ EH1 2EL - ✆ 0131 229 1222 - www.castleterracerestaurant.com - Closed Christmas, New Year, 1 week April, 1 week July, 1 week October, Sunday and Monday*

Cucina

ITALIAN • DESIGN XX A buzzy mezzanine restaurant in a chic hotel, featuring red and blue glass-topped tables and striking kaleidoscope-effect blocks on the walls. Italian dishes follow the seasons - some are classically based and others are more modern.

Menu £ 21 (lunch) - Carte £ 29/57

Town plan: G2-v - *G & V Royal Mile Hotel, 1 George IV Bridge ✉ EH1 1AD - ✆ 0131 220 6666 - www.gandvhotel.com*

Forth Floor at Harvey Nichols

MODERN CUISINE • FASHIONABLE XX A buzzy fourth floor eatery and terrace offering wonderful rooftop views. Dine on accomplished modern dishes in the restaurant or on old favourites in the all-day bistro. Arrive early and start with a drink in the smart cocktail bar.

Menu £ 33 (lunch and early dinner) - Carte £ 34/44

Town plan: G2-z - *30-34 St Andrew Sq ✉ EH2 2AD - ✆ 0131 524 8350 - www.harveynichols.com - Closed 25 December, 1 January and dinner Sunday-Monday*

The Honours

CLASSIC CUISINE • BRASSERIE XX Bustling brasserie with a smart, stylish interior and a pleasingly informal atmosphere. Classical brasserie menus have French leanings but always offer some Scottish dishes too; meats cooked on the Josper grill are popular.

Menu £ 29 (lunch and early dinner) - Carte £ 27/67

Town plan: F2-n - *58A North Castle St ✉ EH2 3LU - ✆ 0131 220 2513 - www.thehonours.co.uk - Closed 24-26 December, 1-2, 9-24 January, 11-15 July, Sunday and Monday*

Mark Greenaway

MODERN CUISINE • INTIMATE XX Smart restaurant located in an old Georgian bank - they store their wine in the old vault. The well-travelled chef employs interesting texture and flavour combinations. Dishes are modern, ambitious and attractively presented.

Menu £ 26 (lunch and early dinner) - Carte £ 42/58

Town plan: F2-b - *69 North Castle St ✉ EH2 3LJ - ✆ 0131 226 1155 (booking advisable) - www.markgreenaway.com - Closed 25-26 December, 1-2 January, Sunday and Monday*

Ondine

SEAFOOD • BRASSERIE XX Smart, lively restaurant dominated by an impressive horseshoe bar and a crustacean counter. Classic menus showcase prime Scottish seafood in tasty, straightforward dishes which let the ingredients shine. Service is well-structured.

Menu £ 25 (lunch and early dinner) – Carte £ 33/78

Town plan: G2-s – *2 George IV Bridge (1st floor) ✉ EH1 1AD – ✆ 0131 226 1888 – www.ondinerestaurant.co.uk – Closed 1 week early January and 24-26 December*

Timberyard

MODERN CUISINE • RUSTIC X Trendy warehouse restaurant; its spacious, rustic interior incorporating wood-burning stoves. The Scandic-influenced menu offers 'bites', 'small' and 'large' sizes, with some home-smoked ingredients and an emphasis on distinct, punchy flavours. Cocktails are made with vegetable purées and foraged herbs.

Menu £ 25 (lunch and early dinner)/55

Town plan: F3-s – *10 Lady Lawson St ✉ EH3 9DS – ✆ 0131 221 1222 (booking essential at dinner) – www.timberyard.co – Closed 1 week April, 1 week October, Christmas, Sunday and Monday*

Aizle

MODERN CUISINE • SIMPLE X Modest little suburban restaurant whose name means 'ember' or 'spark'. Well-balanced, skilfully prepared dishes are, in effect, a surprise, as the set menu is presented as a long list of ingredients – the latest 'harvest'.

Menu £ 45 – tasting menu only

Town plan: H3-z – *107-109 St Leonard's St ✉ EH8 9QY – ✆ 0131 662 9349 – www.aizle.co.uk – dinner only – Closed 1-16 January, 2-17 July, 24-31 December, Monday and Tuesday*

The Atelier

MEDITERRANEAN CUISINE • BISTRO X An attractive little restaurant with bright orange chairs and a stone feature wall. Fresh ingredients are prepared with care, and dishes have French and Italian influences and a subtle modern slant; lunch really is a steal.

Menu £ 10 (lunch) – Carte £ 26/47

Town plan: E3-s – *159 Morrison St ✉ EH3 8AG – ✆ 0131 629 5040 – www.theatelierrestaurant.co.uk – Closed 3 weeks January, 25-26 December and Sunday-Monday*

Bia Bistrot

CLASSIC CUISINE • NEIGHBOURHOOD X A simple, good value neighbourhood bistro with a buzzy vibe. Unfussy, flavoursome dishes range in their influences due to the friendly owners' Irish-Scottish and French-Spanish heritages; they are husband and wife and cook together.

Menu £ 10 (lunch and early dinner) – Carte £ 19/38

Town plan: B3-a – *19 Colinton Rd ✉ EH10 5DP – ✆ 0131 452 8453 – www.biabistrot.co.uk – Closed first week January, second week April, second week July, second week October, Sunday and Monday*

Bon Vivant 

TRADITIONAL CUISINE • WINE BAR X A relaxed wine bar in the city backstreets, with a dimly lit interior, tightly packed tables and a cheery, welcoming team. The appealing, twice daily menu has an eclectic mix of influences; start with some of the bite-sized nibbles.

Menu £ 16 (weekday lunch) – Carte £ 25/38

Town plan: F2-v – *55 Thistle St ✉ EH2 1DY – ✆ 0131 225 3275 – www.bonvivantedinburgh.co.uk – Closed 25-26 December and 1 January*

Café St Honoré

CLASSIC FRENCH • BISTRO Long-standing French bistro, tucked away down a side street. The interior is cosy, with wooden marquetry, mirrors on the walls and tightly packed tables. Traditional Gallic menus use Scottish produce and they even smoke their own salmon.

Menu £15/24 – Carte £31/51

Town plan: F2-r – *34 North West Thistle Street Ln. ✉ EH2 1EA – ✆ 0131 226 2211 (booking essential) – www.cafesthonore.com – Closed 24-26 December and 1-2 January*

Forage & Chatter

MODERN CUISINE • FRIENDLY Follow the narrow staircase down to the basement, where a series of small, rustic rooms and a pretty conservatory await. Appealing Scottish dishes feature many foraged ingredients. Service is engaging and goes the extra mile.

Menu £15 (weekday lunch) – Carte £27/41

Town plan: E2-n – *1A Alva St ✉ EH2 4PH – ✆ 0131 225 4599 – www.forageandchatter.co.uk – Closed 24-26 December, 1-3 January, Sunday and Monday*

Gardener's Cottage

TRADITIONAL CUISINE • RUSTIC This quirky little eatery was once home to a royal gardener. Two cosy, simply furnished rooms have long communal tables. Lunch is light and dinner offers an 8 course set menu; much of the produce comes from the kitchen garden.

Menu £50 (dinner) – Carte lunch £30/40

Town plan: H1-a – *1 Royal Terrace Gdns ✉ EH7 5DX – ✆ 0131 558 1221 (bookings advisable at dinner) – www.thegardenerscottage.co – Closed 25-26 December and 1 January*

Kanpai

JAPANESE • SIMPLE Uncluttered, modern Japanese restaurant with a smart sushi bar and cheerful service. Colourful, elaborate dishes have clean, well-defined flavours; the menu is designed to help novices feel confident and experts feel at home.

Carte £13/40

Town plan: F3-n – *8-10 Grindlay St ✉ EH3 9AS – ✆ 0131 228 1602 – www.kanpaisushiedinburgh.co.uk – Closed Sunday and Monday*

Kim's Mini Meals

KOREAN • SIMPLE A delightfully quirky little eatery filled with bric-a-brac and offering good value, authentic Korean home cooking. Classic dishes like bulgogi, dolsot and jjigae come with your choice of meat or vegetables as the main ingredient.

Carte approx. £18

Town plan: G3-u – *5 Buccleuch St ✉ EH8 9JN – ✆ 0131 629 7951 (booking essential at dinner)*

Purslane

MODERN CUISINE • NEIGHBOURHOOD A cosy, atmospheric basement restaurant made up of just 9 tables. The young chef-owner creates ambitious modern dishes which mix tried-and-tested flavours with modern techniques. Lunch is particularly good value.

Menu £15/35

Town plan: F1-e – *33a St Stephen St ✉ EH3 5AH – ✆ 0131 226 3500 (booking essential) – www.purslanerestaurant.co.uk – Closed 25-26 December, 1 January and Monday*

Seasons

MODERN CUISINE • FRIENDLY An enthusiastic young chef runs this modest wood-clad restaurant. A well-priced set lunch is followed by a 5 or 7 course surprise dinner menu, and cooking is fresh and vibrant. Head downstairs if you fancy a cocktail.

Menu £ 19/40

Town plan: G1-s - *36 Broughton St ✉ EH1 3SB - ✆ 0131 466 9851 - www.seasonstasting.co.uk - Closed 1-7 January, 24-26 December, Monday and Tuesday*

Taisteal

MODERN BRITISH • NEIGHBOURHOOD Taisteal is Irish Gaelic for 'journey' and is the perfect name: photos from the chef's travels line the walls and dishes have global influences, with Asian flavours to the fore. The wine list even has a sake section.

Menu £ 15 (weekdays) - Carte £ 22/37

Town plan: E1-h - *1-3 Raeburn Pl, Stockbridge ✉ EH4 1HU - ✆ 0131 332 9977 - www.taisteal.co.uk - Closed 2 weeks January and Monday*

Wedgwood

MODERN CUISINE • FRIENDLY Atmospheric bistro hidden away at the bottom of the Royal Mile. Well-presented dishes showcase produce foraged from the surrounding countryside and feature some original, modern combinations. It's personally run by a friendly team.

Menu £ 19 (lunch) - Carte dinner £ 32/52

Town plan: H2-a - *267 Canongate ✉ EH8 8BQ - ✆ 0131 558 8737 - www.wedgwoodtherestaurant.co.uk - Closed 1-21 January and 25-26 December*

Hotels

Balmoral

GRAND LUXURY • CLASSIC Renowned Edwardian hotel which provides for the modern traveller whilst retaining its old-fashioned charm. Bedrooms are classical with a subtle contemporary edge; JK Rowling completed the final Harry Potter book in the top suite! Live harp music accompanies afternoon tea in the Palm Court and 'Scotch' offers over 460 malts. Dine on up-to-date dishes or brasserie classics.

188 rooms - †£ 200/645 ††£ 225/645 - ☕ £ 27 - 20 suites

Town plan: G2-n - *1 Princes St ✉ EH2 2EQ - ✆ 0131 556 2414 - www.roccofortehotels.com*

❀ **Number One** - See restaurant listing

Sheraton Grand H. & Spa

GRAND LUXURY • MODERN A spacious hotel with castle views from some rooms - an impressive four-storey glass cube houses the stunning spa. Sleek, stylish bedrooms have strong comforts, the latest mod cons and smart bathrooms with mood lighting. The casual restaurant serves an all-encompassing menu and the bar offers over 50 gins.

269 rooms - †£ 160/675 ††£ 160/675 - ☕ £ 22 - 11 suites

Town plan: F2-v - *1 Festival Sq ✉ EH3 9SR - ✆ 0131 229 9131 - www.sheratonedinburgh.co.uk*

Waldorf Astoria Edinburgh The Caledonian

HISTORIC • DESIGN Smart hotel in the old railway terminus: have afternoon tea on the former forecourt or cocktails where the trains once pulled in. Sumptuous modern bedrooms have excellent facilities; ask for a castle view. Unwind in the UK's first Guerlain spa, then dine in the grand French salon or luxurious brasserie.

241 rooms - †£ 249/619 ††£ 269/639 - ☕ £ 23 - 6 suites

Town plan: F2-x - *Princes St ✉ EH1 2AB - ✆ 0131 222 8888 - www.waldorfastoriaedinburgh.com*

Galvin Brasserie De Luxe • **The Pompadour by Galvin** - See restaurant listing

Prestonfield

LUXURY • PERSONALISED 17C country house in a pleasant rural spot, with an opulent, dimly lit interior displaying warm colours, fine furnishings and old tapestries – it's hugely atmospheric and is one of the most romantic hotels around. Luxurious bedrooms boast a high level of facilities and service is excellent.

23 rooms – £ 220/395 £ 220/395 – 5 suites

Town plan: C3-r – *Priestfield Rd ✉ EH16 5UT – ☎ 0131 225 7800 – www.prestonfield.com*

Rhubarb – See restaurant listing

G & V Royal Mile

LUXURY • DESIGN A striking hotel in a great central location on the historic Royal Mile. Bedrooms on the upper floors have impressive city skyline views. Bold colour schemes, stylish furnishings and clever design features can be seen throughout.

136 rooms – £ 150/300 £ 200/400 – 7 suites

Town plan: G2-v – *1 George IV Bridge ✉ EH1 1AD – ☎ 0131 220 6666 – www.gandvhotel.com*

Cucina – See restaurant listing

Hotel du Vin

LUXURY • DESIGN Boutique hotel located close to the Royal Mile, featuring unique murals and wine-themed bedrooms furnished with dark wood. Guest areas include a whisky snug and a mezzanine bar complete with glass-fronted cellars and a wine tasting room. The traditional bistro offers classic French cooking.

47 rooms – £ 195/355 £ 195/355

Town plan: G3-n – *11 Bristo Pl ✉ EH1 1EZ – ☎ 0131 247 4900 – www.hotelduvin.com/edinburgh*

Howard

TOWNHOUSE • CLASSIC A series of three Georgian townhouses with many characterful original features still in situ; situated in the heart of the New Town. Bedrooms vary in size and have classic furnishings and a contemporary edge; every room is assigned a butler. Formal dining from modern menus in the elegant restaurant.

18 rooms – £ 120/450 £ 140/450 – 3 suites

Town plan: F1-s – *34 Great King St ✉ EH3 6QH – ☎ 0131 557 3500 – www.thehoward.com*

Chester Residence

TOWNHOUSE • CONTEMPORARY A series of peacefully located Georgian townhouses. The luxurious suites come with kitchens and state-of-the-art facilities including video entry and integrated sound systems; the Mews apartments are the best.

23 suites – £ 145/325 – £ 12

Town plan: E2-c – *9 Rothesay Pl ✉ EH3 7SL – ☎ 0131 226 2075 – www.chester-residence.com – Closed 23-26 December*

The Dunstane

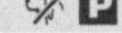

TOWNHOUSE • CONTEMPORARY An impressive house which used to be a training centre for the Royal Bank of Scotland. Guest areas retain original Victorian features and the smart bedrooms have designer touches; some are located across a busy road. Light snacks are served all day in the lounge.

35 rooms – £ 109/229 £ 129/259

Town plan: A3-s – *4 West Coates ✉ EH12 5JQ – ☎ 0131 337 6169 – www.thedunstane.co.uk*

Six Brunton Place

TOWNHOUSE • CONTEMPORARY This late Georgian townhouse – run by a charming owner – was once home to Frederick Ritchie, who designed the One O'Clock Gun and Time Ball. Inside you'll find flagged floors, columns, marble fireplaces and a cantilevered stone staircase; these contrast with contemporary furnishings and vibrant modern art.

4 rooms ☕ – 🚹£ 89 🚹🚹£ 139/199

Town plan: H1-u – *6 Brunton Pl ✉ EH7 5EG*
– ✆ 0131 622 0042 – www.sixbruntonplace.com
– Closed 7-29 December

94 DR

TOWNHOUSE • PERSONALISED Charming owners welcome you to this very stylish and individual hotel in a Victorian terraced house. Bedrooms are well-equipped, there's a retro lounge with an honesty bar and breakfast is served in the conservatory with its decked terrace.

6 rooms ☕ – 🚹£ 90/150 🚹🚹£ 100/225

Town plan: C3-n – *94 Dalkeith Rd ✉ EH16 5AF*
– ✆ 0131 662 9265 – www.94dr.com
– Closed 4-18 January and 25-26 December

23 Mayfield

TRADITIONAL • CLASSIC Lovingly restored Victorian house with a helpful owner, an outdoor hot tub and a rare book collection. Sumptuous bedrooms come with coordinated soft furnishings, mahogany features and luxurious bathrooms. Breakfast is extravagant.

7 rooms ☕ – 🚹£ 99/169 🚹🚹£ 125/199

Town plan: C3-x – *23 Mayfield Gdns ✉ EH9 2BX*
– ✆ 0131 667 5806 – www.23mayfield.co.uk

at Leith

Martin Wishart

MODERN CUISINE • ELEGANT XXX This elegant, modern restaurant is becoming something of an Edinburgh institution. Choose between three 6 course menus – Classic, Seafood and Vegetarian – and a concise à la carte. Top ingredients are used in well-judged, flavourful combinations; dishes are classically based but have elaborate, original touches.

→ Orkney scallops with white asparagus, peas, broad beans and sea rosemary. Squab pigeon with short rib, potato cannelloni, cauliflower and sage sauce. Yorkshire rhubarb with vanilla cream, ginger curd and sorrel granité.

Menu £ 32 (weekday lunch)/85

Town plan: C1-u – *54 The Shore ✉ EH6 6RA*
– ✆ 0131 553 3557 (booking essential) – www.martin-wishart.co.uk
– Closed 25 July-4 August, 25-26 December, 18-19 April, Sunday and Monday

Kitchin (Tom Kitchin)

MODERN CUISINE • DESIGN XX Set in a smart, converted whisky warehouse. 'From nature to plate' is the eponymous chef-owner's motto and the use of natural features like bark wall coverings, alongside the more traditional Harris tweed, reflect his passion for using the freshest and best quality Scottish ingredients. Refined, generously proportioned classic French dishes are packed with vivid flavours.

→ Shellfish cannelloni with crab, celeriac, orange and Newhaven green crab bisque. Peppered loin of Borders roe deer served with rhubarb, root vegetable mash and red wine sauce. Warm apple tart served with Airthrey Kerse Farm vanilla ice cream and caramel sauce.

Menu £ 33 (lunch) – Carte £ 70/87

Town plan: C1-z – *78 Commercial Quay ✉ EH6 6LX*
– ✆ 0131 555 1755 (booking essential) – www.thekitchin.com – Closed 23 December-13 January, 3-7 April, 31 July-4 August, 16-20 October, Sunday and Monday

Norn

MODERN CUISINE • FASHIONABLE XX A young couple run this likeable modern restaurant where the chefs serve their dishes themselves. Creative, intricate cooking showcases produce from small Scottish suppliers along with items they have foraged.

Menu £ 40/65 – tasting menu only

Town plan: C1-a – *50-54 Henderson St ✉ EH6 6DE – ✆ 0131 629 2525 (booking advisable) – www.nornrestaurant.com – dinner only – Closed 26 December-10 January, 17-21 October, Sunday and Monday*

Malmaison

BUSINESS • CONTEMPORARY An impressive former seamen's mission located on the quayside – the first of the Malmaison hotels. The décor is a mix of bold stripes and contrasting black and white themes. Bedrooms are well-equipped and one has a tartan roll-top bath! The restaurant serves grills and European fare.

100 rooms – †£ 95/245 ††£ 95/245 – ☕ £ 14

Town plan: C1-m – *1 Tower Pl ✉ EH6 7BZ – ✆ 0131 285 1478 – www.malmaison.com*

EDNAM – The Scottish Borders ➔ See Kelso

ELGOL – Highland ➔ See Skye (Isle of)

ERISKA (Isle of)

Argyll and Bute – ✉ Oban – Regional map n° **16**-B2

Isle of Eriska

COUNTRY HOUSE • CONTEMPORARY An impressive 19C baronial mansion set in an idyllic spot on a private island and boasting fantastic views over Lismore and the mountains. Open-fired guest areas have a modern country house feel and the spa and leisure facilities are superb. Bedrooms are stylish and well-equipped and some feature hot tubs. Cooking showcases ingredients from the kitchen garden.

23 rooms ☕ – †£ 280/410 ††£ 330/410 – 7 suites

Benderloch ✉ PA37 1SD – ✆ 01631 720371 – www.eriska-hotel.co.uk

EVANTON

Highland – Regional map n° **17**-C2

Kiltearn House

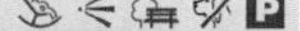

COUNTRY HOUSE • CONTEMPORARY This large sandstone former manse sits in a quiet spot, yet is only a few minutes from the A9. It has a classical sitting room and a conservatory breakfast room; bedrooms are more modern – two have views over Cromarty Firth.

5 rooms ☕ – †£ 60/96 ††£ 84/200

✉ IV16 9UY – South : 1 mi by B 817 on Kiltearn Burial Ground rd – ✆ 01349 830617 – www.kiltearn.co.uk – Closed 25 December

FIONNPHORT – Argyll and Bute ➔ See Mull (Isle of)

FLODIGARRY – Highland ➔ See Skye (Isle of)

FOCHABERS

Moray – Pop. 1 728 – Regional map n° **16**-C1

Trochelhill Country House

COUNTRY HOUSE • CLASSIC Whitewashed Victorian house; well-run by friendly owners who serve tea and cake on arrival. Spacious bedrooms feature modern bathrooms with walk-in showers; two have roll-top baths. Breakfast includes haggis, black pudding and homemade bread.

3 rooms – £ 70 £ 110

IV32 7LN – West : 2.75 mi by A 96 off B 9015
– 01343 821267 – www.trochelhill.co.uk

FORT AUGUSTUS

Highland – Pop. 621 – Regional map n° **17**-C3

Station Road

MODERN CUISINE • INTIMATE XX Light, spacious hotel dining room with views up the Great Glen and a formal feel. It's only open for dinner and offers a 5 course, no-choice set menu. Elaborate modern cooking features adventurous texture and flavour combinations.

Menu £ 55 – tasting menu only

The Lovat Hotel, PH32 4DU
– 01456 459250 (booking essential) – www.thelovat.com
– dinner only – Closed 3 January-6 February, Tuesday-Thursday November-Easter, Sunday and Monday

Brasserie

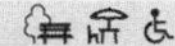

MODERN CUISINE • FRIENDLY X Modern brasserie at the side of a hotel, with a large lawned garden and picnic benches; it offers informal yet surprisingly sophisticated dining. Classically based dishes are given a modern makeover and feature good ingredients.

Carte £ 30/45

The Lovat Hotel, PH32 4DU
– 01456 459250 – www.thelovat.com
– Closed 3 January-6 February, Sunday, Monday and restricted opening in February and March

The Lovat

TRADITIONAL • PERSONALISED A professionally run Victorian house which has been given a bold, stylish makeover. Bedrooms are a mix of the classic – with feature beds and antique furnishings – and the contemporary, with vibrant colours and feature wallpapers.

28 rooms – £ 106/340 £ 119/350

PH32 4DU
– 01456 459250 – www.thelovat.com – Closed 3 January-6 February and restricted opening in February and March

Station Road • **Brasserie** – See restaurant listing

FORT WILLIAM

Highland – Pop. 5 883 – Regional map n° **17**-C3

Inverlochy Castle

MODERN CUISINE • LUXURY XXXX Set within a striking castle in the shadow of Ben Nevis and offering stunning loch views. Two candlelit dining rooms are filled with period sideboards and polished silver. The daily set menu showcases top quality Scottish produce.

Menu £ 67 – tasting menu only

Inverlochy Castle Hotel, Torlundy PH33 6SN – Northeast : 3 mi on A 82
– 01397 702177 (booking essential) – www.inverlochycastlehotel.com
– dinner only

Crannog

SEAFOOD • COSY Popular restaurant with a bright red roof and a colourful boat-like interior; set on the pier above Loch Linnhe – try to get a table by the window. Fresh local fish and shellfish are simply prepared. The 2 course lunch is good value.

Menu £ 19 (lunch) – Carte £ 29/42

Town Pier ✉ PH33 6DB – ✆ 01397 705589 (booking essential) – www.crannog.net – Closed 25-26 December and 1 January

Lime Tree An Ealdhain

MODERN CUISINE • RUSTIC Attractive 19C manse – now an informally run restaurant and art gallery, where the owner's pieces are displayed and two public exhibitions are held each year. Rustic dining room with exposed beams and an open kitchen; cooking is fresh and modern. Simply furnished bedrooms – ask for one with a view of Loch Linnhe.

Carte £ 28/34

9 rooms – †£ 70/135 ††£ 70/135

Achintore Rd ✉ PH33 6RQ – ✆ 01397 701806 – www.limetreefortwilliam.co.uk – dinner only – Closed November, last 3 weeks January and 24-28 December

Inverlochy Castle

GRAND LUXURY • CLASSIC Striking castellated house in beautiful grounds, boasting stunning views over the loch to Glenfinnan. The classical country house interior comprises sumptuous open-fired lounges and a grand hall with an impressive ceiling mural. Elegant bedrooms offer the height of luxury; mod cons include mirrored TVs.

18 rooms – †£ 335/465 ††£ 490/625 – 1 suite

Torlundy ✉ PH33 6SN – Northeast : 3 mi on A 82 – ✆ 01397 702177 – www.inverlochycastlehotel.com

Inverlochy Castle – See restaurant listing

Grange

TOWNHOUSE • PERSONALISED Delightful Victorian house with an attractive garden and immaculate interior, set in a quiet residential area. The beautiful lounge displays fine fabrics and the lovely breakfast room boasts Queen Anne style chairs. Bedrooms are extremely well appointed, with smart bathrooms.

3 rooms – †£ 180 ††£ 180/195

Grange Rd. ✉ PH33 6JF – South : 0.75 mi by A 82 and Ashburn Ln – ✆ 01397 705516 – www.grangefortwilliam.com – Closed November-mid March

FORTINGALL

Perth and Kinross – Regional map n° **16**-C2

Fortingall

TRADITIONAL • PERSONALISED Stylish Arts and Crafts house on a tranquil private estate, boasting lovely country views. The interior is delightful, with its snug open-fired bar and cosy sitting rooms filled with Scottish country knick-knacks. Bedrooms are modern but in keeping with the building's age. Dining is formal and classical.

10 rooms – †£ 130/150 ††£ 190/230

✉ PH15 2NQ – ✆ 01887 830367 – www.fortingall.com

GALSON

GALSON – Western Isles → See Lewis and Harris (Isle of)

GATEHEAD

East Ayrshire – ✉ East Ayrshire – Regional map n° **15**-B2

Cochrane Inn

TRADITIONAL CUISINE • PUB This ivy-covered pub is surprisingly bright and modern inside, with its copper lampshades, coal-effect gas fires and striking contemporary art. It offers a good range of tasty, generously priced dishes; the Express Menu is a steal.

Menu £ 13 (lunch and early dinner) – Carte £ 17/36

45 Main Rd ✉ KA2 0AP – ✆ 01563 570122 – www.costley-hotels.co.uk

GATTONSIDE – The Scottish Borders ➜ See Melrose

GIFFNOCK

East Renfrewshire – Pop. 12 156 – Regional map n° **15**-B1

Catch

FISH AND CHIPS • SIMPLE Modern fish and chip shop with exposed bricks and nautical styling; sit in a booth to take in the action from the open kitchen. Fresh, sustainably sourced fish comes in crisp batter and is accompanied by twice-cooked chips.

Carte £ 18/29

186 Fenwick Rd ✉ G46 6XF – ✆ 0141 638 9169 (bookings advisable at dinner) – www.catchfishandchips.co.uk – Closed 25 December and 1 January

GIGHA (Isle of)

Argyll and Bute – Regional map n° **16**-A3

The Boathouse

SEAFOOD • RUSTIC This 300 year old boathouse is set on a small community-owned island, overlooking the water. Whitewashed stone walls and beamed ceilings enhance the rustic feel. Menus cater for all, centring around fresh seafood and local meats.

Carte £ 23/44

Ardminish Bay ✉ PA41 7AA – ✆ 01583 505123 – www.boathouseongigha.com – Closed November-April

GOOD TIPS!

This former industrial powerhouse has been reborn as a cultural and commercial hub, with a lively dining scene to boot. History is all around: enjoy a stay in the stunning **Blythswood Square** hotel – once the RAC HQ. Modernity comes in the form of creative, cutting-edge restaurants like **Cail Bruich** and Bib Gourmand awarded neighbourhood restaurant, **The Gannet**.

GLASGOW

Glasgow City – Pop. 590 507 – Regional map n° **15**-B1

Restaurants

The Gannet

MODERN BRITISH • RUSTIC X This appealingly rustic restaurant makes passionate use of Scotland's larder and as such, its menus are constantly evolving. Classic dishes are presented in a modern style and are brought to the table by a charming team.

Menu £ 25 (lunch and early dinner) – Carte £ 29/46

Town plan: A2-t – *1155 Argyle St ✉ G3 8TB – ✆ 0141 204 2081 – www.thegannetgla.com – Closed 24-27 December, Sunday dinner, Monday and lunch Tuesday-Wednesday*

Ox and Finch

MODERN BRITISH • DESIGN X A bright, breezy team run this likeable rustic restaurant, with its tile-backed open kitchen and wines displayed in a huge metal cage. The international small plates tempt one and all: cooking centres around old favourites but with added modern twists – and the flavours really shine through.

Carte £ 18/27

Town plan: A2-c – *920 Sauchiehall St ✉ G3 7TF – ✆ 0141 339 8627 (bookings advisable at dinner) – www.oxandfinch.com – Closed 25-26 December and 1-2 January*

Brian Maule at Chardon d'Or

MODERN CUISINE • ELEGANT XXX Georgian townhouse in the city's heart, with original pillars, ornate carved ceilings and white walls hung with vibrant modern art. Generously proportioned, classical dishes have a modern edge and showcase luxurious ingredients.

Menu £ 22 (lunch and early dinner) – Carte £ 46/59

Town plan: C2-b – *176 West Regent St. ✉ G2 4RL – ✆ 0141 248 3801 – www.brianmaule.com – Closed 25 December, 1-2 January, Sunday, Monday and bank holidays*

Bilson Eleven

MODERN CUISINE • INTIMATE XX A bohemian restaurant situated in a small terrace in an eastern suburb; you dine in the house's original drawing room, where the décor blends the old and the new. Cooking is interesting and original with a playful edge.

Carte £ 31/41

10 Annfield Pl, Dennistoun ✉ G31 2XQ - East : 1.5 mi by George St and Duke St - ✆ 0141 554 6259 - www.bilsoneleven.co.uk - dinner only - Closed Christmas-early January, 1 week July, 1 week October, Monday and Tuesday

Blythswood Square

MODERN CUISINE • FASHIONABLE XX Stylish black and white hotel restaurant in the ballroom of the old RAC building, with a zinc-topped bar and Harris Tweed banquettes. Classic menus feature meats from the Josper grill; desserts showcase the kitchen's ambitious side.

Menu £ 25 (lunch and early dinner) - Carte £ 29/56

Town plan: C2-n - *Blythswood Square Hotel, 11 Blythswood Sq ✉ G2 4AD - ✆ 0141 248 8888 - www.blythswoodsquare.com*

Cail Bruich

MODERN CUISINE • INTIMATE XX Smart restaurant with red leather banquettes and low-hanging copper lamps. Menus include a market selection and tasting options; cooking is modern and creative, with BBQ dishes a speciality. Its name means 'to eat well'.

Menu £ 25 (lunch and early dinner) - Carte £ 40/50

Town plan: A1-a - *725 Great Western Rd. ✉ G12 8QX - ✆ 0141 334 6265 (booking advisable) - www.cailbruich.co.uk - Closed 25-26 December, 1-2 January and lunch Monday-Tuesday*

Gamba

SEAFOOD • BRASSERIE XX A cosy bar-lounge and contemporary dining room, tucked away in a basement but well-known by the locals. The appealing menu offers unfussy seafood dishes with the odd Asian influence; lemon sole is a speciality.

Menu £ 20 (lunch and early dinner) - Carte £ 33/60

Town plan: C2-x - *225a West George St. ✉ G2 2ND - ✆ 0141 572 0899 - www.gamba.co.uk - Closed 25-26 December and first week January*

La Parmigiana 

ITALIAN • NEIGHBOURHOOD XX Unashamedly classic in terms of its décor and its dishes, this well-regarded, professionally run Italian restaurant is approaching its 40th birthday. Red walls, white linen and efficient service. Refined cooking delivers bold flavours.

Menu £ 18 (lunch) - Carte £ 30/52

Town plan: B1-r - *447 Great Western Rd, Kelvinbridge ✉ G12 8HH - ✆ 0141 334 0686 (booking essential) - www.laparmigiana.co.uk - Closed 25-26 December, 1 January and Sunday dinner*

Two Fat Ladies in the City

TRADITIONAL CUISINE • CLASSIC DÉCOR XX Intimate restaurant resembling an old-fashioned brasserie, courtesy of its wooden floor, banquettes and mirrors. Dishes are straightforward, with a modern edge, and Scottish seafood is a feature.

Menu £ 16 (lunch and early dinner) - Carte £ 30/44

Town plan: C2-e - *118a Blythswood St ✉ G2 4EG - ✆ 0141 847 0088 - www.twofatladiesrestaurant.com*

Ubiquitous Chip 

MODERN CUISINE • BISTRO XX An iconic establishment on a cobbled street. The restaurant - with its ponds, fountains and greenery - offers modern classics which showcase local ingredients, while the mezzanine-level brasserie serves tasty Scottish favourites.

Menu £ 22 (lunch and early dinner) - Carte £ 33/64

Town plan: A1-n - *12 Ashton Ln ✉ G12 8SJ - ✆ 0141 334 5007 (bookings advisable at dinner) - www.ubiquitouschip.co.uk - Closed 25 December and 1 January*

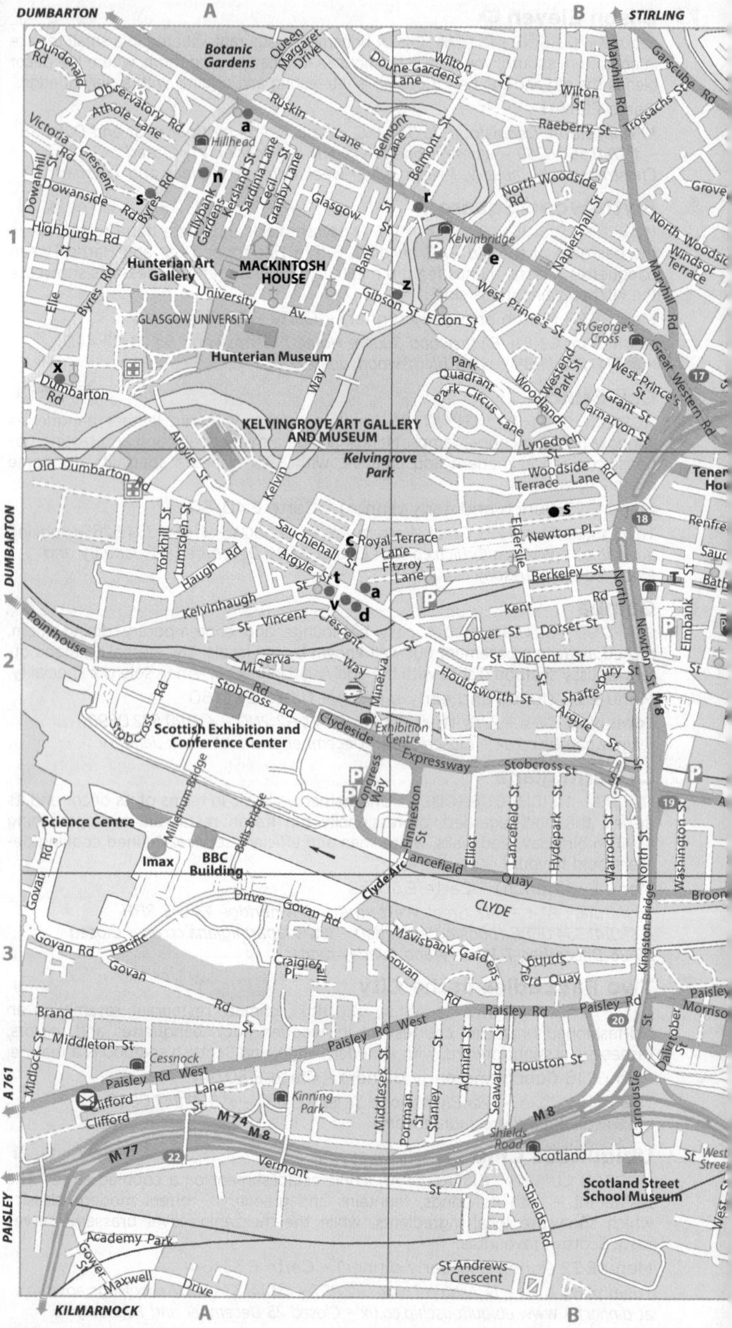

DUMBARTON A B STIRLING

Botanic Gardens
Queen Margaret Drive
Dundonald Rd
Observatory Rd
Athole Lane
Ruskin Lane
Hillhead
Doune Gardens Lane
Wilton St
Belmont Lane
Belmont St
Raeberry St
Maryhill Rd
Garscube Rd
Trossachs St
Victoria Crescent Rd
Dowanhill St
Dowanside Rd
Byres Rd
Lilybank Gardens
Kersland St
Sardinia Lane
Cecil St
Granby Lane
Glasgow St
Bank St
North Woodside Rd
Napiershall St
Grove St
North Woodside Rd
Windsor Terrace
Highburgh Rd
Hunterian Art Gallery
MACKINTOSH HOUSE
Kelvinbridge
Gibson St
Eldon St
West Prince's St
St George's Cross
University Av.
GLASGOW UNIVERSITY
Hunterian Museum
Kelvin Way
Elie St
Dumbarton Rd
Park Quadrant
Park Circus Lane
Woodlands
Westend Park St
West Prince's St
Grant St
Carnarvon St
Great Western Rd
KELVINGROVE ART GALLERY AND MUSEUM
Kelvingrove Park
Lynedoch St
Woodside Terrace Lane
Woodside Rd
Old Dumbarton Rd
Argyle St
Yorkhill St
Lumsden St
Haugh Rd
Sauchiehall St
Royal Terrace Lane
Fitzroy Lane
Eldersile St
Newton Pl.
Berkeley St
Kent Rd
Dorset St
Dover St
North St
Newton St
Elmbank St
Bath St
Renfrew St
Sauchiehall St
Kelvinhaugh St
Vincent Crescent
St Vincent St
Pointhouse Rd
Minerva St
Minerva Way
Houldsworth St
Shaftesbury St
Stobcross Rd
Scottish Exhibition and Conference Center
Clydeside Expressway
Exhibition Centre
Stobcross St
Congress Way
Finnieston St
Lancefield St
Hydepark St
Warroch St
Washington St
Millennium Bridge
Bells Bridge
Science Centre
Imax
BBC Building
Elliot St
Lancefield Quay
Clyde Arc
Govan Rd
Pacific Drive
CLYDE
Kingston Bridge
Broomielaw
Mavisbank Gardens
Spring field Quay
Craigiehall Pl.
Govan Rd
Brand St
Paisley Rd West
Paisley Rd
Morrison St
Dalintober St
Middleton St
Midlock St
Cessnock
Houston St
Admiral St
Seaward St
Middlesex St
Portman St
Stanley St
Carnoustie St
Clifford Lane
Clifford St
Kinning Park
M 74
M 8
M 77
Shields Road
Scotland St
West Street
Vermont St
Shields Rd
Scotland Street School Museum
Academy Park
Gower St
Maxwell Drive
St Andrews Crescent
A761
PAISLEY
DUMBARTON

KILMARNOCK A B

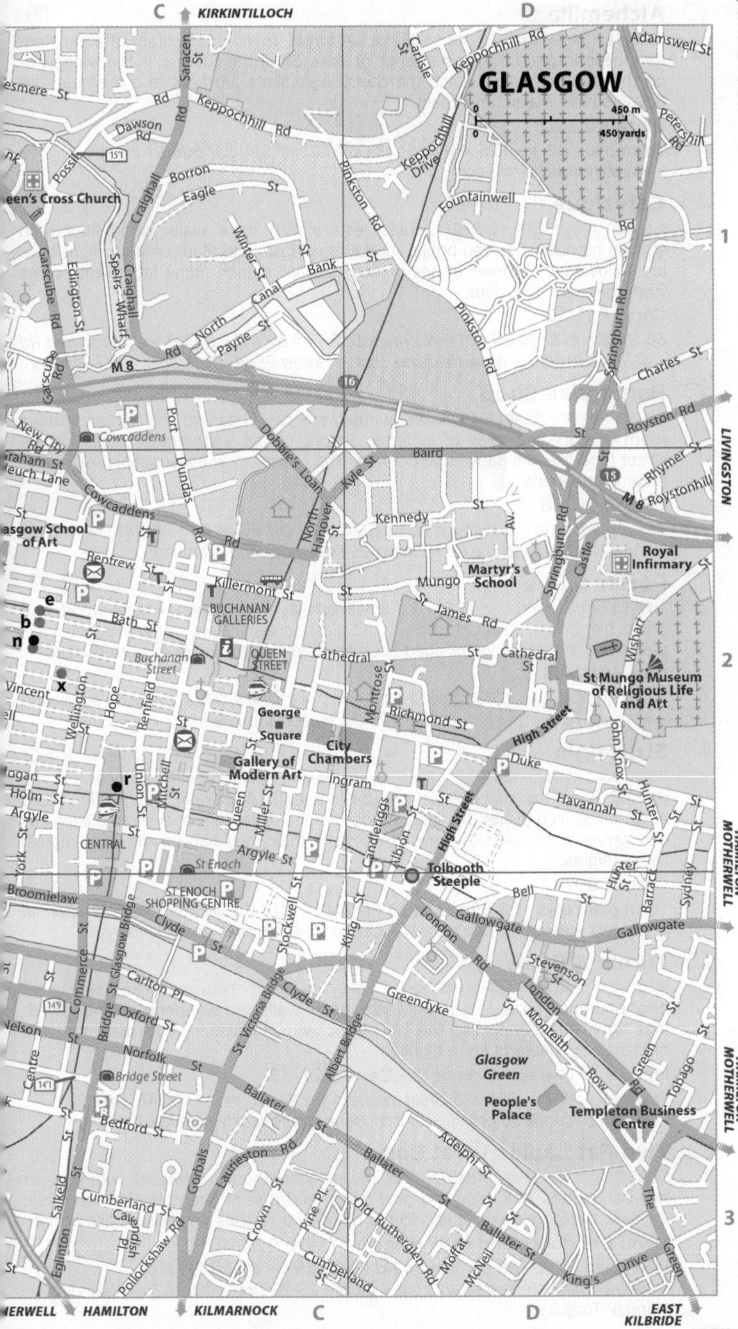
GLASGOW
0
450 m
0
450 yards
C
D
1
2
3
KIRKINTILLOCH
LIVINGSTON
HAMILTON MOTHERWELL
HAMILTON MOTHERWELL
EAST KILBRIDE
HAMILTON
KILMARNOCK
MOTHERWELL
M 8
M 8
Saracen St
Keppochhill Rd
Adamswell St
Petershill Rd
Carlisle St
Dawson Rd
Possil Rd
Borron St
Eagle St
een's Cross Church
Craighall Rd
Speirs Wharf
Garscube Rd
Edington St
Winter St
North Canal Bank St
Payne St
Pinkston Rd
Keppochhill Drive
Fountainwell Rd
Springburn Rd
Charles St
Royston Rd
Rhymer St
Roystonhill
Cowcaddens
New City Rd
Graham St
Buccleuch Lane
Cowcaddens Rd
Port Dundas Rd
Dobbie's Loan
Baird St
Kyle St
North Hanover St
Kennedy St
Glasgow School of Art
Renfrew St
Killermont St
BUCHANAN GALLERIES
Martyr's School
Royal Infirmary
Castle St
Mungo St
James Rd
Bath St
Buchanan Street
QUEEN STREET
Cathedral St
Cathedral St
Wishart St
St Mungo Museum of Religious Life and Art
Vincent St
Wellington St
Hope St
Renfield St
George Square
Montrose St
Richmond St
City Chambers
High Street
Gallery of Modern Art
Duke St
John Knox St
Ingram St
Hogan St
Holm St
Argyle St
Union St
Mitchell St
Queen St
Miller St
Candleriggs
Albion St
High Street
Havannah St
Hunter St
CENTRAL
Argyle St
York St
St Enoch
Tolbooth Steeple
Hunter St
Barrack St
Sydney St
Broomielaw
ST ENOCH SHOPPING CENTRE
Stockwell St
King St
Bell St
Gallowgate
Gallowgate
Clyde St
London Rd
Stevenson St
Carlton Pl.
Commerce St
Glasgow Bridge St
Bridge St
Clyde St
Greendyke St
London Rd
Oxford St
Nelson St
Victoria Bridge
Albert Bridge
Monteith Row
Norfolk St
Centre St
Bridge Street
Glasgow Green
People's Palace
Templeton Business Centre
Green Rd
Tobago St
Ballater St
Bedford St
Adelphi St
Laurieston Rd
Gorbals St
Ballater St
Cumberland St
Cavendish Pl.
Crown St
Pine Pl.
Old Rutherglen Rd
Moffat St
McNeil St
Ballater St
King's Drive
The Green
Salkeld St
Eglinton St
Pollokshaw Rd
Cumberland St
e
b
n
x
r
15
16
151
149
141

Alchemilla

MEDITERRANEAN CUISINE • SIMPLE A sweet, friendly restaurant offering Mediterranean-inspired dishes in a range of sizes. Sit at the counter, in the window or on the mezzanine and watch the chefs. Ingredients are kept to a minimum but flavours have maximum impact.

Carte £ 20/32

Town plan: A2-a - *1126 Argyle St ✉ G3 8TD - ✆ 0141 337 6060 - www.thisisalchemilla.com*

Cafezique

MODERN CUISINE • BISTRO Buzzy eatery with stone walls, wood floors and striking monotone screen prints. All-day breakfasts and Mediterranean light bites are followed by vibrant dishes in two sizes at dinner. Many ingredients come from their deli next door.

Carte £ 21/30

66 Hyndland St ✉ G11 5PT - Northwest : 2.5 mi by A 82, B 808 and Highburgh Rd - ✆ 0141 339 7180 - www.delizique.com - Closed 25-26 December and 1 January

Hanoi Bike Shop

VIETNAMESE • SIMPLE Relaxed Vietnamese café; head to the lighter upstairs room with its fine array of lanterns. Simple, classic Vietnamese dishes include street food like rice paper summer rolls. The charming, knowledgeable team offer recommendations.

Carte £ 20/28

Town plan: A1-s - *8 Ruthven Ln ✉ G12 9BG - Off Byres Rd - ✆ 0141 334 7165 - www.hanoibikeshop.co.uk - Closed 25 December and 1 January*

Porter & Rye

MEATS AND GRILLS • TRENDY Small loft-style operation where wood and bricks blend with steel balustrades and glass screens. Menus offer creative small plates and a good range of aged Scottish steaks, from onglet to porterhouse.

Carte £ 22/55

Town plan: A2-v - *1131 Argyle St ✉ G3 8ND - ✆ 0141 572 1212 (booking advisable) - www.porterandrye.com - Closed 25 December and 1 January*

Stravaigin

INTERNATIONAL • SIMPLE Their motto here is 'think global, eat local'. On the ground floor, the shabby-chic café-bar serves international and subtly spiced Asian-influenced dishes; the intimate downstairs restaurant opens in the evenings and serves more classical fare. They make their own haggis and host regular theme nights.

Carte £ 20/47

Town plan: B1-z - *28 Gibson St. ✉ G12 8NX - ✆ 0141 334 2665 (booking essential at dinner) - www.stravaigin.co.uk - Closed 25 December and 1 January*

Turnip & Enjoy

MODERN BRITISH • NEIGHBOURHOOD You can't help but like this sweet neighbourhood restaurant with its sage green walls and wonderful ceiling mouldings. Service is friendly and the food rustic, with classical flavours presented in a modern way; desserts are a highlight.

Menu £ 19 (weekday dinner) - Carte £ 27/36

Town plan: B1-e - *393-395 Great Western Rd ✉ G4 9HY - ✆ 0141 334 6622 - www.turnipandenjoy.co.uk - Closed Monday and lunch Tuesday-Thursday*

Two Fat Ladies West End

SEAFOOD • NEIGHBOURHOOD Quirky neighbourhood restaurant with red velour banquettes, bold blue and gold décor, and a semi open plan kitchen in the window. Cooking is simple and to the point, and focuses on classical fish dishes.

Menu £ 16 (lunch and early dinner) - Carte £ 27/40

Town plan: A1-x - *88 Dumbarton Rd ✉ G11 6NX - ✆ 0141 339 1944 - www.twofatladiesrestaurant.com - Closed 25-26 December, 1-2 January and Monday-Tuesday*

The Finnieston

SEAFOOD • FRIENDLY Small, cosy pub specialising in Scottish seafood and gin cocktails; with an intriguing ceiling, a welcoming fire and lots of booths. Dishes are light, tasty and neatly presented, relying on just a few ingredients so that flavours are clear.

Carte £ 20/38

Town plan: A2-d - *1125 Argyle St ✉ G3 8ND - ✆ 0141 222 2884 - www.thefinniestonbar.com - Closed 25-26 December and 1 January*

Hotels

Blythswood Square

HISTORIC • DESIGN Stunning property on a delightful Georgian square. Modern décor contrasts with original fittings; bedrooms are dark and moody and the Penthouse Suite features a bed adapted from a snooker table. Afternoon tea is a hit.

100 rooms - £ 150/289 £ 150/289 - 1 suite

Town plan: C2-n - *11 Blythswood Sq ✉ G2 4AD - ✆ 0141 248 8888 - www.blythswoodsquare.com*

Blythswood Square - See restaurant listing

Hotel du Vin at One Devonshire Gardens

TOWNHOUSE • ELEGANT A collection of adjoining townhouses boasting original 19C stained glass, wood panelling and a labyrinth of corridors. It's furnished in dark, opulent shades but has a contemporary country house air. Dine on modern dishes in the elegant oak-panelled restaurant; they also offer wine tastings in the cellar.

49 rooms - £ 109/234 £ 109/234 - £ 18 - 3 suites

1 Devonshire Gdns ✉ G12 0UX - Northwest : 2.5 mi by A 82 (Great Western Rd) - ✆ 0141 378 0385 - www.hotelduvin.com

Dakota Deluxe

BUSINESS • CONTEMPORARY With its black brick façade and box hedges, this boutique hotel wouldn't look out of place in NYC. Sleek, spacious bedrooms have good comforts and the professional staff make it feel like a home-from-home. On the first floor there's a champagne bar; in the basement, classics and grills are brought up-to-date.

83 rooms - £ 135/200 £ 145/210 - 1 suite

Town plan: B2-h - *179 West Regent St ✉ G2 4DP - ✆ 0141 404 3680 - www.glasgow.dakotahotels.co.uk*

Malmaison

BUSINESS • CONTEMPORARY An impressive-looking former Greek Orthodox Church, with moody, masculine décor. Stylish, boldly coloured bedrooms offer good facilities; the best are the brighter duplex suites. The lively glass-roofed basement bar specialises in craft beers and the vaulted brasserie offers a wide-ranging global menu.

72 rooms - £ 90/190 £ 100/200 - £ 15 - 8 suites

Town plan: C2-c - *278 West George St ✉ G2 4LL - ✆ 0141 572 1000 - www.malmaison.com*

Grasshoppers

BUSINESS • DESIGN Located on the 6th floor of the Victorian railway station; its lounge overlooks the largest glass roof in Europe. Stylish, well-designed bedrooms have bespoke Scandinavian-style furnishings, Scottish art and smart, compact shower rooms. Three course suppers are served Mon-Thurs (residents only).

29 rooms - £ 75/105 £ 85/125

Town plan: C2-r - *Caledonian Chambers (6th Floor), 87 Union St ✉ G1 3TA - ✆ 0141 222 2666 - www.grasshoppersglasgow.com - Closed 3 days Christmas*

15 Glasgow

TOWNHOUSE • PERSONALISED Delightful Victorian townhouse on a quiet square. Characterful original features include mosaic floors and ornate cornicing. Spacious bedrooms have top-class furnishings and a subtle Scottish theme. Breakfast is served in your room.

5 rooms – £ 100/160 £ 120/220

Town plan: B2-s – *15 Woodside Pl. ✉ G3 7QL – ✆ 0141 332 1263 – www.15glasgow.com*

GRANDTULLY

Perth and Kinross – Pop. 750 – Regional map n° **16**-C2

Inn on the Tay

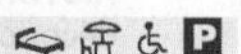

TRADITIONAL CUISINE • FRIENDLY A smart, modern inn on the banks of the Tay. It has a snug bar and a large dining room with superb views over the water. Burgers and gourmet sandwiches fill the lunch menu, while in the evening, satisfying tried-and-tested classics feature. The owners are cheery and welcoming and the bedrooms, comfy and cosy.

Carte £ 20/38

6 rooms – £ 65/70 £ 100/110

✉ PH9 0PL – ✆ 01887 840760 – www.theinnonthetay.co.uk – Closed 25-26 December

GRANTOWN-ON-SPEY

Highland – Pop. 2 428 – Regional map n° **17**-D2

Dulaig

TRADITIONAL • CLASSIC Small, detached, personally run guesthouse, built in 1910 and tastefully furnished with original Arts and Crafts pieces. Modern fabrics and an uncluttered feel in the comfortable bedrooms. Tea and homemade cake on arrival. Communal breakfasts include home-baked bread and muffins.

3 rooms – £ 125/150 £ 165/190

Seafield Av ✉ PH26 3JF – ✆ 01479 872065 – www.thedulaig.com – Closed 18 December-8 January

GULLANE

East Lothian – Pop. 2 568 – Regional map n° **15**-C1

Chez Roux

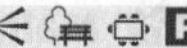

FRENCH • INTIMATE XX Formal restaurant in a classic country house hotel; enjoy an aperitif in the lounge or delightful Jekyll-designed gardens before dining with a view over the Muirfield golf course. Classical French menus have a Roux signature style and feature tried-and-tested classics with a modern edge.

Menu £ 37 (dinner) – Carte £ 29/55

Greywalls Hotel, Duncur Rd, Muirfield ✉ EH31 2EG – Northeast : 0.75 mi by A 198 – ✆ 01620 842144 (bookings essential for non-residents) – www.greywalls.co.uk

La Potinière

TRADITIONAL CUISINE • COSY XX Sweet little restaurant where the two owners share the cooking. The regularly changing menu lists two carefully prepared dishes per course; produce is local or home-grown and their homemade bread is renowned.

Menu £ 22/45

Main St ✉ EH31 2AA – ✆ 01620 843214 (booking essential) – www.lapotiniere.co.uk – Closed January, 24-26 December, Sunday dinner, Monday, Tuesday and bank holidays

Greywalls

COUNTRY HOUSE • CLASSIC A long-standing Edwardian country house by Lutyens, in a superb location beside the Muirfield golf course, overlooking the Firth of Forth. Compact bedrooms are furnished with antiques and the library is particularly cosy. The stunning formal gardens were designed by Jekyll.

23 rooms – £ 94/138 £ 270/407

Duncur Rd, Muirfield ✉ EH31 2EG – Northeast : 0.75 mi by A 198 – ✆ 01620 842144 – www.greywalls.co.uk

Chez Roux – See restaurant listing

HADDINGTON

East Lothian – Pop. 9 064 – Regional map n° **15**-D1

Letham House

COUNTRY HOUSE • CLASSIC A classically proportioned former laird's house dating from 1645. It's been lovingly restored by its current owners in a style which enhances its original features. Luxurious bedrooms have antique furnishings, beautiful fabrics and well-equipped modern bathrooms. Dine communally around a large table: 3 courses of seasonal local produce are tailored to requirements.

5 rooms – £ 100/125 £ 140/205

✉ EH41 3SS – West : 1.25 mi on B 6471 – ✆ 01620 820055 – www.lethamhouse.com

HARRIS

– Highland ➔ See Lewis and Harris (Isle of)

HELENSBURGH

Argyll and Bute – Pop. 14 220 – Regional map n° **16**-B3

Sugar Boat (N)

MODERN BRITISH • BISTRO An appealing, modern all-day bistro. To the front is a café-style area with a marble-topped island bar; behind is the main dining room and an enclosed courtyard. Simple, rustic dishes keep Scottish produce to the fore.

Carte £ 21/31

30 Colquhoun Sq ✉ G84 8AQ – ✆ 01436 647522 – www.sugarboat.co.uk – Closed 25 December

HIGH BLANTYRE

South Lanarkshire – Regional map n° **15**-B1

Crossbasket Castle

HISTORIC BUILDING • PERSONALISED With its 15C origins and sumptuous furnishings, this beautiful castle is a popular spot for weddings. There are elegant drawing rooms, a baronial-style library and an ornately decorated dining room. Bedrooms vary in size and are named after former custodians; the Tower Suite is set over numerous floors.

9 rooms – £ 253 £ 352 – 2 suites

Stoneymeadow Rd ✉ G72 9UE – Southwest : 1 mi by B 7012 – ✆ 01698 829461 – www.crossbasketcastle.com

INNERLEITHEN

The Scottish Borders – Pop. 3 031 – Regional map n° **15**-C2

Caddon View

TOWNHOUSE • PERSONALISED Substantial Victorian house with a large garden and cosy lounge; run by a hospitable couple. Individually decorated bedrooms have modern touches – 'Yarrow' is the most spacious and 'Moorfoot' has the best views. The bright, airy dining room offers a daily set menu of Tweed Valley produce.

8 rooms – £ 50/60 £ 70/120

14 Pirn Rd. ✉ EH44 6HH – ✆ 01896 830208 – www.caddonview.co.uk – Closed 25-26 December

INVERGARRY

Highland – ✉ Inverness – Regional map n° **17**-C3

Glengarry Castle

COUNTRY HOUSE • HISTORIC Family-run Victorian house built in a baronial style and named after the ruined castle in its 60 acre grounds. Two large, open-fired sitting rooms are filled with stuffed wild animals. Classical bedrooms are individually designed; some come with four-poster beds. Dine formally, from a 4 course Scottish menu.

26 rooms – †£ 90/100 ††£ 130/240

✉ PH35 4HW – South : 0.75 mi on A 82 – ✆ 01809 501254 – www.glengarry.net – Closed 5 November-23 March

INVERKEILOR

Angus – ✉ Arbroath – Pop. 902 – Regional map n° **16**-D2

Gordon's

MODERN CUISINE • INTIMATE XX A long-standing, passionately run restaurant with stone walls, open fires and exposed beams. The son works in the kitchen and his mother oversees the service. The concise menu lists carefully prepared classics which use local seasonal produce. Bedrooms are smart, modern and well-kept.

Menu £ 35/65

5 rooms – †£ 110/160 ††£ 110/160

32 Main St ✉ DD11 5RN – ✆ 01241 830364 (booking essential) – www.gordonsrestaurant.co.uk – dinner only and Sunday lunch – Closed January and Monday

INVERNESS

Highland – Pop. 48 201 – Regional map n° **17**-C2

Chez Roux

FRENCH • MINIMALIST XX Smart modern restaurant consisting of three rooms; their walls hung with photos of the Roux brothers' early days. Polished tables are well-spaced and service is professional. The French-inspired menu offers robust, flavoursome dishes.

Menu £ 33/35 – Carte £ 35/55

Town plan: B2-r – *Rocpool Reserve Hotel, 14 Culduthel Rd ✉ IV2 4AG – ✆ 01463 240089 – www.rocpool.com*

Rocpool

MODERN BRITISH • FRIENDLY XX Well-run restaurant on the banks of the River Ness; close to town and popular with the locals. Wide-ranging menus offer vibrant, colourful dishes that are full of flavour and have a distinct Mediterranean edge. The room has a modish feel.

Menu £ 17 (weekday lunch) – Carte £ 26/46

Town plan: A2-b – *1 Ness Walk ✉ IV3 5NE – ✆ 01463 717274 – www.rocpoolrestaurant.com – Closed 25-26 December, 1-3 January and Sunday*

Café 1

MODERN BRITISH • BISTRO X A bustling bistro opposite the castle, with a small bar and two modern dining rooms. There's a good value set lunch and a more elaborate à la carte with an Asian and Mediterranean edge. Pork, beef and lamb come from their own croft.

Menu £ 13 (lunch and early dinner) – Carte £ 25/47

Town plan: B2-e – *Castle St ✉ IV2 3EA – ✆ 01463 226200 – www.cafe1.net – Closed 25-26 December, 1-2 January and Sunday*

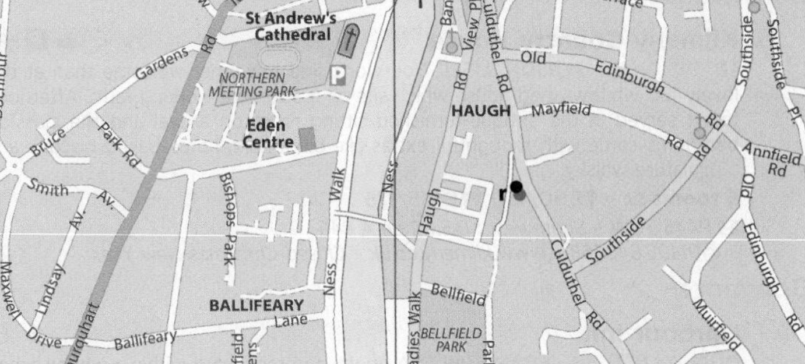

Rocpool Reserve

BUSINESS · DESIGN Stylish boutique hotel with a chic lounge and a sexy split-level bar. Minimalist bedrooms come with emperor-sized beds and are graded 'Hip', 'Chic', 'Decadent' and 'Extra Decadent'; some have terraces, hot tubs or saunas.

11 rooms ☕ – 🚹£ 176/225 🚹🚹£ 215/455

Town plan: B2-r – *14 Culduthel Rd* ✉ *IV2 4AG*
– ✆ *01463 240089* – *www.rocpool.com*

🍴 **Chez Roux** – See restaurant listing

Our selection of restaurants and hotels changes every year, so change your MICHELIN Guide every year!

SCOTLAND

Trafford Bank

HISTORIC · PERSONALISED 19C house with a modern, bohemian style. Original features include a tiled entrance and cast iron banister. Bedrooms come with iPod docks and decanters of sherry. Breakfast arrives on local china and includes haggis and tattie scones.

5 rooms – £ 100/120 £ 100/150

96 Fairfield Rd ✉ IV3 5LL – West : 0.75 mi by A 82 and Harrowden Rd – ✆ 01463 241414 – www.traffordbankguesthouse.co.uk – Closed December and January

at Bunchrew West: 3 mi on A862 ✉ Inverness

Bunchrew House

HISTORIC · CLASSIC Impressive 17C Scottish mansion, in a beautiful spot on the shore of Beauly Firth. Clubby, cosy, open-fired bar and intimate, wood-panelled drawing room. Good-sized, traditionally styled bedrooms; one with a four-poster, another with estuary views. Classical restaurant, with a menu to match and garden views.

16 rooms – £ 176/311 £ 176/311

✉ IV3 8TA
– ✆ 01463 234917 – www.bunchrewhousehotel.com

ISLAY (Isle of)

Argyll and Bute – Regional map n° **16**-A3

Ballygrant

Kilmeny Country House

TRADITIONAL · PERSONALISED You won't find a warmer welcome than at this lovely 18C whitewashed house which sits on a 300 acre working farm. Afternoon tea is served in the antique-furnished sitting room on arrival and the classical bedrooms come with thoughtful extras like binoculars, home-baked biscuits and a miniature whisky.

5 rooms – £ 90/130 £ 135/175

✉ PA45 7QW – Southwest : 0.5 mi on A 846
– ✆ 01496 840668 – www.kilmeny.co.uk – Closed Christmas-New Year

Bowmore

Harbour Inn

MODERN BRITISH · BRASSERIE XX A bright, airy restaurant within a whitewashed inn; ask for a window table for impressive loch views. Lunch offers traditional dishes, while dinner has a more modern edge. Whisky fans should try the tasting menu and whisky flight.

Menu £ 40 (dinner) – Carte £ 22/54

Harbour Inn Hotel, The Square ✉ PA43 7JR
– ✆ 01496 810330 (booking essential) – www.harbour-inn.com – Closed 15 November-15 February

Harbour Inn

INN · COSY The owners of this pretty inn also run the neighbouring distillery. Stylish bedrooms blend the classic and the contemporary, with wood panelling, tartan throws and Islay slate bathrooms. The bar and lounge are full of character.

7 rooms – £ 115 £ 145/175

The Square ✉ PA43 7JR
– ✆ 01496 810330 – www.harbour-inn.com – Closed 15 November-15 February

Harbour Inn – See restaurant listing

Bruichladdich

Regional map n° **27**-A3

Kentraw Farmhouse

FAMILY · CONTEMPORARY An 18C former croft with panoramic loch views; the owner was a local gamekeeper for many years and now runs tours around the island. Spacious bedrooms feature solid oak furnishings – ask for one at the front to wake up to the view.

4 rooms – £ 75/100 £ 100/140

PA49 7UN – North : 1 mi on A 847
– 01496 850643 – www.kentraw.com

Port Charlotte

Port Charlotte

TRADITIONAL · PERSONALISED Waterside hotel packed full of modern art. Large lounge with a wood burning stove and a cosy bar hung with old island photos. Bedrooms display traditional furniture and modern colour schemes; most have a sea view. Good mix of meat and fish dishes in the restaurant.

10 rooms – £ 130/175 £ 185/240

Main St PA48 7TU
– 01496 850360 – www.portcharlottehotel.co.uk – Closed 24-26 December

Port Ellen

Glenegedale House

TRADITIONAL · PERSONALISED This passionately run former factor's house is handy for the airport. It has a boldly decorated lounge, a sunny morning room and stylish bedrooms with funky feature walls. Breakfast is an event – try the porridge with Laphroaig whisky!

4 rooms – £ 90/120 £ 120/160

PA42 7AS – Northwest : 4.75 mi on A 846
– 01496 300400 – www.glenegedalehouse.co.uk – Closed Christmas-New Year

JEDBURGH

The Scottish Borders – Pop. 4 030 – Regional map n° **15**-D2

Willow Court

FAMILY · PERSONALISED Contemporary guesthouse overlooking the rooftops. Comfortable ground floor bedrooms offer a light, stylish space and smart bathrooms. Communal breakfasts feature eggs from their hens. Relax in the conservatory or out on the patio.

3 rooms – £ 75/80 £ 80/90

The Friars TD8 6BN
– 01835 863702 – www.willowcourtjedburgh.co.uk

JURA (Isle of)

Argyll and Bute – Regional map n° **16**-A3

Craighouse

Regional map n° **16**-A3

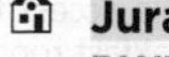

Jura

FAMILY · CLASSIC An 18C drover's cottage on an unspoilt island, which sits in a beautiful spot beside the distillery, looking out over the bay. Bedrooms are simply furnished and those to the front have the view. Menus are traditional (go for the local lobster or langoustines) – and keep an eye out for the murals in the bar.

17 rooms – £ 65/105 £ 100/130

PA60 7XU
– 01496 820243 – www.jurahotel.co.uk – Closed 1 week Christmas

KELSO

The Scottish Borders – Pop. 5 639 – Regional map n° **15**-D2

 Roxburghe

HISTORIC • ELEGANT Characterful Jacobean-style mansion set in extensive parkland and boasting a fly fishing school and a golf course. Plush guest areas display antiques and heirlooms. The 'Feature' bedrooms are luxurious, while those in the courtyard are more modern. Chez Roux offers French-inspired menus.

22 rooms – †£ 222/247 ††£ 222/247 – 2 suites

Heiton ✉ TD5 8JZ – Southwest : 3.5 mi by A 698 – ✆ 01573 450331 – www.roxburghe-hotel.com

at Ednam North: 2.25 mi on B6461✉ Kelso

 Edenwater House

HISTORIC • CLASSIC This delightful house is run by an equally charming couple. Relax in the lovely garden beside the stream or in one of the antique-filled lounges. Bedrooms are individually styled and tastefully furnished. Dine on traditional dishes overlooking the garden or more informally in the wine cellar.

4 rooms – †£ 80 ††£ 98/120

✉ TD5 7QL – Off Stichill rd – ✆ 01573 224070 – www.edenwaterhouse.co.uk – Closed 1 December-12 March

KILBERRY – Argyll and Bute ➜ See Kintyre (Peninsula)

KILCHRENAN

Argyll and Bute – ✉ Taynuilt – Regional map n° **16**-B2

Ardanaiseig

MODERN BRITISH • ELEGANT XX Take time to admire the lovely loch view from the wood-panelled drawing room of this romantic country house before dining in the traditional restaurant. Confidently prepared dishes are classically based with a modern Scottish twist.

Menu £ 50

Ardanaiseig Hotel, ✉ PA35 1HE – Northeast : 4 mi – ✆ 01866 833333 (booking essential) – www.ardanaiseig.com – dinner only – Restricted opening in winter

 Ardanaiseig

COUNTRY HOUSE • PERSONALISED Follow a 4 mile track through azalea-filled grounds and you'll end up at this romantic country house with stunning loch and mountain views. The impressive lounge features Corinthian pillars and the bedrooms are packed with antiques.

19 rooms – †£ 150/220 ††£ 218/298 – 1 suite

✉ PA35 1HE – Northeast : 4 mi – ✆ 01866 833333 – www.ardanaiseig.com – Restricted opening in winter

Ardanaiseig – See restaurant listing

 Roineabhal

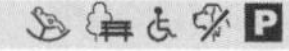

COUNTRY HOUSE • COSY This charming stone and log house was built by the owners themselves. Relax in the open-fired lounge or lovely riverside garden. Bedrooms are immaculate – two are up a spiral staircase and all have access to a roll-top bath with views. Local produce is served in the homely breakfast room. (Min. 2 night stay.)

3 rooms – †£ 85 ††£ 120

✉ PA35 1HD – ✆ 01866 833207 – www.roineabhal.com – Closed November-Easter

KILDRUMMY

Aberdeenshire – Regional map n° **16**-D1

Kildrummy Inn

MODERN BRITISH · COSY Cosy up beside the fire and sample some local whiskies before enjoying dinner in the intimate dining room or bright conservatory. Dishes are original and creative and the sourcing of ingredients is given top priority. Bedrooms have country views and are popular with fishermen, as the inn has a private beat.

Menu £ 35

4 rooms – £ 89/99 £ 89/99

AB33 8QS – Northeast : 0.5 mi on A 97 – 01975 571227 (booking essential) – www.kildrummyinn.co.uk – dinner only and Sunday lunch – Closed January and Tuesday

KILLIECRANKIE – Perth and Kinross ➜ See Pitlochry

KINGUSSIE

Highland – Pop. 1 476 – Regional map n° **17**-C3

Cross at Kingussie

MODERN BRITISH · RUSTIC 19C tweed mill in four acres of wooded grounds. Enjoy drinks on the terrace or in the first floor lounge then head to the dining room with its low beams, antiques and ornaments. Attractively presented cooking is modern British/Scottish. Pleasant, pine-furnished bedrooms have thoughtful extras.

Menu £ 30/55

8 rooms – £ 80/200 £ 100/200

Tweed Mill Brae, Ardbroilach Rd PH21 1LB – 01540 661166 (booking essential at lunch) – www.thecross.co.uk – Closed January and Christmas

KINTILLO – Perth and Kinross ➜ See Perth

KINTYRE (Peninsula)

Argyll and Bute – Regional map n° **16**-B3

Kilberry

Kilberry Inn

REGIONAL CUISINE · INN Remotely set former croft house whose striking red roof stands out against whitewashed walls. Inside you'll find wooden beams, stone walls, open fires and a mix of bare and linen-laid tables. Classic dishes are crafted from carefully sourced local produce and meat and fish are smoked in-house. Modern bedrooms are named after nearby islands; one has an outdoor hot tub.

Carte £ 23/39

5 rooms (dinner included) – £ 140 £ 230

PA29 6YD – 01880 770223 (booking essential at dinner) – www.kilberryinn.com – dinner only and lunch Friday-Sunday – Closed January-mid March, Christmas and Monday

KIRKBEAN

Dumfries and Galloway – Regional map n° **15**-C3

Cavens

COUNTRY HOUSE · PERSONALISED Attractive 18C country house in 20 acres of mature grounds. Relax in the cosy, book-filled Green Room or the elegant drawing room with its grand piano. Luxurious 'Estate' bedrooms boast views over the Solway Firth, while the comfy 'Country' rooms have a simpler style. The linen-clad dining room offers an unfussy daily menu of local produce; complimentary afternoon tea.

7 rooms (dinner included) – £ 150/200 £ 180/270

DG2 8AA – 01387 880234 – www.cavens.com – Closed January-February

KIRKCUDBRIGHT

Dumfries and Galloway – Pop. 3 352 – Regional map n° **15**-B3

Selkirk Arms

TRADITIONAL • PERSONALISED This well-run 18C inn sits in a pretty harbour town and is where Robert Burns wrote the Selkirk Grace in 1794 (in what is now Room 9). Comfy bedrooms have boldly coloured fabrics and throws; some are located in the courtyard. The busy bar is hung with paintings of local scenes and menus are extensive.

16 rooms – £ 90/98 £ 98/115 – 2 suites

High St ✉ DG6 4JG – ✆ 01557 330402 – www.selkirkarmshotel.co.uk – Closed 24-26 December

Gladstone House

TOWNHOUSE • COSY An attractive 18C former merchant's house run by friendly owners. There's a comfy antique-furnished lounge and simple pastel-hued bedrooms with seating areas by the windows where you can take in the rooftop views. Three course dinners use local produce and are tailored around guests' preferences.

3 rooms – £ 70 £ 80

48 High St ✉ DG6 4JX – ✆ 01557 331734 – www.kirkcudbrightgladstone.com – Closed 2 weeks January-February and Christmas

Glenholme Country House

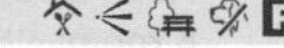

COUNTRY HOUSE • CLASSIC Take in mountain views from this stone house's spacious garden. Inside, it has a cosy, eye-catching style and there's a large book and music library in place of TVs. Bedrooms are themed around Victorian political figures. The dining room features Chinese furnishings and meals are tailored to guests' tastes.

4 rooms – £ 100/110 £ 115/130

Tongland Rd ✉ DG6 4UU – Northeast : 1 mi on A 711 – ✆ 01557 339422 – www.glenholmecountryhouse.com – Closed Christmas-New Year

KIRKWALL → See Orkney Islands (Mainland)

KYLESKU

Highland – Regional map n° **17**-C1

Kylesku

REGIONAL CUISINE • INN Breathtaking views of Loch Glendhu and the mountains make this 17C coaching inn an essential stop-off point. Fresh seafood is the way to go, with langoustines and mussels landed 200 yards away. Relax on the waterside terrace then make for one of the cosy bedrooms; two have balconies with panoramic views.

Carte £ 20/47

11 rooms – £ 75/110 £ 130/180

✉ IV27 4HW – ✆ 01971 502231 – www.kyleskuhotel.co.uk – Closed late November-mid February

LEITH – City of Edinburgh → See Edinburgh

LERWICK → See Shetland Islands (Mainland)

image source/hemis.fr

LEWIS AND HARRIS (ISLE OF)

Western Isles – Regional map n° **17**-A1

LEWIS

Western Isles – Regional map n° **17**-A1

Back

Broad Bay House

LUXURY • CONTEMPORARY Delightful guesthouse with a decked terrace and a garden leading down to the beach. Luxurious interior features an open-plan, Scandinavian-style lounge and a dining area with panoramic views. Modern, oak-furnished bedrooms come with super king sized beds, great extras and sliding doors onto private terraces.

4 rooms – †£ 139 ††£ 179

HS2 0LQ – Northeast : 1 mi on B 895
– 01851 820990 – www.broadbayhouse.co.uk – Closed October-March

Galson

Galson Farm

TRADITIONAL • CLASSIC Welcoming former croft in a wonderfully remote location, boasting views out across the Atlantic. Guest areas are traditional and homely and bedrooms are cosy. The owner also operates the village post office from just inside the porch. Home-cooked meals include lamb and beef from their 60 acre grounds.

4 rooms – †£ 92 ††£ 92/108

South Galson HS2 0SH
– 01851 850492 – www.galsonfarm.co.uk

HARRIS

Western Isles – Regional map n° **17**-A1

Ardhasaig

Ardhasaig House

REGIONAL CUISINE • FRIENDLY XX Purpose-built house that's been in the family for over 100 years. Modern, airy bar-lounge; flag-floored dining room with antique tables and dramatic bay and mountain views. Set menu offers local meats and seafood. Cosy bedrooms; the one in the stone lodge is the best.

Menu £ 55

6 rooms – †£ 60/80 ††£ 70/125

HS3 3AJ
– 01859 502500 (booking essential) – www.ardhasaig.co.uk – dinner only
– Closed November, January and February

Borve

Pairc an t-Srath

FAMILY • PERSONALISED Welcoming guesthouse on a working croft, with views out over the Sound of Taransay. Comfy, open-fired lounge has a chaise longue; the intimate dining room offers delicious home-cooked meals and wonderful vistas. Extremely friendly owners serve tea and homemade cake on arrival. Immaculate bedrooms feature smart oak furniture and brightly coloured Harris Tweed fabrics.

4 rooms ☕ - 🚹£ 54/56 👥£ 108/110

✉ HS3 3HT - ✆ 01859 550386 - www.paircant-srath.co.uk - Closed 2 weeks October-November and Christmas-New Year

Scalpay

Hirta House

TRADITIONAL • PERSONALISED Simple, characterful guesthouse in a small fishing village. Loch and mountain views from the lounge and conservatory. One traditional four-poster bedroom; two more modern rooms - one with a round bed. Nautically themed breakfast room.

3 rooms ☕ - 🚹£ 75/80 👥£ 85/95

✉ HS4 3XZ - ✆ 01859 540394 - www.hirtahouse.co.uk

Scarista

Scarista House

TRADITIONAL • CLASSIC The location is superb - with waves crashing on the beach and views over the mountains - and the caring owners run the place with pride. It has a homely, open-fired library, a first floor drawing room and traditional bedrooms; those in Glebe House are the best. Garden produce features on the classical menu.

6 rooms ☕ - 🚹£ 155/175 👥£ 207/245

✉ HS3 3HX - ✆ 01859 550238 - www.scaristahouse.com - Closed 9 December- 28 February and restricted opening in winter

Tarbert

Ceol na Mara

TRADITIONAL • CLASSIC A homely former crofter's cottage - one of only three on the island to have three storeys. Take in stunning loch views from the lounges. Bedrooms are individually furnished; the two on the top floor open onto a shared sitting area.

3 rooms ☕ - 🚹£ 90/100 👥£ 120/140

7 Direcleit ✉ HS3 3DP - South : 1 mi by A 859 - ✆ 01859 502464 - www.ceolnamara.com

LEWISTON

Highland - Regional map n° **17**-C2

Loch Ness Inn

TRADITIONAL CUISINE • INN There are two parts to this pub: the small Brewery Bar, home to locals and walkers fresh from the Great Glen Way; and the open-plan Lewiston restaurant with its wood burning stove and bright timbered beams. Hearty, robust, flavoursome dishes champion Scottish produce. Bedrooms are spacious and comfortable.

Carte £ 19/42

12 rooms ☕ - 🚹£ 75/95 👥£ 90/120

✉ IV63 6UW - ✆ 01456 450991 - www.staylochness.co.uk

LINLITHGOW

West Lothian - Pop. 13 462 - Regional map n° **15**-C1

Champany Inn

MEATS AND GRILLS • INTIMATE XXX Set in a collection of whitewashed cottages – the traditional restaurant was once a flour mill, hence its unusual shape. The focus is on meat and wine, with 21-day aged Aberdeen Angus beef a speciality. There's also a well-stocked wine shop, a more laid-back 'Chop and Ale House' and 16 tartan-themed bedrooms.

Menu £ 28/43 – Carte £ 47/75

16 rooms – †£ 99/129 ††£ 109/135

Champany ✉ EH49 7LU – Northeast : 2 mi on A 803 at junction with A 904 – ✆ 01506 834532 – www.champany.com – Closed 25-26 December, 1-2 January, Saturday lunch and Sunday

Arden House

LUXURY • MODERN The welcoming owner pays great attention to detail at this purpose-built guesthouse beside a 105 acre sheep farm. Spacious, tastefully styled bedrooms boast modern slate-floored bathrooms and plenty of extras like fresh flowers and magazines. The wide-ranging breakfasts are a highlight.

3 rooms – †£ 78/118 ††£ 89/128

Belsyde ✉ EH49 6QE – Southwest : 2.25 mi on A 706 – ✆ 01506 670172 – www.ardencountryhouse.com – Closed 25-26 December and restricted opening in winter

LOCHALINE

Highland – Regional map n° **17**-B3

Whitehouse

TRADITIONAL CUISINE • FAMILY X Understated wood-panelled restaurant in a remote headland village, run by keen, hands-on owners. The constantly evolving blackboard menu showcases local seafood, game and garden produce. Cooking is pleasingly unfussy and flavoursome.

Menu £ 30/45

✉ PA80 5XT – ✆ 01967 421777 – www.thewhitehouserestaurant.co.uk – Closed November-Easter, Sunday and Monday

LOCHINVER

Highland – ✉ Lairg – Pop. 470 – Regional map n° **17**-C1

Albannach (Colin Craig and Lesley Crosfield)

TRADITIONAL CUISINE • COSY XX Substantial 19C Scottish house in a remote location, boasting exceptional bay and mountain views from the conservatory, terrace and garden. Traditional 5 course dinners rely on top quality local produce, with Scottish beef and seafood from the harbour below the specialities. Contemporary bedrooms are spread about the building; one boasts a private terrace and a hot tub.

→ Mousseline of wild turbot, lobster bisque and langoustine. Highland beef with roots, thyme mash and Amontillado sauce. Citrus soufflé with bitter chocolate ice cream.

Menu £ 78 – tasting menu only

5 rooms (dinner included) – †£ 230/245 ††£ 290/405

Baddidarroch ✉ IV27 4LP – West : 1 mi by Baddidarroch rd – ✆ 01571 844407 (bookings essential for non-residents) – www.thealbannach.co.uk – dinner only – Closed 10 December-16 February and Monday-Wednesday

Chez Roux

FRENCH • INTIMATE XX Romantic restaurant hung with photos of the eponymous brothers, where well-spaced tables take in fantastic bay and mountain views. Regularly changing, classical French menus make use of the wealth of produce on their doorstep.

Menu £ 45 – bar lunch Monday-Saturday

Inver Lodge Hotel, Iolaire Rd ✉ IV27 4LU – ✆ 01571 844496 (bookings essential for non-residents) – www.inverlodge.com – Closed November-April

Caberfeidh

SEAFOOD • COSY An informal lochside sister to the Albannach restaurant, which follows the same ethos of championing fresh local produce. Constantly evolving menus have a seafood slant. The majority of dishes are generously proportioned 'small plates'.

Carte £ 24/41

Main St ✉ IV27 4JY – ✆ 01571 844321 – www.caberfeidhlochinver.co.uk – Closed January, 25 December, Monday in winter and lunch Tuesday-Wednesday

Inver Lodge

TRADITIONAL • PERSONALISED Superbly located on a hillside, overlooking a quiet fishing village. Smart bedrooms have good mod cons and great bay and island views. Relax in the open-fired lounge or billiard room – or try one of their whiskies in the elegant bar.

21 rooms – †£ 165/225 ††£ 225/550

Iolaire Rd ✉ IV27 4LU – ✆ 01571 844496 – www.inverlodge.com – Closed November-April

Chez Roux – See restaurant listing

LOCHRANZA – North Ayrshire ➔ See Arran (Isle of)

LUSS

Argyll and Bute – Pop. 402 – Regional map n° **16**-B2

Loch Lomond Arms

INN • COSY Retaining the warmth and character of an old inn, this hotel offers individual, contemporary bedrooms. 'Lomond' and 'Colquhoun' are the most luxurious: the former has a four-poster bed; the latter, superb views. Wide-ranging menu: dine in the open-fired bar, the relaxed dining room or the more formal library.

15 rooms – †£ 80/130 ††£ 90/190

Main Rd ✉ G83 8NY – ✆ 01436 860420 – www.lochlomondarmshotel.com

MELFORT

Argyll and Bute – Regional map n° **16**-B2

Melfort House

COUNTRY HOUSE • PERSONALISED Enjoy homemade cake in the splendid sitting room or out on the lovely terrace looking over the loch. Bedrooms are furnished with antiques and rich fabrics and one has wonderful water views. The impressive Victorian gardens include two 150yr old monkey puzzle trees. Communal dinners are served by arrangement.

3 rooms – †£ 70/80 ††£ 115/135

✉ PA34 4XD – ✆ 01852 200326 – www.melforthouse.co.uk – Closed Christmas and New Year

MELROSE

The Scottish Borders – Pop. 2 307 – Regional map n° **15**-D2

Burts

INN • CONTEMPORARY Characterful 18C coaching inn on the main square; run by the same family for two generations. Appealing bedrooms blend contemporary furnishings with original features. The cosy bar serves old classics and is a hit with the locals, while the formal dining room offers a mix of modern and traditional dishes.

20 rooms – †£ 78/88 ††£ 145/155

Market Sq. ✉ TD6 9PL – ✆ 01896 822285 – www.burtshotel.co.uk – Closed 6-13 February and 25-26 December

at Gattonside North: 2 mi by B6374 on B6360 ✉ Melrose

Seasons

TRADITIONAL CUISINE • NEIGHBOURHOOD Friendly restaurant run by an experienced couple. The 'Staples' menu arrives in a cookbook and lists favourites such as chargrilled steak; the daily blackboard is more adventurous. Meats are from Melrose and seafood is from Eyemouth.

Menu £ 20 (lunch and early dinner) – Carte £ 20/36

Main St ✉ TD6 9NP – ☎ 01896 823217 – www.seasonsborders.co.uk – dinner only and lunch Friday-Sunday – Closed 3 weeks January, Monday and Tuesday

Fauhope House

HISTORIC • PERSONALISED Charming 19C house by the Tweed, overlooking Melrose – its delightful gardens stretch for 15 acres. The quirkily decorated rooms display an eclectic mix of art and antiques. Bedrooms are very different; some have bold colour schemes.

3 rooms – †£ 90/110 ††£ 130/160

✉ TD6 9LU – East : 0.25 mi by B 6360 taking unmarked lane to the right of Monkswood Rd at edge of village – ☎ 01896 823184 – www.fauhopehouse.com

MEMUS

Angus – Regional map n° **16**-D2

Drovers Inn

CLASSIC CUISINE • COSY An attractive Highland inn in an extremely remote spot, with a delightful beamed interior and a stylish dining room. Well-priced menus make good use of local estate produce. Cooking is traditional, gutsy and boldly flavoured.

Menu £ 20

✉ DD8 3TY – ☎ 01307 860322 – www.the-drovers.com

MOFFAT

Dumfries and Galloway – Pop. 2 582 – Regional map n° **15**-C2

Brodies

REGIONAL CUISINE • NEIGHBOURHOOD XX Large, laid-back, modern eatery that caters for all appetites – serving snacks, light lunches, afternoon tea, more substantial dinners and all-day brunch on Sundays. Cooking has a traditional base and features fresh, local ingredients.

Carte £ 20/36

1-2 Altrive Pl, Holm St ✉ DG10 9EB – ☎ 01683 222870 – www.brodiesofmoffat.co.uk – Closed 25-27 December

Lime Tree

TRADITIONAL CUISINE • COSY XX Small hotel restaurant with a feature fireplace, attractive marquetry and a bay window looking down the valley. Good value menus feature well-judged, attractively presented classics packed with flavour.

Menu £ 29

Hartfell House Hotel, Hartfell Cres. ✉ DG10 9AL – ☎ 01683 220153 (booking essential) – www.hartfellhouse.co.uk – dinner only – Closed 1 week January, 1 week October, Christmas, Sunday and Monday

Hartfell House

TOWNHOUSE • CLASSIC Keenly run house built in 1866 and located in a peaceful crescent. Original features include parquet floors and ornate cornicing. Bedrooms are spacious and traditional and the comfy first floor drawing room has a southerly aspect.

7 rooms – †£ 45/50 ††£ 70/75

Hartfell Cres. ✉ DG10 9AL – ☎ 01683 220153 – www.hartfellhouse.co.uk – Closed 1 week autumn, 1 week January and Christmas

Lime Tree – See restaurant listing

Bridge House

TRADITIONAL • PERSONALISED A classic-looking bay-windowed house in a quiet residential area – the front rooms have views over the hills and valley. Spotlessly-kept bedrooms boast comfy Hypnos mattresses; Munro has a four-poster bed and a great outlook.

7 rooms – £ 57/60 £ 75/80

Well Rd ✉ DG10 9JT – East : 0.75 mi by Selkirk rd (A 708) taking left hand turn before bridge – ✆ 01683 220558 – www.bridgehousemoffat.scot

MUIR OF ORD

Highland – Pop. 2 555 – Regional map n° **17**-C2

Dower House

TRADITIONAL • CLASSIC Personally run, part-17C house with charming mature gardens. Characterful guest areas include an antique-furnished dining room and a small, open-fired lounge with fresh flowers and shelves crammed with books. Comfy bedrooms; one with a bay window overlooking the garden. Traditional, daily set menu.

3 rooms – £ 120/135 £ 145/165

Highfield ✉ IV6 7XN – North : 1 mi on A 862 – ✆ 01463 870090 – www.thedowerhouse.co.uk – Closed November-March

MULL (Isle of)

Argyll and Bute – Pop. 2 800 – Regional map n° **16**-A2

Dervaig

Regional map n° **27**-A2

The Bellachroy

TRADITIONAL BRITISH • INN The 17C Bellachroy sits in a pretty village at the head of Loch Cuin and is the oldest inn on the island. It might look a little shabby from the outside but it's cosy and characterful inside. Go for the ultra-fresh local seafood – maybe scallops from Tobermory or lobster from Croig. Bedrooms are simple.

Carte £ 23/42

7 rooms – £ 55/85 £ 95/130

✉ PA75 6QW – ✆ 01688 400314 – www.thebellachroy.co.uk – Closed Sunday dinner-Wednesday lunch November-Easter

Fionnphort

Ninth Wave

SEAFOOD • CONTEMPORARY DÉCOR XX This remotely set modern restaurant started life as a crofter's bothy and both the décor and the cooking reflect the owners' travels. Seafood plays a key role, with crab, lobster and other shellfish caught by Mr Lamont himself.

Menu £ 48/68

Bruach Mhor ✉ PA66 6BL – East : 0.75 mi by A 849 – ✆ 01681 700757 (booking essential) – www.ninthwaverestaurant.co.uk – dinner only – Closed November-April, Monday and Tuesday

Tiroran

Tiroran House

LUXURY • PERSONALISED The beautiful drive over to this remotely set, romantic Victorian house is all part of the charm. Stylish, antique-furnished bedrooms come with plenty of extras and two lovely lounges look out over 56 acres of grounds which lead down to a loch. Dine from a concise à la carte in the conservatory or cosy dining room. The welcoming owner encourages a house party atmosphere.

10 rooms – £ 120/165 £ 198/245

✉ PA69 6ES – ✆ 01681 705232 – www.tiroran.com – Closed November-mid March

Tobermory

Highland Cottage

TRADITIONAL CUISINE • FAMILY XX Long-standing, personally run restaurant in an intimate cottage, where family antiques and knick-knacks abound. Classical linen-laid dining room and a homely lounge. Traditional daily menu with a seafood base features plenty of local produce. Bedrooms are snug and individually styled.

Menu £ 43

6 rooms – £ 140/155 £ 160/175

Breadalbane St PA75 6PD – via B 8073 – 01688 302030 (bookings essential for non-residents) – www.highlandcottage.co.uk – dinner only – Closed 15 October-1 April

MUTHILL

Perth and Kinross – Pop. 747 – Regional map n° **16**-C2

Barley Bree

CLASSIC CUISINE • RUSTIC X The concise, daily changing menu champions local Scottish produce and creative dishes have a classical base and a modern twist. Have pre-dinner drinks in the modern lounge-bar before dining in the rustic restaurant decorated with fishing memorabilia. Bedrooms are bright and modern.

Menu £ 17 (weekday lunch) – Carte £ 26/48 **s**

6 rooms – £ 70/120 £ 95/160

6 Willoughby St PH5 2AB – 01764 681451 (booking advisable) – www.barleybree.com – Closed 2 weeks July, Christmas, Monday and Tuesday

NAIRN

Highland – Pop. 9 773 – Regional map n° **17**-D2

Boath House

MODERN CUISINE • INTIMATE XX An elegant oval dining room in an early 19C mansion. Well-balanced modern menus showcase the chef's skill and understanding. Cooking is accomplished, with vivid presentation and interesting flavours – and much of the produce is from their garden or orchard. Sit at bespoke oak tables and take in the lake view.

→ Lamb shoulder with pickled walnut, mint and shallot. Halibut with lettuce, dill mayonnaise and braised fennel. Pineapple with caramel and sea buckthorn.

Menu £ 30/70 **s**

Boath House Hotel, Auldearn IV12 5TE – East : 2 mi on A 96 – 01667 454896 (booking essential) – www.boath-house.com

Boath House

HISTORIC • PERSONALISED An elegant 1825 neo-classical mansion framed by Corinthian columns. Inside it cleverly blends contemporary furnishings and original features; most of the modern art is for sale. Bedrooms are elegant and intimate – one has 'his and hers' roll-top baths and some have views over the 20 acre grounds and a lake.

9 rooms – £ 190/260 £ 295/365

Auldearn IV12 5TE – East : 2 mi on A 96 – 01667 454896 – www.boath-house.com

Boath House – See restaurant listing

Cawdor House

TOWNHOUSE • PERSONALISED 19C former manse run by friendly, knowledgeable owners. The cosy lounge has a marble fireplace and bedrooms are clean and uncluttered; original features blend with contemporary styling. Enjoy local bacon and sausages at breakfast.

6 rooms – £ 60/75 £ 75/105

7 Cawdor St IV12 4QD – 01667 455855 – www.cawdorhousenairn.co.uk

NEWPORT-ON-TAY

Fife - Pop. 4 250 - Regional map n° **16**-C2

The Newport

MODERN BRITISH • COSY X The Newport is the place to come for cheery, upbeat service in a great waterside location. It serves colourful, imaginative small plates themed around 'land, sea, garden and ground' and a tasting menu on Friday and Saturday nights.

Carte £ 16/39

4 rooms - £ 100/160 £ 100/160

1 High St. ✉ DD6 8AB - ✆ 01382 541449 (booking essential at dinner) - www.thenewportrestaurant.co.uk - Closed Sunday dinner, Monday and lunch Tuesday

NIGG ➔ See Tain

NORTH BAY - Western Isles ➔ See Barra (Isle of)

NORTH BERWICK

East Lothian - Pop. 6 605 - Regional map n° **15**-D1

Glebe House

FAMILY • PERSONALISED Spacious, welcoming Georgian house with attractive walled gardens and views over the town and sea. It's beautifully furnished inside, with good quality fabrics and antiques. Classically styled bedrooms have lots of extra touches.

3 rooms - £ 95 £ 140

Law Rd ✉ EH39 4PL - ✆ 01620 892608 - www.glebehouse-nb.co.uk - Closed Christmas-New Year and restricted opening in winter

NORTH QUEENSFERRY

Fife - Pop. 1 076 - Regional map n° **16**-C3

Wee Restaurant

TRADITIONAL CUISINE • BISTRO X A likeable quarry-floored restaurant in the shadow of the Forth Rail Bridge; as its name suggests, it's small and cosy. Fresh Scottish ingredients are served in neatly presented, classical combinations. Lunch represents the best value.

Menu £ 16/36 **s**

17 Main St ✉ KY11 1JT - ✆ 01383 616263 - www.theweerestaurant.co.uk - Closed 25-26 December, 1-2 January and Monday

NORTH UIST - Western Isles ➔ See Uist (Isles of)

OBAN

Argyll and Bute - Pop. 8 574 - Regional map n° **16**-B2

Coast

MODERN BRITISH • BRASSERIE XX Busy high street restaurant in a former bank, with a high ceiling, a stripped wooden floor and khaki fabric panels on the walls. Unfussy, modern cooking is well-seasoned and local produce is key. The 'Light Bites' menus are a steal.

Menu £ 18 (lunch and early dinner) - Carte £ 21/45

104 George St ✉ PA34 5NT - ✆ 01631 569900 - www.coastoban.co.uk - Closed January, 25-26 December, Sunday dinner-Monday October-March and Sunday lunch

Manor House

TRADITIONAL · CLASSIC 18C dower house; formerly part of the Argyll Estate. The country house style interior offers traditional comforts, and the spacious lounge and rustic bar boast delightful bay and harbour views. Individually styled bedrooms. Concise daily menu served in the formal dining room.

11 rooms – £ 115/260 £ 125/260

Gallanach Rd. ✉ PA34 4LS – ✆ 01631 562087 – www.manorhouseoban.com – Closed 25-26 December

Glenburnie House

TOWNHOUSE · PERSONALISED A bay-windowed house on the main esplanade, affording great bay and island views. Period features include a delightful staircase and etched glass windows, and antiques abound. Good-sized bedrooms have a subtle contemporary style.

12 rooms – £ 65/75 £ 100/140

Corran Esplanade ✉ PA34 5AQ – ✆ 01631 562089 – www.glenburnie.co.uk – Closed December-February

ONICH

Highland – ✉ Fort William – Regional map n° **17**-B3

Lochleven Seafood Café

SEAFOOD · SIMPLE Simple little restaurant in a stunning lochside spot, looking towards the Glencoe Mountains. Fresh fish and shellfish come from the west coast; the seafood platter is a speciality. Be sure to pay a visit to their adjoining deli and shop.

Carte £ 24/59 **s**

Lochleven ✉ PH33 6SA – Southeast : 6.5 mi by A 82 on B 863 – ✆ 01855 821048 (bookings advisable at dinner) – www.lochlevenseafoodcafe.co.uk – Closed November-March

C. Meier/doc-stock GmbH RM/age fotostock

ORKNEY ISLANDS

Orkney Islands – Pop. 21 349

ISLE OF WESTRAY

Orkney Islands – Regional map n° **18**-A2

Pierowall

 **No 1 Broughton** 

FAMILY · COSY 19C pink-washed house on the waterside, with views over Pierowall Bay and out to Papa Westray. Take in the view from the conservatory or relax in the sauna (on request). Bedrooms are homely. They also offer dry stone walling courses!

5 rooms – £ 50/60 £ 70/80

KW17 2DA
– 01857 677726 – www.no1broughton.co.uk
– Closed 22 December-6 January

MAINLAND

Orkney Islands – Regional map n° **18**-A3

Burray

 **Sands** 

FAMILY · MODERN Converted 19C herring packing store in a small hamlet overlooking the Scapa Flow. Pleasant bedrooms boast smart bathrooms. The bar has a pool table and a dartboard and offers a traditional menu. The dining room serves more refined dishes, which feature island produce and lots of shellfish.

8 rooms – £ 65/90 £ 80/120

KW17 2SS
– 01856 731298 – www.thesandshotel.co.uk

Kirkwall

TRADITIONAL CUISINE · FRIENDLY XX Sit by the large floor to ceiling window or out on the terrace to take in superb panoramic views over the Scapa Flow and the south islands. Traditional menus feature North Ronaldsay lamb, Orkney beef and plenty of fresh seafood from local waters. Homely, well-kept bedrooms have a slight New England edge.

Carte £ 25/42

8 rooms – £ 80/95 £ 120

St Ola KW15 1SF – Southwest : 3 mi on A 964
– 01856 872389 – www.thefoveran.com – dinner only – Restricted opening October-April

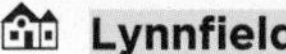

Lynnfield

FAMILY • PERSONALISED An 18C manse which was extended during the war to become an officers' mess. Bedrooms have period Orcadian furnishings and ultra-modern bathrooms. It's close to the Highland Park Distillery and has a wonderful collection of over 360 whiskies; the traditional dining room is also decorated with whisky memorabilia.

10 rooms – †£ 90/120 ††£ 100/165 – 3 suites

Holm Rd ✉ KW15 1SU – South : 1 mi on A 961 – ✆ 01856 872505 – www.lynnfieldhotel.com – Closed 1-7 January and 25-26 December

Stromness

Hamnavoe

TRADITIONAL CUISINE • NEIGHBOURHOOD X Homely restaurant in a backstreet of a sleepy harbourside town; its name means 'Safe Haven' and it has the feel of an old family parlour. Unfussy home cooking utilises fresh market produce and dishes are hearty and full of flavour.

Carte £ 28/40

35 Graham Pl ✉ KW16 3BY – off Victoria St – ✆ 01856 850606 (booking essential) – dinner only – Closed Monday and restricted opening in winter

PEAT INN

Fife – Regional map n° **16**-D2

The Peat Inn (Geoffrey Smeddle)

CLASSIC CUISINE • CONTEMPORARY DÉCOR XXX Whitewashed former pub; now a contemporary restaurant run by a charming team. The smart lounge still has its original log fireplace; ask for a table overlooking the floodlit gardens. Accomplished, classical cooking has subtle modern touches and local ingredients are to the fore. Stylish, split-level bedrooms have plenty of extras and breakfast is served in your room.

→ Potato-crusted cured salmon with chestnut & lemon purée, warm cucumber and oyster cream. Wild Cairngorm roe deer with shallots, braised potatoes, beetroot and carrot. Croustillant of apples and caramel with almond ice cream.

Menu £ 22/50 – Carte £ 33/62

8 rooms – †£ 185/230 ††£ 205/250

✉ KY15 5LH – ✆ 01334 840206 (booking essential) – www.thepeatinn.co.uk – Closed 10 days January, 4 days Christmas, Sunday and Monday

PEEBLES

The Scottish Borders – Pop. 8 376 – Regional map n° **15**-C2

Osso

MODERN CUISINE • FRIENDLY X By day, this is a bustling coffee shop serving a bewildering array of light snacks and daily specials; come evening, it transforms into a more sophisticated restaurant offering a great value, regularly changing menu of well-presented, flavoursome dishes. Service is friendly and attentive.

Menu £ 28 (dinner) – Carte lunch £ 22/33

Innerleithen Rd ✉ EH45 8BA – ✆ 01721 724477 – www.ossorestaurant.com – Closed 1 January, 25 December, dinner Tuesday-Wednesday in winter except December and dinner Sunday-Monday

Be sure to read the section 'How to use this guide'.
It explains our symbols, classifications and abbreviations
and will help you make a more informed choice.

at Eddleston North: 4.5 mi on A703

The Horseshoe

MODERN CUISINE • INN XX Once a roadside inn; now a smart restaurant with elegant tableware and formal service. Sophisticated menus offer well-presented, classically based dishes which keep Scottish produce to the fore. Chic, modern bedrooms are located in the old village schoolhouse and come with pleasing extras.

Menu £ 50 (dinner) – Carte lunch £ 25/35

8 rooms – †£ 70/100 ††£ 100/140

Edinburgh Rd ✉ EH45 8QP – ✆ 01721 730225 – www.horseshoeinn.co.uk – Closed first 2 weeks January, last week June, first week July, Monday and Tuesday

PERTH

Perth and Kinross – Pop. 46 970 – Regional map n° **16**-C2

Deans

TRADITIONAL CUISINE • FRIENDLY XX This is a real family affair, with the father and one son in the kitchen and the mother and the other son out front. It's a smart, modern place with red furnishings and a cocktail bar. Ambitious dishes feature many ingredients.

Menu £ 19/23 (weekday dinner) – Carte £ 26/47

Town plan: A1-c – *77-79 Kinnoull St ✉ PH1 5EZ – ✆ 01738 643377 – www.letseatperth.co.uk – Closed 2 weeks January, 1 week November and Monday*

63@Parklands

MODERN BRITISH • INTIMATE XX An intimate, conservatory-style hotel restaurant decorated in muted shades, with fish-eye mirrors and stag antler lights. Creative dishes are well-presented and showcase the best of Scottish ingredients.

Menu £ 40

Town plan: A2-n – *Parklands Hotel, 2 St Leonard's Bank ✉ PH2 8EB – ✆ 01738 622451 – www.63atparklands.com – dinner only – Closed 26 December-5 January, Tuesday and Wednesday*

63 Tay Street

MODERN BRITISH • INTIMATE XX A well-established riverside restaurant with grey tongue and groove panelling, burgundy chairs and striking exposed stone effect wallpaper. Tersely described modern dishes take their influences from around the globe.

Menu £ 22 (lunch and early dinner) – Carte £ 34/48

Town plan: B2-r – *63 Tay St ✉ PH2 8NN – ✆ 01738 441451 – www.63taystreet.com – Closed 1-8 January, 2-8 July, 26-31 December, Sunday, Monday and lunch Tuesday-Wednesday*

Pig Halle

FRENCH • BISTRO X Lively bistro; its square, marble-floored room tightly packed with tables and dominated by a mirror stencilled with a Paris Metro map. Menus list Gallic favourites. The adjoining deli serves wood-fired pizzas and tasty pastries.

Menu £ 16 (lunch) – Carte £ 21/38

Town plan: B2-s – *38 South St ✉ PH2 8PG – ✆ 01738 248784 – www.pighalle.co.uk – Closed 26 December and 1 January*

Post Box

CLASSIC CUISINE • BRASSERIE X The first Post Office in Perth is a striking building with bright red doors and an atmospheric stone-walled cellar bar. Simply, prepared, classically based dishes are given the occasional modern touch.

Menu £ 18 (lunch and early dinner) – Carte dinner £ 29/44

Town plan: B1-x – *80 George St ✉ PH1 5LB – ✆ 01738 248971 – www.thepostboxperth.co.uk – Closed first 2 weeks January, Sunday and Monday*

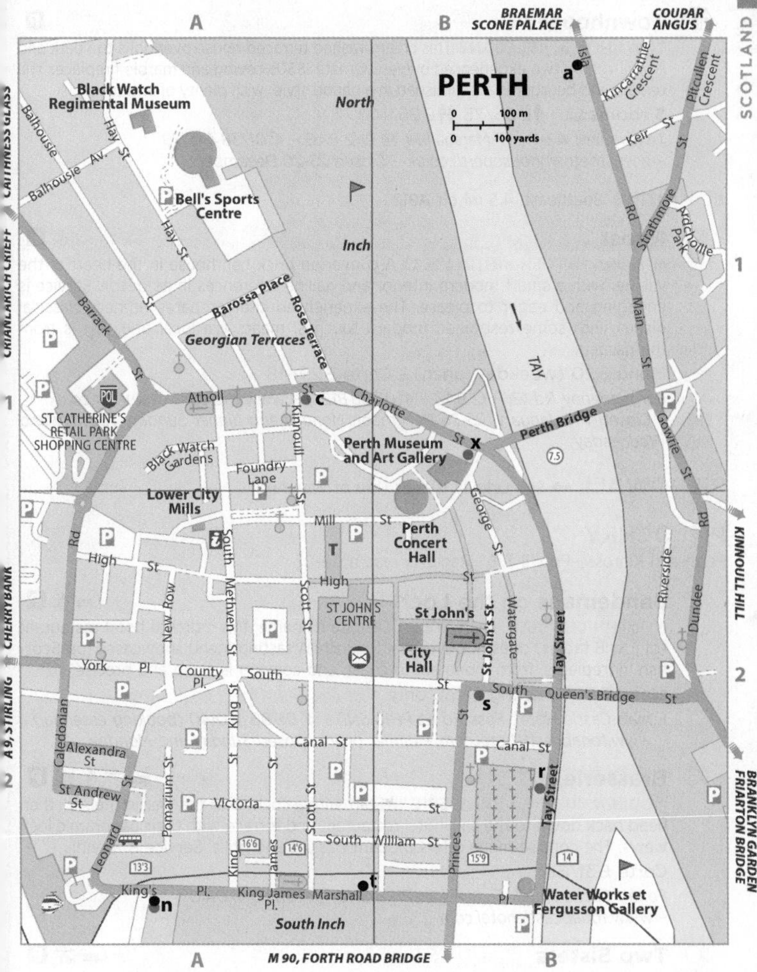

PERTH

A B
BRAEMAR SCONE PALACE
COUPAR ANGUS
0 100 m
0 100 yards
North Inch
Black Watch Regimental Museum
Bell's Sports Centre
Balhousie
Balhousie Av.
Hay St
Barrack St
Barossa Place
Rose Terrace
Georgian Terraces
Atholl St
Charlotte St
Kinnoull St
ST CATHERINE'S RETAIL PARK SHOPPING CENTRE
Black Watch Gardens
Foundry Lane
Perth Museum and Art Gallery
Perth Bridge
Lower City Mills
Mill St
Perth Concert Hall
High St
South Methven St
New Row
Scott St
ST JOHN'S CENTRE
St John's
City Hall
George St
St John's St.
Watergate
Tay Street
York Pl.
County Pl.
South St
Queen's Bridge
Caledonian Rd
Alexandra St
St Andrew St
King St
Pomarium St
Canal St
Victoria St
South William St
James St
Princes St
Leonard St
King's Pl.
King James Pl.
Marshall Pl.
South Inch
Water Works et Fergusson Gallery
Isla Rd
Kincarrathie Crescent
Pitcullen Crescent
Keir St
Strathmore St
Ardchoille Park
Main St
Gowrie St
Riverside
Dundee Rd
TAY
KINNOULL HILL
BRANKLYN GARDEN FRIARTON BRIDGE
M 90, FORTH ROAD BRIDGE
A 9, STIRLING
CHERRYBANK
CRIANLARICH CRIEFF
CAITHNESS GLASS
1
2

Parklands

BUSINESS · MODERN A personally run, extended Georgian house with a contemporary interior. Spacious bedrooms have good facilities and sizeable bathrooms; those to the front have pleasant views over the park. Dine in informal No.1 The Bank or in intimate 63@Parklands.

15 rooms ☕ – 🚹£ 95/150 🚹🚹£ 120/200

Town plan: A2-n – *2 St Leonard's Bank* ✉ *PH2 8EB*
– *✆ 01738 622451*
– *www.theparklandshotel.com*
– *Closed 26 December-5 January*

🍴 **63@Parklands** – See restaurant listing

Townhouse

TOWNHOUSE • ELEGANT This creamwashed terraced house overlooks the park and is well-run by two experienced owners. Ornate 1830s coving and marble fireplaces still remain and bedrooms are furnished in a period style, with plenty of antiques.

5 rooms – £ 65/75 £ 85/140

Town plan: A2-t – *17 Marshall Pl ✉ PH2 8AG – ✆ 01738 446179 – www.thetownhouseperth.co.uk – Closed 23-26 December*

at Kintillo Southeast: 4.5 mi off A912

Roost

MODERN BRITISH • INTIMATE XX A converted brick hen house in the heart of the village, with a smart modern interior and galline references in its décor. Service is engaging and eager to please. The experienced chef prepares refined, classical dishes with some restrained modern touches; meats are local and veg is from the garden.

Menu £ 20 (weekday lunch) – Carte £ 29/48

Forgandenny Rd ✉ PH2 9AZ – ✆ 01738 812111 – www.theroostrestaurant.co.uk – Closed 1-16 January, 25-26 December, Monday and dinner Sunday, Tuesday and Wednesday

PIEROWALL → See Orkney Islands (Isle of Westray)

PITLOCHRY

Perth and Kinross – Pop. 2 776 – Regional map n° **16**-C2

Sandemans on the Loch

MODERN CUISINE • INTIMATE XXX Despite its name, this intimate hotel restaurant (of just 8 tables) does not overlook the loch. A tasting menu showcases top Scottish ingredients, from mountain to coast, and cooking is clean and precise.

Menu £ 75 – tasting menu only

Fonab Castle Hotel, Foss Rd ✉ PH16 5ND – ✆ 01796 470140 (booking essential) – www.fonabcastlehotel.com – dinner only – Closed Sunday and Monday

Brasserie

MODERN CUISINE • BRASSERIE XX Start with a cocktail in the 'Bar in the Air', then head back down to the chic hotel restaurant and terrace with their panoramic loch views. The concise menu offers modern classics and grills. Service is friendly.

Carte £ 31/61

Fonab Castle Hotel, Foss Rd ✉ PH16 5ND – ✆ 01796 470140 – www.fonabcastlehotel.com

Two Sisters

REGIONAL CUISINE • INTIMATE XX Appealing dishes use top Scottish produce and there's a focus on fish, game and steak. Dine amongst fishing memorabilia in the charming bar or in the bright, slightly more formal restaurant of this 17C hotel.

Carte £ 24/47

East Haugh House Hotel, ✉ PH16 5TE – Southeast : 1.75 mi off A 924 (Perth Rd) – ✆ 01796 473121 (booking advisable) – www.easthaugh.co.uk – dinner only and lunch Saturday-Sunday – Closed 1 week Christmas and lunch in winter

Fonab Castle

HISTORIC • CONTEMPORARY This 19C baronial castle offers superb views over the loch to the hills beyond. Bedrooms have a subtly traditional feel and smart bathrooms; the 'Woodland' rooms are more modern and have terraces or balconies.

42 rooms – £ 240/450 £ 240/450 – 4 suites

Foss Rd ✉ PH16 5ND – ✆ 01796 470140 – www.fonabcastlehotel.com

Brasserie • **Sandemans on the Loch** – See restaurant listing

Green Park

TRADITIONAL · CLASSIC Long-standing, family-run hotel on the shore of Loch Faskally; many of its guests return year after year. Well-appointed lounges offer stunning loch and countryside views. Bedrooms vary in style; the largest and most modern are in the newer wing. A traditional dinner is included in the price of the room.

51 rooms (dinner included) – †£ 93/118 ††£ 192/236

Clunie Bridge Rd ✉ PH16 5JY
– ✆ 01796 473248 – www.thegreenpark.co.uk – Closed 17-27 December

Craigmhor Lodge and Courtyard

COUNTRY HOUSE · MODERN Spacious, cosy house just out of town, with an airy breakfast room where local fruits, bacon and sausages are served. Well-kept modern bedrooms are set in the courtyard – some have balconies. Supper hampers can be delivered to your room.

12 rooms – †£ 105/155 ††£ 125/175

27 West Moulin Rd ✉ PH16 5EF
– ✆ 01796 472123 – www.craigmhorlodge.co.uk – Closed Christmas

East Haugh House

TRADITIONAL · PERSONALISED A family-run, 17C turreted stone house in two acres of gardens. Cosy, traditionally appointed bedrooms are named after fishing flies and are split between the house, a former bothy and the old gatehouse.

14 rooms – †£ 85/160 ††£ 85/160

✉ PH16 5TE – Southeast : 1.75 mi off A 924 (Perth Rd)
– ✆ 01796 473121 – www.easthaugh.co.uk – Closed 1 week Christmas

Two Sisters – See restaurant listing

Craigatin House and Courtyard

TOWNHOUSE · MODERN Built in 1820 as a doctor's house; now a stylish boutique hotel. The stunning open-plan lounge and breakfast room centres around a wood burning stove and overlooks the garden. Bedrooms are modern and minimalist.

14 rooms – †£ 99/126 ††£ 109/136

165 Atholl Rd ✉ PH16 5QL
– ✆ 01796 472478 – www.craigatinhouse.co.uk – Closed Christmas

Northlands

TOWNHOUSE · PERSONALISED This guesthouse, set high above the town, was originally named after the large sentinel stone in its grounds. You'll receive a warm welcome and no detail is forgotten; it's tastefully furnished with antiques and Laura Ashley fabrics.

3 rooms – †£ 88/102 ††£ 98/112

Lettoch Rd ✉ PH16 5AZ
– ✆ 01796 474131 – www.northlandsbandb.com – Closed January-February

at Killiecrankie Northwest: 4 mi by A924 and B8019 on B8079 ✉ Pitlochry

Killiecrankie

TRADITIONAL · CLASSIC A whitewashed former vicarage built in 1840 and set in 4.5 acres of mature rhododendron-filled grounds, with a small kitchen garden to the rear. There's a charming open-fired lounge, a snug bar and well-appointed bedrooms which offer everything you might want, including a hot water bottle. Choose between light suppers and traditional dinners. Service is excellent.

10 rooms (dinner included) – †£ 125/145 ††£ 260/320

✉ PH16 5LG
– ✆ 01796 473220 – www.killiecrankiehotel.co.uk – Closed 3 January-23 March

PLOCKTON

Highland – Regional map n° **17**-B2

Plockton Hotel

TRADITIONAL CUISINE • INN A one-time ships' chandlery with a distinctive black exterior and stunning views over Loch Carron to the mountains beyond. Cooking is honest and hearty with a strong Scottish influence, so expect herring in oatmeal or haggis with whisky – and don't miss the Plockton prawns. Simple, comfortable bedrooms.

Carte £ 17/46

15 rooms – £ 50/100 £ 100/150

41 Harbour St IV52 8TN – 01599 544274 – www.plocktonhotel.co.uk

POOLEWE

Highland – Regional map n° **17**-B2

Pool House

FAMILY • PERSONALISED A unique, family-run Victorian house by the water's edge, with a quirky whisky bar in the old billiard room. Bedrooms are all large suites – each individually themed with incredible attention to detail; 'Ashanti' features a 19C marriage bed. The formal restaurant offers a classic seasonal menu.

4 rooms – £ 185/250 £ 250/375

IV22 2LD – 01445 781272 – www.pool-house.co.uk – Closed mid November-mid March

PORT APPIN

Argyll and Bute – Appin – Regional map n° **16**-B2

Airds

MODERN BRITISH • ELEGANT XX An intimate, candlelit country house restaurant with superb loch and mountain views. Classic dishes are presented with a modern edge and much use is made of west coast seafood and local meats, with game a highlight. Don't miss the Mallaig crab or the scallops – and ensure you ask for a table in the window!

Menu £ 22/56 – Carte £ 21/48

Airds Hotel, PA38 4DF – 01631 730236 (bookings essential for non-residents) – www.airds-hotel.com – Closed 28 November-13 December and Monday-Tuesday November-January

Airds

LUXURY • PERSONALISED A characterful former ferryman's cottage fronted by colourful planters and offering lovely loch and mountain views. Two sumptuous, antique-furnished sitting rooms are filled with fresh flowers and magazines. Bedrooms offer understated luxury – ask for one at the front with a waterside view.

11 rooms – £ 145/365 £ 195/415

PA38 4DF – 01631 730236 – www.airds-hotel.com – Closed 28 November-13 December and Monday-Tuesday November-January

Airds – See restaurant listing

PORT CHARLOTTE – Argyll and Bute → See Islay (Isle of)

PORT ELLEN – Argyll and Bute → See Islay (Isle of)

PORTMAHOMACK

Highland – Regional map n° **17**-D2

Oystercatcher

SEAFOOD • BISTRO XX Set in a lovely spot in a tiny fishing village, with lobster pots hanging outside. One formal and one rustic room, with walls crammed with memorabilia. Menus offer fresh seafood in some unusual combinations; the boats that land the fish can be seen by the jetty. Modest bedrooms; nearly 20 choices at breakfast.

Menu £ 40 **s**

3 rooms – £ 54/82 £ 85/115

Main St ✉ IV20 1YB – ✆ 01862 871560 (booking essential) – www.the-oystercatcher.co.uk – dinner only

PORTPATRICK

Dumfries and Galloway – ✉ Stranraer – Pop. 534 – Regional map n° **15**-A3

Knockinaam Lodge

CLASSIC CUISINE • INTIMATE XX Located within a delightful lodge, a traditionally furnished, smartly dressed dining room with delightful sea views (ask for table 5). The four course set menu evolves with the seasons and offers good quality produce – often from their own gardens – cooked in classic combinations.

Menu £ 35/70 – tasting menu only

Knockinaam Lodge Hotel, ✉ DG9 9AD – Southeast : 5 mi by A 77 off B 7042 – ✆ 01776 810471 (bookings essential for non-residents) – www.knockinaamlodge.com

Knockinaam Lodge

COUNTRY HOUSE • PERSONALISED A charming former hunting lodge in a delightfully secluded private cove, with gardens leading down to the sea. Sample their malts in the wood-panelled bar or relax in the country house style drawing room. Bedrooms are furnished with antiques – 'Churchill' boasts a century-old bathtub. Service is detailed.

10 rooms (dinner included) – £ 185/325 £ 300/450

✉ DG9 9AD – Southeast : 5 mi by A 77 off B 7042 – ✆ 01776 810471 – www.knockinaamlodge.com

Knockinaam Lodge – See restaurant listing

PORTAVADIE

Argyll and Bute – Regional map n° **16**-B3

Portavadie

HOLIDAY HOTEL • DESIGN This peaceful lochside complex consists of a marina, self-catering apartments, a small hotel and an impressive spa. Good-sized bedrooms have a modern Scandic style and pleasant views; some have kitchenettes but there's also the choice of a brasserie and an informal dining room with a leather-furnished lounge.

16 rooms – £ 109/149 £ 109/149

Portavadie Marina ✉ PA21 2DA – ✆ 01700 811075 – www.portavadie.com

PORTREE

– Highland → See Skye (Isle of)

RANNOCH STATION

Perth and Kinross – Regional map n° **16**-B2

Moor of Rannoch

FAMILY • COSY This 19C hotel is perched high on the moor and is the ultimate in hiking getaways. The views are delightful, the whole place has a serene feel and wildlife is in abundance. Bedrooms are cosy and the open-fired guest areas come with jigsaws instead of TVs. Rustic home cooking utilises Scottish ingredients.

5 rooms – £ 115 £ 140

✉ PH17 2QA – ✆ 01882 633238 – www.moorofrannoch.co.uk – Closed November-mid February

RATHO

City of Edinburgh – Pop. 1 634 – Regional map n° **15**-C1

Bridge Inn

MODERN CUISINE • PUB A friendly pub on the tow path between Edinburgh and the Falkirk Wheel. The fruit and veg comes from their walled garden, the pork is from their pigs and the eggs are from their chickens and ducks. For a treat, book the private room on their restaurant barge. All of the cosy bedrooms have water views.

Carte £ 25/44

4 rooms – †£ 70/140 ††£ 80/155

27 Baird Rd ✉ EH28 8RU – ✆ 0131 333 1320 – www.bridgeinn.com – Closed 25 December

ST ANDREWS

Fife – Pop. 16 870 – Regional map n° **16**-D2

Rocca

MODERN CUISINE • DESIGN XXX A formal hotel restaurant with designer wallpapers, richly coloured fabrics and great Old Course views. Appealing menus feature a mix of modern Scottish dishes, seafood and grills. Artisan produce is sourced locally.

Carte £ 31/49

Town plan: A1-s – *Rusacks Hotel, Pilmour Links ✉ KY16 9JQ – ✆ 01334 472549 (booking essential) – www.roccarestaurant.com – dinner only – Closed Sunday December-March*

Adamson

MEATS AND GRILLS • BRASSERIE XX A stylish brasserie and cocktail bar set within a house once owned by eminent photographer John Adamson (it was also later the town's Post Office). The wide-ranging menu of tasty dishes includes steaks from the Josper grill.

Menu £ 13 (lunch and early dinner) – Carte £ 22/50

Town plan: A2-v – *127 South St ✉ KY16 9UH – ✆ 01334 479191 – www.theadamson.com – Closed 25-26 December and 1 January*

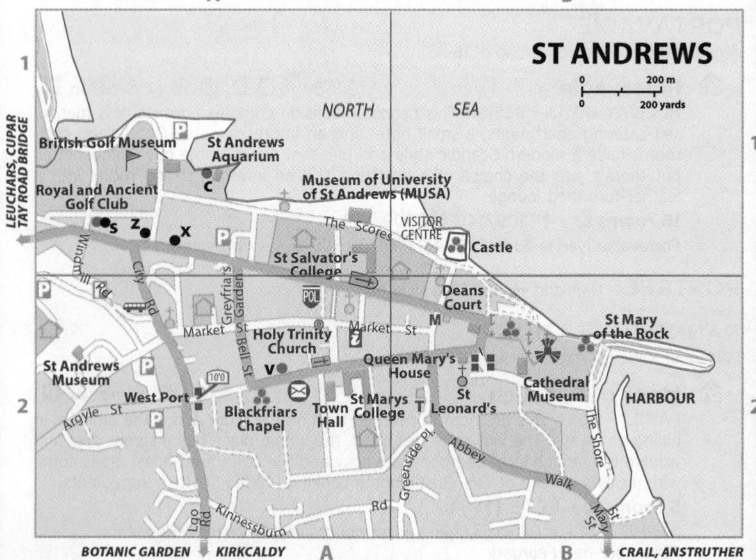

Seafood Ristorante

SEAFOOD • DESIGN XX This striking glass cube offers commanding bay views and is perfect for watching the setting sun. The experienced team bring a modern Italian twist to seafood: choose from cicchetti, fish platters, hearty stews and homemade pastas.

Menu £ 18 (lunch) – Carte £ 31/53

Town plan: A1-c – *Bruce Embankment, The Scores* ✉ *KY16 9AB*
– *✆ 01334 479475* – *www.theseafoodristorante.com*
– *Closed 25-26 December, 1 and 7-14 January*

Grange Inn

TRADITIONAL CUISINE • COSY X A former pub, atop a hill, with great views over the bay. Have an aperitif beside the fire, then head for the stone-walled restaurant with its huge stag's head. The experienced chef serves a menu of tasty, well-prepared classics.

Menu £ 17/45

Grange Rd ✉ *KY16 8LJ – Southeast : 1.75 mi by A 917*
– *✆ 01334 472670 (booking essential)* – *www.thegrangeinn.com*
– *Closed 3 weeks January, Sunday dinner and Monday*

Old Course H. Golf Resort & Spa

LUXURY • CLASSIC A vast resort hotel with an impressive spa, set on a world-famous golf course overlooking the bay. Luxurious guest areas have a subtle Scottish theme and bedrooms are chic, sumptuous and well-equipped. Try their bespoke ales in the Jigger Inn then dine on modern-classics, Josper-grilled meats or seafood.

144 rooms – £ 205/400 ££ 255/429 – 15 suites

Old Station Rd ✉ *KY16 9SP – West : 0.75 mi off A 91 – ✆ 01334 474371*
– *www.oldcoursehotel.co.uk*

Rusacks

LUXURY • PERSONALISED The oldest hotel in St Andrews sits in a commanding position overlooking the 18th green of the Old Course. Original 1846 columns feature in the lobby and a huge array of paintings pay homage to golfing greats. Bedrooms are stylish; choose one with a view. Dine in the pub or formal restaurant.

70 rooms – £ 199/299 ££ 199/299 – 4 suites

Town plan: A1-s – *Pilmour Links* ✉ *KY16 9JQ – ✆ 0344 879 9136*
– *www.macdonaldhotels.co.uk*

Rocca – See restaurant listing

Rufflets Country House

COUNTRY HOUSE • PERSONALISED This country house hotel is surrounded by well-tended gardens and has been owned by the same family since 1952. Inside it's a mix of the old and the new, with original Arts and Crafts features sitting alongside stylish, contemporary bedrooms. Menus offer modern interpretations of classic dishes.

23 rooms – £ 125/275 ££ 150/425 – 2 suites

Strathkinness Low Rd ✉ *KY16 9TX – West : 1.5 mi on B 939 – ✆ 01334 472594*
– *www.rufflets.co.uk* – *Closed 4-24 January*

Fairways

TOWNHOUSE • CONTEMPORARY This tall Victorian building is the closest guesthouse to the Old Course – ask for Room 3 and sit on the balcony overlooking the 18th hole. Bedrooms are contemporary and of a good size. Nothing is too much trouble for the owners.

3 rooms – £ 65/110 ££ 80/140

Town plan: A1-z – *8a Golf Pl.* ✉ *KY16 9JA – ✆ 01334 479513*
– *www.fairwaysofstandrews.co.uk*

Five Pilmour Place

TOWNHOUSE • CONTEMPORARY Victorian terraced house with a surprisingly stylish interior. There's a bright, clubby lounge and a locker room with underfloor heating. Bedrooms have bold feature walls and smart walk-in showers; Room 3 also has a claw-foot bath.

7 rooms - £ 65/135 £ 85/170

Town plan: A1-x - *5 Pilmour Pl. ✉ KY16 9HZ - ✆ 01334 478665 - www.5pilmourplace.com - Closed 12 December-1 March*

ST BOSWELLS

The Scottish Borders - ✉ Melrose - Pop. 1 279 - Regional map n° **15**-D2

Buccleuch Arms

INN • QUIRKY A smart, long-standing coaching inn which offers popular golfing, fishing and shooting breaks. Guest areas have a quirky, shabby-chic style and cosy bedrooms have co-ordinated headboards and soft furnishings. The relaxed, shabby chic bistrot offers classics, grills and afternoon tea.

19 rooms - £ 85/105 £ 105/130

The Green ✉ TD6 0EW - ✆ 01835 822243 - www.buccleucharms.com - Closed 24-25 December

Whitehouse

TRADITIONAL • PERSONALISED Built in 1872 by the Duke of Sutherland, this cosy dower house is equally popular with romantic couples as with walkers, hunters and fishermen. Traditionally furnished bedrooms boast excellent views over the estate and have contrastingly modern bathrooms. Wild salmon and local game feature at dinner.

3 rooms - £ 90/102 £ 140/160

✉ TD6 0ED - Northeast : 3 mi on B 6404 - ✆ 01573 460343 - www.whitehousecountryhouse.com

ST MONANS

Fife - Pop. 1 265 - Regional map n° **16**-D2

Craig Millar @ 16 West End

MODERN CUISINE • FRIENDLY XX A former pub with an attractive interior and a small terrace affording harbour views. 'Land' and 'Sea' tasting menus feature at dinner and cooking is refined and flavoursome. It's run by a charming team.

Menu £ 28/45

16 West End ✉ KY10 2BX - ✆ 01333 730327 (booking essential) - www.16westend.com - Closed Monday-Tuesday and restricted opening October-March

SANQUHAR

Dumfries and Galloway - Pop. 2 021 - Regional map n° **15**-B2

Blackaddie House

MODERN BRITISH • TRADITIONAL DÉCOR XX A stone-built former manse with 16C origins, set by the river. Lunch offers good value classics, while dinner is more elaborate and features original modern cooking; ingredients are luxurious and dishes are well-presented. Bedrooms are named after game birds - ask for 'Grouse', which has a four-poster bed.

Menu £ 40/63

7 rooms - £ 80/100 £ 125/235

Blackaddie Rd ✉ DG4 6JJ - ✆ 01659 50270 (booking essential at lunch) - www.blackaddiehotel.co.uk

SCALPAY - Western Isles ➜ See Lewis and Harris (Isle of)

SCARISTA - Western Isles ➜ See Lewis and Harris (Isle of)

SCRABSTER - Highland ➜ See Thurso

SHETLAND ISLANDS

Shetland Islands - Pop. 21 800 - Regional map n° **18**-B2

MAINLAND

Shetland Islands - Regional map n° **18**-B2

Lerwick

Kveldsro House

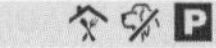

BUSINESS • PERSONALISED Spacious Georgian house hidden in the town centre; its name means 'evening peace'. There's a cosy sitting room with original ceiling mouldings and a comfy bar with views of the islands; bedrooms are traditionally styled. Menus offer mainly island produce; portions are hearty.

17 rooms – £ 115 £ 135

Greenfield Pl ✉ ZE1 0AQ – ✆ 01595 692195 – www.shetlandhotels.com – Closed 25-26 December and 1-2 January

Veensgarth

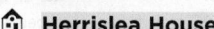

Herrislea House

TRADITIONAL • CLASSIC Large, family-run hotel set just out of town. It has an unusual African hunting theme, with mounted antlers, animal heads and pelts on display. Cosy bedrooms are individually designed and some have valley views. Fresh cooking uses local produce, alongside lamb and beef from their croft.

9 rooms – £ 95/105 £ 115/130

✉ ZE2 9SB – ✆ 01595 840208 – www.herrisleahouse.co.uk – Closed 10 December-10 January

SKYE (Isle of)

Highland - Pop. 10 008 - Regional map n° **17**-B2

Broadford

Tigh an Dochais

BOUTIQUE HOTEL • MODERN Striking house with award-winning architecture, overlooking Broadford Bay and the Applecross Peninsula. Comfy lounge has well-stocked bookshelves. Modern, minimalist bedrooms boast superb views and good facilities, including underfloor heating and plenty of extras. Communal, home-cooked meals by arrangement.

3 rooms – £ 85 £ 105

13 Harrapool ✉ IV49 9AQ – on A 87 – ✆ 01471 820022 – www.skyebedbreakfast.co.uk – Closed November-February

Colbost

Three Chimneys & The House Over-By

MODERN CUISINE • RUSTIC XX Immaculately kept crofter's cottage in a stunning lochside setting. Contemporary art hangs on exposed stone walls in the characterful low-beamed dining rooms. Modern Scottish menus showcase good regional ingredients and seafood from local waters is a highlight. Spacious, split-level bedrooms are stylishly understated and the residents' lounge has a great outlook.

Menu £ 38/65

6 rooms – £ 345 £ 345

✉ IV55 8ZT – ✆ 01470 511258 (booking essential) – www.threechimneys.co.uk – dinner only and lunch April-November – Closed 10 December-19 January

Hillstone Lodge

COUNTRY HOUSE · DESIGN A delightfully located modern house: lots of windows and a pleasant terrace make the most of the fantastic loch and island views, and the immaculately kept bedrooms share the outlook. Breakfast features local bacon and sausages; dinner is served as and when requested, and showcases market seafood and meats.

3 rooms – †£ 100/130 ††£ 120/150

IV55 8ZT
– 01470 511434 – www.hillstonelodge.com
– Closed December and January

Duisdalemore

Duisdale House

TRADITIONAL · PERSONALISED Stylish, up-to-date hotel with lawned gardens, a hot tub and coastal views. Comfortable bedrooms boast bold décor, excellent bathrooms and a pleasing blend of contemporary and antique furniture. Modern cooking makes good use of local produce. Smart uniformed staff.

18 rooms – †£ 188/238 ††£ 238/288 – 1 suite

Sleat IV43 8QW – on A 851
– 01471 833202 – www.duisdale.com

Dunvegan

Roskhill House

COUNTRY HOUSE · CONTEMPORARY Welcoming 19C croft house, in a peaceful location close to the water. Formerly the old post office, the lounge boasts exposed stone, wooden beams and an open fire. Fresh, bright bedrooms have a contemporary edge and smart bathrooms.

5 rooms – †£ 74/90 ††£ 93/108

Roskhill IV55 8ZD – Southeast : 2.5 mi by A 863
– 01470 521317 – www.roskhillhouse.co.uk
– Closed 28 October-1 March

Edinbane

Edinbane Inn

TRADITIONAL CUISINE · COSY This traditional-looking former farmhouse is the perfect place to cosy up by the fire on a misty night. Choose a pub favourite or one of the appealing specials. Come on a Wednesday, Friday or Sunday for the popular music sessions, then stay the night in one of the comfy, cosy, Scottish-themed bedrooms.

Carte £ 24/40

6 rooms – †£ 70/135 ††£ 90/145

IV51 9PW
– 01470 582414 – www.edinbaneinn.co.uk
– Closed 2 January-2 February

Elgol

Regional map n° **17**-B2

Coruisk House

TRADITIONAL CUISINE · SIMPLE This traditional croft house is very remotely set on the west of the island and offers superb views over the hills to the mountains. It's very personally run and seats just 16. Skye produce features in fresh, flavoursome daily dishes. Two simply furnished bedrooms share the stunning outlook.

Carte £ 39/47

5 rooms – †£ 150/250 ††£ 150/250

IV49 9BL
– 01471 866330 (booking essential) – www.coruiskhouse.com
– Closed November-February except 1 week New Year

Flodigarry

Flodigarry

COUNTRY HOUSE • PERSONALISED This 19C house was once Jacobite heroine Flora MacDonald's home. Lawned gardens lead down to the coast and it has excellent panoramic views; stylish designer décor features throughout. The bar is in the old billiard room – look out for the original round windows in the ceiling. Cooking is modern and Scottish.

19 rooms ☕ – 🚹£ 180/350 🚹🚹£ 180/350

✉ IV51 9HZ – ✆ 01470 552203 – www.hotelintheskye.co.uk – Restricted opening in winter

Portree

Scorrybreac

MODERN CUISINE • BISTRO Simply furnished restaurant with distant mountain views and just 8 tables; named after the chef's parents' house, where he ran his first pop-up. Creative modern cooking uses meats from the hills and seafood from the harbour below.

Menu £ 40

7 Bosville Terr ✉ IV51 9DG – ✆ 01478 612069 (booking essential) – www.scorrybreac.com – dinner only – Closed Monday

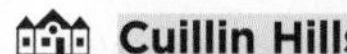

Cuillin Hills

TRADITIONAL • CLASSIC Set in 15 acres of grounds, a 19C hunting lodge offering stunning views over Portree Bay towards the Cuillin Mountains; enjoy top Scottish produce in the restaurant, which shares the outlook. Bedrooms have good facilities – the best are to the front. The stylish open-plan bar serves over 100 malt whiskies.

34 rooms ☕ – 🚹£ 80/220 🚹🚹£ 100/320

✉ IV51 9QU – Northeast : 0.75 mi by A 855 – ✆ 01478 612003 – www.cuillinhills-hotel-skye.co.uk

Bosville

INN • CONTEMPORARY The Bosville sits in an elevated spot overlooking the harbour and the Cuillin Mountains. Stylish bedrooms have locally woven throws and dramatic Skye scenes on the walls. Enjoy a dram by the fire in the lively bar then head for the bistro-style dining room, which showcases the best of Skye's natural larder.

20 rooms ☕ – 🚹£ 85/170 🚹🚹£ 125/180

Bosville Terr ✉ IV51 9DG – ✆ 01478 612846 – www.bosvillehotel.co.uk – Closed Christmas

Marmalade (N)

HISTORIC • ELEGANT Pretty gardens front this elegant 1817 house on the edge of town, which has been returned to its former glory. Stylish bedrooms come in grey hues, with contrastingly colourful throws made by the island's weavers. The comfy bar leads through to a smart brasserie specialising in steak and oysters.

11 rooms ☕ – 🚹£ 125/210 🚹🚹£ 125/310

Home Farm Rd ✉ IV51 9LX – ✆ 01478 611711 – www.marmaladehotel.co.uk

Sleat

Kinloch Lodge

COUNTRY HOUSE • CLASSIC With a loch in front and heather-strewn moorland behind, this 17C hunting lodge affords fantastic panoramic views. It has a traditional country house feel, with antique-filled lounges hung with photos of the Macdonald clan and contemporary bedrooms each themed around a different tartan. Menus mix traditional Scottish elements with some more unusual flavour combinations.

19 rooms (dinner included) ☕ – 🚹£ 200/350 🚹🚹£ 250/450 – 3 suites

✉ IV43 8QY – ✆ 01471 833214 – www.kinloch-lodge.co.uk

Stein

Loch Bay

MODERN CUISINE · SIMPLE X This pretty little crofter's cottage sits in an idyllic hamlet and is a pleasingly simple place with a wood-burning stove and Harris Tweed covered chairs. The experienced chef skilfully prepares intensely flavoured Scottish dishes with French overtones; opt for the well-judged Loch Bay Seafood tasting menu.

➜ Brown crab 'Soup and Sandwich'. Wild trout and prawns with apple & sorrel. Clootie dumpling soufflé.

Menu £ 28/40

1 Macleods Terr, ✉ IV55 8GA – ✆ 01470 592235 (booking essential) – www.lochbay-restaurant.co.uk – Closed January, Christmas, Monday, Sunday dinner and lunch Tuesday and Saturday

Struan

Ullinish Country Lodge

MODERN CUISINE · CLASSIC DÉCOR XX Formal hotel dining room with a traditional, masculine style and a house party atmosphere. The daily changing, 2-choice set menu uses good quality local ingredients; dishes are modern and inventive and combinations are well-judged.

Menu £ 60

Ullinish Country Lodge Hotel, ✉ IV56 8FD – West : 1.5 mi by A 863 – ✆ 01470 572214 (bookings essential for non-residents) – www.theisleofskye.co.uk – dinner only – Closed January and Christmas-New Year

Ullinish Country Lodge

TRADITIONAL · CLASSIC Personally run, 18C former hunting lodge in a windswept location, affording lovely loch and mountain views. The lounge is filled with ornaments and books about the area. Warmly decorated bedrooms boast good facilities and extras.

6 rooms – £ 140/190 ££ 220/270

✉ IV56 8FD – West : 1.5 mi by A 863 – ✆ 01470 572214 – www.theisleofskye.co.uk – Closed January and Christmas-New Year

Ullinish Country Lodge – See restaurant listing

Teangue

Toravaig House

COUNTRY HOUSE · CONTEMPORARY Stylish whitewashed house with neat gardens, set on the road to the Mallaig ferry. Cosy, open-fired lounge with a baby grand piano and heavy fabrics. Individually designed bedrooms boast quality materials and furnishings. The two-roomed restaurant offers a concise, classical menu of island produce.

9 rooms – £ 90/280 ££ 90/280

Knock Bay ✉ IV44 8RE – on A 851 – ✆ 01471 820200 – www.skyehotel.co.uk

SLEAT – Highland ➜ See Skye (Isle of)

SPEAN BRIDGE

Highland – Regional map n° **17**-C3

Russell's at Smiddy House

TRADITIONAL BRITISH · INTIMATE XX Friendly, passionately run restaurant in an appealing Highland village, with a smart ornament-filled lounge and two intimate dining rooms. Tasty dishes use locally sourced ingredients and old Scottish recipes take on a modern style. Cosy, well-equipped bedrooms come with comfy beds and fine linens.

Menu £ 39

5 rooms – £ 95/125 ££ 115/195

Roybridge Rd ✉ PH34 4EU – ✆ 01397 712335 (booking essential) – www.smiddyhouse.com – dinner only – Closed Monday and restricted opening in winter

Corriegour Lodge

TRADITIONAL · COSY A traditional 19C hunting lodge with pretty gardens, set in a great lochside location – they even have their own private beach. Inside there's a homely curio-filled lounge and comfy bedrooms featuring top quality beds, linens and fabrics. Classical dinners comprise 4 courses; every table has a loch view.

11 rooms ☕ – †£ 169/209 ††£ 169/209

Loch Lochy ✉ PH34 4EA – North : 8.75 mi on A 82 – ✆ 01397 712685 – www.corriegour-lodge-hotel.com – Closed 30 October-25 March

Old Pines

TRADITIONAL · COSY A friendly couple run this log cabin style property, which blends well with the Highland scenery. Guest areas are comfy and homely. Feature walls add a splash of colour to the pine-furnished bedrooms and the slate-tiled bathrooms come with underfloor heating. Dining has a classic, dinner party feel.

7 rooms ☕ – †£ 60/80 ††£ 90/120

✉ PH34 4EG – Northwest : 1.5 mi by A 82 on B 8004 – ✆ 01397 712324 – www.oldpines.co.uk – Closed November-Easter

STEIN – Highland ➜ See Skye (Isle of)

STIRLING

Stirling – Pop. 36 142 – Regional map n° **16**-C2

Victoria Square

TOWNHOUSE · ELEGANT Many original features remain in this 19C house, from stained glass to ornate cornicing. Spacious bedrooms have William Morris style wallpapers; some have seating areas, feature beds or views over Victoria Square.

10 rooms ☕ – †£ 70/80 ††£ 80/135

12 Victoria Sq. ✉ FK8 2QZ – ✆ 01786 473920 – www.victoriasquareguesthouse.com – Closed 22-28 December and 1-5 January

West Plean House

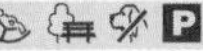

TRADITIONAL · PERSONALISED An attractive house on a working farm, with a long history and a very welcoming owner. It has two classic lounges and warm, traditional bedrooms. Eggs come from their hens and the fruits for the jams, from the garden.

5 rooms ☕ – †£ 66/70 ††£ 99/110

✉ FK7 8HA – South : 3.5 mi on A 872 (Denny rd) – ✆ 01786 812208 – www.westpleanhouse.com – Closed 20 December-8 January

STONEHAVEN

Aberdeenshire – Pop. 11 431 – Regional map n° **16**-D2

Tolbooth

SEAFOOD · RUSTIC XX Stonehaven's oldest building, located on the harbourside: formerly a store, a sheriff's courthouse and a prison. Classic dishes have modern touches; the emphasis being on local seafood, with langoustine and crab the highlights.

Menu £ 20 (weekday lunch) – Carte £ 32/52

Old Pier, Harbour ✉ AB39 2JU – ✆ 01569 762287 – www.tolbooth-restaurant.co.uk – Closed 3 weeks January, 1 week October, 25-26 December, Tuesday October-April and Sunday dinner-Monday

Beachgate House

LUXURY · PERSONALISED Well-run guesthouse looking out over Stonehaven Bay. Super views from well-appointed, first floor lounge. Bedrooms are furnished in a luxurious, modern style. Breakfast includes fresh poached fish or a full Scottish with hen or duck eggs.

5 rooms ☕ – †£ 70/95 ††£ 85/95

Beachgate Ln ✉ AB39 2BD – ✆ 01569 763155 – www.beachgate.co.uk

STRACHUR

Argyll and Bute – Pop. 628 – Regional map n° **16**-B2

Inver

MODERN BRITISH • VINTAGE X A former crofter's cottage and boat store in a beautifully isolated spot on the loch shore. Enjoy afternoon tea sitting in sheepskin covered armchairs in the lounge-bar or take in the view from the vintage-style restaurant, where concise modern menus are led by the finest local and foraged ingredients. Luxurious bothy-style bedrooms in the grounds complete the picture.

Carte £ 22/43

4 rooms – †£ 120 ††£ 160

Strathlaclan ✉ PA27 8BU – Southwest : 6.5 mi by A 886 on B 8000
– ✆ 01369 860537 (booking essential) – www.inverrestaurant.co.uk
– Closed January-mid March, Christmas, Wednesday-Thursday November-December and Monday-Tuesday except bank holidays

Creggans Inn

INN • CLASSIC A well-established inn on the shores of Loch Fyne; the conservatory is a popular spot for taking in the enviable view. Spacious, well-kept bedrooms have traditional décor in keeping with the building's age. Dine in the cosy bar-bistro or the classical restaurant – both serve the same wide-ranging menu.

14 rooms – †£ 115/175 ††£ 130/190 – 1 suite

✉ PA27 8BX
– ✆ 01369 860279 – www.creggans-inn.co.uk
– Closed 2 weeks January and Christmas

STRATHPEFFER

Highland – Pop. 1 109 – Regional map n° **17**-C2

Craigvar

TRADITIONAL • CLASSIC Proudly run by a charming owner, an attractive Georgian house overlooking the main square of a delightful spa village. Traditional guest areas include a comfy lounge and an antique-furnished breakfast room. Spacious bedrooms have a modern edge and plenty of personal touches. Good breakfast selection.

3 rooms – †£ 65/75 ††£ 100

The Square ✉ IV14 9DL
– ✆ 01997 421622 – www.craigvar.com
– Closed 18 December-14 January

STRATHY

Highland – Regional map n° **17**-D1

Sharvedda

FAMILY • PERSONALISED You won't find a warmer welcome than at this remotely located guesthouse on a working croft. Homemade fudge and cake are served on arrival and breakfast is taken in the sunny conservatory, with its wild views over the Pentland Firth.

3 rooms – †£ 60/65 ††£ 80/85

Strathy Point ✉ KW14 7RY – North : 1.5 mi on Strathy Point rd
– ✆ 01641 541311 – www.sharvedda.co.uk
– Closed 25-26 December

STROMNESS

→ See Orkney Islands (Mainland)

STRONTIAN

Highland – Regional map n° **17**-B3

Driftwood Brasserie

MODERN CUISINE • BRASSERIE X An intimate cream wood panelled brasserie in a lochside hunting lodge. The menu covers all bases, from traditional British dishes to Asian fare. Don't miss the West Coast seafood specials or the Ardnamurchan Peninsula venison.

Carte £ 30/48

Kilcamb Lodge Hotel, On A 861 ✉ PH36 4HY
- ✆ 01967 402257 (booking essential at dinner) - www.kilcamblodge.co.uk
- Closed January, 1-14 December and restricted opening in winter

Kilcamb Lodge

COUNTRY HOUSE • TRADITIONAL A charming lochside hunting lodge in an idyllic location, where 22 acres of meadows and woodland run down to a private shore. The traditional interior boasts rich fabrics and log fires yet has a modern edge. Bedrooms 5 and 8 have terrific loch and mountain views. Dine in the brasserie or the formal restaurant.

11 rooms (dinner included) ☕ - 🚹£ 165/385 🚹🚹£ 200/400

On A 861 ✉ PH36 4HY
- ✆ 01967 402257 - www.kilcamblodge.co.uk
- Closed January, 1-14 December and restricted opening in winter

Driftwood Brasserie - See restaurant listing

STRUAN - Highland ➔ See Skye (Isle of)

TAIN

Highland - Pop. 3 655 - Regional map n° **17**-D2

at Nigg Southeast: 7 mi by A9, B9175 and Pitcalnie Rd

Wemyss House

FAMILY • PERSONALISED Remotely set guesthouse run by charming owners; sit in the conservatory extension or on the terrace to enjoy views across the Cromarty Firth to the mountains. The bright Scandic-style interior features bespoke furniture from Stuart's on-site workshop and Christine often plays the grand piano in the cosy lounge.

3 rooms ☕ - 🚹£ 115/120 🚹🚹£ 115/120

Bayfield ✉ IV19 1QW - South : 1 mi past church
- ✆ 01862 851212 - www.wemysshouse.com
- Closed October-Easter

at Cadboll Southeast: 8.5 mi by A9 and B9165 (Portmahomack rd) off Hilton rd✉ Tain

Glenmorangie House

TRADITIONAL • CLASSIC Charming 17C house owned by the famous distillery. Antiques, hand-crafted local furnishings and open peat fires feature; there's even a small whisky tasting room. Luxuriously appointed bedrooms show good attention to detail; those in the courtyard cottages are suites. Communal dining from a classical Scottish menu.

9 rooms (dinner included) ☕ - 🚹£ 195/325 🚹🚹£ 260/450

Fearn ✉ IV20 1XP
- ✆ 01862 871671 - www.theglenmorangiehouse.com
- Closed January

TARBERT - Western Isles ➔ See Lewis and Harris (Isle of)

TARLAND

Aberdeenshire – Pop. 698 – Regional map n° **16**-D1

Douneside House

COUNTRY HOUSE • CLASSIC A castellated baronial mansion set in 7,000 acres and boasting delightful views. Elegant bedrooms feature antiques, Hypnos beds and underfloor-heated bathrooms; it serves as a holiday home for servicemen and ex-servicemen at certain times of the year. The intimate restaurant offers concise, modern menus.

22 rooms – †£ 60/70 ††£ 110/260 – £ 17 – 8 suites

AB34 4UL – North : 1.25 mi by B 9119 (Aberdeen Rd) – 01339 881230 – www.dounsidehouse.co.uk – Closed mid July-August and Christmas

TAYNUILT

Argyll and Bute – Regional map n° **16**-B2

Etive

MODERN BRITISH • INN XX The refurbishment of the Taynuilt Inn was a labour of love for the owner, who transformed it into a relaxed restaurant with comfy lounges, a rustic dining room and a tasting room. Concise menus list fresh, flavoursome, modern dishes of Scottish produce. Well-equipped bedrooms have antique French furnishings.

Menu £ 49

9 rooms – †£ 99/135 ††£ 135/209

PA35 1JN – 01866 822437 (bookings essential for non-residents) – www.taynuilthotel.co.uk – dinner only – Closed Sunday, Monday and restricted opening January-March

TEANGUE – Highland ➜ See Skye (Isle of)

THORNHILL

Dumfries and Galloway – Pop. 1 674 – Regional map n° **15**-B2

Buccleuch & Queensberry Arms

TOWNHOUSE • CONTEMPORARY Smartly refurbished coaching inn, designed by the owner, who also runs an interiors shop. Boldly coloured bedrooms are named after various estates owned by the Duke of Buccleuch and come with eclectic artwork and superb bathrooms. Informal dining options range from bar snacks to a more adventurous à la carte

14 rooms – †£ 65/95 ††£ 95/160 – 1 suite

112 Drumlanrig St DG3 5LU – 01848 323101 – www.bqahotel.com

Gillbank House

TOWNHOUSE • PERSONALISED Red stone house built in 1895; originally the holiday home of the Jenner family of department store fame. A lovely stained glass front door leads to a spacious light-filled interior. The breakfast room has distant hill views and two of the large, simply furnished bedrooms have feature beds; all have wet rooms.

6 rooms – †£ 65/85 ††£ 65/85

8 East Morton St DG3 5LZ – 01848 330597 – www.gillbank.co.uk

Holmhill Country House

COUNTRY HOUSE • PERSONALISED An 18C country house given to Charles Douglas by the Duke of Buccleuch; peacefully set beside the river, in 8 acres of woodland. Spacious bedrooms have great country views; west-facing 'Nith' sees some superb sunsets.

3 rooms – †£ 70/90 ††£ 95/120

Holmhill DG3 4AB – West 0.5mi. by A702 on B 731 – 01848 332239 – www.holmhill.co.uk – Closed Christmas-February

THURSO

Highland – Pop. 7 933 – Regional map n° **17**-D1

Forss House

TRADITIONAL • COSY Traditional Scottish hotel geared towards fishing; they have a 'rod room' and mounted fish sit beside deer heads on the walls. Bedrooms are of a good size – those in 'River House' are the most private with great views. The elegant dining room serves a classic Scottish menu – Scrabster seafood is a speciality.

14 rooms – £102/125 £135/185

Forss KW14 7XY – West : 5.5 mi on A 836 – 01847 861201 – www.forsshousehotel.co.uk – Closed 24 December-4 January

Pennyland House

FAMILY • PERSONALISED Old farmhouse built in 1780; where the founder of the Boys' Brigade was born. Simple, stylishly furnished bedrooms with quality oak furnishings, golf course pictures and modern bathrooms. Open-plan lounge-cum-dining room with harbour views.

6 rooms – £70/80 £80/90

KW14 7JU – Northwest : 0.75 mi on A 9 – 01847 891194 – www.pennylandhouse.co.uk – Closed Christmas and New Year

at Scrabster Northwest: 2.25 mi on A9

Captain's Galley

SEAFOOD • RUSTIC Classic seafood restaurant on the pier, with a vaulted stone dining room and an old chimney from its ice house days. The owner was once a fisherman so has excellent local contacts – he keeps some of his produce in creels in the harbour.

Menu £54

The Harbour KW14 7UJ – 01847 894999 (booking essential) – www.captainsgalley.co.uk – dinner only – Closed 25-26 December, 1-2 January, Sunday and Monday

TIGHNABRUAICH

Argyll and Bute – Regional map n° **16**-B3

Royal An Lochan

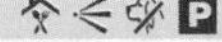

FAMILY • PERSONALISED Spacious 19C hotel located in a peaceful village, overlooking the Kyles of Bute. Comfortable bedrooms; some with excellent outlooks. The characterful bar with its nautical theme serves a snack menu, while the formal conservatory restaurant offers water views and seasonal seafood dishes.

11 rooms – £75/125 £75/150

Shore Rd PA21 2BE – 01700 811239 – www.theroyalanlochan.co.uk

TIRORAN – Argyll and Bute → See Mull (Isle of)

TOBERMORY – Argyll and Bute → See Mull (Isle of)

TORRIDON

Highland – Achnasheen – Regional map n° **17**-B2

Torridon Inn

TRADITIONAL CUISINE • INN Tranquil inn geared towards those who enjoy outdoor pursuits. The timbered bar features stags' antlers and an ice axe; the restaurant overlooks the gardens and loch. Satisfying walkers' favourites mix with more elaborate dishes. Simply furnished, modern bedrooms; the larger ones are ideal for families.

Carte £18/36 **s**

12 rooms – £130/260 £130/260

IV22 2EY – South : 1.5 mi on A 896 – 01445 791242 – www.thetorridon.com – Closed mid-December-January and Monday-Thursday November, February and March

Torridon

TRADITIONAL • CLASSIC A former hunting lodge built in 1887 by Lord Lovelace; set in 40 acres and offering superb loch and mountain views. The delightful interior features wood-panelling, ornate ceilings and a peat fire. Bedrooms are spacious and luxurious, with top quality furnishings and feature baths. The whisky bar has over 350 malts and the smart dining room offers a modern daily menu.

18 rooms – £ 255/460 £ 255/485 – 2 suites

IV22 2EY – South : 1.5 mi on A 896 – 01445 791242 – www.thetorridon.com – Closed January and Monday-Tuesday November-March

TROON

South Ayrshire – Pop. 14 752 – Regional map n° **15**-A2

Tapestry

MODERN BRITISH • ELEGANT XXX A cavernous country house dining room with exposed rafters, huge mirrors and chandeliers – but no tapestries! Interesting set menus feature refined, flavoursome modern dishes that use the best of Scottish produce. Service is formal.

Menu £ 25/45

Lochgreen House Hotel, Monktonhill Rd, Southwood KA10 7EN – Southeast : 2 mi on B 749 – 01292 313343 – www.costley-hotels.co.uk

Lochgreen House

COUNTRY HOUSE • CONTEMPORARY Edwardian country house in a pleasant coastal spot, with sumptuous lounges and a Whisky Room stocked with an extensive range of malts. Bedrooms in the main house are cosy and traditional; those in the extension are more luxurious.

32 rooms – £ 115/165 £ 175/195 – 1 suite

Monktonhill Rd, Southwood KA10 7EN – Southeast : 2 mi on B 749 – 01292 313343 – www.costley-hotels.co.uk

Tapestry – See restaurant listing

TURNBERRY

South Ayrshire – Girvan – Regional map n° **15**-A2

1906

ITALIAN • ELEGANT XXX This understatedly elegant hotel restaurant offers a sense of occasion, courtesy of grand chandeliers, charming service and stunning sea views. Creative, modern Italian cooking is full of flavour and relies on local ingredients.

Menu £ 45 – Carte £ 32/75

Trump Turnberry Hotel, KA26 9LT – On A 719 – 01655 331000 – www.trumpturnberry.com – dinner only

Trump Turnberry

GRAND LUXURY • ELEGANT An iconic Edwardian hotel built around Ailsa golf course. Elegant guest areas have been taken back to their former glory and many of the luxurious bedrooms boast enviable sea views; for something different, stay in the lighthouse. 1906 offers Italian dishes, while Duel in the Sun serves bistro classics.

204 rooms – £ 229/479 £ 259/509 – 4 suites

KA26 9LT – On A 719 – 01655 331000 – www.trumpturnberry.com

1906 – See restaurant listing

UDNY GREEN

Aberdeenshire – Regional map n° **16**-D1

Eat on the Green

MODERN BRITISH • ELEGANT XX An attractive former inn overlooking the village green, with a cosy lounge and two traditionally furnished dining rooms. Well-presented modern dishes change with the seasons and feature vegetables and herbs from their smallholding.

Menu £ 25 (weekday lunch) – Carte £ 34/50

✉ AB41 7RS – ✆ 01651 842337 (booking essential) – www.eatonthegreen.co.uk – Closed Monday and Tuesday

UIST (Isles of)

Western Isles – Pop. 3 510 – Regional map n° **17**-A2

NORTH UIST

Western Isles – Regional map n° **29**-A2

Carinish

Temple View

TRADITIONAL • FUNCTIONAL Victorian house with an uncluttered interior and a homely style. Small bar, sitting room and sun lounge. Simple, comfortable bedrooms: those to the rear have moor views; those at the front overlook the sea or the 13C ruins of Trinity Temple. Cosy dining room offers popular seafood specials.

10 rooms ☕ – 🚹£ 80/85 🚹🚹£ 120/125

✉ HS6 5EJ – ✆ 01876 580676 – www.templeviewhotel.co.uk – Closed Christmas

Langass

Langass Lodge

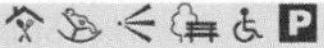

HISTORIC • CLASSIC Victorian former shooting lodge nestled in heather-strewn hills and boasting distant loch views. Bedrooms in the main house are characterful; those in the wing are more modern and spacious, with good views. Eat in the comfy bar or linen-clad dining room from simple, seafood-based menus.

11 rooms ☕ – 🚹£ 95/115 🚹🚹£ 95/155

✉ HS6 5HA – ✆ 01876 580285 – www.langasslodge.co.uk – Closed November-April

Lochmaddy

Hamersay House

TRADITIONAL • CONTEMPORARY Stylish hotel with a sleek, boutique style, a well-equipped gym, a sauna, a steam room and bikes for hire. Chic, modern bedrooms offer good facilities. The forward-thinking owner continually reinvests. Smart bar and dining room; menus display plenty of seafood.

8 rooms ☕ – 🚹£ 95/100 🚹🚹£ 110/140

✉ HS6 5AE – ✆ 01876 500700 – www.hamersayhouse.co.uk

ULLAPOOL

Highland – Pop. 1 541 – Regional map n° **17**-C2

Westlea House

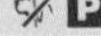

FAMILY • CONTEMPORARY It might look like an ordinary house but inside Westlea has been transformed into a stylish, boutique-style B&B. Individually decorated bedrooms feature bold modern artwork and have a funky feel; two have roll-top baths in the room.

5 rooms ☕ – 🚹£ 45/55 🚹🚹£ 80/105

2 Market St ✉ IV26 2XE – ✆ 01854 612594 – www.westlea-ullapool.co.uk

VEENSGARTH
→ See Shetland Islands (Mainland)

WALKERBURN

The Scottish Borders – Pop. 700 – Regional map n° **15**-C2

Windlestraw

LUXURY • ELEGANT An attractive Arts and Crafts property built in 1906 as a wedding gift for the wife of the mill owner John King Ballantyne. It boasts original fireplaces, old plaster ceilings and great valley views; the bedrooms have been stylishly modernised and guest areas include a plush lounge and a comfy bar. The attractive, wood-panelled dining room offers a daily changing menu.

6 rooms – £ 125/200 £ 175/250

EH43 6AA – On A 72 – 01896 870636 – www.windlestraw.co.uk – Closed 18 December-13 February

WESTRAY (Isle of)
→ See Orkney Islands

WICK

Highland – Pop. 7 155 – Regional map n° **17**-D1

Bord De L'Eau

CLASSIC FRENCH • BISTRO Long-standing riverside bistro run by keen, hands-on owners. Sit in the small conservatory or in the bright dining room, surrounded by French posters and Eiffel Tower prints. Classic Gallic dishes feature plenty of local seafood.

Carte £ 28/41

2 Market St (Riverside) KW1 4AR – 01955 604400 – Closed 25-26 December, 1-2 January, Sunday lunch and Monday

Clachan

FAMILY • PERSONALISED Smart detached house on the edge of town, a short drive from the Queen Mother's former holiday residence, the Castle of Mey. Stylish, well-kept bedrooms blend oak furnishings with tartan fabrics. Black and white photos of the town's herring fishing days decorate the cosy dining room. Extensive breakfasts.

3 rooms – £ 70/78 £ 80/88

13 Randolph Pl, South Rd KW1 5NJ – South : 0.75 mi on A 99 – 01955 605384 – www.theclachan.co.uk – Closed 2 weeks Christmas-New Year

coleenphotography/iStock

WALES

It may only be 170 miles from north to south, but Wales contains great swathes of beauty, such as the dark and craggy heights of Snowdonia's ninety mountain peaks, the rolling sandstone bluffs of the Brecon Beacons, and Pembrokeshire's tantalising golden beaches. Bottle-nosed dolphins love it here too, arriving each summer at New Quay in Cardigan Bay. Highlights abound: formidable Harlech Castle dominates its coast, Bala Lake has a railway that steams along its gentle shores, and a metropolitan vibe can be found in the capital, Cardiff, home to the Principality Stadium and the National Assembly.

Wales is a country which teems with great raw ingredients and modern-day chefs are employing these to their utmost potential; from succulent slices of Spring lamb farmed on the lush mountains and valleys, through to the humblest of cockles; from satisfying native Welsh Black cattle through to abundant Anglesey oysters, delicious Welsh cheeses and the edible seaweed found on the shores of the Gower and known as laverbread.

- Michelin Road maps n° 503 and 713
- Michelin Green Guide: Great Britain

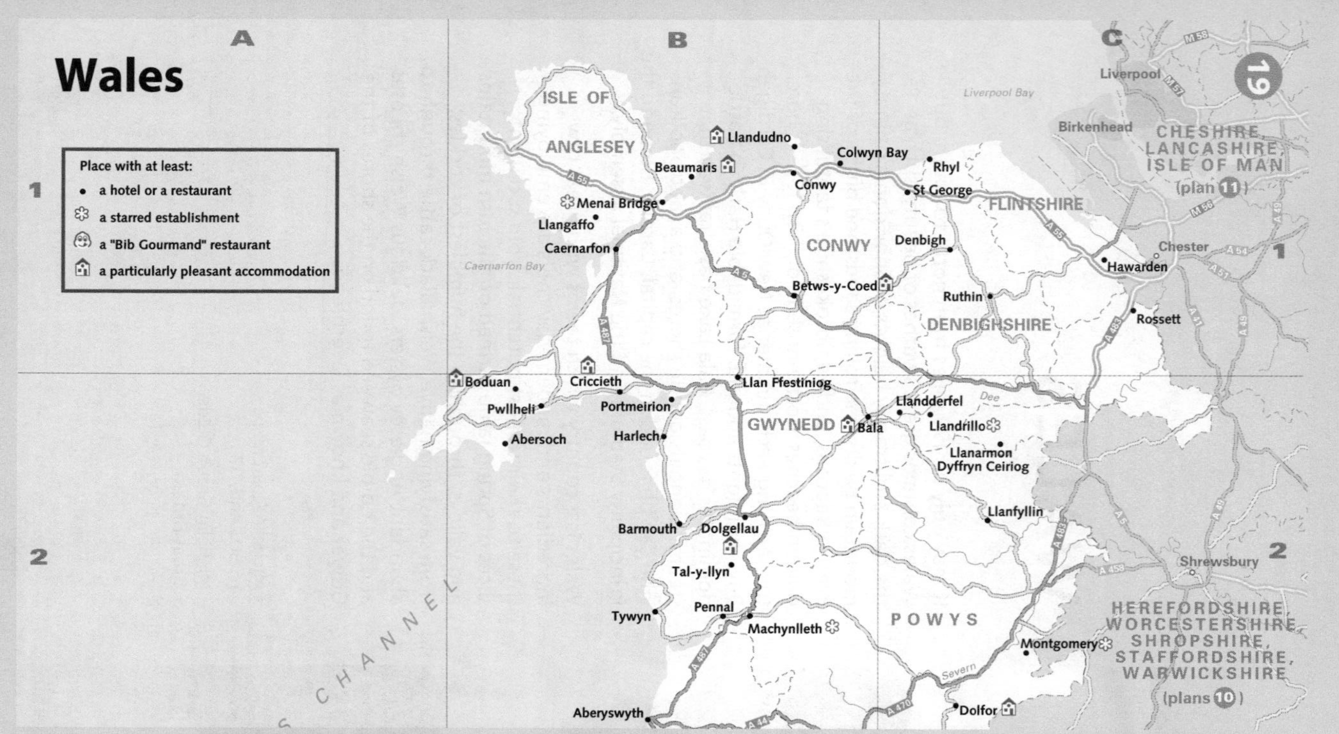
A
B
C
1
2
Wales
Place with at least:
• a hotel or a restaurant
a starred establishment
a "Bib Gourmand" restaurant
a particularly pleasant accommodation
ISLE OF ANGLESEY
Llandudno
Beaumaris
Colwyn Bay
Rhyl
Conwy
St George
Menai Bridge
Llangaffo
Caernarfon
Caernarfon Bay
Liverpool Bay
Liverpool
Birkenhead
CHESHIRE, LANCASHIRE, ISLE OF MAN (plan 11)
19
FLINTSHIRE
CONWY
Denbigh
Chester
Hawarden
Betws-y-Coed
Ruthin
DENBIGHSHIRE
Rossett
Boduan
Criccieth
Llan Ffestiniog
Pwllheli
Portmeirion
Llandderfel
Dee
GWYNEDD
Bala
Llandrillo
Abersoch
Harlech
Llanarmon Dyffryn Ceiriog
Llanfyllin
Barmouth
Dolgellau
Shrewsbury
Tal-y-llyn
Tywyn
Pennal
Machynlleth
POWYS
HEREFORDSHIRE, WORCESTERSHIRE SHROPSHIRE, STAFFORDSHIRE, WARWICKSHIRE (plans 10)
Montgomery
Severn
Aberyswyth
Dolfor
CHANNEL
A 55
A 5
A 487
A 483
A 470
A 458
A 44
A 41
A 49
A 51
A 54
M 56
M 57
M 58

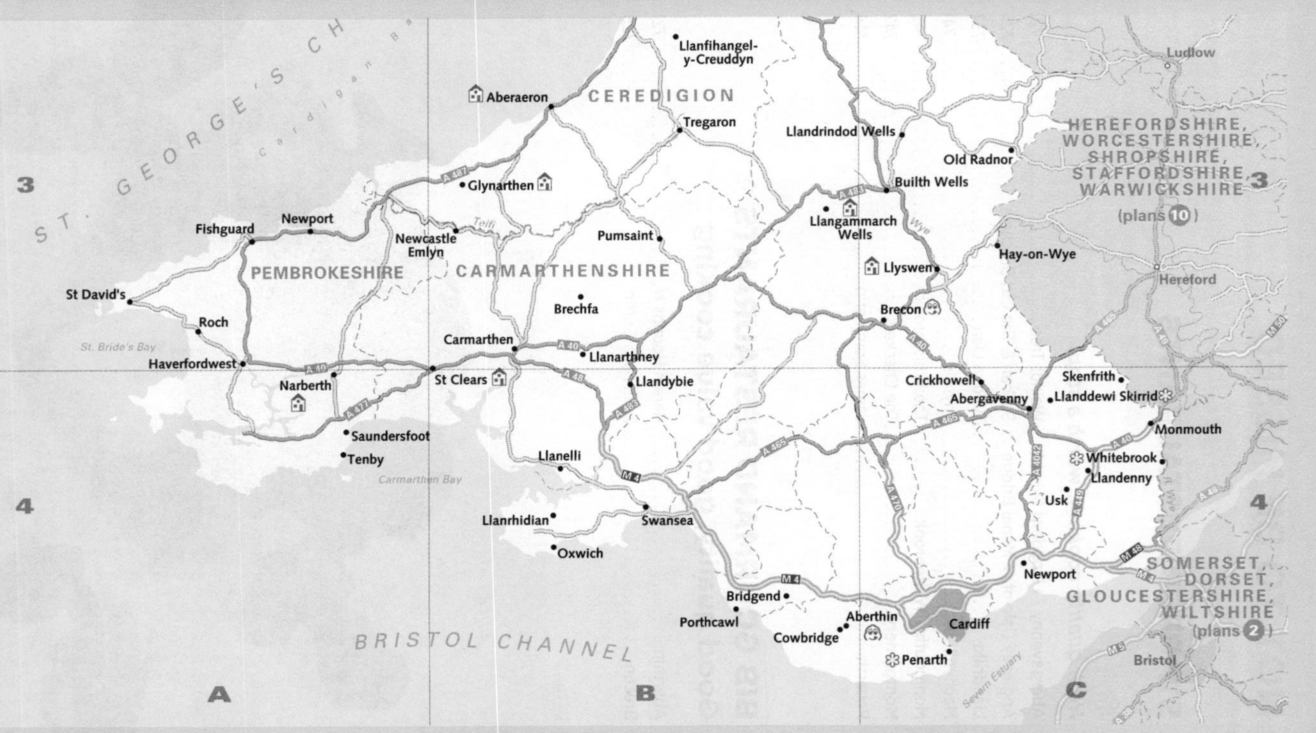

ST. GEORGE'S CH
Cardigan Ba
CEREDIGION
PEMBROKESHIRE
CARMARTHENSHIRE
HEREFORDSHIRE, WORCESTERSHIRE, SHROPSHIRE, STAFFORDSHIRE, WARWICKSHIRE
(plans 10)
SOMERSET, DORSET, GLOUCESTERSHIRE, WILTSHIRE
(plans 2)
BRISTOL CHANNEL
St. Bride's Bay
Carmarthen Bay
Severn Estuary
Teifi
Wye
R. Wye
Llanfihangel-y-Creuddyn
Aberaeron
Tregaron
Llandrindod Wells
Old Radnor
Ludlow
Glynarthen
Builth Wells
Llangammarch Wells
Fishguard
Newport
Newcastle Emlyn
Pumsaint
Hay-on-Wye
Hereford
St David's
Llyswen
Brechfa
Brecon
Roch
Carmarthen
Llanarthney
Haverfordwest
St Clears
Llandybie
Crickhowell
Skenfrith
Narberth
Abergavenny
Llanddewi Skirrid
Monmouth
Saundersfoot
Tenby
Llanelli
Whitebrook
Llandenny
Usk
Llanrhidian
Swansea
Oxwich
Newport
Bridgend
Porthcawl
Aberthin
Cowbridge
Cardiff
Penarth
Bristol
A 40
A 48
A 477
A 487
A 483
A 465
A 470
A 4042
A 449
A 49
A 38
M 4
M 48
M 5
M 50
3
4
A
B
C

NOT TO BE MISSED

STARRED RESTAURANTS

✿

High quality cooking, worth a stop!

BIB GOURMAND RESTAURANTS ☺
Good quality, good value cooking

Michelin

OUR TOP PICKS

Hotels with Spas

It's all about the food

Made their mark

More than just the village pub

Gloriously remote

Cleifiog	(Anglesey (Isle of)/Beaumaris)	722
Coedllys Country House	(St Clears)	747
Old Rectory	(Pwllheli/Boduan)	746
Old Vicarage	(Dolfor)	734
Penbontbren	(Glynarthen)	735

Good value home from home

3 Pen Cei	(Aberaeron)	720
Felin Glais	(Brecon)	725
Firgrove	(Ruthin)	747
Outbuildings	(Anglesey (Isle of)/Llangaffo))	723
Rhedyn	(Builth Wells)	725

Quintessential country houses

Bodysgallen Hall	(Llandudno)	738
Ffynnon	(Dolgellau)	734
Grove	(Narberth)	742
Lake Country House and Spa	(Llangammarch Wells)	740

Special Occasion

Llangoed Hall	(Llyswen)	741
The Swan at Hay	(Hay-on-Wye)	736
Ynyshir	(Machynlleth)	741

ABERAERON ABER AERON

Ceredigion - Pop. 1 422 - Regional map n° **19**-B3

Harbourmaster

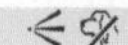

TRADITIONAL BRITISH • INN Vibrant blue inn with a New England style bar-lounge, a modern dining room and lovely harbour views. Choose between the bar menu, a more substantial evening à la carte and daily specials. Smart bedrooms, split between the house and a nearby cottage, are brightly decorated and well-equipped; some have terraces.

Menu £ 28 (dinner) - Carte £ 19/40

13 rooms - £ 75/145 £ 120/265

Quay Par SA46 0BA
- 01545 570755 - www.harbour-master.com
- Closed dinner 24 December-26 December

3 Pen Cei

TOWNHOUSE • PERSONALISED Vibrant blue house on the harbourfront; formerly the Packet Steam Company HQ. Stylish modern bedrooms are named after local rivers: those to the front overlook the water and Aeron has a free-standing bath. Great breakfasts range from fruit salad to smoked salmon and scrambled eggs.

5 rooms - £ 95/150 £ 105/160

3 Quay Par SA46 0BT
- 01545 571147 - www.pencei.co.uk
- Closed 25-26 December

ABERGAVENNY Y-FENNI

Monmouthshire - Pop. 13 423 - Regional map n° **19**-C4

The Court

MODERN BRITISH • CLASSIC DÉCOR XX A country house dining room hung with photos of local scenes. Classic British dishes are given a modern twist and fruit, veg and herbs are from the walled garden. All wines are offered by the glass.

Menu £ 15 (weekdays)/33 - Carte £ 34/54

Llansantffraed Court Hotel, Llanvihangel Gobion NP7 9BA - Southeast : 6.5 mi by A 40 and B 4598 off old Raglan rd
- 01873 840678 (booking essential) - www.thecourtdiningroom.co.uk

Angel

HISTORIC • PERSONALISED A family-run, Georgian coaching inn and outbuildings; characterful guest areas have a modern, shabby-chic feel and bedrooms are a mix of the traditional and the more contemporary. Have afternoon tea in the Wedgewood Room or dine from an all-encompassing menu in the brasserie.

33 rooms - £ 99/168 £ 99/168 - 2 suites

15 Cross St NP7 5EN
- 01873 857121 - www.angelabergavenny.com - Closed 25 December

Llansantffraed Court

HISTORIC • CLASSIC An attractive Grade II listed William and Mary style house with an ornamental lake and a 16C church in its 20 acre grounds. Bedrooms have a restful feel - the corner rooms have both mountain and valley views.

20 rooms - £ 95/135 £ 95/135

Llanvihangel Gobion NP7 9BA - Southeast : 6.5 mi by A 40 and B 4598 off old Raglan rd
- 01873 840678 - www.llch.co.uk

The Court - See restaurant listing

at Llanddewi Skirrid Northeast: 3.25 mi on B4521✉ Abergavenny

Walnut Tree (Shaun Hill)

MODERN BRITISH • COSY A long-standing Welsh institution, set in a wooded valley and always bustling with regulars; start with drinks in the flag-floored lounge-bar. Classic, seasonal dishes are well-priced and refreshingly simple, eschewing adornment and letting the natural flavours of the ingredients speak for themselves.

➜ Veal sweetbreads with sauerkraut and mustard dressing. Sea bass with artichokes, pancetta and salsa verde. Caramel fondant with cherry sorbet.

Menu £ 30 (lunch) – Carte £ 34/55

✉ NP7 8AW – ✆ 01873 852797 (booking essential) – www.thewalnuttreeinn.com – Closed 1 week Christmas, Sunday and Monday

at Cross Ash Northeast: 8.25 mi on B4521

1861

TRADITIONAL BRITISH • COSY A part-timbered former pub; now a cosy, contemporary restaurant named after the year it was built. Classically based cooking has modern twists – much of the fruit and veg is grown by the owner's father.

Menu £ 24/35 – Carte £ 37/50

✉ NP7 8PB – West : 0.5 mi on B 4521 – ✆ 01873 821297 – www.18-61.co.uk – Closed first 2 weeks January, Sunday dinner and Monday

ABERSOCH

Gwynedd – ✉ Pwllheli – Pop. 783 – Regional map n° **19**-B2

Venetia

ITALIAN • BRASSERIE A double-fronted house once owned by a sea captain, with a cosy bar-lounge and a boldly decorated dining room. Cicchetti is followed by classic Italian dishes presented in a distinctly modern style. Chic bedrooms are well-equipped – one has a jacuzzi with a waterproof TV.

Carte £ 21/35

5 rooms – †£ 65/133 ††£ 80/148

Lon Sarn Bach ✉ LL53 7EB – ✆ 01758 713354 – www.venetiawales.com – dinner only – Restricted opening in winter

at Bwlchtocyn South: 2 mi✉ Pwllheli

Porth Tocyn

FAMILY • PERSONALISED High on the headland overlooking Cardigan Bay, a traditional hotel that's been in the family for three generations. Relax in the cosy lounges or explore the many leisure and children's facilities. Homely, modernised bedrooms; some with balconies or sea views. Menus offer interesting, soundly executed dishes.

17 rooms – †£ 115/155 ††£ 115/195

✉ LL53 7BU – ✆ 01758 713303 – www.porthtocynhotel.co.uk – Closed early November-mid March

ABERTHIN

The Vale of Glamorgan – Regional map n° **19**-B4

Hare & Hounds

TRADITIONAL CUISINE • FRIENDLY The chef's passionate desire to make this 300 year old pub the most seasonal in Wales is laudable. Menus change twice daily and produce is from his 3 acre allotment and family farms; he also hunts and forages, so expect plenty of game, mushrooms and hedgerow berries. Cooking is unfussy yet bursts with flavour.

Menu £ 20 (weekday lunch) – Carte £ 24/39

✉ CF71 7LG – ✆ 01446 774892 – www.hareandhoundsaberthin.com – Closed Sunday dinner-Tuesday

ABERYSTWYTH ABERESTUUTH

Ceredigion – Pop. 18 093 – Regional map n° **19**-B2

Gwesty Cymru

TOWNHOUSE • MODERN Grade II listed Georgian townhouse on the seafront, with a brightly painted exterior and a terrace overlooking the bay. Thoughtfully designed modern bedrooms vary in size and décor – all are colour themed, with smart bathrooms. Small, stylish basement bar and dining room; ambitious, adventurous dishes.

8 rooms – †£ 70/165 ††£ 80/165

19 Marine Terr ✉ SY23 2AZ
– ✆ 01970 612252 – www.gwestycymru.com – Closed 23 December-2 January

ANGLESEY (Isle of) SIR YNYS MÔN

Isle of Anglesey – Pop. 68 900 – Regional map n° **19**-B1

Beaumaris

Loft

MODERN BRITISH • ELEGANT XX Formal restaurant under the eaves of an old coaching inn, with a plush, open-fired lounge and an elegant candlelit dining room with exposed beams and immaculately laid tables. Creative modern cooking champions top Anglesey produce.

Menu £ 50

The Bull Hotel, Castle St ✉ LL58 8AP
– ✆ 01248 810329 (booking advisable) – www.bullsheadinn.co.uk – dinner only
– Closed 25-26 December, 1 January and Sunday-Tuesday

Brasserie

TRADITIONAL CUISINE • BRASSERIE X Set overlooking a courtyard, a large brasserie in the old stables of a 17C coaching inn, with a Welsh slate floor, oak tables, a fireplace built from local stone and a relaxed feel. Wide-ranging modern menus feature lots of specials.

Carte £ 20/40

The Bull Hotel, Castle St ✉ LL58 8AP
– ✆ 01248 810329 – www.bullsheadinn.co.uk – Closed 25-26 December and 1 January

The Bull

INN • PERSONALISED Characterful 1670s coaching inn – look out for the old water clock and ducking stool in the bar. Bedrooms in the main house are named after Dickens characters and are traditional; those in the townhouse are more modern and colourful.

25 rooms – †£ 85/105 ††£ 115/185

Castle St ✉ LL58 8AP
– ✆ 01248 810329 – www.bullsheadinn.co.uk – Closed 25-26 December and 1 January

Brasserie • **Loft** – See restaurant listing

Cleifiog

TOWNHOUSE • PERSONALISED Delightful seafront guesthouse overlooking the mountains and the Menai Strait; run by a welcoming owner. Watercolours hang on wood-panelled walls in the cosy, antique-furnished lounge. Comfortable bedrooms have fine linens and large bathrooms. Excellent communal breakfasts feature tasty fresh juices.

3 rooms – †£ 65/95 ††£ 95/125

Townsend ✉ LL58 8BH
– ✆ 01248 811507 – www.cleifiogbandb.co.uk – Closed Christmas-early January

Churchbank

TOWNHOUSE · PERSONALISED Georgian guesthouse with a homely, antique-furnished interior and modern day comforts. Cosy bedrooms look out over the large walled garden and the church opposite; one has a private bathroom. Helpful, amiable owner and hearty breakfasts.

3 rooms – †£ 80/90 ††£ 85/105

28 Church St ✉ LL58 8AB – ✆ 01248 810353
– www.bedandbreakfastanglesey.co.uk

Llangaffo

Outbuildings

TRADITIONAL · PERSONALISED A tastefully converted former barn set close to a prehistoric burial ground and offering fantastic views over Snowdonia. Stylish modern bedrooms come with local artwork and smart bathrooms; for a romantic hideaway, choose the 'Pink Hut' in the garden. Afternoon tea is served in the cosy open-fired lounge and a concise, seasonally led menu in the spacious dining room.

5 rooms – †£ 75 ††£ 100

Bodowyr Farmhouse ✉ LL60 6NH – Southeast : 1.5 mi by B 4419 turning left at crossroads and left again by post box
– ✆ 01248 430132 – www.theoutbuildings.co.uk

Menai Bridge

Sosban & The Old Butchers (Stephen Stevens)

MODERN CUISINE · INTIMATE A brightly painted restaurant displaying Welsh slate and hand-painted tiles from its butcher's shop days. A well-balanced 6-7 course surprise menu offers boldly flavoured modern dishes with original, personal touches, which demonstrate an innate understanding of cooking techniques and flavour combinations.

➜ Celeriac risotto with coffee and Bramley apple. Cefn Llan free range duck with parsnip, yoghurt and liquorice. Rhubarb and custard with almond, wild rice and wood sorrel.

Menu £ 75 – surprise menu only

Trinity House, 1a High St ✉ LL59 5EE – ✆ 01248 208131 (booking essential)
– www.sosbanandtheoldbutchers.com – dinner only and Saturday lunch – Closed January-mid February, Christmas-New Year and Sunday-Wednesday

Dylan's

MODERN CUISINE · FAMILY An old boat yard timber store; now a smart, busy, two-storey eatery by the water's edge, overlooking Bangor. Extensive menus offer everything from homemade cakes and weekend brunch to sourdough pizzas. Find a spot on the terrace if you can.

Carte £ 20/45

St George's Rd ✉ LL59 5DE
– ✆ 01248 716714 (booking advisable) – www.dylansrestaurant.co.uk – Closed 25-26 December

BALA

Gwynedd – ✉ Gwynedd – Pop. 1 974 – Regional map n° **19**-B2

Bryniau Golau

COUNTRY HOUSE · PERSONALISED Original Victorian tiling, plasterwork and fireplaces are proudly shown-off in this elegant house. Bedrooms overlook the lake and mountains: one has a four-poster bed; another, a bath which affords lake views. Their homemade honey features alongside local produce at breakfast.

3 rooms – †£ 90/100 ††£ 110/120

Llangower ✉ LL23 7BT – South : 2 mi by A 494 and B 4931 off B 4403
– ✆ 01678 521782 – www.bryniau-golau.co.uk – Closed December-February

BARMOUTH ABERMAW

Gwynedd – Pop. 2 315 – Regional map n° **19**-B2

Bistro Bermo

TRADITIONAL CUISINE • BISTRO An intimate, personally run bistro with a lively atmosphere. The concise menu follows the seasons and tasty dishes are neatly presented; go for the dry-aged Welsh Black rib-eye, or one of the local fish specials listed on the blackboard.

Carte £ 26/41

6 Church St ✉ LL42 1EW – ✆ 01341 281284 (booking essential) – www.bistrobarmouth.co.uk – dinner only – Closed Sunday, Monday and restricted opening in winter

BEAUMARIS → See Anglesey (Isle of)

BETWS-Y-COED

Conwy – Pop. 255 – Regional map n° **19**-B1

Tan-y-Foel Country House

FAMILY • PERSONALISED Personally run, part-16C country house in 4 acres of grounds, which affords stunning views over the Vale of Conwy and Snowdonia. The snug lounge and breakfast room display traditional features. Modern, individually styled bedrooms have smart bathrooms; the spacious loft room has a vaulted ceiling.

6 rooms – †£ 85/165 ††£ 100/165

✉ LL26 0RE – East : 2.5 mi by A 5, A 470 and Capel Garmon rd on Llanwrst rd – ✆ 01690 710507 – www.tanyfoelcountryhouse.co.uk – Closed January-February and 1 week Christmas

Pengwern

TRADITIONAL • PERSONALISED Cosy Victorian house with stunning mountain and valley views. Warm, well-proportioned bedrooms retain charming original features like the old fireplaces and are named after famous artists who stayed at the house during the 1800s.

3 rooms – †£ 60/70 ††£ 73/84

Allt Dinas ✉ LL24 0HF – Southeast : 1.5 mi on A 5 – ✆ 01690 710480 – www.snowdoniaaccommodation.co.uk – Closed 22 December-3 January

at Penmachno Southwest: 4.75 mi by A5 on B4406 ✉ Betws-Y-Coed

Penmachno Hall

TRADITIONAL • PERSONALISED A former rectory in a pleasant valley location, with delightful views. Cosy lounge, eclectic art collection and lovely mature gardens. Boldly coloured bedrooms contain a host of thoughtful extras. Light supper by arrangement.

3 rooms – †£ 75/100 ††£ 95/100

✉ LL24 0PU – On Ty Mawr rd – ✆ 01690 760410 – www.penmachnohall.co.uk – Closed Christmas-New Year

BODUAN – Gwynedd → See Pwllheli

BRECHFA

Carmarthenshire – Regional map n° **19**-B3

Ty Mawr

TRADITIONAL • TRADITIONAL 16C stone farmhouse in the centre of the village, next to the river. It's personally run and boasts plenty of charm and character, with exposed bricks, wooden beams, open fires and pine-furnished bedrooms. The modern menu has Welsh twists and produce is homemade or from the valley.

6 rooms – †£ 80 ††£ 115/130

✉ SA32 7RA – ✆ 01267 202332 – www.wales-country-hotel.co.uk

BRECON

Powys – Pop. 8 250 – Regional map n° **19**-C3

Felin Fach Griffin

MODERN BRITISH • INN Located in picturesque countryside, a rather unique pub with bright paintwork, colourful artwork and an extremely laid-back atmosphere. The young team are friendly and have a good knowledge of what they're serving. Following the motto 'simple things, done well', dishes are straightforward, tasty and refined. Pleasant bedrooms come with comfy beds but no TVs.

Menu £ 24/29 – Carte £ 27/36

7 rooms – £ 115/140 £ 160/190

Felin Fach LD3 0UB – Northeast : 4.75 mi by B 4602 off A 470 – 01874 620111 – www.felinfachgriffin.co.uk – Closed 25 December and 4 days early January

Felin Glais

TRADITIONAL • COSY 17C stone barn and mill, set in a tranquil hamlet and run with pride. Spacious interior has a pleasant 'lived in' feel; cosy, homely bedrooms have toiletries and linen from Harrods. Large beamed lounge; dine here, at the communal table, or in the conservatory in summer. Lengthy menu – order two days ahead.

4 rooms – £ 95/100 £ 95/110

Aberyscir LD3 9NP – West : 4 mi by Cradoc rd turning right immediately after bridge – 01874 623107 – www.felinglais.co.uk – Closed December and January

BRIDGEND PEN-Y-BONT

Bridgend – Pop. 46 757 – Regional map n° **19**-B4

Leicester's

MODERN CUISINE • INTIMATE XX A friendly team welcome you to this smart hotel restaurant, where striking sculptures are dotted about. Lunch sees a good value, flexible menu, while at dinner you'll find more interesting combinations and eye-catching presentation.

Menu £ 15 (weekday lunch) – Carte £ 29/40

Great House Hotel, High St, Laleston CF32 0HP – West : 2 mi on A473 – 01656 657644 – www.great-house-laleston.co.uk – Closed 24-27 December, Sunday dinner and bank holidays

Great House

HISTORIC • CLASSIC A welcoming 15C listed property; reputedly a gift from Elizabeth I to the Earl of Leicester and once home to the Lord of the Manor. The guest areas have character and bedrooms are comfy – those in the coach house are the most modern.

13 rooms – £ 72/160 £ 90/210

High St, Laleston CF32 0HP – West : 2 mi on A 473 – 01656 657644 – www.great-house-laleston.co.uk – Closed 24-27 December

Leicester's – See restaurant listing

BUILTH WELLS LLANFAIR-YM-MUALLT

Powys – Pop. 2 829 – Regional map n° **19**-C3

Rhedyn

FAMILY • PERSONALISED Former forester's cottage with a small garden and pleasant country views, run by very welcoming owners. Tiny lounge with a bookcase full of local info and DVDs; cosy communal dining room where home-cooked, local market produce is served. Good-sized, modern bedrooms feature heavy wood furnishings, good facilities and quirky touches. Tea and cake are served on arrival.

3 rooms – £ 85 £ 95

Cilmery LD2 3LH – West : 4 mi on A 483 – 01982 551944 – www.rhedynguesthouse.co.uk

BWLCHTOCYN - Gwynedd ➜ See Abersoch

CAERNARFON

Gwynedd – Pop. 9 493 – Regional map n° **19**-B1

Plas Dinas

TRADITIONAL • CLASSIC The former home of Lord Snowdon, set in large gardens and filled with family portraits and antiques. The comfy drawing room has an open fire, a piano and an honesty bar. Smart bedrooms come with good extras and immaculate bathrooms. Traditional dinners are served 5 nights a week.

10 rooms – †£ 109/249 ††£ 109/249

✉ LL54 7YF – South : 2.5 mi on A 487 – ✆ 01286 830214 – www.plasdinas.co.uk – Closed Christmas

at Seion Northeast: 5.5 mi by A4086 and B4366 on Seion rd ✉ Gwynedd

Ty'n Rhos Country House

FAMILY • PERSONALISED Personally run former farmhouse with a large conservatory and a cosy lounge with an inglenook fireplace. Comfortable, modern bedrooms; some have balconies or terraces and others, their own garden. The formal restaurant offers pleasant views over Anglesey; classically based dishes are presented in modern ways.

19 rooms – †£ 90/140 ††£ 145/190

✉ LL55 3AE – Southwest : 0.75 mi – ✆ 01248 670489 – www.tynrhos.co.uk

age fotostock

GOOD TIPS!

Wales' capital combines a rich history with top-class sporting venues, big name shops and a lively cultural scene. This is reflected in our selection, with restaurants like **Park House** – set in a late 19C property built by the founder of modern Cardiff, the 2nd Marquess of Bute – and the ultra-modern, glass-fronted **St. David's Hotel & Spa**.

CARDIFF

Cardiff – Pop. 346 090 – Regional map n° **19**-C4

Restaurants

Park House 

MODERN CUISINE • ELEGANT XXX A striking building overlooking Gorsedd Gardens and designed by William Burgess in the late 1800s; the oak-panelled dining room has a formal air. Each dish is matched with a wine from an impressive list.

Menu £ 18 (lunch) – Carte £ 34/66

Town plan: C1-p – *20 Park Pl.* ✉ *CF10 3DQ*
– *✆ 029 2022 4343 – www.parkhouserestaurant.co.uk*
– *Closed 24-25 December, 1-11 January and Monday*

Asador 44 Ⓝ 

SPANISH • ELEGANT XX A dark, moody restaurant divided into lots of different areas; sit overlooking the Asador, the cheese room or the glass-fronted wine cave. The menu focuses on charcoal-cooked meats and much of the produce is imported from Spain.

Menu £ 17 (weekday lunch) – Carte £ 40/50

Town plan: C1-a – *14-15 Quay St* ✉ *CF10 1EA*
– *✆ 029 2002 0039 (bookings advisable at dinner) – www.asador44.co.uk*
– *Closed Sunday-Monday*

Purple Poppadom 

INDIAN • DESIGN XX Enter via the glass door between the shop fronts and head up to the smart room with bold purple décor. Classic combinations are cooked in a refined modern style and given a personal twist; the seafood dishes are popular.

Menu £ 15 (lunch and early dinner) – Carte £ 19/37

Town plan: B1-n – *185a Cowbridge Rd East* ✉ *CF11 9AJ – 1st Floor*
– *✆ 029 2022 0026 – www.purplepoppadom.com*
– *Closed 25-26 December, 1 January and Monday*

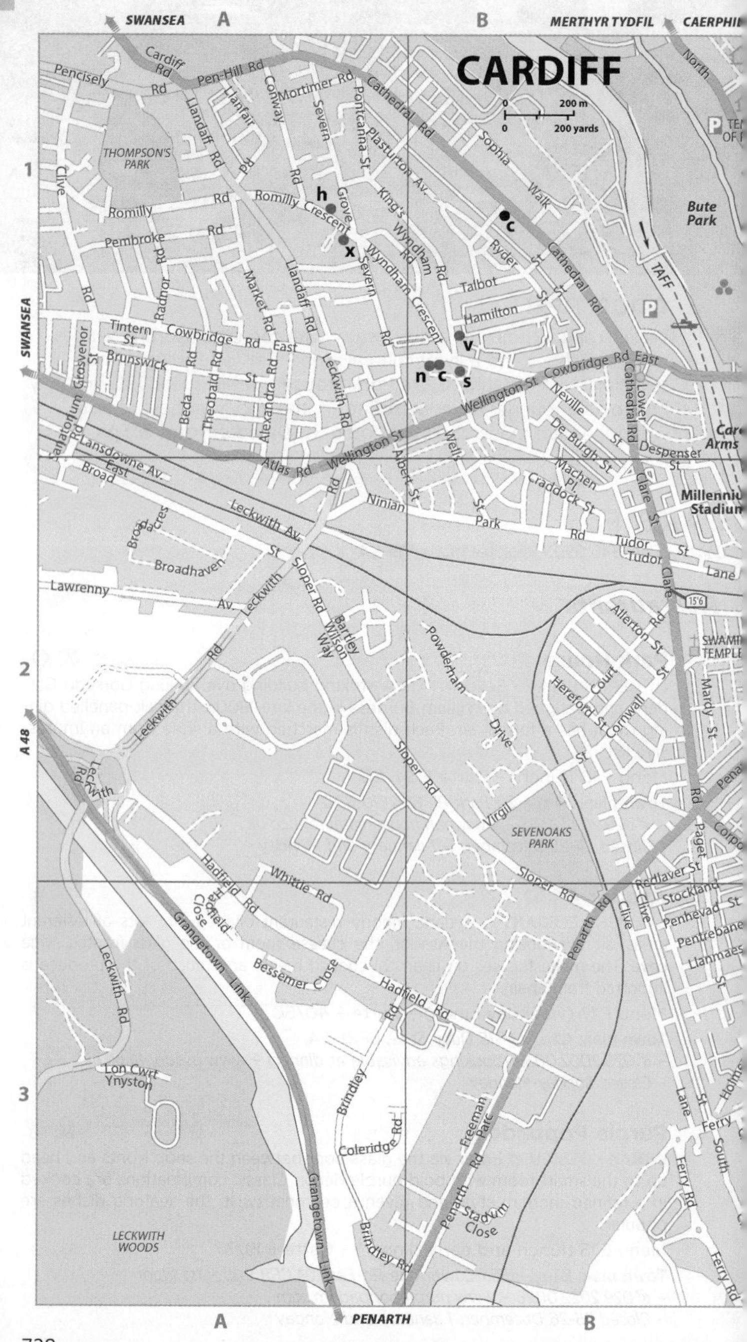
CARDIFF
SWANSEA
MERTHYR TYDFIL
CAERPHI
PENARTH
A 48
A
B
1
2
3
0
200 m
200 yards
THOMPSON'S PARK
Bute Park
SEVENOAKS PARK
LECKWITH WOODS
Millenniu Stadium
SWAMI TEMPLE
TAFF
Cathedral Rd
Cowbridge Rd East
Wellington St
Penarth Rd
Sloper Rd
Leckwith Rd
Grangetown Link
Hadfield Rd
Romilly Crescent
Wyndham Crescent
Clare St
Tudor St
Ferry Rd

C
D
A 48 BRISTOL
CATHAYS
UNIVERSITY COLLEGE
National Museum Cardiff
City Hall
Gorsedd Gardens
Law Courts
Military Museums
ST DAVID'S SHOPPING CENTRE
St John's Church
Central Market
CAPITOL CENTRE
QUEEN ST
CARDIFF NEW SYNAGOGUE
TABERNACL
CALLAGHAN SQUARE
CARDIFF CENTRAL
Bute East Dock
THE RED DRAGON CENTRE
CARDIFF BAY
BUTETOWN
Coal Exchange
Wales Millennium Centre
Pierhead Building
Y Senedd
Techniquest
MERMAID QUAY
Norwegian Church
CARDIFF BAY
HAMADRYAD PARK
CARDIFF BAY WETLANDS RESERVE
CARDIFF YACHT CLUB
TAFF
ROATH DOCK
QUEEN ALEXANDRA DOCK
BRIGEND
1
2
3

Arbennig

REGIONAL CUISINE • SIMPLE Homely neighbourhood bistro with a buzzy feel. Daily baked bread is made to match the dishes on the weekly changing menu. Cooking covers all bases, from soup to steak, and there's a great value set selection available at lunch.

Menu £ 20 (lunch) – Carte £ 27/43

Town plan: A1-h – *6-10 Romilly Cres. ✉ CF11 9NR – ✆ 029 2034 1264 – www.arbennig.co.uk – Closed Sunday dinner and Monday*

'Bully's

FRENCH • NEIGHBOURHOOD A proudly and passionately run neighbourhood bistro decorated with an eclectic array of memorabilia. Menus have a French base but also display some British and Mediterranean touches.

Menu £ 20 (weekday lunch) – Carte £ 29/46

Town plan: A1-x – *5 Romilly Cres. ✉ CF11 9NP – ✆ 029 2022 1905 – www.bullysrestaurant.co.uk – Closed Christmas, Sunday dinner, Monday and Tuesday*

Casanova

ITALIAN • SIMPLE A long-standing Italian restaurant near the stadium. Flavoursome country dishes are a perfect match for the rustic, osteria-style interior; mid-week afternoons they serve an Assaggi (light bites) menu.

Menu £ 18/30

Town plan: C1-c – *13 Quay St ✉ CF10 1EA – ✆ 029 2034 4044 – www.casanovacardiff.co.uk – Closed Sunday and bank holidays*

Chai St

INDIAN • EXOTIC DÉCOR Vibrantly decorated Indian restaurant with a mix of wooden seating; some tables you share. Simple menus focus on thalis, which come with meat, rice, vegetables, naan, poppadoms and raita. Dishes are well-spiced and good value.

Carte £ 11/18

Town plan: B1-s – *153 Cowbridge Rd East ✉ CF11 9AH – ✆ 029 2022 8888 – www.chaistreet.com – Closed 25-26 December*

Chez Francis

FRENCH • SIMPLE Intimate eatery run by an experienced French owner. Dine at tightly packed tables in the narrow bistro or at barrels which act as the bar. All the classics are here from Bayonne ham to coq au vin, roast duck to tarte au citron.

Menu £ 14 (weekday lunch) – Carte £ 23/39

Town plan: B1-c – *185 Cowbridge Rd East ✉ CF11 9AJ – ✆ 029 2022 4959 – www.chez-francis.co.uk – Closed 1 week August, Sunday and Monday*

La Cuina

SPANISH • BISTRO A small, rustic shop conversion with a handful of tables on each level and walls packed with regional delicacies for sale. Authentic Spanish dishes have strong Catalonian influences, with tapas-sized portions served at lunch.

Menu £ 15 (weekday lunch) – Carte £ 28/48

Town plan: B1-v – *11 Kings Rd ✉ CF11 9BZ – ✆ 029 2019 0265 – www.lacuina.co.uk – Closed 3-24 August, 23-27 December and Sunday-Tuesday*

Potted Pig

TRADITIONAL BRITISH • RUSTIC Atmospheric restaurant in a stripped back former bank vault, with brick walls, barrel ceilings and a utilitarian feel. Lesser-known products and cuts of meat are used in robust, tasty dishes. The gin cocktails are a speciality.

Menu £ 12 (weekday lunch) – Carte £ 26/47

Town plan: C1-s – *27 High St ✉ CF10 1PU – ✆ 029 2022 4817 – www.thepottedpig.com – Closed 23 December-3 January, Sunday dinner and Monday*

Hotels

St David's H. & Spa

BUSINESS • MINIMALIST Modern, purpose-built hotel on the waterfront, affording lovely 360° views. Good-sized, minimalist bedrooms have a slightly funky feel; all boast balconies and bay outlooks. Smart spa features seawater pools and a dry floatation tank. Stylish restaurant with superb terrace views serves modern British dishes.

142 rooms – £ 99/175 £ 109/259 – 12 suites

Town plan: D3-a – *Havannah St, Cardiff Bay ✉ CF10 5SD – ✆ 029 2045 4045 – www.principal-hayley.com/thestdavids*

Park Plaza

BUSINESS • MINIMALIST A light, airy hotel with a stylish lounge, extensive conference facilities and a vast leisure centre boasting a smart stainless steel pool and 8 treatment rooms. Stark modern bedrooms come with slate bathrooms. The informal brasserie and bar serve both international dishes and afternoon teas.

129 rooms – £ 89/349 £ 99/359 – £ 13

Town plan: C1-s – *Greyfriars Rd ✉ CF10 3AL – ✆ 029 2011 1111 – www.parkplazacardiff.com – Closed 25-26 December*

Cathedral 73

TOWNHOUSE • CONTEMPORARY Delightful Victorian terraced house on the edge of the city, with boutique furnishings, designer bedrooms and a chauffeur-driven Rolls Royce. Afternoon tea is served in the spacious sitting room and breakfast, in the orangery.

10 rooms – £ 99/250 £ 99/250

Town plan: B1-c – *73 Cathedral Rd ✉ CF11 9HE – ✆ 029 2023 5005 – www.cathedral73.com – Closed 24-27 December*

CARMARTHEN

Carmarthenshire – Pop. 15 854 – Regional map n° **19**-B3

at Llanllawddog Northeast: 8 mi by A485

Glangwili Mansion

FAMILY • MODERN Part-17C mansion rebuilt in a Georgian style, set in a great location on the edge of the forest. The spacious interior features sleek tiled floors, contemporary artwork and bright, bold bedrooms with modern oak furnishings.

3 rooms – £ 90/95 £ 120/140

✉ SA32 7JE – ✆ 01267 253735 – www.glangwilimansion.co.uk – Closed 24-26 December

at Nantgaredig East: 5 mi by A4300 on A4310 ✉ Carmarthen

Y Polyn

TRADITIONAL BRITISH • PUB Small, rustic pub on a busy country road, set close to a stream and boasting pleasant views. Cooking is stout, filling and British at heart, offering satisfying soups, fresh salads, slow-cooked meats and classical puddings.

Menu £ 35 (dinner) – Carte lunch £ 30/41

✉ SA32 7LH – South : 1 mi on B 4310 – ✆ 01267 290000 (booking advisable) – www.ypolyn.co.uk – Closed Sunday dinner and Monday

COLWYN BAY BAE COLWYN

Conwy – Pop. 29 405 – Regional map n° **19**-B1

Bryn Williams at Porth Eirias

MODERN BRITISH • DESIGN X If you're looking for a relaxed, friendly environment, this striking beachside brasserie with faux industrial styling and blue leather banquettes is the place to come. Cooking is pleasingly unfussy and local seafood is to the fore.

Menu £ 20 (weekday lunch) – Carte £ 24/39

The Promenade ✉ LL29 8HH – ✆ 01492 577525 – www.portheirias.com – Closed 25 December

at Rhos-on-Sea Northwest: 1 mi ✉ Colwyn Bay

Plas Rhos House

TRADITIONAL • PERSONALISED Smartly refurbished 19C house with a pleasant terrace, on a small street overlooking the sea. Cosy lounge and bright, cheery breakfast room. Bedrooms have modern bathrooms and thoughtful extras such as chocolates and a decanter of sherry.

5 rooms – †£ 70/80 ††£ 85/110

53 Cayley Promenade ✉ LL28 4EP – ✆ 01492 543698 – www.plasrhos.co.uk – Closed November-April

CONWY

Conwy – Pop. 3 873 – Regional map n° **19**-B1

Signatures

MODERN CUISINE • DESIGN XX Stylish restaurant with elegantly laid tables and a well-versed team – set in a holiday park close to the sea. Brasserie classics and snacks at lunch; more inventive, modern choices at dinner including the chef's 'Signature' dishes.

Menu £ 37 (dinner) – Carte lunch £ 35/46

Aberconwy Resort and Spa ✉ LL32 8GA – Northwest 1.5 mi by A 547 – ✆ 01492 583513 (booking advisable) – www.signaturesrestaurant.co.uk – Closed Monday and Tuesday

at Rowen South: 3.5 mi by B5106

Tir Y Coed

COUNTRY HOUSE • PERSONALISED 'Tir Y Coed' means 'Place in the Trees' and that sums up the lovely location perfectly; ask for a bedroom overlooking the garden if you like wildlife spotting. It has a contemporary country house look and offers good comforts throughout. Seasonal dishes feature produce from the local area.

7 rooms – †£ 120/180 ††£ 135/195

✉ LL32 8TP – ✆ 01492 650219 – www.tirycoed.com

COWBRIDGE Y BONT FAEN

The Vale of Glamorgan – Pop. 3 616 – Regional map n° **19**-B4

Arboreal

MEDITERRANEAN CUISINE • RUSTIC X There's a lively Antipodean vibe at this all-day bar and café, where the chef uses local produce in dishes with a Mediterranean, Asian and North African edge. Bespoke, wood-fired pizzas are a feature and folk music accompanies.

Carte £ 23/40

68 Eastgate ✉ CF71 7AB – ✆ 01446 775093 – www.arboreal.uk.com – Closed first 2 weeks January and Monday

CRICCIETH

Gwynedd – Pop. 1 753 – Regional map n° **19**-B2

Dylan's

MODERN BRITISH • BRASSERIE A striking art deco inspired seafront building designed by Sir Clough Williams-Ellis in the 1950s. Extensive all-day menus offer everything from coffee and cake to seafood specials. Sit in one of two wings or out on the terrace.

Carte £ 20/45

Esplanade ✉ LL52 0HU

– ✆ 01766 522773 – www.dylansrestaurant.co.uk – Closed 25-26 December

Bron Eifion

COUNTRY HOUSE • CONTEMPORARY Characterful country house built in 1883 for a slate merchant; the impressive staircase is constructed from pitch pine he brought back from the USA. Some of the spacious, modern bedrooms have carved Middle Eastern beds. Enjoy bistro dishes to a lovely garden backdrop.

18 rooms – †£ 95/135 ††£ 145/225

✉ LL52 0SA – West : 1 mi on A 497

– ✆ 01766 522385 – www.broneifion.co.uk

CRICKHOWELL CRUCYWEL

Powys – Pop. 2 063 – Regional map n° **19**-C4

Bear

TRADITIONAL BRITISH • INN Well-maintained 15C coaching inn adorned with hanging baskets and full of nooks and crannies. The menu offers honest pub classics alongside more elaborate specials. Sit in the hugely characterful lounge-bar or more formal restaurant.

Carte £ 27/43

Bear Hotel, High St ✉ NP8 1BW

– ✆ 01873 810408 (bookings not accepted) – www.bearhotel.co.uk – Closed 25 December

Bear

TRADITIONAL • COSY Well-known, family-run coaching inn filled with various charming rooms and dating from the 15C. Bedrooms are modern; the most characterful are in the main house and feature beams, four-posters and fireplaces; some have jacuzzis.

36 rooms – †£ 86/145 ††£ 107/182 – 1 suite

High St ✉ NP8 1BW

– ✆ 01873 810408 – www.bearhotel.co.uk – Closed 25 December

Bear – See restaurant listing

CROSS ASH – Monmouthshire ➜ See Abergavenny

CROSSGATES – Powys ➜ See Llandrindod Wells

DENBIGH

Denbighshire – Pop. 8 514 – Regional map n° **19**-C1

Castle House

COUNTRY HOUSE • ELEGANT A Georgian house with Victorian additions; its gardens incorporate the old town walls. Large bedrooms retain their period character and the décor is a pleasing blend of the old and new. The view over the Vale of Clwyd is superb.

4 rooms – †£ 70/140 ††£ 90/180

Bull Ln ✉ LL16 3LY

– ✆ 01745 816860 – www.castlehousebandb.co.uk – Closed Christmas

DOLFOR

Powys - Regional map n° **19**-C2

Old Vicarage

TRADITIONAL • PERSONALISED A 19C red-brick vicarage with a classical, country house style lounge and dining room, and large gardens where they grow the produce used in their home-cooked meals. Cosy bedrooms are named after local rivers and mix period furnishings with bright modern colours. Chutney, preserves and soaps are for sale and afternoon tea is served on arrival.

4 rooms - £ 70/90 £ 95/120

SY16 4BN - North : 1.5 mi by A 483 - 01686 629051 - www.theoldvicaragedolfor.co.uk - Closed Christmas-New Year

DOLGELLAU

Gwynedd - Pop. 2 688 - Regional map n° **19**-B2

Penmaenuchaf Hall

COUNTRY HOUSE • PERSONALISED Personally run Victorian house with wood panelling, ornate ceilings and stained glass windows. Bedrooms blend the traditional and the modern; some have balconies overlooking the lovely grounds, mountains and estuary. Classic dishes are accompanied by a well-chosen wine list.

14 rooms - £ 125/200 £ 180/300

Penmaenpool LL40 1YB - West : 1.75 mi on A 493 (Tywyn Rd) - 01341 422129 - www.penhall.co.uk - Closed 17-21 December and 2-18 January

Ffynnon

TOWNHOUSE • PERSONALISED A spacious Victorian house which once operated as a cottage hospital. Original features and period furnishings abound, offset by stylish modern designs which pay great attention to detail. Keep your wine and snacks in the pantry and enjoy homemade crumpets or pancakes for breakfast. Outdoor hot tub.

6 rooms - £ 95 £ 150/210

Love Ln, off Cader Rd LL40 1RR - 01341 421774 - www.ffynnontownhouse.com - Closed Christmas

at Llanelltyd Northwest: 2.25 mi by A470 on A496

Mawddach

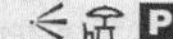

MEDITERRANEAN CUISINE • RUSTIC XX Stylish barn conversion run by two brothers and set on the family farm. The terrace and dining room offer superb views of the mountains and estuary. Unfussy Italian-influenced cooking features lamb from the farm and veg from the garden.

Carte £ 24/43

LL40 2TA - 01341 421752 - www.mawddach.com - Closed 2 weeks November, 1 week January, 1 week spring and Sunday dinner-Wednesday

FISHGUARD

Pembrokeshire - Pop. 3 419 - Regional map n° **19**-A3

Manor Town House

TOWNHOUSE • PERSONALISED Well-run, listed Georgian townhouse, boasting fabulous harbour views. Stylish, elegant lounges and individually designed, antique-furnished bedrooms; some in art deco and some in Victorian styles. Tasty breakfasts; charming owners.

6 rooms - £ 75/95 £ 99/135

11 Main St SA65 9HG - 01348 873260 - www.manortownhouse.com - Closed 24-27 December

GLYNARTHEN

Ceredigion - Regional map n° **19**-B3

Penbontbren

COUNTRY HOUSE • CONTEMPORARY A collection of enthusiastically run converted farm buildings, surrounded by an attractive landscaped garden and 35 acres of rolling countryside. Bedrooms are spacious, stylish and well-equipped and most have a sitting room and patio. The boldly decorated stone-walled breakfast room offers an extensive menu.

6 rooms – †£ 85/99 ††£ 99/125

Glynarthen ✉ SA44 6PE – North : 1 mi taking first left at crossroads then next left onto unmarked lane – ✆ 01239 810248 – www.penbontbren.com – Closed Christmas

HARLECH

Gwynedd – Pop. 1 762 – Regional map n° **19**-B2

Castle Cottage

CLASSIC CUISINE • COSY XX Sweet little cottage behind Harlech Castle, with a cosy yet surprisingly contemporary interior. Start with canapés and an aperitif in the lounge; the table is yours for the evening. Classical menus feature local produce and modern touches. Spacious bedrooms have smart bathrooms and stunning mountain views.

Menu £ 45

7 rooms – †£ 85/125 ††£ 130/175

Pen Llech ✉ LL46 2YL – ✆ 01766 780479 (booking essential) – www.castlecottageharlech.co.uk – dinner only – Closed 3 weeks October-November and Sunday-Wednesday November-February

HAVERFORDWEST HWLFFORDD

Pembrokeshire – Pop. 14 596 – Regional map n° **19**-A3

Lower Haythog Farm

TRADITIONAL • COSY Welcoming guesthouse with mature gardens, part-dating from the 14C and set on a working dairy farm. Cosy bedrooms feature bespoke cherry wood furniture and organic toiletries. Pleasant lounge and conservatory. Aga-cooked breakfasts.

4 rooms – †£ 45/55 ††£ 75/85

Spittal ✉ SA62 5QL – Northeast : 5 mi on B 4329 – ✆ 01437 731279 – www.lowerhaythogfarm.co.uk

Paddock

FAMILY • MODERN Contemporary guesthouse on a working dairy farm. Comfy lounge with books, board games and a wood-burning stove. Modern bedrooms feature chunky wood furniture and sleigh beds made up with Egyptian cotton linen. Home-cooked meals rely on local and market produce; eggs are from their own hens.

3 rooms – †£ 60/65 ††£ 80/85

Lower Haythog, Spittal ✉ SA62 5QL – Northeast : 5 mi on B 4329 – ✆ 01437 731531 – www.thepaddockwales.co.uk

HAWARDEN PENARLÂG

Flintshire – Pop. 1 858 – Regional map n° **19**-C1

Glynne Arms

TRADITIONAL BRITISH • PUB A 200 year old coaching inn opposite Hawarden Castle; owned by the descendants of PM William Gladstone. Choose from bar snacks, steaks from the estate and classical dishes. Regular events include quiz nights and gin tastings.

Carte £ 18/44

3 Glynne Way ✉ CH5 3NS – ✆ 01244 569988 – www.theglynnearms.co.uk – Closed 25 December

HAY-ON-WYE Y GELLI

Powys – Pop. 1 846 – Regional map n° **19**-C3

Garden Room

MODERN BRITISH • CLASSIC DÉCOR XX As its name suggests, the floor-to-ceiling sash windows of this hotel dining room offer great views over the garden. Cooking has an adventurous Scandic style and the chefs come out of the kitchen to explain the dishes.

Menu £ 40

The Swan at Hay Hotel, Church St ✉ HR3 5DQ – ✆ 01497 821188 – www.swanathay.co.uk – dinner only – Closed 2 weeks January, Sunday and Monday

The Swan at Hay

HISTORIC BUILDING • COSY A welcoming 19C coaching inn set in the heart of a pretty town. Relax in the rustic bar or by a wood-burning stove in one of the restful lounges. Bedrooms are cosy with neutral colour schemes; some overlook the garden and hills.

19 rooms – †£ 95/105 ††£ 125/175

Church St ✉ HR3 5DQ – ✆ 01497 821188 – www.swanathay.co.uk – Closed 2 weeks January

Garden Room – See restaurant listing

Bear

TOWNHOUSE • PERSONALISED A listed 16C building which blends the old and the new; it has, over the years, been a private house, a pub and even an antiques shop. The walled garden is something of a hidden gem – relax with a book from their extensive collection.

3 rooms – †£ 55/90 ††£ 80/100

2 Bear St ✉ HR3 5AN – ✆ 01497 821302 – www.thebearhay.com – Closed Christmas and New Year

HOWEY – Powys → See Llandrindod Wells

LLANARMON DYFFRYN CEIRIOG

Wrexham – Regional map n° **19**-C2

Hand at Llanarmon

TRADITIONAL CUISINE • INN Nestled at the head of the Ceiriog Valley, the Hand is ideally located for those who like to get away from it all. Choose a 'Hand Classic' such as mushrooms on toast or pick from 'Today's Choices' like Welsh lamb cutlets with tomato ragout. Bedrooms are modern and there's even a small treatment facility.

Carte £ 21/40

13 rooms – †£ 75/120 ††£ 95/150

✉ LL20 7LD – ✆ 01691 600666 – www.thehandhotel.co.uk

LLANARTHNEY

Carmarthenshire – Regional map n° **19**-B3

Llwyn Helyg

FAMILY • PERSONALISED A striking modern house with marble floors and stylish furnishings. A grand oak staircase leads to luxurious bedrooms with jacuzzi baths and rain showers. Music lovers will appreciate the comfy, well-equipped 'Listening Room'.

3 rooms – †£ 99/115 ††£ 129/155

✉ SA32 8HJ – South : 0.25 mi by the side road across from Wright's – ✆ 01558 668778 – www.llwynhelygcountryhouse.co.uk

LLANDDERFEL

Gwynedd – Pop. 4 500 – Regional map n° **19**-C2

Palé Hall

MODERN BRITISH • ELEGANT XxX Sit in the main room of this hotel restaurant to take in lovely garden views. Dishes are modern with a creative element; the set priced lunch features some lesser-known ingredients, while the main menu has an element of luxury.

Menu £ 37/60

Palé Hall Hotel, Palé Estate ✉ LL23 7PS - ✆ 01678 530285 (bookings essential for non-residents) - www.palehall.co.uk

Palé Hall

COUNTRY HOUSE • PERSONALISED An impressive Victorian house built for industrialist Henry Robertson; its 1920s hydroelectric generator still heats the water. Spacious, elegant rooms boast beautiful marquetry, antique furnishings and ornate design features.

18 rooms - †£ 190/610 ††£ 235/800 - 5 suites

Palé Estate ✉ LL23 7PS - ✆ 01678 530285 - www.palehall.co.uk

Palé Hall - See restaurant listing

LLANDDEWI SKIRRID - Monmouthshire ➜ See Abergavenny

LLANDENNY

Monmouthshire - Regional map n° **19**-C4

Raglan Arms

MODERN CUISINE • PUB Dine by the open fire in the bar or in the bright conservatory which overlooks the spacious terrace. Menus feature a few pub favourites but cooking is very much in the modern vein; dishes take on an extra degree of refinement in the evening.

Menu £ 18 (weekday lunch) - Carte £ 26/39

✉ NP15 1DL - ✆ 01291 690800 - www.raglanarms.co.uk - Closed 24-25 December, Sunday dinner and Monday

LLANDRILLO

Denbighshire - ✉ Corwen - Pop. 1 048 - Regional map n° **19**-C2

Tyddyn Llan (Bryan Webb)

CLASSIC CUISINE • ELEGANT XxX Attractive former shooting lodge in a pleasant valley location, surrounded by lovely gardens and run by a husband and wife team. Spacious country house lounges and a blue-hued, two-roomed restaurant. Hearty, satisfying cooking is based around the classics; tasting menus show the kitchen's talent to the full. Smart, elegant bedrooms offer a good level of facilities.

➜ Griddled scallops with cauliflower purée, pancetta, caper and raisin dressing. Bresse pigeon with wild garlic and bubble and squeak. Rhubarb and champagne trifle.

Menu £ 36/65

13 rooms - †£ 130/160 ††£ 130/190

✉ LL21 0ST - ✆ 01490 440264 (booking essential) - www.tyddynllan.co.uk - dinner only and lunch Friday-Sunday - Closed last 2 weeks January, Monday and Tuesday

LLANDRINDOD WELLS

Powys - Pop. 5 309 - Regional map n° **19**-C3

at Crossgates Northeast: 3.5 mi on A483 ✉ Llandrindod Wells

Guidfa House

TRADITIONAL • COSY A Georgian gentleman's residence with a pleasant garden, a smart breakfast room and a period lounge featuring an original cast iron ceiling rose. Bright, airy bedrooms; the best is in the coach house. Friendly owners serve tea on arrival.

6 rooms - †£ 85/113 ††£ 99/131

Crossgates ✉ LD1 6RF - ✆ 01597 851241 - www.guidfahouse.co.uk

at Howey South: 1.5 mi by A483 ✉ Llandrindod Wells

Acorn Court

FAMILY · PERSONALISED Chalet-style house set in 40 acres, with views over rolling countryside towards a river and lake. Welcoming owner and a real family feel. Spacious, well-kept bedrooms come with good extras. Try the Welsh whisky porridge for breakfast.

3 rooms – †£ 55/92 ††£ 78/92

Chapel Rd ✉ LD1 5PB – Northeast : 0.5 mi – ☎ 01597 823543 – www.acorncourt.co.uk – Closed 23-31 December

LLANDUDNO

Conwy – Pop. 15 371 – Regional map n° **19**-B1

Bodysgallen Hall

COUNTRY HOUSE · HISTORIC A stunning National Trust owned country house in 200 acres of delightful parkland, with a 13C tower and a superb outlook to the mountains beyond. It has a welcoming open-fired hall, a characterful wood-panelled lounge and antique-furnished bedrooms – some in cottages and some affording splendid Snowdon views. The grand dining room serves modern versions of classic dishes.

31 rooms – †£ 165/395 ††£ 185/450 – 21 suites

Royal Welsh Way ✉ LL30 1RS – Southeast : 2 mi on A 470 – ☎ 01492 584466 – www.bodysgallen.com

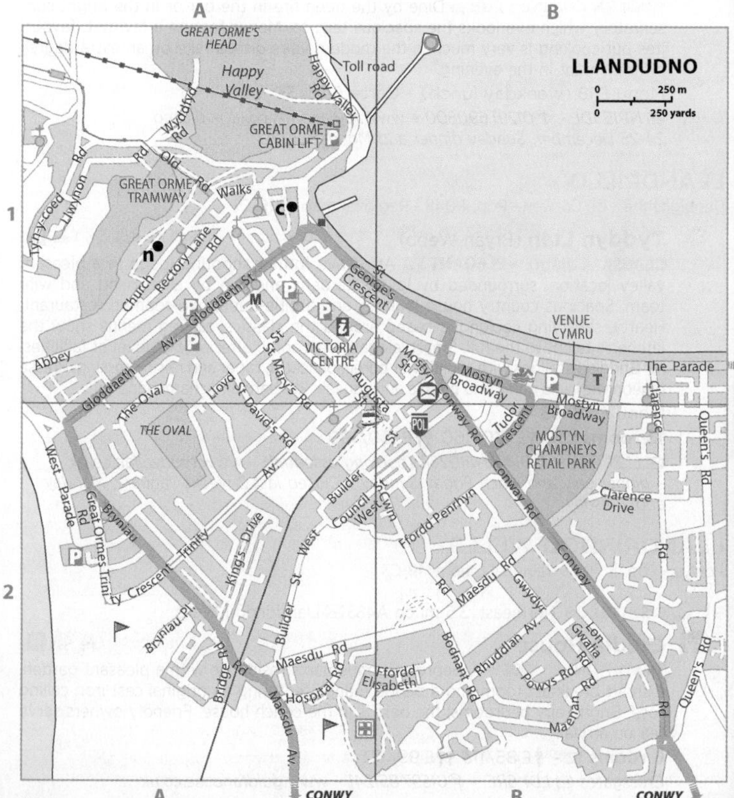

Osborne House

TOWNHOUSE · PERSONALISED Victoriana reigns in this smart townhouse overlooking the bay. Bedrooms are spacious, open-plan suites with canopied beds and lounges; chandeliers cast a romantic glow and marble bathrooms come with double-ended roll-top baths. Breakfast is served in your room. The opulent restaurant offers a wide-ranging menu.

7 rooms – £130/210 £130/210

Town plan: A1-c – *17 North Par ✉ LL30 2LP – ✆ 01492 860330 – www.osbornehouse.co.uk – Closed 16-31December*

Escape Boutique B&B

TOWNHOUSE · DESIGN Attractive Arts and Crafts house with stained glass windows, parquet floors and a chic, modern interior that sets it apart. Stylish lounge and spacious, contemporary bedrooms; those on the top floor have a stunning view of the bay.

9 rooms – £84/134 £99/149

Town plan: A1-n – *48 Church Walks ✉ LL30 2HL – ✆ 01492 877776 – www.escapebandb.co.uk – Closed 18-26 December*

LLANDYBIE

Carmarthenshire – Pop. 2 813 – Regional map n° **19**-B4

Valans

INTERNATIONAL · FRIENDLY XX Run by a local and his wife, a simple little restaurant with a bright red, white and black colour scheme. Fresh, unfussy dishes rely on local produce and offer classical flavours. The 'Lite Lunch' offers some good value options.

Menu £18/25

Primrose House, 29 High St ✉ SA18 3HX – ✆ 01269 851288 (booking advisable) – www.valans.co.uk – Closed 25 December-2 January, Sunday dinner and Monday

LLANELLI

Carmarthenshire – Pop. 43 878 – Regional map n° **19**-B4

Sosban

MODERN CUISINE · ROMANTIC XX Built in 1872 to house a pumping engine for the adjacent docks. It's been impressively restored and has a relaxed lounge-bar and an airy stone-walled dining room. The large menu offers tasty, well-prepared dishes.

Menu £24 (weekday lunch) – Carte £30/46

The Pump House, North Dock ✉ SA15 2LF – ✆ 01554 270020 – www.sosbanrestaurant.com – Closed 25 December, 1 January and Sunday dinner

LLANELLTYD – Gwynedd → See Dolgellau

LLAN FFESTINIOG

Gwynedd – Regional map n° **19**-B2

Cae'r Blaidd Country House

TRADITIONAL · PERSONALISED It's all about mountain pursuits at this alpine-themed guesthouse: the welcoming owners are mountain guides; ice axes, crampons and skis fill the walls; and there's a climbing wall, a drying room and even equipment for hire in the basement. Dine on local produce while taking in the stunning panoramic view.

4 rooms – £55 £90

✉ LL41 4PH – North : 0.75 mi by A 470 on Blaenau Rd – ✆ 01766 762765 – www.caerblaidd.com – Closed January

LLANFIHANGEL-Y-CREUDDYN

Ceredigion – Regional map n° **19**-B3

Y Ffarmers

REGIONAL CUISINE • RUSTIC Life in this remote, picturesque valley revolves around the passionately run village pub. Sit in the locals bar or the homely restaurant which opens onto the garden. Regional and valley produce features in satisfying, original dishes.

Carte £ 21/34

✉ SY23 4LA – ✆ 01974 261275 – www.yffarmers.co.uk – Closed first week January and Sunday dinner-Tuesday lunch

LLANFYLLIN

Powys – Pop. 1 105 – Regional map n° **19**-C2

Seeds

REGIONAL CUISINE • RUSTIC Converted 16C red-brick cottages in a sleepy village; run with pride by a friendly husband and wife team. Cosy, pine-furnished room with an old range and a country kitchen feel. Unfussy, classical dishes and comforting homemade desserts.

Menu £ 26 (dinner) – Carte lunch £ 24/33

5 Penybryn Cottages, High St ✉ SY22 5AP – ✆ 01691 648604 – Closed Thursday in winter and Sunday-Wednesday

LLANGAFFO ➜ See Anglesey (Isle of)

LLANGAMMARCH WELLS

Powys – Regional map n° **19**-B3

Lake Country House and Spa

TRADITIONAL • PERSONALISED Extended, part-timbered 19C country house in 50 acres of mature gardens and parkland, with a pond, a lake and a river. Comfortable lounges and well-appointed bedrooms with antiques and extras; some are set in a lodge. The impressive spa overlooks the river. Breakfast is in the orangery; the elegant restaurant is perfect for a classical, candlelit dinner.

32 rooms – †£ 147/180 ††£ 205/240 – 8 suites

✉ LD4 4BS – East : 0.75 mi – ✆ 01591 620202 – www.lakecountryhouse.co.uk

LLANLLAWDDOG – Carmarthenshire ➜ See Carmarthen

LLANRHIDIAN

Swansea – Pop. 512 – Regional map n° **19**-B4

Fairyhill by Oldwalls

MODERN BRITISH • ELEGANT An attractive Georgian country house with a lake and well-manicured gardens; take it all in from the terrace or the elegant dining room. Modern menus rely on seasonal Gower produce. Spacious bedrooms blend the traditional and the contemporary and come with good facilities.

Menu £ 20/35 – Carte £ 32/48

8 rooms – †£ 180/310 ††£ 200/330

Reynoldston ✉ SA3 1BS – West : 2.5 mi by Llangennith Rd – ✆ 01792 390139 – www.fairyhill.co.uk – Closed October-November

LLYSWEN

Powys – ✉ Brecon – Regional map n° **19**-C3

Llangoed Hall

HISTORIC • PERSONALISED A fine country house beside the River Wye, redesigned by Sir Clough Williams-Ellis in 1910 and restored by the late Sir Bernard Ashley. Delightful sitting rooms and sumptuous bedrooms feature rich fabrics, mullioned windows and antiques; the impressive art collection includes pieces by Whistler. Ambitious modern cooking is led by what's fresh in the kitchen garden.

23 rooms - £ 150/650 £ 150/650

LD3 0YP - Northwest : 1.25 mi on A 470
- 01874 754525 - www.llangoedhall.com

MACHYNLLETH

Powys - Pop. 2 235 - Regional map n° **19**-B2

Ynyshir (Gareth Ward)

CREATIVE • INTIMATE Intimate, Scandic-style restaurant with an open kitchen; set within a beautiful part-Georgian building. The talented chef uses superb local and foraged ingredients to create original dishes with wonderfully balanced flavours; some are finished at the table and for the final course you're invited into the kitchen. Bedrooms have a chic, contemporary country house style.

→ 'Not French onion soup'. Welsh Wagyu. Tiramisu.

Menu £ 40/130 - tasting menu only

10 rooms - £ 136/440 £ 170/550 - 3 suites

Eglwysfach SY20 8TA - Southwest: 6 mi on A 487
- 01654 781209 (booking essential) - www.ynyshir.co.uk
- Closed first week January, Sunday and Monday

MENAI BRIDGE

→ See Anglesey (Isle of)

MONMOUTH TREFYNWY

Monmouthshire - Pop. 10 110 - Regional map n° **19**-C4

#7 Church Street

MODERN BRITISH • FRIENDLY A small, family-run restaurant on a pedestrianised lane in the Old Town. The hard-working chef takes pride in his cooking and even does his own butchery. Dishes are fresh, tasty and very filling - and the homemade cakes in the cabinet are hard to resist. Upstairs, 8 simply furnished bedrooms await.

Menu £ 18 (weekday lunch) - Carte £ 25/46

8 rooms - £ 70/90 £ 110

7 Church St NP25 3BX
- 01600 712600 - www.numbersevenchurchstreet.co.uk
- Closed dinner 24 December-26 December

Stonemill

REGIONAL CUISINE • RUSTIC Attractive 16C cider mill with exposed timbers and an old millstone at the centre of the characterful, rustic restaurant. Good value set menus are supplemented by a more ambitious evening à la carte. Dishes are hearty and classically based.

Menu £ 21/27 - Carte £ 31/48

Rockfield NP25 5SW - Northwest : 3.5 mi on B 4233
- 01600 716273 - www.thestonemill.co.uk
- Closed 2 weeks January, 25-27 December, Sunday dinner and Monday

WALES

at Whitebrook South: 8.25 mi by A466 ✉ Monmouth

The Whitebrook (Chris Harrod)

MODERN BRITISH • INTIMATE XX You'll find this relaxed, intimate, whitewashed property off the beaten track, in a wooded valley. Cooking is modern and understated and menus showcase top quality local and foraged ingredients; descriptions are concise and the elegantly presented dishes are more complex than they first appear. Bedrooms come in muted tones and follow the theme of bringing nature inside.

→ Wye Valley asparagus with hogweed, pine and Tintern mead. Huntsham Farm suckling pig with caramelised celeriac, pear and sorrel. Violet parfait with blueberries, rose and lemon thyme.

Menu £ 35/74

8 rooms – †£ 105/190 ††£ 130/215

✉ NP25 4TX – ✆ 01600 860254 (booking essential) – www.thewhitebrook.co.uk – Closed first 2 weeks January, Monday and lunch Tuesday

MONTGOMERY TREFALDWYN

Powys – Pop. 986 – Regional map n° **19**-C2

The Checkers (Stéphane Borie)

FRENCH • FRIENDLY XX A charming 18C coaching inn set in a hilltop town and run by an enthusiastic Frenchman and his family. Guests are invited to arrive at 7.15pm for aperitifs in the beamed lounge, followed by a tasting menu in the stylish restaurant. Skilfully prepared, classic French dishes are beautifully crafted and flavours pack a punch. Elegant bedrooms are furnished with antiques.

→ Rotolo of river trout with cauliflower purée, toasted almonds and tarragon dressing. Trio of Neuadd Fach pork with pomme mousseline, artichoke and Madeira jus. White chocolate and passion fruit cigarette with strawberries.

Menu £ 65 – tasting menu only

5 rooms – †£ 145/215 ††£ 150/220

Broad St ✉ SY15 6PN – ✆ 01686 669822 – www.checkerswales.co.uk – dinner only – Closed 3 weeks January, 1 week late summer, 25-26 December, Sunday and Monday

NANTGAREDIG – Carmarthenshire → See Carmarthen

NARBERTH

Pembrokeshire – Pop. 2 265 – Regional map n° **19**-A4

Grove

MODERN CUISINE • ELEGANT XX A meal here is thought of as an event: start with a drink in the bar or in one of the lounges, then move on to either the cosy dining room or the orangery overlooking the sheltered courtyard. Refined cooking carefully balances ingredients to create some interesting combinations with original touches.

Menu £ 29/64 **s**

Grove Hotel, Molleston ✉ SA67 8BX – South : 2 mi by A 478 on Herons Brook rd – ✆ 01834 860915 – www.thegrove-narberth.co.uk

Grove

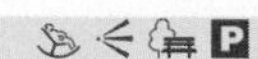

HISTORIC • PERSONALISED Set in 35 acres, in a charming rural location, the Grove comprises a 15C longhouse and a whitewashed property with Stuart and Victorian additions. Bedrooms blend boldly coloured walls and bright fabrics with more traditional furnishings, while the bathrooms boast underfloor heating and deep cast iron baths.

26 rooms – †£ 210/550 ††£ 210/550 – 8 suites

Molleston ✉ SA67 8BX – South : 2 mi by A 478 on Herons Brook rd – ✆ 01834 860915 – www.thegrove-narberth.co.uk

Grove – See restaurant listing

NEWCASTLE EMLYN

Carmarthenshire – Pop. 1 883 – Regional map n° **19**-B3

Gwesty'r Emlyn

INN • CONTEMPORARY This 300 year old coaching inn conceals a surprisingly modern interior. Guest areas include a stylish lounge, a snug bar, a small fitness room and a sauna. Bedrooms are contemporary and well-equipped; one features a glass-covered well. The characterful bistro offers a menu centred around local produce.

29 rooms – †£ 60/80 ††£ 80/120 – 4 suites

Bridge St ✉ SA38 9DU – ☎ 01239 710317 – www.gwestyremlynhotel.co.uk

NEWPORT

Newport – Pop. 128 060 – Regional map n° **19**-C4

Celtic Manor Resort

RESORT • PERSONALISED A vast resort hotel set in 1,400 acres, boasting two floors of function rooms, a shopping arcade, 3 golf courses and an impressive swimming pool and spa. Bedrooms range from Standards to Presidential Suites and from classical to modern in style. The many restaurants offer everything from grills, buffets and carveries to Asian fusion dishes and modern fine dining menus.

332 rooms – †£ 127/343 ††£ 150/380 – 14 suites

Coldra Woods ✉ NP18 1HQ – East : 3 mi on A 48
– ☎ 01633 413000 – www.celtic-manor.com

Follow our inspectors @MichelinGuideUK

NEWPORT TREFDRAETH

Pembrokeshire – Pop. 1 162 – Regional map n° **19**-A3

Llys Meddyg

MODERN CUISINE • RUSTIC XX Centrally located restaurant with a kitchen garden and a slightly bohemian style. Eat in the formal dining room or the characterful, laid-back cellar bar; the owner's father's art is displayed throughout. Cooking showcases local produce in ambitious, complex dishes. Modern bedrooms have a Scandinavian style.

Carte £ 26/41

8 rooms – †£ 80/140 ††£ 100/160

East St ✉ SA42 0SY
– ☎ 01239 820008 – www.llysmeddyg.com
– dinner only – Restricted opening in winter

Cnapan

TOWNHOUSE • PERSONALISED Part-Georgian house in a busy coastal village – keenly run by the 3rd generation of the family. The bar and lounge have a homely feel. Bright bedrooms are compact but well-maintained; ask for one at the back overlooking the garden.

5 rooms – †£ 70/95 ††£ 70/95

East St ✉ SA42 0SY – on A 487
– ☎ 01239 820575 – www.cnapan.co.uk
– Closed January-mid-March and 25-26 December

OLD RADNOR PENCRAIG

Powys – Pop. 400 – Regional map n° **19**-C3

Harp Inn

TRADITIONAL CUISINE • INN This 15C stone inn welcomes drinkers and diners alike. The charming flag-floored rooms boast open fires and beams hung with hop bines and the terrace offers glorious views. 'Seasonality' and 'sustainability' are key, and menus are concise but original. Simple bedrooms come with wonderful views.

Carte £ 20/43

5 rooms – £ 75/80 £ 105/110

LD8 2RH – 01544 350655 – www.harpinnradnor.co.uk – Closed Monday except bank holidays, Tuesday and lunch Wednesday-Thursday

OXWICH

Swansea – Regional map n° **19**-B4

Beach House

MODERN CUISINE • DESIGN XX The former coal store of the Penrice Estate is a charming stone building beside the beach, with a lovely terrace looking out over the bay. Menus range from a good value set lunch to an 8 course tasting menu, and showcase interesting dishes which are full of flavour. The room has a nautical, New England feel.

Menu £ 28 (lunch) – Carte £ 41/59

Oxwich Beach SA3 1LS – 01792 390965 – www.beachhouseoxwich.co.uk – Closed 2 weeks January and Monday-Tuesday

PENARTH

The Vale of Glamorgan – Pop. 27 226 – Regional map n° **19**-C4

James Sommerin

MODERN CUISINE • CONTEMPORARY DÉCOR XX A smart yet laid-back restaurant on the esplanade, which affords panoramic views over the Severn Estuary; five of the sophisticated modern bedrooms share the wonderful outlook. Choose from the à la carte or a customisable 6 or 10 course tasting menu. Confidently executed dishes are hearty and boldly flavoured, with more playful elements appearing in the desserts.

→ Liquid pea ravioli with serrano ham, sage and parmesan. Welsh lamb with broad beans, turnip and cumin. Cherry and almond soufflé with marzipan ice cream.

Carte £ 36/54

9 rooms – £ 130/170 £ 150/190

The Esplanade CF64 3AU – 029 2070 6559 – www.jamessommerinrestaurant.co.uk – Closed 8-12 January and Monday

Pier 64

MODERN CUISINE • FASHIONABLE XX Modern, wood-clad, all-day restaurant, set on stilts in an enviable harbour location. Light, airy interior with a smart bar and huge windows giving every table a view. Accessible menu features plenty of seafood and 28 day dry-aged steaks.

Menu £ 18 (weekday lunch) – Carte £ 24/55

Penarth Marina CF64 1TT – 029 2000 0064 – www.pier64.co.uk – Closed Sunday dinner

Holm House

MODERN BRITISH • DESIGN X This bright, modern room is a complete contrast to the hotel's 1920s façade. Floor to ceiling windows offer sea views and there's an attractive garden terrace. Daily changing dishes are prepared with restraint and accuracy.

Menu £ 24 (weekday lunch) – Carte £ 26/43

Holm House Hotel, Marine Par CF64 3BG – 029 2070 6029 – www.holmhousehotel.com

Mint and Mustard

INDIAN • NEIGHBOURHOOD Fashionable high street restaurant with bare brick walls and exposed ducting. The menu features an extensive selection of vibrantly flavoured curries, tandoor dishes and Keralan-inspired recipes. Ingredients are locally sourced.

Carte £ 18/34

33-34 Windsor Terr ✉ CF64 1AB – ✆ 029 2070 0500 (bookings advisable at dinner) – www.mintandmustard.com – Closed 25 December

Holm House

BOUTIQUE HOTEL • PERSONALISED This characterful Arts and Crafts house sits on the clifftop in a smart residential neighbourhood and looks over the Bristol Channel to the tiny island after which it is named; some of its bedrooms have baths by the window.

12 rooms – £ 90/160 £ 100/170

Marine Par ✉ CF64 3BG – ✆ 029 2070 6029 – www.holmhousehotel.com

Holm House – See restaurant listing

PENMACHNO – Conwy → See Betws-y-Coed

PENNAL

Gwynedd – Regional map n° **19**-B2

Riverside

TRADITIONAL CUISINE • PUB Enter under the 'Glan Yr Afron' (Riverside) sign, then make for the 'Cwtch' with its wood-burning stove. Despite its Grade II listing, it has a bright modern feel. Hearty, no-nonsense pub classics are full of flavour and keenly priced.

Carte £ 20/37

✉ SY20 9DW – ✆ 01654 791285 – www.riversidehotel-pennal.co.uk – Closed 2 weeks January and Monday October-May

PORTHCAWL

Bridgend – Pop. 15 672 – Regional map n° **19**-B4

Foam Edge

TOWNHOUSE • PERSONALISED A smart, modern, semi-detached house – a family home – set next to the promenade, with great views over the Bristol Channel. Spacious, stylish bedrooms offer good facilities. Comfortable lounge and communal breakfasts.

3 rooms – £ 70/80 £ 95/110

9 West Dr ✉ CF36 3LS – ✆ 01656 782866 – www.foam-edge.co.uk – Closed 25 December

PORTMEIRION

Gwynedd – Regional map n° **19**-B2

Portmeirion

HISTORIC • ART DÉCO A unique, Italianate village built on a private peninsula and boasting wonderful estuary views – the life work of Sir Clough Williams-Ellis. Stay in the appealing 1930s hotel or snug, well-appointed bedrooms spread about the village. The art deco style dining room offers a modern international menu.

46 rooms – £ 150/200 £ 150/260 – 22 suites

✉ LL48 6ER – ✆ 01766 770000 – www.portmerion-village.com – Closed 31 August-8 September

PUMSAINT

Carmarthenshire – Regional map n° **19**-B3

Dolaucothi Arms

TRADITIONAL BRITISH • RUSTIC A 500 year old drovers' inn set in the picturesque Cothi Valley; it's a cosy, rustic place with a garden looking out over a river where they have 4 miles of fishing rights. One menu lists pub classics while the second is more adventurous. Bedrooms are comfy and cosy – ask if you want a TV.

Carte £ 18/29

3 rooms – £ 60/70 £ 75/90

SA19 8UW – 01558 650237 – www.thedolaucothiarms.co.uk – Closed 16-29 January, 25-26 December, Tuesday lunch, Monday except bank holidays and midweek lunch November-February

PWLLHELI

Gwynedd – Pop. 4 076 – Regional map n° **19**-B2

Plas Bodegroes

MODERN CUISINE • INTIMATE XX A charming, Grade II listed Georgian house set in peaceful grounds; inside it's beautifully decorated and features an eclectic collection of modern Welsh art. There's a well-chosen wine list and the kitchen uses the best of the local larder to create classic dishes with a contemporary edge. Understated bedrooms are named after trees and have sleek, modern bathrooms.

Menu £ 45

10 rooms – £ 90/150 £ 110/170

LL53 5TH – Northwest : 1.75 mi on A 497 – 01758 612363 (bookings essential for non-residents) – www.bodegroes.co.uk – dinner only and Sunday lunch – Closed January, Sunday dinner except bank holidays and Monday

at Boduan Northwest: 3.75 mi on A497 Pwllheli

Old Rectory

TRADITIONAL • PERSONALISED Lovely part-Georgian family home with well-tended gardens and a paddock. Comfy lounge features a carved wood fireplace; communal breakfasts at a large table include plenty of fresh fruits. Tastefully decorated, homely bedrooms overlook the garden and come with complimentary chocolates and sherry or sloe gin.

3 rooms – £ 85/95 £ 95/115

LL53 6DT – 01758 721519 – www.theoldrectory.net – Closed Christmas

RHOS-ON-SEA – Conwy ➜ See Colwyn Bay

RHYL

Denbighshire – Pop. 25 149 – Regional map n° **19**-C1

Barratt's at Ty'n Rhyl

TRADITIONAL CUISINE • COSY XX Built in 1672 and retaining many original features, including a carved wooden fireplace reputed to have been the top of a bed owned by Catherine of Aragon! The characterful drawing rooms have a cosy, lived-in feel; the dining room, by contrast, is light and airy. Classically based menu. Traditional bedrooms.

Menu £ 40

3 rooms – £ 80 £ 98

167 Vale Rd. LL18 2PH – South : 0.5 mi on A 525 – 01745 344138 (booking essential) – www.barrattsattynrhyl.co.uk – dinner only and Sunday lunch – Closed Sunday and Monday

ROCH

Pembrokeshire – Pop. 463 – Regional map n° **19**-A3

Roch Castle

HISTORIC • DESIGN An intimate 12C castle set over 7 storeys, which has been fully refurbished by its architect owner. It's modern and stylish throughout, from the bedrooms with their quality linens to the fantastic 'Sun Room' with its far-reaching views.

6 rooms – £ 220/260 £ 220/260

SA62 6AQ – 01437 725566 – www.rochcastle.com

ROSSETT

Wrexham – Wrexham – Pop. 2 007 – Regional map n° **19**-C1

Machine House

MODERN BRITISH • RUSTIC This stone-walled barn was once an agricultural machine repair shop and it has retained a characterful, rustic feel. In contrast with the surroundings, dishes are modern, with clearly defined flavours and a creative element.

Menu £ 21/23 – Carte dinner £ 35/47

Chester Rd LL12 0HW – 01244 571678 – www.machinehouse.co.uk – Closed last 2 weeks August, first 2 weeks January, Sunday and Monday

ROWEN – Conwy ➜ See Conwy

RUTHIN RHUTHUN

Denbighshire – Pop. 5 461 – Regional map n° **19**-C1

On the Hill

TRADITIONAL CUISINE • RUSTIC Immensely charming 16C house in a busy market town; a real family-run business. It has characterful sloping floors, exposed beams and a buzzy, bistro atmosphere. The accessible menu offers keenly priced, internationally-influenced classics.

Menu £ 20 (lunch) – Carte dinner £ 25/41

1 Upper Clwyd St LL15 1HY – 01824 707736 (booking essential) – www.onthehillrestaurant.co.uk – Closed 25-26 December, 1 January and Sunday

Manorhaus Ruthin

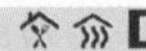

TOWNHOUSE • DESIGN A lovely Georgian manor house which retains plenty of period character despite its contemporary first impression. The stylish lounge is furnished with glass and chrome while the bar has a subtle retro feel; there's even a cinema in the basement. The bright conservatory restaurant serves classic fare.

8 rooms – £ 70/125 £ 85/150

10 Well St LL15 1AH – 01824 704830 – www.manorhaus.com

Firgrove

FAMILY • COSY Attractive stone-built cottage set in stunning gardens. Sit in the snug by the cosy inglenook fireplace in winter or in the delightful plant-filled glasshouse in summer. Two comfortable four-poster bedrooms and a self-contained cottage offer pleasant valley views. The owners join guests for hearty, home-cooked dinners which showcase locally sourced farm produce.

3 rooms – £ 80/120 £ 100/120

Llanfwrog LL15 2LL – West : 1.25 mi by A 494 on B 5105 – 01824 702677 – www.firgrovecountryhouse.co.uk – Closed November-February

ST CLEARS

Carmarthenshire – Pop. 1 989 – Regional map n° **19**-B3

Coedllys Country House

TRADITIONAL • PERSONALISED Lovely country house in a peaceful hillside location, complete with a sanctuary where they keep rescued animals – the hens provide the eggs at breakfast. Guest areas are comfy and traditional and the charming antique-furnished bedrooms have good mod cons and binoculars for bird watchers.

4 rooms – £ 80/85 £ 90/110

Llangynin SA33 4JY – Northwest : 3.5 mi by A 40 turning first left after 30 mph sign on entering village – 01994 231455 – www.coedllyscountryhouse.co.uk – Closed 22-28 December

ST DAVIDS TYDDEWI

Pembrokeshire – ✉ Haverfordwest – Pop. 1 959 – Regional map n° **19**-A3

Cwtch

TRADITIONAL BRITISH • RUSTIC Popular, laid-back restaurant; its name meaning 'hug'. The three rustic dining rooms boast stone walls, crammed bookshelves and log-filled alcoves. Classic British dishes arrive in generous portions and service is polite and friendly.

Menu £ 26/34

22 High St ✉ SA62 6SD – ✆ 01437 720491 (booking advisable) – www.cwtchrestaurant.co.uk – dinner only – Closed January and Monday-Tuesday November-March

Twr y Felin (N)

HISTORIC BUILDING • DESIGN Strikingly restored 19C windmill with a cool, modern interior and over 100 pieces of contemporary art on display. The beautiful watchtower is now part of a 3-storey suite and many of the bedrooms have terraces and bay views. Dine in the dark, sultry restaurant or have snacks in the Gallery.

21 rooms – †£ 190/220 ††£ 190/220 – 2 suites

Caerfai Road ✉ SA62 6QT – ✆ 01437 725555 – www.twryfelinhotel.com

Penrhiw

COUNTRY HOUSE • ELEGANT Built from local red stone and set in 12 acres of gardens offering great country views – a real retreat. Original features have been sympathetically fused with modern designs; the original stained glass door is delightful.

8 rooms – †£ 190/240 ††£ 190/240

✉ SA62 6PG – Northwest : 0.5 mi by A 487 and Quickwell Hill Rd – ✆ 01437 725588 – www.penrhiwhotel.com

Ramsey House

TRADITIONAL • PERSONALISED An unassuming-looking house on the edge of the UK's smallest city. Smart bedrooms have bold feature walls and either coast or country views. The Italian-tiled shower rooms come with bathrobes and L'Occitane toiletries.

6 rooms – †£ 70/130 ††£ 90/130

Lower Moor ✉ SA62 6RP – Southwest : 0.5 mi on Porth Clais rd – ✆ 01437 720321 – www.ramseyhouse.co.uk – Closed January, December and restricted opening November and February

ST GEORGE LLAN SAIN SIÔR

Conwy – Regional map n° **19**-C1

Kinmel Arms

MODERN BRITISH • INN An early 17C stone inn hidden away in a hamlet by the entrance to Kinmel Hall. The open-fired bar is delightful and there's and a lovely pantry selling homemade produce. Menus offer modern British dishes and afternoon tea is a feature. Stylish, contemporary bedrooms have their own kitchenettes for breakfast.

Menu £ 19 (weekday dinner) – Carte £ 16/54

4 rooms – †£ 100/145 ††£ 115/175

The Village ✉ LL22 9BP – ✆ 01745 832207 – www.thekinmelarms.co.uk – Closed 25 December, 1 January, Sunday and Monday

SAUNDERSFOOT

Pembrokeshire – Pop. 2 767 – Regional map n° **19**-A4

Coast

MODERN CUISINE • MINIMALIST Striking modern restaurant; when the weather's right, head for the terrace with its stunning coastal views. Seafood dominates the menu, which ranges from nibbles to a tasting selection. Local produce features in creative dishes.

Menu £ 27 (weekdays) – Carte £ 38/57

Coppet Hall Beach ✉ SA69 9AJ
– ✆ 01834 810800 – www.coastsaundersfoot.co.uk
– Closed 25-26 December, Monday and Tuesday

St Brides Spa

LUXURY • PERSONALISED Located on the clifftop, overlooking the harbour and the bay, is this nautically styled hotel featuring white wood panelling and contemporary Welsh art. The outdoor infinity pool has a great outlook, as do the restaurant and decked terraces. Smart, well-appointed bedrooms come in white and blue hues.

46 rooms – £ 135/210 £ 170/320 – 6 suites

St Brides Hill ✉ SA69 9NH
– ✆ 01834 812304 – www.stbridesspahotel.com

SEION – Gwynedd → See Caernarfon

SKENFRITH

Monmouthshire – Regional map n° **19**-C4

Bell at Skenfrith

CLASSIC CUISINE • PUB Well-run pub in a verdant valley, offering hearty, classical cooking with the occasional ambitious twist and using ingredients from the organic kitchen garden. There's an excellent choice of champagnes and cognacs, and service is warm and unobtrusive. Super-comfy bedrooms have an understated elegance.

Carte £ 30/39

11 rooms – £ 95/130 £ 150/230

✉ NP7 8UH
– ✆ 01600 750235 (booking essential) – www.skenfrith.co.uk

SWANSEA

Swansea – Pop. 179 485 – Regional map n° **19**-B4

Slice

MODERN BRITISH • INTIMATE Sweet former haberdashery in a residential area; the name reflecting its tapered shape. It's run by two friends who alternate weekly between cooking and serving. Precisely prepared, appealing modern dishes are packed with flavour.

Menu £ 29/55

73-75 Eversley Rd, Sketty ✉ SA2 9DE – West : 2 mi by A 4118
– ✆ 01792 290929 (booking essential) – www.sliceswansea.co.uk
– dinner only and lunch Friday-Sunday
– Closed 1 week autumn, 1 week Christmas, Monday-Wednesday

Morgans

BUSINESS • PERSONALISED An impressive Edwardian building by the docks, with a beautiful façade and a charming interior displaying original plasterwork, stained glass windows and a soaring cupola. Bedrooms in the main house are the most spacious. The restaurant boasts a hand-painted mural and a modern menu.

42 rooms – £ 65/250 £ 65/250

Somerset Pl ✉ SA1 1RR
– ✆ 01792 484848 – www.morganshotel.co.uk

TALYLLYN

Gwynedd – ✉ Tywyn – Regional map n° **19**-B2

Dolffanog Fawr

FAMILY · PERSONALISED This homely 18C farmhouse stands in the shadow of Cadair Idris, just up from a lake; kick-back in the hot tub to make the most of the terrific valley views. Modern bedrooms are furnished in solid oak. Breakfast could include Welsh cakes and dinner might feature local lamb or sea trout caught by the owner.

4 rooms – †£ 95 ††£ 100/120

✉ LL36 9AJ – On B 4405 – ☎ 01654 761247 – www.dolffanogfawr.co.uk – Closed November-March

TENBY

Pembrokeshire – Pop. 4 934 – Regional map n° **19**-A4

Salt Cellar

MODERN CUISINE · FRIENDLY XX Four friends own and run this restaurant. It may be in a hotel basement but it's bright and fresh and its pretty terrace over the road offers glorious coastal views. Refined, well-crafted dishes champion local produce.

Menu £ 19 (lunch) – Carte £ 31/42

The Esplanade ✉ SA70 7DU – ☎ 01834 844005 – www.thesaltcellartenby.co.uk – Closed 24-26 December

TREDUNNOCK – Newport ➔ See Usk

TREGARON

Ceredigion – Regional map n° **19**-B3

Y Talbot

TRADITIONAL CUISINE · CLASSIC DÉCOR Originally a drover's inn dating back to the 17C; the bar rooms are where the action is, and the best place to sit. Seasonal menus offer full-flavoured traditional dishes made with Welsh produce. Bedrooms are bright and modern: ask for one of the newest. Oh, and there's an elephant buried in the garden!

Carte £ 22/38

13 rooms – †£ 85/110 ††£ 110/140

✉ SY25 6JL – ☎ 01974 298208 – www.ytalbot.com – Closed 25 December

TYWYN

Gwynedd – Regional map n° **19**-B2

Salt Marsh Kitchen

TRADITIONAL BRITISH · SIMPLE X Sweet little bistro run by a proud, hardworking owner, with distressed wood décor and furnishings. Cooking is honest and generous – the owner is a keen fisherman and will advise you of what's best.

Menu £ 19 (early dinner) – Carte £ 26/36

9 College Grn ✉ LL36 9BS – ☎ 01654 711949 – www.saltmarshkitchen.co.uk – dinner only – Closed January and Monday-Wednesday November-March

USK

Monmouthshire – Pop. 2 834 – Regional map n° **19**-C4

at Tredunnock South: 4.75 mi by Llangybi rd ✉ Newport

Newbridge on Usk

TRADITIONAL BRITISH • **BISTRO** 200 year old inn by a bridge over the River Usk; choose from several dining areas set over two levels or sit on the terrace to have the snack menu. Classic British cooking has a modern twist; sharing plates are popular and include a crumble dessert. The smart, comfortable bedrooms are in a separate block.

Menu £ 16 (weekday lunch) - Carte £ 31/52

6 rooms - £ 69/129 £ 89/169

✉ NP15 1LY - East : 0.5 mi - 01633 451000 - www.celtic-manor.com

WHITEBROOK - Monmouthshire ➜ See Monmouth

Jack Kadaj/iStock

IRELAND

NORTHERN IRELAND

Think of Northern Ireland and you think of buzzing Belfast, with its impressive City Hall and Queen's University. But the rest of the Six Counties demand attention too. Forty thousand stone columns of the Giants Causeway step out into the Irish Sea, while inland, Antrim boasts nine scenic glens. County Down's rolling hills culminate in the alluring slopes of Slieve Donard in the magical Mourne Mountains, while Armagh's Orchard County is a riot of pink in springtime. Fermanagh's glassy, silent lakelands are a tranquil attraction, rivalled for their serenity by the heather-clad Sperrin Mountains, towering over Tyrone and Derry.

Rich, fertile land, vast waterways and a pride in traditional crafts like butchery and baking mean that Northern Ireland yields a wealth of high quality produce: tender, full-flavoured beef and lamb, and fish and shellfish from the lakes, rivers and sea, including salmon, oysters, mussels and crabs. You can't beat an eel from Lough Neagh – and the seaweed called Dulse is a local delicacy not to be missed.

- Michelin Road maps n° 712, 713 and 501
- Michelin Green Guide: Ireland

20 Northern Ireland

A
B
Place with at least:
a hotel or a restaurant
a starred establishment
a "Bib Gourmand" restaurant
a particularly pleasant accommodation
1
2
3
Lough Foyle
Limavady
Londonderry
LIMAVADY
DERRY
STRABANE
Donegal
OMAGH
Lower Lough Erne
FERMANAGH
DUNGANNON
Enniskillen
Lisnaskea
Upper Lough Erne
Monaghan
Lough Allen
REPUBLIC OF IRELAND
(plans 21)
Carrick-on-Shannon
Cavan
Carrickmacross
A
B

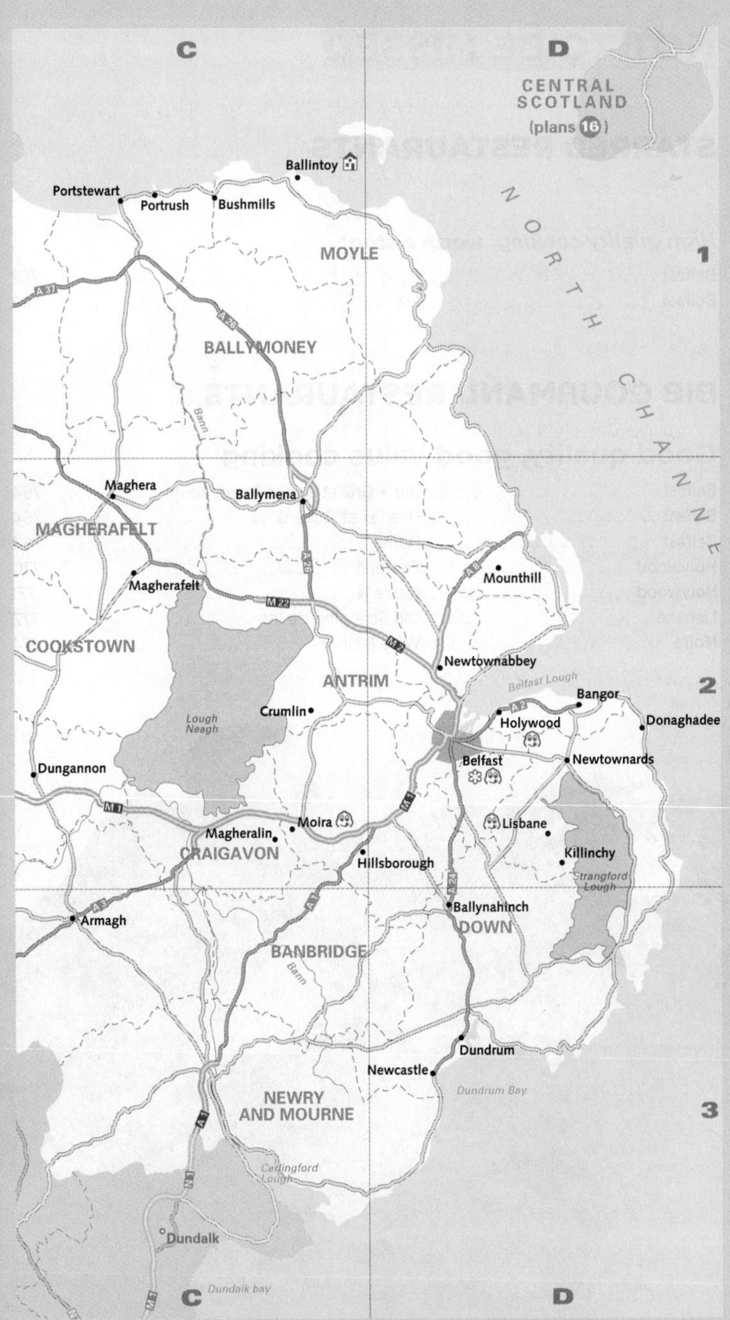
C
D
CENTRAL
SCOTLAND
(plans 16)
NORTH CHANNEL
1
2
3
Ballintoy
Portstewart
Portrush
Bushmills
MOYLE
A 37
A 26
BALLYMONEY
Bann
Maghera
Ballymena
MAGHERAFELT
A 26
A 8
Mounthill
Magherafelt
M 22
COOKSTOWN
M 2
Newtownabbey
ANTRIM
Belfast Lough
Bangor
A 2
Donaghadee
Crumlin
Holywood
Lough Neagh
Belfast
Newtownards
Dungannon
M 1
M 1
Moira
Magheralin
Lisbane
CRAIGAVON
Killinchy
Hillsborough
Strangford Lough
A 24
A 3
A 1
Ballynahinch
Armagh
DOWN
BANBRIDGE
Bann
Dundrum
Newcastle
Dundrum Bay
NEWRY
AND MOURNE
A 1
Carlingford
Lough
M 1
Dundalk
Dundalk bay
M 1
C
D

NOT TO BE MISSED

STARRED RESTAURANTS

✿

High quality cooking, worth a stop!

BIB GOURMAND RESTAURANTS

Good quality, good value cooking

Michelin

OUR TOP PICKS

City hotspots

Likeable locals

A warm welcome awaits

Spa retreats

ANNAHILT EANACH EILTE - Lisburn → See Hillsborough

ARMAGH ARD MHACHA

Armagh - Pop. 15 020 - Regional map n° **20**-C3

Moody Boar

TRADITIONAL CUISINE • BISTRO Set in the old stables of the former Primate of All Ireland's house and surrounded by a vast park; a characterful restaurant with a vaulted ceiling and booths in the old stalls. Classic dishes have personal touches.

Menu £ 18/22 - Carte £ 26/32

Palace Stables, Palace Demense ✉ BT60 4EL - South : 0.5 mi off A 3 - ✆ 028 3752 9678 - www.themoodyboar.com - Closed 25-26 December and Monday

BALLINTOY

Moyle - Regional map n° **20**-C1

Whitepark House

TRADITIONAL • CLASSIC Charming 18C house near the Giant's Causeway, decorated with lovely wall hangings, framed silks and other artefacts from the personable owner's travels. Large, open-fired lounge where cakes are served on arrival. Bright, antique-furnished bedrooms have four-posters or half-testers, and smart modern bathrooms.

4 rooms - £ 85 £ 130

150 Whitepark Rd ✉ BT54 6NH - West : 1.5 mi on A 2 - ✆ 028 2073 1482 - www.whiteparkhouse.com - Closed December and January

BALLYMENA AN BAILE MEÁNACH

Ballymena - Pop. 29 782 - Regional map n° **20**-C2

at Galgorm West: 3 mi on A42

River Room

MODERN BRITISH • INTIMATE Formal, warmly decorated dining room set on the ground floor of a stylishly furnished, whitewashed Victorian manor house, with good views across the River Maine. Refined, classically based cooking and attentive service.

Carte £ 46/56

Galgorm Resort and Spa Hotel, 136 Fenaghy Rd ✉ BT42 1EA - West : 1.5 mi on Cullybacky rd - ✆ 028 2588 1001 - www.galgorm.com - dinner only and Sunday lunch - Closed Monday and Tuesday

Galgorm Resort and Spa

LUXURY • CONTEMPORARY Victorian manor house with newer extensions, set in large grounds. Stylish interior with plenty of lounge space, a huge function capacity and an excellent leisure club with a superb outdoor spa pool. Modern bedrooms boast state-of-the-art facilities; some have balconies. Extensive all-day menus served in characterful Gillies; informal Fratelli offers Italian fare.

134 rooms - £ 155/300 £ 155/300 - 1 suite

136 Fenaghy Rd ✉ BT42 1EA - West : 1.5 mi on Cullybacky rd - ✆ 028 2588 1001 - www.galgorm.com

River Room - See restaurant listing

BALLYNAHINCH

Down - Pop. 5 633 - Regional map n° **20**-D3

Bull & Ram

MEATS AND GRILLS • RUSTIC Stunning Grade I listed former butcher's shop. Sit beneath a herringbone oak ceiling and an old meat-hanging rail, surrounded by original tiling. Meat is the way to go, with beef and lamb dry-aged locally in a Himalayan salt chamber.

Menu £ 14 (lunch) – Carte £ 25/40

1 Dromore St ✉ BT24 8AG – ✆ 028 9756 0908 – www.bullandram.com

BANGOR BEANNCHAR

North Down – Pop. 60 260 – Regional map n° **20**-D2

Wheathill

MODERN CUISINE • NEIGHBOURHOOD 7 Gray's Hill was once known as Wheathill, as it was the route used to transport wheat to the harbour. Choose from hearty, wholesome classics and dishes with an Italian twist. Service is bubbly and the wine list is keenly priced.

Menu £ 18 (early dinner) – Carte £ 22/48

7 Gray's Hill ✉ BT20 3BB – ✆ 028 9147 7405 – www.thewheathill.com – Closed 29 January-4 February, 9-15 July, Sunday dinner, Monday and Tuesday

Cairn Bay Lodge

FAMILY • COSY Set overlooking the bay, a whitewashed Edwardian house decorated with unusual objets d'art. Bedrooms come with plenty of extras and there's also a small beauty facility. The daytime café offers cakes and brunch-type dishes.

8 rooms – †£ 50/60 ††£ 85/100

278 Seacliffe Rd ✉ BT20 5HS – East : 1.25 mi by Quay St – ✆ 028 9146 7636 – www.cairnbaylodge.com

GOOD TIPS!

Optimism abounds in this city, with industry, commerce, arts and tourism all playing a role. With it has come a vibrant and ever-expanding restaurant scene that offers something for everyone, from delis and fish bars to bistros and brasseries. The Cathedral Quarter is the new dining hub attracting the foodies, while **Eipic** and **OX** have brought Michelin Stars.

BELFAST BÉAL FEIRSTE

Belfast – Pop. 267 742 – Regional map n° **20**-D2

Restaurants

✿ Eipic

MODERN CUISINE • ELEGANT XXX An elegant, intimate restaurant featuring a glass-fronted wine room and adjoined by a smart champagne bar. Top quality local ingredients feature on modern, seasonal menus and combinations are original and creative. Flavours are clearly defined and the occasional playful element features too.

➜ Baked beetroot with goat's curd, walnuts and vinegar. Mourne Mountains lamb, sprouting broccoli and wild garlic. Honey cream with rhubarb, raspberries and rosewater.

Menu £ 40/60

Town plan: B2-n – *28-40 Howard St ✉ BT1 6PF*
– *✆ 028 9033 1134 (booking essential) – www.deaneseipic.com*
– *dinner only and Friday lunch*
– *Closed 28 March-3 April, 11-24 July, 25-26 December, 1 January and Sunday-Tuesday*

✿ OX (Stephen Toman)

MODERN BRITISH • BISTRO X Top quality seasonal produce guides the menus at this rustic restaurant; lunch offers a fixed price 3 course selection, while dinner is a daily changing 5 course 'surprise'. Ask for a seat in the old minstrels' gallery to take in views of the river, and arrive early for an aperitif in the Wine Cave.

➜ Salt-cured halibut with buttermilk, almond and cauliflower. Skeaghanore duck with foie gras, chestnuts and quince. Jerusalem artichoke with banana, caramel and pistachio.

Menu £ 20/50

Town plan: B1-m – *1 Oxford St ✉ BT1 3LA*
– *✆ 028 9031 4121 – www.oxbelfast.com*
– *Closed 10-24 July, 24 December-2 January, 3-10 April, Sunday and Monday*

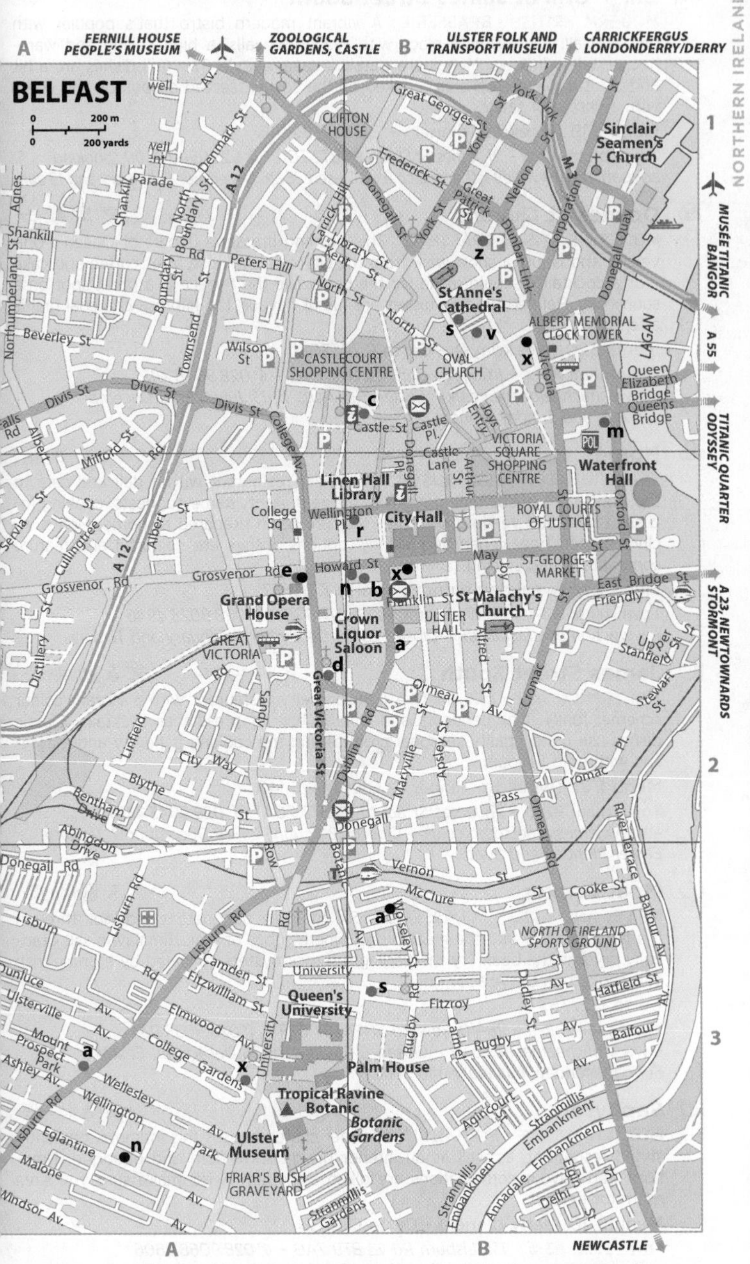
BELFAST
0 200 m
0 200 yards
A
B
1
2
3
FERNILL HOUSE
PEOPLE'S MUSEUM
ZOOLOGICAL
GARDENS, CASTLE
ULSTER FOLK AND
TRANSPORT MUSEUM
CARRICKFERGUS
LONDONDERRY/DERRY
MUSÉE TITANIC
BANGOR
A 55
TITANIC QUARTER
ODYSSEY
A 23, NEWTOWNARDS
STORMONT
NEWCASTLE
CLIFTON HOUSE
Sinclair
Seamen's
Church
St Anne's
Cathedral
ALBERT MEMORIAL
CLOCK TOWER
CASTLECOURT
SHOPPING CENTRE
OVAL
CHURCH
VICTORIA
SQUARE
SHOPPING
CENTRE
Waterfront
Hall
Linen Hall
Library
City Hall
ROYAL COURTS
OF JUSTICE
ST-GEORGE'S
MARKET
Grand Opera
House
Crown
Liquor
Saloon
ULSTER
HALL
St Malachy's
Church
GREAT
VICTORIA
NORTH OF IRELAND
SPORTS GROUND
Queen's
University
Palm House
Tropical Ravine
Botanic
Botanic
Gardens
Ulster
Museum
FRIAR'S BUSH
GRAVEYARD
LAGAN
Queen
Elizabeth
Bridge
Queens
Bridge
Great Victoria St
Donegall Quay
Divis St
Shankill Rd
Grosvenor Rd
Lisburn Rd
Ormeau Rd
Botanic Av.
Donegall Rd
Malone Av.

Bar + Grill at James Street South

MODERN BRITISH • BRASSERIE X A vibrant modern bistro that's popular with one and all. It's a simple place with red brick walls, a high ceiling and warehouse-style windows. Menus are classic brasserie style. The grill dishes are a hit and the succulent steaks are cooked on the Josper, served on boards and come with a choice of sauces.

Menu £ 19 (weekday dinner) – Carte £ 22/46

Town plan: B2-b – *21 James St South ✉ BT2 7GA – ✆ 028 9560 0700 (booking advisable) – www.belfastbargrill.co.uk – Closed 25-26 December, 1 January and 12 July*

Deanes at Queens

MODERN BRITISH • BRASSERIE X This bustling brasserie is part of Queen's University and is just a short walk from the city centre. Those after coffee and cake – or a cocktail – should make for the bar, while the terrace is a great spot on a sunny day. Refined modern dishes are full of flavour; the Mibrasa charcoal grill is a feature.

Menu £ 20 (weekdays) – Carte £ 27/36

Town plan: A3-x – *1 College Gdns ✉ BT9 6BQ – ✆ 028 9038 2111 – www.michaeldeane.co.uk – Closed 5-6 April, 12-13 July, 25-26 December, 1 January and Sunday dinner*

Home

TRADITIONAL BRITISH • RUSTIC X A popular restaurant with a deli and café to the front and a rustic dining room to the rear. As its name suggests, cooking focuses on refined versions of dishes that are often prepared at home. Menus include gluten free, vegan and 'skinny' options; dishes are colourful and feature some interesting spicing.

Menu £ 17 (weekday dinner) – Carte £ 24/37

Town plan: B2-r – *22 Wellington Pl ✉ BT1 6GE – ✆ 028 9023 4946 – www.homebelfast.co.uk – Closed 25-26 December, 1 January and 12 July*

James Street South

MODERN CUISINE • DESIGN XX A light and airy restaurant with a vibrant colour scheme, funky light pendants and a large bar for pre-dinner cocktails. Classic dishes use good quality seasonal produce and the cooking is hearty and masculine with bold flavours.

Menu £ 22 (weekday dinner) – Carte £ 26/49

Town plan: B2-b – *21 James St South ✉ BT2 7GA – ✆ 028 9043 4310 – www.jamesstreetsouth.co.uk – Closed 12-17 July, 25-26 December, 1 January, Easter Monday and Sunday*

Meat Locker

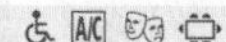

MEATS AND GRILLS • BRASSERIE XX Sit on smart banquettes and look through the large window into the meat fridge, where cubes of pink Himalayan salt gradually dry age the beef. Try the Carlingford rock oysters, followed by a prime Irish cut, cooked on the Asador grill.

Carte £ 27/53

Town plan: B2-n – *28-40 Howard St ✉ BT1 6PF – ✆ 028 9033 1134 – www.michaeldeane.co.uk – Closed 12-13 July, 25-26 December, Easter Sunday-Monday, 1 January and Sunday*

Saphyre

MODERN CUISINE • ELEGANT XX A former church houses this intimate, opulently styled restaurant, as well as an interior design showroom and boutique. Time-honoured flavour combinations are given a modern twist; make sure you save room for dessert.

Menu £ 20 (early dinner) – Carte £ 31/53

Town plan: A3-a – *135 Lisburn Rd ✉ BT9 7AG – ✆ 028 9068 8606 – www.saphyrerestaurant.com – Closed Sunday, dinner Monday-Tuesday and bank holidays*

Shu

MODERN BRITISH • DESIGN XX A well-established neighbourhood restaurant with a modern look and a lively, vibrant atmosphere. Menus are guided by seasonality and the ambitious, modern British dishes have international influences. Good value set price menu.

Menu £ 14/28 – Carte £ 22/42

253 Lisburn Rd ✉ BT9 7EN – Southwest : 1.75 mi on A1 – ☎ 028 9038 1655 – www.shu-restaurant.com – Closed 1 January, 11-13 July, 24-26 December and Sunday

Coppi

MEDITERRANEAN CUISINE • BISTRO X Set on the ground floor of a purpose built property in the Cathedral Quarter. It's big and buzzy, with rustic furnishings and leather booths, and staff are bright and friendly. Good value Italian dishes; start with a selection of cicchetti.

Menu £ 13 (weekday lunch) – Carte £ 20/46

Town plan: B1-z – *St Annes Sq ✉ BT1 2LD – ☎ 028 9031 1959 – www.coppi.co.uk – Closed 25-26 December and 12 July*

Cyprus Avenue Ⓝ

TRADITIONAL CUISINE • NEIGHBOURHOOD X You'll find something to please everyone at this all-day suburban bistro. Head past the cabinet bursting with home-baked goodies, to one of the intimate booths at the back. Dishes are appealing and full of flavour.

Carte £ 19/28

228 Upper Newtownards Rd ✉ BT4 3ET – East : 2.5 mi by A 2 on A 20 – ☎ 028 9065 6755 – www.cyprusavenue.co.uk – Closed 25 December

Deanes Deli

MODERN BRITISH • BISTRO X Glass-fronted city centre eatery. One side is a smart restaurant offering an appealing menu of classical dishes with some Asian and Mediterranean influences; the other side acts as a coffee shop by day and a buzzy tapas bar by night.

Menu £ 19 (early dinner) – Carte £ 21/32

Town plan: B2-a – *42-44 Bedford St ✉ BT2 7FF – ☎ 028 9024 8800 – www.michaeldeane.co.uk – Closed 25-26 December, 12-13 July, 1 January, Sunday and Easter Monday*

Deanes Love Fish

SEAFOOD • ELEGANT X If it comes from the sea, they'll serve it here! A glass ceiling makes it light and airy and the décor has a maritime feel. The à la carte offers three sizes of platter and everything from cod croquettes to lobster. Lunch is good value.

Menu £ 7 (lunch) – Carte £ 19/32

Town plan: B2-n – *28-40 Howard St ✉ BT1 6PF – ☎ 028 9033 1134 – www.michaeldeane.co.uk – Closed Easter Sunday-Monday, dinner 24 December, 12-13 July, 1 January and Sunday*

Ginger Bistro

TRADITIONAL CUISINE • BISTRO X Rustic neighbourhood bistro close to the Grand Opera House. The two rooms feature bright modern artwork and bespoke fish-themed paintings. Good-sized menus feature simply cooked Irish ingredients and display some Asian influences.

Carte £ 24/43

Town plan: A2-d – *7-8 Hope St ✉ BT2 5EE – ☎ 028 9024 4421 – www.gingerbistro.com – Closed Christmas, New Year, Easter, 5 days mid-July, Sunday and lunch Monday-Wednesday*

Hadskis

CLASSIC CUISINE • RUSTIC X This modern conversion is in the up-and-coming Cathedral Quarter. The long, narrow room has an open kitchen, where you can watch the chefs use the latest market produce to prepare globally-influenced dishes and tasty small plates.

Menu £ 20 (early dinner) – Carte £ 25/42

Town plan: B1-s – *33 Donegall St ✉ BT1 2NB – ✆ 028 9032 5444 – www.hadskis.co.uk – Closed 25-26 December, 1 January and 12 July*

Il Pirata

MEDITERRANEAN CUISINE • RUSTIC X Rustic restaurant with scrubbed wooden floors and an open kitchen. Mediterranean-influenced menus offer an extensive range of mainly Italian small plates; 3 or 4 dishes per person (plus dessert) should suffice. Bright, friendly service.

Carte £ 20/30

279-281 Upper Newtownards Rd ✉ BT4 3JF – East : 3 mi by A 2 on A 20 – ✆ 028 9067 3421 – www.ilpiratabelfast.com

Molly's Yard

TRADITIONAL BRITISH • BISTRO X Split-level bistro in a former coach house and stables, with exposed brickwork and a pleasant courtyard. Simple lunches and more ambitious dinners with classical combinations given a personal twist. Fine selection of ales and stouts.

Menu £ 20 (weekdays)/26 – Carte £ 20/44

Town plan: B3-s – *1 College Green Mews, Botanic Ave ✉ BT7 1LW – ✆ 028 9032 2600 (booking essential) – www.mollysyard.co.uk – Closed 11-12 July, 24-26 December, 1 January and Sunday*

Mourne Seafood Bar

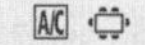

SEAFOOD • BISTRO X This popular seafood restaurant comes complete with a small shop and a cookery school. Blackboard menus offer a huge array of freshly prepared dishes; go for the classics, such as the Carlingford oysters, accompanied by a pint of stout.

Carte £ 20/40

Town plan: B1-c – *34-36 Bank St ✉ BT1 1HL – ✆ 028 9024 8544 (booking essential at dinner) – www.mourneseafood.com – Closed 24-26 December, 1 January, Easter Sunday and 12 July*

Muddlers Club

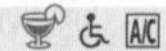

MODERN CUISINE • DESIGN X Tucked away in a labyrinth of passageways is this modern, industrial-style restaurant named after a 200 year old secret society. Cooking shows off local ingredients: starters and mains are rustic, while desserts are more refined.

Carte £ 29/45

Town plan: B1-v – *1 Warehouse Ln ✉ BT1 2DX – (off Waring St) – ✆ 028 9031 3199 (booking advisable) – www.themuddlersclubbelfast.com – Closed 2 weeks July, 1 week Easter, 1-8 January, 24-27 December, Sunday and Monday*

Hotels

Merchant

LUXURY • ELEGANT Former Ulster Bank HQ with an impressive Victorian façade. Plush, intimately styled bedrooms; those in the annexe have an art deco theme. Rooftop gym with an outdoor hot tub and a skyline view; relax afterwards in the swish cocktail bar. British dishes with a Mediterranean edge in the opulent former banking hall. Classic French brasserie dishes and live jazz in Berts.

62 rooms – †£ 170/230 ††£ 180/349 – 2 suites

Town plan: B1-x – *16 Skipper St ✉ BT1 2DZ – ✆ 028 9023 4888 – www.themerchanthotel.com*

Fitzwilliam

LUXURY • CONTEMPORARY Stylish hotel by the Grand Opera House. Smart modern bedrooms have striking colour schemes, contemporary furnishings and good facilities. Have afternoon tea in the lobby, eat informally in the bar or dine on modern Irish dishes in the first floor restaurant. The small function room has great rooftop views.

129 rooms ☕ – 🚹£ 179/199 🚹🚹£ 219/279 – 1 suite

Town plan: A2-e – *Great Victoria St ✉ BT2 7BQ – ✆ 028 9044 2080 – www.fitzwilliamhotelbelfast.com*

Ten Square

BUSINESS • MODERN Hidden behind the historic City Hall is this Grade I listed Victorian hotel. Bedrooms offer a good level of facilities; the newer ones – in a converted office building – are state-of-the-art. The vibrant bar and terrace is a popular spot, as is Jospers restaurant, which serves steaks and grills.

60 rooms ☕ – 🚹£ 105/125 🚹🚹£ 115/225

Town plan: B2-x – *10 Donegall Sq South ✉ BT1 5JD – ✆ 028 9024 1001 – www.tensquare.co.uk – Closed 24-25 December*

Malone Lodge

BUSINESS • MODERN Well-run, privately owned townhouse, in a peaceful Victorian terrace. Smart, spacious bedrooms are spread over various annexes and range from corporate rooms to presidential suites and apartments. State-of-the-art function rooms include a large ballroom. Characterful bar and next door grill restaurant.

102 rooms – 🚹£ 79/139 🚹🚹£ 79/169 – ☕£ 15 – 3 suites

Town plan: A3-n – *60 Eglantine Ave ✉ BT9 6DY – ✆ 028 9038 8000 – www.malonelodgehotelbelfast.com*

Tara Lodge

TOWNHOUSE • CONTEMPORARY Small hotel close to the Botanic Gardens, not far from town. Smart contemporary bedrooms are split between two buildings; go for a 'Signature' room, which comes with bluetooth speakers, hair straighteners and a coffee machine.

34 rooms ☕ – 🚹£ 80/100 🚹🚹£ 90/155

Town plan: B3-a – *36 Cromwell Rd ✉ BT7 1JW – ✆ 028 9059 9099 – www.taralodge.com – Closed 24-27 December*

Ravenhill House

TRADITIONAL • CLASSIC Red-brick Victorian house set in the city suburbs. Bright, homely lounge and wood-furnished breakfast room; colourful bedrooms boast good facilities. Organic breakfasts feature homemade muesli and the wheat for the bread is home-milled.

5 rooms ☕ – 🚹£ 80/140 🚹🚹£ 95/140

690 Ravenhill Rd ✉ BT6 0BZ – Southeast : 1.75 mi on B 506 – ✆ 028 9020 7444 – www.ravenhillhouse.com – Closed January, 27 August-2 September and 20-31 December

BRYANSFORD - Down → See Newcastle

BUSHMILLS MUILEANN NA BUAISE

Moyle – ✉ Bushmills – Pop. 1 343 – Regional map n° **20**-C1

Bushmills Inn

TRADITIONAL • CLASSIC Proudly run, part-17C whitewashed inn that successfully blends the old with the new. The conference room features a state-of-the-art cinema. Up-to-date bedrooms are split between the original house and an extension. Have a drink beside the peat fire in the old whiskey bar before dining on classic dishes.

41 rooms ☕ – 🚹£ 110/320 🚹🚹£ 120/420

9 Dunluce Rd ✉ BT57 8QG – ✆ 028 2073 3000 – www.bushmillsinn.com – Closed 24-25 December

Causeway Lodge

FAMILY • CONTEMPORARY Set inland from the Giant's Causeway, in a peaceful location. Guest areas come with polished wood floors, leather furnishings and artwork of local scenes. Spacious, boutique bedrooms have bold feature walls and a high level of facilities.

5 rooms – £100/140 £100/150

52 Moycraig Rd, Dunseverick ✉ BT57 8TB – East : 5 mi by A 2 and Drumnagee Rd – ✆ 028 2073 0333 – www.causewaylodge.com

CRUMLIN CROMGHLINN

Antrim – Pop. 5 117 – Regional map n° **20**-C2

Caldhame Lodge

FAMILY • PERSONALISED Purpose-built guesthouse near the airport, with a pleasant mix of lawns and paved terracing. Comfy guest areas include a conservatory breakfast room and a lounge filled with family photos. Good-sized, individually decorated bedrooms are immaculately kept and feature warm fabrics and iPod docking stations.

8 rooms – £40/55 £60/100

102 Moira Rd, Nutts Corner ✉ BT29 4HG – Southeast : 2 mi on A 26 – ✆ 028 9442 3099 – www.caldhamelodge.co.uk

DERRY/LONDONDERRY

→ See Londonderry

DONAGHADEE DOMHNACH DAOI

Ards – Pop. 6 856 – Regional map n° **20**-D2

Pier 36

TRADITIONAL CUISINE • PUB This vast, family-run pub sits on the quayside in a picturesque harbour town. There's a smart bar downstairs and, above it, 'Harbour and Company', which has two huge windows overlooking the bay. Choose from pub classics, chargrilled seafood and fantastic wood-fired steaks. Bright bedrooms have a seaside feel.

Carte £20/48

6 rooms – £55/85 £79/119

36 The Parade ✉ BT21 0HE – ✆ 028 9188 4466 – www.pier36.co.uk – Closed 25 December

DUNDRUM DÚN DROMA

Down – Pop. 1 522 – Regional map n° **20**-D3

Buck's Head Inn

SEAFOOD • NEIGHBOURHOOD Have drinks in the lounge of this converted village pub, then sit overlooking the garden or in a cosy booth by the fire. Unfussy lunches are followed by more ambitious dinners; seafood is a strength, particularly mussels.

Menu £30 (lunch) – Carte £22/43

77-79 Main St ✉ BT33 0LU – ✆ 028 4375 1868 – Closed 24-25 December and Monday October-March

Mourne Seafood Bar

SEAFOOD • RUSTIC Friendly, rustic restaurant on the main street of a busy coastal town. Simple, wood-furnished dining room with nautically themed artwork. Classic menus centre around seafood, with oysters and mussels from the owners' beds the specialities.

Carte £16/36

10 Main St ✉ BT33 0LU – ✆ 028 4375 1377 (booking essential) – www.mourneseafood.com – Closed 25 December and Monday-Thursday in winter

Carriage House

TRADITIONAL • CLASSIC Sweet, lilac-washed terraced house with colourful window boxes. Homely lounge with books and local info. Simple, antique-furnished bedrooms; some affording pleasant bay views. Breakfast in the conservatory, overlooking the pretty garden.

3 rooms - £70 £95

71 Main St ✉ BT33 0LU - ☎ 028 4375 1635 - www.carriagehousedundrum.com

DUNGANNON DÚN GEANAINN

Dungannon - Pop. 14 380 - Regional map n° **20**-C2

Grange Lodge

TRADITIONAL • CLASSIC An attractive Georgian country house with well-kept gardens (an ideal spot for afternoon tea!) Antique-furnished guest areas display fine sketches and lithographs. Snug, well-appointed bedrooms are immaculately kept with good extras.

5 rooms - £89/99 £109/119

7 Grange Rd, Moy ✉ BT71 7EJ - Southeast : 3.5 mi by A 29 - ☎ 028 8778 4212 - www.grangelodgecountryhouse.com - Closed 20 December-1 February

ENNISKILLEN INIS CEITHLEANN

Fermanagh - Pop. 13 757 - Regional map n° **20**-A2

Belleek

CLASSIC CUISINE • ELEGANT XX Formal hotel dining room comprising three rooms - two with high ceilings and ornate plasterwork and the third in a glass-fronted cube which offers unrivalled views across the marina. Classic dishes are presented in a modern manner.

Menu £38

Manor House Hotel, Killadeas ✉ BT94 1NY - North : 7.5 mi by A 32 on B 82 - ☎ 028 6862 2200 - www.manorhousecountryhotel.com - dinner only and Sunday lunch

Lough Erne Resort

LUXURY • MODERN Vast, luxurious golf and leisure resort on a peninsula between two loughs. Bedrooms have a classical style and are extremely well-appointed; the suites and lodges are dotted about the grounds. Relax in the beautiful Thai spa or the huge pool with its stunning mosaic wall. Ambitious, contemporary dining and lough views in Catalina; steaks and grills in the clubhouse.

120 rooms - £99/219 £99/219 - 6 suites

Belleek Rd ✉ BT93 7ED - Northwest : 4 mi by A 4 on A 46 - ☎ 028 6632 3230 - www.lougherneresort.com

Manor House

TRADITIONAL • MODERN Impressive yellow-washed manor house overlooking Lough Erne and surrounded by mature grounds. Comfy, stylish guest areas mix the traditional and the contemporary. Bedrooms range from characterful in the main house to smart and modern in the extensions. The formal dining room offers classical cooking and there's a more casual all-day menu served in the old vaults.

79 rooms - £80/135 £90/285 - 2 suites

Killadeas ✉ BT94 1NY - North : 7.5 mi by A 32 on B 82 - ☎ 028 6862 2200 - www.manorhousecountryhotel.com

Belleek - See restaurant listing

GALGORM → See Ballymena

HILLSBOROUGH CROMGHLINN

Lisburn - Pop. 3 738 - Regional map n° **20**-C2

Parson's Nose

TRADITIONAL BRITISH • PUB Characterful Georgian property built by the first Marquis of Downshire; the restaurant above the bar overlooks a lake in the castle grounds. Menus are unashamedly traditional and the daily fish specials are a hit.

Carte £ 20/39

48 Lisburn St ✉ BT26 6AB - ✆ 028 9268 3009 (booking advisable)
- www.theparsonsnose.co.uk - Closed 25 December

Plough Inn

TRADITIONAL CUISINE • PUB Family-run, 18C coaching inn that's three establishments in one: a bar with an adjoining dining room; a café-cum-bistro; and a seafood restaurant. Dishes range from light snacks and pub classics to more modern, international offerings.

Menu £ 24 - Carte £ 24/39

3 The Square ✉ BT26 6AG - ✆ 028 9268 2985
- www.ploughgroup.com/ploughinn - Closed 25-26 December

Lisnacurran Country House

FAMILY • PERSONALISED Homely Edwardian house, where spacious rooms are furnished with antiques. Choose a bedroom in the main house, the former milking parlour or the old barn. Breakfasts are hearty - the homemade soda and potato bread is a must.

8 rooms - †£ 55/60 ††£ 73/85

6 Listullycurran Rd, Dromore ✉ BT25 1RB - Southwest : 3 mi on A 1
- ✆ 028 9269 8710 - www.lisnacurrancountryhouse.co.uk

at Annahilt Southeast: 4 mi on B177 ✉ Hillsborough

Pheasant

TRADITIONAL CUISINE • PUB Dark wood and stained glass give this pub a Gothic look and the Guinness-themed art, warm welcome and laid-back atmosphere add a typically Irish feel. Portions are hearty, lunch is good value and the fishcakes are delicious.

Menu £ 13 (lunch and early dinner) - Carte £ 20/38

410 Upper Ballynahinch Rd ✉ BT26 6NR - North : 1 mi on Lisburn rd
- ✆ 028 9263 8056 - www.thepheasantrestaurant.co.uk - Closed 25-26 December and 12 July

Fortwilliam

TRADITIONAL • CLASSIC Attractive bay-windowed farmhouse with neat gardens, surrounded by 80 acres of land. Homely lounge and a country kitchen with an Aga. Traditional bedrooms have flowery fabrics, antiques and country views; two have private bathrooms.

3 rooms - †£ 50/75 ††£ 75

210 Ballynahinch Rd ✉ BT26 6BH - Northwest : 0.25 mi on B 177
- ✆ 028 9268 2255 - www.fortwilliamcountryhouse.com - Closed 24-27 December

HOLYWOOD ARD MHIC NASCA

North Down - Pop. 12 131 - Regional map n° **20**-D2

Fontana

MODERN CUISINE • NEIGHBOURHOOD XX This smart, modern, first floor restaurant is a favourite amongst the locals; it's accessed down a narrow town centre passageway and decorated with contemporary art. Menus offer British, Mediterranean and some Asian dishes, with local seafood a speciality. A good value set menu is available at dinner.

Menu £ 24 (weekday dinner) - Carte £ 20/37

61A High St ✉ BT18 9AE - ✆ 028 9080 9908 - www.restaurantfontana.com
- Closed 25-26 December, 1-2 January, Saturday lunch, Sunday dinner and Monday

Noble

MODERN CUISINE • NEIGHBOURHOOD Housed in the centre of a busy town, above a health food shop, is this compact little restaurant where the service is warm and genuine and the room has a happy buzz. The good value weekly menu showcases carefully handled local ingredients; for dessert be sure to try the chocolate delice.

Menu £ 20 (lunch and early dinner) – Carte £ 26/31

27a Church Rd ✉ BT18 9BU
– ✆ 028 9042 5655 – www.nobleholywood.com – Closed 24 December-4 January, 10-25 July, Monday-Tuesday and lunch Wednesday

Culloden

BUSINESS • CLASSIC An extended Gothic mansion overlooking Belfast Lough, with well-maintained gardens full of modern sculptures, and a smart spa. Charming, traditional, antique-furnished guest areas have open fires and fine ceiling frescoes. Characterful bedrooms offer good facilities. Classical menus and good views in formal Mitre; wide range of traditional dishes in Cultra Inn.

98 rooms – †£ 240/320 ††£ 280/340 – 3 suites

142 Bangor Rd ✉ BT18 0EX – East : 1.5 mi on A 2
– ✆ 028 9042 1066 – www.hastingshotels.com

Rayanne House

TRADITIONAL • CLASSIC Keenly run, part-Victorian house in a residential area. Homely, antique-filled guest areas. Smart, country house bedrooms with a modern edge; those to the front offer the best views. Ambitious, seasonal dishes in formal dining room; try the Titanic tasting menu – a version of the last meal served on the ship.

10 rooms – †£ 90/100 ††£ 135/145

60 Demesne Rd ✉ BT18 9EX – by My Lady's Mile Rd
– ✆ 028 9042 5859 – www.rayannehouse.com

KILLINCHY

Ards – Regional map n° **20**-D2

Balloo House

CLASSIC CUISINE • PUB Characterful former farmhouse with a smart dining pub feel. Lengthy menus mix hearty pub classics and dishes with international leanings. Pies are popular, as is High Tea, which is served every day except Saturday.

Menu £ 15 (weekday lunch) – Carte £ 20/39

1 Comber Rd ✉ BT23 6PA – West : 0.75 mi on A 22
– ✆ 028 9754 1210 (bookings advisable at dinner) – www.balloohouse.com
– Closed 25 December

LIMAVADY LÉIM AN MHADAIDH

Limavady – Pop. 12 669 – Regional map n° **20**-B1

Lime Tree

TRADITIONAL CUISINE • NEIGHBOURHOOD Keenly run neighbourhood restaurant; its traditional exterior concealing a modern room with purple velvet banquettes and colourful artwork. Unfussy, classical cooking features meats and veg from the village; try the homemade wheaten bread.

Menu £ 26 – Carte £ 28/38

60 Catherine St ✉ BT49 9DB
– ✆ 028 7776 4300 – www.limetreerest.com – dinner only and lunch Thursday-Friday – Closed 25-26 December, Sunday and Monday

LISBANE AN LIOS BÁN

Ards – ✉ Comber – Regional map n° **20**-D2

Old Schoolhouse Inn

MODERN BRITISH • FAMILY X Just a stone's throw from Strangford Lough is this stylish, sumptuous restaurant, which has been passed down from parents to son. Modern dishes are skilfully prepared, full of flavour and use top notch ingredients – including plenty of local seafood and game. Satisfyingly, the chef isn't afraid to prepare some simpler dishes too. Homely bedrooms complete the picture.

Menu £ 20/25 – Carte £ 30/48

8 rooms – †£ 60/70 ††£ 80/100

100 Ballydrain Rd ✉ BT23 6EA – Northeast : 1.5 mi by Quarry Rd on Ballydrain Rd – ✆ 028 9754 1182 (booking essential) – www.theoldschoolhouseinn.com – Closed Monday and Tuesday

Poacher's Pocket

TRADITIONAL BRITISH • PUB Modern-looking building in the centre of a small village; the best seats are in the two-tiered extension overlooking the internal courtyard. Wide-ranging menus offer rustic, hearty dishes; come at the weekend for a laid-back brunch.

Menu £ 13 (weekdays)/23 – Carte £ 16/46

181 Killinchy Rd ✉ BT23 5NE – ✆ 028 9754 1589 – www.poacherspocketlisbane.com – Closed 25 December

LISNASKEA

Fermanagh – Pop. 2 880 – Regional map n° **20**-B3

Watermill Lodge

INN • TRADITIONAL A charming red-brick cottage with a thatched roof conceals a rustic restaurant with a 25,000 litre aquarium and a delightful terrace. From there, superb water gardens lead down to Lough Erne, where airy bedrooms with stone floors and heavy wood furnishings boast terraces looking out over the water.

7 rooms – †£ 59/79 ††£ 89/99

Kilmore Quay ✉ BT92 0DT – Southwest: 3 mi by B 127 – ✆ 028 6772 4369 – www.watermillrestaurantfermanagh.com

LONDONDERRY/DERRY

Derry – Pop. 85 016 – Regional map n° **20**-B1

Browns

MODERN BRITISH • NEIGHBOURHOOD XX The original Browns sits across from the railway station and comes with a plush lounge and an intimate, understated dining room. Dishes are eye-catching and showcase top Northern Irish produce in some interesting combinations.

Menu £ 25 (weekdays) – Carte £ 34/44

1 Bonds Hill, Waterside ✉ BT47 6DW – East : 1 mi by A 2 – ✆ 028 7134 5180 (booking advisable) – www.brownsrestaurant.com – Closed Saturday lunch, Sunday dinner and Monday

Browns In Town

MODERN BRITISH • BRASSERIE X Across the river from the first Browns, is its laid-back bigger sister. A bewildering array of menus offer everything you could want, from light snacks to hearty Irish meats and veg. Cooking is modern and comprises many elements.

Menu £ 25 (weekday dinner) – Carte £ 25/39

Strand Rd ✉ BT48 7DJ – ✆ 028 7136 2889 – www.brownsrestaurant.com – Closed 25 December and Sunday lunch

Harry's

REGIONAL CUISINE • COSY Harry's sits in the shadow of the mighty city walls. Cooking couldn't be more seasonal, with vegetables grown on their 3 acre plot and fish collected from the local fishermen. Unfussy cooking lets natural flavours shine through.

Carte £ 21/37

29-31 Craft Village ✉ BT48 6AY
– ✆ 028 7137 1635 – Closed Sunday and Tuesday-November-May and Monday

Beech Hill Country House

TRADITIONAL • CLASSIC Once a US Marine HQ, this 18C house is now a welcoming hotel and wedding venue. Characterful guest areas feature ornate coving and antiques, and most of the bedrooms have a country house style. Dine overlooking the lake and water wheel – traditional menus use produce from the walled garden.

31 rooms – †£ 95/125 ††£ 160/235 – 2 suites

32 Ardmore Rd ✉ BT47 3QP – Southeast : 3.5 mi by A 6
– ✆ 028 7134 9279 – www.beech-hill.com – Closed 24-25 December

Ramada Da Vinci's

BUSINESS • MODERN The hub of this welcoming hotel is its characterful bar, which was once a pub owned by a local artist. Bedrooms are spacious and modern, the events rooms are stylish and the atmospheric brasserie offers something for everyone. Photos of stars who have stayed here fill the walls.

65 rooms – †£ 59/120 ††£ 59/120 – £ 8

15 Culmore Rd ✉ BT48 8JB – North : 1 mi on A 2 (Foyle Bridge rd)
– ✆ 028 7127 9111 – www.davincishotel.com – Closed 24-25 December

MAGHERA MACHAIRE RÁTHA

Magherafelt – Pop. 3 886 – Regional map n° **20**-C2

Ardtara Country House

COUNTRY HOUSE • CLASSIC Spacious, elegant 19C country house, originally built for a local linen manufacturer. It's set in 8 acres of mature grounds and has a calming, restful air; many period features remain. The intimate wood-panelled restaurant offers a menu of modern classics which feature ingredients foraged for by the chef.

9 rooms – †£ 79/99 ††£ 89/149

8 Gorteade Rd, Upperlands ✉ BT46 5SA
– ✆ 028 7964 4490 – www.ardtara.com – Closed Monday and Tuesday in winter

MAGHERAFELT

Magherafelt – Pop. 8 881 – Regional map n° **20**-C2

Church Street

TRADITIONAL BRITISH • NEIGHBOURHOOD XX Bustling eatery on the main street of a busy country town. The long, narrow room has a mix of bistro, pew and high-backed seating, and there's a second smart room above. Unfussy, classical dishes rely on good quality local produce.

Menu £ 14 (early dinner) – Carte £ 23/38

23 Church St ✉ BT45 6AP – ✆ 028 7932 8083 (booking advisable)
– www.churchstreetrestaurant.co.uk – dinner only and Sunday lunch – Closed 4-14 January, 1 week mid-July, Monday and Tuesday

MAGHERALIN

Craigavon – Pop. 1 403 – Regional map n° **20**-C2

Newforge House 

COUNTRY HOUSE • PERSONALISED A traditional Georgian building with an old linen mill behind and colourful gardens and a meadow in front. Bedrooms are named after former inhabitants of the house and are tastefully furnished with period pieces. Three course dinners are replaced by simpler suppers on Sundays and Mondays.

6 rooms – †£ 90/135 ††£ 130/200

58 Newforge Rd ✉ BT67 0QL – ✆ 028 9261 1255 – www.newforgehouse.com
– Closed 20 December-1 February

MOIRA

Lisburn - Pop. 4 221 - Regional map n° **20**-C2

Wine & Brine

MODERN CUISINE • BISTRO X Local chef Chris McGowan has transformed this fine Georgian house into a bright modern restaurant displaying local art. Top regional ingredients feature in appealing dishes with a comforting feel. As its name suggests, some of the meats and fish are gently brined, using whey from the nearby cheese factory.

Carte £ 26/45

59 Main St ✉ BT67 0LQ - ✆ 028 9261 0500 - www.wineandbrine.co.uk - Closed 2 weeks January, 2 weeks July, Sunday dinner, Monday and Tuesday

MOUNTHILL

Antrim - Pop. 69 - Regional map n° **20**-D2

Billy Andy's

TRADITIONAL BRITISH • RUSTIC It used to be the village store as well as a pub, and although the groceries are gone, this place still seems to be all things to all people. Cooking is filling, with a strong Irish accent. They offer a fine selection of whiskies, there are four modern bedrooms and Saturday music sessions pack the place out.

Carte £ 23/38

4 rooms - **†**£ 40/60 **††**£ 70/90

66 Browndod Rd ✉ BT40 3DX - ✆ 028 2827 0648 - www.billyandys.com - Closed 25-26 December

NEWCASTLE AN CAISLEÁN NUA

Down - Pop. 7 723 - Regional map n° **20**-D3

Vanilla

INTERNATIONAL • NEIGHBOURHOOD XX Contemporary restaurant; its black canopy standing out amongst the town centre shops. The long, narrow room is flanked by brushed velvet banquettes and polished tables. Attractively presented, internationally influenced modern dishes.

Menu £ 21 (lunch and early dinner) - Carte £ 30/45

67 Main St ✉ BT33 0AE - ✆ 028 4372 2268 - www.vanillarestaurant.co.uk - Closed 25-27 December, 1 January and Wednesday dinner in winter

at Bryansford Northwest: 2.75 mi on B180

Tollyrose Country House

FAMILY • PERSONALISED Purpose-built guesthouse beside the Tollymore Forest Park, at the foot of the Mourne Mountains. Simple, modern bedrooms come in neutral hues; those on the top floor have the best views. Lots of local info in the lounge. Friendly owners.

6 rooms - **†**£ 45 **††**£ 75

15 Hilltown Rd ✉ BT33 0PX - Southwest : 0.5 mi on B 180 - ✆ 028 4372 6077 - www.tollyrose.com

NEWTOWNABBEY

Newtownabbey - Pop. 61 713 - Regional map n° **20**-D2

Sleepy Hollow

MODERN CUISINE • RURAL X This remote, passionately run restaurant is a real find, with its rustic rooms, large terrace and cosy hayloft bar! Cooking is contrastingly modern, and the chef prides himself on using seasonal ingredients with a story.

Menu £ 20 (lunch) - Carte £ 26/38

15 Klin Rd ✉ BT36 4SU - Northwest : 1 mi by Ballyclare Rd and Ballycraig Rd - ✆ 028 9083 8672 - www.sleepyhollowrestaurant.com - Closed 25-26 December

NEWTOWNARDS BAILE NUA NA HARDA

Ards – Pop. 28 437 – Regional map n° **20**-D2

Edenvale House

TRADITIONAL • CLASSIC Attractive Georgian farmhouse with a charming owner and pleasant lough and mountain views. It's traditionally decorated, with a comfy drawing room and a wicker-furnished sun room. Spacious, homely bedrooms boast good facilities.

3 rooms – £ 60/65 £ 110

130 Portaferry Rd BT22 2AH – Southeast : 2.75 mi on A 20 – 028 9181 4881 – www.edenvalehouse.com – Closed Christmas-New Year

PORTRUSH PORT ROIS

Coleraine – Pop. 6 640 – Regional map n° **20**-C1

Shola Coach House

TOWNHOUSE • CONTEMPORARY This attractive stone coach house once belonged to the Victorian manor house next door. Inside it's light and airy, with a tasteful contemporary style and modern facilities. Bedrooms are spacious; one is in the colourful garden.

4 rooms – £ 80/125 £ 100/125

110A Gateside Rd BT56 8NP – East : 1.5 mi by Ballywillan Road – 028 7082 5925 – www.sholabandb.com – Closed December and January

PORTSTEWART PORT STIÓBHAIRD

Coleraine – Pop. 7 368 – Regional map n° **20**-C1

Harry's Shack

TRADITIONAL CUISINE • RUSTIC The location is superb: on a sandy National Trust beach, with views across to Inishowen. It's an appealingly simple place with wooden tables and classroom-style chairs. Concise menus wisely let local ingredients speak for themselves.

Carte £ 27/45

118 Strand Rd BT55 7PG – West : 1 mi by Strand Rd – 028 7083 1783 – Closed Sunday dinner and Monday

Strandeen

FAMILY • CONTEMPORARY A great place to escape everyday life: the rooms are light and airy, the atmosphere is serene and the open-plan lounge takes in beach and mountain views. Organic breakfasts feature smoothies, chai porridge and bircher muesli.

5 rooms – £ 100/125 £ 110/125

63 Strand Rd BT55 7LU – 028 7083 3872 – www.strandeen.com

REPUBLIC OF IRELAND

They say that Ireland offers forty luminous shades of green, but it's not all wondrous hills and down-home pubs: witness the limestone-layered Burren, cut-through by meandering streams, lakes and labyrinthine caves; or the fabulous Cliffs of Moher, looming for mile after mile over the wild Atlantic waves. The cities burst with life: Dublin is one of Europe's coolest capitals, and free-spirited Cork enjoys a rich cultural heritage. Kilkenny mixes a medieval flavour with a strong artistic tradition, while the 'festival' city of Galway is enhanced by an easy, international vibe.

This is a country known for the quality and freshness of its produce, and farmers' markets and food halls yield an array of artisanal cheeses and freshly baked breads. Being an agricultural country, Ireland produces excellent home-reared meat and dairy products and a new breed of chefs are giving traditional dishes a clever modern twist. Seafood, particularly shellfish, is popular – nothing beats sitting on the quayside with a bowl of steaming mussels and the distinctive taste of a micro-brewery beer.

- Michelin Road maps n° 712 and 713
- Michelin Green Guide: Ireland

21 Republic of Ireland

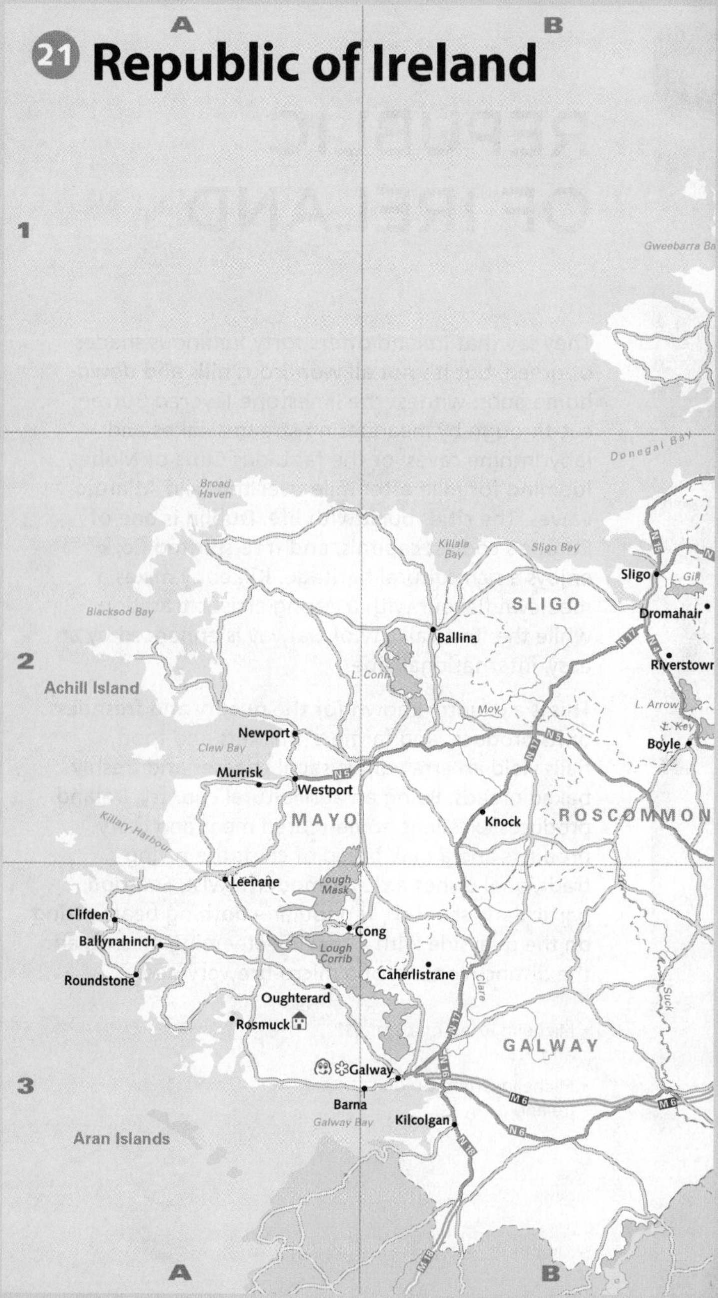

A B

1 2 3

Gweebarra Bay
Donegal Bay
Broad Haven
Killala Bay
Sligo Bay
Blacksod Bay
Sligo
L. Gill
SLIGO
Dromahair
Ballina
Achill Island
Riverstown
L. Conn
L. Arrow
Moy
L. Key
Newport
Clew Bay
Boyle
Murrisk
Westport
MAYO
Knock
ROSCOMMON
Killary Harbour
Leenane
Lough Mask
Clifden
Cong
Ballynahinch
Lough Corrib
Caherlistrane
Roundstone
Clare
Oughterard
Suck
Rosmuck
GALWAY
Galway
Barna
Kilcolgan
Galway Bay
Aran Islands
N5 N15 N17 N4 N16 N18 N6 M6 M18

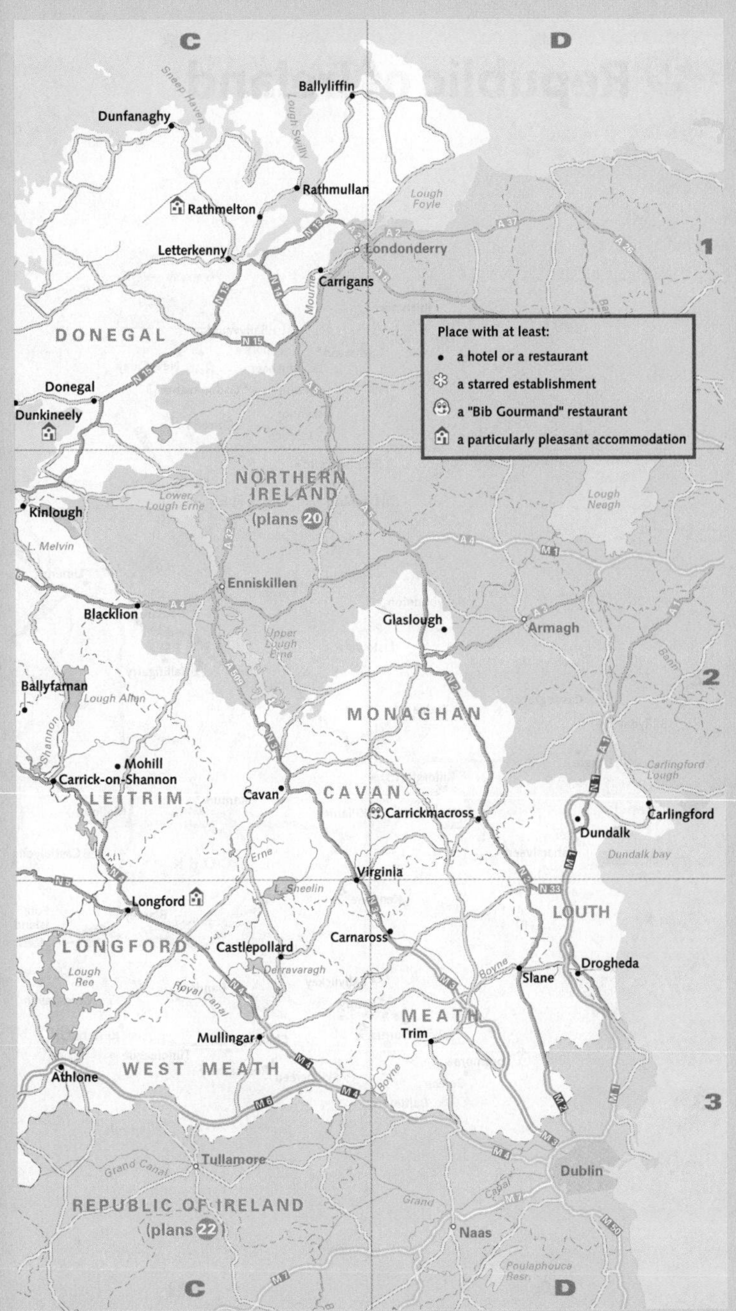
C
D
Ballyliffin
Dunfanaghy
Sheep Haven
Lough Swilly
Rathmullan
Lough Foyle
Rathmelton
Letterkenny
Londonderry
Carrigans
1
DONEGAL
Place with at least:
a hotel or a restaurant
a starred establishment
a "Bib Gourmand" restaurant
a particularly pleasant accommodation
Donegal
Dunkineely
NORTHERN IRELAND
(plans 20)
Lower Lough Erne
Lough Neagh
Kinlough
L. Melvin
Enniskillen
Blacklion
Glaslough
Armagh
Upper Lough Erne
2
Ballyfarnan
Lough Allen
MONAGHAN
Mohill
Carrick-on-Shannon
LEITRIM
Cavan
CAVAN
Carrickmacross
Carlingford Lough
Carlingford
Dundalk
Dundalk bay
Virginia
L. Sheelin
Longford
LOUTH
Carnaross
LONGFORD
Castlepollard
Drogheda
Slane
Lough Ree
L. Derravaragh
Royal Canal
MEATH
Trim
Mullingar
Athlone
WEST MEATH
3
Tullamore
Grand Canal
Dublin
REPUBLIC OF IRELAND
(plans 22)
Naas
Poulaphouca Resr.
C
D

22 Republic of Ireland

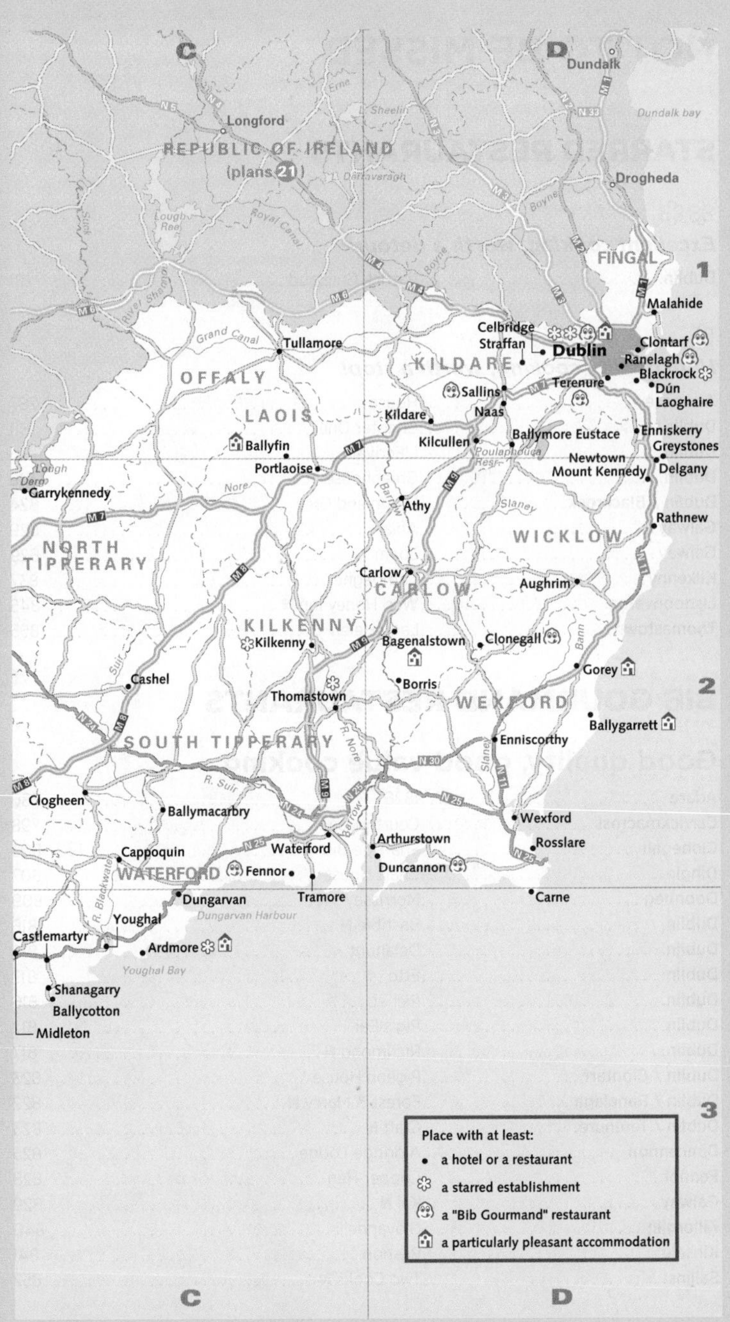
C
D
Dundalk
Dundalk bay
Longford
REPUBLIC OF IRELAND
(plans 21)
Drogheda
FINGAL
1
Malahide
Celbridge
Straffan
Dublin
Clontarf
Ranelagh
Blackrock
Terenure
Dún Laoghaire
Tullamore
KILDARE
OFFALY
Sallins
Naas
LAOIS
Kildare
Enniskerry
Kilcullen
Ballymore Eustace
Greystones
Ballyfin
Newtown Mount Kennedy
Delgany
Portlaoise
Garrykennedy
Athy
Rathnew
WICKLOW
NORTH TIPPERARY
Carlow
CARLOW
Aughrim
KILKENNY
Kilkenny
Bagenalstown
Clonegall
Gorey
Cashel
Borris
2
Thomastown
WEXFORD
Ballygarrett
SOUTH TIPPERARY
Enniscorthy
Clogheen
Ballymacarbry
Wexford
Arthurstown
Rosslare
Cappoquin
Waterford
WATERFORD
Fennor
Duncannon
Tramore
Carne
Dungarvan
Dungarvan Harbour
Youghal
Castlemartyr
Ardmore
Youghal Bay
Shanagarry
Ballycotton
Midleton
3
Place with at least:
a hotel or a restaurant
a starred establishment
a "Bib Gourmand" restaurant
a particularly pleasant accommodation
C
D

NOT TO BE MISSED

STARRED RESTAURANTS

Excellent cooking, worth a detour!

Dublin	Patrick Guilbaud	811

High quality cooking, worth a stop!

Ardmore	House	787
Dublin	Chapter One	811
Dublin	L'Ecrivain	811
Dublin	Greenhouse	816
Dublin / Blackrock	Heron and Grey	824
Galway	Aniar	829
Galway	Loam	829
Kilkenny	Campagne	837
Lisdoonvarna	Wild Honey Inn **N**	845
Thomastown	Lady Helen	855

BIB GOURMAND RESTAURANTS

Good quality, good value cooking

Adare	1826	786
Carrickmacross	Courthouse	798
Clonegall	Sha-Roe Bistro	803
Dingle	Chart House	807
Doonbeg	Morrissey's **N**	809
Dublin	Bastible **N**	816
Dublin	Delahunt	816
Dublin	Etto	817
Dublin	Pichet	816
Dublin	Pig's Ear	817
Dublin	Richmond **N**	817
Dublin / Clontarf	Pigeon House	823
Dublin / Ranelagh	Forest & Marcy **N**	822
Dublin / Terenure	Craft **N**	823
Duncannon	Aldridge Lodge	825
Fennor	Copper Hen	828
Galway	Kai **N**	829
Killorglin	Giovannelli	840
Kinsale	Bastion	841
Sallins	Two Cooks **N**	852

OUR TOP PICKS

Hotels with Spas

Michelin

Notably neighbourhood

Cavistons	(Dun Laoghaire)	826
Courthouse	(Kinlough)	840
Left Bank Bistro	(Athlone)	788
Packie's	(Kenmare)	835
Paradiso	(Cork)	806
Zuni	(Kilkenny)	837

A treat for foodies

Aherne's	(Youghal)	859
Blairscove House	(Durrus)	826
Brabazon	(Slane)	853
The Bulman	(Kinsale)	842
Canteen Celbridge	(Celbridge)	802
Eastern Seaboard	(Drogheda)	810
Inis Meáin Restaurant & Suites	(Aran islands/Inishmaan)	786
O'Grady's on the Pier	(Barna)	794
Old Convent	(Clogheen)	802
Olde Post Inn	(Cavan/Cloverhill)	801
Tannery	(Dungarvan)	826

For golfers

Fota Island	(Fota Island)	828
Inchydoney Island Lodge and Spa	(Clonakilty)	803
Powerscourt	(Enniskerry)	827
Radisson Blu Farnham Estate	(Cavan)	801
Trump International Golf Links and H. Doonbeg	(Doonbeg)	810
Waterford Castle H. and Golf Resort	(Waterford)	857

Little gems

Ballyvolane House	(Castlelyons)	800
Fortview House	(Toormore)	856
Gallán Mór	(Durrus)	827
Kilgraney Country House	(Bagenalstown)	789
Moorfield Lodge	(Rathmelton)	850
Moy House	(Lahinch)	843
Sallyport House	(Kenmare)	836
Shores Country House	(Castlegregory)	800
Viewmount House	(Longford)	846

A sense of grandeur

Ballyfin	(Ballyfin)	791
Hayfield Manor	(Cork)	806
K Club	(Straffan)	854
Merrion	(Dublin)	821
Sheen Falls Lodge	(Kenmare)	836
Shelbourne	(Dublin)	821
Solis Lough Eske Castle	(Donegal)	809

Michelin

The classics

ADARE ÁTH DARA

Limerick - Pop. 1 106 - Regional map n° **22**-B2

1826

MODERN CUISINE • RUSTIC XX This pretty little thatched cottage was built in 1826 and is cosy and characterful, with a wood burning stove and a rustic feel. Interesting, attractively presented dishes use well-sourced ingredients and have subtle modern touches. It's owned by an experienced couple: he cooks and she serves.

Menu €25 (early dinner)/34 - Carte €29/47

Main St - 061 396 004 (booking essential) - www.1826adare.ie - dinner only - Closed last 3 weeks January and Monday-Tuesday

Maigue

TRADITIONAL CUISINE • CLASSIC DÉCOR XX A traditional hotel dining room with a formal feel, named after the nearby river. Menus focus on Irish produce and are firmly rooted in tradition; the trolley offering prime roast rib of beef is a feature.

Carte €27/57 - bar lunch Monday-Saturday

Dunraven Arms Hotel, Main St - 061 605 900 - www.dunravenhotel.com

Dunraven Arms

TRADITIONAL • CLASSIC A charming coaching inn dating from 1792, with classical lounges and a wood-panelled bar; very personally run by the Murphy family. Bedrooms are spacious - ask for one at the front for a more modern feel.

86 rooms - €100/150 €110/260

Main St - 061 605 900 - www.dunravenhotel.com

Maigue - See restaurant listing

ARAN ISLANDS OILEÁIN ÁRANN

Galway - Pop. 1 280 - Regional map n° **22**-B1

Inishmore

Óstán Árann

TRADITIONAL • CLASSIC Comfortable, family-owned hotel with a great view of the harbour. Bustling bar with live music most nights in high season. Spacious, up-to-date bedrooms are decorated in bright colours. Traditional dishes in the wood-floored restaurant.

22 rooms - €80/150 €80/150

Kilronan - 099 61104 - www.aranislandshotel.com - Closed November-February

Ard Einne Guesthouse

TRADITIONAL • COSY Close to the airport, an attractive chalet-style guesthouse set back on a hill and boasting superb views of Killeany Bay; take it all in from the comfy lounge. Uniformly decorated bedrooms have pine furnishings and great outlooks.

6 rooms - €70 €80/90

Killeany - 099 61126 - www.ardeinne.com - Closed November-February

Inishmaan

Inis Meáin Restaurant & Suites

REGIONAL CUISINE • FRIENDLY XX Set on a beautiful island, this futuristic stone building is inspired by the surrounding landscapes and features limed walls, sage banquettes and panoramic views. Cooking is modern, tasty and satisfyingly straightforward, showcasing island ingredients including seafood caught in currachs and hand-gathered urchins. Minimalist bedrooms feature natural furnishings.

Menu €70 - tasting menu only

5 rooms - €250/500 €250/500

- 086 826 6026 (booking essential) - www.inismeain.com - dinner only - Closed October-March and Sunday, 2 night minimum stay

Inisheer

South Aran House

FAMILY · FUNCTIONAL Simple guesthouse on the smallest of the Aran Islands, where traditional living still reigns. With its whitewashed walls and tiled floors, it has a slight Mediterranean feel; bedrooms are homely, with wrought iron beds and modern amenities. Their next door restaurant serves breakfast, snacks and hearty meals.

4 rooms – € 55/60 € 85

– 087 340 5687 – www.southaran.com – Restricted opening in winter

ARDMORE AIRD MHÓR

Waterford – Pop. 435 – Regional map n° **22**-C3

House

CREATIVE · DESIGN XXX Full length windows give every table an impressive coastal view at this smart hotel restaurant. Concise menus showcase local and garden produce and cooking is complex – a host of ingredients are used for each course. Creative dishes combine a good range of flavours and textures and presentation is unique.

➜ Seafood with sea lettuce, pomegranate and cocktail hollandaise. McGrath's lamb, persillade, peas and marsh samphire with lamb Jus. 'Rhubarb 2017', milk crunch, white chocolate and matcha tea.

Menu € 80

Cliff House Hotel, Middle Rd – 024 87800 – www.cliffhousehotel.ie – dinner only – Closed 24-26 December, Tuesday November-February and Sunday-Monday

Cliff House

LUXURY · MODERN Stylish cliffside hotel with a superb bay outlook and a lovely spa. Slate walls, Irish fabrics and bold colours feature throughout. Modern bedrooms have backlit glass artwork and smart bathrooms; some have balconies and all share the wonderful view. Choose from an extensive menu in the delightful bar and on the terrace; the restaurant serves more creative dishes.

39 rooms – € 180/245 € 225/550 – 3 suites

Middle Rd – 024 87800 – www.cliffhousehotel.ie – Closed 24-26 December

House – See restaurant listing

ARTHURSTOWN COLMÁN

Wexford – Pop. 135 – Regional map n° **22**-D2

Harvest Room

MODERN CUISINE · ELEGANT XXX A light, spacious restaurant in keeping with the classic Georgian country house in which it sits; bright rugs and chairs add a modern touch. Classic dishes feature top Irish and kitchen garden produce.

Menu € 65

Dunbrody Country House Hotel, – 051 389 600 (booking essential) – www.dunbrodyhouse.com – dinner only and Sunday lunch – Closed 9 January-12 February, 16-26 December and Monday-Tuesday except July-September

Dunbrody Country House

COUNTRY HOUSE · ELEGANT A part-Georgian hunting lodge with a charming period feel and welcoming open peat fires. It was once owned by the Marquis of Donegal and now celebrity chef Kevin Dundon runs his cookery school here.

16 rooms – € 125/195 € 190/320 – 6 suites

– 051 389 600 – www.dunbrodyhouse.com – Closed 9 January-12 February,16-26 December and Monday-Tuesday October-June

Harvest Room – See restaurant listing

ATHLONE BAILE ÁTHA LUAIN

Westmeath – Pop. 15 558 – Regional map n° **21**-C3

Kin Khao

THAI • FRIENDLY Vivid yellow building with red window frames, hidden down a side street near the castle. The upstairs restaurant is decorated with tapestries and there's a good selection of authentic Thai dishes – try the owner's recommendations.

Menu € 10 (weekday lunch)/20 – Carte € 27/43

Abbey Ln. – ✆ 090 649 8805 – www.kinkhaothai.ie – dinner only and lunch Wednesday-Friday and Sunday – Closed 25 and 31 December

Left Bank Bistro

INTERNATIONAL • FRIENDLY Keenly run, airy bistro with rough floorboards, brick walls and an open-plan kitchen. Extensive menus offer an eclectic mix of dishes, from light lunches and local fish specials to tasty Irish beef and even Asian-inspired fare.

Menu € 20 (dinner) – Carte € 32/45

Fry Pl – ✆ 090 649 4446 – www.leftbankbistro.com – Closed 1 week Christmas, Sunday and Monday

Thyme

REGIONAL CUISINE • FRIENDLY Welcoming corner restaurant with candles in the windows; set next to the river and run by a chatty, personable team. Hearty, flavoursome dishes are a mix of the traditional and the modern. Local suppliers are listed on the menu.

Menu € 25/30 – Carte € 31/49

Custume Pl., Strand St – ✆ 090 647 8850 – www.thymerestaurant.ie – dinner only and Sunday lunch – Closed 24-26 December, 1 January and Good Friday

Shelmalier House

TRADITIONAL • PERSONALISED Well-run guesthouse with neat gardens, homely décor and strong green credentials. Relax in the sauna then head for one of the comfy bedrooms – Room 1 is the best. Extensive breakfasts often include a daily special such as pancakes.

7 rooms – € 50 € 80/85

Retreat Rd., Cartrontroy – East : 2.5 km by Dublin rd (N 6, junction 9) – ✆ 090 647 2245 – www.shelmalierhouse.com – Closed December-February

at Glasson Northeast: 8 km on N55 ✉ Athlone

Wineport Lodge

LUXURY • DESIGN A superbly located hotel where the bedroom wing follows the line of the lough shore and each luxurious room boasts a balcony or a waterside terrace (it's worth paying the extra for the Champagne Suite). The outdoor hot tubs make a great place to take in the view. Extensive menus utilise seasonal produce.

30 rooms – € 120/210 € 160/400

Southwest : 1.5 km – ✆ 090 643 9010 – www.wineport.ie – Closed 23-26 December

Glasson Stone Lodge

FAMILY • PERSONALISED Smart guesthouse built from local Irish limestone. Pine features strongly throughout; bedrooms boast thoughtful extras and locally made furniture – Room 4 is the best. Breakfast includes homemade bread and fruit from the garden.

6 rooms – € 45 € 70

– ✆ 090 648 5004 – www.glassonstonelodge.com – Closed November-April

ATHY BAILE ÁTHA Í

Kildare – Pop. 8 218 – Regional map n° **22**-D2

Green Barn

ORGANIC • DESIGN A charming, shabby-chic shop and café with a laid-back vibe, set in the grounds of an early Georgian villa. It has an admirable organic ethos and overlooks the kitchen garden which informs the unfussy, rustic menu.

Carte € 22/47

Burtown House & Gardens - Northeast : 8 km off N 78 - ✆ 059 862 3865 - www.burtownhouse.ie - lunch only and Friday-Sunday dinner - Closed Monday and Tuesday except bank holiday Mondays

AUGHRIM EACHROIM

Wicklow - Pop. 1 364 - Regional map n° **22**-D2

Strawberry Tree

ORGANIC • ELEGANT Ireland's only certified organic restaurant. It's formal, with an intimate, atmospheric feel, and is set on a village-style hotel estate. Menus feature wild and organic ingredients sourced from local artisan suppliers.

Menu € 65

Brooklodge Hotel, Macreddin Village - North : 3.25 km - ✆ 0402 36444 - www.brooklodge.com - dinner only - Closed 24-25 December and Monday October-April

Armento

ITALIAN • BISTRO Informal Italian restaurant set in a smart hotel on a secluded 180 acre estate. Southern Italian menus feature artisan produce imported from Armento and pizzas cooked in the wood-fired oven.

Menu € 35

Brooklodge Hotel, Macreddin Village - North : 3.25 km - ✆ 0402 36444 - www.brooklodge.com - dinner only - Closed 24-25 December and Tuesdays October-April

Brooklodge H & Wells Spa

SPA AND WELLNESS • CLASSIC Sprawling hotel in 180 peaceful acres in the Wicklow Valley. Flag-floored reception, comfy lounge, informal café and pub. Smart, modern bedrooms with large bathrooms; some in an annexe, along with the conference rooms. State-of-the-art spa.

86 rooms - € 100/140 € 120/200 - 18 suites

Macreddin Village - North : 3.25 km - ✆ 0402 36444 - www.brooklodge.com - Closed 24-25 December

Strawberry Tree • **Armento** - See restaurant listing

BAGENALSTOWN MUINE BHEAG

Carlow - Pop. 2 775 - Regional map n° **22**-D2

Kilgraney Country House

COUNTRY HOUSE • PERSONALISED Georgian country house which adopts a truly holistic approach. Period features blend with modern, minimalist furnishings and the mood is calm and peaceful. It boasts a small tea room, a craft gallery and a spa with a relaxation room, along with pleasant herb, vegetable, zodiac and monastic gardens.

7 rooms - € 120/135 € 170/240

South : 6.5 km by R 705 (Borris Rd) - ✆ 059 977 5283 - www.kilgraneyhouse.com - Closed November-February and Monday-Wednesday

Lorum Old Rectory

COUNTRY HOUSE • TRADITIONAL A welcoming, double-gabled stone rectory built in 1863, set in a lovely spot at the foot of the Blackstairs Mountains. The traditional interior is decorated with antiques; ask for Room 3 with its 4-poster bed and double-aspect views. Enjoy homemade bread and preserves at breakfast and garden produce at dinner.

4 rooms - € 100 € 160

Kilgraney - South : 7 km by R 705 (Borris Rd) - ✆ 059 977 5282 - www.lorum.com - Closed December-January

BALLINA BÉAL AN ÁTHA

Mayo – Pop. 10 490 – Regional map n° **21**-B2

Library

MODERN CUISINE • ELEGANT XX Start with a drink in the bar, which is fitted out with original pieces from a 16C Spanish galleon, then head for the dramatic candlelit dining room. Seasonal modern dishes include fillet of beef flambéed on a sword at the table!

Menu € 35 (weekdays) – Carte € 47/60

Belleek Castle Hotel, Northeast : 2.5 km by Castle Rd – ✆ 096 22400 – www.belleekcastle.com – dinner only – Closed 1 January-13 February

Mount Falcon

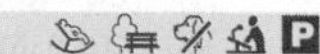

HISTORIC • ELEGANT Classic former shooting lodge built in 1876, with golf, cycling, fishing and archery available in its 100 acre grounds. Choose between characterful bedrooms in the main house and spacious, contemporary rooms in the extension. The restaurant is located in the old kitchens and serves elaborate modern dishes.

32 rooms – € 150/200 € 160/260 – 2 suites

Foxford Rd – South : 6.25 km on N 26 – ✆ 096 74472 – www.mountfalcon.com – Closed 25 December

Belleek Castle

HISTORIC • ELEGANT An imposing castellated property built on the site of an old medieval abbey and surrounded by 1,000 acres of parkland. An amazing array of characterful rooms come complete with open fires, ornate panelling, antiques and armour.

10 rooms – € 135/185 € 170/270

Northeast : 2.5 km by Castle Rd – ✆ 096 22400 – www.belleekcastle.com – Closed 1 January-13 February

Library – See restaurant listing

BALLINGARRY BAILE AN GHARRAÍ

Limerick – Pop. 527 – Regional map n° **22**-B2

Mustard Seed at Echo Lodge

TRADITIONAL • CLASSIC This cosy former convent is surrounded by well-kept gardens and filled with antique furniture, paintings, books and fresh flowers. Bedrooms in the main house have period styling, while those in the former school house are brighter and more modern. Dinner is an occasion – the two grand rooms are candlelit and have gilt mirrors; cooking is elaborate and boldly flavoured.

16 rooms – € 90/160 € 130/320

– ✆ 069 68508 – www.mustardseed.ie – Closed mid-January-early February and 24-26 December

BALLSBRIDGE DROICHEAD NA DOTHRA – Dublin → See Dublin

BALLYBUNION BAILE AN BHUINNEÁNAIGH

Kerry – Pop. 1 354 – Regional map n° **22**-A2

Teach de Broc Country House

FAMILY • MODERN A purpose-built house by the Ballybunion golf course, with a spacious open-plan lounge and bar and eye-catching modern Irish art. Good-sized bedrooms have smart bathrooms; those at the front looks towards the links. The simple bistro-style dining room serves a wide-ranging menu.

14 rooms – € 90/130 € 120/160

Link Rd – South : 2.5 km by Golf Club rd – ✆ 068 27581 – www.ballybuniongolf.com – Closed November-mid-March

Tides

FAMILY • PERSONALISED Generously sized bedrooms, superb views and welcoming hosts are the draw at this purpose-built guesthouse. Quiz David about the local area in the comfy lounge and, at breakfast, enjoy Doreen's pancakes.

7 rooms - € 80/150 € 100/180

East : 1.75 km. by R 551 on R 553 - 086 600 0665 - www.ballybunionhotels.com - Closed December-January

BALLYCOTTON BAILE CHOITÍN

Cork - Pop. 476 - Regional map n° **22**-C3

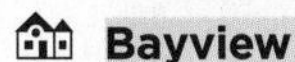

Bayview

FAMILY • PERSONALISED This superbly located hotel sits in an elevated spot overlooking the bay and the island opposite. Many of the spacious, understated bedrooms have Juliet balconies and you can sit in the garden and watch the fishing boats come in. Menus are modern and ambitious; ask for a seat by the window.

35 rooms - € 92/212 € 92/212 - €15

- 021 464 6746 - www.thebayviewhotel.com - Closed November-Easter

BALLYDAVID BAILE NA NGALL

Kerry - Dingle - Regional map n° **22**-A2

Gorman's Clifftop House

FAMILY • CLASSIC Purpose-built house in a wonderfully rural location, offering superb views out across Ballydavid Head and the Three Sisters. It's family run and has a lovely homely feel. Bright, spacious bedrooms have good facilities; those to the front share the view. The concise menu features home-cooked local produce.

8 rooms - € 95/110 € 130/165

Slea Head Dr, Glashabeg - North : 2 km on Feomanagh rd. - 066 915 5162 - www.gormans-clifftophouse.com - Closed mid October-mid March

BALLYFARNAN BÉAL ÁTHA FEARNÁIN

Roscommon - Pop. 205 - Regional map n° **21**-C2

Kilronan Castle

HISTORIC BUILDING • CLASSIC Impressively restored castle with characterful sitting rooms, a library and a palm court; wood panelling, antiques and oil paintings feature throughout. Smart leisure club and hydrotherapy centre. Opulent red and gold bedrooms offer a high level of comfort. The formal dining room serves a classical menu.

84 rooms - € 99/179 € 109/209

Southeast : 3.5 km on Keadew rd - 071 961 8000 - www.kilronancastle.ie

BALLYFIN AN BAILE FIONN

Laois - Pop. 633 - Regional map n° **22**-C1

Ballyfin

GRAND LUXURY • HISTORIC An immaculate Regency mansion built in 1820 and set in 600 acres. The interior is stunning, with its cantilevered staircase, breathtaking ceilings and restored antiques. The library features 4,000 books, the drawing room is decorated in gold leaf and the bedrooms are luxurious. Produce grown in the kitchen garden informs the dishes served in the dining room.

20 rooms - € 380/620 € 590/1250 - 3 suites

- 057 875 5866 - www.ballyfin.com - Closed January

BALLYGARRETT BAILE GHEARÓID

Regional map n° **22**-D2

Clonganny House

COUNTRY HOUSE • ELEGANT Close to the coast you'll find this Georgian manor house, which has been stylishly and comfortably refurbished. Bedrooms are located in the old coach house and have a wonderfully classical style: all feature handmade and antique furnishings and open onto private terraces overlooking the garden. The formal linen-laid dining room offers a traditional set priced menu.

4 rooms – € 150/180 € 180/200

Southwest : 4.5 km. by R 472 – ✆ 053 948 2111 – www.clonganny.com

BALLYLICKEY BÉAL ÁTHA LEICE

Cork – ✉ Bantry – Regional map n° **22**-A3

Seaview House

TRADITIONAL • CLASSIC Well-run Victorian house that upholds tradition both in its décor and service. It has a pleasant drawing room, a cosy bar and antique-furnished bedrooms – some with sea views. Classic dishes are served at polished tables laid with silver tableware. The attractive gardens lead down to the shore.

25 rooms – € 105/140 € 140/185

– ✆ 027 50073 – www.seaviewhousehotel.com – Closed late November-early April

BALLYLIFFIN BAILE LIFÍN

Donegal – Pop. 461 – Regional map n° **21**-C1

Ballyliffin Lodge

TRADITIONAL • MODERN Remote hotel with well-kept gardens, affording a superb outlook over the countryside to the beach. Bedrooms offer good facilities; ask for one facing the front. Relax in the lovely spa and pool, or enjoy afternoon tea with a view in the lounge. Informal, bistro-style dining, with international menus.

40 rooms – € 83/124 € 114/196

Shore Rd – ✆ 074 937 8200 – www.ballyliffinlodge.com – Closed 24-26 December

BALLYMACARBRY BAILE MHAC CAIRBRE

Waterford – ✉ Clonmel – Pop. 132 – Regional map n° **22**-C2

Glasha Farmhouse

TRADITIONAL • CLASSIC A large farmhouse between the Knockmealdown and Comeragh Mountains. Guest areas include a comfy lounge, airy conservatory and pleasant patio. Bedrooms are immaculately kept and some have jacuzzis. The welcoming owner has good local knowledge. Meals are home-cooked, with picnic lunches available.

6 rooms – € 70 € 100

Northwest : 4 km by R 671 – ✆ 052 613 6108 – www.glashafarmhouse.com – Closed December

BALLYMORE EUSTACE AN BAILE MÓR

Kildare – Pop. 872 – Regional map n° **22**-D1

Ballymore Inn

TRADITIONAL CUISINE • PUB Remote village pub with a deli selling home-made breads, pickles, oils and the like. The owner promotes small, artisan producers, so expect organic veg, meat from quality assured farms and farmhouse cheeses. Portions are generous.

Menu € 23 (weekday lunch)/33 – Carte € 33/50

– ✆ 045 864 585 – www.ballymoreinn.com

BALLYNAHINCH BAILE NA HINSE

Galway – ✉ Recess – Regional map n° **21**-A3

Owenmore

MODERN CUISINE • INTIMATE XX Within a 17C country house you'll find this bright, elegant restaurant which looks out over the river and the estate. Modern dishes are delicate and subtly flavoured. In winter, end the evening with a drink beside the marble fireplace.

Menu €70 **s**

Ballynahinch Castle Hotel, – ✆ 095 31006 (booking essential) – www.ballynahinchcastle.com – dinner only

Ballynahinch Castle

TRADITIONAL • CLASSIC Dramatically located on the Wild Atlantic Way, amongst 450 acres of woodland, with a salmon fishing river in front and the mountains behind. Relax by a peat fire in one of the cosy sitting rooms. Bedrooms have a country house style.

45 rooms – €175/340 €185/450 – 3 suites

– ✆ 095 31006 – www.ballynahinchcastle.com

Owenmore – See restaurant listing

BALLYVAUGHAN BAILE UÍ BHEACHÁIN

Clare – Pop. 258 – Regional map n° **22**-B1

Gregans Castle

MODERN CUISINE • ELEGANT XX Have an aperitif in the drawing room of this country house hotel before heading through to the restaurant (ask for a table close to the window, to take in views stretching as far as Galway Bay). Interesting modern dishes have clean, clear flavours and showcase the latest local produce. Service is attentive.

Menu €75 **s**

Gregans Castle Hotel, Southwest : 6 km on N 67 – ✆ 065 707 7005 (booking advisable) – www.gregans.ie – dinner only – Closed 5 November-15 February

Gregans Castle

FAMILY • PERSONALISED Well-run, part-18C country house with superb views of The Burren and Galway Bay. The open-fired hall leads to a cosy, rustic bar-lounge and an elegant sitting room. Bedrooms are furnished with antiques: two open onto the garden; one is in the old kitchen and features a panelled ceiling and a four-poster bed.

21 rooms – €175/210 €245/280 – 4 suites

Southwest : 6 km on N 67 – ✆ 065 707 7005 – www.gregans.ie – Closed 5 November-15 February

Gregans Castle – See restaurant listing

Ballyvaughan Lodge

TRADITIONAL • PERSONALISED Welcoming guesthouse with a colourful flower display and a decked terrace. The vaulted, light-filled lounge features a locally made flower chandelier; bedrooms boast co-ordinating fabrics. Breakfast uses quality, farmers' market produce.

11 rooms – €50/60 €80/100

– ✆ 065 707 7292 – www.ballyvaughanlodge.com – Closed 23-28 December

BALTIMORE DÚN NA SÉAD

Cork – Pop. 347 – Regional map n° **22**-A3

Mews (N)

MODERN CUISINE • INTIMATE X Two friends own this cosy, rustic restaurant. Ingredients collected each morning inform the daily set menu and the wholesome, flavour-packed dishes arrive in succession for sharing. Lesser known wines and local spirits accompany.

Menu €65 – tasting menu only

– ✆ 028 20572 (booking essential) – www.mewsrestaurant.ie – dinner only – Closed October-March, Sunday except bank holidays and Monday-Tuesday April-June.

Casey's of Baltimore

FAMILY • CLASSIC Extended 19C pub with a terracotta façade, well located near the seashore. Comfy lounge and simple pine-furnished bedrooms with good facilities. You're guaranteed a warm welcome from the family owners. The restaurant and beer garden overlook the bay; classical menus, and traditional music at the weekend.

14 rooms – € 90/120 € 90/180

East : 0.75 km on R 595 – 028 20197 – www.caseysofbaltimore.com – Closed 20-26 December

BANDON DROICHEAD NA BANDAN

Cork – Pop. 1 917 – Regional map n° **22**-B3

Poachers

TRADITIONAL CUISINE • PUB Sit in the cosy bar, the small snug or the dining room under the eaves. Dishes are boldly flavoured and local seafood is the star of the show – you'll always find fish landed at Union Hall and crabs from Courtmacsherry.

Menu € 22/35 – Carte € 24/41

Clonakilty Rd – Southwest : 1.5 km on N 71 – 023 884 1159 – www.poachers.ie – Closed 25 December

BANTRY BEANNTRAÍ

Cork – Regional map n° **22**-A3

O'Connors

SEAFOOD • BISTRO X Well-run harbourside restaurant, with a compact, bistro-style interior featuring model ships in the windows and modern art on the walls. The menu focuses on local seafood, mostly from the small fishing boats in the harbour.

Carte € 25/49

Wolf Tone Sq – 027 55664 (booking essential) – www.oconnorsbantry.com – dinner only – Closed Tuesday-Wednesday November-April

BARNA BEARNA

Galway – Pop. 1 878 – Regional map n° **21**-B3

Upstairs @ West

MODERN CUISINE • INTIMATE XX Stylish first floor restaurant in a smart boutique hotel, with a chic champagne bar, booth seating and a moody, intimate feel. Seasonal menus offer ambitious, innovative dishes, showcasing meats and seafood from the 'West' of Ireland.

Menu € 33 (weekdays) **s** – Carte € 33/59 **s**

Twelve Hotel, Barna Crossroads – 091 597 000 – www.westrestaurant.ie – dinner only and Sunday lunch – Closed Monday and Tuesday

O'Grady's on the Pier

SEAFOOD • RUSTIC X In winter, sit in the cosy, rustic downstairs room; in summer, head out onto the terrace or up to the bright first floor with its superb views across the harbour and Galway Bay. Classical dishes showcase fresh local seafood.

Carte € 29/53

– 091 592 223 – www.ogradysonthepier.com – Closed 24-26 December

Twelve

BUSINESS • MODERN An unassuming exterior hides a keenly run boutique hotel complete with a bakery, a pizza kitchen and a deli. Stylish, modern bedrooms have large gilt mirrors, mood lighting and designer 'seaweed' toiletries; some even boast cocktail bars! Innovative menus in Upstairs @ West; modern European dishes in The Pins.

48 rooms – € 90/150 € 99/159 – 10 suites

Barna Crossroads – 091 597 000 – www.thetwelvehotel.ie

Upstairs @ West – See restaurant listing

BARRELLS CROSS - Cork ➜ See Kinsale

BLACKLION AN BLAIC

Cavan - Pop. 229 - Regional map n° **21**-C2

MacNean House

CREATIVE • ELEGANT XXX A stylish restaurant in a smart townhouse, with a chic lounge, a plush dining room and a cookery school. The 8 course tasting menu offers attractively presented, ambitious dishes which use complex techniques and feature many different flavours and textures. Bedrooms are a mix of modern and country styles.

Menu €85 - tasting menu only

19 rooms - €96 €134/192

Main St - 071 985 3022 (booking essential) - www.macneanrestaurant.com - dinner only and Sunday lunch - Closed January, Monday and Tuesday

BLACKROCK Dublin ➜ See Dublin

BLARNEY AN BHLARNA

Cork - Cork - Pop. 2 437 - Regional map n° **22**-B3

Square Table

FRENCH • COSY XX Sweet restaurant with a warm, welcoming, neighbourhood feel. Menus offer French-influenced dishes crafted from Irish produce; the early evening menu is good value. It's proudly and enthusiastically run by twins Tricia and Martina.

Menu €29 - Carte €31/46

5 The Square - 021 438 2825 (booking essential) - www.thesquaretable.ie - dinner only and Sunday lunch - Closed last 2 weeks January, first week February, Sunday dinner, Monday and Tuesday

BORRIS AN BHUIRÍOS

Carlow - Pop. 646 - Regional map n° **22**-D2

Clashganny House

CLASSIC CUISINE • INTIMATE XX Hidden away in a lovely valley, this early Victorian house is the setting for the realisation of one couple's dream. The modern restaurant is split over three rooms; appealing menus balance light options with more gutsy dishes.

Menu €35

Clashganny - South : 5 km by R 702 and R 729 - 059 977 1003 - www.clashgannyhouse.com - dinner only and Sunday lunch - Closed 24-26 December, Sunday dinner and Monday-Tuesday

1808 N

MODERN CUISINE • BISTRO X The Step House hotel's restaurant is an appealing bistro deluxe with lots of mahogany, red leather banquettes and French doors opening onto the garden. Modern menus use the best of Irish produce. Service is relaxed and friendly.

Carte €24/42

Step House Hotel, Main St - 059 977 3209 - Closed 15 January-10 February and Monday-Tuesday

Step House

TOWNHOUSE • PERSONALISED A small heritage village is home to this family-run Georgian townhouse. Sizeable modern bedrooms - many with mountain outlooks - are set at the top of a striking staircase; the suite has a huge terrace and a panoramic view.

20 rooms - €110/130 €150/400 - 1 suite

Main St - 059 977 3209 - www.stephousehotel.ie - Closed 15 January-10 February

1808 - See restaurant listing

BOYLE MAINISTIR NA BÚILLE

Roscommon – Pop. 1 459 – Regional map n° **21**-B2

Lough Key House

HISTORIC · CLASSIC Welcoming Georgian house with a neat garden and mature grounds, located next to Lough Key Forest Park. Homely guest areas are filled with antiques and ornaments; bedrooms in the original house are the best, with their antique four-posters and warm fabrics. You're guaranteed a warm Irish welcome.

6 rooms – € 49/59 € 89/98

Southeast : 3.75 km by R 294 on N 4 – 071 966 2161 – www.loughkeyhouse.com – Closed 7 November-29 March

Rosdarrig House

FAMILY · PERSONALISED Neat house on the edge of town, close to the abbey; the friendly owners offer genuine Irish hospitality. Guest areas include two homely lounges and a linen-laid breakfast room. Simply furnished bedrooms overlook the colourful garden.

5 rooms – € 45/50 € 75/80

Carrick Rd – East : 1.5 km on R 294 – 071 966 2040 – www.rosdarrig.com – Closed November-March

CAHERLISTRANE CATHAIR LOISTREÁIN

Galway – Regional map n° **21**-B3

Lisdonagh House

COUNTRY HOUSE · CLASSIC Ivy-clad Georgian house with lough views. The traditional country house interior boasts eye-catching murals and open-fired lounges. Antique-furnished bedrooms have marble bathrooms; the first floor rooms are brighter. The grand dining room offers 5 course dinners and simpler suppers.

9 rooms – € 90/120 € 140/180

Northwest : 4 km by R 333 off Shrule rd – 093 31163 – www.lisdonagh.com – Closed December-April

CAHERSIVEEN CATHAIR SAIDHBHÍN

Kerry – Pop. 1 168 – Regional map n° **22**-A2

Quinlan & Cooke

SEAFOOD · BRASSERIE X 'QC's, as the locals call it, is an atmospheric restaurant with a nautical theme. Seafood-orientated menus offer unfussy classics and more unusual daily specials; the family also own a local fish wholesalers. Stylish, well-equipped bedrooms are in a townhouse and mews; breakfast is brought to your room.

Carte € 29/53

11 rooms – € 80/149 € 99/169

3 Main St – 066 947 2244 (booking advisable) – www.qcbar.com – Closed Monday-Wednesday in winter and Sunday lunch

CAPPOQUIN CEAPACH CHOINN

Waterford – Pop. 759 – Regional map n° **22**-C2

Richmond House

TRADITIONAL CUISINE · TRADITIONAL DÉCOR XX Imposing Georgian house built in 1704 for the Earl of Cork and Burlington, and filled with family curios. Have a drink in the cosy lounge before heading to the cove-ceilinged dining room. Cooking is classically based; be sure to try the delicious local lamb. Cosy bedrooms are decorated in period styles.

Menu € 33/55

9 rooms – € 60/80 € 110/140

Southeast : 0.75 km on N 72 – 058 54278 – www.richmondhouse.net – dinner only – Closed Christmas-New Year and Monday-Thursday January-February

CARAGH LAKE LOCH CÁRTHAÍ

Kerry – Regional map n° **22**-A2

 **Ard-Na-Sidhe**

COUNTRY HOUSE • CLASSIC 1913 Arts and Crafts house on the shores of Lough Caragh, surrounded by mountains. A subtle modernisation has emphasised original features such as oak-panelled walls and leaded windows; bedrooms are smart and contemporary. The restaurant offers classic dishes with modern twists.

18 rooms – † € 190/300 †† € 210/320

– ✆ 066 976 9105 – www.ardnasidhe.com – Closed 9 October-20 April

 **Carrig Country House**

TRADITIONAL • CLASSIC A wooded drive leads down to this Victorian former hunting lodge on the lough shore. The cosy, country house interior comprises traditionally furnished guest areas and individually decorated bedrooms with antique furnishings. Take in beautiful mountain views from the dining room.

17 rooms – † € 125/155 †† € 190/390

– ✆ 066 976 9100 – www.carrighouse.com – Closed November-February and mid-week in low season

CARLINGFORD CAIRLINN

Louth – Pop. 1 045 – Regional map n° **21**-D2

Bay Tree

MODERN CUISINE • FRIENDLY XX Keenly run neighbourhood restaurant fronted by bay trees and decorated with branches and hessian. Attractively presented, well-balanced modern dishes feature herbs and salad from the garden and seafood from nearby Carlingford Lough. Service is polite and organised, and the bedrooms are warm and cosy.

Menu € 28 (weekday dinner)/35 – Carte € 31/47

7 rooms – † € 65/70 †† € 89/99

Newry St – ✆ 042 938 3848 (booking essential) – www.belvederehouse.ie – dinner only and Sunday lunch – Closed 24-26 December and Monday-Tuesday October-May

 **Carlingford House**

TRADITIONAL • PERSONALISED Early Victorian house close to the old ruined abbey; the owner has lived here all her life. Smart, understated bedrooms have good mod cons and are immaculately kept. Pleasant breakfast room; tasty locally smoked salmon and bacon.

5 rooms – † € 75/100 †† € 100

– ✆ 042 937 3118 – www.carlingfordhouse.com – Closed 3 January-1 February

CARLOW CEATHARLACH

Carlow – Pop. 13 698 – Regional map n° **22**-D2

 **Barrowville Town House** 

TOWNHOUSE • ELEGANT Attractive Georgian house on the main road into town. Comfortable, characterful drawing room with heavy fabrics, period ornaments and a grand piano. Breakfast is in the conservatory, overlooking the pretty garden. Spacious, brightly decorated bedrooms offer a good level of comfort and modern facilities.

7 rooms – † € 45/70 †† € 70/120

Kilkenny Rd – South : 0.75 km on R 448 – ✆ 059 914 3324 – www.barrowville.com – Closed 24-26 December

CARNAROSS CARN NA ROS

Meath – ✉ Kells – Regional map n° **21**-D3

Forge

TRADITIONAL CUISINE • RUSTIC XX Stone-built former forge in rural Meath; its atmospheric interior features flagged floors and warm red décor. Two fairly priced menus offer hearty dishes made from local produce, with some of the veg and herbs taken from the garden.

Menu € 30 (early dinner)/48 – Carte € 37/49

Pottlereagh – Northwest : 7 km by R 147 and N 3 on L 7112 – ✆ 046 924 5003 – www.theforgerestaurant.ie – dinner only and Sunday lunch – Closed 1 week February, 1 week July, 24-26 December, 1 January, Sunday dinner, Monday and Tuesday

CARNE

Wexford – Regional map n° **22**-D3

Lobster Pot

SEAFOOD • PUB Popular pub filled with a characterful array of memorabilia. Large menus feature tasty, home-style cooking. Fresh seafood dishes are a must-try, with oysters and lobster cooked to order being the specialities. No children after 7pm.

Carte € 26/60

Ballyfane – ✆ 053 913 1110 – www.lobsterpotwexford.ie – Closed 1 January-10 February, 24-26 December, Good Friday, Monday and Tuesday

CARRICKMACROSS CARRAIG MHACHAIRE ROIS

Monaghan – Pop. 1 978 – Regional map n° **21**-D2

Courthouse

REGIONAL CUISINE • RUSTIC X Relaxed, rustic restaurant featuring wooden floors, exposed ceiling rafters and bare brick; ask for table 20, by the window. Great value menus offer carefully prepared, flavourful dishes which are a lesson in self-restraint – their simplicity being a key part of their appeal. Friendly, efficient service.

Menu € 27 (weekdays) – Carte € 28/43 **s**

1 Monaghan St – ✆ 042 969 2848 (booking essential) – www.courthouserestaurant.ie – dinner only and Sunday lunch – Closed 1 week January, 1 week June, 25-26 December, Good Friday, Monday except bank holidays and Tuesday

Nuremore

MODERN CUISINE • ELEGANT XXX Traditional split-level dining room within a well-established Victorian hotel. Formally set, linen-laid tables are well-spaced and service is attentive. Menus showcase luxurious seasonal ingredients and dishes are stylishly presented.

Menu € 35

Nuremore Hotel, South : 2.25 km by R 178 on old N 2 – ✆ 042 966 1438 – www.nuremore.com – dinner only and Sunday lunch

Nuremore

COUNTRY HOUSE • PERSONALISED Long-standing Victorian house with extensive gardens and a golf course. Classical interior with a formal bar and a comfy lounge serving three-tiered afternoon tea. Good leisure facilities. Peaceful bedrooms; many have rural views.

72 rooms – € 100/120 € 120/180

South : 2.25 km by R 178 on old N 2 – ✆ 042 966 1438 – www.nuremore.com

Nuremore – See restaurant listing

Shirley Arms

INN • MODERN An early 19C coaching inn, which forms part of the Shirley Estate and sits beside the Courthouse Square. Bedrooms are surprisingly modern; those in the original house are slightly more characterful. There's a welcoming bar, an informal bistro and, for private parties, a stylish bar-cum-nightclub.

25 rooms – € 95/105 € 120/130

Main St. – 042 967 3100 – www.shirleyarmshotel.ie – Closed 25-26 December and Good Friday

CARRICK-ON-SHANNON CORA DROMA RÚISC

Leitrim – Pop. 3 980 – Regional map n° **21**-C2

St.George's Terrace

MODERN CUISINE • ELEGANT XXX Start with drinks in the plush bar of this imposing Victorian building before moving into the boldly decorated main dining room with its high ceiling and chandelier. Well-balanced cooking has seasonal Irish produce at its heart.

Carte € 35/50

St George's Terr. – 071 961 6546 – www.stgeorgesterrace.com – dinner only and Sunday lunch – Closed 2 weeks January, 1 week October, 24-27 December, Monday and Tuesday

Oarsman

TRADITIONAL CUISINE • PUB Traditional family-run pub set close to the river and filled with pottery, bygone artefacts and fishing tackle; it's a real hit with the locals. Flavoursome cooking uses local produce. The upstairs restaurant opens later in the week.

Menu € 23 (weekdays)/40 – Carte € 31/52

Bridge St – 071 962 1733 – www.theoarsman.com – Closed 25-27 December, Good Friday and Sunday-Monday October-April

CARRIGANS AN CARRAIGAIN

Donegal – Pop. 336 – Regional map n° **21**-C1

Mount Royd

TRADITIONAL • PERSONALISED Traditional, creeper-clad house in a quiet village. It's immaculately kept throughout, from the snug lounge and pleasant breakfast room to the four cosy bedrooms – one of which opens onto a terrace overlooking the well-tended gardens and fountain. Tasty, locally smoked salmon features at breakfast.

4 rooms – € 40/45 € 75

– 074 914 0163 – www.mountroyd.com – Closed 1 week Christmas and restricted opening in winter

CASHEL CAISEAL

South Tipperary – Pop. 2 275 – Regional map n° **22**-C2

Chez Hans

TRADITIONAL CUISINE • TRADITIONAL DÉCOR XX A long-standing family-owned restaurant in an imposing former Synod Hall built in 1861. There's a good value set price menu midweek and a more interesting à la carte of classic dishes at the weekend.

Menu € 33 (weekdays) – Carte € 41/58

Rockside, Moor Ln. – 062 61177 (booking essential) – www.chezhans.net – dinner only – Closed last week January, 1 week Easter, 24-26 December, Sunday and Monday

Cafe Hans

TRADITIONAL CUISINE • FRIENDLY X Located just down the road from the Rock of Cashel; a vibrant, popular eatery set next to big sister 'Chez Hans' and run by the same family. Sit at closely set tables amongst an interesting collection of art. Tasty, unfussy lunchtime dishes are crafted from local ingredients. Arrive early as you can't book.

Menu € 15 - Carte € 20/33

Rockside, Moore Lane St - ☎ 062 63660 (bookings not accepted) - lunch only - Closed 2 weeks late January, 1 week October, 25 December, Sunday and Monday

Baileys of Cashel

TOWNHOUSE • MODERN Used as a grain store during the Irish famine, this Georgian house conceals a cosy lounge with a library and contrastingly spacious, contemporary bedrooms. The penthouse has superb views of the famous rock. Enjoy live music and classic dishes in the cellar bar or modern European cooking in the restaurant.

20 rooms - € 70/85 € 110/120

42 Main St - ☎ 062 61937 - www.baileyshotelcashel.com - Closed 23-28 December

Aulber House

FAMILY • PERSONALISED Within walking distance of the Rock of Cashel and the 13C Cistercian abbey ruins. A bespoke mahogany staircase leads to a galleried landing and many rooms have king-sized beds. Unwind in the gazebo in the beautiful gardens.

11 rooms - € 50/85 € 85/95

Deerpark, Golden Rd - West : 0.75 km on N 74 - ☎ 062 63713 - www.aulberhouse.com - Closed November-February

CASTLEGREGORY CAISLEÁN GHRIAIRE

Kerry - Pop. 243 - Regional map n° **22**-A2

Shores Country House

LUXURY • ELEGANT This modern guesthouse is set in a beautiful elevated position between the mountain and the beach and is run by a gregarious owner. Some of the stylish bedrooms have antique beds and all have good attention to detail. There's a great choice at breakfast, including wonderful fruit cocktails and homemade cakes.

6 rooms - € 55/140 € 70/150

Conor Pass Rd, Cappateige - Southwest : 6 km on R 560 - ☎ 066 713 9195 - www.shorescountryhouse.com - Closed 2 December-10 January

CASTLELYONS CAISLEÁN Ó LIATHÁIN

Cork - Pop. 292 - Regional map n° **22**-B2

Ballyvolane House

FAMILY • PERSONALISED Stately 18C Italianate mansion surrounded by lovely gardens, lakes and woodland; children can help feed the hens, collect the eggs, pet the donkeys or go on a tractor tour. Comfy guest areas and bedrooms match the period style of the house, and family antiques and memorabilia feature throughout. The walled garden and latest farm produce guide what's on the menu.

6 rooms - € 150 € 200/240

Southeast : 5.5 km by Midleton rd on Britway rd - ☎ 025 36349 - www.ballyvolanehouse.ie - Closed 24 December-4 January and restricted opening in winter

CASTLEMARTYR BAILE NA MARTRA Cork

Cork - Pop. 1 277 - Regional map n° **22**-C3

Bell Tower

ITALIAN • LUXURY XXX A bright, formally laid restaurant set on the ground floor of a 17C manor house, with traditional décor and plenty of windows overlooking the attractive gardens. Classic dishes with a modern twist from an experienced team.

Menu € 65 **s** - Carte € 50/70 **s** - bar lunch

- 021 421 9000 - www.castlemartyrresort.ie - Closed Monday and Tuesday October-March

Castlemartyr

COUNTRY HOUSE • MODERN Impressive 17C manor house in 220 acres of grounds, complete with castle ruins, lakes, a golf course and a stunning spa. Luxurious bedrooms have superb marble bathrooms. Look out for the wonderful original ceiling in the Knight's Bar. Franchini's offers an extensive Italian menu; the Bell Tower is more formal.

103 rooms - € 179/240 € 179/240 - 28 suites

- 021 421 9000 - www.castlemartyrresort.ie

Bell Tower - See restaurant listing

CASTLEPOLLARD BAILE NA GCROS

Westmeath - Pop. 1 042 - Regional map n° **21**-C3

Lough Bishop House

TRADITIONAL • PERSONALISED Charming 18C farmhouse on a tranquil, south-facing hillside. The hospitable owners and their dogs greet you, and tea and cake are served on arrival in the cosy lounge. Simple bedrooms have neat shower rooms and no TVs. Communal dining - home-cooked dishes include meats and eggs from their own farm.

3 rooms - € 65/100 € 130/195

Derrynagarra, Collinstown - South : 6 km by R 394 taking L 5738 opposite church and school after 4 km - 044 966 1313 - www.loughbishophouse.com - Closed Christmas-New Year

CAVAN AN CABHÁN

Cavan - Pop. 3 649 - Regional map n° **21**-C2

Radisson Blu Farnham Estate

LUXURY • DESIGN Set in extensive parkland and boasting every conceivable outdoor activity and an impressive spa. Original Georgian features are combined with contemporary furnishings and the luxurious bedrooms offer superb views. Traditional menus feature local, seasonal ingredients and afternoon teas are a speciality.

158 rooms - € 160/260 € 160/350 - 4 suites

Farnham Estate - Northwest : 3.75 km on R 198 - 049 437 7700 - www.farnhamestate.com

Cavan Crystal

BUSINESS • MODERN Modern hotel next to the Cavan Crystal factory, with an impressive atrium, a stylish lounge-bar and red and black bedrooms in a uniform design. It comes with good meeting and leisure facilities and is popular for spa breaks. The contemporary first floor restaurant serves attractively presented modern dishes.

85 rooms - € 55/125 € 75/190

Dublin Rd - 049 436 0600 - www.cavancrystalhotel.com

at Cloverhill North: 12 km by N3 on N54 Belturbet

Olde Post Inn

TRADITIONAL CUISINE • RUSTIC XX Enjoy a fireside aperitif in the flag-floored bar or the wood-framed conservatory of this red-brick former post office. The well-established restaurant serves traditional dishes made with Irish produce, wherein classic flavour combinations are given a modern twist. Bedrooms are contemporary.

Menu € 63

6 rooms - € 65/70 € 110/130

- 047 55555 - www.theoldepostinn.com - dinner only and Sunday lunch - Closed 24-27 December, Monday and Tuesday

CELBRIDGE

Kildare – Pop. 17 262 – Regional map n° **22**-D1

Canteen Celbridge

MODERN CUISINE · FRIENDLY A local chef and his endearing French wife have created this relaxed, understated restaurant, where abstract art stands out against grey walls. Well-crafted dishes are boldly flavoured and Irish produce takes centre stage.

Menu € 25 (weekdays) – Carte € 45/54

4 Main St – 01 627 4967 (booking advisable) – www.canteencelbridge.com – dinner only and Saturday lunch – Closed first week January, last week August, first week September, 25-26 December, Sunday and Monday

CLIFDEN AN CLOCHÁN

Galway – Pop. 2 056 – Regional map n° **21**-A3

Mitchells

SEAFOOD · BISTRO A long-standing, family-run restaurant. It's set over two floors and decorated with regional prints and seascapes. They offer a huge array of traditional seafood dishes; local prawns, mussels and oysters all feature.

Menu € 29 (weekdays) – Carte € 30/52

Market St – 095 21867 – www.mitchellsrestaurantclifden.com – Closed November-15 March

Quay House

TOWNHOUSE · QUIRKY A former harbourmaster's house and monastery on the quayside, overlooking the river. The quirky, bohemian-style interior is crammed with memorabilia, paintings and pictures. Breakfast takes place in the leafy conservatory.

16 rooms – € 80/110 € 135/160

Beach Rd – 095 21369 – www.thequayhouse.com – Closed November-March

Sea Mist House

TRADITIONAL · COSY Step back in time at this creeper-clad house, which was built in 1820 and is the owner's family home. Original features are enhanced by interesting paintings; the only TV is in the lounge. Enjoy honey from their bees at breakfast.

4 rooms – € 55/80 € 80/110

– 095 21441 – www.seamisthouse.com – Closed November-March

CLOGHEEN AN CHLOICHÍN

South Tipperary – Pop. 491 – Regional map n° **22**-C2

Old Convent

MODERN CUISINE · CHIC A very personally run restaurant in a former convent set on the edge of the village. The candlelit former chapel with its delightful original stained glass windows is where dinner is served. The set 8 course daily changing menu features original, modern dishes. Smart, comfortable bedrooms have good quality linens; help yourself to goodies from the pantry.

Menu € 65 – tasting menu only

7 rooms – € 150/200 € 175/225

Mount Anglesby – Southeast : 0.5 km on R 668 (Lismore rd) – 052 746 5565 (booking essential) – www.theoldconvent.ie – dinner only – Closed 7 January-1 February, 2 weeks August, 23-26 December, Sunday except before bank holidays and Monday-Thursday

CLONAKILTY CLOICH NA COILLTE

Cork – Pop. 4 000 – Regional map n° **22**-B3

Gulfstream

MODERN CUISINE • CHIC Contemporary New England style restaurant set on the first floor of a vast hotel and offering superb views over the beach. Modern menus highlight produce from West Cork and feature plenty of fresh local seafood.

Carte € 52/64

Inchydoney Island Lodge and Spa Hotel, South : 5.25 km by N 71 following signs for Inchydoney Beach – ☎ 023 883 3143 – www.inchydoneyisland.com – dinner only and Sunday lunch – Closed 24-25 December

Deasy's

TRADITIONAL CUISINE • COSY An appealing pub in a picturesque hamlet, offering lovely views out across the bay. Its gloriously dated interior is decorated with maritime memorabilia. Menus are dictated by the seasons and the latest catch from the local boats.

Menu € 32 (early dinner) – Carte € 32/47

Ring – Southeast : 3 km – ☎ 023 883 5741 – Closed 24-26 December, Good Friday, Sunday dinner, Monday, Tuesday and restricted opening in winter

Inchydoney Island Lodge and Spa

SPA AND WELLNESS • MODERN Superbly located on a remote headland and boasting stunning views over the beach and out to sea; all of the contemporary bedrooms have a balcony or terrace. The impressive spa boasts a seawater pool and 27 treatment rooms. Dine in the modern restaurant or nautically styled bistro-bar.

67 rooms – € 158/250 € 158/250 – 4 suites

South : 5.25 km by N 71 following signs for Inchydoney Beach – ☎ 023 883 3143 – www.inchydoneyisland.com – Closed 24-25 December

Gulfstream – See restaurant listing

CLONEGALL CLUAIN NA NGALL

Carlow – Pop. 245 – Regional map n° **22**-D2

Sha-Roe Bistro

TRADITIONAL CUISINE • FRIENDLY A welcoming 17C former coaching inn set in a picturesque village; it's a simple place with a relaxed, intimate feel and candlelit tables in the evenings. Menus offer carefully presented, unfussy dishes with clear flavours and a classical base. Sourcing of local and farmers' market ingredients is paramount.

Carte € 32/45

Main St – ☎ 053 937 5636 (booking essential) – www.sha-roebistro.ie – dinner only and Sunday lunch – Closed January, 1 week April, 1 week October, Sunday dinner, Monday and Tuesday

CLONTARF CLUAIN TARBH – Dublin → See Dublin

CLOVERHILL DROIM CAISIDE – Cavan → See Cavan

CONG CONGA

Mayo – Pop. 178 – Regional map n° **21**-A3

George V

MODERN CUISINE • ELEGANT A visit to the stunning wine cellars is a must at this grand, sophisticated hotel restaurant, where wood-panelling and Waterford Crystal chandeliers set the tone. Classic French flavours are delivered using subtly modern techniques.

Carte € 65/83

Ashford Castle Hotel – ☎ 094 954 6003 – www.ashfordcastle.com – dinner only

Cullen's at the Cottage

TRADITIONAL CUISINE • BISTRO XX Set within the grounds of Ashford Castle is this pretty little thatched cottage with an attractive landscaped terrace and lovely views. It has a stylish, subtly rustic look and a relaxed feel. Menus list appealing classics.

Carte € 34/58

Ashford Castle Hotel, – ✆ 094 954 5332 – www.ashfordcastle.com – Closed November-March

Ashford Castle

HISTORIC BUILDING • ELEGANT Hugely impressive lochside castle surrounded by extensive grounds; try archery, falconry, clay pigeon shooting or zip-lining; take to the water; or relax with loch views in the spa. Handsome guest areas display plenty of historic splendour and bedrooms are sumptuously appointed. Dine in the stone cellars in Dungeon, casually in Cullen's or formally in elegant George V.

83 rooms – € 265/575 € 285/595 – 5 suites

– ✆ 094 954 6003 – www.ashfordcastle.com

George V • **Cullen's at the Cottage** – See restaurant listing

The Lodge at Ashford Castle

BOUTIQUE HOTEL • CONTEMPORARY The attractive Georgian sister to Ashford Castle sits within its grounds and offers lovely views of Lough Corrib. Some of its stylish bedrooms are duplex; the sumptuous Lake View Suites come with bespoke furnishings and great outlooks. Wildes offers a creative fixed price menu; the Quay bar serves simpler fare.

64 rooms – € 130/280 € 150/300 – 12 suites

The Quay – Southeast : 2.25 km by R 345 off R 346 – ✆ 094 954 5400 – www.thelodgeac.com – Closed 24-25 December and midweek in winter

CORK CORCAIGH

Cork – Pop. 119 230 – Regional map n° **22**-B3

Orchids

MODERN CUISINE • ELEGANT XXX Sophisticated formal dining room in a well-appointed country house. Pillars dominate the room, which is laid with crisp white tablecloths. Menus offer refined dishes with some modern twists.

Menu € 69

Hayfield Manor Hotel, Perrott Ave, College Rd – Southwest : 2 km by R 608 – ✆ 021 484 5900 (booking essential) – www.hayfieldmanor.ie – dinner only – Closed Sunday and Monday

Les Gourmandises

CLASSIC FRENCH • ELEGANT XX Smart, contemporary restaurant which is proudly run by experienced owners – he cooks and she looks after the service. Accomplished dishes have a classic French heart and original Irish twists. The set menus represent good value.

Menu € 33 (weekdays)/48

Town plan: B2-v – *17 Cook St – ✆ 021 425 1959 (booking essential) – www.lesgourmandises.ie – dinner only – Closed Sunday and Monday*

Greenes Ⓝ

MODERN CUISINE • FRIENDLY XX Head down the alleyway at the side of the Isaacs Hotel, towards the waterfall, to access this formal yet friendly restaurant. The chef is a local and uses his cooking to showcase ingredients from West Cork producers.

Menu € 33 – Carte € 39/62

Town plan: B1-s – *48 McCurtain St – ✆ 021 455 2279 (bookings advisable at dinner) – www.greenesrestaurant.com – Closed 23 December- 2 January*

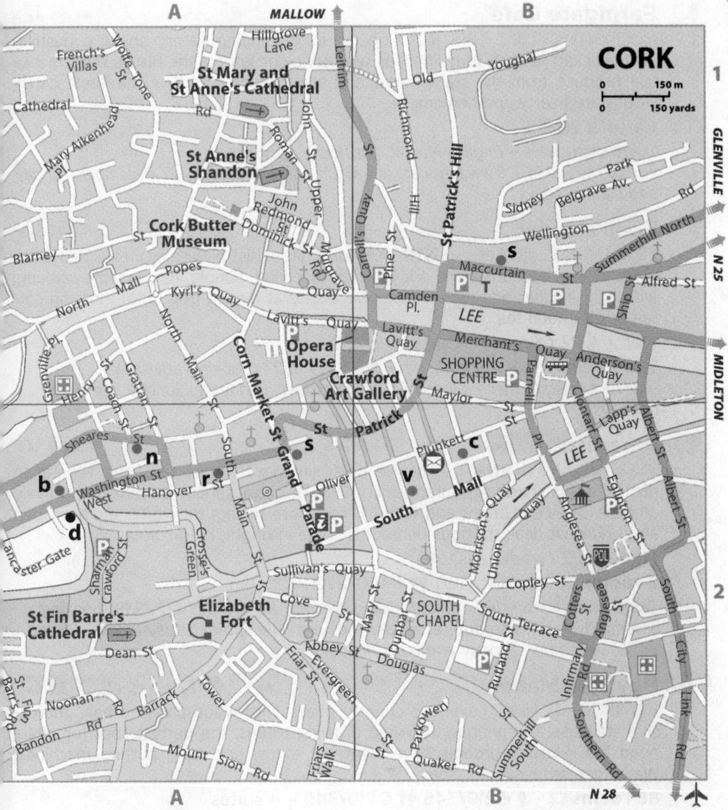

CORK

0 150 m
0 150 yards

A B 1 2
MALLOW
GLENVILLE
N 25
MIDLETON
N 28

St Mary and St Anne's Cathedral
St Anne's Shandon
Cork Butter Museum
Opera House
Crawford Art Gallery
St Fin Barre's Cathedral
Elizabeth Fort
SHOPPING CENTRE
SOUTH CHAPEL
LEE

French's Villas
Wolfe Tone St
Hillgrove Lane
Cathedral Rd
Mary Aikenhead Pl.
John St Upper
Roman St
John Redmond St
Dominick St
Mulgrave Rd
Blarney St
Popes Quay
North Mall
Kyrl's Quay
Lavitt's Quay
Camden Pl.
Leitrim St
Carroll's Quay
Pine St
Richmond Hill
St Patrick's Hill
Old Youghal Rd
Park Rd
Sidney Belgrave Av.
Wellington Rd
Summerhill North
Maccurtain St
Alfred St
Ship St
Merchant's Quay
Anderson's Quay
Lapp's Quay
Maylor St
Parnell Pl.
Clontarf St
Albert St
Grenville Pl.
Henry St
Coach St
Grattan St
North Main St
Corn Market St
Grand Parade
St Patrick St
Sheares St
Washington St West
Hanover St
South Main St
Oliver Plunkett St
South Mall
Morrison's Quay
Union Quay
Anglesea St
Eglinton St
Lancaster Gate
Sharman Crawford St
Crosse's Green
Sullivan's Quay
Cove St
Copley St
South Terrace
Cotters St
Mary St
Dunbar St
Abbey St
Douglas St
Friar St
Evergreen St
Rutland St
Infirmary Rd
South City Link Rd
Dean St
St Finbarr's Rd
Noonan Rd
Barrack St
Tower St
Bandon Rd
Mount Sion Rd
Friars Walk
Parkowen
Quaker Rd
Summerhill South
Southern Rd

Perrotts

MODERN CUISINE • BRASSERIE XX A conservatory restaurant overlooking the gardens of a luxurious country house. It's smart but comfortably furnished, with an adjoining wood-panelled bar. The menu offers a modern take on brasserie classics.

Carte € 43/57

Hayfield Manor Hotel, Perrott Ave, College Rd – Southwest : 2 km by R 608 – ✆ 021 484 5900 – www.hayfieldmanor.ie – Closed 25 December

Rachel's

TRADITIONAL CUISINE • FRIENDLY XX The service is friendly and energetic at this rustic, industrial-style restaurant and sultry piano bar. Flavoursome, generously proportioned dishes use garden and farm ingredients – go for a dish cooked in the wood-fired oven.

Carte € 35/50

Town plan: A2-r – *28 Washington St – ✆ 021 427 4189 (booking advisable) – www.rachels.ie – dinner only and Sunday lunch – Closed Sunday dinner*

The sun's out? Enjoy eating outside on the terrace: .

Farmgate Café

REGIONAL CUISINE • BISTRO Popular, long-standing eatery above a bustling 200 year old market; turn right for self-service or left for the bistro. Daily menus use produce from the stalls below and are supplemented by the latest catch. Dishes are hearty and homemade.

Carte € 20/35

Town plan: A2-s - *English Market (1st floor), Princes St - ✆ 021 427 8134 - www.farmgate.ie - lunch only - Closed 25-27 December, Sunday and bank holidays*

Fenn's Quay

TRADITIONAL CUISINE • BISTRO Modest little bistro with whitewashed brick walls, closely set tables and a loyal local following. Simple, flavoursome cooking, with light lunches and more substantial dishes at dinner; pop in for morning coffee or afternoon tea.

Menu € 27 (dinner) - Carte € 27/50

Town plan: A2-n - *5 Sheares St - ✆ 021 427 9527 (booking advisable) - www.fennsquay.net - Closed 24-27 December, 1 January, Sunday and bank holidays*

Paradiso

VEGETARIAN • INTIMATE They've been serving creative, satisfying vegetarian dishes at this stylish restaurant since 1993. The atmosphere is intimate yet lively and the service is bright and friendly. For those dining, they offer a dinner, bed and breakfast deal; spacious bedrooms come in bright, bold colours.

Menu € 22 (weekdays)/40

2 rooms - € 140/180 € 140/220

Town plan: A2-b - *16 Lancaster Quay, Western Rd - ✆ 021 427 7939 (booking essential) - www.paradiso.restaurant - dinner only and Saturday lunch - Closed 24-27 December, Sunday and bank holidays*

Hayfield Manor

HISTORIC • CLASSIC Luxurious country house with wood-panelled hall, impressive staircase and antique-furnished drawing rooms; the perfect spot for afternoon tea. Plush bedrooms have plenty of extras, including putting machines. Well-equipped residents' spa.

88 rooms - € 219/345 € 219/345 - 4 suites

Perrott Ave, College Rd - Southwest : 2 km by R 608 - ✆ 021 484 5900 - www.hayfieldmanor.ie

Orchids • **Perrotts** - See restaurant listing

Lancaster Lodge

BUSINESS • MODERN Purpose-built hotel next to the River Lee and within easy walking distance of the town centre. Spacious, bright bedrooms with bold fabrics and modern artwork; the executive suites have whirlpool baths. A good choice for the business traveller.

48 rooms - € 99/169 € 99/189 - €13

Town plan: A2-d - *Lancaster Quay, Western Rd - ✆ 021 425 1125 - www.lancasterlodge.com - Closed 23-26 December*

CORROFIN CORA FINNE

Clare - Pop. 689 - Regional map n° **22**-B1

Fergus View

FAMILY • PERSONALISED This charming house takes its name from the nearby river and offers pleasant country views from its front rooms. Bedrooms are immaculately kept and the welcome is warm - it's been in the family for four generations.

5 rooms - € 53/55 € 78/80

Kilnaboy - North : 3.25 km on R 476 - ✆ 065 683 7606 - www.fergusview.com - Closed November-February

CROSSHAVEN BUN AN TÁBHAIRNE

Cork – Pop. 2 093 – Regional map n° **22**-B3

Cronin's

SEAFOOD • PUB A classic Irish pub filled with interesting artefacts. It's been in the family since 1970 as is now run by the 3rd generation. Unfussy seafood dishes feature local produce. The limited opening restaurant offers more ambitious fare.

Carte € 17/31

1 Point Rd – 021 483 1829 – www.croninspub.com – Closed 25 December and Good Friday

DELGANY DEILGNE

Wicklow – ✉ Bray – Pop. 6 682 – Regional map n° **22**-D2

Pigeon House

MODERN BRITISH • BISTRO X This former pub now houses a bakery, a deli and a large restaurant complete with a counter of homemade cakes. Breakfast morphs into coffee, then into lunch and dinner; you can have anything from a bacon sarnie to duck liver parfait.

Carte € 28/47

The Delgany Inn – 01 287 7103 – www.pigeonhouse.ie – Closed 25-26 December and Monday and dinner Tuesday

DINGLE AN DAINGEAN

Kerry – Pop. 1 965 – Regional map n° **22**-A2

Chart House

REGIONAL CUISINE • RUSTIC X This characterful former boathouse sits in a pleasant quayside spot. The charming open-plan interior features exposed stone and stained glass, and the room has a cosy, intimate feel. Seasonal local ingredients feature in rustic, flavoursome dishes and service is friendly and efficient.

Menu € 32 – Carte € 35/48

The Mall – 066 915 2255 (booking essential) – www.thecharthousedingle.com – dinner only – Closed 2 January-12 February, 22-27 December and Monday October-April

Global Village

TRADITIONAL CUISINE • BISTRO XX A homely restaurant with a laid-back feel. Despite having visited 42 countries, the chef likes to keep things local, with meat and vegetables from the peninsula. The local fish dishes are fantastic.

Menu € 35 **s** – Carte € 35/52 **s**

Upper Main St – 066 915 2325 – www.globalvillagedingle.com – dinner only – Closed January-February and restricted opening in winter

Idás

MODERN CUISINE • NEIGHBOURHOOD XX This rustic, slate-faced restaurant is found in the heart of town. Creative modern cooking uses produce from the Dingle Peninsula. The chef-owner, Kevin, went to art school and it shows in the presentation.

Menu € 40/60

John St – 066 915 0885 (booking essential) – www.idasdingle.com – dinner only – Closed January-mid February, Tuesday in winter and Monday

Out of the Blue

SEAFOOD • RUSTIC X Its name is perfectly apt: not only is it painted bright blue, but this simple harbourside restaurant keeps its focus firmly on ingredients that come from the sea. Menus are decided each morning, based on the latest local catch.

Carte € 39/57

Waterside – 066 915 0811 (booking essential) – www.outoftheblue.ie – dinner only and Sunday lunch – Closed mid November-February

Castlewood House

COUNTRY HOUSE · GRAND LUXURY Spacious house overlooking the bay. Modern bedrooms come with whirlpool baths and extras like robes and chocolates. The hot and cold breakfast options are extensive; don't miss the bread and butter pudding.

12 rooms – € 100/220 € 150/240

The Wood – Northwest : 1 km on R 559 – 066 915 2788 – www.castlewooddingle.com – Closed 6-27 December and 6 January-13 February

Greenmount House 

FAMILY · PERSONALISED Well-run hotel in an elevated position above the town, with views of the hills and harbour; take it all in over a delicious breakfast. Lounges are comfy and bedrooms are modern; some have balconies or small terraces.

14 rooms – € 60/150 € 80/160

Upper John St, Gortonora – by John St. – 066 915 1414 – www.greenmounthouse.ie – Closed 16-27 December

Heatons 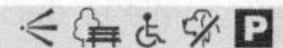

FAMILY · PERSONALISED Large, family-run house close to town, where a warm welcome is guaranteed. Most bedrooms have sea views and some have whirlpool baths. Comprehensive breakfasts include homemade pancakes, omelettes and Drambuie porridge.

16 rooms – € 64/97 € 88/133

The Wood – Northwest : 1 km. on R 559 – 066 915 2288 – www.heatonsdingle.com – Closed 2 January-1 February

DONEGAL DÚN NA NGALL

Donegal – Pop. 2 607 – Regional map n° **21**-C1

Harvey's Point 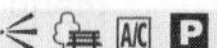

MODERN CUISINE · CHIC XXX A formal, traditional restaurant set within a family-owned country house hotel; its semi-circular windows afford delightful views of the lough. Classic dishes make use of local Donegal produce and are presented in a modern manner.

Menu € 65

Harvey's Point Hotel, Lough Eske – Northeast : 7.25 km. by N 15 – 074 972 2208 – www.harveyspoint.com – dinner only – Closed Wednesday July-October

Cedars 

TRADITIONAL CUISINE · INTIMATE XX Stylish, modern restaurant in a 17C castle close to the lough, with romantic booths to the rear and a slate terrace boasting views over the lawns and woodland. Small menu with international influences, but Donegal produce to the fore.

Menu € 55 – Carte € 46/66

Solis Lough Eske Castle Hotel, Northeast : 6.5 km by N 15 – 074 972 5100 – www.solishotels.com/lougheskecastle – dinner only and Sunday lunch

Harvey's Point 

FAMILY · CLASSIC A sprawling, family-run hotel in a peaceful loughside setting, with traditional guest areas and huge, very comfortable, country house style bedrooms – all offer a high level of facilities and most have lovely countryside outlooks.

64 rooms – € 99/360 € 198/480

Lough Eske – Northeast : 7.25 km. by N 15 – 074 972 2208 – www.harveyspoint.com

Harvey's Point – See restaurant listing

Solis Lough Eske Castle

LUXURY • CLASSIC Beautifully restored 17C castle, surrounded by 43 acres of sculpture-filled grounds. There's a fantastic spa and a swimming pool overlooking an enclosed garden. Bedrooms are a mix of contemporary and antique-furnished; go for a Garden Suite.

96 rooms – € 230/380 € 230/380 – 1 suite

Northeast : 6.5 km by N 15 – 074 972 5100 – www.solishotels.com/lougheskecastle

Cedars – See restaurant listing

Gateway Lodge

FAMILY • MODERN A modern property set close to town. Bedrooms are simply furnished, offer good value for money and have very comfortable beds; some are located in a two-storey annexe. Extensive breakfasts feature produce from the local butcher. Light lunches are followed by modern dinners in the café-style restaurant.

24 rooms – € 59/89 € 79/129

Lough Eske Rd – 074 974 0405 – www.thegatewaydonegal.ie – Closed 23-27 December

Ardeevin

FAMILY • COSY Friendly, brightly painted house set in peaceful gardens and boasting beautiful views over Lough Eske; personally run by the friendly owner. Warm, pleasantly cluttered guest areas are filled with ornaments and curios. Individually designed bedrooms display quality furnishings and thoughtful extras.

4 rooms – € 50 € 85

Lough Eske, Barnesmore – Northeast : 9 km by N 15 following signs for Lough Eske Drive – 074 972 1790 – www.ardeevinguesthouse.co.uk – Closed November-19 March

DONNYBROOK DOMHNACH BROC – Dublin → See Dublin

DOOLIN DÚLAINM

Clare – Regional map n° **22**-B1

Cullinan's

CLASSIC CUISINE • TRADITIONAL DÉCOR XX This brightly painted house is located in the heart of The Burren and its cosy dining room's full-length windows look out over the countryside and the River Aille. Local ingredients like Doolin crab or Burren lamb feature in classic dishes which are full of flavour. Bedrooms are cosy and contemporary.

Menu € 30 (weekdays) – Carte € 36/48

10 rooms – € 60/90 € 80/125

– 065 707 4183 (booking essential) – www.cullinansdoolin.com – dinner only – Closed November-March, Sunday and Wednesday

DOONBEG AN DÚN BEAG

Clare – Pop. 272 – Regional map n° **22**-B2

Morrissey's

SEAFOOD • PUB Smartly refurbished pub in a small coastal village; its terrace overlooks the river and the castle ruins. The menu may be simple but cooking is careful and shows respect for ingredients; locally caught fish and shellfish feature heavily and the crabs in particular are worth a try. Bedrooms are modern – two overlook the river – and they have bikes and a kayak for hire.

Carte € 26/45

5 rooms – € 50 € 100

– 065 905 5304 (bookings not accepted) – www.morrisseysdoonbeg.com – dinner only and Sunday lunch – Closed January, February and Monday-Tuesday January-May

Trump International Golf Links and H. Doonbeg

LUXURY • DESIGN Smart resort complex owned by Donald Trump. Stylish, sumptuous bedrooms and suites are spread about the grounds: some are duplex and feature fully fitted kitchens; all have spacious marble bathrooms and are extremely comfortable. Ocean View offers fine dining with a pleasant outlook over the sea, while Trump's, in the golf clubhouse, serves a traditional menu.

75 rooms – € 190/320 € 190/320

Northeast : 6 km on N 67 – 065 905 5600 – www.trumpirelandhotel.com – Closed Sunday-Thursday November-February

DROGHEDA DROICHEAD ÁTHA

Louth – Pop. 30 393 – Regional map n° **21**-D3

Eastern Seaboard

INTERNATIONAL • BISTRO A lively industrial style bistro; its name a reference to its location within Ireland and also a nod to the USA, which influences the menus. Share several small plates or customise a hearty main course with your choice of sides.

Carte € 22/41

1 Bryanstown Centre, Dublin Rd – Southeast : 2.5 km by N 1 taking first right after railway bridge – 041 980 2570 – www.glasgow-diaz.com – Closed 25-26 December and Wednesday

The Kitchen

WORLD CUISINE • BISTRO Glass-fronted riverside eatery. By day, a café serving homemade cakes, pastries, salads and sandwiches; by night, a more interesting, mainly Eastern Mediterranean menu is served, with influences from North Africa and the Middle East.

Menu € 30/50 – Carte € 31/42

2 South Quay – 041 983 4630 – www.kitchenrestaurant.ie – Closed 25-27 December and Monday-Tuesday

Scholars Townhouse

TOWNHOUSE • CLASSIC 19C former priest's house: now a well-run, privately owned hotel with smart wood panelling and ornate coving featuring throughout. Appealing bar and cosy lounge; comfortable, well-kept bedrooms. Dine on classically based dishes under an impressive mural of the Battle of Boyne.

16 rooms – € 65/139 € 65/139

King St – by West St and Lawrence St turning left at Lawrence's Gate – 041 983 5410 – www.scholarshotel.com – Closed 25-26 December

DROMAHAIR

Leitrim – Pop. 748 – Regional map n° **21**-B2

Luna

INTERNATIONAL • FRIENDLY A delightful little cottage on the main road of a sleepy village; the loughside drive over from Sligo is beautiful. It might have a neighbourhood feel but the food has global overtones, from the South of France and Tuscany to Asia.

Carte € 26/46

Main St – 071 913 4332 – dinner only – Closed January and Sunday

Z. Steger/age fotostock

GOOD TIPS!

The Celtic Tiger is back, with a purr if not yet a roar, and the capital's food scene continues to show signs of hotting up. A resurgence in informal dining has seen good value neighbourhood restaurants like **Craft**, **Richmond** and **Bastible** become popular – and these sit happily alongside the city's collection of Michelin Stars.

DUBLIN BAILE ÁTHA CLIATH

Dublin – Pop. 527 612 – Regional map n° **22**-D1

Restaurants

✿✿ Patrick Guilbaud (Guillaume Lebrun)

MODERN FRENCH • ELEGANT XxxX A truly sumptuous restaurant in an elegant Georgian house; the eponymous owner has run it for over 35 years. Accomplished, original cooking uses luxurious ingredients and mixes classical French cooking with modern techniques. Dishes are well-crafted and visually stunning with a superb balance of textures and flavours.

→ Blue lobster ravioli with coconut-scented lobster cream, toasted almonds and curry dressing. Wicklow lamb glazed in coriander mojo with shiitake, cauliflower and lamb jus. Guanaja chocolate and peanut parfait.

Menu € 60/120

Town plan: G3-e – *21 Upper Merrion St ✉ D2*
– ☎ 01 676 4192 (booking essential)
– www.restaurantpatrickguilbaud.ie
– Closed 17 and 30 March, 25-31 December, Sunday, Monday and bank holidays

✿ Chapter One (Ross Lewis)

MODERN CUISINE • INTIMATE XxX Good old-fashioned Irish hospitality meets with modern Irish cooking in this stylish basement restaurant beneath the Writers Museum. The series of interconnecting rooms have an understated elegance and striking bespoke art hangs on the walls. Boldly flavoured dishes showcase produce from local artisan producers.

→ Charred mackerel with Clarinbridge oysters, apple and lovage. Wild turbot, walnut crust and poached pear with kohlrabi. Flavours & textures of Irish milk and honey.

Menu € 40/75 **s**

Town plan: F1-r – *The Dublin Writers Museum, 18-19 Parnell Sq ✉ D1*
– ☎ 01 873 2266 (booking essential)
– www.chapteronerestaurant.com
– Closed 2 weeks August, 2 weeks Christmas, Sunday, Monday and bank holidays

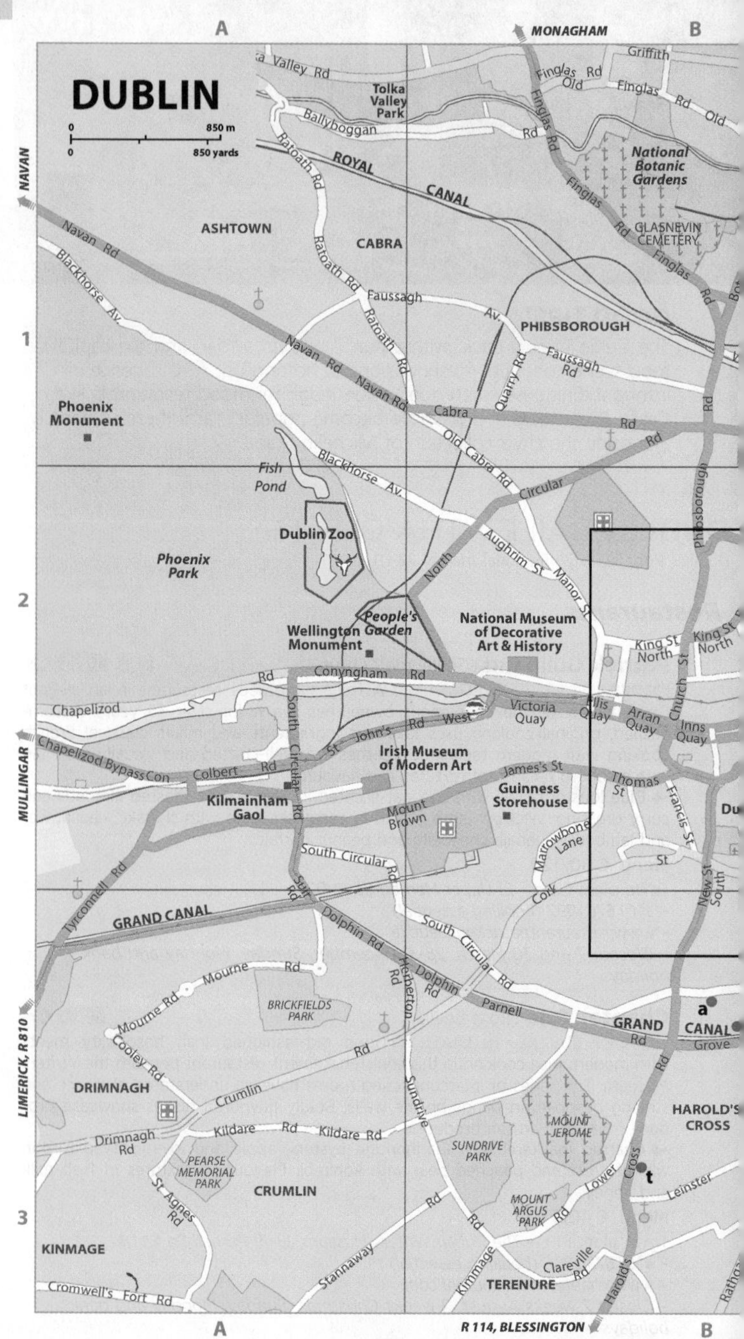
DUBLIN
0
850 m
0
850 yards
A
B
1
2
3
MONAGHAM
NAVAN
MULLINGAR
LIMERICK, R 810
R 114, BLESSINGTON
ASHTOWN
CABRA
PHIBSBOROUGH
Tolka Valley Park
National Botanic Gardens
GLASNEVIN CEMETERY
ROYAL CANAL
Phoenix Monument
Fish Pond
Dublin Zoo
Phoenix Park
People's Garden
Wellington Monument
National Museum of Decorative Art & History
Irish Museum of Modern Art
Kilmainham Gaol
Guinness Storehouse
GRAND CANAL
BRICKFIELDS PARK
DRIMNAGH
PEARSE MEMORIAL PARK
CRUMLIN
KINMAGE
SUNDRIVE PARK
MOUNT JEROME
MOUNT ARGUS PARK
TERENURE
HAROLD'S CROSS
Navan Rd
Blackhorse Av.
Ratoath Rd
Ballyboggan Rd
Finglas Rd
Faussagh Av.
Quarry Rd
Cabra Rd
Old Cabra Rd
North Circular Rd
Aughrim St
Manor St
Conyngham Rd
Chapelizod
Chapelizod Bypass
Con Colbert Rd
South Circular Rd
St John's Rd West
Victoria Quay
Ellis Quay
Arran Quay
Inns Quay
James's St
Thomas St
Francis St
Mount Brown
Marrowbone Lane
Church St
King St North
Phibsborough Rd
New St South
Tyrconnell Rd
Dolphin Rd
Herberton Rd
Mourne Rd
Cooley Rd
Crumlin Rd
Drimnagh Rd
Kildare Rd
St Agnes Rd
Cromwell's Fort Rd
Stannaway Rd
Kimmage Rd
Sundrive Rd
Parnell Rd
Grove Rd
Harold's Cross Rd
Lower Rd
Leinster
Clareville Rd
Cork St
a
t

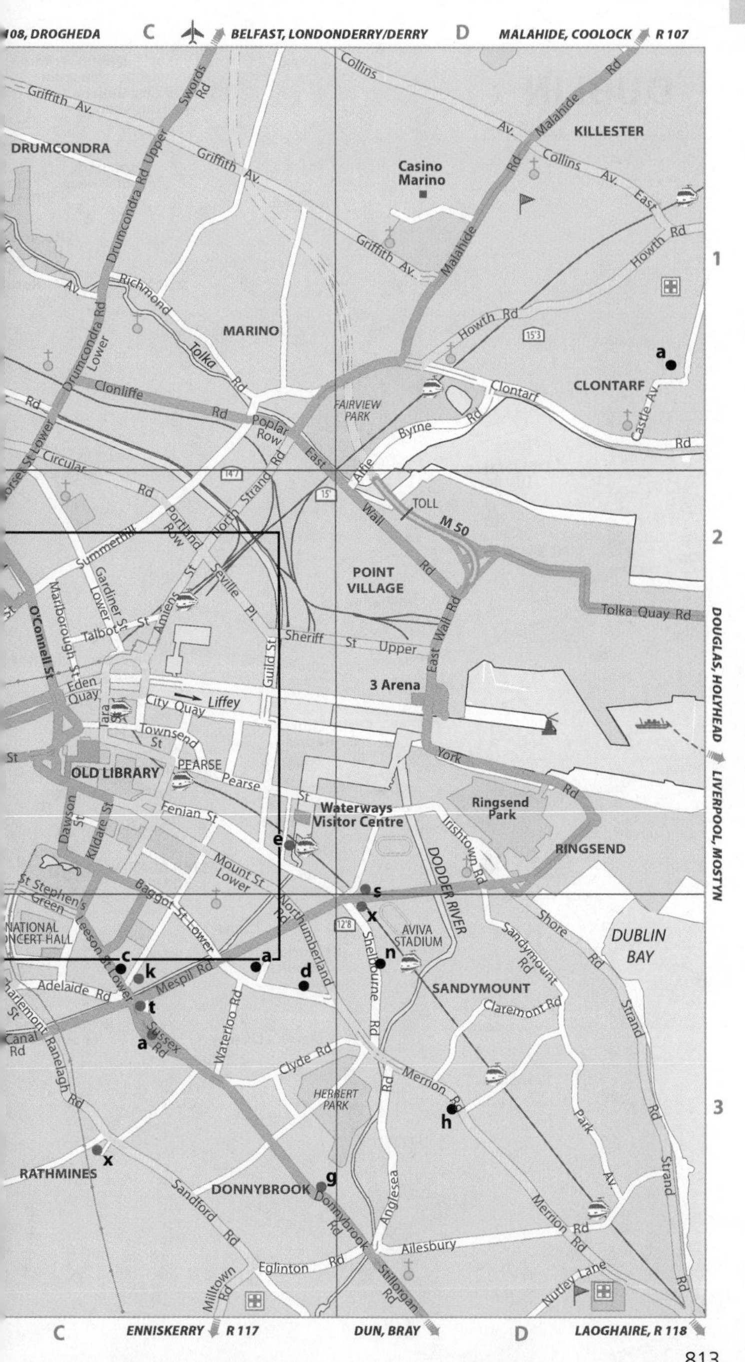
108, DROGHEDA
C
BELFAST, LONDONDERRY/DERRY
D
MALAHIDE, COOLOCK
R 107
DRUMCONDRA
KILLESTER
Casino Marino
MARINO
CLONTARF
FAIRVIEW PARK
POINT VILLAGE
M 50
TOLL
3 Arena
Liffey
OLD LIBRARY
Waterways Visitor Centre
Ringsend Park
RINGSEND
AVIVA STADIUM
SANDYMOUNT
DUBLIN BAY
DODDER RIVER
HERBERT PARK
RATHMINES
DONNYBROOK
NATIONAL CONCERT HALL
DOUGLAS, HOLYHEAD
LIVERPOOL, MOSTYN
1
2
3
C
ENNISKERRY
R 117
DUN, BRAY
D
LAOGHAIRE, R 118

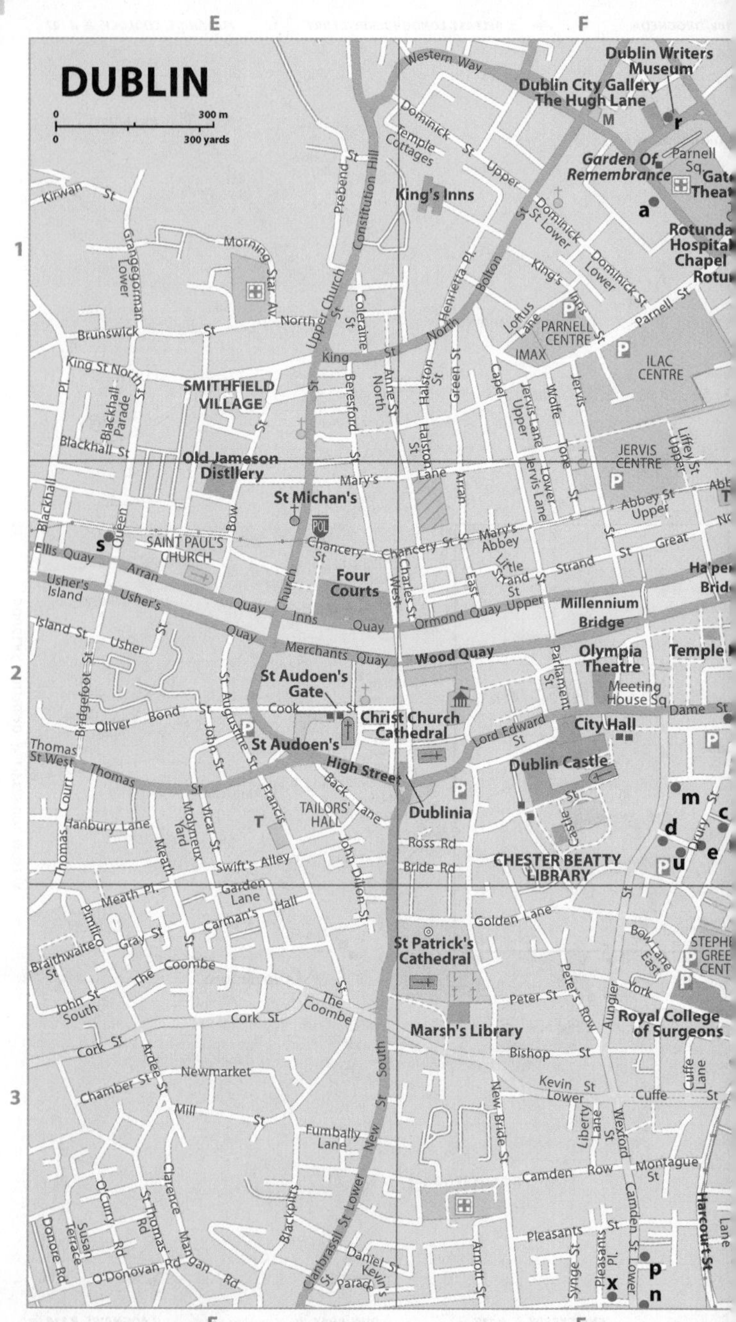

DUBLIN
0
300 m
0
300 yards
E
F
1
2
3
Dublin Writers Museum
Dublin City Gallery The Hugh Lane
Garden Of Remembrance
Parnell Sq.
King's Inns
Rotunda Hospital Chapel
PARNELL CENTRE
IMAX
ILAC CENTRE
SMITHFIELD VILLAGE
Old Jameson Distillery
JERVIS CENTRE
St Michan's
SAINT PAUL'S CHURCH
Four Courts
Millennium Bridge
Wood Quay
Olympia Theatre
Meeting House Sq
St Audoen's Gate
Christ Church Cathedral
City Hall
St Audoen's
High Street
Dublin Castle
TAILORS' HALL
Dublinia
CHESTER BEATTY LIBRARY
St Patrick's Cathedral
Marsh's Library
Royal College of Surgeons
Western Way
Dominick St Upper
Temple Cottages
Constitution Hill
Prebend St
Kirwan St
Grangegorman Lower
Morning Star Av.
Brunswick St North
King St North
Upper Church St
Coleraine St
Henrietta Pl.
Bolton St
Dominick St Lower
King's Inns St
Loftus Lane
Parnell St
Beresford St
Anne St North
Halston St
Green St
Capel St
Jervis Lane Upper
Wolfe Tone St
Jervis St
Liffey St Upper
Blackhall Parade
Blackhall Pl.
Blackhall St
Halston Lane
Arran St East
Jervis Lane Lower
Abbey St Upper
Mary's Lane
Mary's Abbey
Chancery St
Chancery Pl.
Little Strand St
Strand St Great
Queen St
Bow St
Ellis Quay
Arran Quay
Usher's Island
Usher's Quay
Inns Quay
Ormond Quay Upper
Charles St West
Church St
Merchants Quay
Island St
Usher St
Bridgefoot St
St Augustine St
Oliver Bond St
John St
Cook St
Lord Edward St
Parliament St
Dame St
Thomas St West
Thomas St
Back Lane
Castle St
Thomas Court
Hanbury Lane
Molyneux Yard
Vicar St
Francis St
John Dillon St
Ross Rd
Bride Rd
Meath St
Swift's Alley
Meath Pl.
Garden Lane
Carman's Hall
Pimlico
Gray St
Braithwaite St
The Coombe
Golden Lane
Bow Lane East
Drury St
Aungier St
York St
Peter St
Peter's Row
John St South
Cork St
Ardee St
Newmarket
Chamber St
Mill St
Bishop St
Kevin St Lower
Cuffe Lane
Cuffe St
New Bride St
Liberty Lane
Wexford St
Fumbally Lane
New St South
Camden Row
Montague St
Harcourt St
O'Curry Rd
St Thomas' Rd
Clarence Mangan Rd
Blackpitts
Clanbrassil St Lower
Donore Rd
Susan Terrace
O'Donovan Rd
Daniel St
Kevin's Parade
Arnott St
Pleasants St
Synge St
Pleasants Pl.
Camden St Lower
M
T
POL
a
c
d
e
m
n
p
r
s
u
x

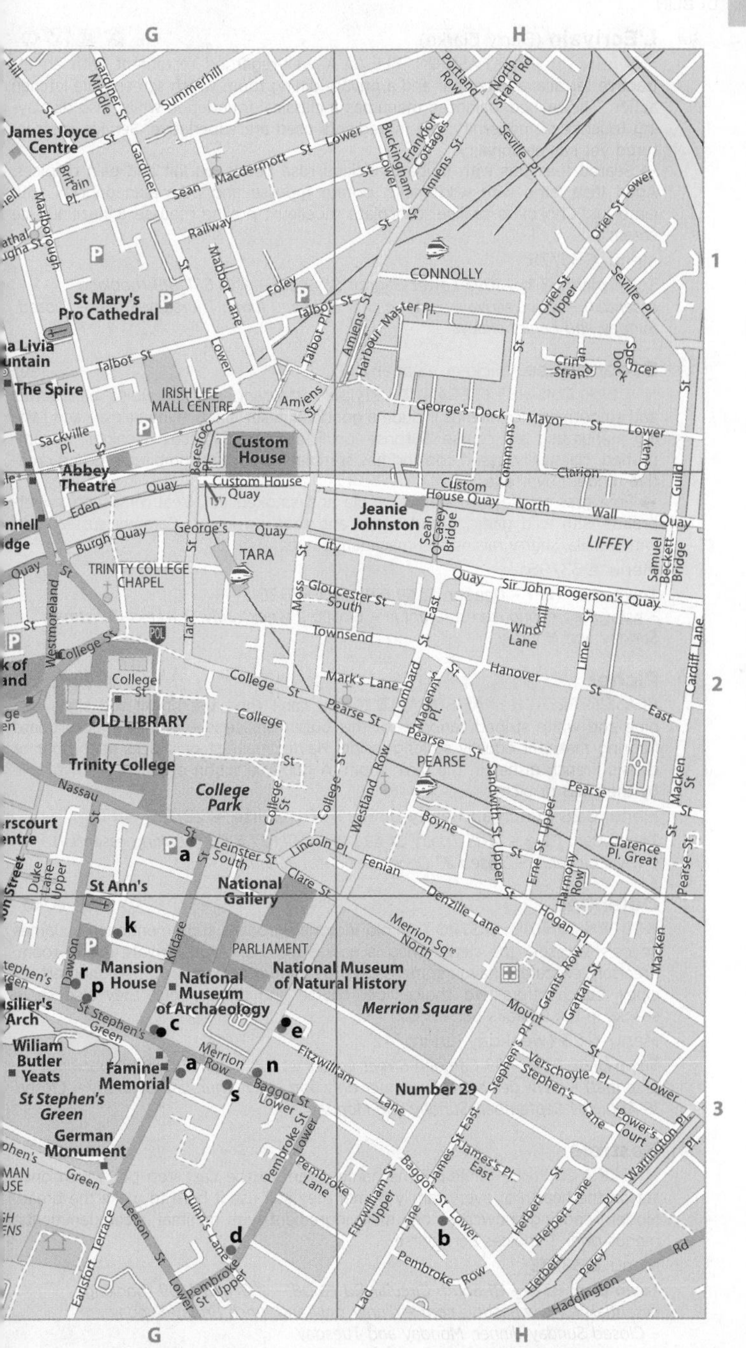
G
H
1
2
3
James Joyce Centre
St Mary's Pro Cathedral
The Spire
IRISH LIFE MALL CENTRE
Custom House
Abbey Theatre
CONNOLLY
Jeanie Johnston
LIFFEY
TARA
TRINITY COLLEGE CHAPEL
OLD LIBRARY
Trinity College
College Park
PEARSE
St Ann's
National Gallery
PARLIAMENT
Mansion House
National Museum of Archaeology
National Museum of Natural History
Merrion Square
Number 29
Famine Memorial
Wiliam Butler Yeats
St Stephen's Green
German Monument
Summerhill
Gardiner St Middle
Gardiner St
Sean Macdermott St Lower
Railway St
Mabbot Lane
Talbot St
Amiens St
Custom House Quay
Eden Quay
Burgh Quay
George's Quay
City Quay
Sir John Rogerson's Quay
North Wall Quay
Sean O'Casey Bridge
Samuel Beckett Bridge
Westmoreland St
College St
Townsend St
Pearse St
Hanover St East
Nassau St
Leinster St South
Clare St
Merrion Sq North
Fitzwilliam Lane
Baggot St Lower
Pembroke St Lower
Leeson St Lower
Earlsfort Terrace
Kildare St
Dawson St
Mount St Lower
Haddington Rd
G
H

L'Ecrivain (Derry Clarke)

MODERN CUISINE · FASHIONABLE XXX A well-regarded restaurant with an attractive terrace, a glitzy bar and a private dining room which screens live kitchen action. The refined, balanced menu has a classical foundation whilst also displaying touches of modernity; the ingredients used are superlative. Service is structured yet has personality.

→ Seared foie gras with rhubarb, pickled rose petals, parfait and pain d'épices. Aged Irish lamb with wild garlic, potato mousse and parmesan gnocchi with lamb jus. Chocolate praline, chocolate moelleux, praline mousse & hazelnut ice cream.

Menu € 35/75

Town plan: H3-b - *109a Lower Baggot St ✉ D2 - ✆ 01 661 1919 (booking essential) - www.lecrivain.com - dinner only and lunch Thursday-Friday - Closed Sunday and bank holidays*

Greenhouse (Mickael Viljanen)

MODERN CUISINE · ELEGANT XXX Stylish restaurant with turquoise banquettes and smooth service. Menus include a good value set lunch, midweek set and tasting menus and a 5 course 'Surprise' on Friday and Saturday evenings. Accomplished, classically based cooking has stimulating flavour combinations and creative modern overtones.

→ Foie gras royale with walnut, apple and smoked eel. Veal rump and sweetbreads with wild garlic, broad beans and roasting juices. Caramel custard tart with vanilla, sherry raisins and macadamia nuts.

Menu € 33/95

Town plan: G3-r - *Dawson St ✉ D2 - ✆ 01 676 7015 - www.thegreenhouserestaurant.ie - Closed 2 weeks July, 2 weeks Christmas, Sunday and Monday*

Pichet

CLASSIC FRENCH · FASHIONABLE XX You can't miss the bright red signs and blue and white striped canopies of this buzzy brasserie – and its checkerboard flooring makes it equally striking inside. Have breakfast or snacks at the bar or classic French dishes in the main room. A good selection of wines are available by the glass or pichet.

Menu € 28 (lunch and early dinner)/50 - Carte € 28/53

Town plan: F2-g - *14-15 Trinity St ✉ D2 - ✆ 01 677 1060 (booking essential) - www.pichet.ie - Closed 25 December and 1 January*

Delahunt

MODERN CUISINE · BISTRO X An old Victorian grocer's shop mentioned in James Joyce's 'Ulysses'; the clerk's snug is now a glass-enclosed private dining room. Precisely executed, flavoursome dishes are modern takes on time-honoured recipes. Lunch offers two choices per course and dinner, four; they also serve snacks in the upstairs bar.

Menu € 23 (weekday lunch)/42

Town plan: F3-p - *39 Camden Street Lower ✉ D2 - ✆ 01 598 4880 (booking essential) - www.delahunt.ie - dinner only and lunch Thursday-Saturday - Closed 15 August-1 September, Sunday and Monday*

Bastible

MODERN CUISINE · SIMPLE X The name refers to the cast iron pot which once sat on the hearth of every family home; they still use it here to make the bread. Modern cooking showcases one main ingredient with minimal accompaniments; menus offer 3 choices per course.

Menu € 38/45

Town plan: B3-a - *111 South Circular Rd ✉ D8 - ✆ 01 473 7409 (booking essential) - www.bastible.com - dinner only and lunch Friday-Sunday - Closed Sunday dinner, Monday and Tuesday*

Etto

MEDITERRANEAN CUISINE • RUSTIC X The name of this rustic restaurant means 'little' and it is totally apt! Blackboards announce the daily wines and the lunchtime 'soup and sandwich' special. Flavoursome dishes rely on good ingredients and have Italian influences; the chef understands natural flavours and follows the 'less is more' approach.

Menu € 28 (weekday lunch) – Carte € 29/44

Town plan: G3-s – *18 Merrion Row ✉ D2 – ✆ 01 678 8872 (booking essential) – www.etto.ie – Closed Sunday and bank holidays*

Pig's Ear

MODERN CUISINE • BISTRO X Well-established restaurant in a Georgian townhouse overlooking Trinity College. Floors one and two are bustling bistro-style areas filled with mirrors and porcine-themed memorabilia; floor three is a private room with a Scandinavian feel. Good value menus list hearty dishes with a modern edge.

Menu € 22 (lunch and early dinner)/27 – Carte € 28/48

Town plan: G2-a – *4 Nassau St ✉ D2 – ✆ 01 670 3865 (booking essential) – www.thepigsear.ie – Closed first week January, Sunday and bank holidays*

Richmond (N)

MODERN CUISINE • NEIGHBOURHOOD X A real gem of a neighbourhood restaurant with a rustic look and a lively feel; sit upstairs for a more sedate experience. The vibrant, gutsy dishes change regularly – apart from the Dexter burger and rib-eye which are mainstays; on Tuesdays they serve a good value tasting menu where they try out new ideas.

Menu € 23/33 – Carte € 31/48

Town plan: B3-r – *43 Richmond Street South – ✆ 01 478 8783 (booking advisable) – www.richmondrestaurant.ie – dinner only and brunch Saturday-Sunday – Closed Monday*

Forty One

MODERN CUISINE • ELEGANT XXX Intimate, richly furnished restaurant on the first floor of an attractive, creeper-clad townhouse, in a corner of St Stephen's Green. Accomplished, classical cooking features luxurious Irish ingredients and personal, modern touches.

Menu € 35 (lunch) – Carte dinner € 63/78

Town plan: G3-a – *41 St. Stephen's Grn. ✉ D2 – ✆ 01 662 0000 (booking advisable) – www.restaurantfortyone.ie – Closed 27 July-16 August, 25-26 December, Sunday and Monday*

One Pico

MODERN CUISINE • ELEGANT XXX Stylish modern restaurant tucked away on a side street; a well-regarded place that's a regular haunt for MPs. Sit on comfy banquettes or velour chairs, surrounded by muted colours. Modern Irish cooking offers plenty of flavour.

Menu € 25 (weekday lunch)/49

Town plan: G3-k – *5-6 Molesworth Pl ✉ D2 – ✆ 01 676 0300 – www.onepico.com – Closed bank holidays*

Amuse

MODERN CUISINE • FRIENDLY XX Modern, understated décor provides the perfect backdrop for the intricate, innovative cooking. Dishes showcase Asian ingredients – including kombu and yuzu; which are artfully arranged according to their flavours and textures.

Menu € 29 (weekday lunch)/65

Town plan: G3-r – *22 Dawson St ✉ D2 – ✆ 01 639 4889 (booking advisable) – www.amuse.ie – Closed 2 weeks Christmas-New Year, last week July, first week August, Sunday and Monday*

Bang

MODERN CUISINE • BISTRO XX Stylish restaurant with an intimate powder blue basement, a bright mezzanine level and a small, elegant room above. There are good value pre-theatre menus, a more elaborate à la carte and tasting menus showcasing top Irish produce.

Menu € 25 (early dinner)/50 – Carte € 40/63

Town plan: G3-a – *11 Merrion Row ✉ D2*
– *✆ 01 400 4229 – www.bangrestaurant.com – dinner only – Closed Christmas and bank holidays*

Dax

FRENCH • BISTRO XX Clubby restaurant in the cellar of a Georgian townhouse near Fitzwilliam Square. Tried-and-tested French dishes use top Irish produce and flavours are clearly defined. The Surprise Menu best showcases the kitchen's talent.

Menu € 32 (weekday lunch)/39 – Carte € 47/68

Town plan: G3-d – *23 Pembroke St Upper ✉ D2*
– *✆ 01 676 1494 (booking essential) – www.dax.ie – Closed 25 December-4 January, 7-14 August, Saturday lunch, Sunday and Monday*

Fade St. Social - Restaurant

MODERN CUISINE • BRASSERIE XX Have cocktails on the terrace then head for the big, modern brasserie. Dishes use Irish ingredients but have a Mediterranean feel; they specialise in sharing and wood-fired dishes, and use large cuts of meat such as chateaubriand.

Menu € 35 (lunch and early dinner) – Carte € 33/88

Town plan: F2-u – *4-6 Fade St ✉ D2*
– *✆ 01 604 0066 – www.fadestsocial.com – dinner only and lunch Thursday-Saturday – Closed 25-26 December and 1 January.*

Mr Fox (N)

MODERN CUISINE • INTIMATE XX In the basement of a striking Georgian house you'll find this light-hearted restaurant with a lovely tiled floor and a small terrace. The charming team present tasty international dishes, some of which have a playful touch.

Menu € 22 (weekdays) – Carte € 33/48

Town plan: F1-a – *38 Parnell Sq. West ✉ D1*
– *✆ 01 874 7778 – www.mrfox.ie – Closed Sunday, Monday and bank holidays*

Pearl Brasserie

CLASSIC FRENCH • BRASSERIE XX Formal basement restaurant with a small bar-lounge and two surprisingly airy dining rooms; sit in a stylish booth in one of the old coal bunkers. Intriguing modern dishes have a classical base and Mediterranean and Asian influences.

Menu € 25 (lunch) – Carte € 44/66

Town plan: G3-n – *20 Merrion St Upper ✉ D2*
– *✆ 01 661 3572 – www.pearl-brasserie.com – Closed 25 December and Sunday*

Peploe's

MEDITERRANEAN CUISINE • COSY XX Atmospheric cellar restaurant – formerly a bank vault – named after the artist. The comfy room has a warm, clubby feel and a large mural depicts the owner. The well-drilled team present Mediterranean dishes and an Old World wine list.

Menu € 32 (lunch) – Carte € 41/65

Town plan: G3-p – *16 St Stephen's Grn. ✉ D2*
– *✆ 01 676 3144 (booking essential) – www.peploes.com – Closed 25-26 December, Good Friday and lunch bank holidays*

Saddle Room

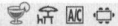

MEATS AND GRILLS • ELEGANT XX Renowned restaurant with a history as long as that of the hotel in which it stands. The warm, inviting room features intimate gold booths and a crustacea counter. The menu offers classic dishes and grills.

Menu € 23 (weekday lunch) – Carte € 40/85

Town plan: G3-c – *Shelbourne Hotel, 27 St Stephen's Grn. ✉ D2 – ✆ 01 663 4500 – www.shelbournedining.ie*

Suesey Street

MODERN CUISINE • INTIMATE XX An intimate restaurant with sumptuous, eye-catching décor, set in the basement of a Georgian townhouse; sit on the superb courtyard terrace. Refined, modern cooking brings out the best in home-grown Irish ingredients.

Menu € 25 (weekday dinner)/48 – Carte € 44/58

Town plan: C3-k – *26 Fitzwilliam Pl ✉ D2 – ✆ 01 669 4600 – www.sueseystreet.ie – Closed 25-30 December, Saturday lunch, Sunday and Monday*

Camden Kitchen

CLASSIC CUISINE • BISTRO X A simple, modern, neighbourhood bistro set over two floors; watch the owner cooking in the open kitchen. Tasty dishes use good quality Irish ingredients prepared in classic combinations. Service is relaxed and friendly.

Menu € 24/27 – Carte € 28/50

Town plan: F3-x – *3a Camden Mkt, Grantham St ✉ D8 – ✆ 01 476 0125 – www.camdenkitchen.ie – Closed 24-26 December, Sunday and Monday*

Drury Buildings

ITALIAN • TRENDY X A hip, laid-back 'New York loft': its impressive terrace has a retractable roof and reclaimed furniture features in the stylish cocktail bar, which offers cicchetti and sharing boards. The airy restaurant serves rustic Italian dishes.

Menu € 24/28 – Carte € 30/53

Town plan: F2-e – *52-55 Drury St ✉ D2 – ✆ 01 960 2095 – www.drurybuildings.com – Closed 25-26 December*

Fade St. Social - Gastro Bar

INTERNATIONAL • FASHIONABLE X Buzzy restaurant with an almost frenzied feel. It's all about a diverse range of original, interesting small plates, from a bacon and cabbage burger to a lobster hot dog. Eat at the kitchen counter or on leather-cushioned 'saddle' benches.

Menu € 30 (early dinner) – Carte € 24/35

Town plan: F2-u – *4-6 Fade St ✉ D2 – ✆ 01 604 0066 (booking essential) – www.fadestreetsocial.com – dinner only and lunch Saturday-Sunday – Closed 25-26 December and 1 January*

Fish Shop N

SEAFOOD • RUSTIC X A very informal little restaurant where they serve a daily changing seafood menu which is written up on the tiled wall. Great tasting, supremely fresh, unfussy dishes could be prepared raw or roasted on the wood-fired oven.

Menu € 39/55 – tasting menu only

Town plan: E2-s – *6 Queen St ✉ D7 – ✆ 01 430 8594 (booking advisable) – www.fish-shop.ie – dinner only – Closed Sunday-Tuesday and bank holidays*

l'Gueuleton

CLASSIC FRENCH • BISTRO X Rustic restaurant with beamed ceilings, Gallic furnishings, a shabby-chic bistro feel and a large pavement terrace. Flavoursome cooking features good value, French country classics which rely on local, seasonal produce. Service is friendly.

Menu € 29/38 – Carte € 39/52

Town plan: F2-d – *1 Fade St ✉ D2 – ✆ 01 675 3708 – www.lgueuleton.com – Closed 25-26 December*

Locks

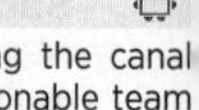

MODERN CUISINE • BISTRO Locals love this restaurant overlooking the canal - downstairs it's buzzy, while upstairs is more intimate, and the personable team add to the feel. Natural flavours are to the fore and dishes are given subtle modern touches; for the best value menus come early in the week or before 7pm.

Menu € 30/35 (weekday dinner) - Carte € 36/55

Town plan: B3-s - *1 Windsor Terr ✉ D8 - ✆ 01 416 3655 (booking essential) - www.locksrestaurant.ie - dinner only and lunch Friday-Sunday - Closed Sunday dinner and Monday*

La Maison

CLASSIC FRENCH • BISTRO Sweet little French bistro with tables on the pavement and original posters advertising French products. The experienced, Breton-born chef-owner offers carefully prepared, seasonal Gallic classics, brought to the table by a personable team.

Menu € 22 (weekday dinner) - Carte € 21/56

Town plan: F2-c - *15 Castlemarket ✉ D2 - ✆ 01 672 7258 - www.lamaisonrestaurant.ie - Closed 25-27 December and 1-2 January*

Osteria Lucio

ITALIAN • INTIMATE Set under the railway arches and run by two experienced chefs. Robust, rustic dishes showcase local produce, alongside ingredients imported from Italy; sit by the bar to watch pizzas being cooked in the wood-oven.

Menu € 23 (early dinner) - Carte € 25/54

Town plan: C2-e - *The Malting Tower, Clanwilliam Terr ✉ D2 - ✆ 01 662 4198 - www.osterialucio.com - Closed 25-29 December and bank holiday Mondays*

Pickle (N)

INDIAN • FASHIONABLE It might not look much from the outside but inside the place really comes alive. Spices are lined up on the kitchen counter and dishes are fresh and vibrant; the lamb curry with bone marrow is divine. Try a Tiffin Box for lunch.

Menu € 50 - Carte € 25/56

Town plan: F3-n - *43 Camden St ✉ D2 - ✆ 01 555 7755 - www.picklerestaurant.com - Closed Monday and lunch Saturday-Sunday*

Rustic Stone

MODERN CUISINE • FASHIONABLE Split-level restaurant offering something a little different. Good quality ingredients are cooked simply to retain their natural flavours and menus focus on healthy and special dietary options; some arrive on a sizzling stone.

Menu € 30/40 - Carte € 33/63

Town plan: F2-m - *17 South Great George's St ✉ D2 - ✆ 01 707 9596 - www.rusticstone.ie - Closed 25-26 December and 1 January*

Saba

THAI • FASHIONABLE Trendy, buzzy restaurant and cocktail bar. Simple, stylish rooms have refectory tables, banquettes and amusing photos. Fresh, visual, authentic cooking is from an all-Thai team, with a few Vietnamese dishes and some fusion cooking too.

Menu € 14 (weekday lunch)/35 - Carte € 19/47

Town plan: F2-k - *26-28 Clarendon St ✉ D2 - ✆ 01 679 2000 - www.sabadublin.com - Closed 25-26 December*

Taste at Rustic by Dylan McGrath

ASIAN • RUSTIC Dylan McGrath's love of Japanese cuisine inspires dishes which explore the five tastes; sweet, salt, bitter, umami and sour. Ingredients are top-notch and flavours, bold and masculine. Personable staff are happy to recommend dishes.

Menu € 45/55 - Carte € 34/120

Town plan: F2-m - *17 South Great George's St ✉ D2 - (2nd Floor) - ✆ 01 526 7701 (booking advisable) - www.tasteatrustic.com - dinner only - Closed 25-26 December, 1 January, Sunday and Monday*

Hotels

Shelbourne

GRAND LUXURY • CLASSIC A famed hotel dating from 1824, overlooking St Stephen's Green; this is where the 1922 Irish Constitution was signed. It has classical architecture, elegant guest areas, luxurious bedrooms and even a tiny museum. The lounge and bars are the places to go for afternoon tea and drinks.

265 rooms – € 259/750 € 259/750 – €29 – 19 suites

Town plan: G3-c – *27 St Stephen's Grn.* ✉ *D2* – *01 663 4500*
– *www.theshelbourne.ie*

Saddle Room – See restaurant listing

Merrion

TOWNHOUSE • CLASSIC A Georgian façade conceals a luxury hotel and a compact spa with an impressive pool. Opulent drawing rooms are filled with antique furniture and fine artwork – enjoy 'Art Afternoon Tea' with a view of the formal parterre garden. Stylish bedrooms have a classic, understated feel and smart marble bathrooms. Dine from an accessible menu in the barrel-ceilinged bar.

142 rooms – € 505/635 € 525/656 – €29 – 10 suites

Town plan: G3-e – *Upper Merrion St* ✉ *D2* – *01 603 0600*
– *www.merrionhotel.com*

Fitzwilliam

BUSINESS • MODERN Stylish, modern hotel set around an impressive roof garden. Contemporary bedrooms display striking bold colours and good facilities; most overlook the roof garden and the best have views over St Stephen's Green. The bright first floor brasserie offers original Mediterranean-influenced menus.

139 rooms – € 200/495 € 220/509 – €22 – 3 suites

Town plan: F3-d – *St Stephen's Grn* ✉ *D2* – *01 478 7000*
– *www.fitzwilliamhotel.com*

Number 31

TOWNHOUSE • DESIGN A very quirky, individual property: it's classically styled around the 1960s and features a striking sunken lounge. Most of the stylish bedrooms are found in the Georgian house across the terraced garden.

21 rooms – € 120/220 € 160/300

Town plan: C3-c – *31 Leeson Cl.* ✉ *D2* – *01 676 5011* – *www.number31.ie*

at Ballsbridge

Chop House

MEATS AND GRILLS • PUB Imposing pub close to the stadium, with a small side terrace, a dark bar and a bright, airy conservatory. The relaxed lunchtime menu is followed by more ambitious dishes in the evening, when the kitchen really comes into its own.

Menu € 35 – Carte € 31/55

Town plan: D3-x – *2 Shelbourne Rd* ✉ *D4* – *01 660 2390*
– *www.thechophouse.ie* – *Closed Saturday lunch*

Old Spot

TRADITIONAL CUISINE • PUB The appealing bar has a stencilled maple-wood floor and a great selection of snacks and bottled craft beers, while the relaxed, characterful restaurant filled with vintage posters serves pub classics with a modern edge.

Menu € 22 (weekdays)/45 – Carte € 28/55

Town plan: D2-s – *14 Bath Ave* ✉ *D4* – *01 660 5599* – *www.theoldspot.ie*
– *Closed 25-26 December and Good Friday*

InterContinental Dublin

LUXURY • CLASSIC Imposing hotel bordering the RDS Arena. Elegant guest areas, state-of-the-art meeting rooms and impressive ballrooms boast ornate décor, antique furnishings and Irish artwork. Spacious, classical bedrooms have marble bathrooms and plenty of extras. A wide-ranging menu is served in the bright, airy restaurant.

197 rooms – † € 285/550 †† € 285/550 – ☕ €28 – 58 suites

Town plan: D3-h – *Simmonscourt Rd. ✉ D4 – ✆ 01 665 4000 – www.intercontinental.com/dublin*

Dylan

TOWNHOUSE • DESIGN An old Victorian nurses' home with a sympathetically styled extension and a funky, boutique interior. Tasteful, individually decorated bedrooms offer a host of extras; those in the original building are the most spacious. The stylish restaurant offers a menu of modern Mediterranean dishes and comes complete with a zinc-topped bar and a smartly furnished terrace.

44 rooms ☕ – † € 250/450 †† € 350/550

Town plan: C3-a – *Eastmoreland Pl ✉ D4 – ✆ 01 660 3000 – www.dylan.ie*

Ariel House

TOWNHOUSE • CLASSIC Close to the Aviva Stadium and a DART station; a personally run Victorian townhouse with comfy guest areas and antique furnishings. Warmly decorated bedrooms have modern facilities and smart bathrooms – some feature four-posters.

37 rooms ☕ – † € 99/250 †† € 99/290

Town plan: D3-n – *50-54 Lansdowne Rd ✉ D4 – ✆ 01 668 5512 – www.ariel-house.net – Closed 22 December-4 January*

Pembroke Townhouse

TOWNHOUSE • CLASSIC Friendly, traditionally styled hotel set in 3 Georgian houses. Small lounge with honesty bar and pantry. Sunny breakfast room offering homemade bread, cakes and biscuits. Variously sized, neutrally hued bedrooms; go for a duplex room.

48 rooms – † € 99/350 †† € 99/375 – ☕ €15

Town plan: C3-d – *88 Pembroke Rd ✉ D4 – ✆ 01 660 0277 – www.pembroketownhouse.ie – Closed 2 weeks Christmas-New Year*

at Donnybrook

Mulberry Garden

MODERN CUISINE • COSY XX Delightful restaurant hidden away in the city suburbs; its interesting L-shaped dining room set around a small courtyard terrace. Choice of two dishes per course on the weekly menu; original modern cooking relies on tasty local produce.

Menu € 49

Town plan: C3-g – *Mulberry Ln ✉ D4 – off Donnybrook Rd – ✆ 01 269 3300 (booking essential) – www.mulberrygarden.ie – dinner only – Closed Sunday-Wednesday*

at Ranelagh

Forest & Marcy (N)

MODERN CUISINE • FASHIONABLE X There's a lively buzz to this lovely little wine kitchen with high-level seating. Precisely prepared, original dishes burst with flavour; many are prepared at the counter and the chefs themselves often present and explain what's on the plate. All of the carefully chosen wines are available by the glass.

Menu € 45 – Carte € 36/48

Town plan: C3-a – *126 Leeson St Upper ✉ D4 – ✆ 01 660 2480 (booking essential) – www.forestandmarcy.ie – dinner only and lunch Friday-Saturday – Closed 24 December-10 January, 22 August-5 September and Monday-Tuesday*

Brioche

MODERN CUISINE • CHIC A lovely bistro with an open kitchen, in the buzzy, village-like Ranelagh district. Attractive, modern dishes use top Irish ingredients and many have playful touches. Pleasingly, brioche is served at the start of every meal.

Menu € 38 (weekday dinner) – Carte € 39/61

Town plan: C3-x – *51 Elmwood Ave Lower ✉ D6 – ✆ 01 497 9163 – www.brioche.ie – Closed 25-27 December, 1 January, Sunday dinner, Monday and Tuesday*

Forest Avenue

MODERN CUISINE • NEIGHBOURHOOD This rustic neighbourhood restaurant is named after a street in Queens and has a fitting 'NY' vibe. Elaborately presented tasting plates are full of originality and each dish combines many different flavours.

Menu € 32 (weekday lunch)/60

Town plan: C3-t – *8 Sussex Terr. ✉ D4 – ✆ 01 667 8337 (booking essential) – www.forestavenuerestaurant.ie – Closed last 2 weeks August, 25 December-10 January, 11-16 April, Sunday-Tuesday and lunch Wednesday*

at Rathmines

Zen Sichuan

CHINESE • ELEGANT Long-standing family-run restaurant, unusually set in an old church hall. At the centre of the elegant interior is a huge sun embellished with gold leaf. Imaginative Chinese cooking centres around Cantonese and spicy Sichuan cuisine.

Menu € 28 – Carte € 18/35

Town plan: C3-z – *89 Upper Rathmines Rd ✉ D6 – ✆ 01 497 9428 – www.zensichuan.com – dinner only and Friday lunch – Closed 25-27 December*

at Terenure

Craft (N)

MODERN CUISINE • NEIGHBOURHOOD A busy southern suburb plays host to this neighbourhood bistro. Concise menus evolve with seasonal availability and the lunch and early evening menus really are a steal. Dishes are modern and creative with vibrant colours and fresh, natural flavours. Sweet service from a local team completes the experience.

Menu € 27 (early dinner) – Carte € 24/45

Town plan: B3-t – *208 Harold's Cross Rd ✉ D6W – ✆ 01 497 8632 – www.craftrestaurant.ie – dinner only and lunch Friday-Sunday – Closed 1 week Christmas-New Year, Sunday dinner, Monday and Tuesday*

at Clontarf Northeast: 5.5 km by R 105 ✉ Dublin

Pigeon House

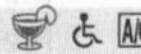

MODERN CUISINE • NEIGHBOURHOOD Slickly run neighbourhood bistro that's open for breakfast, lunch and dinner. It's just off the coast road in an up-and-coming area and has a lovely front terrace and a lively feel. Cooking is modern and assured. The bar counter is laden with freshly baked goodies and dishes are full of flavour.

Menu € 27 (dinner) – Carte € 30/47

11b Vernon Ave ✉ D3 – East : 1km by Clontarf Rd on Vernon Ave (R808) – ✆ 01 805 7567 – www.pigeonhouse.ie – Closed 25-26 December

Fishbone (N)

SEAFOOD • NEIGHBOURHOOD A friendly little restaurant opposite the Bull Bridge, with a cocktail bar at its centre and a glass-enclosed kitchen to the rear. Prime seafood from the plancha and charcoal grill is accompanied by tasty house sauces.

Menu € 18 (weekday lunch)/38 – Carte € 29/57

324 Clontarf Rd ✉ D3 – East : 1.5 km on Clontarf Rd – ✆ 01 536 9066 – www.fishbone.ie – Closed 25-26 December

Clontarf Castle

BUSINESS • HISTORIC A historic castle dating back to 1172, with sympathetic Victorian extensions; well-located in a quiet residential area close to the city. Contemporary bedrooms are decorated with bold, warm colours and many have four-poster beds. The restaurant offers local meats and seafood in a medieval ambience.

111 rooms – € 200/400 € 220/420

Town plan: D1-a – *Castle Ave. ✉ D3 – ✆ 01 833 2321 – www.clontarfcastle.ie*

at Blackrock Southeast : 7.5 km by R 118

Heron & Grey (Damien Grey)

MODERN CUISINE • FRIENDLY X A homely, candlelit restaurant in a bohemian suburban market; it's personally run by Heron – who leads the service – and Grey, who heads the kitchen. Irish ingredients feature in intensely flavoured dishes which are full of contrasting textures and tastes. The set 5 course dinner menu changes every 2 weeks.

→ Langoustine with seawater and fennel. Dashi, scallop and pak choi. Yuzu with nasturtium and amaretto.

Menu € 63 – tasting menu only

Blackrock Market, 19a Main St – ✆ 01 212 3676 (booking essential) – www.heronandgrey.com – dinner only and Sunday lunch – Closed 2 weeks late August, 2 weeks Christmas-New Year and Sunday dinner-Wednesday

at Foxrock Southeast : 13 km by N 11 ✉ Dublin

Bistro One

TRADITIONAL CUISINE • NEIGHBOURHOOD XX Long-standing neighbourhood bistro above a parade of shops; run by a father-daughter team and a real hit with the locals. Good value daily menus list a range of Irish and Italian dishes. They produce their own Tuscan olive oil.

Menu € 29 (weekdays) – Carte € 27/57

3 Brighton Rd ✉ D18 – ✆ 01 289 7711 (booking essential) – www.bistro-one.ie – Closed 25 December-3 January, 3 April, Sunday and Monday

at Dundrum South : 7.5 km by R 117 ✉ Dublin

Ananda

INDIAN • EXOTIC DÉCOR XX Its name means 'bliss' and it's a welcome escape from the bustle of the shopping centre. The stylish interior encompasses a smart cocktail bar, attractive fretwork and vibrant art. Accomplished Indian cooking is modern and original.

Menu € 20/28 – Carte € 33/67

Sandyford Rd, Dundrum Town Centre ✉ D14 – ✆ 01 296 0099 – www.anandarestaurant.ie – dinner only and lunch Friday-Sunday

at Sandyford South : 10 km by R 117 off R 825✉ Dublin

China Sichuan

CHINESE • FASHIONABLE XX A smart interior is well-matched by creative menus, where Irish produce features in tasty Cantonese classics and some Sichuan specialities. It was established in 1979 and is now run by the third generation of the family.

Menu € 16 (weekday lunch) – Carte € 26/57

The Forum, Ballymoss Rd. ✉ D18 – ✆ 01 293 5100 – www.china-sichuan.ie – Closed 25-27 December, Good Friday, lunch Saturday and bank holidays

DUNCANNON DÚN CANANN

Wexford – Pop. 328 – Regional map n° **22**-D2

Aldridge Lodge

COUNTRY • FRIENDLY XX This attractive house is set in a great rural location and run by cheery owners. The constantly evolving menu offers tasty home-made bread and veg from the kitchen garden. The focus is on good value fish and shellfish (the owner's father is a local fisherman), with some Asian and fusion influences. Homely bedrooms come with hot water bottles and home-baked cookies.

Menu € 35/40 **s**

3 rooms - € 45/55 € 90/110

South : 2 km on Hook Head rd
- ✆ 051 389 116 (booking essential) - www.aldridgelodge.com
- dinner only - Closed 3 weeks January, 24-28 December, Monday and Tuesday

DUNDALK DÚN DEALGAN

Louth - Pop. 31 149 - Regional map n° **21**-D2

Rosemount

FAMILY • COSY An attractive dormer bungalow fronted by a delightful flower-filled garden. The welcoming owners serve tea and cake on arrival and a freshly cooked breakfast the next morning. The lounge is warmly decorated and the individually styled, spotlessly kept bedrooms feature fine fabrics and modern facilities.

12 rooms - € 50/55 € 75/80

Dublin Rd - South : 2.5 km on R 132
- ✆ 042 933 5878 - www.rosemountireland.com
- Closed 22-27 December

at Jenkinstown Northeast: 9 km by N52 on R173

Fitzpatricks

TRADITIONAL CUISINE • PUB A hugely characterful pub on the coast road, at the foot of the mountains, featuring beautiful flower displays and a wealth of memorabilia. Extensive menus list hearty, flavoursome dishes; specialities include local steaks and seafood.

Menu € 35 - Carte € 30/45

Rockmarshall - Southeast : 1 km
- ✆ 042 937 6193 - www.fitzpatricks-restaurant.com
- Closed 25 December

DUNDRUM DÚN DROMA - Dún Laoghaire-Rathdown → See Dublin

DUNFANAGHY DÚN FIONNACHAIDH

Donegal - ✉ Letterkenny - Pop. 312 - Regional map n° **21**-C1

Mill

TRADITIONAL CUISINE • FRIENDLY XX Converted flax mill on the waterside, with lovely garden edged by reeds and great view of Mount Muckish. Homely inner with conservatory lounge and knick-knacks on display throughout. Antique-furnished dining room has a classical Georgian feel. Traditional menus showcase seasonal ingredients and fish features highly. Cosy, welcoming bedrooms come in individual designs.

Menu € 40

7 rooms - € 70/110 € 100/150

Southwest :0.75 km on N 56
- ✆ 074 913 6985 - www.themillrestaurant.com
- dinner only - Closed December-mid March

DUNGARVAN DÚN GARBHÁN

Waterford – Pop. 7 991 – Regional map n° **22**-C3

Tannery

MODERN CUISINE • FRIENDLY XX Characterful 19C stone tannery, close to the harbour; they also run the cookery school here. Have small plates at the counter or head upstairs to the bright restaurant. Attractively presented, classically based dishes use good seasonal ingredients. Stylish bedrooms are in a nearby townhouse.

Menu € 33 (weekdays) – Carte € 39/55

14 rooms – € 65/80 € 105/140

10 Quay St – via Parnell St – 058 45420 – www.tannery.ie – dinner only and lunch Friday and Sunday – Closed last 2 weeks January, 25-26 December, Sunday dinner except July-August, Monday and Good Friday

DUNKINEELY DÚN CIONNAOLA

Donegal – Pop. 375 – Regional map n° **21**-C1

Castle Murray House

TRADITIONAL • COSY This extended former farmhouse is perched on a hillside and affords lovely bay and mountain views. The small knick-knack filled bar and flag-floored lounge have a traditional feel. Bedrooms are contrastingly modern and stylish – those to the front share the view; go for the one with the huge roof terrace.

10 rooms – € 120/150 € 120/160

St John's Point – Southwest : 1.5 km by N 56 on St John's Point rd – 074 973 7022 – www.castlemurray.com – Closed December-February

DUN LAOGHAIRE DÚN LAOGHAIRE

Dún Laoghaire-Rathdown – Pop. 23 857 – Regional map n° **22**-D1

Rasam

INDIAN • EXOTIC DÉCOR XX The scent of roses greets you as you head up to the surprisingly plush lounge and contemporary restaurant. Fresh, authentic dishes come in original combinations – they dry roast and blend their own spices.

Menu € 24 (weekdays) – Carte € 32/53

18-19 Glasthule Rd, 1st Floor (above Eagle House pub) – 01 230 0600 – www.rasam.ie – dinner only – Closed 25-26 December and Good Friday

Cavistons

SEAFOOD • BISTRO X A landmark restaurant in town, where guests come for fresh, carefully cooked fish and shellfish brought in by the local boats – go for the scallops or lobster when they're in season. Plans are afoot to move to larger premises.

Menu € 21 – Carte € 28/52

58-59 Glasthule Rd – 01 280 9245 (booking essential) – www.cavistons.com – lunch only and dinner Thursday-Saturday – Closed Sunday and Monday

DURRUS DÚRAS

Cork – Pop. 334 – Regional map n° **22**-A3

Blairscove House

MODERN CUISINE • ELEGANT XX Charming 18C barn and hayloft, just a stone's throw from the sea, with fantastic panoramic views, pretty gardens, a courtyard and a lily pond. Stylish bar and stone-walled, candlelit dining room. Starters and desserts are in buffet format, while the seasonal main courses are cooked on a wood-fired chargrill. Luxurious, modern bedrooms are dotted about the place.

Menu € 60 **s**

4 rooms – € 220/260 € 220/260

Southwest : 1.5 km on R 591 – 027 61127 (booking essential) – www.blairscove.ie – dinner only – Closed 4 November-15 March, Sunday and Monday

Gallán Mór

COUNTRY HOUSE · PERSONALISED Proudly run guesthouse named after the 3,500 year old standing stone in its garden; set in a lovely rural location overlooking Dunmanus Bay and Mizen Head. Bedrooms have warm fabrics, good facilities and handmade wooden beds. The delightful owners welcome you with homemade cake beside the wood-burning stove.

4 rooms – € 75/100 € 110/130

Kealties – West : 5.5 km. on Ahakista rd – 027 62732 – www.gallanmor.com – Closed October-March. Minimum 2 nights stay.

ENNIS INIS

Clare – Pop. 24 253 – Regional map n° **22**-B2

The Cloister

MODERN BRITISH · HISTORIC XX Set in the medieval quarter of a historic town and once part of a 13C friary, this restaurant's combination of classic architecture and modern-day bling is an impressive sight. Traditional dishes have subtle modern overtones.

Menu € 25 (dinner) – Carte € 28/51

Abbey St – 065 686 8198 – www.cloister.ie – Closed 25 December, Good Friday and Monday

ENNISCORTHY INIS CÓRTHAIDH

Wexford – Pop. 2 842 – Regional map n° **22**-D2

Monart

SPA AND WELLNESS · GRAND LUXURY Comprehensively equipped destination spa in 100 acres of beautifully landscaped grounds; a haven of peace and tranquility. The Georgian house with its contemporary glass extension houses spacious, stylish bedrooms with a terrace or balcony. The Restaurant serves light, modern dishes; the minimalistic Garden Lounge offers global dishes in a more informal environment.

70 rooms – € 169/595 € 258/595 – 2 suites

The Still – Northwest : 4.75 km by N 30 on L 6124 – 053 923 8999 – www.monart.ie – Closed 11-27 December

ENNISKERRY ÁTH AN SCEIRE

Wicklow – Pop. 1 811 – Regional map n° **22**-D1

Powerscourt

GRAND LUXURY · CLASSIC Impressive curved building overlooking Sugar Loaf Mountain, featuring stylish guest areas, luxurious bedrooms, state-of-the-art conference facilities and a superb spa; outdoor activities include archery and falconry. Sika offers modern, formal dining, while the plush lounge-bar serves a concise menu of classics. McGills is a traditional Irish pub with a menu to match.

194 rooms – € 185 € 200 – 92 suites

Powerscourt Estate – West : 1.5 km by Powerscourt rd – 01 274 8888 – www.powerscourthotel.com

FANORE

Clare – Regional map n° **22**-B1

Vasco

MODERN CUISINE · SIMPLE X Remotely set restaurant opposite the seashore, with a minimalist interior and a glass-screened terrace. The keen owners collect the latest produce on their drive in; the daily menu ranges from sandwiches and cake to soup and light dishes.

Carte € 26/46

Craggagh – West : 1 km on R 477 – 065 707 6020 – www.vasco.ie – Closed October-mid March, Sunday-Monday and dinner Tuesday-Wednesday

FENNOR FIONNÚIR

Waterford – Regional map n° **22**-C2

Copper Hen

TRADITIONAL CUISINE • RUSTIC A likeable little restaurant located above a pub, with rustic décor and a brightly coloured fireplace; set on the coast road from Tramore to Dungarvan. Keenly priced menus offer fresh, hearty, unfussy classics and service is enthusiastic and efficient. The owners raise their own pigs.

Menu € 27

Mother McHugh's Pub – ✆ 051 330 300 – www.thecopperhen.ie – dinner only and Sunday lunch – Closed 2 weeks September, 1 week January, 25-26 December, Sunday dinner, Monday and Tuesday

FOTA ISLAND OILEÁN FHÓTA

Cork – Regional map n° **22**-B3

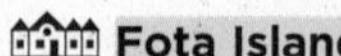

Fota Island

LUXURY • DESIGN A resort hotel set within Ireland's only wildlife park. Extensive business and leisure facilities include a golf course and a state-of-the-art spa. Bedrooms are spacious and well-appointed, and most have island views. The stylish restaurant offers modern takes on classical dishes.

131 rooms – € 120/250 € 135/265 – 8 suites

– ✆ 021 488 3700 – www.fotaisland.ie – Closed 25 December

FOXROCK CARRAIG AN TSIONNAIGH – Dún Laoghaire-Rathdown

→ See Dublin

Michelin

GOOD TIPS!

When you think Galway, you think music. An effervescent spirit and a non-conformist attitude helped to put music at the heart of the city. A need to do their own thing is also adopted by the city's restaurants which are an eclectic bunch, from the ground-breaking **Loam** to rustic tapas bar, **Cava Bodega**, and elegant Japanese restaurant, **Raw**.

GALWAY GAILLIMH

Galway - Pop. 75 529 - Regional map n° **21**-B3

Restaurants

✿ **Loam** (Enda McEvoy)

CREATIVE • **MINIMALIST** XX A large basement with industrial styling; the focus here is on the quality of the ingredients, which grow in the fertile local loam. The talented chef understands his craft and produces modern, understated dishes with pure flavours. Choose from the 2-3 course fixed price menu or the 7 course tasting menu.

➜ Mackerel with radish and golden beetroot. Lamb with turnip and ramson. Chanterelle and hazelnut.

Menu € 40/70

Geata na Cathrach, Fairgreen Rd - Northeast : 2 km by R 336 - ✆ 091 569 727 - www.loamgalway.com - dinner only - Closed Sunday and Monday

✿ **Aniar** (JP McMahon)

CREATIVE • **SIMPLE** X Both the room and the cooking have a back-to-nature ethos. Aniar means 'From the West' and this is where most of the produce comes from: the 3 set menus are only confirmed once all of the day's ingredients have arrived. Contrasts in texture and temperature play their part in delicate, Scandic-style dishes.

➜ Oyster with cucumber and arrowgrass. Monkfish with sea strawberry, woodruff and malt. Sorrel and buttermilk.

Menu € 55/110 - tasting menu only

Town plan: A2-a - *53 Lower Dominick St - ✆ 091 535 947 (booking essential) - www.aniarrestaurant.ie - dinner only - Closed 25-26 December and Sunday-Tuesday*

Kai

MEDITERRANEAN CUISINE • **NEIGHBOURHOOD** X A laid-back eatery with a gloriously cluttered interior and a bohemian feel; the owners run it with real passion. Morning cakes morph into fresh, simple lunches and are followed by afternoon tea and tasty dinners. Concise menus list fresh, vibrant dishes and produce is organic, free range and traceable.

Carte € 34/42

Town plan: A2-x - *22 Sea Rd- ✆ 091 526 003 (booking essential) - www.kaicaferestaurant.com - Closed Sunday-Monday in winter and bank holidays*

GALWAY

N 59, CLIFDEN
N 84, CASTELBAR
N 17, SLIGO
LEENANE
R 336, BARNA, SALTHILL
ARAN ISLANDS

Salmon Weir Bridge
Catholic Cathedral
FRANCISCAN FRIARY
Eyre Square Kennedy Park
Bank of Ireland Building
CORRIB SHOPPING CENTER
Lynch's Castle
St Nicholas
IRISH THEATRE
EYRE CENTRE
O'Brien Bridge
DRUID THEATRE
COMMERCIAL DOCK
DUN AENGUS DOCK
Spanish Arch
Galway City Museum
CLADDAGH
GALWAY BAY
SOUTH PARK
Nimmo's Pier

0 — 100 m
0 — 100 yards

Raw

JAPANESE • INTIMATE XX An elegant, modern restaurant on the 4th floor of a smart hotel. As its name suggests, almost everything is raw. Most dishes are fish-based and they specialise in sushi and sashimi to order. The 'tuna tataki' is particularly tasty.

Menu € 40 – Carte € 30/54

Radisson Blu Hotel and Spa, Lough Atalia Rd – Northeast : 2 km by R 336 – ✆ 091 538 212 (booking essential) – www.sushiinthesky.ie – dinner only – Closed 24-26 December, Sunday and Monday

Prices quoted after the symbol 🚹 refer to the lowest rate for a single room in low season, followed by the highest rate in high season. The same principle applies to the symbol 🚹🚹 for a double room.

Seafood Bar @ Kirwan's

SEAFOOD • BRASSERIE XX Well-regarded, long-standing restaurant with a large terrace, in an old medieval lane. Lively brasserie atmosphere, with dining on two levels. Modern menus have a classical base; most dishes consist of tasty seafood – go for the specials.

Carte € 30/57

Town plan: B2-s – *Kirwan's Ln*
– ✆ 091 568 266 – www.kirwanslane.com
– Closed 25-26 December and Sunday lunch

Vina Mara

MODERN CUISINE • BISTRO XX Bistro-style restaurant in the heart of the city, with a rich Mediterranean colour scheme. Modern Irish cooking has a fresh style, clearly defined flavours and relies on quality local ingredients; vegetarians are also well-catered for.

Carte € 31/53

Town plan: B2-n – *19 Middle St*
– ✆ 091 561 610 – www.vinamara.com
– Closed 25-27 December and Sunday

Ard Bia at Nimmos

MEDITERRANEAN CUISINE • COSY X Pleasingly cluttered, atmospheric riverside restaurant, where tables occupy every space; it's open all day but it's at night that it really comes alive. Sourcing is paramount and dishes take their influences from across the Med.

Carte € 35/50

Town plan: B2-u – *Spanish Arch*
– ✆ 091 561 114 (booking essential at dinner) – www.ardbia.com
– Closed 24-28 December

Cava Bodega

SPANISH • TAPAS BAR X This split-level tapas bar – with its reclaimed wood tables – has a rustic, neighbourhood feel; sit downstairs to watch the chefs in the open kitchen. It's all about sharing: choose around 3 dishes each and a Spanish beer or wine.

Carte € 18/34

Town plan: B2-b – *1 Middle St*
– ✆ 091 539 884 – www.cavarestaurant.ie – dinner only and lunch Saturday-Sunday – Closed 25-26 December

Il Vicolo N

ITALIAN • BISTRO X Start with an aperitif on the riverside terrace before dining in the characterful cellars of this old mill, whose exposed stone walls provide the perfect backdrop for the rustic cuisine. Cicchetti makes up the core of the menu.

Carte € 29/51

Town plan: A2-v – *The Bridgemills, O'Brien's Bridge*
– ✆ 091 530 515 – www.ilvicolo.ie – dinner only and lunch Saturday-Sunday
– Closed 25-26 December and Monday September-April

Le Petit Pois

FRENCH • FAMILY X Whitewashed walls are offset by brightly coloured lights and a dresser bursting with produce. Equally colourful French dishes showcase Irish produce and are packed with flavour; at dinner try the tasting menu with matching wines.

Menu € 40/60 – Carte € 35/49

Town plan: B1-c – *Victoria Pl – ✆ 091 330 880 – www.lepetitpois.ie*
– dinner only – Closed Sunday and Monday

Oscar's Seafood Bistro

SEAFOOD • INTIMATE A long-standing bistro in a bohemian part of the city. Striking red banquettes line the walls and it has an intimate feel. The chef has a passion for seafood and his menus mix classic recipes with his own creations.

Menu € 19 (weekday dinner) - Carte € 27/54

Town plan: A2-s - *Dominick St - 091 582 180 - www.oscarsbistro.ie - dinner only - Closed 1-16 January and Sunday except bank holidays*

Hotels

Radisson Blu H. & Spa

BUSINESS • MODERN Corporate hotel overlooking a lough, with a striking atrium, vast meeting facilities and a spa with a thermal suite and salt cave. Bedrooms are spacious and modern - the 5th floor rooms have balconies and share a business lounge. Marina's offers international dishes; Raw serves sushi and raw meats.

261 rooms - € 145/450 € 155/450 - 4 suites

Lough Atalia Rd - Northeast : 2 km by R 336 - 091 538 300 - www.radissonhotelgalway.com

Raw - See restaurant listing

G

LUXURY • DESIGN A smart design hotel on a small retail park, with distant views of the bay and mountains from the striking atrium's oversized window. Vibrantly coloured guest areas include blue and pink lounges and a seductive purple restaurant. Spacious bedrooms are more calming, as is the impressive thermal spa.

101 rooms - € 150/370 € 160/380 - 2 suites

Wellpark, Dublin Rd - Northeast : 3 km by R 336 and R 338 - 091 865 200 - www.theghotel.ie - Closed 23-26 December

The House

TOWNHOUSE • DESIGN This unassuming hotel sits in a great central spot, close to the Spanish Arch and the Latin Quarter. Both the guest areas and the bedrooms are decorated in stylish, eye-catching colour schemes; for a quieter stay ask for a room on a higher floor. The laid-back restaurant offers a small menu of classics.

40 rooms - € 89/225 € 99/380 - 1 suite

Town plan: B2-e - *Lower Merchants Rd - 091 538 900 - www.thehousehotel.ie - Closed 25-26 December*

Ardawn House

TRADITIONAL • COSY Set by the stadium, with the city just a stroll away. A small lounge leads to a breakfast room laid with silver-plated cutlery and bedrooms are clean and fresh with modern fabrics. The owners are friendly and helpful.

8 rooms - € 60/180 € 90/200

College Rd. - Northeast : 2.25 km. by R 336 on R 339 - 091 568 833 - www.ardawnhouse.com - Closed 15-27 December

GARRYKENNEDY

North Tipperary - Regional map n° **22**-C2

Larkins

TRADITIONAL CUISINE • PUB Thatched pub in a charming loughside location. The traditional interior boasts original fireplaces and old flag and timber floors - and plays host to folk music and Irish dancers. Unfussy dishes feature plenty of fresh seafood.

Carte € 26/42

- 067 23232 - www.larkins.ie - Closed 25 December, Good Friday, Monday-Tuesday and Wednesday-Friday lunch November-April

GLASLOUGH GLASLOCH

Monaghan - ✉ Monaghan - Regional map n° **21**-D2

Castle Leslie

HISTORIC BUILDING • HISTORIC Impressive castle set in 1,000 acres of parkland: home to the 4th generation of the Leslie family. Ornate, comfortable, antique-furnished guest areas and traditional, country house style bedrooms. Dine in Snaffles restaurant in the grounds.

20 rooms - € 190/370 € 210/390

Castle Leslie Estate - 047 88100 - www.castleleslie.com - Closed 22-27 December

Lodge at Castle Leslie Estate

HISTORIC • CONTEMPORARY An extended hunting lodge to the main castle, with contrastingly stylish bedrooms. Unwind in the Victorian treatment room or charming open-fired bar - or hire an estate horse from the excellent equestrian centre and explore the 1,000 acre grounds. The mezzanine restaurant offers modern Mediterranean fare.

29 rooms - € 160/180 € 180/200 - 1 suite

- 047 88100 - www.castleleslie.com

GLASSON - Westmeath ➜ See Athlone

GOLEEN AN GÓILÍN

Cork - Regional map n° **22**-A3

Heron's Cove

TRADITIONAL • PERSONALISED Long-standing guesthouse hidden away in a pretty location, with views over a tiny harbour. Bedrooms are tidy and pleasantly furnished: all overlook the waterfront and most have a balcony - if you're lucky you might see herons at the water's edge. The busy restaurant offers seasonal menus of local produce.

5 rooms - € 60/90 € 80/150

The Harbour - 028 35225 - www.heronscove.com - Closed Christmas-New Year and restricted opening in winter

GOREY GUAIRE

Wexford - Pop. 3 463 - Regional map n° **22**-D2

The Duck

REGIONAL CUISINE • FRIENDLY The Duck is a smart, rustic bistro which sits within the grounds of a grand country house, next to a superb kitchen garden which informs its menu. Sit on the wonderful terrace with a glass of wine and dine on unfussy, global cuisine.

Carte € 30/59

Marlfield House Hotel, Courtown Rd - Southeast : 1.5 km on R 742 - 053 942 1124 - www.marlfiledhouse.ie - Closed 3-16 January and Monday-Tuesday October-April except Christmas

Marlfield House

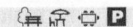

COUNTRY HOUSE • ELEGANT Well-appointed, period-style bedrooms look out over the large grounds of this attractive Regency house. Various sitting and drawing rooms have a homely, classical feel and all are packed with antiques, oil paintings and curios. Have afternoon tea in the garden while watching the peacocks wander by, then dine in the conservatory restaurant or the terrace café and bar.

19 rooms - € 105/125 € 250/670

Courtown Rd - Southeast : 1.5 km on R 742 - 053 942 1124 - www.marlfieldhouse.com - Closed 3-16 January and Monday-Tuesday October-April

The Duck - See restaurant listing

GREYSTONES NA CLOCHA LIATHA

Wicklow – Pop. 10 173 – Regional map n° **22**-D1

Chakra by Jaipur

INDIAN • EXOTIC DÉCOR XX An elegant, intimate restaurant with bold décor, unusually set within a shopping centre. Interesting dishes represent the country from north to south. Spicing is delicate, flavours are refined and desserts are a highlight.

Menu € 24/30 – Carte € 29/52

Meridian Point Centre (1st floor), Church Rd – 01 201 7222 – www.jaipur.ie – dinner only and Sunday lunch – Closed 25 December

theatre lane (N)

MODERN CUISINE • BISTRO X A relaxed, bijoux, bistro-cum-brasserie tucked away above the theatre. Simple lunches are centred around free range rotisserie chicken. Dinner really steps things up a gear, with a concise menu of unfussy modern dishes.

Menu € 33 (dinner) – Carte lunch € 23/26

Theatre Ln. Hillside Rd – 01 255 7294 (booking essential at dinner) – www.theatrelane.com – Closed 25-26 December, Monday-Wednesday, Thursday lunch and Sunday dinner

HAROLD'S CROSS ➜ See Dublin

INISHEER ➜ See Aran Islands

INISHMAAN INIS MEÁIN - Galway ➜ See Aran Islands

INISHMORE ÁRAINN - Galway ➜ See Aran Islands

JENKINSTOWN BAILE SHEINICÍN - Louth ➜ See Dundalk

KANTURK CEANN TOIRC

Cork – Pop. 2 263 – Regional map n° **22**-B2

Glenlohane

HISTORIC • CLASSIC A Georgian country house set in 260 acres – it has been in the family for over 250 years. Traditional interior hung with portraits and paintings. Colour-themed bedrooms; 'Blue' has an antique four-poster and bathtub. Cosy library and drawing room. Open-fired dining room for home-cooked communal dinners.

3 rooms – € 120 € 220

Southeast : 4 km. by R 576 (Mallow rd) and R 580 on L1043 – 029 50014 – www.glenlohane.com

KENMARE NEIDÍN

Kerry – Pop. 2 175 – Regional map n° **22**-A3

Park

CLASSIC CUISINE • ELEGANT XXX Start with canapés in the lounge then move on to the elegant dining room of this luxurious hotel. Silver candelabras, cloches and gueridon trolleys all feature and service is top-notch. Classically based dishes have a modern touch and local ingredients are kept to the fore.

Menu € 70 – Carte € 42/75

Park Hotel, – 064 664 1200 (booking advisable) – www.parkkenmare.com – dinner only – Closed 2 January-16 February and 10-22 December

Lime Tree

CLASSIC CUISINE • RUSTIC XX A 19C property that's taken on many guises over the years. The characterful interior has exposed stone walls, an open fire and even its own art gallery. Flavoursome, classical dishes utilise quality local ingredients.

Menu € 45

Shelbourne St.
– ✆ 064 664 1225 – www.limetreerestaurant.com – dinner only – Closed January-March and weekdays October-December

Mulcahys

MODERN CUISINE • INTIMATE XX Come for cocktails and snacks in the bar or settle in for the evening in the intimate restaurant. Unfussy dishes utilise Irish ingredients, including local fish, which is used in the sushi. For dessert, try the tarte Tatin for two.

Carte € 29/50

Main St – ✆ 064 664 2383 – www.mulcahyskenmare.ie – dinner only – Closed 24-26 December, Tuesday and Monday and Wednesday October-April

Boathouse Bistro

SEAFOOD • BRASSERIE X Converted boathouse in the grounds of Dromquinna Manor; set on the waterside, overlooking the peninsula and mountains. It has a nautical, New England style and a laid-back vibe. Simple, appealing menus focus on seafood.

Carte € 27/64

Dromquinna – West : 4.75 km by N 71 on N 70
– ✆ 064 664 2889 (booking advisable) – www.dromquinnamanor.com – Closed December-mid-February, mid-week February, March & November and Monday-Wednesday in October

Mews N 

MODERN CUISINE • BISTRO X Owners Gary and Maria provide a warm welcome at this cosy, intimate, three-roomed restaurant. Many different ingredients combine to create colourful dishes with rich flavours. There's plenty of choice, including daily specials.

Menu € 30 (early dinner) – Carte € 30/50

Henry Ct, Henry St
– ✆ 064 664 2829 (booking essential) – www.themewskenmare.com – dinner only – Closed January-mid February and Sunday-Thursday November, December and March

Packie's

TRADITIONAL CUISINE • RUSTIC X Popular little restaurant in the town centre, with two rustic, bistro-style rooms, exposed stone walls, tiled floors and an interesting collection of modern Irish art. Cooking is honest, fresh and seasonal; the seafood specials are a hit.

Carte € 24/50

Henry St – ✆ 064 664 1508 (booking essential) – dinner only – Closed first 2 weeks February, Monday September-May and Sunday

Park

GRAND LUXURY • CLASSIC One of Ireland's most iconic country houses sits in the town centre and looks out over wonderful gardens to the bay and the hills. It's elegantly furnished, with a charming drawing room, a cosy cocktail lounge and tastefully styled bedrooms. The stylish spa adds a modern touch.

46 rooms – € 135/310 € 405/540

– ✆ 064 664 1200 – www.parkkenmare.com – Closed 2 January-16 February and 10-22 December

Park – See restaurant listing

Sheen Falls Lodge

LUXURY • PERSONALISED Modern hotel in an idyllic spot, where the waterfalls drop away into the bay. It has a welcoming wood-fired lobby, a lovely indoor swimming pool and well-appointed bedrooms overlooking the falls. Unusually, the restaurant serves a brasserie menu on the upper level and more refined dishes on the lower level.

68 rooms - € 165/400 € 195/430 - 11 suites

Southeast : 2 km. by N 71 - 064 664 1600 - www.sheenfallslodge.ie - Closed January

Brook Lane

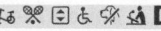

BUSINESS • MODERN Personally run hotel close to the town centre. Bedrooms range from 'Deluxe' to 'Luxury'; the latter have impressive fabric headboards and specially commissioned handmade furniture. The informal bar-bistro offers classic Irish and seafood dishes and hosts regular live music events.

21 rooms - € 75/120 € 110/200

Gortamullen - North : 1.5 km. by N 71 on N 70 - 064 664 2077 - www.brooklanehotel.com - Closed 23-27 December

Sallyport House

FAMILY • CLASSIC Unassuming 1930s house; its charming interior packed with antiques and Irish art. Pleasant lounge with local information. Breakfast is served from the characterful sideboard and features pancakes, stewed fruits and smoked salmon. Traditionally furnished bedrooms are immaculately kept and boast water views.

5 rooms - € 90/95 € 120/140

South : 0.5 km. on N 71 - 064 664 2066 - www.sallyporthouse.com - Closed November-March

KILCOLGAN CILL CHOLGÁIN

Galway - Oranmore - Regional map n° **21**-B3

Moran's Oyster Cottage

SEAFOOD • COSY An attractive thatched pub hidden away in a tiny hamlet - a very popular place come summer. It's all about straightforward cooking and good hospitality. Dishes are largely seafood based and oysters are the speciality.

Carte € 28/49

The Weir - Northwest : 2 km. by N 18 - 091 796 113 - www.moransoystercottage.com - Closed 24-26 December and Good Friday

KILCULLEN

Kildare - Pop. 3 473 - Regional map n° **22**-D1

Fallon's

TRADITIONAL BRITISH • FASHIONABLE You'll find plenty of happy locals in the snug, the modern dining room, the conservatory and, in the evening, the rustic, pastel-coloured bistro. Flavoursome dishes are generously proportioned; save room for a homemade dessert.

Carte € 27/51

Main St - 045 481 260 - www.fallonb.ie - Closed 25 December and Monday

KILDARE CILL DARA

Kildare - Pop. 8 142 - Regional map n° **22**-D1

Harte's

CLASSIC CUISINE • RUSTIC Have a local artisan beer in the snug open-fired bar or kick things off with a gin tasting board; then move on to tasty, well-prepared dishes with modern twists in the small restaurant with its large mirrors and exposed brick walls.

Menu € 26 (weekdays) - Carte € 28/42

Market Sq - 045 533 557 - www.harteskildare.ie - Closed Monday except bank holidays

KILKENNY CILL CHAINNIGH

Kilkenny - Pop. 24 423 - Regional map n° **22**-C2

Campagne (Garrett Byrne)

MODERN BRITISH · FASHIONABLE XX Stylish, relaxed restaurant with vibrant, contemporary art and smart booths, hidden close to the railway arches, away from the city centre. Modern cooking has a classic base, and familiar combinations are delivered with an assured touch. Popular early bird menu. Well-run, with friendly, efficient service.

→ Foie gras with pineapple chutney, moscatel jelly, candied walnuts and toasted brioche. Pithivier of Aylesbury duck with white turnip, cabbage and Madeira. Hot chocolate soufflé tart with Horlicks ice cream.

Menu € 34 (lunch and early dinner) **s** - Carte € 37/58 **s**

5 The Arches, Gashouse Ln - ✆ 056 777 2858 (booking advisable) - www.campagne.ie - dinner only and lunch Friday-Sunday - Closed 2 weeks January, 1 week July, Sunday dinner and Monday

Ristorante Rinuccini

ITALIAN · CLASSIC DÉCOR XXX Set in the basement of a townhouse and named after the 17C papal nuncio, this family-owned restaurant is well-known locally. Classic Italian cuisine with homemade ravioli a speciality. Some tables have views through to the wine cellar.

Menu € 29 (lunch and early dinner) - Carte € 31/50

1 The Parade - ✆ 056 776 1575 - www.rinuccini.com - Closed 26-27 December

Anocht

MODERN CUISINE · DESIGN XX Set above the Design Centre in an old 1760s grain store is this daytime café, which morphs into an intimate candlelit restaurant at night. Colourful, creative dishes are full of flavour; influences range from the Med to Asia.

Menu € 29 (early dinner) - Carte € 34/44

1st floor, Kilkenny Design Centre, Castle Yard - ✆ 056 772 2118 (booking advisable) - www.anochtrestaurant.ie - dinner only - Closed Monday-Wednesday, Sunday July-September and bank holidays

Zuni

MODERN BRITISH · BRASSERIE XX To the front is a small café and a continental-style bar; behind is a sleek, light-filled restaurant with leather panels dividing the tables. Eclectic modern menus rely on local ingredients and desserts are a highlight. Comfortable bedrooms are decorated in black and white.

Menu € 30 (early dinner) - Carte € 30/46

13 rooms - € 60/120 € 75/170

26 Patrick St - ✆ 056 772 3999 - www.zuni.ie - Closed 25-26 December

Foodworks

TRADITIONAL CUISINE · FRIENDLY X A former bank in the town centre: its bright, fresh look is a perfect match for the style of cooking. Unfussy dishes use top local produce, including fruit and veg from the experienced chef-owner's farm.

Menu € 23 (early dinner) - Carte € 25/46

7 Parliament St - ✆ 056 777 7696 - www.foodworks.ie - Closed 25-26 December and Sunday

Butler House

TOWNHOUSE · ELEGANT A welcoming Georgian townhouse in the city centre, with great views over the garden towards the impressive castle. Sizeable, simply furnished bedrooms have modern oak furnishings and a Scandic feel; ask for one to the rear.

13 rooms - € 80/175 € 120/195

15-16 Patrick St. - ✆ 056 776 5707 - www.butler.ie - Closed 23-29 December

Rosquil House

FAMILY • PERSONALISED Modern, purpose-built guesthouse on the main road out of the city. Leather-furnished lounge filled with books and local information; spacious, comfortable bedrooms and a smart, linen-laid breakfast room. Extensive buffet breakfasts with a cooked daily special; omelettes feature. Experienced, welcoming owners.

7 rooms – € 65/90 € 80/120

Castlecomer Rd – Northwest : 1 km – 056 772 1419 – www.rosquilhouse.com – Closed 3-27 January and 24-27 December

KILLARNEY CILL AIRNE

Kerry – Pop. 12 740 – Regional map n° **22**-A2

Panorama

MODERN CUISINE • FASHIONABLE XXX Large, formal restaurant set within a luxurious hotel. Panoramic windows afford superb views across the lough to the mountains. Creative modern menus follow the seasons and use the very best Irish produce.

Carte € 34/65

Europe Hotel, Fossa – West : 5.75 km. by Port Rd on N 72 – 064 667 1300 – www.theeurope.com – dinner only – Closed 9 December-January, Sunday dinner and restricted opening November, February and March

Park

TRADITIONAL CUISINE • ELEGANT XXX Elegant hotel restaurant with chandeliers, ornate cornicing and a pianist in summer. Classically based menus use some modern combinations; Irish meats are a feature and the tasting menu is a highlight.

Carte € 56/76 – bar lunch

Town plan: B1-k – *Killarney Park Hotel, – 064 663 5555 – www.killarneyparkhotel.ie – Closed 24-27 December*

Brasserie

INTERNATIONAL • BRASSERIE XX Set in a sumptuous lakeside hotel; a modern take on a classical brasserie, with water and mountain views – head for the terrace in warmer weather. The accessible all-day menu ranges from salads to steaks.

Carte € 34/53 **s**

Europe Hotel, Fossa – West : 5.75 km. by Port Rd on N 72 – 064 667 1300 (bookings not accepted) – www.theeurope.com – Closed 9 December-1 February

Europe

GRAND LUXURY • MODERN A superbly located resort boasting stunning views over the lough and mountains. It has impressive events facilities and a sublime three-level spa. Bedrooms are lavishly appointed; some overlook the water.

187 rooms – € 200/350 € 220/370 – 6 suites

Fossa – West : 5.75 km. by Port Rd on N 72 – 064 667 1300 – www.theeurope.com – Closed 9 December-1 February

Panorama • **Brasserie** – See restaurant listing

Aghadoe Heights H. and Spa

LUXURY • DESIGN An unassuming hotel with stunning views over the lakes, mountains and countryside. It boasts an impressive spa and a stylish cocktail bar which comes complete with an evening pianist. Bedrooms are spacious and many have balconies or terraces. The split-level restaurant makes the most of the views.

74 rooms – € 105/280 € 180/310

Northwest : 4.5 km. by N 22 off L 2109 – 064 663 1766 – www.aghadoeheights.com – Closed 24-26 December and weekdays November-April

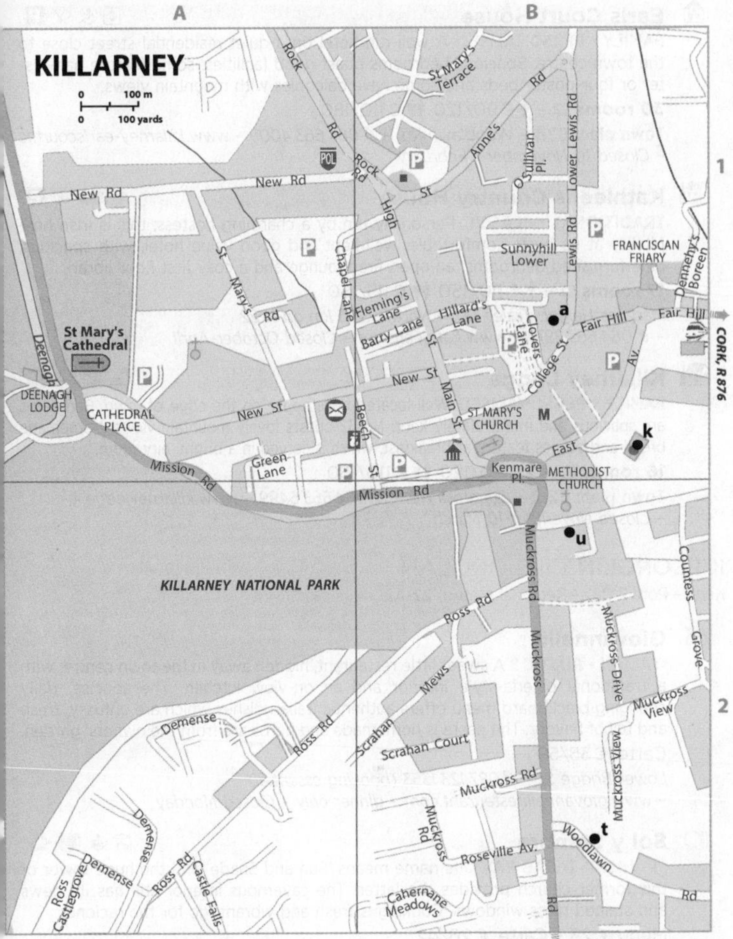

Killarney Park

LUXURY • CLASSIC A well-versed team run this smart hotel, with its plush library and lavish drawing room. Bedrooms mix modern furnishings with original features. Lunch and afternoon tea are served in the clubby, wood-panelled bar.

67 rooms – € 225/570 € 255/570 – 6 suites

Town plan: B1-k – *064 663 5555 – www.killarneyparkhotel.ie – Closed 24-27 December*

Park – See restaurant listing

Fairview

TOWNHOUSE • PERSONALISED Stylish house in the centre of town, with a leather-furnished lounge and modern bedrooms with marble-tiled bathrooms. The Penthouse has a 4-poster, a whirlpool bath for two and mountain views from the balcony.

29 rooms – € 70/200 € 90/250

Town plan: B1-a – *College St.*

– *064 663 4164 – www.killarneyfairview.com – Closed 24-25 December*

Earls Court House

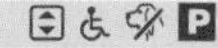

FAMILY • PERSONALISED A well-run hotel on a quiet residential street close to the town centre. Spacious bedrooms boast good facilities: some feature half-tester or four-poster beds and some have balconies with mountain views.

30 rooms - € 90/120 € 110/180

Town plan: B2-t - *Woodlawn Rd. - 064 663 4009 - www.killarney-earlscourt.ie - Closed 10 November-1 February*

Kathleens Country House

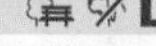

TRADITIONAL • CLASSIC Personally run by a charming hostess: this is Irish hospitality at its best! Comfortable, well-kept and good value hotel, with spacious, pine-furnished bedrooms, an open-fired lounge and a cosy first floor library.

17 rooms - € 110/150 € 115/150

Madams Height, Tralee Rd. - North : 3.75 km on N 22 - 064 663 2810 - www.kathleens.net - Closed October-April

Killarney Lodge

FAMILY • PERSONALISED Well-located guesthouse on the edge of town. Bedrooms are spacious and immaculately kept; No. 12 boasts lovely mountain views. Homemade bread and scones feature at breakfast, which is served in a bright, airy room.

16 rooms - € 90/120 € 110/150

Town plan: B2-u - *Countess Rd. - 064 663 6499 - www.killarneylodge.ie - Closed November-10 March*

KILLORGLIN CILL ORGLAN

Kerry - Pop. 2 082 - Regional map n° **22**-A2

Giovannelli

ITALIAN • RUSTIC A sweet little restaurant, hidden away in the town centre, with a traditional osteria-style interior and an on-view kitchen. The concise, daily changing blackboard menu offers authentic Italian dishes which are unfussy, fresh and full of flavour. The pasta is homemade and herbs are from the owners' garden.

Carte € 35/59

Lower Bridge St - 087 123 1353 (booking essential) - www.giovannellirestaurant.com - dinner only - Closed Monday

Sol y Sombra

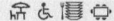

SPANISH • TAPAS BAR Its name means 'Sun and Shade' and the huge tower of this former church provides the latter! The cavernous interior still has its pews and stained glass windows. Cooking is fresh and vibrant: go for the raciones.

Menu € 28 - Carte € 26/42

Old Church of Ireland, Lower Bridge St - 066 976 2347 - www.solysombra.ie - dinner only and Sunday lunch - Closed 7 January-2 February and Monday-Tuesday in winter

KINLOUGH CIONN LOCHA

Leitrim - Pop. 1 018 - Regional map n° **21**-C2

Courthouse

ITALIAN • BISTRO Boldly painted former courthouse with a pretty stained glass entrance. The Sardinian chef-owner creates extensive seasonal menus of honest, authentic Italian dishes; local seafood and some imported produce feature. The atmosphere is informal and the service, friendly. Simply styled bedrooms offer good value.

Menu € 30 (early dinner) - Carte € 30/50

4 rooms - € 40/55 € 80/90

Main St - 071 984 2391 (booking essential) - www.thecourthouserest.com - dinner only and Sunday lunch - Closed Monday and Wednesday in winter and Tuesday

KINSALE CIONNE TSÁILE

Cork – Pop. 2 198 – Regional map n° **22**-B3

Bastion

MODERN CUISINE • FRIENDLY X A small wine-bar-cum-bistro run by a keen young couple. Modern cooking relies on Irish produce but has Mediterranean influences. Dishes are tasty, carefully prepared and often have an innovative, playful element. The bar serves prosecco on tap, as well as prosecco cocktails.

Menu € 45 – Carte € 32/56

Town plan: A1-n – *Market St*
– *☎ 021 470 9696 (booking advisable)*
– *www.bastionkinsale.com*
– *dinner only and Sunday lunch*
– *Closed last 2 weeks January, first 2 weeks February, Monday and Tuesday*

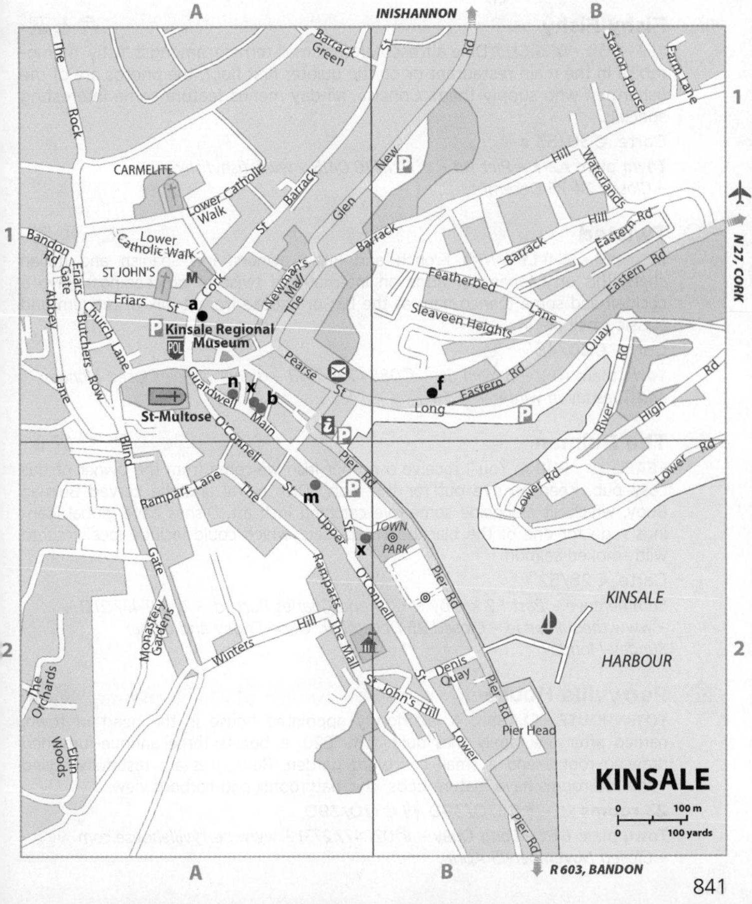

Finns' Table

REGIONAL CUISINE • FRIENDLY XX Behind the bright orange woodwork lie two attractive rooms – one with colourful banquettes, the other in powder blue with wine box panelling. Meat is from the chef's family farm and everything from bread to ice cream is homemade.

Menu € 35 (early dinner) – Carte € 36/61

Town plan: A1-b – *6 Main St – ✆ 021 470 9636 – www.finnstable.com – dinner only – Closed November, Christmas, Sunday-Thursday January-mid March and Tuesday-Wednesday*

Max's

SEAFOOD • COSY XX An efficiently run, two-roomed restaurant on a quaint main street, with a simple yet smart rustic style – a spot well-known by the locals! The unfussy, classical seafood menu offers plenty of choice; try the tasty 'Fresh Catches'.

Menu € 25 (early dinner) – Carte € 33/49

Town plan: A2-m – *Main St – ✆ 021 477 2443 (booking advisable) – www.maxs.ie – dinner only – Closed Christmas, Sunday, Monday and Thursday September-May and bank holidays*

Fishy Fishy

SEAFOOD • DESIGN X Dine alfresco on the small terrace, amongst 'fishy' memorabilia in the main restaurant or on the quieter first floor; the photos are of the fishermen who supply them. Concise, all-day menus feature some interesting specials.

Carte € 30/53 **s**

Town plan: A2-x – *Pier Rd – ✆ 021 470 0415 – www.fishyfishy.ie – Closed 24-26 December*

Twisted

SPANISH • SIMPLE X With French and Fijian owners and Spanish and Italian chefs, this arty tapas bar adds an international twist to proceedings. Have a cocktail and some Iberico ham at the bar or choose from a mix of modern and classic small plates.

Carte € 30/45

Town plan: A1-x – *5 Main St – ✆ 086 4774 2148 – dinner only – Closed Monday and Tuesday in winter*

The Bulman

SEAFOOD • PUB You'll receive a proper Irish welcome from the owner of this cosy pub. Keep an eye out for the Moby Dick mural and the carved Bulman Buoy, which sit alongside some eye-catching Irish art. Dishes have global leanings – go for one of the blackboard specials, which could include locally cured wild smoked salmon.

Carte € 28/52

Summercove – East : 2 km by R 600 and Charles Fort rd. – ✆ 021 477 2131 – www.thebulman.ie – Closed 25 December, Good Friday and dinner Sunday-Monday

Perryville House

TOWNHOUSE • CLASSIC A luxuriously appointed house in the heart of town, named after the family that built it in 1820. It boasts three antique-furnished drawing rooms and a small courtyard garden. Bedrooms are tastefully styled – the top rooms have feature beds, chic bathrooms and harbour views.

23 rooms – € 170/390 € 170/390

Town plan: B1-f – *Long Quay – ✆ 021 477 2731 – www.perryvillehouse.com – Closed November-15 April*

Old Presbytery

TOWNHOUSE • CLASSIC 18C building which once housed priests from the nearby church – a few ecclesiastical pieces remain. Bedrooms feature Irish pine furniture and either brass or cast iron beds; Room 6 has a roof terrace. Breakfasts are comprehensive.

9 rooms – € 70/130 € 95/150

Town plan: A1-a – 43 Cork St. – 021 477 2027 – www.oldpres.com – Closed mid November-mid February

at Barrells Cross Southwest: 5.75 km on R600 ✉ Kinsale

Rivermount House

FAMILY • PERSONALISED Spacious, purpose-built dormer bungalow overlooking the countryside and the river, yet not far from town. It has a distinctive modern style throughout, with attractive embossed wallpapers and quality furnishings. Bold, well-appointed bedrooms display high attention to detail and have immaculate bathrooms.

6 rooms – € 70/100 € 95/140

North : 0.75 km on L 7302 – 021 477 8033 – www.rivermount.com – Closed November-mid-March

KNOCK AN CNOC

Mayo – Pop. 811 – Regional map n° **21**-B2

*Hotels see : **Cong** SW : 58 km by N 17, R 331 R 334 and R 345*

LAHINCH AN LEACHT

Clare – Pop. 642 – Regional map n° **22**-B1

Moy House

COUNTRY HOUSE • ELEGANT An 18C Italianate clifftop villa, overlooking the bay and run by a friendly, attentive team. Homely guest areas include a small library and an open-fired drawing room with an honesty bar; antiques, oil paintings and heavy fabrics feature throughout. Individually designed, classical bedrooms boast good extras and most have views. Formal dining is from a 5 course set menu.

9 rooms – € 150/200 € 165/395

– 065 708 2800 – www.moyhouse.com

LEENANE AN LÍONÁN

Galway – ✉ Clifden – Regional map n° **21**-A3

Delphi Lodge

COUNTRY HOUSE • PERSONALISED A former shooting lodge of the Marquis of Sligo, in a lovely loughside spot on a 1,000 acre estate. Bright, simple bedrooms with smart bathrooms. 'Special Experience' days, free bike hire and a large walkers' drying room. Communal dining from a set menu; guests are encouraged to mingle in the drawing room.

13 rooms – € 140/160 € 230/280

Northwest : 13.25 km by N 59 on Louisburgh rd
– 095 42222 – www.delphilodge.ie – Closed November-February

LETTERKENNY LEITIR CEANAINN

Donegal – Pop. 15 387 – Regional map n° **21**-C1

Browns on the Green

MODERN CUISINE • FRIENDLY XX Situated on the first floor of a golf club but with views of the mountains rather than the course. A cosy lounge leads into the intimate modern dining room. Refined dishes are modern interpretations of tried-and-tested classics.

Menu € 11 (lunch) – Carte € 32/50

Letterkenny Golf Club, Barnhill – Northeast : 5.75 km by R 245
– 074 912 4771 (booking advisable) – www.brownsrestaurant.com – Closed 25-26 December, Good Friday, Monday and Tuesday

Lemon Tree (N)

REGIONAL CUISINE • FAMILY XX This established family-run restaurant sees brother, sisters and cousins all working together to deliver surprisingly modern dishes which draw from Donegal's natural larder. The early evening set dinner menu is good value.

Menu € 25 (early dinner) - Carte € 28/43

32 Courtyard Shopping Centre, Lower Main St - ✆ 074 912 5788 - www.thelemontreerestaurant.com - dinner only - Closed 24-26 December

LIMERICK LUIMNEACH

Limerick - Pop. 57 106 - Regional map n° **22**-B2

Sash

TRADITIONAL CUISINE • BRASSERIE XX A relaxed, modern bistro with a feature wall of pictures and mirrors, set on the first floor of a boutique hotel - it's named after the type of window found in houses of this era. Menus are wide-ranging.

Menu € 35 (weekday dinner) - Carte € 31/51

Town plan: A2-a - *No.1 Pery Square Hotel, Pery Sq - ✆ 061 402 402 - www.oneperysquare.com - dinner only and lunch Saturday-Sunday - Closed Monday*

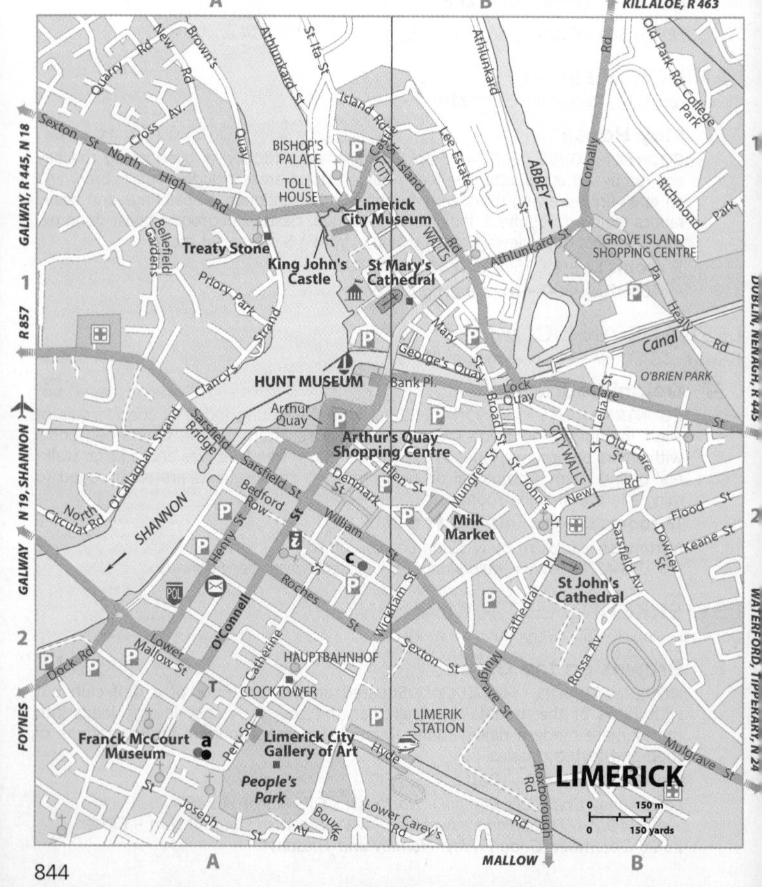

Cornstore

TRADITIONAL CUISINE • BISTRO Head past the bar and up to the larger, more comfortable first floor restaurant to enjoy carefully prepared, traditional cooking. Dry-aged Irish steaks form the core of the menu; seafood also plays a part – and a cocktail is a must!

Menu € 30 (weekday dinner) – Carte € 28/50

Town plan: A2-c – *19 Thomas St – 061 609 000 – www.cornstore.com*

No 1. Pery Square

TOWNHOUSE • CONTEMPORARY A charming boutique townhouse in the Georgian Quarter, with a superb spa and a spacious drawing room overlooking the gardens. Choose a luxurious 'Period' bedroom or more contemporary 'Club' room.

20 rooms – € 135/165 € 165/250 – 1 suite

Town plan: A2-a – *Pery Sq – 061 402 402 – www.oneperysquare.com – Closed 25-26 December*

Sash – See restaurant listing

LISCANNOR LIOS CEANNÚIR

Clare – Pop. 129 – Regional map n° **22**-B1

Vaughan's Anchor Inn

SEAFOOD • PUB A characterful family-run pub in a small fishing village. Nautical memorabilia lines the walls and along with the impressive fish tank, gives a clue as to the focus of the menu, where locally sourced seafood underpins the cooking. Bright, stylish bedrooms are hung with photos of local sights.

Carte € 27/60

7 rooms – € 90/120 € 90/120

Main St – 065 708 1548 – www.vaughans.ie – Closed 24-25 December

LISDOONVARNA LIOS DÚIN BHEARNA

Clare – Pop. 739 – Regional map n° **22**-B1

Wild Honey Inn (Aidan McGrath)

CLASSIC CUISINE • INN This personally run inn started life as an 1860s hotel, so it may not look much like a pub, but once inside it's warm, cosy and full of pubby character. Two weekly changing fixed price menus have a classical French base and showcase the county's produce in neat, confidently prepared dishes which are packed with flavour. Comfy bedrooms have a fittingly traditional feel.

→ Black pudding and foie gras terrine with apple. Wild turbot with green beans, roasted artichoke, tomatoes and tapenade velouté. Basque tart with poached plums and vanilla cream.

Menu € 40/50

14 rooms – € 80/100 € 120/130

South : 0.5 km on Ennistimon rd – 065 707 4300 – www.wildhoneyinn.com – dinner only – Closed November-February, Tuesday-Wednesday October, March and April and Sunday-Monday

Sheedy's Country House

FAMILY • CLASSIC Set in the centre of the village and run by the 3rd generation of the family. Relax in the comfy library, the Lloyd Loom furnished sun lounge or the traditional bar. Spacious, well-kept bedrooms have floral fabrics and good facilities. A classic menu is offered in the dining room, where service is exacting.

11 rooms – € 90/130 € 130/180

– 065 707 4026 – www.sheedys.com – Closed October-Easter

LISTOWEL LIOS TUATHAIL

Kerry – Pop. 4 205 – Regional map n° **22**-B2

Allo's Bistro

TRADITIONAL CUISINE • COSY X Former pub dating back to 1873; now a simple, well-run and characterful restaurant. Series of homely rooms and friendly, efficient service. Wide-ranging menus rely on regional produce, with theme nights on Thursdays and an adventurous gourmet menu Fri and Sat evenings. Individual, antique-furnished bedrooms.

Carte € 31/46

3 rooms – † € 70/100 †† € 70/100

41-43 Church St – ✆ 068 22880 (booking essential) – www.allosbarbistro-townhouse.com – Closed Sunday and Monday except bank holidays

LONGFORD AN LONGFORT

Longford – Pop. 8 002 – Regional map n° **21**-C3

VM

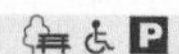

MODERN CUISINE • TRADITIONAL DÉCOR XXX Formal hotel restaurant in the old stables of a Georgian house. The smart, rustic dining room has stone-faced walls and overlooks a Japanese garden. Cooking is interesting, modern and original, and orchard and garden produce features.

Menu € 65

Viewmount House Hotel, Dublin Rd – Southeast : 1.5 km by R 393 – ✆ 043 334 1919 – www.viewmounthouse.com – dinner only and Sunday lunch – Closed 29 October-7 November, Sunday dinner, Monday and Tuesday

Viewmount House

COUNTRY HOUSE • CLASSIC Set in 4 acres of mature grounds, a welcoming Georgian house with a charming period feel – original features include an ornate vaulted ceiling in the breakfast room. Bedrooms are traditionally styled, furnished with antiques and have good modern facilities; opt for a duplex room. The breakfasts are delicious.

12 rooms – † € 75/100 †† € 150/170

Dublin Rd – Southeast : 1.5 km by R 393 – ✆ 043 334 1919 – www.viewmounthouse.com – Closed 29 October-7 November

VM – See restaurant listing

MALAHIDE MULLACH ÍDE

Fingal – Pop. 15 846 – Regional map n° **22**-D1

Bon Appetit

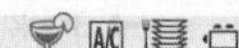

MODERN CUISINE • BRASSERIE XX Smart Georgian terraced house near the harbour. The intimate, dimly lit bar offers cocktails and tapas; below is a modern brasserie with a lively atmosphere. Modern dishes have a classical French base; the steaks are a highlight.

Menu € 24 (lunch) – Carte dinner € 35/57

9 St James's Terr. – ✆ 01 845 0314 – www.bonappetit.ie – dinner only and lunch Friday-Sunday – Closed 25 December and Monday

Jaipur

INDIAN • ELEGANT XX A friendly basement restaurant in a Georgian terrace. The origins of the tasty, contemporary Indian dishes are noted on the menu. The monkfish with lime, ginger, coriander root & fried okra is a speciality.

Menu € 22 (early dinner) – Carte € 26/49

5 St James's Terr – ✆ 01 845 5455 – www.jaipur.ie – dinner only and Sunday lunch – Closed 25 December

Old Street

MODERN BRITISH • CHIC A pair of converted cottages house this delightful split-level restaurant which features a stylish cocktail bar with a lovely panelled ceiling and designer touches. The experienced team carefully craft appealing modern dishes.

Menu € 29 - Carte € 32/55

Old St - 01 845 5614 - www.oldstreet.ie - Closed 1-7 January , 25-26 December and Monday

MALLOW MALA

Cork – Pop. 8 578 – Regional map n° **22**-B2

Longueville House

HISTORIC • CLASSIC A part-Georgian manor house overlooking Dromaneen Castle and built in William and Mary style. It boasts a lovely stone-tiled hall, a superb flying staircase, a stunning drawing room and well-appointed bedrooms furnished with antiques. Traditional menus use produce from the garden and estate.

20 rooms - € 85/195 € 189/455

West : 5.5 km by N 72 - 022 47156 - www.longuevillehouse.ie - Closed 24-27 December, Monday-Tuesday and restricted opening in winter

MIDLETON MAINISTIR NA CORANN

Cork – Pop. 3 733 – Regional map n° **22**-C3

Farmgate Restaurant & Country Store

REGIONAL CUISINE • SIMPLE A friendly food store with a bakery, a rustic two-roomed restaurant and a courtyard terrace. Lunch might mean soup, a sandwich or a tart; dinner features regional fish and meats – the chargrilled steaks are popular. Cakes served all day.

Carte € 21/32

Broderick St, Coolbawn - 021 463 2771 (bookings advisable at dinner) - www.farmgate.ie - Closed 24 December-3 January, Sunday and Monday

Sage

REGIONAL CUISINE • BISTRO A passionately run restaurant with a rustic feel. Hearty, classical cooking is full of flavour – ingredients are sourced from within a 12 mile radius and their homemade black pudding is a must. To accompany, try a biodynamic wine or artisan beer. The next door Greenroom café serves lighter dishes.

Menu € 30 (early dinner) - Carte € 28/49

The Courtyard, 8 Main St - 021 463 9682 (bookings advisable at dinner) - www.sagerestaurant.ie - Closed 25-27 December and Monday

MOHILL MAOTHAIL

Leitrim – Pop. 928 – Regional map n° **21**-C2

Lough Rynn Castle

LUXURY • HISTORIC 18C country house with superb gardens and peaceful grounds; popular for weddings. Numerous lounges and a baronial hall with original parquet flooring and an impressive fireplace. Large, well-appointed bedrooms – those in the main house are the most characterful. Formal dining room; ambitious French cuisine.

44 rooms - € 89/175 € 99/195

Southeast : 4 km by R 201 off Drumlish rd - 071 963 2700 - www.loughrynn.ie

Lough Rynn Country House

FAMILY • PERSONALISED Purpose-built stone house in a peaceful country setting, boasting lovely views over Lough Rynn – three of the homely bedrooms share the view and one has a small balcony. There's a comfy lounge and a cottagey breakfast room, and the delightful owner welcomes guests with home-baked scones or muffins.

4 rooms – € 55 € 110

Southeast : 3.5 km. by R 201 off Drumlish rd – 087 922 8236 – www.loughrynnbandb.ie

MULLINGAR AN MUILEANN GCEARR

Westmeath – Pop. 9 414 – Regional map n° **21**-C3

Marlinstown Court

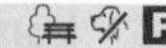

TRADITIONAL • COSY Clean, tidy guesthouse close to the N4; a very homely, personal option for staying away. The light, airy lounge opens into a pleasant pine-furnished breakfast room overlooking the garden. Bedrooms are simply and brightly decorated.

5 rooms – € 45/60 € 80/100

Dublin Rd – East : 2.5 km on Dublin Rd off N 4 (junction 15) – 044 934 0053 – www.marlinstowncourt.com – Closed 23-27 December

MURRISK MURAISC

Mayo – Pop. 235 – Regional map n° **21**-A2

Tavern

TRADITIONAL CUISINE • PUB A vibrant pink pub where the friendly team make you feel at home; the collection of rolling pins and vintage signs gives it a quirky edge. Fresh ingredients feature in generous, classic dishes; shellfish is from the nearby bay.

Carte € 24/46

– 098 64060 – www.tavernmurrisk.com – Closed 25 December and Good Friday

NAAS AN NÁS

Kildare – Pop. 20 713 – Regional map n° **22**-D1

Vie de Châteaux

CLASSIC FRENCH • BISTRO X A smart modern bistro with a great terrace overlooking the old harbour. The keenly priced menu of carefully cooked, fully flavoured Gallic dishes will evoke memories of holidays in France; save room for 'Les Mini Desserts'.

Menu € 26 (lunch) – Carte € 33/53

The Harbour – 045 888 478 (booking essential) – www.viedechateaux.ie – Closed 24 December-2 January, lunch Monday, Tuesday, Saturday and bank holidays

at Two Mile House Southwest: 6.5 km by R448 on L 2032

Brown Bear

MODERN BRITISH • BRASSERIE XX Set in a sleepy village, the Brown Bear comprises a locals' bar and a clubby bistro with tan leather booths and candlelit tables. Ambitious dishes are creatively presented and full of flavour. Service is smooth and assured.

Menu € 25 (early dinner) – Carte € 32/52

– 045 883 561 – www.thebrownbear.ie – dinner only and lunch Saturday-Sunday – Closed 24-27 December, Monday and Tuesday

NEW QUAY BEALACLUGGA

Clare – Regional map n° **22**-B1

Linnane's Lobster Bar

SEAFOOD • PUB A simple but likeable place, with peat fires and full-length windows which open onto a terrace. They specialise in fresh seafood; watch the local boats unload their catch, some of which is brought straight to the kitchen.

Carte € 23/57

New Quay Pier – 065 707 8120 – www.linnanesbar.com – Closed 25 December, Good Friday and Monday-Thursday November-17 March

Mount Vernon

COUNTRY HOUSE • PERSONALISED Charming whitewashed house with a pretty walled garden, set close to the beach and affording lovely views. Antiques and eclectic curios fill the guest areas; spacious bedrooms have their own personalities – two open onto a terrace. Simply cooked dinners rely on fresh, local produce. Warm, welcoming owners.

5 rooms – € 90/135 € 190/230

Flaggy Shore – North : 0.75 km on coast rd – 065 707 8126 – www.mountvernon.ie – Closed November-March

NEWPORT BAILE UÍ FHIACHÁIN

Mayo – Pop. 616 – Regional map n° **21**-A2

Newport House

HISTORIC • CLASSIC A delightful 1720s creeper-clad mansion with lovely gardens and river views – they also own neighbouring Lough Beltra, so many guests come to fish. The stunning staircase, topped by a domed cupola, leads up to traditional, antique-filled bedrooms. Dine beneath family portraits and an elegant chandelier.

14 rooms – € 130/175 € 220/290

– 098 41222 – www.newporthouse.ie – Closed November-18 March

NEWTOWNMOUNTKENNEDY BAILE AN CHINNÉIDIEH

Wicklow – Pop. 2 548 – Regional map n° **22**-D2

Druids Glen H. & Golf Resort

RESORT • CLASSIC Hidden away in the countryside but just 30mins from Dublin, you'll find this smart resort hotel and its two championship golf courses – along with a great spa and a vast array of other leisure facilities. The delightful bar overlooks the 13th hole and the appealing restaurant has a lovely terrace too.

145 rooms – € 155/250 € 165/405 – 11 suites

– 01 287 0800 – www.druidsglenresort.com

OUGHTERARD UACHTAR ARD

Galway – Pop. 1 333 – Regional map n° **21**-A3

Currarevagh House

TRADITIONAL • CLASSIC Classically furnished Victorian manor house set in 180 loughside acres and run by the same family for over 100 years. It has a pleasingly 'lived-in' feel and offers a real country house experience. Have afternoon tea by the fire or take a picnic out on their boat; set dinners offer unfussy, flavoursome dishes.

12 rooms – € 75/95 € 140/190

Northwest : 6.5 km on Glann rd – 091 552 312 – www.currarevagh.com – Closed November-February

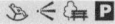

Railway Lodge

COUNTRY HOUSE • RURAL An elegantly furnished house in a remote setting, with lovely views across the countryside. Bedrooms come with stripped pine furnishings and a keen eye for detail. The charming owner offers great local recommendations.

4 rooms – € 50/60 € 100/110

West : 0.75 km by Shannapheasteen rd taking first right onto unmarked road – 091 552 945 – www.railwaylodge.net

PORTLAOISE PORT LAOISE

Laois – Pop. 20 145 – Regional map n° **22**-C2

 **Ivyleigh House** 

TOWNHOUSE • CLASSIC Traditional listed Georgian property in the city centre, run by a welcoming owner. Comfy lounge and communal dining area, with antiques and ornaments displayed throughout. Good-sized bedrooms are decorated in a period style. Homemade breads, preserves, muesli and a Cashel blue cheesecake special at breakfast.

6 rooms – € 75/80 € 110/160

Bank Pl, Church St – 057 862 2081 – www.ivyleigh.com – Closed 12 November-1 April except Christmas and New Year

RAMELTON RÁTH MEALTAIN

Donegal – Pop. 1 212 – Regional map n° **21**-C1

 **Moorfield Lodge** 

FAMILY • CONTEMPORARY Striking, modern house run by a welcoming owner. Bright, stylish bedrooms with underfloor heating, floor to ceiling windows and Egyptian cotton sheets. Room 1 has its own terrace, a double jacuzzi bath and a TV built into the bathroom tiles. Communal breakfasts are served around an antique table.

3 rooms – € 140/200 € 140/200

Aughnagaddy Glebe, Moorfield – 074 989 4043 – www.moorfieldlodge.com

Ardeen

TRADITIONAL • CLASSIC A Victorian house on the edge of the village, with peaceful gardens and a river nearby. Welcoming owner and homely, personally styled interior. Open-fired lounge with local info; communal breakfasts. Simple, well-kept bedrooms without TVs.

5 rooms – € 45/55 € 90

bear left at the fork in the village centre and left at T-junction – 074 915 1243 – www.ardeenhouse.com – Closed October-May

RANELAGH – Dublin → See Dublin

RATHMINES RÁTH MAONAIS – Dublin → See Dublin

RATHMULLAN RÁTH MAOLÁIN

Donegal – Letterkenny – Pop. 518 – Regional map n° **21**-C1

Cook & Gardener 

CLASSIC CUISINE • FAMILY XX Formal hotel restaurant comprising several interconnecting rooms. Daily menus list the best of what's in season, including produce from the house's original walled kitchen garden. Classic cooking is presented in a modern manner.

Carte € 34/57

Rathmullan House Hotel, North : 0.5 mi on R 247 – 074 915 8188 – www.rathmullanhouse.com – Closed 2 January-2 February and restricted opening in winter

 **Rathmullan House** 

TRADITIONAL • CLASSIC Family-run, part-19C house set next to Lough Swilly. Bedrooms in the original house have a fitting country house style; those in the extension are more modern and come with balconies or private terraces overlooking the gardens.

34 rooms – € 90/125 € 180/280

North : 0.5 mi on R 247 – 074 915 8188 – www.rathmullanhouse.com – Closed 2 January-2 February and restricted opening in winter

Cook & Gardener – See restaurant listing

RATHNEW RÁTH NAOI

Wicklow – ✉ Wicklow – Pop. 2 964 – Regional map n° **22**-D2

Brunel

IRISH • ELEGANT XX Spacious, elegant restaurant in a hotel extension, overlooking the gardens: named after the builder of the Great Eastern ship on which Captain Halpin sailed. Flavoursome, traditional dishes use the best Wicklow ingredients.

Menu € 37 – Carte € 40/55

Tinakilly House Hotel, On R 750 – ✆ 0404 69274 – www.tinakilly.ie – dinner only and Sunday lunch – Closed 24-26 December

Tinakilly House

HISTORIC • CLASSIC A substantial Victorian house in extensive grounds which stretch to the seashore: built for Captain Robert Halpin. Original features include an impressive staircase. Spacious, classically furnished bedrooms; some have four-posters.

52 rooms – € 89/140 € 90/170 – 1 suite

On R 750 – ✆ 0404 69274 – www.tinakilly.ie – Closed 24-26 December

Brunel – See restaurant listing

RIVERSTOWN BAILE IDIR DHÁ ABHAINN

Sligo – Pop. 374 – Regional map n° **21**-B2

Coopershill

TRADITIONAL • CLASSIC Magnificent Georgian house run by the 7th generation of the same family; set on a working farm within a 500 acre estate. Spacious guest areas showcase original furnishings – now antiques – and family portraits adorn the walls. Warm, country house style bedrooms. Formal dining amongst polished silverware.

8 rooms – € 151/175 € 202/250

– ✆ 071 916 5108 – www.coopershill.com – Closed November-March

ROSMUCK

Regional map n° **21**-A3

Screebe House (N)

MODERN CUISINE • INTIMATE XX An airy hotel dining room overlooking the sea. The concise à la carte features top ingredients in modern combinations, while the 12 course tasting menu offers creative, sophisticated dishes with contrasting textures and tastes.

Carte € 49/72

Screebe House Hotel, Notheast : 9 km by R 1204 on R 340 – ✆ 091 574 110 (bookings essential for non-residents) – www.screebe.com – dinner only – Closed 1 December-15 February, Monday, Tuesday and weekdays in winter

Screebe House (N)

COUNTRY HOUSE • CLASSIC An old Victorian fishing lodge in a stunning spot on Camus Bay; it has the look of a country house and a friendly, laid-back atmosphere. Enjoy tea by the fire in the sitting room or a beer beneath an enormous stag's head in the bar. Understated bedrooms feature good quality furnishings and character beds.

10 rooms – € 140/160 € 185/320

Northeast : 9 km by R 1204 on R 340 – ✆ 091 574 110 – www.screebe.com – Closed 1 December-15 February, Monday, Tuesday and weekdays in winter

Screebe House – See restaurant listing

ROSSCARBERY ROS Ó GCAIRBRE

Pop. 534 – Regional map n° **22**-B3

Pilgrim's

MODERN CUISINE • RUSTIC It's been a guesthouse and the village bookshop among other things, but this cosy, proudly run restaurant has always kept its name. The concise daily menu lists generously proportioned dishes prepared from local and foraged ingredients. The depth of flavours and the warm hospitality really stand out.

Carte € 31/43

6 South Sq – ✆ 023 883 1796 (booking advisable) – www.pilgrims.ie – dinner only and Sunday lunch – Closed January-17 March, Tuesday-Wednesday in winter, Sunday dinner and Monday

ROSSLARE ROS LÁIR

Wexford – Pop. 1 547 – Regional map n° **22**-D2

Kelly's Resort

FAMILY • PERSONALISED It started life in 1895 as a beachfront 'refreshment house'; now it's a sprawling leisure-orientated hotel run by the 4th generation of the Kelly family. An impressive collection of contemporary art is displayed throughout the guest areas and well-appointed bedrooms. Formal 'Beaches' has an appealing menu and an exceptional wine list; La Marine serves brasserie classics.

126 rooms – € 88/131 € 176/262

– ✆ 053 913 2114 – www.kellys.ie – Closed December-mid February

ROUNDSTONE CLOCH NA RÓN

Galway – Pop. 245 – Regional map n° **21**-A3

O'Dowds

SEAFOOD • COSY The blue exterior and proximity to the harbour give a clue as to this pub's speciality: simply prepared, super fresh seafood – much of it landed just outside the door. It's been run by the same family for over 100 years.

Carte € 23/54

– ✆ 095 35809 (booking advisable) – www.odowdsseafoodbar.com – Closed 25 December

SALLINS

Pop. 5 283 – Regional map n° **22**-D1

Two Cooks

IRISH • NEIGHBOURHOOD This delightful restaurant on the first floor of a residential parade is run by – you've guessed it – two chefs; he cooks while she keeps things running smoothly out front. The main menu is supplemented by a good value set selection on Wednesdays and Thursdays. Cooking is honest and well-judged.

Menu € 38 (weekdays) – Carte € 39/45

Canal View – ✆ 045 853 768 – www.twocooks.ie – dinner only and Sunday lunch – Closed 15-31 January, 16-30 August, 25-26 December, Sunday dinner and Monday-Tuesday

SANDYFORD ÁTH AN GHAINIMH

→ See Dublin

SHANAGARRY AN SEANGHARRAÍ

Cork – ✉ Midleton – Pop. 414 – Regional map n° **22**-C3

Ballymaloe House

FAMILY • CLASSIC With its pre-18C origins, this is the very essence of a country manor house. Family-run for 3 generations, it boasts numerous traditionally styled guest areas, comfortable, classical bedrooms and a famed cookery school. The daily changing fixed price menu offers local, seasonal produce.

29 rooms ☕ – 👤 € 205/315 👥 € 255/315

Northwest : 3 km on R 629 – ✆ 021 465 2531 – www.ballymaloe.ie – Closed 7 January-4 February and 24-28 December

SKIBBEREEN AN SCIOBAIRÍN

Cork – Pop. 2 568 – Regional map n° **22**-B3

Good Things @ Dillon's Corner Ⓝ

MODERN CUISINE • SIMPLE X Carmel Somers' restaurant and cookery school sits within an old grocery store and has a pleasant café feel during the day. Dishes range from modern Irish to those with Mediterranean and Middle Eastern leanings; local produce abounds.

Carte € 30/49

68 Bridge St – ✆ 028 51948 (booking essential at dinner) – www.goodthingscafe.com – Closed Sunday, Monday and dinner Tuesday-Wednesday

Liss Ard

HISTORIC • PERSONALISED With 150 acres of grounds – including a lake – this 200 year old manor house, stables and lodge create an idyllic rural retreat. Inside they're surprisingly modern with sleek furnishings and a minimalist Swiss/German style. Staff are friendly and daily menus are led by the availability of local produce.

25 rooms ☕ – 👤 € 79/120 👥 € 99/295

Liss Ard Estate, Castletownsend Rd – Southeast : 2.5 km on R 596 – ✆ 028 40000 – www.lissardestate.com – Closed November-March

SLANE BAILE SHÁINE

Meath – Pop. 1 349 – Regional map n° **21**-D3

Brabazon

MODERN CUISINE • RUSTIC XX Relaxed, rustic restaurant in the former piggery of a delightful manor house. Sit at a painted wooden table by the fire or out on the terrace overlooking the landscaped courtyard. Contemporary cooking uses top quality ingredients.

Menu € 25/40 – Carte € 27/59

Tankardstown Hotel, Northwest : 6 km by N 51 off R 163 – ✆ 041 982 4621 – www.tankardstown.ie/dining/brabazon – dinner only and Sunday lunch – Closed 24-27 December and Monday-Tuesday

Tankardstown

COUNTRY HOUSE • CONTEMPORARY A fine Georgian manor house with a lavish interior, set up a sweeping tree-lined drive. Bedrooms in the main house are furnished with antiques; those in the courtyard are more modern and come with kitchens. Have afternoon tea in the cottage, wood-fired pizzas in Cellar or contemporary dishes in Brabazon.

25 rooms ☕ – 👤 € 105/360 👥 € 210/360 – 6 suites

Northwest : 6 km by N 51 off R 163 – ✆ 041 982 4621 – www.tankardstown.ie – Closed 24-27 December

Brabazon – See restaurant listing

Conyngham Arms

FAMILY • PERSONALISED 17C coaching inn on the main street of a small but busy town. It has a laid-back feel, an appealing shabby-chic style and a lovely hidden garden. Some of the bedrooms have feature beds and all come with coffee machines and freshly baked biscuits from their nearby bakery. Dine in the bar, with its open kitchen.

15 rooms – € 59/99 € 89/139

– 041 988 4444 – www.conynghamarms.ie – Closed 25-26 December

SLIGO SLIGEACH

Sligo – Pop. 17 568 – Regional map n° **21**-B2

Montmartre

CLASSIC FRENCH • BISTRO XX Smart, modern restaurant in the shadow of the cathedral, with a tiled exterior and wooden blinds. The French chefs prepare classic Gallic menus which follow the seasons. The all-French wine list features interesting, lesser-known wines.

Menu € 24 – Carte € 26/52

Market Yard – 071 916 9901 – www.montmartrerestaurant.ie – dinner only – Closed 7-30 January, Sunday except before a bank holiday and Monday

Hargadons Bros

TRADITIONAL CUISINE • RUSTIC Hugely characterful pub with sloping floors, narrow passageways, dimly lit anterooms and a lovely "Ladies' Room" complete with its own serving hatch. Cooking is warming and satisfying, offering the likes of Irish stew or bacon and cabbage.

Carte € 22/43

4-5 O'Connell St – 071 915 3709 (bookings not accepted) – www.hargadons.com – Closed Sunday

Tree Tops

TRADITIONAL • PERSONALISED An unassuming whitewashed house in a residential area, with immaculately kept bedrooms, a cosy lounge and a smart buffet breakfast room overlooking the garden. The chatty, welcoming owners have an interesting Irish art collection.

3 rooms – € 75 € 75

Cleveragh Rd – South : 1.25 km by Dublin rd – 071 916 2301 – www.sligobandb.com – Closed Christmas-New Year

SPANISH POINT RINN NA SPÁINNEACH

Clare – Milltown Malbay – Regional map n° **22**-B2

Red Cliff Lodge

FAMILY • COSY A thatched cottage in a superb spot on the headland; later extensions have created a U-shaped arrangement around a cobbled courtyard. Smart, spacious bedrooms come with kitchenettes and great views over the beach

6 rooms – € 90/150 € 120/190

South : 0.75 mi – 065 708 5756 – www.redcliffIodge.ie – Closed October-Easter, midweek April-May and Monday

STRAFFAN TEACH SRAFÁIN

Kildare – Pop. 635 – Regional map n° **22**-D1

K Club

GRAND LUXURY • CLASSIC A golf resort with two championship courses, an extensive spa and beautiful formal gardens stretching down to the Liffey. The fine 19C house has elegant antique-filled guestrooms and luxurious bedrooms. Elegant Byerley Turk serves a 6 course tasting menu; grand River Room offers refined classics; Legends has a brasserie menu; and K Thai serves Thai and Malaysian fare.

134 rooms – € 229/429 € 229/429 – 16 suites

– 01 601 7200 – www.kclub.ie

Barberstown Castle

COUNTRY HOUSE • HISTORIC This 13C castle with Georgian and Victorian extensions is set within 20 acres of grounds and makes a popular wedding venue. Large, luxurious country house bedrooms feature good facilities; many have four-poster beds and garden outlooks. Dine from French menus in the Georgian house and stone keep.

55 rooms - € 135/200 € 180/240

North : 0.75 km - 01 628 8157 - www.barberstowncastle.ie - Closed January-February and 24-26 December

TERENURE

→ See Dublin

THOMASTOWN BAILE MHIC ANDÁIN

Kilkenny - Pop. 2 273 - Regional map n° **22**-C2

Lady Helen

MODERN CUISINE • ROMANTIC XXX Sited within an impressive Georgian house is this grand, luxurious restaurant which looks out over the estate and the River Nore. Ambitious, visually impressive modern dishes are precisely prepared and ingredients come from the estate, the county and the coast; for the full experience go for the tasting menu.

→ Potato and truffle ravioli with duck egg yolk and rosemary velouté. Rabbit with langoustine, sweet onion and lemon tortellini. Passion fruit with mango and coconut sponge.

Menu € 75/99

Mount Juliet Estate, West : 5.5 km by R 448 on L 4206 - 056 777 3000 (booking essential) - www.mountjuliet.ie - dinner only - Closed Sunday-Monday

Mount Juliet Estate

HISTORIC • CLASSIC Within this Irish Estate's 1,500 acres you can enjoy fishing, falconry, horse riding and golf. The house was built in the 1700s and is a fine example of Georgian architecture, with original stuccowork and hand-carved fireplaces. Well-appointed bedrooms have a period style; ask for a River Nore view.

32 rooms - € 179/270 € 189/280 - 2 suites

West : 5.5 km by R 448 on L 4206 - 056 777 3000 - www.mountjuliet.ie

Lady Helen - See restaurant listing

Abbey House

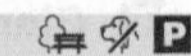

TRADITIONAL • COSY Attractive whitewashed Victorian house with a neat, lawned garden and a friendly, hospitable owner; set opposite the ruins of Jerpoint Abbey. Traditionally styled lounge with plenty of local info. Simple bedrooms with antique furniture.

6 rooms - € 60/80 € 90/100

Jerpoint Abbey - Southwest : 2 km on R 448 - 056 772 4166 - www.abbeyhousejerpoint.com - Closed December-February

TIMOLEAGUE

Cork - Pop. 323 - Regional map n° **22**-B3

Dillon's

MODERN CUISINE • BISTRO X A former pub-cum-grocer's named after its first owner. The original bar counter and shelves remain and the room has a homely feel. Flavoursome dishes are eye-catchingly presented and make good use of local ingredients.

Carte € 30/57

Mill St - 023 886 9609 (booking essential) - www.dillonsrestaurant.ie - dinner only - Closed Sunday dinner, Wednesday and Thursday

TOORMORE AN TUAR MÓR

Cork – ✉ Goleen – Pop. 207 – Regional map n° **22**-A3

 **Fortview House** 

FAMILY • PERSONALISED Well-kept guesthouse on a 120 acre dairy farm, run by a very bubbly owner. It has a rustic, country feel courtesy of its stone walls, timbered ceilings, coir carpets and aged pine furniture. Breakfast is an event, with home-baked scones and bread, eggs from their hens and other local products all featuring.

3 rooms – € 50 € 100

Gurtyowen – Northeast : 2.5 km on R 591 (Durrus rd) – 028 35324 – www.fortviewhousegoleen.com – Closed October-April

TRALEE TRÁ LÍ

Kerry – Pop. 20 814 – Regional map n° **22**-A2

 **Grand** 

TOWNHOUSE • TRADITIONAL Opened in 1928 and located in the heart of this bustling town. It has a small first floor lounge and modern bedrooms. The traditional bar – once the post office – is a popular spot and offers hearty all-day dishes. The classical dining room serves a mix of Irish specialities and more global fare.

48 rooms – € 60/100 € 80/200

Denny St – 066 712 1499 – www.grandhoteltralee.com – Closed 25 December

 **Brook Manor Lodge** 

TOWNHOUSE • PERSONALISED Spacious detached house with a bright conservatory breakfast room and views to the Slieve Mish Mountains; perfect if you like golf, hiking or fishing. Bedrooms are immaculate – those at the back have the view.

7 rooms – € 90/99 € 99/170

Fenit Rd, Spa – Northwest : 3.5 km by R 551 on R 558 – 066 712 0406 – www.brookmanorlodge.com – Closed November-March

TRAMORE TRÁ MHÓR

Waterford – Pop. 9 722 – Regional map n° **22**-C2

 **Glenorney** 

TRADITIONAL • CLASSIC Smart cream house with pretty gardens, set on a hill overlooking the bay. Bedrooms are well-kept and the book-filled sun lounge is a good place to relax. At breakfast they serve pancakes, French toast and homemade preserves.

6 rooms – € 50/80 € 90

Newtown – Southwest : 1.5 km by R 675 – 051 381 056 – www.glenorney.com – Closed November-mid March

TRIM BAILE ÁTHA TROIM

Meath – Pop. 1 441 – Regional map n° **21**-D3

 **Trim Castle** 

BUSINESS • MODERN Modern family-run hotel opposite the castle, complete with a café, a homeware shop and a delightful roof terrace with a great outlook. Good-sized bedrooms come in contemporary hues – those to the front share the view. Dine in the bar or opt for classic European dishes in the stylish first floor restaurant.

68 rooms – € 75/165 € 75/180

Castle St. – 046 948 3000 – www.trimcastlehotel.com

Highfield House

TOWNHOUSE • PERSONALISED Substantial 18C stone house close to the river and the oldest Norman castle in Europe. Well-appointed lounge and breakfast room, boldly coloured bedrooms and a delightful terraced courtyard. Comprehensive breakfasts; scones on arrival.

10 rooms – € 58/65 € 90/95

Castle St – 046 857 7115 – www.highfieldguesthouse.com – Closed 21 December-2 January

TULLAMORE TULACH MHÓR

Offaly – Pop. 11 346 – Regional map n° **22**-C1

Blue Apron

CLASSIC CUISINE • BISTRO X Friendly, engaging service sets the tone at this intimate restaurant, which is run by an enthusiastic husband and wife team. All-encompassing menus offer generous, flavoursome dishes that are prepared with care and understanding.

Menu € 28 (weekdays) – Carte € 26/56

Harbour St – 057 936 0106 – www.theblueapronrestaurant.ie – dinner only – Closed 2 weeks August, 24 January-7 February, 24-27 December, Monday and Tuesday

TWO MILE HOUSE → See Naas

VIRGINIA ACHADH AN IÚIR

Cavan – Pop. 2 282 – Regional map n° **21**-C3

St Kyrans

CLASSIC CUISINE • DESIGN XX This rurally set restaurant may look plain from the outside but it's a different story on the inside. The smart linen-laid restaurant offers breathtaking views over Lough Ramor and the menu lists classic dishes with an Irish heart and hints of modernity. Five of the modern bedrooms have water views.

Menu € 25 (weekdays) – Carte € 31/48

8 rooms – € 60/90 € 120/140

Dublin Rd – South : 2.25 km. on N 3 – 049 854 7087 – www.stkyrans.com – Closed 23-28 January, Christmas, Good Friday, Monday and Tuesday.

WATERFORD PORT LÁIRGE

Waterford – Pop. 46 732 – Regional map n° **22**-C2

La Bohème

FRENCH • INTIMATE XX Characterful candlelit restaurant in the vaulted cellar of a Georgian house. The French chefs offer an array of Gallic dishes and daily market specials – the simpler dishes are the ones to choose. Service is friendly.

Menu € 26 (early dinner)/36 – Carte € 34/59

2 George's St – 051 875 645 (booking essential) – www.labohemerestaurant.ie – dinner only – Closed 25-27 December, Sunday except bank holidays and Monday

Waterford Castle H. and Golf Resort

HISTORIC BUILDING • CLASSIC An attractive part-15C castle set on a charming 320 acre private island in the river. The carved stone and wood-panelled hall displays old tapestries and antiques, and the beautiful dining room boasts a delightful hand-carved fireplace. Elegant, classical bedrooms have characterful period bathrooms.

19 rooms – € 99/179 € 158/298 – 5 suites

The Island, Ballinakill – East : 4 km by R 683 and private ferry – 051 878 203 – www.waterfordcastleresort.com – Closed 7 January-2 February and 24-26 December

WESTPORT CATHAIR NA MART

Mayo – Pop. 5 543 – Regional map n° **21**-A2

La Fougère

CLASSIC CUISINE • ROMANTIC XXX Spacious hotel restaurant with a large bar, several different seating areas and huge windows offering views to Croagh Patrick Mountain. The three menus feature fresh, local produce, including langoustines from the bay below. Formal service.

Menu € 52

Knockranny House Hotel & Spa, Castlebar Rd, Knockranny – East : 1.25 km on N 5 – ✆ 098 28600 (booking advisable) – www.knockrannyhousehotel.ie – dinner only – Closed 24-26 December

Idle Wall

REGIONAL CUISINE • COSY X The sun dial by the front door marks the old 'idle wall', where local dockworkers used to sit and wait for employment at the harbour below. Menus continually evolve as the experienced chef sources the latest artisan produce. It's a sweet place, with wonky timbers and charming country and boating memorabilia.

Menu € 25 – Carte € 32/55

The Quay – ✆ 098 50692 – www.theidlewall.ie – dinner only – Closed February and Monday

An Port Mór

CLASSIC CUISINE • COSY X Tucked away down a small alleyway and named after the chef's home village. The compact interior has a shabby-chic, Mediterranean-style. Local produce is showcased in elaborate dishes and seafood specials are chalked on the blackboard.

Menu € 24 (early dinner) – Carte € 33/48

Brewery Pl, Bridge St – ✆ 098 26730 – www.anportmor.com – dinner only – Closed 24-26 December, Sunday in winter and Monday

Sheebeen

TRADITIONAL CUISINE • PUB Pretty pub with lovely bay and Croagh Patrick views. Hearty, unfussy dishes feature shellfish and lobsters from the bay, and lamb and beef from the fields nearby. Sit outside, in the rustic bar or in the first floor dining room.

Carte € 26/46

Rosbeg – West : 3 km on R 335 – ✆ 098 26528 – www.croninssheebeen.com – Closed 25 December, Good Friday and weekday lunches November-mid March

Knockranny House H. & Spa

FAMILY • PERSONALISED Modern hotel in an elevated position overlooking the town, mountains and bay, and furnished in a contemporary yet classical style. Large, smart bedrooms offer excellent comforts; some have marble bathrooms or four-poster beds. Superb spa.

97 rooms – † € 90/155 †† € 110/185 – 10 suites

Castlebar Rd, Knockranny – East : 1.25 km on N 5 – ✆ 098 28600 – www.knockrannyhousehotel.ie – Closed 24-26 December

La Fougère – See restaurant listing

WEXFORD LOCH GARMAN

Wexford – Pop. 19 913 – Regional map n° **22**-D2

Greenacres

TRADITIONAL BRITISH • BISTRO X Set over 3 floors, with a bistro, deli, wine store, bakery and art gallery. Wide-ranging menu of classic dishes, with daily fish specials. Amazing choice of wine from around the world, with some sensational vintages in the private salon.

Menu € 38 (dinner) – Carte € 36/48

Selskar – ✆ 053 912 2975 – www.greenacres.ie – Closed 25-27 December and Sunday except October-December

La Côte

SEAFOOD • NEIGHBOURHOOD X On the main promenade of a historic town, you'll find this welcoming, personally run restaurant comprising two homely rooms. Local seafood is at the heart of the good value menu - check the blackboard for the day's recommendations.

Menu € 29 (early dinner)/34

Custom House Quay - 053 912 2122 - www.lacote.ie - dinner only - Closed 2 weeks January, Sunday and Monday

Killiane Castle

COUNTRY HOUSE • ELEGANT A 17C house and 14C castle on a family-owned dairy farm. Individually decorated, antique-furnished bedrooms look out over the surrounding farmland; wood-panelled Room 2 is the best. Breakfast includes homemade bread and yoghurt, while the 3 course dinners showcase their own beef, pork and vegetables.

8 rooms - € 80/95 € 120/150

Drinagh - South : 5.5 km by R 730 off N 25 - 053 915 8885 - www.killianecastle.com - Closed mid December-mid February

YOUGHAL EOCHAILL

Cork - Pop. 6 990 - Regional map n° **22**-C3

Aherne's

SEAFOOD • FRIENDLY XX A traditional place dating from 1923, keenly run by the 2nd and 3rd generations of the same family. Have lunch in one of the bars or dinner in the restaurant. Seafood is from the local boats and hot buttered lobster is a speciality. Some of the antique-furnished bedrooms have balconies.

Menu € 35 - Carte € 24/45 - bar lunch

13 rooms - € 85/110 € 120/210

163 North Main St - 024 92424 - www.ahernes.com - Closed 23-27 December

Walter Raleigh

FAMILY • PERSONALISED It might not look it but this immaculately kept hotel is over 300 years old. It's named after the one-time mayor of Youghal, who would have approved of the charming way it is run. Enjoy breakfast on the balcony overlooking Blackwater and dinner in the traditional bar or restaurant.

39 rooms - € 95/120 € 120/150

- 024 92011 - www.walterraleighhotel.com - Closed 25-26 December

MICHELIN

MICHELIN

MICHELIN

MICHELIN

MICHELIN

Tyres wear
more quickly
on short urban
journeys.

TRUE!

You tend to accelerate and brake more often when driving around town so your tyres work harder!
If you are stuck in traffic, keep calm and drive slowly.

Tyre pressure only affects your car's safety.

FALSE!

Driving with underinflated tyres (0.5 bar below recommended pressure) doesn't just impact handling and fuel consumption, it will shave 8,000 km off tyre lifespan.
Make sure you check tyre pressure about once a month and before you go on holiday or a long journey.

If you only encounter **winter weather from time to time** - *sudden showers, snowfall or black ice -* **one type of tyre** *will do the job.*
?
TRUE!
The revolutionary **MICHELIN CrossClimate** - the very first summer tyre with winter certification - is a practical solution to keep you on the road whatever the weather.

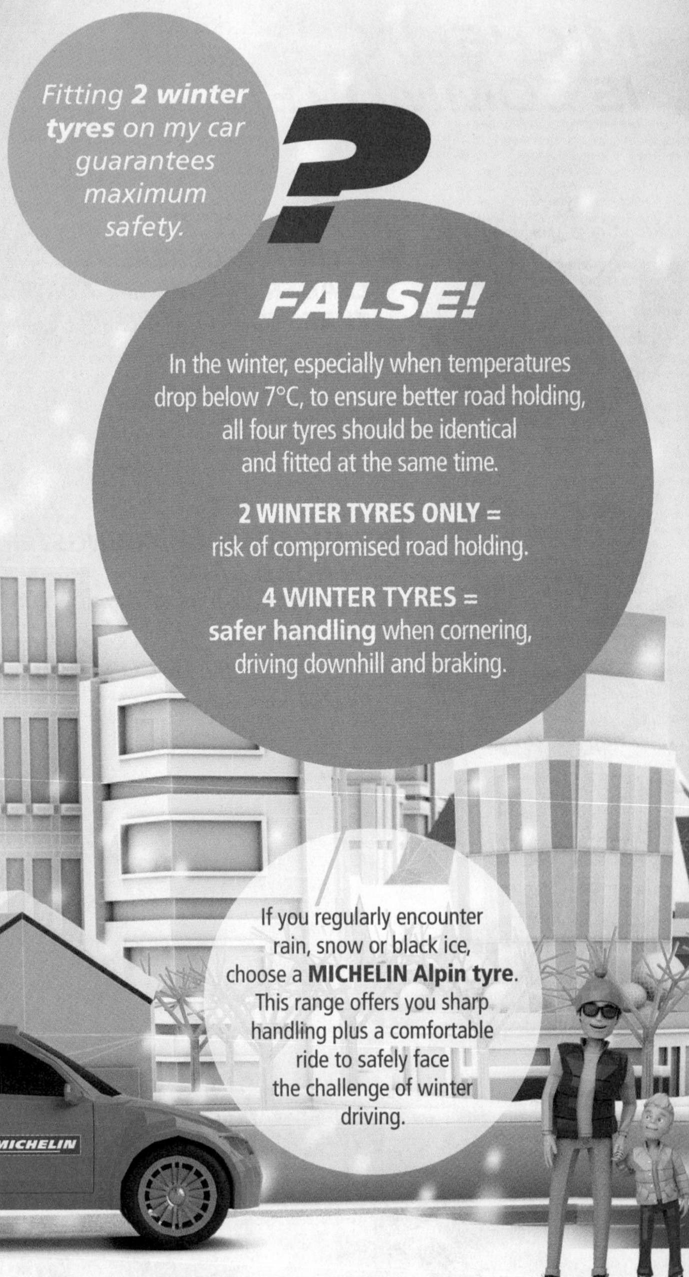
Fitting **2 winter tyres** on my car guarantees maximum safety.
?
FALSE!
In the winter, especially when temperatures drop below 7°C, to ensure better road holding, all four tyres should be identical and fitted at the same time.
2 WINTER TYRES ONLY = risk of compromised road holding.
4 WINTER TYRES = **safer handling** when cornering, driving downhill and braking.
If you regularly encounter rain, snow or black ice, choose a **MICHELIN Alpin tyre**. This range offers you sharp handling plus a comfortable ride to safely face the challenge of winter driving.
MICHELIN

MICHELIN IS COMMITTED

MICHELIN IS **GLOBAL LEADER IN FUEL-EFFICIENT TYRES** FOR LIGHT VEHICLES.

EDUCATING OF YOUNGSTERS IN ROAD SAFETY, NOT FORGETTING TWO-WHEELERS. LOCAL ROAD SAFETY CAMPAIGNS WERE RUN IN **16 COUNTRIES** IN 2015.

QUIZ

1 TYRES ARE BLACK SO WHY IS THE MICHELIN MAN WHITE?

Back in 1898 when the Michelin Man was first created from a stack of tyres, they were made of natural rubber, cotton and sulphur and were therefore light-coloured. The composition of tyres did not change until after the First World War when carbon black was introduced. But the Michelin Man kept his colour!

2 FOR HOW LONG HAS MICHELIN BEEN GUIDING TRAVELLERS?

Since 1900. When the MICHELIN guide was published at the turn of the century, it was claimed that it would last for a hundred years. It's still around today and remains a reference with new editions and online restaurant listings in a number of countries.

3 WHEN WAS THE "BIB GOURMAND" INTRODUCED IN THE MICHELIN GUIDE?

The symbol was created in 1997 but as early as 1954 the MICHELIN guide was recommending "exceptional good food at moderate prices". Today, it features on the MICHELIN Restaurants website and app.

If you want to enjoy a fun day out and find out more about Michelin, why not visit the l'Aventure Michelin museum and shop in Clermont-Ferrand, France:

www.laventuremichelin.com

INDEX OF TOWNS

C — Page

D — Page

E — Page

F Page

G Page

L — Page

M Page

T — Page

INDEX OF MAPS

TOWN PLAN KEY

Sights

- Hotels
- Restaurants

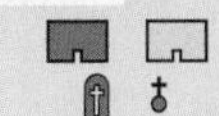

Place of interest
Interesting place of worship

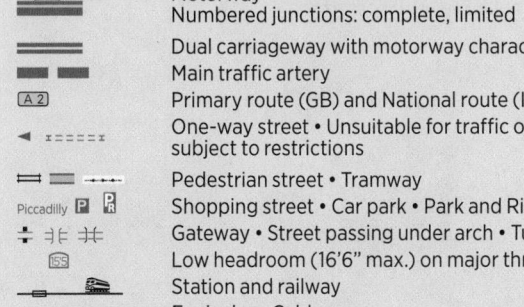

Roads

M 1 — Motorway
Numbered junctions: complete, limited

Dual carriageway with motorway characteristics
Main traffic artery
A 2 — Primary route (GB) and National route (IRL)
One-way street • Unsuitable for traffic or street subject to restrictions
Pedestrian street • Tramway
Piccadilly — Shopping street • Car park • Park and Ride
Gateway • Street passing under arch • Tunnel
15'5 — Low headroom (16'6" max.) on major through routes
Station and railway
Funicular • Cable-car
B — Lever bridge • Car ferry

London

Borough • Area
Borough boundary
Congestion Zone • Charge applies Monday-Friday 07.00-18.00
Nearest Underground station to the hotel or restaurant

Various signs

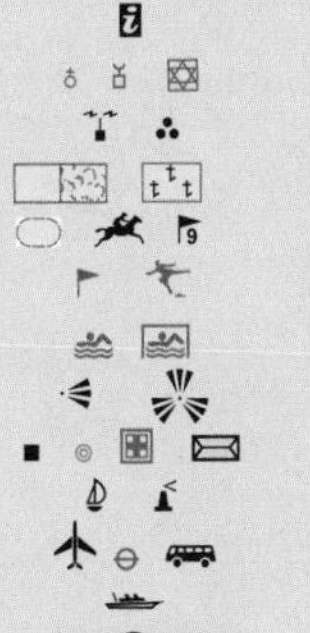

Tourist Information Centre
Church/Place of worship • Mosque • Synagogue
Communications tower or mast • Ruins
Garden, park, wood • Cemetery
Stadium • Racecourse • Golf course
Golf course (with restrictions for visitors) • Skating rink
Outdoor or indoor swimming pool
View • Panorama
Monument • Fountain • Hospital • Covered market
Pleasure boat harbour • Lighthouse
Airport • Underground station • Coach station
Ferry services: passengers and cars
Main post office
Public buildings located by letter:
C H J — County Council Offices • Town Hall • Law Courts
M T U — Museum • Theatre • University, College
POL. — Police (in large towns police headquarters)